the BERKELEY guides
THE BUDGET TRAVELER'S HANDBOOK

CRITICAL ACCLAIM FOR
THE BERKELEY GUIDES

"[The Berkeley Guides are] brimming with useful information for the low-budget traveler — material delivered in a fresh, funny, and often irreverent way." —*The Philadelphia Inquirer*

"...hip, blunt and lively....these Cal students boogie down and tell you where to sleep in a cowboy bunkhouse, get a tattoo and eat cheap meals cooked by aspiring chefs." —*Atlanta Journal Constitution*

"...Harvard hasn't yet met 'On the Loose's' pledge to plant two trees in Costa Rica for every one felled to print its books—a promise that, given the true grit of these guides, might well mean a big new forest in Central America." —*Newsweek*

"[The Berkeley Guides] offer straight dirt on everything from hostels to look for and beaches to avoid to museums least likely to attract your parents...they're fresher than Harvard's Let's Go series." —*Seventeen*

"The books are full of often-amusing tips written in a youth-tinged conversational style." —*The Orlando Sentinel*

"So well-organized and well-written that I'm almost willing to forgive the recycled paper and soy-based ink." —*P.J. O'Rourke*

"These guys go to great lengths to point out safe attractions and routes for women traveling alone, minorities and gays. If only this kind of caution weren't necessary. But I'm glad someone finally thought of it." —*Sassy*

"The very-hip Berkeley Guides look like a sure-fire hit for students and adventurous travelers of all ages. This is real budget travel stuff, with the emphasis on meeting new places head on, up close and personal....this series is going to go places." —*The Hartford Courant*

"The guides make for fun and/or enlightening reading." —*The Los Angeles Times*

"The new On the Loose guides are more comprehensive, informative and witty than Let's Go." —*Glamour*

ATLANTIC
OCEAN

NOR
Bergen

SCOTLAND

NORTHERN
IRELAND

Edinburgh

North
Sea

DENM

Belfast

IRELAND   Irish
           Sea   G R E A T
Dublin   B R I T A I N

Cork   WALES

Cardiff   ENGLAND

London   The Hague

English Channel

Brussels
BELGIUM

Paris
LUXEMBOURG

F R A N C E

Lyon

Marseille   Nice

Madrid   ANDORRA

Barcelona

PORTUGAL

Lisbon

S P A I N

Sevilla   Granada

Gibraltar
Tangier

Rabat

MOROCCO

Fès

HOLLAND
Amsterdam

Rotterdam

G

Bon

Frankfu

Zürich
Bern   S
SWITZERLAND

LIECH

Milan

Monte Car
Flor

Corsica

Sardinia

Balearic
Islands

Mediterranean Sea

Ty

ALGERIA

0   400 miles

0   600 km

TUNISIA

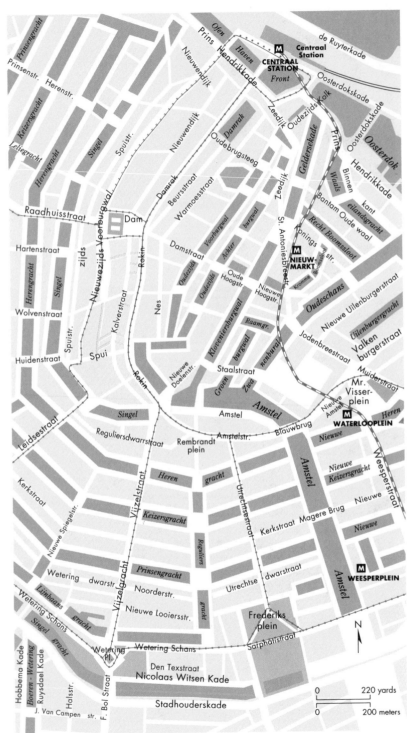

Amsterdam

4

Berlin

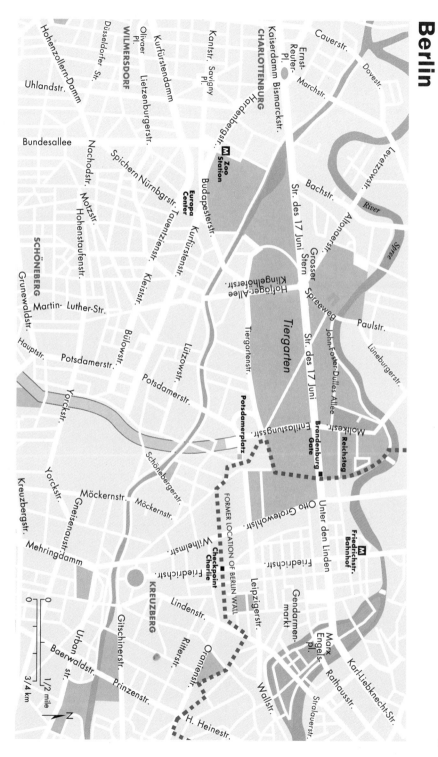

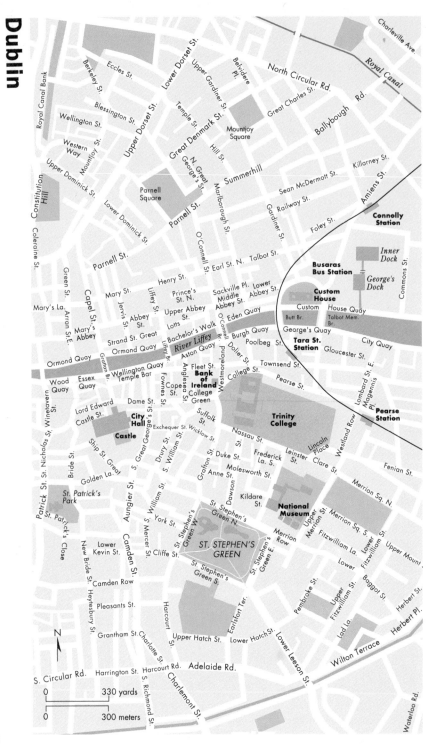

Dublin

Madrid

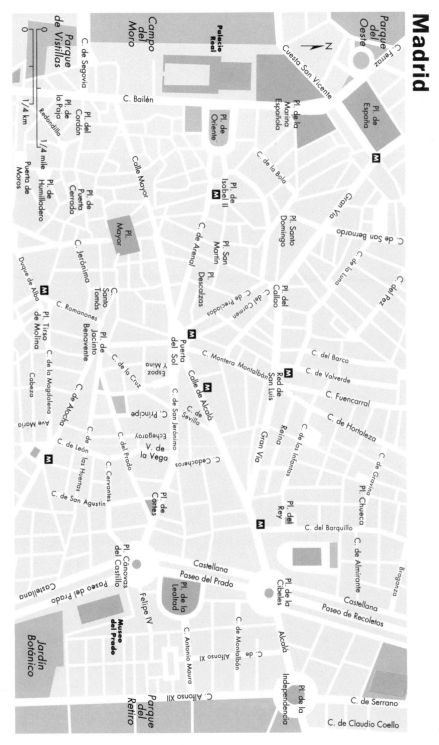

Regent's Park

Inner Circle

Outer Circle End

Albany St.

Hampstead Rd.

Euston Station

Euston Rd.

Gower

Maida Vale

Abbey Rd.

Abercorn Pl.

Grove End Rd.

Circus Rd.

Wellington Rd.

Prince Albert Rd.

Hall Rd.

St. John's Wood Rd.

Lisson Grove

Outer Circle

Chester Rd.

Park Rd.

Balcombe St.

Dorset Square

Telecom Tower

B

Tottenham Cou

Clifton Rd.

Bloomfield Rd.

Edgware Rd.

Harrow Rd.

Marylebone Flyover

Marylebone Rd.

Gt. Portland St.

Portland Pl.

Harley St.

Bishop's Bridge Rd.

Paddington Station

Praed St.

Sussex Gdns.

Seymour Pl.

Gloucester Pl.

Baker St.

Marylebone High St.

Wigmore St.

Berners St.

Queensway

Craven Hill

Edgware Rd.

BAYSWATER

Bayswater Rd.

N. Carriage Dr.

Manchester Square

Duke St.

Oxford Oxford Circus

SOHO

Regent St.

Brewer St.

Bayswater Rd.

Oxford St.

Grosvenor Square

Brook St.

New Bond St.

Grosvenor St.

Berkeley Square

Royal Academy

Piccadilly Circus

Kensington Gardens

Round Pond

Hyde Park

The Serpentine

U.S. Embassy

Sth. Audley St.

Park Lane

Curzon St.

Dover St.

Jermyn St.

St. James's

Pall Mall

The

St. James Park

Kensington Palace

W. Carriage Dr.

S. Carriage Dr.

Kensington Rd.

Kensington Gore

Kensington Rd.

Kensington Rd.

Piccadilly

Green Park

Constitution Hill

Knightsbridge

Grosvenor Pl.

Birdcage

Buckingham Palace

Palace Gate

Gloucester Rd.

Prince Consort Rd.

Exhibition Rd.

Royal Albert Hall

KNIGHTSBRIDGE

Brompton Rd.

Sloane St.

Pont St.

Cadogan Pl.

Belgrave Square

Eaton Square

Buckingham Palace Rd.

Victoria Station

Victoria

Wilton Rd.

Cromwell Rd.

Queen's Gate

South Kensington Museums

SOUTH KENSINGTON

Old Brompton Rd.

Fulham Rd.

Sloane Ave.

Sydney St.

Old Church St.

Oakley St.

CHELSEA

Sloane Ave.

King's Rd.

Pimlico Rd.

Warwick Way

Lupus St.

Vauxh

Belgrave Rd.

Redcliffe Gdns.

Finborough Rd.

Fulham Rd.

Beaufort St.

Cheyne Walk

Albert Br.

Battersea Br.

Royal Hospital Rd.

Chelsea Embankment

River Thames

Chelsea Br. Rd.

Chelsea Br.

Grosvenor

Nine

Battersea Park

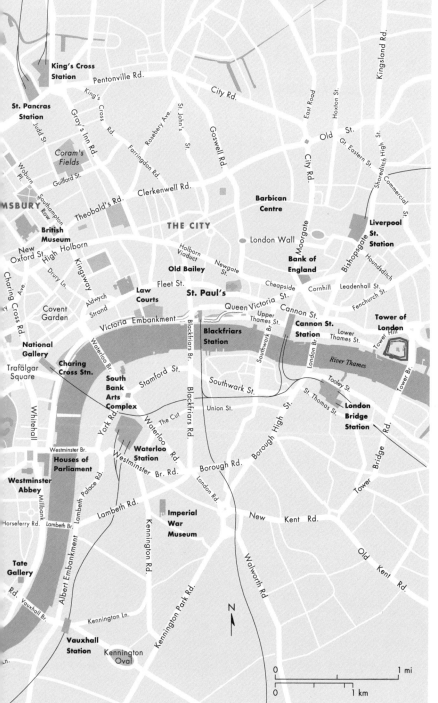

London

King's Cross Station

St. Pancras Station

Pentonville Rd.

City Rd.

King's Cross Rd.

Gray's Inn Rd.

Judd St.

Rosebery Ave.

St. John's St.

Goswell Rd.

East Road

Hoxton St.

Old St.

Kingsland Rd.

Gt. Eastern St.

Shoreditch High St.

City Rd.

Commercial St.

Coram's Fields

Woburn Pl.

Guilford St.

Southampton Row

Theobald's Rd.

Clerkenwell Rd.

THE CITY

Barbican Centre

Liverpool St. Station

MSBURY

British Museum

New Oxford St.

High Holborn

Holborn Viaduct

London Wall

Moorgate

Bishopsgate

Houndsditch

Charing Cross Rd.

Drury Ln.

Kingsway

Newgate St.

Old Bailey

Bank of England

Cheapside

Cornhill

Leadenhall St.

Fenchurch St.

Aldwych

Fleet St.

Law Courts

St. Paul's

Queen Victoria St.

Cannon St.

Covent Garden

Strand

Victoria Embankment

Blackfriars Br.

Upper Thames St.

Cannon St. Station

Lower Thames St.

Tower of London

National Gallery

Waterloo Br.

Blackfriars Station

Southwark Br.

London Br.

River Thames

Tower Hill

Trafalgar Square

Charing Cross Stn.

South Bank Arts Complex

Stamford St.

Southwark St.

Tooley St.

Tower Br.

Whitehall

York Rd.

Waterloo Rd.

The Cut

Blackfriars Rd.

Union St.

St. Thomas St.

London Bridge Station

Westminster Br.

Waterloo Station

Borough High St.

Bridge Rd.

Houses of Parliament

Westminster Br. Rd.

Borough Rd.

Tower

Westminster Abbey

Lambeth Palace Rd.

London Rd.

New Kent Rd.

Old Kent Rd.

Horseferry Rd.

Lambeth Br.

Lambeth Rd.

Imperial War Museum

Millbank

Albert Embankment

Kennington Rd.

Walworth Rd.

Tate Gallery

Rd.

Vauxhall Br.

Kennington Ln.

Kennington Park Rd.

N

Vauxhall Station

Kennington Oval

0 .... 1 mi

0 .... 1 km

Munich

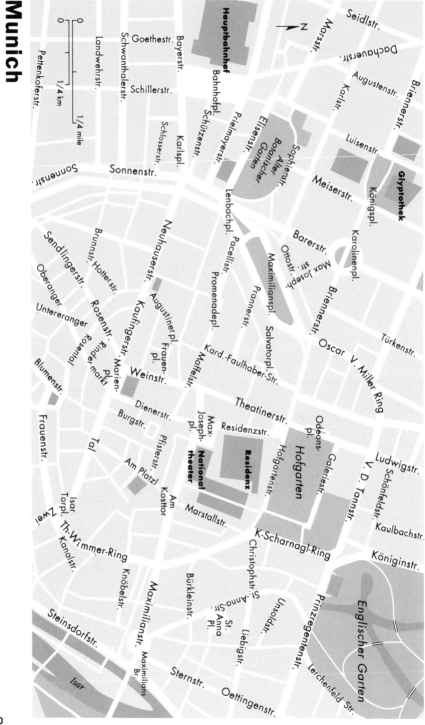

Prague

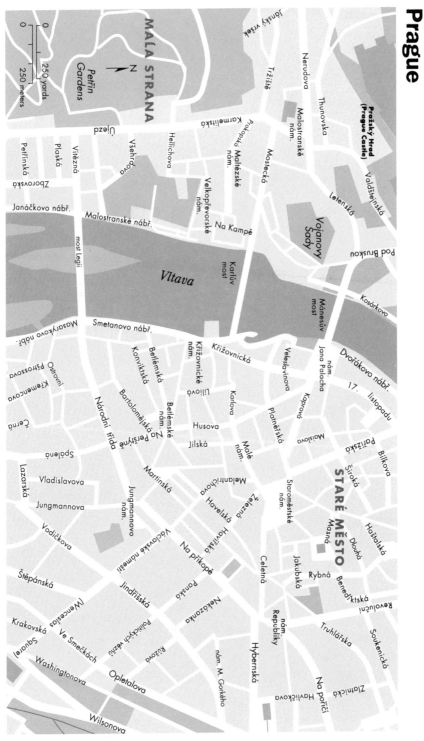

Paris

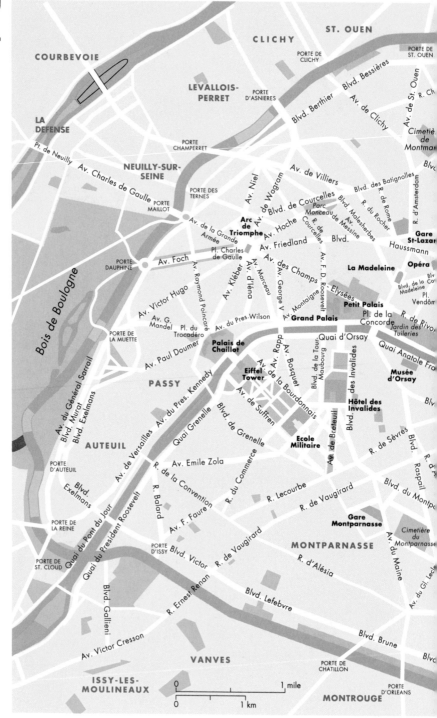

ST. OUEN

CLICHY

COURBEVOIE

PORTE DE
CLICHY

PORTE DE
ST. OUEN

LEVALLOIS-
PERRET

PORTE
D'ASNIERES

Blvd. Berthier

Av. de Clichy

Av. de St. Ouen

R. Ch.

Blvd. Bessières

LA
DEFENSE

PORTE
CHAMPERRET

Cimetiè
de
Montmar

Pt. de Neuilly

Av. Charles de Gaulle

NEUILLY-SUR-
SEINE

Blvd

PORTE DES
TERNES

Av. de Villiers

Blvd. des Batignolles

Av. Niel

R. de Rome

R. d'Amsterdam

PORTE
MAILLOT

Av. de Wagram

Blvd. de Courcelles

Blvd. Malesherbes

R. du Rocher

R. d'Amsterdam

Av. de la Grande
Armée

Arc
de
Triomphe

Parc
Monceau

Av. de Messine

R. de
Courcelles

Gare
St-Lazar

Av. Hoche

Haussmann

PORTE
DAUPHINE

Av. Foch

Pl. Charles
de Gaulle

Av. Friedland

Blvd.

Av. Kléber

Av. d'Iéna

Av. des Champs

La Madeleine

Opéra

Av. Victor Hugo

Av. Raymond Poincaré

Marceau

Av. George V

Av. F. D. Roosevelt

-Elysées

Petit Palais

Blvd. de la Co
Madeleine

Blv

Pl.
Vendôn

Av. G.
Mandel

Pl. du
Trocadéro

Av. du Pres. Wilson

Av. Montaigne

Grand Palais

Pl. de la
Concorde

R. de Rivo

Jardin des
Tuileries

Bois de Boulogne

PORTE DE
LA MUETTE

Av. Paul Doumer

Palais de
Chaillot

Quai d'Orsay

Quai Anatole Fra

Musée
d'Orsay

PASSY

Eiffel
Tower

Av. Rapp

Av. Bosquet

Blvd. de la Tour-
Maubourg

des Invalides

Blv

Av. du Général Sarrail

Blvd. Murat

Blvd. Exelmans

Av. du Pres. Kennedy

Av. de la Bourdonnais

Av. de Suffren

Hôtel des
Invalides

Blvd.

R. de Sèvres

Blvd.

R. d'A

AUTEUIL

Av. de Versailles

Quai Grenelle

Blvd. de Grenelle

Ecole
Militaire

Av. de Breteuil

PORTE
D'AUTEUIL

Av. Emile Zola

R. de la Convention

R. du Commerce

R. Lecourbe

Blvd. du Montp

Blvd.
Exelmans

R. Balard

Blvd.
Raspail

PORTE DE
LA REINE

R. de Vaugirard

Gare
Montparnasse

Cimetière
du
Montparnasse

PORTE DE
ST. CLOUD

Quai du Pont du Jour

Quai du Président Roosevelt

PORTE
D'ISSY

Blvd. Victor

R. de Vaugirard

MONTPARNASSE

Av. du Maine

R. d'Alésia

Av. du Gl. Lecle

Blvd. Gallieni

R. Ernest Renan

R. F. Faure

Blvd. Lefebvre

Av. Victor Cresson

VANVES

PORTE DE
CHATILLON

Blvd. Brune

Blv

ISSY-LES-
MOULINEAUX

MONTROUGE

PORTE
D'ORLEANS

0   1 mile

0   1 km

Paris

Rome

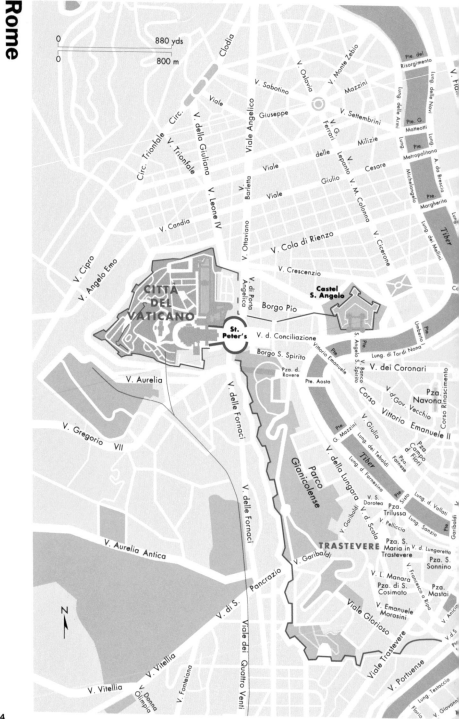

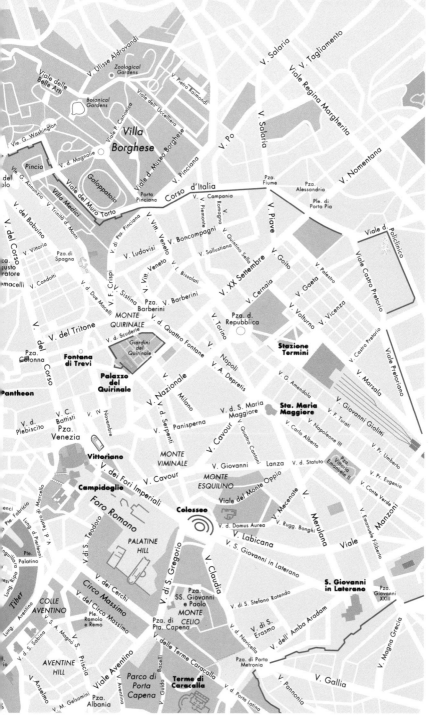

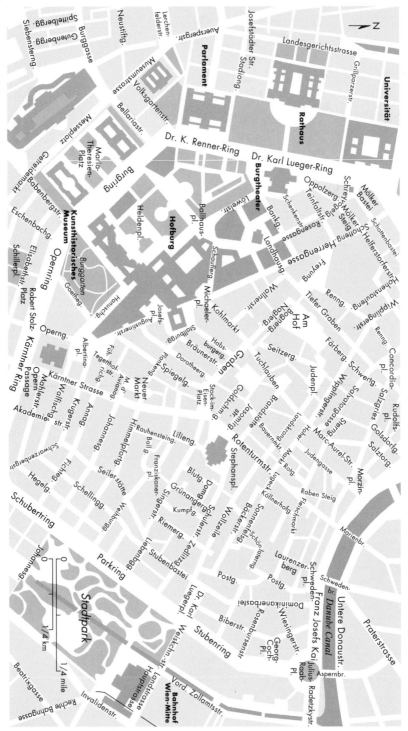

Vienna

The BERKELEY guides

THE BUDGET TRAVELER'S HANDBOOK

EUROPE

ON THE LOOSE 1995

WRITTEN BY BERKELEY STUDENTS IN COOPERATION WITH THE
ASSOCIATED STUDENTS OF THE UNIVERSITY OF CALIFORNIA

EUROPE ON THE LOOSE

Editors: Baty Landis, Lisa Roth, AnneLise Sorensen, Sharron Wood
Editorial Coordinators: Laura Comay Bloch, Sharron Wood
Executive Editor: Scott McNeely
Production Editors: Ellen Browne, Janet Foley, Laura M. Kidder, Dawn Lawson, Tracy Patruno, Linda K. Schmidt
Map Editor: Bob Blake
Cartographers: David Lindroth, Inc.; Eureka Cartography
Creative Director: Fabrizio La Rocca
Text Design: Tigist Getachew
Cover Design and Illustration: Rico Lins

SPECIAL SALES

Contents

We Go Where You Go.

Lowest student/budget airfares anywhere

International Student ID Cards
International Youth ID Cards
Eurail and Britrail passes
issued on the spot

Hostel Cards
Work Abroad Programs
Travel Gear and Guidebooks
Expert travel advice

Call for a FREE Student Travels magazine.

Amherst, MA
413-256-1261
Ann Arbor, MI
313-998-0200
Atlanta, GA
404-377-9997
Austin, TX
512-472-4931
Berkeley, CA
510-848-8604
Bloomington, IN
812-330-1600
Boston, MA
617-266-1926
Boulder, CO
303-447-8101
Cambridge, MA
617-497-1497
617-225-2555

Chapel Hill, NC
919-942-2334
Chicago, IL
312-951-0585
Columbus, OH
614-294-8696
Dallas, TX
214-363-9941
Davis, CA
916-752-2285
Denver, CO
303-571-0630
Evanston, IL
708-475-5070
La Jolla, CA
619-452-0630
Long Beach, CA
310-598-3338
714-527-7950

Los Angeles, CA
310-208-3551
818-905-5777
Miami, FL
305-670-9261
Minneapolis, MN
612-379-2323
New Haven, CT
203-562-5335
New Orleans, LA
504-866-1767
New York, NY
212-661-1450
212-666-4177
212-254-2525
Palo Alto, CA
415-325-3888
Philadelphia, PA
215-382-0343

Pittsburgh, PA
412-683-1881
Portland, OR
503-228-1900
Providence, RI
401-331-5810
Salt Lake City, UT
801-582-5840
San Diego, CA
619-270-6401
San Francisco, CA
415-421-3473
415-566-6222
Santa Barbara, CA
805-562-8080
Seattle, WA
206-632-2448
206-329-4567

Tempe, AZ
602-966-3544
Washington, DC
202-337-6464

London, Britain
(071) 437.7767
Munich,Germany
(089) 395 022
Paris, France
(1) 44.55.55.65
Singapore
(65) 738-7066
Tokyo, Japan
(3) 3581 5517

For U.S. cities not listed, call: 1-800-2-COUNCIL (1-800-226-8624)

America's oldest and largest student travel organization!

Council Travel is a travel company of the Council on International Educational Exchange

What the Berkeley Guides Are All About

Three years ago, a motley bunch of U.C. Berkeley students spent the summer traveling on shoestring budgets to launch a new series of guidebooks—the *Berkeley Guides*. We wrote the books because, like thousand of travelers, we had grown tired of the outdated attitudes and information served up year after year in other guides. Most important, we thought a travel guide should be written by people who know what cheap travel is all about.

You see, it's one of life's weird truisms that the more cheaply you travel, the more you inevitably experience. You're bound to experience a lot with the *Berkeley Guides,* because we believe in living like bums and spending as little money as possible. You won't find much in our guides about how a hotel blends mauve curtains with green carpet. Instead, we tell you if a place is cheap, clean (no bugs), and worth the cash.

Coming from a community as diverse as Berkeley, we also wanted our books to be useful to *everyone,* so we tell you if a place is wheelchair accessible, if it provides resources for gay and lesbian travelers, and if it's safe for women traveling solo. Many of us are Californians, which means most of us like trees and mountain trails. It also means we emphasize the outdoors in every *Berkeley Guide,* from info on hiking to tips on protecting the environment. To further minimize our impact on the environment, we print our books on recycled paper using soy-based inks, and we plant two trees for every one we use.

Most important, these guides are for travelers who want to see more than just the main sights. We find out what local people do for fun, where they go to eat, drink, or just hang out. Most guidebooks lead you down the tourist trail, ignoring important local issues, events, and culture. In the *Berkeley Guides,* we give you the information you need to understand what's going on around you— whether it's the latest on a student protest in France or yet another government scandal in London or Rome.

The Berkeley Guides began by covering Eastern Europe, Mexico, California, and the Pacific Northwest and Alaska. During the first year of research, our student writers slept in whorehouses in Mexican border towns and landed bush planes above the Arctic Circle. The second year was no different: Our writers weathered guerrilla attacks in the Guatemalan Highlands, motorcycle wrecks in Ireland, and a strange culinary concoction in Belize known as "greasy-greasy." The result was five new guidebooks, covering Central America, France, Germany, San Francisco, and Great Britain and Ireland. This year, one writer got an ulcer, one lost her skirt on a moped, one survived a bus plunge, while another spent hours digging through a dumpster to find a lost manuscript batch. Bloodied but unbowed, the *Berkeley Guides* brings you four new guidebooks, covering Europe, Italy, Paris, and London, not to mention completely revised, updated editions of our first- and second-year guides.

We've done our best to make sure the information in the *Berkeley Guides* is accurate, but time doesn't stand still: prices change, places go out of business. Call ahead when it's really important, assuming, of course, that the place has a phone. We really appreciate feedback from our readers—we want to hear about your latest find, a new scam, whatever. Write to the editors at 515 Eshleman Hall, University of California, Berkeley, CA 94720.

Thanks to You

Putting together a guidebook that covers more than 25 countries is no easy task. From figuring out how to mail manuscript from Morocco to getting the lowdown on the bar scene in Barcelona, our writers and editors relied on helpful souls along the way. We'd like to thank the following people—as well as the hundreds of others whom our writers met briefly on the road—for their advice and encouragement.

The Aamodt family (Sjoa, Norway); Poul Arnedal (Copenhagen, Denmark); Reina Ascherman (Brussels, Belgium); Anja Auhuber (Innsbruck, Austria); Laura Ballingall (Swansea University, Wales); Stevie Bergsmann (Linz, Austria); Harold Bernaert (Utrecht, Netherlands); Michael Bernstein (Ann Arbor, MI); Rose Brandt (Northridge, CA); Mathias Brixa (Innsbruck, Austria); William Bold (Washington, D.C.); Paul Burgin (San Diego, CA); Patxi Fernández Castillo (Burgos, Spain); Julian Cohen (Miami, FL); Joaquim Rocha da Cunha of the Portuguese National Tourist Office; Allan J. Davies (Lindosa, Portugal); Ed R. DeGraf (Rotterdam, Netherlands); Pedro Diaz (Sevilla, Spain); Gabriela Deubler (Salzburg, Austria); Lutgart, Marjan, Katrien, and Gilbert Devillers (Antwerp, Belgium); Melissa Edison (Dallas, TX); Mahairas Eiaggenos (Sámos, Greece); Gabrielle Fink (Innsbruck, Austria); Feargal Fitzpatrick (Dublin, Ireland); Al Fleming (Madison, WI); Anna-Lisa French (Palos Verdes, CA); Jorge Romaní de Gabriel (Santiago de Compostela, Spain); Jim and Jane Gierlich (Hermosa Beach, CA); Esther Haas and the rest of the Sleep-In crew (Rotterdam, Netherlands); Wolela Haile (Oslo, Norway); Petra Hanelt (Vienna, Austria); Peter Hanley (Pamplona, Spain); José Luis Expósito Haro (Granada, Spain); Christine Heiss (Innsbruck, Austria); Steen Henriksen (Skagen, Denmark); Ingrid Hickey (Terrigal, Australia); Thijs Hoeffnagel and Karen Holla (Amsterdam, Netherlands); Roswitha "Wiwi" Hofmann (Vienna, Austria); Florian Holzer, editor of *Wien, wie es ißt*, and *Falter-Zeitschrift* (Vienna, Austria); Anto Howard (Dublin, Ireland); Kokkalis Ilias (Sámos, Greece); C. Ireland (Costa Rica); Steve Isaacs (Copenhagen, Denmark); Hejle Jacobsen (Copenhagen, Denmark); Hans de Kiefte and Marjet Aarsen (Haarlem, Netherlands); Frau and Oskar Kienast (Vienna, Austria); Josh Kirshner (Nashville, TN); Sallyann Klutz (Pittsburgh, PA); Ilse Korhonen (Salzburg, Austria); Martá and Ted Krassney (Barcelona, Spain); Matt Krupt and Jennifer Rhodes (McLean, VA); Erling Kuernevik (Norway); Soren Larsen, Ole Mortensen, and Jacob Mariaga (Århus, Denmark); Eva Larsson (Lund, Sweden); Frank Lee (Birmingham, England); Rhonda Kae Lesinski (Fresno, CA); Elizabeth Levings (Manchester, England); Ada Limón (Somona, CA); Sandi Litchi (Richmond, CA); Nicole Löcse (Chemnitz, Germany); Antonio Lucas (Luxembourg City, Luxembourg); James and Ann MacKeen (Los Angeles, CA); Amy Marinelli (Aptos, CA); Julian Abad Marigil of the Ministerio de Turismo (Spain); Darren Marks (Sydney, Australia); Lee Lai May (Hong Kong); Claire McSwen and Dan O'Rourke (Amsterdam, Netherlands); Dr. Jeffrey Michael Mercer (Lagos, Spain); David Michaels (Darmstadt, Germany); Professor Adrienne Miller (Berkeley, CA); Lars Mogelberg (Copenhagen, Denmark); Marja Murray of the Finnish National Tourist Board (Los Angeles, CA); Briand Nelson (Christiania, Denmark); Andreas Nottebohm (Mallorca, Spain); May Olsen (Cascais, Portugal); Antonio Padilla (Barcelona, Spain); Julie Paul (Pittsburgh, PA); Robert Pirsig (New York, NY); Wilfredo Ramirez (Madrid, Spain); Tanya Riener (Feldkirchen, Austria); Siubhan Richmond (Los Angeles, CA); Birgit Rigi (Laxenburg, Austria); Margit Robin (Innsbruck, Austria); Carlos Alberto Goncalves Rodrigues (Sintra, Portugal); Pedro Roig-Martinez (Mallorca, Spain); Audun Schei and family (Mjølfjell, Norway); Fritz Seidl (Retz, Austria); Alison Selfridge (Khánia, Greece); David Sinclair (Paris, France); Eivind Skjerven and Bjørn Kjetil Lindvik of Stryn Fjell-Og Breførarlag (Stryn, Norway); the Solberg family (Sjoa, Norway); Elizabeth, Hans and Kåre Holter Solbjell (Oslo, Norway); Kurt Sørensen (Fredericia, Denmark); Hassan Sorrike (The Hague, Netherlands); Cynthia Stoal (Rotterdam, Netherlands); Markus Stofer and Claudia Roth (St. Gallen, Switzerland); John Stoker (Pamplona, Spain); Joe "Balloon Guy" Stratman (Cypress, CA); Dr. K. C. Strehorn (New York, NY); Lars Svaerdpill and Finn Hemmelso (Copenhagen, Denmark); the founders of the Svenska Tourist Föerening (STA); Peter Terwogt (The Hague, Netherlands); Peder Tholstrup (Copenhagen, Denmark); Ulaf and everyone at Use-It (Oslo, Norway); Jess Lawrence Weinstein (Portland, OR); Jacki and Gavin Wesson (Sydney, Australia); Charlie Williams (Barcelona, Spain); Jasper Winn (the Netherlands).

We'd particularly like to thank Kathy Schindelheim and Werner Kunz of Balair, Joe Zucker of Lufthansa, Mr. Moussaoui of Royal Air Maroc, Gloria Mello of Tap Air Portugal, and Dagobert Scher of Rail Europe for their generous help in getting our writers to the ends of the earth (and back).

We'd also like to thank the Random House folks who helped us with cartography, page design, and production: Bob Blake, Ellen Browne, Fionn Davenport, Denise DeGennaro, Janet Foley, Tigist Getachew, Laura M. Kidder, Fabrizio La Rocca, Dawn Lawson, Tracy Patruno, Linda Schmidt, Bob Shields, and John Shostrum.

Finally, we'd like to thank Andrew Barbour, the former executive editor of the *Berkeley Guides*. After three years in the trenches, Andrew set out on a year-long odyssey through Africa; so far he's contracted malaria, been stung by a poisonous fish, gotten stuck in an Algerian minefield, and traveled roads in Zaire that were far more stressful than any disease.

Berkeley Bios

Behind every restaurant review, train schedule, and cheap thrill in this book lurks a student writer. Sixteen writers signed on for the summer, fanning out over Europe, Turkey, and Morocco. Every two weeks they sent their manuscript back to a four-woman editorial team in Berkeley, who whipped it into shape.

The Writers

After spending two months biking through the rain to write for *The Berkeley Guide to Great Britain and Ireland 1994,* **Andy Brandt** knew exactly where he wanted to go the following summer: the south of Spain. Despite sweltering heat, a severe shortage of any food item *not* containing pork, a Cadíz innkeeper who caused an uproar over a missing ashtray, and a "misplaced" manuscript batch, he blazed his way across Andalucía, the Costa del Sol, the Communidad Valenciana, and the Balearic Islands. A U.C. Berkeley graduate, he is currently applying to graduate schools in Journalism (Northwestern, are you listening?).

Despite her yearly pledge to "finally spend a summer at home on the beach," **Marisa Gierlich** once again traveled around Europe for the Berkeley Guides (she wrote for *The Berkeley Guide to France 1994*). Now that she has completed her degree in English, written the Sweden chapter for this book, and spent a few weeks in and around Rome working on *The Berkeley Guide to Italy 1995,* she continues her quest to discover the true meaning of responsible tourism and the role of guidebooks in its development. Her other life goal is to cover all of Sweden's mountain ranges on foot before she dies. Just to get warmed up, she's about to travel to the Yukon and British Columbia, then spend a few months trekking through the Rockies in Montana.

Christine Gomez allegedly smoked (but never, ever inhaled) lots of funny-looking cigarettes in Amsterdam . . . all for the sake of research, of course. She was an editor for the Berkeley Guides last year, but she prefers to be out there in the field meeting all the crazy people of the world. As she puts it, "everyone is this close (small space between index finger and thumb) to just losing it—it's great." When not out mingling, she was happiest hopping onto one of those crappy Dutch bikes and careening through sand dunes, heath land, and forest trails. Christine is currently a slave at an ad agency.

Pamela Harris, a political theory student at U.C. Berkeley, could never quite believe that traipsing across Spain was her summer job. She was especially happy that she would be able to cash in on all those years of high school Spanish. The laugh was on her, though, when she sat under the knife of a macho hairdresser in Salamanca: Pam had never learned to say "blunt cut, layered underneath," and ended up with a kind of chin-length shag, feathered on the sides. Very attractive. Her travels peaked in Santiago de Compostela, where she arrived in time to catch a glimpse of the king, queen, and president of Spain, and basically lose herself completely in the revelry surrounding the Feast of Saint James.

Reading one too many treatises by Plato during her studies as a rhetoric major finally prompted **Dawn MacKeen** to jet off and explore the Grecian lands for herself. Scooters became her favorite form of transportation around the islands, but she soon learned that Greece wasn't the best place for novices—twice she wiped out on the rocky roads. Luckily, a few locals scraped her off the ground and rushed her to two different Greek doctors. She eventually returned safely to the Berkeley office, proudly displaying her scars.

Amy McConnell, who skipped her own graduation to get a jump on Denmark, credits her discoveries about the country to the friendly Danes who took her under their wing. She swears that Americans are revered in Denmark, which is why she was able to hook up with a military sergeant who brought her up to speed on Danish defense; an American expatriate who let her share his apartment for two weeks; and three university students in Århus who gave her the scoop on local nightlife. She also spent a night with a goose farmer in the Funen countryside, strolled Jutland's northernmost beaches with a lighthouse keeper in Skagen, and traveled hundreds of miles in a truck full of Danish herring.

After graduating with a degree in social science, writer **Sean McFarland** flew off to Portugal for a summer of adventure. After reading about a remote youth hostel near Porto, he headed straight for what he thought would be paradise. Three bus rides and two hitches later, he found himself walking up a lonely mountain in the middle of nowhere. Mild insanity already setting in, he was talking with a herd of goats when a truck pulled up. When Sean asked about the elusive hostel in careful Portuguese, the driver replied, with a perfect British accent, that the hostel had been closed for five years. However, the travel fairy was looking after Sean, and the English chap, who was living in the now-defunct hostel, put him up at his farm for a week of dry BBC, weak tea, and strong brandy. After finishing the Portugal chapter, Sean hitched across Europe twice, finally returned to the States, and is now planning a career in meditation.

One of the challenges **Corey Nettles** faced while writing for the Berkeley Guides was to digest the fact that, although she was writing part of the chapter on Spain, most of the people she met did not even consider themselves Spanish, but rather Catalan, Asturian, or Basque. Some of her highlights include hiking in the Pyrenees, the celebration of Los San Fermínes in Pamplona, and her favorite city—Barcelona. After two months of bus and train hopping (and suffering a bus breakdown in the middle of Aragon's barren plains), Corey thought she had the transportation thing down pat. Her opinion changed when, at the end of her trip, she came within minutes of missing her flight home after sleeping through her train stop. Unbowed, Corey spends her days scheming how to get back to Spain.

Meir Rinde found Moroccans frustratingly, though understandably, cynical about their homeland; one of the friendlier Tangier hustlers, after five or six beers, warned him "trust no one in this country." After a trip that included his initiation to backpacking, and to Pepto-Bismol and other curatives, he escaped to the comfort of his hippie co-op in Berkeley. Meir says Morocco was a humbling experience and hasn't exactly been advising his friends to visit. ("Why not Egypt? At least it's got pyramids.") He's willing to admit, though, that those who are cool enough to ignore his advice might actually enjoy the place. He graduated with a degree in English in May 1994 and plans to go into academia or journalism.

When the editors of the Europe book found out that **David Poole** had missed the application deadline because he was recuperating from malaria, which he had picked up in Guatemala the previous month, they decided to bend the rules and meet this character. Perhaps the best traveled of the Berkeley Guides writers, having visited five continents and 36 countries, David wasn't fazed in the least by his assignment in Turkey, even when he got bristle burn from all the times he was obliged to greet Turkish men with a kiss on either cheek. After finishing his stint, David bade us and U.C. Berkeley "cheerio" before traveling across the Middle East and returning to his home in Lancaster, England.

Frustrated in Finland was how **Adam S. Ruderman** often found himself. No master of the Finnish tongue, he was a perennial loser in the verbal sparring bouts of which he is so fond. On one occasion at the tourist office in Rovaniemi, the good lady behind the desk made a critical aside to her colleague regarding the tattered, unshaven American before her. Unable to defend himself, Adam was rescued by a spunky little Finn with thick glasses and a thick accent, a reporter from the Rovaniemi daily writing her weekly "who's visiting our town" column. She had found her subject: the out-of-place American. After a brief interview, this Nordic journalist explained how, in all her years in this Arctic Circle town, she had never come across an American. "Are you lost?" she inquired with pity. "I guess so," thought Ruderman, who hadn't seen a fellow Yank in two months of Finnish travels, "and it's pretty cool."

After the matriarchy of the Berkeley Guides packed him off to Greece with some mild words of encouragement and a sack of brownies, **Oliver Schwaner-Albright,** a potential architect who diverts himself by pursuing a B.A. in art history from U.C. Berkeley, tried to follow his friend's advice to "stay arrogant" while, dehydrated and filthy, he trekked through Istanbul, Athens, and the north of Greece. After conquering the peaks of Mt. Olympus wearing a pair of black Converse low-tops and a typewriter strapped to his back, he was shipped off to Bulgaria, where he mastered a third alphabet, made a phone call for $2/5$ of a cent, and learned to nod his head to tell someone "no." He recently returned to Europe to update *The Berkeley Guide to France* and co-write *The Berkeley Guide to Paris.*

Ever since **Trisha Smith** discovered that water freezes when the temperature is low enough, she's been seeking the many forms of frozen H_2O. It was only natural that she chose to cover Norway, where Europe's largest slab of ice lurks above fjords carved by ancient glaciers. Trisha made friends with a couple of Norwegian trolls, but the reindeer were more elusive, always disappearing in the mist or behind a crag before she could make contact. Trisha's future plans are predictably vague. She is hoping to hop a sailboat and work her way through the Caribbean. She is aware that ice is scarce in this part of the world.

When the Berkeley Guides editors asked **Zak Smith** to write the chapters on Belgium and Luxembourg, he was happy to forgo a summer working at the university law library in favor of listening to Tchaikovsky in Brussels's Grand Place. Early in his trip, Zak thought that spending the night with a vomiting bunk-mate in a Belgian hostel was the worst thing that would happen during his two-month stint. He was wrong. A few weeks later he traveled to the Netherlands to visit a cousin, who's a nun in a remote convent. Thinking he would get some work done while he waited to see her, Zak took out his manuscript, but it was gone. Big problem. Zak eventually found the missing manuscript in a train station trash can, only a little worse for wear. Zak returned to Berkeley to finish a double major in political science and history, which will hopefully take him back to Europe in the field of international relations.

Having traveled extensively in the East, Southeast Asia, and India, **Katherine Stechschulte** embarked on a fearless journey to . . . Switzerland. At first she had trouble adapting to the hyper-efficient country: She missed many trains because she didn't realize they actually ran on time, and she had trouble washing her hands until she figured out that most sinks turned themselves on automatically. Having mastered the art of traveling in an overdeveloped country, she had a remarkable time discovering the Swiss mountains, lakes, and rivers. Upon return, Katherine started her graduate studies in architecture.

Last in Austria as a twelve-year-old, **Jay Tate,** a political science graduate student, was surprised at how many of the places that he remembered as decayed and declining had put on a new face. Jay had looked forward to do some June glacier skiing, but had to postpone this plan indefinitely when he trashed his knee on a train door in Innsbruck. He spent the next few weeks swallowing pink ibuprofens big enough for a horse. Hitchhiking even short distances suddenly seemed like a good idea. Trading directions for a short lift within Vienna turned into a couple of hours of broken Russian, Spanish, and German with the self-described "King of the Gypsies"—who's got Slovakian business cards to prove it. Just as the trip ended, hyper-vigilant metropolitan police pulled up to order the innocent pair of address-exchangers out of the car to pose the burning question: "Do you have any weapons?"

Finally, we'd like to put in a word for the writers and updaters who worked on the Berkeley Guides to France, Germany, Great Britain and Ireland, Italy, and Eastern Europe, whose work made this massive tome possible: Mary Bahr, Boyce Brown, Christy Collins, Colleen Cotter, Heidi Craig, Michael D'Amato, Helen Dorra, Peter Edwards, April Gertler, Michael Guenza, Pilar Guzman, Veronica Gushin, Karyn Krause, Les Kruger, Helen Lenda, Greg Magnuson, Virginia Matzek, Alyson McCleave, Ann McDevitt, Scott McNeely, Suzette Olsen, Virginie Pelletier, Geraldine Poon, Terrence Priester, Mark S. Rosen, Julie Ross, Rashmi Sadana, Linda Shing, Shelly Smith, Laini Taylor, Christopher Van Bebber, Oliver Wilken, and Betsy Wilkins.

The Editors

A New Orleans native majoring in English at U.C. Berkeley, **Baty Landis** kept up spirits during long nights spent in the less-than-ventilated editorial offices by pinching saggy elbows and singing inventive variations of "Davy Crockett." Early in the summer she let the writers know that she responded well to gifts, and consequently received chocolate from the writer in Austria, chocolate from the writer in Belgium, chocolate from the writer in Switzerland, and a flag on a toothpick from one of the writers in Greece. After serving her time editing accounts of other people's adventures, Baty offered herself a promotion and is now updating *The Berkeley Guide to France* and co-writing *The Berkeley Guide to Paris*.

After many stationary months editing and listening to countless stories about the benefits of Port wine and the intensity with which Spaniards pursue nocturnal activities, **Lisa Roth** surfaced from her cluttered Berkeley office and hightailed it abroad. After visiting Israel, she stopped in Europe for three months to hang out with Berkeley Guides writers who couldn't get enough of their travels and never came home. Lisa also got a chance to practice all four of the languages she knows at a French ski station in the Catalan Pyrenees with Spanish friends and a Hungarian cousin. Refreshed and seeking more character-building experiences, Lisa's back in San Francisco making her living as a travel writer.

AnneLise Sorensen had so much fun editing *The Berkeley Guide to Central America,* she returned to edit the Europe book. Feeling vaguely like Napoleon, AnneLise and her co-editors stood over a table covered with a huge map of Europe and divvied it up with a red marker. Charged with the formidable task of plotting itineraries, assigning chapter lengths, and figuring out how to get the computer to print that little circle above the A in Århus, AnneLise and her colleagues spent many a wee hour drinking cheap red wine and staring out at the million-dollar view from the office balcony. Tired of experiencing the sights and sounds of Europe through her trusty writers, AnneLise is now preparing to travel to Ireland and Northern Ireland to update *The Berkeley Guide to Great Britain and Ireland,* steeling herself for the seven weeks of Guinness and cabbage that lie ahead. When she returns, AnneLise plans on becoming a mover and shaker in the magazine industry.

A self-proclaimed Europhile in a city where studying dead white men is considered tragically unhip and politically suspect, **Sharron Wood** decided to spend her second year at the Berkeley Guides working as an editor for the guide to Europe. A bit of a masochist, she is now working for the Guides as Editorial Coordinator. She plans to stay at her desk only until the Berkeley Guides starts working on a guide to the Arctic Circle; she has dibs on the archipelago of Svalbard and Franz Josef Land (take a look at your atlas). Just in case that book never materializes, she's planning to study Finnish, learn how to play the hardanger fiddle, and develop a taste for pickled herring so she can travel to Finland and Scandinavia at the first opportunity.

We'd also like to thank the editors of the Great Britain and Ireland, France, Germany, Italy, and Eastern Europe books, for handing us edited, cut, and clean copy at a moment's notice: Nina Goldschlager, Christine Gomez, Nicole Harb, Alison Huml, Karyn Krause, Chelsea Mauldin, Emily Miller, Melanie Montaverde, Caitlin Ramey, and Mark S. Rosen.

What to do when your *money* is done traveling before you are.

Don't worry. With MoneyGram,℠ your parents can send

you money in usually 10 minutes or less to more than

15,500 locations in 75 countries. So if the money you

need to see history becomes history, call us and we'll

direct you to a MoneyGram agent closest to you.

USA: 1-800-MONEYGRAM • Canada: 1-800-933-3278
France: (331) 47-77-70-00 • Germany: (0049) Ø*-69-21050
England: (44) Ø*-71-839-7541 • Spain: (91) 322 54 55
When in Europe, contact the nearest American Express Travel Service Office.

MoneyGram℠
INTERNATIONAL MONEY TRANSFERS.

BASICS

1

If you've ever traveled with anyone before, you know there are two types of people in the world: the planners and the nonplanners. You also know that travel brings out the very worst in both groups: Left to their own devices, the planners will have you goosestepping from attraction to attraction on a cultural blitzkrieg, while the nonplanners will invariably miss the flight, the train, and the point. We try to take a middle ground, providing you with the resources to figure out your itinerary, without planning your every step. And, whichever camp you belong in, *always*, *always* remain flexible. Companies go out of business, prices inevitably go up, and sooner or later you're going to miss a train connection. If you wanted predictability, you should have stayed home.

Planning Your Trip

USEFUL ORGANIZATIONS

GOVERNMENT TOURIST OFFICES Government tourist offices can answer general questions about travel in their country or refer you to other organizations for more information. Try to be as specific as possible when writing to request information (e.g., I'm a 26-year-old budget traveler interested in hiking and skiing in Norway in May of next year) or you may just end up with a stack of glossy brochures about expensive tours to Monte Carlo or shopping expeditions in London. If you can get someone to answer questions over the phone, so much the better. The offices are usually staffed by natives of the country they represent.

➤ **AUSTRIAN TOURIST INFORMATION OFFICE** • **United States** (500 5th Ave., 20th Floor, New York, NY 10110, tel. 212/944–6880). **Canada** (1010 Sherbrooke St. W, Suite 1410, Montreal, Quebec H3A 2R7, tel. 514/849–3709). **United Kingdom** (30 St. George St., London W1R 0AL, tel. 0171/629–0461).

➤ **BELGIAN NATIONAL TOURIST OFFICE** • **United States** (745 5th Ave., Suite 714, New York, NY 10151, tel. 212/758–8130). **United Kingdom** (Premier House, 2 Gayton Rd., Harrow, Middlesex HA1 2XU, tel. 0181/861–3300).

➤ **BRITISH TOURIST AUTHORITY** • **United States** (551 5th Ave., 7th Floor, New York, NY 10176, tel. 212/986–2266). **Canada** (94 Cumberland St., Suite 600, Toronto, Ontario M5R 3N3, tel. 416/925–6326). **United Kingdom** (Thames Tower, Black's Rd., Hammersmith, London W6 9EL, tel. 0181/846–9000).

1

➤ **BULGARIAN TOURIST OFFICE** • United States (Balkan Holidays, 41 E. 42nd St., Suite 508, New York, NY 10017, tel. 212/573–5530). **United Kingdom** (18 Princes St., London W1R 7RE, tel. 0171/499–6988).

➤ **CEDOK CZECH AND SLOVAK TRAVEL BUREAU** • United States (10 E. 40th St., Suite 3604, New York, NY 10016, tel. 212/689–9720). **United Kingdom** (17–18 Old Bond St., London W1X 4RB, tel. 0171/629–6058).

➤ **DANISH TOURIST BOARD** • United States (Box 16617, Beverly Hills, CA 90209, tel. 213/936–0975). **Canada** (Box 115, Station N, Toronto, Ontario M8V 3S4, tel. 416/823–9620). **United Kingdom** (Sceptre House, 169–173 Regent St., London W1R 8PY, tel. 0171/734–2637).

➤ **FINNISH TOURIST BOARD** • United States (655 3rd Ave., Suite 1810, New York, NY 10017, tel. 212/949–2333). **Canada** (1200 Bay St., Suite 604, Toronto, Ontario M5R 2A5, tel. 416/964–9159). **United Kingdom** (66–68 Haymarket, London SW1Y 4RF, tel. 0171/839–4048).

➤ **FRENCH GOVERNMENT TOURIST OFFICE** • United States (610 5th Ave., New York, NY 10020, tel. 212/757–1125). **Canada** (1981 McGill Collège Ave., Suite 490, Montreal, Quebec H3A 2W9, tel. 514/288–4264). **United Kingdom** (178 Piccadilly, London W1V 0AL, tel. 0171/491–7622).

➤ **GERMAN NATIONAL TOURIST OFFICE** • United States (122 E. 42nd St., 52nd Floor, New York, NY 10168, tel. 212/661–7200). **Canada** (175 Bloor St. E, Suite 604, Toronto, Ontario M4W 3R8, tel. 416/969–1570). **United Kingdom** (Nightingale House, 65 Curzon St., London W1Y 7PE, tel. 0171/495–3990).

➤ **GREEK NATIONAL TOURIST ORGANIZATION** • United States (645 5th Ave., 5th Floor, New York, NY 10022, tel. 212/421–5777). **Canada** (1233 Rue de la Montagne, Montreal, Quebec H3G 1Z2, tel. 514/871–1535). **United Kingdom** (4 Conduit St., London W1R 0DJ, tel. 0171/734–5997).

➤ **HUNGARIAN TRAVEL BUREAU (IBUSZ)** • United States (1 Parker Plaza, Suite 1104, Fort Lee, NJ 07024, tel. 201/592–8585). **United Kingdom** (Danube Travel Ltd., 6 Conduit St., London W1R 9TG, tel. 0171/493–0263).

➤ **IRISH TOURIST BOARD** • United States (757 3rd Ave., New York, NY 10017, tel. 212/418–0800). **Canada** (160 Bloor St. E, Suite 934, Toronto, Ontario M4W 1B9, tel. 416/929–2777). **United Kingdom** (Ireland House, 150 New Bond St., London W1Y 0AQ, tel. 0171/493–3201).

➤ **ITALIAN GOVERNMENT TOURIST OFFICE (ENIT)** • United States (630 5th Ave., Suite 1565, New York, NY 10111, tel. 212/245–4822). **Canada** (1 Place Ville Marie, Suite 1914, Montreal, Quebec H3B 3M9, tel. 514/392–6206). **United Kingdom** (1 Princes St., London W1R 8AY, tel. 0171/408–1254).

➤ **LUXEMBOURG NATIONAL TOURIST OFFICE** • United States (801 2nd Ave., New York, NY 10017, tel. 212/370–9850). **United Kingdom** (122–124 Regent St., London W1R 5FE, tel. 0171/434–2800).

➤ **MOROCCAN TOURIST OFFICE** • United States (20 E. 46th St., Suite 1201, New York, NY 10017, tel. 212/557–2520). **Canada** (2001 Rue Université, Suite 1460, Montreal, Quebec H3A 2A6, tel. 514/ 842–8111). **United Kingdom** (205 Regent St., London W1R 7DE, tel. 0171/437–0073).

➤ **NETHERLANDS BOARD OF TOURISM** • United States (355 Lexington Ave., 21st Floor, New York, NY 10017, tel. 212/370–7367). **Canada** (25 Adelaide St. E, Suite 710, Toronto, Ontario M5C 1Y2, tel. 416/363–1577). **United Kingdom** (25–28 Buckingham Gate, London SW1E 6LD, tel. 0171/630–0451).

➤ **NORTHERN IRELAND TOURIST BOARD** • **United States** (2551 5th Ave., 7th Floor, New York, NY 10176, tel. 212/922–0101 or 800/326–0036). **Canada** (111 Avenue Rd., Toronto, Ontario M5R 3J8, tel. 416/925–6368).

➤ **NORWEGIAN TOURIST BOARD** • **United States** (655 3rd Ave., New York, NY 10017, tel. 212/949–2333). **United Kingdom** (Charles House, 5–11 Lower Regent St., London SW1Y 4LR, tel. 0171/839–6255).

➤ **POLISH NATIONAL TOURIST OFFICE (ORBIS)** • **United States** (500 5th Ave., New York, NY 10110, tel. 212/867–5011). **United Kingdom** (82 Mortimer St., London W1N 7DE, tel. 0171/580–8028).

➤ **PORTUGUESE NATIONAL TOURIST OFFICE** • **United States** (590 5th Ave., 4th Floor, New York, NY 10036, tel. 212/354–4403). **Canada** (2180 Yonge St., Toronto, Ontario M4S 2B9, tel. 416/250–7575). **United Kingdom** (22–25 Sackville St., London W1X 1DE, tel. 0171/494–1441).

➤ **ROMANIAN NATIONAL TOURIST OFFICE** • **United States** (342 Madison Ave., Suite 210, New York, NY 10173, tel. 212/697–6971). **United Kingdom** (17 Nottingham Pl., London W1M 3RD, tel. 0171/224–3692).

➤ **SPANISH NATIONAL TOURIST OFFICE** • **United States** (665 5th Ave., New York, NY 10022, tel. 212/759–8822). **Canada** (102 Bloor St. W, Suite 1400, Toronto, Ontario M5S 1M8, tel. 416/961–3131).

➤ **SWEDISH TOURIST BOARD** • **United States** (655 3rd Ave., New York, NY 10017, tel. 212/949–2333). **United Kingdom** (29–31 Oxford St., 5th Floor, London W1R 1RE, tel. 0171/437–5816).

➤ **SWISS NATIONAL TOURIST OFFICE** • **United States** (608 5th Ave., New York, NY 10020, tel. 212/757–5944). **Canada** (154 University Ave., Suite 610, Toronto, Ontario M5H 3Y9, tel. 416/971–9734). **United Kingdom** (Swiss Centre, 1 New Coventry St., London W1V 8EE, tel. 0171/734–1921).

➤ **TURKISH TOURIST OFFICE** • **United States** (821 U.N. Plaza, New York, NY 10017, tel. 212/687–2194). **United Kingdom** (170–173 Piccadilly, 1st Floor, London W1V 9DD, tel. 0171/734–8681).

STUDENT TRAVEL ORGANIZATIONS Student Travel Australia (**STA**) has 120 offices worldwide and offers low-price airfares to destinations around the globe. STA also offers the American Youth Hostels card (*see below*), the ISIC (International Student Identity Card), the IYC (International Youth Card), and the ITC (International Teacher Card), as well as their own STA Travel Card (about $6) for recent graduates, which proves eligibility for some travel discounts. Write or call one of the following offices for a slew of free pamphlets on services and rates, or info on the STA nearest you. *United States: 5900 Wilshire Blvd., Suite 2100, Los Angeles, CA 90036, tel. 213/937–1150. United Kingdom: Priory House, 6 Wrights Lane, London W8 6TA, tel. 171/938–4711. Australia: 224 Faraday St., Carlton, Melbourne Victoria 3053, tel. 3/347–6911. New Zealand: 10 High Street, Box 4156, Auckland, tel. 9/309–9723.*

Council on International Educational Exchange (**CIEE**) (205 E. 42nd St., New York, NY 10017, tel. 212/661–1414) is a nonprofit organization dedicated to the pursuit of work, study, and travel abroad. Through its two subsidiaries, Council Travel and Council Charter, CIEE offers budget-travel services, including discounted airfares, rail passes, accommodations, and guidebooks. **Council Travel** is an international network of travel agencies that specializes in the diverse needs of students, youths, and teachers. They also issue American Youth Hostels card, the ISIC, the IYC, and the ITC. At least 30 Council Travel offices serve the budget traveler in the United States, and there are about a dozen in Britain, France, and Germany.

TOP 5 Ways to Save Money While Traveling

5. Ship yourself in a crate marked "Livestock." Remember to poke holes in the crate.

4. Board a train dressed as Elvis and sneer and say "The King rides for free."

3. Ask if you can walk through the Channel Tunnel.

2. Board the plane dressed as an airline pilot, nod to the flight attendants, and hide in the rest room until the plane lands.

1. Bring a balloon to the airline ticket counter, kneel, breathe in the helium, and ask for the kiddie fare.

But if you're serious about saving money while you're traveling abroad, just get an ISIC--the International Student Identity Card. Discounts for students on international airfares, hotels and motels, car rentals, international phone calls, financial services, and more.

Travel CUTS (Canadian Universities Travel Service, Ltd.) (187 College St., Toronto, Ontario M5T 1P7, tel. 416/979–2406) is a full-service travel agency that sells discounted airline tickets to Canadian students and issues the ISIC, IYC, and hostel cards. Their 25 offices are on or near college campuses. Call weekdays 9–5 for information and reservations.

Educational Travel Center (ETC) (438 N. Francis St., Madison, WI 53703, tel. 608/256–5551) sells tickets to students and real people for low-cost flights (most departing from Chicago) within the continental United States and around the world. ETC claims to beat student and charter fares. They also issue hostel cards. For more details, request their free brochure, "Taking Off."

Hostelling International (HI) (Box 37613, Washington, DC 20013, tel. 202/783–6161), formerly the IYHF, is the umbrella group for a number of national youth hostel associations. Membership in any national youth hostel association (*see below*) allows you to stay at an HI-affiliated hostel at member rates (about $10–$22 per night). Members also have priority if the hostel is full and are eligible for discounts on rail and bus travel around the world. Travelers of any age can join one of the following hostel organizations and stay in hostels worldwide for the same price or only a few dollars more than those under 26.

The Highs and the Lows

The following are the average daily maximum and minimum temperatures (in degrees Fahrenheit) for some European cities:

	Jan.	Mar.	May	July	Sept.	Nov.
Amsterdam	40/34	47/38	61/50	70/59	65/56	47/41
Athens	55/44	60/46	77/61	92/73	84/67	66/53
Brussels	40/30	51/36	65/46	73/54	69/51	48/38
Bucharest	34/19	50/30	74/51	86/60	78/52	49/35
Budapest	34/25	50/36	72/52	82/61	73/54	46/37
Copenhagen	36/28	41/31	61/46	71/57	64/51	45/38
Dublin	46/34	51/37	60/43	67/52	63/48	51/39
Helsinki	26/17	34/23	56/44	73/57	56/46	39/30
Lisbon	57/46	63/50	71/55	81/63	79/62	63/52
London	43/36	50/38	62/47	71/56	65/52	50/42
Madrid	47/35	59/41	70/50	87/63	77/57	55/42
Munich	35/23	48/30	64/45	74/55	67/48	44/33
Oslo	28/19	39/25	61/43	72/55	60/46	38/31
Paris	43/34	54/39	68/49	76/58	70/53	50/40
Prague	36/25	46/32	66/46	75/55	68/50	46/36
Rome	52/40	59/45	74/56	87/67	79/62	61/49
Sofia	35/25	50/33	69/50	81/60	70/52	48/37
Stockholm	30/23	37/26	58/43	71/57	60/49	40/34
Turkey	46/37	51/38	69/53	82/65	76/61	59/48
Vienna	34/25	47/30	67/50	76/60	68/53	45/37
Warsaw	32/22	42/28	67/48	75/58	66/49	42/33

A one-year membership with **American Youth Hostels (AYH)** (Box 37613, Washington, DC 20013, tel. 202/783-6161) costs about $25 for adults age 18-55 (renewal $25) and $10 for those under 18 (renewal $10). Other national hostel associations include **Canadian Hostelling Association (CHA)** (1600 James Naismith Dr., Suite 608, Gloucester, Ontario K1B 5N4, tel. 613/748-5638); **Youth Hostel Association of England and Wales (YHA)** (Trevelyan House, 8 St. Stephen's Hill, St. Albans, Herts. AL1 2DY, England, tel. 01727/55215); **Australian Youth Hostels Association (YHA)** (Box 61, Strawberry Hills, Sydney 2012, New South Wales, tel. 02/212-1266); and **Youth Hostels Association of New Zealand (YHA)** (Box 436, Christchurch 1, tel. 03/799-970).

STUDENT AND TEACHER ID CARDS

The **International Student Identity Card (ISIC)** entitles students 12 years of age and older to special discounts at museums, theaters, sports events, and many other attractions. If purchased in the United States, the $16 cost for the popular ISIC card also buys you limited sickness and accident insurance, emergency medical evacuation insurance, and access to a 24-hour international, toll-free hotline for assistance in medical, legal, and financial emergencies. In the United States, apply to STA or CIEE offices (see Student Travel Organizations, above); in Canada, the ISIC is available for C$12 from Travel CUTS (see Student Travel Organizations, above). In the United Kingdom, students with valid university IDs can purchase the ISIC at any student union or student-travel company. Applicants must submit a photo as well as proof of current full-time student status, age, and nationality.

The **Go 25: International Youth Travel Card (IYC)**, formerly known as the FIYTO (Federation of International Youth Travel Organisations) card, is issued to travelers (students and nonstudents) under age 26 and provides services and benefits similar to those given by the ISIC card. The $16 card is available from the same organizations that sell the ISIC. When applying, bring a passport-size photo and your passport as proof of your age.

The $17 **International Teacher Identity Card (ITIC)**, sponsored by the International Student Travel Confederation, is available to teachers of all grade levels, from kindergarten to graduate school. The services and benefits you get when buying the card are similar to those for the two previous cards. When you buy the card, ask for the International Teacher Identity Card Hardbook, which has all the details.

HOW MUCH IT WILL COST

Even in the most expensive European countries (France, Germany, Great Britain, Switzerland, and the Scandinavian countries), budget travelers will rarely spend more than $50-$60 a day, less if they're willing to rough it a bit. But, happily, if you have a EurailPass in hand, all it takes is a few hours on a train to get to somewhere much cheaper. Although prices in Eastern Europe are rising steadily, you can stay in cities like Prague and Budapest for about $20-$30 a day. Greece and Turkey are also big travel bargains. Though you may spend 24 hours on a bone-jarring bus or train to get here, once you arrive you're unlikely to spend more than $20-$25 a day in Turkey, $30-$35 in Greece. For each chapter, we have given a ballpark figure of how much it costs to travel in that country, as well as the exchange rate for that country's currency at press time. Check the financial section of a major newspaper or call your local bank's international department for the latest exchange rates.

WHEN TO GO

Most travelers descend on Europe in the summer, when school is out and the weather is warm. Although it may be the best time to come if you want to bask on the beach or hike around the north, you will be faced with crowds, the highest prices of the year, and possibly the hostility of locals who are tired of the tourist infestation. Winter means relative solitude everywhere except at the winter resorts, but the availability of services may be lower, the daylight hours are distressingly few in the north, and bad weather can leave you huddling by the radiator in your hotel room (*if* your hotel room has a radiator, that is). If you actually get to choose when you travel, you can't beat late spring and early fall for a happy balance; crowds and prices are moderate, and the weather is generally good.

PASSPORTS AND VISAS

Travelers from outside Europe will need a passport to visit any of the countries in this book, and travelers from United Kingdom will need either a passport or a Visitor's Passport (good for Western European travel only) to visit a foreign country. Visas, government passport stamps that authorize you to stay in the country for a certain period of time, are not often required for visitors from the United States, Canada, the United Kingdom, Australia, or New Zealand who are staying in any one country for less than three months; exceptions are noted in the Basics sections of the appropriate chapters. Countries that require visas will sometimes issue them on the spot upon entry; with other countries, you have to apply to the relevant consulate several weeks before leaving home. Eastern Europe keeps flip-flopping on its visa requirements, so talk to the embassy or consulate in your home country before leaving on your trip.

If you plan to stay in any one country for more than three months, you'll almost certainly need a visa; talk to that country's consulate before you leave home. If you didn't plan to stay, but just can't bear to leave your hostel in the mountains or your new Euro-boyfriend, contact the country's immigration officials or local police well before your three months are up.

One more bureaucratic note: Having certain visas in your passport is frowned upon when entering certain other countries. This is not generally a problem for European travelers, but if you are planning on visiting Israel and might want to visit an Arab country (like Morocco) in the future, ask that the Israeli visa be placed on a separate piece of paper (and not actually in your passport), so you can remove it before you hit customs in Morocco. With the Israeli stamp you *might* be denied entrance to Morocco entirely. The same goes for entering Greece with a visa from Cyprus.

OBTAINING A PASSPORT Do not put this off. The wheels of bureaucracy often grind slowly, so apply for a passport as soon as you start planning your trip.

➤ **U.S. CITIZENS** • First-time applicants, those whose most recent passport was issued more than 12 years ago or before they were 16, those whose passports have been lost or stolen, and travelers between the ages of 13 and 17 (a parent must also accompany them) must apply for a passport in person. Other renewals can be taken care of by mail. Apply at one of the 13 U.S. Passport Agency offices a *minimum* of five weeks ahead of your departure. For fastest processing, apply between August and December. If you blow it, you can have a passport issued within five days of departure if you have your plane ticket in hand. This method will probably work, but if there's one little glitch in the system, you're out of luck. Local county courthouses, many state and probate courts, and some post offices also accept passport applications.

Have the following items ready when you go to get your passport:

• A completed passport application (form DSP-11), available at courthouses, some post offices, and passport agencies.

• Proof of citizenship (certified copy of birth certificate, naturalization papers, or previous passport issued in the past 12 years).

• Proof of identity with your photograph and signature (for example, a valid driver's license, employee ID card, military ID, student ID).

• Two recent identical, 2"-square photographs (black-and-white or color head shots).

• A $55 application fee for a 10-year passport, $30 for those under 18 for a five-year passport. First-time applicants are also hit with a $10 surcharge. If you're paying cash, exact change is necessary; checks or money orders should be made out to Passport Services.

For more information or an application, contact the Department of State Office of Passport Services (tel. 202/647–0518) and dial your way through their message maze.

Those lucky enough to be able to renew their passports by mail must send a completed Form DSP-82 (available from a Passport Agency); two recent, identical passport photos; their current passport (less than 12 years old); and a check or money order for $55 ($30 for those under 18). Send everything to the nearest Passport Agency. Renewals take from three to four weeks.

Passport applications can be picked up at U.S. post offices, at federal or state courts, and at the U.S. Passport Agency in Boston, Chicago, Honolulu, Houston, Los Angeles, Miami, New Orleans, New York, Philadelphia, San Francisco, Seattle, Stamford, CT, and Washington, DC.

➤ **CANADIAN CITIZENS** • Canadians should send a completed passport application (available at any post office or passport office) to the Bureau of Passports (Suite 215, West Tower, Guy Favreau Complex, 200 René Lévesque Blvd. W, Montreal, Quebec H2Z 1X4, tel. 514/283–2152). Include C$35, two recent, identical passport photographs, the signature of a guarantor (as specified on the application), and proof of Canadian citizenship (original birth certificate or other official document as specified). You can also apply in person at regional passport offices in many locations, including Edmonton, Halifax, Montreal, Toronto, Vancouver, and Winnipeg. Passports have a shelf life of five years and are not renewable. Processing takes about two weeks by mail and five working days for in-person applications.

➤ **U.K. CITIZENS** • Passport applications are available through travel agencies, a main post office, or one of six regional passport offices (in London, Liverpool, Peterborough, Belfast, Glasgow, and Newport). The application must be countersigned by your bank manager or by a solicitor, barrister, doctor, clergyman, or justice of the peace who knows you personally. Send or drop off the completed form; two recent, identical passport photos; and a £15 fee to a regional passport office (address is on the form). Passports are valid for 10 years (five years for those under 18) and take about four weeks to process.

➤ **AUSTRALIAN CITIZENS** • Australians must visit a post office or passport office to complete the passport application process. A 10-year passport for those over 18 costs AUS$76, and the under-18 crowd can get a five-year passport for AUS$37. For more information, call toll-free in Australia 008/02–60–22 weekdays during regular working hours.

➤ **NEW ZEALAND CITIZENS** • Passport applications can be found at any post office or consulate. Completed applications must be accompanied by proof of citizenship, two passport-size photos, and a letter from a friend confirming the applicant's identity. The fee is NZ$50 for a 10-year passport. Processing takes about three weeks.

LOST PASSPORTS If your passport is lost or stolen while you are traveling, you should immediately notify the local police and nearest embassy or consulate (addresses are given in each chapter). A consular officer should be able to wade through some red tape and issue you a new one, or at least get you back into your country of origin without one. The process will be slowed up considerably if you don't have some other forms of ID on you, so you're well advised to carry any other forms of ID (a driver's license, a copy of your birth certificate, a student ID) separate from your passport, and tuck a few copies of the front page of your passport in your luggage and your traveling companion's pockets.

A United States embassy or consulate will usually only issue a new passport in emergencies. In nonemergency situations, the staff will affirm your affidavit swearing to U.S. citizenship, and this paper will get you back to the United States. The British embassy or consulate requires a police report, any form of identification, and three passport-size photos. They will replace the passport in four working days. Canadian citizens face the same requirements as the Brits, but you must have a guarantor with you: someone who has known you for at least two years, lives within the jurisdiction of the consulate or embassy, and is a mayor, practicing

Fortunately, when you travel on Rail Europe, there are some sights you'll miss.

No goofy hats. No big sunglasses. No plaid shirts with striped shorts. Instead, on Rail Europe, you'll experience Europe the way Europeans do. You'll enjoy scenic countryside no one else can show you. And meet unique and interesting people. In short, you'll explore Europe the way it was meant to be explored. When it comes to visiting 33 European countries, get real. Go Rail Europe. Because traveling any other way could end up showing you some pretty dreadful sights. To learn more, call your travel agent or 1-800-4-EURAIL. (1-800-438-7245)

Rail Europe

Europe. To the trained eye.

lawyer, notary public, judge, magistrate, police officer, signing officer at a bank, medical doctor, or dentist. Since most travelers do not know anyone fitting this description, there is also the option of paying an officer of the consulate/embassy to be your guarantor—proving once again that throwing enough money at a problem usually makes it go away. A replacement passport usually takes five working days. New Zealand officials ask for two passport-size photos, while the Australians require three, but both can usually replace a passport in 24 hours.

TRAIN PASSES

Train passes can be a great deal if you are covering a lot of ground in a short period of time and can save you time standing in lines waiting to buy tickets. However, you have to choose your pass carefully to avoid spending more on rail travel than you did to fly to Europe in the first place.

Before plunking down hundreds of dollars on a pass you should consider several issues. First, add up the prices of the rail trips you plan; some travel agents have a manual that lists ticket prices, or you can call Rail Europe at 800/438–7245. Good luck getting through. If you are under 26, subtract about 30% from that number; you can probably save about that much buying a BIJ ticket in Europe (see Getting Around, in Staying in Europe, below). If the number you get is more than or roughly equal to the price of a pass that would suit your needs, you should probably spring for the pass.

If you're under 26 years of age on your first day of travel, it's always a better deal to get a youth pass of some sort (Europass Youth, Eurail Youth Flexipass, or Eurail Youthpass). Youth passes are always good only for second-class travel. If you're 26 or over on your first day of travel, you're not eligible for a youth pass, and you will have to buy one of the (much more expensive) passes good for first-class travel. Travelers 26 and older might do better buying individual second-class tickets.

Be sure to buy your rail pass before leaving home. They are technically not available once you arrive in Europe, though you might be able to buy one for a slightly inflated price at some discount travel agencies in big European cities. Also, if you have firm plans to go to Europe next year, you might want to look into buying your pass this year (you have six months from the date of purchase to start using it), since prices go up each year on December 31. The following passes are available from student travel organizations (see above), many travel agents, and Rail Europe (tel. 800/438–7245).

Don't be suckered in by Rail Europe's claim that the **EurailPass,** valid for unlimited first-class train travel through 17 countries (Austria, Belgium, Denmark, Finland, France, Germany, Greece, Hungary, Italy, Luxembourg, Netherlands, Norway, Portugal, Republic of Ireland, Spain, Sweden, and Switzerland) is "the best buy in rail travel." Unless you want to practically live on the train, it's probably not worth your while. It's available for periods of 15 days ($498), 21 days ($648), one month ($798), two months ($1,096), and three months ($1,398). If you're under 26, the **Eurail Youthpass** is a better deal. One or two months of unlimited second-class train travel cost $578 or $768, respectively. Fifteen days of unlimited travel will cost you $398.

A **Eurail Saverpass** costs a little less than a comparable EurailPass. A pass good for 15 days of first-class travel is $430, for 21 days $550, and for one month $687. This pass requires that a minimum of two people each buy a Saverpass and travel together at all times. Between April 1 and September 30, there is a three-person minimum.

Unlike the EurailPass and Eurail Saverpass, which are good for unlimited travel for a certain period of time, the Eurail Flexipass allows you to travel for five, 10, or 15 days within a two month period. The Flexipass is valid in the same countries as the EurailPass. You can buy five days of travel for $348, 10 days for $560, and 15 days for $740. The under-26 crowd can get the second-class **Eurail Youth Flexipass,** good for five days ($255), 10 days ($389), or 15 days ($540).

The **Europass** (first-class) and the **Europass Youth** (second-class), good only for travel in Italy, France, Switzerland, Germany, and Spain, are the latest things to hit the market. With these passes you can travel for five days in three contiguous countries ($280, $198 second-class), for eight days in four contiguous countries ($394, $282 second-class), or for 11 days in all five countries ($508, $366 second-class). In all cases, the days of travel can be spread out for up to two months, and you can add up to two extra travel days ($38 each, $28 second-class) to the first two passes, up to four extra travel days to the pass good in all five countries.

As well as the above passes, which are good in a number of countries, there are dozens of other passes that are good for travel only within a single country or within a certain region (Scandinavia or Eastern Europe, for example). Information on these passes is given in the Basics section of individual chapters. Call the country's government tourist office (*see* Useful Organizations, *above*) to find out how to buy these passes.

MONEY

Cash never goes out of style, but traveler's checks and major credit cards are usually the safest and most convenient way to pay your way while on the road. Depending on the length of your trip, strike a balance among the three. You can exchange your traveler's checks for local currency in most Western European cities, and many upscale establishment will take plastic. If you're going to Eastern Europe or other remote locations, though, it doesn't hurt to have some extra U.S. dollars stashed away; many Eastern European establishments prefer or even demand cash, and changing traveler's checks outside urban areas may be tough. Protect yourself by carrying your stash in a money belt or necklace pouch (available at luggage or camping stores) and by keeping accurate records of traveler's checks' serial numbers, credit-card numbers, and emergency phone numbers for reporting loss or theft of your cards or checks.

You lose money every time you exchange currency, so try to avoid changing so much of your money to foreign currency that you end up having to exchange it back as you leave the country.

CHANGING MONEY The best place to exchange your cash or traveler's checks into the local currency varies from country to country; we've given suggestions in the Basics sections of each chapter. Sometimes you'll get the best rates at a post office, sometimes at a bank, and occasionally at a private exchange office. When you think you've found a fabulous exchange rate, ask if they charge a commission; some places take up to 5% off the top, though 2%–3% is more common. It helps to exchange money during regular business hours when you have the greatest number of options.

It's always cheaper to buy a country's currency in that country, rather than at home. In other words, you'll get a better deal buying Spanish pesetas in Spain than at your bank in the United States. However, it's still a good idea to change $30 or so into foreign currency before you arrive in a country in case the exchange booth at the train station or airport at which you arrive is closed or has an unbearably long line.

TRAVELER'S CHECKS Traveler's checks may look like play money, but they work much better. They can sometimes be used for purchases in the same way as a personal check, but usually you'll have to exchange them into the local currency before spending them. You can buy traveler's checks at most banks and credit unions. American Express traveler's checks are still the most widely accepted brand.

Card members can order **American Express** traveler's checks in U.S. dollars and six foreign currencies by phone, free of charge if you've got a gold card, or for a 1% commission with your basic green card. AmEx also issues **Traveler's Cheques for Two,** checks that can be signed and used by either you or your traveling companion. At their Travel Services offices (about 1,500 around the world), you can usually buy and cash traveler's checks, write a personal check in exchange for traveler's checks, report lost or stolen checks, exchange foreign currency, and have mail held (just have it addressed to your name and the office's address). Ask for the "American Express Traveler's Companion," a handy little directory of their offices. *Tel. 800/221–7282 in the U.S. and Canada.*

11

Citibank and other banks worldwide issue **Citicorp** traveler's checks in U.S. dollars and some foreign currencies. For 45 days after you buy the checks, you have access to the 24-hour International S.O.S. Assistance hotline, which can provide English-speaking doctor, lawyer, and interpreter referrals; assistance with loss or theft of travel documents; traveler's-check refund assistance; and an emergency message center. *Tel. 800/645–6556 in the U.S. or 813/623–1709 collect from outside the U.S.*

If you don't have an AmEx gold card, you can still get American Express Traveler's Checks fee free with an AAA membership. Talk to the cashier at your local AAA office.

MasterCard International traveler's checks, issued in U.S. dollars only, are offered through banks, credit unions, and foreign-exchange booths. Call for information about acceptance of their checks at your travel destination and for the local number to call in case of loss or theft. *Tel. 800/223–7373 in the U.S. or 609/987–7300 collect from outside the U.S.; 447/ 335–02–995 toll-free or 07/335–02–995 collect in Europe.*

As a sponsor of the '92 Olympics, **Visa** boosted its name recognition and acceptance worldwide. Checks are available in at least 10 currencies. *Tel. 800/227–6811 in the U.S. and Canada for refund referral service, 415/574–7111 collect from outside the U.S.*

➤ **LOST OR STOLEN CHECKS** • Unlike cash, traveler's checks, once lost or stolen, can be replaced or refunded *if* you keep the purchase agreement and a record of the checks' serial numbers. Common sense dictates that you keep the purchase agreement separate from your checks. Caution-happy travelers will even give a copy of the purchase agreement and checks' serial numbers to someone back home. Most traveler's checks issuers promise to refund or replace lost or stolen checks in 24 hours. Who knows? You might get lucky. In a safe place—or several safe places—record the toll-free or collect telephone number to call in case of emergencies.

CREDIT CARDS Major credit cards are accepted in larger towns and tourist haunts and sometimes in small towns and rural areas as well. Check merchants' windows for the card logos. Don't rely too heavily on your plastic, though; many small restaurants and shops operate on a cash-only basis. Still, credit cards can be fabulously helpful in an emergency or to buy that pair of obscenely expensive Italian shoes to take home. And, when you're really strapped, you can usually take your Visa, MasterCard, or American Express into a bank and walk out with a cash advance (*see* Getting Money from Home, *below*).

GETTING MONEY FROM HOME Provided there's money at home to be had, there are at least seven ways to get it: (1) Have it sent through a commercial bank that has a branch in the town where you're staying. Unless you have an account with that bank, you'll have to go through your own bank, and the process will be slower and more expensive. (2) If you're an American Express cardholder, cash a personal check at an American Express office for up to $1,000 every 21 days, usually given in traveler's checks rather than cash. (3) **Express Cash** allows American Express cardholders to withdraw up to $1,000 every 21 days from their personal checking accounts via ATMs. Each transaction carries a 2% fee, with a minimum charge of $2 and a maximum of $6. Apply to AmEx for a personal identification number (PIN) at least two to three weeks before departure. Call 800/CASH–NOW for an application. (4) An **American Express MoneyGram** can be a dream come true if you can convince someone back home to go to an American Express MoneyGram agent, fill out the necessary form, and transfer cash to replenish your empty wallet. Fees vary according to the amount of money sent but average about 8%–10%. You have to get the transaction reference number from your sender back home and show ID when picking up the money. For locations of American Express MoneyGram agents in the United States, call 800/543–4080; overseas call collect 303/980–3340. (5) **MasterCard** and **Visa** cardholders can get cash advances from many banks, even in small towns. The commission for this service is usually only a few dollars, but interest on the advance generally starts accumulating immediately—there's no month's grace period like there is when you make purchases with your card. If you get a PIN number for your card before you leave home, you might even be able to make the transaction with an

This guidebook teaches you how to budget your money.

This page is for slow learners.

We all make mistakes. So if you happen to find yourself making a costly one, call Western Union. With them you can receive money from the States within minutes at any of our European locations. Plus, it's already been converted into the appropriate currency.

Just call our numbers in Austria 0222 892 0380, Belgium 02 753 2150, Denmark 800 107 11, Finland 9 800 20440, France 161 43 54 46 12, Germany 069 2648201, 0681 933 3328, Greece 01 687 3850, Ireland 1 800 395 395*, Italy 02 95 457 305, Netherlands 06 0566*, Poland 2 231 7008, Spain 93 301 1212, Sweden 020 741 742, United Kingdom 0 800 833 833*, or if you are in the United States 1 800 325 6000*.

And since nobody's perfect, you might want to keep these numbers in your wallet, for those times when nothing else is in there.

WESTERN UNION | MONEY TRANSFER

The fastest way to send money worldwide.[SM]

* Toll free within country.

ATM machine. (6) Have funds sent through **Western Union** (tel. 800/325–6000). Have someone take cash, a certified cashier's check, or a healthy MasterCard or Visa to a Western Union office. The money will reach the requested destination in two business days but may not be available for several more hours or days, depending on the whim of the local authorities. (7) In extreme emergencies (arrest, hospitalization, or worse), there is one more way U.S. citizens can receive money overseas: by setting up a **Department of State Trust Fund.** A friend or family member sends money to the Department of State, which then transfers the money to the U.S. embassy or consulate in the city in which you're stranded. Once this account is established, you can send and receive money through Western Union, bank wire, or mail, all payable to the Department of State. For information, talk to the Department of State's Citizens' Emergency Center (tel. 202/647–5225).

➤ **CASH MACHINES** • ATMs are popping up all over Europe, and they can be a real lifesaver if you luck into one at the right time. Unfortunately, it's very difficult to get anyone to tell you if your little piece of plastic (whether a bank card linked to your checking or savings accounts or a credit card) will work in any European ATMs. It very likely will, but your bank may be quite clueless. It can't hurt to ask, though.

Many foreign ATMs won't accept PINs (personal identification numbers) with more than four digits, so you may want to reprogram your PIN if it's long. If you know your PIN number as a word, learn the numerical equivalent before you leave, since some ATM keypads show no letters, only numbers.

LUGGAGE

Like new shoes, fully packed luggage should be broken in: If you can't tote your bag all the way around the block at home, it's going to be worse than a ball and chain in Europe. Lockers and baggage check rooms are available in most airports, train, and bus stations, but you'll save time and money if you can easily carry your belongings with you.

Bags with a long strap (preferably wide and padded) can be worn across your body to distribute weight and minimize vulnerability to bag-snatching. This method will still result in aching shoulders if the bag is too heavy. If you plan to be doing a lot of walking, a backpack's your best bet.

BACKPACKS By distributing the weight of your luggage across your shoulders and hips, backpacks ease the burden of traveling. You can choose among four types of packs: day packs (best for short excursions), external-frame packs (for longer travels or use on groomed trails), internal-frame packs (for longer travels across rougher terrain), and travel packs (hybrid packs that fit under an airline seat and travel well in cities or the backcountry). Although external frames achieve the best weight-distribution and allow airspace between you and your goodies, they're more awkward and less flexible than packs with an internal frame. Since an external frame backpack will run you about $100–$225 (internal frames are about $50 more), be sure to have it fitted correctly when you buy it. Check to see that it is waterproof, or bring an extra waterproof poncho to throw over it in downpours. The disadvantage of packs is that you can't disguise 'em—you're branded as a foreign, student traveler. And in cities, especially on public transportation, you may have a hard time negotiating yourself and your pack through doorways or down crowded aisles.

The Sleep Sheet Defined: Take a big sheet. Fold it down the middle the long way. Sew one short side and the long, open side. Turn inside out. Get inside. Sleep.

WHAT TO PACK

As little as possible. Besides the usual suspects—clothes, toiletries, camera, a Walkman, and a good book, bring along a day pack or some type of smaller receptacle for stuff; it'll come in handy not only for day excursions but also for those places where you plan to stay for only one or two days. You can check heavy, cumbersome bags at the train or bus station (or leave it at your hotel or hostel) and carry only the essentials with you while you look for lodging.

BEDDING If you're planning to stay in hotels, you won't need to bring any bedding. Hostels require that you use a sleep sheet, and, though many rent them, some don't. If you have a backpack, consider a sleeping mat that can be rolled tightly and strapped onto the bottom of your pack; these make train- and bus-station floors a tad more comfy.

CLOTHING Smart—and not terribly fashion-conscious— travelers will bring two outfits and learn to wash clothes by hand regularly. At the very least, bring comfortable easy-to-clean clothes. Bring several T-shirts and one sweatshirt or sweater for cooler nights. Socks and undies don't take up too much room, so throw in a couple extra pairs. Obviously, those traveling in winter or in the north will need clothes they can layer for warmth, and some sort of rain gear. While you don't want to be caught unprepared for the weather, it might be better to resort to buying a sweater in Norway than to tote around an expedition-weight parka for a month before realizing you're never going to make it north of Belgium.

Before tossing a blow-dryer into your bag, consider that European electrical outlets pump out 220 volts, enough to explode or implode American appliances. If you absolutely must have that electric toothbrush, you need a converter that matches your appliance's wattage and the outlet's current. In addition to taking up precious packing space, a converter costs about $15.

Packing light does not mean relying on a pair of cut-off shorts and a tank top to get you through any situation. Shorts, if not frowned upon, will almost certainly brand you as a foreigner in many countries. And you may find that Europeans dress a little more formally than Americans. Also, travelers who plan on visiting churches, especially in southern Europe, should take at least one modest outfit. Italians are especially strict, often insisting that women cover their shoulders and arms.

Shoes may be your best friend or worst foe: A sturdy pair of walking shoes or hiking boots (broken in before your trip) and a spare pair (probably sandals) allow you to switch off and give your tootsies a rest. Plastic sandals or thongs protect feet on hostile shower floors and are also useful if you're camping or beach-hopping.

TOILETRIES Use a separate, waterproof bag to pack your toiletries; the pressure on airplanes can cause lids to pop off and create instant moisturizer slicks inside your luggage. Bring all the paraphernalia you need to conduct chemical warfare on your contact lenses, if you wear them, though you should be able to find supplies in Western European cities. Bring some toilet paper with you and have some in your pockets at all times; public rest rooms never seem to have any. Finally, bring insect repellent, sunscreen, and lip balm from home.

LAUNDRY For the average traveler, hotel rooms are the best place (and certainly the cheapest) to do laundry. A bring-your-own laundry service includes a plastic bottle of liquid detergent or soap (powder doesn't break down as well), a rubber drain cover, about six feet of clothesline (enough to tie to two stable objects), and some plastic clips (bobby pins or paper clips can substitute). Porch railings, shower curtain rods, bathtubs, and faucets can all serve as wet-laundry hangers if you forget the clothesline. Be sure to bring an extra plastic bag or two for still-damp laundry and dirty clothes. When doing laundry in a hotel room, be tidy and discreet. Many hotel owners are understandably edgy about the thought of your wet socks dripping on their centuries-old wooden floors.

CAMERAS AND FILM Keep film as cool as possible, away from direct sunlight or blazing campfires. If your camera is new, or new to you, shoot and develop a few rolls before leaving home to avoid spoiling travel footage with prominent thumb shots or miscalculated f-stops. The smaller and lighter the camera, the better, unless you're a photo artiste. Pack some lens tissue and an extra battery for cameras with built-in light meters. Consider splurging on a $10 skylight filter to protect your lens and reduce haze in your photos.

On a plane trip, unprocessed film is safest in your carry-on luggage—ask security to inspect it by hand. (It helps to keep your film in a plastic bag, ready for quick inspection.) Inspectors at American airports are required by law to honor requests for hand inspection, so don't be afraid to demand your rights (if you've got no contraband hiding in your luggage, that is). All airport scanning machines used in U.S. airports are safe for any number of scans from five to 500, depending on the speed of your film. The higher the film speed, the more susceptible it is to damage. The effects are cumulative, so you don't have to worry until you pass the five-scan mark.

MISCELLANEOUS Stuff you might not think to take but will be damn glad to have: (1) extra day pack for valuables or short jaunts, (2) flashlight, (3) Walkman, (4) pocket knife, (5) water bottle, (6) sunglasses, (7) several large zip-type plastic bags (useful for wet swimsuits, towels, leaky bottles, and stinky socks), (8) travel alarm clock, (9) needle and small spool of thread, (10) batteries, and (11) some interesting books.

CUSTOMS AND DUTIES

Going through customs when you arrive in Europe is usually pretty painless. The officials will check your passport and have you fill out a form, but often won't touch your luggage unless you look too shady or their dogs have caught a whiff of something interesting in your bags. If you bring any expensive equipment with you from home, such as cameras or video gear, carry the original receipt or register it with customs before leaving home (in the United States ask for U.S. Customs Form 4457). Otherwise, you may end up paying duty on your return.

U.S. CUSTOMS Like most government organizations, the U.S. Customs Service enforces a number of mysterious rules that presumably make sense to some bureaucrat somewhere. You're unlikely to have run-ins with customs as long as you *never* carry any illegal drugs in your luggage. When you return to the United States, you have to declare all items you bought abroad, but you won't have to pay duty unless you come home with more than $400 worth of foreign goods, including items bought in duty-free stores. For purchases between $400 and $1,000, you have to pay 10%. You also have to pay tax if you exceed your duty-free allowances: 1 liter of alcohol or wine, 100 non-Cuban cigars or 200 cigarettes, and one bottle of perfume. A free leaflet about customs regulations, "Know Before You Go," gives tedious details about customs regulations. Write to the U.S. Customs Service (Box 7407, Washington, DC 20044, tel. 202/647–0518) and ask for the publication by name.

CANADIAN CUSTOMS Exemptions for returning Canadians depend on how long you've been out of the country; for two days out, you're allowed to return with C$100 worth of goods; for one week out, you're allowed C$300 worth. Above these limits, you're taxed 20% (more for items shipped home). In any given year, you're allowed only one $300 exemption. Duty-free limits are 50 cigars, 200 cigarettes, 2.2 pounds of tobacco, and 40 ounces of liquor—all must be declared in writing upon arrival at customs and must be with you or in your checked baggage. To mail back gifts, label the package "Unsolicited Gift–Value under $40." For more scintillating details, request a copy of the Canadian Customs brochure "I Declare/Je Déclare" from Revenue Canada Customs and Excise Department (Connaught Bldg., 3rd Floor, 555 MacKenzie Ave., Ottawa, Ontario K1A OL5, tel. 613/957–0275).

U.K. CUSTOMS Travelers age 17 or over who return to the United Kingdom from France and other European Union (formerly European Community) countries may bring back the following duty-free goods, provided they were *not* bought in a duty-free shop: 300 cigarettes or 150 cigarillos or 75 cigars or 400 grams of tobacco, 1.5 liters of alcohol over 22% volume or 5 liters of alcohol under 22% volume, 5 liters of still table wine, 75 grams of perfume, ³⁄₈ liters of eau de toilette, and other goods worth up to £250. For more information, contact the customs office.

AUSTRALIAN CUSTOMS Australian travelers 18 and over may bring back, duty free: 1 liter of alcohol, 250 grams of tobacco products (equivalent to 250 cigarettes or cigars), and other articles worth up to $AUS400. If you're under 18, your duty-free allowance is $AUS200. To avoid paying duty on goods you mail back to Australia, mark the package

So, you're getting away from it all.

Just make sure you can get back.

AT&T Access Numbers
Dial the number of the country you're in to reach AT&T.

*AUSTRIA†††	022-903-011	*GREECE	00-800-1311	NORWAY	800-190-11
*BELGIUM	0-800-100-10	*HUNGARY	00◇-800-01111	POLAND†◆²	0◇010-480-0111
BULGARIA	00-1800-0010	*ICELAND	999-001	PORTUGAL†	05017-1-288
CANADA	1-800-575-2222	IRELAND	1-800-550-000	ROMANIA	01-800-4288
CROATIA†◆	99-38-0011	ISRAEL	177-100-2727	*RUSSIA† (MOSCOW)	155-5042
*CYPRUS	080-90010	*ITALY	172-1011	SLOVAKIA	00-420-00101
CZECH REPUBLIC	00-420-00101	KENYA†	0800-10	S. AFRICA	0-800-99-0123
*DENMARK	8001-0010	*LIECHTENSTEIN	155-00-11	SPAIN •	900-99-00-11
*EGYPT¹ (CAIRO)	510-0200	LITHUANIA◆	8◇196	*SWEDEN	020-795-611
*FINLAND	9800-100-10	LUXEMBOURG	0-800-0111	*SWITZERLAND	155-00-11
FRANCE	19◇-0011	F.Y.R. MACEDONIA	99-800-4288	*TURKEY	00-800-12277
*GAMBIA	00111	*MALTA	0800-890-110	UKRAINE†	8◇100-11
GERMANY	0130-0010	*NETHERLANDS	06-022-9111	UK	0500-89-0011

Countries in bold face permit country-to-country calling in addition to calls to the U.S. **World Connect℠** prices consist of **USADirect®** rates plus an additional charge based on the country you are calling. Collect calling available to the U.S. only. *Public phones require deposit of coin or phone card. ◇Await second dial tone. †May not be available from every phone. †††Public phones require local coin payment through the call duration. ◆Not available from public phones. • Calling available to most European countries. ¹Dial "02" first, outside Cairo. ²Dial 010-480-0111 from major Warsaw hotels. ©1994 AT&T.

Here's a travel tip that will make it easy to call back to the States. Dial the access number for the country you're visiting and connect right to AT&T. It's the quick way to get English-speaking AT&T operators and can minimize hotel telephone surcharges.

If all the countries you're visiting aren't listed above, call **1 800 241-5555** for a free wallet card with all AT&T access numbers. Easy international calling from AT&T. **TrueWorld Connections.**

AT&T

All the Best Trips Start with Fodor's

"Australian goods returned." For more rules and regulations, request the pamphlet "Customs Information for Travellers" from a local Collector of Customs (Collector of Customs, GPO Box 8, Sydney NSW 2001, tel. 02/226–5997).

NEW ZEALAND CUSTOMS Travelers over age 17 are allowed, duty-free: 200 cigarettes or 250 grams of tobacco or 50 cigars or a combo of all three up to 250 grams, 4½ liters of wine or beer, one 1,125ml bottle of spirits, and goods with a combined value up to $NZ700. For details, ask for the pamphlet "Customs Guide for Travellers" from a New Zealand consulate or any customs office.

STAYING HEALTHY

There are few serious health risks associated with travel in Europe. The U.S. Centers for Disease Control warns of a tick-borne encephalitis problem in Central and Eastern European countries, but if you avoid tramping through wooded areas and drinking unpasteurized milk, you should be fine. Many travelers, though, suffer from mild diarrhea and nausea. It's more often caused by stress and changes in diet than any nasty bacteria in the water. In general, common sense prevails. Get plenty of rest, watch out for sun exposure, don't drink water from a river, eat balanced meals—do we sound like your mother yet?

FIRST-AID KIT You may spend your entire trip thinking your first-aid kit is nothing but extra bulk. However, if you get seasick on the way to Greece or slice your pinkie with your Swiss Army knife in the Alps, you'll be glad to have even the most basic first-aid kit, with items like Dramamine, sunscreen, antacid, bandages, antiseptic, tweezers, and aspirin. Needless to say, this list can become much more elaborate; add to it based upon your own individual frailties. However, self-medication should only be relied on for short-term illnesses; seek professional help if any symptoms persist or worsen. Don't expect to get prescriptions filled abroad; get any you might need filled at home and bring an ample supply with you.

HEALTH AND ACCIDENT INSURANCE Some general health-insurance plans cover health expenses incurred while traveling, so review your existing health policy (or your parent's policy, if you're a dependent) before leaving home. Most university health-insurance plans stop and start with the school year, so don't count on school spirit to pull you through. Canadian travelers should check with their provincial ministry of health to see if their resident health-insurance plan covers them on the road. Budget- and student-travel organizations, such as STA and CIEE (*see* Student Travel Organizations, *above*), and credit-card conglomerates also sometimes include health-and-accident coverage with the purchase of an ID or credit card. If you buy an ISIC card, you're automatically insured for $100 a day for in-hospital sickness expenses, $3,000 for accident-related medical expenses, and $10,000 for emergency medical evacuation. For details, request a summary of coverage from CIEE (INS Dept., 205 E. 42nd St., New York, NY 10017–5706). Several private companies also offer coverage designed to supplement existing health insurance for travelers, and travel agents often provide travel-insurance information and sell policies.

Carefree Travel Insurance (Box 310, 120 Mineola Blvd., Mineola, NY 11501, tel. 516/294–0220 or 800/323–3149) is, in fact, pretty serious about providing coverage for emergency medical evacuation and accidental death or dismemberment. It also offers 24-hour medical phone advice.

International SOS Assistance (Box 11568, Philadelphia, PA 19116, tel. 215/244–1500 or 800/523–8930) provides emergency evacuation services, worldwide medical referrals, and medical insurance.

Travel Assistance International (1133 15th St., NW, Suite 400, Washington, DC 20005, tel. 202/331–1609 or 800/821–2828) offers emergency evacuation services and 24-hour medical referrals.

Travel Guard (1145 Clark St., Stevens Point, WI 54481, tel. 715/345–0505 or 800/782–5151) provides an insurance package that includes coverage for sickness, injury (or untimely death), lost baggage, and trip cancellation. You can choose from an advance purchase ($19), super advance purchase ($39), or a megaplan for trips up to 180 days (8% of your travel costs).

PRESCRIPTIONS Bring as much as you need of any prescription drugs as well as your prescription (packed separately). Ask your doctor to type the prescription and include the following information: dosage, the generic name, and the manufacturer's name. To avoid problems clearing customs, diabetic travelers carrying syringes should have handy a letter from their physician confirming their need for insulin injections.

To be on the safe side, bring condoms from home. Do you really want to trust your life to 5¢ Bulgarian condoms that tend to fall apart when you open the package?

CONTRACEPTIVES AND SAFE SEX Some European countries have been hit extremely hard by the AIDS crisis, and no country is free of the disease. Condoms are widely available in pharmacies in most European countries, though they are of questionable quality in some areas. If you forgot to bring some from home, look for familiar, hopefully reliable brands, available in Western European and Scandinavian countries. You may have to ask for condoms (they're often kept behind the counter), and you might get leered at if you're a woman buying condoms in the south.

The pill, IUDs, and diaphragms are available in most Western European countries, but you have to go to a doctor for a prescription, and it's hardly the sort of thing you'd want to do on a vacation.

PRECAUTIONS

PROTECTING YOUR VALUABLES If there's something you would really hate to lose, leave it at home. That way, the most valuable possessions you'll have with you are your passport, traveler's checks, air and rail tickets, and possibly some medications. These things aren't very bulky, so save yourself a lot of stress and keep them on you in a neck or waist pouch. If you opt for a neck pouch, wear it *under* your clothing, not just swinging in the breeze where any half-witted thief can loop it over your silly neck. Waist pouches are best worn under clothes, too, with the zipper zipped and facing your body.

Once you've got that valuable passport, rail pass, and money in your money belt, don't take it off—not on trains, not in hostels, not even in the shower (well, okay—but just for a minute). Those travelers in the next bed are not necessarily above grabbing your stuff while you sleep. Be especially careful on trains. If you're sleeping in a *couchette* (second-class bunk), use your luggage as a pillow or a teddy bear and get real cozy with it. In regular cars, don't drift off when your bag is on the rack over your head; it's much too simple for someone to sweep it down and hop off at the next stop.

DRUGS AND ALCOHOL Drug consumption and possession are almost always punishable by fines or a jail sentence, and trying to transport drugs across borders is just asking to be extradited or imprisoned. Keep in mind that border officials don't do *random* searches—they specifically select the scruffier backpackers. But even if you dress to the hilt specifically to cross the border, you never know when there will be dogs waiting to nail you. Drug *sale* is also a big no-no—if you're caught, you'll go to jail for sure. If you get busted for drugs (or breaking any other law), your embassy might say a few sympathetic words but cannot give you one iota of legal help. You're on your own.

WOMEN TRAVELERS

Women traveling in Europe get a mixed bag of reactions. To grossly generalize, women are treated extremely well in the north. Men have figured out that harassing women is not okay, and many big cities have women's resource centers and rape crisis organizations. In the south, and especially in Greece, Turkey, Morocco, and southern Italy, men will often hiss or whistle at women or follow them for short distances. Western women traveling alone are often considered easy, or even worse; one of our writers was offered 2,000 drachmas by a Greek man who wanted to sleep with her. As well as taking commonsense precautions (not walking in isolated areas at night, not telling men where they're staying), women should not advertise their singleness, maybe saying they are meeting a boyfriend later.

GAY AND LESBIAN TRAVELERS

Although many big cities like Amsterdam and Paris have a visible and happening gay scene, most of Europe, and especially vehemently Catholic countries, has a dim view of homosexuality. Homosexuality is technically illegal in a few countries (including Romania), but for the most part gay travelers will face no worse than a frosty reception. Contact the following organizations before leaving home for more info on your destination, or talk to the gay and lesbian organizations we list in individual chapters to find out about the scene. Another resource is *Are You Two . . . Together? The Gay and Lesbian Travel Guide to Europe*, by Pamela Brandt and Lindsy Van Gelder (Random House, 1991). This and other books for gay and lesbian travelers can be found at any good travel bookstore.

The Fraternal Order of Gays (FOG) Travel Service (304 Gold Mine Dr., San Francisco, CA 94131, tel. 415/641–0999) arranges tours and can make bookings.

International Gay Travel Association (IGTA) (Box 4974, Key West, FL 33041, tel. 800/448–8550) is a nonprofit organization of 387 members worldwide that provides listings of member agencies.

International Lesbian and Gay Association (ILGA) (81 rue Marché au Charbon, 1000 Brussels 1, Belgium, tel. 32/2–502–2471) is a good source of info on conditions, specific resources, and hot spots in any given country.

RESOURCES FOR THE DISABLED

Accessibility may soon have an international symbol if an initiative begun by the Society for the Advancement of Travel for the Handicapped (SATH) catches on. *H,* a bold, underlined, capital H, is the symbol that SATH is publicizing for hotels, restaurants, and tourist attractions to indicate that the property is wheelchair accessible. Reviews in this book indicate when properties are wheelchair accessible.

Some countries have organizations to disseminate information to disabled travelers and have taken steps to insure that trains and hotels are accessible. In other countries, however, the tourist organizations don't know what to say when asked about accessibility. It never hurts to call the country's government tourist agency (*see* Useful Organizations, *above*) and ask about relevant publications and organizations, but it's also important to contact an organization that knows a bit about travel for the disabled (*see below*). While awareness of the needs of travelers with disabilities increases every year, budget opportunities are harder to find. Always ask if discounts are available, either for you or for a companion.

Many trains and train stations in Western Europe are wheelchair accessible, though many in more remote locations are not. Call Rail Europe (tel. 800/438–7245) for information about accessibility where you will be traveling.

ORGANIZATIONS **Flying Wheels Travel** (143 W. Bridge St., Box 382, Owatonna, MN 55060, tel. 800/535–6790 or 800/722–9351 in MN) arranges cruises, tours, and vacation travel itineraries.

Mobility International USA (MIUSA) (Box 3551, Eugene, OR 97403, tel. 503/343–1284 for voice and TDD) is an internationally affiliated, nonprofit organization that coordinates exchange programs for disabled people around the world and offers information on accommodations and organized study programs for their members. Membership ($20 annually) gives you discounts on publications, services, MIUSA travel and educational programs, and a free quarterly newsletter. Nonmembers may subscribe to the newsletter for $10.

Moss Rehabilitation Hospital's Travel Information Service (1200 W. Tabor Rd., Philadelphia, PA 19141–3009, tel. 215/456–9603; TDD 215/456–9602) provides information on tourist sights, transportation, accommodations, and accessibility in destinations around the world. You can request and receive information by state or by country for a $5 postage and handling fee. They also provide toll-free telephone numbers for airlines with special lines for the hearing-impaired.

The Society for the Advancement of Travel for the Handicapped (347 5th Ave., Suite 610, New York, NY 10016, tel. 212/447–7284, fax 212/725–8253) is a nonprofit educational group that works to inform and educate people about travel for the disabled. Annual membership costs $45, or $25 for students and senior citizens, and entitles you to a quarterly newsletter that details new tours, tourism guides, resources, and late-breaking political advances for the disabled. Members can also request information about a specific destination; send $2 and a stamped, self-addressed envelope.

Travel Industry and Disabled Exchange (**TIDE**) (5435 Donna Ave., Tarzana, CA 91356, tel. 818/368–5648) publishes a quarterly newsletter and a directory of travel agencies and tours targeted for disabled travelers. The annual membership fee is $15.

PUBLICATIONS *Access to the World: A Travel Guide for the Handicapped,* by Louise Weiss, is highly recommended for its worldwide coverage of travel boons and busts for the disabled. It's available from Henry Holt & Co. (tel. 800/247–3912) for $12.95; the order number is 0805001417.

The Itinerary (Box 2012, Bayonne, NJ 07002, tel. 201/858–3400) is a bimonthly travel magazine for the disabled. It's not available in bookstores, so get your one-year subscription for $10.

Twin Peaks Press (Box 129, Vancouver, WA 98666, tel. 206/694–2462 or, for orders, only 800/637–2256) publishes *Travel for the Disabled,* which offers helpful hints as well as a comprehensive list of guidebooks and facilities geared to the disabled. Their *Directory of Travel Agencies for the Disabled* lists more than 350 agencies throughout the world. Each is $19.95 plus $2 ($3 for both) shipping and handling. Twin Peaks also offers a "Traveling Nurse's Network," which puts disabled travelers in touch with registered nurses to aid and accompany them on their trip. Travelers fill out an application that Twin Peaks matches to nurses' applications in their files. The rest of the arrangements, such as destination and nurse's pay, are left to the traveler. An application is $10.

RESOURCES FOR PEOPLE OF COLOR

The situations that people of color will face in Europe vary widely from country to country, and there is no umbrella organization that provides information and resources on the subject. In more cosmopolitan areas, people of color will rarely attract attention. In more remote locations, curiosity far outweighs prejudice—the constant attention can be annoying, but usually doesn't blossom into full-fledged antagonism. An African-American writer in Romania wrote, "Out in the country, I was like someone from Mars; people were too amazed to be upset."

In countries where racism against African immigrants is common, locals may not understand or care that you haven't immigrated from Africa, and they may be somewhat antagonistic. In most places, though, locals see African-Americans as Americans first and foremost. If you find yourself in a sticky situation, it may be best to emphasize that you are an American (or a Briton, or an Australian) traveling through the country.

WORKING ABROAD

If you are a citizen of an EU country, you can usually go to work in any other EU country without a lot of hassle. If you're not from an EU country, it's going to be tougher. Unemployment in many European countries is high, and locals are often reluctant to give jobs to foreigners. Plenty of people find short-term jobs teaching English, waiting tables, or doing seasonal agricultural work, though this usually isn't exactly legal. To do it the official way, you need to get a prospective employer to vouch that she absolutely, positively needs you, and not a native, to fill the position. With this endorsement you can get the needed work permit and a visa. For more information on the process and job opportunities, look at some of the following publications. **World Trade Academy Press** (50 E. 42nd St., Suite 509, New York, NY 10017, tel.. 212/697–4999) publishes *Looking for Employment in Foreign Countries* ($16.50 plus $3.50 shipping). **Addison Wesley** publishes *International Jobs: Where They Are, How to Get Them* for $12.45. Call 800/447–2226 to order. **InterExchange, Inc.** (161 6th Ave., New York, NY 10013, tel. 212/9240–0446) is a nonprofit organization that produces pamphlets on work-abroad programs, including resort work, farm work, and English teaching.

If you're a student, the easiest way to arrange work in Europe is through **CIEE**'s Work Abroad and International Voluntary Service Departments (205 E. 42nd St., New York, NY 10017, tel. 212/661–1414, ext. 1130). CIEE arranges work permits for a price and publishes resource books on work opportunities. Check out CIEE's publication *Work, Study, Travel Abroad: The Whole World Handbook* to learn about all the red tape you're going to face.

VOLUNTEER PROGRAMS **Service Civil International/International Voluntary Service** works for peace and international understanding through two- to three-week work camps in the United States (fee: $35), Europe (fee: $75), and Eastern Europe (fee: $100). You must be 16 or older to participate in U.S. camps, 18 or older for the European camps. *Innisfree Village, Rte. 2, Box 506, Crozet, VA 22932, tel. 804/823–1826.*

Volunteers for Peace sponsors two- to three-week international work camps in the United States, Europe, Africa, Asia, and Central America for around $125. If you're interested, send for their **International Workcamp Directory** ($10), which lists more than 800 opportunities. *43 Tiffany Rd., Belmont VT, 05730, tel. 802/259–2922.*

The Council on International Educational Exchange arranges short- and long-term voluntary service in the United States and abroad. *Volunteer!* ($8.95 + shipping and handling) is a comprehensive guide to volunteering around the world. *205 E. 42nd St., New York, NY 10017, tel. 212/661–1414.*

STUDYING ABROAD

Studying in another country is the perfect way to scope out a foreign culture, meet locals, and improve your language skills. You may choose to study through a U.S.-sponsored program, usually through an American university, or to enroll in a program sponsored by a European organization. Do your homework; study programs vary greatly in expense, academic quality, exposure to language, amount of contact with local students, and living conditions. Tap into the resources below.

Working through your local university is the easiest way to find out about study-abroad programs in Europe. Most universities have staff members to distribute information on programs at European universities, and they might be able to put you in touch with program participants.

The **American Institute for Foreign Study/American Council of International Studies** (313 E. 43rd St., New York, NY 10017, tel. 800/237–4636; 102 Greenwich Ave., Greenwich, CT 06830, tel. 800/727–2437; in Boston, tel. 617/421–9575; in San Francisco, tel. 800/222–6379) and the **Council on International Educational Exchange (CIEE)** (University Programs Dept., 205 E. 42nd St., New York, NY 10017, tel. 212/661–1414) manage study-abroad programs at various European universities. The **Experiment in International Living/School for International Training** (**EIL**) (Kipling Rd., Box 676, Battleboro, VT 05302, tel. 800/451–4465) offers the Semester Abroad Program. The **Institute of International Edu-**

cation (IIE) (809 U.N. Plaza, New York, NY 10017, tel. 212/883–8200) publishes two comprehensive guides: *Academic Year Abroad* and *Vacation Study Abroad.*

Coming and Going

Flexibility is the key to getting a serious bargain on airfare. If you can play around with your departure date, amount of luggage carried, and return date, you will probably save money. You should also stay flexible about the city to which you fly; it's difficult to generalize about fares, but flights to London are usually the cheapest, followed by flights to Paris, Brussels, Frankfurt, and Amsterdam. If you have a rail pass of some sort, you'll might save money by flying into one of these cities and hopping on the train to where you really want to go. On your fateful departure day, remember that check-in time for international flights is a long two hours before the scheduled departure. For an in-depth study of tackling plane travel, consult *The Airline Traveler's Guerilla Handbook,* by George Albert Brown (Blake Publishing Group, 320 Metropolitan Sq., 15th St., NW, Washington, DC 20005; $14.95).

BUYING A TICKET Although airline tickets may be your biggest single expense, planning ahead can save you hundreds. Options include charter flights, flying standby, student discounts, courier flights, and APEX (Advance Purchase Excursion) and Super-APEX fares; read on to help get through this maze.

When your travel plans are still in the fantasy stage, start studying the travel sections of major Sunday newspapers: Courier companies, charter flights, and fare brokers often list incredibly cheap flights. Many newspapers also publish a chart of destinations and the current lowest fares available with major carriers. Travel agents, who have access to computer networks that show the lowest fares before they're advertised, are another obvious resource. Budget travelers are the bane of travel agents, though, whose commission is based on the ticket prices. Try travel agencies on or near college campuses; they often cater to this pariah class.

Hot tips when making reservations: If the reservation clerk tells you that the least expensive seats are no longer available on a certain flight, ask to be put on a waiting list. If the airline doesn't keep waiting lists for the lowest fares, call them on subsequent mornings and ask about cancellations and last-minute openings—airlines trying to fill all their seats sometimes add additional cut-rate tickets at the last moment. When setting travel dates, remember that off-season fares can be much lower and there will also be fewer people vying for the inexpensive seats at those times. Ask which days of the week are the cheapest to fly. Finally, even when you have your ticket in hand, call a few days before the flight to confirm your spot.

APEX tickets may be the simplest way to go; if you know exactly when you want to go and it's not tomorrow (or the next day, or the next . . .), then just buying your ticket ahead can save you a bundle and guarantee you a seat. Regular APEX fares normally apply to tickets bought at least 21 days in advance; you can get Super-APEX fares if you know your travel plans at least a month in advance. Here's the catch: If you cancel or change your plans, you'll pay a penalty, usually $50–$100.

CONSOLIDATORS AND BUCKET SHOPS Consolidator companies, also known as bucket shops, buy blocks of tickets at wholesale prices from airlines trying to fill flights. Check out any consolidator's reputation with the Better Business Bureau before starting; most are perfectly reliable, but it's better to be safe than sorry. Then register with the consolidator and, usually in conjunction with their staff, work up a list of possible destinations and departure dates. The week before you leave, the consolidators will contact you and give you a list of the flights they think they can get you on. You're obligated to accept one of these flights, even if it wasn't your first choice. If you don't, the consolidators probably won't put too much effort into getting you on another flight.

It goes without saying that you can't be too choosy about which city you fly into. Other drawbacks: Consolidator tickets are often not refundable, and the flights to choose from often feature indirect routes, long layovers, and undesirable seating assignments. If your flight is delayed or canceled, you'll also have a tough time switching airlines. As with charter flights, you risk taking a huge loss if you change your travel plans, but at least you'll be on a regularly scheduled flight with less risk of cancellation than on a charter (*see below*). If possible, pay with a credit card, so if your ticket never arrives, you don't have to pay. Bucket shops generally advertise in newspapers—be sure to check restrictions, refund policies, and payment conditions.

Airhitch (2790 Broadway, Suite 100, New York, NY 10025, tel. 212/864–2000; 1341 Ocean Ave., Suite 62, Santa Monica, CA 90401, tel. 310/458–1006) was created by and for students (although others can use it) to provide low-price, last-minute seats on airplanes bound for Western Europe. One-way tickets to Europe from the East Coast cost $169; from the West Coast, $269; and from selected points in between, $229. If you plan to use Airhitch, though, be forewarned: Some people have been left languishing in the airport for days waiting for an available flight home.

Other well-known consolidators are **Access International** (101 W. 31st St., Suite 1104, New York, NY 10001, tel. 212/465–0707 or 800/825–3633), **UniTravel** (1177 N. Warson Rd., Box 12485, St. Louis, MO 63132, tel. 314/569–2501 or 800/325–2222), and **Up & Away Travel** (141 E. 44th St., Suite 403, New York, NY 10017, tel. 212/972–2345). **Sunline Express** (607 Market St., San Francisco, CA 94105, tel. 415/541–7800 or 800/786–5463) is a fare broker that specializes in bargain fares to Mexico but also deals in fares to Europe. Again, check travel sections for more listings.

STANDBY AND THREE-DAY-ADVANCE-PURCHASE FARES Flying standby is almost a thing of the past. The idea is to purchase an open ticket and wait for the next available seat on the next available flight to your chosen destination, but most airlines have dumped standby policies in favor of three-day-advance-purchase youth fares, which are open only to those under 25 and (as the name states) only within three days of departure. Return flights must also be booked no earlier than three days prior to departure. Three-day-advance works in the off-season, when flights aren't usually jam-packed, and the savings are substantial, but you might be waiting for weeks to get a flight in the summer.

There are also a number of brokers that specialize in discount and last-minute sales, offering savings on unsold seats on commercial carriers and charter flights, as well as tour packages. If you're desperate to get to Paris by Wednesday, try **Last Minute Travel Club** (tel. 617/267–9800).

CHARTER FLIGHTS Charter flights have vastly different characteristics, depending on the company you're dealing with. Generally speaking, a charter company either buys a block of tickets on a regularly scheduled commercial flight and sells them at a discount (this is the prevalent form in the United States) or may lease the whole plane and then offer relatively cheap fares to the public (most common in the United Kingdom). Although they subject you to a few potential drawbacks (infrequent flights, restrictive return-date requirements, lickety-split payment demands), a charter company may offer the cheapest ticket at the time you want to travel, especially during high season, when advance-purchase fares are most expensive. Make sure you find out a company's policy on refunds should a flight be canceled by either yourself or the airline. Summer charter flights fill up fast and should be booked a few months in advance.

You're in much better shape when the company is offering tickets on a regular commercial flight. After you've bought the ticket from the charter folks, you generally deal with the airline directly. When a charter company has chartered the whole plane, things get a little sketchier: Bankrupt operators, long delays at check-in, overcrowding, and flight cancellation are fairly common. You can minimize risks by checking the company's reputation with the Better Business Bureau and taking out enough trip-cancellation insurance to cover the operator's potential failure.

The following list of charter companies is by no means exhaustive; check newspaper travel sections for more extensive listings: **DER Tours** (Box 1606, Des Plaines, IL 60017, tel. 800/782–2424), **Travel Charter** (1120 E. Long Lake Rd., Troy, MI 48098, tel. 313/528–3570 or

800/521–5267), **Travel CUTS** (187 College St., Toronto, Ont. M5T 1P7, tel. 416/979–2406), and **Council Charter** (tel. 212/661–0311 or 800/800–8222).

STUDENT DISCOUNTS Student discounts on airline tickets are offered through **CIEE,** the **Educational Travel Center, STA Travel,** and **Travel CUTS** (*see* Student Travel Organizations, *above*). Keep in mind that you will *not* receive frequent-flier mileage for discounted student, youth, or teacher tickets. For discount tickets based on your status as a student, youth, or teacher, have an ID when you check in that proves it: an International Student Identity Card, Youth Identity Card, or International Teacher Identity Card.

COURIER FLIGHTS A few restrictions and inconveniences are the price you'll pay for the colossal savings on airfare offered to air couriers, the travelers who accompany letters and packages between designated points. Restrictions include luggage limitations (check-in luggage space is used for the freight you're transporting, so you take carryons only), limited stays of a week or two, and often a limit of one courier on any given flight.

Now Voyager (74 Varick St., Suite 307, New York, NY 10013, tel. 212/431–1616) connects 18-and-over travelers scrounging for cheap airfares with companies looking for warm bodies to escort their packages overseas. Flights in the summer and over school holidays are in high demand, so try to book two months in advance. Departures are from New York, Newark, Houston, or Miami; destinations may be in Europe, Asia, or Mexico (City, that is). Most flights are one week in length, with round-trip fares ranging from $150 on up. A nonrefundable $50 registration fee, good for one year, is required. Call for current offerings.

Check newspaper travel sections or the yellow pages of your phone directory for other courier companies, or mail away for a telephone directory that lists companies by the cities to which they fly. Send a self-addressed, stamped envelope to **Pacific Data Sales Publishing** (2554 Lincoln Blvd., Suite 275-I, Marina Del Rey, CA 90291). **A Simple Guide to Courier Travel** gives tips on flying as a courier. Send $17.95 (includes postage and handling) to Discount Travel (Box 331, Sandy, UT 84091) or call them at 800/344–9375.

TAKING LUGGAGE ABOARD You've heard it a million times. Now you'll hear it once again: Pack light. U.S. airlines allow passengers to check two pieces of luggage, neither of which can exceed 62 inches (length + width + height) or weigh more than 70 pounds. If your airline accepts excess baggage, it will probably charge you for it. Foreign-airline policies vary, so call or check with a travel agent before you show up at the airport with one bag too many.

If you're traveling with a pack, tie all loose straps to each other or onto the pack itself, as they tend to get caught in luggage conveyer belts. Put valuables like cameras and important documents in the middle of packs, wadded inside clothing, because outside pockets are extremely vulnerable to probing fingers.

Anything you'll need during the flight (and valuables to be kept under close surveillance) should be stowed in a carryon bag. Foreign airlines have different policies but generally allow only one carryon in tourist class, in addition to a handbag and a bag filled with duty-free goodies. The carry-on bag cannot exceed 45 inches (length + width + height) and must fit under the seat or in the overhead luggage compartment. Call for the airline's current policy. Passengers on U.S. airlines are limited to one carry-on bag, plus coat, camera, and handbag (women get a break here). Carry-on bags must fit under the seat in front of you; maximum dimensions

Bikes in Flight

Most airlines will ship your bike, provided it is dismantled and packed in a box sold for around $10 by many airlines. Domestic flights charge bike-toting travelers about a $45 fee, more if the bike is the third piece of luggage. International travelers can usually substitute a bike for the second piece of checked luggage at no extra charge; otherwise, it will cost $100 extra.

are 9 x 45 x 22 inches. Hanging bags can have a maximum dimension of 4 x 23 x 45 inches; to fit in an overhead bin, bags can have a maximum dimension of 10 x 14 x 36 inches. If your bag is too porky for compartments, be prepared for the humiliation of rejection and last-minute baggage check.

Staying in Europe

GETTING AROUND

If you're really interested in seeing Europe cheaply, trains are the way to go. If you're short on time and want to go to the edges of the continent (to Turkey, Helsinki, or northern Norway, for example), seriously consider flying if you don't want to spend a hell of a lot of time on trains, buses, and ferries.

BY TRAIN European trains vary from the sublime to the ridiculous. In France, Germany, Switzerland, and Scandinavia the trains are almost unfailingly clean and punctual. The farther south and east you go, however, the more unreliable and crowded trains generally get. In certain places in Greece, Turkey, and Eastern Europe, the rickety trains take so long to get to their destination you might as well walk. Prices generally correspond to efficiency. You'll pay about $50 to travel a few hundred miles in France, about $10 to travel the same distance in Hungary. For the most part, though, European trains are a budget traveler's godsend, toting passengers across the continent in good time at relatively good prices.

Before you leave home, you should consider buying a rail pass (*see* Train Passes, in Planning Your Trip, *above*). These passes give you either unlimited travel for a certain period of time, or a certain number of days of travel taken within a two-month period. If you have opted not to buy a pass, you still shouldn't have to pay full price for train tickets very often. If you're spending a lot of time in one country, a country-specific rail pass (described in the Basics section of many chapters) may be a good deal. Another often-overlooked option is the *Billet International de Jeunesse* (International Youth Ticket), usually known as a **BIJ** or **BIGE** ticket. Travelers under the age of 26 can buy an international train ticket for about 30% off the regular second-class fare and make unlimited stops along the way for up to two months. BIJ tickets are available at budget travel agencies like Wasteels in major cities all over Europe. Look under the heading Bucket Shops in this book for likely candidates.

Most trains have first- and second-class compartments, but the difference in comfort is minimal on almost all routes. Get second-class tickets unless you want to waste money and hang out with the business travelers with laptop computers. If you're taking an overnight train, however, pay about $17 for a *couchette*, or second-class bunk. Couchettes are usually six to a compartment. It's not the Ritz, and if all six bunks are filled it's going to be pretty crowded, but six to eight hours of sleep in the prone position can do wonders for your disposition the next day. Even if you don't want to, you may be required to pay the supplement for a couchette on some overnight trains.

To make yourself as comfortable as possible while traveling, bring a bottle of water and some food. Food and drinks sold on the train are expensive (and not very good), and it's amazing how many friends you can make with a baguette, some Brie, and bottle of wine in your bag.

As soon as you tell anyone you are taking an overnight train, they will immediately regale you with stories of all the people they know who were robbed while sleeping on the train. Thefts do occur, but if you take some precautions, you shouldn't let that spoil a good night's sleep. Never, ever leave your luggage unattended, even if it means schlepping your backpack to the bathroom, and sleep with your money and passport strapped to your body and your luggage under your arm. Just pretend it's your significant other. Leaving it up on the luggage rack while you snore is asking for someone to grab it and run.

BY BUS Although the European train network is extensive, at times you'll find that buses are the only way to go. You might also find that in Great Britain, Ireland, Turkey, and parts of Eastern Europe, buses are either significantly cheaper than trains or much quicker and more comfortable. We tell you the best way to go in each country chapter of this book. The big difficulty in long-distance bus travel is finding the right company. In many big cities, a chaos of companies serves different routes; talk to the tourist office or a local budget travel agency to navigate the murky waters of bus schedules.

BY CAR In Europe, trains and buses are so efficient and rental cars are so expensive that few budget travelers resort to driving a car during their vacation. If you're traveling with a group, however, and trying to cover an area poorly served by public transportation, you might find that renting a car is the easiest and even the cheapest way to go (even though gas can cost $4 a gallon). Timid drivers should be wary of renting a car. Signs and bewildering traffic rules vary from country to country, and navigating in a country where you may not even know the alphabet, much less the language, can unnerve even hardened L.A. drivers. If you accept the challenge, invest in some good road maps and seek out alternative main roads (to help avoid speed-demon drivers and hefty tolls charged on many main thoroughfares).

Discount travel agencies in major cities are usually the best places to look for bargain airfares, discount train tickets, and long-distance bus schedules. You'll find the names and addresses of these places under the heading Bucket Shops in the Basics section of most large cities in this book.

Drivers with licenses issued by an EU country are not required to get an **International Driver's Permit (IDP)**. U.S., Canadian, and Australian licenses are valid in a few European countries, but it's best to go ahead and get an IDP if you plan on driving; it might make things a little easier if you're pulled over for a traffic violation, and some car rental companies will require that you have one. The IDP is available through the American and Canadian Automobile Associations. AAA charges about $16 for a license, $10 if you bring your own passport photos when you apply. Those who aren't members of AAA will pay a few dollars more. Call your local office for info on the application process. You should be able to get an IDP on the spot at most AAA locations in about 15 minutes.

RENTAL CARS Rental rates vary widely and usually include unlimited free mileage and standard liability coverage. Most major car-rental companies are represented in Europe, including **Avis** (tel. 800/331–1212, 800/879–2847 in Canada, 0181/848–8765 in the United Kingdom); **Budget** (tel. 800/527–0700); **Hertz** (tel. 800/654–3131, 800/263–0600 in Canada, 0181/679–1799 in the United Kingdom); and **National** (tel. 800/227–7368, 0181/950–4080 in the United Kingdom). You can expect a discount of about 15%–30% if you call ahead and reserve a car.

Other sources of savings are the several companies that operate as wholesalers—companies that do not own their own fleets but rent in bulk from those that do. Rentals through such companies must be arranged and paid for before you leave home. Among them are **Auto Europe** (Box 1097, Camden, ME 04843, tel. 207/236–8235, 800/223–5555, or 800/458–9503 in Canada); **Connex International** (23 N. Division St., Peekskill, NY 10566, tel. 914/739–0066, 800/333–3949, or 800/843–5416 in Canada); **Europe by Car** (mailing address: 1 Rockefeller Plaza, New York, NY 10020; walk-in address: 14 W. 49th St., New York, NY 10020, tel. 212/581–3040 or 212/245–1713); **Foremost Euro-Car** (5430 Van Nuys Blvd., Suite 306, Van Nuys, CA 91401, tel. 818/786–1960 or 800/272–3299); and **Kemwel** (106 Calvert St., Harrison, NY 10528, tel. 914/835–5555 or 800/678–0678). Their rates are even better in summer, when business travel is down. Always ask for all the fine-print details (required deposits, cancellation policies, etc.) in writing.

BY PLANE Flying from one European city to another is often a costly process, but it can save you heaps of time on trains, buses, and ferries if you are headed for remote areas. Most Western European countries have good internal services linking the capital city with major business and industrial centers, though these may be the least useful flights for budget travelers. In countries such as Sweden, Norway, Greece, and to some extent the United Kingdom, air service is a vital link between main cities and remote island or mountain communities and are often subsidized by the government. In Greece, for example, you can fly very inexpensively between Athens and the islands—though not *between* the islands.

Before booking a flight, consider the alternatives. Sometimes if you add the time you'll need to get to and from the airport, inevitable flight delays, and the time spent waiting for luggage, you'll realize flying won't save you that much time. Flights are probably best left for long hauls.

If you've chosen to fly, talk to budget travel agencies in major towns, listed in this book under the heading Bucket Shops. If you're under 25, you may be in luck. Many European airlines offer bargain one-day-advance-purchase or standby tickets to travelers 24 and under. Always ask about youth discounts when booking a flight with a European airline.

PHONES

Phones systems range from the ultra-efficient to the barely functional. In most Western European countries you can call home by calling an AT&T, MCI, or Sprint operator (phone numbers are given in country Basics), calling collect, or buying some sort of phone card to insert in a public phone. Calling collect is the most expensive route; you'll pay a charge of almost $6 just to set up the call. If you can call using another method, do. Often the easiest method is finding a telephone office (often located in or near the post office), where you can call from a phone booth assigned to you and pay later (occasionally even with a credit card). In less-developed countries, you can probably get through, but you may have to wait hours to get a connection and suffer through frequent disconnections and bad sound quality. The foibles of each country's phone system are detailed in the country Basics.

To call one of the countries that we cover from the United States or Canada, dial 011, then the country code (listed for each of the countries we cover in the country Basics section), then the area code and phone number. In most cases, you should omit the first number in the area code (often a 0, 1, or 9). These first digits are generally used only when calling long distance from elsewhere within that country. When calling from Great Britain, follow the same procedure, but substitute 010 for the 011. In Ireland, use 16; in Australia, use 0011; and in New Zealand, 00.

To call home from one of the countries that we cover, follow the directions given in the country Basics. The country code for the United States and Canada is 1; for Great Britain, 44; for Ireland, 353; for Australia, 61; and for New Zealand, 64.

MAIL

When sending letters or postcards home, mark it with the words "air mail" and the local equivalent (*par avion* in French, *mit Luftposte* in German, *por avion* in Spanish); par avion will do if you don't know the local name. Your mail should make it home in about one week to two months; 10 days is about average. Mail from the United States to Europe usually travels a little faster and arrives in about a week.

In most countries you can receive mail in major post offices. Addressing mail to the recipient (preferably in capital letters) with the name of the city, the postal code, and the words POSTE RESTANTE will get the mail where you want it to go. Add the local equivalent of poste restante if possible; it's *lista de correos* in Spanish, *fermo posta* in Italian, and *postlagernde briefe* in German. Whenever you want to pick up held mail, take your passport or other photo ID and some money; usually you have to pay a small, per-letter fee to pick up mail. Any other relevant information is covered in the Basics section of each country chapter.

If you are an American Express cardmember, it might be easier to have mail sent to the nearest American Express office. They, too, might charge a small fee every time you ask for mail. American Express puts out the "American Express Traveler's Companion," with the addresses of all their offices abroad.

WHERE TO SLEEP

Lodging will probably be your second-largest expense after transportation, but in most places your options are wide open. It's a far cry from the United States, where your only options are usually a bland freeway-side motel or a posh, expensive hotel. If you're arriving in Europe during high season, you might want to make reservations for the first few nights you'll be there to save you the stress of looking for a cheap place on a few hours of sleep. If you're in a bind, the local tourist office can usually book rooms, sometimes for a small fee. They can't work miracles in high season, however, and are sometimes less than enthusiastic about catering to budget travelers.

HOTELS Hotels usually aren't a bad deal if you have one or two traveling companions. Double rooms at budget hotels are rarely more than $60, even in the more expensive countries like Great Britain and Switzerland. In the least expensive countries, like Greece, doubles are closer to $15 a night. Don't expect to have your bed turned down and your every whim catered to; most budget hotels are small places with simple facilities. The least expensive rooms usually don't have a shower or toilet attached; you'll have to share the bathroom down the hall with everyone else, and sometimes have to pay a few dollars to take a shower. Think of it as a good opportunity to get to know your fellow travelers. In this book, "with bath" means that a hotel room has an attached toilet and bath or shower. The price categories refer to a double room, without bath (if available).

For a smaller, family-run place, look for signs advertising a pension, guest house, private room, bed-and-breakfast, or any foreign-language equivalent (*see* Where to Sleep in the Basics section of each country). These are generally (but not always) cheaper than hotels and can sometimes offer a more intimate experience. In general, though, budget B&Bs tend to be pretty utilitarian and not the cozy, chintz-decorated homes you were expecting.

HOSTELS Hostels are usually good deals for solo travelers, especially since single rooms are often expensive and difficult to find. On the downside, hostels are sometimes overrun with groups of vacationing children, are often on the outskirts of town, and frequently have strict curfews (often around midnight) and daytime lockouts (especially oppressive in towns like Barcelona, where nightlife doesn't even get started until the wee hours).

The usual hostel setup is single-sex dorms with four to 40 beds, in anything from an atmospheric Renaissance castle to a prisonlike cement building. In Scandinavia, where hotels tend to be astronomically expensive, hostels tend to be nicer and often have double and triple rooms as well as dorm beds. Here you'll find more families and adult travelers than in hostels in the south. A breakfast, often just bread or a pastry and coffee, is often included in the price. Dinner, and occasionally lunch, are also served for a small price at some hostels. The food may be bland and institutional, but often a hostel dinner is the cheapest hot meal in town.

At least half the hostels you'll run across, designated in this book with the abbreviation HI, are affiliated with Hostelling International (*see* Useful Organizations, *above*). Many of these hostels require guests to be members of a national hostel organization; nonmembers are not allowed to stay at some hotels, and are required to pay a small supplement at others. Some hostels will sell you a hostel membership on the spot, but many won't. If you plan to stay in hostels, pick up a card at a student travel agency (*see* Useful Organizations, *above*) before leaving home. There are no age restrictions for buying hostel cards or staying in hostels, though travelers under 26 might get priority if the hostel is full.

Hostelling International has recently set up the computerized **International Booking Network (IBN),** which makes it possible to reserve a bed at more than 200 HI hostels worldwide. Unfortunately, only hostels in major Western European cities belong to the network; more remote ones do not. To make reservations before leaving the United States, call Hostelling International (tel. 202/783–6161), give them the details about where and when you want to stay, and give them your credit-card number. You'll pay the price of a night's stay in the hostel plus a booking fee of $5. You can also reserve through the network while you're on the road. Every time you stay at a hostel that belongs to the network, they'll make reservations for you at the next hostel on your route; again, you'll pay up front in the local currency.

Hostels that are not affiliated with Hostelling International are as varied as the affiliated ones. They sometimes offer the advantage of not enforcing a curfew or lockout and occasionally the disadvantage of being a bit dirtier or less organized than HI hostels.

CAMPING Europeans seem to have a strange affinity for camping in shady parking lots on the outskirts of town. If you don't mind camping with several dozen caravanning families and their dogs, you can save a bundle by staying in campsites, which generally cost $1–$10 a night, depending on the country. If you prefer to camp in a location that has more trees than people, all is not lost, however. Caravanners generally stick pretty close to the cities, and they never make it to remote wilderness and mountain areas.

Before packing loads of camping gear, seriously consider how much camping you will actually do versus how much trouble it will be to haul around your tent, sleeping bag, stove, and all your other junk. Unless you have some great backwoods adventures in mind, it may not be worth it.

OTHER OPTIONS Formed in the aftermath of World War II, **Servas** is a membership organization that enables you to arrange a stay with host families. Servas is dedicated to promoting peace and understanding around the globe. Becoming a member makes you eligible for their host list directory for any country you desire. Servas is not for tourists or weekend travelers; peace-minded individuals who want more than a free bed can write or call for an application and an interview. You can arrange a stay with a Servas host or host family in advance or just try your luck when you reach the country. Membership is $45 per year, and a onetime deposit of $15 is required. *In the United States: 11 John St., Room 407, New York, NY 10038, tel. 212/267–0252; in Canada: 229 Hilcrest Ave., Willowdale, Ontario M2N 3P3, tel. 416/221–6434; in the United Kingdom: Anne Greenbough, Box 1035, Edinburgh EH3 9JQ; in New Zealand: Leo Palmer, 24 Rahiri Rd., Mount Eden, Auckland 4, tel. 09/630–6279.*

AUSTRIA

By Jay Tate

2

Although 98% of Austrians are ethnic Germans, they take their reputation for cosmopolitanism seriously and want very much to be considered a cultural superpower. Classical music flourishes year-round in festivals all over the country; drama and dance on Vienna's stages is still some of the world's best; and opera continues to thrive in Salzburg, Innsbruck, Graz, Linz, and especially Vienna.

It's not surprising that Austria has such an expansive outlook when you consider that it was once part of the enormous Austro-Hungarian Empire, which in the 18th century spread all the way east to the Russian Empire. Until the Austro-Hungarian Empire collapsed in 1918, Austria served as a bridge between the east and west. Massive resources were funneled from throughout the empire into Vienna, the imperial capital, making the country's wealth of Renaissance and Baroque art and architecture possible.

In 1955, Austria signed the Treaty of Permanent Neutrality to end the Allied occupation after World War II. After this event, Vienna, which had been a center of world culture even into the 1920s, slid to the status of cultural backwater, cut off from Eastern Europe, yet blocked from participating fully in Western Europe. With the recent dismantling of the Iron Curtain, however, Austria has reestablished important ties with Bohemia, Moravia, Hungary, and other Eastern European regions, resulting in a flood of new art galleries, restaurants, and immigrants, including refugees from the war in the former Yugoslavia. And, despite the fact that Austria is still best known as for its traditional attractions, like its historic architecture and classical music, the political and economic transformation is inspiring some changes. For example, the new director of the world-famous Salzburg Summer Festival, Gerard Mortier, has been trying to shake up the traditional programs established by Herbert van Karajan, but still has to avoid alienating too many of the wealthy but often musically conservative visitors who provide so much of the festival's support.

Lest you fear that all your days in Austria be spent in museums and at concerts, you should know that the splendor of Austria's geographical setting rivals its artistic sophistication. Bike trails sweep the country, along the famous Donau (Danube River) and from the relatively flat Vorarlberg in the west to the Alpine region of Tirol. So when you're overwhelmed by Vienna and all those sights that pack a powerful historical wallop, remember that there are plenty of tiny Austrians towns that are just too adorable to be taken very seriously.

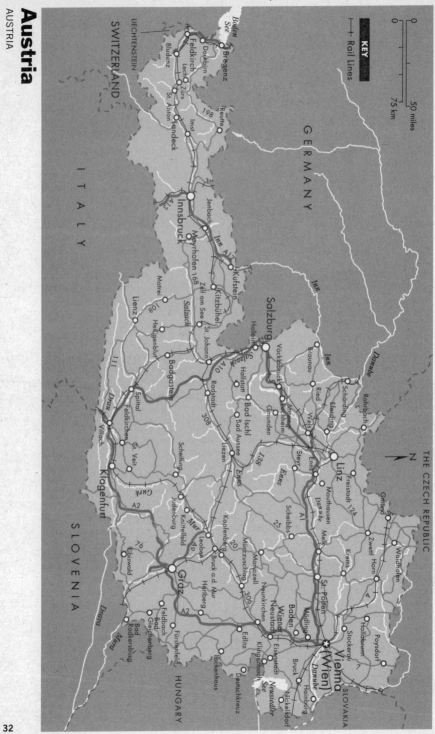

Basics

MONEY $1 = 11.7 Austrian schillings and 1 Austrian schilling = 8.5¢. The schilling is divided into 100 gröschen. Banks are generally open Monday–Wednesday and Friday 8–12:30 and 1:30–3, Thursday 8–5. Bank commissions on traveler's checks are atrocious—you're better off at an American Express office or a post office. Train stations in all major cities have *Geldwechsel* (money-exchange) offices that offer reasonable rates. Cash-exchange machines have so far been spotted only in Vienna, Salzburg, and Innsbruck.

➤ **HOW MUCH WILL IT COST** • Vienna, Salzburg, and Innsbruck, in that order, are Austria's most expensive cities, but even they aren't outrageous. Throughout Austria a hostel bed costs 120AS–140AS; rooms in private houses cost 150AS–210AS per person, up to 500AS or more in Vienna. Pension prices generally start around 300AS per person. Cheap restaurant lunches start around 50AS, dinners around 80AS. In general, if you stay in hostels, you can stay for $40 a day or less. In resort towns, including Innsbruck, ask at your hotel or the tourist office about the **Visitor's Card,** which gives you a discount of 10%–20% at local swimming pools, saunas, ski lifts, bowling alleys, and other attractions. Ten-percent **tips** are included in restaurant and taxi bills, but a smaller tip on top of that is customary.

COMING AND GOING It's a good thing that getting to and from Austria by train is so easy, because flying into Vienna is prohibitively expensive. For standby flights out of Austria, check with **OKISTA-Reisen** (Türkenstr. 4, Vienna, tel. 0222/310–8886). **Austrian Airlines** (tel. 0222/71799 in Vienna) is the national airline.

GETTING AROUND EurailPasses are good on all Austrian trains and on most ferries on the Donau (Danube River).

➤ **BY TRAIN** • If you don't have a EurailPass, you might want to get one of the national rail passes. For four days of travel within Austria during a 10-day period, pick up the second-class **Rabbit Card** (1,130AS) or, for travelers under 26, the **Rabbit Card Junior** (700AS). The **Bundesnetzkarte** (3,600AS) is good for a month of second-class travel on all Austrian trains. With a single ticket for a trip of more than 70 km, you can get off and on along the way for up to four days; with a round-trip ticket (*Rundreisen*), you can do the same for a period of two months. Round-trip tickets cost as much as two one-ways. Anyone under 26 buying a ticket should ask for an *ermäßigte Bahnkarte* (discount train ticket).

➤ **BY BUS** • Buses are slower and more expensive than trains, but you might need them in Austria's forested interior. Ask the tourist office or bus station for a *Fahrpläne Bundesbus* regional schedule.

➤ **BY FERRY** • A cruise on the Donau from Passau, Germany across the Austrian border and through Linz, Melk, and Krems to Vienna takes 11 hours and is free with a EurailPass, 1,100AS without one. During spring and fall ferries run only two–three times per week (and may be canceled if the water level is too high), and between November and March they don't run at all. For helpful maps and information about trips on the Donau, contact **Niederösterreich Information** (Heidenschluß 2, A-1010 Vienna, tel. 0222/533–3114, ext. 34).

➤ **BY BIKE** • More than 170 train stations rent bicycles for 90AS per day, 45AS if you have a train ticket from that day or the previous evening. Mountain bikes (250AS per day) are sometimes available but rent out fast; call the station to reserve ahead. Best of all, you can rent a bike at one station and drop off at another, or rent from ferry offices along the Donau (same prices) and leave the bike at another ferry port.

➤ **HITCHING** • Hitching in Austria is so-so. German and Italian tourists and Eastern European commuters are all good sources of rides. **Mitfahrzentrale** (tel. 0222/715–0060 in Vienna) pairs riders with drivers for a fee based on the distance traveled; a ride from Vienna to Salzburg costs around 200AS. The service has many more prospective riders than drivers, so call a few days in advance.

WHERE TO SLEEP Austria has some of the nicest **hostels** anywhere. Showers and sheets are often included, though breakfast often is not. Hostels usually charge about 130AS–140AS for a dorm bed; hostels that belong to Hostelling International (HI) charge an extra 30AS or so for nonmembers. *Privatzimmer* (rooms in private homes) are common in touristed towns and are often your next cheapest option. Usually you pay per room and can share your space with as many people as you like (within reason). Breakfast is sometimes included. A *Gasthof* or *Gasthaus* is a simple country inn that almost always serves breakfast and often other meals. A *Frühstückpension* (bed-and-breakfast) is a little cheaper, and a plain old *Pension* is cheaper still. **Hotels** usually, though not always, have goodies like telephones and TVs in the rooms, include breakfast in the price, and are more expensive than a Gasthof or Pension. Tourist offices often reserve rooms at no charge.

FOOD Most of Austria is still dining in the 19th century. Beef, pork, and sausages are everywhere, most cheaply at *Würstelstand* (sausage vendors). *Imbisstube* (snack bars), often found at city markets, are cheap places for soup. University *Mensas* (cafeterias) are generally the cheapest spots for a meal, and some of their stuff is even edible. Meats are often breaded and fried as *Schnitzl,* the most famous version of which is Wiener schnitzl, traditionally made with veal. Austrian specialties not likely to be in your German pocket dictionary include *Pfannkuchen* (pancakes), *Knödel* (dumplings), *Nockerl* (small dumplings), *Marillen* (apricots), and *Erdapfeln* (potatoes). Restaurants have a nasty habit of serving bread or appetizer plates without telling you that a *Gedeck* (charge) will apply—ask before you dig in. For dessert, *Strudel* (thin pastry wrapped around a filling) comes in all varieties, including apple (*Apfelstrudel*), cream cheese (*Topfenstrudel*), and cherry (*Kirschenstrudel*). **Cafés** are a huge part of Austrian life, though their food can be a rip-off. The popular *Portion Kaffee* is a small pot of coffee served with a pot of hot milk and a glass of water. Finally, wine lovers may find themselves spending lots of time in *Heurigen,* Austria's answer to the pub, where you can get light meals to go with delicious Austrian white wines.

VISITOR INFORMATION Even the smallest town usually has a tourist office (*Verkehrsverein* or *Verkehrsamt*) with at least one staff member who speaks English. Visitors with disabilities should check with the **Osterreichischer Zivilinvalidenverband** (Lange Gasse 60, A-1080 Vienna, tel. 0222/408–5505) for information.

PHONES Country code: 43. For local telephone information, dial 16; for long-distance information, dial 08. Coin-operated telephones, which take one-, five-, or 10-schilling coins, are everywhere, and phones that take the *Telefon Wertenkarte,* a phone card available at any post office or tobacco shop, are common in the major cities. Post offices have booths for phone-first, pay-later calls. To phone first and pay much later, call AT&T USA Direct (tel. 022–903–011), MCI (tel. 022–903–012), or Sprint (tel. 022–903–014).

MAIL Post offices are generally open weekdays 8–noon and 2–6, Saturday 8–11. The German term for poste restante is *Postlagernde Briefe.* Many post offices also have phone booths where you can make a long-distance call and pay when you are done. Buy stamps at tobacco shops to avoid standing in line.

EMERGENCIES Dial 133 for the **police,** 144 for an **ambulance,** and 122 for the **fire department.** Even emergency calls require at least 1AS in pay phones. Pharmacies rotate the thankless task of remaining open all night; to find the nearest one, consult a newspaper or, in Vienna, call 1550.

LANGUAGE Ninety-eight percent of all Austrians are ethnic Germans and speak a German dialect. Throughout the country *Grüß Gott* and *Servus* replace *Guten Tag* as a greeting; *Auf Wiederschauen* is more common than *Auf Wiedersehen* for good-bye. Most Austrians in the tourist industry speak English, though they may do it grudgingly.

Vienna

European culture and civilization owes a huge debt to Vienna (Wien), longtime center of the Habsburg Empire and pet project of the medieval Babenberg dynasty. Thanks to the Habsburg clan, Vienna has some of the most magnificent Baroque architecture in Europe, but the city's current layout actually derives more from the period following the Prussian defeat of Austria in 1866. After their decisive loss in the Austro-Prussian war, the Viennese tried to ignore their country's military failures and declining influence abroad by means of unprecedented expenditures at home. **Jugendstil** (Art Nouveau), a brightly colored, antitraditional artistic movement popular between around 1900 and World War I, was one product of this trend toward domestic spending and an emphasis on the arts. Two world wars later, Vienna has slid even farther to the political margins and seems almost like a beautiful museum, frozen in time, as though in mourning for the loss of its past prominence.

Amazing remnants of all Vienna's major cultural movements are lovingly preserved within the city, making this one of the big Culture Stops on a European tour. Nightlife here is not what it is in Paris or Madrid, but by the end of the day you'll be too worn down to go out, anyway. Luckily, the city's musical tradition, which slumped with Austrian politics earlier this century, is back, and possibilities for calm musical evenings more than fill the nightlife void.

BASICS

VISITOR INFORMATION **Central Tourist Office.** *1010 Kärntner Str. 38, near the Staatsoper, tel. 0222/513–8892. Open daily 9–7.*

Jugend-Info Wien can score cut-rate tickets for clients under 27 and gives anyone information on Vienna events. *1010 Dr.-Karl-Renner-Ring/Bellaria Passage, tel. 0222/526–4627. Below ground at U3 Volkstheater stop. Open weekdays noon–7, Sat. 10–7.*

Contact **Rosa Lila Villa Lesbian & Gay House** for information about the "*Szene*" in Vienna or anywhere else in Austria. *1060 Linke Wienzeile 102, tel. 0222/568150. Open weekdays 5–8 PM.*

AMERICAN EXPRESS *1010 Kärntner Str. 21–23, tel. 0222/51540. Open weekdays 9–5:30, Sat. 9–noon.*

BUCKET SHOPS Go to **OS Reisen** for plane, train, and bus tickets—cheap. *1010 Reichsratsstr. 13, tel. 0222/588–6238.*

EMBASSIES AND CONSULATES **Australia.** *1040 Mattiellistr. 2, tel. 0222/512–8580. Open weekdays 8:45–1 and 2–5.*

Canada. *1010 Dr.-Karl-Lueger-Ring 10, tel. 0222/533–3691. Open weekdays 8:30–12:30 and 1:30–3:30.*

United Kingdom. *1030 Jaurèsgasse 10, tel. 0222/713–1575. Open weekdays 9:15–noon and 2–4.*

United States Consulate. *1010 Gartenbaupromenade 2, tel. 0222/31339. Open weekdays 8:30–noon and 1–3:30, phones staffed until 5 PM.*

United States Embassy. *1090 Boltzmanngasse 16, tel. 0222/31339; 0222/319–5523 or 0222/319–5524 in an emergency. Open weekdays 8:30–5.*

PHONES AND MAIL Telephones and telegram and telex services are available at the main telephone office daily 6 AM–midnight at Börseplatz 1, near Schottenring. When calling Vienna from outside Austria, drop the 0222 area code and replace it with 1.

Post-restante mail should go to Hauptpostamt, Barbaragasse 2, A-1010 Wien, Postlagernde Briefe. The office is open 24 hours a day; pick up mail at entrance one. The post offices next to the West, Süd, and Franz-Josef train stations are also open 24 hours and have phones and currency exchange. Postal codes correspond to the Bezirke (*see* Getting Around, *below*). The postal code in the first Bezirk is A-1010, in the second A-1020, and so on.

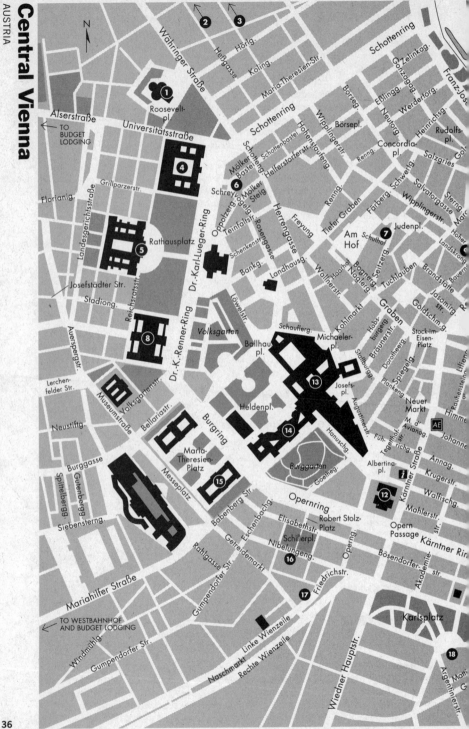

N

Alserstraße
← TO BUDGET LODGING

Universitätsstraße

Währinger Straße

Roosevelt-pl.

① ② ③

Heßgasse Hörlg.

Koling.

Maria-Theresien-Str.

Schottenring

Schottenring

Gonzagag. Zelinkog.

EßIingg. Neutorg. Werdertorg.

Heinrichsg.

Rudolfs-pl.

Salzgries

Börsepl.

Börseg.

Wipplingerstr.

Hohenstaufeng.

Helferstorferstr.

Renng.

Concordia-pl.

Schwertg.

Salvatorgasse Wipplingerstr.

④

Grillparzerstr.

Florianig.

Landesgerichtsstraße

Rathausplatz

⑤

Josefstädter Str.

Reichsratsstr.

Stadiong.

Auerspergstr.

Lerchen-felder Str.

Neustiftg.

Burggasse

Gutenbergg. Spitelbergg.

Siebensterng.

Mariahilfer Straße

← TO WESTBAHNHOF AND BUDGET LODGING

Windmühlg.

Gumpendorfer Str.

Museumstraße

Volksgartenstr.

⑧

Bellariastr.

Marta-Theresien-Platz

⑮

Messeplatz

Babenberg Str.

Rahlgasse Str.

Getreidemarkt

Eschenbachg.

Gumpendorfer Str.

Nibelungeng.

Schillerpl.

⑯

Friedrichstr.

⑰

Linke Wienzeile

Naschmarkt

Rechte Wienzeile

Wiedner Hauptstr.

Mölker Bastei

Schotteng. Schottenbastei

Schrey. ⑥ Mölker Steig

Oppolzerg.

Teinfaltstr.

Rosengasse

Schenkenstr.

Bankg.

Löwelstr.

Volksgarten

Dr.-Karl-Lueger-Ring

Dr.-K.-Renner-Ring

Burgring

Heldenpl.

Ballhaus-pl.

Schauflerg.

Michaeler-pl.

⑬

Josefs-pl.

⑭

Hanuschg.

Burggarten

Goetheg.

Herrengasse

Landhausg.

Freyung

Tiefer Graben

Wallnerstr.

Renng.

Farberg.

Am Hof

Schulhof

⑦ Judenpl.

Landskrong.

Bogner Seitzerg.

Naglerg.

Hoher M.

Tuchlauben

Brandstätte

Bauern

Jasomirg. str.

Graben

Goldschm.g.

Stock-im-Eisen-Platz

Habs-burgerg.

Bräunerstr.

Dorotheerg.

Spiegelg.

Plankeng.

Stallburgg.

Augustinerstr.

Führ.

Tegetthof. richg.

Albertina-pl.

Neuer Markt

M. d. Avianog.

AE

Annag.

Krugerstr.

Walfischg.

Mahlerstr.

Opernring

Robert Stolz-Platz

Elisabethstr.

Opernpass.

Kärntner Straße

Johanne

Himme

Lilien

Rauhenstein

Opern Passage

Bösendorferstr.

Akademie-str.

Kärntner Rin

Karlsplatz

⑱

Argentiniers

Mah

G

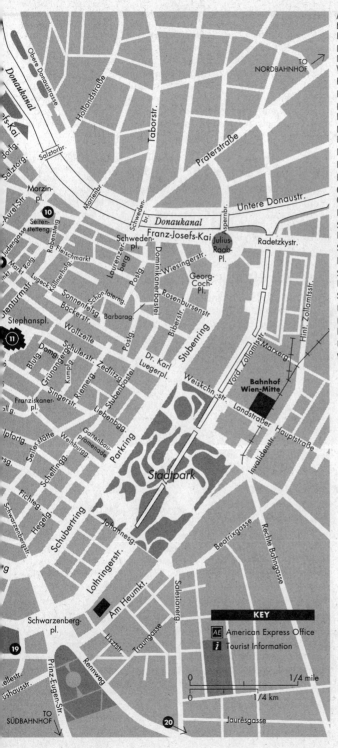

Akademie der bildenden Künste, 16

Historisches Museum der Stadt Wien, 19

Hofburg, 13

Karlskirche, 18

Kunsthistorisches Museum, 15

Museum Moderner Kunst, 3

Neue Hofburg, 14

Parlament, 8

Pasqualatihaus, 6

Österreichische Galerie, 20

Rathaus, 5

Secession Building, 17

Staatsoper, 12

Ruprechtskirche, 10

Sigmund Freud Haus Museum, 2

Stephansdom, 11

Uhrenmuseum, 7

Underground Roman ruins, 9

Universität, 4

Votivkirche, 1

KEY

AE American Express Office

i Tourist Information

0   1/4 mile

0   1/4 km

COMING AND GOING

BY TRAIN Vienna has two major train stations. **Westbahnhof,** in the west of town, sends trains to western Austria, most of western Europe, and Hungary. Frequent destinations include Munich (4½ hrs, 660AS), Salzburg (3 hrs, 380AS), and Budapest (3 hrs, 310AS). The station closes between 1:15 AM and 4 AM. The **Südbahnhof,** in the south of town, has connections to Austria, Italy, Eastern Europe, and Berlin. Regular trains go to Venice (8 hrs, 610AS), Budapest (3 hrs, 210AS), Prague (4 hrs, 400AS), and Krakow (7 hrs, 440AS). The station closes 1 AM–4 AM. There are two lesser stations to the north (**Franz-Josefs Bahnhof** and **Wien Nord**), plus a central station (**Wien Mitte**), from which shuttles to the airport leave most frequently. For rail information, dial 1717 from Vienna or call 0222/580–033–999.

BY BUS Most international buses pass through **Wien Mitte** (1030 Marxergasse, tel. 0222/71101 or 0222/71107), the best place to pick up schedules and make inquiries.

BY PLANE Flights arrive at the airport in Schwechat, about 20 km southeast of Vienna. For airport info, call 0222/711–102–231. Schnellbahn 7 (see Getting Around, below) leaves Wien Nord at least every hour between 5 AM and 9 PM and passes through Wien Mitte on the way to the airport (22AS). Airport buses (tel. 0222/580–033–369; 20 min, 60AS) leave every 20 minutes between 6:30 AM and 11:30 PM from the city air terminal next to the Hilton Hotel in the third Bezirk, hourly between 5:40 AM and midnight from Südbahnhof (20 min, 60AS) and Westbahnhof (35 min, 60AS). Buy tickets on the bus.

BY FERRY Ferries to Krems (5¾ hrs, 3¾ hrs downstream, 325AS) and points farther up the Donau leave Vienna daily at 8 AM during summer. Reservations are a good idea: Without one, get to the ferry terminal at least an hour in advance. The ferries are run by **DDSG Donaureisen** (1024 Handelskai 265, tel. 0222/217500). Ferries dock at the Reichsbrücke Schiffarszentrum near the U1 Vorgartenstraße stop.

HITCHING If you have the foresight to plan in advance, call Mitfahrzentrale (see Austria Basics, above) a few days before you want to travel. If not, for Salzburg and other points west ride U4 to the end of the line at Hütteldorf; A1 Westautobahn is the freeway for you. On weekdays, a free bus leaves from the Staatsoper (see Worth Seeing, Ringstraße, below) every hour for Shopping Center Süd, near an entrance to the southbound A2 Südautobahn; on weekends, you have to pay for the same bus trip (every 30 min, 30AS). To go east, take U3 to the end at Erdberg; walk a bit in the same direction and turn left to the cloverleaf. To head north, ride U1 to Vienna International Center and walk back to the cloverleaf entrance to A22 Donauuferautobahn.

GETTING AROUND

Vienna is as neatly laid out as a box of sweets and is best explored on foot. The city is divided into 23 Bezirke, or districts. The densely packed area within and around the 7-km **Ringstraße,** a roughly circular boulevard which goes by the name Franz-Josefs-Kai and nine names ending in "ring," is the first district; the second district is the Prater amusement park area across the Donaukanal (Danube Canal). The third through ninth districts run counterclockwise from south to north around the first district, while districts 10 and up edge outward to the Wienerwald (Vienna Wood). Many addresses in this chapter include the Bezirk number before the street address (1010 refers to the first district, 1020 to the second, and so on).

BY U-BAHN, STRABENBAHN, SCHNELLBAHN, AND BUS Vienna's **U-Bahn** (subway) covers only major routes; each line is designated by a number (U1, U2, etc.). Many areas are covered instead by **Straßenbahn** (trams), while **buses** generally start from the terminus of, and have the same number as, a corresponding Straßenbahn, except that bus numbers tack on an "A" or "B." **Schnellbahn** (local trains) are rarely called for within the city, but the frequent connections between Südbahnhof, Wien Mitte, and Wien Nord sometimes come in handy, and EurailPasses are valid. The whole system goes into cardiac arrest around midnight. After that, you have to rely on night buses (25AS, no passes valid) leaving every half-hour from Schwedenplatz and cruising by the bus stops marked with an "N." For questions about city transportation, call **Wiener Verkehrsbetriebe** (tel. 0222/587–3186 or 0222/512–4227).

Single tickets, good on all public transportation for an hour after validation, cost 20AS, a Fier-Streifenkarte (strip of four) 60AS. Bargain passes, ranging from the 45AS day pass to the 125AS week pass, are sold at transit windows, tobacco shops, and some tourist offices. Automated ticket machines at stations also sell 24-hour and 72-hour passes.

BY TAXI Night, weekend, and holiday fares are 25AS plus 12AS per km or 4AS per minute. At all other times the distance charge is 11AS per km. Add 10AS if you phone for a taxi or have luggage. To arrange a pickup, call 0222/1718, 0222/31300, or 0222/91091.

BY BIKE The West, Süd, and Nord train stations rent bikes for 45AS per day to rail ticket holders, 90AS per day otherwise. The Ringstraße has wide bicycle lanes and is accessible from the train stations by cycling routes. The Wien Nord station is convenient to the Prater recreation area and is a good departure point for hooking up with the main Donau cycling road. *Logbuch Radwege Wien* (100AS), available in bookstores, is a detailed map of all 460 km of bike roads past the sights of Vienna.

WHERE TO SLEEP

Lodging in Vienna is substantially more expensive than elsewhere in Austria. Nonetheless, even the dinkiest rooms are almost always clean. *Privatzimmer* (200AS–1,000AS per room) are not much cheaper than other forms of accommodation, and demand for these rooms, often nicer than those at pensions, far exceeds supply. To book a private room the day you arrive, contact the **Tourismusverband** (tel. 0222/211–1466); make advance bookings through **Verkehrsbüro** (1010 Friedrichstr. 7, tel. 0222/588000). Either way, a stay of at least two days is usually expected. The various tourist offices will book pension or hotel rooms for a 35AS fee or give you the excellent *Hotels & Pensionen* brochure. Most of the hotels below are in the sixth, seventh, and eighth Bezirke, just west of the center. If you've gotta be central, try the **Hotel Pension City** (1010 Bauernmarkt 10, tel. 0222/533–9521; singles 600AS, doubles 900AS–1,100AS), a block northeast of Stephansdom. To be near Nordbahnhof, stay in **Wilhelmshof** (1020 Kleine Stadtgutgasse 4, off Nordbahnstr., tel. 0222/214–5521; singles from 320AS, doubles from 530AS). A piddly breakfast is usually included in the price of the hotel or pension room.

➢ **UNDER 500AS • Esterhazy.** Rock-bottom price for a Vienna pension: singles 270AS–300AS, doubles 470AS–500AS. Grungy, with shower and toilet in the hall. Good transportation nearby, and within walking distance of the Ringstraße. *1060 Nelkengasse 3, off Mariahilfer Str., tel. 0222/587–8505.*

Fünfhaus. Near Westbahnhof. Enormous, uncarpeted rooms with sofas. Basic doubles only 470AS, 550AS with shower and toilet; breakfast 35AS. Some of the rooms are around the corner at Grangasse 8. *1150 Sperrgasse 12, tel. 0222/892–3545. From Westbahnhof take Mariahilfer Str. 10 min south, turn right on Sperrgasse.*

➢ **UNDER 600AS • Hargita.** Small, bright, family-run pension feels more like a home (you cross the breakfast room to visit the loo). Singles 400AS–450AS, doubles 500AS–650AS, 800AS with bath. Prices drop 100AS in winter and are never completely firm. *1070 Andreasgasse 1, tel. 0222/526–1928. From Westbahnhof, walk 10 min east on Mariahilfer Str.*

Holzwarth. Just south of Westbahnhof. Cozy rooms, mostly doubles. Popular with German and French tourists. Courtyard is home to trees, flowers, and birds. Singles 410AS–510AS, doubles 570AS–770AS. *1150 Lichtgasse 2–4, tel. 0222/892–2032.*

Hospiz. Simple, clean YMCA rooms with sinks for men and women, just far enough from West-bahnhof to be quiet. Singles 320AS, doubles 560AS, 640AS with shower, slightly cheaper in winter. Drop your sleeping bag on an exercise mat in the gym for 170AS. *1070 Kenyongasse 15, tel. 0222/931304. From Westbahnhof, cross Neubaugürtel and go 1 more block.*

➤ **UNDER 700AS • Kraml.** Satisfied folks come out of this classy, family-run establishment in an alley near Westbahnhof. Generous breakfast. Single 260AS, doubles 610AS–750AS; discounts for long stays. *1060 Brauergasse 5, tel. 0222/587–8588. 15 min from Westbahnhof: walk down Mariahilfer Str., turn right on Otto Bauer, left on Königsegg, and right on Brauergasse.*

Tangra. Simple, modern furnishings in surprisingly bright, fresh rooms, all with bath, toilet, and telephone, some with TV. Singles 250AS–350AS, doubles 650AS. *1070 Mariahilfer Str. 58, tel. 0222/526–1306. From Westbahnhof, walk 20 min up Mariahilfer Str. or take U3 to Kirchengasse. AE, V.*

HOSTELS **Hotel Ruthensteiner (HI).** Five-minute walk from Westbahnhof. Some guests complain of dirt and brusque management. Beds 125AS–200AS. *1150 Robert-Hamerling-Gasse 24, tel. 0222/834693 or 0222/830–8265. From Westbahnhof, go west on Mariahilfer Str., left on Palmgasse, and right on Robert-Hamerling-Gasse.*

Hotel Zöhrer. Only 29 beds in central, sunny hostel with a courtyard. Breakfast, sheets, and kitchen privileges all included. Beds 160AS. *1080 Skodagasse 26, just off Alserstr., tel. 0222/430730. From Westbahnhof, take Straßenbahn 5 to Skodagasse; from Südbahnhof, Bus 13A to Skodagasse.*

Jugendgästehaus Hütteldorf-Hacking (HI). In a spiffy green area a 15- to 20-minute walk from the western end of the U4 line. Lots of groups. Beds 140AS. *Schloßberggasse 8, tel. 0222/877–0263. Take U4 to Hüttledorf, then Bus 53B. Midnight curfew, lockout 9–4.*

Jugendgästehaus Wien Brigittenau (HI). Largest hostel in town, which means way too many school groups. North of center. Beds 140AS. *Friedrich-Engels-Pl. 24, tel. 0222/332–82940. From Franz-Josefs-Bahnhof, Straßenbahn 35A to Friedrich-Engels-Pl.*

Jugendherberge Wien Myrthengasse/Neustiftgasse (HI). Vienna's most centrally located pair of hostels, in historic buildings with comfy lounges and courtyards. Book ahead. Breakfast included. Beds 140AS, members only. *Myrthengasse 7 and Neustiftgasse 85, tel. 0222/523–6316. From Westbahnhof, walk 10 min north on Neubaugürtel, turn right on Neustiftgasse; Myrthengasse is 10 min up. 1 AM curfew, lockout 9–noon, wheelchair access, laundry.*

Schloßherberge am Wilhelminenberg (HI). Beautiful hostel on Vienna's green outskirts. Transportation here is less than convenient. Beds in cheery quads with bath 200AS. *1160 Savoyen-str. 2, tel. 0222/458–503–700. Take U6 to Thalinstr., then Straßenbahn U6 to end of Thalin-str., then Bus 46B or 146B to Maroltingerstr.*

STUDENT HOUSING June through September student dorms are converted into bare but well-maintained **Saisonhotels,** often staffed by enthusiastic students. **Alsergrund** (1080 Alserstr. 33, tel. 0222/433–2317 or 0222/512–7493) and **Auersperg** (1080 Auerspergstr. 9, tel. 0222/432–5490 or 0222/512–7493) both feature sparkling singles from 350AS and doubles from 560AS near Rathausplatz. **Auge Gottes** (1090 Nußdorfer Str. 75, tel. 0222/342585; singles 275AS, doubles 460AS–550AS) and **Hans Döbling** (1090 Gymnasi-umstr., tel. 0222/347631; singles from 300AS, doubles from 550AS) are less central but are near Franz-Josefs Bahnhof and cheaper than other Saisonhotels. **Josefstadt** (1080 Buch-feldgasse 16, tel. 0222/435211, ext. 22 or 0222/512–7493; singles 400AS, doubles 620AS) sits two blocks directly behind ye olde Rathausplatz. All rooms have private bath.

FOOD

Most of the restaurants listed below are in the first Bezirk, where you'll likely spend most of your days, but if you're staying west of the center, you shouldn't have problems finding reasonable meals closer to home. You'll find chain grocery stores even within the historic first

Bezirk—there's a **Billa** (Singerstr. 6, tel. 0222/512–9250) just around the corner from Stephansdom. The city's largest open-air market, **Naschmarkt** (off Karlspl., bet. Linke Wienzeile and Rechte Wienzeile; open weekdays 7–6, Sat. 7–1), has cheap eats as well as Eurojunk with variable souvenir potential. Find weekday Mensa meals at the **Universität** (1010 Universitätsstr. 7, tel. 0222/434594) and **Akademie der bildenden Künste** (*see* Worth Seeing, *below*); consult the tourist office's *Youth Scene* magazine for a complete list.

➤ **UNDER 80AS • Einstein.** This big-time student hangout behind the Universität serves up everything from Continental breakfast (40AS) to cheap, complete meals (Wiener schnitzl with potato salad 60AS) and beers on tap. Lots of outdoor tables. *1010 Rathauspl. 4, tel. 0222/422626. U2: Rathaus. Open weekdays 7 AM–2 AM, Sat. 10 AM–2 AM, Sun. 10 AM–midnight.*

Restaurant Bukarest. A shrine to Romania's favorite spice, paprika. Both Romanian and Viennese specialties on the enormous menu of almost 100 items. Everything's inexpensive and good. Salads 30AS, soups 30AS–40AS. *1010 Bräunerstr. 7, bet. Graben and the Hofburg, tel. 0222/512–3763.*

➤ **UNDER 100AS • Esterhazy Keller.** Pop down to check out this cavernous Heurige even if you don't eat here. Medieval-style wine cellar with 10AS–40AS sausages, breads, and salads. *1010 Haarhof 1, tel. 0222/533–3482. U3: Herrengasse. Closed weekends and several weeks in summer.*

Vinissimo. Try some of Austria's incredible Riesling and dessert wines (20AS–50AS per glass) over a constantly changing menu of reinterpreted Austrian and Italian dishes, like risotto with Japanese seaweed (90AS) or ginger soup with prawns (35AS). Waiters happily discuss the menu in perfect English. Outdoor terrace in back. *1060 Windmühlgasse 20, tel. 0222/586488. Closed Sat. dinner and Sun.*

➤ **UNDER 120AS • Noodles & Company.** Homemade pasta (80AS–100AS) and minestrone (40AS) in a classy joint below the famous Künstlerhaus, a former center of the conservative art world. Live piano music until 2 AM, food served till 4 AM. *1010 Karlspl. 5, bet. Künstlerhaus and the Musikverein, tel. 0222/505–3839. Closed Sat. lunch. AE, V.*

➤ **UNDER 150AS • Vollwert-Restaurant Lebenbauer.** Central Vienna's most stylish vegetarian restaurant has a long wine list and delicious nibble plates (unadvertised fee of 25AS). Main dishes around 110AS. *1010 Teinfaltstr. 3, tel. 0222/533–5556. U3: Herrengasse. Closed Sat. dinner and Sun. AE, V.*

➤ **UNDER 250AS • Plachutta.** Elegant restaurant on a quiet corner harbors master preparers of traditional Viennese beef. Vegetable plate (95AS) available for the vegetarian friend you drag with you. Meat dishes from 175AS. Cover charge of 35AS added to each table's bill. *1010 Wollzeile 38, tel. 0222/512–1577. U3: Stubentor. Wheelchair access.*

CAFES Social life in turn-of-the-century Vienna revolved around café meetings over newspapers, the latest gossip, and a Portion Kaffee (*see* Austria Basics, Food, *above*), which will run you 40AS–50AS at any of the following establishments. **Demel** (Kohlmarkt 14, tel. 0222/533–6020) has everything you ever wanted to taste in chocolate—except you can't afford it. Originally decorated by modernist renegade Adolf Loos, **Café Museum** (1010 Friedrichstr. 6, tel. 0222/565202) is popular with local students and isn't a bad place to eat (dishes 20AS–50AS). Television crews come to the classic old **Cafe Sperl** (1060 Gumpendorfer Str. 11, tel. 0222/564158) when the assignment calls for a Vienna coffeehouse. You can play pool for 60AS per hour. **Café-Restaurant Willendorf** (1060 Linke Wienzeile 102, tel. 0222/587–1789) is Vienna's leading gay café, though straights are welcome; Rosa Lila (*see* Visitor Information, *above*) has its headquarters in the building.

WORTH SEEING

The first Bezirk, roughly outlined by the Ringstraße, contains most of Vienna's major sights. Buy *Vienna A to Z* (30AS) from the tourist office for a concise, building-by-building intro to more than 300 attractions.

THE ALTSTADT In the 1st century AD, the Romans built a fort called Vindobona near the Donau; the walls stood along modern-day Tiefer Graben, Naglergasse, Graben, and the tiny Kramergasse/Rotgasse Alley northeast of Stephansplatz. Marcus Aurelius wrote his famous *Meditations* here while directing successful military operations against Germanic tribes; a street through the center of the old outpost area where he later died bears his name. The fort was revived under Charlemagne in 799 and became the Babenberg family residence in 1156. With the help of literally tons of gold paid in 1196 to buy the release of Richard I ("the Lionheart"), the Babenberg court began to attract artists and poets from much of Europe, and the city of Vienna grew up and out from the fort. The aisle and lower tower of the humble **Ruprechtskirche** (Judengasse) are among the few visible fragments of the Babenberg cultural explosion. A few buildings surviving from the Middle Ages dot the area, presenting sometimes startling contrasts to the city's prevailing Baroque style. Descend the stairs inside Hoher Markt 3, which leads a double life as a bakery and entrance to the **underground Roman ruins** (tel. 0222/535–5606; admission 15AS; open Tues.–Sun. 9–12:15 and 1–4), where the excavated remains of two Roman houses are on display in a minimuseum.

STEPHANSDOM In 1258, Ottokar II of Bohemia, who had conquered Vienna just six years earlier, ingratiated himself to his new subjects by ordering the construction of a new and much-improved version of St. Stephan's Cathedral, formerly a small, fire-prone Romanesque church. The Habsburgs booted Ottokar out in 1279 but continued the construction he had begun. You can take an elevator to the top of the Stephansdom's 449-foot south tower, walk up the never-completed north tower, and visit the catacombs, accessible only by guided tour, where little bronze cases cushion the precious innards of notable Habsburgs. Each little special excursion costs around 20AS. *Stephanspl. 1, tel. 0222/515–52526. Guided tours Mon.–Sat. at 10:30 and 3, Sun. at 3; evening tours June–Sept., Sat. at 7 PM.*

HOFBURG Palace of the ruling Habsburgs from 1278 until their fall in 1918, the Hofburg grew to become as sprawling and confused as the empire over which it presided. The 2,600-odd rooms house dozens of government offices and several of Vienna's weightiest sights. Exploring the whole complex would take at least a day; if you have less than that, skip the well-known but rather glum **Kaiserappartements** (Imperial Apartments), which aren't worth the 65AS for admission, 40AS students.

Don't skip the **Schatzkammer** (Treasury Room), with its 1,000 years of crowns, relics, and vestments, including those of the Holy Roman Empire with which Napoleon adorned himself in 1804 (Room 11). The "Short Guide" brochure (10AS), available in the bookstore, gives the lowdown on every last sumptuous item. *Admission: 60AS, 30AS students. Open Wed.–Mon. 10–6.*

The **Hofburgkapelle** (Hofburg Chapel) is home to the famous Wiener Sängerkraben (Vienna Boys' Choir), where both Haydn and Schubert wowed their elders. Limited free standing room is available to hear the choir sing 9:15 AM Sunday mass late September through June. For seats (50AS–220AS), write eight weeks in advance to Hofmusikkapelle, Hofburg, A-1010 Vienna. Any leftovers go on sale each Friday at the chapel at 5 PM.

Catch the intricate prancing of the Lipizzaner stallions during training sessions at the **Spanish Riding School** (Spanische Reitschule, tel. 0222/533–9032; admission 70AS). The horses of the school are away from late June through August but otherwise can usually be seen Tuesday–Saturday at 10 AM; check with the tourist office since there are plenty of exceptions. Actual performances (200AS–700AS, standing room 160AS) sell out months in advance; write to Spanische Reitschule, Hofburg, A-1010 Vienna. The American Express office (*see above*) sometimes has a few last-minute tickets, but expect a 20%-plus service charge.

The astounding collections of the **Nationalbibliothek** (National Library) include musical manuscripts by the masters, almost 200,000 examples of papyrus, and a **Globensammlungen** (admission 10AS), a collection of 199 globes. Habsburg book collections were first gathered together under Emperor Karl VI in the library's **Prunksaal** (admission 40AS, 20AS students), a magnificent Baroque showpiece of a library. *Josefspl. 1, tel. 0222/53410. Main desk open weekdays 9–7:45, until 3:45 PM mid-July–Aug., Sat. 9–1.*

A young and impressionable Hitler lived in Vienna just before World War I when the **Neue Hofburg,** the newest wing of the palace, was being completed. A quarter of a century later, in 1938, when the Nazis rolled in unopposed to annex Austria, Hitler chose the balcony of the Neue Hofburg to announce to an enthusiastic (and carefully orchestrated) crowd the entry of his native land into the German Reich. Four different collections, all excellent, are now on display inside this behemoth: the **Ephesus Museum,** with acquisitions excavated from this famous lost city by the Aegean Sea; the **Collection of Musical Instruments,** including pianos belonging to Beethoven, Brahms, and Schumann; the **Collection of Weapons** (admission to all three 30AS); and the vast ethnological museum, the **Museum für Volkerkunde** (admission 30AS).

KARLSKIRCHE Emperor Karl VI decided to celebrate the end of a plague epidemic in 1713 by commissioning an extraordinary Baroque church in honor of St. Charles Borromeo, a Milanese archbishop famous for his work with plague victims. St. Karl is the subject of the decorations on the twin pillars outside the church, of the ascent depicted at the high altar, and of the ceiling frescoes (also look for the angel who's setting fire to a copy of Luther's Bible!). Gustav and Alma Mahler exchanged rings and said "Ja" here in 1902. *Karlspl.*

RINGSTRAßE This ambitious piece of city planning, based around a single street that encircles the center of Vienna, was the Habsburg Empire's extravagant final effort to buy off the grumbling middle class with great gobs of Kultur while, behind the scenes, tightening the autocratic screws loosened by the Revolution of 1848. The elaborate **Votivkirche,** built to celebrate a failed assassination attempt against the emperor in 1853, set the aren't-we-lucky-to-have-the-Habsburgs tone implicit in Ringstraße monumentalism. Within 30 years, costly buildings for virtually all the major cultural and political institutions had been erected on the Ringstraße, each a revival of some earlier architectural style considered symbolic of the building's function. Thus the **Staatsoper** (State Opera House) is neo-Italianate, the **Universität** neo-Renaissance, the **Parlament** neo–ancient Greek, the **Rathaus** (City Hall) neo–tradeguild. Artists soon found the heavy emphasis on tradition oppressive, and in 1898 the **Secession Building** (1010 Friedrichstr. 12, tel. 0222/587–5307; admission 30AS, 15AS students), which today features only Klimt's *Beethoven Frieze* between special exhibitions, began to display controversial works by Klimt and other artists in direct defiance of Ringstraße taste. Within only a few years, Klimt's Jugendstil became the new orthodoxy.

Phantoms of the Opera

The construction of the Staatsoper took a heavy toll on those involved. The building's foundation was laid before the surrounding street had been completed, and the street wound up being higher than planned. Somewhat suspect history has it that Emperor Franz-Josef innocently noted that the building was a bit low to the ground, and that his disapproval was more than the poor architects, Eduard van der Nüll and August Sicard von Sicardsburg, could take. Within months, Nüll had committed suicide and Sicardsburg had died of "heartbreak" (technically, it was a stroke), prompting the horrified emperor to limit all subsequent aesthetic pronouncements to "Es war sehr schön, es hat mich sehr gefreut" ("It was very nice, it pleased me very much").

➤ **KUNSTHISTORISCHES MUSEUM (MUSEUM OF FINE ARTS)** • Housing one of the world's great art collections, this 19th-century home to centuries of Habsburg artistic acquisitions is also Vienna's best-preserved example of budget-busting Ringstraße architecture. The extravagant central staircase alone, smothered by priceless works, sums up the museum's grand and essentially traditional view of art. The **Gemäldegalerie** (Picture Gallery) includes major works by Raphael, Titian, Rubens, the cryptic Lorenzo Lotto, Velázquez, Caravaggio, Vermeer, Van Dyck, Rembrandt, and Bruegel. The **Kunstkammer** (Art Room) boasts an enormous collection of ornate miniature sculptures, metalwork, and specially commissioned artistic objects such as Cellini's dizzyingly elaborate *Saliera*, a golden salt shaker. The **Antikensammlung** (Collection of Greek and Roman Antiquities) is one of the world's leading collections of ancient Western art. *1010 Burgring 5, tel. 0222/52177. Take U2 to Mariahilfer Str. Admission: 95AS, 45AS students. Open Tues.–Sun. 10–6.*

SCHONBRUNN Austria's answer to Versailles, done up in spiffy yellow by Empress Maria Theresa, daughter of Karl VI and mother of Marie Antoinette, the Schönbrunn palace has grounds so vast that occupying armies have used it as their headquarters. Admission to the park, which has a terrific hilltop view and lots of wooded pathways, is free, and the grounds are open daily from 6 AM to dusk. In the **Schauräume** (Imperial Apartments), a six-year-old Mozart played for Maria Theresa in the Hall of Mirrors. The apartment chambers contain everything from Bohemian chandeliers to Chinese lacquerwork and miniature Persian and Indian woodcuts. *Tel. 0222/811–13239. Take U4 to Schloß Schönbrunn. Admission: 80AS. Tours daily 8:30–5, until 4:30 Nov.–Mar.*

The Akademie der bildenden Künste twice denied admission to a prospective art student named Adolf Hitler.

Inside the palace, the **Wagenburg** (tel. 0222/877–3244; admission 30AS) displays all kinds of wheels for royals: coaches, carriages, sleighs, and the imperial hearse. The **Butterfly House** (tel. 0222/877–5087, ext. 406; admission 35AS) is also very cool. Flit in and check it out.

OTHER MUSEUMS **Akademie der bildenden Künste (Academy of Fine Arts).** Here you'll find an impressive Old Masters collection, including *The Last Judgment* by Hieronymus Bosch. *1010 Schillerpl. 3, tel. 0222/588–16225. Admission: 30AS, 15AS students. Open Tues., Thurs., Fri. 10–2; Wed. 10–1; weekends 9–1.*

Historisches Museum der Stadt Wien (Vienna Historical Museum). Take advantage of this excellent intro to the city, which displays archaeological finds, paintings by leading artists, and objects ranging from toys and games to weaponry. *1040 Karlspl., tel. 0222/505–8747. Admission: 30AS, 10AS students. Open Tues.–Sun. 9–4:30.*

Museum Moderner Kunst (Museum of Modern Art). Almost everyone in the 20th-century pantheon of painterly heroes is represented here. Traditionalists can ignore the canvases and stare at the 18th-century frescoes on the ceiling. *Liechtenstein Palace, 1090 Fürstengasse 1, tel. 0222/341259 or 0222/346306. Admission: 30AS, 15AS students. Open Wed.–Mon. 10–6.*

Österreichische Galerie (Austrian Gallery). This collection is housed in the Belvedere Palace, whose grounds ooze imperial splendor. The upper palace is devoted to turn-of-the-century Vienna rebels Gustav Klimt, Egon Schiele, and Oskar Kokoschka, while the lower palace houses the leading collection of Austrian Baroque art. *1030 Prinz-Eugen-Str. 27, tel. 0222/784–1580. Admission: 60AS. Open Tues.–Sun. 10–5.*

Sigmund Freud Haus Museum. This was home and office to the father of modern psychoanalysis from 1891 until he was persuaded to flee the Nazis in 1938. Beyond a few pieces of original furniture, the main attraction is the scores of original documents; a comprehensive binder details the importance of each room and document. *1090 Berggasse 19, tel. 0222/319–1596. Take U2 to Schottentor. Admission: 60AS, 40AS students. Open daily 9–4.*

Uhrenmuseum. This surprisingly interesting collection of Austrian clocks spans three floors and includes a 1699 working timepiece from Stephansdom. Ask permission to set the big clocks in clattering motion. *1010 Schulhof 2, tel. 0222/533–2265. Admission: 30AS, 10AS students. Open Tues.–Sun. 9–4:30.*

CHEAP THRILLS Every summer night at around 9 PM, the Rathaus becomes the stage for **free opera films.** Lots of cheap food and drink stands are set up nearby, and it makes for a fun time even if you don't watch the opera.

Believe it or not, the Donau is clean enough to swim in, and the banks east of town host a major beach scene. On the south end of **Donauinsel** (take U1 to Donauinsel), a long, thin island in the Donau, you'll find waterskiing, the world's longest water slide, and lots of topless sunbathers. Rent bikes and Rollerblades below the Donauinsel U-Bahn stop. Music lovers should take Straßenbahn 71 (to the Tor II stop) to the **Zentralfriedhof** (Central Cemetery; 1110 Simmeringer Hauptstr. 234; open May–Aug., daily 7–7, shorter hrs off-season), where Beethoven, Schubert, Gluck, Hugo Wolf, Brahms, and Johann Strauss the Elder and Younger all rest in Section 32A. Schönberg is in Section 32C.

FESTIVALS Musical festivals take place almost year-round in Vienna. Before you buy tickets for any of them, ask about student discounts. The biggie, worth planning a vacation around, is the **WienerFestwochen** (tel. 0222/586–1676) during May and June, when plays, operas, exhibitions, and other events seem to fill every hall in town.

AFTER DARK

BARS *Weinkeller* (wine cellars) serve cheap food with white wine; **Esterhazy** (*see* Where to Sleep, *above*) and **Zwölf Apostel-keller** (1010 Sonnenfelsgasse 3, tel. 0222/512–6777), northeast of Stephansplatz off Rotenturm, are two good ones. Many of Vienna's bars and night spots are jammed into the tiny alleys around Seitenstettengasse and Rabensteig. Plenty of student spots, not surprisingly, are behind the Universität in the eighth Bezirk, particularly on Florianigasse. **Krah Krah** (1010 Rabensteig 8, tel. 0222/638193), with a young, rowdy, college scene, serves 55 different beers. Smoke-filled **Café Alt Wein** (1010 Bäckerstr. 9, tel. 0222/512–5222) has cheap eats, beer, and wine and is a trendy see-and-be-seen spot. Gay bars are mostly on Linke Weinzeile in the sixth Bezirk.

CLASSICAL MUSIC While its literature wilted under censorship and its painting and architecture languished in sterile academicism, Vienna became the fountainhead of western music—what Brahms called "the musician's holy city." Thanks to state subsidies, a supportive public, and millions of visitors each year, this tradition continues to be vigorously maintained. *Studentenplatz/Restplatz* (student tickets; 50AS) and *Stehplatz* (standing-room tickets; 20AS–50AS) are available at all national halls.

Beethoven Memorials

Beethoven inhabited several dozen dwellings around Vienna, spending winters at Innere Stadt (Inner City) addresses like the Pasqualatihaus (1010 Mölker Bastei 8, tel. 0222/535–8905). His summers were usually spent north of the city, such as at 1190 Probusgasse 6 (tel. 0222/375408), where in 1802 he wrote his Heiligenstädter Testament in poignant rage at his increasing deafness. Take Straßenbahn 37, and on the way to or from this house, stop off at the Eroicahaus (1190 Döblinger Hauptstr. 92, tel. 0222/369–1424), where he composed most of his Third Symphony. Admission to each of the houses is 15AS, and they are open Tuesday–Sunday 9–12:15 and 1–4:30.

The 19th-century **Staatsoper** (1010 Opernring 1, tel. 0222/514–442–960), where major operas play, has long been the heart of music in Vienna. When not playing there, the Vienna Philharmonic can be heard at the **Musikverein** (1010 Karlspl. 6, tel. 0222/658–2190), while the Vienna Symphony Orchestra appears most often at the **Konzerthaus** (1010 Lothringerstr. 20, tel. 0222/712–1211). First-rate opera is also performed at the **Volksoper** (1090 Währinger Str., tel. 0222/514–443–318), while ballets and musicals (100AS–1,000AS) take place at **Theater An der Wien** (1060 Linke Wienzeile 6, tel. 0222/588–30237) and **Raimund-Theater** (1060 Wallgasse 18, tel. 0222/599770).

JAZZ AND ROCK MUSIC Jazz has a wide following in Vienna, so consult the journal *Falter* for the latest. **Jazzland** (1010 Franz-Josefs-Kai 29, tel. 0222/533–2575), the granddaddy of Vienna jazz clubs, is still going strong. **Volksgarten** (1010 Heldenpl., tel. 0222/630518; cover 50AS–100AS; closed Tues.–Wed. and Sun) is a major disco, while **U4** (1120 Schönbrunner Str. 222, tel. 0222/858318; closed Sun.) and **The Tunnel** (1080 Florianigasse 39, tel. 0222/423465) are great places for live bands (around 100AS).

THEATER Vienna's theater is rivaled only by that in London and Berlin, and cheap tickets abound. The traditional **Burgtheater** (1010 Dr.-Karl-Lueger-Ring) and the more modern **Akademietheater** (1030 Lisztstr. 1) and **Volkstheater** (1070 Neustiftgasse 1, tel. 0222/932–776) have student tickets at 50AS, as does **Theater in der Josefstadt** (1080 Josefstädter Str. 24–26, tel. 0222/402–5127). All four are closed in July and August, but **avant-garde theater** is performed year-round and is often more fun for the Germanically challenged, anyway (most tickets 120AS–300AS, about 50AS students); **die theater Künstlerhaus** (1010 Karlspl. 5, tel. 0222/587–0504) and anything organized by **WUK** (1090 Währinger Str. 59, tel. 0222/401210) are young and fun. Consult *Falter* for other venues.

Near Vienna

MARIAZELL

Draw a squiggly line across the map of Austria and you'll get an idea of what to expect on the winding train ride through cornfields, rolling meadows, and craggy Alpine tunnels that finally lands you in Mariazell, whose **Basilika** (tel. 03882/2595; open daily 6 AM–8 PM, free tours upon request) is the most important Catholic pilgrimage destination in Austria. In the 14th century, King Ludovicus I of Hungary donated an altar to the Virgin in thanks for help in defeating the Turks, and the place became a hot spot for the Christian faithful. Ludwig's gift and those from many other monarchs are displayed in the **Schatzkammer** (admission 15AS, 5AS students; open weekdays 10–noon and 2–3, weekends 10–3) upstairs in the basilica. The Habsburgs, in particular, were staunch supporters of this remote holy place and commissioned the magnificent altars by Fischer von Erlach. The Gothic **Glockenturm** (Bell Tower; admission 10AS; open Tues.–Fri. 10–12:15 and 2–3:30, weekends 10–12:15 and 1–4) offers views of the town and surrounding valley. Saturday evenings (8:30 PM) bring the famous *Lichterprozession*, a candlelit parade. For more information on the town, talk to **Tourismusverband Mariazell** (Hauptpl. 13, tel. 03882/2366).

COMING AND GOING If the train ride weren't pilgrimage-slow, Mariazell would definitely be best visited as a day trip. Unfortunately, the **Mariazellerbahn** ride takes 3½ hours (195AS) from Vienna's Westbahnhof, and it leaves Mariazell for the last time around 5:30 PM. The Mariazell **Bahnhof** is actually in the town **St. Sebastian**, but walk five minutes uphill and you're in Mariazell. An **express post bus** (tel. 03882/2166) leaves once daily (4:15 PM) from the lower level of Mariazell's post office building for Wien Mitte and is actually a bit faster than the train (2¾ hrs, 170AS), but rail passes aren't valid.

WHERE TO SLEEP AND EAT Look for ZIMMER FREI signs advertising bed-and-breakfasts along the road from the Bahnhof. Roll out of bed into morning mass at **Salvatorheim** (Abt.-Severin-Gasse 7, tel. 03882/2216; doubles 350AS–400AS), on the road behind the basilica. Mariazell's small, noisy **HI Jugendherberge** (Fischer-von-Erlach-Weg 2, tel. 03882/2669;

dorm beds 120AS, doubles with bath 340AS, members only) attracts lots of kids with its sports facilities. Follow Wiener Neustadterstraße south from Hauptplatz.

The Donau Valley

Austria's Donau Valley was a wine-producing region under the Celts even before the Romans arrived and began planting vines of their own. Today the valley has been romanticized by legend and by reality—this is where Richard the Lionheart was locked in a dungeon for years, and where marvelous castles and abbeys suddenly appear at a turn in the road. The Donauuferbahn train line follows the Donau upstream all the way to St. Valentin, a 20-minute train ride short of Linz. With a single Vienna–Salzburg ticket, you can make as many stops as you want for up to four days; with a round-trip ticket, you can do the same for up to two months. The **Donau Radweg,** Austria's most famous bike trail, which goes from Passau, Germany through Linz, Melk, Krems, and Vienna, and on to Bratislava in Slovakia, is at its best in spring. But perhaps the best way to get into the Donau spirit is to let your EurailPass take you on a **ferry,** perhaps from Krems to Melk (3 hrs, 240AS without pass). For other possibilities, get in touch with **Donau Cruises** (DDSG Donaureisen, off Hauptpl., tel. 0732/783607) in Linz.

Linz

Linz an der Donau is one of those towns that lives under a shadow. Nearby Vienna gets all the fame and glory, while Linz, home to a lot of the area's factories, gets dissed with jokes (like "Linz rhymes with Provinz"). All the while, though, it's quietly making significant contributions to the nation's culture. The astronomer Johannes Kepler taught at Linz's university, which now bears his name; the talents of composer Anton Bruckner developed while he played the organ at the Alter Dom; the poet Rainer Maria Rilke attended the Handelschule on Rudigierstraße; and the philosopher Ludwig Wittgenstein went to the old Realschule (just a year after Adolf Hitler dropped out). Austria's third-largest city, underrated Linz has a well-preserved *Altstadt* (Old City) and excellent museums, and it just may be the very best place to dip into Austrian urban culture beyond the widening gyre of tourists from Vienna.

BASICS The staff at **Freudenverkehrszentrale** (Hauptpl. 4, tel. 0732/1770) will happily call hotels for you at no charge. In the train station by the exchange window is a free hot-line telephone (dial 1777) to the office. The **American Express** office (Bürgerstr. 14, tel. 0732/669013; open weekdays 9–5:30, Sat. 9–noon) has the usual services.

GETTING AROUND Linz's main strip, **Landstraße,** runs north from the Hauptbahnhof to **Hauptplatz,** the focal point of town. You could walk it in 30–40 minutes, or take Straßenbahn 3. Hauptplatz is north of most of the sights, the Donau is just north of Hauptplatz, and the university is north of the Donau. Rent bikes from the station or from **Rad Verleih** (Hauptpl. 33, tel. 0732/330550), where mountain bikes are 120AS per day.

WHERE TO SLEEP AND EAT There are few, if any, Privatzimmer in Linz. The smallest, most central, and nicest hostel in town is the **HI Jugendherberge** (Kapuzinerstr. 14, tel. 0732/782720; beds 115AS); there's no curfew or lockout, and the price includes sheets and shower, but no breakfast. From the station, take Straßenbahn 3 to Taubenmarkt and walk left on Promenade, which becomes Klammstraße, to Kapuzinerstraße. Showers in every room and a bar are pluses at the more remote **HI Jugendgästehaus** (Stanglhofweg 3, tel. 0732/664434; singles 280AS, doubles 360AS); from the station, take Bus 45 to Stadion. The simple **Goldenes Dachl** (Hafnerstr. 27, tel. 0732/675480; singles 220AS, doubles 440AS) is a 15-minute walk from the station going right on Bahnhofstraße to Volksgartenstraße, then left on Wurmstraße, and right on Hafnerstraße.

The Saturday market on Hauptplatz is a good place to pick up snacks, and the small streets of the Altstadt near the Schloßmuseum (*see* Worth Seeing, *below*) hide lots of reasonable cafés and restaurants. **S'Kist'l** (Altstadt 17, tel. 0732/784545; closed Sun.) has a Heurige-style buffet (25AS–70AS) and 25 different beers. It draws artsy types until 2 AM. For an incredibly sweet Linzer torte (25AS) or other elegant dessert nibbles, stop in at **Philipp Wrann** (Landstr. 70, tel. 0732/773288). The bar **Wohin "Bar bei Hans"** (Starheubergstr. 11, tel. 0732/278075) draws lesbian and gay natives and visitors.

WORTH SEEING A trip to Linz would be wasted without stops in at least a few of the city's fantastic museums. In the castle up the hill from Hauptplatz is **Schloßmuseum Linz**, an earthy and appealing collection spanning all aspects of daily life along the Donau from the Middle Ages to the turn of the century. Displays on folk art, pottery, musical instruments, cider making, domestic architecture, and 18th-century science all have their own rooms. *Tummelpl. 10, tel. 0732/774419. Admission: 25AS. Open Tues.–Fri. 9–5, weekends 10–4.*

Picking up where the Schloßmuseum leaves off, the **Neue Galerie der Stadt Linz** is across the river on the second floor of a shopping mall. All the early modern Austrian greats are here, including Klimt, Kubin, and Albin Egger-Lienz. *Blüttenstr. 15, tel. 0732/239–33600. Admission: 40AS, 20AS students. Open Mon.–Wed. and Fri. 10–6, Thurs. 10–10, Sat. 10–1.*

The composer Anton Bruckner served as cathedral organist for a dozen years at the 17th-century **Alter Dom** (open daily 7–noon and 3–7), a distinctive building that was the main cathedral in town during Linz's heyday. Just up the hill from the Schloßmuseum is the small, well-restored **Martinskirche,** which dates back to 799 and is thought to be the oldest church in Austria.

For a view of the city, head north across the Donau to the top of Pöstlingberg; Ride Straßenbahn 3 to Bergbahnhof Urfahr, then walk up or ride about 3 km on the **Pöstlingbergbahn** (22AS, 35AS round-trip, tel. 0732/280–17577); the climb is so steep that it made the *Guinness Book of World Records.*

NEAR LINZ

Adolph Hitler often announced plans to make his native Linz a center of German culture, but he had no qualms about establishing **KZ Lager,** the main concentration camp in Austria, only half an hour down the Donau at **Mauthausen.** The site includes a small museum and memorials to the more than 110,000 who died here, but the value of a visit here lies more in the significance of the space than in the quality of the displays. The camp is a 5-km, signposted walk from the Mauthausen train station; post buses (tel. 0732/1671) from Linz drop you nearer the camp. *Tel. 07238/2269. Admission: 15AS. Open Feb.–mid-Dec., daily 8–4.*

Krems

At the downstream end of the Wachau, the Donau's most invitingly scenic and historic stretch, Krems is a good starting or stopping point for exploration of the entire Donau Valley. The town itself is pretty lazy and quiet, but fortunes made by trade along the river have led to the construction of lots of elaborate, medieval buildings. The lovingly restored Altstadt, bisected by the east–west Landstraße, sits in the shadow of the Gothic **Piaristenkirche;** Martin Johann "Kremser" Schmidt, the town's most famous artist, did all the altarpieces here as well as the frescoes in the nearby Baroque **Pfarrkirche St. Veit** (Pfarrpl.). The **Dominikanerkirche** (Theaterpl. 8–9, tel. 02732/84927), which is no longer used as a church, houses the excellent **Historisches Museum der Stadt Krems** and the **Weinbaumuseum** (admission to both 20AS; open Tues.–Sat. 9–noon and 2–5, Sun. 9–noon), which has displays on the region's wine culture.

To stay in Krems overnight, crash at **HI Jugendherberge** (Ringstr. 77, tel. 02732/83452; beds 150AS; closed Nov.–Mar.) or the fitness-room-equipped **Kolping-Gästehaus** (Ringstr. 46, tel. 02732/83541; doubles 550AS, dorm beds 180AS), both in the Altstadt. Or get in touch with the **tourist office** (Undstr. 6, tel. 02732/82676) about Privatzimmer.

Graz

Austria's second-largest city is a university town and industrial center that takes a casual, almost offhand interest in tourism—it's an ordinary city where the locals are reasonably nice but won't try to sweet talk you out of your tourist buck. Known since the 19th century as "Pensionopolis" for the many retirees attracted to its mild weather, low cost of living, and cultural offerings (opera, theater, music festivals), Graz also has an extensive Innere Stadt, or Altstadt, where the historic buildings share streets with lively night spots. A slow walk up the hill and through the streets is worth the effort for the architecture you'll discover and the views from the top.

BASICS

VISITOR INFORMATION *Herrengasse 16, tel. 0316/835241. Open weekdays 9–7, Sat. 9–6, Sun. 10–5.*

AMERICAN EXPRESS *Hamerlinggasse 6, A-8010 Graz, tel. 0316/817010.*

COMING AND GOING

Graz is 2½ hours by train from Vienna, four hours from Salzburg. The **Hauptbahnhof** is a 30-minute walk or a short Straßenbahn ride (Tram 1, 3, 6, 7, or 14) west of the active Innere Stadt; Hauptplatz and Herrengasse mark the very center. The university area starts just up the hill from the Innere Stadt, on the other side of Glacisstraße. For a **taxi**, call 0316/2801.

WHERE TO SLEEP AND EAT

Rooms at rock-bottom prices lurk just behind the train station in **Pension Kügerl-Lukas** (Wagner-Biro-Str. 8, tel. 0316/52590; doubles 400AS). The entry and stairwell look like those of a tenement, but the rooms are clean. The front desk—also a local bar—stays open 24 hours. Five minutes down the road in front of the station is the cheerier **Hotel Strasser** (Eggenberger Gürtl 11, tel. 0316/913977; doubles 500AS). Near Schloß Eggenberg but consequently far from everything else, **"Alt Eggenberg" Wagenhofer** (Baiernstr. 3, tel. 0316/56615; doubles 500AS–550AS) has only rooms with bath. From the station, take Straßenbahn 1. In a serene setting a 20-minute walk from the train station, the **Jugendgästhaus** (Idhofgasse 74, tel. 0316/914876; beds 130AS–160AS; closed Dec. 22–Jan. 7) has four- and six-person dorm rooms. From the station, walk down Annenstraße three blocks, then turn right on Idhofgasse.

The **Hauptplatz market** of fruits, fast food, and other goodies is open weekdays 7–6, Saturdays until about 2. The most central grocery store is **Hornig** (Hans-Sachs-Gasse 9, off Herrengasse, tel. 0316/825–2520). Lots of student hangouts on Harrachgasse and Zinzendorfgasse provide good values, though the best area in the evening to eat, get coffee, or find a bar is a block off Herrengasse, near the tourist office. **Cosa Nostra** (Hans-Sachs-Gasse 10; closed Tues.) is an exceptionally friendly place where you can fill up on unlimited fresh pizza bread with your reasonably priced Italian meal. The best salad bar (13AS per 100 grams) for miles is at **Mangold's Vollwertrestaurant** (Grieskai 10, on the west bank of river, tel. 0316/918002; closed Sat. dinner and Sun.).

WORTH SEEING

The tourist office has a sentimentally written but useful "city walk" map for exploring the Innere Stadt. The Baroque interior of the **Domkirche** is especially worth a look.

Graz gets its name from an old Slavic word meaning fort, and its enormous **medieval arsenal,** on display at the Landzeughaus, is of mind-numbing proportions—3,300 suits of armor, 7,800 firearms, 2,275 swords, and so on. *Herrengasse 16, tel. 0316/53264. Admission: 25AS, students free. Open Apr.–Oct., weekdays 9–5, weekends 9–1.*

A walk up to the crumbling **Schloßberg**—not to be confused with the Schloß Eggenberg—gives the best views of the city, particularly around sunset; up there you'll find a bell tower, the town's funky clock tower, and a fairytale stone staircase for the walk down. For a castle in much better condition, take Straßenbahn 7 across town to the early 17th-century **Schloß Eggenberg** (tel. 0316/53264, ext. 11; admission 25AS; open Apr.–Oct., daily 10–4) and adjoining "Wildpark," a popular hangout among peacocks. The rich Baroque **Prunkräume** (State Apartments) are the palace's leading attraction, but interesting archaeological finds and an extensive coin collection are also on display.

The **Landesmuseum Joanneum,** named after its founder Archduke Johann, was one of the first public museums in Europe. The collection is housed in many locations in and outside Graz, but the principal part of the collection, including works by Pieter Brueghel the Elder and Lucas Cranach the Elder and Younger, appears here. *Museumgebäude Neutorgasse 45, tel. 0316/801–74770. Admission: 25AS, students free. Open weekdays 10–5, weekends 10–1.*

Salzburg

 Salzburg sags under a weighty musical tradition. Wolfgang Amadeus Mozart was born and raised here, but he eventually rejected Salzburg for Vienna because the so-called patronage of the ruling archbishop was getting him nowhere. But Mozart's disgust with his hometown didn't quite start a trend, and big-name musicians have continued to make this a tour stop. The 1964 filming of *The Sound of Music* in and around Salzburg sealed the city's musical reputation. Summer is the best time to visit if you want to find everything open or go to the city's big music festival, though you won't exactly have the place to yourself—horrendous crowds pour in to see this small town with big culture. The **Salzburger Sommer Festspiele** (tel. 0662/844501), held the last week of July through the end of August, packs in incredible quantities of music with incredibly few price breaks for students; tickets generally start at 200AS–300AS.

BASICS

VISITOR INFORMATION Information Hauptbahnhof (tel. 0662/871712 or 0662/873638; open July–Aug., Mon.–Sat. 8:15 AM–9:30 PM, shorter hrs off-season) in the train station has lots of maps and brochures and will find you lodging for a 30AS fee. **Information Mozartplatz** (Mozartpl. 5, tel. 0662/847568; open Easter–Sept., daily 9–8, shorter hrs off-season) provides the same services and also sells performance tickets. **Information der Salzburger Land Tourismus** next door has regional information.

AMERICAN EXPRESS *Mozartpl. 5, tel. 0662/842501. Open weekdays 9–5:30, Sat. 9–noon.*

MAIL **Hauptpostamt.** *Residenzpl. 9, tel. 0662/844–12116. Open weekdays 7–7, Sat. 8–10 AM. Postal code A-5010.*

COMING AND GOING

Trains leave Salzburg's station (tel. 0662/1717), a 20-minute walk north of the center, frequently for Vienna (3 hrs, 380AS) and Munich (2 hrs, 280AS), daily for Zürich (6 hrs, 800AS), Venice (6½ hrs, 440AS), Prague (8 hrs, 450AS), and Paris (10 hrs, 1,540AS). To hook up with drivers headed your way, call **Mitfahrzentrale.** *W. Philharmonikergasse 2, tel. 0662/841327. Open Mon.–Thurs. 9–noon and 2–5, Fri. 9–noon.*

GETTING AROUND

The Salzach River swoops down through town, and virtually everything you want to see clings to its banks. Northeast of the central river area is the mountain **Kapuzinerberg,** where you'll find good hiking trails, but the more interesting mountain is **Mönchsberg,** the home of the Hohensalzburg Fortress southwest of the river. An elevator called the **Mönchsbergaufzug**

(Gstättengasse 13, tel. 0662/205–51180) whisks people to the top of the Mönchsberg for 15AS, 23AS round-trip. If you need a **taxi,** call 0662/8111 or 0662/661066.

BY BUS A ride costs 20AS if you buy a ticket on the bus, 16AS if you buy it from a dispensing machine at major bus stops. A book of five tickets (a *Fünf Stück*) from a tobacco shop costs 65AS, a 24-hour pass 27AS. Buses 5, 51, and 55 travel between the Hauptbahnhof and the Altstadt. Most buses run 6 AM–11 PM.

BY BIKE Consider bagging the *Sound of Music* tours, renting a pair of wheels from the office at the train station (tel. 0662/715–415–427), and exploring Salzburg on your own. Bike roads crisscross town and grace both riverbanks; look for the blue dashed lines on the tourist office's free "Hotelplan" map or invest in their bike map (80AS). To rent mountain bikes (150AS per day), try **Activ Reisebüro** (Kaigasse 21, tel. 0662/891148).

WHERE TO SLEEP

Hostels in Salzburg are plentiful, varied, and well run. The tourist office will book a room in a pension or hotel for 30AS or give you a list of Privatzimmer. Summer student housing, located mostly on Linzer Gasse, is nice but surprisingly expensive; the only affordable dorm is **Institut St. Sebastian** (Linzer Gasse 41, tel. 0662/871386 or 0662/882606; doubles 360AS, dorm beds 120AS). If you must have a green and peaceful spot, try **Gasthof Uberfuhr** (Ignaz-Reider-Kai 43, tel. 0662/23010), a riverside family inn a 20-minute walk south of the Altstadt. From the Bahnhof, take Bus 1 or 2 to Hanuschplatz, then Bus 49 to Überfuhrstraße/Mandigasse, and head left for five minutes to the river. The campground **Camping Gnigl/Ost** (Parscher Str. 4, tel. 0662/644143; 20AS per tent, 30AS per person; closed Sept.–May 15) is readily accessible by Bus 27 or 29 from Mirabellplatz to Minnesheimstraße.

➢ **UNDER 500AS** • **Junger Fuchs.** Narrow halls and low ceilings lend a potentially claustrophobic feel and sometimes transmit the voices of fellow guests with exceptional clarity, but this place is central and cheap. The proprietor doesn't take to Americans. Singles 240AS, doubles 360AS–380AS. *Linzer Gasse 54, tel. 0662/875496. 20-min walk from train station; go under tracks on Rainer Str., left on Franz-Josef-Str., right on Wolf-Dietrich-Str., and right again on Linzer Gasse. Showers 15AS.*

Pension Elisabeth. Cheapest place near the station, so call ahead. Plain but clean. Singles 280AS–320AS, doubles 400AS, 480AS with shower. *Vogelweiderstr. 52, tel. 0662/871664. Cross to back of station, go over tracks and through drive at nearby #12 (Lastenstr., but don't bother looking for the name) to Breitenfelderstr. and follow to Vogelweiderstr.*

➢ **UNDER 600AS** • **Bergland.** Eighteen completely charming rooms, buffet breakfast, TV, phone, and delightful owner who pours drinks in a cozy bar. Minimum stay of two days unless a room opens late. Singles with shower 400AS, doubles without 520AS. *Rupertgasse 15, tel. 0662/872318. Left out of station, turn left under tracks to Gabelsbergerstr., take Bayernhamerstr. at fork, and turn left on Rupertgasse (15 min). Reservations advised.*

Pension Adlerhof. Bland, but an easy three-minute walk from the station. Singles 360AS, doubles 530AS. If they're full try nearby **Jahn** (Elisabethstr. 31, tel. 0662/871405). *Elisabethstr. 25, tel. 0662/875236. Go straight out of station and left on Elisabethstr.*

HOSTELS **Gasthaus Bürgerwehr.** Salzburg's smallest and freshest hostel: A friendly couple welcomes guests to magnificent mountaintop views of all Salzburg. Always fully booked by noon; reservations accepted one day in advance. Beds 110AS. *Mönchsberg 19C, tel. 0662/841729. From station, Bus 1 to Gstättengasse at Mönchsbergaufzug. Take elevator (13AS), then head right briefly downward, through the stone arch, and make a sharp loop left up the hill. 1 AM curfew, showers 10AS. Closed mid-Oct.–Apr.*

Haunspergstraße (HI). Well-equipped hostel an easy walk from the train station. No groups. Pool table, table tennis, Foosball. Beds 140AS, including sheets, shower, and breakfast. *Haunspergstr. 27, tel. 0662/875030. Walk straight out of the station 3–4 blocks and turn right right on Haunspergstr. Midnight curfew, lockout 2–5, laundry. Closed Sept.–June.*

International Youth Hotel. Americans and Australians down beers at one of the rowdiest bars in Salzburg. Free *Sound of Music* showings daily at 1:30 PM; book *Sound of Music* tours at a discount. All rooms reassigned every morning; show up just before 10 AM for the best choice. Beds 120AS–140AS, doubles 320AS. *Paracelsusstr. 9, tel. 0662/879649. From station, turn left, turn left under tracks on Gabelsbergerstr., then turn right on Paracelsusstr. Laundry, showers 10AS, luggage storage.*

Jugendgästehaus Salzburg (HI). Salzburg's largest hostel, just outside the Altstadt. Spacious lawn, jaunty multicolored interior. Beds 130AS–180AS, including breakfast, shower, and sheets; doubles 450AS. Reservations accepted in writing or by fax only. *Josef-Preis-Allee 18, tel. 0662/842–6700 or 0662/846857, fax 0662/841101. From station, Bus 5 or 55 to just across river. Midnight curfew, lockout 9–11 AM, laundry, wheelchair access.*

Jugendherberge Aigen (HI). Newly renovated hostel with lots of plants, 15- to 20-minute walk from Altstadt. All rooms bright and sparkling. Beds 140AS (170AS nonmembers), including breakfast, sheets, shower, locker in room. Reception open 7–9 AM and 5–midnight. Checkout by 8:45 AM. *Aigner Str. 34, tel. 0662/23248. From station, Bus 51 to Mozartsteg, then Bus 49 to Finanzamt, then walk 200 meters on Aigner Str. Midnight curfew.*

Jugendherberge Glockengasse (HI). Centrally located at base of Kapuzinerberg. Nice staff, clean, but with rules that might have been written by Captain von Trapp. Beds 120AS first night, 110AS additional nights. Rates include breakfast, shower, sheets, and locker, but beds come 12 to a room. *Glockengasse 8, tel. 0662/876241. Walk left out of station, left under tracks, on Gabelsbergerstr., right on Bayerhamerstr. to the mountain (20 min). Midnight curfew, lockout 9–3:30. Closed mid-Oct.–Apr.*

Plainstraße (HI). Mellow and even kinda classy hostel. Beds 140AS (160AS nonmembers); rates include breakfast, sheets, and shower. All rooms doubles, triples, and quads. *Plainstr. 83, tel. 0662/50728. Walk straight out of station 2–3 blocks and turn right on Plainstr. Midnight curfew, lockout 9–5. Closed Sept.–June.*

FOOD

Steer clear of the Altstadt if you're tight on cash, and join the locals at the cheaper joints across the river. Unless you make the super but Thursday-only **Schrannemarkt** (by Stephanskirche; open until 1 PM), buy fruits and vegetables at **Grüner Markt** (open weekdays 6–6, Sat. 6–1) in front of **Kollegienkirche** (Universitätspl.). Three blocks from the train station, **Steierischen Weinstuben** (St. Julien-Str. 9, tel. 0662/874790) serves working-class Salzburgers hot meals (40AS–175AS) and hosts live traditional music until 3 AM. Weekdays, hit **Uni-Cafe** (Sigmund-Haffner Gasse 11, near Staatsbrücke, tel. 0662/24139) for filling cafeteria lunches (35AS–50AS) in slick art-deco surroundings.

The chocolate manufacturers Fürst (Brodgasse 13, at Alter Markt, tel. 0662/843759) are the creators of famous chocolate balls known as "Salzburger Mozartkugeln," with a miniportrait of Mozart on the wrapper.

➤ **UNDER 100AS • Humboltstube.** Varied salad buffet (40AS–110AS) served on a plaza dramatically dwarfed by the sheer mountain face nearby. Good place for two people to split a *Salzburger Nockerl* (giant dessert dumpling; 100AS). *Gstättengasse 6, tel. 0662/843171. At base of Mönchsbergaufzug in the Altstadt.*

Peperone Pizzaria. The waiters are fun, and the pizzas (60AS–90AS) are fantastic—especially the Sicilian. Yummy take-away slices 25AS. *Gaisbergstr. 12, near Mönchsberg elevator at end of Griesgasse, tel. 0662/641468.*

➤ **UNDER 150AS • Bürgerwehr-Einkehr.** View of entire valley from friendly, traditional mountain Gasthof surroundings. The food is average: salads 70AS, Wiener schnitzl with potatoes and mixed salad 100AS. *Mönchsberg 19C, tel. 0662/841729. From Anton-Neumayr-Pl. at end of Griesgasse, take elevator (13AS) or walk up from Toscaninihof. Closed mid-Oct.–Apr.*

Mandarin I. Wildly overdecorated interior, garden area out back. Weekdays, lunch special plus soup 70AS. Mandarin duck with rice and vegetables (110AS) is an excellent dinner. *Schallmooser Hauptstr. 15, north side of Kapuzinerberg, tel. 0662/875703.*

CAFES **Cafe Bazar** (Schwarzstr. 3, near Staatsbrücke, tel. 0662/874278; closed evenings and Sun.) is a classy traditional café near the Salzach; the vegetable omelets (60AS) are delicious. **Galerie Cafe "la femmerie"** (Markus Sitticus Str. 17, off Rainerstr., tel. 0662/871639; open Wed.–Sat. 10 PM–midnight) is an easygoing lesbian café run by the local Frauenkulturzentrum (Women's Culture Center).

WORTH SEEING

In the pristine Altstadt south of the Salzach River, the brooding **Hohensalzburg Fortress** on the hill and the airy Italianate **Residenz** of the archbishops below compete for aesthetic dominance. The best-preserved old-city streets are **Getreidegasse**, where Mozart was born, and **Linzer Gasse,** Getreidegasse's continuation across the river. Since Salzburg was long a bishopric, it's not surprising that the Altstadt is dominated by religious buildings. The Baroque **Dom** (tel. 0662/845295; admission 25AS, 10AS students; open mid-May–mid-Oct., daily 9–5), a magnificent venue for organ concerts, was commissioned by Archbishop Markus Sitticus. Mozart was baptized here as an infant in 1756, and returned later in life to play the organ. After the church was built, archaeologists decided to excavate the Roman ruins underneath it, so the old structure has an even older layer poking out from underneath. A combination entrance ticket to the excavations, the Museum Carolino Augusteum (*see below*), and the Bürgerspital Spielzeugmuseum (*see below*) costs 60AS, 20AS students. Behind the Dom, **Stiftskirche St. Peter,** a luxurious Romanesque-turned-rococo church, marks the site of St. Rupert's 7th-century monastery, which grew to become the city of Salzburg.

The manicured **Mirabellgarten,** just off the river and bordering the Altstadt, was the site of both prince-archbishop intrigues and goofy games of do-re-mi; today *Sound of Music* tours (280AS) use it as their point of departure. The two major companies offering the approximately four-hour tour are **Panorama Tours** (Mirabellpl., near St. Andrä-Kirche, tel. 0662/874029) and **Salzburg Sightseeing** (Mirabellpl. 2, tel. 0662/881616); both strike out daily at 9:30 AM and 2 PM. If you just want to take in the highlights, **Schloß Leopoldskron** and **Schloß Frohnburg**, the houses used in filming the movie, are an easy bike ride south of the center of town.

HOHENSALZBURG FORTRESS Originally built in 1077, the stark Hohensalzburg was substantially enlarged in the early 1500s by Archbishop Leonhard "The Turnip" von Keutschach. Take the 50-minute English-language tour (25AS, 15AS students in addition to admission) if you want an account of the torture chamber and other details of castle life. To get here, you can walk up about 20 minutes or take the Festungsbahn (cable car) for 18AS. *Mönchsberg 34, tel. 0662/804–22123. Admission without tour: 20AS, 10AS students. Open Apr.–Sept., daily 8–7; Oct.–Mar., daily 8–6.*

While walking through the Hohensalzburg Fortress, keep your eyes peeled for 58 tiny turnip drawings, reminders of the fortress's 16th-century resident Archbishop Leonhard "The Turnip" von Keutschach.

MOZART'S GEBURTHAUS As an adult the great composer preferred Vienna, complaining that audiences in his native city were no more responsive than tables and chairs. Still, home is home, and this was Mozart's—when not on one of his frequent trips abroad—until the age of 17. The 1760 clavichord used by the child prodigy is here, as well as the 1780 piano he used later on. Joseph Lange's famous unfinished portrait of the composer hangs nearby. *Getreidegasse 9, tel. 0662/844313. Admission: 50AS, 35AS students. Open June–Aug., daily 9–7; Sept.–May, daily 9–6.*

HEILBRUNN A summer palace 4 km south of the Salzburg Altstadt, Schloß Heilbrunn was built between 1613 and 1619 by Archbishop Markus Sitticus. The merry archbishop used his **Wasserspielen** (Water Garden) to amuse and humiliate his guests; a 45-minute tour gives you a look at some of his tactics (tip: wear a raincoat). Tickets for the tour also include admission to the bright yellow **Schloß,** which houses some artwork worth a look. The evening tours offered in July and August every hour from 5 to 10 PM (minimum 10 people) are the most magical way to see the water works, though you can't get student discounts. *Tel. 0662/826372 or 0662/820003. From station, Bus 55. Admission: 48AS, 24AS students under 26. Open Apr. and Oct., daily 9–4:30; May–Sept., daily 9–5.*

OTHER MUSEUMS **Bürgerspital Spielzeugmuseum (Toy Museum).** This place displays a remarkable collection of toys from a time before Nintendo and professional sports. *Bürgerspitalgasse 2, tel. 0662/847560. Admission: 30AS, 10AS students. Open Tues.–Sun. 9–5.*

Museum Carolino Augusteum. Romp through Salzburg history from Iron Age artifacts to 19th-century paintings by native son Hans Makart in this classy local museum. Friday evening concerts in the Roman Hall cost 270AS, 135AS students. *Museumpl. 1, tel. 0662/843145 or 0662/645561. Admission: 40AS, 15AS students. Open Tues. 9–8, Wed.–Sun. 9–5.*

AFTER DARK

Many of Salzburg's bars and other night spots cluster around Museumplatz (at the base of Mönchsberg) in the Altstadt, just across the river on Imberstraße, and behind that on narrow Steingasse. A tasty homemade brew called Weißbier (30AS) is served at **Die Weisse** (Virgilgasse 9, north of Kapuzinerberg, tel. 0662/872246); giant pretzels are 18AS. **Urban Keller** (Schallmooser Haupstr. 50, tel. 0662/870894; cover usually 80AS) books the best jazz in town, while Austrian grunge and other antipretentious groups play, usually for free, at **Schneitl-Musik Pub** (Bergstr. 5/7, off Linzer Gasse, tel. 0662/878678). **Kupferpfandl Cafe Club 2000** (Paracelsusstr. 14, north of Gabelsbergerstr., tel. 0662/75760) is a popular gay bar. For late-night spaghetti (70AS–90AS), hit **Andreas Hofer** (Steingasse 65, tel. 0662/872769), a candlelit wine bar across Mozartsteg Bridge from the Altstadt.

Near Salzburg

SALZBERGWERKE

For ages, the Salzbergewerke (salt mines) of Hallein, 16 km south of Salzburg, were the basis of Salzburg's wealth and power. Tours of the mines involve donning cave gear, slipping down miners' slides, and chugging along on a little train—amusing, if not terribly informative. From Salzburg, take a train or bus to Hallein, then walk to the Salzbergbahn cableway and take it up. *Tel. 06245/5285, ext. 15. Admission with round-trip cableway fare: 185AS. Open May–mid-Oct., daily 9–5.*

THE SALZKAMMERGUT

The region east of Salzburg known today as the Salzkammergut is Austria's lake district. When the imperial family joined in the 19th-century European craze for salt baths and put a particular stamp of approval on Bad Ischl, nearby lake resort towns started emphasizing their own saline characteristics until eventually all towns within about 50 km came to be grouped under one name. The lakes are surrounded by generally flat terrain to the north and by increasingly dramatic mountains as you head south. Attnang-Puchheim, on the main Vienna–Salzburg line (1 hr from Salzburg, 2½ hrs from Wien Westbahnhof), is where you transfer to enter the Salzkammergut from the north.

For 60 years, **Bad Ischl** was the summer vacation spot of choice of Emperor Franz-Josef. If you come to the Salzkammergut at all, you'll probably stop here, if only because it's the most convenient transfer point in the area. And as a transfer point, it's not bad—a small, easy, and lighthearted place, encircled by the Ischl and Traun rivers. A tour of the **Kaiservilla** (Kaiserpark, tel. 06132/23241; tour in English 70AS), a wedding present from Franz-Josef's parents, takes you by his spartan bedroom and the study and desk where he signed a declaration of war against Serbia that exploded into World War I. Take the **Salzbergwerke tour** (tel. 06132/239–4831; admission 115AS; open May 10–June, daily 9–4, July–Sept., daily 10–5) to learn about the huge role salt has played in the Salzkammergut. For info and help finding a place to sleep, head left out of the station to **Kurdirektion** (Bahnhofstr. 6, tel. 06132/27757 or 06132/23520). The 120AS beds at **HI Jugendgästenhaus** (Am Rechensteg 5, tel. 06132/66577) include breakfast, sheets, and shower, but the hostel fills up early. The much cheaper **HI Jugendherberge Pfarrheim** (Auböckpl. 6C, tel. 06132/34838; beds 50AS; closed mid-Sept.–mid-June) skips the breakfast and charges 10AS extra for sheets.

The town of **Hallstatt** not only has the world's oldest salt mines, it's also the most drop-dead gorgeous lakeside village in the Salzkammergut. Hallstatt's **Salzbergwerke tour** (115AS; open June–mid-Sept., daily 9:30–4:30, May and mid-Sept.–mid-Oct., daily 9:30–3) is arguably the best in the Salzkammergut because of the lakeside location; ride the Salzbergbahn (85AS round-trip) from the base of town to the mine. The **Prähistorisches Museum** (Seestr.; admission 35AS, 20AS students; open daily 9:30–6) gives you the lowdown on how ancient salt mines actually worked. Hourly trains from Bad Ischl (30 min, 70AS) drop you off at the Hallstatt Hauptbahnhof, where you can pick up a ferry (40AS round-trip, passes not valid) to shuttle you across the Hallstätter See to the village (last ferry either way about 6 PM). The tourist office **Tourismus Verband** is at Seestraße 169 (tel. 06134/208), and Hallstatt's welcoming **HI hostel** (Salzbergstr. 50, tel. 06134/279 or 06134/681; beds 90AS; closed Oct.–Apr.) is an easy 10-minute walk along Seestraße to Salzbergstraße.

Innsbruck

A focal point of the Austrian Renaissance, imperial residence off and on following the coronation of Maximilian I in 1493, and political capital of the quintessentially Alpine province of Tirol, Innsbruck came to world attention in 1964 and again in 1976 as host to the Winter Olympics. Since then, travelers have woken up to the fact that this is one of the most beautifully situated and exciting cities in Austria. Traditional Tirolean culture, evident in the excellent Tirol Folk Museum and in the streets of the almost completely preserved Altstadt, is supplemented by an opera house, a major university, and frequent, if slightly wacky, events like candle-carrying scuba divers in the River Inn or a carefully choreographed concert using all the church bells in the Inn Valley.

BASICS

VISITOR INFORMATION The train station has a **Hotel Information** office (tel. 0512/583766; open daily 8 AM–10 PM) that specializes in room bookings (30AS fee). The **Innsbruck Information Office** (Burggraben 3, tel. 0512/5356; open Mon.–Sat. 8–7, Sun. 8–6, shorter hrs off-season) books rooms and handles event tickets. The tourist office (tel. 0512/59850) upstairs is worth a stop if you need more detailed info. A **Tirol-Info office** (Wilhelm-Greil-Str. 17, tel. 0512/532–0170) has a mountaineering expert available to answer questions 8:30–6 Thursdays and Fridays.

AMERICAN EXPRESS *Brixner Str. 3, tel. 0512/582491. Open weekdays 9–5:30, Sat. 9–noon.*

CONSULATE United Kingdom. *Matthias-Schmid-Str. 12/I, tel. 0512/588320. Open weekdays 9–noon.*

MAIL The Hauptpostamt never closes. *Maximilian Str. 2, tel. 0512/5000.*

COMING AND GOING

Innsbruck is a major European crossroads. It's about three hours from Salzburg, five hours from Vienna, two hours from Munich, four hours from Zurich, and four hours from Venice.

The **Altstadt,** where historic attractions and night spots are clustered, is a 10-minute walk from the train station. Single **bus** or **Straßenbahn** tickets cost 18AS—four tickets cost 44AS—so the 23AS Tageskarte, good for a day of travel in central Innsbruck, is a great deal. The card is available at the train station, the tourist office (where you can also pick up a 10AS route map), or

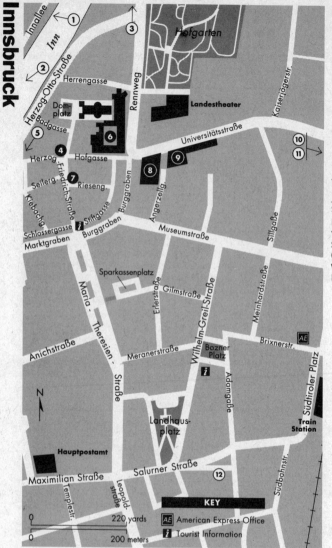

Sights ●

Goldenes Dachl, **4**

Hofburg, **6**

Hofkirche, **8**

Stadtturm, **7**

Tiroler
Volkskunst-
museum, **9**

Lodging ○

Gasthof
Innsbrücke, **2**

Internationales
Studentenhaus, **5**

Jugendherberge
Innsbruck, **10**

Jugendherberge
St. Nicolas, **1**

Pension Stoi, **12**

Torten-Arneus-
Schwedenhaus
(HI), **3**

Volkshaus
Innsbruck, **11**

KEY

AE American Express Office

i Tourist Information

---

a tobacco shop. A **cable car** runs from 20 minutes north of the Hofgarten to the top of the Nordkette Mountains for 280AS. For a **taxi,** call 0512/1718. For mountain bikes (180AS–250AS per day), check out **City-Mountain bike rental** (Innstr. 95, tel. 0512/286515).

WHERE TO SLEEP

The tourist office will give you a complete list of Privatzimmer, but Innsbruck's pensions and Gasthofs are more convenient. For cheap lodging July to mid-September, call the **Internationales Studentenhaus** (Rechengasse 7, tel. 0512/59477) for information about the more than 500 rooms available in student dorms.

➤ **UNDER 600AS** • **Gasthof Innsbrücke.** The riverside location is so convenient you might forget about the street noise. Doubles without bath 440AS. Better-equipped rooms with bath (700AS) are also better furnished. *Innstr. 1, tel. 0512/281934. From Bahnhof, Bus A or K.*

Pension Paula. The cheapest pension in the hills. Singles from 300AS, simple doubles 460AS–560AS, lux doubles (including private bath and balcony) 600AS. Reserve ahead in summer and December. *Weiherburggasse 35, tel. 0512/292262. From station, take St. Nicholas K bus to Schmelzergasse, walk a few steps up the hill on Schmelzergasse, turn right on Weiherburggasse.*

➤ **UNDER 700AS** • **Pension Stoi.** Quiet, spotless, bright rooms only five minutes' walk from the station. Triples and quads have great balconies. Few singles 440AS, doubles 600AS. *Salurner Str. 7, tel. 0512/585434. On a small unnamed street left off Salurner Str.*

HOSTELS To reach Innsbruck's oldest, cheapest hostel, **Jugendherberge Innsbruck** (Reichenauer Str. 147, tel. 0512/46179; beds 130AS first night, 100AS additional nights), take Bus O toward Olympiscle Dorf to Campingplatz-Jugendherberge. **Jugendherberge St. Nicholas** (Innstr. 95, tel. 0512/286515; beds 120AS first night, 100AS additional nights) is more convenient to the Altstadt and the hills but gets expensive with extras: Showers cost 10AS, breakfast 45AS. Take Bus K to Innstraße. **Volkhaus Innsbruck** (Radetzkysteade 47, tel. 0512/466682; beds 100AS per night) is in the same area as Jugendherberge Innsbruck; take Bus R to St. Pirmin/Volkhaus. The popular **HI Torten-Arneus-Schwedenhaus** (Rennweg 17B, tel. 0512/585814; beds 100AS) is open July and August only.

FOOD

The cheapest food in Innsbruck is at the university cafeterias scattered around campus and at **Imbiss Station** trucks on Goldenes Dachl plaza and near the Triumphforte gate at the corner of Maria-Theresien-Straße and Salurner Straße. Do your grocery shopping at **M-Preis supermarkets,** near the train station on Salurner Straße or on the corner of Reichenauer Straße and Andechsstraße. Restaurants catering to students are clustered on and near Innrain, just across the river from the Altstadt. **Salute Pizzaria** (Innrain 37), for example, has 22 kinds of pizza going for 30AS–90AS and noodle dishes from 50AS.

➤ **UNDER 100AS** • **Churrasco.** Italian restaurant by the River Inn with a view of the Nordkette Mountains. Tasty minestrone 40AS, pizza or calzone 70AS–110AS, spinach tortellini 100AS. *Innrain 2, tel. 0512/586398. Wheelchair access.*

Philippine. As in Philippine Welser, wife of Archduke Ferdinand II. Vegetarian restaurant with friendly staff, healthy food, enormous pots of tea. Unusual spaghetti dishes 80AS, wok-fried vegetables 145AS. Convenient to train station. *Templestr. 2, tel. 0512/589157. Closed Sun.*

Schnitzlparadies. Cheap yet classy place to sample variations on Austria's most famous main course: schnitzl (around 80AS). Live piano music Tuesdays and Thursdays. *Innrain 25, tel. 0512/572972. Closed Sun.*

➤ **UNDER 150AS** • **Weißes Rößl.** Excellent Altstadt source of traditional Tirolean fare, in warm second-floor rooms of a 1410 Gasthof. Wiener schnitzl with salad 120AS, Apfelstrudel the way grandma used to make it 30AS. *Kiebachgasse 8. Closed Sun.*

CAFES Cafés are concentrated in the Altstadt near the Goldenes Dachl, but the best student cafés line Innrain near the university. **Hofgarten Café/Restaurant** (tel. 0512/588851), in the center of Innsbruck's public park, is a major weekend meeting place, often featuring free live music. Try the peppery ribs (75AS). **Ebi's Uni Cafe Bistro** (Innrain 55, tel. 0512/573949) is a premier student café, complete with cheap drinks and snacks and a balcony facing the university.

WORTH SEEING

The principal sight in Innsbruck is the medieval Altstadt, where the narrow tower **Stadtturm** (Herzog-Friedrich-Str. 21; admission 20AS, 10AS students) provides a view of it all—if you can see over the heads of other travelers, that is. The **Hofburg** (Rennweg 1; admission 30AS, 10AS students), where the imperial family lived off and on following 1493, was completely renovated in the 18th century; the room where Franz I died was converted into a chapel. **Dom zu St. Jacob,** to the rear of the castle, features impressive Baroque frescoes and an altar with Lucas Cranach's *Mariahilfbild* (Intercession of the Virgin).

The **Goldenes Dachl** (Golden Roof), a mansion built between 1497 and 1500 to celebrate Emperor Maximilian I's second marriage, to Maria Blanca Sforza of Milan, stands at the northern end of Herzog-Friedrich-Straße and was the first building in Austria to be built in Renaissance, rather than Gothic, style. The **Olympiamuseum** (tel. 0512/5360; admission 22AS, 11AS students) inside has paraphernalia from the 1964 and 1976 Winter Olympics.

HOFKIRCHE Emperor Maximilian I wrote prolifically on the importance of building monuments to oneself, and the Hofkirche is the practical application of this doctrine. Constructed by his grandson Ferdinand I between 1553 and 1563, the church contains an impressive marble cenotaph decorated with reliefs picturing scenes from the emperor's life. The tiny Silberne Chapel upstairs contains the tomb of Archduke Ferdinand II (the pious kneeling posture was his own idea) and his wife. The **Tiroler Volkskunstmuseum** (combined admission with Hofkirche 50AS) next door displays Tirolean cultural artifacts including kitchenware, dowry furniture, period clothing, and enormous cowbells. *Universitätsstr. 2, tel. 0512/584302. Admission: 20AS. Open daily 9–5.*

SCHLOß AMBRAS Tiroleans begrudgingly allowed Archduke Ferdinand II's marriage to commoner Philippine Welser, but the thought of the ill-matched couple living within the city limits was a bit more than they could take, so Ferdinand fixed up a little 10th-century château for his honey outside town. The upper castle, completed in 1556, now houses a collection of Habsburg portraits. The **Kunst und Wunderkammer** displays precious metals, Chinese craftwork, scientific instruments, and a portrait of an astonishingly hairy man and his children. *Tel. 0512/48446. From station, take Straßenbahn 6 or free shuttle bus to Schloß Ambras. Admission: 60AS, 30AS students. Open Apr.–Oct., Wed.–Mon. 10–5.*

AFTER DARK

Innsbruck supports a good range of night spots, most of them in or near the Altstadt. On any given summer night, check for free happenings at the **Goldenes Dachl,** the **Hofgarten Café** (*see above*), or the **university,** where parties on Wednesday or Thursday nights from 10 PM have cheap beer. **Treibhaus** (Angerzellgasse 8, tel. 0512/586874) is easily the best place for live music, and there's usually no cover to see local bands. **Dom-Café Bar** (Pfarrgasse 3, tel. 0512/57353) draws a slightly older crowd, while the nearby **Büro Cafe Bar** (Badgasse 1, tel. 0512/575633) and **Zoo Club** (Maria-Theresien-Str.; closed Sun.–Mon.) are brighter, trendier places for a drink or light snack. **Alte Piccolo Bar** (Seilergasse 1, tel. 0512/582163) in the Altstadt is a central gay bar.

A full schedule of opera and other classical music, dance, and drama is performed at the **Tiroler Landestheater** (Rennweg 2, tel. 0512/52074, ext. 4); standing-room tickets are 50AS, seats start at 70AS, and a half hour before a performance all seats drops to 70AS for students.

KITZBUHEL

A mining village once upon a time and a health resort since the 19th century, the town of **Kitzbühel,** an hour east of Innsbruck, has built a reputation as one of the best places for skiing on the planet. The compact little valley town of less than 9,000 inhabitants is also one of the world's more efficient operations for extracting money from tourists. Fortunately, a network of mostly Australian ski bums devoted to the place supports a small network of cheap hotels and restaurants. Ride Austria's first cable car, the **Hahnenkamm** (tel. 05356/58510), to the start of several hiking trails. **Tourismusverband** (Hinterstadt 18, tel. 05356/2155 or 05356/2272) doesn't book rooms but does give you lodging suggestions. You should thank the Australian expatriate community for the few cheap sleeps in town, including the 120AS beds at **House Malkenecht** (10 Sportsfeld, tel. 05356/72034). For drinks, company, or information about what's happening in Kitzbühel, head for the popular pub **The Londoner** (Franz-Reisch-Str., tel. 05356/71428).

BELGIUM

3

By Zak Smith

The most obvious difference between Belgium's two very distinct population groups—the Flemish in the north and the Walloons in the south—is language: Northerners speak Flemish, a Dutch dialect, and southerners speak French. But you'll notice differences in everything from architecture to politics. The two regions don't even share a common history: Each has been controlled by different royal families (from Burgundy, Spain, Vienna, and elsewhere) at various periods. A mild war of independence with the Netherlands in 1830 established the new country, but Belgium hasn't developed a national identity that supersedes regional loyalties. In fact, the country recently transformed itself into a federation composed of Flanders, Wallonie, and Brussels, and a significant number of Flemish and Walloons want two completely separate countries. Luckily, Belgium's political problems haven't led to any kind of violence, and the chances of this country becoming the next Yugoslavia, torn apart by civil war, are slim.

It's ironic that a country at risk of breaking up should be at the center of the effort to unify all Europe, but Belgium is home to the European Commission, where most decisions affecting the European Union are made. Most Belgians would honestly like to see their EU neighbors come together. Their all-too-vivid memories of World Wars I and II, in which Belgium was completely ravaged, have left them believing that the only secure future lies in a unified Europe.

Belgium's most appealing city and the darling of the tourist industry is the old-fashioned Brugge in the west. The capital, Brussels, is the site of the most powerful EU institutions, and Antwerp is a wonderful city, alive with music and the legacy of Peter Paul Rubens. To the southeast lie the hills and forests of the Ardennes, where nature still reigns supreme, though the hills ooze with memories of World War II.

Basics

MONEY $1 = 32 Belgian francs and 10 Belgian francs = 30¢. The Belgian franc is very stable and is also accepted throughout Luxembourg. Banks are generally open weekdays 9–noon and 2–4 and offer the best exchange rates; the American Express offices in Brussels and Antwerp are also competitive. Bureaux de change and most train stations can change your money at more convenient times, but they offer less favorable rates and charge fees.

➤ **HOW MUCH IT WILL COST** • Belgium's food and lodging are expensive (hotel doubles start at 1,200BF), but low transportation costs balance them out. If you travel with a

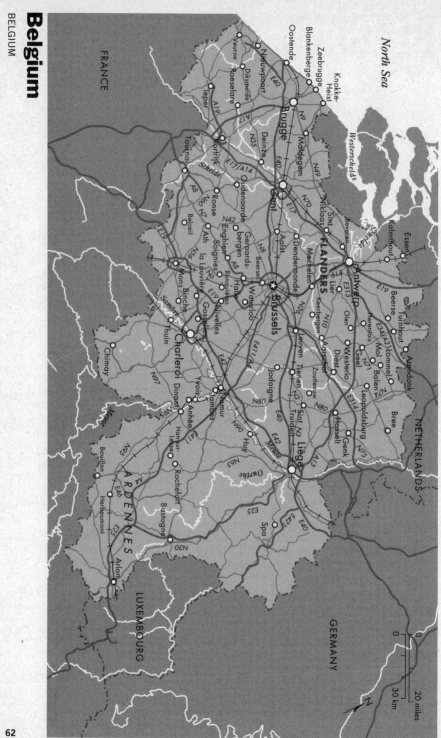

North Sea

Westerschelde

FRANCE

NETHERLANDS

GERMANY

LUXEMBOURG

Knokke-
Heist

Oostende
Blankenberge
Zeebrugge

Nieuwpoort
Veurne
Diksmuide
Roeselare
Ieper

Brugge
Maldegem
Deinze
N35

Tournai
Kortrijk
Ronse
Oudenaarde
Gerards-
bergen
Beloeil
Ath
Enghien
Soignies
Ronquières
Mons
Binche
la Louvière
Nivelles
Gosselies
Charleroi
Thuin
Chimay

Gent
Aalst
Dendermonde
Halle
Waterloo
Mechelen
Kembergen
Aarschot
Zoutleeuw
Jodoigne
Tienen
Leuven
Sint
Niklaas
Beveren

Brussels

Antwerp
Lier
Olen
Herentals
Geel
Mol
Balen
Leopoldsburg
Bree
Genk
Hasselt
Sint
Truiden
Liège
Spa

Kalmthout
Essen
Beerse
Turnhout
Arendonk

Namur
Yvoir
Anhée
Dinant
Tambes
Bouillon
Herbeumont
Arlon
Bastogne
Rochefort
Hamoir-
lesse

ARDENNES
Ourthe
Meuse
Huy

Sambre

Scheldt

FLANDERS

20 miles

30 km

partner and stay in hotels, figure at least $45 a day to get by; if you sleep in hostels, you can keep it closer to $35.

GETTING AROUND Because Belgium is small, train travel within the country is never very expensive. Trains run almost everywhere, except in the Ardennes, where you'll have to use the bus. In other regions, it's silly to travel by bus—you don't save that much money, and trains are much more efficient.

➤ **BY TRAIN** • If you plan to spend more than a couple days here and don't have a EurailPass, national rail passes can help keep fares low. The **Benelux Tourrail Pass** costs 3,780BF (2,860BF under 26) and is good for five days of travel within a 17-day period in Belgium, the Netherlands, and Luxembourg. The **Belgium Tourrail Pass** offers the same deal in Belgium for 1,800BF (1,350BF under 26). A **Half-Fare Card** is good for a month and costs 550BF. But the best deal for people under 26 is the Belgian **Go Pass,** which costs 990BF and is good for eight one-way trips anywhere in the country.

➤ **BY BUS** • Two Belgian bus companies handle travel within and between cities: DeLIJN in Flanders and TEC in Wallonie. Tickets for one system are not good on the other, but national passes are valid on both, and EurailPasses can be used for bus travel between cities.

➤ **BY BIKE** • Biking is a good way to get around the country and is popular with residents as a mode of transportation. Many roads have bike lanes, and the terrain is easy to tackle almost everywhere but in the Ardennes. The best part about biking here is that you can rent bikes from most train stations for about 150BF per day and return the bike to any other station that rents.

WHERE TO SLEEP Belgium's well-run and extremely popular **hostels** are good places to meet outdoorsy European travelers. Hostels normally charge around 350BF per night (100BF more for nonmembers at HI hostels) and include a shower and breakfast; sheets often cost 100BF extra. The privacy of a **hotel** double will run you at least 1,200BF, including breakfast and showers. Some **universities** rent out rooms in the summer—check into this option in Gent, especially. **Camping** is popular and very cheap throughout Belgium (around 300BF for two people), but the campgrounds are rarely centrally located.

FOOD In most budget restaurants, you'll pay about 400BF for such regional favorites as boiled mussels (in the north) and saucy meat dishes (in the south). Dessert lovers should keep a sharp eye on the budget, because it's easy to go overboard on scrumptious waffles and *pralines* (chocolates). Go into a **Léonidas** chocolate store in any town and ask for a sample box to taste some inexpensive bits of heaven. Wash it all down with one of Belgium's hundreds of inexpensive beers. Basic varieties start at around 40BF a bottle, while the delicious national specialty *kriek,* a cherry-flavored beer, costs about 90BF.

The most popular Belgian dish is the cheapest—the humble frites (french fries), served in every restaurant and home with mayonnaise or ketchup.

PHONES AND MAIL Country code: 32. Most of Belgium's phones use cards (sold at newsstands and post offices), though some accept coins. Local calls cost 10BF, and a three-minute call to the United States or Australia will cost $4 or $6, respectively. To reach AT&T's USA Direct line, dial 078–11–00–10 from any phone; for MCI, dial 078–11–00–12.

Mail service in Belgium is reliable, and post offices are easy to find; they're often near the train station and they display a red horn symbol. It costs 32BF to send a postcard or lightweight letter to the United States.

LANGUAGE Most Belgians speak English, but even your most bumbling stab at the native language will be appreciated. That's easier said than done in Flanders, where the language is Flemish, a Dutch dialect spoken by only five million people in the world. Luckily, the Flemish are even more willing and able to speak English than the Walloons to the south (whose native tongue is French).

Brussels

There's something about this city that just doesn't click. Given that Brussels (Bruxelles in French, Brussel in Flemish) is not just the Belgian capital but also the headquarters of the European Union, a bustling center for bureaucrats, lobbyists, and Euro-politicians, you'd think it would have plenty of sights and a lively cultural scene. But somehow it flops as a sightseeing destination, and it's not a particularly hip place to hang out. Maybe it's because Brussels is a city in limbo. What was once just the capital of Belgium is becoming the capital of Europe, and the city is struggling with the transformation. It's already an autonomous region in the Belgian federation, equal in status to Flanders and Wallonie and recognizing both French and Flemish as official languages.

In all fairness, Brussels is worth seeing; it's just that you could see it all in a day or two. The Grand' Place is amazing, filled with 15th- and 17th-century gilded buildings that you could gaze at for hours. There are also plenty of museums to fill a couple days, though many are a testament to Belgium's not-so-pleasant colonial past.

BASICS

VISITOR INFORMATION The **Tourism and Information Office of Brussels** (Hôtel de Ville, Grand' Place, tel. 02/513–89–40; open daily 9–6) may be housed in an amazing building, but the staff doesn't know a thing about budget travel. After you've bought their great map and city guide (100BF), move on to **Infor Jeunes** (27 rue du Marché aux Herbes; open weekdays noon–5:30). Their written info is all in French, but some of the employees speak English. Brussels also has a **regional tourist office** (63 rue du Marché aux Herbes, tel. 02/504–03–09; open Mon.–Sat. 9–6, Sun. 1–5, longer hrs in summer) with general information on Belgium.

AMERICAN EXPRESS *2 pl. Louise, tel. 02/512–17–40. Metro: Louise. Open weekdays 9–5, Sat. 9:30–noon.*

CHANGING MONEY The best place to exchange money is at **Petercam Securities** (19 pl. Ste-Gudule, tel. 02/213–05–11; open weekdays 9–5). It's filled with clients carrying suspiciously huge wads, sometimes bags, of money—but who's asking questions when they give great rates and charge no commission? For late-night exchange, you'll have to resort to awful rates at the train stations or the bureaux de change near the Grand' Place.

EMBASSIES **Australia.** *6 rue Guimard, tel. 02/231–05–00. Open weekdays 9–noon.*

Canada. *2 av. Tervuren, tel. 02/735–80–40. Open weekdays 9–noon and 2–4.*

United Kingdom. *85 rue d'Arlon, tel. 02/287–62–17. Open weekdays 9:30–12:30 and 2:30–4:30.*

United States. *25 blvd. du Regent, tel. 02/513–38–30. Open weekdays 9–noon.*

MAIL For postal service on Saturday, go to the office (open weekdays 9–5, Sat. 9–noon) on the second floor of the Centre Monnaie shopping center, close to the Grand' Place and next to the De Brouckere Metro stop.

COMING AND GOING

BY TRAIN Brussels is served by three main stations, all of which store luggage, change money, and hook up with the Metro. **Gare du Nord** (85 rue du Progrès) handles northern and eastern destinations, including Antwerp (30 min, 575BF), Amsterdam (3 hrs, 1,010BF, 900BF under 26), and Köln (3 hrs, 1,000BF, 810BF under 26), as well as trips to and from the Brussels airport. The station's in a seedy part of town, but you can walk to the main shopping streets and many hostels. **Gare du Midi** (2 rue de France), or **Zuidstation** in Flemish, lies in a run-down area and is the busiest of the three stations, handling southern and western destinations like Paris (3 hrs, 1,400BF, 1,150BF under 26) and London (7 hrs with ferry) via Oostende (1 hr, 410BF). From the station, Trams 52 and 55 will take you to

Bourse, near the Grand' Place. All trains that stop at **Gare Centrale** (2 carrefour de l'Europe) also stop at Midi and/or Nord, but Centrale is right by the Grand' Place and is perfect for luggage storage (open 4:30 AM–1 AM). For all Brussels train information, call 02/219–26–40.

BY PLANE **L'Aéroport de Bruxelles National** (tel. 02/722–31–11) is in the suburb of Zaventem, 14 km northeast of the city center. More than 50 airlines serve over 1,000 destinations from the airport, and, increasingly, charter and other cheap transatlantic flights have been stopping here. Getting into Brussels from the airport is a snap: Between 6 AM and 11:30 PM, take the train (20 min, 80BF) to Gare du Nord or Gare Centrale. Just be sure to buy a ticket before you get on or they'll slap you with extra fees.

GETTING AROUND

If you try to cover Brussels by instinct, you're bound to get lost. Pick up a map and use a combination of walking and **STIB** (Société des Transports Intercommunaux Bruxellois), the extensive public transit system. Metros, trams, and buses all run on the same tickets: A single ticket costs 50BF, a day pass 200BF, and a 10-journey card 290BF. All three are sold at any Metro station; on buses you can only buy single tickets. The two system-information offices (Rogier and Gare du Midi Metro stations; open weekdays 8:30–5:15, Sat. 9:30–5:30) both give out free Metro maps. Venturing into the Flemish suburbs north of the city involves Flanders's public transportation system, DeLIJN; to get to the southern suburbs, you'll have to use the Walloon TEC. **Taxis** are expensive but necessary when public transit closes down at 12:30 AM. Hailing one is rarely a problem; just be sure to get an approximate price quote from your driver before taking off.

WHERE TO SLEEP

Brussels offers everything from international chains to sleazy one-nighters to a plethora of hostels. The two main lodging areas are the **city center,** between Gare Centrale and Gare du Nord, and **St-Gilles** to the south, near Gare du Midi. Prices for a hotel double run 900BF–1,800BF, and a double in a hostel hits the bottom of that range; in both cases, breakfast is usually included.

CITY CENTER Stay in the city center if you want to be close to sights and shopping. The area near the Gare du Nord is a red-light district; women walking here should prepare themselves for catcalls and the like.

If all else fails, the Gare du Midi has a stinky lounge open all night—just say you're waiting for a train.

➤ **UNDER 1,200BF** • **Hôtel du Grand Colombier.** Dumpy-looking building on a filthy side street off shopping avenues. Inside it's much neater, though it looks like they hit the local wallpaper store's going-out-of-business sale— each room has a different design, and some have more than one. Singles and doubles from 900BF. *8–10 rue du Colombier, tel. 02/217–96–22. From Gare du Nord, south on rue du Progrès, which becomes blvd. Adolphe Max; left on rue du Finistère and right on rue du Colombier. AE, MC, V.*

➤ **UNDER 1,500BF** • **Hôtel Elysée.** Tiny reception, narrow staircase and corridors, but all the saved space goes into the rooms. Just a hop, skip, and a jump from Grand' Place, overlooking a nice little square with a weekend market. Singles and doubles from 1,375BF. *4 rue de la Montagne, tel. 02/511–96–82. Metro: Gare Centrale. AE, MC, V.*

Pacific Sleeping. Paint splotches and wild-animal photos frankly don't work as decor, but the little beds are piled high with thick comforters. Breakfast (included) comes with an omelet. Paul, the multilingual owner, goes out of his way to take care of you. Singles 850BF; doubles, triples, and quads 700BF per person; showers 100BF. *57 rue Antoine Dansaert, tel. 02/511–84–59. Metro: Bourse.*

rue du Canal

Porte de
Flandre

r. du Grand Hospice

r. de Laeken

quai au Bois à Brûler

quai aux Briques

r. du Pont

Canal de Charleroi

ch. de Ninove

porte et pl. de Ninove

bd. Barthélémy

r. de Flandre

r. Antoine Dansaert

r. Notre Dame du Sommeil

r. de la Senne

r. Rempart des Moines

pl. du Béguinage

bd. Emile

pl. de
Brouckère

r. des Fabriques

pl.
Ste Catherine

Aug. Orts

Marché aux Porcs

rue des Cyprès

r. du Sureau

Anspach

r. du Fossé-aux-L

pl. et Th.
de la
Monnaie

Pont de la
Carpe

pl. du
Jardin aux Fleurs

r. Pletinckx

pl. de la
Bourse

Marché aux Poulets

r. Grétry

r. des Bouchers

r. 't Kint

Artevelds

r. des
Riches Claires

pl.
St-Géry

r. aux Herbes

r. du Marché aux Herbes

pte. de
Flandre

r. de la Senne

r. Camusel

r. Van

r. des Jetons

Jules van
Praet

ptc. de
Flandre

porte
d'Anderlecht

r. d'Anderlecht

r. du Midi

Grand'
Place

r. de la
Montagn

r. de la Violette

Infante
Isabella St

ch. de Mons

bd. R. Poincaré

r. de Cureghem

bd. Anspach

r. des Midi

r. de l'Etuve

Lombard

i

Gare
Centrale

r. Ollier

r. Plantin

r. du Vautour

Verdure

pl. de
Anneessens

r. des
Foulons

Champagne

r. du

r. des Bogards

r. des Alexiens

Chêne

14

r. St-Jean

pl. de
l'Albertine

Canter

r. Brogniez

2

sq.
R. Pequelir

bd. Maurice Lemonnier

pl.
Rouppe

r. du Poinçon

r. d'Accolay

pl. de
Dinant

bd. de l'Empereur

r. Lebeau

sq. de
l'Aviation

r. de
St-Esprit

9

Rollebeek

r. des
Pigeons

15

pl. Bara

bd. Jamar

pl. de la
Constitution

av. de Stalingrad

r. Terre-Neuve

r. du Miroir

r. Blaes

r. Haute

bd. de l'Europe

r. du Lavoir

r. des Tanneurs

r. St-Ghislain

r. des Capucins

r. des Minimes

r. Ernest Allard

r. de la Régence

r. des Petits

Car

Gare
du
Midi

av. Fonsny

av. de l'Argonne

bd. du Midi

av. de la Porte de Hal

r. de Russie

r. de
l'Economie

r. des Renards

r. de la Bostère

r. Pierémans

r. Haute

pl.
Poelaert

r. aux Laines

pl. du
Grand Cerf

r. d'Angleterre

r. de Hollande

r. de Montserrat

Quatre Bras

Waterloo

r. Emile Féron

r. Fontainas

av. Jean Volders

8

Henri Jaspar

r. Bosquet

18

bd. de
l'av. de la
Louise

Toison d'Or

AE

av. Louise

r. des Chevaliers

r. des Drapiers

r. Keyenveld

ch. de Forest

ST-GILLES

r. Berckmans

r. Jourdan

12

Capouillet

17

pl.
Stéphanie

TO
WATERLOO

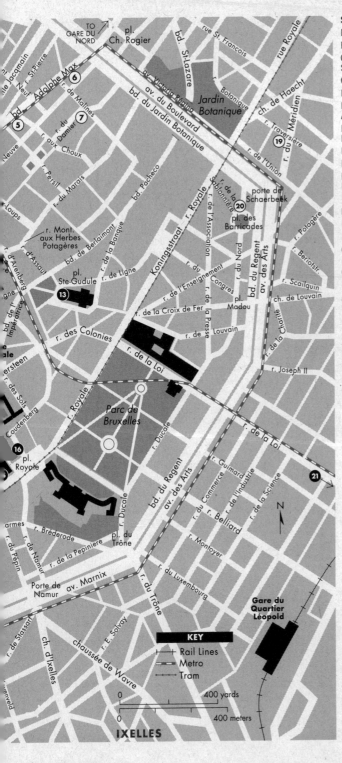

Sights ●

Bourse, **4**

Bruparck, **1**

Cathédrale
St-Michel, **13**

Grand' Place, **10**

Manneken-Pis, **14**

Musée d'Art
Ancien, **15**

Musée d'Art
Moderne, **16**

Musée Grueuze, **2**

La Porte de Hal, **8**

Royal Art and
History Museum, **21**

Lodging ○

Bruegel (HI), **9**

Bruswell, **7**

CHAB, **19**

Hôtel du Grand
Colombier, **5**

Hôtel Elysée, **11**

Jacques Brel
(HI), **20**

Le Gascogne, **6**

Les Bluets, **12**

Pacific Sleeping, **3**

Résidence Duke of
Windsor, **17**

Résidence
Osborne, **18**

KEY

⊦⊦ Rail Lines

═══ Metro

⊦⊦ Tram

0   400 yards

0   400 meters

➤ **UNDER 1,800BF** • **Le Gascogne.** Stuck between a sex shop and a peep show, but surprisingly high-class. On the main shopping street near Gare du Nord. Prices are high—singles 1,300BF, doubles 1,800BF—but where else can you get blankets made from red stuffed-animal fur? *137 blvd. Adolphe Max, tel. 02/217–69–62. From Gare du Nord, south on rue du Progrès, which becomes blvd. Adolphe Max. AE, MC, V.*

ST-GILLES You'll need to use the Metro to reach most sights from this residential area south of town. The hotels here are often family-owned and are a little more personable than those downtown.

➤ **UNDER 1,200BF** • **Résidence Osborne.** Welcoming, spacious rooms in two buildings across the street from each other. Congenial staff. Singles 900BF, doubles 1,100BF, showers 100BF. *67 rue Bosquet, tel. 02/537–92–51. Metro: Hôtel des Monnaies. AE, MC, V.*

➤ **UNDER 1,500BF** • **Les Bluets.** Too much furniture cramps the rooms, but hotel is well-kept by a brisk, businesslike proprietress. Singles 1,150BF, doubles 1,350BF. *124 rue Berckmans, tel. 02/534–39–83. Metro: Hôtel des Monnaies. AE, MC, V.*

➤ **UNDER 1,800BF** • **Résidence Duke of Windsor.** Each room has private bath, and the friendly sixty something proprietress strives for a family atmosphere. Five rooms only, all with 19th-century furnishings and all worth the splurge. A no-smoking establishment. Singles 1,250BF, doubles 1,650BF. *4 rue Capouillet, tel. 02/539–18–19. Metro: Hôtel des Monnaies. Written reservations only.*

HOSTELS **Bruegel (HI).** Stone's throw from Manneken-Pis and within sight of Gare Centrale. TV room gets MTV and CNN. Very modern; the only thing missing is large lockers for backpacks, so watch your goods. Small lockers available. Dorm beds 400BF (sheets 120BF), singles 650BF, doubles 1,100BF. *2 rue de St-Esprit, tel. 02/411–04–36. Metro: Gare Centrale. Midnight curfew, lockout 10–2, wheelchair access.*

Bruswell. Formerly called Sleepwell. Extremely helpful, concerned staff seems to be cleaning constantly. Bring your own sheets or you'll sleep under their oversize napkins. Great location five minutes from Gare du Nord, near shopping streets and Metro. Dorm beds 300BF (sheets 100BF), singles 500BF, doubles 850BF. *Rue du Damier, tel. 02/218–50–50. From Gare du Nord, south on rue du Progrès, left on rue de Malines, right on rue du Damier. 1 AM curfew, lockout 10–4, luggage storage.*

CHAB. Temperamental hot water in showers. Has a pool table and sculpted-frog fountains. Lame staff, but the place is orderly. Dorm beds 350BF (sheets 80BF), singles 600BF, doubles 1,000BF. *8 rue Traversière, tel. 02/217–01–58. Metro: Botanique. 2 AM curfew, lockout 10–4, laundry, luggage storage. MC, V.*

Jacques Brel (HI). Modern, with a shower in each room. Nice courtyard; bar below serves food. Grand' Place is a 15-minute walk. Beds 400BF (sheets 120BF), singles 650BF, doubles 1,100BF. *30 rue de la Sablonnière, tel. 02/218–01–87. Metro: Botanique. 1 AM curfew, lockout 10–2, laundry, wheelchair access.*

FOOD

There are so many restaurants in Brussels that it's hard to sift out the good from the bad. The famous **rue des Bouchers** near the Grand' Place is nothing but restaurants, all of them specializing in seafood. Even if you can't afford to eat here, walk through just to see the displays of food. For a cheap dinner, look to the city's ethnic restaurants. The two best areas to try are the **city center** and the **Ixelles** neighborhood, southeast of the center.

CITY CENTER Streets filled with restaurants fan out from the Grand' Place; in general, the farther down these streets you go, the better the restaurants become. For the poor man's version of rue des Bouchers, try **rue du Marché aux Fromages,** one block south of the Grand' Place and lined with Greek restaurants. For cheap crêpes, head for **La Fleur de Blé Noir** (55 rue de l'Enseignement, tel. 02/218–55–06), serving lunch only (except Friday night). A meal costs around 250BF.

➤ **UNDER 300BF** • **Da Kao.** Great deal near the Bourse: tiny Vietnamese restaurant with Asian knickknacks on the walls. *38 rue Antoine Dansaert, tel. 02/512–67–16. Metro: Bourse. Closed Sun.*

➤ **UNDER 500BF** • **Plaka.** One of the best on the Greek strip near the Grand' Place. Eat inside amid Greek memorabilia, or get it to go and picnic on the Grand' Place. Very crowded despite two stories of seating. *6 rue du Marché aux Fromages.*

IXELLES Locals come to this artsy neighborhood, which spreads southeast of the Porte de Namur, to eat, shop, and escape the tourist crowds.

➤ **UNDER 500BF** • **Le Paradoxe.** Lots of plants and natural wood. Good, earthy vegetarian food; "suggestions du jour" is the cheapest way to go. Live music (usually piano) most nights. The owners run a grain and natural-foods shop next door. *329 chaussée d'Ixelles, tel. 02/649–89–81. Metro: Porte de Namur. Closed Sun.*

Restaurant Indochine. Chatty owner, hanging plants and bamboo decor, and good, cheap Vietnamese food. *58 rue Lesbroussart, tel. 02/649–96–15. Metro: Porte de Namur; walk 20 min south on chaussée d'Ixelles or take Bus 71. Closed Sun.*

Shezan. Traditional Indian and Pakistani food in an atmosphere of Indian art and music. *120 chaussée de Wavre, tel. 02/512–94–95. Metro: Porte de Namur. Wheelchair access. Closed Mon.*

WORTH SEEING

Brussels aspires to be Belgium's center of art, culture, and history, and while it's no Paris, it makes a decent showing. The city has plenty of museums, most near Metro stops and many adjoining big parks that are great for picnics. The main cathedral, **Cathédrale St-Michel,** is best viewed from the outside, where the Gothic towers gleam white after a recent cleaning that removed centuries of grime. The cathedral took more than 300 years to complete, but for all that work there's not much to see inside. Another landmark is the **Bourse,** a magnificent stock exchange built in 1871 on a scale that Brussels's stock trading has never quite justified. Perhaps the most famous sight in all of Brussels, though, is the **Manneken-Pis,** a statue of a little boy peeing his heart out a few blocks off the Grand' Place (down rue Charles Buls, which becomes rue de l'Etuve). The city likes to dress him up in little Manneken-Pis clothes appropriate to the season and various holidays.

GRAND' PLACE Some fans insist the Grand' Place is the most beautiful square in Europe. It's surrounded by architectural wonders, each with a history. Legend has it that the **Hôtel de Ville**'s 15th-century architect committed suicide when he saw that the completed building had an off-center tower. Most of the other buildings surrounding the Grand' Place were built between 1695 and 1700, after Louis XIV of France had bombarded and destroyed earlier structures. Look for the exact construction dates in gold digits at the top of each building. In No. 9, nicknamed **Le Cygne** (The Swan), Karl Marx and Friedrich Engels whipped out the *Communist Manifesto* in 1848. The **Musée de la Ville de Bruxelles** (tel. 02/511–27–42; admission 80BF; open weekdays 10–12:30 and 1:30–5, weekends 10–1) traces the city's evolution, showcasing the artwork of less-than-famous locals along the way. The most bizarre displays are of the costumes for the Manneken-Pis.

In the evenings, the Grand' Place becomes a magnet for anyone who wants to drink. Couples and groups pack into the popular cafés lining the square and gaze up at the gilded buildings between sips.

When you've had enough sightseeing, you may be tempted to join the crowds for a drink at a café on the square. You'll pay half the price, though, if you choose a café a couple blocks away. From late April to early October and again around Christmas, the Grand' Place brightens up with nightly **music and light shows,** starting at 11 PM until mid-August, at 10 PM after that. The shows celebrate a different composer each year.

MUSEES DES BEAUX-ARTS Two museums of fine art display early and modern works. The **Musée d'Art Ancien** houses works from the 15th to 19th centuries and has an entire room devoted to Brueghel, as well as a ton of Rubens's paintings and sketches. The collection of 19th-century art is disappointing. *3 rue de la Regence, tel. 02/508–32–11. Metro: Parc. Admission free. Wheelchair access. Open Tues.–Sun. 10–noon and 1–5.*

The **Musée d'Art Moderne** covers the 20th century and features an interesting collection of contemporary Belgian art. Sports fans will enjoy the portrait of Wayne Gretzky by Andy Warhol. *1–2 pl. Royale, tel. 02/508–32–11. Metro: Parc. Admission free. Wheelchair access. Open Tues.–Sun. 10–1 and 2–5.*

LA PORTE DE HAL Once a main gate of a protective wall around Brussels, the Porte de Hal dates from the 14th century and today houses a folklore museum. The building itself is impressive, with a long, hollowed-out circular stairwell. The museum is still being filled with folklore goodies; presently it houses old-fashioned toys. Most eye-catching is the 19th-century Maison de Poupée, a dollhouse that took 10 years to build. *Blvd. du Midi, tel. 02/534–25–52. Metro: Porte de Hal. Admission: 80BF, 30BF students. Wheelchair access. Open Tues.–Sun. 10–5.*

MUSEE GUEUZE This small working brewery still makes its Lambic with equipment bought secondhand in 1937. The process takes place from mid-October to mid-May only, but you can visit and get free samples year-round. *56 rue Gheude, tel. 02/520–28–91. Metro: Lemonnier. Admission: 70BF. Open weekdays 8–4:30, Sat. 9:30–1; longer weekend hrs mid-Oct.–mid-May.*

ROYAL ART AND HISTORY MUSEUM Although the Belgians didn't "acquire" as much ancient art as the British during the colonial period, they still have an impressive collection of Egyptian and Byzantine works. One special treat in this museum is the lace room, which has some huge, extraordinary pieces of lace. Also interesting is the scale model of ancient Rome. *10 Parc du Cinquantenaire, tel. 02/741–72–11. Metro: Schuman. Admission free. Open Tues.–Fri. 9:30–5, weekends 10–5.*

BRUPARCK The official guide to Brussels calls Bruparck "Europe's Leisure Capital." Don't buy it. The only redeeming attraction at this amusement park north of town is the theater complex **Kinepolis** (tel. 02/478–04–50), which no movie fan should miss. The 29 cinemas have huge screens, the latest sound systems, and armchairs for each person. All films are shown in their original language and start at 8 and 10:30 PM. Admission is 200BF, 170BF for students. To reach Bruparck, take Metro line 1A to Heysel.

AFTER DARK

This isn't the most jumping city: Public transportation stops running at midnight, drinks and covers are expensive, and most bars just aren't that cool. Movies are a good option; they're almost always shown in the original language, to avoid conflicts over whether to dub them into French or Flemish. Major cinemas are at Bruparck (*see above*), **City 2** (rue Neuve), and **Porte de Namur** (av. de la Toison d'Or). Admission runs around 200BF, but students often get discounts.

At **La Canne à Sucre** (12 rue des Pigeons, tel. 02/513–03–72), you can listen to Caribbean music and try one of more than 200 rum-based cocktails (250BF). Cheaper is **Taverne Falstaff** (17–23 rue Henri Maus, near the Bourse, tel. 02/511–98–77), where you can drink beer (around 100BF) and sit on the covered terrace. The eerie **Le Cercueil** (rue Haring, off Grand' Place), where the decor involves funerary bouquets and coffins serve as tables, is an interesting place for one drink (two would clean out your wallet). **Flanagans** (55 Cantersteen, across from Gare Centrale, tel. 02/502–52–88) has live rock Thursday–Sunday; at the daily happy hour (8:30–10 PM) beers are 40BF and hard alcohol is 100BF. For dancing, try **Le Garage** (16 rue Duquesnoy, off pl. St-Jean, tel. 02/512–66–22), open every night after 11 PM. Sunday is gays only.

Near Brussels

WATERLOO Besides being a popular Abba song, Waterloo is a small Belgian town 20 km south of Brussels where a great battle was fought on June 18, 1815. At the battle, Napoleon led 72,000 French troops against the duke of Wellington's 68,000 Allied troops and Field Marshal Gebhard von Blücher's 45,000 Prussian troops. Napoleon drove off Blücher but was unable to do the same to Wellington. By the end of the battle, Napoleon had lost 25,000 men, Wellington 15,000, and Blücher 8,000.

Today you can visit the battlefield as well as several monuments and museums, none of which is exciting enough to make the trip from Brussels worthwhile unless you're a major history buff. At **Musée Wellington** (147 chaussée de Bruxelles, tel. 02/354–78–08), you'll see illuminated maps of the battle. From there you can head out to the battlefield, where the best view is from the **Butte du Lion** (254 rte. du Lion, tel. 02/385–19–12), a huge mound with a steep and skinny staircase. If you want to make a day of Waterloo, buy the combination ticket (300BF, 230BF students), which covers all attractions. Otherwise, individual museum admissions cost about 120BF.

➤ **COMING AND GOING** • Trains leave Brussels's Gare Centrale every hour for Waterloo (30 min, 90BF). Waterloo's town center is 1 well-marked km from the station. To get to the battlefield, 8 km from the center, you have to take a bus to Le Lion; catch Bus W across the street from the Wellington Museum.

Flanders

Flanders is flat. Much like its neighbor, the Netherlands, the northwestern half of Belgium is characterized by geographic monotony. Fortunately, the Flemish are not as boring as their region. They're the friendliest of the Belgians, and they usually enjoy speaking English with travelers (though, as always, you should ask first). In fact, most Flemish can chat with you in English, French, Flemish, or German, although French would be their last choice—a strong separatist movement has developed here, perhaps as a result of the region's recent economic success. Historically, Flanders has been the poorer part of Belgium, but since World War II its industrial base has helped it surpass Wallonie in wealth

Flanders vs. Wallonie: And the Winner Is . . .

In 1993, the Belgian Parliament officially made Belgium a three-part federalist state, composed of French-speaking Wallonie, Flemish-speaking Flanders, and bilingual Brussels. As many separatists—especially from Flanders—pushed for an out-and-out split between the regions, King Baudouin I, whom both sides liked and respected, provided a stabilizing force. Just a few weeks after Parliament set up the federalist state, however, Baudouin died at the age of 62. Most citizens thought his energetic young son Philippe would become the country's sixth king, but instead Baudouin's brother Albert was pressured into taking the throne, because the feds thought an older, more experienced man could do a better job of keeping the country unified. It remains to be seen whether they made the right decision, since the Flemish separatist movement is still going strong.

and population. This area also contains the nation's most interesting sights, especially in the towns of Brugge and Antwerp.

Brugge

Brugge (Bruges), just 70 km from the Belgian coast, offers a taste of pre–World War II Europe—the Europe many travelers imagine when their trips are still in the planning stages. The streets are cobblestone, canals snake everywhere, and almost every building looks like it dates from the 15th or 16th century, even when it doesn't. Simply put, Brugge is one of the most beautiful cities in Europe. If you have time for only one stop in Belgium, make this it.

Residents have accepted Brugge's role as a tourist town; they keep their city clean and treat travelers well, and in the process they've made themselves wealthy off tourist dollars. Guided tours, though they may seem cheesy, are one of the best ways to learn about the history of Brugge and Flanders. A couple of agencies in town make them lots of fun. Try the **Back Road Bike Company** (meeting point outside the tourist office, tel. 050/34–30–45), which takes groups on bike treks in the region surrounding Brugge and appeals mostly to the hostel crowd; the English-language tours run 400BF–450BF.

BASICS Send mail at the **post office** (5 Markt, tel. 050/33–14–11). Brugge's postal code is 8000. During peak season lots of little visitor information offices come out of hibernation, but the **main tourist office** is open year-round. *11 Burg, tel. 050/44–86–86. Open May–Sept., weekdays 9:30–6:30, weekends 10–noon and 2–6:30; Oct.–Apr., Mon.– Sat. 10–noon and 2–6:30.*

Because this city is in Flemish-speaking Flanders and not French-speaking Wallonie, its correct name is Brugge (pronounced broo-huh), not Bruges (broozh). If you call it Bruges in front of a Flemish separatist, you'll surely get your pronunciation corrected, and you may get a political lecture to boot.

GETTING AROUND Brugge revolves around the central **Markt,** which is surrounded by bustling streets and canals. The perimeter of town is lined with a series of forgotten parks—good escapes from the sightseeing masses. The best park is **Minnewater** (Lake of Love), in the southern part of town. The most romantic way to get around Brugge would be to row through the canals, but the waterways are reserved for tourist boats. The next best thing is biking or walking. Both are a cinch, since Brugge, like all of western Flanders, is flat as a board. When you're bushed or rushed, take the **bus** (40BF). The info booth for the DeLIJN bus system is at the **train station,** on Stationsplein about 2 km south of the town center.

➤ **BY BIKE** • Biking through town is great; just watch out for dazed tourists and aggressive bus drivers. As long as you have a train ticket of some kind, you can rent a one-speed bike at the train station for 150BF per day. **Popelier Eric** (14 Hallestr., near Markt, tel. 050/34–32–62; open 9–9) rents three-speeds for 250BF a day.

WHERE TO SLEEP Most of Brugge's lodging is packed into the central and western parts of town. Some cushy four-star hotels run down-to-earth annexes across the street or around the corner. The very best deals are the hostels, but the hotels listed below offer more privacy for not too much more money (unless you're a single traveler). They all book up quickly, so reserve ahead.

➤ **UNDER 1,500BF** • **Het Geestelijk Hof.** Huge rooms—some guests cram a bunch of companions in when nobody's looking. Quiet area, but close to major sights. Doubles from 1,300BF, breakfast included. No singles. *2 Heilige Geeststr., tel. 050/34–25–94. AE, MC, V.*

'T Keizershof. Pleasant rooms with flower boxes in every window. Just three minutes from the station. Owners and their friendly dog like it quiet. Cheapest in Brugge: singles 950BF, doubles 1,200BF. *126 Oostmeers, tel. 050/33–87–28. Laundry.*

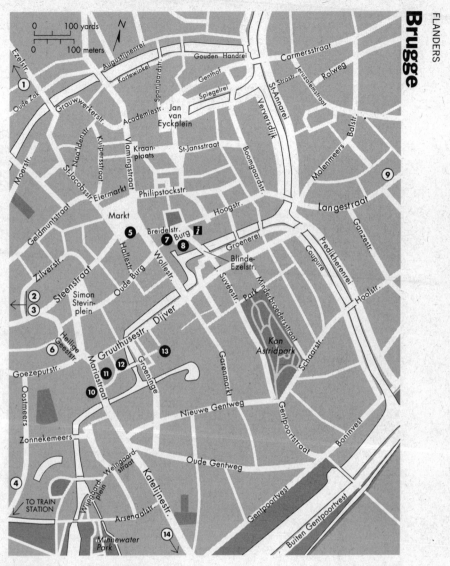

➤ **UNDER 1,800BF** • **Pension Imperial.** Near main shopping street. Ritzy look, owned by still ritzier neighboring hotel. Singles 1,250BF, doubles 1,550BF with breakfast. *28 Dweersstr., tel. 050/33–90–14. From station, go north (left) on Buiten Begijnenvest, which becomes Koning Albertlaan; at 't Zand, turn right on Zuidzandstr. and left on Dweersstr.*

➤ **HOSTELS** • **Bauhaus International Youth Hotel.** So-so location but right-on price: dorm beds 300BF, doubles 900BF. Party image means many guests overlook disorganization and dirt. If you want to join Americans in a spring-break mood, this place and its loud, smoky bar are for you. *135–137 Langestr., tel. 050/34–10–93. From station, Bus 6 or 16 to Bauhaus. AE, MC, V.*

Europa International Youth Hostel (HI). Near station, but 15 minutes from the center. Almost too peaceful. Managers would earn a Brownie button for broom and sponge use. Beds 350BF–450BF, 450BF–550BF nonmembers; sheets 120BF. *143 Baron Ruzettelaan, tel. 050/35–26–79. From station, Bus 2 to 2nd stop. Lockout for some rooms 10–1. Luggage storage, wheelchair access. Closed mid-Dec.–early Jan.*

Passage. Best location of all Brugge hostels. Proprietress is brisk, businesslike, hawk-eyed, and occasionally friendly. Tidy but not sterile. Beds 350BF–400BF, 5% discount for HI members. *26 Dweersstr., tel. 050/34–02–32. Follow directions to Pension Imperial (see above). Luggage storage. AE, MC, V.*

Snuffel. A hostel with a cause: All profits go to local homeless youth. Helpful staff can point you to good sights or at least to the info stand they've created. Not too central, but near laundry, supermarket, and great restaurant (*see* Food, *below*). Dorm beds 350BF, doubles 900BF, quadruples 1,400BF, sheets 60BF. *47–49 Ezelstr., tel. 050/33–31–33.*

➤ **CAMPGROUNDS** • The closest campground to town is **St.-Michiel** (55 Tillegemstr., tel. 050/38–08–19), in a crowded field surrounded by trees and inhabited by wandering chickens. The campground and on-site restaurant are open year-round. One or two people with a tent pay 250BF–350BF, showers included; from the station, take Bus 7. If St.-Michiel is full, take Bus 66B to Loppem Drop, where you'll find **Lac Loppem** (Lac 10, tel. 050/82–42–62; 200BF per site, 90BF per person).

FOOD It's hard to find affordable meals in Brugge. Avoid restaurants on or near the Markt at dinner; cheaper and more authentic cuisine is farther from the center. During the day, though, many expensive restaurants in the center turn into tearooms, setting up outside tables where you can join other travelers and shoppers for a drink and maybe a waffle. Fresh fruit and vegetable markets take place Wednesday mornings on the Burg and Saturday mornings on 't Zand and Beursplein. You can also try the hostels listed above for a meal; all have restaurants with good food at budget prices.

➤ **UNDER 300BF** • **De Bretoen Pannekoeken.** Variety of hearty meals; crêpes start at about 150BF. Homey atmosphere is enhanced by culinary knickknacks on the walls. Five minutes from the Markt and worth every step. *4 Ezelstr., near Snuffel hostel, tel. 050/34–54–25. Wheelchair access. Closed Tues.*

Restaurant Ganzespel. Nicky whips up a typical Flemish menu of her choice every day. This is a good place to try *waterzooï*, a creamy chicken soup. When the menu's meaty, vegetarians can ask for a special omelet (200BF). Bland surroundings, but good food and music. Menus at 225BF and 400BF. *37 Ganzestr., near Langestr., tel. 050/33–12–33. Closed Mon.–Tues.*

➤ **UNDER 500BF** • **L'Estaminet.** Locals rave about the filling spaghetti, potent drinks, and blues music. Interesting variations on the *croque* (grilled cheese sandwich) start at 150BF. Covered terrace faces Kon Astridpark. *5 Park, tel. 050/33–09–16. Wheelchair access. Closed Mon., Tues., and Nov.*

WORTH SEEING For a great view of Brugge, climb to the top of the 13th-century **Belfort** (admission 80BF, 60BF students; open daily 9:30–5, shorter hrs off-season), on the Markt in the center of town. On the nearby Burg, you can enter the Gothic Hall of the gorgeous **Stadhuis** (Town Hall) for 40BF. Also on the Burg, don't miss the extravagant **Heilig-Bloed**

Basiliek (Basilica of the Holy Blood), built to enshrine the vial containing Christ's blood. The **Heilig-Bloed Museum** inside the church charges 20BF admission, but it's worth it if you're into holy relics.

➤ **ONZE-LIEVE VROUWEKERK** • Brugge has loads of churches, but the Church of Our Lady, built between the 13th and 15th centuries, has an edge: It offers a chance to see a Michelangelo masterpiece—the exquisite *Madonna with Child*—without trekking all the way to Italy. Also interesting are the colorfully carved mausoleums of Charles the Bold and his daughter Mary, but you have to pay 30BF to see them. *Cnr. of Gruuthusestr. and Mariastr. Closed for services daily 11:30–2:30.*

If you're on a shopping kick, buy relatively cheap lace on Breidelstraat, which connects the Markt to the Burg. The lace is often handmade in the city, but ask to be sure.

➤ **GROENINGE MUSEUM** • The most prized pieces in this extensive collection of 15th- to 20th-century Flemish art are works by the Flemish Primitives. Jan van Eyck's *The Virgin with the Canon* contains amazingly rich colors, and Pieter Pourbus's *The Last Judgement* is fearfully gripping. *12 Dijver, tel. 050/33–99–11. Admission: 130BF, 100BF students. Open Apr.–Sept., daily 9:30–5; Oct.–Mar., Wed.–Mon. 9:30–12:30 and 2–5.*

➤ **GRUUTHUSE MUSEUM** • The aristocratic family who lived in this house during the 15th century had a royal monopoly on *gruut,* an important ingredient in beer. Today their former home displays a mix-and-match art collection and shows you how aristocratic families lived during the 1400s. *17 Gruuthusestr., tel. 050/33–99–11. Admission: 100BF, 70BF students. Open Apr.–Sept., daily 9:30–12:30 and 2–5; Oct.–Mar., Wed.–Mon. 9:30–12:30 and 2–5.*

➤ **MEMLING MUSEUM** • This brilliant collection of paintings by 15th-century local boy Hans Memling is housed in the former St.-Jans Hospital, where Memling spent time convalescing after being wounded in France. *38 Mariastr., tel. 050/33–25–62. Admission: 130BF, 70BF students. Open Apr.–Sept., daily 9:30–5; Oct.–Mar., Thurs.–Tues. 9:30–noon and 2–5.*

AFTER DARK After the shops have closed at about 6, the city seems to die. Hard-core partyers can seek out a few lively nightspots on **Eiermarkt,** near the Markt, but the crowd here is pretty young—as in early high school. For a cool blues bar, try **Vino Vino** (15 Grauwwerkersstr., north of the Markt). With luck you might hit one of their Spanish theme nights, when the bar serves up *tapas* (Spanish appetizers) and plays Spanish tunes. The Passage, Bauhaus, and Snuffel hostels (*see* Where to Sleep, *above*) have bars, each with a different scene. The rowdiest is the Bauhaus, which draws a frat crowd; locals favor Passage.

NEAR BRUGGE: THE COAST

The Belgian coast is short, but it contains several remarkably distinct small towns. An international crowd flocks to cosmopolitan Oostende. The favorite of the Belgians themselves, ritzy Knokke-Heist, can intimidate the hell out of a budget traveler; but it's worth a stop if only to marvel at Belgian beach culture. For a quieter beach experience, try the tiny industrial town of **Zeebrugge**—good for shy types who don't like to flaunt their stuff in front of all Belgium.

None of these towns is more than a 20-minute train ride from Brugge; in fact, many budget travelers bike from Brugge to the coast (about ½ hr) and between the individual towns. Otherwise, a single tram runs the length of the Belgian coast, making it easy to visit at least a couple of towns in a day. Tram trips start around 40BF.

OOSTENDE This coastal city in western Flanders tries to do it all and nearly succeeds. It's Florida's Palm Beach, a medieval European town, a bit of New Jersey's Atlantic City, and Amsterdam's Red Light District all mixed up and thrown onto the Belgian coast. Older Belgians and Brits flock to the luxurious hotels overlooking the ocean. Families show up, the kids playing on the beach while the parents take romantic walks on the promenade. And at night, when the elderly lock themselves away and the parents put the kiddies to bed, the young set hits the bars.

Oostende started as a humble fishing village, but by the 19th century the Belgian royal family had chosen it as their second residence, and since then the town has been a first-rate seaside resort. The best thing to do here is tool around the streets, parks, and beach, preferably on a warm, sunny day. If that sunny day gets *too* warm, find cool relief in **St.-Petrus-en-Pauluskerk** (St. Peter and Paul Church), facing the train station. The church was built early in this century, and the best thing about it is the cubist-influenced stained glass. The **Museum voor Schone Kunsten** (Wapenplein, tel. 059/80–53–35; admission 50BF, 25BF students; closed Tues.), on the main square between the station and the beach, has an admirable collection of works by Oostende native James Enser, along with pieces by other local artists. The **tourist office** (2 Monacoplein, 15 min northwest of station, tel. 059/70–11–99) can help you out with the rest of Oostende's museums.

➢ **WHERE TO SLEEP AND EAT** • Oostende's restaurants cater to wealthy vacationers, so get to know the streetside *frieten* (french fry) stands. The burgers look questionable, but the locals gobble 'em up; and it's hard to screw up fries. You can get dinner for 250BF and a bed for 400BF at the busy and friendly **HI hostel** (82 Langestr., near Wapenplein, tel. 059/80–52–97). Or try **Hotel Ariel** (1A Adolf Buylstr., off Wapenplein, tel. 059/70– 08–37). The outside needs paint and the inside needs air freshener, but you can open a window and sleep easy in a 1,600BF double.

KNOKKE-HEIST Knokke-Heist is actually a conglomeration of five small towns: Heist, Duinbergen, Albertstrand, Knokke, and Het Zoute. Together, the towns offer 14 km of beautiful beach, with the street **Zeedijk** and a boardwalk running along the entire length. As far as Belgians are concerned, Knokke-Heist is the beach with the most. Here locals turn sunbathing into an art, putting out chairs and sectioning off their own private bits of sand with spikes and canvas. From the boardwalk, it's quite a sight to see a beach so neatly partitioned by a canvas grid, but that's Belgium for you. Of course, you *can* simply throw your towel down on the beach; just be sure it's not invading the personal sand swatch of your neighbor.

Trekking along the boardwalk is the best way to get around, but if your feet are weary you can take the coastal **tram** (about 40BF), which follows **Elizabetlaan** through Knokke-Heist. Tourism is the main industry here, and the streets are packed with hotels, restaurants, and shops. As you move from Heist toward Knokke, the cost of food and lodging rises, though the entire area is overpriced.

➢ **WHERE TO SLEEP AND EAT** • You can kill two birds with one stone at **Ter Heis** (210 Zeedijk Heist, on the boardwalk, tel. 050/51–18–95; closed Oct.–Easter), a great deal for summer food and lodging. A full meal costs around 300BF; a double room is 1,500BF.

Gent

When you step out of St.-Pietersstation in Gent (Ghent) and see the industrial nightmare in front of you, you might be tempted to hop right back on the train. Count your blessings—the presence of ugly, pragmatic buildings near the station means fewer downtown, a good couple of km away. In fact, Gent's Oude Stade (Old Town) recently underwent a face-lift, a sign of its increasing popularity as a tourist destination. New and improved tourist quarters, van Eyck's Northern Renaissance masterpiece *The Adoration of the Mystic Lamb,* and a huge student population streaming through the cafés along St.-Pietersnieuwstraat make the town a fun stop.

BASICS **Visitor Information** is available at the Town Hall (Botermarkt, tel. 09/224–15–55; open Mar. 14–Nov. 14, daily 9:30–6:30, shorter hrs off-season). Send mail at the **main post office** (16 Korenmarkt, tel. 09/225–20–34; open weekdays 8–8, Sat. 9–noon). Gent's postal code is 9000.

GETTING AROUND The Three Towers (*see* Worth Seeing, *below*) that mark the center of town lie within a five-minute walk of each other along a curved road. To get to the center from the train station, take Bus 12 to Korenmarkt. From there it's easy to hoof it, but just in case you don't feel up to it, DeLIJN runs trams between 5:30 AM and 11:30 PM.

WHERE TO SLEEP Hotels aren't that pricey if you're traveling with a partner—doubles cost about 1,200BF—but single travelers get reamed. Luckily, in 1993 a hostel finally opened up in Gent. The hostel and the town's best hotels are around the Three Towers; university housing is closer to the station.

Flandria Hotel. Elegant rooms, but the manager's a jerk. Great location near St.-Baafs. Singles 1,200BF, doubles 1,300BF. *3 Barrestr., tel. 09/223–06–26. From tourist office, take Neder-polder; go left on Kwaadham and right on Barrestr.*

Hotel De IJzer. The cheapest hotel in Gent. Doors squeak, but otherwise rooms are okay. Heavy traffic outside, elderly crowd plays billiards in the bar below. Singles and doubles 1,150BF. *117 Vlaanderenstr., tel. 09/225–98–73. From tourist office, head south to St.-Baafspl.; then southeast on Limburgstr., which becomes Vlaanderenstr. 2:30 AM curfew.*

➤ **HOSTEL • De Draecke (HI).** Brand-spanking-new and in the center, but so far lacks personality. Private toilet and shower in each room. Members 350BF, nonmembers 450BF, sheets 120BF. *11 St.-Widostr., tel. 09/233–70–50. From Korenmarkt, take Drabstr. and veer right onto J. Breydelstr., follow through name changes, right on Braderstr., right on St.-Widostr. 11 PM curfew, lockout 10–5.*

➤ **STUDENT HOUSING • Universitaire Homes.** From mid-July through late September this office will set you up in a single room near the university (south of the city center) for 500BF, breakfast and shower included. Buildings on Stalhof have the best location. *6 Stalhof, tel. 09/222–09–11. From station, Bus 9, 70, or 90 to Overpoort. 1 building (Home Fabiola) with wheelchair access.*

Vooruit (23 St.-Pieters-nieuwstr., tel. 09/225–10–44) used to be a Socialist Party meeting place; today it's just a theater and music hall with a cool café where you can watch the culture hounds of Gent come and go.

FOOD Near the Three Towers, along Mageleinstraat and St.-Niklaasstraat, you'll find lots of restaurants targeting tourists and any locals who can afford to shop nearby. The cheapest meals in town are on the student strip, south of the city center along St.-Pietersnieuwstraat. At **Studenten-voorzieningen Cafeteria** (45 St.-Pietersnieuwstr., tel. 09/264–70–62; open mid-Sept.–June, weekdays 8–8), you can eat for 150BF and meet local students. The nearby pizzerias and *frituurs* (french-fry stands) are also good places to fill growling stomachs. If you're desperate for vegetarian food, make the trek to **De Appelier** (47 Citadellaan, tel. 09/221–67–33; closed Sat.), where you can feast for less than 300BF. Walk south past all the student joints on St.-Pietersnieuwstraat and turn left on Citadellaan.

La Rustica. Student favorite 10 minutes from Korenmarkt. Nondescript building harbors delicious pizzas (150BF–250BF) and big bowls of pasta in rich sauces (around 250BF). *154 St.-Pietersnieuwstr., tel. 09/233–07–08. Closed Sat. lunch and Sun.*

WORTH SEEING Gent draws most of its tourists with its landmark Three Towers, of which one is a bell tower and two belong to churches. Visit the 14th-century **Belfort** (bet. E. Braun-pl. and St.-Baafspl., tel. 09/233–39–54; admission 80BF, 40BF students; open daily 10–12:30 and 2–5:30) to get a great view of the city and see a room filled with old bells, which you can play if nobody's looking. Of the Three Towers, **St.-Niklaaskerk** (bet. Koren-markt and E. Braunpl.; open daily 10–11:45 and 2–5) has sustained the most damage over the years as a result of wars and fires; what you visit nowadays has been restored in a major way. **St.-Baafskathedraal** (St.-Baafspl.; open 9:30–noon and 2–6) is the best tower to visit because it houses one of van Eyck's finest paintings, *The Adoration of the Mystic Lamb* (admission to painting 50BF and worth every franc). The rest of the cathedral includes a Rubens painting and a magnificent oak and marble pulpit.

➤ **HET GRAVENSTEEN** • This castle has been around since 1180, and it shows. Come here when you feel like crawling around broken walls, not when you want painstakingly restored rooms. Some rooms and areas are marked to show their original purpose, and a former prison now houses period coins and torture devices. *St.-Veerleplein, north of Korenmarkt, tel. 09/225–93–06. Admission: 80BF, 40BF students. Open daily 9–5:15.*

AFTER DARK Nightlife centers around that ultimate student row, St.-Pietersnieuwstraat, where each bar seems to attract a different type of student. For dancing try **Pole Pole** (158 St.-Pietersnieuwstr., tel. 09/233–21–73), a hopping club with an African theme. If you stop by **De Sloef** (226 St.-Pietersnieuwstr.) in the afternoon, you'll probably find students playing Risk; board games are a popular pastime along this strip, and what better way to get to know someone than over a friendly little game of world domination?

Antwerp

Unlike Brugge, which banks its future on the attractions of the past, Antwerp lives for the moment. It, too, has a rich past, but it's also a city on the move that has been constantly growing since the late 1800s. Antwerp's port ranks as one of the 10 busiest and most important in the world, and half of the world's finished diamonds come from here. Antwerp wasn't always so successful. It went through two centuries of poverty when the port closed between 1648 and 1863, and it suffered during the Napoleonic Wars. Even in hard times, though, Antwerp remained culturally exciting. It was the home of Rubens and is thus heir to many of his best works; and spurts of wealth over the years produced a beautiful cathedral and the Grote Markt. Today live music performances go on all the time, on the streets, in bars, and in cafés.

BASICS The **visitor information** office (15 Grote Markt, tel. 03/232–01–03) is open Monday–Saturday 9–7:45 and Sunday 9–4:45. The **American Express** office (21 Frankrijklei, tel. 03/232–59–20) is open weekdays 9–5:30 and Saturday 9–noon. To get there from the station, take De Keyserlei and turn left on Frankrijklei.

GETTING AROUND The most populous city in Belgium, Antwerp sprawls along the Schelde River and into the countryside. Luckily, all the sights are crunched into the Oude Stade (Old Town), so you shouldn't need the tram and bus much, except to get to the budget lodging. The train station is east of the city center—take Tram 2 from the station to reach Groenplaats, just south of the Grote Markt.

➤ **BY TRAM AND BUS** • As always, **DeLIJN** runs a comprehensive system of buses and trams, which are referred to as the Metro when they run underground. You can buy regular tickets (40BF) on board, but you can only get day passes at a DeLIJN office; the two most convenient are at Groenplaats and at Premetrostation Diamant, near the train station. You can find maps of routes and stops in DeLIJN offices and at certain stops; some drivers also carry maps.

WHERE TO SLEEP Solo travelers get a better deal here than in most cities: Single rooms often run under 800BF (doubles go for around 1,200BF). Most budget accommodations lie south of the Grote Markt, though a few places are near the train station. If you're in a bind, the sterile **Internationaal Zeemanshuis** (21 Falconrui, tel. 03/232–16–09; doubles 1,750BF) should be able to find you a space in one of 100 rooms.

➤ **UNDER 1,200BF** • Sleep Inn. Cheapest, friendliest hotel in town, a short distance from the Fine Arts Museum and a downtown-bound tram. Chatty old proprietor's family has been here since the Hapsburg era. Singles 500BF, doubles 1,000BF. *1 Bolivarpl., tel. 03/237–37–48. From station, follow De Keyserlei to Frankrijklei and take Bus 1 to Bolivarpl. Laundry, wheelchair access.*

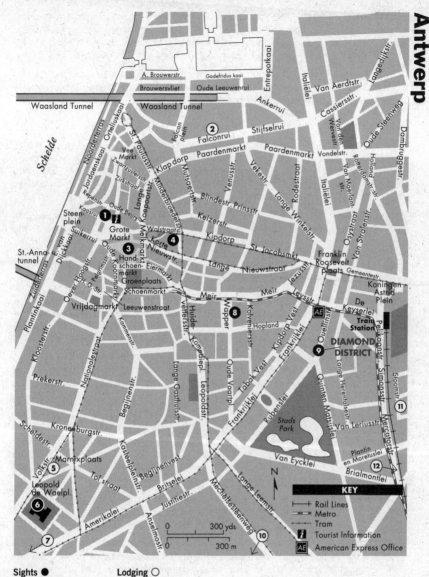

Scale:
0 — 300 yds
0 — 300 m

KEY

╫ Rail Lines
▭▭ Metro
‥‥‥ Tram
🛈 Tourist Information
AE American Express Office

Sights ●

Grote Markt, 1

Hendrik
Conscienceplein/
St.-Carolus
Borromeus, 4

Koninklijke Musea
voor Schone
Kunsten, 6

Provinciaal
Diamantmuseum, 9

Rubenshuis, 8

Onze-Lieve
Vrouwekathedraal, 3

Lodging ○

Boomerang
International Youth
Hostel, 5

Internationaal
Zeemanshuis, 2

New International
Youth Hotel, 12

Op Sinjoorke
(HI), 10

Scoutel, 11

Sleep Inn, 7

➤ **UNDER 1,500BF** • **New International Youth Hotel.** Matronly old woman runs clean, cheery place that must have been designed for a Minotaur; just hope you don't have to find your way out in an emergency. Fifteen-minute walk from the station. Singles 800BF, doubles 1,200BF, dorm beds 400BF, sheets 100BF. *256 Provinciestr., tel. 03/230–05–22. From station, take Pelikaanstr. south along tracks, left on Provinciestr.*

Scoutel. Directions: Drop capsule on ground, add water, up pops insta-hotel. Bare white walls but private bath in every room. Very close to the station. Doubles 1,500BF, 1,300BF under 25. *3 Stoomstr., tel. 03/226–46–06. From station, exit left on Pelikaanstr., left at Lange Kievitstr., right on Stoomstr. Check-in until 6 PM only.*

➤ **HOSTELS** • **Boomerang International Youth Hostel.** The best hostel in Antwerp, though the interior decorator must have been tripping. Bathrooms newly renovated; hopefully they'll replace the mattresses next. Fifteen-minute walk from Grote Markt. Dorm beds 350BF, dorm sheets 100BF, singles and doubles 1,000BF. *49 Volkstr., tel. 03/238–47–82. From station, Bus 23 to Leopold de Waelpl., northeast on Volkstr.*

Op Sinjoorke (HI). Cheapest deal in town, not counting the bus fare you need to get here. It's built on the site of former city defenses; the beautiful surroundings include a partial moat. Otherwise modern, with a typical HI crowd. Dorms, singles, and doubles 350BF per person for members, 450BF for nonmembers, sheets 120BF. Work three hours, stay for free. *2 Eric Sasselaan, tel. 03/238–02–73. From station, Bus 18 to C. Huysmanslaan. Lockout 10–5, laundry, wheelchair access. Closed mid-Dec.–early Jan.*

FOOD Antwerp's Oude Stade is the best place in the city to grab a meal. You may have to shell out a few francs more than in other Belgian towns, but you're paying for some of the best food in the country. The main restaurant street is **Oude Koornmarkt,** off Grote Markt, but the whole area has potential. Antwerp also has a great café scene, and many coffeehouses become roaring bars at night.

➤ **UNDER 500BF** • **Atlantis.** Vegetarian fare, with many varieties of spaghetti and omelets as well as soy burgers and some traditional Belgian dishes adapted to veggie standards. Full meal about 300BF. *6 Korte Nieuwstr., east of Grote Markt, tel. 03/234–05–17. Closed weekend lunches and Tues.*

Pasta. Smell of pesto grabs you as soon as you walk in. Be sure to go to upstairs restaurant (entrance on Pelgrimstr.), which is cheaper and has a partial glass ceiling that affords an awesome view of the cathedral. Most pasta dishes 350BF or less; all are good and come with scrumptious Italian bread. *32 Oude Koornmarkt, off Grote Markt, tel. 03/233–17–76. Closed weekend lunches.*

Ulcke Van Zurich. Steak and potatoes cooked to order, at fair prices—around 440BF for a meal. Dark wood adds to hearty steak-house atmosphere. *50 Oude Beurs, north of Grote Markt, tel. 03/234–04–94. Wheelchair access. Closed weekend lunches.*

WORTH SEEING Entering Antwerp means entering the world of Peter Paul Rubens, who made the city his home. Residents are thrilled by the artist's legacy, especially the sketches and paintings he left behind. In **Onze Lieve Vrouwekathedraal** (Handschoenmarkt, tel. 03/231–30–33; admission 60BF; open weekdays 9–6, Sat. 9–3, Sun. 1–4), you can see what are arguably his best works: the two triptychs *The Raising of the Cross* (1610) and *The Descent from the Cross* (1612). The huge paintings contribute to the overall power of the 14th-century cathedral, which contains art dating from the 14th century to the present.

For more Rubens, visit the **Koninklijke Musea voor Schone Kunsten** (1–9 Leopold de Waelpl., tel. 03/238–78–09; admission free; open Tues.–Sun. 10–5), which has an entire room filled with his works, including *Venus Frigida* (1614), one of his few paintings with a non-Christian theme. Rubens is only one of several Northern Renaissance stars honored here; van Eyck, in particular, gets lots of wall space. To round off the Rubens experience, wander around the **Rubenshuis** (9 Wapper, tel. 03/232–47–47; admission 75BF; open Tues.–Sun. 10–5). This well-preserved home where the artist spent the last 25 years of his life holds a portion of his private collection, including his *Self-Portrait* (1625–1628) and works by some of his pupils. If you want to see still more, the tourist office has a "Rubens' Walk" pamphlet and map that direct you to buildings containing his works.

But Rubens isn't all there is to Antwerp. The streets of the Oude Stade are packed with sights and incredible architecture, most notably around the gilded **Grote Markt.** The Diamond District near the train station contributes a big chunk of the city's wealth. Mounds of diamonds are displayed at **Provinciaal Diamantmuseum** (31–33 Lange Herentalsestr., tel. 03/231–86–45; admission free; open daily 10–5). Diamond-cutting demonstrations are given Saturdays 2–5 and by request during the week.

CHEAP THRILLS A great place to relax is on the peaceful square **Hendrik Conscience-plein,** which faces the magnificent facade of the church of St.-Carolus Borromeus. For a distant view of town, follow **St.-Annatunnel,** a pedestrian tunnel, under the river to the pathways and parks of the residential area on the other side. The five-minute walk through the tunnel is kind of creepy when you think of all the water above you—especially when you see some of it seeping through sinister cracks. More soothing is the peaceful **sculpture garden** in the suburb of Mortsel; from Groenplaats, take Bus 26.

AFTER DARK Antwerp has a fantastic nightlife. It's such a musical city that you can almost always find a live show. **De Muze** (15 Melkmarkt, near Grote Markt, tel. 03/226–01–25) is a great place for live or recorded jazz and De Koninck beer: Natives call this Antwerp brew *Bolleke,* or "small bowl," after the glass it's usually served in. **De Muziek-doos** (12 Ernest van Dijckkaai), on the river near the Grote Markt, appeals to a grungier crowd; street performers pass in and out all night. If you're itching to dance, try **Paradox** (25 Waalsekaai, near Koninklijke Musea voor Schone Kunsten, tel. 03/237–99–52), which has a different dance theme every Saturday night and doubles as a daytime café.

Leuven

For a taste of the ongoing political struggle between the Flemish and the Walloons, consider the recent history of the Catholic University of Leuven (Louvain). Although it's in the Flemish region of Brabant and most of its students are Flemish, the university's language of instruction was French from its founding in 1425. In 1968, as student protests and riots swept through Europe, students in Leuven demanded not only free speech but also a switch to Flemish instruction. They won; today classes at the university are taught in Flemish, and the students have settled back down to drinking the locally brewed Artois beer and hanging loose in this architecturally beautiful, cheerful town.

BASICS There's a **visitor information** office in the Grote Markt (1A Naamsestr., tel. 016/21–15–39; open weekdays 8–3, weekends 10–3, closed Sun. Nov.–Feb.). The **post office** (1 Smolderspl. tel. 016/22–75–23; open Mon.–Thurs. 9–6, Fri. 9–7, Sat. 9–noon) can take care of your mailing needs.

GETTING AROUND Leuven is bordered on the east by low hills, but all the attractions in town are on flat land and you should have no problem walking around. To reach the town center from the train station, follow Bondgenotenlaan. To venture out of the center, take DeLIJN (317 Diestsestr., tel. 016/22–50–98); tickets start at 40BF. Biking is also an option—rent from the station for 150BF a day.

WHERE TO SLEEP AND EAT University students can find cheap long-term lodging, but travelers are stuck in expensive hotels. Camping is the best deal here. **Schoolbergen** (58 Sneppenstr., tel. 016/25–59–69) offers sites for 135BF per person plus 100BF per tent, and summer-camp-style dorm rooms for 200BF–250BF per bed. Take Bus 2 from the station and tell the driver that Schoolbergen is your destination. If you have a little more cash, try the convenient **Hotel La Royale** (6 Martelarenpl., across from station, tel. 016/22–12–52; singles 850BF, doubles 1,550BF). The rooms need new carpets, but the first floor has a wonderful sitting room.

What Leuven lacks in lodging it makes up for in cheap, filling food. In the Oude Markt you'll find more than 40 bars, many of which are also popular student restaurants. For one of the best vegetarian meals in Belgium, try **Lukemieke** (55 Vlamingenstr., across from Stadspark, tel. 016/22–97–05); meals (250BF) are served in the colorful garden in back when the weather permits.

WORTH SEEING Leuven's **Stadhuis** is a late-Gothic marvel, world-famous for its intricate sculpture and six white spires. Museums are a great deal if you get the 50BF pass (20BF students) to all four collections in town. Two of them really aren't worth seeing, but the **Stedelijk Museum voor Religeuze Kunst** (St.-Pieterkerk, Grote Markt, tel. 016/22–69–06; open Mon.–Sat. noon–5, Sun. 2–5, closed Mon. Oct. 15–Mar. 15) has a neat collection of old embroidered priests' garments, and the **Stedelijk Museum Vander Kelen-Mertens** (6 Savoyestr., tel. 016/22–69–06; open Tues.–Sat. 10–5, Sun. 2–5) features restored salons in Renaissance, Baroque, and rococo styles. The tourist office's city map covers all the sights and tells the architectural history of various university buildings built between the 16th and 20th centuries. One of the nicest is the **Arenberg Castle** (Kardinaal Mercierlaan), a 20-minute walk out of town, whose grounds are perfect for Frisbee and picnicking.

Wallonie

The people of Wallonie speak French and share much of their cultural heritage with their French neighbors to the south. Fortunately, they don't share the notorious French rudeness. Walloons are nearly as hospitable as the Flemish to English-speaking travelers. And you have to give the Walloons a break, because they're still trying to deal with their relatively new position of political and financial inferiority to Flanders. Generally, this is the less interesting of Belgium's two regions—the cities don't have half the allure of Antwerp or Brugge—but the hills and forests of the Ardennes to the east make Wallonie a major destination for outdoor thrill seekers.

Liège

The largest city in Wallonie was originally a diocese and principality of the Holy German Empire, and industrial Liège has kept its religious overtones. In fact, the only real reason to come here is if you're especially taken with churches, or if you're on your way into the Ardennes.

Some humorous choir stalls in the Eglise St-Jacques poke fun at the church's religious order. Look close to see monkeys dressed in popes' hats reading the Bible.

Eglise St-Jean (pl. Xavier Neujean, tel. 041/23–70–42; open Mon.–Sat. 3–5:45, Sun. 10:30–1, and in summer 7:30–9) has several amazing 13th-century wood sculptures. **Eglise St-Jacques** (pl. St-Jacques), a Benedictine abbey, was built between the 12th and 16th centuries. The church's floral-painted ceilings are notable. A treasury full of silver, gold, and ivory sculptures is the best reason to visit **Cathédrale St-Paul** (pl. de la Cathédrale; admission to treasury 40BF; open daily 7:30–12:30 and 2–6, shorter hrs off-season). To round out the religious experience, check out the **Fonts Baptismaux de St-Barthélemy** (pl. St-Barthélemy, tel. 041/23–49–98; admission 80BF, 30BF students; open Tues.–Sat. 10–1 and 2–5, Sun. 2–5), a giant brass tub crafted in the 12th century. For many years, this was the only font in town from which the sacrament of baptism could be given.

VISITOR INFORMATION *92 Féronstrée, tel. 041/21–92–21. Open weekdays 9–6, Sat. 10–4, Sun. 10–2.*

COMING AND GOING Once you're in the center, Liège isn't hard to cover on foot; but the train station is a 20-minute hike or a 36BF bus ride from the middle of town. If you take a TEC (tel. 041/67–00–64) bus to Liège instead of the train, you'll be dropped at a more central location.

WHERE TO SLEEP AND EAT When you exit the train station you'll see a variety of hotels, but hold off until you get nearer the center. The shabby rooms at **New Val Hostel** (21 rue des Augustins, tel. 041/23–46–53; doubles 850BF, dorm beds 350BF), halfway between the center and the station, are about the best you can do in Liège. To get here from the station, take Bus 1 or 4 to Charlemagne. If you exit the same bus at rue Darchis, you'll reach the giant rooms of **Pension Darchis** (18 rue Darchis, tel. 041/23–42–18; doubles 1,400BF).

Three restaurant-packed streets are rue Pont-d'Avroy, rue St-Gilles, and rue du Pot d'Or. When the midnight munchies hit, turn to **Le Vaudree II** (149 rue St-Gilles, tel. 041/23–18–80), which is open all night and offers 42 beers on tap and 980 bottled. A meal costs about 450BF, but hearty sandwiches are less.

Mons

The town of Mons, 60 km southwest of Brussels, grew around a small monastery founded in the 7th century by Ste-Waudru, the daughter of a count of the Hainaut province. Today the best sight in town is the **Ste-Waudru Collegiate Church,** a Gothic church begun in 1450 by a female chapter of her followers. Also worth a gander is the hideous **belfry,** which Victor Hugo proclaimed was redeemed only by its intimidating size. Mons has maintained a small-town feel, despite its recent emergence as an economic and cultural center in a newly industrialized Wallonie. You could spend a relaxing day just enjoying the town's narrow cobblestone roads and elegant, if grimy, 17th-century buildings.

VISITOR INFORMATION *22 Grand' Place, tel. 065/33–55–80. Open June–Sept., Mon.–Sat. 9–6:30, Sun. 10–6:30; shorter hrs off-season.*

GETTING AROUND Buses don't run through the center, but at least everything worthwhile is smooshed together. The train station is northeast of and downhill from the center; to get to Grand' Place, take rue de la Houssière past Ste-Waudru Church, and follow rue des Clercs from there.

WHERE TO SLEEP AND EAT Mons doesn't have much cheap housing. In July and August **M. et Mme. Rousseau J.** (5 rue des Belneux and 61 blvd. Kennedy, tel. 065/33–80–72) offer 1,100BF doubles near the center. Reserve ahead for the small, frilly **Hôtel St-Georges** (15 rue des Clercs, tel. 065/31–16–29; doubles 1,200BF), a block away from the Grand' Place. Rooms facing the street have an awesome view of the belfry.

The Grand' Place is the best place to start a hunt for a meal; the surrounding streets are packed with restaurants and cafés. For local cuisine and murals that celebrate Mons's history and culture, come to **No Maison** (21 Grand' Place, tel. 065/34–74–74), where meals start at 350BF.

Namur

Namur, the compact gateway to Luxembourg and the Ardennes, sits at the convergence of the Sambre and Meuse rivers, below cliffs that support the 2,000-year-old **Namur Citadelle** (tel. 081/22–68–29). The entrance price for the citadel is steep (195BF), so if you fork it over be sure you get your money's worth—crawl all over the site on your own, take in the historical slide show, and follow a couple of the many tours, which may or may not be given in English. The best tour is of the underground passages. The *téléférique* (cable car) up to the citadel is a rip-off; walking up is a much better idea.

The **tourist office** (sq. de l'Europe Unis, tel. 081/22–28–59) can elaborate on the various tours, as can the **Auberge de Jeunesse de Namur "Félicien Rops" (HI)** (8 av. Félicien Rops, tel. 081/22–36–88; dorm beds 335BF, doubles 820BF). The hostel offers discounted kayaking tickets as well as a bed for the night. To get here, take Bus 3 or 4 from the station. At mealtime try one of the many restaurants on the streets around Eglise St-Jean. **Au Passe Simple** (33 rue Fossés-Fleuris, tel. 081/23–14–31) offers a huge selection of salads and meals for around 350BF.

The Ardennes

Nowadays the Ardennes may seem like just a huge, hilly forest, perfect for playing in the woods and along rivers. But about 50 years ago these hills, which stretch from France through south-eastern Belgium and Luxembourg into Germany, were the site of some serious fighting. Several battles of World War II, including the Battle of the Bulge, were fought in this now-tranquil landscape, and you'll see monuments to the Allied war effort all over.

Professor Wells at England's Birmingham University has argued that William Shakespeare's play "As You Like It" was set in the Ardennes, not the forest of Arden in Britain, as most editions suggest.

Today, kayaks, hiking trails, and caves, not monuments and statues, are the main attractions of the Ardennes. The forest is also home to countless old **citadels** guarding rivers and strategic passes. Most communities have turned their local citadels into money-making museums, charging about 200BF for a visit that normally includes tours in French and Flemish. One of the best tours is in the town of Bouillon, at a feudal **château** (tel. 061/46–62–57; admission 140BF) dating from the 11th century. It once belonged to Godfrey of Bouillon, leader of the first Crusade and later king of Jerusalem.

COMING AND GOING The best way to get into the Ardennes is to take the train from Brussels to Namur (1½ hrs, 300BF) or to Liège (1½ hrs, 350BF). These two cities have tourist offices and train stations to help you plan further.

GETTING AROUND The Ardennes cover much of Wallonie. They're served by the bus system TEC, which comes in handy since trains aren't too thorough in the region. A little planning ahead can go a long way with TEC, considering that some towns aren't served at all on Sundays and most send off only a few buses per weekday. Serious bikers can avoid the buses and tackle the hills and river valleys on two wheels—although the region is large by Belgium's standards, you're never far from the next small town.

WHERE TO SLEEP The more popular towns in the Ardennes have a variety of hotels that range from the merely expensive to the absolutely outrageous—expect to pay at least 1,400BF for a double room. A better way to sack out around here is at one of the half-dozen or so well-located hostels, including one in Bastogne and one in Bouillon (16 rte. du Christ, tel. 061/46–81–37) located high on a hill overlooking a château and a river. The Namur hostel (*see* Namur, *above*) can give you info about any of them.

OUTDOOR ACTIVITIES The most popular activities in the Ardennes are hiking, biking, and kayaking. The region is crisscrossed with rivers, and many towns have **kayak rental shops** that'll give you six hours on a river for around 500BF. Kayaking is easier after it's rained enough to raise the water levels. Finding **bike rentals** can be hard in the Ardennes. Train stations usually rent three-speeders, which don't quite cut it in these hills. Check with kayaking companies or the nearest tourist office. **Hiking** in the region is organized on a town-by-town basis, so some areas have well-developed hiking trails and maps, while others leave you on your own.

Finally, this is a chance to explore the **caves and grottoes** in such towns as Dinant and Han-sur-Lesse. Some of the caves provided shelter for prehistoric peoples, who left behind their tools, bones, and cave paintings, now on display. Other caves are worth seeing for their huge underground caverns, streams, or mini-lakes. A visit to a cavern can cost anywhere from 300BF to 500BF.

BULGARIA 4

By Christopher Van Bebber and Oliver Schwaner-Albright

To most Westerners, Bulgaria is an enigmatic place that provokes shrugs and looks of confusion. None of this is helped by the fact that virtually everything here is written in Cyrillic script, which looks to the untrained eye like something conceived in a Gothic nightmare. Even worse, Bulgarians tend to nod their heads to indicate "no" and shake their heads to indicate "yes." Unless you're careful, this unique custom can wreak havoc on your sense of reality; be sure to get oral confirmation from train and bus conductors when you ask a question. Otherwise, you may end up in Romania.

There's an ancient Bulgarian proverb that warns, "God forbid you live in an interesting time," but Bulgaria has been anything but dull since the 1989 revolution. Despite some political reform and advances toward a market economy, the legacy of Bulgaria's Communist dictators—particularly of former party boss Todor Zhivkov—is formidable: a stagnant economy, rising environmental problems, deep ethnic distrust, and a people frustrated after 45 years of abuse. Many Bulgarians believed the "miracle" of Westernization would bring prosperity overnight. But as time wears on, it's obvious that meaningful reform may take years to implement, perhaps decades to succeed. Bulgaria is hardly grim, but you will encounter some of the grosser long-term effects of Communist mismanagement.

On the upside, prices in Bulgaria are comparable with those in the rest of Eastern Europe, and for $30 a day you can live like royalty. Even if you're traveling on a maxed-out credit card, you won't feel shortchanged. Sofia, the capital, has long been overlooked by the backpack set, which means places like Rila, Plovdiv, and Veliko Tuřnovo in the Balkan Mountains have been *way* overlooked. The same can't be said of the somewhat flashy and resort-dominated Black Sea coast, but then again, it still ain't no Club Med.

Basics

MONEY $1 = 56 leva and 10 leva = 17¢. Each lev (plural leva) is divided into 100 stotinki. Banks in Bulgaria are generally open Monday–Saturday 9–noon and 2–5. You can only exchange traveler's checks at tourist offices, banks, and major hotels in the big cities. The latter, however, often charge a $5 transaction fee. Avoid the dicey black market and watch out for counterfeit notes (check for a lion watermark on your large bills). You shouldn't have to pay for anything except plane tickets and sometimes lodging in U.S. currency, so don't get duped.

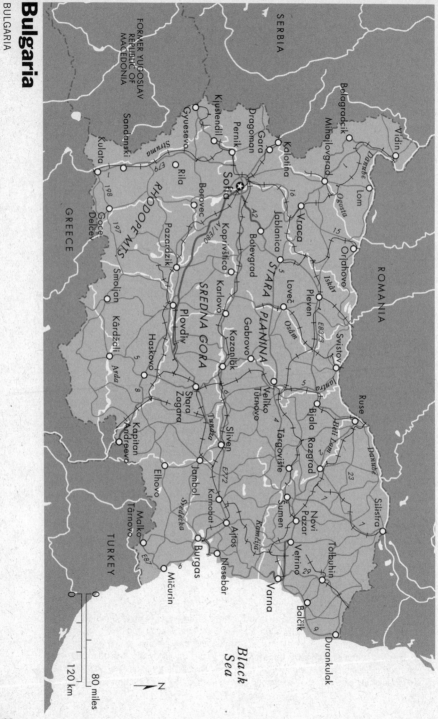

SERBIA

FORMER YUGOSLAV
REPUBLIC OF
MACEDONIA

Belagradcik

Vidin

Mihajlovgrad

Danube

Gara
Dragoman

Kalotina

Lom

Ogosta

Gyueshevo

Kjustendil

Pernik

Sofia

Vraca

Orlahovo

ROMANIA

16

Kulata

198

Rila

Borovec

Jablanica

15

Iskar

Sandanski

197

Goce
Delčev

RHODOPE MTS

Pazardzik

A1/E80

A2

Botevgrad

Koprivštica

Loveč

Pleven

Svistov

E83/3

Osam

GREECE

Strumo

E79

Smoljan

Kärdžali

Arda

Haskovo

5

8

SREDNA GORA

Plovdiv

Karlovo

Kazanlàk

Gabrovo

STARA PLANINA

Veliko
Tärnovo

Jantra

5

Bjala

Razgrad

Ruse

Beli Lom

Danube

23

Stara
Zagara

6

Sliven

Targovište

4

Kamčija

2

Elhovo

Kapitan
Andreevo

Jambol

Tundža

E772

Karnobat

Aitos

Sumen

Novi
Pazar

Silistra

Malko
Tärnovo

E87

Sredečka

Burgas

Nesebär

Vetrino

29

Tolbuhin

1

Mičurin

Varna

Balčik

9

Durankulak

Black Sea

N

0   0

80 miles

120 km

➤ **HOW MUCH IT WILL COST** • Prices in Bulgaria are on the rise, but relax—you can still fill your stomach for a few dollars a day. Museum admission and entertainment costs are negligible. Living modestly to well will cost you about $25 a day, including lodging.

VISAS AND ENTRY REQUIREMENTS U.S. citizens need only a passport for stays under 30 days. For longer visits you'll need a visa, issued at a Bulgarian border or airport for $68 (in hard currency) or at the Bulgarian Embassy (1621 22nd St. NW, Washington, DC 20008, tel. 202/387–7969). The whole process takes about two weeks. Non-U.S. citizens must purchase a visa at an embassy or at the Bulgarian border, even on short visits. For more info contact the Bulgarian Consulate (187 Queensgate, London SW7, tel. 0171/581–3144). No immunizations are required to enter Bulgaria.

COMING AND GOING

➤ **BY TRAIN** • EurailPass, InterRail, and most East European rail passes don't do diddly in Bulgaria, and neither do student IDs and sweet smiles. Fortunately, prices are relatively low. Sofia is the main rail hub, with direct international connections to Bucharest, Athens, and Istanbul. Train fares from Athens and Istanbul hover around $90 each way, and may be comparable with airline fares. If you're traveling through Romania, you must purchase a Romanian travel visa (approximately $36) even if you're only passing through.

➤ **BY PLANE** • **Balkan Airlines** (in U.S., tel. 212/573–5530), the Bulgarian state carrier, has flights from various European hubs to Sofia, but the prices vary wildly. **American Airlines, Lufthansa,** and **Swiss Air** have connections from Canada and the United States to Sofia via Frankfurt, Milan, and Zurich.

Per capita, Bulgarians are the world's seventh-largest group of moviegoers. Not surprisingly, you'll find theaters in even the smallest village. Movies are always subtitled, not dubbed, and cost around $1.

GETTING AROUND Take the bus: It's faster and more efficient than the train and only a fraction more expensive. Both will be crowded in summer, especially in August when all Europe is on vacation. Trains, like buses, will stop in even the most remote towns. Express trains travel on some major routes (for example, Sofia–Varna). Train tickets usually go on sale an hour before departure. To avoid long lines at ticket windows, buy tickets in advance at **Rila Railway Bureau,** which has offices in larger cities.

WHERE TO SLEEP Whenever possible stay in private accommodations, be it a family home or private hotel. At dumpy state-run establishments foreigners pay as much as $100–$150 per night. Dream on, bloodsuckers. Hostels are another option, but they tend to be more grungy and no cheaper than private rooms. University dorms are sometimes open in summer and charge $2–$5 for beds; inquire at an Orbita tourist office for lists of participating universities. There are about 100 campsites ($2–$5 per night) scattered throughout Bulgaria, many concentrated on the Black Sea coast.

FOOD Most grocery stores carry only the basics, and since the purchase of bread is a daily ritual, expect to line up for it. Bulgarian tap water is safe to drink, but be wary of undercooked meat; consider requesting your food *dobre opechen* (well done). No surprise, the diet in Bulgaria is meat-heavy, with skewered, sausaged, or grilled *kebapcha* (pork) topping the list. The national dish is *bop* (lentil soup), while Middle Eastern influences are evident in *tarato,* a soup of yogurt and cucumber. Veggies note: A *shopska* salad, composed of tomato, cucumber, and *cirene* (a popular cheese), is tasty and available in most restaurants. For dessert try *palatscinka,* a delicious crepe with a nut filling. The *smetkata* (bill) won't be brought until you ask for it, and always check the addition.

VISITOR INFORMATION **Orbita,** the national student-travel organization, arranges stays in private homes and some hostels. They also operate hotels of their own, some run-down and expensive, others affordable and akin to youth hostels. **Balkantourist** can also arrange rooms in private homes and campgrounds, but don't let them steer you to an expensive government-owned hotel.

PHONES **Country Code: 359.** Local calls cost 20 stotinki. Phone-card telephones are popping up everywhere, and post offices sell cards. However, there are two types of cards *and* two types of card phones. Use the black cards for domestic calls on the more common orange-colored phones. The smaller cards with decorative pictures can be used on the newer (and more reliable) silver phones for calls throughout Europe. Still, it's easiest to make calls from telephone offices adjacent to most post offices. Just enter a booth, make the call, and pay at the counter as you leave. To call collect, try to say *"zatiachna smetka telefonen razgovar."* Calls to the United States cost $2 a minute; European calls cost about 30 leva a minute.

MAIL Post offices are big, easy to find, and conveniently located. They have late hours and, at least in big cities, are often open on weekends. Letters to Europe can take as long as two weeks to arrive, and letters to the United States can take anywhere from two weeks to two months.

LANGUAGE Bulgarian is a Slavic language that uses the Cyrillic alphabet, which means that signs, newspapers, and billboards will look totally weird to Westerners. If you speak Russian, you're in luck: It's the nation's second-most-common language. German and French are also widely spoken, with English coming in a distant but increasingly prominent fifth.

Sofia
Long overlooked by bargain-hunting backpackers, historic Sofia is ripe for discovery. Compared with other European capitals, prices are cheap, the people friendly, and the atmosphere relaxed. Despite its bland Soviet-inspired architecture, Sofia has Roman churches, Ottoman mosques, and yellow-brick roads crowded with all sorts of characters—even the occasional dancing bear led by a mandolin player. If you're an outdoorsy type, Sofia is ringed by the Balkan Mountains to the north and the Ljulin range to the west; Mt. Vitoša, a year-round playground, is on the city's doorstep. Of course, the Communists left Sofia with some godawful monuments and a decaying urban infrastructure. But since 1989 the capital of Bulgaria has definitely regained some of its former funk. The moral of the story: Visit now before Sofia gets "discovered" by hipsters in search of another Prague to exploit.

BASICS

VISITOR INFORMATION **Balkantourist** charges $12 per person for private rooms that are usually clean and centrally located. Other services include guided tours and currency exchange. *Alexander Stambolijski 27, tel. 02/87–29–67 or 02/88–52–56. Open daily 8 AM–9 PM (until 10 PM in summer).*

Pirin Travel Agency, across the street from **Orbita,** provides info and hostel bookings. *Alexander Stambolijski 30, tel. 02/87–05–79. Open weekdays 9–6.*

AMERICAN EXPRESS **InterBalkan,** the best American Express office in the city, changes traveler's checks for no commission, and holds cardholder mail. *Pl. Sveta Nedelya. Open weekdays 8–8, Sat. 8–1:30.*

EMBASSIES

➤ **UNITED STATES** • The **U.S. Embassy** (Alexander Stambolijski 1, tel. 02/88–48–01; open weekdays 9–5) broadcasts CNN daily 1 PM–2 PM. The **U.S. Consulate** is open to Americans for travel info. *Kapitan Andreev 1. From pl. Sveta Nedelya take Tram 9 south 2 stops to Evlogi Georgiev, then walk south 2 blocks on bul. Cerni Vräh. Open weekdays 9–5.*

➤ **UNITED KINGDOM** • Citizens of Great Britain, Canada, Australia, and New Zealand *must* register at the **British Embassy** for stays in Bulgaria longer than a month. *Bul. Marsăl Tolbuhin 65, tel. 02/87–83–25, after-hrs tel. 02/87–95–75. Open Mon.–Thurs. 8:30–5:30, Fri. 8:30–1.*

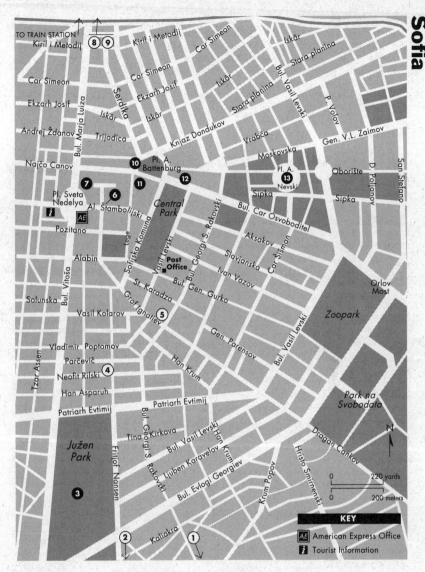

Sights ●

Bulgarian Jewish
Exhibition, **6**

Hram-pametnik
Alexander
Nevski, **13**

Naroden Dvorets na
Kulturata, **3**

Natzionalen
Archeologicheski
Musei, **11**

Natzionalna
Hudozhestvena
Galeria, **12**

Partiyniyat Dom, **10**

Sveti Georgi
Rotonda, **7**

Lodging ○

Hotel Edelweis, **8**

Hotel Niky, **4**

Hotel Orbita, **2**

Hotel Sevastopol, **5**

Hotel
Srednagorad, **9**

Slavianska
Beseda, **1**

PHONES AND MAIL If you dial "9" first and act like a guest, you can make local calls from the lobby of the **Sheraton** (pl. Sveta Nedelya 2). Make international calls 24 hours a day from the **phone office** (Stefan Karadzha 6) half a block west of the central post office. Ask for the international cashier to avoid getting stuck in a line for domestic calls. The **central post office** has some phones for local calls. *Bul. General Gurko 2, near Central Park. Enter on Vasil Levski bet. Sveta Karadzha and bul. General Gurko. Open daily until 8:30.*

COMING AND GOING

Navigating Sofia can be frustrating if you're not armed with a current map—more than 400 streets and squares have been renamed since 1991. One of the city's main arteries is **bulevard Marija Luiza** (formerly Georgi Dimitrov), which runs south from Gare Centrale Sofia to **ploschdat Sveta Nedelya** (Holy Sunday Church Square). Bulevard Marija Luiza becomes bulevard Vitoša south of here and continues past the teeming Naroden Dvorets na Kulturata (National Palace of Culture).

BY TRAIN From the behemoth **Gare Centrale Sofia** (bul. Marija Luiza), take Tram 1, 7, 14, or 15 south toward the city center; buy tickets on the lower level. Make international rail reservations inside the station at the **Rila International Travel Office** (open daily 8–6:30); advance tickets for domestic trips are sold at their office on ploschdat Slaveikov 8 (tel. 02/87–57–42). On the station's main level, **Balkantourist** (open 7 AM–9 PM) exchanges money and arranges accommodations.

BY BUS Get tickets and directions to Sofia's four major bus terminals at the **Comprehensive Travel Office** in the basement of Naroden Dvorets na Kulturata (*see* Worth Seeing, *below*; bus information, tel. 02/59–31–06). To reach the **international bus station** (General Hristo Mihajlov 23, tel. 02/52–50–04), take Tram 19 past Hristo Botev and walk the remaining two blocks. **East Terminal** (tel. 02/45–30–14) serves Plovdiv, Svilengrad, and Borovice; take Tram 14 or 19 southeast of the city, past Park na Svobodata. **Ovca Kupel** (West Terminal, tel. 02/55–30–47) serves Blagoevgrad, Melnik, Sandanski, and the Rila Monastery; take Tram 5 from ploschdat Sveta Nedelya. **Pirdop Terminal** (pl. Pirdop, tel. 02/45–30–14) serves northern destinations.

BY PLANE Sofia's **airport** is 13 km northeast of the city. Downtown Sofia is easily accessible by Bus 84 from outside the terminal (about 20 min). Or, for about $6, hail a taxi (tel. 02/72–06–72 or 02/79–80–35).

WHERE TO SLEEP

The best bargains are private accommodations arranged through Balkantourist; for about $12 you'll score a centrally located room in far better condition than the city's hotels. For information on seasonal hostels or to reserve space in advance, contact **Pirin Travel Agency** (*see* Visitor Information, *above*). If everything is full, there are dozens of comfortable, private hotels in the southern suburb of Simeonovo (take Bus 67), among them one run by friendly hotelier **Andro Galev** (10 Bor St., tel. 02/635–1506).

CENTRAL SOFIA **Hotel Niky.** Family-run hotel with spotless rooms a few blocks from bulevard Vitoša. Manager speaks English. Toilets down the hall. Singles $20, doubles $30. *Neofit Rilski St. 16, tel. 02/51–19–15. Restaurant.*

Hotel Orbita. Plain, clean rooms with radios and views of Mt. Vitoša. A short tram ride from center. Popular disco downstairs. Breakfast included. Singles $22, doubles $34. *James Baucher 76, tel. 02/66–89–97. Tram 9 past Južen Park to J. Baucher St. 130 rooms. Restaurant.*

Hotel Sevastopol. Aging hotel with decent-size rooms, TV in lobby, musty carpets, and some English-speaking staff. Breakfast included. Singles $13, doubles $22. *Bul. G. S. Rakovski 116, tel. 02/87–59–41. Tram 1, 7, or 15 from Gare Centrale to pl. Sveta Nedelya, then 2 stops on Tram 2 or 14. 57 rooms.*

Slavianska Beseda. Large, immaculate rooms with bathtubs and phones. Friendly staff speaks English. Doubles $30. *Slavianska St. 3, tel. 02/88–04–41. Tram 9 from Gare Centrale to pl. Alexander Nevski, then walk south on Pariž and turn right on Slavianska.*

NEAR GARE CENTRALE SOFIA **Hotel Edelweis.** Small and grimy rooms filled with old furniture and street noise. Singles $8, doubles $12, payable in leva only. *Bul. Marija Luiza 79, tel. 02/83–54–31. Tram 1, 7, or 15 from Gare Centrale. Restaurant.*

Hotel Srednagorad. Bring earplugs, because half of these scummy cubicles face a busy intersection. Singles $9, doubles $12. *Bul. Marija Luiza 60, tel. 02/83–53–11.*

HOSTEL **Hotel Jubileina.** Operated by Pirin, this hotel-like complex has two-, three-, and four-person rooms and is worth the 20-minute trip. Bathrooms are communal. $7 per night. *Rizhki Prohod St. 1, tel. 02/20–49–91 or 02/20–50–14. From Gare Centrale take Bus 77 or Tram 4.*

CAMPGROUNDS If you have a car, **Vranya Campground** (tel. 02/78–12–13) is 9 km southeast of town on Highway E80. Otherwise, to reach **Tschernya Kos** (tel. 02/57–11–29) on Highway E79, 11 km southwest of the city, take Tram 5 to the last stop and then hop on Bus 57, 58, or 59.

FOOD

Prices in central Sofia can get outrageous, so check out the café scene on bulevard Vitoša, where ice cream and coffee fetches a reasonable 25¢. The boulevard's hippest hangout is **Café Espresso** (bul. Vitoša 37), followed closely by the part café, part cabaret (shows start around 9:30 PM) **Havana Café** (bul. Vitoša 27).

Budapest. Hearty Hungarian food, excellent service, and reasonable prices. Try the goulash ($2.50) or the beef-filled pancake ($2). *Bul. G. S. Rakovski 145, tel. 02/87–27–50. 1 block south of main post office. Lunch and dinner only.*

Bulgaria. Downstairs in the historic Grand Hotel Bulgaria, with a live band and dance floor. Moderate prices for traditional fare and a formal atmosphere. *Pl. A. Battenburg, northwest corner of Central Park, tel. 02/87–02–02.*

Kitai. Tasty Bulgarian take on Chinese food, in the shadow of Alexander Nevsky statue. Huge entrees $1–$2.50. *Sipka St. 6, tel. 02/46–51–29. South of pl. Alexander Nevsky. Closed daily 2:30–6.*

Pizzeria Venezia. Bulgaria's finest wood-oven-baked pizzas ($1–$3), best topped with a Czech pilsner ($1). Sit elbow-to-elbow with locals. *Benkovski 12, tel. 02/87–63–64. North of pl. Alexander Nevsky.*

Restaurant King. Family-run place (they have 10 kids) that specializes in Middle Eastern food. Stuff yourself with falafel (12 leva) and dolma sandwiches (15 leva). *Denkoglu 38, ½ block east of bul. Vitoša, tel. 02/81–39–69.*

WORTH SEEING

In a pinch Sofia can be covered in a hectic day, though there's plenty to fill up a longer stay. One downer is that Sofia's eyeball-popping National Museum of History (bul. Vitoša 2, tel. 02/88–41–60) is temporarily closed for renovations.

BULGARIAN JEWISH EXHIBITION This exhibit chronicles the history of Bulgarian Jews, and focuses on how they were saved from Nazi persecution. Ask for the recorded commentary in English. *Bul. Alexander Stambolijski 50, top floor of bank building on Pl. Văzraždane. Admission: 6 leva, 3 leva students. Open Sun.–Fri. 10–4.*

HRAM-PAMETNIK ALEXANDER NEVSKY The domed, neo-Byzantine Alexander Nevsky Memorial Church was completed in 1912 as a memorial to the 200,000 Russian soldiers who died fighting for Bulgaria's liberation from the Turks in 1878. You're not permitted to wander during the morning service (9:30–10:30), so catch an evening service when the choir—which includes members from the National Opera—sings from the balcony. *Pl. Alexander Nevsky. Open Wed.–Mon. and Sat. 10:30–4:30. Sat. service at 6 PM.*

NARODEN DVORETS NA KULTURATA Known to Sofians as the NDK (National Palace of Culture), this monstrous cultural center in Južen Park is dominated by a modern sculpture commemorating the 1,300th anniversary of Bulgaria's nationhood. Constructed in 1981, the futuristic building is used mainly for conventions, concerts, films, and congresses. The large **garden** has become a popular hangout in the evening. The basement of the palace features a number of shops, disco, bowling alley, and transportation office. Take the elevator from the basement to the top-floor **Panorama Café** and enjoy the view.

On summer weekends there's a worthwhile crafts market in the northwest corner of Central Park. Look for the stands near the former mausoleum of Georgi Dimitrov, Bulgaria's first communist leader.

NATZIONALEN ARCHEOLOGICHESKI The worthwhile National Museum of Archaeology sits inside the quadrangular, nine-dome Mehmet Pasha's Great Mosque, built in 1494. Exhibits of jewelry, vases, and frescoes trace Bulgarian culture from antiquity to the Middle Ages. *Pl. A. Battenburg, tel. 02/88–24–05. Admission: 10 leva. Open Tues.–Sat. 10–noon and 1:30–6, Sun. 2–6.*

NATZIONALNA HUDOZHESTVENA GALERIA The National Art Gallery, housed in a neo-Baroque palace, hosts traveling exhibits as well as its own collection of mainly Bulgarian work. Also inside is the comatose National Ethnographic Museum. *Bul. Car Osvoboditel, 1 block east of pl. A. Battenburg, tel. 02/88–35–59. Admission: 20 leva, 5 leva students. Open Wed.–Mon. 10–12:30 and 1:30–6.*

PARTIYNIYAT DOM The mammoth Party House, a legacy of the Stalin years, now houses the offices of Bulgaria's three major political parties—the UDF, the TDP, and the BSP. Still visible outside are the black scars of a fire that broke out during a 1990 student rally. *Pl. A. Battenburg. Open weekdays 9–5.*

SVETI GEORGI ROTONDA Hidden in the Sheraton's courtyard is one of Sofia's oldest structures, St. George's Church. Built in the 4th century as a Roman rotunda, it was destroyed by the Huns, rebuilt by Justinian, and turned into a mosque by the Turks before being restored as a church. Remains of other Roman buildings can be seen nearby. *Courtyard of Sheraton Hotel, pl. Sveta Nedelya. Open daily 10:30–1 and 3–5:30.*

AFTER DARK

In the evening, throngs of young people mill about the cafés on the southern end of bulevard Vitoša, near the National Palace of Culture. Around 10 PM the crowds disperse to one of a dozen clubs where drinking and dancing last until the wee hours. **Orbi Lux** in the Hotel Orbita (*see* Where to Sleep, *above*) is considered the coolest disco in the country.

Whatever you're eating or drinking, don't forget to say masrovo (cheers).

DANCING Most clubs don't open until 9 or 10 PM and don't close until dawn. Most also charge a cover of about $1. Near the Grand Hotel Sofia, **Angel Club** (pl. Narod no Sarine 9) has an underground (literally) dance floor and a number of bars. **Disco NDK** (in basement of the National Palace of Culture) is a teenage hangout with dance floors and a cheap cover. **Sevastopol** (bul. G. S. Rakovski 116, at Graf Ignatiev), in the Sevastopol Hotel, is one of the capital's more popular haunts.

MUSIC If you want to hear the classics, check with major hotels or at the ticket offices of concert halls. For advance tickets—about $1 each—go to the kiosk (tel. 02/87-15-88) at 2 ploschdat A. Battenburg. Concerts are held at 7:30 PM in the **Bulgaria Concert Hall** (Aksavkov St. 1, tel. 02/87-40-73), the **Slaveikov Concert Hall** (pl. Slaveikov, tel. 02/88-23-49), and the **National Palace of Culture.** For jazz, try **Frankie's Jazz Club,** a small joint near the American library off bulevard Vitoša.

NEAR SOFIA

RILA MONASTERY The famous **Rila Monastery,** hidden in the imposing Rila Mountains 100 km south of Sofia, was founded in the 10th century by Ivan of Rila (876–946). As you make the ascent through a steep, narrow, forested valley, it's easy to understand why Ivan settled on this remote location for his religious pursuits. Still, Ivan built what was—and still is—the largest monastery in Bulgaria, thereby attracting all sorts of plunderers and treasure seekers. The monastery's fortresslike appearance reflects this turbulent history; **Hreylu's Tower** (1345), adjacent to the church, is now the oldest standing part of the structure, and its rugged stonework contrasts markedly with the elegance of the surrounding complex. Inside the monastery is a collection of religious artifacts spanning more than 1,000 years, plus a sarcophagus containing Ivan's embalmed body. The monastery is open daily with services at 8 AM and 5 PM; guided tours in several languages cost $1. The **museum** (admission 5 leva, 2 leva students; open daily 8–5) at the rear of the monastery features old icons, ancient manuscripts, and the Rila Cross, a 16-inch cross carved with over 1,500 minute figurines. Legend has it that a monk named Raphael did the carving over a 12-year period, after which he went blind.

➢ **COMING AND GOING** • A direct bus from Sofia's Ovca Kupel station departs daily at 8 AM and arrives at the monastery around 11 AM. Aside from a small post office and the new Bank for Agricultural Credit (behind the monastery), most tourist services can be had in the Riletz Hotel (*see below*).

➢ **WHERE TO SLEEP** • Lodging options near the monastery are limited. During July and August the crowds can be heavy, so arrive early, or call ahead for reservations. The monastery itself offers 250 cozy beds to travelers, but at $12 a person, it ain't for charity's sake. Register in room 65 (in far corner from front gate), and remember that the doors are locked at 11 PM sharp. The modern **Riletz Hotel** (main road, ⅔ km behind monastery, tel. 21–06) has 90 large rooms with views of the mountains, and clean bathrooms; doubles cost $26. The showerless hostel to the rear of the monastery, **Touristicheski Spalnia,** has 25 beds in a dungeon-like vault for $6 a night. To reach **Camping Bor,** follow the signs behind the monastery ⅔ km down the road. You'll soon see a dozen bungalows (doubles $12) and a pitch for tents ($1 per tent and $2 per person).

Central Bulgaria

As travelers shoot across Bulgaria on an express train from Sofia to the Black Sea coast, some wistfully contemplate the fields of roses and rugged mountains that make up central Bulgaria. Follow your instincts and don't be afraid to forsake a Black Sea suntan in favor of exploring **Plovdiv** or the famed **Valley of Roses,** an area 100 km east of Sofia that produces 70% of the world's rose oil. **Kazanlǎk** is the "Capital of the Rose," with its rose museum and research garden, and is served by frequent trains; local buses service smaller cities like **Koprivtica.** Even if you're set on the Black Sea coast, consider a brief stop in the ancient village of **Veliko Tǔrnovo.**

Plovdiv

From afar, industrial Plovdiv is an unsightly mess that gives no indication of charm. But beyond the bland high-rise apartment blocks is Old Plovdiv, a well-preserved, 19th-century neighborhood that is quickly becoming Bulgaria's center of bohemian chic: The combination of a cosmopolitan university and winding cobblestone streets has spawned art galleries, bars, and antiques shops. Some of its Roman ruins—Plovdiv is built atop the ancient Roman settlement of Trimontium—have been excavated and put into use as markets and cafés, further adding to the city's ambience.

BASICS The local Balkantourist office, **Pauldin Tourist** (bul. Bulgaria 34, tel. 032/55–38–48; open daily 8 AM–9 PM), changes money and is your best bet for arranging rooms (until 5 PM). It's a hike from the stations, but the staff speaks a little English and may be able to arrange accommodations over the phone. **Orbita** (Vazrazdane 79, tel. 032/23–23–00; open weekdays 8:30–noon and 1–5:30) is closer but less helpful. Look for it before the tunnel when coming from Plovdiv's stations.

COMING AND GOING As Bulgaria's second-largest city, Plovdiv is easily reached from all corners of the country. The nearby **train station** (tel. 032/22–27–29) and **bus terminal** (tel. 032/77–76–07) are a 10-minute walk from the center, or you can take Bus 36 downtown; it departs from the traffic circle opposite the stations.

WHERE TO SLEEP Plovdiv is short on cheap hotels, especially during its May, late-September, and October festivals. Aside from private rooms, inquire at Orbita (*see above*) about summer university housing (from $4 per person). Or book ahead at the excellent **Touristcheski Dom** (Aleko Konstantinov 5A, 2 blocks from pl. Vazrazdane, tel. 032/23–32–11; doubles $15), an eight-room hotel set in a restored Greek mansion in the heart of Old Plovdiv. No one speaks English, so try booking through Orbita. The aged **Bulgaria Hotel** (Patriarch Evtimij 13, tel. 032/22–60–64) has a central location and charges $35 per double. From the train station take Bus 27 or 37 to the tunnel on Vazrazdane. The **Leipzig Hotel** (bul. Ruski 76, tel. 032/23–22–50), just four blocks from the train station, is comparable to the Bulgaria in quality and price but is easier to find.

FOOD The best traditional Bulgarian restaurants are in Old Plovdiv, notably the superb **Paldin Restaurant** (Tseretelev 3, tel. 032/23–17–20). Dine outdoors at this landmark eatery, or in its dark, musty tavern. From Knias Alexander take Maksim Gorki and turn right at Tseretelev. Also in the old city, **Trakijski Stan** (Paldin 5, tel. 032/22–45–10) balances hearty Bulgarian food with loud Top 40 music.

WORTH SEEING Plovdiv's major attraction is its old town, built atop the three hills that inspired the town's Roman name, Trimontium. Wandering the narrow cobblestone streets you'll see restored houses, museums, churches, and scads of ancient fortified walls. Behind the post office near the central square, notice the **Forum of Philoppolis** and other dilapidated Roman ruins. Near the Marica River off 6 Septemvri, two blocks from Knias Alexander, the **Archeological Museum** (pl. Soedinenie 1, tel. 032/22–43–39; admission 10 leva; open Tues.–Sun. 9–12:30 and 2–5:30) has three halls containing prehistoric, Roman, and medieval displays. The **Mosque of Djoumaya Djamiya** (at the end of Knias Alexander) was built in the 14th century by order of Sultan Murad II. It's still used and is open from first to last prayer, except during services. Remember to remove your shoes at the door. Built in the 2nd century AD, the **Roman amphitheater** was only recently discovered when a landslide removed part of the hill. It's the largest amphitheater in Bulgaria, seating 3,000 people, and is used regularly for performances in summer.

Veliko Tŭrnovo

Built along the banks of the Yantra River, the old homes of Veliko Tŭrnovo are carved deep into a hillside under the shadow of dramatic limestone cliffs. Since the town's layout follows the twisting Yantra River, getting around can be confusing. Try orienting yourself by Veliko Tŭrnovo's two major landmarks: the triangular **Maika Bulgaria Square** on the west side of town, and **Tzarevets Hill** to the east. Also useful are city maps from **Balkantourist** (Etur Hotel, tel. 062/2–81–65; open daily 10–noon and 3–8), whose English-speaking staff arranges private accommodations ($8 per night) and changes currency at fair rates.

COMING AND GOING Veliko's **train station** (tel. 062/2–02–30) is on the opposite side of the Yantra River from the city center, near Sveta Gora Park. Buses 4 and 13 depart every 20 minutes from the station for downtown. From the **bus station** (Nikola Gabrovski, tel. 062/4–08–09) just south of the city center, Buses 7, 10, 11, and 14 run regularly to the city center.

WHERE TO SLEEP The **Orbita Hotel** (Hristo Botev 15, tel. 062/2–03–91) has the cheapest beds in town at $1.30 per night. It's on the fourth floor of the Orbita Youth Complex; from the bus station take Buses 7, 10, 11, or 14. For something more upscale—doubles cost $26—head to the **Yantra Hotel** (pl. Velcho Vassera, off D. Blagoev, tel. 062/2–03–91) in the Varusa District. Half of its 78 mongo rooms have views of Tzarevets Hill, and the on-site restaurant is excellent. The **Etur Hotel** (Ivailo 2, off Hristo Botev, tel. 062/2–68–51) is central—it houses the Balkantourist office—but overpriced at $21 for singles and $26 for doubles. Still, the views aren't half bad and the staff is generally friendly.

➢ **CAMPGROUNDS** • **Boliarski Stan Campground.** Trees shield the wood bungalows ($2 doubles) from nearby high-rise apartments. Friendly management runs a good on-site restaurant. From town take Bus 11 for 4 km to the Varna–Sofia junction and follow signs. *Tel. 062/4–18–59. Closed Nov.–May.*

FOOD There are plenty of excellent eating spots in Veliko Tŭrnovo, especially along the streets Vasil Levski and Georgi Dimitrov. For outstanding Bulgarian cuisine, head to the family-run, no-name **restaurant** (Tsarkaloyan 1; open daily 11–11) down from pl. Maika Bulgaria; the prices are criminally low. The family-run **Samovodska Krachma** (Rakovska 31; open daily 10–11) offers a limited menu dominated by grilled meat. The *nadenitza* (home-made sausage with all the trimmings; 10 leva) are real tasty.

WORTH SEEING Veliko Tŭrnovo's most prominent landmark is **Tzarevets Hill,** with its fort, church, and palace. The hill is almost completely enclosed by a loop in the Yantra, and you cross over to the site on a narrow stone bridge built in the 17th century by the Turks. The summit itself is dominated by **Ascension Patriarchal Church** (admission 20 leva, 10 leva students; open daily 9–7), which offers great views. In front of Tzarevets Hill is **Assenovtsi Park,** with its monument to the reestablishment of the Bulgarian kingdom. Across the footbridge behind the Interhotel lies a large three-story, brown-brick building containing the **State Art Museum** (admission 10 leva; open Tues.–Sun. 10–6) and its top-rate collection of modern Bulgarian art.

Valley of Roses

Between Sofia and the Black Sea is the famed Valley of Roses, the cradle of Bulgaria's rose-oil industry (pound per pound, rose oil is more valuable than gold). Kazanlăk, in the heart of the region, is the "Capital of the Rose," with its rose museum and garden. More intriguing is Koprivštica, a town that falls firmly in the "cute and cobblestone" category.

KAZANLĂK

This town of 60,000 draws its fame from the precious attar (a fancy name for rose oil) culled from local roses, which is then sold around the world for the manufacturing of perfume. A visit to Kazanlăk needn't take long: Tour the Museum of Roses, examine the murals of the 2,200-year-old Thracian tomb, and, if you're here in early June, catch folk dancing at the **International Rose Festival,** held next to the Rose Museum. There's not much else to see or do in this strangely pleasant industrial town, which stinks of roses in summer.

COMING AND GOING Kazanlǎk lies on a major rail route between Sofia and Burgas. Service is frequent, with connections to many cities. Head to the town center from the **train station** (tel. 0431/2–20–12) by walking up Rozova Dolina. The **bus station** (tel. 0431/2–23–83), opposite the railroad depot, serves Plovdiv as well as local destinations.

WHERE TO SLEEP Your best bet is a private room arranged through Balkantourist, which has a desk inside **Hotel Rose** (pl. Svobodata, tel. 0431/2–72–10). If that doesn't pan out, try the **Kazanlǎkska Roza Campground/Motel** (tel. 0431/2–42–39), 3 km from town toward Sipka (take Bus 5 or 6). You can either rent a bungalow for $9 or stay in the motel for $11. More expensive and convenient is **Hotel Zornista** (tel. 0431/2–23–84; doubles $30), perched on a hill overlooking Kazanlǎk. Walk from the station toward town, turn right, cross the river, turn left, and walk a few blocks to the stairs leading to the Thracian tomb; follow the trail for about 15 minutes.

WORTH SEEING **Historical Museum.** A worthwhile museum near the central square, with finds from the ancient Thracian city of Seuthopolis, and artifacts typical of the local rose-oil industry. *Kiril Imotodi 9, tel. 0431/2–80–66. Walk 1 block on Iskar from pl. Svobodata. Admission free. Open daily 8–noon and 1–5:30.*

Rose Museum and Research Institute. Walk away with reams of rose trivia, such as that pickers must start work at dawn to preserve the unique fragrance of attar, and that 2,000 rose petals yield just one gram of rose oil. *Take Bus 5 from bus station. Admission free. Open May–Oct., daily 8:30–5:30.*

Thracian Tomb. The original 4th-century BC Thracian tomb is closed to the public and kept at a constant temperature, but an exact replica has been constructed behind it. To reach the tomb, cross the river and climb the stairs into the park. *Tel. 0431/2–47–50. Open daily 8–noon and 1–5:30.*

KOPRIVŠTICA

Koprivštica is perhaps the most significant of Bulgaria's museum towns—not the least because the first shots in Bulgaria's war for independence against the Turks were fired here on April 20, 1876. More than a century later, the town remains virtually intact and unchanged; even today, transport on Koprivštica's cobblestone streets is mostly by foot or horse-drawn cart. Architecturally speaking, it exhibits the various styles developed during the National Revival period in a half-dozen noted homes (now open as museums). Koprivštica can be seen in a day, but you may be tempted to splurge and stay in one of its luxurious old mansions.

COMING AND GOING The station lies on the Sofia–Burgas line, but not all trains stop, so make sure *yours* does. At the train station, catch the bus that meets every train and carries passengers 10 km to town; buy your ticket (about 1 leva) from the driver. The **bus station** (tel. 997184/21–33) is up the road from the city center and has a posted schedule for all trains and buses.

WHERE TO SLEEP For about $18 you can either stay in a charmless room in the small **Hotel Koprivštica** (tel. 997184/21–82) or in a luxurious guest house—with timber floors, woven rugs, and traditional furniture—rented through the hotel's reception desk. Of the four available houses, the Shuleva House has private baths and, like the Drehlekova House, is adjacent to the stairs leading to the Hotel Koprivštica. The town's cheapest beds ($3) are at **Tourescheski Spalnia Voivodenets** (tel. 997184/21–45); the old brown building near the central square is clean and has large dorm-style rooms.

WORTH SEEING Admission to all the house museums can be had with a single ticket (10 leva), available at any of the sites.

Georgi Benkovski House. Built in 1831 with some interesting 19th-century National Revival architectural touches: a stone-laid lower floor with a salon and a wood-beam second floor with an open veranda. Inside are artifacts and displays on Benkovski and other revolutionaries. *Jako Dorosiev 5. Open Wed.–Mon. 7:30–noon and 1:30–5:30.*

Lyuben Karavelov House. Inside is an exhibit on the writing career of Lyuben Karavelov (1843–1876), with copies of his works and other memorabilia. *Bul. Anton Ivanov 39. Open Wed.–Mon. 7:30–noon and 1:30–5:30.*

Todor Kableshkov House. Also representative of the National Revival style, this house was built in 1845 and has since been turned into a museum of the April Uprising. Exhibits document the activities of Todor Kableshkov and his fellow revolutionaries. *Todor Kableshkov 8. Open Tues.–Sun. 7:30–noon and 1:30–5:30.*

Black Sea Coast

Bulgaria may be a country shaped by the collision of East and West, but locals claim that the Black Sea coast has been shaped by Balkantourist alone. The company has attempted to create an Eastern version of the French Riviera with flashy resorts and beach sports. **Varna** in the north and **Burgas** in the south are the only coastal towns with train service and therefore serve as transit hubs for the coastal resorts and the region's small, untouristed fishing villages.

Varna

Bulgaria's third-largest city, Varna has dominated the Black Sea coast for almost three millennia. These days, sailors from around the world lend the city a cosmopolitanism rarely found in Bulgaria. The central part of town, with its well-kept beach and gardens, is hidden from the high-rise apartments southwest of the port. The main activities here are swimming, beach bumming, and water sliding (one goes straight into the ocean). Even so, Varna is best remembered as a major transport hub (with rail service to Istanbul and Athens).

BASICS **Balkantourist** has three branches in Varna, though the office across from the train station (tel. 052/22–56–30; open daily 8–6) is the most helpful; the staff exchanges money, books private rooms ($6 a person), and provides free maps.

COMING AND GOING The train station, **Gare Centrale,** is by the harbor; make the ⅓-km walk north to town or grab Bus 41. The **bus station** (Vladislav Varnenčik 159, tel. 052/44–83–49) is 4 km from town and accessible on Bus 1, 22, or 41.

WHERE TO SLEEP The best accommodations in Varna are private rooms arranged through Balkantourist (*see above*). The cheapest hotel, **Hotel Musala** (Musala 3, tel. 052/22–39–25), is off the main square—ploschdat 9 Septemvri—and charges $30 for bland doubles. **Hotel Odessa** (bul. Slivnica 1, tel. 052/22–82–381) is the nicest of the bargain hotels and is close to the beach. The little old ladies at the desk speak English and charge $33 for singles, $45 for doubles.

WORTH SEEING Restaurants, stores, and cafés abound on bulevard Knjaz Boris I, a pedestrian street that intersects with bulevard Slivnica before it runs down to the beach. Bulevard Primorski runs from the gardens past the beach to the train station (watch out for pickpockets here). Most museums in Varna are open Tuesday–Sunday from 10 to 5.

Ethnographic Museum. The architecture of this old wood building is as engaging as the collection of peasant clothes and tools inside. *22 Panagjurishte, tel. 052/22–00–98. Admission: 20 leva, 5 leva students.*

Museum of Art and History. Don't miss this one, with artifacts from a 3rd-century-BC necropolis discovered in 1972 near Varna. Display cases show the graves just as they were found, with many gold adornments still on the skeletons. *Bul. Marija Luiza, tel. 052/23–04–23. Admission: 25 leva, 5 leva students.*

Roman Thermae. The substantial remains of ancient Roman baths are definitely worth a visit. Built at the end of the 2nd century AD, the baths were in use up to the end of the 3rd century. *Han Krum, off bul. Knjaz Boris I. Admission: 10 leva, 2 leva students.*

NEAR VARNA

ALADZHA MONASTERY It costs a mere 5 leva to enter Aladzha's 13th-century **Skalen Manastir** (Rock Monastery), chipped laboriously out of the surrounding limestone cliffs by monks who lived in the caves nearby. Across from the monastery, **Louna Sresta** offers expensive game dishes and nightly folk shows at 9:30 PM. Bus 29 departs from in front of Varna's cathedral for Aladzha (20 min); check with Balkantourist for departure times. The wooded area around the monastery is perfect for hiking, or you can head to the beach on a windy 4-km road that overlooks the Black Sea. At the end of it all is **Zlatni Pjasăci** and its small beach.

Burgas

The youngest city on the Black Sea coast, Burgas has few historical sights and should service only as a travel hub to nearby Sozopol and Mičurin and a place to change money. As always, **Balkantourist** has solid exchange rates and accepts traveler's checks, and arranges private accommodations for $8 per night. The most helpful branch (tel. 056/4–55–53; open daily 8–6) is opposite the bus station.

COMING AND GOING There's no direct rail service to Varna or Istanbul from Burgas's only **train station** (pl. Vassil Kolarov, tel. 056/4–50–22), but trains do run several times daily to Sofia and Plovdiv, and once a day to Veliko Tŭrnovo. The train station is next to the **Jug** (South) bus station (tel. 056/4–56–31) and the port.

WHERE TO SLEEP **Briz Hotel.** A pleasant dump opposite the train station. Singles $9, doubles $12. *Pl. Vassil Kolarov, tel. 056/3–61–80. 100 rooms. Restaurant.*

Park Hotel. Best value for your money. Clean rooms with bath and balconies. Close to the beach. Singles $17, doubles $25. *North Seaside Gardens, tel. 056/31–4–55. Take Bus 4 from town center. 130 rooms. Restaurant.*

Primorets Hotel. Helpful English-speaking staff and rooms that sparkle. Decent downstairs restaurant. *Liliana Dimitrova 1, near seaside gardens, tel. 056/44–1–17. 125 rooms, some w/bath.*

NEAR BURGAS

SOZOPOL The village of Sozopol, 35 km south of Burgas, is the haunt of fishermen, artists, and Bulgarian tourists. Sozopol's cobblestone alleys are lined with traditional houses, so it's got a pleasant Olde Worlde feel. If it's a beach you're after, stop by the small, sandy strand below the park, or head to the larger beach below the new town. Frequent buses run between Burgas and Sozopol, and three or four times a day farther south to Mičurin.

If you're looking for a hotel, try **Hotel Toptin** (tel. 995514/1852) or **Hotel Radik** (tel. 995514/1706), two family-run places opposite one another on bulevard Republikska, near Balkantourist. Both have clean rooms for under $10. Private accommodations arranged through **Balkantourist** (Ropotamo 28, tel. 995514/251), in the new town, are cheaper ($6 per person). The office is open daily 8–8 in summer, weekdays 8–4 off-season.

MICURIN The stone-fringed beaches of Mičurin, a tiny fishing village 65 km south of Burgas, are perfect for snorkeling. The road south from Mičurin passes forests, fields of corn, grapes, and wildflowers—prime hiking territory. **Cooptourist,** near the bus station, books private accommodations ($7 per person), changes money, and is open daily 8–8 (closed daily for lunch in off-season). The **Chaika Hotel,** just up from the bus station, offers small, clean rooms with a hall shower for $3. Aside from the cafés, many families operate small restaurants out of their homes.

CZECH REPUBLIC AND SLOVAKIA

5

By Helen Lenda and Christopher Van Bebber

I went with a Prague acquaintance to her country house, and at the train station her dog was issued a funky little ticket with DOG penciled on it in Czech. It was so humane and yet so practical—but you get used to that. In the musical notes of the people's speech, the generosity they show each other in daily life, and in the peaceful towns their ancestors built, there's something surprisingly harmonious about the Czech Republic and Slovakia.

It is surprising that Czechs and Slovaks are so placid after 50 years of foreign domination—by the Nazis from 1938 to 1945 then the Soviets until 1989—and the recent dissolution of their union. Between the world wars the Czechs and Slovaks were spliced together to form Czechoslovakia, one of the most prosperous democratic nations in Europe before Hitler took over. The union survived under the Soviets, but Slovaks became increasingly disgruntled at being second-class citizens in a country ruled by Czechs. There was a bloodless split on January 1, 1993, but, except for the fact you have to change money as you travel from one country to the other, you would hardly notice that you are crossing an international border.

While the Slovaks are floundering in attempts to find their political feet, the Czech Republic has a conscientious leadership and an educated population that attract foreign investment. The latter's promise is striking when you consider that someone like Václav Havel, the most important Czech author of the 60s and 70s, was named president. When Havel articulates the need for a society based on human dignity and needs, people here listen.

Basics

MONEY $1 = 29 Czech koruny and 10 Czech koruny = 34¢. $1 = 30 Slovak koruny and 10 Slovak koruny = 33¢. The unit of currency in the Czech Republic is the koruna (crown), abbreviated Kč, which is divided into 100 haleru (hellers). New coins and notes were gradually put into circulation in 1993. Slovakia is also slowly phasing in new money, Slovak crowns, abbreviated SK. Until the switch is complete, Czech and Slovak currency may still be differentiated only by stickers affixed to the corner of the bills. In both countries, check your bills carefully to avoid old currency (clerks sure do).

Although the buildings of the Czech Republic and Slovakia survived World War II unscathed, the Soviets left their mark. The countries look as if everybody—except for an army of cement workers on drugs—simply left for 50 years.

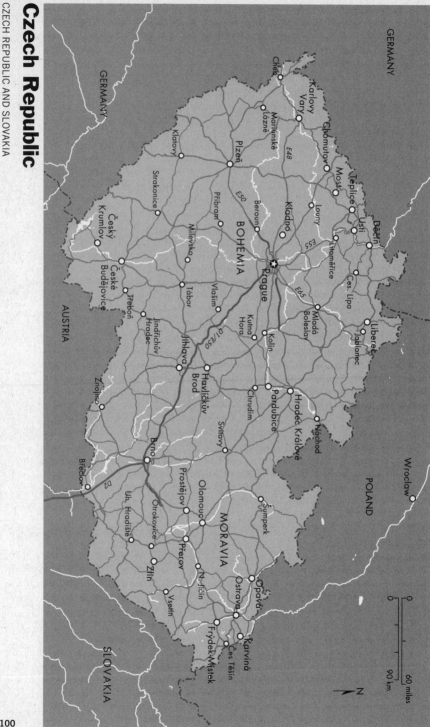

Czech Republic

CZECH REPUBLIC AND SLOVAKIA

Your best bet is to brave the lines and change money on weekdays at state banks, which charge 2% commission and sometimes do credit card cash advances. The new crop of fast-exchange windows, like Chequepoint, skim an extortionate 9% off the top; hotels may rob you of even more. All that's left of the black market are small-time swindlers looking to give you worthless money.

➤ **HOW MUCH IT WILL COST** • Prices in the Czech Republic and Slovakia are catching up with those in the West, but they still have a way to go. By seeking cheap lodging alternatives like rooms in private homes ($10–$20 per person), hostels ($5–$15), and university dorms ($5–$10), you can keep your daily budget well below $40 in big cities. Transportation costs, however, are higher here than in most other Eastern European countries. In 1993 the Czech Republic matched Slovakia's tripling of train fares. Before you hop on a train heading west, check tourist offices in Prague for names of private bus lines charging half the train fare.

VISAS AND ENTRY REQUIREMENTS Americans and Brits may enter the Czech Republic and Slovakia for 90 days without a visa. Canadians, Australians, and New Zealanders must apply for 30-day visas before entering.

COMING AND GOING Trains are the most common way of reaching the Czech Republic and Slovakia, although InterRail and EurailPasses are not accepted here. If you're headed straight to the Czech Republic or Slovakia from the United States, though, you might save some aggravation and money by flying directly to Prague or Bratislava. **ČSA** (545 5th Ave., Suite 1101, New York, NY 10017, tel. 212/682–5833), the state airline, has direct flights from New York to Prague (with a free connection to Bratislava) four times per week ($900) and from Toronto and Montréal (more than $1,000) every Saturday. You'll probably get a better deal with one of the Western airlines currently serving Prague, which include **British Airways, KLM,** and **Air France.**

GETTING AROUND The state runs **CSD** (the railroad) and **CSAD** (the bus system). As a rule, trains are slow and uncomfortable. Buses are slightly more expensive and often crowded, but uncrowded buses are more comfortable than trains. On the signs in major train stations, *rychlík* (express trains) are listed in red and *osobný vlak* (local trains) in black. Schedules are posted on all train platforms; *odjezd* and *příjezd* mean "departures" and "arrivals," respectively. In larger stations, domestic and *mezinarodní* (international) tickets are sold at separate locations.

The bus system is thorough; even small towns have a bus terminal with a ticket office and numbered platforms with schedules posted for every route. When reading them, remember that a crossed-hammer logo above a bus itinerary means "work days only" (no weekend service); "s" means the bus runs Saturday; "n" indicates Sunday service.

WHERE TO SLEEP Hotels charge about $30–$40 per double, but informal **pensions** and **private rooms** charging only $10–$20 per person are springing up everywhere: Look for ZIMMER FREI and PRIVAT ZIMMER signs, or inquire at tourist agencies. Hostelling International (HI) runs more than 20 **hostels** with beds that go for as little as $2.50 with an HI card; all hostels have showers and kitchen facilities. A common lodging option in the Czech Republic and Slovakia is the **ubytovna,** designed to house workers. If you have a student ID, try staying in university dorm rooms open in July and August; inquire at local ČKM offices (*see* Visitor Information, *below*) for up-to-date information.

FOOD You'll find many reasons to love the Czech Republic and Slovakia, but food will not be one of them. The food is straightforward: It'll fill you up, stick to your ribs, and go easy on your budget. The all-time Czech classic is *vepřo-knedlo-zelí* (pork, dumplings, and cabbage), and the Slovak favorite is *hulušky* (potato dumplings with sheep cheese). Chicken is usually gross; look instead for roasted *kachna* (duck). A safe bet for a cheap, digestible meal is *vepřový řízek* (Wiener schnitzel). Vegetarians may have to settle for pickled carrots, cabbage, peas, and lots of rice, potatoes, or omelets. In Czech, *bez masa* means "without meat." The best places to go for rock-bottom budget meals are *pivnici* (beer halls) and cafeteria-style *bufets.* Head to a *cukrárna* (sweet shop) or *kavárna* (café) afterward to top off your meal.

For drinks, Moravian wine is the best and most expensive the country has to offer. The most popular aperitifs (about 20 Kčs per glass) are *slivovice* (plum brandy), *becherovka* (herb liqueur), and Slovakia's *borovička,* a ginlike drink derived from juniper berries. And, of course, there's beer. On the morning after, you'll need *kava* (coffee), *presso* (espresso), or *čaj* (tea), which never come decaffeinated.

BUSINESS HOURS Bank hours are Monday 7:30–5 and Tuesday–Friday 7:30–noon. Private and hotel exchange offices are open daily, often late into the evening. **Museums** are generally open Tuesday–Friday 9–5. Some are closed November through April. **Stores** are open week-days 9–6 (grocery stores often open at 6 AM); most close at noon on Saturday and almost all are closed Sunday. Some **food shops** stay open on Sunday and during the evening.

VISITOR INFORMATION Čestovní Kancelăr Mládeže (ČKM), the youth travel bureau, will help you find budget accommodations (including way cheap university dorms) and point you to inexpensive activities.

Use a public phone and run the risk of dialing the right number and reaching the wrong person; reaching two people at once, neither of whom you know; or finding the muffled background conversation more interesting than your own.

Čedok, the Czech and Slovak state travel agency, is slowly—too slowly—losing its monopoly on tourism. Staff members are usually more into booking rooms than answering questions. You'll find branches all over the Czech Republic and Slovakia, as well as in New York and London. *10 E. 40th St., New York, NY 10016, tel. 212/689–9720; 17–18 Old Bond St., London W1X 4RB, tel. 071/629–6058.*

PHONES Country code: 42. The Czech Republic and Slovakia still share a country code, and both have introduced phones that accept cards. Purchase cards at tobacco shops and some post offices. You can call the United States collect or with a telephone card by dialing **AT&T USA Direct** (tel. 00–420–00101) and speaking to a U.S. operator. Direct international calls are made by dialing 00, then the country code, then the rest, with no pauses. If you can't find a working pay phone, check the post office.

MAIL Letters to North America usually take one to two weeks, letters to the United Kingdom just a few days. Postage for letters to North America is 9 Kčs, for postcards 6 Kčs. Letters to Europe are 6 Kčs, postcards 5 Kčs.

Prague
The history of Prague (Praha in Czech) is evident in its layout: The city has a medieval center, modern communist outskirts, and architecture from every major period and style in between. Prague's buildings, unlike those in many Eastern European cities, survived World War II undamaged. The city is a testament to Europe's architectural history. Prague's cultural vibrance greets you at every turn of the cobblestone streets, in the sculptures, colorful roofline frescoes, clever concert posters, talented street musicians, and roaring beer halls. It's no wonder that young Americans have flocked to Prague in search of the Left Bank of the '90s. Unfortunately, they've started to wear their welcome thin. Prices have risen so drastically that Czechs can only watch while tourists feast in the restaurants they used to frequent in the city center.

BASICS

VISITOR INFORMATION **American Hospitality Center** (Na Můstku 7, off Václavské nám., tel. 02/262–045; open summer, daily 10–10, daily 9–9 off-season) is a great resource for maps, lodging information, and contact with other travelers; besides, **Chicago's Famous Pizza** is in back. There's a counter staffed by English speakers at **Čedok** (Na příkopě 18, near Nám. Republiky Metro, tel. 02/212–7111; open weekdays 8:30–6, Sat. 8:30–12:30), which distributes info on lodging, tours, and car rentals. For other Čedok locations, *see* Where to Sleep, *below.*

Prague Information Service (PIS) can give you the latest on events and sells concert tickets and maps from three locations. *Staroměstské nám. 22, Staré Město, tel. 02/224–453; Panská 4, tel. 02/224–311; Na příkopě 20, tel. 02/223–411. All open daily 10–6.*

AMERICAN EXPRESS **American Express**'s office on Václavské náměstí is handy if you're a cardholder: You can cash a check or withdraw cash from a 24-hour automatic-teller machine outside. *Václavské nám. 56, tel. 02/229–487, fax 02/261–504. Metro: Muzeum. Open weekdays 9–5, Sat. 9–3.*

EMBASSIES **Canada.** *Mickiewiczová 6, Hradčany, tel. 02/326–941; after hours, 02/312–0251. Tram 22 or 18 uphill to Chotkovy Sady, then follow Mickiewiczová. Open weekdays 8–noon and 2–4.*

United Kingdom. *Thunovská 14, Malá Strana, tel. 02/533–347. Open weekdays 9–noon and 2:45–4.*

United States. *Tržiště 15, Malá Strana, tel. 02/536–641. Metro to Malostranská, then Tram 22 to Malostranské nám. Open weekdays 8–1 and 2–4:30.*

PHONES AND MAIL For telephone assistance, dial 120. International calls can be made 24 hours a day from the **main post office** (Jindřišská 14, tel. 02/264–193; mail service 7 AM–11 PM). From a private phone, dial 0133 to get in touch with an operator.

COMING AND GOING

BY TRAIN Most trains to Prague stop at **Hlavní nádraží** (Wilsonova 80, tel. 02/235–3836), the city's main station. **Nádraží: Holešovice** station (Arnoštovská ul.; Metro: Nádraží Holešovice) is served by trains from Berlin, among other major European cities. International trains not terminating in Prague will often deposit you at Holešovice. The Metro's Line C connects the two train stations. Most trains stopping at **Masarykovo nádraží** are going to or coming from Bohemia and Brno. The station is near Náměstí Republiky on Hernská ulice; to get there, take the Metro to Náměstí Republiky. **Smíchovské nádraží** (Křižova ul., Metro: Smíchovské nádraží) is a stop on some domestic routes west (like Karlštejn Castle) and south.

BY BUS Buses leaving from **Florenc Bus Terminal** serve most domestic and international destinations. If you're traveling to other cities in Bohemia, buses are usually a more convenient and scenic option than trains. *Tel. 02/221–4459. Metro: Florenc Terminal. Open daily 5 AM–11 PM.*

BY PLANE **Ruzyně Airport** (tel. 02/367–760 or 02/367–814), 15 km northwest of the center, always has long lines, so get there early. A **ČSA bus** departs from the front of the terminal every half-hour for the Dejvická Metro station and Náměstí Republiky (15 Kčs, daily 6–6). Bus 119 from Dejvická (4 Kčs) makes the trip more frequently but stops more often along the way. Suspect a rip-off if a **taxi** ride costs more than $7.

GETTING AROUND

Pick up the bargain *plán města* (city map) from any bookstore or *tabak* (tobacco shop); it's an indispensable guide to transportation and the city streets. The Metro, bus, and tram lines serve the city thoroughly and cheaply. All three require a 4 Kčs ticket; there are no transfers. Yellow vending machines dispense single-use tickets in Metro stations; tabaks and some newsstands sell sheets of 10 (no discount); and red machines dispense 24-hour tickets (25 Kčs). Long-term passes are sold at the counter marked DP in the I.P. Pavlova Metro station (open weekdays 7–10 AM and 2–6 PM, Sat. 7–10 AM) and at the Muzeum Metro station (4-day pass $3.00, 5-day $3.50, 1-month $7.00).

BY SUBWAY The Metro system consists of three lines, which form a triangle around the center of the city. **Line A** runs east to west; **Line B** runs southwest to northeast; and **Line C** connects to the two biggest railway stations and extends far to the south. Get your ticket

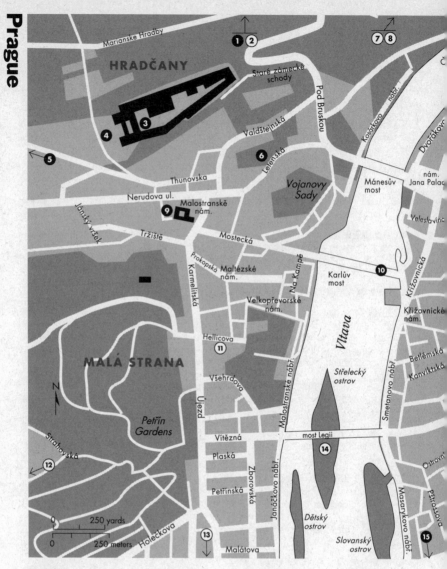

HRADČANY

Marianske Hradby

Staré zámecké schody

Valdštejnská

Pod Bruskou

Kozánkovo nábř.

Dvořákovo

Staré zámecké schody

Thunovska

Letenská

Vojanovy Sady

Mánesův most

nám. Jana Palac

Nerudova ul.

Malostranské nám.

Velestavinc

Jánský vršek

Tržiště

Mostecká

Na Kampě

Karlův most

Karmelitská

Prokopská

Maltézské nám.

Křižovnická

Velkopřevorské nám.

Křižovnické nám.

Hellicova

MALÁ STRANA

Vltava

Betlémská

Všehrdova

Malostranské nábř.

Střelecký ostrov

Konviktská

N

Újezd

Petřín Gardens

Smetanovo nábř.

Strahovská

Vítězná

most Legii

Ostrovn'

Plaská

Zborovská

Pstrossova

Petřínská

Janáčkovo nábř.

Dětský ostrov

Masarykovo nábř.

0 250 yards

0 250 meters

Holečkova

Malátova

Slovanský ostrov

Sights ●

Anežský Klášter, **19**
Belvedere Summer Palace, **1**
Chrám sv. Mikulše, **9**
Karlův Most, **10**
Hradčanské náměstí, **4**
Loreto Church, **5**
Národní Muzeum, **36**
Novoměstská radnice, **28**

Palác Kultury, **35**
Pražský Hrad, **3**
Staroměstská radnice, **20**
Staronová Synagóga, **18**
Starý Židovský Hřbitov, **16**
Státní Židovský Muzeum, **17**
Týn Church, **23**
Vyšehrad, **15**
Wallenstein Palace, **6**

Lodging ○

AVE Ltd. Travel Agency, **34**
Bonsai Privat, **7**
Čedok, **32**
Charles' University Dorms, **29**
Džbán, **2**
EESTEC Dorms, **12**
Hostel Braník (HI), **13**
Hostel Ostrov, **14**
Hostel Sokol, **11**
Hotel Axa, **27**

Hotel Hybernia, **30**
Kolej 17 listopadu, **24**
Kolej Jednota, **31**
Pension Unitas, **21**
Penzion Troja, **8**
Pragotur, **26**
Prague Suites, **22**
Tour Hotel, **33**
Ubytovna ČSPLO, **25**

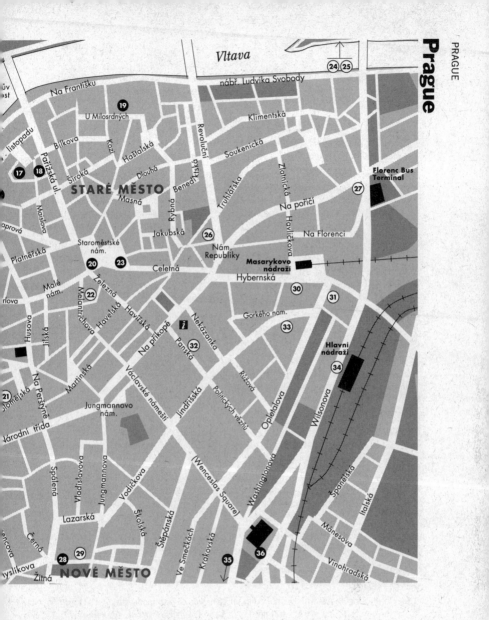

Vltava

nábř. Ludvíka Svobody

(24)(25)

Na Františku

Na Františku

U Milosrdných (19)

Klimentská

Bílkova

Kozí

Haštalská

Soukenická

listopadu

Pařížská ul.

Široká

Dlouhá

Zlatnická

Florenc Bus Terminal

(17) (18)

STARÉ MĚSTO

Masná

Benediktská

Truhlářská

Na poříčí

(27)

aprová

Maiselova

Rybná

Havlíčkova

Na Florenci

Platnéřská

Jakubská

(26)

Nám. Republiky

Masarykovo nádraží

Staroměstské nám.

(20) (23)

Celetná

Hybernská

Malé nám.

Železná

(30)

(31)

rlova

Melantrichova

Havelská

Havířská

Husova

(22)

Nekázanka

Gorkého nam.

(33)

Na příkopě

Panská

(32)

Hlavní nádraží

Martinská

Václavské náměstí

Jindřišská

Růžová

Opletalova

(34)

(21)

loměřická

Na Perštýně

Jungmannovo nám.

Policických vězňů

Wilsonova

Národní třída

Španělská

Spálená

Vladislavova

Jungmannova

Vodičkova

(Wenceslas Square)

Washingtonova

Italská

Lazarská

Školská

Štěpánská

Ve Smečkách

Krakovská

Mánesova

Čená

(28) (29)

NOVÉ MĚSTO

(35)

(36)

Vinohradská

ysíkova

Žitná

punched before you enter; each ticket is valid for one hour of travel. The Metro runs daily 5 AM–midnight.

BY BUS AND TRAM Buses and trams run 24 hours, but service is reduced after 11 PM. Every stop has a map of the *nočný provoz* (night routes) and a fairly reliable schedule.

WHERE TO SLEEP

ACCOMMODATION SERVICES Accommodation offices abound in Prague—most will set you up in a private home for $12–$25. The main operators are listed below.

AVE Ltd. Travel Agency. Rooms in hostels or private homes in the suburbs go for $15 and up. *Hlavní nádraží, tel. 02/236–2560 or 02/236–3075; open daily 6 AM–11 PM. In Nádraží Holešovice, tel. 02/807–505; open daily 6 AM–10 PM, off-season, daily 7 AM–8 PM. Ruzyně airport, tel. 02/334–3106; open daily 7 AM–10 PM. Ul. 5. května, tel. 02/426–994; open daily 10–6.*

Čedok. Doubles in private homes go for $35 with breakfast; hotel doubles start at $50. Credit cards are accepted. *Panská 5, tel. 02/225–657 or 02/227–004; open weekdays 9–9, Sat. 9–4, Sun. 9–2. Rytířská 16, tel. 02/263–697; open weekdays 9–6, Sat. 9–2. Pařížská, tel. 02/231–6978; open weekdays 9–6, Sat. 9–2. Ruzyně airport, tel. 02/367–802; open weekdays 8–8, Sat. 8–6, Sun. 8–5.*

Pragotur. One of the city's largest accommodation services, Pragotur arranges rooms in central private homes for $15, rooms in outlying dorms for $10, and hotel doubles for $22 and up. *U Obecního domu 2, off Nám. Republiky, tel. 02/232–5128. Open weekdays 8–7, Sat. 9–6, Sun. 9–3.*

Prague Suites. Affiliated with the American Hospitality Center, Prague Suites specializes in long-term rentals but also offers short-term stays in private homes for $15–$20 per person. Credit cards are accepted. *Melantrichova 8, tel. 02/267–770 or 02/269–384, fax 02/266–179. Metro: Můstek. Open 24 hrs.*

HOTELS Despite the deluge of travelers that comes to Prague every year, you should have no trouble finding a place to rest your weary head. If you find yourself in the boonies, remember that buses can get you into the center quickly from most outlying neighborhoods.

➤ **NEAR HLAVNI NADRAZI** • This area is not rich in historical sights but is well connected to the rest of Prague by Metro and tram. Most of the hotels have recently undergone face-lifts and, consequently, price-lifts. Those listed below charge less than $25 for a double.

Hotel Axa. Recently renovated hotel with direct tram service to Václavské náměstí just outside the door. *Na poříčí 40, tel. 02/232–7234. Metro: Nám. Republiky. Restaurant, bar.*

Hotel Hybernia. Basic, clean rooms five minutes from main train station, across the street from Masarykovo nádraží. *Hybernská 24, tel. 02/220–431. Restaurant, bar.*

Tour Hotel. Small hotel with plain rooms, dingy hallways, and moderate prices. Made popular by its proximity to main train station. Dorm beds ($9) also offered. *Gorkého nám. 21, tel. 02/235–9917.*

➤ **STARE MESTO** • Rooms in the center of this historic area are exorbitant, with the exception of the place below.

Pension Unitas. Originally a convent, then a prison. You can sleep in Václav Havel's former cell if you reserve far enough ahead. Twelve rooms are former cells, the other 39 are in the less oppressive old convent area. Doubles $35, including ample breakfast. *Bartolomějská 9, tel. 02/232–7700. Metro: Národní třída. Reservations advised.*

➢ **SUBURBS** • In the Troja neighborhood north of the center, many pensions line the quiet streets above the main road to the Castle Troja. Take Bus 112 from the Nádraží Holešovice Metro to the Trojská stop and look for PENSION and PRIVAT signs. Among the quiet old villas here is **Bonsai Privat** (Nad Kazankou 21, tel. 02/840–863), a homey bed-and-breakfast, and **Penzion Troja** (Nad Kazankou 26, tel. 02/6641–1081), across the street. Both run about $18 per person.

HOSTELS **Hostel Braník (HI).** A few km from the center. A good, clean choice in the busy summer months. Dorm beds $10, including breakfast. *Vrbova 1233, Braník, tel. 02/462–641. Metro to Smíchovské nádraží, then Bus 198 4 stops. Reception open 24 hrs.*

Hostel Ostrov. Central summer hostel on an island in the Vltava River. Dorm beds only $6, but the toilets are outdoors. *Střelecký ostrov 336, tel. 02/201–243. Tram 6, 9, 17, 18, or 22 to Národní Divadlo, walk to center of Legii bridge, take stairs to island. Café. Reception open 24 hrs.*

Hostel Sokol. Cheapest bed in central Prague, between the Vltava River and Malá Strana. Summer hostel with dorm beds for $6; you'll pay an 18 Kčs fine to be let in after 12:30 AM. *Hellicova 1, tel. 02/534–551, ext. 397. Tram 12 or 22 from Malostranská Metro to Hellicova and follow signs. Lockout 10 AM–3 PM. Closed Oct.–May.*

Ubytovna ČSPLO. Hidden in industrial Holešovice, 10 minutes from the center near the Vltava River. Grungy exterior but clean on the inside. Beds in doubles or triples $10 first night, $8 thereafter. *Ul. Var hulikové, tel. 02/802–912. From Holešovice Metro, walk west along Vrbenského, cross bridge to Přívozní; turn left, walk to end, turn left again; look for sign on right. Kitchen facilities. Reception open 24 hrs.*

STUDENT HOUSING **Charles' University Dorms.** Central office for university dorms. Beds in central dorm rooms, available in July and August, are $10. September–May, rooms 30 minutes from center are $5. *Rezinická 17, tel. 02/290–073. Metro: Můstek. Office up 2 flights, Room 24. Open Mon.–Thurs. 7:15–4, Fri. 7:15–2:30.*

EESTEC Dorms. Mid-July–late August, basic dorm doubles in the suburbs $3 per person. *Kolej Strahov, Spartakiádní ul., tel. 02/350–670. Bus 217 from Dejvická Metro to 6th ul., near apartment blocks.*

Kolej 17 listopadu. In dismal industrial area across river from Holešovice, 15 minutes from center. Dorm beds, available only July and August, are $10. *Ul. Patková 3, tel. 02/848–525. Bus 112 from Holešovice Metro to Pelc/Tyrolská. Kitchen facilities.*

Kolej Jednota. Close to main train station. July and August, beds in two-, three-, and four-person rooms $11 per person, including breakfast. September–June, office in lobby arranges pensions for $11–$14. *Opletalova 38, tel. 02/223–543.*

CAMPGROUNDS Most campgrounds are open April–October, and reservations are recommended for bungalows but not for tent sites. The tourist brochure *Praha Camping* lists campgrounds around the city. There is a series of small campgrounds along Trojská ulice, easily reached by Bus 112.

Džbán. Three km from city on shore of small lake. Peaceful tent sites ($3.50 per tent plus $3.50 per person) and small bungalows ($6.50 per person) on a large field. Well connected to city by tram and bus. *Nad lávkou 3, Vokovice, tel. 02/396–006. Tram 26 from Dejvická Metro. Showers, food store. Closed Oct.–Apr.*

FOOD

If you avoid the restaurants in Prague's center and head out of town a tram stop or two, you'll see lower prices and more Czechs. *Vinárny* (wine cellars) and pivnici serve snacks and sometimes full meals and are popular gathering places from 6 PM to 10 PM. For fresh produce, try the open-air **market** on Havelská in Staré Město. You'll find everything you need in the **Krone**

Supermarket (cnr. of Václavské nám. and Jindřišská; Metro: Můstek), open daily. At all of the following places a full meal comes to $5 or less.

STARE MESTO Head to the Staré Město for classic Czech meals and other ethnic food. Compare menus to avoid paying inflated prices: The price of beer can double within a few blocks.

Kavárna Hogo Fogo. Hip place covered in surrealist art. Attracts locals and foreigners alike. English menu features soups, salads, spaghetti, and fried cheese. *Salvatorská 4. Metro: Staroměstská.*

Pizzeria Kmotra. Orgasmic large pizzas and calzones ($2–$3) served in cozy cellar. Sit near the oven to watch the chef work his magic. *V Jirchářích 12, tel. 02/206–435. Metro: Národní třída. Reservations advised.*

Restaurace U Supa. Just off Staroměstské náměstí. A comfortable restaurant with good, solid Czech food and four kinds of beer on tap. *Celetná 22, tel. 02/223–042. Closed daily 3 PM–4 PM.*

NOVE MESTO Hotel restaurants abound on Václavské náměstí. As you get farther from the city center, it may take more time to find a restaurant, but it will be less touristed and cheaper.

Akropolis. Popular hangout between Žižkov and Vinohrady neighborhoods. Aqua walls, suspended canoe, and aquariums make you feel like you're underwater. Cheap beer, fish, and meat dishes. *Cnr. of Kubelíkova and Vita Nejedlého. Metro: Jiřího z Poděbrad.*

FX Cafe. Small, artsy place above Radost nightclub open 22 hours (8 AM–6 AM) a day. Plenty of American expats will make you feel right at home. Great apple pie $1.50, Greek salads $1.75. *Bělehradská 120, tel. 02/251–210. Metro: I.P. Pavlova.*

Mayur Indian Snack Bar. Sniff your way here for some of the best curries ($2) and tandoori dishes ($3) in Prague. Attached restaurant has longer menu and higher prices. Reserve ahead or come early. *Stepanská ul., off Václavské nám, tel. 02/236–9922. Metro: Muzeum.*

HRADCANY **U Cerného Vola.** Genuine Czech beer hall. Great prices, lively atmosphere, medieval-looking murals, and Velkopopovické beer make this a worthy stop. Light meals $1.50–$3. *Loretanská 1, at Loretanské nám., up from castle.*

CAFES Kavárny serve a variety of coffees, alcoholic drinks, light dishes, and indulgent desserts. The enormous, thoroughly art nouveau **Café Nouveau** (Obecní Dům, at Nám. Republiky) has live jazz in the evening. The smoky, crowded **Kavárna Velryba** (Opatovická 24; Metro: Národní třída) draws literary types; it's hidden on a backstreet near the edge of Staré Město. The **U Zeleného Caje** (Nerudova 19, Hradčany, up from Malostranské nám.; closes at 7) is a very '90s place with a few small dishes and about 50 varieties of tea—mostly herbal, of course.

WORTH SEEING

Prague is crammed with glorious monuments and museums; fortunately, the most famous are within walking distance of the Vltava River's majestic curve between Malá Strana and Staré Město.

PRAZSKY HRAD Surrounded by museums and monuments, Pražský Hrad (Prague Castle) presides serenely over Prague's medieval core like royalty surveying the color guard. Its ensemble of sharp spires and rooflines is the city's defining landmark and the symbolic center of the country. You can buy individual tickets for each of the sights within the castle or purchase an inclusive ticket at any of the ticket offices for $2.50 ($1.25 students). Most of the castle's attractions are open May–September, Tuesday–Sunday 9–5, and October–April, Tuesday–Sunday 9–4. Inquire at Vikářská ulice 37 (behind the cathedral) for info and guided tours.

You can enter the enormous castle complex at **Hradčanské náměstí** (Castle Square), accessible by Nerudova ulice, or by taking the **Radnické schody** (New Castle Steps), which lead up from Thunovska. Crowds gather daily at the imposing main gate to watch the noontime changing of the guard. Inside the gate is the first of three courtyards around which the castle complex is arranged.

On the opposite side of the complex, the **Staré zamecké schody** (Old Castle Steps) lead down to the Malostranská Metro; you can beat the herds of tourists and enter the castle here (turn left after you exit the Metro, walk past Valdštejnská ulice, then turn left again). This route leads you past the **Lobkovický Palác** (Jiřská 3; open Tues.–Sun. 10–6), now a museum of Czech and Moravian history.

The **Hradní galérie** (Castle Gallery) is housed in a former stable in the second courtyard and contains works by Rubens, Titian, and Tintoretto that were once owned by Bohemian kings. In the opposite corner of the courtyard is the **Kaple svatého Kříže** (Chapel of the Holy Cross), which contains religious artifacts from the cathedral treasury and the coat of arms of St. Wenceslas. A passage leads from this courtyard to the **Powder Bridge** and magnificent **Royal Gardens** (admission 5 Kčs, 2 Kčs students).

➢ **CHRAM SV. VITA** • St. Vitus's Cathedral, begun in the 14th century but not finished until the early 20th, dominates the castle complex's third courtyard. Its Gothic and neo-Gothic buttresses and towers dwarf the rest of Prague's 100 spires. Inside, fight the crowds for a look at the brilliant **Chapel of Václav,** built on the site of the tomb of this great king, and check out the **crypt** (admission 20 Kčs, 10 Kčs students), where several other Czech kings are buried. In the main hall, note the spectacular modern stained glass, particularly the window designed in 1931 by Alfons Mucha in the **New Archbishops' Chapel**. You can also climb the cathedral's tower (admission 8 Kčs, 5 Kčs students) for a view of the city.

➢ **KRALOVSKY PALAC** • The seat of Czech political power since the 9th century, the Royal Palace sits high on a ridge that has protected it for more than 1,000 years. Wide Romanesque fortifications were added during the 12th century and are now the setting for the **Garden on the Ramparts** and summer concerts. In the 15th century King Vladislav ordered the construction of the most memorable addition, the immense **Vladislavský sál** (Vladislav Hall). This late-Gothic hall was built with a wide staircase that enabled knights to bring their horses up for jousting sessions. The defenestration room is where imperial governors rebelling against Catholic rule were tossed out the window by Czech nobility in 1618, sparking the Thirty Years' War. *Admission: 30 Kčs, 15 Kčs students.*

Look for Václav Havel around the castle's first courtyard—this is the place you're most likely place to catch a glimpse of the playwright/politician.

➢ **BAZILIKA AND KLASTER SV. JIRI** • Across the courtyard from Královský Palác is the first convent in Bohemia, St. George's Basilica and Convent, constructed in the 10th century. The Romanesque interior dates from the 1140s, when it was rebuilt after a devastating fire. Concerts are often held in the church, and the **National Gallery** next door holds a permanent display of Bohemian art from the Gothic to Baroque eras. *Admission: 10 Kčs, 5 Kčs students.*

After St. George's, head into the **Zlatá ulička** (Golden Lane), where a row of tiny houses was built into the castle walls in 1541; these houses have been home to artists and artisans over the centuries. One of the houses served briefly as Franz Kafka's quarters (it's well marked). At the end of the lane is **Daliborka,** the castle dungeon.

HRADCANY This neighborhood surrounding Pražský Hrad is packed with sights—and tourists. Among the well-preserved buildings outside the Hrad on Hradčanské náměstí are the Baroque **Arcibiskupský palác** (Archbishop's Palace) and the **Sternberk Palace** (admission 40 Kčs, 10 Kčs students; open Tues.–Sun. 10–6), with paintings from the Middle Ages to the 18th century. The **Vojenské muzeum** (Military Museum; admission 20 Kčs, 10Kčs students; open May–Oct., Tues.–Sun. 10–6), in the 16th-century section of the **Schwarzenberg Palota** (Schwarzenberg Palace), shows the development of weapons until 1918.

West of Hradčanské náměstí is the **Loreto Church** (Loretanské nám. 7; admission 30 Kčs, 20 Kčs students; open Tues.–Sun. 9–12:15 and 1–4:30), named for the Italian town to which the Virgin Mary's house in Nazareth was supposedly transported by angels to save it from the infidels. Behind the church is the opulent, Baroque **Church of the Nativity of Our Lord**; upstairs is the dazzling Loreto treasury, with relics from the 17th and 18th centuries.

BELVEDERE SUMMER PALACE A short hike from Hradčany, in the gardens east of Prague castle, is the Belvedere Summer Palace, with its "singing fountain": You can hear sounds like voices when you sit under its metal bowl. Designed by Italian architects during the 1550s, the palace was Prague's first taste of Renaissance architecture and is now used as a gallery space for changing art exhibits. *Mariánskéhradby ul. Admission: 10 Kčs, 5 Kčs students. Open Tues.–Sun. 10–6.*

MALA STRANA Below the Prague Castle lie the Renaissance and Baroque palaces of Malá Strana (the Lesser Quarter), home primarily to museums and government offices. The center of Malá Strana is the square **Malostranské náměstí,** dominated by **Chrám sv. Mikuláše** (Church of St. Nicholas). Built in 1755, the church is one of the best examples of Baroque architecture in Prague.

The magnificent **Wallenstein Palace** contains an art gallery and peaceful gardens with bronze casts of statues (the Swedes carted off the originals at the end of the Thirty Years' War). Frescoes decorate the immense Baroque stage, focal point of the gardens and the setting for summer concerts. *Entrance gate at Letenská 10. Walk south from Malostranská Metro and turn right. Gardens open May–Sept.*

KARLUV MOST Built during the 14th century by Charles IV, Karlův Most (Charles Bridge) was the only bridge in Prague for almost 500 years (there are 17 today). Used in earlier centuries as a marketplace, the bridge is now a lively pedestrian zone filled with tourists, musicians, and vendors.

Ironically, you can thank Adolf Hitler for the State Jewish Museum's excellent collection: He planned to open a museum here documenting the practices of what he had hoped would be an extinct people.

STARE MESTO The Staré Město (Old Town) radiates from Staroměstské náměstí, an enormous, lively square. Every hour a crowd gathers beneath the clock tower of the 14th-century **Staroměstská radnice** (Old Town Hall; admission 20 Kčs, 10 Kčs students; open May–Oct., Tues.–Sun. 9–6; Nov.–Apr., Tues.–Sun. 9–5) to watch its mechanical parade of figures. Behind the hall is the grand **Kostel sv. Mikuláše** (St. Nicholas's Church). Across the square is another church, the somber **Týn Church,** housing the tomb of the astronomer Tycho Brahe. Next door is the **House by a Stone Bell**; its Baroque facade was removed to reveal the original Romanesque construction. The house offers art exhibits by day and concerts by night.

At the other end of Staré Město, close to where Revoluční meets the river, is the **Anežský Klášter** (St. Agnes's Convent). This meticulously restored early Gothic convent was founded in 1233. Aside from the architecture, the convent is worth visiting for its collection of 19th-century Czech paintings and drawings. *Anežská ul., tel. 02/231–4251. Metro: Nám. Republiky. Admission: 40 Kčs, 10 Kčs students. Open Tues.–Sun. 10–6.*

JOSEFOV Northwest of Staroměstské náměstí along Pařížskà ulice is Josefov, the old Jewish ghetto of Prague. The area was the center of the Jewish community from the 10th century to World War II, but almost all of Prague's Jews fled or were murdered during the Holocaust. The **Staronová Synagóga** (Old-New Synagogue; Maislova ul. and Bílkova) was constructed in 1270 in the early Gothic style and called new. In the 16th century, when other synagogues were being built in Prague, it was given the name "Old-New" to distinguish it from newer synagogues. Across the alley are the rich collections of the **Státní Židovský Muzeum** (State Jewish Museum; admission 30 Kčs, 15 Kčs students; open Sun.–Fri. 9–5).

Farther down the street is the **Starý Zidovský Hřbitov** (Old Jewish Cemetery), where more than 12,000 tombs were laid between 1439 and 1787; as available space diminished, new graves were laid in as many as 12 layers. *Admission: 80 Kčs, 30 Kčs students. Open spring–fall, Sun.–Fri. 9:30–1 and 1:30–5:30; winter, Sun.–Fri. 9:30–1 and 1:30–4:30.*

Near the cemetery, the **Umlecko-Prumyslove Muzeum** displays the largest glass collection in the world, as well as porcelain, furniture, coins, and measuring instruments. Inside the museum is an artsy, smoky cafe. *Ul. 17 listopadu 2, tel. 02/232–000. Metro: Staroměstská. Admission: 20 Kčs, 10 Kčs students. Open Tues.–Sun. 10–6.*

NOVE MESTO The Nové Město (New Town) is predominantly commercial, with busy shopping and business areas. Its focal point is **Václavské náměstí** (Wenceslas Square), a long, broad boulevard that has been a center of political action, including the Prague Spring of 1968 and the '89 Velvet Revolution. At the top of Václavské náměstí stands the **Národní Muzeum** (National Museum), a stately neo-Renaissance structure that contains exhibits on history, zoology, and mineralogy. The interior alone is worth a peek for its lavish frescoes and statues. *Metro: Muzeum. Open Tues.–Sun. 10–5.*

Several blocks west is **Karlovo náměstí**, with the Gothic **Novoměstská radnice** (New Town Hall). Mobs tossed several Catholic councillors out the window of the hall in 1419, thus beginning the Hussite Revolution. Also on the east side of the square, at the corner of Ječná ulice, is the Baroque **St. Ignatius Church** and, at the south end, the mysterious **Faust's House.** It's said that Dr. Faust was dragged off to hell through the laboratory ceiling after making his deal with the devil.

Since the Renaissance, Czechs have had a strange way of settling a score—they'd simply throw you out the window. Thus there was the Defenestration of 1419, which led to the Hussite Revolution, not to mention the defenestrations of 1422 and 1430.

VYSEHRAD Clinging on an almost sheer rock face rising from the bank of the Vltava River, **Vyšehrad** is a medieval citadel several km from the Staré Město. This is where the Premyslid tribe founded the first Czech dynasty during the 11th century. The Romanesque **Rotunda of St. Martin** and extensive walls are reminders of Vyšehrad's former prominence. Many important Czech cultural figures are buried here in the **Slavín Cemetery,** including the composers Dvořák and Smetana. *Metro: Vyšehrad.*

To the east lies the modern **Palác Kultury** (Palace of Culture), a sprawling complex of concert halls, restaurants, and a movie theater. Ask at the box office for information about the jazz festivals and ballet and drama performances that often take place here. *Tel. 02/ 422–116. Box office open weekdays 9–1 and 2–7:30; open weekends 1 hr before performance.*

TROJA PALACE AND ZOO A 17th-century frescoed palace surrounded by a formal garden, Troja now contains an exhibit of 18th- and 19th-century Czech paintings. Across the street from the palace is the extensive Troja Zoo. *Troja Palace, U trojského zámku. Bus 112 from Holešovice Metro. Palace admission: 40 Kčs, 20 Kčs students. Open Tues.–Sun. 10–5. Zoo admission: 20 Kčs, 5 Kčs students. Open daily 9–7.*

AFTER DARK

Your best sources for the latest nightlife information are the English-language newspapers. The *Prague Post* covers a broad range of the city's cultural activities; *Prognosis* is a better bet for the current hot spots.

Although you can take always attend live music or theater performances, settling down with a good drink and a sociable crowd at any pivnice or vinárna may be the best way to pass the evening.

BEER HALLS Stained cardboard coasters, drab yellow decor, wood paneling, smoke, and conversation—Prague's beer halls merit a visit as much for the atmosphere as for the fine beer. Many beer halls brew their own beer; for good beer and tables full of merry foreigners, try **U Fleků** (Kremencova II, Staré Město) or **U sv. Tomáše** (Letenská 12, Malá Strana). In general, beer halls close at 10 or 11, so start early.

CLASSICAL MUSIC Chamber music and other **classical concerts** are performed in churches throughout the city. Look for the booklets "Cultural Events" and "This Month in Prague" in tourist offices and bookstores for complete listings. You can buy tickets at the offices of individual theaters, at ticket outlets such as **Bohemia Ticket International** (Na příkopě 16, tel. 02/228–738, Metro: Mustek), or through **Tiketpro**—call 02/311–8780 and use your Visa card to pay for tickets. Or stop by one of these outlets: **Prague Information Service** (Na příkopě 20), **Lucerna** (Štěpánská 61), or **Reduta Jazz Club** (Národní třída 20).

JAZZ AND ROCK MUSIC **AghaRTA Jazz Centrum.** Live acts, including some of Prague's best up-and-coming jazz artists. *Krákovská 5, tel. 02/224–558. Metro: Muzeum or I.P. Pavlova. Cover from $1.50.*

Club America. One of Prague's few gay and lesbian bars. Plays a variety of hard rock and rap. *Petřínská 5. Cover from $1.75.*

Radost. Caters to a hip international crowd with a mix of modern rock and dance tracks. Czech and English poetry readings Sunday at 6. *Bělehradská 120. Metro: I.P. Pavlova.*

Near Prague

KRIVOKLAT HRAD

It's easy to imagine medieval castle life at Křivoklát Castle, which doesn't suffer from the tourist hordes and picture-perfect restoration of some of the other castles near Prague. Křivoklát was founded during the 11th century and rebuilt several times after fires repeatedly wrecked the place. The castle contains one of the least-altered late-Gothic chapels in Bohemia, as well as the 80-foot-long **King's Hall.** On summer weekends you'll be transported to the Renaissance as a duel is performed in the courtyard. To get here, take the train from Smíchovské nádraží to Beroun, and change to a train to Křivoklát (2 hrs). *Tel. 313/98120. English or German tour: $3, $1.50 students. Open May–Sept., Tues.–Sun. 9–5; Oct.–Apr., Tues.–Sun. 9–3.*

HRADEC KRALOVE

A 2½-hour train ride from Prague's Hlavní nádraží or Smíchovské nádraží, Hradec Králové is the historic center of eastern Bohemia. At its core is an old town that dates to the 10th century; the old town's **Velké náměstí** (Big Square) is true to its name—it stretches several blocks. At one end stands the Gothic **Church of the Holy Spirit**; during services, the only time you can enter, you can gaze at the exquisite stained glass above the altar and at the coats of arms on the ceiling. On the opposite side of the square is the **Galerie moderního umění** (Gallery of Modern Art; admission 6 Kčs, 3 Kčs students; open Tues.–Sun. 9–noon and 1–6), which contains an impressive collection of 20th-century Czech art. A few blocks from Velké náměstí is the **Muzeum Východních Cech** (Museum of East Bohemia; Elíščino nábřeží 465; admission 10 Kčs, 5 Kčs students; open Tues.–Sun. 9–noon and 1–5), in a building designed by Jan Kotěra, a leader of Czech modern architecture. The exterior of the Art Nouveau building is worth seeing whether or not you care for the exhibits inside—19th- and 20th-century household artifacts and fashions, and a model of historic Hradec Králové. Many castles and historic villages lie just a few kilometers away, making Hradec Králové a handy base. **Čedok** (Gočarova 63, tel. 049/32–321; open Mon., Wed., and Fri. 8–4, Tues. 8–5, Thurs. 9–6, Sat. 9–noon) has info on the town and its environs and can arrange private rooms and exchange currency. To get here from the station, turn right on Puškinova, walk to the intersection, and turn left on Gočarova.

WHERE TO SLEEP AND EAT Hotel doubles in Hradec Králové start at about $20 and skyrocket from there. The shabby **Hotel Paříž** (Baťkovo nám. 552, tel. 049/32631), near the station, and the less-than-appealing **Hotel Stadión** (Komenského 1214, tel. 049/23911) charge less than $25 for doubles. Take Bus B from the station to get to the latter. In July and August, **dorms** (Na kotli, tel. 049/25644) southeast of town have beds for $3; take Bus 2 and look for the brick building just past the intersection of Brněnská and Sokolská. The large **Camp Stříbrný Rybník** (Lhotecká silnice, east of town, tel. 049/615–591; closed Oct.–Apr.) has quadruple bungalows for $7 and rents bikes. Take Bus 17 from town.

Southern Bohemia

With its rolling green hills, medieval towns and castles, and hearty food and drink, southern Bohemia conjures up a comfortable travel dream. Although it was torn apart in the religious tumult of the Thirty Years' War (1618–48), the area has survived the upheavals of the last three centuries comparatively unscathed. Even four decades of Communist rule touched southern Bohemia with a relatively light hand, leaving behind fewer concrete boxes and smokestacks than in most other areas of Eastern Europe.

Ceské Budějovice

Ceské Budějovice, the major city of southern Bohemia, is home to Budvar beer, better known by its German name, Budweiser; much of the town is devoted to the beer's production. The large, drab **Budvar brewery** is accessible only to groups; you can join one through **Čedok** (Nám. Přemysla Otakara II 21, tel. 038/38428; open weekdays 9–6, Sat. 9–noon). At its heart, though, Ceské Budějovice is pretty much the same town that was built in the 13th century. At the southwest corner of the main square, **náměstí Přemysla Otakara II,** stands the Baroque **city hall,** with its striking dragon rainspouts. A few steps from the central fountain, look for a small five-sided stone with a cross known as the **Bludný Kámeň** (Wandering Stone). Legend has it that anyone who steps over the stone after 9 PM will get lost at night. A short walk west of the square brings you to the 14th-century **Dominican Monastery,** the oldest preserved building in town. Northeast of the square is the 17th-century **Kostel sv. Mikuláše** (St. Nicholas's Church) and the neighboring **Cerná Věž** (Black Tower; nám. Přemysla Otakara II; admission 6 Kčs, 4 Kčs students; open May and June, Tues.–Sun. 10–6; July and Aug., daily 10–7; Sept.–Nov., Tues.–Sun. 9–5). The tower survived the great fire of 1641 that blackened it. You can climb its 252 steps for a view.

Are Bohemians from Bohemia?

To the English-speaking world, the word "bohemian" conjures up ideas of artsty types living in unconventional lifestyle; few people even have a clue that Bohemia is a region covering the greater part of the the the Czech Republic. No one is quite sure how the word got its popular meaning, but there are at least a few theories. One legend has it that the bizarre proto-hippie activities of one Hussite splinter ground, the Adamites—who engaged in free love and nudist rituals—provided great fodder for an anti-Czech campaign by the Vatican, and over time, "bohemian" became synonymous with "wacko" in several languages. Another common explanation is that the French thought Gypsies came from Bohemia, and they applied the name to vagabond-artsy types who populated Paris in the last century.

COMING AND GOING There are excellent **train** connections to Prague (3 hrs) and all southern Bohemian destinations. The **bus** terminal across the street from the train station sends express buses four times a day to Prague (2 hrs). From the train station, take the underground passageway to Žižkova and follow it to the main square (a 15-min walk).

WHERE TO SLEEP AND EAT Central hotels like **Hotel Grand** (Nádražní 27, tel. 038/36591) and **Hotel Zvon** (nám. Přemysla Otakara II 28, tel. 038/55361) have decent, if plain, doubles for $30. **Pension JVN** (Na Mlýnské stoce 7, tel. 038/232–7700) and the **Super Penzion Oppus** (tel. 038/52030) next door have more character for the same money. You can also arrange private rooms through **Čedok** (*see above*), but the cheapest beds are in the two hostels open in July and August: **Domov Mládeže** (tel. 038/45309; doubles $10) is a 10-minute bus ride northeast of town; take Bus 14 to the last stop. The second hostel, **Kolej Vš Zemědělské** (Studentská 13, tel. 038/40251), has lumpy beds for $3.50 in a triple, $4 in a double. You pay only $1.50 with an ISIC card. Take Bus 13 to Branišovská.

To relish the spirit of southern Bohemia, stop at **Masné Krámy** (Krajinská 13 at Hroznová, tel. 038/32652) for a foaming half-liter and a heavy plate of pork. For relief from the usual pork and dumplings, try **Čínská Restaurace** (Hroznova 18, 2 blocks from main square), a Chinese place with a large selection of beef, fish, chicken, and vegetable dishes from about $4.

Ceský Krumlov

None of the surrounding towns and villages will prepare you for the stunning beauty of Ceský Krumlov's majestic, haunting castle or its narrow, twisting streets surrounded by the swirling Vltava River. Although it's now experiencing extensive renovation and a deluge of German tourists, Ceský Krumlov has a magical allure. Visit the **Městské Museum** (City Museum; Horní ul. 152) for a crash course in the town's history; above the museum are the Gothic **St. Vít Church** and the Renaissance **Jesuit School**, excellent examples of Bohemian craftsmanship. Perched on a crag, the proud **Rožmberk Castle** (admission 60 Kčs, 30 Kčs students; open May–Aug., daily 7:45–noon and 12:45–4; Sept., Tues.–Sun. 8:45–noon and 12:45–4; Oct. and Apr., Tues.–Sun. 8:45–noon and 12:45–3) rivals any castle in the country in size and splendor. Follow the winding carriage passage to the ticket office, where tours commence. Connected to the castle by a covered bridge is the 1766 rococo theater, one of the oldest in Europe. In the adjacent garden, next to the Bellarie Pavilion, summer performances are offered on a revolving stage.

Ceský Krumlov is easily reached from Ceské Budějovice by **train** or **bus** in 45 minutes. To reach town from the stations, walk downhill to the right and left over the bridge (10 min). On your way to the old town, you'll pass **Čedok** (Látran 79, tel. 0337/2189 or 0337/3444; open fall–winter, Mon. 9–5, Tues., Wed., and Fri. 9–4, Thurs. 10–6, summer, also Sat. 9–noon) on the corner. The staff speaks English and has scads of info on current events and lodging.

WHERE TO SLEEP AND EAT Hotels here are expensive and full in summer. Thank your lucky stars if you get one of the $25 doubles at the homey **Hotel Krumlov** (Nám. Svornosti 14, tel. 0337/22558). Fortunately, private rooms are plentiful and central. You can make arrangements with **Čedok** or **CTS** (Látran 67, tel. 0337/2821; open in season, daily 9–1 and 1:30–7; off-season, Mon.-Sat. 9–1 and 1:30–7). You can call to see if there's space in the scummy hostel, **Ubytovna Slavoj** (Chvalšinská 233, tel. 0337/3961; beds $2), a 10-minute walk northeast of town.

For excellent fresh food try **Belarie** (Dlouhá 96), a small restaurant overlooking the river. In a former Jesuit college on a hill opposite the castle is **Hotel Růže** (Horní 153, tel. 0337/22–45), which serves the fanciest food around. Both serve meals for less than $10.

Western Bohemia

Western Bohemia is rich and fertile like the south, but unlike its neighbor, it's riddled with tourists and industry. There are well-worn paths to the spa towns Karlovy Vary and Mariánské Lázně (Marienbad); the towns continue to draw people with their healing waters and exquisite crystal and porcelain. The legendary brews of the gritty industrial city Plzeň (Pilsen) have satisfied rich and poor alike, as have *oplatky* (sweet wafers), an irresistible delicacy of the region.

Plzeň

Plzeň (Pilsen) is a gray, industrial town best known for its beer. You can sample the famous brew at the **Plzensky Prazdroj** (Pilsen-Urquell Brewery; Ul. V Prazdroje 7, near train station; admission 30 Kčs). Tours of the brewery leave from the main gate weekdays at 12:30. For weekend tours, call 019/55626. The **Pivovarské muzeum** (Brewery Museum; Veleslavínova 6; admission 30 Kčs, 15 Kčs students; open Tues.–Sun. 10–6), in a 16th-century former pub, has a variety of historical implements as well as an authentic, chilly cellar. If you're getting heady from the beer-related attractions, dry out on the main square, **náměstí Republiky,** where you can gaze at the ornate **city hall,** the enormous **synagogue,** and **Chrám sv. Bartoloměja** (St. Bartholomew's Church), with underground catacombs and the largest tower in the region. Also on the square, the **West Bohemian Ethnographic Museum** (admission 6 Kčs, 3 Kčs students; open Tues.–Sun. 9–5) has surprisingly extensive exhibits on daily life in the region since the 15th century.

Plzeň sits on the main **train** line to Prague. Trams to town stop around the corner from the station; Trams 1 and 2 pass the brewery on their way to town. The **bus station** (Přemyslova) is at the west end of town. To reach the center, walk to the tram stop along Přemyslova and take Tram 1 or 2 toward Bory or walk for 15 minutes.

WHERE TO SLEEP AND EAT Plzeň has few hotels, all expensive and run by less-than-friendly management. The elegant **Slovan** (Smetanovy sady 1, tel. 019/33551; doubles from $35) is the best deal of the three central hotels. Private rooms ($12 per person) can be arranged through **Čedok** (Prešovská 10, tel. 019/221–444; open weekdays 9–noon and 1–5, Sat. 9–noon) or **ČKM** (Dominikánska 3; open Mon.–Thurs. 9–noon and 1–5, Fri. 9–noon and 1–4). **Bílá Hora** (tel. 019/35611) is a campground with four-bed bungalows ($18) and tent sites near a lake in a northern suburb; take Bus 20 or 39 from downtown to its terminus.

Beer may be plentiful in Plzeň, but restaurants are not. Several snack bars offer quick, inexpensive Czech food—try the **Bistro,** with outside seating on the main square. **Pivnice,** around the corner from the brewery museum, is a no-nonsense beer hall serving frothy mugs and traditional food.

Mariánské Lázně

Set in a forested valley, Mariánské Lázně, better known as Marienbad, retains the elegance that bewitched the great German poet Goethe. He came here 13 times to enjoy the mineral waters and his mistress. Start a walk around town at the impressive **colonnade,** a wrought-iron extravaganza dating from 1889, where patients fill their *becher* (special spouted spa cups) with mineral water every morning and afternoon. At one end, a musical fountain plays its heart out every odd hour, beginning at 7 AM and finishing at 9 PM. The newly renovated **Křížový pramen** (Cross Spring) is at the upper end of the colonnade. A walk through the park brings you to **Rudolph and Ferdinand's Springs.** They're named after King Rudolph II and King Ferdinand V, and each spring is housed in its own monumental building. To complete your cure, take one of the marked **spa walks,** following one of several colored trails. Or, if you're a serious spa goer, visit the **Ustřední Lázně** (Masarykova 22, tel. 0165/2170), where you can indulge in a mineral bath for about $12 or a massage for about $15. The small **Russian Orthodox church** on Ruská is worth a short detour; it was built in 1900 and used by the Russian nobility.

VISITOR INFORMATION Čedok can arrange accommodations in private homes and local hotels. *Třebízského 2/101, tel. 0165/2254. Open weekdays 8–noon and 12:30–5, Sat. 8 AM–11 AM.*

COMING AND GOING The train station is a stop on the major train route between Plzeň and Prague. To reach town from the station, catch Bus 5 in front of the station or use your feet; turn right outside the station, then left onto Hlavní třída and continue for a half-hour into the center of town.

WHERE TO SLEEP The central hotels are not cheap, but there are plenty of alternatives. Two hotels, **Kossuth** (Ruská 77, tel. 0165/2861) and the preferable **Europa** (Třebízského 101, tel. 0165/2064) are both former workers' spas and charge less than $25 per double. The best deal in town is CKM's plush **Juniorhotel Krakonoš** (Zádub 53, tel. 0165/2624), on a tree-lined ridge above town. It costs only $8 per person with an ISIC or HI card, $25 per double without; take Bus 12 from downtown. **Domov Mládeže** (Ruská 217/50, tel. 0165/2731) is central and cheap ($2.50 with student ID), but beds are available only in July and August and occasionally on weekends throughout the year.

Karlovy Vary

Set in a winding river valley, the world-renowned spa town Karlovy Vary (Karlsbad in German) exudes cosmopolitan confidence. From Peter the Great to J. S. Bach, from Casanova to Karl Marx, everybody who's been anybody has stopped in Karlovy Vary to sample its waters. Open for business since 1401, the town still receives as many patients as tourists at its 12 hot springs.

The **central town,** straddling the Teplá River just above its juncture with the Ohře River, is the major attraction. Stroll along the riverbanks between the concrete high-rise sanatorium **Thermal** at one end and Grandhotel Pupp at the other to get a feel for the town. On the hill above Thermal is a thermal pool (20 Kčs per hour); inquire at Thermal. Wander down the river from Thermal to sample the bubbling waters at various springs. At the central spring, **Vřídlo,** you can watch the geyser shoot skyward or watch patients fill their becher from taps in the adjacent hall. Those wanting further treatments should ask at one of the spa hotels; massages run $20 and up. Also sharing the waterfront is the 1736 **Kostel sv. Maří Magdaleny** (Church of Mary Magdalene). The **Grandhotel Pupp** (Stará louka), founded in 1701, is a remarkable, white, ornate sprawl, the site of centuries of personal and political intrigue. Behind it, a **funicular** (5 Kčs–7 Kčs; open daily 10–6) heads up the hill, stopping at two lookouts.

Instead of paying for an expensive spa treatment, pick up a plastic becher for 1 Kč at a souvenir shop, and go around sampling the healing waters from various springs.

VISITOR INFORMATION Čedok has two branches where you can exchange money and arrange lodging. *Karla IV (downtown), tel. 017/26110. Moskevská 2, near stations, tel. 017/22226. Both open Tues., Thurs., and Fri. 8–noon and 1–4; Mon. and Wed. 8–noon and 1–6; Sat. 8–noon.*

COMING AND GOING The main **train station** is far from town, across the River Ohře; take Bus 11 downtown. A smaller station, which serves Mariánské Lázně, is closer to the center and near the major **bus station** at Koněvova 2. Buses offer better service than do trains between Karlovy Vary and Prague or Plzeň. The bus station is within easy walking distance of the town and the Tržnice city bus center; as you leave the station, turn left and walk away from the river.

WHERE TO SLEEP Hotels here are plentiful but costly. ČKM's extremely comfortable **Juniorhotel Alice** (Pětiletky 1, tel. 017/24–848; $8–$12 per person) in the woods south of town is the best deal around; take Bus 7 from the city bus center. Nearby is **Autocamping Březova** (Slovenská 9, tel. 017/251–012), a well-equipped campground with tent sites ($3 per tent plus $2.50 per person) and bungalows (doubles and triples $45). Ask **Čedok** about private accommodations ($16–$25 per person), or try one of the pensions along the main pedestrian corridor, which have doubles for about $30: **Penzion Elefant** (Stará Louka 30, tel. 017/23406) and **Penzion U Tří Mouřenínu** (Stará Louka 2, tel. 017/25195).

Moravia

The relatively untouristed green, rolling hills and quiet medieval cities of Moravia are a good place to wind down after a visit to tourist-clogged Prague. Here you can explore the limestone caves of the Moravský Kras, the small towns of the highlands to the west, and the Czech Republic's best wine-growing region south of Brno. For a more urban experience, Brno, with its 19th-century architecture and bustling inner city, has enough sights to occupy a traveler for a couple of days; in fact, Brno is sopping up some of the overflow of expatriates in Prague.

Brno

If you can resist the temptation to compare Brno to Prague, the city has a lot to offer. A great deal of work is going into refurbishing the city center, and the effect is dramatic; Brno buzzes with activity and the comings and goings of Western expatriates who have recently flocked to the town. Brno became the rich industrial heartland of the Austrian empire in the 18th and 19th centuries. In keeping with conservative tastes of the 19th century, classical architecture predominates; some of the most outstanding avant-garde architects of the day, including Adolf Loos, Johann Pieter Oude, and later Ludwig Mies van der Rohe, designed buildings for Brno.

VISITOR INFORMATION Čedok's two branches sell city maps and help find rooms in private homes, hotels, and dorms. *Divandelní ul. 3, tel. 05/25466; open weekdays 9–5, Sat. 9–noon. Nádražni 2a, near station, tel. 05/24904; open June–Sept., weekdays 9–6; Oct.–May, weekdays 9–5, Sat. 9–noon.*

ČKM Student Travel Bureau can arrange lodging in dorms and private homes. Avoid the currency-exchange counter. *Ceska ul. 11, tel. 05/23641. Open weekdays 9–noon and 1–4.*

COMING AND GOING The **train station** (tel. 05/27564), at the southern end of the city center, has frequent service to Prague (4 hrs) and Bratislava (2 hrs). To get to the center of town, walk north along Masarykova ulice. The **bus station** (Oputěná ul.) is south of the town center and a five-minute walk from the train station. To reach the city center, follow the CSD signs for the train station, then head north on Masarykova ulice.

WHERE TO SLEEP AND EAT Most of Brno's hotels are concentrated around the Pěší Zone in the city center but are pricey. Your cheap options include private rooms or summer dorms arranged by Čedok or ČKM. Without a doubt, the hostel **Ubytovna Teplarny** is the best deal, with mongo rooms for $3 per person. Every two rooms share a kitchen, TV room, and spotless bathroom. The hostel is across from a monstrous factory; from the train station take Tram 4 or 10 one stop to Vlhká, continue one block in the direction of the tram, and turn left on Spitalka. Near the Church of St. John, **Hotel Astoria** (Novobramská ul. 3, tel. 05/22541 or 05/27526) packs foreigners into decently clean rooms. Singles are $19, doubles $25, $38 with bath; breakfast is included. Walk 10 minutes northeast from the train station. A few blocks north of Náměstí Svobody is **Hotel Avinon** (Ceská 20, tel. 05/27606), a tidy hotel on top of a loud disco. Come prepared with earplugs or dancing shoes. Singles are $22, doubles $33, breakfast included.

Founded in 1552, **Pivnice Stopkova** (Ceska ul. 5, off Nám. Svobody) serves filling dinners of sausage, kraut, and potatoes for less than $3; walk upstairs for a more upscale meal. **Cernohorská plvnice** (Kapucinske nám. 1) is an aged Czech beer hall with vaulted ceilings, solid wooden tables, and tons of locals and expats-in-the-know guzzling different kinds of *černy* (dark beer) on tap. Get in line at **Aida** (Orlí 4, off Masarykova ul.) for the best ice cream cone around.

WORTH SEEING Masarykova ulice runs north–south through the center of Brno, straight through Náměstí Svobody, the central square. The Gothic **Dóm na Petrove** (Cathedral of Sts. Peter and Paul) sits on **Petrov Hill,** overlooking the city from the southwest corner. Next door is the **Kapucínské Klaster** (Capuchin Monastery; open Tues.–Sat. 9–11:45 and 2–6, Sun. 11–11:45 and 2–4:45), with a 17th-century crypt in which bodies were buried and dried by air channeled through 60 vents; enter through the door marked KAPUCINSKA HROBKA. Down the hill (east) is the **Zelný trh** (Cabbage Market), filled with vendors hawking produce, flowers, and whatever else they can get their hands on.

Just off the Zelný trh is the **Stará radnice** (Old Town Hall; Radnická ul.; admission 2 Kčs, 1 Kč students; open daily 9–5). Built by master builder Antonín Pilgram in 1510, it is the oldest secular building in the city. You can climb the clock tower of the hall for good views of the old town. A few blocks away is the 16th-century **Nová radnice** (New Town Hall; Dominikánske nám.), which was used as a center for the Moravian parliament for many years and even today holds administrative offices. Summer concerts are held in the courtyard.

Originally constructed for Premysl King Ottakar II during the 13th century, **Spilberk hrad** (Spilberk Castle) still broods over Brno. There is no direct path to the castle; just follow your instincts (or detailed map) upward and west, and you'll get there. Recently, the torture devices once used at the prison have been reproduced. One of the prisoners' cells is left open and unlighted, so you can climb in and contemplate life in the slammer. Ask for a pamphlet in English for a self-guided tour of the castle. *Admission: 20 Kčs, 10 Kčs students. Open Oct.–May, Tues.–Sun. 9–5; June–Sept., Tues.–Sun. 9–6.*

CHEAP THRILLS Brno is in the midst of the fertile southern-Moravian wine country. Try to get to one of the small villages—Bzence, Strašnice, Mikulor, and Velka Pavlovice are a few—where people make their own wine and store it in cellars called *sklepy.* The sklepy are recognizable by the doors buried in hillsides. Try knocking on a few doors—if anyone's home, they'll usually invite you in to sample and buy some wine. September and October, the harvest months, are especially festive.

NEAR BRNO

MORAVSKY KRAS One hour north of Brno is the region **Moravský Krás** (Moravian Karst), known for its complex system of limestone caves. Four caves are open to the public, including the **Punkevní caves,** which feature a boat ride on an underground river. The **Macocha gorge,** part of the Punkevní tour, is 455 feet deep; legend says it's named for an evil stepmother who attempted to kill her stepson by throwing him into the abyss. The caves are surrounded by wonderful forests with well-marked trails, including a ⅔-km hike from the Macocha gorge to the Punkevní caves. The other caves are several kilometers apart but are easily covered by bike, car, or the bus tour (about 5 hrs) that leaves from the bus station in Blansko. Frequent buses (1 hr) travel from Brno's bus station to Blansko. *Tour admission: $2. Caves open daily 7:30–3:30. Tours May–Sept., daily at 8 AM and 11 AM.*

Olomouc

One of the most attractive and lively towns in northern Moravia, Olomouc is a good place to visit if you want to fraternize with students outside the capital. Olomouc's Palacký University is recognized as one of Moravia's foremost (along with Brno's). Its active student center is *the* place to mingle with students and can be found through a gate at the corner of Křížkovského and Wurmova, northeast of Náměstí Republiky. Olomouc is known not only for its university but also for its superb annual horticulture exhibition, **Flora Olomouc,** which occurs in May, and for its well-preserved historical monuments and buildings, including a number of churches and other ecclesiastical buildings.

VISITOR INFORMATION Čedok books rooms in hotels, hostels, and private homes, exchanges currency, and sells helpful English brochures (10 Kčs). *Horní nám. 2, tel. 068/28831. Open weekdays 8–noon and 1–5, Sat. 9–noon.*

ČKM sells ISIC cards for $7 and can arrange accommodations in hotels or dorms in the summer. *Denisova 4, west of Nám. Republiky, tel. 068/29009. Open weekdays 9–noon and 1–5, Sat. 9–noon.*

COMING AND GOING The **train station** (Jeremenkova ul., tel. 068/476–2175) is at the eastern end of town, on the routes of Trams 3, 4, and 5. Frequent trains depart southward toward Brno. Just south of the train station is the **bus depot** (Sladkovského ul., tel. 068/33291), where you can catch buses to small villages of the region. Trams 4 and 5 connect the bus station with town.

WHERE TO SLEEP AND EAT You'll get a better deal in Olomouc's dorms, hostel, or private rooms than in the shabby hotels. In July and August the cheapest beds are in the **student dorms** (Třída 17 listopadu 52, tel. 068/23841, ext. 721), a 15-minute walk southeast of the center; $2.50 gets you a bed in a double. Don't worry about reservations—the 24-hour reception staff will tell you there is a "sea of rooms." Take Tram 4 or 5 to Zižkovo náměstí, turn left on Třída 17 listopadu, and look for the grassy field on the left. The office is in the single-story building. At the hostel **Ubytovna Sport** (Plavecký Stadión, Legionářská 11, tel. 068/413–181), right above a swimming pool 10 minutes from the city center, clean singles cost $3.50, doubles $13, and triples $14. Take Tram 4 or 5 to Náměstí Národních hrdinů, then walk north to the far side of swimming building. A 10-minute walk from the city center, **Hotel Gol** (Legionářská 12, tel. 068/28617; doubles $25) is a new place with clean, well-lighted rooms. Take Tram 4 or 5 to Náměstí Národních hrdinů; then walk north past the Legionnaires' building and turn right.

For a city of its size, Olomouc has relatively few restaurants. **Hanácká Restaurace** (Dolní nám.) is the place to go for Moravian specialties in a smoke-free environment. There is a pleasant **café** (cnr. of Wurmova and Křížkovského; closed weekend lunch) in the university student center. In summer, drinks are served on the terrace.

WORTH SEEING The Horní náměstí (Upper Square) is dominated by the large **town hall,** which was built as a merchant's house in 1261. The tower dates from 1607 and is presently under reconstruction; no one can say when it will be done. North of the square off Opletalova ulice is the Gothic **Chrám sv. Mořice** (Cathedral of St. Moritz; ul. 8 května). The Baroque interior was crowned by the Czech Republic's largest organ (2,311 pipes) in 1745. This is the site of the annual International Organ Festival in September. One block north of St. Moritz stands the **Church of the Immaculate Conception**; its frescoes, which date from 1500, were discovered during the 1983 restoration.

Massive, neo-Gothic **Dóm sv. Václava** (St. Wenceslas Cathedral; Václavské nám) is noteworthy for its three naves and the unusual decoration covering the vaulted ceiling. The cathedral was a Romanesque basilica during the 12th century and underwent major neo-Gothic reconstruction in the late-19th century; many Gothic and Baroque ornamentations were added in between. The stairs to the left of the altar lead to the **crypt** (open May–Sept., Mon.–Thurs. and Sat. 9–noon and 1–5, Fri. 1–5, Sun. 11–5), where you can check out richly embroidered bishops' robes and accessories. Next door is the **Premsylid Palace** (admission 16 Kčs, 8 Kčs students; open May–Sept., daily 9–noon and 1–5; Oct.–Apr., weekends 9–noon and 1–5), which dates from the 13th century and is famous for its carved Romanesque windows on the second floor. Tours (English text available) last a half-hour.

Slovakia

On January 1, 1993, Slovakia celebrated an ambivalent New Year. The date marked the formal split of Czechoslovakia into the Czech Republic and Slovakia; for the first time in more than a millenium, Slovakia was an independent nation. To some, the split seemed inevitable. Rural Slovaks had never quite fit in with the more cosmopolitan Czechs, and Slovakia has a look and feel that's very different from Bohemia and Moravia. In Bratislava, so close to the Czech Republic border, the differences are subtle enough to escape notice. Yet as you move eastward through Slovakia, certain things stand out: The mountains are higher and more rugged, the villages more rural and timeless. In the High Tatras Mountains, block-long farm villages preside humbly over the rolling countryside.

Bratislava

Slovakia's capital, Bratislava, holds few apparent charms for the traveler: It is an awkward city that lacks the striking beauty of Prague or the grandeur of Vienna. Bratislava's brooding castle and massive modern bridge mix awkwardly, reflecting a clash of styles and eras. The city has more than its share of crumbling factories and high-rise apartment buildings, and even the winding streets of the Staré Mesto (Old Town) and the handsome castle on the hill look tired and worn. Still, Bratislava is worth at least a day's exploration: If you look beyond the urban ills, you'll find a few compelling sights and an excellent jazz scene.

BASICS Čedok (Stúrova ul. 13, tel. 07/52834; open weekdays 9–6, Sat. 9–noon) changes money and grudgingly dispenses maps and brochures. Check with **Slovakturist** (Panská ul. 13, tel. 07/335–722; open Mon. 9:30–5:30, Tues.–Fri. 9–4) if you're heading for the mountains. The hip, English-speaking staff at **ČKM** (Hviezdoslavovo nám. 16, tel. 07/331–607; open Mon. and Wed. 10–5:30, Tues. 9–4, Thurs. 9–4:30, Fri. 9–5:30) may be the most helpful people you'll find in Slovakia.

➤ **EMBASSY** • **United States.** *Hviezdoslavovo 4, tel. 07/335–932.*

➤ **PHONES AND MAIL** • The **main post office** (Nám. SNP 35; open weekdays 7 AM–8 PM, Sat. 7–2, Sun. 9–noon) is on Bratislava's main square. Come here to make calls from the **phone office** (open weekdays).

COMING AND GOING Trains leaving from the **main train station** (Dimitrovovo nám., tel. 07/48275) serve most major European destinations, including Prague (5½ hrs), Vienna (1 hr), and Budapest (3 hrs). Trams 1 and 13 depart from the lower level and head into town. The long-distance **bus depot** is on Mlynské nivy (tel. 07/212–734 or 07/63212). Allow plenty of time to purchase a ticket before you board. From the depot take Bus 215 or 220 downtown. From Bratislava's **airport,** east of the city, you can get relatively inexpensive service to Prague and other major European cities. To reach downtown from the airport, take the CSA bus or Bus 24.

WHERE TO SLEEP

To find a cheap hotel room in Bratislava you'll have to head to the burbs; however, with the excellent tram and bus service, it should take no more than 20 minutes to reach the historic center of town from your hotel. The best lodging deals in Bratislava are the hostels and private rooms. Visitor-information bureaus (*see above*) arrange accommodations in private rooms and some hostels, so pay a visit.

Two good hotel options in the suburbs charge less than $30 per double. **Hotel Tourist** (Ondavská 5, tel. 07/653–556) has clean, no-frills singles for $20, doubles for $30, both with bath. Reservations are required in summer. Take Tram 22 to Bajskalá, walk south, make the first right (on Prešovska), and the next right (on Ondavská). The small **Flóra** (Senecká Cesta, tel. 07/214–122; singles $17, doubles $22) is near a lake. Take Tram 2 from the train station to the last stop (40 min). Near Flóra, **Zlaté Piesky Campground** (tel. 07/214–145) has four-bed bungalows for $11 year-round. Summer tent sites are $1 per tent and $2 per person.

Slovakia

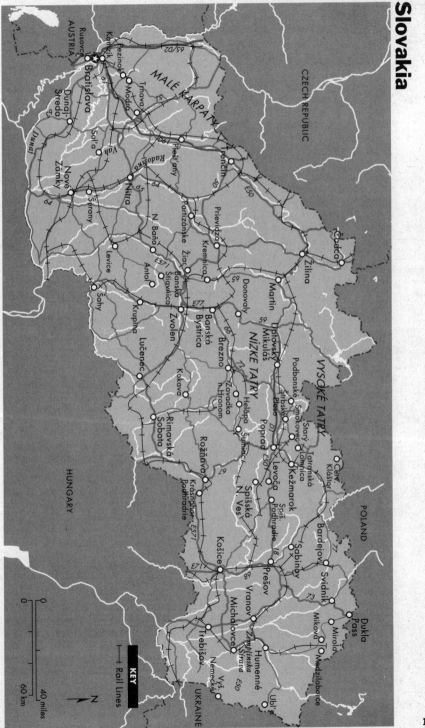

SLOVAKIA

CZECH REPUBLIC

AUSTRIA

Rusovce
Kamzík
Pezinok
Modra
Bratislava
Trnava
Dunaj-Streda
Šaľa
(Dunaj)
Nové Zámky
Šurany
Nitra
Levice
Anol
N. Baňa
Šahy
Krupina
Lučenec
Rimavská Sobota
Kokava
Parížzánske
Partizánske
Prievidza
Kremnica
Žiar
Banská Štiavnica
Zvolen
Banská Bystrica
Brezno
Zvadka
n.Hronom
Hel'pa
Šumiac
Rožňava
Krásnohor
Podhradie
MALÉ KARPATY
Pieš'any
Radošina
Trenčín
E50
Čadca
Žilina
Donovaly
Martin
Liptovský Mikuláš
NIZKÉ TATRY
Podbanské
Štrbské Pleso
Tatranská Lomnica
Starý Smokovec
Poprad
VYSOKÉ TATRY
Červ. Kláštor
Kežmarok
Spišské Podhradie
Levoča
Spiš.
Spišská N. Ves
Košice
E571
E71
POLAND
Bardejov
Sabinov
Svidník
Prešov
Vranov
Michalovce
Trebišov
Vyš. Nemecké
Humenné
Zemplínska Šírava
Medzilaborce
Miková
Mirol'
Dukla Pass
Ubl'a
UKRAINE

HUNGARY

KEY
⊢—⊣ Rail Lines

N

0   40 miles
0   60 km

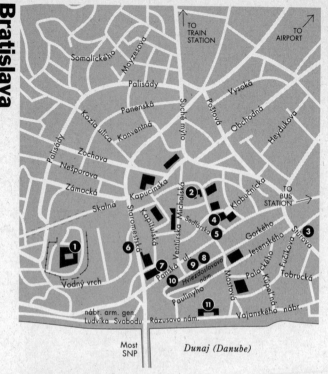

BIS, **5**
Čedok, **3**
ČKM, **10**
Dom sv. Martina, **7**
Hrad, **1**
Mirbach Palace, **2**
Palffy Palace, **9**
Múzeum Hodín, **6**
Slovenská Národná
Galéria, **11**
Slavakoturist, **8**
Stará radnica, **4**

Dunaj (Danube)

HOSTELS AND STUDENT HOUSING **Ineks.** Cement-block building with mushy beds in singles and doubles ($5 per person). Lounge with fridge and TV on each floor. *Nobelova 16. Tram 7 to end of line, then walk toward overpass and make first right (on Nobelova); hostel is set off street in high rise.*

Sputnik Juniorhotel ČKM. Sleep to the pounding beat of the disco downstairs. Clean and friendly. Only $7 with ISIC or HI card; without, singles $17, doubles $26. Check at ČKM for vacancies. *Drieňová ul. 14, tel. 07/238-000. Bus 22 from train station to Bajskalá, then walk 300 meters on Drieňová.*

Ustav Vzdelávania v Stavebníctve. At the foot of Kamzík hill with a view of the city and tranquil forest. Fills up with tour groups. Bed in small single or double $10. *Bardošová ul. 33, tel. 07/375-212. Bus 44 from train station or Bus 211 from bus station to Bardošová and walk ½ km.*

FOOD

Food is cheap, although variety and quality are sometimes lacking. Wine cellars and beer halls have limited menus but stay open later than restaurants. **Veľkí Františkáni** (Františkánske nám. 10) is a large, trendy wine cellar serving local wine drawn straight from barrels. **Pivovarská Reštaurácia** (Križna 26), known to hard-core beer lovers as "Stein," is full of men who look like they never leave their bar stools. Take Tram 2, 4, 6, or 9 to Legionárska.

Kaviareň Amadeus. Well-prepared, reasonably priced ($1.60–$3) Slovak food in cellar restaurant. Elegant upstairs café, with piano music some evenings. *Obchodná 68, off Poštova from Nám. SNP. Open daily 10 AM–11 PM.*

Restaurácia Pod Batou. Small, lively restaurant where you can fill up on cheap, spicy Slovak food. Try pork wrapped in a potato pancake on a bed of veggies ($2.50). *Baštou Bástova ul. 3, tel. 07/331–765. From Michael's Gate, make 1st right; it's in courtyard on left. Open daily 11 AM–midnight.*

Terno. Hidden on the fourth floor of Dom Odievania (House of Clothing) on main square. Pass the sleazy lounge to get to a terrace café with a superb rooftop view and interesting variations on Slovak cuisine. *Nám. SNP 29, tel. 07/334–792. Open Mon. 10–7, Tues.–Fri. 8–7, Sat. 8–1.*

TV Restaurant. Climb Kamzík hill north of the city and take the elevator (5 SK) up the TV tower to this revolving restaurant. Try the "turkey chest filled up with ham in wined sauce" ($3), "sterilized salad," or other wonders of translation. *Kamzík. Electric Bus 213 to last stop, then walk 20 min. Open Tues.–Thurs. 11–8, Fri.–Sat. 11–9, Sun. 11–8.*

WORTH SEEING

The center of Bratislava, bordered by the massive castle on the hill and **Most SNP,** the space-age bridge just below it, is on the northern bank of the Danube. What's left of the capital's **Staré Město** (Old Town) is huddled to the east of the castle.

At the center of Staré Mesto is the historic **Stará radnica** (Old Town Hall; Hlavné nám.; admission 10 SK, 5 SK students; open Tues.–Sun. 10–5), with a sunny courtyard and a **museum** housing a number of gruesome implements. The hall was built in 1430 by the town's first mayor, who was determined to build the most spectacular house of the day with its own fortifications. He succeeded. Ask about the summer concerts and theater performances that take place here.

Slovakia's central repository of art, the **Slovenská Národná Galéria** (Slovak National Gallery; Rázusovo nám.; admission 10 SK, 5 SK students) lies along the banks of the Danube. In the 1970s the sober 18th-century building grew an astonishingly awkward red-metal wing, a crippling aesthetic blow. Pop inside anyway to see the small collection of modern Slovak works. Around the corner is the **Dessewffy Palace,** housing more of the national collection; the second and third floors have the most engaging exhibits. Additional collections are exhibited at two other locations in Staré Mesto: **Mirbach Palace** (Františkánske nám. 11), displaying 18th- and 19th-century art, and the recently renovated **Palffy Palace** (Panská ul. 9), with modern art. *All museums open Tues.–Sun. 10–5.*

One look at Bratislava's **hrad** and you won't wonder why locals refer to this stocky, square building as an upturned table. The castle dominates the hill above the city, leaving a firm imprint on its skyline. Three impressive gates lead into the grounds, which offer good views, pleasant lawns, and summer concerts. The main building houses a museum with some moderately interesting exhibits on the history of the region. The temporary exhibits are generally excellent. *From Staré Mesto walk through underpass by cathedral and up Beblavého ul., or take electric Bus 213, 216, or 217 to rear entrance. Admission: 15 SK, 6 SK students. Open Tues.–Sun. 9–5.*

Separated from the castle by the new highway is the **Dóm sv. Martina** (St. Martin's Cathedral). This 15th-century Gothic church served from 1563 to 1830 as the coronation site for Hungarian monarchs, as the crown on top of the church tower testifies. Roughly between the castle and cathedral, the narrow, rococo **Múzeum Hodín** (Clock Museum; Zidovská ul. 1; admission 8 SK, 4 SK students; open Wed.–Mon. 10–5) earns a mention in many architecture textbooks as one of the best remaining examples of rococo architecture in Central Europe. It was built on such a small lot that it's only 7 feet wide at the base, although it widens as it goes up. Inside are three floors of clocks.

CHEAP THRILLS

In summer a peaceful nook in the center of the city is transformed into the **Citáreň Cervený Rak** (Reading Garden of the Red Crayfish). Take advantage of the red-wire chairs and little tables set up under the trees, and read, stroll, or take in an occasional concert or poetry reading. *Michalská ul. 24, next to Farmaceutické Múzeum. Open May–Oct., Mon.–Sat. 10–6.*

AFTER DARK

Check with the city info office, **BIPS** (Laurinská ul. 1, tel. 07/333–715), for the latest listings of special events, including a schedule of concerts at sites like the **Johann Hummel Museum** (Klobučnicka ul. 2, near Nám. SNP; open Tues.–Sun. 10–5).

MUSIC Bratislava is *the* place for classical-music and opera buffs who are cheap and don't plan ahead. Tickets are only $1–$2 and are easily purchased the day of the performance. Opera productions take place in the **Slovenské Národne Divadlo** (Slovak National Theater; Hviezdoslavovo nám. 1, tel. 07/51146) and usually begin at 7. You can buy advance tickets from the box office behind the theater on Jesanského ulice (open weekdays noon–4) or purchase your ticket 30 minutes before the performance at the theater. The Slovak Philharmonic performs at the **Reduta** (Palackého 2, tel. 07/333–3513, ext. 227). The box office in front of the concert hall is open weekdays 1–5.

Venues featuring other sorts of live music are slowly springing up. Check out the club whose name says it all: the **Rock, Pop, Jazz Klub** (Jakubova nám. 12, tel. 07/59844); it's a happening place that books Slovak and Czech rock bands and an occasional jazz show. University clubs **V-Klub** (Nám. SNP 12, tel. 07/50458), **V-Klub Steps** (Panenská ul. 25, tel. 07/330–865), and the disco-oriented **Klub Junior** (Palackého 7, tel. 07/332–625) are also popular stops.

Banská Bystrica

Locals will tell you that Banská Bystrica is at the geographic center of Europe. Whether or not this is true, Banská Bystrica, encircled by hills and mountains, is certainly at the heart of Slovakia. The town prospered during the Middle Ages as a mining center but is best known as the home of the Slovak National Uprising (alias SNP) against the Nazis in 1944. You can pay homage to the SNP by visiting the engaging **Múzeum SNP** (off Stefana Moyzesa ul.; admission 10 SK, 5 SK students; open Tues.–Sun. 8–6), in a remarkable split building that locals describe as a potato cut in half. The main square, **Námestie SNP**, features a number of remarkable houses, including that of the **Thurzo** family. The genuine Renaissance graffiti on the outside was added during the 16th century, when the family's wealth was at its height. Today the building houses the **municipal museum** (Nám. SNP 31; admission 8 SK; open Sun.–Fri. 9–noon and 1–5). Across the street is the **Benický House,** which houses an art gallery. At the top of the square, **Dóm Panny Márie** (Cathedral of the Virgin Mary), built in 1492, features a carved-wood altar by Master Pavol of Levoča and remaining bits of the city fortifications. You'll find Banská Bystrica's **Čedok** (Trieda SNP, tel. 088/42575; open weekdays 9–6, Sat. 9–noon) on the walk from the stations to the center of town. **Slovaktourist** (open weekdays 9–5, Sat. 8–noon) has an office just off the square at Dolná ulice 5. If you're headed to the Tatras, reserve accommodations through this agency.

COMING AND GOING The train and bus stations are next to each other a little way out of town. Trains serve Bratislava and Prague two or three times daily and Košice once. Buses serve the region more thoroughly and efficiently. To reach downtown take Bus 1, 2, or 4 or follow Ulice 29 augusta to Čedok. Turn left and walk 10 minutes or so, bearing right after the Muzeum SNP.

WHERE TO SLEEP AND EAT If the places below are full, Čedok can find you a room. In a pleasant older building, ČKM's **Hotel Junior** (Národná ul. 12, 1 block off Námestie SNP, tel. 088/23367) is a hotel and a hostel. In the hostel, singles are $7, doubles $9, and triples $12. Across the street is the **Hotel Národný Dom** (Národná ul. 11, tel. 088/23737; singles

$15, doubles $24). Clean rooms include a shower, telephone, and breakfast. In a high rise on the outskirts of town, the **PSP Hotel** (Hámor 15, tel. 088/25624) offers clean, sunny rooms for $12 per single and $18 per double. Take Bus 24 from the stations to Medeny Hamor.

Slovenská Pivnica (Lazovná 18, tel. 088/53717; open daily 10–10) is a popular restaurant in a cellar off the main square. The superb traditional Slovak fare is worth the wait for a table. **Copaline Baquette** (Nám. SNP) is a favorite of expatriates, who chow down on baguette sandwiches (20 SK) or divine *čoko,* a bread-and-chocolate concoction.

The High Tatras

Ask the average Slovak where you should go in her country, and she will invariably say **Vysoké Tatry** (the High Tatras). These mountains cut a jagged path along the Slovak-Polish border and offer excellent hiking and skiing (lift tickets are only $5). All trails are well marked and color-coded but go ahead and pick up a green "Vysoké Tatry" map (45 SK), published by Harmanec.

Although the Tatras range is relatively compact (only 32 km from end to end), its peaks seem just as wild and beautiful as the Alps. The High Tatras comprise 20 peaks (Mt. Gerlach, at 8,758 feet meters, is the tallest) and 35 glacial lakes that, according to legend, can impart the ability to see through doors and walls to anyone who bathes in them. Summer is the rainiest season: Come prepared to get wet, or be miserable. Thunderstorms generally roll in late in the afternoon, so begin hiking early.

You cannot camp inside the Tatran National Park (TANAP), so you have to base yourself at one of the three resorts—Strbské Pleso to the west, Starý Smokovec in the middle, and Tatranská Lomnica to the east—or commute from Poprad. It's possible to stay in mountain *chata* (huts) within the park, but you must make reservations far in advance. Check with the central **Čedok** office in Starý Smokovec (*see below*) or Slovaktourist in Bratislava (*see above*).

POPRAD

The bleak, concrete sprawl of Poprad serves as base for the majestic peaks rising to the northwest of town. The markets offer a greater selection at lower prices than you'll find in the mountains. In a pinch you can stay in Poprad and commute to the hiking trails. Near the train station, the large, comfortable rooms at the **Európa** (Wolkrová ul. 3, tel. 092/32744; singles $5, doubles $9) might induce you to skip the overpriced mountain campgrounds.

Don't worry about purchasing a 10 SK hiking pass. Just head out and you'll run into a ranger who will ask optimistically, "Do you have your pass yet?" You can buy one on the spot without a fine.

Poprad's **train station** (Wokrová ul., tel. 092/32509) is well connected to the rest of the country. The bus station across the street has connections to all surrounding towns and large cities. To get into town, take a bus from Platform 4, or walk 20 minutes away from the tracks and cross the river. Electric trains running to the Tatras resorts leave from the right of the bus station. Your first stop for information should be the extremely helpful **Poprad Information Agency** (Nám. sv. Egida 58, on main square, tel. 092/63636 or 092/457–271; open weekdays 9–noon and 1–5, Sat. 9–noon). The English-speaking staff sells maps and brochures on the Tatras and will arrange private rooms.

TATRANSKA LOMNICA

The easternmost of the three main Tatras resorts, Tatranská Lomnica has the most campgrounds and some of the best skiing. Though this isn't the best spot to begin hikes in the Tatras, the wealth of accommodations makes it a good place to stay. **Čedok** (tel. 0969/967–428; open weekdays 8:30–4), in the Lomnica Hotel, can change money. Trains arrive from Poprad, and local electric trains arrive from Starý Smokovec.

Tatranská Lomnica is littered with hotels, but many are on the pricey side. Ask at Čedok about private rooms. **Hotel Družba** (tel. 0969/967–7613), a modern hotel close to the slopes and trailheads, is an excellent value: Singles are $10 and doubles $20. To get here, walk east from the station; it's just off the main road from Poprad. A small, family-run pension, the **Penzión Bělín** (tel. 0969/967–778) is one of the best deals in the Tatras: Clean, inviting rooms are $6 per person. Definitely the best of the Lomnica campgrounds, **Tatranec** (tel. 0969/967–704) is only a 10-minute walk from town. Tent sites are $1.50 plus $1.50 per person. Doubles in the motel go for $15, four-bed bungalows for $28. From Lomnica, hike 10 minutes downhill on the road to Poprad.

STARY SMOKOVEC

Starý Smokovec, the oldest and most centrally located Tatras resort, is also the most charming. To top it off, it's the starting point for some of the best hikes around. Every 45 minutes from 6:30 AM to 11 PM an electric train runs from Poprad to Starý Smokovec, with stops in Tatranská Lomnica and Strbské Pleso. **Čedok** (Nám. 22, tel. 0969/2702; open weekdays 8–6, Sat. 9–12:30), next to the train station, can exchange money and arrange accommodations.

The electric train that runs between Starý Smokovec and Tatranská Lomnica also serves nearby places to crash. **Juniorhotel ČKM** (Horný Smokovec, tel. 0969/2661), in the forest, is two stops away by electric train. In high season, book in advance or hope for cancellations. Rooms are $8 with an HI card. Nearby is the pleasant **Hotel Sport** (tel. 0969/2361; singles $16, doubles $26); from the train stop, cross the tracks and road and walk five minutes to the hotel. **Tatracamp Pod Lesom** (Dolný Smokovec, tel. 0969/2406) is a large campground with tent sites, bungalows, showers, and cooking facilities. Rates are $1.75 per person and $1.75 per tent. Take a train from Starý Smokovec to Pod Lesom.

STRBSKE PLESO

The westernmost of the Tatras resorts has excellent facilities and offers the best access for an ascent of Rysy Peak, one of the most memorable hikes in the Tatras. The friendly branch of Čedok (Strbské Pleso, tel. 0969/92111; open weekdays 9–4) is next to the train station. Here you can change money, get information, and arrange lodging.

Strbské Pleso has several hotels, though most are out of the budget traveler's range. Head to the village of Tatranská Strba, down the hill and connected to the resort by a special train, for cheaper rooms. The clean **Pensión Novospol** (Zeleničná č. 18, tel. 0969/92512) is a short walk from Tatranská Strba's train station; singles go for $10 and doubles for $15. The large, clean rooms with baths in the new **Hotel Nezábudka** (tel. 0969/92838) are a definite bargain (singles $9, doubles $15); from the station, walk uphill five minutes toward Strbské Pleso.

DENMARK

By Amy McConnell

6

Perched inconspicuously between Scandinavia and the Continent, with 5 million people spread among 500 islands, Denmark is a tiny but vital country with one of the friendliest populations in the world. Although most people know little about Denmark (other than pastries and Vikings), Danes exhibit no resentment or inferiority complex. In fact, Danes are remarkably receptive to visitors—especially Americans. The Danes' affinity for the English-speaking world shows up in everything from their impeccable command of English to their music, fashion, and movie preferences.

Despite American influences, Danes are vehemently protective of their culture and language, as proven by the 1992 Maastricht Treaty referendum, in which Denmark shocked the world and sent the EC into a panic by voting against union with Europe. Although a slight majority of Danes finally approved the EC's amendments, most agree that it was important to force "those Netherlandish authorities" to remember that even the smallest country has a voice.

That everyone must be heard is Denmark's golden rule, and it shows up most strongly in the country's economic policies. One-third of its GNP goes to social services, and generous unemployment benefits—collected by about 12% of the population—ensure that you'll see very few down-and-out Danes. The social-welfare system is also responsible for the country's strict labor regulations. With a 38-hour work week and five weeks of paid vacation per year, the Danes seem to wallow in free time.

Danes joke about two things: their country's high tax rate and its undeniably flat landscape. The latter, however, is no joke: One of Denmark's highest hills stands at a wee 450 feet.

With so much leisure time, Danes can concentrate on the really important things in life—like soccer. In Denmark, people follow soccer scores as if they were a matter of life and death: When Denmark's soccer team won the European Cup in 1992, the streets of Copenhagen were more crowded than they were on the day Denmark was liberated from the Germans in World War II.

Such national pride is typical of the Danes, who celebrate the accomplishments of their fellow countrymen as if they were one happy Nordic family. Danes describe their country as *hyggelit* (pronounced *hoog*-ly), which means something like "small and cozy" and has to do with such simple pleasures as drinking and chatting with friends. Hyggelit is what a visit to Denmark is all about: nothing fancy, nothing overwhelming, and as predictably pleasant as vanilla ice cream.

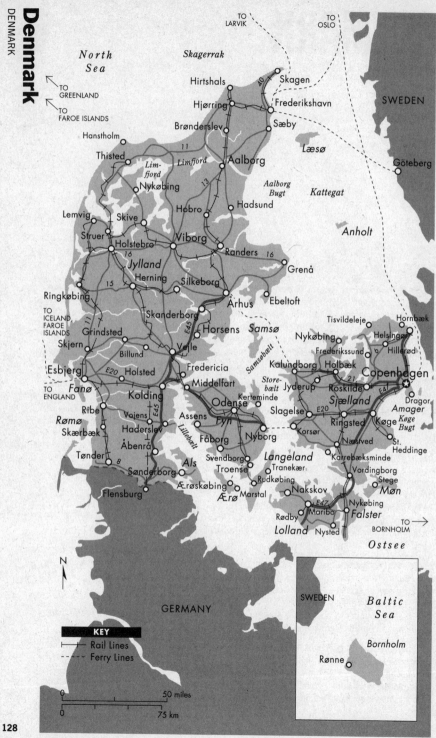

Denmark

North Sea

TO GREENLAND

TO FAROE ISLANDS

Skagerrak

TO LARVIK

TO OSLO

Hirtshals

Skagen

40

SWEDEN

Hjørring

Frederikshavn

Brønderslev

Sæby

Hanstholm

Læsø

Göteberg

Thisted

11

Limfjord

Aalborg

Limfjord

Nykøbing

13

Aalborg Bugt

Kattegat

Hobro

Hadsund

Lemvig

Skive

Anholt

Struer

Holstebro

Viborg

Randers

16

16

Jylland

Herning

Silkeborg

Grenå

15

Ringkøbing

Skanderborg

Århus

Ebeltoft

TO ICELAND FAROE ISLANDS

Grindsted

Samsø

Tisvildeleje

Hornbæk

Skjern

11

Billund

Vejle

Horsens

E45

Nykøbing

Helsingør

Hillerød

Frederikssund

Samsøbælt

Kalundborg

Holbæk

Copenhagen

Esbjerg

E20

Holsted

Fredericia

Storebælt

Jyderup

Roskilde

E4

21

Fanø

Kolding

Middelfart

Slagelse

Sjælland

Dragor

TO ENGLAND

Kertemined

Korsør

E20

Ringsted

Amager

Køge Bugt

Ribe

Vojens

Assens

Odense

Fyn

Nyborg

Køge

Rømø

Haderslev

Lillebælt

Fåborg

Næstved

St. Heddinge

Skærbæk

Åbenrå

Svendborg

Langeland

Karrebæksminde

Tønder

8

Als

Troense

Tranekær

Vordingborg

Stege

Ærøskøbing

Rudkøbing

Møn

Sønderborg

Ærø

Marstal

Nakskov

Flensburg

Nykøbing

E47

Falster

TO BORNHOLM

Rødby

Maribo

Lolland

Nysted

Ostsee

N

GERMANY

KEY

— Rail Lines

--- Ferry Lines

SWEDEN

Baltic Sea

Bornholm

Rønne

0   50 miles

0   75 km

Basics

MONEY US$1=6.70 kroner (abbreviated 6.70kr) and 10kr=$1.50. Changing money in Denmark is always expensive; the minimum exchange fee for traveler's checks is 40kr. Unless you're an American Express cardholder (in which case you can cash traveler's checks for free at Copenhagen's American Express office), banks are the best place to change money. Most are open Monday–Wednesday and Friday 9:30–4, Thursday 9:30–6. Oddly enough, it's cheaper to withdraw money directly from your bank back home via ATMs, which are found in all of Denmark's cities and many larger towns. ATMs typically accept Cirrus-affiliated bank cards, Visa, and MasterCard.

➢ **HOW MUCH IT WILL COST** • Despite high prices and taxes, Denmark is not impossibly expensive as long as you stick to hostels and campgrounds and don't overdo it at cafés and restaurants. Hostels usually cost 60kr–75kr, campgrounds 40kr. All-you-can-eat lunch specials go for 25kr–50kr, an average dinner 50kr–100kr (no tip is necessary). One-way train trips to most Danish cities are 130kr–250kr without a EurailPass. Intracity buses rarely cost more than 10kr. Beer in cafés and bars costs 15kr–20kr. Live music is often free, but some clubs charge up to 100kr covers.

COMING AND GOING DSB (Danish State Railways) honors EurailPass and InterRail. For those without rail passes, the train isn't always the best way to go. Youths (defined by DSB as anyone under 26) and students are eligible for many cheap flights, and buses are sometimes a good deal, too.

➢ **BY TRAIN** • Trains in Denmark are comfortable and *always* on time. The main route to Copenhagen is via Hamburg (6 hrs, 370kr, 305kr youth). You can also get to Copenhagen via Berlin (8 hrs, 300kr, 255kr youth). Nordturist and ScanRail passes, both good for travel within Scandinavia, are valid on DSB. The **Nordturist Pass** (1,930kr, 1,450kr youth), available and valid only in Scandinavia, entitles the holder to 21 days of unlimited train travel. **ScanRail,** also available in Scandinavia but 20% cheaper in your home country, entitles you to four days of travel within 15 days (1,050kr, 2nd class), nine days of travel within three weeks (1,775kr), or 14 days within one month (2,475kr). Buy Nordturist from local DSB ticket offices and ScanRail from your favorite travel agency; try STA in the United States (tel. 212/477–7166 or 510/642–3000) or the United Kingdom (tel. 071/937–9921).

➢ **BY FERRY** • Ferries, which connect most of the Scandinavian islands, are a part of almost all train rides in and around Denmark—and trains drive right on board. Nordturist and ScanRail passes include many free or half-price ferry crossings; EurailPass and InterRail include a few free crossings and some 20%–30% discounts.

The ferry is a popular way to go from Denmark to Malmö (45 min, 85kr), Stockholm (9 hrs, 500kr, 350kr youth, including train fare), Oslo (16 hrs, 405kr–515kr, 295kr students), and London (26 hrs, 785kr including train fare).

➢ **BY BUS** • Inter-European buses aren't the most pleasant way to travel, but they're cheap and not much slower than trains. **Eurolines** (Reventlowsgade 8, Copenhagen, tel. 33–25–95–11) has buses to Hamburg (7 hrs, 200kr, 165kr youth), London (26 hrs, 398kr), and most other cities in Europe. Reserve a seat one week in advance. Rail passes are not valid on buses, and bicycles aren't allowed.

➢ **BY PLANE** • People under 26 and students of any age can find dirt-cheap flights through discount-travel organizations; cheap flights, however, are practically nonexistent for nonstudents over the age of 26. Sample youth fares include London (2 hrs, 595kr), Paris (2 hrs, 870kr), and Rome (2 hrs, 1,185kr), among other major European cities. In Copenhagen call **Royal Scandinavian Air**'s discount-flight department (tel. 32–32–68–88), or, for the best savings, try a bucket shop.

GETTING AROUND You can travel almost everywhere in Denmark by train, although some areas in Jylland, including Billund, are accessible only by bus. Otherwise, there's little reason to take long-distance buses within Denmark. They cost nearly as much as trains and aren't nearly as pleasant.

➤ **BY TRAIN** • Hourly trains link Sjælland with Fyn and Jylland. Rail passes cover the cost of all ferry crossings, but not the 30kr cost of a seat reservation, which is mandatory for all second-class ticket holders. Discounted fares are available on certain "cheap days" (usually Tues., Wed., Thurs. and Sat.) for train rides of more than 100 km. In general, intercity trips rarely cost more than 200kr.

➤ **BY BIKE** • Extensive bike paths and quiet side roads make Denmark an ideal cycling country. Bikes are allowed on most trains for free and on ferries for a small charge; on interregional buses it's a good idea to reserve bike space in advance. You can rent bikes all over Denmark for 35kr–50kr per day or 200kr–250kr per week. Each of Denmark's 14 counties publishes its own cycling map with information on campsites and bike-repair shops. Before hitting the roads with your two-wheeler, pick up the helpful *Denmark By Bicycle* from Copenhagen Tourist Information (*see* Visitor Information in Copenhagen, *below*).

WHERE TO SLEEP *Vandrerhjem* (youth hostels) and campgrounds are the budget traveler's staples in Denmark—cheap and pleasant. Some of the bigger cities also have summer sleep-ins, where everyone crashes in a temporary dorm for about the same price as a hostel. Rooms can be booked in private homes throughout Denmark for about 200kr–275kr for a double. Hotels rarely cost less than 450kr per double; *sømandshjem* (seaman's hotels) are usually the cheapest.

FOOD Restaurants exist more for the sake of tourists than for Danes, most of whom prefer to eat at home. The most affordable restaurants are ethnic—Italian, Greek, Indian, and Chinese. Look for *tilbud* (fixed-price specials) and *aftensmenu* (50kr–75kr dinner specials). For some typical Danish grub, try *smørrebrød* (an open-face Danish sandwich) or *syld* (marinated herring) on *rugbrød* (dark, thinly sliced rye bread). Wash it all down with beer or *schnapps* (strong, clear liquor served ice-cold).

BUSINESS HOURS Banks are generally open Monday–Wednesday 9:30–4 and Thursday 9:30–6. Museums are open Tuesday–Sunday from 10 to 4 or 5. Stores are open Sunday–Thursday from 9 or 10 to 5:30 or 6, Friday from 9 or 10 to 7 or 8, and Saturday from 9 or 10 to noon or 2.

FESTIVALS AND HOLIDAYS Major public holidays in Denmark are New Year's Day, Easter Sunday and Monday, Christmas Eve, Christmas Day, and Boxing Day (Dec. 26). Major annual festivals include the 10-day **Copenhagen Jazz Festival** (early July), the four-day **Roskile Festival** of rock music (late June or early July), the **Århus International Jazz Festival** (mid-July), and the **Central Fyn Festival** of folk and rock (late June).

PHONES Country Code: 45. Cities in Denmark do not have telephone codes, so no matter where you are, just dial the eight-digit phone number. In public phone booths, use 1kr for local calls (insert money *after* the phone is answered), or 5kr–10kr for long-distance calls. Local rates are half-price Monday–Saturday 7:30 PM–8 AM and all day Sunday. For local directory assistance dial 118.

All about Salted Fish, Pickles, and Beets

The best-known Danish dish is smørrebrød—the ubiquitous open-face sandwich. In olden times, fishermen used to pile salted fish and other delicacies on bread because it was cheap. Then, during an energy crisis in the 1770s, the government encouraged everyone to eat cold lunches, which made smørrebrød the meal of choice. Since then it has become an increasingly elaborate dish, piled high with smoked salmon, pickles, eggs, beets, remoulade (relish), and every other conceivable foodstuff—constrained only by the physics of stacking.

To call other parts of Europe, dial 009 + country code + area code + telephone number. Directory assistance for all of Europe is 113. Calls cost 3kr per minute to Scandinavia and 3.30kr–6kr to the rest of Europe. To dial the United States direct or collect, call AT&T (tel. 8001–0010), MCI (tel. 8001–0022), or Sprint (tel. 8001–0877). Direct-dial calls to the United States cost 10kr per minute or 8kr per minute between 11 PM and 8 AM. To place a collect call through a Danish operator, dial 115; for general phone help (bad lines, disconnections), dial 140.

MAIL Post offices, generally open weekdays from 9 or 10 to 5 or 6, Saturday 9–noon, run a speedy mail service. Letters and postcards to the United States, Canada, Australia, and New Zealand cost 5kr, to Great Britain 3.75kr. In Copenhagen you can receive poste restante at **Use It** (*see* Visitor Information in Copenhagen, *below*).

EMERGENCIES Dial 112 for **fire, police,** or **ambulance.** You can get emergency medical treatment from the casualty wards of most hospitals 24 hours a day, free of charge. Denmark's *apoteks* (pharmacies) are open weekdays 9–5:30, Saturday 9–1. A few have extended hours; check the telephone directory for specifics.

LANGUAGE Virtually all Danes speak impeccable English and are more than willing to use it. If you're intent on leaving your English at home, try German, which most Danes also speak. Or go out on a limb and say *tak* (thank you), *tak for det* (a chummier version of thanks), or *unskyld* (excuse me). Other useful words are *øl* (beer), *vandrerhjem* (youth hostel), and *slot* (castle).

WOMEN TRAVELERS That Denmark is ruled by a queen, not a king (and that its best-known monument is not a warrior but a little mermaid), is indicative of how women are treated here. If you do run into problems as a woman traveler, or if you simply crave information about Danish women's issues, there's a national women's organization called **Dansk Kvindesamfund** (Copenhagen K, Niels Hemmingsensgade 10, 3rd floor, tel. 33–15–78–37).

Denmark's well-loved monarch, Queen Magrethe II, has little influence in the social-democratic parliament, but her presence qualifies Denmark as the oldest monarchy in the world, dating from AD 800.

GAY AND LESBIAN TRAVELERS Denmark was the first country to legalize domestic partnerships for gays and lesbians, and the spirit of tolerance lives on. **LBL,** the National Danish Organization for Gays and Lesbians (Knabrodstræde 3, Copenhagen C, tel. 33–11–37–84) owns and runs the Pan Club chain of gay bars and cafés throughout Denmark. LBL also publishes *Pan Bladet* magazine (free in gay bars and cafés), which has articles on gay issues plus listings of gay bars, discos, and organizations throughout Denmark.

DISABLED TRAVELERS Travel in Denmark is relatively easy for people with disabilities. Wheelchairs have access to most restaurants, some hotels and hostels, and all DSB trains. Intercity trains require wheelchair reservations, but local trains don't. Metropolitan trains (S-bahns) have a wheelchair ramp in the front car; ask the conductor for assistance. **Dansk Handicap Forbund** (National Handicap Organization, Hans Knudsens Plads 1A, Copenhagen C, tel. 39–29–35–55) publishes *Access in Denmark: A Travel Guide for the Disabled,* which will help you prepare for your trip.

Copenhagen

With more than a fifth of Denmark's population and more than half of the country's businesses, schools, and museums, Copenhagen (København in Danish) is a booming cosmopolitan center. The city's café culture, nightlife, liberal laws, and generous student discounts make it a haven for the young. Particularly in summer, the city throbs with action as Danes flock outdoors to enjoy their few months of sunshine. In the city center, pedestrian streets and the Nyhavn canal turn into a massive orgy of bicycles, boats, and beer whenever the sun shines. The music scene, too, is surprisingly good, featuring several annual summer festivals as well as regular live bands in cafés and parks.

Originally called København (Merchants' Harbor), Copenhagen retains the feeling of an intimate harbor. Seventeenth-century palaces and churches (and even a 12th-century castle) sidle up to canals filled with rickety boats; timbered houses, ancient street signs, and cobbled sidewalks evoke the city's medieval past. The ever-visible sea, ancient throughway for Viking ships, counterbalances Copenhagen's prim tourist-oriented quarters, while fresh air and soul-stirring vistas make this an eminently livable place.

*FAIL-SAFE WAYS TO
MAKE DANISH FRIENDS*
• *Offer a beer* • *Criticize the
Swedes* • *Compliment the
Danish Soccer League*
• *Offer another beer*

BASICS

VISITOR INFORMATION Be sure to pick up the invaluable info/entertainment guide, *Copenhagen This Week,* from the helpful English-speaking staff at **Copenhagen Tourist Information.** For 13kr they'll book you a private room. *Bernstorffsgade 1, across from train station, tel. 33–11–13–25. Open Apr. 22–May, daily 9–6; June–Sept. 19, daily 9–8. Accommodation service: tel. 33–12–28–80.*

Use It, a youth-oriented service in the Huset building (a cultural/youth center with two discos, a café, and a cinema) provides free accommodations services, a message and ride board, poste restante, free baggage storage for a day (10kr each additional day), free brochures, and free contraceptives. *Rådhusstræde 13, east of Rådhuspladsen, tel. 33–15–65–18. Open mid-June–mid-Sept., daily 9–7; mid-Sept.–mid-June, weekdays 10–4.*

AMERICAN EXPRESS *Amagertorv 18, tel. 33–12–23–01. Open weekdays 9–5, Sat. 9–2.*

BUCKET SHOPS **Kilroy Travel Denmark** issues ISIC and FIYTO/Go 25 Youth Cards and gives advice on budget travel to students and youths. *Skindergade 28, tel. 33–11–00–44. Open mid-May–mid-June, Mon.–Wed. and Sat. 10–5, Thurs. 10–7, Sun. 10–1; shorter hrs off-season.*

CHANGING MONEY Several bureaux de change line the Strøget, the pedestrian-only mall in the city center. Some banks change money outside banking hours for a hiked-up fee (35kr). To withdraw cash, you can use the red "Konatanten" ATMs found on virtually every street corner. Most of them accept Cirrus cards, as well as MasterCard and Visa if you have a PIN number. **Unibank** ATMs are open daily 8 AM–10 PM.

EMBASSIES **Australia.** *Kristianiagade 21, tel. 35–26–22–44. Open weekdays 9–noon.*

Canada. *Kristen Bernikowsgade 1, tel. 33–12–22–99. Open weekdays 8:30–4:45.*

United Kingdom. *Kastelvej 40, tel. 35–26–46–00. Open weekdays 9–5.*

United States. *Dag Hammarskjolds Allé 24, tel. 31–42–31–44. Open weekdays 8:30–5.*

PHONES AND MAIL You can make long-distance calls at the **Telecom Center** in the central train station. Photocopying, telegram, and telefax services are also available. *Tel. 33–14–20–00. Open weekdays 8–6, weekends and holidays 9–9.*

Main post office. *Tietgensgade 37, behind train station, tel. 33–33–89–00. Open weekdays 10–6, Sat. 9–1. Postal code: 1500.*

COMING AND GOING

BY TRAIN All trains stop at the central train station, **Hovedbanegården** (tel. 33–14–17–01), across from the Tivoli Gardens' main entrance and a few blocks southwest of Rådhuspladsen, where the Strøget begins. Domestic trains head to Århus (4 hrs, 200kr), Odense (2½ hrs, 130kr), Fredericia (3 hrs, 166kr), and most other parts of Denmark. International trains go to Stockholm (8 hrs, 495kr), Oslo (11 hrs, 595kr), Hamburg (5 hrs, 370kr), and most major European cities.

BY BUS From Rådhuspladsen, Bus 953 goes to Humlebæk (40 min, 33kr) and Elsinore (1 hr, 33kr), Bus 923 to Roskilde (1 hr, 33.25kr).

BY FERRY The ferry to **Oslo** (16 hrs, 405kr–515kr, 605kr–715kr with a cabin) leaves daily at 5 PM from Kvæsthusbroen 1, near Nyhavn. You can buy tickets on the day of departure at the ferry building (tel. 33–11–22–55, open daily 8:30–5); Bus 28 from the city center will drop you there. Hourly catamarans to **Malmö, Sweden** (45 min, 85kr), leave from the corner of Nyhavn and Havnegade (tel. 33–12–80–88, departures daily 6 AM–1 AM). Ferries to the island of **Bornholm** (7 hrs, 174kr, 311kr with a cabin) leave from Kvæsthusbroen 2 (tel. 33–13–18–66) twice daily in summer and once a day the rest of the year. Ferries to **Swinoujście, Poland** (10 hrs, 280kr, 230kr youth, 50kr–130kr extra for a cabin), leave five times per week from Nordre Toldbod 12A (tel. 33–11–46–45).

BY PLANE Copenhagen's **Kastrup Airport** offers domestic (tel. 32–32–68–48) and international flights (tel. 32–32–68–68). All domestic destinations—most reachable in less than an hour—cost 350kr on standby for those under 26. Youth-discount tickets to Stockholm, Oslo, and Hamburg cost 650kr; to Frankfurt and London, 800kr. To reach the airport, take Bus 9, 13, or 36 (30 min, 13kr) from Rådhuspladsen, or the direct SAS bus (20 min, 28kr) from the central train station.

GETTING AROUND

The S-bahn (metro) serves central destinations, and buses cover the outskirts. The **Copenhagen Card** entitles you to free travel by S-bahn and bus within Copenhagen, plus free admission to almost all museums and sights. A one-day pass costs 120kr, a two-day pass 200kr, a three-day pass 250kr. Buy them at tourist offices, hotels, travel agencies, or the train station.

BY SUBWAY All rail passes (EurailPass, InterRail, ScanRail) entitle you to free travel on metropolitan S-bahn trains, which run every three to five minutes 5:30 AM–2:30 AM. Tickets (9.50kr from machines marked BILLETAUTOMAT at every subway and train station) are valid for one hour and can be used on buses as well as on the subway. *Rabatkorts* (rebate cards), 70kr for 10 tickets or 65kr for a 24-hour pass, are available at subway stations and on the bus; be sure to stamp your card when you board the train or bus. The central station provides subway information (tel. 33–14–17–01) and maps.

BY BUS Bus tickets are interchangeable with S-bahn tickets, so you can use the same tickets for both. Although buses are slower than the S-bahn, their routes are more extensive, and they run all night (after 1 AM, bus tickets cost an additional 9.50kr). Most buses stop at Rådhuspladsen or the train station. Route maps (5kr) are available at all subway stations. For bus information in English call 36–45–45–45.

BY BIKE Bicycles, which you can rent by the day or week on virtually every corner, are an especially practical way to get around: For 11kr you can bring them on subways during the week 6:30 AM–8:30 AM and 3:30 PM–5:30 PM, all day on weekends. **Dan Wheel** (Colbjørnsensgade 3, 2 blocks southwest of railway station, tel. 31–21–22–27) has the cheapest bike rental, at 35kr per day and 165kr per week, with a 200kr deposit.

WHERE TO SLEEP

The cheapest options (hostels, campgrounds, and sleep-ins) are a considerable distance from the center but are well run and easily reached by train, bus, or bike. Most budget hotels line the streets that branch south and west from the train station. Another option is renting a room in a private house (260kr per night), which usually requires a 10- to 15-minute trek from the city center; book through the tourist office for a small fee (13kr per person).

HOTELS

➤ **UNDER 500KR • Hotel Jørgensen.** Close to the Strøget. Dorm beds 89kr–98kr (wimpy breakfast included). Victorian-style doubles 395kr–460kr or 550kr–650kr with bath (huge buffet breakfast included). Ask for a room on the sunny south side. Bring your own sheet if

KEY

i Tourist Information

Rail Lines

N

Tagensv.

Nørre Al.

Mølleg.

Elmeg.

Fælledv.

Blegdamsv.

Ravnborg

Sortedam

Dronning Louises Bro.

Peblinge Dossering

Blegdamsv.

Sortedams

Sortedam

Øster Søg.

Fredensbro.

Fredensg.

Blegdamsv.

Dossering

Sø

Øster Søg.

Øster

Øster Farimagsg.

Dag Hammarskjölds Al.

Stockholmsg.

Rigensg.

Sølvg.

Øster
Anlæg

Botanisk
Have

Kongens
Have

Kronprinsesseg.

Adelg.

Gother

Griffenfeldsg.

Nørrebrog.

Blågårdsg.

Åboulevard

Rosenørns A.

Gyldenløvesg.

Vester Søg.

Nørre Søg.

Jørgens Sø

Sankt

Svineryggen

Vodroffsv.

Gammel Kongev.

Vesterbrog.

Vester Farimagsg.

Kampmannsg.

Nyropsg.

Vesterport

Axeltorv.

Vester Voldg.

H.C. Andersens Blvd.

Hammerichsg.

Vendersg.

Nansensg.

Nørre Farimagsg.

Nørre Voldg.

Ørsteds
Parken

Israels
Pl.

Fiolstr.

Frederiksborg

Gothersg.

Øster Voldg.

Åbenrå

Nørreport
Station

Købmagerg.

Landemærket

Vognmagerg.

Gammelmønt

Pilestræde

Ny Østerg.

Kr. Bernikg.

Øster Voldg.

Nørregade

Larsbjørnsstr.

Sankt Peders Str.

Vester Voldg.

Vesterg.

Frederiksberggg.

Kattesundet

Narreg.

Krystalg.

Nørregade

Vimmelsk.

Gammel
torv

Nytorv

Nyg.

Nyg.

Knabrostræde

Kompagnistr.

Kbmagerg.

Hyskenstr.

Læderstr.

Amagertorv

Højbro

Østerg.

Bremerholm

Kronprinsensg.

Valkendorfsg.

SLOTSHOLMEN

Niels
Hemmingsg.

Gammel Strand

Christiansborg
Slotsplads

Holmen

Vindelbrog.

Rådhusstr.

Farverg.

Kompagnistr.

Tøjhusgade

Frederiksholms Kanal

Christians Brygge

Rådhus
Pl.

Tivoli

Bernstorffsg.

Central
Railway
Station
(Hovedbanegården)

Dantes
Plads

Ny Vesterg.

H.C. Andersen Blvd.

Vester Voldg.

Vester

Niels Brocks G.

Colbjørnsensg.

Tietgensg.

Halmtorvet

Isteds.

Hambrosg.

Amager Blvd

Langebro

Langgade

Vesterbrog.

① ② ③ ④ ⑤ ⑥ ⑧ ⑮ ⑯ ⑰ ⑱ ⑲ ⑳ ㉑ ㉒ ㉓ ㉔ ㉕ ㉖ ㉗ ㉘ ㉙ ㉚

i i i

0   440 yds

0   400 m

Copenhagen

Sights

Amalienborg Plads, **10**

Assistens Kierkegaard, **1**

Carlsberg Brewery, **29**

Christiania, **13**

Christiansborg Slot, **15**

Erotica Museum, **25**

Frihedsmuseet, **9**

The Little Mermaid, **7**

National Museet, **16**

Ny Carlsberg Glyptotek, **24**

Rosenborg Slot, **8**

Rundetårn, **19**

Statens Museet for Kunst, **6**

Strøget, **17**

Tivoli, **23**

Vor Freslers Kirke, **14**

Lodging

Absalon Campground, **26**

Bellahøj Camping, **3**

City Public Hostel, **27**

Copenhagen Hostel, **30**

Copenhagen Sleep-in, **5**

Hotel Jørgensen, **20**

Ibsens Hotel, **22**

KFUK's YMCA Interpoint, **18**

KFUM's Soldaterjhem, **21**

Lyngby Hostel, **4**

Mermaid Hotel, **11**

Saga Hotel, **28**

Sømandshjemmet Bether, **12**

Vandrehjem Bellahøj, **2**

you stay in a dorm, or rent one for 30kr. *Rømersgade 11, tel. 33–13–81–86. Laundry, luggage storage, bike rental (50kr per day). AE, MC, V.*

Mermaid Hotel. Small but clean rooms between Kongens Nytorv and Havengade. Warning: 18 rooms on each floor share two showers, so get up early to avoid lines. Doubles 430kr (including buffet breakfast). *Peder Skramsgade 19, tel. 33–13–48–82. Bus 27 from train station.*

Saga Hotel. It's in a sleazy part of town but less than five minutes from the central train station. Doubles 300kr–520kr, 400kr–800kr with bath. *Colbjørnsensgade 18–20, tel. 31–24–49–44. Luggage storage. AE, MC, V.*

➤ **UNDER 650KR • Ibsens Hotel.** A family-run place with charm. Friendly proprietors, homey feeling, each room unique. Doubles 600kr (breakfast included). Free bike loan for guests. *Vendersgade 23, near Nørreport station, tel. 33–13–19–13. AE, MC, V. Closed Dec. 23–Jan. 2.*

Sømandshjemmet Bethel. A seaman's hotel with the best view in Copenhagen; be sure to ask for a room that overlooks Nyhav Canal. Doubles (all with private bathrooms) 575kr, breakfast included. *Nyhavn 22, tel. 33–13–03–70. Bus 27 from central train station. MC, V.*

HOSTELS **City Public Hostel.** The most convenient hostel in town: a 10-minute trek from the train station and center. Cozy lounge with alpine-lodge look. Beds 95kr. *Absalonsgade 8, tel. 31–31–20–70. Kitchen facilities. Closed Oct.–Apr.*

Copenhagen Hostel. In a big, beautiful park 15 minutes from center of town. Dorm beds 60kr. *Vejlands Allé 200, tel. 32–52–29–08. Bus 46 from central station. Kitchen facilities. Closed Dec. 20–Jan. 2.*

KFUM's Soldaterhjem. A cross between a hotel and a hostel, with 10 private, basic rooms (doubles 325kr), two shared bathrooms, and a public lounge area. Used mostly by students and young Danish Royal Guards. Rooms on south side look onto Rosenborg Castle. *Gothersgade 115, 1 block south of Nørreport S-bahn station, tel. 33–15–40–44.*

Lyngby Hostel. For nature lovers, families, and peace seekers who don't mind the hour trek from Copenhagen. In Dyrehaven Deer Park near the town of Lyngby-Tårbæk. Beds 60kr. *Rådvad 1, tel. 42–80–30–74. S-bahn to Lyngby, then Bus 182 or 183 to Hjortekær and walk 2 km (follow signs). Curfew 11 PM, luggage storage, kitchen facilities.*

Vandrerhjem Bellahøj (HI). Next to a prime picnic area, with grassy hills and a pond. Lots of amenities make up for inconvenient location 15 minutes by bus from center. Beds 60kr, 82kr nonmembers, sheets 30kr. *Herbergvejen 8, tel. 31–28–97–15. Bus 2 Bellahøj (not Bus 2 Brøshøj Plads) from Rådhuspladsen to Hvildevej. Lockout 10–4, laundry, luggage storage. Closed Jan.*

SLEEP-INS AND CAMPGROUNDS **Absalon Campground.** Geared toward the long-term caravan camper, offering a miniature golf course, kitchen, market, showers, and laundry facilities. Choose tent sites (42kr) or dollhouselike cabins (160kr–195kr). Highway and housing projects nearby spoil any semblance of nature. *Korsdalsvej 132, tel. 31–41–06–00. S-bahn B or L to Brønbyøster, then walk through Nygårds Plads, turn right on Nykæ and left on Brønbyøstervej. AE, MC, V.*

Bellahøj Campground. Not a camping experience, just a place to crash. Reception open 24 hours. Sites 40kr. *Hvidkildevej 66, tel. 31–10–11–50. Bus 2 Bellahøj to Hvildevej. Shower, kitchen facilities, café, store.*

Copenhagen Sleep-In. A huge skating rink divided into dorms with no real walls, often noisy at night. Bring your own sleeping bag or cough up 40kr for sheet-and-blanket rental. Dorm beds 85kr, doubles 240kr, singles 120kr (breakfast included with singles and doubles). Next to Fælledparken. *Per Henrik Lings Allé 6, tel. 35–26–50–59. S-bahn A, B, or C to Nordhavn or Østerport station. Lockout noon–4, luggage storage, kitchen facilities. Closed Sept.–June.*

KFUK's YWCA Interpoint. Crash in a big 18th-century ballroom divided into single-sex "cabins," all a stone's throw from Round Tower and University Cathedral. Interpoint pass required (25kr, valid 1 yr); buy it here. Bring a sleeping bag. 60kr per person, breakfast included. *Store Kannikestræde 19, tel. 33–11–30–31. Open July–Aug. 23.*

FOOD

True Danish meals are hard to find in restaurants; the closest you'll get is smørrebrød, which can get pricey. However, Copenhagen has scads of cheap ethnic restaurants and atmospheric cafés, especially in Nørrebro and Vesterbro. If you're on the go, *Pølser* stands sell skinny red hot dogs (19kr) that you won't find anywhere outside Denmark; stands selling falafel and gyros (30kr) are also common. The biggest **outdoor market** (open weekdays 8–5) is at Israels Plads, just west of the Nørreport station.

UNDER 50KR **Govinda.** Hare Krishna–run, cafeteria-style vegetarian restaurant with unbelievably delicious food. All-you-can-eat buffet for 30kr includes soup, rice, a vegetable dish, salad, and chutney. *Nørre Farimagsgade 82, near Nørreport station, tel. 33–33–74–44.*

Kashmir Indian Restaurant. All-you-can-eat Indian lunch buffet costs a mere 39kr. A pretty good deal at night, too, with tandoori specials (60kr–75kr) and curries (50kr–60kr). Even Queen Magrethe II chowed here once. *Nørrebrogade 35, near Dronning Louises bridge, tel. 35–37–54–71.*

Urtens Cafe. Relaxed vegetarian restaurant with fresh seasonal grub; gorge on salads (30kr–45kr), nut burgers (45kr), or quiche (55kr). Also try the organic market next door. *Larsbjørnstræde 18, 2 blocks north of Rådhus Pl., tel. 33–15–03–52. Closed Sun.*

UNDER 75KR **Cafe Krasnapolsky.** Quite possibly the most trendy café and bar in Copenhagen, with an ultradiverse crowd of fashion models, tourists, and regulars. The chef adds a sophisticated touch to such standards as lasagna (50kr) and smørrebrød (38kr). Dancing Thursday nights. *Vestergade 10, 1 block north of Rådhus Pl., tel. 33–32–88–00.*

Crazy Time. Between 11 and 4 you'll pay 60kr for a main course plus all the pasta, salad, beer, and wine you can consume within 60 minutes. Or pay 111kr for 111 minutes of gluttony between 4 and 11. The food's decent, the atmosphere loud and impersonal, but it's great if you want to get stuffed. *Østergade 26, near Kongens Nytorv, tel. 33–14–73–33.*

Færgecafeen. Danish food, Danish crowd, Danish music right on the Christianshavn canal. Sunday's all-you-can-eat brunch (59kr) consists of a huge smørrebrød "kolt bord" spread across the pool table. *Strandgade 50, tel. 31–54–46–24.*

Pasta Basta. A classy Slotsholmen eatery that's loved by all Copenhageners. All-you-can-eat cold-pasta bar costs 69kr, wine 10kr per glass. Warm pastas and other entrées 60kr–130kr. *Valkendorfsgade 22, tel. 33–11–21–31. Closed Sun.*

WORTH SEEING

With Baroque palaces and beer breweries, canal communities, a free-love-and-drug commune, and museums of outer space and erotica, Copenhagen rates high on the hip meter. Most attractions are in or near the center, so walking is the best way to get around. If you don't feel like walking, hop on Bus 6, which takes you past most major sights. A more picturesque option are the canal tours (50 min, 15kr) offered by **Netto Boats** (half the price and just as good as the competing Canal Tours). Between April 25 and September 30, they leave every half-hour between 10 and 5 from Holmens Kirke and Nyhavn.

AMALIENBORG PLADS This octagonal plaza with four palaces—one each for the queen (a flag hangs in front when she's home), her mother, the prince, and the guards—was never intended as a royal residence. It was built in 1754 for the four richest families of Copenhagen, but when a fire destroyed Christiansborg Palace at the end of the 18th century the royalty took over Amalienborg as "temporary housing" and never left. The changing of the guard (daily at noon) is most elaborate in winter.

CARLSBERG BREWERY The Carlsberg tour gives you background on J. C. Jacobsen, who founded the original Carlsberg Brewery in 1847, and on his son Carl, who founded the more modern Ny Carlsberg Brewery in order to meet the public's growing demand for beer. On the tour you'll see both breweries, which merged in 1906, and the world's largest beer-bottle collection (10,473 unique bottles). At the tour's end, you can sample as much Carlsberg as you like. Drink up, 'cause no bottles leave the room. *Ny Carlsbergvej 140, tel. 33–27–13–14. Bus 6 or 18 from Radhusen Pl. Admission free. Tours weekdays 11–2.*

CHRISTIANSBORG SLOT Christiansborg Slot, which stands on the spot where Bishop Absalon built a fortress in 1167 (marking the birth of Copenhagen), originally served as the royal residence but now houses the parliament, the supreme court, and the royal reception rooms, all accessible to the public. **Ruinerne af Absalons Borg** (Prins Jørgen's Gård 1, off Vinderbrogade, tel. 33–92–64–92; admission 12kr, 5kr students; open May–Sept., daily 9:30–3:30; shorter hrs off-season) is a vast cavern of crumbling rocks with detailed explanations of the three stages of the castle's history. Take a guided tour of the **parliament chambers** (Christiansborg Slotsplads, enter from Vestergade and turn left; admission free; daily tours Feb.–Dec. at 11 and 3, Aug. 16–31 at 11, 1, and 3) to see the country's first three constitutions and the rooms where the Folketing (People's Parliament) meets. Tours fill up fast and are limited to 35 people; stop by after 9 AM to reserve your space.

You must don special non-scuff slippers before touring 16 of the 600 or so **De Kongelige Repræsentationslokaler** (Royal Reception Rooms), where you'll see the queen's throne and rows of royal portraits. *Christiansborg Slotsplads. Enter from Ny Vestergade and turn right. Admission: 27kr, 12kr students with ISIC cards. Tours June–Aug., Tues.–Sun. at 11, 1, and 3; less frequent off-season.*

THE LITTLE MERMAID You must be in a poetic frame of mind to appreciate the little lump of bronze that sits at the entrance to Copenhagen's harbor. Dedicated to the city in 1913 by Carl Jacobsen (of Carlsberg Breweries fame), *Den Lille Havfrue* (The Little Mermaid) is the legendary subject of Hans Christian Andersen's tale about the mermaid who tries to be human (because she's in love with a prince, of course). Sadly, she only partially succeeded: Now she's stuck with legs and feet but no voice, forever doomed to be the object of fawning tourists and Kodak moments.

ROSENBORG SLOT This Dutch Renaissance castle is a treasure chest of royal Danish history. Built in 1596 for King Christian IV, it was abandoned 100 years later when Frederick III and his big ego came along, demanding a larger and grander residence. Now a museum, Rosenborg displays the crown jewels and a few castle rooms; the best is the king's "winter room," thought to be the oldest art gallery in Europe. *Øster Volgade, tel. 33–15–32–86. Admission to palace and treasury, 35kr; to treasury only, 25kr. Open daily 10–3 (until 4 in summer).*

RUNDETARN The views of Copenhagen from the Round Tower are reason enough to mount this circa-1642 astronomical observatory (the oldest functioning observatory in Europe). Look for the king's monogram and motto, REGNA FIRMAT PIETAS (PITY STRENGTHENS EMPIRE), in the famous wrought-iron balustrade. *Købmagergade 52A, tel. 33–93–66–60. Admission: 12kr. Open June–Aug., Mon.–Sat. 10–8, Sun. noon–8; shorter hrs off-season.*

TIVOLI Inspired by the 18th-century pleasure gardens of London, Paris, and Vienna, Tivoli Gardens is a miniature city of concert pavilions, gardens, rides, and restaurants, and the setting for frequent, free, outdoor music and drama performances. The rides (8kr–16kr each, 70kr for 5–10, 250kr for all 25) range from roller coasters to a flying-trunk tour of Hans Christian Andersen's fairy tales. At night the gardens are lighted by colored bulbs and sometimes fireworks. *Vesterbrogade 3, across from central train station, tel. 33–15–10–01. Open daily 10 AM–midnight.*

NEIGHBORHOODS

CHRISTIANIA Ten minutes from the center of what brochures call "Wonderful, Wonderful, Copenhagen" lies a commune of people who don't find it so wonderful. In fact, they think it sucks, which is why they've created a self-governed community in which they can live as they please. It all started in 1972, when a group of squatters discovered some recently abandoned military barracks near the island of Amager; they tore down the walls and moved in. They built new houses, created their own shops, organized their own government, and made their own rules, one of which was to legalize drugs. For many years Copenhagen refused to supply the community with electricity or water, but Christianians survived and thrived, using wood stoves, importing water, and creating workshops to produce everything they needed. Today Christiania is a highly organized, fully recognized commune with grocery stores, cafés, a theater, day-care centers, and a local radio station. The city no longer opposes Christiania's existence, especially since the commune instituted its own cleanup of hard drugs in 1979.

Residents say they can live in Christiania without ever going into Copenhagen—except once a month, to pick up their social-welfare checks.

Residents are surprisingly tolerant of people visiting Christiania. Guided walking tours (15kr, daily at 3 PM) regularly parade through the car-free community, but go on your own if you want to meet commune dwellers. Tours leave from the playground to the right of the main entrance on **Prinsenssgade**; or pick up a free map at the grocery store for a self-guided tour.

CHRISTIANSHAVN Occupying the small island between Copenhagen and Amager, Christianshavn has a look and mood all its own. The area was nothing but water until 1618, when King Christian IV commissioned Dutch engineers to build a commercial harbor here. The result is a rampart-enclosed, Dutch-style canal community (nicknamed "Little Amsterdam") with some of the city's best-preserved 17th-century houses and courtyards. Walk along **Strandgade,** the waterfront promenade, to see Christianshavn's oldest, most beautiful homes. **Vor Frelsers Kirke** (Our Savior's Church, Sankt Annæ Gade 25, tel. 31–57–27–98; open daily 9:30–4:30) has an exterior spiral staircase you can climb for 10kr, a live carillon demonstration (listen for the bells Saturday at 3 and Sunday at noon), and the largest organ in Copenhagen. In July the church puts on free organ concerts; call ahead for times.

NYHAVN Now a picturesque canal community, Nyhavn (which means "New Harbor") was once the sailors' red-light district, full of taverns, tattoo shops, and Swedes who came over to get their fill of cheap, legal liquor (at the time booze was outlawed in Sweden). Nyhavn was also the favorite residence of Hans Christian Andersen, who lived near the royal theater. Particularly on a sunny day, a walk among Nyhavn's canal-side houses is an unbeatable experience; cafés roll out their portable bars, and the beer flows.

OLD COPENHAGEN Sometimes called the Latin Quarter, the oldest and liveliest part of Copenhagen lies within the streets Nørre Volgade, Vester Vølgade, Gothersgade, and Ostergade. The district's hard-to-miss **Rådhuspladsen** (Town Hall Square) was built in 1900 in a neo-Renaissance style; it sports a bust of Bishop Absalon, the father of Copenhagen, over the main door. A few blocks up the Strøget are Gammeltorv and Nytorv, two twin squares that dominate the heart of medieval Copenhagen. If you want to stroll Old Copenhagen, head down Købmagergade, a much nicer pedestrian street than the crowded Avenues streets nearby.

MUSEUMS

EROTICA MUSEUM This museum's sex-oriented paintings, wax figures, postcards, and photos put Madonna's book *Sex* to shame, reminding the world that Denmark was the first country to "liberate" pornography, in 1968. The first floor, with soporific images of erotica in antiquity, is only a warm-up for the increasingly graphic exhibits that follow, including wax images of venereal skin diseases and S&M videos. *Vesterbrogade 31, tel. 31–31–40–90. Admission: 45kr. Open May–Sept., daily 10–9; Oct.–Apr., daily noon–6.*

FRIHEDSMUSEET Built in the 1950s by the Danish Resistance Movement, this museum documents Denmark's unsuccessful attempt to stay neutral during World War II, as well as the Danes' spontaneous effort to hide Jews until they could be transported to Sweden and safety. The exhibits are in English, as are some tours (June–Aug., Tues., Thurs., Fri., Sun. at 2; May, Thurs. and Sun. at 2). *Churchillparken, tel. 33–13–77–14. Admission free. Open May–mid-Sept., Tues.–Sat. 10–4, Sun. 10–5; shorter hrs off-season.*

NATIONAL MUSEET This two-year-old museum is less than thrilling, although it does have a huge, somewhat interesting collection of prehistoric artifacts—from Bronze Age tools and weapons to Viking longboats and a few Renaissance antiquities. The saving grace is a permanent "please touch" exhibit for the blind, about the peoples of Greenland, with Eskimo recordings and lots of fur to feel. *Ny Vestergade 10, between Christiansborg Slot and Tivoli Gardens, tel. 33–13–44–11. Admission: 30kr, 20kr students. Open Tues.–Sun. 10–5.*

NY CARLSBERG GLYPTOTEK In addition to its classical treasures, the museum (founded by Carl Jacobsen of Carlsberg Brewery) has a sizable collection of impressionist art, including many works by Degas and Gauguin. *Dante's Plads 7, east of Tivoli Gardens, tel. 33–91–10–65. Admission: 15kr, students free. Open May–Aug., daily 10–4; Sept.–Apr., weekdays noon–3, Sun. 10–4.*

STATENS MUSEET FOR KUNST Denmark's state museum has something for everyone: old art, modern art, paintings, sculptures, and sketches by the famous and obscure. Despite its impressive holdings—you'll find work by Matisse, Picasso, Rembrandt, and Rubens, to name a few—the collection feels jumbled and somewhat sterile. The temporary exhibitions (on Max Ernst and Fernard Léger, for example) are often worthwhile. *Sølvgade 48–50, tel. 33–91–21–26. Admission: 20kr. Open Tues.–Sun. 10–4:30.*

AFTER DARK

Most of the city's bars, cafés, and clubs are just west of the Strøget and in Nørrebro. If you're tight on funds, there's often free music in parks and cafés; check *Gaffa* or *The Neon Guide,* free in most cafés and at Huset's information desk (*see* Visitor Information, *above*).

Copenhagen's annual, 10-day **jazz festival** begins on the first Friday in July and features some of the best jazz musicians in the world. Sessions take place on street corners, in cafés, along the water, and in parks—and many are free. For information and tickets, call the festival office (Kjeld Langesgade 4A, tel. 33–93–20–13).

CAFES AND BARS When Copenhagen's first Parisian-style café opened in 1976, it was such a success that countless others have followed. **Cafe Sommersko** (Kronprinsensgade 6, off Købmagerg., tel. 33–14–81–89) is still one of the most popular, with huge open windows, a Mediterranean atmosphere, and great homemade food (sandwiches 27kr). There's a more alternative crowd at **Cafe Rust** in Nørrebro (Guldbergsgade 8, tel. 35–37–72–83), which has free live music every night. The hip, tiny, student-filled **Cafe Funke** (Skt. Hans Torv, tel. 31–36–17–41) also has free live music; get there early for a seat. **Cafe Floss** (Larsbjørnstræde 10, tel. 33–11–67–45) two blocks north of Rådhus Pladsen, boasts three kinds of grappa, an extra-late happy hour (until 10:30), and a serious drinking crowd of postpunks, models, and musicians. You'll find 65 varieties of whiskey (25kr–125kr) plus absinthe (which has been outlawed since the early 1900s in most countries) at **Krut's Karport** (Øster Farimagsgade 12, near Botanical Gardens, tel. 35–26–86–38), where there's free live jazz on Sunday at 3 PM.

The gay and lesbian **Pan Cafe** (Knabrostræde 3, tel. 33–11–37–84); off the Strøget, has a coffee and cocktail bar and a disco (admission free to 50kr); Thursday and Friday are women's nights. The nearby ultrapopular **Sebastian Cafe** (Hykenstræde 10, tel. 33–32–22–79) has a bulletin board with gay news and events and changing art exhibits upstairs. The **Cosy Bar** (Studiestræde 24, tel. 33–12–74–27) is *the* after-hours place for gays; it opens at 11 PM.

CLUBS AND DISCOS Copenhagen has a regular schedule of free outdoor concerts during summer—the sort of events that happily blend good music, a clear sky, and lots of beer. At **Fælledparken** in Østerbro, jazz and rock bands play every Thursday, Friday, and Saturday from 8 PM to 10 PM. Afterward, the 100-year-old **Pavilionen Cafe** in the middle of the park becomes an after-hours disco (at least until 5 AM). Smaller, more hyggelit concerts happen every Saturday from 2 PM to 7 PM at **5'Øren,** a seaside park in Amager, 20 minutes from Copenhagen on Bus 5, 9, 12, 13, or 37.

At the Pavilionen Cafe, ask for a free blanket at the bar and watch the sunrise from Fælledparken.

Banan Republikken A/S. Caribbean-style café/bar/restaurant with world music, reggae, salsa, and an ethnic crowd. Daily menu features superbly prepared Caribbean dishes (70kr–90kr). *Nørrebrogade 13, near Dronning Louises bridge, tel. 35–36–08–30. Cover 40kr.*

Copenhagen Jazz House. A huge place that hosts some of the biggest names in jazz. It's jazz till midnight, then disco (30kr cover) till dawn. *Niels Hemmingsgade 10, 2 blocks south of Rundetårn, tel. 33–15–26–00. Cover 50kr–100kr. Closed Sun. and Mon.*

Loppen. Christiania's concert house, with rock, jazz, pop, and fusion. Free concerts every Wednesday and Thursday at 9 PM. Take Bus 8 from the city center. *Loppehygningen, Christiania, tel. 31–57–84–22.*

Musikkafe'en. Mainstream rock, soul, funk, reggae, and jazz on the third floor of Huset, with a disco Friday and Saturday from 2 AM to 5 AM. *Rådhusstræde 13, tel. 33–15–20–02. Cover 30kr–70kr. Closed June.*

Sofie's Kælder. Danish bebop in a cellar by the Christianshavn canal. *Sofiegade 1, tel. 31–54–29–45. No cover.*

10'eren. A small club with local bands. Jam sessions Friday and Saturday after midnight. *Nørre Volgade 2, near Nørreport Station, tel. 33–32–10–87. No cover. Closed Sun.*

Near Copenhagen

DRAGØR Just one hour from Copenhagen is the colorful fishing village of **Dragør,** which dates from the Middle Ages. With its half-timbered yellow cottages and cobbled streets, it looks like a set for *Babette's Feast,* with a scenic harbor to boot. The tiny **Dragør Museum** (Havnepladsen, tel. 32–53–41–06; admission 10kr, students free) has an impressive collection of model ships. Dragør's other draw is the ferry to Sweden (23kr one-way, 23kr extra for bikes), which leaves hourly from the ferry station, **Dragør Limhamn Overfarten** (tel. 32–53–36–70). The quickest way to Dragør from Copenhagen is Bus 73, which leaves every 20 minutes from Kongens Nytorv and the Nørreport S-bahn station.

HELSINGØR It's hard to say who holds more sway in this Riviera-like port town—Hamlet or Holgar the Dane. Hamlet is said to have killed his mother in **Kronborg Slot** (supposedly the model for Elsinore Castle in Shakespeare's *Hamlet*), while Holgar the Dane, whose massive stone likeness looms in the castle's dungeon, will allegedly rise from the dead if ever Denmark needs him in battle. Lesser known but still worthwhile is **Sankt Maria's Kirke** (Sankt Annagade 38, tel. 49–21–17–74), said to be the best-preserved monastery in northern Europe. Its comical frescoes are sure to win over even the most ardent atheist. Helsingør's **tourist information office** (Havnepladsen 3, tel. 49–21–13–33), across from the train station, is open weekdays 9:30–7 and, in summer only, Saturday 10–6.

Helsingør is so close to Sweden you can practically touch it. Two ferry lines make the 25-minute crossing to Helsinborg (Sweden) every 20 minutes. **Sundbusserne** (tel. 49–21–35–45; 17kr one-way, 8.50kr for bikes) is the cheapest, but **Scanlines** (tel. 29–26–26–40; 20kr one-way, 20kr for bikes) operates all night long.

➤ **WHERE TO SLEEP AND EAT** • Once a count's summer home, **HI Helsingør Vandr-erjhem** (Nørdre Strandvej 24, tel. 49–21–16–40) is now a first-rate hostel with family-size rooms (128kr), dorm rooms (beds 64kr–84kr), and a backyard beach. From Copenhagen take the train to Marienlyst station. The **Kammer Kaffeen** (Havnepladsen 1, tel. 42–29–00–52), next to the tourist office, has a lively atmosphere and good, cheap food.

HUMLEBÆK The **Louisiana Museum of Modern Art** (tel. 42–19–07–19; admission 45kr, 35kr students), in Humlebæk, has an awesome, unconventional display of modern sculptures (including works by Henry Moore, Max Ernst, Alberto Giacometti, and others) and paintings in an outdoor setting that's a masterpiece in itself. Transparent glass walls give drop-dead views of the sea and surrounding lush countryside, blurring the distinction between nature and art. Humlebæk is about 35 km from Copenhagen; take the train from Helsingør or Copenhagen (less than 15kr) or Bus 733 from Hillerød (19kr).

ROSKILDE Once upon a time, Roskilde was the medieval capital of Denmark, evidenced today by the ancient churches and monasteries you see everywhere. Most impressive is the huge **Roskilde Domkirke.** The architecture, which spans five centuries, is as varied as the royal tombs housed inside. The most ornate belongs to Denmark's favorite king, Christian IV; it's surrounded by life-size murals and a Thorvaldsen sculpture. *Domkirkepladsen. Admission: 10kr. Open June–Aug., Mon.–Sat. 9–4:45, Sun. 12:30–4:45; shorter hrs off-season.*

Every year on the last weekend in June, Roskilde hosts an immensely popular rock festival; for 550kr you're treated to dense crowds and four days of nonstop rock.

Not as old but perhaps more intriguing is the **Vikingeskib-shallen** (Viking Ship Museum), which displays five Viking wrecks unearthed near Roskilde and expertly pieced together. Don't miss the 15-minute film (in English) that shows how the painstaking excavation was completed. *Strandengen, tel. 42–35–65–55. Admission: 28kr, 18kr students. Open June–Aug., daily 11–5; shorter hrs off-season.*

➤ **COMING AND GOING** • Perched on the western tip of Sjælland, Roskilde is a popular stopover for those headed to Fyn and Jylland. InterCity trains, which require 30kr reservations, board the ferry directly; otherwise, you can take a regular train to Korsør and board the ferry yourself. Roskilde's **tourist information office** (Gullandstræde 15, tel. 42–35–27–00; open weekdays 9–7, Sat. 9–5, Sun. 10–2; shorter hrs off-season) rents bicycles for 50kr per day.

➤ **WHERE TO SLEEP AND EAT** • At the **Roskilde Campground** (Baunehøjvej 7, tel. 46–75–79–96), 4 km from town on Bus 602, you can camp for 40kr or sleep in a cabin or plush apartment for about 150kr. Sandwiched between a beach and green fields, it feels like a vacation resort. You can also crash at the **HI hostel** (Hørhusene 61, tel. 42–35–21–84), 3 km from town on Bus 601 or 604. If you're here for the Roskilde music festival, try the special campground set up for ticket holders.

Fyn

The island of Fyn is said to be the most Danish part of Denmark: small, farm-filled, friendly, and tranquil. The main city, Odense, is a far cry from a metropolis, even if it does tout itself as the birthplace of Hans Christian Andersen. Still, Fyn's tiny, castle-dotted islands are magical, and the Danish sun seems to shine more often in Fyn than anywhere else, making it the most popular part of Denmark for biking and camping.

Odense

The birthplace of Hans Christian Andersen and the biggest city on Fyn, Odense is an odd cross between a provincial village and a cultural hot spot. Tucked among its redbrick streets (many of which are lined with kitschy plastic flags of Andersen) are several surprisingly progressive art museums, theaters, and cafés. Still, if you don't have the stomach for quaintness and quietness, you might very well find this town as unenticing as Andersen did (he left as soon as he was able); one or two days here is plenty.

BASICS The Odense **tourist information office** is in the Rådhuset (city hall). From the train station, walk south on Jernbanegade and turn left on Vestergade. In addition to booking accommodations (25kr per person), the staff coordinates a "Meet the Danes" program (also offered in Aalborg, Arhus, and Roskilde): With 24 hours' advance notice, they will set you up with some friendly Danish folks for free. *Tel. 66–12–75–20. Open mid-June–Aug., Mon.–Sat. 9–7, Sun. 11–7; Sept.–mid-June, weekdays 9–5, Sat. 10–1.*

COMING AND GOING Odense's main train station, **Bånegarden** (Østre Stationsvej 27, tel. 66–12–10–13), is on the northern edge of town, a 10-minute walk from the city center. InterCity trains, which require 30kr seat reservations, offer the fastest service from Copenhagen (2½ hrs); the train boards the ferry directly.

GETTING AROUND Although most of the town is easily seen on foot, several sights and most budget accommodations are best reached by bus or bike. The main bus-departure points are the train station and Klingenberg (the city-hall square). Bus rides, which you pay for when you get off, generally cost 5kr–10kr; **tourist passes** (25kr) are valid for 24 hours of bus travel within Odense and can be purchased at the train station, the tourist office, and some kiosks. Another option is the 100kr **Adventure Pass** (available at the train station, tourist office, and hostel), which gives you two days of free travel in and around Odense, plus free admission to most museums and sights. For general **bus info,** dial 66–11–71–11.

WHERE TO SLEEP **Odense Hostel.** Two km from city center in a quiet, Mr. Rogers–type neighborhood. A converted manor house with guest kitchen (bring your own plates and utensils), TV room, and laundry. Dorm beds 64kr, two- and four-person rooms 192kr–288kr. *Kragsbergvej 121, tel. 66–13–04–25. Bus 61 or 62 to Kragsbergvej. Closed Dec. and Jan.*

Yde's Hotel. Cheapest hotel in town. Cute, tiny, quiet doubles without bath are 390kr (buffet breakfast included). Five-minute walk from train station. *Hans Tausensgade 11, tel. 66–12–11–31. From station head west on Østre Stationsvej, turn at second left.*

➤ **CAMPGROUND • DCU Camping.** Close to idyllic Fruens Bøge park and the Fyn Village Museum—but far from everything else. Grass and trees compensate for highway noise. Swimming pool, guest kitchen, small market. Sites 42kr, cabins 160kr (195kr in summer). *Odensevej 102, tel. 66–11–47–02. Bus 41, 91, or 92 from Klingenberg, or take the Svendborg-bound train to Fruens Bøge. Laundry, showers. Closed Sept. 27–Mar. 25.*

FOOD Most cafés and restaurants are on or near Vestergade and Brandt's Passage, although the outlying streets contain a few high-quality feeding holes.

Blomsten. A tiny, publike place where regulars come for good, cheap Mexican food. Tostadas 20kr, burritos 35kr. Student discount on beer (1kr–2kr for a half-pint). *Dronningensgade 29, between Odinsgade and Thorsgade, tel. 65–91–05–08. Closed Sun.*

Cafe Cuckoo's Nest. A relaxed place with an extra-friendly staff and an outdoor patio. Sandwiches 24kr–30kr, omelets 46kr. *Vestergade 73, next to Brandt's Passage, tel. 65–91–57–87.*

Spisehuset Trianglen. A three-story building with Mongolian barbecue (79kr), French fondue (89kr), all-you-can-eat pizza and pasta (45kr). All come with salad bar. *Vintapperstræde 4, off Vestergade, tel. 66–12–92–02. Closed Mon.–Sat. 3 PM–5 PM. No Sun. lunch.*

WORTH SEEING If crowds, cobbled streets, and low houses with lace curtains give you the creeps, stay clear of **Brandt's Passage,** off Vestergade. This heavily boutiqued walking street adds a new, unwanted meaning to the word quaint.

➤ **BRANDT'S KLÆDEFABRIK • ** Without this cultural gold mine, Odense would seem unforgivably provincial. Once a cloth mill, the Klædefabrik now houses museums, galleries, and shops. The **Danske Presse Museet** (Danish Printing Museum, tel. 66–12–10–20; admission 15kr; open weekdays 10–5, weekends 11–5) vividly demonstrates the history and present state of the printing trade, with workshops for printing, bookbinding, and papermaking.

The Museet for Fotokunst (Museum of Photographic Art, tel. 66–13–78–16; admission 20kr; open Tues.–Sun. 10–5) and Kunsthallen (Art Gallery) mount first-rate exhibits. The book shop downstairs is a good place to browse. *Brandt's Passage 37–43, tel. 66–13–79–02. Admission to all 4 museums: 40kr. Open weekdays 10–5:30, weekends 10–5.*

➤ **HANS CHRISTIAN ANDERSEN HUS** • If you came to Odense just for this, woe is you. The Hans Christian Andersen House (Hans Jensens Stræde 37–45, tel. 66–13–13–72; admission 20kr; open June–Aug., daily 9–6; shorter hrs off-season), in the building where he was supposedly born, fancies itself a "literary museum," but the collection of Hans' photographs, letters, books, and possessions sheds no great light on the author or his work. Even more depressing is the **H. C. Andersens Barndomshjem** (Munkmøllstræde 3–5, tel. 66–13–13–72; open Apr.–Sept., shorter hrs off-season), Andersen's childhood home. The highlight is a 30-second guided tour of the three tiny rooms where Andersen and his large family lived and worked. Yawn.

➤ **KUNST MUSEET** • Its colorful, rich collection of Danish art includes modern and abstract pieces on the ground floor and, upstairs, pastoral paintings by the famous Fyn Group of painters—worth a look. *Jernbanegade 13, tel. 66–13–13–72. Admission: 15kr. Open Sun.–Tues. and Thurs.–Sat. 10–4, Wed. 10–4 and 7–10.*

➤ **MØNTERGARDEN** • This 18th-century housing complex is filled with exhibits on Odense's urban and cultural history from the Viking age to the 20th century. Everything from church architecture to Renaissance interiors to turn-of-the-century costumes is on exhibit. *Overgade 48–50, tel. 66–13–13–72. Admission: 15kr. Open daily 10–4.*

AFTER DARK Odense has a decidedly unprovincial nightlife. **The Boogie Dance Café** (Nørregade 21, tel. 66–44–00–39) is a popular rock discotheque. **Musikhuset** (Arkaden, Vestergade 68, tel. 66–14–09–01) plays rock, jazz, and blues, with karaoke Monday and Wednesday at 10 and Friday and Saturday at 10:30. The **Pan Cafe/Disco** (Sankt Anna Gade 4, 2nd floor, tel. 66–13–19–48) draws a mostly gay crowd.

NEAR ODENSE

EGESKOV SLOT The inconvenience of getting to the isolated Egeskov Slot, the so-called "floating castle," only adds to its mystery. The admission is unusually high (90kr), but if you're into castle architecture, hunting trophies, and labyrinthine gardens, it's definitely worth it. Egeskov means "oak forest" and refers to the stand of trees felled in about 1540 to form the piles on which the rose-stone structure was built (that's what you get for building a castle in the middle of a lake). A ticket gives you access to all the gardens, a short series of rooms, and a museum which houses historical airplanes, cars, motorcycles, and carriages. To reach the castle, take the Odense–Svendborg train to Kværndtup (40 min, 35kr), and either walk 2 km down Bøjdenvej or wait for the hourly bus. *Egeskov Slot, Egeskovgade 18, tel. 62–27–10–16. Open June–Aug., daily 9–6; May and Sept., daily 10–5.*

KERTEMINDE Here's an old, untarnished-by-tourists fishing village with tiny, top-quality museums. Langegade, the main street, is lined with colorfully painted cottages and shops, old-fashioned street signs, and an old apotek with real apothecary jars. **Farvergården** (Langegade 8, tel. 65–32–37–27; admission 10kr; open Mar.–Oct., daily 10–4), the town museum, is the best place to see what 18th-century Danish houses looked like. Kerteminde's real treasure, though, is the **Johannes Larsen Museet** (Møllebakken 14, tel. 65–32–37–27; admission 25kr, 20kr students), with an abundant collection of Larsen's paintings displayed in his studio and gardens, which he built and landscaped himself. Five km away is Kerteminde's other main draw, **Ladby Skibbet** (Vikingevej 123, tel. 65–32–16–67; admission 15kr, 10kr students), an excavated Viking ship that contains the only entombed Viking chief ever found in Denmark (he's still here, along with his 11 horses and four hunting dogs). The **tourist information office** (Strandgade 1B, tel. 65–32–11–21; open mid-June–Aug., Mon.–Sat. 9–5; shorter hrs off-season) has plenty of info on the area. To reach Kerteminde, take Bus 890 or 885 (30 min, 24kr) from Odense's train station.

Ærø

If you spend much time on the island of Ærø, it's hard to deny that the tiny town of **Ærøskøbing** occupies the most delectable corner of Denmark, with fresh sea air, vivid contrasts (green fields, blue sea), and a divine sense of isolation and age. Ærøskøbing is also a cultural hot spot (or warm spot, anyway), with an annual jazz festival—the third-largest in Denmark—in July. The festival is sponsored by **Cafe Andelen** (Søndergade 28A, tel. 52–52–17–11), the lifeblood of Ærøskøbing's music, art, cinema, and café scene. The café serves a killer rhubarb pie they call "rar bar bar" (don't try to pronounce it until you've had a few drinks); the stuff's so popular that Politiken, Denmark's largest newspaper, bought the rights to the recipe. Equally popular is the **Flaskeskibsmuseet** (Bottle Ship Museum, Smedegade 22; admission 10kr; open daily 10–4), with an amazing collection of ships in bottles—all pieced together by Peter "Bottle" Jacobsen, a sailor.

Ærøskøbing's **tourist information office** (Kirkestræde 29, tel. 62–53–19–60; open mid-June–Aug., weekdays 9–4, Sun. 9–noon) will direct you to either the small beachside **hostel** (Smedevejen 13, tel. 62–52–10–44; beds 65kr; closed Nov.– Mar.) or the scenic **campground** (Sygehusvejen, tel. 62–52–18–54; sites 36kr; closed Oct.–Apr.). They'll also help you find a cheapish B&B—expect to pay 175kr for a double. At the **Waffelbageri** (Vestergade 45) there's usually a line of people waiting to buy the "Ærøskøbing special"—walnut ice cream topped with maple syrup and served in a waffle cone (14kr). At night head for the harborside bar **Arrebo** (Vestergade 4, tel. 62–52–21–58), which has nightly live music in summer (mostly blues and '70s tunes).

COMING AND GOING **Svendborg,** one hour from Odense by train, is the most practical starting point for Ærø island. The ferry harbor in Svendborg is down Frederiksgade, just east of the train station. Another option is the ferry from Fåborg to Søby (1 hr), which is timed to meet the bus to Ærøskøbing. It's a good idea to ask the skipper to notify the bus driver that there's a passenger on board, since ferries sometimes run late. Most ferry trips cost 80kr round-trip. If you're only planning a day trip to Ærø, consider a **one-day bus-and-ferry pass** (114kr), available at Odense's train station.

Jylland
The **Jylland (Jutland) peninsula, the only part of Denmark attached to mainland Europe, is the largest of Denmark's regions, with two-thirds of its population. The landscape is more dynamic and diverse than that of any other part of Denmark, with vast moors and sand dunes, the country's best beaches and highest "mountains" (read *hills*), and the famous meeting point off Skagen of the Baltic and North seas. There's a special student flavor to Århus, Denmark's second-largest city, and a pleasant stench of beer in Aalborg, which has the longest stretch of bars and discotheques in the country. Best of all, Jylland is less touristed than Sjælland and Fyn, giving you the chance to hang with locals and discover the true meaning of hyggelit.

Århus

Århus, Denmark's second-largest city and home to a major university, brims with student activity and café culture; it also hosts two popular annual festivals, one for jazz in July and one for civic pride (and beer drinking) in September. Thanks to its ripe old age—Århus was first settled by Vikings, who called it *Aros*, an Old Norse word meaning *river mouth*—the city has two 13th-century cathedrals, an Old Town whose streets and buildings date from the 16th century, and one of Denmark's best prehistory museums. The **tourist information office** (tel. 86–12–16–00; open late June–early Aug., daily 9–8; shorter hrs off-season), in the Rådhuset, provides maps and B&B listings.

COMING AND GOING The **train station** (tel. 86–18–17–33), on the city center's southern edge, has trains to Copenhagen (4–5 hrs, 130kr–200kr), Odense (2 hrs, 95kr–118kr), Aalborg (1½ hrs, 78kr–95kr), Fredericia (1 hr, 77kr), Viborg (1 hr, 65kr), and Silkeborg (1 hr,

47kr). The **bus station** (Fredensgade 45, tel. 86–12–86–22), east of the train station, serves Copenhagen (4½ hrs, 130kr), Aalborg (2 hrs, 94kr), Viborg (2 hrs, 68kr), and Silkeborg (1 hr, 42kr).

GETTING AROUND When riding the buses, enter at the rear, and buy your ticket from the automatic machine on board. Each ticket (12.50kr) is valid for unlimited bus travel, plus transfers, for two hours. The **tourist multiride ticket** (45kr), valid on all buses for 24 hours, also gets you free sightseeing tours. Better yet, rent a bike (50kr per day) at **Asmussen G Cykelsportcenter** (Fredensgade 54, near train station, tel. 86–19–57–00).

WHERE TO SLEEP If you're short on cash, a good choice is the central, cheap **Århus Summer Sleep-In,** where dorm beds cost 75kr–80kr. The location frequently changes; call 86–25–71–88 or contact the tourist office for up-to-date info.

Eriksen's Hotel. About a block west of the train station. Clean and cozy. Doubles 380kr. *Banegårdesgade 6–8, tel. 86–13–62–96. MC, V.*

Windsor Hotel. If Eriksen's is full, resolute hotel goers may have to make do with this second-rate option. Small but clean doubles (380kr) come with breakfast. *Skolebakken 17, tel. 86–12–33–00.*

➢ **HOSTEL** • **Århus Vandrerhjem.** Idyllic surroundings (in the woods near a beach) make up for the 3-km trek from the city center. Beds 70kr. *Marienlundsvej 10, tel. 86–16–72–98. Take Bus 1, 6, 9, 16, 56, or 58. Laundry, luggage storage, kitchen facilities. Closed mid-Dec.–mid-Jan.*

➢ **CAMPGROUND** • **Blommehaven Campground.** A nature lover's dream, in the heart of Marselisborg Forest, with a deer park, wooded trails, and a beach. Campsites cost 40kr and are nicely hedged by rose bushes; cabins 250kr. Clean, modern bathrooms. *Ørneredevej 35, tel. 86–27–02–07. Bus 19. Kitchen, bike rental, minimarket. Closed Oct.–Mar.*

FOOD As a university town, Århus is loaded with affordable, atmospheric eating spots, including good ethnic restaurants and an endless assortment of cafés where 35kr buys a light meal, 10kr a full breakfast.

Den Blåparaply. All-you-can-eat pizza and salad for 29kr (35kr Fri. and Sat. after 5), pita sandwiches (27kr), and sandwiches (from 20kr). *Frederiksgade 73, near train station, tel. 86–18–12–65. BYOB. No Sun. lunch.*

Husets Cafe/Restaurant. In the heart of the Huset complex (*see* Worth Seeing, *below*), where you'll often find concerts, exhibitions, and interesting people. The menu includes daily specials (45kr), eggplant Parmesan (60kr), meal-size salads (25kr–35kr), and sandwiches (20kr). *Vesterallé 15, tel. 86–12–27–95.*

Kulturgyngen Restaurant. Friendly people prepare ethnic dishes as part of a government-funded social project for the unemployed. Diverse lunch menu includes Indian dahl (15kr), hummus plate (35kr), and sandwiches (20kr). Dinner menu limited to a single daily special (45kr). *Mejlgade 53, tel. 86–19–22–55. BYOB. Closed Sun.*

Legoland

The rumors are true: Legoland exists. So stop what you're doing and hop on the first train to Vejle, then Bus 912 to Billund (30 min, 30kr), where you'll be rewarded with scaled-down versions of cities, towns, and villages, as well as working harbors and airports (complete with sound effects), even a miniature Statue of Liberty—all built with millions of tiny Lego bricks. Lego means "play well" in Danish, but don't get caught fiddling with the goods. Admission to Legoland is 95kr, and the park is open May–September, daily 10–8. For more info, call 75–33–13–33.

WORTH SEEING Don't leave Århus without visiting **Huset** (Vesterallé 15, tel. 86–12–27–95; open weekdays 9–9), an arts-and-crafts studio where the public is invited to practice woodworking, batik, photography, and computer programming; you pay for materials only. **Århus Koncerthus** (Thomas Jensens Allé, tel. 86–13–43–44; open daily 11–9), whose huge foyer is made entirely of glass, hosts scads of free art exhibits and daytime performances. Between June 22 and August 6, the brewery **Ceres Bryggerierne** offers 5kr guided tours (Tues. and Thurs. at 9, Wed. at 2) with free beer at the end. Get tickets at the tourist information office.

➤ **ÅRHUS KUNST MUSEET** • There's a little of everything here: classical paintings from the Danish golden age, Danish works from the 1900s, some German canvases, and even a few Warhols. When you get bored, ponder the postwar architecture of C. F. Møller, who designed this and other simple brick buildings around town. *Vennelystparken, tel. 86–13–52–55. Admission: 20kr. Open Tues.–Sun. 10–5.*

➤ **DEN GAMLE BY** • You could spend all day exploring Århus's Old Town, a reconstructed village that features 65 half-timbered houses, shops, and a mill, all meticulously re-created with period interiors. Admit it: It's a nifty idea to wander through functioning workshops and fully furnished historic houses. It's also right next to the Botanic Gardens, a good place to relax with a beer. *Viborgvej, tel. 86–12–31–88. Admission: 40kr, 32kr students. Open June–Aug., daily 9–6; shorter hrs off-season.*

➤ **KVINDEMUSEET** • With temporary homemade exhibits about safety at night, sexuality, and other female concerns, this four-story building is more a women's center than a museum. The café upstairs serves light lunches (10kr–15kr) and often has piano concerts on Sunday afternoons. *Domekirkeplads 5, tel. 86–13–61–44. Admission: 10kr. Open June–mid-Sept., daily 10–5; shorter hrs off-season.*

➤ **MOESGÅRD FOLKHISTORISK MUSEET** • Among Denmark's innumerable prehistory museums, this one stands out as the resting place of the Grauballe Man, whose skin and hair have been miraculously preserved since his death in 80 BC. He was found in 1952 in a peat bog, where tannic acids prevented his decay; now he lies in a case, looking somewhat prunelike but nonetheless human. The museum's other highlight is its 6-km "prehistoric trackway"—a scenic path that winds through the woods along a river, with Viking burial sites and a Stone Age temple as side attractions. To reach the museum, take Bus 19 from the train station or city center. *Højberg, tel. 86–27–24–33. Admission: 25kr, 15kr students. Open May–mid-Sept., daily 10–5; shorter hrs off-season.*

AFTER DARK If you're a café hound, head for the streets around Studsgade and Rosensgade; the oldest and most adored café here is the artsy **Casablanca** (Rosensgade 12, tel. 86–13–55–11). **Cafe Smaglos,** the "Tasteless Café" (Klostertorv 7, tel. 86–13–51–33), has an odd assortment of knickknacks, mismatched chairs, and customers. The **Pan Cafe** (Jægergårdsgade 42, tel. 86–13–43–80; cover 40kr) is the local gay and lesbian hangout.

The pamphlet "What's On in Århus," available at the tourist office, lists local clubs and discos, as does the flyer "Ugen Ud," found in most cafés. Dependable music cafés include **Kulturgyngen** (Mejlgade 53, tel. 86–19–22–55; cover 30kr and under), which has live alternative music and occasional jam sessions. Århus's biggest discotheque is **Blitz** (Klostergade 34, tel. 86–19–10–99; cover 40kr–120kr; closed Sun.–Wed.), with a regular disco on the ground floor and an alternative disco (mostly hip-hop) below; live bands rock in the upstairs bar.

NEAR ÅRHUS

VIBORG If you're looking for that perfect blend of history and outdoor beauty, scurry to Viborg. King Knud (in 1027) and King Christian V (in 1665) were crowned here, and the town retains the majestic look of its glory days, with a twin-tower cathedral, cobblestone squares, and lush gardens. Viborg is also at the center of one of Denmark's greenest landscapes: North of Viborg, placid Limfjord borders moors, beech forests, fir groves, and heather-clad hills. Hikers should take the 5-km bike or bus ride (try Bus 712 to Dollerup) to the **Hald** region, rife with glacially formed hills, towering forests, and teardrop lakes. Self-guided hiking brochures are available at Viborg's tourist office.

South of Viborg lie Lake Søndersø and **Forstbotanisk Have**; the latter's wooded nature trails surround the pleasant **Viborg Hostel** (Vinkelvej 36, tel. 86–67–17–81; closed Dec.), where dorm rooms cost 35kr and family-size rooms 64kr–84kr. Also here is **DCU Camping Viborg** (Vinkelvej 36B, tel. 86–67–13–11; closed Apr.–Sept); sites cost 38kr, cabins 160kr plus 38kr per person. To reach either, take Bus 707 from Viborg's train station.

SILKEBORG One hour by train from Århus, Silkeborg, in the heart of Denmark's Lake District, is paradise for outdoorsy folks. It has one of the most scenic forests in Denmark, a river that's great for canoeing, an annual riverboat jazz festival in late June, and a sailing regatta in early August. In Silkeborg's city center, the **Silkeborg Museum** (Hovegårdsvej, tel. 86–82–14–99; admission 20kr, open daily 10–5) is the resting place of Grauballe Man's two peatbog friends, the Tollund Man and the Elling Woman, plus a host of Iron Age artifacts. Next, try canoeing down the **Remstrup Å River** with a rented canoe (45kr for one hour) from the shop at Remstrupvej 41 (tel. 86–82–35–43). Row down the river to **Himmelbjerg,** Denmark's tallest "mountain" (more like a large hill), which affords a dramatic view of lakes and pine forests. The river runs between the trail-filled Dronningstolen Forest and Indelukket Park, where you'll find one of Denmark's best museums, **Silkeborg Museum of Art** (Gudenåvej 7–9, tel. 86–82–53–88; admission 20kr; open April–Oct., Tues.–Sat. 10–5; shorter hrs off-season). It's a huge and varied collection that merits several hours of perusal. Too idyllic to be true, the **Silkeborg Hostel** (Ahåvevej 55, tel. 86–82–36–42; beds 35kr; closed Dec.–Feb.) has dorm rooms overlooking the river, and lots of smaller 60kr–75kr family rooms.

Aalborg

Aalborg has a charming 16th-century look, hearty nightlife, and a fjord-side setting that makes it a primo place to while away a few stress-free days. The only tourists you'll meet are those on their way to Norway or Sweden or off to explore the banks of nearby Limfjord, northern Jylland's famed waterway.

The best starting point is **Rådhus Torv** (Town Hall Square), where the elaborate, five-story **Jens Bangs Stenhus** (Jens Bang's Stone House) stands as a testament to the egotism of the 16th-century bourgeoisie. Despite his wealth and best efforts, Bang was never elected to the town council; this fact is illustrated by the sculpted caricature on the house's south facade, where he's sticking his tongue out at the rococo **Rådhus** (Town Hall), the most beautiful building in Aalborg.

North of the city in Nørresundby is **Lindholm Høje** (Vendilavej 11, tel. 98–17–55–22; museum admission 20kr; open June–Aug., daily 10–7), a Viking burial ground and museum—a must for anyone even remotely interested in the Vikings. With 700 graves marked by stones that form triangles, ovals, and ships, the site can be awesome if you block out the tourists around you and imagine the place 1,000 years ago. The museum will help you do just that, with great archaeological displays illustrating the Vikings' lifestyle, work habits, and burial customs. To get here, take Bus 6 from the train station or city center.

COMING AND GOING The **train station** (tel. 98–16–16–16) offers service to Copenhagen (7 hrs, 175kr–219kr plus 30kr mandatory seat reservation), Arhus (1 hr 20 min, 78kr–95kr), and Frederikshavn (1 hr, 53kr). The adjacent **bus station** has buses to Copenhagen (5½ hrs, 165kr) and Esbjerg (3½ hrs, 156kr). Buy tickets on the bus.

GETTING AROUND Most of Aalborg is walker-friendly, with a network of pedestrian streets branching east and west off Østerågade, which leads from the train station to the city center. The famous Jomfru Ane Gade, where you'll find most restaurants, bars, and discotheques, is just off Bispensgade in the city center. Within Aalborg, most local buses (10kr) leave from Nytorv (the central square); buy your ticket (valid for 1 hr) from the driver. If you're staying for a few days, buy a discounted bus pass from the bus station or the centrally located **tourist**

office (Østerågade 8, tel. 98–12–60–22; open June–Aug., weekdays 9–5, Sat. 9–4; shorter hrs off-season).

WHERE TO SLEEP The **Fjordparken Hostel and Campground** (Skydebanevej 50, tel. 98–11–60–44) are inconveniently but beautifully located next to Limfjord, in the northwest corner of town. The hostel has 60kr dorm beds and 279kr–396kr family-size rooms; the campground has 40kr sites and 175kr–235kr cabins. Campers can use all of the hostel facilities, including the kitchen, minimarket, laundry, and cafeteria. Bus 8 from the bus station will bring you here. Aalborg's cheapest hotel is the **Aalborg Sømandshjem** (Østerbro 27, tel. 98–12–19–00), where clean doubles cost 440kr. From the bus station or city center take Bus 1 or 2.

Frederikshavn

Frederikshavn is a humdrum transport center with frequent ferry service to Norway and Sweden, and trains to major European destinations. The three ferry stations, clustered around Havnepladsen (south of the train station), are **Læsø Færgen** (tel. 98–42–83–00), with frequent express catamarans to Göteborg, Sweden (1 hr 45 min, 75kr, reservations advised); **Stena** (tel. 98–20–02–00), with slower ferries to Göteberg (3 hrs, 90kr) and daily ferries to Oslo (9 hrs, 320kr–410kr, 115kr extra for sleeping cabins) and Moss; and **Larvik** (tel. 98–42–14–00), with daily ferries to Larvik, Norway (6 hrs, 320kr, 100kr extra for cabins). The **HI Frederikshavn Hostel** (Buhlsvej 6, 2 km from train station, tel. 98–42–14–75; closed Dec.) is peaceful and pleasant, with 53kr dorm beds and family-size rooms from 65kr–78kr per person.

Skagen

Skagen lies at the northernmost tip of Jylland, where the Skagerrak and Kattegat seas meet (and where mighty North Sea winds blow). Until the 1800s, only hardy Skagen fishermen eked out a fragile living here, despite drifting sands that invaded their fields, wrecked ships, and even buried a church. In the early 1900s, new rail lines and a harbor transformed the town, whereupon Scandinavian painters descended. They were drawn by Skagen's dunes and moors and by the unique light reflected off the meeting seas. Today Skagen is a holiday resort full of first-rate museums, second-rate galleries, picturesque yellow houses, and the same craggy shoreline that has braved the sea for centuries.

Skagen's best attraction, the landscape, is free. For a wet and wild experience, walk north along the beach to the point where the Kattegat Sea meets the Skagerakk Sea in an endless clashing of waves. While you're here, look for the grave of Holgar Drachmann, the best known of the Skagen painters, whose spirit (and corpse) is forever enshrined in one of the northernmost dunes. To sample Skagen-inspired art, visit the **Skagen Museet** (Brøndumsvej 4, tel. 98–44–64–44; admission 25kr; open June–Aug., daily 10–6; shorter hrs off-season).

COMING AND GOING You can get to Skagen only by way of Frederikshavn on privately owned trains (40 min) and buses (1 hr). Both cost 30kr, and rail passes are not valid. The **tourist office** (Sankt Laurentii Vej 22, tel. 98–44–13–77; open June–Aug., Mon.–Sat. 9–5; shorter hrs off-season), conveniently located inside the train and bus station, can book you a room in a private home for a 25kr booking fee.

WHERE TO SLEEP AND EAT The **Skagen Hostel** (Højensvej 32, tel. 98–44–13–56; beds 75kr; telephone reservations 9–11 and 5–7; closed Dec.–Jan.) is 5 km from town, in Gammel Skagen; take Bus 79 from the train station. Infinitely more convenient is the informal **sleep-in** (Oddevej 11, tel. 98–45–16–48) at the home and art gallery of Orla Andersen, who will let you crash on his floor for 75kr (kitchen and shower included). He also has four doubles that each costs 300kr. Skagen's hotels are pricey; the cheapest is **Skagen Sømandshjem** (Østre Strandevej 2, near the harbor, tel. 98–44–25–88), where clean doubles go for 230kr. **Grenen Camping** (Fyrvej 16, tel. 98–44–25–46; closed Sept.–Apr.) is the most convenient campground, with 42kr campsites and 140kr cabins (plus 42kr a person). Take Bus 990 from town. Skagen's restaurants, too, are expensive. **Theater Caféen** (Sankt Laurentii Vej 63, tel. 98–44–66–80) will give you the biggest bang for your buck, with all-you-can-eat lunch (39kr) and dinner (99kr) deals and a 25% discount for early birds.

Esbjerg

People come to Esbjerg to catch a ferry for England or the Faroe Islands. **DFDS Scandinavian Seaways** (Englandskagen, tel. 75–12–48–00) has ferries to Harwich (18 hrs, 620kr–920kr, including bed) and Newcastle (22 hrs, same price). **Smyril Line** serves the Faroe Islands (2 days, 1,290kr, including bed) and Iceland (4 days, 890kr, including bed). **DSB** (tel. 75–12–00–00) runs ferries to Fanø (20 min, 10kr). InterCity trains from Copenhagen and Fredericia go directly to the ferry harbor. If you arrive at the train station, take Bus 5 from the adjacent **bus station** (tel. 75–12–33–77) to the harbor.

Ribe

Ribe, founded by Vikings in about AD 780, is the oldest and best-preserved town in Denmark, with a cathedral, a striking monastery, and a slew of inns and houses. For an unbeatable introductory view, climb the redbrick tower of the 12th-century **Ribe Domkirke** (Torvet, tel. 75–42–06–19; admission 5kr; open June–Aug., Mon.–Sat. 10–6, Sun. noon–6; shorter hrs off-season), which stands on the site of one of Denmark's first churches, built by Bishop Angsar in AD 860. Outside the cathedral in the main square you'll find Denmark's oldest inn, **Weis' Stue** (tel. 75–42–07–00), with farm tables, biblical frescoes, and pewter mugs from 1700. From here you can join the night watchman on his rounds (June–Aug. at 8 PM and 10 PM, May and Sept. at 10 PM); by lantern light he rambles through Ribe, singing and stopping at various points to give a little town history in Danish and English.

Although you could wander Ribe's medieval streets all day, save time for **Sankt Catherine's Kirke and Abbey** (Sankt Catherine Plads, tel. 75–42–05–34; admission free; open daily 10–noon and 2–5). Founded in 1228 by the Black Friars of the Dominican order, it was one of few churches to survive the Reformation. **Hans Tausen's Hus** (Skolegade; admission 15kr; open June–Aug., daily 10–6; shorter hrs off-season), former home of Ribe's first Lutheran bishop, is now a first-rate museum of Viking artifacts. Ribe's **tourist information** (Torvet 3–5, tel. 75–42–15–00), in a 16th-century merchant's house, provides a free leaflet on accommodations in private homes.

WHERE TO SLEEP AND EAT Ribe's **HI hostel** (Sankt Pedersgade 16, tel. 75–42–06–20; closed Dec. and Jan.) is on a quiet street two minutes from the city center. Four-bed rooms cost 71kr–84kr per person. Ribe's **campground** (Farupvej, tel. 75–41–07–77), in the woods 1½ km from town, has campsites (40kr) and cabins (85kr plus 40kr per person). Ribe's most relaxed eatery is **Cafe Nikolaj** (Sankt Nicolajgade 6, tel. 75–42–42–03), where locals come to play backgammon, listen to jazz, or hang out in the riverside garden. Sandwiches, salads, and pastas go for 20kr–30kr.

FINLAND

By Adam Ruderman

Though the reserved Finns won't embrace you, Finland will: It wraps you in overwhelming birch forests that push into the city borders, and then releases you into a jigsaw-puzzle landscape of more than 180,000 lakes. Finland used to be one of the most expensive tourist destinations in Europe, but it is now eminently affordable—fortunate for visitors but not for the Finns. The economy has suffered greatly with the collapse of the Soviet Union, Finland's neighbor to the east and formerly its major export market. It is ironic that after 45 years of tightrope walking between the capitalist West and the communist East, Finland survived the Cold War politically only to fail economically.

No stranger to adversity, Finland was dominated by its nearest neighbors, Sweden and Russia, for centuries. After more than 600 years of Swedish rule and 100 years under the czars, the country bears many traces of these two cultures, including a small Swedish-speaking population and a number of Russian Orthodox churches. But Suomi (Finnish for "Finland") remains stubbornly individualistic—it's one of the few countries that shared a border with the Soviet Union in 1939 and retained its independence. Maybe this melancholy self-sufficiency is the result of the battle against brutal winters, or maybe it comes from the country's turbulent political past; whatever the reason, the Finns have made the philosophy of *sisu*—resilience in the face of inevitable hardship—a national credo.

Basics

MONEY $1 = 5.23 markkaa and 1 markka = 19¢. The Finnish unit of currency is the markka (FIM), consisting of 100 penniä. You can exchange traveler's checks and currency in banks (open weekdays 9:15–4:15), airports, train stations, and big hotels. Banks offer the best rates, and most towns have at least one bank with a 24-hour automatic teller machine. Credit cards are accepted at big hotels, at almost all restaurants and stores, and at some budget accommodations.

➤ **HOW MUCH IT WILL COST** • In 1990 Finland was one of the world's most expensive countries, but a recession in November 1991 lowered prices dramatically. Now almost everything aside from food and alcohol is affordable. A local phone call costs FIM 2, a 100-km train trip roughly FIM 45, and a double room in a mid-range hotel about FIM 250. If you stay in hostels, you can get by on FIM 200 per day with no problem, and with a rail pass you can spend even less. You're not expected to tip for services; if your cab driver lugs your bags around or the waitperson is wonderful, an extra 5% is plenty.

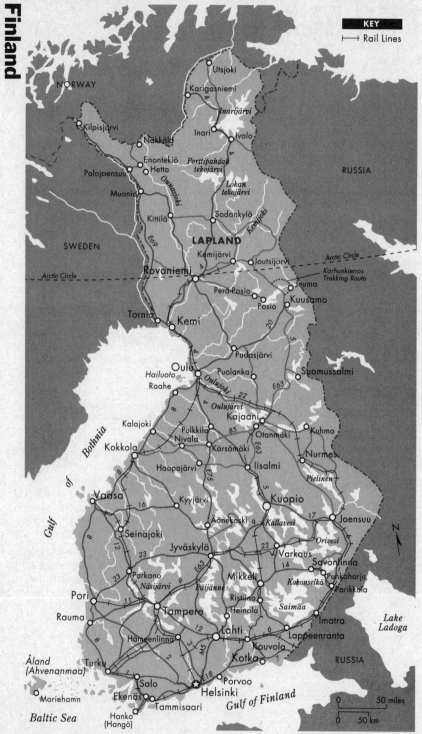

KEY

⊢——⊣ Rail Lines

NORWAY

Utsjoki

Karigasniemi

Inarijärvi

Kilpisjärvi

Näkkälä

Inari   Ivalo

RUSSIA

Enontekiö
Hetta

*Porttipahdan
tekojärvi*

Palojoensuu

Ounasjoki

Muonio

*Lokan
tekojärvi*

Kittilä

Sodankylä

Kemijoki

LAPLAND

SWEDEN

Kemijärvi

E69

Joutsijärvi   *Arctic Circle*

*Karhunkierros
Trekking Route*

Arctic Circle

Rovaniemi

Jeuma

Perä-Posio

Posio   Kuusamo

Tornio

Kemi

20

Pudasjärvi

5

Suomussalmi

4

Oulu

Puolanka

Hailuoto

Oulujoki

E63

Raahe

22

Oulujärvi

Kajaani

Kalajoki

Pulkkila

85

Kuhmo

Kokkola

Nivala

Otanmäki

Kärsämäki

E63

Nurmes

8

Haapajärvi

Iisalmi

E75

Pielinen

Vaasa

Kyyjärvi

5

Kuopio

17

16

Äänekoski

9   *Kallavesi*

Joensuu

N

Seinäjoki

8

12

Jyväskylä

23

Orivesi

23

E63

Varkaus

Savonlinna

Parkano

9

Mikkeli

14

Punkaharju

23

Näsijärvi

Päijänne

Kokonselkä

Parikkala

Pori

11

Ristiina

Saimaa

Rauma

Tampere

Heinola

Imatra

*Lake
Ladoga*

8

12

Lahti

6

Lappeenranta

Hämeenlinna

3

M5

Kouvola

Turku

2

Kotka

1

RUSSIA

*Åland
(Ahvenanmaa)*

Salo

E18

Porvoo

Mariehamn

Ekenäs

☆
Helsinki

Baltic Sea

Hanko
(Hangö)

Tammisaari

Gulf of Finland

0   50 miles

0   50 km

Gulf

of

Bothnia

COMING AND GOING Finland is in the European boonies, and getting here is an arduous task. The quickest, most direct route is across the Baltic Sea by ferry; most people depart from Stockholm, Sweden. You can get to Finland with a EurailPass, but taking strictly trains means a heinous journey through northern Sweden.

The ships that sail the Baltic are luxurious, cheap, and festive. **Silja Line** (in Stockholm, tel. 08/222–140; in Helsinki, tel. 90/180–4555 or 90/18–041) sails twice daily from Stockholm to Turku (11 hrs; mid-June–mid-Aug. FIM 150, FIM 115 students; off-season FIM 90, FIM 65 students) and once daily to Helsinki (14 hrs; mid-June–mid-Aug. FIM 285, FIM 250 students; off-season FIM 225, FIM 200 students). For Eurailers, Silja trips are discounted; check with the ferry office for specifics. **Viking Line** (in Stockholm, tel. 08/743–6400; in Helsinki, tel. 90/12–351) sails from Stockholm to Helsinki (late June–early Sept. FIM 160, students and rail-pass holders FIM 110; off-season FIM 80, students and rail-pass holders FIM 55) and from Stockholm to Turku via Mariehamn (late June–early Sept. FIM 132, students and rail-pass holders FIM 88; off-season FIM 66, students and rail-pass holders FIM 44).

GETTING AROUND What little railway Finland has is punctual and efficient, but the train system is inadequate for extensive travel. Fortunately, the highways are well maintained, and buses travel 90% of them.

➢ **BY TRAIN • Valtion Rautatiet (VR)** (Vihonkatu 13, Helsinki, tel. 90/7071), the national railway, runs a tight, clean, high-tech ship. Especially good are connections along the Helsinki–Tampere–Turku triangle. One of the three main lines can get you as far north as Kolari or Kemijärvi in Lapland (via Oulu from Helsinki), and traveling east to Moscow or St. Petersburg is a snap. Connections to Sweden are cumbersome and always involve switching trains. The InterRail pass and EurailPass are good for unlimited travel in Finland, and you can buy a Finnrail pass at all major stations, entitling you to unlimited train use for eight days (FIM 470), 15 days (FIM 730), or 22 days (FIM 920).

➢ **BY BUS •** Buses are a must for any traveler hoping to get off the beaten track. Eurail-Passes and Finnrail passes aren't valid on buses, but a Student Coach Discount Card (FIM 30), available at any station, gets you a 30% discount on all fares. Another option is the Coach Holiday Ticket (FIM 300), good for 1,000 km of travel throughout Finland within two weeks. All bus fares are nationally determined, and price hikes are frequent. The 165-km ride from Turku to Helsinki costs about FIM 75. Buy tickets at the station or on board. For questions about long-distance bus travel, call 9600–4000.

➢ **BY PLANE •** Some domestic fares on **Finnair** (in Helsinki, tel. 90/818–800) are quite cheap, especially in July. The Finnair Holiday Ticket (US$300, US$250 for those under 25) allows unlimited domestic air travel for 15 days. If you want to visit northern Lapland but don't fancy traveling 1,200 km on the ground, inquire about the Helsinki–Ivalo airfare (round-trip about FIM 900, FIM 700 for those under 24).

➢ **BY BIKE •** Great call. Finland is essentially mountainless, the main roads are excellent, the minor roads are deserted, the camping regulations are liberal, and June and July offer extended daylight hours. You can rent a bike for FIM 20–FIM 50 per day and throw it on trains and most long-distance buses.

WHERE TO SLEEP The cost of sleeping in Finland varies greatly, depending on your needs. Technically, you could get away without paying a penni, since Finland's "everyman's right" grants legal permission to temporarily pitch a tent anywhere that's not obstructive or on private property (try the abandoned farms and farmhouses all over the countryside). **Campgrounds** have reasonably priced cottages, and throughout Lapland you'll find cheap or free **wilderness huts** with bunk beds and even firewood, where you can come and go as you please. Most **hotels** offer weekend discounts, and hostels in Finland are cheaper than in the rest of Western Europe. The Finnish youth-hostel association, **Suomen Retkeilymajajärjestö (SRM)**, is a member of Hostelling International. Prices for all HI hostels listed below are for members; if you don't have a membership card, expect to pay FIM 15 more.

FOOD As usual, pizzas, burgers, and sausages are among the cheapest options. You're best off getting your authentic-cuisine fix at lunch; dinner prices for Finnish dishes run high. Specialties include *poro* (reindeer) and *graavilohi* (pickled salmon); in summer, look for *ravut* (crayfish) at restaurants flying crayfish flags. *Olut* (beer) is big in Finland and comes in three classes. Class I, the cheapest and weakest, is treated like soda, although its alcohol content is on a par with that of U.S. beer. Class IV is the most potent (there's no Class II).

BUSINESS HOURS Stores are generally open weekdays 9–5 and Saturday 9–1 or 9–2. Almost everything is closed Sunday, although *kioski,* which sell only basics (cigs, soda, cookies) are usually open daily until 11 PM.

PHONES **Country code: 358.** Some phone booths accept FIM 1 or FIM 5 coins, but more accept only phone cards, which you can buy at post offices. A local call costs FIM 2 for two minutes, and a call to the United States or Australia is FIM 5.40 per minute. For FIM 4, you can use a special pay-after-you-call booth at the post office. The cheapest times to call internationally are weeknights 10 PM–8 AM and weekends. For international information, call 92020. The access code for AT&T USA Direct is 9800–100–10; MCI's code is 9800–102–80.

Finland is in the process of "internationalizing" its phone system, so numbers and area codes change frequently. Call telephone information at 118 for the latest.

EMERGENCIES The emergency number is 112 for an **ambulance** or the **fire** department, 100–22 for the **police.**

LANGUAGE Finnish is not a Scandinavian but a Finno-Ugric language, related to Estonian and distantly to Hungarian. Finns realize their language is obscure; most start learning English before they get their first pimple, and tourist information is generally published in English. Many Finns also speak Swedish, the primary language in some areas along the western coast.

WOMEN TRAVELERS Finland's major feminist organization, **Naisasialiitto Unioni** (Bulevardi 11A, Helsinki, tel. 90/643–158), is the best resource for female travelers.

GAY AND LESBIAN TRAVELERS Of the Scandinavian countries, Finland is the least accepting of homosexuality, and open affection, even in the capital city, is unheard of. For more info, contact **Seta Ry** (Oikokatu 3, Helsinki, tel. 90/135–8302).

Helsinki

Despite perceptions to the contrary in the United States, Finland is not populated by fur-clad ice-cave dwellers. It's a modern techno-nation, and nowhere is that more apparent than in Helsinki, the country's largest, most cosmopolitan, and most pretentious city. The youth here embrace cheesy retro-Americana, from bolo ties and muscle cars to acid wash and feathered hair; the older folks are cool and casual and don't leave home without the cellular phone.

It all started for Helsinki in about 1550, when King Gustav I, ruler of the Swedish-Finnish empire, uprooted the then-humble market town from the mouth of the Vantaa River and replanted it on the Gulf of Finland at its present location, in the hope that it would become a bustling trade mecca. In 1812, after Russia annexed Finland, Czar Alexander I declared Helsinki the new capital. He also decided the city needed a more stately style, so he called on Carl Ludvig Engel, who designed Helsinki's magnificent neoclassical buildings. The city now contains about one-sixth of Finland's population, and its suburbs sprawl across several peninsulas.

BASICS

VISITOR INFORMATION The **City Tourist Office** sells the invaluable **Helsinki Card** (one-day FIM 80, two-day FIM 105, three-day FIM 125), good for unlimited local transport, admission to all museums, and a variety of other discounts. Many hotels also sell the card.

Pohjoisesplanadi 19, tel. 90/169–3757. Open mid-May–mid-Sept., weekdays 8:30–6, Sat. 8:30–1; off-season, weekdays 8:30–4.

Hotellikeskus (in train station, tel. 90/171–133) will find you a room in a private home for a fee of FIM 10 or in a hotel for FIM 5. It also sells the Helsinki Card. The **Finnish Tourist Board** (Eteläesplanadi 4, tel. 90/4030–1300), across from the City Tourist Office, answers questions about tours and long-distance travel and has tons of info on camping and biking routes.

AMERICAN EXPRESS Services include personal-check cashing, mail holding, and lost-card replacement for members. *Pohjoisesplanadi 2, tel. 90/18–551. Open weekdays 9–5.*

CHANGING MONEY It's best to change money in the airport or at a bank, to avoid the stiff commission charged by hotels. After hours, though, hotels may be your only choice. Larger places like the **Arctia Hotel Marski** (Mannerheimintie 10, tel. 90/68–061), one block west of the train station, are the best bet.

EMBASSIES **Canada.** *Pohjoisesplanadi 25B, tel. 90/171–141. Open Mon.–Thurs. 8:30–4, Fri. 8:30–1:30.*

Great Britain. *Itäinen Puistotie 17, tel. 90/661–293. Open weekdays 9–noon.*

United States. *Itäinen Puistotie 14B, tel. 90/171–931. Open weekdays 9–noon.*

PHONES AND MAIL The main post office, near the train station, has poste restante, pay-after-you-phone booths, money exchange, and phone cards and stamps for sale. *Mannerheimintie 11, tel. 90/195–5117. Open weekdays 9–5. Telephone center open weekdays 9 AM–10 PM, Sat. 10–4. Poste restante office open weekdays 8 AM–9 PM, Sat. 9–6, Sun. 11–9. Postal code 00100.*

COMING AND GOING

The **train station** (tel. 90/101–0115) is in the city center, next to the main post office. Eight trains travel between Helsinki and Turku daily (2 hrs 15 min, FIM 90). The **long-distance bus station** (tel. 90/9700–4000) is nearby, across Mannerheimintie from the post office on Salomonkatu. Helsinki is connected to Stockholm by two ferry lines: **Viking** (Katajanokan Terminaali, tel. 90/12–351) and **Silja** (Olympia Terminaali, tel. 90/180–4555 or 90/18–041). Silja also goes to Travemünde, Germany.

The **Helsinki-Vantaa airport** (tel. 90/82–771) is in the town of Vantaa, about 20 km from Helsinki. Sirola Bus 615 (FIM 14) connects the airport with Platform 12 at the train station. Finnair buses (FIM 20) are quicker and go to the Finnair City Bus Terminal, next to the train station. Yellow airport taxi-vans will take you anywhere in Helsinki for a flat rate of FIM 50.

GETTING AROUND

Helsinki's suburbs sprawl, but most sights, hotels, and eats are within walking distance of one another on a single peninsula. The main street, **Mannerheimintie,** runs roughly north–south and intersects the other major street, **Aleksanterinkatu,** one block south of the train station. Most sights are within a few blocks of these streets and the **Esplanadi** strolling park, off the south end of Mannerheimintie.

If you're not up for a walk, **trams** are a good option; they serve the city center better than **buses,** which are most helpful in the suburbs. Tram 4 takes you north up Mannerheimintie or east of the city center to the Katajanokka neighborhood. Tram 3T can get you to southeastern Helsinki, including Kaivopuisto. Most buses and trams pass through the Mannerheimintie and Aleksanterinkatu intersection. The **ferry** to the island fortress of Suomenlinna is also a part of the city's public transportation system. Tickets on all city transport lines cost FIM 9 and can be used for one hour of unlimited transfers. Buy tickets from drivers; get maps from the tourist office or from the Rautatientori Metro station under the train station. The city's one Metro line is not too useful for visitors.

Helsinki

FINLAND

Taivallahti

Taivalsaari

Sibeliuksen
puisto

Töölönlahti

Eläintarhantie

Kaisan.

Klu
Glo

Hietaniemi
Cemetery

Pohjoinen Hesperiank.

Eteläinen Hesperiank.

Museok.

Apollonk.

Temppelik.

Nervanderink.

Arkadiank.

Lapinlahti

Hietaniemenk.

Eteläl Rautatiek.

Long-
Distance
Bus Station

Train
Station

City B
Statio

Mikonk.

Aleks

Keskusk.

Salomonk.

Urho
Kekkosenk.

Simonk.

Kaivok

Mannerheimintie

Länsiväylä

Lapinlahdentie

Pohj Rautatiek.

Runebergsgatan

Malmink.

Lapinlahdenk.

Lastenkodink.

Fredrikink.

Yrjön.

Annank.

Porkkalank.

Itämerenk.

Ruoholahden

Ruoholahdenk.

Abrahamink.

Eerikink.

Kalevank.

Lönnrotink.

Albertink.

Uudenmaank.

Pie
Roobe

Ruoholahti

Köydenpunojank.

Hietalahdenk.

Hietalahdenranta

Sandviksk.

Mallask.

Iso

Bulevardi

Roobertink.

Roobertink.

Punavuorenk.

Jääkärink.

Hietalahti

Merimiehenk.

Pursimiehenk.

Sepänk.

Telakkak.

Munkkisaarenk.

Tehtaankatu

Hernesaarenk.

Rehbinderintie

Skepparegatan

Lai

Ehrensvard Tiegatan

Merikatu

Mer

156

Sights ●
Ateneum, **11**
Eduskuntatalo, **6**
Hietaniemi beach, **3**
Kansallismuseo, **5**
Kauppatori, **15**
Presidentinlinna, **16**
Senaatintori, **14**
Seurasaari, **1**
Suomenlinna, **17**
Temppeliaukion
kirkko, **4**
Tuomiokirkko, **12**
Uspenskin
katedraali, **18**

Lodging ○
Eurohostel (HI), **20**
Finn, **10**
Kallio Hostel, **8**
Kongressikoti, **13**
Lönnrot, **9**
Pension Regina, **19**
Satakuntatalo, **7**
Stadionin
Retkeilymaja (HI), **2**

N

Siltavuoren-
satama

Sörnäistensatama

Pohjoissatama
(North Harbor)

KATAJANOKKA

Eteläsatama
(South Harbor)

Valkosaari

Luoto

Ryssänsaari

Pikkuluoto

KEY

AE American Express
    Office

i Tourist Information

├─┤ Rail Lines

Kaivopuisto

Merisatama

0   1/4 mile

0   1/4 km

WHERE TO SLEEP

Helsinki offers plain hotels and posh ones and little in between. The lower-end places may be bland, but they're not grimy, and most are less than 10 minutes' walk from the train station and city center. Many hotels offer discounts on weekends.

➤ **UNDER FIM 250 • Kongressikoti.** Hallways are stinky, but luckily rooms aren't. Proprietress usually bails at 5 PM, so call ahead if you'll be late and need her to wait. All rooms share bath. Singles FIM 120, doubles FIM 200, breakfast included. Discount for stays of more than two nights. *Snellmaninkatu 15, tel. 90/135–6839. Kitchenette.*

Lönnrot. Good location, really cool staff. Singles FIM 160, doubles FIM 220, all with sinks and phones, none with bath. *Lönnrotinkatu 16, tel. 90/693–2590. AE, MC, V.*

➤ **UNDER FIM 350 • Finn.** All rooms have telephones, toilets, and TVs; most have showers. Housekeeping is a bit lax. Singles FIM 250, doubles FIM 300. *Kalevankatu 3, tel. 90/640–904. MC, V.*

Pension Regina. In the happening Kaivopuisto area south of the city center, between the Baltic Sea and a hip dance bar. Elderly Regina won't answer the door unless you call first. Singles FIM 200, doubles FIM 300, none with bath. *Puistokatu 9, tel. 90/656–937. Tram 3T to Puistokatu.*

Satakuntatalo. Suites with three to five rooms share shower, toilet, phone, and kitchen. Houses students all winter. Singles FIM 200, doubles FIM 270, triples FIM 300. *Lapinrinne 1, tel. 90/695–851. Laundry. AE, MC, V.*

HOSTELS **Eurohostel (HI).** Long halls, white-box rooms, annoying timed showers. Singles FIM 145, doubles FIM 190, triples FIM 275, breakfast FIM 25. *Linnankatu 9, tel. 90/664–452. Tram 2 or 4 to Katajanokka. Laundry, wheelchair access, kitchen, free sauna.*

Kallio Hostel. Slightly cramped and creaky, but personable. Often full, since there are only 30 beds. Beds FIM 50. *Porthaninkatu 2, tel. 90/992–590. Take Metro north to Hakaniemi. 2 AM curfew, lockout 10:30–11, laundry, kitchen, free lockers. Closed Sept.–mid-May.*

Stadionin Retkeilymaja (HI). Huge, crowded, and ugly, but cheap. Bike rental FIM 40 per day. Dorms FIM 45, doubles FIM 100, sheets FIM 20, breakfast FIM 25. *Pohjoinen Stadiontie 3B, tel. 90/496–071. Tram 3T north to Olympic Stadium, or 20-min walk north on Mannerheimintie. 2 AM curfew, lockout 10–4, laundry, kitchen facilities, lockers FIM 3.*

FOOD

You won't find many bargains in Helsinki, but the cheap, fresh fish is an exception. **Kauppatori** (Market Square) is jammed with umbrella-covered stands selling anything recently pulled out of the water, raw or cooked, daily 7–2 (later in summer). You'll also find fruits, veggies, baked goods, and handicrafts here or in **Kauppahalli** (Market Hall), which faces the square and is open weekdays 8–5, Saturday 8–2. In the morning townsfolk turn out in full force to down vast quantities of *lihapiirakka* (FIM 11), a pastry filled with beef and rice. Other smart shopping ideas include the discount markets underneath the train station (**Alepa** and **Pirkka** are the best deals) and the deli cases in the basement of the behemoth department store **Stockmann's** (cnr. of Mannerheimintie and Pohjoisesplanadi). University cafeterias offer just what you'd expect from dorm food—and plenty of it—for FIM 18–FIM 22. Try **Porthania** (Hallituskatu 13, at Fabianinkatu) or the cellar-dwelling **Alibi** (Hietaniemenkatu 14), a block from Perho Mechelin (*see below*).

➤ **UNDER FIM 40 • Happy Days.** A Finnish stab at Tex-Mex. Chicken burger (FIM 38) and tuna sandwich (FIM 21), both with fries, are good bets. Late afternoons, especially Thursday–Sunday, the patio is packed with Finns getting ripped. *Pohjoisesplanadi 2, tel. 90/657–700. Open daily 11 AM–4 AM, food until 11 PM. Wheelchair access.*

Kappeli. Popular among Finnish yuppies. Pizza downstairs (FIM 30–FIM 40) in hearty portions, beer upstairs and outside. *Eteläesplanadi 1, across from tourist office, tel. 90/179–242. Open daily 9–4.*

Perho Mechelin. Daily lunch deal (FIM 35) includes meat, veggies, salad, soup, and drink. Specialties are *stekt gös* (fried perch; FIM 42) and *pasta med lax och rökt renskek* (pasta with salmon and reindeer; FIM 35). Beer is overpriced. *Mechelininkatu 7, tel. 90/493–481. From Mannerheimintie, west on Arkadiankatu, left on Mechelininkatu.*

Salaattipiste. They serve only salads (FIM 20–FIM 35): Make your own or let them do it for you. *Hietalahdenkatu 10, tel. 90/607–422. From Mannerheimintie, walk down Lönnrotinkatu, left on Hietalahdenkatu. Open weekdays 9–3, Sat. 10–1.*

➤ **UNDER FIM 50 • Konstan Möljä.** Very small, very popular, and very Finnish. All-you-can-eat lunch buffets (FIM 42, FIM 50–FIM 59 on weekends) include fresh fish or meat, salad, bread, soup, and drink. *Hietalahdenkatu 14, tel. 90/694–7504. From Mannerheimintie, walk down Kalevankatu, right on Hietalahdenkatu. Open weekdays 11–4, weekends noon–6.*

WORTH SEEING

Get a feel for the city by walking on the north esplanade, **Pohjoisesplanadi,** cruising through **Kauppatori** (Market Square), or checking out the harbor. Most sights are within 3 km of the train station. The tourist office's detailed booklet "Helsinki on Foot" is helpful for background info on sights.

SENAATINTORI When Helsinki became a capital city, the Russians invited Berliner Carl Ludvig Engel, who had worked extensively in St. Petersburg, to design the buildings around the Senaatintori, (Senate Square). The graceful square is dominated by the unique **Tuomiokirkko,** a Lutheran cathedral designed by Engel in 1830 but later augmented with four green, conical towers to support the weight of its bells. The university and state council buildings around Senaatintori are also Engel's neoclassical creations. His buildings give the square a Russian feel, and you'll see other signs of Russian influence, like the statue of Czar Alexander II in front of the cathedral. In fact, so Eastern is the atmosphere that several Hollywood films, including *Reds, Gorky Park,* and *White Nights,* used this square as the site for their Russian scenes.

CHURCHES Besides the cathedral on Senaatintori (*see above*), Helsinki has two holy houses that merit a look. The ultramodern **Temppeliaukion kirkko** (Lutherinkatu 3, tel. 90/494–698), tucked away in a labyrinth of streets west of the train station, is carved from solid rock and topped with a copper dome. The church has English services Sunday at 2. The gaudy ornaments inside the redbrick cathedral **Uspenskin katedraali** (Kanavakatu 1, tel. 90/634–267; open Tues.–Fri. 9:30–4, Sat. 9–noon, Sun. noon–3) are distinctly Russian. The upstairs terrace offers a great view of the city.

GOVERNMENT BUILDINGS The 200 members of Finland's Eduskunta (Parliament) meet, quarrel, and make laws in the austere **Eduskuntatalo** (Parliament House) at Mannerheimintie 30. It was built in 1930 entirely by hand. The 1818 **Presidentinlinna** (President's Palace) at Pohjoisesplanadi 1 has been the official pad of the Finnish president since 1919; Mauno Koivisto, the current chief, took up residence in 1982. A few feet away, around the corner, is the **Päävartio** (Main Guard Post). Catch the changing of the guard and a small parade Tuesday and Friday at 1.

MUSEUMS Helsinki has more than 50 museums, and the Helsinki Card (*see* Visitor Information, *above*) gets you into most of them for free. The **Kansallismuseo** (National Museum) embraces Finnish culture and history, displaying everything from northern handicrafts to souvenirs of Russia's reign over Finland, including Czar Al's throne from 1809. *Mannerheimintie 34, tel. 90/40–501. Admission: FIM 10. Open daily 11–4.*

The **Ateneum,** Finland's largest art museum, contains Finnish and foreign art from the 18th century to the present. It has works by all the national greats (most of whom you probably haven't heard of). *Kaivokatu 2–4, tel. 90/173–361. Admission: FIM 10. Open Tues. and Fri. 9–5, Wed. and Thurs. 9–9, weekends 11–5.*

SEURASAARI This island west of the city, connected to the mainland by a footpath, is a popular place for a picnic, a stroll, or a date with a favorite novel. You can examine transplanted Finnish country dwellings and farmhouses in the Open-Air Museum, or **Ulkomuseo** (admission FIM 10, FIM 5 students; open June–Aug., Thurs.– Tues. 11–5, Wed. 11–7; May–Sept., weekdays 9–3, weekends 11–5). Tuesday, Thursday, and weekend evenings in summer, the island sees folk dances (tel. 90/484–234 for times; admission FIM 20). To reach Seurasaari, take Bus 24 from the Swedish Theater, at the junction of Mannerheimintie and the Esplanadi, to the end of the line.

SUOMENLINNA The fortress of Suomenlinna, on a small cluster of islands in Helsinki's harbor, was an active military installation until 1973, when it became a city park. The fortress makes a great day trip, with six museums; the retired, tourable World War II sub *Vesikko;* a summer theater (tel. 90/718–622); a public beach; and endless catacombs, bunkers, and rusting artillery. Bring along some beer and food and head for the easternmost point to watch the huge ferries pass. You can reach the island by public ferry (FIM 9) from Helsinki's port, near Kauppatori. Ferries leave every 20–30 minutes from 6:20 AM to 1:30 AM.

CHEAP THRILLS

At the park **Kluuvi,** northeast of the train station, you might see people playing *pesäpallo,* a distinctly Finnish version of American baseball. The areas bordering the Eläintarhanlahti waterway are popular with sunbathers and drinkers, as is the beach **Hietaniemi** (on the peninsula west of where Arkadiankatu dead-ends). The park **Sibeliuksen puisto,** northwest of the city center, is hip and mellow, and **Kaivopuisto,** south of the city center on the water (take Tram 3T) rocks with frequent outdoor concerts in summer. Check the tourist office's "Helsinki This Week" for events.

AFTER DARK

Helsinki's students stick around after finals in mid-May, making this *the* happening city during summer. Young Finns are usually hyper-stylized and coolly reserved, but nights out reveal a more relaxed side. Drinking and entrance ages are enforced, although women tend to be treated with leniency. To avoid stiff beer prices, hit up one of the state-run liquor stores, called **Alko** (Mannerheimintie 1 or Salomonkatu 1; open Mon.–Sat.), and take your purchases to one of the spots listed below. People also drink at Suomenlinna and on the cathedral steps, although alcohol is legally forbidden in public places.

Café Engel. Named for the architect responsible for Senaatintori. Mellow, somber students down cappuccino (FIM 14), espresso (FIM 11), beer (FIM 13.50), and pastries. *Aleksanterinkatu 26, across from Tuomiokirkko, tel. 90/652–776. Open weekdays 9 AM–midnight, Sat. 9:30 AM–midnight, Sun. 11–6.*

Cantina West. Live music on three floors. Overpriced food and overdone southwest U.S. decor, but a tragically hip nightspot anyway. Must be 22. Cover FIM 15 on weekends. *Kasarmikatu 23, ½ block from Eteläesplanadi, tel. 90/622–1500.*

Kaivo. Helsinki's most happening spot. A restaurant and music bar with meals for about FIM 40, occasional live music (but usually a DJ), and a friendly crowd. Minimum age is 24 (leniency and lots of it for women). FIM 30 cover on weekends. *Puistotie, northeast side of Kaivopuisto Park, tel. 90/177–881. Open Wed.–Sat. 9 PM–4 AM for dancing; terrace open summer, daily 11 AM–2 PM.*

Prunni and **Zetor.** Dance bars 30 feet apart. Both trendy, both dark, both swarming with hormones. Minimum age is 22. Beers FIM 20–FIM 25. *Kaivopihaplaza, off Mannerheimintie just north of Aleksanterinkatu, tel. 90/665–960 and 90/666–966, respectively.*

The Southwest

The southwest is Finland's quiet, hard-working agricultural region, dotted with farms and fields. Cities along the Gulf of Bothnia have industrialized since World War II, but the rest of the region remains steadfastly rural. The liveliest town is Turku, one of Finland's major ports and the site of two universities. The Åland Islands, west of Turku, offer great outdoor activities, especially bike tours.

Turku

The proud citizens of Turku feel some animosity toward Helsinki. After all, Turku used to be capital of Finland. It was home to the country's first university, and Michael Agricola, bishop of Turku, ushered the Reformation and Lutheranism into Finland. But over the span of just a few years (beginning in 1812), Turku lost its status as the capital, the university moved to Helsinki, and the town suffered a catastrophic fire. Today things look brighter: Turku's port, the number-one gateway to Finland from the Baltic, is thriving, and students at two local universities breathe life into the town. During summer vacation the pace slows, but the July Ruisrock Festival (featuring rock music) and the August Music Festival liven things up. You can reach Turku by train from Helsinki (2 hrs 15 min, FIM 90) or by ferry from Stockholm. **Viking Line** (tel. 921/63–311) and **Silja Line** (tel. 921/652–244) sail twice daily.

BASICS The **tourist office** (Käsityöläiskatu 3, tel. 921/233–6366; open weekdays 8–4) has tons of brochures in English. **American Express** (Aurakatu 14, tel. 921/610–611) has a desk at Area Travel, a half-block north of the market square. The **post office** (Humalistonkatu 7, tel. 921/63–117) contains a tiny telephone center where you can make long-distance calls and pay afterward.

WHERE TO SLEEP The nuns at **St. Birgittas Convent Guesthouse** (Ursininkatu 15A, tel. 921/501–910; singles FIM 180, doubles FIM 280) run a sterile, piously quiet place; scripture instruction is available. The **Hotel Astro** (Humalistonkatu 18, tel. 921/511–800; doubles FIM 200) has cheap, sweaty rooms circa 1970 and great hourly rates. Run by a cute older couple, **Turisti Aula** (Käsityöläiskatu 11, tel. 921/233–4484) offers smaller doubles in the same price range. Bus 8 makes the 10-km trek twice hourly to Ruissalo Island, site of a **campground** (tel. 921/589–249; FIM 30 per person; closed Sept.–May) surrounded by trim forests and beaches, including a nude one.

➤ **HOSTEL** • **Turun Kaupungin Retkeilymaja (HI).** Near the ferry terminals, 15-minute walk from the train station. Dorms FIM 35, singles FIM 95, doubles FIM 110, breakfast FIM 17. *Linnankatu 39, tel. 921/316–578. From station, walk down Käsityöläiskatu and turn right on Linnankatu, or take Bus 3. 2 AM curfew, lockout 10–3, laundry, wheelchair access, kitchen facilities.*

FOOD For fish, bread, fruits, veggies, and nonedible tourist kitsch, head for the outdoor **kauppatori,** or market square (open Mon.–Sat. 8–2), and the **kauppahalli,** or market hall (cnr. of Linnankatu and Aurakatu; open weekdays 8:30–5, Sat. 8–2). **Greenway** (Yliopistonkatu 28, tel. 921/516–566) serves veggie stews, salads, and yogurt at lunch weekdays and Saturday for FIM 75 per kilo. For a burger, try the ultra-popular **Hesburger** chain (Kristiinankatu 9) across from the market square in the Hansa shopping center. **Pinella** (Porthanin Puisto, above Tuomiokirkko bridge, tel. 921/311–102) offers a Finnish menu, with meals for about FIM 45 and a patio on the river for sun worshipers. On sunny afternoons and evenings, people traipse back and forth between Pinella and **Donna,** a stationary bar-boat ½ km west that specializes in beer and so-called *gin,* a gin-and-grapefruit-soda concoction (FIM 20).

WORTH SEEING Although locals joke that their town introduced culture to Finland and hasn't seen any since, Turku has some worthwhile attractions. If you're committed to seeing everything, pick up "Two Walking Tours in Turku" from the tourist office. More historically than visually interesting, **Turun Linna** (Turku Castle) has stood at the mouth of the Aurajoki River since 1280, undergoing renovations aplenty. There is a small **historical museum** at the site (admission FIM 15; open in summer, daily 10–6, off-season, daily 10–3).

Luostarinmäki, an artisans' colony and the sole survivor of the 1827 fire, has been turned into an open-air handicrafts museum with old-style craft and smith shops. *Tel. 921/620–350. Cross bridge on Aurakatu, turn left on Luostarinkatu. Admission: FIM 15. Open late Apr.–early Sept., daily 10–6; mid-Sept.–mid-Apr., Tues.–Sun. 10–3.*

Dating from the 13th century, **Turun Tuomiokirkko** (Tuomiokirkkotori 20, tel. 921/510–651) is the granddaddy of Finland's cathedrals and home of the national religion, Evangelical Lutheranism. The adjacent cathedral museum houses relics and a photo essay tracing the church's development. Free concerts are held here Tuesday at 8 PM in summer.

AFTER DARK At night, head for **Apteekki** (Kaskenkatu 1, tel. 921/502–595), a friendly pub in a former apothecary shop, with drug drawers intact. Or try the **Old Bank** (Aurakatu 3, tel. 921/515–700), with marble pillars and yuppies. At **1957** (Eerikinkatu 12, tel. 921/519–574) you can catch Finnish rock or jazz nightly. **Börs Club** (Kauppiaskatu 6, tel. 921/637–381; cover FIM 40 Sat.), a few doors down, is Turku's hottest dance club.

NEAR TURKU

RAUMA Rauma is the third-oldest city in Finland, and UNESCO has chosen its **old town,** full of medieval dwellings and shops, as a World Heritage Site. Ten buses a day make the 92-km trip (about 1 hr 40 min) north from Turku's bus station to Rauma for FIM 50 (FIM 60 for express service). Rauma's **tourist office** (tel. 938/344–551) is at Valtakatu 2.

The town's only budget lodging options are **HI Poroholman Retkeilymaja** and **Poroholman Camping,** which share a reception area. Dorm beds cost FIM 30, doubles are FIM 130, and camping is FIM 30 per person. *Poroholman leirintäalue, 2 km from bus station, tel. 938/224–666. From tourist office, west on Valtakatu, cross tracks, left on Syväraumankatu, left on Urheilukatu. Closed Sept.–May 14.*

Mariehamn and the Åland Islands

Composed of more than 6,000 islands—most smaller than the ferries that sail around them—the Ålands (pronounced OH-lands) lie midway between Finland and southern Sweden in the Baltic Sea. The Ålands are officially Finnish, but residents speak Swedish and identify culturally with Sweden. Most businesses accept Finnish markaa and Swedish kronor.

Ålanders, descended from Swedes, harbor no love for mainland Finns. They're Finnish citizens, but the islands' government devises its own laws, prints stamps, and flies a flag.

Named by Czar Alexander II after his wife, Maria, **Mariehamn** (population 11,000) is the only town in the island group; it lies along a narrow peninsula on the southern tip of the main island. The Storagatan/Norra Esplanaden, lined with linden trees, connects the harbors on the eastern and western sides of town. The **Åland Museum** (Storagatan, tel. 928/25–400), New European Museum of the Year in 1982, presents the area's history and culture. Also look for the **Åland Art Museum,** in the same building. A few minutes east of the museums lies **Lilla Holmen,** a beach and park accessible by footbridge and renowned for its peacocks.

Bridges and free ferries connect the islands. Biking is a great way to tour the area: You'll find flat, floral bike paths all over, and wherever you pedal you're never far from the sea. Mariehamn's **tourist office** (Storagatan 11, tel. 928/27–300) has bike-route maps and ferry schedules, and can help you find accommodations.

COMING AND GOING Mariehamn is a port of call for daily **Silja Line** ferries from Stockholm (5½ hrs; in season FIM 80, FIM 60 students and rail-pass holders; off-season FIM 50, FIM 40 students and rail-pass holders) and Turku (6 hrs; FIM 50, FIM 40 students and rail-pass holders). **Viking Line** also sails to Mariehamn from Stockholm (FIM 50, FIM 35 students) and Turku (in season FIM 115, FIM 80 students; off-season FIM 55, FIM 30 students).

In Mariehamn, **Ro-No Rent** (Osterhamn, eastern harbor, tel. 928/12–820; Västerhamn, western harbor, tel. 928/12–821) rents bikes for FIM 25 per day, FIM 125 per week. You can also pick up a Windsurfer, boat, or dune buggy here. Local buses depart from Mariehamn's **bus station,** at Strandgatan and Styrmansgatan near the eastern harbor.

WHERE TO SLEEP AND EAT Tourists raid the Ålands in summer, and cheap digs are few. The aptly named **Botel Alida** (anchored at Osterleden and Styrmansgatan, tel. 928/13–755) is a hotel on a boat, offering closets for two for FIM 140. **Strandnäs Hotel** (Godbyvägen, tel. 928/21–511) and **Adlon Sleepover** (Hamngatan 7, tel. 928/15–300) are plain hotels that won't break the bank, with singles and doubles for about FIM 220 and FIM 320, respectively. Weekdays between 9 and 5, the **Ålandsresor** (Storagatan 9, tel. 928/28–040; doubles FIM 150) books rooms in private homes. **Camping Gröna Udden** (Osternäsvägen, tel. 928/19–041), 1 km south of Storagatan and Lilla Holmen, offers cheap sites for FIM 10 per person mid-May through August.

For affordable eats, try the markets in the center of town or **Dixie Burger and Chicken Grill** (Ålandsvägen 40). **F.P. von Knorring** (Osterhamn, tel. 928/16–500) offers lunches on an anchored ship for less than FIM 40; dinner runs an additional FIM 10–FIM 20. Splurge at the restaurant in the posh **Hotel Arkipelag** (Strandgatan 31, tel. 928/13–309), where fine meals go for FIM 70–FIM 90 and a bar and disco open up after dinner.

The Lake Region

A map of Finland looks a little tattered in the southeast, like a curtain with cat-claw scratches. Here a seemingly endless series of rivers, lakes, canals, and inlets breaks up the landscape. Tiny cabins, vacation homes for thousands of Finns, surround the lakes. Somehow the railways of the Lake Region skirt the water obstacles, connecting a garland of larger cities: Tampere, Jyväskylä, Kuopio, Savonlinna, and Lahti. Water buses, cruise ships, and canoes are the most common means of transportation, and hiking and biking are good bets for a leisurely tour. The Lake Region is popular, but there's room for everybody; enough canoe routes, hiking paths, and hostels exist that you can feel relatively isolated as you travel.

Tampere

On the Lake Region's western edge, 175 km north of Helsinki, Tampere languished for years as a tiny trading post, a 4-km stretch of land between Lake Näsijärvi to the north and Lake Pyhäjärvi to the south. The town's big break came in 1820, when itinerant Scottish businessman James Finlayson harnessed the raging Tammerkoski rapids, which run through the city, to power his spinning mill. This act turned Tampere into the country's industrial center, specializing in textiles and garnering the dubious title "the Manchester of Finland." In the early 20th century, after Lenin's 1905 residential stint in Finland, communism flourished; and Tampere served as the Reds' capital during the 1918 Finnish Civil War.

Nowadays light industry and the service sector predominate. The Tammerkoski rapids are lined with fishermen and shopping malls rather than factories, and the only signs of communism are in the **Lenin-Museo,** or Lenin Museum (Hämeenpuisto 28, tel. 931/127–313). The **Amurin Työläiskort-telimuseo,** or Amuri Museum (Makasiininkatu 12, tel. 931/141–633; admission FIM 10; open mid-May–mid-Sept., Tues.–Sat. 9–5, Sun. 11–5), presents 100 years of incredibly well preserved workers' housing, and **Verkaranta** (Verkatehtaankatu 2, tel. 931/503–414;

admission free; open weekdays 9:30–6, Sat. 9–2, Sun. noon–7) displays handicrafts in a former factory. Depending on the staff's mood, you may get to spin something yourself on the upstairs loom. One of the least-visited museums in Finland, the **Finnish Ice Hockey Museum** (tel. 931/124–200) in the *Jäähalli* (Ice Rink) also hosts games.

Särkänniemi, a small peninsula jutting into Lake Näsijärvi 2 km northwest of the train station, offers an amusement park, aquarium, planetarium, art museum, children's zoo, and 551-foot observation tower, all with separate admission prices ranging from FIM 10 to FIM 30 (a FIM 100 general-admission pass gets you into everything). **Viikinsaari Island,** a 30-minute boat ride across Lake Pyhäjärvi, has beaches and raucous dancing on summer evenings. You can cruise either of Tampere's lakes for up to 10 hours; check with the tourist office for timetables and routes.

BASICS The **tourist office** (Verkatehtaankatu 2, tel. 931/126–652), on the eastern shore of the Tammerkoski south of Hämeenkatu, sells fishing licenses (FIM 35) and clarifies confusing lake-cruise schedules. **American Express** (Area Travel, Hämeenkatu 7A, tel. 931/235–360) provides limited services, including members-only mail holding, traveler's-check sales, and lost-card assistance.

COMING AND GOING Frequent trains run to Tampere from Helsinki (2 hrs, FIM 80) and Turku (2½ hrs, FIM 72). The train station is east of the Tammerkoski rapids at the end of Hämeenkatu, the main boulevard. Crammed with shops and banks, this street runs 1½ km between the train station and the tree-lined street Hämeenpuisto. Hämeenkatu crosses the Tammerkoski rapids at Hämeensilta Bridge. All local buses stop at Keskustori, the central square, ¾ km west of the train station on Hämeenkatu.

WHERE TO SLEEP Tampere has three cheap hostels, all clean, large, and uncrowded in summer. If you can't get a spot at one, try **Sportmotel** (Vuorentaustantie 5, tel. 931/444–281; doubles FIM 300), **Kauppi** (Kalevanpuistotie 2, tel. 931/535–353; doubles FIM 280), or **Victoria** (Itsenäisyydenkatu 1, tel. 931/242–5111; doubles FIM 300), in ascending order of luxury.

Domus (HI). A combination hostel and summer hotel. The latter offers kitchen and bath in each room, plus free sauna, free laundry, bike rental, and a friendly staff. Beds FIM 50, with breakfast and sheets FIM 80; doubles FIM 230. *Pellervonkatu 9, tel. 931/550–000. Follow Itsenäisyydenkatu, which becomes Sammonkatu, east from station, and turn left on Joukahaisenkatu; or take Bus 25. Wheelchair access. MC, V. Closed Sept.–May.*

Hostel Uimahallin Maja (HI). Often a family scene. Smell of smoke pervades. Beds FIM 70, singles FIM 125, doubles FIM 210, breakfast included. *Pirkankatu 10–12, tel. 931/229–460. Follow Hämeenkatu from station, right on Hämeenpuisto, left on Pirkankatu.*

NNKY Retkeilymaja (HI). Very close to the train station, this YMCA hostel is clean as can be. Beds FIM 40, singles FIM 90, doubles FIM 140, sheets FIM 25, breakfast FIM 25. *Tuomiokirkonkatu 12A, tel. 931/225–446 or 931/235–900. From station take Hämeenkatu, first right on Tuomiokirkonkatu. Reception open daily 8–10 and 4–midnight, kitchen. Closed Sept.–May.*

FOOD Pihvinki (Hallituskatu 22, tel. 931/148–082) offers hearty, home-cooked Finnish lunches for less than FIM 50. **Meidän Muori** (Rautatienkatu 16, tel. 931/244–6126), in Hotel Tampere, is great for soups and salads. Weekday lunches (FIM 35) are excellent at **Ohranjyvä** (Näsilinnankatu 15, tel. 931/127–217), and in the evening an intellectual crowd gathers here for beer. In Hotel Ilves, **Amarillo** (Hatanpään valtatie 1, tel. 931/133–131) offers decent meals (FIM 50) and a raging nighttime bar. **Freetime** (in Koskikeskus Mall, tel. 931/134–585) is another hot spot, but the outdoor **Pub Rosendahl** (Pyynikintie 13, tel. 931/244–1504) seems to be the undisputed king, especially on summer evenings.

Savonlinna

On a series of islands linked by bridges, Savonlinna (population 29,000) is small enough to get a grip on. Home to one of Scandinavia's best-preserved medieval forts, this town wows tourists, packing them in most prodigiously during July's annual **Opera Festival,** a month of evening concerts at locales in and around the city. You can order tickets by mail or phone (contact Opera Festival, Olavinkatu 35, 57130 Savonlinna, tel. 957/514–700) for FIM 200–FIM 500. Many concerts take place in the open-air theater at **Olavinlinna Castle.** Built in 1475 to protect the Swedish-Finnish empire's eastern border, the castle has seen many battles in its day but has been well preserved. Get there by way of a 50-meter bridge that spans Lake Pihlajavesi, southeast of the city center. Admission is FIM 14; the castle is open daily 10–5 from June to mid-August and daily 10–3 off-season.

Check with the **tourist office** (Puistokatu 1, off Olavinkatu, tel. 957/273–492) for lake-cruise schedules; the best is the Heinävesi route, which leaves Savonlinna's port and calls at Heinävesi village (FIM 145). The tourist office has excellent info on the entire region. Savonlinna lies off the main rail lines. Four trains run daily from Helsinki toward Joensuu; get off in Parikkala and transfer to Savonlinna. The central train station, Savonlinna-Kauppatori, is near the tourist office, one block north of Olavinkatu, the town's main artery.

WHERE TO SLEEP AND EAT Savonlinna is busy in summer, especially during the July Opera Festival. To find accommodations fast, let the tourist office reserve space for you. They'll probably suggest **HI Malakias** (Pihlajavedenkuja 6, tel. 957/23–283; doubles FIM 210; closed Sept.–June), 2 km west of the tourist office (follow Olavinkatu to Tulliportinkatu to Savonkatu). Buses 2 and 3 cruise Olavinkatu if you're too lazy to walk. **HI Vuorilinna Hostel** (Kylpylaitoksentie, tel. 957/57–500) is open only in June and the last three weeks of August. The prices are the same as at Malakias, but the location is better: behind the casino on the casino island, across the footbridge north of the market square. **Hospits Hotel** (Linnankatu 20, tel. 957/22–443; doubles FIM 220), near Olavinlinna Castle south of Olavinkatu, is a step up in comfort.

Cheap fruits, veggies, and cooked fish are peddled at the **market square,** south of Olavinkatu next to the Haapasalmi canal. You can get a homemade lunch for FIM 40 at **Lounaskahvila Annukka** (Olavinkatu 33, tel. 957/514–342), near the market square. **Majakka** (Satamakatu 11, tel. 957/21–456), a popular Finnish restaurant and pub, offers FIM 40–FIM 50 meals. **Snellman** (Olavinkatu 31, tel. 957/13–104) charges a high FIM 50–FIM 70 per meal, but it's worth the splurge. In the same building, **Nelson Pub** (tel. 957/273–104) is the place to go for an aperitif.

Northern Finland

Northern Finland is often called Europe's last wilderness, a region of vast forests, fells, and great silences. The Arctic Circle bisects the area; to the south, the port town of Oulu is surrounded by farmland, and the Kuusamo region blends Lapland's tundra with the waterways of the Lake Region. Hikers trek north to experience summer's midnight sun and the aurora borealis, leaving the train behind at Kemijärvi.

Lonely fells are punctuated only by the occasional herd of reindeer, and in winter the sun may not rise for several weeks.

The trekking gets hardest in Finland's most mountainous region, along the Norwegian border in western Lapland. The city of Rovaniemi provides the best access to western Lapland and to Sweden and Norway. Beyond the puny villages of Ivalo and Inari, north of Lake Inarinjärvi, the trees thin out and then disappear, and you'll see why Lapland is often referred to as "the other Finland"—the cultivated south bears no resemblance to this place.

Oulu

Although you wouldn't go out of your way to visit Oulu, this port town and transportation hub on the Gulf of Bothnia offers an eclectic nightlife, as well as some provocative museums and several islands. Oulu became important in the mid-18th century as a center for tar trading. It was a rough town back then; the sailors, a rowdy bunch fond of stabbing games, believed a man was only as good as his latest scar. Today the tar industry is gone, but paper and pulp help the economy thrive—you can't miss the reek of the paper factory south of the city center. The sailors are also gone, but Oulu's youth have kept their grungy spirit alive, favoring faded tattoos, leopard-skin seat covers, and greasy hair.

The **Zoological Museum** (Linnanmaa, tel. 981/353–611; admission free; open June–Aug., Tues.–Sun. 11–3, Sept.–May, Sun. 11–3 and by appointment), near the university, houses photo and taxidermy displays on Finnish wildlife and is adjacent to the two glass pyramids of the **botanical gardens.** You can learn the story of tar at the **Ainola Provincial Museum** (Ainola Park, tel. 981/375–200; admission FIM 5, FIM 2 students; open June–Aug., Mon.–Thurs. 10–6, Sat. 10–3, Sun. 11–8, shorter hrs off-season). To the west is **Tietomaa** (Nahkatehtaankatu 6, tel. 981/377–911), a sprawling science center with exhibits on aerodynamics, magnetics, and electricity. The FIM 55 admission price is worth it if you have a few hours.

Trains from Helsinki and Turku run to Oulu six to eight times daily (7 hrs, FIM 225). Within town, you'll need a bus only to reach the campground or **Turkansaari,** an island 14 km from Oulu on the Oulujoki River (take the water bus, FIM 60 round-trip). A great day trip, the island features preserved 19th-century buildings, an open-air museum, and plenty of summer festivals, including Tar-Burning Day. Usually held in late June, this festival lasts an entire week and is the busiest time of the year for the helpful staff at Oulu's **tourist office** (Torikatu 10, tel. 981/314–1295).

WHERE TO SLEEP AND EAT Affordable accommodation is practically an oxymoron in Oulu. June 2 through August, the **HI Välkkylä** (Kajaanintie 36, tel. 981/377–707 or 981/311–5247) is open for bare-bones dorm living at FIM 65 per bed. Doubles are FIM 160, breakfast FIM 25. Turn right as you leave the train station, right again on Rautatienkatu, and right on Kajaanintie. **Apollo** (Asemakatu 31, tel. 981/374–344; doubles FIM 280) and **Turisti** (Rautatienkatu 9, tel. 981/375–233; doubles FIM 260) are convenient hotels. **Eden Spa Hotel** (Vellamontie 10, tel. 981/550–4100) is too pricey to stay at but offers a beach, pool, and sauna to nonguests for FIM 50 per day. Bus 5 will take you a few km northwest to **Nallikari Camping** (FIM 30 per person, cabins FIM 230; closed Oct.–Apr.), next to lovely beaches along the Gulf of Bothnia.

Rock Club 45 (Saaristonkatu 12, tel. 981/311–5202) and **Madison** (Hallituskatu at Isokatu, tel. 981/374–522) serve beers (FIM 25) and meals (FIM 40–FIM 50) to youthful crowds. You can get a pizza for FIM 30 at **Novto** (Asemakatu 17, tel. 981/377–876). The undisputed hot spot for eating and drinking on warm afternoons and evenings is **Jumpru** (Kauppurienkatu 6). Try the **Never Grow Old Reggae Bar** (Lefkunpuisto 3, tel. 981/113–936) or **Kantakrouvi** (Uusikatu 23, tel. 981/224–355) for skanking grooves and danceable tunes, respectively.

Rovaniemi

A small metropolis 900 km north of Helsinki, Rovaniemi, the "Gateway to Lapland," is actually 300 km south of the nearest Sami (Lapp) village. Nonetheless, Rovaniemi's wealth of tourist information and its good rail connections to the south (12 hrs from Helsinki, FIM 260) make it the best headquarters for trips into Lapland. Otherwise it's a drab industrial city, which was nearly destroyed by retreating German troops in 1944.

Having little to boast about in their own town besides a few blah museums, the staff at the **tourist office** (Aallonkatu 1, tel. 960/346–270) offers tons of info on travel in Lapland, including hiking, canoeing, camping, and biking literature. **Arctic Circle Tours** (Koskenkylä, tel. 960/369–146) leads hiking, fishing, biking, and rafting trips for up to four days in the vicinity of Rovaniemi. If you're interested, call in advance to set something up, and plan to pay about

FIM 100 for night hiking and FIM 375 for a day of rafting (the owner is open to negotiation). **Lapin Safarit** (Lapland Safaris, Harrikatu 2–4, tel. 960/312–304) runs trips north of Rovaniemi. Although these trips are more touristy, they're a little cheaper than Arctic Circle Tours and don't require a minimum number of people. Boat cruises to the reindeer farm (*see below*) go for FIM 180, rafting on the Raudanjoki rapids is FIM 220, a three-hour mountain-bike excursion costs FIM 200 (bikes included), and a romantic summer-night boat cruise runs FIM 95.

Don't even think about coming to the Arctic Circle without visiting **Santa Claus Village,** destination of more than a half-million letters annually. Nine kilometers north of Rovaniemi (Bus 8 weekdays, Bus 10 weekends), the village shops and Santa's office (open summer, daily 8–8, winter, daily 9–5) entertain tourists and preach goodwill. Along the same route is a **reindeer farm,** where visitors pet and ride the indigenous deer; call 960/384–150 for an appointment.

WHERE TO SLEEP AND EAT For singles under FIM 150 and doubles at FIM 200, try one of two small pensions, **Matka-Kalle** (Asemieskatu 1, tel. 960/20–130) or **Outa** (Ukkoherrantie 16, tel. 960/312–474). Another FIM 50 will get you a room at the larger, centrally located **Aakenus** (Koskikatu 47, tel. 960/22–051). Rovaniemi's **HI Tervashonka** (Hallituskatu 16, tel. 960/344–644; beds FIM 45) is dull and smoky, with bathrooms in the hall, showers in the basement, and a FIM 25 breakfast. To get there, turn right out of the train station and walk down Hallituskatu to Rovakatu. Check-in is 6:30 AM–10 AM and 5 PM–10 PM. **Ounaskoski Camping** (Jäämerentie 1, tel. 960/345–304; FIM 30 per person), on the eastern shore of the Ounaskoski River, is open from June through August.

Carnivores can try reindeer casserole at **Torikeidas** (Lapinkävijäntie 3, tel. 960/23–630). **Oppipoika** (Korkalonkatu 33, tel. 960/20–321) is a splurge, but the chef, a professor at the culinary college, cooks great reindeer dishes for about FIM 50.

Lapland

The largest of Finland's 12 provinces, Lapland is a vast wilderness of tundra, trees, and natural parks, covering a third of the country. In summer you'll have to brave swarms of mosquitoes (consult a Finnish pharmacist for repellent) and the midnight sun (the 24-hour day starts on about June 6 north of Rovaniemi), but you'll be rewarded with excellent trekking, fishing, and canoeing.

Karhunkierros

The granddaddy of all trekking routes in Finland, the 75-km Karhunkierros (Bear's Ring) offers hikers a four- to six-day trip over spectacular, diverse Finnish topography. The trail zigzags along the Kitkajoki and Oulankajoki rivers, skims the Russian border, and meanders past awesome waterfalls. The Karhunkierros is often crowded, but it makes a good warm-up for more demanding treks in western Lapland, and you'll find plenty of campsites and wilderness huts along the way.

The village of Juuma, 50 km north of Kuusamo, makes a great base from which to take off along the route, with places to stay the night, eat, phone, and mail postcards. You can get here by bus (FIM 56) from Kuusamo, which is connected to Helsinki by rail. The Kuusamo tourist office (Torangintaival 2, tel. 989/850–2910) can provide trekking info, including a map with the route's wilderness huts. These free and sometimes crowded huts are scattered every 10 km–15 km along the route; some lack cots, so bring a sleeping pad. In summer, tent camping is another popular option.

From Rovaniemi, the region's transport hub (*see above*), two buses daily run north along the Swedish border and then head 30 km inland to **Hetta;** one bus continues north across the border to Kautokeino for Norwegian connections. Hetta's **tourist office** (tel. 9696/51–261), large for the region, can direct you on the popular 26-km trek to the Sami village of **Näkkälä.** Also look here for info on canoe rentals for one- to seven-day journeys down the Ounasjoki River.

Farther north is **Kilpisjärvi,** with the highest terrain in Finland. You can reach the town by bus every day from Hetta (change in Palojoensuu) or from Rovaniemi via Kittilä. Kilpisjärvi's main attractions are fantastic multiday treks. The **Kilpisjärven Retkeilykeskus** (tel. 9696/77–771) is a trekking center that brings hikers together and provides maps. Ask the staff about the limited lodging in the **HI Peeran Retkeilykeskus** (tel. 9696/2659; beds FIM 45), in a hard-to-find location about 20 km south of town.

Route E75 rambles north from Rovaniemi to the towns of Ivalo and Inari. Several buses a day (and plenty of thumbers) travel this road. On the way, you pass through Saariselkä, 30 km south of Ivalo, which is home to **Urho Kekkonen National Park,** one of Finland's most popular trekking parks. The routes are crowded, easy, well marked, and laden with wilderness huts. Get more info at the park's **tourist office** (tel. 9693/46–241).

Farther along the bus route, modern **Ivalo** is northern Lapland's major town. You can get regional information at the **tourist office** (tel. 9697/12–521), at the bus terminal, and at the airport, which offers daily flights to Helsinki (FIM 630). Forty kilometers farther north is **Inari,** site of the country's best museum on Lapland, the **Saamelaismuseo** (Sami Museum). Inari's **tourist office** (tel. 9697/51–193) shares its roof with the town's bank, across the street from the bus depot and ½ km from the **HI Kukkula** (tel. 9697/51–244; beds FIM 25, doubles FIM 110; closed Oct.–Dec.). Continuing along Route E75 you'll reach **Karigasniemi,** on the Norwegian border, home to **Kevo Natural Park.** A 70-km, four-day (minimum) trek runs through the Kevo River Gorge. Stay at the **HI Välimäen Retkeilymaja** (tel. 9697/61–188; beds FIM 35) before or after the trek.

FRANCE 8

Travelers on the Eurail trail would be hard pressed to avoid stopping in France.
One of the largest countries in Europe, France sits squarely in the middle of Western Europe, and, according to many of the French and assorted Francophiles, France might just as well be the center of the universe.

France has been a center of European intellectual life ever since the founding of the Sorbonne in Paris in the 13th century. Over the next few centuries, the entire Western world began to adopt the French language and aspects of French culture. Then, with the French Revolution of 1789 and Napoleon's frolic over the European continent, France established herself as a world political, as well as cultural, power—a fact the proud French obviously have not forgotten, although the rest of the world may have.

In more recent years, the tables have turned, and foreign cultures have been invading France. Young French people often emulate foreigners in the way they dress, the music they listen to, and even in their manner of speaking. The French pay exorbitantly for American clothes in thrift stores; old American Levis are the current fashion passion. Buskers sing Bob Dylan tunes in the streets and American blues bands brood in the bars. The French even give their night-clubs pseudo-English names: Le Crazy Boy, Le Nickel Chrome, Studio Circus, Le Manhattan, La Locomotive. Increasingly, the French are abandoning baguettes for Big Macs; there are currently more than 100 McDonald's in France, including a 400-seater on the Champs-Elysées.

But the French also fear the movement toward what Europeans call the Coca-Cola civilization. The older generation in particular sees the infiltration of American fads and the country's integration into the European Union (formerly the European Community) as eroding traditional French ways of life. If they aren't bemoaning the decline of traditional French music, they worry about what one writer has called "the Cheez Whiz factor," the decline of the production of pungent regional cheese. Apparently, young French people as well as the Americans and the Germans who eat French cheese prefer blander, creamier varieties. When Euro Disney opened in April 1992, the French gnashed their teeth and wondered what the world was coming to. Would Parisians actually strap on mouse ears by day and sleep in a hotel with a Wild West theme by night? It seems like they won't, and Euro Disney is reportedly losing $1 million a day.

Paris in particular illustrates the tension between the veneration of tradition and the interest in foreign cultures. To travel outside Paris and into the tiniest towns, though, is to see France in a purer form, with all its regional variations. In the south you'll find lots of recent immigrants, especially Algerians, who sometimes face hostility from members of the Front National, France's increasingly strong ultraright party. In the southwest, along the Spanish border, the

ENGLAND

*La Manche
(English Channel)*

Calai

Boulogne

Cherbourg

Fécamp

Etretat

Dieppe

Ami

Le Havre

Arromanches

Honfleur

Rouen

*Ile de
Bréhat*

Bayeux

Caen

Seine

*Ile
d'Ouessant*

Perros-Guirec

Roscoff

Mont
St-Michel

St-Malo

Giverny

Versailles

Brest

Morlaix

St-Brieuc

Dinan

Fougères

Chartres

Quimper

Rennes

O

Concarneau

Vitré

Le Mans

Cham

Lorient

Vannes

Angers

Blois

Quiberon

Belle-Ile

Nantes

Saumur

Loire

Tours

**ATLANTIC
OCEAN**

Poitiers

Ile de Ré

Niort

La Rochelle

Saintes

Limoges

Bay of Biscay

Angoulême

Périgueux

Bordeaux

Sarlat

Brive-la-
Gaillarde

Garonne

Dordogne

Rocamado

Langon

Cahors

Montauban

Albi

Bayonne

Pau

Tarbes

Toulouse

Biarritz

St-Jean-Pied-
de-Port

Carcassonne

N

—— Rail Lines

0   50 mi

0   75 km

S P A I N

ANDORRA

170

BELGIUM

Lille

Arras

Cambrai

St-Quentin

éns

Beauvais

LUXEMBOURG

Reims

Metz

Paris

Châlons-sur-Marne

Nancy

Saverne

Rhine

GERMANY

Troyes

Strasbourg

léans

Calmar

Auxerre

Mulhouse

ord

Vézelay

Belfort

Bourges

Clamecy

Dijon

Besançon

Beaune

Nevers

SWITZERLAND

Montluçon

Mâcon

Saône

Bourg-en-Bresse

Rhône

Clermont-Ferrand

Lyon

Annecy

Chamonix

Vienne

Voiron

Chambéry

ITALY

Aurillac

Le Puy

Grenoble

Rhône

Rodez

Montélimar

Millau

Orange

Nîmes

Avignon

Menton

MONACO

Arles

Aix-en-Provence

Nice

Monte Carlo

Montpellier

Cannes

Antibes

St-Raphaël

Narbonne

Marseille

St-Tropez

Perpignan

Toulon

Mediterranean Sea

Corsica

Basque people preserve their culture and their unique language, Euskaldunak, in the face of trends toward centralization. Alsace-Lorraine, on the eastern edge of France, is almost as German as it is French; and in Brittany, one of the last regions to be incorporated into France, people still occasionally speak Breton and celebrate their Celtic heritage with riotous get-togethers.

France's geography is as diverse as the people who inhabit it. The Riviera attracts an international jet-set crowd to its famous strips of sand, while the rocky coasts of Brittany and Normandy are inhabited mostly by the region's farmers and young European travelers who take advantage of the great hiking. Both the Pyrénées at the Spanish border and the Alps at France's eastern edge offer skiing and mountain biking to the people who are willing to venture off the Eurail trail. The flat farmland of the north doesn't have a lot in the way of dramatic vistas, but this is where you'll find many reminders of the two world wars. In the small towns of these regions you won't find many sights on the dramatic Eiffel Tower scale, but you will find plenty of residents who are willing to listen to your fumbling French and show you what living in France is all about.

Basics

MONEY $1 = 5.4 francs and 1 franc = $.18. The units of currency in France are the franc and the centime (1 franc = 100 centimes). We give prices with the franc value first, then the franc symbol (F), then the centime value, if any (e.g., 5F40). You might, however, also see prices given with a comma separating the number of francs and centimes (e.g. 5,40F).

Banks are usually open on weekdays from about 9 to 5, but they sometimes close for an hour or two between noon and 2. Crédit Agricole banks are occasionally open on Saturday instead of on Monday. Bank exchange rates are usually pretty good, but check to see if they charge a commission (sometimes 10F–20F). The rates at bureaux de change vary wildly, but are sometimes as good as those at the bank. For late-night transactions, check out the train stations and the most touristed areas of the city you can find, but expect to pay for not thinking ahead.

ATM machines are popping up all over France and sometimes take regular credit cards as well as bank cards. Call your bank's department of international banking to find out if your little piece of plastic will work in any French ATMs.

➢ **HOW MUCH IT WILL COST** • You can do France for about $40–$50 a day (plus transportation expenses), less if you're really frugal, more if you want to splurge on French goodies. Hotels are not a big problem for budget travelers; singles in one- or no-star hotels cost 120F–250F, doubles 200F–300F. Hostels cost anywhere between 50F and 100F per night and charge 20F–50F for a meal. A three-course meal at a cheap but good restaurant usually costs 50F–90F; lunch prices are toward the lower end. In most cafés, brasseries, and restaurants the service is *compris* (included), so they can be as rude to you as they want and still not get stiffed. Going out after dinner is how you can really go broke fast. Cover charges for nightclubs range from 60F to 120F and usually include one drink. Drinks in clubs are outrageously expensive—about 50F each—but a beer in a bar goes for 20F–40F. Train rides cost approximately 30F–50F per half-hour, a little less on long hauls; you can cross the country for about 400F–500F, less with student discounts.

GETTING AROUND **Buses,** slightly less expensive and significantly slower than the trains, are generally used only to fill in the gaps left by the rail lines. Buy tickets for short distances when you board the bus. For greater distances, you can buy the tickets in advance at the bus station.

➢ **BY TRAIN** • The railway system in France is fast, extensive, and efficient. For long distances, it's better to take the lightning-fast TGV trains. They require a reservation, which usually costs around 36F. All French trains have first- and second-class cars; second-class cars are perfectly comfortable and more likely to be filled with people you might like to talk to. First-class sleeping cars are expensive, but second-class *couchettes,* bunks that come six to

More Europe for less money.

To see the real insider's Europe, take to the roads.

To save money with the insider's car plan, call Eurodrive.

Our *low, tax-free rates* on comfortable, brand-new cars are truly all-inclusive and can save you hundreds of dollars off rental car costs.

Your own Renault car: your direct link to the "insider's" Europe of charming villages, family-run hotels, and lower prices.

Eurodrive benefits include:

- Low, tax-free rates for trips from 23 days to 6 months
- Unlimited mileage • Full insurance coverage good in 25 countries
- Minimum age of only 18 years
- Wide range of brand-new, fuel-efficient cars
- 24-hour roadside service • Thousands of satisfied customers

---

RENAULT *EURODRIVE*

l'Europe en Liberté

The Alternative to Car Rental

Call 1-800-221-1052

From Western states, call 1-800-477-7116
650 First Avenue, New York, NY 10016

Travel Agent inquiries welcome

a compartment, cost only an additional 90F. For most long-haul nighttime trips you are required to reserve a couchette or sleeping car.

EurailPasses are good in France, but if you're staying within the country, the **French Flexipass** is a better deal. A four-day pass ($175 in first class, $125 in second) can be used on any four days within a 15-day period. You can add up to five additional days for $38 a day first class, $27 second class. Take care of buying rail passes before you leave home. Once you're in France, French Flexipasses are not available, and EurailPasses are only sparsely so—try Blue Marble travel agency (tel. 1/42–36–02–34) in Paris.

Various discount cards, applicable mostly during the off-peak blue and white periods, rather than peak red period, are also available. Those under 26 years of age can get discounts with the **Carte Carrissimo.** This card gives a 50% discount during the blue period and a 20% discount during the white period, not only to the cardholder, but to as many as three companions (on condition that they, too, are under 26). The 190F card gives discounts on four tickets purchased within one year's time. The 390F card gives discounts on eight tickets under the same conditions as above. The **Carte Couple** (free) gives one person of a male-female couple a 50% discount during the blue period.

➤ **HITCHING** • In regions where American travelers are scarce (like the north), displaying a U.S. flag over your pack might help you get a ride. For organized (and expensive) hitching, contact **Allostop,** an organization that links up hitchers and riders for a membership fee (about 230F) plus roughly 30F–70F per ride. Contact their main office in Paris (tel. 1/42–46–00–66) for information and locations of branch Allostop offices.

WHERE TO SLEEP The French rate their **hotels** by the star system, ranging from no stars to four. The number of stars indicates the percentage of rooms equipped with bath or other amenities but may not be a good indication of how nice the place is. Room prices should be listed near the hotel's front door or on the wall behind the reception desk. Rooms marked *e.c.* offer only running water; rooms marked *douche* have a shower in the room; and rooms marked *douche/WC* or *bain/WC* have a shower and a toilet, or a bath and toilet in the room. *Petit dejeuner compris* means that breakfast is included in the price of the room.

Hotels are a good deal if you are traveling in twos or threes, but **hostels** are often a better deal for solo travelers. Hostels tend to be inconveniently located on the edge of town, but a few are housed in spectacular old abbeys or châteaux and are worth the trek. Hostels are officially supposed to charge 39F–45F per night, 16F for sheets, and 17F for breakfast and hold reception hours 7:30 AM–8 PM. Prices and hours vary, though, according to the whims of the managers— expect to pay 50F–100F for a bed plus 16F for sheets.

Another cheap alternative, especially in rural areas, is the **gîte d'étape.** Like hostels, gîtes usually feature dorm rooms and community showers, occasionally housed in fantastic rustic buildings. Although they are often technically reserved for hikers, budget travelers can often wheedle their way in. Some gîtes cost as little as 30F a night, but some cost up to 60F.

Some French schools rent out beds in their university **dorms** as soon as the students leave for the summer. The dorms tend to be bland and institutional, but they are sometime inhabited by real, live French students. To get a spot in one of these student dorms, contact the local **Centre Régional des Oeuvres Universitaires** (**CROUS**). We have given local CROUS telephone numbers for many towns.

Camping in France is not for those who seek peaceful seclusion among trees and streams; it's more for those who like nestling up to a family-filled caravan in a shady parking lot on the outskirts of town. Prices range from 14F per person to 60F per person. In general, showers are included and the bathroom are kept clean, but fire pits and barbecue grills are rarities.

FOOD It's not by chance that France is known as one of the culinary capitals of the world. Whether it's a 15F crêpe from a sidewalk stand at 2 AM or a 50F menu at the traditional 8 PM dinner hour, the food you find in France is good. Take care budget travelers—this is not the place to starve yourselves!

When eating out, look for the words *menu* or *prix fixe,* which generally point you to three- or four-course meals served at a special rate, often 50F–100F. The biggest money-saver, though, is eating your big meal in the middle of the day, when prices are often reduced by about a third. Restaurants operate in two shifts: Lunch is served around noon–2 and dinner around 6–11. To avoid paying 15F for bottled water, which the waiter will inevitably try to serve, order simply a *carafe d'eau* (i.e. tap water). Don't forget wine, which comes by the carafe or by the glass and usually costs less than 20F in budget restaurants.

If you don't want to go all out on a traditional French meal, look for ethnic restaurants (especially Chinese and Vietnamese) and pizzerias, both of which tend to be less expensive. Still cheaper grub can be found at sandwich and crêpe stands, which offer quick fixes for 12F–20F; order a traditional dessert crêpe or a *crêpe salée* (savory crêpe), filled with stuff like cheese, ham, or mushrooms. Bars and brasseries are good places to eat lunch and are also good spots to find sandwiches (12F–30F) and *salad composée* (28F–40F) at all hours.

Supermarkets are plentiful and offer the best prices for your basics, but small *boucheries* (butcher shops) and *fromageries* (cheese shops) will sell you *jambon* (ham) and different cheeses by the slice for about the same price. *Charcuteries* are generally delis that offer fresh salads and take-out stuff like quiche or lasagna that is sold by weight for pretty good prices.

HOLIDAYS AND FESTIVALS Bastille Day, celebrated on July 14, is France's biggest national celebration. Parades and fireworks mark the anniversary of the storming of the famous state prison in 1789, in the early days of the French Revolution. Other days when you can expect most businesses to close are: January 1, Easter Monday, May 1 (Labor Day), May 8 (VE Day—a new holiday that's not observed as widely as the others), Ascension Day (five weeks after Easter), the Monday after Pentecost, August 15 (Assumption Day), November 1 (All Saints' Day), November 11 (Armistice Day), and December 25.

BUSINESS HOURS Most museums are closed one day a week (usually Tuesday) and on national holidays. Normal opening times are from 9:30 to 5 or 6, often with a long lunch break between noon and 2. Large stores in big towns are open from 9 or 9:30 in the morning until 6 or 7 in the evening, without a lunch break. Smaller shops often open an hour or so earlier and close a few hours later, but they often close for a lengthy lunch break in between.

PHONES **Country Code: 33.** Public phones are never far away in France; you will find them at post offices and often in cafés. All French phone numbers have eight digits; an area code (16) is required *only* when calling from Paris to any place in the country outside Paris. When calling from anywhere other than Paris to Paris, dial 1, then the eight-digit number.

Almost all French phones nowadays accept only the ***télécarte,*** a handy little card you can buy at *tabacs* (tobacco shops), post offices, or Métro stations; it costs 40F for 50 units or 96F for 120 units. The digital display on the phone counts down your units while you're talking and tells you how many you have left when you hang up. Old-fashioned phones will take 50-centime, 1F, 2F and 5F coins. You can find local phone directories in all post offices; many post offices now also have directories on the computerized service Minitel. For local and national directory assistance, dial 12 on any phone.

To dial direct to another country, dial 19, then the country code, area code, and number. To use an AT&T calling card or to talk to their international operators, dial 19–00–11. You can call collect by dialing 12 for the operator and saying "*en PCV*" ("on pay say vay").

MAIL France's postal system is relatively efficient; mail takes about four to 10 days to make its way to the United States. It costs about 5F to send a letter, a little less to send postcards. Buy stamps in tabacs unless you're already headed toward a post office. Most local post offices also hold mail that is marked POSTE RESTANTE for up to 15 days. Have your pen pals address your letter with your last name first, preferably in capital letters, and make sure they include the postal code, given for most towns in this book.

EMERGENCIES Dial 17 for the **police,** 15 for an **ambulance,** and 18 for the **fire department.** For nonemergency situations, look in the phone directory for the number of the *commissariat* or the *gendarmerie,* both referring to the local police station.

Most pharmacies close at 7 or 8 PM, but the *commissariat de police* in every city has the list of the *pharmacies de garde,* the pharmacists on call for the evening. This is an emergency-only service, and you may have to go to the commissariat (rather than just telephone) to get the name. Pharmacies de garde are also often printed in the newspaper or posted on the doors of closed pharmacies.

LANGUAGE The French study English for a minimum of four years at school, so you can almost always find someone with a good grasp of the language. Starting every conversation with a few polite phrases in French will make people more willing to speak to you in English.

Paris

Paris is one of the most written about, raved about, and spat upon cities in the entire world. Droves of people have come for hundreds of years looking to inject their lives with beauty, glamour, culture, scandal, and romance. They have sung about Paris, painted her, found themselves, lost their religion, and learned how to eat well and smoke too much.

Paris is a city for sensualists. The leering gargoyles hanging over heavy doors, the smell of freshly baked croissants, the pulse of jazz through overcrowded streets, the young and old couples making out along the Seine, and that first sip of wine to start off the evening all are part of the Parisian obsession with the physical world. Paris voluptuaries explore the city during the late-night and early morning hours, when the boutiques are blessedly dark and the footsteps of party stragglers echo through the streets. When day breaks, though, Paris puts her face on. Fashionable 85-year-old matrons parade their freshly coiffed Pekingese pooches past boutique windows, spruced-up facades of medieval buildings, and artfully arranged *boulangerie* (bakery) and *pâtisserie* (pastry shop) displays. Cafés fill up, and the strong, dark coffee starts to pour, wiring up the professionals seated at little bitty tables packed along the sidewalks. All the while, tourists sweep through town, trying to see in a week what locals haven't seen in a lifetime.

All this action can be overwhelming, and you might feel this is a place where people were meant to shop, not live. But whatever Paris's shortcomings, you and a few hundred thousand other travelers will come to her in awe and admiration again this year, and will revel in an atmosphere as heady and full-bodied as a good French wine.

BASICS

VISITOR INFORMATION The multilingual staff at Paris's main tourist office, the **Office de Tourisme de Paris** (127 av. des Champs-Elysées, 8e, tel. 1/49–52–53–54; open daily 9–8), will book you a room at a not-so-cheap hotel (180F–350F) for a 20F fee. The branch offices, at the Eiffel Tower (open May–Sept. only) and each of the train stations, also book rooms and distribute brochures. For 24-hour information in English on the week's cultural events, call 1/49–52–53–56.

The **Accueil des Jeunes en France** (Reception Center for Young People in France), or AJF, is more in tune with the backpack set. These friendly folks book budget accommodations for 10F, sell ISIC cards, and can find you cheap train fares for a 20F fee. The offices are:

Beaubourg. *119 rue St-Martin, 4e, tel. 1/42–77–87–80. Métro: Rambuteau. Open summer, Mon.–Sat. 9–6; shorter hrs off-season.*

Gare du Nord. *10e, tel. 1/42–85–86–19. Métro: Gare du Nord. Open June–Oct., daily 8 AM–10 PM; Mar.–May, daily 9:30 AM–6:30 PM.*

Quartier Latin. *139 blvd. St-Michel, 5e, tel. 1/43–54–95–86. Métro: Port Royal. Open weekdays 10–1 and 1:30–6.*

AMERICAN EXPRESS Hot tip: There's a free toilet downstairs. *11 rue Scribe, 9e, tel. 1/47–77–77–07. Métro: Opéra. Open weekdays 9–5:50.*

BUCKET SHOPS **Nouvelles Frontières.** *Central office: 63 blvd. des Batignolles, 8e, tel. 1/43–87–99–88. Métro: Villiers. Open Mon.–Sat. 9–7, Thurs. until 8:30.*

Council Travel. *49 rue Pierre Charron, 8e, tel. 1/44–95–95–75; Métro: Franklin D. Roosevelt. 31 rue St-Augustin, 2e, tel. 1/42–66–20–87; Métro: Opéra. 51 rue Dauphine, 6e, tel. 1/43–25–09–86; Métro: Odéon. 16 rue de Vaugirard, 6e, tel. 1/46–34–02–90; Métro: Luxembourg.*

CHANGING MONEY During business hours you can get good rates at the banks along avenue de l'Opéra and the Champs-Elysées. The bureaus at the train stations stay open until at least 8 PM and have slightly worse rates. For late-night transactions, visit the 24-hour **Chequepoint** office (152 Champs-Elysées, 8e), or use one of the automated cash-exchange machines that are popping up all over.

EMBASSIES **Australia.** *4 rue Jean-Rey, 15e, tel. 1/40–59–33–00. Métro: Bir-Hakeim. Open weekdays 9–noon.*

Canada. *35 av. Montaigne, 8e, tel. 1/44–43–29–00. Métro: Franklin Roosevelt. Open weekdays 8:30–noon.*

New Zealand. *7 ter rue Léonard de Vinci, 16e, tel. 1/45–00–24–11. Métro: Victor Hugo. Open summer, 8:30–1 and 2–5:30, Fri. until 2.*

United Kingdom. *35 rue du Faubourg St-Honoré, 8e, tel. 1/42–66–91–42. Métro: Madeleine. Open weekdays 9:30–1 and 2:30–6.*

United States. *2 av. Gabriel, 8e, tel. 1/42–96–12–02. Métro: Concorde. Open weekdays 9–6.*

EMERGENCIES While regular pharmacy hours are about 9 to 7 or 8, **Pharmacie Derhy** (84 av. des Champs-Elysées, 8e, tel. 1/45–62–02–41) is open 24 hours. The **Hôpital Americain** (63 blvd. Victor-Hugo, Neuilly-sur-Seine, tel. 1/46–41–25–25) and the **Hôpital Anglais** (3 rue Barbès, Levallois, tel. 1/46–39–22–22) are both about a 45-minute ride outside Paris.

ENGLISH BOOKS AND NEWSPAPERS Pick up a copy of the monthly *Free Voice,* available at English-language bookstores, some restaurants, and the American Church (65 quai d'Orsay, 7e, tel. 1/47–05–07–99). English-language bookstores carry *France-USA Contacts,* which has all sorts of classified listings in English and French.

Shakespeare and Company (37 rue de la Bûcherie, 5e) and **Tea and Tattered Pages** (24 rue Mayet, 6e, tel. 1/40–65–94–35) are both havens for expatriates looking to buy used books and socialize with other Anglophones.

PHONES AND MAIL The central post office, the **Hôtel des Postes** (52 rue du Louvre at rue Etienne-Marcel, 1er, tel. 1/40–28–20–00) is open 24 hours. All post offices in Paris accept poste restante mail, but this is the place the mail will end up if it is just addressed to you, poste restante, Paris.

Almost all **phones** around Paris accept only the télécarte phone card, sold at tobacco stores. To make calls within the city, dial only the eight-digit number. To dial other French towns from Paris, you have to dial 16 before the eight-digit number; to call Paris from outside the city, dial 1 first.

COMING AND GOING

BY TRAIN Six train stations serve Paris; all have cafés, newsstands, bureaux de change, lockers for luggage, and tourist offices, and all connect to the Métro system. Trains run to Amsterdam (370F), Copenhagen (1001F), and other northern destinations from the **Gare du Nord** (10e). Trains leave **Gare de Lyon** (12e) for southern spots like Lyon (279F), Lausanne (290F–350F), and Rome (536F). **Gare d'Austerlitz** (13e) serves the southwest, including Bordeaux (285F), Toulouse (329F), and Madrid (670F). Trains from **Gare Montparnasse** (15e) head to Brittany and southwest France; daily trains run to Bordeaux (285F), Brest (298F), and Biarritz (349F). The smaller **Gare de l'Est** (10e, tel. 1/45–82–50–50) shoots trains eastward to Frankfurt (404F), Prague (829F), and Vienna (923F); and the **Gare St-Lazare** (9e) serves Normandy and London (350F–470F). Call 1/45–82–50–50 for all train information.

BY BUS **Eurolines** (3 av. de la Porte de la Villette, 19e, tel. 1/40–38–93–93) offers international bus service only. Buses may be slightly cheaper than trains but are usually slower.

BY PLANE Paris is served by two international airports: **Orly** is 14 km south of Paris, and **Charles de Gaulle** (also called **Roissy**) lies 23 km northeast of town. The handiest way to get to town from either airport is on an **Air France bus.** Buses depart from the terminals for Paris every 12–15 minutes 6 AM–11 PM. The bus from Charles de Gaulle (48F) stops at the Air France office at Porte Maillot, not far from the Arc de Triomphe, and the one from Orly (32F) runs to Invalides. You can pick up the Métro from both these points. Signs near the baggage pickup at both airports list many other transportation options.

GETTING AROUND

The Rive Gauche (Left Bank) refers to the part of the city roughly south of the Seine and includes the Sorbonne and a number of youthful, bustling neighborhoods. The Rive Droite (Right Bank), north of the Seine, is traditionally more elegant. Between the two banks you have the Ile de la Cité, where you'll find Cathédrale Notre-Dame, and the smaller Ile St-Louis.

To figure out the zip code of any point in Paris, just tack the arrondissement number onto the digits 750. For example, the zip code in the first arrondissement is 75001, in the 16th 75016.

Once you have the left and right banks figured out, move on to the *arrondissements,* or districts, numbered 1 to 20. Arrondissements 1 through 8 are the most central and contain most of the big tourist attractions, while the 9th through 20th spiral outward toward the outskirts of the city. If you plan to stay longer than a few days, buy a detailed map at a newspaper kiosk or bookstore.

BY METRO Every city should have public transportation that's as efficient as the Métro, whose stations are rarely more than a 10-minute walk from where you are. Thirteen Métro lines crisscross Paris; any station or tourist office can give you a map of them all. Métro lines are marked in the station both by number and by the names of the stops at each end of the line; find the name of the terminus toward which you want to travel, and follow the signs. To transfer to a different line, look for orange CORRESPONDENCE signs and for the line number and terminus you need. The blue and white signs that say SORTIE (exit) will lead you back above ground.

Métro trains run daily from 5:30 AM; the last train departs at 12:30 AM. Individual tickets cost 6F50, but *carnets* (books of 10 tickets) are only 39F. For longer stays, you can get an unlimited weekly pass (*carte jaune*) for 59F or an unlimited monthly pass (*carte orange*) for 209F.

Several Métro stations also act as **RER** stations; the RER rail system extends into the Paris suburbs, and the four main lines show up on Métro maps. You can use normal Métro tickets on them, unless you plan to leave the city boundaries. In this case, buy a separate ticket at the ticket booth.

BY BUS There are maps of the bus system at all bus stops; all 63 lines run Monday–Saturday 6:30 AM–8:30 PM, with limited service until 12:30 AM and all day on Sunday. The *Noctambus* (night bus) service runs 10 lines hourly 12:30 am–5:30 AM; all lines start at Châtelet, and all stops served by Noctambus have a yellow and black sign with an owl on it. For bus information, call 1/43–46–14–14.

Métro tickets are accepted on the buses. Theoretically you need two tickets, but you probably won't get caught if you travel with only one. Stamp your ticket in the machine at the front of the bus.

BY TAXI Trying to hail taxis on the street is difficult; find a major hotel or a makeshift taxi stand in a well-traveled part of the city. If you call for a taxi (try **Taxis Radio 7000,** tel. 1/42–70–00–42, or **Taxis Bleus,** tel. 1/49–36–10–10), you have to pay an additional fee for pickup.

BY BOAT During the summer, the Seine is full of *bateaux mouches* (tourist boats) that travel up and down the river, offering a running commentary in five languages. The boats' bright lights make people living along the river mad as hell, but they do show off the city at its glitziest. Board the boat for a 1¼-hour tour (30F, 40F after 8 PM) at the Pont de l'Alma. A less touristy but more expensive alternative is the **Batobus,** (tel. 1/45–56–06–25), a small boat-bus that runs between the Eiffel Tower and the Hôtel de Ville from April to September. There are five stations along the way, and you pay 12F for each station you pass, or you can get a 60F day pass that permits you to get on and off the boats all day long.

WHERE TO SLEEP

During the summer, rooms in the center of the city and in Montmartre fill up fast, but hotels near the train stations or at the edge of town nearly always have space. The tourist offices or AJF (*see* Visitor Information, *above*) will find you something in a pinch, but they can't work miracles in high season.

QUARTIER LATIN Although this student-oriented quarter in the fifth arrondissement borders the Ile de la Cité, you can still find some cheap sleeps here, especially on **rue Gay-Lussac** and the area between **rue des Ecoles** and **boulevard St-Germain.** Unfortunately, most of the hotels here are extremely popular; reserve a month ahead for all the following places if at all possible.

➤ **UNDER 200F • Hôtel des Alliés.** On the far edge of the fifth arrondissement in a working-class area. Sunny rooms with funky light fixtures look as if they were trapped in time in 1971. Singles 130F–150F, doubles 165F. *20 rue Berthollet, 5e, tel. 1/43–31–47–52. Métro: Gobelins.*

➤ **UNDER 250F • Hôtel le Central.** Friendly Spanish family offers small rooms with showers. On a tiny square near rue Mouffetard and the Panthéon. Singles 160F–180F, doubles 210F–240F. *6 rue Descartes, 5e, tel. 1/46–33–57–93. Metro: Maubert-Mutualité or Cardinal-Lemoine.*

➤ **UNDER 300F • Hôtel des Carmes.** Kitschy lobby, but big clean rooms. Reserve ahead for the cheaper, showerless rooms. Doubles 260F–420F. *5 rue des Carmes, 5e, tel. 1/43–29–78–40. Métro: Maubert-Mutualité. Wheelchair access.*

Hôtel du Progrès. Pleasant, British, multilingual proprietress. Spacious doubles with nice touches like big wood armoires. Play starving expatriate in a tiny 148F single. Doubles 240F–330F. *50 rue Gay-Lussac, 5e, tel. 1/43–54–53–18. Métro: Luxembourg. Wheelchair access.*

➤ **UNDER 325F • Hôtel Esmeralda.** Welcoming management, rooms decorated with gauzy curtains and wood furniture. The Cathédrale Notre-Dame is about five steps away. Hugely popular; often booked way in advance. Several singles only 150F per night. Doubles w/bath 310F. *4 rue St-Julien-le-Pauvre, 5e, tel. 1/43–54–19–20. Métro: St-Michel.*

ST-GERMAIN-DES-PRES Although the area around St-Germain-des-Prés has been gentrified into unconsciousness, a good number of cheap hotels have held on, retaining a bit of the atmosphere that originally attracted poor bohemians like yourself.

➤ **UNDER 200F • Hôtel des Médicis.** Sorta funky, run-down budget traveler's hangout. Solo travelers sometimes share a room if all the singles are full. Singles and doubles 140F–160F. *214 rue St-Jacques, 5e, tel. 1/43–29–53–64. Métro: Luxembourg.*

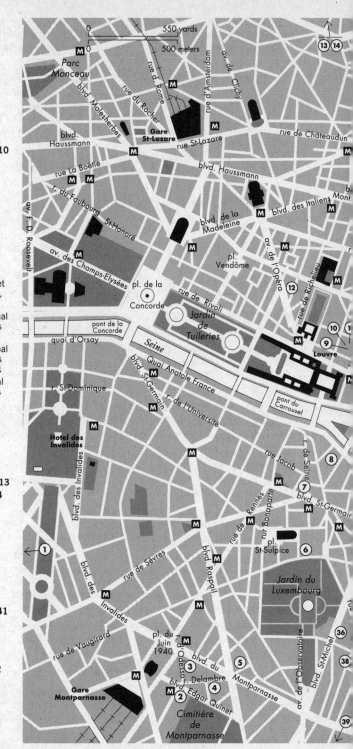

Paris Lodging

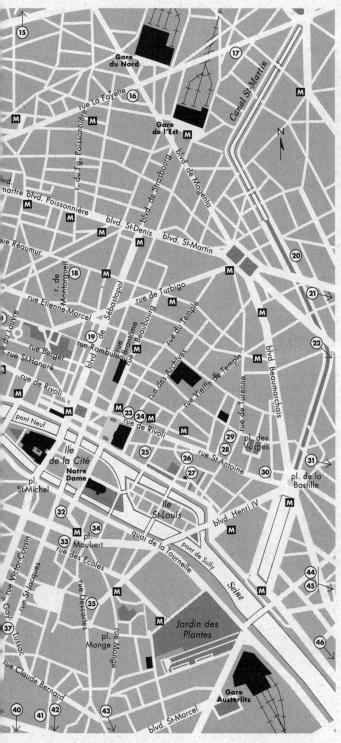

Hôtel Esmeralda, **32**
Hôtel le Central, **35**
Hôtel le Fauconnier, **27**
Hôtel le Fourcy, **26**
Hôtel Maubuisson, **25**
Hôtel Métropole Lafayette, **17**
Hôtel Pratic, **28**
Hôtel Rivoli, **24**
Hôtel Tholozé, **14**
Idéal Hôtel, **15**
Luna-Park Hôtel, **21**
Maison des Arts et Metiers, **39**
Maison des Clubs Unesco de Paris, **42**
Maison d'Etudiants, **9**
Modern's Hôtel, **45**
Three Ducks Hostel, **1**
Université de Paris Foyer International des Etudiantes, **36**

➤ **UNDER 250F** • **Hôtel des Académies.** Near Gare Montparnasse on a quiet street full of art stores and students. Decorated with art posters and flowered wallpaper. Singles 150F–200F, doubles 230F, w/shower 280F. *15 rue de la Grande-Chaumière, 6e, tel. 1/43–26–66–44. Métro: Vavin.*

➤ **UNDER 300F** • **Hôtel de Nesle.** A bohemian backpacker haven. Each individually decorated room has a theme pertaining to the history of France. Singles 200F, doubles 260F. *7 rue de Nesle, 6e, tel. 1/43–54–62–41. Métro: Odéon or St-Michel.*

Hôtel du Petit Trianon. Amazingly located, ramshackle little gem with all the street life you can stand right outside your front door. Singles 200F, doubles 300F, w/shower 320F. *2 rue de l'Ancienne Comédie, 6e, tel. 1/ 43–54–94–64. Métro: Odéon.*

MONTPARNASSE This is a great walking neighborhood, with a skyscraper, a train station, a cemetery, and Hemingway's old haunts nearby. The streets near the central area, especially **rue d'Odessa** and **rue Delambre,** are literally lined with one-star and no-star hotels.

➤ **UNDER 275F** • **Celtic-Hôtel.** On a small, interesting street. Decent, quiet rooms with real wood armoires. Doubles 200F, w/shower 240F–260F. *15 rue d'Odessa, 14e, tel. 1/43–20–93–53. Métro: Montparnasse or Edgar-Quinet.*

Hôtel Domance. Calm, quiet hotel, a two-minute walk from Montparnasse train station. Welcoming proprietress, dark lobby, and genuinely pretty rooms. Singles 200F, doubles w/shower 250F. *17 blvd. Edgar Quinet, 14e, tel. 1/43–20–63–15. Métro: Edgar Quinet.*

➤ **UNDER 325F** • **Hôtel Delambre.** Artist André Bréton's former home. If you have a sensitivity to certain color schemes, let them know in advance. Singles 250F, doubles w/bath 320F. *14 rue Delambre, 14e, tel. 1/43–20–66–31. Métro: Edgar Quinet.*

LES HALLES AND BEAUBOURG There's no area of Paris quite like Les Halles, with its blend of punk stores, hustlers, street musicians, and packs of pouty young people. It's not exactly tranquil, but it's near Paris's museums and raging nightlife.

➤ **UNDER 300F** • **Grand Hôtel de Besançon.** Clean, fairly quiet, and practically in the center of Paris. Rooms on the street get sun but more noise. Singles and doubles w/bath 280F–320F. *56 rue de Montorgueil, 2e, tel. 1/42–36–41–08. Métro: Les Halles.*

Hôtel de la Vallée. Come for the most bohemian of Parisian experiences; prostitutes and punk rockers hang out near the front door. Near lots of cheap food stands. Singles and doubles 220F–300F. *84 rue St-Denis, 1er, tel. 1/42–36–46–99. Métro: Châtelet-les-Halles.*

LE MARAIS This one-time home of aristocrats evolved into the home of Paris's tenements, and it's now considered the home of the hip. Although this neighborhood in the fourth arrondissement is between the pricey Ile de la Cité and Beaubourg, its little winding streets still harbor a number of small no-star hotels.

➤ **UNDER 150F** • **Hôtel Rivoli.** Not many decorative touches or frills, but decent and cheap. Rooms facing rue de Rivoli can be noisy, so ask for one overlooking the smaller street. Singles and doubles 130F, w/shower 160F–190F. *44 rue de Rivoli, 4e, tel. 1/42–72–08–41. Métro: Hôtel-de-Ville.*

➤ **UNDER 250F** • **Grand Hôtel du Loiret.** Really well-located old hotel is appealing in its shabbiness. Singles 150F–200F, doubles w/shower 250F. *8 rue des Mauvais-Garçons, 4e, tel. 1/48–87–77–00. Métro: Hôtel-de-Ville.*

Hôtel Pratic. Mismatched decor in clean, quiet rooms. Ask for a north room that looks out on the place St-Marché. Singles 180F, doubles 220F, 260F w/bath. *9 rue d'Ormesson, 4e, tel. 1/48–87–80–47. Métro: St-Paul.*

➤ **UNDER 400F** • **Grand Hôtel Jeanne-d'Arc.** Large, pretty rooms look like a room at grandma's house—if you have a French grandma, that is. All rooms have telephone, toilet, and bath or shower. Doubles 360F–425F. *3 rue Jarente, 4e, tel. 1/48–87–62–11. Métro: St-Paul. Wheelchair access.*

BASTILLE The Bastille, spreading over the 11th, 12th, and 4th arrondissements, is becoming increasingly hip. Ethnic neighborhoods harbor plenty of cheap hotels, cool cafés, reasonably priced restaurants, and Paris's up-and-coming artists.

➤ **UNDER 200F** • **Hôtel de la Herse d'Or.** Cavernous entryway leads to simple rooms. Managers often chat with their friends in the cozy lobby/dining area. Singles and doubles 190F, 250F–270F w/bath. *20 rue St-Antoine, 4e, tel. 1/48–87–84–09. Métro: Bastille.*

Luna-Park Hôtel. A little run-down, but convenient, safe, and near cheap food. An easy walk from Père Lachaise cemetery. Singles and doubles 170F–200F. *1 rue Jacquard, 11e, tel. 1/48–05–01–21. Métro: Parmentier.*

9TH AND 10TH ARRONDISSEMENTS The main draw of this area is its proximity to the Gare de l'Est and Gare du Nord. There aren't any major attractions here, but if you just want to drag your sorry ass into the nearest bed after that 36-hour ride from Istanbul, the following places will seem like heaven.

➤ **UNDER 150F** • **Hôtel Métropole Lafayette.** Smack in the middle of the street in a lively part of the 10th. It's loud, but also cheap, clean, and run by managers with a sense of humor. Singles and doubles 100F–250F. *204 rue La Fayette, 10e, tel. 1/46–07–72–69. Métro: Louis Blanc or Gare de l'Est.*

➤ **UNDER 200F** • **Hôtel du Brabant.** Clean and peaceful rooms with wood furniture, a tiny tiled sink and bidet area, and marble faux-fireplaces. Welcoming proprietor takes a lot of tour groups. Doubles 190F. *18 rue des Petits Hotels, 10e, tel. 1/47–70–12–32. Métro: Gare du Nord or Gare de l'Est.*

MONTMARTRE This area north of the city center is a crazy mix of sex shops, tourist traps, and old-style Paris. Although not exactly centrally located, it's a great base if you want a concentrated taste of many of the city's personalities.

➤ **UNDER 150F** • **Hôtel Tholozé.** Basic but good-size rooms with lumpy beds. Grumpy management doesn't speak English but rents some of the cheapest rooms in Montmartre. Triples (300F) and quads (350F) are a good deal. Singles and doubles 120F–180F. *24 rue Tholozé, 18e, tel. 1/46–06–74–83. Métro: Abbesses.*

➤ **UNDER 200F** • **Idéal Hôtel.** With 120F singles, it's a great deal for solo travelers, even though your hosts may need a gentle reminder to replenish the toilet paper. Doubles from 160F. *3 rue des Trois Frères, 18e, tel. 1/46–06–63–63. Métro: Abbesses.*

➤ **UNDER 250F** • **Hôtel André Gill.** Quiet hotel in a courtyard. Kitsch-o-rama lobby precedes clean and pleasant rooms, some with stained-glass windows. Doubles 240F. *76 rue des Martyrs, 18e, tel. 1/42–62–48–48. Métro: Pigalle or Abbesses. Wheelchair access.*

GARES DE LYON AND AUSTERLITZ From the Gare de Lyon, head straight on **rue de Lyon** and veer off on all the little streets that intersect it to shop around for a hotel. From either Gare de Lyon or Gare Austerlitz, try quiet, carless **rue d'Austerlitz,** which is packed with cheap, clean hotels.

➤ **UNDER 200F** • **Hôtel de Marseille.** Service is good at this family-run place that couldn't be closer to the Gare de Lyon. Doubles 170F–270F. *21 rue d'Austerlitz, 12e, tel. 1/43–43–54–22. Métro: Gare de Lyon.*

Modern's Hôtel. A few doors down from the Hôtel de Marseille (*see above*). Clean, quiet, and well run. Singles and doubles 130F–210F. *11 rue d'Austerlitz, 12e, tel. 1/43–43–41–17. Métro: Gare de Lyon.*

HOSTELS AND FOYERS Even at the height of tourist season you ought to be able to find a room in one of Paris's many hostels or the similar *foyers.* Both hostels and foyers are a mixed lot; some are rather spartan while others are more upscale, housed in great historic buildings. They're a good option if all the cheapest hotels in the city are booked or if you're traveling solo.

➤ **HOSTELS** • There are two **HI hostels** in Paris, three in the summer, when a dorm within the Cité Universitaire opens. If you want to buy a hostel card (100F) or a sleep sack, or get the lowdown on hostels throughout France, stop by one of Paris's three **FUAJ** offices. *27 rue Pajol, 18e, tel. 1/46–07–00–01; Métro: La Chapelle. 10 rue Notre-Dame de Lorette, 9e, tel. 1/42–85–55–40; Métro: Le Peletier. 9 rue Brantôme, 3e, tel. 1/48–04–70–40; Métro: Châtelet/Les Halles.*

Auberge de Jeunesse d'Artagnan. Enormous, spotless place only steps away from Père Lachaise. Loud and crowded in summer, with an intensely social bar and cafeteria. Beds with breakfast and sheets 100F–125F. *80 rue Vitruve, off rue Davout, 20e, tel. 1/43–61–08–75. Métro: Porte de Bagnolet. Lockout 10–2, laundry, wheelchair access.*

Auberge de Jeunesse Jules Ferry. Come early and be ready to socialize. Cheap food and groceries are nearby but breakfast is included in the 100F price. Bring your own sheets. *8 blvd. Jules-Ferry, 11e, tel. 1/43–57–55–60. Métro: République. Lockout 10–2, luggage lockers 5F.*

Maison des Arts et Métiers. Open mid-July to mid-September only. Ugly concrete building on a wooded campus. Three-night minimum. Singles 100F. *1 av. Pierre-Masse, 14e, tel. 1/42–53–51–44. Métro/RER: Cité Universitaire. 60 beds. 1 AM curfew, sheets 20F.*

Three Ducks Hostel. Boisterous private hostel; no card required. Crowded, mostly with Americans; book ahead between May and October by sending payment for the first night. Beds 85F (in rooms for two–six). *6 pl. Etienne-Pernet, 15e, tel. 1/48–42–04–05. Métro: Commerce. 1 AM curfew, lockout 11–5, laundry next door, kitchen facilities.*

➤ **FOYERS** • You can't book ahead at **UCRIF foyers,** so show up as early as you can at your foyer of choice or inquire about space at the **Centrale de Réservation** (20 rue J.J. Rousseau, 1er, tel. 1/42–36–88–18 or 1/40–26–66–43), a few blocks north of the Louvre. UCRIF's standard foyer is set up in rooms of one to eight beds with free showers, TV lounges, and study rooms. Beds in dorms cost about 100F per night with breakfast; add 10F–40F to stay in a single or double. All have a 2 AM curfew, a 9 AM–2:30 PM lockout, 10F luggage lockers, and 50F meals. The foyers are open to those between 18 and 35 years of age.

BVJ Centre International de Paris/Les Halles. *5 rue du Pelican, 1er, tel. 1/40–26–92–45. Métro: Louvre.*

BVJ Centre International de Paris/Louvre. *20 rue J.J. Rousseau, 1er, tel. 1/42–36–88–18. Métro: Louvre, Châtelet-les-Halles, or Palais Royal.*

BVJ Centre International de Paris/Opera. *11 rue Thérèse, 1er, tel. 1/42–60–77–23. Métro: Pyramides or Palais Royal.*

BVJ Centre International de Paris/Quartier Latin. *44 rue des Bernardins, 5e, tel. 1/43–29–34–80. Métro: Maubert-Mutualité.*

Set up in medieval aristocratic palaces and 18th-century hôtels, the **MIJE foyers** are nicer than most hotels you're likely to stay in. Conveniently situated in the Marais, near Notre-Dame, and near Les Halles, the foyers have rooms of two to eight beds; 115F per night includes sheets and breakfast. Telephone reservations aren't taken, but you can reserve in person one week in advance or show up soon after 7 AM on the morning you want to stay. All have a 1 AM curfew, enforce a lockout between noon and 2 PM, and serve 50F meals. The maximum stay is seven nights. The Hôtel le Fauconnier (*see below*) distributes information about the MIJE foyers and takes care of group reservations.

Hôtel le Fauconnier. *11 rue du Fauconnier, 4e, tel. 1/42–74–23–45. Métro: St-Paul.*

Hôtel le Fourcy. *6 rue de Fourcy, 4e, tel. 1/42–74–23–45. Métro: St-Paul.*

Hôtel Maubuisson. *12 rue des Barres, 4e, tel. 1/42–74–23–45. Métro: St-Paul or Hôtel-de-Ville.*

Some other foyers run by different organizations are:

Centre d'Accueil et d'Animation Paris, 20ème. Dorm beds 97F, singles 136F. *46 rue Louis Lumière, 20e, tel. 1/43–61–24–51. Métro: Porte de Bagnolet.*

Centre International de Séjour de Paris Kellermann. Dorm beds 97F, singles 140F–170F. *17 blvd. Kellermann, 13e, tel. 1/44–16–37–38. Métro: Porte d'Italie. Wheelchair access.*

Centre International de Séjour de Paris Maurice Ravel. Dorm beds 97F, singles 143F. *6 av. Maurice Ravel, 12e, tel. 1/44–75–60–00. Métro: Porte de Vincennes. Wheelchair access.*

Foyer International d'Accueil de Paris Jean Monnet. Dorm beds 115F, singles 240F. *30 rue Cabanis, 14e, tel. 1/45–89–89–15. Métro: Glacière. Wheelchair access.*

Maison des Clubs Unesco de Paris. Dorm beds 110F, singles 150F. *43 rue de la Glacière, 13e, tel. 1/43–36–00–63. Métro: Glacière.*

STUDENT HOUSING CROUS opens some of its student residences to travelers during the summer. Singles and doubles usually cost 62F–75F; meals served in university restaurants cost 24F. The three best (i.e., least institutional) are listed below. To find out what's available, go to the central CROUS office on the ground floor of the Résidence Jean Sarrailh. *39 av. Georges Bernanos, 5e, tel. 1/40–51–36–00. Métro: Port Royal. Office open weekdays 9–5.*

Association des Etudiants Protestants de Paris. Large, old foyer across from Jardin de Luxembourg. Dorm beds 75F, singles 93F, doubles 172F. No lockout or curfew, and you can stay a whole five weeks. Show up early; the office opens at 8:45, and they don't take reservations. *46 rue de Vaugirard, 6e, tel. 1/43–54–31–49. Métro: Mabillon or St-Sulpice. Kitchen facilities.*

Maison d'Etudiants. A fabulous mansion with a flower-filled courtyard and beds for 100F a night. Three-night minimum stay. Near the Louvre. *18 rue J.J. Rousseau, 1er, tel. 1/45–08–02–10. Métro: Louvre. Luggage storage. Reception open 11 AM–6:30 PM. Closed Sept. 15–June 15.*

Université de Paris Foyer International des Etudiantes. Old wood and iron building with a rooftop terrace, theater, and cafeteria. Singles only, 154F per night with breakfast. *93 blvd. St-Michel, 5e, tel. 1/43–54–49–63. Métro: Port Royal. Laundry facilities, kitchen.*

FOOD

To find out how the Parisians eat so well, shop at the *boulangeries* (bakeries), *boucheries* (butcher shops), and *pâtisseries* (pastry shops) found in every residential area of the city. Then, stop by the outdoor markets to finish your grocery shopping. A combination of stands and permanent shops are set up at the south end of **rue Mouffetard** (5e), on **rue de Buci** (6e), on **rue Lepic** in Montmartre, on **rue Daguerre** (14e), at **place Monge** (5e) and on **rue d'Aligre** (12e), near Bastille.

Monoprix and **Prisunic,** two large, budget department store chains, have supermarkets inside. The Prisunic (109 rue de la Boétie, 8e, tel. 1/42–25–27–46) on the Champs-Elysées stays open until midnight; Monoprix (there's one at 21 av. de l'Opéra) stores are open Monday–Saturday 9–8.

Baguettes and cheese are okay for a while, but don't forget to treat yourself to a real meal every now and then. Try traditional French fare at one of the city's ubiquitous bistros, or go out for great ethnic food, especially Moroccan and Vietnamese. The homesick can even find Chicago pizza and New York bagels.

QUARTIER LATIN The large student population ensures that there are plenty of reasonable restaurants here, especially off **rue de la Montagne Ste-Geneviève. Rue Mouffetard,** which winds its way down from the Panthéon, is also a good, though more touristy, street. During the day, students and professors eat inexpensive meals at brasseries around the **Faculté des Sciences** (Métro: Jussieu). Avoid jacked-up prices by staying off boulevard St-Michel.

Al Dar. A deli attached to a Lebanese restaurant. Sandwiches 20F, plates featuring falafel 24F, and chicken sausage 39F–50F. *8–10 rue Frédéric Sauton, 5e, tel. 1/43– 25–35–62. Métro: Maubert-Mutualité.*

For the best ice cream and sorbet in Paris (9F–12F a scoop), head to Berthillon (31 rue St-Louis-en-l'Ile) on the Ile St-Louis. Be adventurous and try chestnut, ginger, lychee, or rose-petal ice cream.

Le Jardin des Pâtes. Fresh pasta (44F–69F) made from corn, wheat, rice, or rye served with sublime sauces. *4 rue Lacépède, 5e, tel. 1/43–31–50–71. Métro: Monge. Closed Mon., except in Aug.*

La Petite Légume. Vegetarian restaurant with many vegan dishes. Grains with mixed vegetables 38F, miso soup 28F, vegetarian platter (tofu, salad, vegetables, rice, and dried fruits) 60F. *36 rue des Boulangers, 5e, tel. 1/40–46–06–85. Métro: Jussieu. Closed Mon.*

ST-GERMAIN-DES-PRES The area around place St-Germain-des-Prés is a curious mix of students, street performers, tourists, and people who go shopping for a living. Good streets to scope out include **rue Monsieur-le-Prince,** where you'll find many Japanese and Chinese restaurants, and **rue des Cannettes,** near place St-Germain-des-Prés.

Le Coffee Parisien. Serves *real* brunch, like eggs Benedict (70F), pancakes (50F), and eggs Florentine (65F), as well as burgers and big salads. *7 rue Perronot, 7e, tel. 1/40–49–08–08. Métro: St-Germain-des-Prés. Closed Aug.*

Cosi. Combine a fancy sandwich (30F–46F) on fresh-baked focaccia, a glass of wine (14F–20F), modern decor, and opera music in the background, and voilà: French delicatessen. *54 rue du Seine, 6e, tel. 1/46–33–35–36. Métro: Odéon.*

Orestias. Friendly Greek family shouts at you and each other while serving up a substantial three-course meal featuring grilled meats and desserts like flan or baklava for 44F. *4 rue Grégoire-de-Tours, 6e, tel. 1/43–54–62–01. Métro: Odéon. Closed Sun.*

MONTPARNASSE Montparnasse is near St-Germain-des-Prés and, by association, gets to charge high prices, but also has lots of fast food. Many people from Brittany have settled in this area, so crêperies are particularly popular here.

Café Pacifico. Crowded with hip mescal drinkers in a neo-Californian setting. Snacks are free and drinks are half-price weekdays 6–7:30; the 72F lunch menu is another good bet. *50 blvd. Montparnasse, 15e, tel. 1/45–48–63–87. Métro: Montparnasse-Bienvenue. Open Tues.–Sun. noon–2 AM. Closed late Aug.*

Crêperie du Manoir Breton. Local joint where staff in traditional Breton clothing serve a 57F menu of dinner, dessert crêpes, and cider, wine, juice, or beer. *18 rue d'Odessa, bet. blvd. Montparnasse and blvd. Edgar Quinet, 14e, tel. 1/43–35–40–73. Métro: Montparnasse-Bienvenue. Wheelchair access.*

New York Speed Rabbit. Homesick Americans eat deep-dish pizza (52F–82F for two people), "Malibu salad" (coleslaw with chicken, cheese, and corn, 39F) and frozen yogurt (34F). Get food to go, or call for free delivery. *47 blvd. Montparnasse, 6e, tel. 1/45–44–28–81. Métro: Montparnasse-Bienvenue. Wheelchair access.*

NEAR THE CHAMPS-ELYSEES Prices here are higher than high, but try **Rue du Colisée,** off the Champs-Elysées, for cheaper Greek sandwiches and cafés. Otherwise, pack a picnic for the Parc de Monceau.

Chicago Pizza Pie Factory. Cure homesickness with some Chicago pizza and a few happy-hour half-price drinks (daily 6–8) while watching baseball and football games. *5 rue de Berri, 8e, tel. 1/45–62–50–23. Métro: George V.*

LES HALLES AND BEAUBOURG This area has everything from Kentucky Fried Chicken to Greek food, crêpes, and American-style eateries. Take-out stands, especially North African and Greek, sell food for bargain-basement prices. Classier joints are closer to the Beaubourg center.

Dame Tartine. A restaurant-cum-art-gallery next to the Beaubourg center and facing the Stravinsky Fountain. Serves *tartines* (open-faced sandwiches); the 30F *poulet aux amandes* (chicken with almonds) is the best. *2 rue Brisemiche, 3e, tel. 1/42–77–32–22. Métro: Rambuteau or Les Halles. Wheelchair access.*

Panini Sandwiches à Emporter. Panini's fresh hot sandwiches are a step above your average street fare. Try the Napoli (14F), grilled with mozzarella cheese and tomatoes. *65 rue Rambuteau, 3e, tel. 1/40–29–08–98. Métro: Rambuteau. Wheelchair access.*

LE MARAIS The Marais has more restaurants than you could eat your way through in a year, from falafel stands in the Jewish district (especially along **rue des Rosiers**) to tapas bars and ritzy vegetarian restaurants. To discover restaurants so off-the-beaten-track that even we haven't found them, poke around **rue Vieille du Temple, rue du Temple,** and **rue des Francs-Bourgeois.**

Chez Marianne. A restaurant/deli that serves Jewish specialties from Central Europe and Israel. Sampler platters (55F–75F) let you try stuff like herring in cream sauce, egg salad, hummus, and baba ghanouj. *2 rue des Hospitalières-St-Gervais, 4e, tel. 1/42–72–18–86. Métro: St-Paul.*

Le Gamin de Paris. Candlelight and accommodating service accompany appetizers (22F–60F) and main dishes like beef fillets with shallots (86F) and roast duck with figs and raisins (86F). Weekday lunch special costs 44F. *49 rue Vieille du Temple, 4e, tel. 1/42–78–97–24. Métro: St-Paul. Reservations required for dinner.*

BASTILLE The Bastille area is one of the best for wandering around and finding reasonably priced, potentially trendy restaurants. **Rue de la Roquette** is lined with wine bars, Tex-Mex stands, and pizza joints. **Rue Oberkampf** is good for Greek and North African sandwich shops and excellent couscous.

La Canaille. Rabble-rousers came to this artsy joint to eat, drink, and sing protest songs in the '60s. The singing is on the wane, but the generous 80F lunch and 90F dinner menus offer lots of choices. *4 rue Crillon, 4e, tel. 1/42–78–09–71. Métro: Sully-Morland or Bastille. Closed weekend lunch.*

Le Temps des Cérises. A co-op named after "The Time of Cherries," a song whose words you can read off the restaurant walls. Squeeze in with the locals for a 58F menu. *31 rue de la Cérisaie, 4e, tel. 1/42–72–08–63. Métro: Sully-Morland. Closed Sat. dinner, Sun., and Aug.*

9TH AND 10TH ARRONDISSEMENTS The ninth and 10th arrondissements include some of the ritziest streets of Paris and a few of sleaziest. Eating around the Opéra can be unbearably pricey, but at the edges of the 10th, the food gets more affordable and the streets more deserted.

Chez Papa. Boisterous waitresses serve southwestern French food to crowds of rowdy patrons. *Boyardes,* huge bowls of salad packed with potatoes, egg, and ham, cost a piddling 36F–38F; piping hot *escargots papa* are 49F. *206 rue Lafayette, 10e, tel. 1/42–09–53–87. Métro: Louis Blanc.*

Hollywood Canteen. Young James Dean wanna-bes serve Gary Cooper and Marilyn Monroe burgers (25F–40F) with cherry Cokes (16F). Sunday brunch (65F) includes bacon and eggs, pancakes, and waffles. Other Hollywood Canteens Americanize the first, fifth, eighth, ninth, and 11th arrondissements. *18 blvd. Montmartre, 9e, tel. 1/42–46–46–45. Métro: Montmartre. Wheelchair access. Open daily 9 AM–2 AM.*

MONTMARTRE AND PIGALLE Montmartre overflows with reasonably priced restaurants of all kinds, especially along **rue des Trois Frères,** which winds down to boulevard de Rochechouart. **Rue Lepic,** leading north from place Blanche, has some of the best food shops in the city. The area around Pigalle in the ninth arrondissement is packed with fast-food chains both all-American and North African. As you head south from Pigalle, especially along **rue Montmartre,** you'll see lots of Greek restaurants and little markets.

Haynes. The first American restaurant in Paris, serving up soul food and southern fried chicken (65F) to expatriates since 1949. *3 rue Clauzel, 9e, tel. 1/48–78–40–63. Métro: St-Georges. Closed Sun.–Mon. and Aug.*

La Pignatta. More of a deli than a restaurant. Fresh pizzas for two 30F–40F, hot sandwiches on focaccia 18F–22F. *4 rue des Abbesses, 18e, tel. 1/42–55–82–05. Métro: Abbesses.*

CAFES Cafés are required to post a *tarif des consommations*—a list that includes prices for the basics: *café* (regular coffee), *café crème* (coffee with hot milk), *demi pression* (beer), and *vin rouge* (red wine). They list two prices, one *au comptoir* (at the counter) and the other *à terrasse* (seated at a table). If you just need a quick cuppa java, take it at the counter and save yourself a lot of money. If you have a rendezvous, take it at the table and hang out as long as you like. People have written entire masterpieces in cafés over one tiny little cup of coffee. Or maybe two.

Au Père Tranquille (cnr. of rue Pierre Lescot and rue des Prêcheurs in Les Halles, 4e, tel. 1/45–08–00–34) is flashy and expensive (with 15F coffee), but its terrace is one of the more inviting places around Les Halles to have a drink. The unusually cheery proprietress at **Brulerie de l'Odéon** (6 rue Crébillon, 6e, tel. 1/43–26–39–32; closed Sun. and Aug.) serves gourmet coffees (8F) and teas in an old-fashioned café. Across the street from the Jardin du Luxembourg, **Café au Petit Suisse** (9 rue Corneille at rue Vaugirard, 6e; closed Sun. and Aug.) nurtures students, starving writers, and other locals. Café is 8F. **Les Enfants Gâtés** (43 rue des Francs-Bourgeois, 4e, tel. 1/42–77–07–63) features low lights, ceiling fans, and easy chairs—a great location for literary types who pretend to be inspired by Parisian cafés. Café is 15F, pastries 40F. A *salon du thé* (tea salon) inside one of the largest mosques in Europe, **La Mosquée** (19–39 rue Geoffroy-St-Hilaire, 5e, tel. 1/43–31–18–14) is intricately tiled and decorated with Moroccan wood carvings and tapestried benches. Café or sweet mint tea goes for 9F. Garrulous waiters, an old wooden mirrored bar, and outdoor seating among the cherry trees attract lots of university students to **La Palette** (43 rue de Seine, 6e, tel. 1/43–26–68–15) at night. Café is 8F. **La Pause** (41 rue de Charonne, 11e, tel. 1/48–06–80–33) is visited by a significant but not overwhelming contingent of types who ride their motorcycles on the sidewalk. An outdoor terrace overlooks rue de Charonne. Café is 7F50, sandwiches 21F–29F.

WORTH SEEING

The center of the city is quite walkable, and Parisian street life—its glamour, its leisurely pace, its little piles of doggie doo on sidewalks—is an important element of any visit to Paris. Try to make time for a little aimless wandering and some late-night or early morning exploring. Afterward you'll probably become one of those stereotypical people who rave about how beautiful Paris is—as if we didn't know.

ARC DE TRIOMPHE Never one particularly renowned for his subtlety or his modesty, Napoleon I commissioned this monument to his military prowess. In 1815, when Napoleon met his Waterloo, the Arc de Triomphe was only half-finished, but it was completed in 1836. Rude's *La Marseillaise,* depicting the uprising of 1792, resides here, along with a bunch of 19th-century sculptures. An unknown soldier is buried underneath the monument, and some city employee lights a flame on his grave every day at 6:30 PM. Climb the Arc for a view of Paris as Baron Haussmann must have envisioned it—from far above. *Pl. Charles de Gaulle-Etoile. Métro: Charles de Gaulle-Etoile. Admission: 31F, 20F students. Open Sun.–Thurs. 10–5:30, Fri. 10–9:30.*

BASILIQUE DU SACRE-COEUR Also known as the Taj Mahal of Paris or That Huge White Thing on the Hill, Sacré-Cœur is a mix of Romanesque and Byzantine architecture, with saints, gargoyles, and crosses thrown in for good measure. It annoys purists, but so do a lot of Parisian landmarks. You might want to wait before you make your own judgment until dusk, when the bleached facade begins to glow pink. *35 rue du Chevalier de la Barre, tel. 1/42–51–17–02. Métro: Anvers. Admission to tower: 15F. Open summer, daily 9–7; winter, daily 9–6.*

CENTRE BEAUBOURG The Beaubourg, otherwise known as the **Centre National d'Art et de Culture Georges-Pompidou,** is easily recognizable: It's the huge structure that looks like God turned it inside out, then went to town on it with her Crayolas. The building displays all the machinations that are usually safely hidden away; the water mains are green, the air-conditioning ducts blue, and the electricity cables yellow, just as they appear on architectural drawings.

The **B.P.I.** (Bibliothèque Publique de l'Information), a two-level library in the Centre Beaubourg, has books, videos, newspapers, and magazines from all over the world. The **Musée National d'Art Moderne** (*see* Museums, *below*) on the third and fourth floors has the largest collection of modern art in the world. Then you've got the **C.C.I.** (Centre de Création Industrielle), which features temporary exhibits on architecture and environmental design, and the **Salle Garance,** which hosts all kinds of film festivals and nightly movies. And, finally, in front of the center, sword swallowers, mimes, fire jugglers, and scruffy types with guitars compete for attention and francs. *Pl. Georges-Pompidou, tel. 1/44–78–12–33. Métro: Rambuteau. Admission to building free; museum: 30F, 20F under 25, free Sun. 10–2; Salle Garance: 25F; contemporary galleries: 20F. One-day pass for entire center: 57F, 40F under 25. Open Mon. and Wed.–Fri. noon–10, weekends 10–10.*

EIFFEL TOWER Stuck safely at the western end of the city, where Parisians don't have to deal with it too often, the Eiffel Tower bristles with television and radio transmitters. It was its potential as a radio antenna, rather than its beauty, that prevented it from being torn down in the early 1900s. Gustave Eiffel built the thing for the 1889 World's Fair, and it has since served as a weather tower during World War II and the chosen place of suicide for more than 350 people. Nowadays it's a source of wonder for legions of visitors, especially at night when it's entirely lit up. Try visiting early in the morning or late at night to avoid hour-plus lines. *Champ de Mars, 7e, tel. 1/45–50–34–56. Métro/RER: Champ de Mars. Admission (elevator): 18F to 1st level, 35F to 2nd level, 52F to top. Admission (stairs): 10F to 2nd level. Open daily 9 AM–11 PM, until midnight July–Aug.*

City Planner Baron Haussmann Put Paris Before the People

When Napoléon III wasn't out waging war with Otto von Bismarck, he was turning Paris inside out with the help of his formidable city planner, Baron Haussmann. Napoléon, an Anglophile, visited London and fell in love with the orderly parks and the wide boulevards. The wheels in his head started turning; he wanted to create a Paris with green spaces and city squares, a Paris for which he would be remembered and revered. He would turn the medieval town with tiny, winding, congested streets into a city of grand boulevards. Haussmann shared Napoléon's love for the Imperial Order and not a little bit of his megalomania—he was just the man for the job.

From 1853 to 1870, Paris was a huge construction site. Entire neighborhoods were razed and 36 wide boulevards were added. One of the main motivations for creating the wide boulevards was so that the police could more easily suppress worker revolts. New buildings lined the boulevards in an imperious and monotonous style (good examples are on the avenue de l'Opéra), English-style parks were created, and the city began its life as the aesthetic extravaganza you see today.

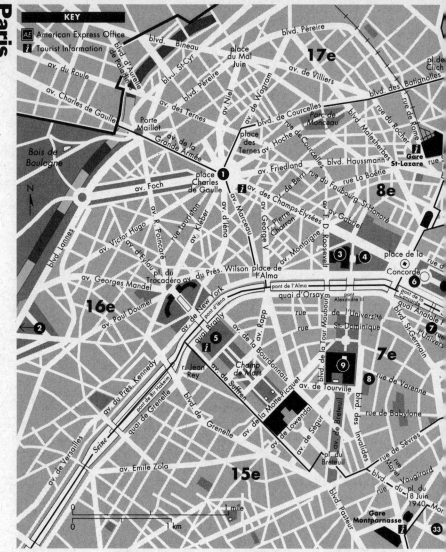

KEY

AE American Express Office

i Tourist Information

17e

8e

16e

7e

15e

Bois de Boulogne

N

Arc de Triomphe, **1**

Basilique du Sacré-Cœur, **24**

Centre Beaubourg, **22**

Cité des Sciences et de l'Industrie, **25**

Ecole Nationale des Beaux-Arts, **13**

Eglise St-Germain-des-Prés, **14**

Eiffel Tower, **5**

Forum des Halles, **23**

Grand Palais, **3**

Hôtel Carnavalet, **28**

Hôtel des Invalides, **9**

Hôtel de Ville, **21**

Institut du Monde Arabe, **31**

Jardin des Tuileries, **11**

Louvre, **12**

Montparnasse Cemetery, **33**

La Mosquée, **32**

Musée de Cluny, **18**

Musée de l'Orangerie, **6**

Musée d'Orsay, **7**

Musée Marmottan, **2**

Musée Picasso, **27**

Musée Rodin, **8**

Notre-Dame, **20**

Opéra, **10**

Palais de Justice, **19**

Palais du Luxembourg, **15**

Panthéon, **16**

Père Lachaise Cemetery, **26**

Petit Palais, **4**

Place de la Bastille, **30**

Place des Vosges, **29**

Sorbonne University, **17**

Paris

HOTEL DES INVALIDES Built by the warmongering Louis XIV in 1674 to house all the soldiers wounded during his various military campaigns, Invalides now houses more recently wounded soldiers as well as a tomb, a church, and a few museums (one with an enormous collection of guns, cannons, tanks, and other toys; the other holds Napoleon's souvenirs). The tomb of Napoleon Bonaparte is housed in the Eglise du Dôme. Here the little megalomaniac is ensconced in five coffins, one inside the next, to keep him nice and cozy. *Pl. des Invalides, tel. 1/44–42–37–70. Métro: Invalides. Admission to museums and tomb: 32F, 22F students. Admission to church free. Open Apr.–Oct., daily 10–6; Nov.–Mar., daily 10–5.*

LOUVRE The Musée du Louvre—at various times a fortress, a royal residence, a community of bums and prostitutes, and a storehouse for the "souvenirs" collected by Napoleon as he rampaged around Europe—is now one of the undisputed queens of museums, with everything from Oriental antiques to the crown jewels. Pick up a color-coded map in the central lobby if you want any chance of finding your way around the museum's three enormous wings. Current renovations, scheduled to be completed in 1995, will almost double the size of the museum; be sure to bring your compass and extra water supply. *34–36 quai du Louvre, 1er, tel. 1/40–20–50–50 or 40–20–51–51 for recorded information. Métro: Louvre or Palais-Royale. Wheelchair access. Admission: 35F, 20F ages 18–25, under 18 free; general admission on Sun.: 20F. Open Thurs.–Sun. 9–6, Mon. and Wed. until 10 PM.*

If you really wanna do the Louvre for tourists, here it is: da Vinci's La Joconde (a.k.a. the Mona Lisa), under her protective layer of plastic and surrounded by many more layers of tourists, is in the Denon wing, section five on your map. Go to it, champ.

MUSEE D'ORSAY Rescued from the wrecking ball by adamant historical conservationists in the late 1970s, this cavernous former train station built in 1900 opened in 1986 as the city's official museum of Impressionist-era art. The Orsay is a bit overwhelming, especially on Sundays when millions of weekend art critics jockey for the best angle from which to really *feel* that Monet. The ground floor can provide you with a bit of historical context for all you'll see on the floors above. The third floor features the impressionists in full flower, including Monet, Manet, Degas, and Renoir. *1 rue de Bellechasse, 7e, tel. 1/40–49–48–14 or 45–49–11–11 for recorded information. Métro/RER: Musée d'Orsay. Admission: 32F, 20F students, under 18 free. Open Tues., Wed., Fri., and Sat. 10–6, Thurs. 10–9:45, Sun. 9–6.*

NOTRE-DAME Here it is in all its Gothic majesty, playground for Quasimodo and first stop on the itinerary of every self-respecting tourist—the fantastic medieval Cathédrale Notre-Dame. Consecrated way back in 1182, she suffered some indignities in 1789 when revolutionaries rampaged through, destroying all signs of aristocracy in the cathedral and decapitating all 28 of the statues of the Israeli kings that stand over the main doors. Then, in the mid-1800s, the church gained her rightful aesthetic space when Haussmann destroyed some of her little neighbor houses and created a big plaza from which to view her. If you're lucky enough to catch it on a sunny day, you can enjoy the diffused light cast by the rose windows. The enormous organ rumbles during free Sunday concerts and masses. Speaking of masses, the summer crowds are terrible, so do yourself a favor and come at 7 AM or so. *Tel. 43–26–07–39. Métro: Cité. Admission to tower: 26F, 20F students and senior citizens.*

OPERA The Opéra, perhaps the most pompous of all Parisian buildings, was built by Charles Garnier after he defeated hundreds of other architects in a competition for the building's design in 1861. Today, the Opéra Garnier sits in the middle of place de l'Opéra, wreaking all manner of aesthetic havoc on innocent passers-by. Those who spring for the admission fee can climb the ornate stairway and check out the auditorium, whose ceiling was repainted by Marc Chagall in 1964. For the full experience, plan to attend an event here, which can cost as little as 30F, though is much more likely to cost at least 100F. *Pl. de l'Opéra, 9e, tel. 1/47–42–57–50. Métro: Opéra. Admission: 28F, 15F students. Open daily 11–4:30, closed occasionally for rehearsals.*

PERE LACHAISE CEMETERY The biggest cemetery in Paris and one of the most famous anywhere, Père Lachaise is the final resting place of Molière, la Fontaine, Colette, Frédéric Chopin, Gertrude Stein, and Alice B. Toklas. Maps that pinpoint the most famous of the dearly departed are on sale near the main entrance for 10F. Jim Morrison's graffiti-decorated tombstone is the easiest to find; arrows spray-painted on other people's graves mark the way. Oscar Wilde's adoring fans leave pink triangles, flowers, and love notes, all watched over by a huge angel who lost his testicles after some complained he was indecent. *Blvd. de Ménilmontant, 20e. Métro: Père Lachaise. Open spring–fall, daily 8–6; winter, daily 8–5.*

Grab a bottle of wine and the one you love (or a temporary substitute) and head out over the Seine on the pedestrian Pont des Arts, where musicians, artists, and other young partiers flock to watch the sun go down behind the Eiffel Tower and come up over Notre-Dame.

NEIGHBORHOODS

BASTILLE In 1789, angry revolutionaries stormed the notorious Bastille prison; today the **July Column,** topped by the gilded statue of Freedom, stands in its place on **place de la Bastille.** The area around the former prison site is now witnessing a revolution of a different sort: gentrification. Art galleries, bars, and clubs are taking the place of machine shops and craftspeople, and nightlife is hopping in the many bars, discos, and restaurants. In addition, the area has tiny alleyways, or *passages,* that harbor ancient and crumbling storefronts, abandoned machinery, and other glimpses of Paris that usually remain well-hidden. Especially fun streets for daytime wandering are **rue de Charonne** and **rue du Faubourg-St-Antoine.** At night, check out **rue de la Roquette** and **rue de Lappe.**

LES HALLES AND BEAUBOURG When a 19th-century market hall was torn down in 1968, shopping mall developers moved in, creating what you see today: the **Forum des Halles,** Europe's largest underground shopping mall, a multilevel, soulless structure populated with young, pouty Parisians. Despite the indignities that this region has suffered, the streets around the Forum des Halles retain a bit of their traditional marketplace atmosphere. In the daytime, the streets fill up with funky students and street musicians, beer-drinking punk rockers, wide-eyed tourists, and patrons of the porn shops that have sidled in on the edges of the district. Don't miss **rue St-Denis,** one of the oldest streets in Paris, which now bustles day and night with street performers and café patrons. You're also likely to find itinerant musicians at the fanciful **place Igor-Stravinsky** next to the Centre Beaubourg (*see* Worth Seeing, *above*).

ILE DE LA CITE AND ILE ST-LOUIS When you go to see Notre-Dame, don't give into the see-and-flee mode of sightseeing. There are plenty of other things to see on the Ile de la Cité, even though the island might look like a monotonous chunk of concrete at first sight. The **Crypte Archéologique** (tel. 43–29–83–51), right in front of the cathedral, details the history of the Ile de la Cité with diagrams and photographs; the area once consisted of tiny winding streets, churches, street stalls, and houses before Baron Haussmann razed them all. Behind Notre-Dame, near the garden, is the **Mémorial de la Déportation,** a striking tribute to the 200,000 French people who died in Nazi concentration camps. The walls are lined with moving quotations by famous French poets, philosophers, and writers.

Also on the Ile de la Cité, inside the **Palais de Justice, Sainte-Chapelle** blvd. du Palais, 1er; admission 26F, 17F students and seniors) is regularly cited by visitors as one of the most stunning chapels in Paris, made sublime by the abundance of stained glass. In the mid-13th century, the pious medieval king Louis IX bought the alleged crown of thorns and a part of *the* Cross from some shady guys on a street corner in Constantinople, and built Sainte-Chapelle to house the relics. Next to Sainte-Chapelle, the **Conciergerie** (admission 26F, 17F students, 40F joint ticket with Sainte-Chapelle) was first used as a royal palace but later became a prison. Inside you'll see the huge **Salle des Pas Perdus** and **Chambre Dorée,** where Louis IX once resided, before he was decapitated. For the ultimate irony, see the cell where Marie Antoinette spent her last days and where Robespierre (one of her most vehement critics) would spend his last preguillotine hours less than one year later.

In the 17th century, some developers, in a spectacular capitalistic move, joined the two small islands that form the Ile St-Louis and proceeded to build town houses on them. From that time through the early 1900s, the island was occupied by artists, writers, and intellectuals of various stripes. As you wander around the ultrabourgeois neighborhood, keep an eye out for the plaques that are posted on various buildings describing who lived here when. An especially somber one, mounted at 19 quai de Bourbon: "Here lived Camille Claudel, sculptor, 1899–1913. Then ended her brave career as an artist and began her long night of internment" (in an insane asylum).

LE MARAIS One of the few areas in central Paris left untouched by Baron Haussmann, the Marais has retained its tiny, labyrinthine streets, which still hold surprises, from glimpses of medieval alleys to restored faces of old boulangeries and brasseries. Many of the Marais's hôtels, or aristocratic residences, hide beautiful courtyards behind their big doors and fancy facades; some hôtels house exhibits and are open to the public. See especially the **Hôtel Carnavalet** (23 rue de Sévigné), now a museum of Parisian history with a brilliant exhibit on the French Revolution. The 16th-century building, which once housed the French writer Madame Sévigné, was decorated by the same sculptors who worked on the Louvre. The **Jewish quarter,** centered around rue des Rosiers and rue des Ecouffes, has endured centuries of growing pains since the 1100s and offers a glimpse of some of the most enduring traditions in the city, as well as the best kosher food in Paris. The area between the Seine and the rue de Rivoli, behind the **Hôtel de Ville,** is beautifully packed with old hôtels and tiny green spots; farther north, around the rue Vieille du Temple and the rue des Francs Bourgeois, you've hit the land of quaint restaurants and the oldest square in Paris, the **place des Vosges.** Built in the early 17th century by Henri IV to be a royal residence, the place's most famous later inhabitant was Victor Hugo, who is memorialized in a museum here. People don't just come here 'cause it's old, though—it's also hip. The **rue Ste-Croix-de-la-Brétonnerie** is the center of gay life in Paris, with bars, bookstores, and many gay-owned businesses.

MONTMARTRE Rising above the city on the highest hill in Paris is Montmartre, site of the Basilique du Sacré-Cœur (*see* Worth Seeing, *above*) and home to a once-thriving artistic community. Even now, after many of the artists who once established themselves here headed for cheaper quarters, even after sleek tour buses have delivered hordes of tourists to its tiny streets, Montmartre remains first and foremost a village where a special breed of Parisian lives and socializes and has a drink or three in the evening.

At the top of the hill, near **place du Tertre,** lived the artists and writers. Today, aggressive third-rate painters fill the touristy square, taking advantage of the area's artistic heritage. Real artists live northwest of place du Tertre in million-dollar homes on **avenue Junot.** The little alley at number 25 is probably one of the most picturesque in Paris. Down the hill is the **Bateau Lavoîr** (13 pl. Emile Goudeau), the artists' colony where Picasso, Braque, Gris, and others had studios. One block south is the **place des Abbesses,** a tranquil old plaza with one of the two remaining Art Deco Métro entrances designed by Charles Garnier.

The cabarets, at the bottom of the hill near **place Pigalle** and **place de Clichy,** provided new heights of titillation for the artists and criminals who used to live in the area, as well as for Quartier Latin students and bourgeois couples who decide to slum it for an evening. The **Moulin Rouge** (pl. Blanche), immortalized by Toulouse-Lautrec in his paintings, still cashes in on Paris's reputation as a city of sin and hosts tacky, Vegas-style night shows.

MONTPARNASSE Most people know Montparnasse as an area of wide boulevards and famous cafés; Hemingway, Henry Miller, Picasso, Sartre, and Lenin all showed up in Montparnasse's cafés and villas to create or philosophize. Something of them remains in the **Montparnasse Cemetery,** on plaques in front of houses, and carved into the tables of bars they frequented. The **boulevard de Montparnasse** has the most cafés of historical/literary interest, including Hemingway's favorite haunt, **La Closerie de Lilas** (171 blvd. du Montparnasse); Picasso's favorite hangout, **Le Select** (99 blvd. du Montparnasse); and **Le Dome** (108 blvd. du Montparnasse), where Sartre used to go with Simone de Beauvoir at least three times a week.

South of boulevard du Montparnasse, the quarter grows increasingly working class and multi-cultural. The tiny streets within the triangle formed by **rue Raymond Losserand, rue d'Alésia** and **avenue du Maine,** with their modern low-income housing complexes and cheap, neighborhood cafés and restaurants, offer a view of Paris you're not going get at the Eiffel Tower. The area between Métro Alésia and the Parc du Montsouris has dead-end alleys and unexpected spots of green.

QUARTIER LATIN The center of French intellectual life for more than 700 years, the Latin Quarter has drawn the intellectually restless, the politically discontented, the artistically inspired, and those who like to hang out with them to its universities, cafés, garrets, and alleys, almost since the beginning of time. The prestigious **Sorbonne University,** established in 1253, was the first university in Paris, and it drew students and professors from all over Europe to its hallowed halls and contemplative courtyards. Even though the Latin Quarter is not exactly undiscovered territory, its spirit refuses to die. The presence of the ever-functioning Sorbonne, as well as the **Ecole Nationale des Beaux-Arts,** guarantees that the quarter remains youthful, creative, and relatively liberal.

Especially rewarding journeys may include the labyrinth of streets between place Maubert and boulevard St-Michel near the Seine, the **place St-Michel** (a meeting spot for tourists), and the tiny streets that head toward **carrefour de l'Odéon** (a meeting spot for French students). Don't miss the **rue St-André-des-Arts,** a pedestrian street lined with crêperies, postcard shops, and a good experimental cinema. The **rue de la Montagne-Ste-Geneviève,** which winds behind the **Panthéon,** is one of the oldest streets in Paris and is lined with a number of buildings that date from the Middle Ages.

ST-GERMAIN-DES-PRES Centered around the oldest church in Paris (the **Eglise St-Germain-des-Pres**), St-Germain's traditional cultural and intellectual life has, of late, been diffused by the arrival of too many boutiques. Descending into one of the area's little bars, now populated by boys in sportscoats and girls in Hermès scarves, it's hard to imagine that they once pulsed with the primal beats of the *babacool* (beatnik) generation. An old babacool haunt that still has some life in it is the club **Tabou** (33 rue Dauphine, 6e), which was founded by singer Juliette Greco and jazz trumpeter Boris Vian to accommodate their friends the Zazous, another group of funky, free-lovin' folk.

Among the narrow streets to check out, especially interesting are **rue de Seine** and **rue de Buci** with their open-air street markets; little **rue Visconti,** which once contained Paris's Protestant ghetto; and the area around **rue Jacob** and **rue des Sts-Pères,** which contains most of the area's art galleries. Also sit for a minute in the periodically tranquil **place de Furstemberg,** reportedly named "My Favorite Plaza in Paris" by more people than any other.

MUSEUMS

So you wanna go to a museum? You've come to the right place. In addition to the biggies, Paris has many small, quirky museums devoted to a single artist, writer, or deviant strain of thought. The **Espace Montmartre Dalí** (11 rue Poulbot, 18e, tel. 1/42–64–40–10) has flamboyant photos of the artist himself, as well as his paintings and sculptures. Honoré de Balzac once lived in the **Maison de Balzac** (47 rue Raynouard, 16e, tel. 1/42–24–56–38; admission 17F, 9F students), and he left behind a bunch of letters and original manuscript. See the memorabilia of writer and bohemienne George Sand at the **Musée de la Vie Romantique** (16 rue Chaptal, 9e, tel. 1/48–74–95–38), housed in the former studio of painter Ary Scheffer. Devoted to the history of torture instruments, **Les Martyrs de Paris** (Porte du Louvre in Forum des Halles, 1er, tel. 1/40–28–08–96; admission 43F, 32F students) includes a reenactment of the beheading of Louis XVI and various acts of torture.

Many museums have a reduced admission charge on Sundays and close either Monday or Tuesday. If you really want to knock yourself out, get a **Carte Musées et Monuments.** This museum pass gives you unlimited access to the permanent collections of 65 museums and monuments in and around Paris. Buy it at museums, big Métro stations, or any tourist office; a one-day pass costs 60F, a three-day 120F, and a five-day 170F.

CITE DES SCIENCES ET DE L'INDUSTRIE This museum is a mammoth orgy of everything industrial and scientific, inviting you to play with, test out, or just marvel at its many exhibits. The magnificent spherical steel Géode cinema in front of the exhibit building houses the largest projection screen in existence. Tickets for films at the Géode (usually nature flicks) are 55F, 37F students. *Parc de la Villette, 30 av. Corentin-Cariou, 19e, tel. 1/40–05–70–00, 1/40–05–80–00 for recorded information. Métro: Porte de la Villette. Admission: 45F, 35F under 26. Open Tues.–Sun. 10–6.*

GRAND PALAIS AND PETIT PALAIS Intended, like the Eiffel Tower, to be temporary additions to the Parisian landscape for the 1900 World Exposition, these domed Art Deco extravaganzas dodged the wrecking ball. The Grand Palais became an exhibition hall for big-time traveling exhibitions. The Petit Palais, across the street, features 18th- and 19th-century French furniture, Greek pottery, tapestries, and paintings by Courbet, Millet, Delacroix, and minor impressionists. *Av. Winston Churchill, 8e. Métro: Champs-Elysées. Grand Palais: tel. 1/44–13–17–30. Admission: 42F, 29F students. Open Wed.–Mon. 10–8. Petit Palais: tel. 1/42–65–12–73. Admission: 26F, 14F students. Open Tues.–Sun. 10–5:40.*

INSTITUT DU MONDE ARABE Like the Beaubourg Center, the Institut du Monde Arabe is more than a museum: It's a monstrous, multimedia, Arab-French cultural center with a museum, a library, a cinema, and temporary exhibits. The **museum** (admission 25F), on the seventh floor, has an impressive collection of Arab-Islamic art dating from the pre-Muslim era to the present. The library on the third floor offers books and magazines on Arab culture. Pick up information on temporary art exhibits, dances, lectures, debates, and musical events at the ticket office. Also check out the south wall, which is covered with 240 *moucharabiehs* (thin metal plates with classic Arab designs cut out of them) whose openings adjust themselves automatically to the changing intensity of the sun. *1 rue des Fossés-St-Bernard, 5e, tel. 1/40–51–38–38. Métro: Jussieu. Admission: 40F. Open Tues.–Sun. 10–6.*

LOUVRE *See* Worth Seeing, *above.*

MUSEE DE CLUNY Located on the site of ancient Roman baths, this museum features a large collection of medieval artifacts, including a stunning tapestry collection. Six tapestries entitled *The Lady and the Unicorn* depict a refined lady demonstrating the five senses to her unicorn friend. *Pl. du Painlevé, 5e, tel. 1/43–25–62–00. Métro: Cluny-la Sorbonne. Admission: 26F, 17F students and Sun. Open Wed.–Mon. 9:15–5:45.*

MUSEE MARMOTTAN This former hôtel particulier in the posh and tranquil 16th arrondissement features late 19th- and early 20th-century artists but is best known for its Monets, including the famous *Soleil Levant,* which caused Monet's critics to dub his style "impressionism" with a degree of cynicism that is lost on us today. Upstairs you'll find some Renoirs, Sisleys, and more Monets, including caricatures he did of famous Parisians. *2 rue*

La Mosquée

La Mosquée (39 rue Geoffrey St-Hilaire, 5e, tel. 1/45–35–97–33; admission 15F, 10F students), one of the largest mosques in Europe, has been a center of the Muslim community since the 1920s. Take a tour (in French) or inspect the intricately tiled courtyard and tearoom (see Cafés, below) on your own. For a decadent experience, spend an afternoon at the hammam (admission 60F–70F, towel rental 10F), the Turkish baths in the mosque. After all, how many chances do you get to lie around naked, listening to Arabic music and drinking mint tea? Women are admitted on Monday, Wednesday, Thursday, and Saturday, men on Friday and Sunday. The baths are closed in August.

Louis-Boilly, 16e, tel. 1/42–24–07–02. Métro: Muette. Admission: 35F, 15F students. Open Tues.–Sun. 10–5:30.

MUSEE NATIONAL D'ART MODERNE This airy museum on the third and fourth floors of the Beaubourg (*see* Worth Seeing, *above*) is the largest modern-art museum in the world. In fact, the collection is so big that only a fifth of it is shown at any one time. Inside, a phantasmagoria of pieces awaits—from Matisse to Picasso, Braque to Léger, Kandinsky to Dalí to Warhol to art so new that the paint is hardly dry. *Pl. Georges-Pompidou, 4e, tel. 1/44–78–12–33. Métro: Rambuteau. Admission: 30F, 20F students and senior citizens, free Sun. before 2 PM. Open Mon. and Wed.–Fri. noon–10, weekends 10–10.*

MUSEE DE L'ORANGERIE This collection of impressionist and post-impressionist paintings, including works by Manet, Renoir, Cézanne, Modigliani, Matisse, and Sisley, is displayed in a series of small, peaceful rooms. The bottom floor is devoted to Monet's *Nymphéas* (Water Lilies), huge tableaus inspired by the ponds in Monet's gardens at Giverny. *Pl. de la Concorde, 8e, tel. 1/42–97–48–16. Métro: Concorde. Admission: 26F, 17F students and Sun. Wheelchair access. Open Wed.–Mon. 9:45–5:15.*

The Musée de la Sculpture en Plein Air (Open Air Sculpture Museum) at the edge of the Jardin des Plantes near the Pont d'Austerlitz is an ideal place to hang out among modern sculptures and kick back to contemplate the murky depths of the Seine.

MUSEE D'ORSAY See Worth Seeing, *above.*

MUSEE PICASSO Located in a beautiful hôtel particulier in the heart of the Marais district, this museum remains one of the most popular in Paris and one of the most pleasurable to tour; its chronological layout is accompanied by biographical information, adding another dimension to an already excellent collection of paintings. *5 rue de Thorigny, 4e, tel. 1/42–71–25–21. Métro: St-Paul. Admission: 26F, 16F students. Open Wed.–Mon. 9:30–6.*

MUSEE RODIN Along with the Museum of Modern Art and the Picasso Museum, the Rodin Museum remains one of the most consistently praised by people who can't stand museums. The collection of sculptures by Auguste Rodin (1840–1917), in the 18th-century **Hôtel Biron,** sends visitors into paroxysms of dreaminess. Acres of gardens around the hôtel feature 200 varieties of roses as well as some of Rodin's most famous sculptures. *77 rue de Varenne, 7e, tel. 1/47–05–01–34. Métro: Varenne. Admission: 26F, 17F students and Sun., 4F gardens only. Open Tues.–Sun. 10–6.*

PARKS AND GARDENS

More than 350 spots of green dot the city, from large *bois* (woods) to tiny, manicured lawns with maybe a tree and a wizened old man with a beret and a cane. Not only do Parisian gardens offer a place to sit, but they can also liven up your day with bizarre little dog-walking scenes or encounters with old ladies who know all the pigeons personally.

BOIS DE BOULOGNE This 2,200-acre wooded area just west of Paris is what makes the city livable for a lot of people. Landscaped by Baron Haussmann in the 1850s at the request of Napoleon III, the Bois de Boulogne is speckled with lakes and ponds and lined with trails. One of the nicest things Napoleon III ever planned, "Le Bois" has several small gardens and the **Musée des Arts et Traditions Populaires** (6 rte. du Mahatma-Gandhi), which contains artifacts related to rural activities in preindustrial environments. Toward the northwest, the **Parc Bagatelle** has spectacular flowers, as well as ponds, peacocks, and a special fountain for lovers. Admission to the park is 6F.

Buses traverse the Bois du Boulogne during the day (Bus 244 from Porte Maillot), but the Métro goes only to the fringe: Alight at Porte Dauphine (east), Les Sablons (north), or Porte d' Auteuil (south). Avoid the Bois at night, when it becomes a different sort of playground, populated with hookers and hoodlums.

JARDIN DU LUXEMBOURG Okay, so it may not be the greenest of Parisian parks, but if you head away from the center you'll get away from the gravel and find some shadier areas as well as some very nice fountains and flowers. And it's certainly popular with lots of Sorbonne students and little boys and girls in full Sunday dress sailing miniature boats in the fountain. At the north end of the park is the **Palais du Luxembourg,** built, like the park, for Marie de' Medici, widow of Henri IV, at the beginning of the 17th century. Today it's the site of the French Senate and is not open to the public. Near the palace is the pleasantly tree-entangled area around the **Fountain of the Medici.** A statue of Pan, merrily playing his flute and standing on a pig carcass, will guard over you through all manner of debauchery. *6e. Métro/RER: Luxembourg.*

On the west end of the Jardin des Tuileries, the place de la Concorde saw many a monarch and revolutionary lose their head during the Revolution, including Louis XVI, Marie Antoinette, Robespierre, and Danton. Nowadays it sees about a billion cars zooming around, of all things, its Egyptian obelisk, which was given to France by the Pasha Mohammed Ali in 1831.

JARDIN DES PLANTES King Louis XIII first conceived of this park in 1626, intending it to become "The King's Garden of Medicinal Herbs." Today it's the city's official botanical garden and houses more than 10,000 varieties of plants (all tidily placed in little rows and labeled, of course), a zoo, an aquarium, a natural history museum, and lots of students playing hooky from the nearby university. With the Gare d'Austerlitz right along its southern edge, this park is a great place if you have a long wait for your train. *5e. Métro: Jussieu, Monge, or Gare d'Austerlitz. Admission to museums: 12F–25F. Park open daily dawn–dusk.*

JARDIN DES TUILERIES Besides offering a place to rest your weary feet after your walk down the Champs-Elysées, the Jardin des Tuileries—strategically located between the place de la Concorde and the Louvre—gives you a good view of city planning, Haussmann-style. In one direction, you can look straight down the Champs-Elysées all the way to the Arc de Triomphe. In the other direction, you'll see a long, orderly expanse of garden between you and the Louvre. This meticulous planning is carried down to the smallest details of the park. André le Nôtre, the guy who designed the obsessively ordered gardens at Versailles, planned the placement of every pathway and statue. The Musée de l'Orangerie, a small museum featuring late impressionist paintings, is in the southwest corner of the park (*see* Museums, *above*). *1er. Métro: Tuileries.*

AFTER DARK

If you don't go out at night during your stay in Paris, you're depriving yourself big time. Even if you don't want to dress up or spend a lot of money, many nighttime activities are entirely gratis, from listening to a lone saxophonist wail away by the river to running around streets made mystical by that peculiar light the street lamps emit at 3 AM.

BARS **La Bastide.** This small, funky bar in the heart of the Bastille is a haven for young scruffy types. The steady flow of jazz and blues music and occasional kitschy '60s tunes encourage all kinds of sing-alongs. Beer is 10F, 14F after 10 PM; cocktails 26F, 30F after 10 PM. *Rue de Lappe, 11e, tel. 1/47–00–26–72. Métro: Bastille.*

Le Birdland. A small intimate bar with a big jazz collection, Birdland caters to a crowd of varying ages with cocktails and beer, Thelonious, and Charlie until 6 AM. *20 rue Princesse, 6e, tel. 1/43–26–97–59. Métro: Mabillon.*

Café Au Vieux Paris. Song sheets are passed out and audience participation is *not* optional. The songs come mostly from the '30s, '40s, and '50s, and if you look closely (or drink enough), you may see the ghost of Edith Piaf. *72 rue de la Verrerie, 4e. Métro: Hôtel de Ville. Open Tues.–Sat. Closed Aug.*

Café de la Plage. World music, soul, funk, blues, and jazz tracks accompany 18F–32F beers and 20F aperitifs at this Franco-British bar in the Bastille area. The crowd is young and congenial, and aspires to be in a band. *59 rue de Charonne, 11e, tel. 1/47–00–91–60. Métro: Ledru-Rollin.*

Le Central. This casual, friendly bar in the Marais is one of the most established gay men's bars in Paris, attracting an older crowd of regulars as well as tourists. Women are welcome but rare. Disco hits are on the stereo. *33 rue Vieille-du-Temple, 4e, tel. 1/48–87–99–33. Métro: Hôtel de Ville.*

Flann O'Brien. Live Irish music (to which you are strongly encouraged to sing along) accompanies pints of frothy Guinness (20F–37F). *6 rue Bailleul, 1er, tel. 1/42–60–13–58. Métro: Louvre.*

La Paillotte. Nurse a carefully chosen cocktail (38F) and gaze deep into somebody's eyes in this dark, jazzy joint in the Quartier Latin. The owner has one of the best jazz collections in Paris. *45 rue Monsieur-le-Prince, 6e, tel. 1/43–26–45–69. Métro: Odéon. Open until dawn. Closed Sun. and Aug.*

Le Piano Vache. Lots of university students come here to rest heavy elbows on the tables, chain smoke, and solve the world's problems. *8 rue Laplace, 5e, tel. 46–33–75–03. Métro: Cardinal Lemoine.*

Subway. Subtle decorative touches like tires hanging from the ceiling and iron bars make this all-men's bar in the Marais feel just like home. A fairly young, trendy crowd frequents this industrial wonderland. *35 rue Ste-Croix-de-la-Bretonnerie, 4e, tel. 1/42–77–41–10. Métro: St-Paul.*

DANCE CLUBS **Le Balajo.** The granddaddy of the Paris discos keeps 'em coming back to the same hyper-kitschy decor and mix of rock-and-roll, salsa, and disco. *9 rue de Lappe, 11e, tel. 1/47–00–07–87. Métro: Bastille. Cover 100F–120F. Closed Tues., Thurs., and Sun.*

Chez Moune. The nightly striptease is performed for women, by women: Men are allowed only if extremely well-behaved. The club also has women-only tea dances on Sunday afternoon. *54 rue Pigalle, 9e, tel. 1/45–26–64–64. Métro: Pigalle.*

Kat Privilege. The only full-time lesbian disco in Paris lays down a variety of tunes (house, funk, mainstream rock) for a diverse crowd. Drinks are a whopping 60F. *3 Cité Bergère, 9e, tel. 1/42–46–50–98. Métro: Montmartre. Closed Sun. and Mon.*

Keur Samba. The music ranges from zouk (Antilles) to soukous (African) to American hip-hop and house at this pumping, expensive disco near the Champs-Elysées. *79 rue de la Boétie, 8e, tel. 1/43–59–03–10. Métro: St-Augustin.*

Le Palace. This super '80s extravaganza disco remains popular through flights of fashion and the fickleness of disco patrons. The crowd is unpretentious, and the music is a solid mix of disco-house. *8 rue du Faubourg Montmartre, 9e, tel. 1/42–46–10–87. Métro: Montmartre.*

Lesbian Nightlife

Although gay life in Paris is based in the Marais, lesbian life is much less visible and is subject to the whims of fashion; bars and clubs surface and split the scene as fast as you can say "what's your number." For up-to-date information on the scene in Paris, contact the Maison des Femmes (tel. 1/43–48–24–91), a feminist/lesbian resource center, or Archives Lesbiennes (tel. 1/48–05–25–89).

Rex Club. A disco playing techno, hip-hop, and thrash funk/rock, and a live music venue featuring garage/rock bands, the Rex provides a much needed outlet for all those rockers who are about to be genteeled to death. *5 blvd. Poissonnière, 2e, tel. 1/42–36–83–98. Métro: Bonne Nouvelle. Closed Aug.*

CINEMAS Both Paris entertainment weeklies, *L'Officiel des Spectacles* and *Pariscope*, have comprehensive film listings. The plush, new cinemas often play American films a few months after they appear in the United States. The biggest and flashiest is **Gaumont Grand Ecran** (30 pl. d'Italie, 13e, tel. 1/45–80–77–00); other new cinemas are in Les Halles, near the Opéra, and along the Champs-Elysées. Full-price tickets cost from 35F to about 50F. Discounts are sometimes available for students and senior citizens, and for everyone on Mondays and sometimes on Wednesdays; on weekends and holidays, everyone has to pay full price.

The older, funkier theaters tend to be cheaper and have a more offbeat selection. These small cinemas tend to congregate in the fifth and sixth arrondissements, near boulevard St-Michel, Odéon, and St-Germain-des-Prés.

JAZZ This town has loved jazz for as long as jazz has been around. Although vestiges of Paris's jazz scene remain, you will be hard pressed to find a truly divey, truly cheap, truly *jazzy* place within city limits. This said, there's some fine music to be heard in Paris, and in many places you can stay all night for the price of a drink, a 25F–100F drink, that is. Most jazz clubs are located in Châtelet, Les Halles, St-Germain, and the Latin Quarter.

Le Baiser Salé. At this bar in Châtelet, the small, hot room upstairs is the perfect venue for small, hot ensembles. Music is mostly fusion and Afro-jazz—an especially good bet in Paris. First drinks cost 65F and up. *58 rue des Lombards, 1er, tel. 1/42–33–37–71. Métro: Châtelet.*

Le Caveau de la Huchette. This classic *cave* has been serving up swing and Dixieland since the 1950s, and still sees a young, wholesome crowd swing dancing like it's going out of style. Entrance costs 55F, 65F Fridays, 70F Saturdays; students pay 50F during the week. *5 rue de la Huchette, 5e, tel. 1/43–26–65–05. Métro: St-Michel.*

L'Eustache. This small, classic café/bar in Les Halles is well-loved by young Parisians without a lot of money. Jazz plays three nights a week at 10 and goes till 2:30 AM; drinks are 38F and up. *37 rue Berger, 1er, tel. 1/40–26–23–20. Métro: Les Halles.*

The Lionel Hampton Room. Internationally famous names pass through this large, slick hotel bar, catering to an upscale, older crowd. The exceptional music will take some of the sting out of the 130F price per drink. *Hôtel Meridien, 81 blvd. Gouvion-St-Cyr, 17e, tel. 1/40–68–30–42. Métro: Porte Maillot.*

WORLD MUSIC On any given night in Paris you can listen to live zouk, soukous, Jamaican reggae, North African raï (Arabic blues), Brazilian salsa, Argentine tango, and various hybrid forms, like rap-raï and Afro-jazz. Radio Nova is an excellent multicultural radio station (101.5 FM), and the **Maison d'Amérique Latin** (217 blvd. St-Germain, tel. 1/49–54–75–00) is a good information source on Latin music. *Le Guide Actuel du Paris Mondial,* available at Fnac stores, is devoted exclusively to world cultural life in Paris.

La Chapelle des Lombards. This hot bar has consistently high-quality Latin music, zouk, and African music. The bar attracts a racially mixed crowd that has a really good time. Cover is 100F. *19 rue de Lappe, 11e, tel. 1/43–57–24–24. Métro: Bastille.*

Les Trottoirs de Buenos Aires. This bar features nightly live Argentine tango for a happy older crowd of swinging dancers. *37 rue des Lombards, 1e, tel. 1/40–26–28–58; Métro: Châtelet. Closed Aug.*

CLASSICAL MUSIC *Pariscope* has a complete list of all classical music events and their cost: *entrée libre* means free. The Louvre, the Musée d'Orsay, and the Centre Beaubourg have concert spaces that feature cheap or free lunchtime concerts and more expensive nighttime music. Many churches and cathedrals also have frequent classical music concerts, often free.

For opera, you have a couple of choices. The old **Opéra Garnier** provides an opulent setting for programs that increasingly feature more ballet and less opera. The **Opéra Bastille** (120 rue de Lyon, tel. 1/44–73–13–00), which opened in 1989, is the building in Paris that is most widely accepted as being objectively ugly. Nevertheless, the acoustics are good, productions are lavish, and its opening has helped Paris to regain its reputation as a first-class opera town.

Ile-de-France

There are four reasons you might want to explore the Ile-de-France, the region surrounding Paris: (1) You're a real history buff and want to see where Louis XVI, Marie Antoinette, Joan of Arc, and Napoleon and Josephine hung out; (2) you're hoping to find artistic inspiration by exploring the haunts of Monet, Renoir, Rodin, and Hugo; (3) you want to hear what Donald Duck sounds like speaking French; (4) you're experiencing cultural overload in Paris and need to escape. If any or all of this sounds good, the Ile-de-France is worth exploring. A 50F ticket and an hour on the train or bus is all it takes to get out of Paris and into the playground of France's rich and famous.

Versailles

Louis XIII began the château at Versailles as his hunting lodge, but when Louis XIV, the Sun King, converted the château from a weekend retreat to the headquarters of his government between 1661 and 1710, he didn't cut any corners. The architects Louis Le Vau and François Mansart designed everything his royal acquisitiveness could want, from a chapel to the throne room dedicated to Apollo, the king's mythical hero. J. A. Gabriel later added an opera house so Louis XV could be entertained at home without troubling himself to mingle with the populace.

If you don't feel like dealing with crowds, or if you don't have any money left but still want to say that you've been to Versailles, head straight back behind the château to the gardens. This is where you'll find Versailles's famous fountains, which spout only on Sundays at 3:30 (when admission to the garden is 19F), and on selected Saturday nights for the **Fêtes de Nuit,** when the fountains come to life with music and lights. The section of the garden nearest the château is done in 17th-century French fashion; in other words, it's regimented and ordered, designed by André Le Nôtre to demonstrate his command over Mother Nature. Move farther away from the château to discover hundreds of acres of gardens, and lose the less adventurous tourists huddling around the fountains in the safety of the château's shadow.

In the northwest corner of the gardens are the smaller châteaux, the **Grand Trianon** (admission 20F, 13F students) and the **Petit Trianon** (admission 12F, 8F students), which have been used as guest houses for everyone from Napoléon I to Richard Nixon. Although you can go inside, there's not much here, and the visit is particularly anticlimactic if you've just toured the big château. Behind the Petit Trianon is the **Hameau de la Reine** (Hamlet of the Queen), a collection of cottages where Marie Antoinette came to get away from her getaway and play peasant.

It's hard to tell which is larger at Versailles—the château that housed 20,000 of Louis XIV's courtiers, or the mass of tour buses and visitors standing in front of it—so arrive at 9 AM sharp, when the château opens. Better yet, call 30–84–75–99, listen to the tour schedule (in English), and choose a time—with luck you may not have to wait in line at all. Pick up the small brochure available at the information tent at the gates of the château to figure out the system once you arrive. *Admission: 40F, 26F students, under 18 free. Tours: additional 22F–40F. Open May–Sept., Tues.–Sun. 9–6:30; Oct.–Apr., Tues.–Sun. 9–5:30.*

COMING AND GOING The cheapest way to get to Versailles from Paris is to take the **Métro** to Invalides and the yellow RER C line the rest of the way. One Métro ticket plus 6F50 covers the trip and drops you at the Gare Rive Gauche on avenue Général de Gaulle, just three well-marked blocks from the château.

Chartres

In the late 9th century, Charles the Bald presented Chartres with the tunic of the Virgin Mary, turning the city into a hot spot for the Christian faithful. The magnificent Gothic cathedral was built in the 12th and 13th centuries, after the existing church had burned to the ground in the 11th century, leaving Mary's wardrobe miraculously intact.

The cathedral and its 21,500 square feet of glass have been painstakingly preserved through seven centuries of wars. Malcolm Miller, who could be an extra on an "Addams Family" episode, gives tours in English Monday–Saturday at noon and 2:45. For an additional 20F that might be better spent elsewhere, you can climb the cathedral's northern tower for a view of the city. Organ recitals are given on Sundays in July and August at 4:45 PM free of charge, though definitely not free of tourists. The well-stocked **Office de Tourisme** (pl. de la Cathédrale, tel. 37–21–50–00) in front of the cathedral rents Walkmans (35F for one or two people) for a 1½-hour, self-guided tour of the town and cathedral.

If you venture outside the cathedral, you'll discover that one side of Chartres is beautifully designed and historic; the other side, bland, awkward, and modern. To see the historic side, follow the **route touristique** behind the cathedral. Clearly marked with shiny gold signs, the route winds through old Chartres on narrow streets. If you stray from the tourist route, though, you're slapped into reality by boring modern houses and tasteless apartment buildings.

COMING AND GOING Hourly trains make the 50-minute, 63F train trip from Paris's Gare Montparnasse. Chartres's **train station** (tel. 37–36–30–76) is within walking distance of the cathedral. A nifty light-up map in the station shows you exactly where to go.

WHERE TO SLEEP AND EAT The **HI Auberge de Jeunesse** (23 av. Neigre, tel. 37–34–27–64; beds 59F, 75F nonmembers) is the only affordable place to crash in Chartres. Its ugly exterior is only a facade; inside, it is clean, comfortable, and quiet. The hostel lies at the bottom of the old town, across the river from the cathedral, a well-marked 20-minute walk from the train station or five-minute trip on Bus 3.

Most restaurants are overpriced and plagued by tourists. Wander around the pedestrian zone, especially on rue Noël Ballay, rue du Cygne, and rue du Bois-Merrain Marceau, until you find a sandwich that looks appealing. Or try **Crêperie la Poêle Percée** (7 rue Poêle Percée, tel. 37–21–60–70) for cheap crêpes, *galettes* (pancakes), and salads.

Giverny

In 1880, a young Claude Monet moved to the small town of Giverny, on the edge of a forest. In the almost half-century he lived here, Monet painted his most famous works in and of Giverny. Of course, he didn't just choose a spot, set up camp, and pick up his paintbrush—Giverny itself is a work of art that Monet spent several years perfecting before he began reproducing it on canvas. He planted colorful checkerboard gardens, installed a water-lily pond, put up a Japanese bridge, and finally decorated the interior of the house to match it all. For the full effect, come midweek in the morning to avoid the crush. *Tel. 32–51–28–21. Admission: 25F gardens, 35F gardens and house. Open Apr.–Oct., Tues.–Sun. 10–6.*

Trains leave every couple of hours from Paris's Gare St-Lazare for the 50-minute, 60F ride to Vernon; buses meet the trains and whisk you away to Giverny for another 11F. If you have time and energy, the 6-km walk from Vernon to Giverny along the Seine is worthwhile, and not just because you'll save 11F. The **Office de Tourisme** (36 rue Carnot, tel. 32–51–39–60) has informative brochures on Monet's stay at Giverny and trail maps for hiking and biking in the surrounding forest.

Euro Disney

It's controversial, it's expensive, and it's a hell of a lot of fun. If you bite the bullet and spend the 308F50 (250F for admission and 58F50 on the RER), you'll see what Disney has learned from 50 years of experience—the "cast members" are friendly, the grounds are spotless, and the rides are detailed right down to the smell of bread coming out of Snow White's kitchen window. New stuff—like Alice's Curious Labyrinth, a trippy maze of hedges and Wonderland characters—vouch for the inexhaustible creativity of the Disney company. Although Disney brings an international flair to the park with Adventureland's Middle-Eastern Grand Bazaar and Fantasyland's Alsatian village, it's definitely still more "Disney" than "Euro." The American Wild West and Roaring '20s themes seem to find their way into everything.

See the picnic area between the RER station and the park's main entrance? Use it. It would be silly to spend the same amount that you would at a nice Parisian restaurant for a sandwich and drink. If you're looking for the cheapest eats in the park, head for the carts in Adventureland and Frontierland. *Take RER line A to Marne-la-Vallée/Chessy, tel. 49–41–49–41. Admission: 250F, 175F ages 3–12. Open weekdays 9–7, weekends and in summer until 11 PM.*

The Loire Valley **If Brittany is stubbornly** independent and Paris is arrogantly cosmopolitan,

then the Loire Valley is France pure and simple. The region was Joan of Arc's first battleground, playground of the Valois kings, and the center of French Renaissance architecture. The many châteaux of the Loire Valley range from medieval fortresses to Renaissance country homes, and they don't skip a beat in between. Builders, digging into hillsides to create the Renaissance homes demanded by trendy dukes and counts, left in their wake two other unique sights of the region: *caves champignonnières* (mushroom cellars), where more than 70% of France's edible fungi grow on the walls, and *maisons troglodytiques,* cave homes whose chimneys and weathervanes poke ridiculously out of the ground. Today, swarms of visitors come to the region to see these freaky houses along with the literally hundreds of châteaux, none of them far from the Loire's banks.

Forget about traveling between the châteaux by train or public bus—the lines radiate from major towns like Orléans and Tours. To see lots of châteaux in little time without your own wheels, you'll have to deal with private bus companies out of Tours and Blois that organize daylong tours. If you have two or three traveling companions, it might be worthwhile to rent a car. If not, the best transportation is by bike; the countryside is pretty flat, and the châteaux are within easy reach. Expect to pay at least 50F a day for bikes in the major towns, as much as 80F in smaller villages. A good map like Michelin #6 will help you stay off the congested main routes.

Orléans

Much of Orléans is consecrated to the Maid of Orléans, Joan of Arc, who came to liberate the city from the English during the Hundred Years' War in 1429. Her statue, her name, her presence are everywhere. But you don't have to have a consuming passion for Joan to want to visit here; the town makes a comfy base for exploring the châteaux nearby. While you're in town, though, you might as well visit the **Cathédrale Ste-Croix,** where stained-glass windows tell Joan's life story, and the **Maison de Jeanne d'Arc** (3 pl. de Gaulle, tel. 38–79–22–22; admission 10F, 5F students), which displays neat dioramas of scenes from Joan's life.

COMING AND GOING Trains run frequently from Paris's Gare d'Austerlitz (82F), Blois (47F), and Tours (82F). The **station** (tel. 38–53–50–50) is four blocks from the center of town and is attached to the local and regional bus services and the **tourist office** (pl. Albert 1er, tel. 38–53–05–95). The **Les Aubrais** train station is a 10-minute ride away on a free *navette* (shuttle) that leaves from the more centrally located station.

WHERE TO SLEEP Budget accommodations are easy to find. A 15-minute walk from the station is the bright **Hôtel Coligny** (80 rue de la Gare, tel. 38–53–61–60; doubles 110F–140F), with some of the cheapest rooms in town. The **Hôtel Etoile d'Or** (25–27 pl. du Vieux Marché, tel. 38–53–49–20; doubles 140F) is slightly dumpy but centrally located. The **HI hostel** (14 rue du Faubourg Madeleine, tel. 38–62–45–75; beds 47F) is the best deal in town. Take Bus B toward Paul Bert to Jean Jaurès. **Camping Municipal d'Olivet** (rue du Pont Bouchet, tel. 38–63–53–94) has gorgeous, wooded sites on the Loiret River.

FOOD Orléans's main dining area is the lively, pedestrian **rue de Bourgogne**, where traditional French cuisine rubs elbows with African, Middle Eastern, and Asian dishes. For American food with a French-Creole accent, go to **Le Mississipi** (68 rue Bannier, tel. 38–53–39–00), with three daily lunch specials between 40F and 58F. The **Georges V** (in Les Halles Châtelet, tel. 38–53–08–79) is the town's most popular bar.

NEAR ORLEANS

Les Rapides du Val de Loire and **CTDL** operate bus lines between Orléans and towns not served by rail. They all leave from the bus station (tel. 38–53–94–75) next to the train station. Remember to call them *autocars* or *cars* rather than buses when asking for info.

Abandoned in 1956 by the bankrupt owner, the **Château de Chamerolles** (tel. 38–39–84–66; admission 25F) was practically in ruins when it was taken over by the county and carefully restored. Now the château looks brand spanking new and houses the **Musée des Parfums,** which you can see on an unguided tour through several centuries of sweet smellies. Visits are leisurely, gardens and benches are everywhere, and you can help yourself to the fresh fruit and flowers in the rooms! CTDL runs a few buses daily from Orléans to Chilleurs-aux-Bois for about 36F; from there, it's a shady 2-km walk to the château.

Blois

For all its size, Blois is a pretty sleepy town. Other than the château, there's very little to see or do in the city itself. But the area around Blois is densely packed with châteaux, and lodging and food are reasonable. If Blois is a bit of a snooze, it snores comfortably and conveniently.

The architecturally jumbled **Château de Blois** covers every major style from Gothic to Baroque. Look for François I's famous salamander logo on the **staircase** and in the **François I wing.** The king chose the symbol because the salamander was believed to spit forth the fires of good and put out the fires of evil. Notice also his wife's emblem, the ermine, and that of his mother, the swan (purity) pierced by an arrow (sin).

COMING AND GOING Several trains a day stop at Blois's **station** (tel. 54–55–31–00) from Orléans (47F) and Tours (47F). The **tourist office** (3 av. Jean-Laigret, tel. 54–74–06–49) is a short walk from the train station. For **bike rental,** call **Cycles Le Blond** (44 levée des Tuileries, tel. 54–74–30–13) or **Yamaha Sports-Moto-Cycles** (6 rue Henri Drussy, tel. 54–78–02–64).

WHERE TO SLEEP AND EAT A stone's throw from the Eglise St-Nicolas, the **Hôtel St-Nicolas** (2 rue de Sermon, tel. 54–78–05–85) and the **Hôtel Viennois** (5 quai Amedée Coutant, tel. 54–74–12–80) are the best deals in town, with singles and doubles for 110F–150F. The spotless **HI hostel** (18 rue de l'Hôtel Pasquier, tel. 54–78–27–21) is 7 km outside Blois, and the last bus out (Bus 4 toward Les Grouets) runs at 7:30.

Good, cheapish restaurants of every type cover the pedestrian quarter around the château and the old part of town around the cathedral. **La Jeune France** (62 rue Denis Papin, tel. 54–78–07–44) serves huge, delicious salads and seafood platters for less than 50F.

Most châteaux around Blois are bikeable; pick up the pamphlet "Effeuillez Blois" from the tourist office or ask at the bike shop about good routes. Pack a picnic lunch and plan to return to Blois for the night; rooms in château towns are unreasonably expensive.

It's hard to believe that the **Château de Chambord** (tel. 54–20–31–32; admission 31F, 20F students), a two-hour bike ride upriver from Blois, was built as a hunting lodge—all 440 rooms, 365 chimneys, and 5,500 acres of park and forest. François I started work on Chambord in 1519 and never took a break, even when he was so broke he couldn't ransom his sons out of Spain and had taken to melting down his subjects' silverware. The immensity of the château means you could leave without seeing some of the best parts, but try to find the **terrace** upstairs, where hundreds of chimneys form a veritable city skyline, and the double helix **staircase,** almost undoubtedly designed by Leonardo da Vinci.

Twenty km south of Blois along D765, the **Château de Cheverny** (tel. 54–79–96–29; admission 29F, 20F students) isn't as overwhelming as the château at Chambord. Although the exterior is dignified and not too inviting, the interior is warm and homey. Even with its priceless Delft vases, Gobelin tapestries, and Persian embroideries, it feels lived in. And, whadayaknow, it *is*—check out the photos of the count's family by the entrance; the real-life versions are just upstairs.

Tours

Tours, at the halfway point between Orléans and Angers, is an unhappy medium. Filled with ugly concrete high rises, it lacks the intimacy of smaller cities and the excitement of larger ones. At night, it crawls with the students who make up a tenth of the city's population, but by day it's just another polluted, industrial town. But don't knock Tours too hard; the city has heaps of cheap sleeps and eats, and the surrounding area is home to the most famous châteaux of the Loire Valley.

That said, there are a *few* things worth seeing in Tours. Classical music fills the Gothic **Cathédrale St-Gatien,** and the stained-glass windows, some of which date back to the 13th century, fill the building with light. In the creaky rooms of what used to be the archbishop's residence, the **Musée des Beaux-Arts** (18 pl. François Sicard, tel. 47–05–68–73) holds a few goodies, including a tiny Rembrandt you can hardly see behind its security glass. The **Musée du Gemmail** (7 rue du Mûrier, tel. 47–61–01–19) features stunning works of art made from layers of broken colored glass lit from behind.

COMING AND GOING Trains run frequently from Paris (151F) and Orléans (82F). The **tourist office** is in the Hôtel de Ville, across from the train station and to the left. Tickets on **Fil Bleu,** the city bus service, cost 6F20 and are good for an hour. Most buses pass place Jean Jaurès, and run until about 10 PM. Rent good-looking 10-speeds at **Montaubin** (2 rue Nationale, tel. 47–05–62–27).

WHERE TO SLEEP Tours has plenty of dirt-cheap hotels, "dirt" being the operative word here. The diviest places cluster around the train station on rue Edouard Vaillant. Try the pretty plush **Hôtel Regina** (2 rue Pimbert, tel. 47–05–25–36) behind the Grand Théâtre or the **Hôtel Val de Loire** (33 blvd. Heurteloup, tel. 47–05–37–86), just around the corner from the train station. Both have doubles for about 120F–170F. The loud and scummy **HI hostel** (Parc de Grandmont, tel. 47–25–14–45) has beds for 60F. Take Bus 1 toward Joue Blotterie or Bus 6 toward Chambray II. **Le Foyer** (16 rue Bernard Palissy, tel 47–05–38–81), off place de la Gare, has 65F beds in comfy double rooms and is a better option than the hostel for those aged 16–25.

FOOD Tours's cheap restaurants cater to the student population around **place Plumereau** (place Plume to locals). At the popular **Les Fondues** (25 pl. du Grand Marché, tel. 47–61–49–69), a full meal including wine costs you 62F. After dinner, Tours's students hang out in the bars around place Plume. **L'Excalibur** (35 rue Briçonnet, tel. 47–64–76–78), Tours's most popular disco, plays music videos in a 12th-century setting.

NEAR TOURS

Welcome to the Land of the Big-Name Châteaux! **Les Rapides de Touraine** runs private buses from Tours to some of the châteaux. Cheap accommodations around here are about as easy to find as an ice cube in your Evian; stick to Tours and Chinon as home bases.

For a short, outdoorsy excursion, bike about 10 km downriver from Tours to visit the world-renowned gardens (admission 24F) of **Villandry.** First planted in 1536, the gardens were uprooted in the 18th century when they went out of style, but redone in 1906. The **château** (tel. 47–50–02–09; admission 13F) is worth popping into to get a better view of the gardens from the upstairs windows.

CHINON The **Château de Chinon** (tel. 47–93–13–45; admission 23F, 16F students), once a favorite home of English kings, is now a crumbling shell of a fortress on the northwest edge of Chinon's centre ville. The imposing château was almost done in by Cardinal Richelieu, who took stones from Chinon rather than lugging in new materials to build his own château 20 km away. The state has since reconstructed a couple of rooms, but their efforts at authenticity are pretty sorry. One original piece is the Marie-Javelle, a bell that has been rung every half-hour since 1399, and, legend says, of its own accord at each of Joan of Arc's victories.

A few daily **trains** and **buses** go from Tours 50 km downstream to Chinon (42F). From the train station, follow the river downstream and hang a right at the statue of Rabelais to reach the town center. Chinon's **tourist office** (tel. 47–93–17–85) is at 12 rue Voltaire.

➤ **WHERE TO SLEEP AND EAT** • Reserve ahead at the hostel and plan on picnicking if you want to stay the night. Beds cost 42F at the **HI Auberge de Jeunesse, Centre d'Accueil** (rue Descartes, tel. 47–93–10–48), a five-minute walk from the train station. Place Jeanne d'Arc hosts the Thursday **market.**

CHATEAU D'AZAY-LE-RIDEAU At first glance, the turrets, moat, and thick walls of the château at Azay-le-Rideau (tel. 47–45–42–04; admission 26F, 17F ages 18–25) make it seem like a defensive stronghold; tax collector Gilles Berthelot designed the château in 1518 and tried to give his new-money palace an old-money air by adding feudal touches. He never got to enjoy the château, though; the corrupt financier fled to Italy before it was finished to avoid being hanged. The château's unusual *L*-shape is in fact only half of a planned quadrangle. Inside the château, don't miss the tapestries—18th-century marvels that were never exposed to light and have retained their vibrant colors.

Several daily trains and buses bounce 30 km down the Loire from Tours to Azay for 42F. Buses drop you right by the château; from the train station, you've got a 2-km walk along the D57.

CHATEAU DE CHENONCEAU The design of the graceful Château de Chenonceau (tel. 47–23–90–07; admission 40F, 25F students) was overseen entirely by women. After Catherine Briçonnet built the château from 1513 to 1521, Henri II's mistress, Diane de Poitiers, ordered gardens and a bridge across the Cher for easy access to her hunting grounds. Henri's wife, Catherine de Médicis, kicked Diane out and ordered her *own* gardens and tacked galleries onto the bridge. In 1589, the château passed to Henri III's widow, Louise de Lorraine. In mourning until the day she died, Louise did her second-floor room in black and gray and decorated it with skulls and thorns.

Five **trains** arrive from Tours (32F) every day. The château is about 1 km from the train station. The **tourist office** is right outside the château.

Angers

The cost of living in Anjou's calm capital is higher than it is farther up the Loire, but between the château, museums, and marvelous tapestries, Angers offers plenty to fill up a day's visit. The **Château d'Angers** (tel. 41–87–43–47) looks like a photo negative; the forbidding black walls are made of *ardoise,* a strong slate usually saved for château rooftops, while the towers are topped with the white tufa stone usually seen in château walls. With a guide, you can tour the **logis royal,** which shelters some good 14th- to 17th-century tapestries, but that's just a warmup for the stunning **Tenture de l'Apocalypse,** housed next door in a 20th-century addition (admission 31F, 20F students). The oldest preserved tapestry in the world, this 14th-century wool- and gold-thread masterpiece depicts John the Evangelist's narration of the Book of Revelation. The **tourist office** (tel. 41–23–51–11) is just outside the château on place Kennedy.

COMING AND GOING Trains arrive from Tours (77F) and Paris (192F). The **city bus** system, COTRA, is efficient, but generally only necessary for trips into the suburbs. Pick up a map at the tourist office and buy your 6F ticket from the driver.

WHERE TO SLEEP AND EAT You should have no problem finding a room in Angers year-round. **Hôtel des Lices** (25 rue des Lices, tel. 41–87–44–10) and **L'Avenue** (9 rue Jean Boudin, tel. 41–88–92–42) both have clean rooms starting at 105F for a double. The ritzy HI hostel, the **Centre Accueil du Lac de Maine** (49 av. du Lac de Maine, tel. 41–22–32–10), has 58F beds in quadruples as well as more expensive singles and doubles; there's a **camp-ground** (tel. 41–73–05–03) in the same complex. Take Bus 6 toward Val de Maine or Bouchemaine. Beds are 55F at the **Foyer des Jeunes Travailleurs** (rue Darwin, tel. 41–72–00–20). Take Bus 8 to CFA.

Angers's pedestrian quarter around place du Ralliement is chock-full of restaurants, pizzerias, crêperies, and cafés. The popular **Le Spirit Factory** (14–16 rue Bressigny, tel. 41–88–50–10) serves mussels (49F–65F) upstairs and homemade beer downstairs. Your best bet for cheap eats, though, is the market at **Les Halles** (rue Plantaganêt).

NEAR ANGERS

SAUMUR Saumur is unusual among Loire cities in that its beautifully restored **château** (tel. 41–51–30–46; admission 32F, 23F students) is not half as interesting as the town itself. Cafés line the cobblestone street, several wineries offer tastings of local wines, and the Saumur cavalry school, the **Ecole Nationale d'Equitation** (tel. 41–50–21–35), puts on very popular 60F demonstrations throughout the summer. From April through September, you can visit the school and watch students work out in the arena for half-price. Saumur's **tourist office** (pl. de la Bilange, tel. 41–51–03–06) can direct you to **Fontevraud-l'Abbaye,** where Henri II, Eleanor of Aquitaine, and Richard the Lionheart's tombs rest.

About 10 **trains** arrive daily from both Angers and Tours for about 51F. Although Saumur makes an easy day trip, stay at the modern **Centre de Séjour, Auberge de Jeunesse** (rue de Verdun, tel. 41–67–45–00; beds 44F) if you want a more leisurely visit. Head into the side streets behind quai Carnot and quai des Etats-Unis for great little cafés and restaurants.

Brittany

You can get an idea of what Brittany is all about just by looking at a map of France. A rugged peninsula jutting out into the Atlantic off the western coast of France, Brittany boasts wave-battered crags and smooth, sunny beaches, all accessible by hundreds of windswept footpaths. Off the coast, dozens of islands lure you into unexpectedly long stays. Inland, what was once a huge forest is now a world of rolling farmland and forgotten villages.

Brittany's geographic isolation mirrors its cultural separateness from the rest of France. Brittany wasn't even part of France until 1532, when Anne de Bretagne, duchess of Brittany, keeled over after having linked Brittany to France by marrying two French kings in succession. Since then, the relationship between France and Brittany has been rocky. The Bretons, descendants of 5th-century refugee Celts, have resisted the pull of French culture, preserving a language and customs all their own.

Genealogical trivia: Jack Kerouac is a direct descendant of the dukes of Brittany.

Brittany's most exported food is the *galette,* a thin buckwheat pancake; in theory, they're only filled with butter or eggs and sausage, but in practice, anything goes. *Crêpes* are just flimsier galettes, made of wheat flour and filled with, in general, things that are bad for you: sugar, butter, honey, or chocolate. Brittany's dependence on seafood shows in their *kauteriad* (sometimes spelled *côteriade*), a distinctive fish soup, and *saumon fumé,* smoked salmon. *Kouign* are delectable sugar cakes, while *kouign amann* are the same thing with butter. The local drink, *cidre* (cider), comes in *brut* (dry) and *doux* (sweet) versions.

Rennes

Only a handful of medieval streets survived Rennes's disastrous 1720 fire, and now heartless modern buildings fill the city. The remaining half-timbered houses, though, now buzz with 40,000 students during the school year—the streets around place Ste-Anne are jammed with immensely popular student bars. Near the medieval buildings and looming over one end of rue des Portes Mordelaises, the **Cathédrale St-Pierre** is a gloomy but visually rich 19th-century church. The **Palais de Justice** (pl. du Parlement, tel. 99–25–49–00) is the only one of Rennes's large buildings to have survived the 1720 fire; the ornate interior looks like a miniature Versailles.

VISITOR INFORMATION *Pont de Nemours, tel. 99–79–01–98. Train station branch: tel. 99–53–23–23.*

COMING AND GOING Trains leave from the **Gare SNCF** (tel. 99–65–50–50) for Paris (2 hrs, 246F–300F), Nantes (2 hrs, 104F), and St-Malo (1 hr, 61F). Regional buses leave from the **bus station** (blvd. Magenta, tel. 99–30–87–80) just up the street. **City buses** are plentiful, though most of Rennes is walkable. Buy single tickets for 5F50 from the driver or *carnets* (books) of 10 tickets for 36F70 from the stand (tel. 99–79–37–37) on place de la République.

WHERE TO SLEEP AND EAT Many cheap hotels cluster around the train station. **Hôtel Hermine** (doubles 95F–110F) is the slightly cheaper and scruffier annex to the prim **Hôtel Joffre** (6 rue Maréchal Joffre, tel. 99–79–37–74; doubles from 120F). Register for either with the kind woman at the Joffre. **Hôtel Riaval** (9 rue de Riaval, tel. 99–50–65–58; doubles 108F–155F) is one of the cheapest hotels in town and usually has rooms at the last minute. Rennes's picturesque **HI hostel** (10–12 canal St-Martin, tel. 99–33–22–33) has beds for 63F–103F. From the station, take Bus 2 in the summer, Bus 20 or 22 the rest of the year, and get off at rue St-Malo. Call **CROUS** (7 pl. Hoche, tel. 99–36–46–11) for info on staying in one of Rennes's dozen university residences. **Camping des Gayeulles** (rue Professeur Maurice Audin, tel. 99–36–91–22), right next to the Parc des Bois, charges 11F for a tent plus 12F per person.

Rennes has tons of ethnic restaurants (including Polish, Moroccan, and Lebanese), and crêperies are all over the place, particularly around place Ste-Anne. The elaborately decorated **Crêperie Ar Pillig** (10 rue d'Argentré, tel. 99–79–53–89) has galettes for 10F–39F and crêpes for 10F–31F. **Le Jardin des Plantes** (32 rue St-Melain, tel. 99–38–74–46) serves large dinners for 69F–85F in a half-timbered house.

NEAR RENNES

The area around Rennes attracts visitors interested in the remnants of Brittany's medieval past: Many of France's best fortress towns are clustered here, glaring suspiciously out over the rolling farmland. **Vitré,** just 30 minutes away from Rennes by train, has a castle with massive towers and a well-preserved medieval walled town that spreads out from the castle's gates. **Fougères**'s enormous castle, surrounded by a loop of the Nançon River, is in ruins after having been used as a quarry by 18th-century builders. Buses make the one-hour trip from Rennes hourly (43F). A few minutes farther away by bus or train, the northern coast makes an easy day trip from Rennes.

ST-MALO Thrust out into the sea, bound to the mainland only by tenuous man-made causeways, St-Malo is famous for its *intra muros* (within the walls), a fortified section of town on a near-island. Although much of the intra muros was reconstructed after World War II, sections of the ramparts date from the 13th century and are worth a wander. At low tide you can easily walk to the **Fort National,** a massive fortress accessible only by guided tour, and the **Grand Bé,** an island where the French author Châteaubriand was entombed.

➢ **COMING AND GOING** • Train arrive from Rennes (1 hr, 61F) at the **train station** (tel. 99-65-50-50), a 15-minute walk from the old walled town. Several different **bus** companies run buses from the station just south of Porte St-Vincent. Right next door, the **Office de Tourisme** (tel. 99-56-64-48) gives out information on bus and ferry schedules.

➢ **WHERE TO SLEEP AND EAT** • In summer call ahead, even to the hostel. **Hôtel de l'Europe** (44 blvd. de la République, tel. 99-56-13-42) and **Hôtel de l'Océan** (pl. 11 Novembre, tel. 96-39-21-51) both have doubles for 110F and up. At the comfortable **HI hostel** (37 av. du Père Umbricht, tel. 99-40-29-80), beds are 64F-78F. From the station, take Bus 5 to "Auberge." The intra muros restaurants are overpriced and tacky without exception. The city's cheapest choice is pizza; pizzerias lurk around every corner. Rue Jacques Cartier, along the landward side of the city's ramparts, has several cheap snack places stuck in between the tourist traps.

DINAN Dinan is one of the best-preserved medieval towns in Brittany. Seven-hundred-year-old ramparts tower on steep hillsides that slope down to the Rance River, and medieval buildings line rue de l'Apport, place des Merciers, place des Cordeliers, and rue de la Poissonnerie. Climb the **Tour de l'Horloge,** at the intersection of rue de l'Horloge and rue de l'Apport, for a view of the big picture. The **Office de Tourisme** (6 rue de l'Horloge, tel. 96-39-75-40), just down the street from the Tour de l'Horloge, can hook you up with Monsieur Castel, who gives great 25F tours of Dinan in French only.

➢ **COMING AND GOING** • Trains arrive at the art deco **train station** (tel. 96-39-22-39) from Rennes (1 hr, 64F) and other major towns in Brittany. **CAT** (tel. 96-39-21-05) and **TAE** buses (tel. 99-50-64-17) connect Dinan to St-Malo, Dinard, and other nearby towns.

➢ **WHERE TO SLEEP AND EAT** • **Hôtel du Théâtre** (2 rue Ste-Claire, tel. 96-39-06-91), right next to the tourist office, has one single for 80F and doubles for 105F-150F. A 30-minute walk from the train station or the center of town, the friendly **HI hostel** (Vallée de la Fontaine des Eaux, Moulin de Méen, tel. 96-39-10-83) has beds and cots in a tent outside for 46F. Sites at the **campground** next door are 24F. From town, walk downstream along the Rance on rue du Quai and look for a sign on the left.

The Hundred Years' War

Most of the châteaux in Brittany were built during the Hundred Years' War, which (surprise!) spanned 116 years. Between 1337 and 1453, the French and the English killed one another at a pretty good clip, especially after they learned how to use gunpowder. All this self-destructive fervor was inspired by a continuing conflict over who belonged on which throne and who owed allegiance to whom. King Edward III of England kicked off the war by making a claim to the French throne. After Edward's death in 1377, the fighting died down until Joan of Arc appeared on the scene in 1429, claiming God had told her to deliver Orléans from the English. After the French whipped up on the weary English at Orléans, they proceeded to kick some British butt all over the country until the English held only the coastal town of Calais and the French had unified the rest of France.

Many of Dinan's restaurants and good crêperies line rue du Petit Fort, from the Porte du Jerzual down to the riverbank. For reasonable pizza (27F–45F) and lots of vegetarian options, try **La Pergola** (5 rue de la Chaux, tel. 96–39–64–34). Those in the know go to **Bar au Prélude** (20 rue Haute-Voie, tel. 96–39–06–95) for cheap food (under 50F) and live music until 1 AM.

Côtes d'Armor

To the west of Dinan along Brittany's northern coast, the tourist towns fall behind, the coastline gets wilder and weirder, and the people tend to be friendlier and more curious about foreigners. Ties to Brittany's ancient Celtic culture are strong here in the northern half of Basse Bretagne (Deep Brittany); elders speak Breton, and Irish pubs replace French cafés.

The northern coast is traditionally divided into three color-coded sections: the **Côte d'Emeraude** (Emerald Coast), stretching from St-Malo to St-Brieuc; the **Côte de Granit Rose** (Pink Granite Coast), which includes Paimpol, the Ile de Bréhat, and Perros-Guirec; and the **Ceinture Dorée** (Gilded Belt), which curves around the little-visited northwestern tip of Brittany. Most coastal towns provide ample opportunities for playing sand sloth in the summer and for hiking along the coast year-round.

Perros-Guirec is the best place to scope out the pink granite boulders of the region and lounge on an idyllic crescent of white sand enclosed by plunging hills. About four daily buses arrive from **Lannion,** a town on the Paris–Brest rail line that has one of the few youth hostels (tel. 96–37–91–28) near the coast. The Sentier des Douaniers footpath leads from Perros-Guirec through fern forests, past cliffs and amazing pink granite boulders, to the beach at **Ploumanach.**

A few miles inland, snuggled down at the bottom of a valley, is **Morlaix,** a near-obligatory stop on the way to or from Brest. Stop here to see *maisons à lanterne,* houses with richly sculpted facades that are products of a 16th-century architectural rage centered here. Staying at Morlaix's **HI hostel** (3 rte. de Paris, tel. 98–88–13–63), you can take your time visiting nearby **Carantec,** where you'll find one of the most popular postcard subjects in Brittany, the Château du Taureau, a barren castle-island in the middle of the bay.

BREST

Allied bombs flattened Brest during World War II, and whitewashed concrete buildings sprang up all over town in the '50s and '60s. There's not a lot for travelers to see here, but Brest's **Océanopolis** (Port de Plaisance, tel. 98–34–40–40), a huge aquarium and museum, is worth your time. Cough up the 50F, 40F for those under 25, and you'll painlessly learn all sorts of things about marine life and ocean dynamics. Brest's other main drawing card is that it's the pickup point for ferries to the windswept Ile d'Ouessant and the Crozon peninsula. The **tourist office** (8 av. Georges Clémenceau, tel. 98–44–24–96) can help you unravel ferry schedules.

COMING AND GOING TGV and regular **trains** travel to Brest's station (tel. 98–80–50–50) from Paris several times a day for 334F. Trains also connect Brest to Morlaix (49F), Rennes (164F), and Quimper (76F). The regional **bus station** (tel. 98–44–46–73) is across from the train station. From the Port de Commerce, the **Penn ar Bed** ferry company (tel. 98–80–24–68) runs ferries to the Ile d'Ouessant and other islands. Most of the **local bus** lines radiate from place de la Liberté. An hour-long trip costs 6F.

WHERE TO SLEEP AND EAT Lodging is cheap, easy to find, and generally low-quality. The rooms at the **Hôtel Bar du Musée** (1 rue Couédic, tel. 98–44–70–20; doubles 105F) are a little frayed, but basically comfy. The airy, modern **HI hostel** (rue Kerbriant, Port de Plaisance du Moulin Blanc, tel. 98–41–90–41; beds 61F) has lots of amenities, and it's close to a beach. Take Bus 7 from the train station to the end, turn left uphill, and follow the signs.

Head to rue Jean Macé for inexpensive meals with the locals. **Le Soleil d'Or** (4 rue Graveran, tel. 98–43–61–94) is a friendly vegetarian restaurant with 43F main dishes.

NEAR BREST

ILE D'OUESSANT The Ile d'Ouessant, isolated from the mainland by 20 km of waves and treacherous tides, resembles many other Breton islands: it's small, windswept, and rocky. You can bike around the island and admire its craggy coast, compact farmhouses, and thousands of sheep. The trip out to the far western point rewards you with a view of wave-torn boulders, several ruined outposts, and glimpses of the island's seals and rare birds.

Penn ar Bed ferry company (*see* Brest, *above*) charges 162F for a round-trip ticket from Brest. Ferries leave on this 2½-hour jaunt daily from the dock in Brest at 8:30 AM, and pull away from the island at 5 PM, 6:30 PM on Sundays. Since the ferry only gives you six hours on the island, consider staying overnight. Hotels cluster in **Lampaul**, the town at the island's center, an 8F bus ride from the port. Try the **Hôtel de l'Océan** (tel. 98–48–80–03) or the **Hôtel de la Duchesse Anne** (tel. 98–48–80–25), both with doubles for 150F. At the entrance to Lampaul, the **tourist office** (tel. 98–48–85–83) has maps and ferry info.

The Southern Coast

From Quimper to Nantes, Brittany's kaleidoscopic southern coast is one of the most popular vacation spots in France. Traditional crowd-pullers, the twisting streets and tottering medieval houses of Quimper furnish rich postcard material. At the northern edge of the Golfe du Morbihan, **Vannes** draws tourists like flies to its considerable vieille ville, bordered by a long stretch of ramparts, towers, and gates. The coast's sunny beaches, though, especially those at Quiberon, are the real reason to come here. Nobody beats Belle-Ile's sea-bound beauty: The island's sandy beaches and tormented coast have inspired more than one poet. The small towns of **Quimperlé** and **Auray** have modest vieille villes and summertime festivals, while Concarneau maintains a quintessentially Breton fishing port in the face of massive tourist invasions. Neolithic menhirs sprinkle the whole region, but the densest concentration line the fields outside **Carnac.**

QUIMPER

Quimper has all the amenities of a standard Breton tourist town: a medieval town center, a soaring cathedral, and a pleasant river. The requisite **vieille ville** extends from the doorsteps of the St-Corentin church along rue Kéréon to place Terre-au-Duc, and north toward place avenue Beurre. The vast 13th- to 15th-century **Cathédrale St-Corentin** remains very much in use by fervent *quimperois,* giving the candlelit vaults a meditative air. To the side of the cathedral, the **Palais des Evêques** (1 rue du Roi Gradlon, tel. 98–95–21–60) leads to a small garden and the extremely modest remains of the town's ramparts. The helpful staff at the **Office de Tourisme** (pl. de la Résistance, tel. 98–53–04–05) leads summertime guided tours of Quimper for 20F, 15F students.

COMING AND GOING Several trains daily leave for Brest (76F) and for Nantes (164F) from the **train station** (tel. 98–90–50–50). A chaos of **bus companies** crisscross the region. Check the schedules posted in the parking lot of the train station for info. Most of the local bus lines converge near the Odet river next to the vieille ville, and a ticket costs 5F70.

WHERE TO SLEEP AND EAT Few hotels in Quimper are cheap; those that are, are quickly booked. **Hôtel Pascal** (19 av. de la Gare, tel. 98–90–00–81; doubles from 140F) has clean, drab rooms just across the street from the train station. Or, brave the moldy bathrooms at the otherwise okay **Hôtel Celtic** (13 rue Douarnenez, tel. 98–55–59–35). Simple and clean, the **HI hostel** (6 av. des Oiseaux, tel. 98–55–41–67; beds 42F) backs onto a forest 2 km from the train station. Take Bus 1 toward Penhars to the Chaptal stop. Reservations are highly recommended. **Camping Municipal** (tel. 98–90–62–02), right behind the hostel, is overrun with RVs and charges 23F per person and 38F per site.

Several late-night crêperies huddle on rue du Frout behind the Cathédrale St-Corentin. The permanent covered market, **Les Halles,** is bordered by rue St-François and rue Astor. A couple of great bars and crêperies stay open late on rue Ste-Catherine. The **Céili Pub** (4 rue Aristide Briand, tel. 98–95–17–61) attracts locals with Breton and Irish music and drink.

CONCARNEAU

The hordes of summertime tourists come to Concarneau to see its island fortress, small and disappointing considering all the ballyhoo. A better reason to come here is to delve into the area's fishing industry for a real taste of Breton maritime life. Start at the fantastic **Musée de la Pêche** (rue Vauban, tel. 98–97–10–20), a striking museum on fishing boats and techniques. The 30F admission includes access to two trawlers. Next, watch the unloading of fish that takes place on the docks behind the big warehouse on quai Carnot, Sunday–Wednesday, midnight–6 AM. Catch 40 winks, then return for the morning *criée,* or fish auction, Monday–Thursday 7–9 AM.

To get to Concarneau, take a **Caoudal bus** (tel. 98–97–35–31) from Quimper (22F) or Quimperlé (30F). If you want to stay the night, go to the great **youth hostel** (quai de la Croix, tel. 98–97–03–47) that sidles right up to the coast near the **Plage des Sables Blancs.** Beds cost 42F per night.

QUIBERON

The Presqu'ile de Quiberon is a 15-km stretch of rough coastal cliffs and beaches joined to the mainland by a hair's breadth of sand. Though in many ways similar to other crowded and pricey beach towns, Quiberon's spectacular coast and its port, with departures for the islands of Belle-Ile, Hoedic, and Houat, will be of interest to the the adventurous traveler. An 18-km footpath follows the dramatic western coast, dubbed the **Côte Sauvage.** Beaches ring the coast like pearls, and the **Grande Plage** is the most popular. The **Office de Tourisme** (7 rue de Verdun, tel. 97–50–07–84) has info on rentals of Windsurfers and kayaks.

COMING AND GOING Trains only make it to Quiberon from July to early September. Otherwise, **TTO** buses (tel. 97–47–29–64) and **Bayon Transports** (tel. 97–24–26–20) run several buses daily from nearby towns like Carnac (21F) and Auray (34F). Buses stop at the train station.

WHERE TO SLEEP AND EAT Cheap hotels are hard to come by. The **Hôtel Bon Acceuil** (6 quai de l'Houat, tel. 97–50–07–92) has unremarkable doubles for 110F–135F, and the **HI hostel** (45 rue du Roch Priol, tel. 97–50–15–54) has 50 beds that go for 43F. Campsites are 23F.

Most of Quiberon's restaurants post a nearly identical 69F menu of seafood and a Breton dessert. For less money you can eat at one of the ubiquitous crêperies or across from the station at the **Armor Express** (tel. 97–30–42–26), where a fishy main dish is 41F.

Nantes

The writer Stendhal remarked of 19th-century Nantes, "I hadn't taken 20 steps before I recognized a great city." Since then, the river that flowed around the upper-crust Ile Feydeau has been filled in and replaced with a rushing torrent of traffic, and now major highways cut through the heart of the town. Still, the unlucky Ile Feydeau, surrounded and bisected by highways, still preserves the tottering 18th-century mansions built with wealth from Nantes's huge slave trade. Nantes's 15th-century **Château des Ducs de Bretagne** (pl. Marc Elder, tel. 40–41–56–56), a heavily fortified castle built by the dukes of Brittany, is also still in relatively good shape, despite having lost an entire tower during a gunpowder explosion in 1800. The 15th-century **Cathédrale St-Pierre** (pl. St-Pierre) has had a tougher time of it. It was damaged during the Revolution, had its windows blown out from the château's 1800 gunpowder explosion, was bombed by Allies in 1944, and had its roof completely burned up in 1972. Despite all this abuse, its immense height and airy interior make it one of France's best. Nantes's many museums are skippable, but at least the **Musée des Beaux-Arts** (10 rue Georges Clemenceau, tel. 40–41–91–25) even has huge Rubens hanging above the sinks in the bathroom. West of the centre ville on Bus Route 21, the entertaining **Musée Jules Verne** (3 rue de l'Hermitage, tel. 40–69–72–52) is, happily, heavy on pictures and light on actual facts about Verne, who spent his life in Nantes.

VISITOR INFORMATION *Pl. du Commerce, tel. 40–47–04–51.*

COMING AND GOING Nantes's **train station** (tel. 40–08–50–50) is a 10-minute walk from the vieille ville. Trains leave for Paris almost hourly (254F) and for Rennes (104F) seven times daily. **Cariane Atlantique** (5 cour 5e Otages, tel. 40–20–46–99) runs regional buses.

Trams and local buses tote you around town, though all the major sights and most of the cheap lodgings are clustered within the vieille ville. The ticket stand at the Commerce tram stop has free maps of the bus and tram systems. One ticket, good for an hour on both tram and bus, is 7F; five tickets are 27F; and 10 are 50F.

WHERE TO SLEEP AND EAT Nantes has lots of cheap hotels around the centre ville. The **Hôtel Surcouf** (41 rue Richebourg, tel. 40–74–17–25; doubles 86F–240F) is a stone's throw from the château. At the **Hôtel St-Daniel** (4 rue du Bouffay, tel. 40–47–41–25; doubles 125F–150F), some rooms overlook a garden behind the Ste-Croix church. The modern and antiseptic **HI hostel** (2 pl. de la Manufacture, tel. 40–20–57–25), a 20-minute walk from the sights, charges 50F–60F a night. From the train station, turn right on boulevard Stalingrad and follow the tram tracks to the end of the manufacturing plant and turn left. The less convenient **Centre Jean-Macé** (90 rue du Préfet Bonnefoy, tel. 40–74–55–74) and the **Foyer des Jeunes Travailleurs Porte Neuve** (1 rue Porte-Neuve, tel. 40–20–00–80) also house young travelers for 52F and 63F, respectively. **Camping du Val de Cens** (21 blvd. du Petit Port, tel. 40–74–47–94) has pleasant spots right on the edge of a forest for 20F per site plus 15F per person.

The pedestrian areas around place du Bouffay and place Ste-Croix are the best places to look for student-oriented restaurants. Place du Bouffay is also home to a market that dates back to the 16th century. **La Crêperie Jaune** (1 rue des Echevins, tel. 40–47–15–71) is always jammed with students who order the 50F *pavé nantais,* a big galette stuffed with ham, cheese, and veggies. **Le Petit Bacchus** (5 rue Beauregard, tel. 40–47–50–46) serves great menus (50F, 70F, and 98F) in cozy, low-ceilinged rooms. **Rue Scribe,** near place Graslin, is the spot par excellence for late-night bars.

Normandy
Every summer, bus loads of tourists swarm through Normandy's medieval city of Rouen, the magnificent rock island of Mont St-Michel, and the popular seaside resorts along the northern coast. All three areas merit the attention, but they have little in common with the rest of isolated and inward-looking Normandy. Away from the hordes of vacationing Brits and Parisians, travelers can happily lose themselves in the region's cliff-lined coast, apple orchards, and green countryside, where a crowd is a Norman farmer with his herd of brown-and-white cows.

From Normandy's ubiquitous cows come creamy Camembert, Livarot, and Pont l'Evêque **cheeses,** all named after towns in the region; any dish *à la Normande* is served with a cheese-and-cream sauce. Fiery **calvados** brandy is drunk before, during, and after meals, as well as with coffee. Calvados comes in handy when you're stuffed with the rich regional food; simply take a swig to burn a *trou normand* (Norman hole) in your stomach and make more room. The restaurants love it.

Rouen

With many monuments, churches, and medieval streets, Rouen is a living, open-air museum as well as a busy industrial port city of about a half-million people. Corneille and Flaubert both lived here, and Victor Hugo nicknamed Rouen the "City of One Hundred Spires," referring to its church-crowded skyline. The city was heavily bombed during World War II, but parts of the medieval town of the Rive Droite (the right bank of the Seine) miraculously survived, and the rest has been reconstructed.

Joan of Arc once asked the question, "Oh Rouen, art thou then my final resting place?" In short, yes it was. She was held captive in the still-standing Tour Jeanne d'Arc and was burned at the stake on May 30, 1431, on the place du Vieux Marché.

BASICS The English-speaking staff at the **Office de Tourisme** (25 pl. de la Cathédrale, tel. 35–71–41–77) dispenses armloads of brochures. The **American Express** office (1–3 pl. Jacques Lelieur, off rue Général Leclerc, tel. 35–98–19–80) is the only one in Normandy. Pick up poste restante mail at the central **post office** (45 rue Jeanne d'Arc, tel. 35–08–73–73). The postal code is 76000.

COMING AND GOING The station (tel. 35–98–50–50) is on place Bernard-Tissot at the far northern end of rue Jeanne d'Arc, about a 10-minute walk north of the center of town. Trains travel to and from Paris's Gare St-Lazare (95F), Caen (112F), and Le Havre (65F). **Compagnie Normande d'Autobus** runs regional buses from the **bus station** (rue des Charettes, tel. 35–71–23–29) on the north bank of the Seine.

Like Paris, Rouen is divided by the Seine. The medieval section of town is on the Rive Droite. The old town is relatively compact and walkable. Call **Allo le bus** (tel. 35–52–52–00) for information about bus routes; bus tickets are 4F50 each and a carnet of 10 is 31F80. Buy single tickets from the driver, carnets from a tabac.

WHERE TO SLEEP Prices on the Left Bank are not particularly cheap, so go ahead and stay on the right, closer to all the sights. **Hôtel Normandy** (47 rue du Renard, tel. 35–71–13–69; doubles 62F–82F), the cheapest hotel, is about a 20-minute walk from the station. The convenient **Hôtel du Sphynx** (130 rue Beauvoisine, tel. 35–71–35–86), just north of the town center, and the **Hôtellerie du Vieux Logis** (5 rue Joyeuse, tel. 35–71–55–30) are slightly more upscale. On the Rive Gauche, the institutional and generally unpleasant hostel **Centre de Séjour** (118 blvd. de l'Europe, tel. 35–72–06–45) has beds in recently renovated rooms for 54F50. Take Bus 12 or Bus 5 from the station to the St-Julien stop.

FOOD Most Rouen restaurants are pricey, but for minimum bucks, there's always the open-air market at place St-Marc Friday–Sunday. Just off place de la Cathédrale, **Natural** (3 rue du Petit Salut, tel. 35–98–15–74) serves vegetarian food like risotto with mushrooms (35F), and tartes (45F), lunch only. **Au Temps des Cerises** (51 rue Basnages, tel. 35–89–98–00) features filling dishes made with Normandy cheeses. Menus are 58F for lunch or 120F for dinner.

WORTH SEEING The most important sights lie close together between place du Vieux Marché and St-Maclou and can be covered on a walking tour. Built and rebuilt between the 12th and 16th centuries, the Cathédrale de Notre-Dame (pl. de la Cathédrale) is now undergoing restoration to make it whiter-than-white. When the current restorations are complete you will be able to climb to the top of the **Gros Horloge** (rue du Gros Horloge; admission 11F, students free) to see a small clockworks museum and a knockout view of the city. The magnificent Flamboyant Gothic **Eglise St-Ouen** (pl. du Général de Gaulle) is all that remains of an ancient abbey founded by Benedictine monks during the Carolingian era. The aesthetic merits of the odd **Eglise Jeanne d'Arc** (pl. du Vieux Marché), completed in 1979, are debatable; the shape of the roof is *supposed* to evoke the flames of Joan's fire, while the stained-glass windows contrast with the church's modern architecture. Built in 15th-century Flamboyant Gothic style, the **Eglise St-Maclou** (pl. Barthélémy) has beautifully carved wooden doors from 1552. Across the street and to the left is the fantastically decorated **Aître St-**

Maclou (186 rue Martainville), a 16th-century half-timbered house that originally served as a charnel house, a building where they dump the bodies of the dearly departed. The more-interesting-than-it-sounds ironworks museum, **Musée le Secq des Tournelles** (Eglise St-Laurent, rue Jacques Villon), displays intricate wrought-iron objects like keys, coffeemakers, and weapons.

AFTER DARK The hip hang out until 2 AM at the super-popular **Café Leffe** (36 pl. des Carmes, tel. 35–71–93–30). **Le Nickel Chrome** (26 rue St-Etienne de Tonneliers, tel. 35–15–37–37) is très chic, with rock, jazz, and blues starting around 11.

NEAR ROUEN

If you travel northwest from Rouen through the lush Seine valley, you pass through the almost-undisturbed ruins of abbeys and churches in the towns that border the **Forêt de Brotonne.** Regional buses from Rouen following the **Route des Abbayes** will drop you off in most of these tiny towns. Continuing farther northwest you reach the coast, with its white chalk cliffs and popular fishing and resort towns. In the 19th and early 20th centuries, these French versions of British bathing resorts attracted writers and artists like Maupassant, Proust, Monet, and Braque.

Etretat is perhaps the most attractive of the towns along the "Alabaster Coast," which stretches from Le Havre to Dieppe. Although the promenade along the pebbly beach is congested with seedy cafés and *frites* (french fry) stands, the town is justly famous for its magnificent cliff arches that jut into the ocean. The price of food and hotels here means Etretat works best as a day trip; buses traveling from Fécamp, Dieppe, and Le Havre frequently stop here.

FECAMP Fécamp is more hick and smells fishier than Dieppe (*see below*), but the small seaport attracts hordes of visitors on sunny summer days. As well as sporting chalk cliffs and rocky beaches, this is also the site of the Baroque **Benedictine Palace and Distillery** (110 rue Alexandre le Grand, tel. 35–10–26–00), which produces the sharp, sweet Benedictine liqueur and offers tours complete with a sample for 25F. The **tourist office** (113 rue Alexandre le Grand, tel. 35–28–51–01) is across the street from the Benedictine Palace.

➤ **COMING AND GOING** • Several trains daily run to Dieppe (97F), Paris (141F), and Rouen (63F) from the **train station** (tel. 35–28–24–82). **Auto Car Gris** (8 av. Gambetta, tel. 35–28–16–04) runs buses to Etretat several times a day for 25F.

➤ **WHERE TO SLEEP AND EAT** • Fécamp's hotels are cheap for a coastal town. The **Hôtel Moderne** (3 av. Gambetta, tel. 35–28–04–04) has simple doubles without shower for 110F–130F. The **HI hostel** (rue du Commandant Roquigny, tel. 35–29–75–79; beds 40F, campsites 25F), open summers only, is in a small house on a hill overlooking the town. On the cliffs south of town, the **Camping de Reneville** (tel. 35–28–20–97) has beautiful views and costs 34F a night for two people and a tent. Look along the quay for relatively inexpensive brasseries, or try **Bar des Halles** (1 pl. Bellet), a brasserie that serves good omelets or fish soup for 20F–25F.

DIEPPE Dieppe is your typical seaside resort, filled with French and British weekenders who sunbathe, shop on the Grande Rue, or have a go at the card tables. Although the town was largely rebuilt after World War II, it still has some historic neighborhoods, especially around the **Eglise St-Jacques,** a mossy 14th-century building with Renaissance carvings. The beach is bordered by a neatly trimmed **lawn,** where Allied troops attempted a landing on August 19, 1942, and lost more than half their 6,000 troops. Overlooking town from the cliffs to the northwest, a 15th-century **château** offers a view of Dieppe's guano-covered rooftops; inside, a worthwhile museum (admission 25F) houses paintings, maps, and African ivory carvings. For more info, talk to the friendly folks at the **tourist office** (quai du Carénage, tel. 35–84–11–77).

➤ **COMING AND GOING** • The **train station** (tel. 35–84–20–71) runs daily trains to Rouen (50F). **Sealink** (tel. 35–84–80–54) ferries make the four-hour 160F run to Newhaven in England from the *gare maritime* at quai Henri IV. You can reach the main sights in town

FRANCE

on foot, but buses can save you a long uphill haul to the youth hostel. The **Société des Transports Urbains Dieppois** (tel. 35–84–49–49) distributes bus schedules at 1 place Ventabren, off quai Duquesne.

➤ **WHERE TO SLEEP AND EAT** • Hotels here are not cheap and are crowded during July and August. **Hôtel de la Jetée** (5 rue de l'Asile Thomas, tel. 35–84–89–98; doubles 120F–180F) has clean, attractive rooms, some with a bit of an ocean view. If it's full, try **Hôtel au Grand Duquesne** (15 pl. St-Jacques, tel. 35–84–21–51; doubles 150F–180F). The **HI hostel** (48 rue Louis Fromager, tel. 35–84–85–73) is southwest of town. Take Bus 2 to the Château Michel stop.

Café and brasserie prices tend to be cheaper farther away from the quay. **Restaurant les Tourelles** (43 rue du Cdt. Fayolle, tel. 35–84–15–88) serves good seafood and traditional Norman cuisine; lunch and dinner menus are 51F and 61F. Weekly markets sell food on Grande Rue and place Nationale all day Saturday and on Tuesdays and Thursdays 8–1.

Caen

Like many towns in the region, Caen was reduced to rubble by artillery and bombing in 1944 when the Allied troops descended on the town to recapture it from the Germans. Still, two magnificent abbeys survived the war. When William the Conqueror blew his chance to get into heaven by marrying his cousin, Mathilda of Flanders, he had the **Abbaye aux Hommes** (tel. 31–30–42–01) constructed to atone for his sins. The nave and towers remain from the original 11th-century abbey church, **Eglise St-Etienne.** Mathilda promised to do her part in the expiation process when she married her cousin, and so founded the **Abbaye aux Dames** (off blvd. de la République, tel. 31–06–98–98). It's less ornate than the Men's Abbey but it's still a fine example of Romanesque architecture. Normandy war museums are legion, but **Mémorial: Un Musée pour la Paix** (Esplanade Eisenhower, tel. 31–06–06–44), its one *peace* museum, is special; one gallery is dedicated to Nobel Peace Prize winners. Admission is 53F, 44F for students. For more info on Caen's sights, stop by the **tourist office** (pl. St-Pierre, tel. 31–86–27–65).

COMING AND GOING The **train station** (tel. 31–83–50–50), south of town on place de la Gare, has trains to Paris (153F), Rouen (112F), and Bayeux (29F). Regional buses leave from the **bus station** (tel. 31–44–77–44) right next to the train station. Caen's centre ville is easy to get around on foot, but the city **bus system,** CTAC, has an office on 11 boulevard Maréchal Leclerc (tel. 31–85–42–76) and an information booth near the train station. Tickets, available from the driver, are 5F50 each.

WHERE TO SLEEP AND EAT Head up avenue du 6 Juin and look for hotels around place de la Résistance. The **Hôtel Auto-Bar** (40 rue de Bras, a block south of rue St-Pierre, tel. 31–86–12–48; doubles 98F) has clean, no-frills rooms conveniently located near the town's museums. In an old stone and wood building, the **Hôtel St-Etienne** (2 rue de l'Académie, tel. 31–86–35–82; doubles 120F–160F) has small, comfortable rooms. As usual, the **HI hostel** (68 rue Eustache Restout, tel. 31–52–19–96; beds 65F) is a hassle to get to, but the two- and four-person rooms are nice. Take Bus 5 or 17 from the station or the centre ville to Fresnel. The **Camping Municipal** (Rte. de Louvigny, tel. 31–73–60–92) is open June–September and costs 15F per person and 8F per tent. Take Bus 13 from the centre ville.

Cafés and brasseries cluster in the **quartier Vaugueux** and on **rue de Geôle** near the château. **La Petite Auberge** (17 rue des Equipes d'Urgences, off rue St-Jean near pl. de la Résistance, tel. 31–86–43–30) serves delicious traditional Norman food for less than 75F.

NEAR CAEN

Northeast of Caen stretches the **Côte Fleurie** (Flowered Coast), a string of ritzy resort towns between Honfleur and Cabourg. The population of the small beach towns here triples in the summer, when French and foreign tourists come to spend money on overpriced cocktails and luxury hotels. West of the Côte Fleurie, the beaches attract travelers for another reason: Here thousands of Allied troops arrived in the 1944 D-Day landings, a turning point of World War II.

East of Trouville, **Honfleur** is one of the prettiest and most interesting of the little seaside towns along the Côte Fleurie. Unlike many towns in Normandy, it was untouched by World War II and much of its Renaissance architecture remains intact. Buses from Caen, Le Havre, and many towns in between arrive at Honfleur's **Bus Verts** station (pl. de la Porte-de-Rouen, tel. 31–89–28–41). The **tourist office** (pl. Arthur Boudin, tel. 31–89–23–30) might be able find you a less-than-extravagant spot in a guest house.

BAYEUX Most travelers to Bayeux don't pay much attention to the town's magnificent **Gothic cathedral** or historic houses of the vieille ville. They're too busy making a beeline for its famous 11th-century **tapestry** (Centre Guillaume le Conquérant, tel. 31–92–05–48), which depicts William the Conqueror's invasion of England. Actually a linen embroidery, the work narrates Will's trials and victory over his cousin Harold in 58 amusing, embroidered scenes. Admission is 28F, 13F for students. Consult the **tourist office** (1 rue des Cuisiniers, tel. 31–92–16–26) for info on Bayeux's lesser-known attractions, and for help in arranging a visit to the nearby D-Day landing beaches.

➤ **COMING AND GOING** • Trains run to Caen (29F) and Paris (164F) from Bayeux's **train station** (tel. 31–92–80–50). **Bus Verts** (tel. 31–92–02–92) has buses to Caen and to Arromanches in the summer only. To get to the centre ville from the train station, turn left on RN13 and follow the signs.

➤ **WHERE TO SLEEP AND EAT** • The 100F doubles at **Hôtel de la Gare** (26 pl. de la Gare, tel. 31–92–10–70) are small and a little dingy but generally comfortable. Jean-Marc, the owners' son, leads informative tours (100F) to the D-Day beaches in English. The **Auberge de Jeunesse, Family Home** (39 rue Général de Dais, tel. 31–92–15–22) has beds for 75F and up. From the station, follow the FAMILY HOME signs or take the "Auberge" minibus.

Crêperies surround the cathedral; brasseries and pizzerias are on rue St-Jean. **Café Inn** (67 rue St-Martin, tel. 31–21–11–37) looks like an English country house and serves dainty salads and sandwiches for 15F–32F.

D-DAY BEACHES In the predawn darkness of June 6, 1944, thousands of U.S. and British paratroopers dropped from the sky along an 80-km stretch of coast west of Cabourg during "Operation Overlord." Their mission was to blow up river crossings, sever enemy communications, and distract the Germans so they would be unable to attack the seaborne assault troops due to land later that morning on five beaches: Omaha, Utah, Sword, Gold, and Juno. After successfully gaining control of Normandy, the Allied troops swept through France. The events and consequences of this momentous invasion are immortalized in many museums and cemeteries in Arromanches and on the nearby beaches.

Arromanches, a town on Gold Beach, is the best place to see the remains of Port Winston, one of the concrete ports where Allied troops unloaded their supplies during the invasion. The **Musée de Débarquement,** overlooking the ocean, provides a detailed account of the construction of Port Winston, as well as the usual collection of Allied invasion paraphernalia. West of Arromanches, overlooking Omaha Beach, the moving **St-Laurent cemetery** is covered with endless rows of white crosses and stars of David. West of Omaha Beach is **Pointe du Hoc,** where American Rangers scaled the 100-foot cliffs to destroy the German artillery that threatened troops landing on the Omaha and Utah beaches.

➤ **COMING AND GOING** • Unless you have a car, the D-Day beaches are best visited on a bus tour from Bayeux. **Bus Fly** (tel. 31–22–00–08) leaves from the hostel or the tourist office, while smaller **Normandy Tours** (tel. 31–92–10–70) leaves from Bayeux's Hôtel de la Gare (*see Bayeux, above*). Both tour companies charge about 100F per person and conduct tours in French and English.

Mont St-Michel

Acting as a homing signal to every traveler in France, Mont St-Michel is a 264-foot mound of rock topped by a delicate abbey that looms a few hundred yards off the coast. The causeway from the mainland leads over a flat, sandy bay bed at low tide, but the waters roll almost to the causeway's edge when the tide rises. You approach the Mont's maze of chambers and spires via a single winding street that seethes with human activity. To avoid as much misery as possible, try to visit off-season; the crowds are almost unbearable in July and August.

A lively guided tour (tel. 33–60–14–14) that costs 32F, 21F for students, takes you through the impressive abbey and the abbey church, as well as the **Merveille**, a 13th-century, three-story collection of rooms and passageways. The 52F tour (41F students) includes the delicate **Escalier de Dentelle** (Lace Staircase) and **pre-Roman church.** Between mid-June and September, light and music shows are held Monday–Saturday 10 PM–midnight. Nearly the entire abbey is at your disposal then, guide-free and magically lit up. Admission is 60F, 35F for students. The **tourist office** (tel. 33–60–14–30) on the left behind the first gate as you enter town can give you more information.

COMING AND GOING STN buses (tel. 33–60–00–35) run the 6 km from Pontorson, the nearest town served by train. The buses take you directly to the Porte du Roi main gate in 15 minutes for 20F. To avoid crowds on the way up to the abbey, go through the Gendarmerie gateway to the left of the main entrance.

WHERE TO SLEEP Reserve, reserve, reserve, or sleep in a nearby town like Pontorson or Avranches. The simple, clean doubles at the **Hôtel du Mouton Blanc** (Grande Rue, tel. 33–60–14–08) are the cheapest on the Mont, starting at 200F, but are usually booked far in advance. The **Hôtel St-Aubert** (rte. de Mont-St-Michel, tel. 33–60–08–74; doubles 250F–350F) is 2 km from the Mont. The nearest campground, **Camping du Mont** (tel. 33–60–09–33), is often crowded in summer. It costs 13F per person and 11F per tent or car. Many people visiting the Mont stay in Avranches's **HI hostel** (15 rue du Jardin des Plantes, tel. 33–58–06–54; beds 50F).

Champagne and the North

Lacking the easy charm of most of the country, this region seduces relatively few tourists from Paris and the rest of France. The flat farmland doesn't have a lot in the way of dramatic vistas, but the vineyards of Champagne add a sparkle to the region. Each year, millions of bottles of bubbly pour down thirsty throats in Reims and Epernay while thousands of travelers tour the champagne houses and their moldy chalk cellars.

Reims

Most of Reims's historic buildings were flattened during World War I, but the city is home to some of the biggest names in champagne production. Hundreds of chalky tunnels serve as the damp and moldy berth for millions of bottles of champagne. Most champagne houses offer free tours, complete with a sample and a propaganda blitz at the end. **Mumm** (34 rue du Champ de Mars, tel. 26–49–59–70) is the closest to the centre ville, but its frequent English tours tend to be huge and bland. The slide show at **Pommery** (5 pl. du Général Gouraud, tel. 26–61–62–55) is one of the worst, but their moldy tunnels were excavated by the Romans about 2,000 years ago. **Taittinger** (9 pl. St-Niçaise, tel. 26–85–45–35) has even better tunnels, but there's a 15F fee for a tour.

When you're done at the champagne houses, stagger over to Reims's huge **Cathédrale de Notre-Dame.** Decorated with obvious glee by some 13th-century cutups, the facade features stern saints alternating with giggling angels. Devoid of the video-camera crowd that infests the cathedral, the **Basilique St-Remi** (53 rue St-Simon, tel. 26–04–07–70) swallows you up in its hangarlike nave. For your daily art fix, visit the **Musée de Beaux-Arts** (8 rue Chanzy, tel. 26–47–28–44), with a small but stimulating collection that includes a room of Corot and Jacques-Louis David's *La Mort de Marat*.

VISITOR INFORMATION *2 rue Guillaume de Machault, next to the cathedral, tel. 26–47–25–69.*

COMING AND GOING The **train station** (tel. 26–88–50–50), about a 10-minute walk from the center of town, runs trains to Paris's Gare de l'Est (1½ hrs, 103F) and Epernay (20 min, 30F). **STDM Trans-Champagne** (tel. 26–65–17–07) and **RTA** (tel. 23–68–03–41) both provide bus transportation around the region. **Transports Urbains de Reims** (6 rue Chanzy, tel. 26–88–25–38) runs the city buses (5F); all stop in front of the train station.

WHERE TO SLEEP AND EAT Place Drouet d'Erlon and rue de Thillois, just across the park from the train station, harbor a number of cheap hotels. Bright, pleasant doubles at the **Hôtel Linguet** (14 rue Linguet, tel. 26–47–31–89) are 80F–130F. **Hôtel St-Andre** (46 av. Jean Jaurès, tel. 26–47–24–16), northeast of place Aristide Briand, rents some of its doubles for 89F–195F. Reserve in advance for the 63F beds at the **HI hostel** (Parc Léo Lagrange, tel. 26–40–52–60), 20 minutes from the station. From the station, cross the park and turn right onto boulevard Général Leclerc, cross the Pont de Vesle, take the first left onto chaussée Bocquaine, and look for the CENTRE INTERNATIONAL DE SEJOUR sign. If they're full, call the **Foyer ARPEJ** (66 rue de Courcelles, tel. 26–47–46–52) or the **Résidence Gérard Philipe** (2 rue Gérard Philipe, tel. 26–85–21–00).

What's the Secret of Good Champagne? Ask the Riddler

Dom Pérignon, a blind 17th-century Benedictine monk, was the first to discover the secret of bubbly production. Today, champagne is not made so differently from the way he did it 300 years ago. Chardonnay, Pinot Noir, and sometimes Pinot Meunier grapes ferment separately and are then mixed into each house's distinctive blend and bottled. Left upside down in chilly underground tunnels, the heavy-walled bottles are frequently turned by "riddlers," men who spend three years learning exactly how to turn bottles in order to nudge the sediment down into the neck. After a while the bottles are opened, the sediment shoots out, a small quantity of liqueur is added, and the corks are tied down for good with wire. It takes about three years of fermentation to produce the proper level of fizz, alcohol, and taste.

Irritatingly, champagne costs about as much in Champagne as it does in Chicago, but there are a couple of ways to get some cheaply. Wine stores can usually recommend excellent but unknown champagnes for around 70F–80F, half the price of the big names. Vin mousseux, méthode champenoise, *a slightly inferior product, doesn't conform to the champagne cartel's strict regulations; a bottle can be had for 35F–40F.* Vin crémant *is the cheapest of the imposters, what Hydrox are to Oreos, and not particularly good.*

Place Drouet d'Erlon harbors cafés, bars, tearooms, and pizzerias and couscous joints that charge around 35F–50F for a main dish. The **Os et l'Arête** (15 rue du Colonel Fabien, tel. 26–04–63–12), around the corner from the youth hostel, serves a 54F menu with pizza as the main dish.

Troyes

If you're the sort that goes for dusty old medieval buildings, Troyes could be your cup of café crème. Troyes is most famous for its 16th-century half-timbered houses that festoon rue Roger Salengro and cluster near the Hôtel de Vauluisant and the Eglise St-Jean. The **tourist office** (16 blvd. Carnot, tel. 25–73–00–36), on the square in front of the station, conducts walking tours of Troyes's historic streets daily at 3 PM for 35F, 17F50 students.

Troyes's churches are also worth a visit. Most impressive is the **Cathédrale St-Pierre et St-Paul** (pl. St-Pierre), where Flamboyant Gothic flames lick the outlandish facade. One of the town's most interesting museums is the **Musée d'Art Moderne** (pl. St-Pierre, tel. 25–80–57–30), displaying works by Degas and Braques. A single 20F ticket gets you access to this and most of Troyes's other museums.

COMING AND GOING Trains run almost hourly from Paris to Troyes's **train station** (tel. 25–73–50–50). Take an **STDM Trans-Champagne** bus (tel. 26–65–17–07) to other towns in the region if you don't want to take a detour through Paris. Several **city buses** (6F) stop in front of the tourist office.

WHERE TO SLEEP AND EAT The elegant **Hôtel de Paris** (54 rue de la Monnaie, tel. 25–73–11–70), in the heart of the old town, has two singles and lots of doubles from 120F. The **Hôtel Butat** (50 rue Turenne, tel. 25–73–77–29) is only slightly more expensive. The **HI hostel** (Chemin Ste-Scholastique, Rosières, tel. 25–82–00–65) is 7 km from Troyes. Take Bus 6 from the tourist office to the end of the line, turn right, and follow the signs for 2 km. Call ahead to the **Maison Notre-Dame en l'Isle** (8 and 10 rue de l'Isle, tel. 25–80–54–96) where folks of all ages stay in a beautiful 16th-century convent for 65F a head.

Reasonable restaurants freckle Troyes's old town. The outdoor tables of pricey crêperies and pizzerias clog the pedestrian streets around Eglise St-Jean. Waiters proudly produce exotic concoctions as sitar music and incense waft through the air at **Soleil de l'Inde** (33 rue de la Cité, down the street from the cathedral, tel. 25–80–75–71), where full menus are about 45F–70F.

Calais

You'll end up passing through Calais if you take the train through the new Eurotunnel from France to England, but that doesn't mean you have to stay. Little tempts tourists to pause for long here; the town's sole claim to fame is the Rodin bronze, *The Burghers of Calais.*

Should you be stuck here for the night, try the **Hôtel du Littoral** (71 rue Aristide Briand, tel. 21–34–47–28; doubles 100F–190F). **Maison pour Tous/Point Acceuil Jeunes** (81 blvd. Jacquard, tel. 21–34–69–53) has mattresses in big common rooms, a kitchen, and badminton facilities; 45F gets a spot (35F under 26).

To get out of town, talk to **Sealink** (2 pl. d'Armes, tel. 21–34–55–00), **P & O Ferries** (Car Ferry Terminal, tel. 21–46–10–10), or **Hoverspeed** (Hoverport, tel. 21–96–67–10) about frequent ferry crossings to England.

Boulogne

A hop, skip, and hydroplane from the south coast of England, Boulogne suffers from an overload of British day-trippers. Still, the town's fine walled **vieille ville,** high above the port, is worth stopping for. For a dizzying panorama of the whole area, wheeze your way up the 13th-century **belfry**; access is free through the **Hôtel de Ville.** The **Office de Tourisme** (quai de la Poste, tel. 21–31–68–38) adeptly dispenses info about the town and transportation options.

COMING AND GOING Most trains leave from the **Gare Boulogne-Ville** (tel. 21–80–50–50) in the center of town, but some leave for Paris from the **Gare Maritime,** near the ferry terminal. Trains head north to Calais (1 hr, 37F) and south through Amiens to Paris (3 hrs, 158F). The ferry terminal lies just across the river from central Boulogne. Talk to **Hoverspeed** (tel. 21–30–27–26) or **P & O European Ferries** (tel. 21–46–04–40) for info on frequent hovercrafts and ferries to Dover.

WHERE TO SLEEP AND EAT Cheap places to spend a night in Boulogne include **Hôtel le Castel** (51 rue Nationale, tel. 21–31–52–88) and the **Hôtel Hamiot** (1 rue Faidherbe, tel. 21–31–44–20), where doubles run about 110F. The **HI hostel** (36 rue de la Porte Gayole, tel. 21–31–48–22) has 60F beds in cramped, institutional rooms. The **Université d'Eté** dorm (69 rue Repaire, tel. 21–99–77–77; bed 60F), open to travelers in July and August only, is much more fun.

Tourist restaurants line the streets. Prices aren't particularly high, but the quality of the food rarely justifies the cost. The Wednesday and Saturday **markets** that fill up place Dalton are a better choice.

Alsace-Lorraine

Although the two regions are almost always grouped together, Alsace and Lorraine actually have distinct personalities. Alsace is more German, more exciting, and more popular, with welcoming towns that cater to tourists without being touristy. Most Lorraine towns are poorer than their Alsace neighbors and hardly know what to do with tourists; they're fine if you want to get a taste for everyday village life, but otherwise they don't have much to offer. The notable exception is Nancy, a good-time university town with enough sights to keep you busy for a week.

Strasbourg

Few cities are as multicultural as Strasbourg, which edges right up to the German border among mountains and vineyards. Although Germany has the upper hand as far as architecture and food go, with timbered houses and heavy, sauerkraut-laden dishes, the presence of the Council of Europe and European Parliament draws a pan-European crowd to the city. Visiting Middle Eastern markets and art museums filled with painting by French Impressionists, the diverse young *strasbourgeoisie* hang out happily together.

BASICS The **branch tourist offices** (pl. de la Gare, tel. 88–32–51–49; pont de l'Europe, tel. 88–61–39–23) have similar services as the **main office** (17 pl. de la Cathédrale, tel. 88–52–28–28). The **American Express office** (31 pl. Kléber, tel. 88–75–78–75) has the best exchange rates in town. The main **post office** (5 av. de la Marseillaise, tel. 88–23–44–00) also exchanges money at fair rates.

COMING AND GOING Trains speed from the **station** (tel. 88–22–50–50) to Lyon, into Germany, and to Paris's Gare de l'Est (259F). You can cover most of the town on foot, but local buses (7F, or 25F50 for a carnet of five) leave from the train station.

WHERE TO SLEEP An easy walk from the train station, the **Hôtel le Colmar** (1 rue du Maire Kuss, tel. 88–32–16–89; doubles from 130F) has spiffy, sometimes noisy rooms. Closer to the center of town, the **Hôtel Michelet** (48 rue du Vieux Marché aux Poissons, tel. 88–32–47–38; doubles 130F–210F) is regularly swamped by budget travelers. The **HI Auberge de Jeunesse "René Cassin"** (9 rue de l'Auberge de Jeunesse, tel. 88–30–26–46), 2 km from the train station, charges 64F–156F per bed; camping out back costs 40F. From the train station, take Bus 3, 13, or 23. The **CIARUS dorm** (7 rue Finkmatt, tel. 88–

32–12–12) isn't cheap (beds are 71F–171F), but it's filled with cool people from all over the world. From the train station, take Bus 10 headed toward avenue des Vosges.

FOOD Lots of young people find cheap eats in the winding streets behind the cathedral. **Place Austerlitz** has an outdoor vendor scene as well as some nice cafés and restaurants. **Flam's** (29 rue des Frères, tel. 88–36–36–90) does *tarte flambées,* thin-crusted pizzalike things, for 29F–36F. **Au Petit Pêcheur** (3 pl. du Corbeau, tel. 88–36–11–49) offers the same Alsatian cuisine served across the bridge but for half the price. Daily specials are about 42F, a three-course meal 50F. At the **Salon de Thé Christian** (10 rue Mercière, tel. 88–22–12–70) tearoom, devote yourself to the blueberry tart (12F).

WORTH SEEING At the heart of Strasbourg, the red-stone **Cathédrale de Notre-Dame** impresses even Parisians. The spire reaches 471 feet, making it the highest in France and the second-highest in Europe. Every day at 12:30 PM little apostles march past a likeness of Christ and a rooster crows in the **Astronomical Clock** at the cathedral's far right end. Most of Strasbourg's other major sights radiate from the cathedral. Be sure to pass through La Petite France, a historic Alsatian neighborhood just southwest of the centre ville, with Renaissance buildings that have survived plenty of wars. Also spend time in the vieille ville south of place Gutenberg, where imposing buildings tower on all sides. It's hard to spend much time in Strasbourg, though, without passing by a horde of museums. The **Palais Rohan** (2 pl. du Château, tel. 88–52–50–00; admission 22F, 8F students), built in the 1700s as a royal residence, is worth visiting in its own right, but it also houses three fun museums: the **Musée Archéologique,** the **Musée des Arts Décoratifs,** and the **Musée des Beaux-Arts.** Each charges 15F, 8F students. Right next to the Palais Rohan and near the cathedral is the **Musée de l'Oeuvre Notre-Dame** (3 pl. du Château, tel. 88–32–06–39; admission 15F, 8F students). Artists working on the cathedral during the 14th and 15th centuries used this building as a workshop; the statues and stained-glass windows that didn't make the cut stayed here. The adjoining **Musée d'Art Moderne** (5 pl. du Château, tel. 88–32–48–95) covers all the important movements in modern art from the 19th century to the 1960s.

AFTER DARK Most bars are cover-free, but expect to pay 20F–25F for a beer and up to 50F for mixed drinks. Put on your bomber jacket if you're headed for **Bar les Aviateurs** (12 rue des Soeurs, behind the cathedral, tel. 88–36–52–69), where posters pay homage to pilots. The neon-lit **La Java** (6 rue du Faisan, behind the cathedral, tel. 88–36–34–88) runs its own record label and plays music on the cutting edge.

NEAR STRASBOURG

Around Strasbourg are both rich green fields and vineyards and the wild forests of the Vosges Mountains, just begging to be hiked. The main attraction of many towns near Strasbourg is their proximity to these mountains; **Saverne,** on the northern tip of the mountains, is pretty dull on its own but nearly irresistible as the gateway to the Parc Naturel Regional des Vosges du Nord.

Colmar, 40 km southwest of Strasbourg, is not an immediately attractive town, thanks to World Wars I and II, but calm canals wind through **La Petite Venise** (Little Venice), an area of bright Alsatian houses with colorful shutters and window boxes just south of the centre ville. Hotels in town are expensive, so you probably won't want to stay longer than a day. If you're using Colmar as a base for exploring the region, though, you can stay at the **HI Auberge de Jeunesse Mittelhart** (2 rue Pasteur, tel. 89–80–57–39) or the **Maison des Jeunes de la Culture** (17 Camille-Schlumberger, tel. 89–41–26–87). The **Office de Tourisme de Colmar et de sa Région** (4 rue des Unterlinden, tel. 89–41–02–29) offers information on Colmar and the surrounding area.

Nancy

Nancy is one of the most underrated cities in France; most tourists pass by, thinking it's a deadbeat town. Nancy is alive and well, thank you, and has been since the 11th century, when Gérard d'Alsace built a fortified castle here. Today, it's a fantastically lively, friendly, and beautiful city of some 106,000 on the Meurthe River, near the Vosges Mountains.

Life revolves around the huge place Stanislas, which is bordered by the spacious **Musée des Beaux-Arts** (tel. 83–37–65–01; admission 20F, free on Wed. for students), the **Hôtel de Ville,** the **Opéra,** outdoor cafés, fountains, and a triumphal arch. Ask at the **tourist office** (14 pl. Stanislas, tel. 83–35–22–41) for info about Nancy's myriad museums and free listings of goings-on around town.

COMING AND GOING Lots of trains arrive from Paris (201F) and Strasbourg (104F) at the **station** (tel. 83–56–50–50). Nancy is fairly spread out, but the central area is doable on foot. **Allô bus** (tel. 83–35–54–54) runs buses (6F50) all over the city and to the 'burbs.

WHERE TO SLEEP The best place to stay is near the town center. The **Hôtel de la Poste** (56 pl. de la Cathédrale, tel. 83–32–11–52; doubles 115F–155F) edges right up to the cathedral. Closer to the train station, **Hôtel Foch** (8 av. Foch, tel. 83–32–88–50; doubles 125F–190F) has a shabby reception area, but okay rooms. The **HI Auberge de Jeunesse, Château de Remicourt** (149 rue de Vandoeuvre, Villers, tel. 83–27–73–67; beds 45F) is in a castle 4 km from town. Take Bus 26 to the Remicourt stop. **Camping Brabois** (N74 in Villers-Les-Nancy, tel. 83–27–18–28) is on the border of a forest; you can rent a site April–October for 13F per person and 6F per tent. Take Bus 26 or Bus 46 to Cottages.

Nightlife in Nancy usually flatlines by 2 AM, but Le Blueberry Jazz Bar (22 rue Gustave Simon, tel. 83–35–13–11) plays techno until the wee hours. Le Ch'timi (17 pl. St-Epvre) serves 150 different beers; sit down across from the Basilique St-Epvre and try to keep the church in focus.

FOOD Reasonably priced restaurants line **rue des Maréchaux** and **rue St-Dizier.** A fresh-food **market** goes on all day Tuesday–Saturday at place Henri Mengin. Just one of the great restaurants on Grande Rue, **Mezcalito** (no. 49, tel. 83–32–22–17) whips up a variety of lunchtime salads for less than 30F. The specialty at the hip **Café-Restaurant du Théâtre** (11 rue des Maréchaux, tel. 83–32–14–62) is the 65F osso buco; salads cost 32F–50F.

Burgundy

Except for a few better-known spots like Dijon, Cluny, and Beaune, Burgundy attracts relatively few tourists despite its almost overwhelming richness of art; many Burgundian towns show off killer Romanesque cathedrals despite their sort of small-town hickness. Away from the towns spread expanses of vineyards and beautiful countryside. The Morvan Park alone preserves 3,500 square km of countryside smack-dab in the middle of the region.

Auxerre

During the hot, slow days of summer, Auxerre feels almost like a beach town without a beach, with its colorful shop awnings, friendly, unhurried locals, and tourists wearing khaki and sunglasses. But the giant cathedral and churches rising above a sea of red-tile roofs and old stone houses remind you that you're in Burgundy. On the northeastern side of the Morvan Forest, Auxerre is the major transportation hub for northern Burgundy, but even here you can give up all hopes of moving anywhere very quickly. Slow down to a mosey with the *auxerrois* and take time to enjoy the sights.

COMING AND GOING The **train station** (tel. 86–46–93–94) sends daily trains to Paris (2½ hrs, 117F) and Dijon (2 hrs, 121F). The **tourist office** (1–2 quai de la République, tel. 86–52–06–19) can hook you up with private bus companies.

WHERE TO SLEEP AND EAT Finding cheap sleeps is pretty easy; the best deals are the hostels, both near the centre ville. At the **Foyer des Jeunes Travailleurs** (16 av. de la Résistance, tel. 86–46–95–11), you can crash in a private room for 75F, 70F with a hostel card. From the station, walk five minutes down avenue de la Résistance. The **Foyer des Jeunes Travailleuses** (16 blvd. Vaulabelle, tel. 86–52–45–38) offers 75F singles. The former is technically for men, the latter for women, but both will accept anyone. Otherwise, try the **Hôtel de la Porte de Paris** (5 rue St-Germain, tel. 86–46–90–09), north of the centre ville.

Chow down at the grill and pizzeria **La Tour d'Orbandelle** (34 pl. des Cordeliers, tel. 86–52–31–46) or the traditional Burgundian **Hôtel-Restaurant du Commerce** (5 rue René Schaeffer, tel. 86–52–03–16), where menus start at 58F.

WORTH SEEING Start your exploration at the **Abbatiale St-Germain** (pl. St-Germain), whose star attraction is the tour of the crypts, with their superb 9th-century Carolingian frescoes. The abbey convent building houses the **Musée St-Germain,** which has good exhibits of prehistoric and Gallo-Roman art. There's an 18F fee for the tour and access to the museum, but students get in free. The **Cathédrale St-Etienne** (pl. St-Etienne) features a Flamboyant Gothic facade with damaged but still interesting portal carvings. For 10F you can see 12th- to 13th-century manuscripts and enamels in the **treasury** as well as a rare fresco of Christ on horseback in the medieval **crypt.**

NEAR AUXERRE

With beautiful views of the surrounding fields and a superb basilica, the Basilique Ste-Madeleine, **Vézelay** sees an awful lot of visitors for a tiny town of 500. Even so, this pretty little medieval village that served as the takeoff point for the Second and Third Crusades during the 12th century is really worth visiting. If the crowds get to you, try pretending they're religious pilgrims and just part of the scenery.

You can take one of five daily **trains** (1 hr) from Auxerre as far as Sermizelles; from there, catch one of two daily **Cars de la Madeleine** buses (tel. 86–33–25–67) to travel the remaining 50 km to Vézelay. Return to Auxerre for the night, or reserve ahead at the **Centre des Rencontres Internationales** (rue des Ecoles, tel. 86–33–26–73) or the posh **HI hostel** (rte. de l'Etang, tel. 86–33–24–18) in Vézelay.

Dijon

Dijon is more than just the wine-mustard capital of the world. With a population of almost 130,000, Dijon is Burgundy's only real city and an important industrial center and transportation hub, with a huge train station and a TGV line to Paris. Also home to a large university, the city has enough young blood to give it a happening nightlife year-round.

For centuries an insignificant Roman colony called Divio, Dijon became the capital of the duchy of Burgundy in the 11th century and acquired most of its important art treasures during the 14th and 15th centuries; the city's churches, the ducal palace, and one of the finest art museums in France remain as impressive evidence of the powerful Burgundian dukes' patronage of the arts. For brochures on the town's history and sights, go to the **tourist office** (pl. Darcy, tel. 80–43–42–12).

COMING AND GOING Frequent trains zoom to Paris (1½–3 hrs, 186F), Lyon (2 hrs, 132F), and Strasbourg (4 hrs, 201F) from the **station** (tel. 80–41–50–50). The **TRANSCO bus station** (rue des Perrières, tel. 80–42–11–00) is next door. STRD **city buses** cost 5F per ride; there's an information booth on place Grangier (tel. 80–30–60–90). Rent two-wheel transportation at **Travel'Car** (28 blvd. de la Marne, tel. 80–72–31–00) or **OK-Bike** (134 av. V. Hugo, tel. 80–55–34–28).

WHERE TO SLEEP AND EAT Scope out the sleep scene in the centre ville. The **Hôtel du Théâtre** (3 rue des Bons Enfants, tel. 80–67–15–41; doubles 88F–145F), south of place de la République; the **Hôtel du Lycée** (28 rue du Lycée, tel. 80–67–12–35; doubles 115F–190F), just northeast of the centre ville; and the **Hostellerie du Sauvage** (64 rue Monge, tel. 80–41–31–21; doubles 160F–300F) are all good bets. The 60F dorm beds and 140F singles at the **Centre de Rencontres Internationales** (1 blvd. Champollion, tel. 80–71–32–12), 4 km outside town, are merely okay; from place de la République, take Bus 5 toward Epirey. If you're in a bind, call **CROUS** (3 rue du Docteur Maret, tel. 80–40–40–40) for info on university housing. The large **Camping du Lac** (3 blvd. Chanoine Kir, tel. 80–43–54–72), a half-hour walk west of town (or Bus 12 from the station), costs 4F per tent plus 8F50 per person.

Plenty of good restaurants hide among the tourist traps. Pizzerias and crêperies are always in style—check avenue Foch. The adventurous order escargots (33F) or frogs' legs sautéed with Provençal spices (65F) at **Restaurant le St-Vincent** (79 rue Jeannin, tel. 80–67–36–54). **La Cathédrale** (pl. Ste-Bénigne, tel. 80–30–42–10) is a popular student bar with a view of the cathedral.

WORTH SEEING A 15F card, available at any museum, gets you into all the museums in town, but you needn't bother with it if you have a student ID card, which will get you into all museums free. At the **Musée des Beaux-Arts** you can see a well-displayed collection of cubist art. The spectacular *salle des gardes* (guards' room) contains the richly decorated tombs of Burgundy bigwigs. The museum is housed in the 17th-century **Ancien Palais des Ducs de Bourgogne** (pl. Ste-Chapelle, tel. 80–74–52–70). The **Musée Archéologique** (5 rue du Docteur Maret, tel. 80–30–88–54; admission 12F, students free) is one of the most impressive in the region; the rare wood and stone sculpture and pottery are in excellent condition.

Three churches in town merit a visit. The 13th- to 14th-century **Cathédrale St-Bénigne** (pl. St-Bénigne) presents an austere facade, but a colorful roof pattern and a 300-foot, 19th-century spire lighten the effect. The choir inside the **Eglise St-Michel** (pl. St-Michel) has some fine 18th-century wood carvings. The Gothic **Eglise Notre-Dame,** north of the ducal palace, houses an 11th-century statue of the *Vierge Noire* (Black Virgin) and a tapestry commemorating Dijon's 1944 liberation from German occupation.

NEAR DIJON

Burgundy's most famous **vineyards** stretch south of Dijon all the way to Mâcon. Throughout this killer countryside, small towns with big wine names attract tourists with their cellars and wine tastings. You can visit the area by TRANSCO bus or by bike, but if you're simply looking for cheap or free wine tasting, you'll find a visit to Beaune much more efficient.

Towns near Dijon also contribute to Burgundy's reputation for spectacular church architecture. The tiny town of **Cluny** clusters around its famous abbey, which was founded in 909. The abbey basilica, a symbol of the order's vast wealth and power, was built between 1088 and 1130, but was ransacked and pillaged during the 16th-century Wars of Religion between the Protestants and Catholics. Today, visitors from all over the world leave the abbey grumbling in various languages, "Is this all that's left?" but informative guided tours (26F, 17F students), leaving from the Musée Ochier (tel. 85–59–12–79), give you an idea of what the abbey originally looked like.

BEAUNE Beaune, about 20 minutes away from Dijon by train, is bedecked with art on its surface and wine cellars on its underside. Most visitors come to see the **Hôtel Dieu** (rue de l'Hôtel Dieu, tel. 80–24–45–00; admission 27F, 21F students), which shows off colorfully patterned roof tiles and a medieval courtyard. Chancellor and tax collector Nicolas Rolin, hoping to get a ticket to heaven, founded this hospital in 1443; it now houses several large galleries. Across from the Hôtel Dieu, at the **Marché aux Vins** (tel. 80–22–27–69), 80F plus a 10F deposit gets you a wine-tasting cup and free rein among 50 bottles of wine. If you want to do the wine thing full force, the **tourist office** (pl. de la Halle, tel. 80–22–24–51) has a handout describing the various *caves* (cellars) and what they have to offer.

Lyon

Lyon is a city of ups and downs. One minute you think you're in shitsville; the next you can't see past all the fancy restaurants and boutiques. Lyon's size makes it possible to find anything you want in terms of food and lodging, from dirt cheap (and scummy) to elegant, like the Hôtel Cours des Loges in Vieux Lyon, where the Oriental rugs are outdone only by the gold-plated toilet seats. You can find some of the best cuisine in France at world-renowned Paul Bocuse and then rock till 4 AM in a sleazy bar next to a kebab stand run by a toothless guy named Omar.

Easy access to the Alps and to the Beaujolais is what tempts many visitors to set up camp here. Lyon itself may be no place to commune with nature, but the pristine Alps are only an hour away by train, and the city is the best place in the region to catch trains and airplanes, visit museums, and pig out on some of the country's best cuisine.

BASICS

VISITOR INFORMATION The main **Office de Tourisme** on place Bellecour has a train information booth where you can buy tickets and make reservations. Branches in Vieux Lyon near St-Jean Cathedral on Fourvière Hill and in Gare de Perrache all have the same weekday hours as the main office but close for the weekend. For real nitty-gritty info, pick up the 7F weekly *Lyon Poche*, available at any tabac. *Tel. 78–42–25–75. Open June 15–Sept. 15, weekdays 9–7, Sat. 9–6, Sun. 10–6; Sept. 15–June 15, weekdays 9–6, Sat. 9–5, Sun. 10–5.*

AMERICAN EXPRESS *6 rue Childebert, 2e, tel. 78–37–40–69. Open May–Sept., weekdays 9–noon and 2–6:15, Sat. 9–noon. Currency exchange until 5:30 PM only.*

MAIL Poste restante mail addressed to R. P. Lyon 69002 goes to the central post office on the corner of rue de la Charité and rue Alphonse Fochier. The tourist office map pinpoints all the smaller branches. Lyon's postal code is 6900 followed by the number of the arrondissement (*see* Getting Around, *below*).

COMING AND GOING

Across the Rhône from the Presqu'ile, the modern **Gare Part Dieu** serves major destinations in France and Italy. The smaller **Gare de Perrache** services most of the same towns as Part-Dieu but has fewer international trains. Both stations have a Thomas Cook change bureau, an SOS Voyagers office, 25F luggage lockers, and 15F20 showers. The Part-Dieu station also has a tourist office. More fashion than function, the art-deco **Gare St-Paul** is at the base of Fourvière Hill in Vieux Lyon.

The modern **Aéroport International de Lyon Satolas** (tel. 72–22–72–21) is 30 km east of town. To get to town from the airport, hop on a **Satobus.** The bus makes frequent trips to Gare de Perrache and Gare Part-Dieu for 45F a pop.

GETTING AROUND

Lyon is divided into three sections by the Rhône and the Saône rivers. **Vieux Lyon** is on the west side of the Saône at the bottom of Fourvière Hill. Between the two rivers, the **Presqu'ile** can be covered on foot. The northern part of the Presqu'ile ascends steeply through run-down streets to the **Croix-Rousse** district. The city is subdivided into nine arrondissements; the first and second are on the Presqu'ile, and Vieux Lyon is in the fifth.

Lyon's four Métro lines make a tick-tack-toe grid across the city. Automated dispensers in each station spit out 7F tickets and 39F booklets of six. Trains run 5 AM–midnight. Lyon's **TCL buses** are more efficient and cost the same. On both the bus and the Métro, stamp your ticket in the orange machine when you board. Pick up bus maps at the TCL office across from the Part-Dieu station or on the ground floor of the Perrache station.

WHERE TO SLEEP

Most cheap hotels are concentrated around Gare de Perrache; the farther north from the station you go, the nicer the hotels get until you hit place des Terreaux, where they start getting sleazy again. The Part-Dieu neighborhood doesn't offer much in the way of accommodations, which is no biggie since there's not much to see around it anyway. Lyon is no place in which to pitch a tent. If you want to camp, get out into the Alps.

SOUTH OF PLACE BELLECOUR The southern end of the Presqu'ile is your best bet for lodging. Gare de Perrache is handy, and pedestrian rue Victor Hugo has plenty of grab-a-bite eateries. It's pretty dead at night, though, so if you go out carousing, you'll have a long stagger home.

➤ **UNDER 150F • Hôtel le Beaujolais.** Scuzzy hallways but clean, simple rooms and proximity to train station make up for it. Register at the bar downstairs. Doubles 125F–155F. *22 rue d'Enghien, 2e, tel. 78–37–39–15. Métro: Perrache.*

➤ **UNDER 200F • Hôtel Vaubecour.** Well-worn but clean rooms with flowered wallpaper and antique furniture. Young business travelers far outnumber backpackers. Doubles 135F–165F. *28 rue Vaubecour, 2e, tel. 78–37–44–91. Métro: Ampère.*

➤ **UNDER 250F • Hôtel Alexandra.** The first hotel recommended by locals; bougainvillea-lined staircase, newly refurnished rooms, ideal location, cheery service. Doubles from 220F. *49 rue Victor Hugo, 2e, tel. 78–37–75–79. Métro: Ampère.*

NORTH OF PLACE BELLECOUR Between place Bellecour and place des Terreaux lies a chic shopping district where budget hotels are clean and quiet. The other side of place des Terreaux is a different world. Lively bars and cheap eats make this area fun, but it's borderline dangerous at night.

➤ **UNDER 200F • Hôtel le Terme.** Behind place des Terreaux. Dark, spacious rooms with TVs and phones. Grimy hall showers are free. Doubles 168F–215F. *7 rue St-Catherine, 1er, tel. 78–28–30–45. Métro: Hôtel de Ville.*

HOSTEL **Auberge de Jeunesse (HI).** A great hostel in the middle of a concrete hell, 30 minutes outside town. Sunny common area, TV room, and rooftop deck are open all day. Ask for Rooms 12–28 to avoid noise. Reception open 7–11:30 AM and 5:30–11:30 PM. The last bus from Part-Dieu leaves at 10:36 PM. Beds 45F. *51 rue Roger Salengro, Vénissieux, tel. 78–76–39–23. From Part-Dieu, take Bus 36 to Vivani-Joliot-Curie, walk left under PARIS/MARSEILLE freeway sign, and look right. 116 beds. 11:30 PM curfew, lockout 10–5:30, laundry, breakfast 17F, kitchen facilities.*

FOOD

Roll up your sleeves—it's time to *eat!* Dining is Lyon's most popular pastime. The city's *bouchons* (bistros) are known throughout France for their gastronomical goodies such as *quenelles* (sort of fake sausages made with flour, eggs, and fish) and *salade lyonnaise* (with bacon, croutons, and a poached egg on top). Stands sell *donner-kebabs* (gyro-like concoctions with spicy lamb) all over town. **Les Halles** (102 cours Lafayette, just west of Part-Dieu) houses fresh-food vendors, but the real action is at the daily morning **market** along quai Tilsitt on the east bank of the Saône.

PRESQU'ILE The Presqu'ile is the city's ritziest eating district. Many restaurants line rue Mercière and place des Terreaux.

Le Glabat Bar. Mom and pop serve generous 40F daily specials with potatoes and veggies to a crowd of casual regulars. *28 rue des Remparts d'Ainay, 2e, tel. 78–42–73–55. Closed Sun.*

Le Pâtisson. Vegetarian restaurant with a subdued atmosphere; a heaping plate of grub with dessert is 55F for lunch, 80F for dinner. *17 rue Port-du-Temple, 2e, tel. 72–81–41–71. Closed weekends.*

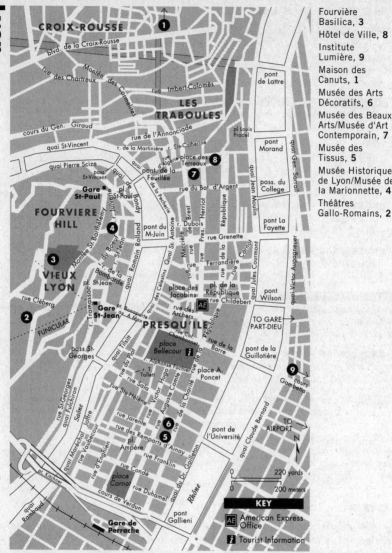

CROIX-ROUSSE

blvd. de la Croix-Rousse

Montée des Carmelites

rue des Chartreux

rue Imbert-Colomès

LES TRABOULES

cours du Gén. Giraud

rue de l'Annonciade

quai St-Vincent

r. de la Martinière

r. Ste-Catherine

pl Louis Pradel

quai Pierre Scize

pass. St-Vincent

pont de la Feuillée

r. d'Algérie place des Terreaux

Gare St-Paul

pl. St-Paul

rue du Bat. d'Argent

FOURVIERE HILL

pont du M-Juin

r. Dubois

r. Brest

Herriot

rue Grenette

VIEUX LYON

rue Cléberg

pl. St-Jean

place des Jacobins

rue Ferrandière

pl. de la République

rue Childebert

FUNICULAR

Gare St-Jean

PRESQU'ILE

rue des Archers

pass St-Georges

place Bellecour

rue de la Barre

TO GARE PART-DIEU

pont de la Guillotière

rue Alphonse Fochier

place A. Poncet

pont Wilson

cours Gambetta

rue Ste-Sala

rue Ste-Hélène

rue Jarente

rue des Remparts d'Ainay

pont de l'Université

TO AIRPORT

pl. Ampère

rue Franklin

place Carnot

rue Condé

rue Duhamel

cours de Verdun

pont Gallieni

Gare de Perrache

Rhône

Fourvière Basilica, **3**

Hôtel de Ville, **8**

Institute Lumière, **9**

Maison des Canuts, **1**

Musée des Arts Décoratifs, **6**

Musée des Beaux-Arts/Musée d'Art Contemporain, **7**

Musée des Tissus, **5**

Musée Historique de Lyon/Musée de la Marionnette, **4**

Théâtres Gallo-Romains, **2**

220 yards

200 meters

KEY

AE American Express Office

i Tourist Information

VIEUX LYON Rue St-Jean is filled with "traditional" lyonnais restaurants, suspiciously filled with Bermuda-shorts-clad tourists. The restaurants north of place St-Jean are worth a shot, though.

Au Vieux Forneau. Scrounge up 94F for a hearty traditional buchon meal with salade lyonnaise, tender quenelles de brochette, and tangy lemon tarts. Classy place with marble tables and high ceilings. *1 rue Tramassac, 5e, tel. 78–37–06–42. Closed Mon. and Aug.*

NEAR PART-DIEU This area has lots of cheery neighborhood cafés and mercifully few tourists.

Pizzeria Totila. Mushrooms, peppers, artichokes, and olives top off the delicious pizza Totila (43F); pasta is covered with flavorful sauces. Filled with locals who chat with the staff. *10 rue Prof. Weill, 6e, tel. 78–52–95–74. Closed Sun.*

Le Verdi. Yuppie patrons feast their way through lunch hour on big, fresh salads, thin-crust pizzas, and generous desserts, all served with artistic flair. Trendy neon decor suits the high-priced pastas. Pizza 40F. *13 blvd. des Brotteaux, 6e, tel. 72–74–29–53.*

WORTH SEEING

Most sights in Lyon are on the Presqu'ile or in Vieux Lyon. Get a feel for the city by walking along the narrow cobblestone alleys and beautiful old courtyards of Vieux Lyon. **Traboules**, covered passageways originally built to protect silk from the elements as silk weavers carried it from place to place, connect streets within the Croix Rousse and Vieux Lyon. Many are just run-down alleys with roofs, but others pass through beautiful Renaissance courtyards. The classier traboules lie along rue St-Jean and rue Juiverie. Students hang out on the southern part of the Presqu'ile, especially on **place Bellecour; place des Terreaux** is another fun hangout spot and home to the **Hôtel de Ville.** Above town, on the Fourvière Hill, the Grand Théâtre and Odéon of the **Théâtres Gallo-Romains** (17 rue Cléberg, tel. 78–25–94–68) have a seating capacity of 4,500 and are the oldest Roman theaters in France, built in 15 BC by the emperor Augustus. The extensive, well-preserved ruins are used each summer for theatrical performances.

FOURVIERE BASILICA This sinister-looking Roman Catholic church is only the most recent of several places of worship that have sat on the top of Fourvière Hill since the Romans settled here. Built in 1870 and dedicated to the Virgin Mary, the church's marble and wood carvings in the main basilica and underground vault require sitting-time to absorb. *Open daily 8–noon and 2–6.*

MUSEUMS The **Musée des Beaux-Arts** (Palais St-Pierre, pl. des Terreaux, 1er, tel. 78–28–07–66; admission 20F, 10F students), France's largest collection of art after the Louvre, is housed in a 16th-century abbey. The collection of Egyptian artifacts discovered by local archaeologists is almost worth a museum in itself. In the same building, the **Musée d'Art Contemporain** holds temporary exhibits of works by current artists from around the world.

The **Musée des Tissus** (34 rue de la Charité, 2e, tel. 78–37–15–05; admission 20F, 10F students, Wed. free) has info on every aspect of silk from the worms to the weaving process, where Lyon comes into the picture; all the silk once worn by French royalty was woven in Lyon. To see some looms at work, visit the **Maison des Canuts** (12 rue d'Ivry, 4e), where a very hands-on staff makes sure you get your 6F worth. Next door to the Musée des Tissus and on the same admission ticket, the **Musée des Arts Décoratifs** chronicles the development of Lyon's decorative arts.

The **Institute Lumière** (25 rue du Premier Film, 8e, tel. 78–00–86–68; admission 25F, 10F students) displays loads of funky projection inventions, old stereoscopes, and some of the first animated cartoons. Films are shown on site October–June. Exotic, costumed puppets from around the world, some created by puppet pioneer Laurent Mourguet, live in the **Musée de la Marionnette** (Hôtel Gadagne, pl. du Petit-Collèe, tel. 78–42–03–61). In the same building, the **Musée Historique de Lyon** traces Lyon's history from the Middle Ages to the 18th century through pottery, paintings, furniture, and antique playing cards.

AFTER DARK

Bars and clubs start rockin' around 11 PM and don't stop until the roosters crow. The bars in the alleys around place des Terreaux fill up with students; the "alternative" scene is north of place des Terreaux, on the way up the Croix Rousse hill. **The Look Bar** (2 rue du Palais de Justice, tel. 78–37–38–94) looks like an English pub on the outside but serves fruity drinks and plays 1980s tunes. **Phoebus** (22 rue Poteau, 1er, tel. 78–39–49–29) is a good weekend spot to hear live rock and jazz groups and drunken, singing French people.

Near Lyon

LE BEAUJOLAIS All it takes is 50F for a train trip north and about 120F for a bike to have the whole Beaujolais wine region at your feet. The northern section of the Beaujolais, near **Belleville,** is where the premier wines come from. Literally hundreds of caves lie in this area where you can taste 10 different appellations of wine ranging from the light Fleurie to the more coarse Morgon. Twenty km south, near **Villefranche-sur-Saône,** the concentration of caves gives way to golden towns built of *pierre dorées,* soft, golden-colored stones that come out of the local hillsides. Just west of Villefranche-sur-Saône, the hilltop village of **Oingt** offers a bird's-eye view of the surrounding vineyards. Entirely built from soft golden stone, the town's winding pathways that lead up to a medieval tower and church are home to many art *ateliers* (workshops) and current exhibitions. Belleville and Villefranche-sur-Saône are both on the Lyon–Dijon train line. Olivier Marguin (165 rue de la République, tel. 74–66–35–51) rents bikes in Belleville.

VIENNE If you do nothing but climb up to Notre Dame de Pipet and look out over the red-tiled roofs of the Rhône Valley, you'll be happy you made this 20-minute train trip from Lyon. Every turn seems to reveal another ancient church, a view of crumbling Roman walls, or an archaeological sight. Vienne's landmark attraction is the 1st-century **Théâtre Romain,** the largest of its kind in France. Stop by the **tourist office** (cours Brillier, tel. 74–85–12–62) for info about the July Jazz à Vienne festival that fills the theater.

The **HI hostel** (11 quai Riondet, tel. 74–53–21–97, beds 58F) is ideally situated on the Rhône, next to the tourist office, but has a ridiculously early 10 PM curfew. Buy baguettes and sandwiches along pedestrian **rues Marchande** and **des Clercs.**

The Alps

How do you introduce the Alps? **"Majestic snow-**capped peaks," "craggy ledges and rocks," "flowery wooden chalets," "rugged mountain people" . . . all the clichés apply. You can still find traditional villages framed by massive granite peaks rising up in the background, but the Alpine landscape has changed over the past 20 years. The lifestyle in many towns has gone from agricultural to tourist industrial, thanks to the explosion of skiers, mountain climbers, hikers, and bikers who make the Alps their playground. Change isn't always for the worse; along with condo-filled ski stations comes a plethora of budget accommodations and a raging nightlife.

BASICS

WHERE TO SLEEP As well as hotels and hostels, the Alps have plenty of gîtes d'étape (*see* France Basics, *above*) and **collectives,** which offer hostel-like accommodations, but usually only for people staying at least a week. Along the marked routes traversing the Alps, you can get a dorm bed for less than 50F a night at **refuges.** These are ideal if you do long-distance hikes or want to do an overnight hike but don't have the camping gear. The tourist office at your point of departure will have a list of the refuges for the route you want to take. Most of the **campgrounds** in the Alps are caravan-free, but you can often avoid their crowds of tents by pitching a tent elsewhere and using the campground showers for about 10F.

OUTDOOR ACTIVITIES Some of the best **skiing** in the world is done at Chamonix, Les Arcs, and Val d'Isère, but big prices (at least 150F for a lift ticket) reflect the big operations. For better prices (about 100F), head to a smaller station like Valloire or St-Véran. **Cross-country skiing** might be the most enjoyable way to really see the Alps. All it takes is equipment (75F–100F per day) and a strong set of lungs. In the summer, **mountain bikers** take over the cross-country ski trails. Look for the little yellow bicycle sign pointing you toward a VTT Circuit (mountain biking trail), or ask for maps at any local bike shop, where bikes go for 80F–120F a day. For the truly short of funds, **hiking** is the best way to see the Alps. Two major routes, the Grande Randonnée (GR) and the Grand Traversée des Alpes (GTA), lead from town to town passing refuges on the way.

Grenoble

Sitting at the confluence of the Isère and Drac rivers and within spitting distance of the Alps (if the wind's at your back), Grenoble has been attracting nature lovers since the first settler pitched a tent here around the 1st century BC. Recently, the city has expanded so quickly that today it's hard to see the rugged peaks through the thick smog that hangs over the valley floor. Down in the midst of that smog, Grenoble bustles with the spirit of a university town that has a good number of immigrants from North Africa and the Middle East.

The ancient village of St-Hugues used to be a separate community but is now part of Grenoble's vieille ville and is lined with antiques shops and artists' galleries. The rest of the vieille ville, distinguished by bits and pieces of the Roman walls that used to enclose it, is a collection of small squares (place de Gordes, place St-André, and place aux Herbes) filled with open markets in the morning and beer-drinking students in the afternoon and evening. Sixteenth-century pedestrian streets connecting the squares hold modern shops and boutiques. Looming over all the action is the spirit of Stendhal, the 19th-century writer who remains the town's most celebrated citizen. The **tourist office** (14 rue de la République, tel. 76–42–41–41) distributes an itinerary that directs you to all the town's Stendhal-related sights. Hiking enthusiasts should make a beeline for the **Maison de la Randonnée** (7 rue Voltaire, tel. 76–51–76–00) to find out about the many day hikes from Grenoble.

COMING AND GOING The **train station** (tel. 76–47–50–50) serves the Alps region and sends frequent trains to Paris, Nice, and Marseille. Regional buses leave from the **bus station** (tel. 76–87–90–31), right next to the train station. The 21 efficient lines of Grenoble's **TAG buses** (7F) cover every corner of the city, many leaving from place Victor Hugo. TAG also runs **trams** that take the same tickets. Flat Grenoble is perfect for biking, and bike lanes run along the sides of most main streets. The **Mistral Shop** (13 pl. Ste-Claire, tel. 76–51–11–50), across from the tourist office, rents bikes for about 80F a day.

WHERE TO SLEEP Cheap hotels cover the area between the train station and place Victor Hugo, but most of the ones near the station have jacked-up prices. The happy little man who runs the **Hôtel Lakanal** (26 rue des Bergers, tel. 76–46–03–42; doubles 125F–180F) keeps his small rooms tidy and his bathrooms sparkling. A half-block from the train station, the '70s-style **Alpazur Hôtel** (59 av. Alsace-Lorraine, tel. 76–46–42–80; doubles 152F–168F) is run by a helpful family with an English-speaking son. Fifteen minutes south of town, the well-equipped **HI hostel** (18 av. Grésivaudan, Eschirolles, tel. 76–09–33–52) is a good place in which to meet fellow travelers, but you'll have to put up with shoe-box-size dorm rooms and the 11 PM curfew, cut shorter by the 9 PM last bus from town. Take Bus 1 or 8 from the center of town to the Quinzaine stop.

FOOD The small streets between place Notre-Dame and place St-André are littered with hole-in-the-wall restaurants that fix filling sandwiches for less than 25F. The eateries that fill place Grenette have outdoor tables where you can snack on a sandwich or pizza. **Le Valgo** (2 rue St-Hugues, off pl. Notre-Dame, tel. 76–51–38–85) serves up specialties of the Hautes Alpes (Upper Alps) family-style, on calico-covered tables in a cozy wooden room or outside. The *oreilles d'ânes* (donkeys' ears) ravioli are well worth the 45F. The lively **Café de la Table Ronde** (7 pl. St-André, tel. 76–44–51–41) is supposedly the second-oldest café in France, established in 1739. Stendhal used to come here to get hyped on coffee, which today is about the only affordable thing on the menu. After dark, locals head to the English-style **King Charly Pub** (12 rue Sault, tel. 76–47–29–72) for a 13F half-pint.

WORTH SEEING When you want to get above Grenoble's urban smog, head up to the Bastille, a maze of walls and stairways at the foot of the Chartreux Mountains. Constructed at the beginning of the 19th century to replace an old hillside fortress that was decaying under the weight of time and battle, the Bastille now houses a pretty good **ancient car museum** and an **exposition museum** with changing exhibits. Travel up to the Bastille via the 30F *téléphérique* (cable car) that runs daily 10 AM–midnight, and hoof it back down along the Montée de Chalmont footpath that winds through gardens and onto a flower-lined cobblestone path.

On the hill below the Bastille, housed in the ancient convent of Ste-Marie-d'en-Haut, the **Musée Dauphinois** (30 rue Maurice Gignoux, tel. 76–87–66–77) has two floors of changing exhibits and two floors of permanent displays on life in the Alps. The **Musée de Peinture et de Sculpture** (pl. Lavalette) has a surprisingly large collection of Renaissance, Impressionist, and modern art.

CHEAP THRILLS The **Chartreuse distillery** (10 blvd. Edgar Kofler, tel. 76–05–81–77), 20 minutes north in Voiron, is the single place in the world where the famous green 110-proof liquor is produced; only three monks are entrusted with the secret formula, which Marshall d'Estrées originally gave to the monastery in 1605 as a "health elixir." The tour is all in French, but you don't need any language skills to taste the potent stuff. You *do* need 32F for round-trip bus fare to Voiron on VFD.

Chamonix

In the Haute-Savoie between the Swiss and Italian borders, this rugged mountain town laden with tourists and their related fluff boasts the highest peak in the Alps—the 15,781-foot Mont Blanc. Lots of people come just to ride the Aiguille du Midi cable car to the 12,602-foot mark, take lots of pictures, and buy tacky T-shirts and souvenirs. The real heart of the town, though, is in the people who don't have time to take pictures while they're scaling the mountain's face. The **Maison de la Montagne** (pl. de l'Eglise, tel. 50–53–03–40) will help hikers out with maps, weather reports, and other info. The lively folks at the **Office de Tourisme** (pl. de l'Eglise, tel. 50–53–00–24) is better for info on Chamonix itself.

COMING AND GOING Chamonix's centrally located **train station** (tel. 50–66–50–50) serves Grenoble (4 hrs, 159F), Geneva (2½ hrs, 124F), and Annecy (2½ hrs, 95F). Once you're in Chamonix, transportation is easy on foot or by local 6F60 buses that loop around town.

WHERE TO SLEEP AND EAT Chamonix is chock-full of cheapish hotels, but the best place to stay is outside town away from the tourist throngs. The **HI hostel** (tel. 50–53–14–52), south of town in Pèlerins, offers dorm beds in a big ski chalet at the foot of the Bossons glacier for 68F per person. If you aren't up to the 15-minute walk, Pèlerins is on the train line. **Le Chamoniard Volant** (45 rte. de la Frasse, tel. 50–53–14–09) and **La Montagne** (789 promenade des Crémeries, tel. 50–53–11–60) both offer dorm beds for 60F–65F per night in wooden chalets surrounded by the Bois du Bouchet, within walking distance of the train station. In the center of town, the **Ski Station** (rte. des Moussoux, tel. 50–53–20–25) charges 50F for a bunk in a large dorm room and 5F for three minutes of hot water in the shower.

Every bar and restaurant in Chamonix seems to offer "authentic" fondue or raclette for 60F–90F per person. If you're in the mood for something different, though, try the chicken tandoori at the cozy **Bumblebee Bistro** (65 rue des Moulins, tel. 50–53–50–03).

Annecy

If someone got rid of all the neon-clad tourists, Annecy would almost be paradise. Even with the tourists, this is an amazingly picturesque village at the edge of a dazzling mountain lake in the Haute-Savoie. If you get here before July or after mid-September, you'll have the flower-lined canals to yourself and avoid paying hiked-up full-season prices. At the same time, though, you'll miss a hopping summer nightlife and illuminated water shows and concerts on the lake and canals.

When you're ready for some sights, head up to the 14th-century **château** that houses the regional museum of art and archaeology, to the old **prisons** in the Palais de l'Isle that house exhibits on the history of Annecy, or to the **Haute-Savoie museum.** Three churches and **Cathédrale St-Pierre** fill the streets with the ringing of bells on every hour. The high-tech **tourist** office (1 rue Jean Jaurès, in the Centre Bonlieu, tel. 50–45–00–33) leads daily guided visits of the town for 32F.

COMING AND GOING Trains run regularly to Chamonix (2½ hrs, 90F), Grenoble (2 hrs, 82F), and Lyon (2 hrs, 108F) through Annecy's centrally located **station** (tel. 50–66–50–50). **Frossard** (tel. 50–45–73–90), **Crolard** (tel. 50–45–08–12), and **Francony** (tel. 50–45–02–43) run regional buses from the gare routière right next to the train station.

WHERE TO SLEEP AND EAT If you've got a few extra francs on you, forgo the out-of-the-way **HI hostel** (16 rte. de Semnoz, tel. 50–45–33–19) and head for the aptly named **Central Hôtel** (6 bis rue Royale, tel. 50–45–05–37), which has rooms for two, three, or four people at 190F–250F.

You'll find fondue and raclette in almost every restaurant in the vieille ville, with sandwich stands and pizza joints for those who want to go with an old standby. Since the cuisine doesn't range much in quality, go for atmosphere. **Captain Pub** (11 rue de Pont Morens, tel. 50–45–79–80) turns into a friendly bar after 10 PM, and **Le Vieux Necy** (3 rue Filaterie, tel. 50–45–01–57), near Eglise St-Maurice, draws local youth eager to guzzle any liquid set in front of them.

Provence

What many visitors remember best about Provence is the light. The sunlight here is vibrant and alive, bathing the vineyards, olive groves, and fields full of lavender and sunflowers with an intensity that captivated Cézanne and van Gogh. Bordering the Mediterranean and flanked by the Alps and the Rhône River, Provence attracts hordes of visitors, especially during frequent summer festivals. Fortunately, many of the tourists are siphoned off to the beaches along the Riviera, which is a part of Provence but whose jet-set image somehow doesn't fit in with the rest of the region.

Avignon

When you look at Avignon from a distance, all you see is the tremendous Papal Palace. Look up Avignon in any history book and you will find popes. Somewhere in Avignon a soap shop is probably selling a pope on a rope. So what's the big deal with popes in this town? In 1309, Pope Clement V shifted the seat of the papacy from Rome to Avignon; Avignon remained the capital of Christendom until 1377. During the Avignon papacy, artists attached themselves to the papal entourage and the arts flourished.

Avignon is built along the Rhône River and encircled by 14th-century city walls. Although the streets that lead to the main historical sites teem with tourist and cars, away from the Palais des Papes, the narrow, cobbled streets are serene. Every July and August, during the renowned

The Mistral: It's an Ill Wind That Blows

If you come to Provence in late autumn or early spring, bring your windbreaker. The infamous mistral is a bitterly cold, dry wind that comes sweeping down from the north whenever a low pressure weather system develops over the Mediterranean. The temperature can drop dramatically in just a matter of minutes. Supposedly, the extensive network of expressways has lessened the mistral's effect, but then the snow was always deeper and colder when our parents had to walk to school. Many roads, fields, and towns have wind-breaks of closely planted trees or stone walls to give some shelter from the fierce wind.

Festival d'Avignon, there is a performance of some kind on nearly every corner, and it's almost impossible to find a cheap place to stay.

VISITOR INFORMATION The multilingual staff at the **main tourist office** (41 cours Jean-Jaurès, tel. 90–82–65–11) will happily load you down with shiny brochures; the annex is at the entrance to the Pont St-Bénézet. **Nouvelles Frontières** (33 rue Carnot, tel. 90–82–31–32) sells student discount tickets.

COMING AND GOING From Avignon's **train station** (tel. 90–82–50–50), trains go all over Provence and to Paris (4 hrs on the TGV, 357F). The **bus station** (5 av. Monclar, tel. 90–82–07–35), right next door, sends buses to many nearby towns. Walking is the best way to traverse Avignon's narrow streets, but **Transhumance** (tel. 90–95–57–81) rents bicycles through the tourist office at the train station.

WHERE TO SLEEP AND EAT Most of the cheap hotels are bunched on two streets, **rue Perdiguier** and **rue Joseph Vernet.** The rustic **Hôtel St-Roch** (9 rue Paul Mérindol, tel. 90–82–18–63; doubles 195F–280F), just outside the city walls, has a cozy living room and a garden with tables. The best dorm deal in Avignon is the huge **Foyer Bagatelle** (Ile de la Barthelasse, tel. 90–86–30–39; beds 54F), a 15-minute walk from the center of town. Take Bus 10 from the main post office to the Ile de la Barthelasse, an island in the Rhône River. The **Squash Club** (32 blvd. Limbert, tel. 90–85–27–78) is dirty but really cheap (46F per person). From the train station, go east along the ramparts to boulevard Limbert; the entrance is in an alley. You'll find several campgrounds on the Ile de la Barthelasse, including one at the Foyer Bagatelle.

For affordable food, look beyond the shiny tourist traps near the Palais des Papes. Lots of good restaurants line **rue des Lices** and **rue des Teinturiers.** You can buy produce at the large **indoor market** on place Pie (Tues.–Sun. mornings). Eat a full Provençal meal at the artsy **Le Petit Comptoir** (52 rue des Lices, tel. 90–86–10–94) for 55F. The folks at the family-owned **L'Etoile** (96 rue Philonarde, tel. 90–86–31–85) dish out the best couscous in the city for 40F. For some after-dinner intoxication, go to place des Corps Saints, where **Koala Bar** and **Les Celestins** are popular hangouts.

WORTH SEEING Most sights cluster around the colossal **Palais des Papes** (pl. du Palais, tel. 90–27–50–73; admission 30F, 22F students) where six Avignon popes held court. The Great Court, where visitors arrive, forms a link between the severe Palais Vieux (Old Palace) built by Pope Benedict XII, a member of the Cistercian order, and the more decorative Palais Nouveau (New Palace), courtesy of the artsy Pope Clement VI. Guides conduct tours of the austere interior in English daily at 10 AM and 3 PM for 43F, 34F students. Near the Palais des Papes, the mostly Romanesque **Cathédrale Notre-Dame des Doms** sports many incongruous extras that have been appended throughout the centuries. Added in 1859, the huge, awkward statue of the Virgin Mary dwarfs the cathedral's bell tower. For a quick change of scenery, go beyond the cathedral to the **Rocher des Doms,** a large park with fountains, ponds, peacocks, swans, and a small café. Built in the 14th century, the **Petit Palais** (pl. du Palais, tel. 90–86–44–58; admission 18F, 9F students, free Sun.) used to be a residence for cardinals and archbishops, but now it's a museum housing an outstanding collection of Italian paintings and avignonais sculpture and painting.

NEAR AVIGNON

Small and quiet nearby towns make fantastic day trips. Go to **Fontaine-de-Vaucluse** for its natural beauty; the star attraction of this small village, 50 minutes from Avignon by bus (22F), is a fountain, believed to be the source of the emerald-green Sorgue River. Scientific types reckon the fountain is fed by a underground stream that is, in turn, fed by rainwater from the Vaucluse Plateau. For a lazy, wine-drinking fiesta, head to **Châteauneuf-du-Pape,** a small hillside town, just a half-hour bus ride (18F50) from Avignon. The 13 million bottles of wine they produce here each year can be very expensive, but you can taste it for free in the *caves de dégustation* (wine-tasting cellars) that are on practically every street.

`ORANGE` Orange is a small, busy town, with most of the activity focused around the narrow, cobbled streets of the centre ville. Its two spectacular Roman monuments, the Théâtre Antique and the Arc de Triomphe, are incongruent with the dimensions of the city. The enormous, semicircular **Théâtre Antique** (pl. des Frères Mounet, tel. 90–51–17–60; admission 25F, 20F students) in the center of town is one of the best examples of a Roman theater in existence. Built during Augustus's reign in AD 1, the theater still has its large statue of the emperor. On the northern side of town, the magnificent Arc de Triomphe was built in the 1st century on the ancient **Via Agrippa,** the road that used to link Lyon with Arles. Dedicated to the celebration of empire, the monument is composed of three archways and decorated with images of warfare.

Orange is only 30 minutes and 27F away from Avignon by train, so there's not much point in spending the night. The tourist annex (pl. des Frères Mounet), across from the Théâtre Antique, is more centrally located than the **main tourist office** (cours Aristide Briand, tel. 90–34–70–88).

Arles

Arles's small vieille ville is filled with residential pockets where time seems to have stood still since 1888, when Vincent van Gogh immortalized the city in his paintings. Arles actually manages to live up to the beauty of van Gogh's renditions (and capitalizes on them with ubiquitous "Vince" T-shirts), but the town's biggest tourist attractions are the Roman theater and amphitheater, built by Roman colonists who came to Arles in 46 BC.

`COMING AND GOING` The **train station** (90–82–50–50) harbors a **tourist office annex** (tel. 90–49–36–90); the **main tourist office** (tel. 90–18–41–20) is on esplanade des Lices. The **bus station** (tel. 90–49–38–01) faces the train station on avenue Paulin Talabot. All you need to get around the vieille ville is your feet, but you can rent bicycles at **Collavoli** (15 rue du Pont, tel. 90–96–03–77) or at the train station.

`WHERE TO SLEEP AND EAT` Many well-maintained hotels in the vieille ville offer singles and doubles for 100F–200F. The friendly multilingual management will check you in at **Le Galoubet** (18 rue du Dr. Fanton, 1 block north of pl. du Forum, tel. 90–96–25–34; doubles 140F–170F). Van Gogh memorabilia decorates the well-furnished **Lou Gardien** (70 rue du 4 Septembre, tel. 90–96–76–15; doubles 160F), a couple of blocks north of place du Forum. An uptight staff presides over the **HI hostel** (20 av. Maréchal Foch, tel. 90–96–18–25; beds 75F the first night, 62F thereafter), a five-minute walk from the center of town. From the train station, take Bus 4 and transfer to Bus 3 on boulevard des Lices. **Camping City** (rte. De Crau, tel. 90–93–08–86) is just over 1 km from the city center and costs 15F per site plus 16F per person. From the center of town, take Bus 2 or follow the signs to Pont de Croix.

Stay away from the overpriced restaurants on the central boulevard des Lices; **place du Forum, place Voltaire,** and the narrow streets leading away from them are better bets for bustling cafés and restaurants. For a quick fix of crêpes or pizza, go to **rue Hôtel de Ville.** One block north of place du Forum, **Vitamine** (16 rue du Dr. Fanton, tel. 90–93–77–36) is often busy; the good-size salads (16F–70F) and pasta dishes (28F–42F) are worth the wait.

`WORTH SEEING` A 44F ticket (31F students), available at all the attractions, gets you into all of Arles's sights. The **Arènes** (Rond-Point des Arènes; admission 15F, 9F students), a 2nd-century Roman amphitheater, holds up to 20,000 spectators during the bullfights and concerts that take place here in the summer. Not much is left of the **Théâtre Antique** (rue due Cloître; admission 15F, 9F students), a Roman theater built during Augustus's reign in the 1st century BC. The semicircular seating tiers still stand, but only two columns and a few stumps remain of the stage. A huge pile of stone and brick constitutes the ruins of the **Thermes de Constantin** (rue Dominique-Maisto, by rue du 4 Septembre; admission 15F, 9F students), 4th-century Roman baths. The size of the structure is impressive, but it's difficult to tell which parts belong to the original and which parts have been reconstructed.

A 17th-century chapel houses the **Musée d'Art Chrétien** (rue Balze, near Hôtel de Ville; admission 12F, 7F students), a superb collection of 4th-century Christian sarcophagi. From inside the museum you can descend into the **Cryptoporticus,** an underground gallery that used to form the base of a Roman forum. The Provençal poet Frédéric Mistral used his 1904 Nobel Prize money to establish the **Musée Arlaten** (rue de la République; admission 15F, 10F students), a museum of ethnography where attendants clothed in Provençal costume provide commentary on the exhibits.

Aix-en-Provence

If you come to Aix, bring your credit cards and nice clothes, because it's not easy being a traveling scumbag amid all this bourgeois luxury. Come to this city to see its impressive architecture, elegant fountains, and to join all those fashionable folks for whom café-going and boutique-shopping are a way of life. On the other hand, if you're trying to avoid snobbery and Parisian prices, Aix is probably not for you.

The museums and churches in Aix are overshadowed by the city itself; the **tourist office** (2 pl. du Général de Gaulle, tel. 42–16–11-61) shows off the town with guided tours in English or French for 45F. The leafy boulevard **cours Mirabeau** is lined with 17th- and 18th-century *hôtels particuliers* (aristocratic town houses), which now house banks and private offices. Luxurious fountains grace every square; the main one is the **Fontaine de la Rotonde** on place du Général de Gaulle, at the west end of cours Mirabeau.

If it's a rainy day, visit the **Atelier Paul Cézanne** (9 av. Paul Cézanne, tel. 42–21–06–53; admission 13F, 7F students), a house-studio where impressionist Paul Cézanne lived in the 1890s. The 17th-century Archevêché (Archbishop's Palace) is home to the Tapestry Museum, the **Musée des Tapisseries** (28 pl. des Martyrs de la Résistance, tel. 42–23–09–91; admission 12F, 9F students). A striking series of 17 tapestries made in Beauvais illustrates the adventures of Don Quixote. Aix's most interesting museum is the **Fondation Vasarély** (av. Marcel Pagnol, tel. 42–20–01–09; admission 35F, 20F students), displaying 42 "mural integrations" by a Hungarian artist that manipulate color and space in innovative ways.

COMING AND GOING The **train station** (pl. Victor Hugo, tel. 42–26–09–95) runs hourly trains to Marseille (30 min, 34F). One block west of la Rotonde, the **bus station** (rue Lapierre, tel. 42–27–17–91) is filled with a zillion independent bus companies. Most of the sights are within central Aix, where walking is the best way to get around.

WHERE TO SLEEP AND EAT If the hostel is full, you're screwed—only a handful of hotels cost less than 200F, and even those are overpriced. The **Hôtel Paul** (10 av. Pasteur at north entrance of centre ville, tel. 42–23–23–89; doubles 179F–189F) and the **Hôtel Vigouroux** (27 rue Cardinale near Musée Granet, tel. 42–38–26–42; doubles 200F–220F), open to travelers summers only, are about as good as it gets. The staff has guests goose-stepping around the **HI hostel** (3 av. Marcel Pagnol, tel. 42–20–15–99), but beds are only 75F for the first night and 65F thereafter. From la Rotonde, take Bus 12. April through August, stop by **CROUS Cité des Gazelles** (38 av. Jules Ferry, tel. 42–26–33–75) weekdays for info on the 44F beds in university dorms just south of the centre ville.

Small, cheap holes-in-the-wall are hard to come by. **Place Ramus** and the adjacent **rue de la Verrerie, rue Félibre Gaut,** and **rue des Marseillais** are overrun by medium-priced restaurants of all types. Fresh produce is available daily at the open-air **market** on place Richelme. Fight for a table outside at **Lauranne Passion** (7 pl. Ramus, tel. 42–27–46–46) to get your 55F fill of healthy greens. After dark, the young and hip hang out on place Richelme, place de l'Hôtel de Ville, and place des Cardeurs.

Marseille

This huge, polluted city circumvents touristy niceties and pursues its own problem-ridden existence with little regard for those in search of the picturesque. The Mediterranean's largest port, Marseille is plagued with social conflict, political corruption, drugs, and crime. Racial tension has followed on the heels of recent waves of immigration. If you're longing for glamour or Parisian sophistication, Marseille will probably not cut it. But if you're sick of seeing busloads of tourists, Marseille can be a great place to see a French port city in action.

BASICS The **visitor information** annex at the train station (tel. 91–50–59–18) shares duties with the main office (4 la Canebière, tel. 91–54–91–11). Nearby, the **American Express** office (39 la Canebière, tel. 91–13–71–21) has the usual cardmember services. Pick up poste restante mail at the main **post office** (1 pl. Hôtel des Postes, cnr. of rue Colbert and rue Barbusse, tel. 91–90–31–33; postal code 13001).

COMING AND GOING Marseille's enormous **train station** (tel. 91–08–50–50), at the northern end of the centre ville, is a 20-minute walk from the Vieux Port and about a 10-minute walk from most budget hotels. The **bus station** (tel. 91–08–16–40) is at the east end of the train station. **SNCM** (61 blvd. des Dames, tel. 91–56–32–00) sends ferries to Corsica, Sardinia, and North Africa. The **Aéroport Marseille Provence** is 25 km from Marseille. **Transports Routiers Passagers Aériens** runs frequent buses between the airport and the train station for 39F.

GETTING AROUND Marseille is divided into 16 arrondissements. The Vieux Port, the surrounding centre ville, and the main street, **la Canebière,** make up the city's nerve center. La Canebière separates the poorer areas to the north from the more chic neighborhoods to the south. Many of the points of interest are clustered around the Vieux Port, but you'll have to use public transportation to get from one end of town to the other. Pick up a map of bus and Métro lines at the tourist office or at the RTM (Réseau de Transport Marseillais) **info desk** (6–8 rue des Fabres, tel. 91–91–92–10). Tickets, available at bus terminals and Métro stations, cost 8F and are valid for both bus and Métro trips.

WHERE TO SLEEP You can rub elbows with the down and out for around 50F per night at the really cheap, dilapidated hotels on **rue du Théâtre Français** and the intersecting **rue Mazagran.** On **allées Léon Gambetta,** a 10-minute walk from the train station, you'll find cleaner places for 80F–120F. Rooms at the **Hôtel de Bourgogne** (31 allées Léon Gambetta, tel. 91–62–19–49; doubles from 150F) are unusually bright, large, and clean. Rooms at the **Hôtel Sphinx** (16 rue Sénac, tel. 91–48–70–59; doubles 116F–160F) are well-tended by the friendly proprietor, and the prices are hard to beat. From the train station, take boulevard d'Athènes and go left on la Canebière to rue Sénac. The **Auberge de Jeunesse Bonneveine** (47 av. Joseph-Vidal, tel. 91–73–21–81; beds 59F) is near the beach and has no curfew. From the train station, take the Métro to rond point du Prado, then take Bus 44. A 19th-century château has been converted into the beautiful **Auberge de Jeunesse de Bois-Luzy** (67 av. de Bois-Luzy, tel. 91–49–06–18; beds 42F). Take Bus 6 from place de la Libération. The campgrounds in Marseille have been closed—they had too many problems with theft. As for roughing it, don't—it's dangerous.

FOOD Eats are cheap in Marseille, but the food-stand fare is greasy and unappetizing. The largest concentration of restaurants and cafés is at the Vieux Port. Restaurants on **quai de Rive Neuve** offer good deals, and many feature the city's fish-stew specialty, bouillabaisse. For pizza, sandwich, and produce stands, go to **rue de Rome** and the side streets to the east. The happening bar scene is at **cours Honoré d'Estienne d'Orvès** and **place aux Huiles,** by the Vieux Port, and **cours Julien,** near the train station.

WORTH SEEING You won't see the spirit of Marseille behind a glass case in a museum or under the vaulted dome of a church, but rather in its crowded, dirty streets and markets. The museums are numerous, but not all sparkle with brilliance. The cultural center **Centre de la Vieille Charité** (2 rue de la Charité, tel. 91–56–28–38), in a restored 17th-century hospice, is probably the sight most worth your time. Permanent collections include the **Musée d'Archéologie Méditerranéenne,** which displays primarily Egyptian and Celto-Ligurian artifacts. Admission to temporary exhibits is 20F, 15F students, temporary and permanent exhibits 25F, 15F students. The 17th-century Hôtel de Montgrand houses the **Musée Cantini** (19 rue Grignan, tel. 91–54–77–75; admission 15F, 7F50 students), an excellent collection of modern art. The permanent display includes works of the fauvist, cubist, and surrealist movements.

The most imposing structure of Marseille's cityscape, the 19th-century **Basilique de Notre-Dame de la Garde** (blvd. A. Aune) overlooks the city from a limestone cliff and is topped by a statue of the Virgin Mary. The building's interior is colorfully decorated with murals and mosaics. Take Bus 60 from cours Jean Ballard, just south of quai des Belges. The **Abbaye St-Victor** (rue Sainte) was built in the 5th century in honor of St-Victor, the patron of sailors and millers. The abbey was destroyed in the 10th century during the Saracen invasion and rebuilt in the 11th and 12th centuries with an emphasis on fortification. In the spooky underground **crypt,** you can see what's left of the 5th-century abbey, as well as pagan and Christian sarcophagi.

NEAR MARSEILLE

When you have to start scraping Marseille's urban grime from under your fingernails, it's time for a day trip to **Cassis,** the town Virginia Woolf referred to as paradise on earth during her stay here. Originally a fishing village, the tiny port is now an upscale beach town filled with restaurants, tourist shops, and expensive villas. You can hike, climb the white cliffs, snorkel in the sea, then snooze on the sand. The best way to come to Cassis is by **bus,** because the train station is 3 km from town. The ride from Marseille takes 40 minutes and costs 20F. If you plan to stay overnight, the only cheap sleep is the **Auberge de Jeunesse** (tel. 42–01–02–72), a one-hour walk from Cassis. It's in the middle of nowhere and there are no buses, so you'll need to get a map from the **tourist office** (pl. Baragnon, tel. 42–01–71–17) to figure out how to get here.

The Riviera
Also known as the Côte d'Azur, the French Riviera is a narrow stretch of Mediterranean coastline that extends from St-Tropez to Menton, near the Italian border. For decades the Riviera has been the playground of Europe, conjuring up images of wealth, sandy beach resorts, and all that is chic. In reality, the beaches are mostly small and pebbly (at least those east of Antibes), the area is overdeveloped and crowded, the movie stars have headed to more secluded areas, and it's horribly expensive.

Nevertheless, the sun, the sidewalk cafés, the smell of sand and water, and the sight of aloof expatriates with money still hold a sublime allure. Life along the coast revolves around the beach; people come to the Riviera to get horizontal and maximize UV exposure. Some beaches are public and free; on many others, you have to pay a fee (30F and up), which buys you a plot of sand and an umbrella.

St-Tropez

All summer long in St-Tropez, the fashion-conscious stroll between crowded cafés around the harbor, while the yacht-club types look on from their decks and floating bars. Budget travelers are not made to feel welcome: The restaurants and hotels are outrageously priced; it's hard to get to the beaches; and there aren't even any places to store your backpack for the day.

Still, if you dream of sharing a patch of sand with the glitterati, we don't want to rain on your parade, even if the big, sandy beaches are far from town and mostly private. **Plage des Granier** is the only public beach within easy walking distance of town, but it's small and crowded. From here, you can take a path that passes **Plage des Salins** (4 km from St-Tropez) and ends up at **Plage de Pampelonne** (8 km from St-Tropez), both of which are divided into alternating private and public plots of sand. The most convenient way to find the sand that's right for you is to rent a moped (*see* Coming and Going, *below*). Otherwise, SODETRAV buses make the short trek from the bus station to the Plage de Pampelonne (15 min, 15F) three times a day Monday–Saturday. The two **tourist offices** have tons of brochures and a hotel reservation service. One office faces the port on quai Jean Jaurès (tel. 94–97–45–21) and the other is at the bus station (23 av. du Général-Leclerc, tel. 94–97–41–21).

COMING AND GOING The closest you can get to St-Tropez by train is St-Raphaël, about 25 km away. From here, you can either take a pretty 1½-hour trip on a **SODETRAV** bus (tel. 94–54–62–36 in St-Tropez or 94–95–24–82 in St-Raphaël) for 78F round-trip, or a 50-minute boat trip with **Les Bateaux Bleus** (Vieux Port de St-Raphaël, tel. 94–95–17–46) for 100F round-trip. To get around town, go to **Azur Motor Sport** (10 rue Joseph-Quaranta, tel. 94–97–77–20) or **Location Vélos-Motos, Louis Mas** (5 rue Quaranta, tel. 94–97–00–60), both near place des Lices, to rent a bike or moped.

WHERE TO SLEEP AND EAT You're much better off sleeping elsewhere and visiting St-Tropez for the day. If you stay, your best bets are the peaceful **Hôtel Lou Cagnard** (18 av. Paul Roussel, tel. 94–97–04–24 or 94–97–09–44; doubles 250F–390F) or the often-booked **Hôtel Les Chimères** (Port du Pilon, tel. 94–97–02–90; doubles from 200F), near the bus station.

Get ready to gnaw on bread and cheese, because it's damned expensive to eat here. The vieille ville is a better option than the port for reasonably priced sandwiches, salads, and the like. **Bar San Carlo** (50 rue Général Allard) is a hip hangout that's rough around the edges but serves good sandwiches and drinks; a hamburger with fries is 30F.

St-Raphaël

Between the red cliffs of the Massif de l'Esterel and the high, rocky Massif des Maures, St-Raphaël is a simple town with sandy beaches, marinas, and a casino. It's a good base from which to explore the surrounding area since it's well-served by public transportation and has more affordable hotels than other places along the Riviera.

COMING AND GOING Trains from all over the Riviera stop at the St-Raphaël-Valescure **train station** (pl. de la Gare, tel. 94–91–50–50 for information or 94–22–39–19 for reservations). The **tourist office** (le Stanislas, rue Waldeck-Rousseau, tel. 94–82–15–68) is outside the train station. The bus station is directly behind the train station. **Forum Cars** (tel. 94–95–16–71) and **SODETRAV** (tel. 94–95–24–82) serve other towns on the Riviera. **Les Bateaux Bleus** (tel. 94–95–17–46) ferries leave from St-Raphaël's Vieux Port for St-Tropez, Port-Grimaud, Fréjus, and the Iles-de-Lérins.

WHERE TO SLEEP AND EAT The one-star hotels in St-Raphaël tend to be pretty dingy, but you can do quite well for just a few dollars more. On the Vieux Port, **Hôtel le Touring** (1 quai Albert 1er, tel. 94–95–01–72) has rooms with a nice view but no shower for 150F for one or two people. **Hôtel des Pyramides** (77 av. Paul-Doumer, tel. 94–95–05–95), east of the train station and within view of the beach, has doubles with sink for 170F and a single for 90F. The **Centre International du Manoir** (chemin de l'Escale, tel. 94–95–20–58; beds 90F) is 5 km from St-Raphaël in the suburb of Boulouris. Buses and trains go to Boulouris every 30 minutes from the bus and train stations.

St-Raphaël has a plethora of snack stands, pizzerias, crêperies, and fine restaurants along its oceanfront. Across from the train station, **Christie's Pâtissier** (40 rue Waldeck-Rousseau, tel. 94–40–55–30) sells ready-to-eat foods, and **Pizza Côte d'Azur** (blvd. Jean Moulin, tel. 94–19–09–19) delivers pizzas (38F–100F) anywhere in St-Raphaël or Fréjus. Open Tuesday–Sunday, a morning outdoor **market** (rue de la République, behind the bus station) sells nuts and olives, as well as the usual produce.

Cannes

Conspicuous consumption, extravagant nightlife, and a host of wanna-bes characterize this Riviera hot spot, which has been attracting the well-to-do since the mid-1800s. Today, this resort town is probably most famous for its **Film Festival**, when Hollywood's luminaries blow into town and try to eclipse all the intellectual European filmmakers dressed in black. Held in May, the festival attracts an insane number of people, as do all the music and performing arts events that take place in the following months. All the pretensions aside, Cannes is probably a better destination for budget travelers than equally glamorous St-Tropez, because it's less insular and isolated—you and your grubby backpack won't stick out as much.

Besides the amusement of the whole *scene* in Cannes, there isn't much to see. An elegant, palm tree-lined promenade called **la Croisette** borders the beach. At one end of the promenade is the modern **Palais des Festivals** (Festival Hall), a summer casino, and the **Vieux Port,** where old pleasure boats are moored. At the other end is a winter casino and a modern harbor for some of the most luxurious yachts in the world. All along the promenade you'll find chichi cafés, expensive boutiques, and luxury hotels. Speedboats and water-skiers glide by the long, narrow beach lined with bathers soaking up the sun and the atmosphere.

Cannes's beach has private sections with neat rows of mattresses and colored parasols where you can swim for about 120F. To the west of the umbrella section and past the Vieux Port is the public **Plage du Midi. Plage Gazagnaire,** east of the new harbor, is also a good public beach. **Le Suquet,** Cannes's old quarter, rises on a hill on the other side of the Vieux Port. With narrow streets and a more down-to-earth atmosphere, it's a pleasant respite from the glitz.

BASICS The biggest and best tourist office is the **Cannes Direction Générale du Tourisme** (esplanade Président Georges Pompidou, tel. 93–39–01–01), inside the Palais des Festivals on boulevard de la Croisette. The branch office (tel. 93–99–19–77) at the train station is less helpful, but they will give you a list of hotels and make reservations. Younger travelers go to the **Cannes Information Jeunesse** (5 quai St-Pierre, tel. 93–68–50–50) for job listings and information on excursions, sports, hostels, and camping. The **American Express Bank** (cnr. of blvd. de la Croisette and rue Buttura) and the **Am Ex Voyages/Exchange office** (8 rue des Belges, near rue Notre-Dame, tel. 93–38–15–87) both offer currency exchange. Go to the latter for travel service, moneygrams, bill payment, lost cards, and mail service.

COMING AND GOING The Marseille–Ventimiglia train passes through Nice (29F) and Antibes (11F) and arrives at Cannes's **train station** (tel. 93–99–50–50) every half-hour. Don't get off at the Cannes-la-Bocca stop or you'll be stranded in the suburbs. Regional buses leave the bus station (tel. 93–39–31–37) attached to the train station and from the station on place de l'Hôtel-de-Ville (tel. 93–39–18–71), which also offers local service. Maps at the bus stops around town explain the local lines. Rent bicycles at the train station, mopeds at **Garage Mistral** (14 rue Georges Clémenceau, tel. 93–39–33–60).

WHERE TO SLEEP Cannes takes pity on the poor traveler by having lots of budget hotels within walking distance of the train station. Spotless doubles start at 184F at the **Hôtel du Nord** (6 rue Jean Jaurès, tel. 93–38–48–79), which is in view of the train station. The homey **Hôtel le Florian** (8 rue Commandant-André, tel. 93–39–24–82; doubles 200F) is near the beach and boulevard de la Croisette. Two blocks from the train station, **Atlantis Hôtel** (4 rue du 24 Août, tel. 93–39–18–72; doubles 190F–230F) is a cut above your average budget hole-in-the-wall—try to book ahead. In Cannes's western suburb of la Bocca, accessible by train, is the campground **Caravaning Bellevue** (67 av. Maurice Chevalier, tel. 93–47–28–97). Police rarely patrol Cannes's beaches and public gardens at night, so they're a pretty good bet for sleeping under the stars.

FOOD Prices are never going to be low in Cannes, but the cafés and restaurants farthest from the beach are usually the cheapest. You can buy sandwiches, crêpes, and pastries along the beach, as well as in the pedestrian zone of **rue Meynadier.** For lively atmosphere and a mix of high and low prices, walk along the packed row of restaurants, bistros, and trendy spots in Le Suquet, Cannes's old town. Look for **Bar au Petit Palace** (20 rue Suquet, tel. 93–39–99–18), with its moustached regulars; **Chez Mamichette** (11 rue St-Antoine, tel.

93–39–49–62), with outdoor tables and a view of the water; or **R.E.R. Caffé** (21 rue St-Antoine, tel. 93–39–30–32), a hangout for the young. **Le Santorin** (av. Jean Jaurès, tel. 93–38–18–96) is popular with locals because of its good selection of pastas (about 40F) and salads (30F–35F).

AFTER DARK Cannes's rich and famous bump and grind, drink themselves silly, gamble, and otherwise spend a lot of money to keep up appearances. Average Joes, though, go to the movies—a less expensive specialty of Cannes. **Les Arcades** (77 rue Félix Faure, tel. 93–39–00–98), **Olympia** (5 rue d'Antibes, tel. 93–39–13–93), and **Star** (98 rue d'Antibes, tel. 93–39–11–79) show European and American films. Locals go to **Studio Circus** (48 rte. de la République, tel. 93–38–32–98) to dance the night away. The smart ones bring their own alcohol and just pay the 100F cover, which is standard in most Riviera discos. **Disco 7** (7 rue Rouguière, off rue Félix Faure, tel. 93–39–10–36), attracting a predominantly gay crowd, features a transvestite show and holds AIDS benefit nights.

NEAR CANNES

ANTIBES In winter, the view of the snow-covered Alps from Antibes is spectacular, but it's a view that few visitors here ever see—Antibes is a summer resort first and foremost. In summer, the town explodes with festivals, and huge crowds drive prices through the roof. Street artists and musicians take over the public squares lined with expensive boutiques, and beach sports take over the beautiful sandy beaches. Pablo Picasso liked sunny Antibes so much that he stayed for a while. Now the **Musée Picasso** (pl. Marijol, tel. 92–90–54–20; admission 20F, 10F students) displays his art at the seaside Château Grimaldi, where Picasso spent six prolific months.

Twenty minutes and 20F from Nice, Antibes's **train station** (av. Robert-Soleau, tel. 93–33–63–51 or 93–99–50–50) is only a block or so from the beach. Signs lead you from the train station to the **Maison du Tourisme** (11 pl. du Général-de-Gaulle, tel. 93–33–95–64). Regional buses leave from the **bus station** (1 pl. Guynemer, tel. 93–34–37–60). To get to Cannes or Nice, or to catch local buses, wait at the different posts on **place du Général-de-Gaulle**. If you're going to spend the night, go to the **Relais International de la Jeunesse "Caravelle 60"** (rte. de la Garoupe, tel. 93–61–34–40). It's a wonderful, cheap place to stay but it's located in Cap d'Antibes, a long walk from anything but the beach. Buses run out to Cap d'Antibes almost every hour, 8 AM–7 PM.

Nice

Nice is both the best and the worst city on the French Riviera. Nowhere else along the Côte d'Azur can you find such cheap rooms and food, including all sorts of authentic ethnic dishes. Trains from Nice speed to spots all along the Mediterranean Coast, making this a great base for day trips, but tons of museums, a long pebbly beach, a pedestrian quarter, and a hopping nightlife are enough to keep any traveler in town for a while.

At the same time, though, you have to contend with big-city crime and grime—Nice is five times the size of Cannes—but you also reap the rewards of its diversity, size, and energy. Rich retirees from Paris and northern France share the streets with thousands of immigrants from Africa, as well as Kurds, who live in Nice's most dilapidated quarters. Many of the French residents don't consider the city's growing diversity a plus. Nice is a stronghold of Jean Le Pen and his neofascist Front National party, which wants to rid France of its large immigrant population.

BASICS The **tourist office** (tel. 93–87–07–07) next to the train station will reserve you a hotel room for 10F–20F. The office near the beach (5 av. Gustave V, tel. 93–87–60–60) specializes in excursions and after-dark activities but isn't so hip on accommodations. The **American Express** office (11 Promenade des Anglais, at rue du Congrès, tel. 93–16–53–53) does the usual Am Ex thing. Pick up mail at the **post office** at 23 avenue Thiers (tel. 93–88–55–41). The postal code is 06000.

COMING AND GOING Nice's **train station** (tel. 93–87–50–50 for information or 93–88–89–93 for reservations) is on the north edge of town and serves many towns along the Riviera. Trains from Paris take more than eight hours unless you pay for a reservation on the TGV, which zips to Nice in about half the time. Buses leave Nice's **bus station** (Promenade du Paillon, on the edge of Vieux Nice, tel. 93–80–84–84) regularly for points all along the Riviera. Planes arrive at the **Aéroport Nice-Côte d'Azur.** Buses run between the airport and the bus station daily from 5 AM to 7 PM; Bus 23 runs to the train station from 8 to 6.

GETTING AROUND Nice lies between the train station to the north and the **Baie des Anges** (Angel Bay) to the south. **Place Masséna** is the main square; to the east is the old part of town, known as **Vieux Nice,** and to the west is the newer section. Everything you'd want to see in Nice, with the exception of the Roman ruins and the Musée Matisse, is within walking distance, but the city is also well served by buses. Buy tickets for **SUN** buses at the central station at 10 avenue Félix Faure or at the Bus Masséna information center (Parc-Autos de la place Masséna, tel. 93–16–52–52). Tickets cost 8F. If you're willing to brave the traffic, rent a bike or moped at **Nicea Location Rent** (9 av. Thiers, tel. 93–82–42–71), across from the train station. Bicycles go for 120F plus a hefty deposit; mopeds start at 150F a day.

WHERE TO SLEEP Nice thrives on tourists, and hotel managers do everything they can to make it cheap and easy to stay here. All the hotels listed below are in the budget hotel area just south of the train station, just 10 minutes away from the beach. If the area's packed, go north and check out **avenue Malaussena.**

Americans swarm to the **Hôtel Belle Meunière** (21 av. Durante, tel. 93–88–66–15), where spartan rooms go for minimum bucks; one single is 75F, doubles are 150F–250F, and dorm spaces are a bargain 70F. The staff jokes with the mostly French clientele and whoever else comes by at the **Hôtel Interlaken** (26 av. Durante, tel. 93–88–30–15; doubles 195F in summer, 130F winter) just outside the train station. The bathrooms are cramped, but the rooms have high ceilings and French doors and shutters. The staff treats the guests like family at the **Hôtel du Centre** (2 rue de Suisse, tel. 93–88–83–85; doubles from 186F), which is equipped with extras like TVs in the rooms. Down a little alley, the **Hôtel le Gervais** (19 rue Alsace-Lorraine, tel. 93–88–25–15; doubles 152F) is quiet and colorfully decorated, but the alley gets spooky at night. The comfy rooms, the cool terrace on the fifth floor, and a communal TV room make the **Hôtel Idéal Bristol** (22 rue Paganini, tel. 93–88–50–72; doubles 174F) popular.

Lots of Americans socialize at the **HI hostel** (rte. Forestière du Mont-Alban, tel. 93–89–23–64; beds 60F). At 5 PM the staff posts a list of how many beds are left for the night, but if you want a spot during summer, it's best to arrive early in the morning. Take Bus 14 from place Masséna. There's usually room in the **Relais International de la Jeunesse "Clairvallon"** (26 av. Scudéri, tel. 93–81–27–63; beds 70F) after the other hostel is full. Guests have access to the tennis courts, gardens, and the pool. Check in at 5 PM. Take Bus 15 from place Masséna to the Scudéri stop. **Les Collinettes** (3 av. R. Shuman, tel. 93–97–06–64 or 93–86–71–98) is a girls' school that's open to both sexes during the summer. Private rooms are 100F a night. **Centre Hébergement Jeunesse Magnan** (31 rue Louis-de-Coppet, tel. 93–86–28–75) is near Florida Plage. A bed will cost you only 50F.

If you end up roughing it at the train station, beware that it attracts cockroaches in their human and insect forms. Nice's beach is long, so you may be able to stay one step ahead of police if they patrol.

Just outside Nice, **Terry Camping** (768 rte. de Grenoble, St-Isadore, tel. 93–08–11–58) has lots of amenities. Depending on the season, tent sites cost 22F–44F for one or two people. Take Bus 700 from the bus station in Nice.

FOOD The outdoor **market,** held every morning at cours Saleya, is a gold mine for the backpack set, but when you're ready to do your taste buds right, head for Vieux Nice. Restaurants here serve the usual seafood dishes, pasta, and pizza, but also look for local specialties like *socca* (chickpea porridge) and *pissaladière* (anchovies and olives in a pastry crust). If you decide to branch out, you'll find Mexican, Algerian, Tunisian, and every other type of cuisine imaginable. *Tapas* (Spanish appetizers) come with a *rapido* (shot) of tequila for 70F at the popular **Pauline Tapas** (14 rue E-et-P

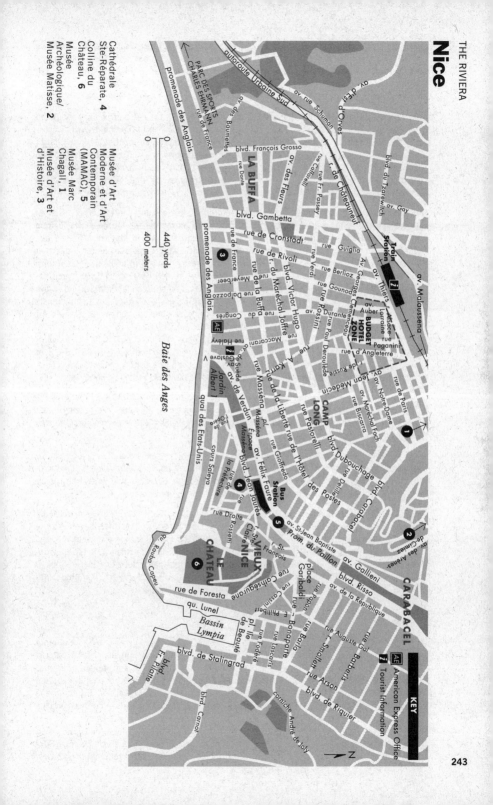

Cathédrale
Ste-Réparate, **4**
Colline du
Château, **6**
Musée
Archéologique/
Musée Matisse, **2**

Musée d'Art
Moderne et d'Art
Contemporain
(MAMAC), **5**
Musée Marc
Chagall, **1**
Musée d'Art et
d'Histoire, **3**

0

440 yards

400 meters

Baie des Anges

KEY

AE American Express Office

7 Tourist Information

Tiranty, off av. Jean Médecin, tel. 93–80–12–44). **Le Claridge** (av. Jean Médecin, bet. rue de la Suisse and rue d'Alsace-Lorraine) is a crêperie, pizza parlor, bar, and café all rolled into one. Crêpes run 20F–25F, pizzas about 40F. **Nissa Socca** (5 rue Ste-Réparate, tel. 93–80–18–35) is a great place to try niçois specialties. The house ravioli is a deal at 38F and comes with a huge basket of bread.

WORTH SEEING Also called the Vieille Ville, **Vieux Nice** is the old part of town, bounded by boulevard Jean-Jaurès to the north and west and cours Saleya to the south. Within Vieux Nice, **Place Rosetti** is home to the **Cathédrale Ste-Réparate,** a 17th-century church with an immense working organ and incredibly ornate stained-glass windows. The **Colline du Château** (Castle Hill) bounds Vieux Nice to the east. The castle that was once there has long since crumbled, but the hill is worth a climb for its spectacular view of Nice. Take the stairs at the turning point of the quai des Etats-Unis or the elevator for 5F (elevator runs daily 9–6).

In **Cimiez,** a hilly area north of the town center, are public gardens and the remains of a **Roman arena.** Amid the ruins, a 17th-century villa houses two museums: the **Musée Archéologique** (160 av. des Arènes-de-Cimiez, tel. 93–81–59–57) and the **Musée Matisse** (164 av. des Arènes-de-Cimiez, tel. 93–81–08–08). The Musée Matisse pays homage to painter and former resident Henri Matisse, who settled here after World War I and lived in this former hotel until his death in 1954. Marc Chagall also spent his last years on the Riviera; the **Musée Marc Chagall** (av. Dr-Ménard, tel. 93–81–75–75; admission 26F, 17F students and on Sun.) displays his works, many of which draw themes from Jewish-Russian folklore. Environmentalists shouldn't miss the conservation library next door. Whoever built the god-awful **Musée d'Art Moderne et d'Art Contemporain** (promenade des Arts, tel. 93–62–61–62; admission free) must have been on something, but inside you'll find Andy Warhol classics and other avant-garde treasures. The **Musée d'Art et d'Histoire** (65 rue de France, tel. 93–88–06–22 or 93–88–11–34; admission free), on the other hand, is housed in a gorgeous villa that was once home to the Massénas, one of Napoleon Bonaparte's pet families. Today it's home to a museum of regional culture and niçois history.

CHEAP THRILLS In Nice, the cheapest thrill of all is obvious: the beach. For a laugh, walk along Promenade des Anglais and check out the private beaches, where people spend money to lie on what they consider to be a superior patch of pebbles.

If you're lucky enough to be in Nice during the last couple of weeks before Lent, you're in for a great time—or a little piece of misery, depending on how you feel about streets filled with music and partying at all hours of the night. Parades, feasts, dancing, and general frenzy are all part of **Carnival,** Nice's version of which is famous throughout France.

AFTER DARK Live music (usually reggae) and dancing last until 12:30 every night at **Le Dynamo** (3 rue Paganini, tel. 93–87–09–00). For a pub atmosphere, try **Chez Wayne** (15 rue de la Préfecture, tel. 93–13–46–99); the live blues bands that play here are well worth the 20F cover. **Zodiac** (6 passage E. Negrin, tel. 93–87–78–87) and **Quartz's** (18 rue du Congrès, tel. 93–88–88–87) attract a mostly gay crowd, though many clubs in Nice are mixed. **Salle Emeraude** (rue Papon near rue Emmanuel Philibert, tel. 93–89–88–55) is a blue-collar billiards hall where locals play snooker and "American" pool for money.

NEAR NICE

If you think Nice's beaches are nice, invest in a short bus or train ride to one of the more secluded surrounding villages and found out what being a sand sloth is really about. Just east of Nice, **Villefranche-sur-Mer** is a great place to laze with the French and Italians who have already discovered this near-perfect spot. Fabulous mansions crowd together on cliffs above a beautiful cove. The niçois are known to escape here on their midday breaks—the train ride is only 6 minutes and 8F. A 20-minute bus ride east of Nice, chic **St-Jean** sits on **Cap-Ferrat,** a jagged peninsula whose mountains rise steeply from the sea. This has long been a favorite spot for movie scenes and stars; a couple of James Bond movies were filmed here, and actor David Niven's former home is on a street bearing his name. Go south on the Promenade Maurice-Rouvier, which runs along the edge of the peninsula, and you'll stumble upon reasonable pizzerias, ice-cream parlors, and cafés on the promenade of the plage de St-Jean. Keep trekking around the peninsula's tip and you'll reach a wooded area, where a beautiful path leads along the outermost edge of the Cap. The beaches at **Cap d'Ail,** even though they're rocky, are perfect for stretching out and forgetting about civilization. For the more social, a sandy section has chairs and umbrellas for rent and beachside restaurants. Food and lodging are as extortionate here, but Cap d'Ail's prize is the Relais International de la Jeunesse "Thalassa" (rte. de la Mer, tel. 93–78–18–58; beds 72F the first night, 60F thereafter), a great youth hostel right on the beach. All this beachside fun is an easy 20-minute train or bus ride from Nice.

PEILLON We of the late-20th century like to think we perfected the science of engineering, but when you see Peillon, one of the most perfectly perched of France's *village perchés,* you realize that some attitude adjustment is in order. Less than a half-hour inland from Nice, the fortified medieval town of Peillon is literally carved out of the cliffs.

At the entrance of Peillon is the town's main attraction, the **Chapelle des Pénitents Blancs** (Chapel of the White Penitents). To get here, take the bus from Nice; the train leaves you several steep kilometers below below the town's entrance. Hikers can climb from Peillon to **Peille** (one hour from Nice by bus), an even remoter, smaller version of Peillon. The *sentier* (footpath) that connects the two is an old Roman trading path that takes about two hours to hike. For camping, **La Laune** (Moulins de Peillon, tel. 93–79–91–61) is open June–September.

Monaco

Cross the high rises of Hong Kong with the amusement-park feel of Disneyland, add a royal touch, and there you have Monaco—all 473 acres of it. Presided over by Prince Rainier III, Monaco is Europe's last constitutional autocracy, but for travelers' purposes the tiny principality may as well be part of France. Monaco's famed Monte Carlo Casino used to be the principality's big breadwinner, but these days banking, media, and tourism keep the coffers full. Budget travelers beware, though: Monaco is not a place to eat or sleep, unless you can squeeze into the exceptional youth hostel.

BASICS Ask at the **tourist office** (2a blvd. des Moulins, Monte Carlo, tel. 92–16–61–16) for *Bienvenue!,* a monthly guide of useful information. To get to this office or the **American Express** office (35 blvd. Princesse Charlotte, tel. 93–25–74–45), take Bus 1, 2, or 4 to the Casino-Tourisme stop.

COMING AND GOING Monaco's **train station** (tel. 93–87–50–50 for information or 93–88–89–93 for reservations) is 20 minutes (15F) west of Nice; trains run between the two every half-hour.

On a high, rocky promontory that extends to the sea is the old town of **Monaco-Ville,** one of five sections of Monaco. Most of the attractions worth seeing are in this area, an easy walk from the train station. Below and east of the promontory is **la Condamine,** the commercial harbor area with apartments and businesses. Next over is **Monte Carlo,** the modern gambling town, and then **Le Larvatto,** a swimming resort with artificial beaches. **Fontvieille** is the industrial district by the port.

Six bus lines travel to all the major points of interest in Monaco. The 8F50 fare includes a transfer good for 30 minutes. A card for four rides costs 18F; 28F50 gets you eight trips. You can buy cards and get a bus map from **Compagnie des Autobus de Monaco** (3 av. Président J. F. Kennedy, tel. 93–50–62–41).

WHERE TO SLEEP The hostel is the only good deal in Monaco. One block northeast of the train station, the **HI Centre de la Jeunesse Princesse Stephanie** (24 av. Prince Pierre, tel. 93–50–83–20; beds 60F) may be the nicest hostel on the Riviera and, not surprisingly, it's often full. Check-in is 9:30–10:30 AM; arrive early to get your numbered ticket. The maximum stay is five nights, one night during peak periods. If you can't get in here, you're best off sleeping in nearby Nice, Cap d'Ail, or Antibes. If you can't stand the thought of leaving the principality's royal ground and the hostel is full, try **Hôtel Cosmopolite** (4 rue de la Turbie, tel. 93–30–16–95; doubles from 160F).

FOOD A daily outdoor **market** near the station lessens your chances of starving in such an expensive place. A lot of the cheaper restaurants and take-out stands are in the old section of Monaco. For a sit-down crêpe or pizza for less than 50F, try **Crêperie-Pizzeria du Rocher** (12 rue C. Félix Gastaldi, tel. 93–30–09–64). The la Condamine area is good for crêpe stands and cafés serving sandwiches and pizzas at fair prices. **LAM Traiteur** (4 rue de la Turbie, tel. 93–30–88–88), near the youth hostel, serves hot, fresh Chinese and Vietnamese food for 25F–50F. Monaco suffers from a seriously snobby social scene, but the English barman at **Maky's Pub** (57 rue Grimaldi, tel. 92–16–12–40) can commiserate over how overdeveloped the whole place is. The pub serves some good food and turns into a piano bar at night.

WORTH SEEING Set in a carefully manicured sculpture garden, the **Casino de Monte Carlo** (pl. du Casino, tel. 92–16–21–21) is the most famous building on the Riviera and has been featured in countless films. If you're over 21, have your passport, and are dressed in something other than sandals and shorts, you can enter the main gambling hall, the American Room. The Salons Privées (private rooms) are for high rollers and require jacket and tie, money for admission, and confidence. The **Le Café de Paris** (pl. du Casino, tel. 92–16–20–20) casino is across the street.

The **Palais du Prince** (admission 25F) is up on the rock in Monaco-Ville. A 40-minute guided tour takes you through lavish state rooms furnished with priceless antiques and paintings. The private apartments where the family lives are off-limits. In front of the main entrance on **place du Palais,** you can watch the daily changing of the guard at 11:55 AM. Also in Monaco-Ville, the **cathedral** (4 rue Colonel Bellando de Castro, tel. 93–30–88–13) contains the tombs of former princes of Monaco. Pay homage to the great Hitchcock heroine Grace Kelly at the tomb inscribed "Gracia Patricia."

The **Musée Océanographique** (av. St-Martin, tel. 93–15—36–00; admission 60F, 30F students) is the real reason to come to Monaco. Prince Albert I founded the Oceanographic Museum in 1910 to display objects he brought back from his journeys of deep-sea exploration. The museum has an amazing aquarium, exhibits describing wonders of the ocean, and research laboratories. In the elegant conference hall you can watch a film by Jacques Cousteau, director of the museum from 1957 to 1988. Come early to avoid crowds; it opens at 9:30 October–March, at 9 April–September.

The Southwest

After you spend some time in this region that borders Spain and reaches up the Atlantic coast toward Brittany, the term "the south of France" takes on new meaning. This western half of France's south is less expensive and less pretentious than the Riviera and has a lot to offer the adventurous traveler in the way of natural beauty and historic sites. The region is a mix of coastal playgrounds, dry, vine-covered terrain, rolling hills in the Dordogne and Lot River valleys, and precipitous mountain slopes in the Pyrénées. Although Bordeaux bustles like the big city it is, once you head into the quiet country villages or climb into the mountains, you'll find yourself switching into a relaxed Mediterranean mode.

Despite all this, the region lacks any real blockbuster sights. Unless you're continuing on to Spain, it may not be worth the effort to get here. Then again, if you want to get away from the Euro Disney crowd, this is the place to be. The southwest is about as off the beaten track as France gets.

Languedoc-Roussillon

Spend a few days in this region and you'll be sipping red wine and taking afternoon siestas before you know it. Dozens of beaches line the Mediterranean, from the swampy Camargue just east of Montpellier to Cap Cerbère at the Spanish border. Inland Languedoc-Roussillon, with its dry climate, may seem like one big vineyard: The vine thrives here, and its inhabitants thrive off it.

CARCASSONNE

Carcasonne's **Cité**, the fortified upper town, looks like the greatest sand castle ever built that didn't wash away. The 13th-century charm of the Cité is best appreciated from afar. Once you enter the city walls, 20th-century tourism takes over and tourist traps flank each cobblestone street. The ville basse, across the Aude River from the Cité, is where you'll find the train station, several cheap hotels, and the main **tourist office** (15 blvd. Camille Pelletan, on sq. Gambetta, tel. 68–25–07–04).

Since the town is so tourist-oriented, signs point you in all the right directions. **La Porte Narbonnaise** is the main entrance to the Cité and just inside the gate you'll find a **tourist office annex** (tel. 68–25–68–81). Walking around the ramparts and the Cité is free, but if you want a 45-minute guided tour of the **Château Comtal,** the last inner bastion, built in the 12th century, it will cost you 26F, 17F for students. Don't miss a cool respite in the funky **Basilique St-Nazaire,** featuring gargoyles on the outside and a stunning display of 14th- to 16th-century stained glass.

COMING AND GOING Trains travel from the **station** (tel. 68–71–79–14) to Toulouse (50 min, 69F) and Marseille (3 hrs, 193F). You can easily walk to the Cité in about a half-hour, but the last 15 minutes uphill are hellish. Local Bus 4 (4F90) runs twice an hour from the train station to the Cité, except on Sundays.

WHERE TO SLEEP AND EAT Cheap hotels are in the ville basse; try the **Hôtel le Cathare** (53 rue Jean Bringer, tel. 68–25–65–92; doubles from 160F) or the **Hôtel St-Joseph** (81 rue de la Liberté, tel. 68–25–10–94; doubles 100F). If you want to stay within the Cité, the modern **hostel** (rue de Vicomte Trencavel, tel. 68–25–23–16) is a good choice. Take Bus 4 from the train station and follow the signs. The campground **Campeole la Cité** (D104, tel. 68–25–11–77) offers a great view of the Cité from the banks of the Aude River for about 36F–48F per person. Take Bus 5 from the train station.

Inside the medieval walls, several outdoor restaurants fill place Marcou, just inside the Porte Narbonnaise and to the left. **Le Vieux Four** (2 rue St-Louis), a small restaurant on a quiet alley, has crêpes for about 25F–35F.

MONTPELLIER

Montpellier is smack in the middle of the Mediterranean coastline, a five-hour train ride from Paris, Nice, and Barcelona. There aren't any blockbuster sights here, but there are a whole lot of students (55,000—one-fourth of the city's population), as well as a vibrant nightlife and many cultural events. From June to September, when many of the students are away, Montpellier plays host to festivals of music, theater, and dance.

The 1,000-year-old history of Montpellier is best revealed by its hodgepodge of architectural styles. The historic centre ville is characterized by 17th- and 18th-century **hôtels particuliers,** especially along rue de la Loge, rue de l'Argenterie, rue St-Guihlem, and rue des Etuves. At the intersection of rue Foch and boulevard Professeur Louis Vialleton is Montpellier's version of the **Arc de Triomphe.** It may not be as grand as the one in Paris, but then there aren't 10 lanes of traffic encircling it either. Past the arch is the **promenade du Peyrou;** the statue in the center of this park is of the Sun King, Louis XIV. Notice that the king's stirrups are missing. When the sculptor realized this blunder, he committed suicide. If you continue to the end of the park, you'll find the **Château d'Eau,** a Corinthian temple, and the terminal for **les Arceaux,** an 18th-century aqueduct made up of 53 arches. On a clear day, the view from here is spectacular. At the center of it all is the classy **place de la Comédie,** known fondly as l'Oeuf, a reference to its egg shape. It's anchored at one end by the impressive **Opéra-Bastille.** The other end branches out into the expansive **esplanade de Charles de Gaulle** to the north and **le Triangle** to the east, where you'll find **le Polygone,** an American-style shopping center. Behind le Polygone is **Antigone,** Montpellier's official nod to the future. A neoclassical symmetrical wonder, it was designed by architect Ricardo Bofill to house low- to middle-income families. By comparing this structure with the 13th-century **Tour de la Babote,** also in the centre ville, you get a good sense of the range of historical influences in Montpellier. You can get a detailed map of the notable architecture or take a guided tour from the tourist office.

VISITOR INFORMATION *Just off pl. de la Comédie in le Triangle, tel. 67–58–67–58.*

COMING AND GOING Frequent trains go to Paris (5 hrs, 373F), Toulouse (2 hrs, 163F), and Barcelona (5 hrs, 308F). The **train station** (tel. 67–58–50–50) is just a few minutes' walk from place de la Comédie in the centre ville. The **bus station** (rue Jules Ferry, tel. 67–92–01–43) is next door to the train station. The historic centre ville is a pedestrian's paradise, but **SMTU** (23 rue Maguelone, tel. 67–22–87–87) runs local buses (6F) for the weary. The benevolent organization **Vélos pour tous** (Kiosque Bosc, esplanade de Charles de Gaulle, tel. 67–02–27–23) rents bikes by the day for *free!*

WHERE TO SLEEP Just about all the budget hotels in Montpellier are in the centre ville. On a quiet street just off the main square, **Hôtel des Etuves** (24 rue des Etuves, tel. 67–60–78–19; doubles 144F–184F) has large rooms at the top of a narrow, spiral staircase. The **Hôtel le Nice** (14 rue Boussairolles, tel. 67–58–42–54; doubles 120F–180F) is also near the main square. Though located in the centre ville, the **HI hostel** (2 impasse de la Petite Corraterie, off rue des Ecoles Laïques, tel. 67–60–32–22; beds 75F) is kind of hard to find. Take Bus 3, 5, 6, 9, or 16 from the train station to boulevard Louis Blanc unless you're feeling really energetic.

FOOD Produce is sold at the **market** on place Jean Jaurès and the neighboring Halles Castellane daily until noon. If you decide to take advantage of the ambience of the centre ville, go to **rue des Ecoles Laïques** where you'll find ethnic restaurants at bearable prices. A beer and an enchilada at the colorful **Restaurant Tapas** (4 rue des Ecoles Laïques, tel. 67–52–86–89) will cost you less than 50F. If you're in the mood for crêpes, head to the serene **place de St-Roch** or the livelier **place St-Côme** and adjoining **rue Jules Latreille.** Jazz music plays in the background at **Le Feu Follet** (10 rue du Petit St-Jean, tel. 67–60–95–04), where a 69F menu includes meat that has been grilled on a wood-burning fire in the middle of the restaurant. If you want to hang with local students and rabble-rousers, head to the bars on **place Jean Jaurès.** To dance into the night, head to the animated **Rockstore** (20 rue de Verdun, tel. 67–58–70–10). The cover charge ranges from free (weekdays 11–11:30 PM) to about 50F.

TOULOUSE

Just 97 km from the Spanish border, laid-back Toulouse is influenced by its warm Mediterranean neighbor. The city also has a well-preserved Roman heritage; the ubiquitous redbrick buildings have earned Toulouse its nickname, la Ville Rose (the pink city). To soak up the history of Toulouse, walk around its well-preserved centre ville. Built at the end of the 11th and beginning of the 12th centuries, the **Basilique St-Sernin** (rue du Taur) is the largest Romanesque building in France. The church is named after the early Christian martyr Saturnin, former bishop of Toulouse. When Saturnin refused to take part in a bull sacrifice in AD 257, the Romans tied him to a bull's horns. The nearby 14th-century church of **Notre-Daum du Taur** was built on the spot where St-Saturnin was dragged to his death. A masterpiece of southern Gothic architecture, **Les Jacobins** (pl. des Jacobins; admission to cloisters 7F, students free) usually plays second fiddle to St-Sernin Basilica but is really just as impressive. In summer, the cloisters provide an atmospheric setting for the city's music festival.

The city's largest museum, the **Musée des Augustins** (21 rue de Metz, tel. 61–22–21–82; admission 10F, students free) has an impressive display of Roman sculpture and religious paintings, as well as works by Murillo and Rubens. For more modern artwork, stop by the **Château d'Eau** (pl. Laganne, tel. 61–42–61–72; admission 10F, 5F students), a fascinating photo gallery and research center that was built in 1822, the same year that Nicéphore Nièpce obtained the first permanent photographic images.

VISITOR INFORMATION *Donjon du Capitole, rue Lafayette, tel. 61–11–02–22.*

COMING AND GOING Trains connect Toulouse to Carcassonne (1 hr, 69F), Perpignan (1½ hrs, 139F), and Paris (8 hrs, 350F). The **train station** (tel. 61–62–50–50 or 61–62–85–44 for reservations) is next door to the **regional bus station** (tel. 61–48–71–84). The main square of the centre ville is **place du Capitole,** a good 15-minute walk from the train station. Take Bus 22 (7F) if you don't want to walk. The new Métro system (tel. 61–41–70–70) has two lines; the more helpful one runs from the train station to the center of town. The 7F tickets are good for transfers onto buses as well.

WHERE TO SLEEP Just off Toulouse's main square, the **Hôtel du Grand Balcon** (8 rue Romiguières, tel. 61–21–48–08) is a two-star hotel with one-star prices. Stay in Antoine de St-Exupéry's old room for only 125F a night. On a cozy, narrow lane in the centre ville, the **Hôtel Croix-Baragnon** (17 rue Croix-Baragnon, tel. 61–52–60–10; doubles 165F) has polished, modern rooms that overlook the red rooftops of Toulouse. The bathrooms leave a lot to be desired at the noisy **HI hostel** (125 rue Jean Rieux, tel. 61–80–49–93), but the price is right—only 39F a night. From the train station, take Bus 14 to place Depuy, then cross the street and take Bus 22 (Gonin-la Terrasse) and watch for the signs. Camping at **Municipal du Pont de Rupe** (av. des Etats-Unis, tel. 61–70–07–35), 6 km from Toulouse, costs about 40F per person. Take Bus 10 from place Jeanne d'Arc.

FOOD Avoid the snobby restaurants on place du Capitole and head down one of the many alleys that fan out from it. **Rue du Taur** has several snack bars and crêperies, and **rue des Lois** has cheap ethnic eateries. Place St-Georges hosts an outdoor fruit and vegetable **market** Tuesday–Sunday. Get food to go at **Paella Chaude** (78 rue Jean Rieux, near hostel, tel. 61–34–65–37), a paella paradise that sells the stuff for 67F per kilogram. With funky lace-covered lamps and a wooden interior, **Le Sherpa** (46 rue du Taur, tel. 61–23–89–29) serves excellent salads (25F–30F) and crêpes (20F–28F) all day. Toulouse hipsters gather in the bars on **place St-Georges.** To have a *pastis* with the local rugby players, stop by **Le Pastis O** on place St-Pierre.

The Basque Region

The Basque people live in the region that stretches from Bayonne across the Pyrénées to Bilbao in Spain and retain a distinct culture that is neither French nor Spanish. Although some Basques support ETA, a group that struggles for Basque political autonomy, Basque militancy isn't as much of a factor in France as it is in Spain, where travelers are warned to stay away from government buildings, which are occasionally bombed. The French Basque seem content to set themselves apart by performing their local dances, playing *pelote* (jai alai) or its variant *cesta punta,* eating *pipérades* (omelets with tomatoes and green peppers), and drinking *izarra* (a bright green liqueur). What most clearly sets the Basques apart, however, is their language, which is unrelated to any other known language; the Basques call themselves the Euskaldunak, the Basque speakers. **Biarritz** and **Bayonne** are the largest and most easily accessible of the French Basque towns, but smaller places like peaceful **St-Jean-Pied-de-Port** and the coastal villages of **Bidart** and **Guéthary** are more characteristic of the region.

BIARRITZ

Biarritz isn't quite what it used to be. During the 19th century, the Spanish and French nobility graced the beach resort's posh villas and palaces, but now this Basque city caters to a flood of wealthy international tourists. If you're just looking for a patch of sand on which to bask, you'll do better farther south, but for a glimpse of the high life, a day or two in Biarritz does the trick.

After catching some rays on the beach, it's fun to join the tourists on the **Rocher de la Vierge,** an impressive rock formation just southwest of the Grande Plage. The bridge connecting it to the mainland is made from a piece of metal from the Eiffel Tower. Then, for a good look at the Atlantic and a view of the rocky Basque coast, walk north to the 241-foot lighthouse near Anglet. You can go inside for free from 10 to noon and 2 to 5 (until 6:30 in summer).

COMING AND GOING Trains travel to Biarritz from Bordeaux (2 hrs, 136F) and Toulouse (4 hrs, 193F). Plenty of trains roll into Biarritz's **train station,** La Négresse (tel. 59–23–15–69), in the summer, but during the off-season most go only as far as Bayonne. From Bayonne, hop on Bus 2 in front of the station and you'll be in Biarritz in under an hour. Bus 2 also takes you from the Biarritz train station to the Hôtel de Ville. The **Comité du Tourisme et des Fêtes** (Sq. d'Ixelles, tel. 59–24–20–24), up the street from the Hôtel de Ville, churns out the usual maps and hotel list.

WHERE TO SLEEP Be prepared to fight for one of the few double rooms under 200F. To find the cheaper hotels near the ocean, follow **rue Mazagran** down the center of the peninsula toward the Port Vieux beach. In the center of the main tourist area, the **Hôtel de la Marine** (1 rue des Goëlands, off rue Mazagran past pl. St-Eugene, tel. 59–24–34–09; doubles from 160F) is popular with surfers. The very official patronne at **Hôtel des Pyrénées** (3 rue de Gascogne, tel. 59–24–20–22; doubles 160F) prefers written reservations but will give you a large, stylish room without one if there's space. Near the beach and only 1 km from the train station, **Biarritz Camping** (28 rue d'Harcet, tel. 59–23–00–12) costs 20F per person and 23F per tent site. From the station, take the bus marked LA NAVETTE DES PLAGES.

FOOD If you follow rue Mazagran past place St-Eugene toward Port Vieux, you'll pass some snack bars and relatively inexpensive restaurants. **Le Ketchup** (41 bis rue Mazagran, tel. 59–24–70–75) serves everything from hamburgers to *poulet basquaise* (Basque chicken) until 3 AM. The big 45F lunch and dinner menus attract a lot of locals to **Le Petit Grill** (13 av. Verdun, off pl. Clémenceau, tel. 59–24–15–80), a five-minute walk from the Hôtel de Ville. For picnic goodies, head to the covered **market** Les Halles, open daily 7–1.

Bordeaux

As big as Bordeaux is, as famous as it is, and as prosperous as it is, there should be more to see and do here. Although the city is culturally diverse and has a fast-paced nightlife, Bordeaux is like Paris without the good stuff. The city is blackened with soot, crowded with cars, and blighted by seedy neighborhoods. Although it's in the middle of one of the finest wine-growing areas in the world, many of the vineyards surrounding Bordeaux are not all that scenic and most are tough to get to without a car. But if you're enough of an oenophile to know that Lafite-Rothschild, Latour, and Mouton-Rothschild wines are all grown hereabouts, then the area might be worth a detour.

BASICS The **tourist office** (12 cours du 30 Juillet, tel. 56–44–28–41) is near the Grand Théâtre. Have poste restante mail sent either to the **American Express** office (14 cours de l'Intendance, tel. 56–81–70–02) or the **post office** (52 rue Georges Bonnac, tel. 56–48–88–88; postal code 33000).

COMING AND GOING Bordeaux is a major rail hub; trains travel from here to Paris (285F) and many French and Spanish cities. The **train station** (tel. 56–92–50–50) is about a 45-minute walk from the the the centre ville, in a scuzzy area full of sex shops and cheap hotels. Efficient city buses (7F50) are useful for getting away from the station; take Bus 7 or 8 to the centre ville. Bus maps are available at the tourist office, the train station, or the **bus station** (25 rue Marchand, 57–57–88–88).

WHERE TO SLEEP AND EAT There are a few decent hotels and a good youth hostel near the train station, but be wary of the neighborhood after dark. The spic-and-span **Hôtel Lion d'Or** (38 pl. André Meunier, tel. 56–91–71–62; doubles 120F–145F) is by far the nicest affordable hotel near the station. The centre ville is generally a better bet. You can't do better than the **Hôtel d'Amboise** (22 rue de la Vieille Tour, tel. 56–81–62–67; doubles 90F–110F), a cheerily decorated place near place Gambetta. The funky **Hôtel St-François** (22 rue du Mirail, opposite the Grosse Cloche, tel. 56–91–56–41; doubles 118F–168F), with its spiral stairway and decorative orange flowers, was obviously decorated by someone with a sense of humor. The **HI hostel** (22 cours Barbey, off cours de la Marne, tel. 56–91–59–51) is a pretty friendly place but has a cruelly early lockout (9:30–6) and a strictly enforced 11 PM curfew. The **Maison des Etudiantes** (50 rue Ligier, tel. 56–96–48–30; singles 47F students, 67F nonstudents) is a much better deal than the hostel and is near the centre ville. It accepts women only, except in July and August. Take Bus 7 or 8 from the station to the Bourse du Travail stop, then walk to rue Ligier from there.

FOOD It's a cinch to eat cheaply in Bordeaux if you're not picky; sidewalk stands around place Gambetta will sell you a kebab-stuffed baguette, greasy fries, and a Coke for 25F. Right next to the cathedral, the **Brasserie le Musée** (37 pl. Pey Berland, tel. 56–52–99–69) serves salad, roast chicken, dessert, and wine, all for 52F. Discover a local delicacy at **Francs Délices** (54 rue de la Devise, tel. 56–52–28–22), where the 88F menu includes foie gras.

WORTH SEEING Bordeaux doesn't have too many blockbuster sights; it relies on the nearby vineyards and beaches to draw visitors. Bordeaux's tourist world revolves around place Gambetta. Just down cours de l'Intendance from the place is the **Grand Théâtre** (pl. de la Comédie), an enormous building that inspired Charles Garnier's opulent Opéra in Paris. The 25F guided tour (20F students), arranged through the tourist office, takes you up into the nosebleed seats for a look at the magnificent ceiling. Just north of the theater, the Monument aux Girondins commemorates the bravery of the local party that fought to suppress an aristocratic counterrevolution during the French Revolution. There are no actual Girondins depicted on the statue, but Liberty is on top, the Republic is tossing out the vices of the monarchy on one side, and Bordeaux is frolicking in democratic harmony with the Garonne and Dordogne rivers on the other.

The **Musée d'Aquitaine** (20 cours Pasteur, tel. 56–10–17–58; admission 15F, 8F students, free Wed.) is one of the city's best museums, taking you on a trip through human history, with an emphasis on daily life. The terrific prehistoric section reproduces the famous Lascaux cave paintings in part. Named for a famous World War II resistance fighter, the **Musée Jean Moulin** (pl. Jean Moulin, tel. 56–10–15–80; admission free) probes a past that many French are reluctant to discuss, displaying souvenirs of collaborationist France, like an election poster for a candidate with the Anti-Semitic Party, as well as the usual stuff about the heroism of the Resistance. Each year the **Musée d'Art Contemporain** (7 rue Ferrère, tel. 56–44–16–35; admission 30F, 20F students and under 26, free noon–2 PM) promotes four artists, who use the huge expanse to do anything they want. It's very cutting edge.

AFTER DARK Night owls start off around 9 PM in the cafés around place de la Victoire; **Chez Auguste** (3 pl. de la Victoire, tel. 56–91–77–32) is the super-popular student stop. After spending the night dancing, real diehards head back to place des Capucins for the 2 AM

For Budget Travelers, Bordeaux Wines Can Be Sour Grapes

The Bordeaux region produces some stellar wines with astronomical prices. The Médoc region that stretches northwest of Bordeaux produces some of the most famous labels in the world, including Mouton-Rothschild, Lafite-Rothschild, and Latour. Across the Gironde estuary are the Côtes de Blaye and Côtes de Bourg regions; Entre-Deux-Mers is to the south.

Many of the regions, especially the flat, dusty Médoc, have nothing of interest to show their visitors except bottles of their product. The Bordeaux tourist office arranges trips to many of the local vineyards, although the Château Mouton-Rothschild is conspicuously absent from these tours. If you're determined to go it alone, the Maison du Vin (1 cours du 30 Juillet, tel. 56–00–22–66) can tell you how to get to many of the vineyards by bus or just give you a taste of the wines so you can save yourself the trip.

opening of the bars there. **Le Rhodes** (22 pl. des Capucins, tel. 56–91–42–31) is the most popular bar in the weird nocturnal world of place des Capucins. **Le Gentry** (13 rue Georges Bonnac, tel. 56–48–11–13) is a friendly gay pub with 10F beers. **La Palmeraie** (22 quai de la Monnaie, tel. 56–94–07–52) is a bar where Bordeaux's African population gets together for a *soirée black*.

NEAR BORDEAUX

The Entre-Deux-Mers (Between Two Seas) region actually lies between two rivers, the Garonne and the Dordogne. Just southeast of Bordeaux, the area is dotted with tiny medieval towns and crumbling castles that overlook orderly rows of vines. In the fortified town of **Cadillac,** the Château de Cadillac (tel. 56–62–69–58; admission 20F, 13F students) is a medieval/Renaissance castle that's been in bad shape since a group of women prisoners nearly burned the place down in 1928. Its 22 monumental fireplaces were so large that building them used up the marble from several quarries in the Pyrénées. One of the most interesting places in Entre-Deux-Mers is the hilltop town of **St-Macaire,** where crumbling ivy-covered ramparts date from the 12th and 13th centuries. Tourists jostle through the narrow streets of the medieval town of **St-Emilion,** grabbing for the famous red wines and scrumptious macaroons that bear the town's name. Ignore them and revel in the magnificent hillside views and visit the marvelous Eglise Monolithe, a church completely carved out of the side of a cliff. All three towns are accessible by Citram bus from Bordeaux.

The Dordogne and Lot River Valleys

After its descent from the mountains in the Massif Central, the Dordogne River makes its way westward through Bordeaux before spilling into the Atlantic. The Lot River makes a similar journey about 40 km to the south. Maintained by peasant farmers for centuries, the rolling countryside in this area is chock-full of riverside châteaux, medieval villages, and prehistoric sites. Towns like **Périgueux** have a smattering of Roman monuments and regional history museums. The region is honeycombed with dozens of *grottes* (caves) that are filled with prehistoric drawings, etchings, and carvings. The green lushness of the area gives way to dry, vineyard-covered expanses, especially as the rivers approach the Atlantic Ocean. Biking is one of the most popular ways to see the region, but be prepared for a lot of hills.

SARLAT

Tucked among the hills 6 km from the Dordogne River, Sarlat is a bustling tourist center that, in certain areas, manages to preserve its small-town atmosphere. To get a sense of old Sarlat, venture off the main pedestrian artery, **rue de la République,** along some of the narrow paths of soft golden-colored brick lined with 16th- and 17th-century buildings. The commercial center of town lies on the east side of rue de la République, featuring cafés, restaurants, and a thousand or so wine and foie-gras shops. Unfortunately, in July and August, the streets are so packed with tourists that a walk through town is more like a rugby scrum. To find out about getting out of town to the surrounding châteaux, talk the **tourist office** (pl. de la Liberté, tel. 53–59–27–67) off the main square.

COMING AND GOING   Trains from Bordeaux arrive at Sarlat's **station** (rte. de Souillac, tel. 53–59–00–21), a half-hour walk from town. Pick up a copy of "Guide Pratique" from the tourist office for info on **SNCF buses** that cover the area. The accommodating couple at **Sarlat Sport** (rue Jean Leclaire, off av. de Selves, tel. 53–59–33–41) rents bikes for about 90F a day.

WHERE TO SLEEP AND EAT   In summer, be sure to have a reservation before setting foot in Sarlat. Superbly located on the quiet side of the vieille ville, the **Hotel des Recollects** (4 rue Jean Jacques, tel. 53–59–00–49; doubles 155F–165F) is the cheapest place in town, with charming rooms and attentive proprietors. Most of the year the rustic, relaxed **HI hostel** (36 bis av. de Selves, tel. 53–59–47–59 or 53–30–21–27) is open only to groups, but individuals are welcome from July 1 to October 15. Campers pay 23F per person to pitch a tent out back. Walk 10 minutes from rue de la République to avenue Gambetta, then veer left onto avenue de Selves.

The budget dining scene is disappointing, but markets and boulangeries line rue de la République. With some of the cheapest menus in town (50F, 70F, and 90F), **Le Commerce** (rue Alberic Cahuet, just off rue de la République, tel. 53–59–04–26) dishes up a saucy *cassoulet* (a meaty casserole with beans) and other regional specialties.

ROCAMADOUR

The medieval village of Rocamadour hangs dramatically on the edge of a cliff, 1,500 feet above the Alzou River gorge. Rocamadour became famous in 1166 when chroniclers recorded the miraculous discovery of the body of St-Amadour under a sanctuary; pilgrims have been coming ever since. Only 30 people actually live in Rocamadour, but 1.5 million tourists and pilgrims visit each year. If you want to have a look at the seven sanctuaries and the crypt, take one of the free guided tours that leaves from the **Chapel of Notre-Dame.**

COMING AND GOING Half the drama of Rocamadour is figuring out how to get here. The Rocamadour-Padirac **train station** (tel. 65–33–63–05) connects directly with Toulouse (1½ hrs, 132F). The hour-long walk from the station to town takes you down the steep gorge and then up to the village. Bus excursions also arrive from Souillac, Sarlat, and Brive.

Between the train station and town you'll pass L'Hospitalet, a tourist center on a plateau about 1 km from Rocamadour. The **tourist office** (tel. 65–33–62–59) in L'Hospitalet is open year-round, while the office in the actual village (rue Piétonne, tel. 65–33–62–80) is open only July–September.

WHERE TO SLEEP AND EAT It's not easy to find a room for less than 200F in Rocamadour, and without a reservation it's nearly impossible. Not a bargain, but located in the middle of the rock, **Hôtel le Globe** (rue Piétonne, tel. 65–33–67–73) has doubles with shower and telephones for 180F. Farther from the village, but next to the train station, **Hôtel des Voyageurs** (tel. 65–33–63–19) offers very basic doubles for 110F.

The only commercial street, rue Piétonne, has everything from crêpe stands to restaurants with 180F menus. Try **Chez Anne-Marie** (tel. 65–33–65–81) on the far end of rue Piétonne and eat the 55F lunch menu on the cliff-side terrace.

La Rochelle

By some miracle of climate, the coastline here gets nearly as much sun as the Côte d'Azur. But in an area where the main attractions are sun and sand, the port city of La Rochelle adds a dose of culture to an otherwise hedonistic vacation. Eighteenth-century stone houses line the cour des Dames, a spacious avenue that circles the historic harbor where two 14th-century towers stand sentinel. Inland, a massive stone gate marks the entrance to the narrow streets of the old town. The port's famous towers, historic houses, and museums draw visitors all year, but summer is particularly crowded because of the city's proximity to the beaches of nearby Ile de Ré and the popular six-day Francofolies music festival the second week in July.

During the Renaissance, La Rochelle was one of the best-fortified ports in France. The only entrance from the sea was between the heavily guarded towers, the **Tour de la Chaîne** and the **Tour St-Nicolas**; a chain was passed between them at night to bar enemy passage. Unfortunately, that didn't keep Cardinal Richelieu from attacking this longtime Protestant stronghold in 1627, leaving 23,000 people dead from starvation after a yearlong siege. Tour St-Nicolas's labyrinthine passageways and multilayered fortifications open onto spectacular views of the port. Continue along the ramparts to the **Tour de la Lanterne,** now known as the Tour des Quatre Sergents in honor of four sergeants imprisoned here in the late 1800s. Admission to the Tour St-Nicolas and Tour de la Lanterne is 20F, 16F students; admission to the Tour de la Chaîne is 18F.

La Rochelle's enjoyable **Musée Maritime** (Bassin des Chalutiers, tel. 46–50–58–88; admission 36F, 18F under 14) displays three to five ships, depending on which ones are in port at the moment. None of them are too spruced up for the tourist trade, so you can appreciate just how messy, smelly, and cramped the quarters are on a working ship. Keeping with La Rochelle's maritime theme, the **aquarium** (Port des Minimes, tel. 46–44–00–00; admission 39F) displays its eels, seahorses, piranhas, and various fish in large tanks that try to approximate the critters' natural habitats. Kids of all ages will dig the tide pools and the re-creation of the Amazon rain forest. The **tourist office** (pl. de la Petite Sirène, tel. 46–41–14–68) offers a complete guide to the city and makes hotel reservations for 10F.

COMING AND GOING La Rochelle is a major stop on the rail line between Nantes (119F) and Bordeaux. You can also come from Paris (244F) via Poitiers (100F). The hostel and campgrounds are outside town; to get there, you need to take the green **Autoplus** bus (8F). Most buses run from the main bus station on place de Verdun. You don't have to go near a bus to see the city's main sights, though, many of which encircle the old harbor. In summer, a boat service called the **Passeur Autoplus** (4F) takes you from cours des Dames to the museums near La Ville en Bois, the section of town south of the historic port. In addition, a **Bus de Mer** water bus (10F) picks passengers up from the cour des Dames and drops them in Port des Minimes, the port south of La Ville en Bois.

WHERE TO SLEEP AND EAT If you show up during the Francofolies without a hotel reservation, be prepared to sleep in the streets. The friendly managers at **Hôtel de la Paix** (14 rue Gargoulleau, tel. 46–41–33–44; doubles 140F–200F) spoil you with great rooms in an 18th-century house. Smack-dab in the center of town, the **Hôtel Henri IV** (31 rue des Gentils-hommes, behind Hôtel de Ville, tel. 46–41–25–79; doubles from 140F) opens onto a cobblestone square frequented by mimes and jugglers. Two km south of the train station, the **HI hostel** (av. des Minimes, tel. 46–44–43–11; beds 64F–95F) looks and feels like a factory. If you don't get a room, you might snag a 28F space in the campground behind. Take Bus 10 from avenue de Colmar (1 block from the train station) to the Lycée Hôtelier stop.

Avoid the restaurants with expensive dockside views along cours des Dames; instead, trek inland to the pedestrian part of rue du Temple or stick to the not-so-chichi quai du Gabut side of the harbor. **Le Plaisance** (av. des Minimes, tel. 46–44–41–51) serves better-than-average pizzas, salads, and light seafood dishes for less than 50F.

NEAR LA ROCHELLE

ILE DE RE Linked by bridge to La Rochelle, Ré is an island for everyone. Over 50 km of beaches, an ornithological reserve, a citadel, a museum, a lighthouse, and great seafood all wait at the end of a 9F ride across the **Pont de Ré.** Vineyards sweep over the eastern part of the island, and oyster beds lie beneath the shallow waters to the west.

The town of **St-Martin** is a good place to start a day trip. Stop by the **tourist office** (av. Victor Bouthillier, tel. 46–09–20–06) for a map of the island. The town's beach, **Plage de la Cible,** is just on the other side of the grass-covered citadel.

A few kilometers to the southwest, the town of **La Couarde** has great beaches and windsurfing. Rent boards and other equipment at **Locasud,** next to the Grande Plage parking lot, or at **Tou's'loue,** next to the marketplace. All the way at the end of Ré, the beaches in **Les Portes** are icky at low tide, but you'll have them all to yourself. A better beach is the **Plage de la Conche des Baleines,** backed by dunes and pine trees. Climb the **Phare des Baleines** lighthouse for a great view of the island.

COMING AND GOING La Rochelle's Bus 1 takes you as far as the Sablanceaux beach in **Rivedoux,** just at the tip of Ré (9F). That's okay for an appetizer, but if you really want to see the island, hop a **Ré Bus** (tel. 46–09–20–15) in La Rochelle or any island town and explore farther. Fares for the Ré Bus range from 10F to 42F50.

WHERE TO SLEEP AND EAT Ré is such a convenient day trip from La Rochelle that there's little reason to stay overnight in the expensive hotels, unless you have a reservation at the excellent **Hôtel Le Sully** (19 rue du Marché, St-Martin, tel. 46–09–26–94), an old house in the pedestrian quarter of St-Martin with 180F doubles. Campgrounds are everywhere; try **Camping de la Prée** (tel. 46–29–51–04) in Les Portes, where up to three people can stay for 55F. For food, either bring a picnic or shell out megabucks for seaside seafood. Thirty flavors of homemade Italian-style ice cream are scooped up at the corner stand on the St-Martin docks.

GERMANY   9

Every German can tell you where he or she was on the night of November 9,
1989, when the news spread that the Berlin Wall was open. Like the assassination of John F.
Kennedy, it's a moment permanently branded on the memory of a nation. The euphoric mood
that prevailed directly after the fall of the Berlin Wall, however, has vanished. Five years after
the country was officially reunified, on October 3, 1990, emotions about unification, especially among Easterners, are mixed. Whereas the political and bureaucratic structures of West
Germany were quickly introduced into the former German Democratic Republic (GDR), the
economic and psychological gap has yet to be overcome. For the average West German, unification has largely meant an increased tax burden, as state resources are siphoned off to support and modernize eastern Germany. For East Germans, nearly every aspect of their lives has
changed. Unification has meant a huge surge in unemployment, and many East Germans, long
used to a cradle-to-grave welfare system, are struggling to cope with the demands of a free-
market economy.

For travelers, unification means easy access to a part of Germany that is in many ways more
"German" than the rest of the country. A trip to the East German countryside is not only a trip
to the core of Prussia, the most powerful and important of the German states of the 19th century, but also a trip into Germany's past. Although many changes have taken place over the last
five years, some of the smaller towns look as if time has stood still for the last 60 years: Cobbled streets are lined with lime trees, wrought-iron fences surround ramshackle buildings, and
ads push products that no longer exist. Sadly, urban planners ruined the outskirts of many
towns with high rises that look even uglier and shabbier than their Western counterparts. But
most of the historic centers—if not destroyed by World War II—remain untouched.

Traveling through Germany you will find that the people in the countryside still look very "German," whereas you will see lots of "foreign" faces in cities like Berlin, Frankfurt, and Munich.
Whether they want to or not, Germans have to face the phenomenon of an increasingly multicultural population. "Foreigners" today comprise 8% of Germany's population of 78 million.
Most of these were recruited from southern and southeastern Europe during the economic
booms of the '60s and early '70s. In terms of its Turkish population, Berlin is the world's third-
largest city, after Istanbul and Ankara.

As Germany's economy has soured and the social costs of reunification have soared, some Germans have become increasingly hostile to the presence of these minorities, whom they accuse
of stealing jobs. Over the last few years, gangs of neo-Nazi skinheads have attacked foreign-
worker hostels, Turkish families, and other minorities. This rising anti-immigrant sentiment
has led the government to tighten the asylum laws, which had been the most liberal in Europe. 257

BELGIUM

FRANCE

LUX.

Aachen

Bonn

Köln

Siegen

Trier

Koblenz

Mosel

Rhine

Marburg

SWITZERLAND

Rhein

Saarbrücken

Bad Kreuznach

Ludwigshafen

Wiesbaden

Mainz

Darmstadt

Frankfurt-am-Main

Main

Alsfeld

Bad Hersfeld

Fulda

Eisenach

Ilmenau

Erfurt

Weimar

Rheinfelden

Freiburg

Black Forest

Offenburg

Speyer

Mannheim

Heidelberg

Würzburg

Thüringer Wald

Suhl

Meiningen

Saalfeld

Gera

Baden-Baden

Karlsruhe

Heilbronn

Rothenburg-o-d-Tauber

Bamberg

Coburg

Hof

Bayreuth

Mündlberg

Plauen

Zwickau

Konstanz

Bodensee

Tuttlingen

Tübingen

Stuttgart

Biberach

Ulm

Neu-Ulm

Fürth

Nürnberg

Chemnitz

Friedrichshafen

Ravensburg

Wangen

Memmingen

Danube

Augsburg

Isar

Regensburg

Dresden

Füssen

Garmisch-Partenkirchen

BAVARIAN ALPS

Munich

Bad Reichenhall

Straubing

Deggendorf

CZECH REPUBLIC

Mittenwald

Inn

Berchtesgaden

Passau

Danube

AUSTRIA

Germany

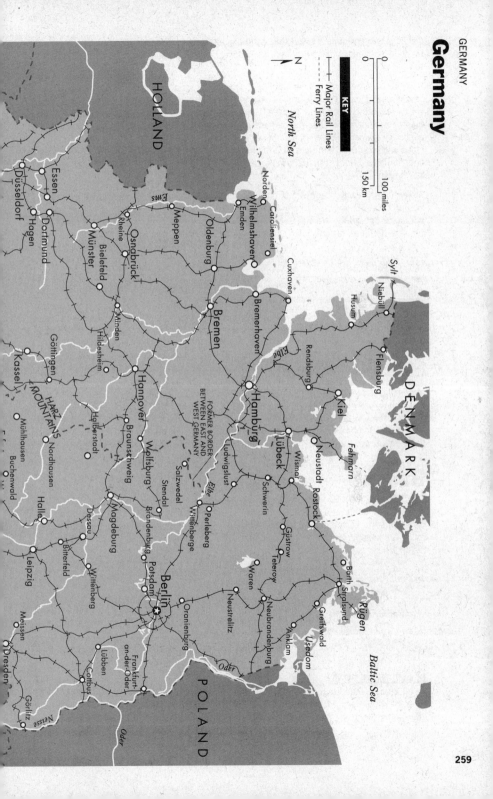

Critics of the government assert that, by changing the asylum laws, the government has caved in to the demands of the radical right while doing little to condemn the violence against minorities.

Regardless of the desires of the rabid right, multiculturalism is here to stay. Nowadays, the fast food of choice in Germany is as likely to be a kebab as a bratwurst, and in many towns travelers can take their pick from Chinese, Greek, and Italian restaurants. At the same time, Germany's traditional folk culture is on the wane; regional dresses have disappeared from daily life almost everywhere—Bavarian lederhosen and dirndls are among the few exceptions. The big cities still have their traditional fun-fairs like Hamburg's *Dom,* Stuttgart's *Cannstatter Wiesn,* and Munich's *Oktoberfest,* but to get an impression of less commercialized traditions you must travel to the countryside.

Increasingly, though, German folk traditions are becoming the domain of tourist villages and kitsch culture. Today, particularly in the big cities, there is a cultural backlash reminiscent of the heady days of the Weimar Republic, the emergence of a broad and diverse *Alternativkultur,* with Berlin as its undisputed capital. In today's Germany, drama-therapy groups offer healing through action, body therapists offer healing through massage, Zen-based meditations or aura readings promise to establish inner balance, and the "lonely hearts" pages list a huge number of gay ads and coming-out groups.

Germans, who were famous for being workaholics, are now champions of leisure. The average German worker has a 38-hour week, six weeks of annual vacation, plus 12 national holidays.

Yet don't expect all Germans to be warm, fuzzy, and exuberant. Most Americans who spend time here complain about German rudeness, whether behind the steering wheel, in shops, or in restaurants—almost any social setting, in fact. Germans display little of the outgoing friendliness of Americans, and, as a result, it can be difficult for visitors to fit in. Don't be surprised if you go to parties and nobody introduces him- or herself. You might talk to people for two hours and never find out their names. But that's completely normal. It's also normal to be very critical. Don't praise the nice decoration, the great food, or the music too much—as an American, you will be automatically classified as superficial. Be nasty instead and complain about everything. It sounds weird, but that's what the Germans do.

Basics

MONEY $1 = DM1.59 and DM1 = 62¢. 100 Pfennig make up 1 mark. Deutsche Marks are about as stable as a currency can get; in fact, the stability of other European currencies is measured in comparison to the Deutsche Mark. Banks generally give the best rates when you're exchanging. Post offices are another good outlet for cash, as are ATMs through the Cirrus and Plus systems.

Visas are not required for U.S., Canadian, U.K., Australian, and New Zealand citizens for stays up to three months in Germany.

➤ **HOW MUCH IT WILL COST** • In small towns, hotel doubles can go for as low as DM40, but in a city like Frankfurt you'd be hard-pressed to find one under DM90. If you don't have a train pass, set aside some cash for Germany's expensive rail network. Within cities, transportation costs about DM2.50 per ride or DM8 for a day pass. As for tipping, service is generally included at restaurants, so simply round up to the nearest mark. Taxis are the same.

COMING AND GOING The ultra-efficient trains of this country are the envy of and example for all Europe. EuroCity (EC) trains connect Frankfurt and a few other major German cities to other major European destinations. The only problem is price, unless you have a EurailPass, InterRail, or Deutsche Bundesbahn (DB) train pass (*see below*).

➤ **BY PLANE** • Considering that Frankfurt's airport is the second largest in Europe, it's a popular first stop for many travelers. Traveling onward from Germany ain't cheap, but if your next stop is, say, Athens or Seville, it's worth a phone call or two to check on the latest air rates. Try **Lufthansa** (tel. 069/6907–1222), Germany's national airline.

GETTING AROUND InterCity (IC) and InterCity Express (ICE) trains connect most German cities, and all trains claim Frankfurt as their hub. The system is so extensive that you'll rarely have to turn to any other form of transport, even for tiny towns. **EurailPass** and **InterRail** are accepted on all trains. Also worthwhile is Deutsche Bundesbahn's (DB) **Junior Flexipass,** available from train stations and travel agencies to anyone under 26. The pass entitles you to free second-class train travel—as well as travel on most Europabus and DB buses plus some ferries—for a preset number of days within a 30-day cycle: a five-day pass costs $138, a 10-day pass $188, a 15-day pass $238. To purchase DB rail passes before leaving the United States, contact **DER Tours** (tel. 800/782–2424).

Buses are marginally cheaper than trains, but less reliable. The only real alternative to the trains is the handy, country-wide *Mitfahrgelegenheit* (ride-share) service; almost all towns have an office where you can match up with drivers going your way. You just pitch in for gas and a few extra marks for your spot. However, buyer beware: The cost of ride sharing often matches the equivalent train fare, so do some comparison shopping. **Hitching** is popular in Germany; generally, just stand by the Autobahn in the direction you want to go with a sign stating your hoped-for destination.

As for public transport, the **U-Bahn** (subway network) is the most useful; it runs throughout the center of a city, usually stopping near the main sights. Tickets cost about DM3. If you plan on riding the U-Bahn frequently in a single day, invest in a *Tageskarten* (day pass); they're available from most subway and train stations. Germany's **S-Bahn** is a wider-reaching system, most useful for getting to hostels or sights in the suburbs. EurailPasses are valid on the S-Bahn, though *not* on the U-Bahn. Finally, **trams** generally follow U-Bahn routes and hit many of the same spots. All three of these systems share the same tickets, and you can buy them either from the driver or from *Fahrscheine* machines next to many stops. Authorities have recently been using undercover controllers to bust freeloaders, so watch out. An on-the-spot fine costs DM60.

WHERE TO SLEEP By far the cheapest option are *Jugendherbergen* (youth hostels), where beds in dorm rooms go for around DM20 (for those under 27) or DM27 (for those over 27). Conditions vary wildly, however: In Bavaria, for instance, people over 27 are not allowed to stay, period. Additional costs include sheets (DM3–DM6) and sometimes showers (DM1–DM3). Breakfast is almost always free. The cheapest hotels run DM35–DM55 for singles and DM55–DM100 for doubles, depending on the size of the city and whether you want a private shower. Facilities for guests in rooms *ohne Dusche* (without shower) are usually in the hallways. A night's stay at a *Campingplatz* (campsite), found in most small towns and near most big cities, runs about DM4–DM7 per person and DM3.50–DM6 per tent. Almost all tourist offices can book you a *Privatzimmer* (room in a private home), some of which require a two- or three-night minimum stay, at DM25–DM50 plus a fee of about DM5. **Student housing,** when available, tends to go for DM20–DM40 a head.

It's a little-known but important fact that most of Germany's youth hostels have keys they'll lend out for a deposit (about DM40). In other words, curfews are bogus.

FOOD One of the best ways to save money in Germany is to shop at local markets or grab a bite at a street-side *Imbiß* stand, the German equivalent of a greasy-spoon diner. Most offer wurst (sausage) and fries—or ethnic specialties like curry and falafel—for under DM10. Assembling a meal from the various markets and shops is cheaper still. Bakery bread runs from DM2 for a simple baguette to DM4.50 for a hearty loaf of wheat bread. A Coke is 80 pfennigs, a can of beer DM1.20, and a cheap bottle of wine DM5.

FESTIVALS AND HOLIDAYS If festivals are your thing, September and October are the best months to visit Germany: Harvest festivals bust out all over the place, not least of all in Munich, where the world-famous **Oktoberfest** draws hundreds of thousands of international beer-guzzlers. If you happen to arrive in December and you're just aching for some quaintness, don't miss the **Christmas markets** of some of the smaller towns as well as the biggies. Germany's premier **film festival** takes place in Berlin during February. In July, one of the major annual musical events in the world takes place in Bayreuth: the **Richard Wagner Festival.**

VISITOR INFORMATION It would take some detective work to find a German town without a tourist office; they live for that organized tour and glossy brochure crap. Use the offices mainly to get maps and help with accommodations; they'll almost always book you a hotel room or private room for a DM5 fee.

EMERGENCIES In an emergency, dial 110 for the **police,** 112 for an **ambulance.** These numbers do not require coins at pay phones.

PHONES Country Code: 49. Germany's phone system is modern, efficient, and easy to use—at least, that's the case west of Berlin. The system in eastern Germany is still a wee bit antiquated and connections to and from the former Communist areas are often poor. Many phones don't accept coins, so if you'll be making lots of calls, invest in a telephone card (DM12 and up), available at post offices and many currency-exchange agencies. **Local phone calls** run 30 pfennig for the connection plus DM1 or so every couple minutes. Most phone booths have instructions in English. You can make **international calls** from phone booths marked with the silhouette of a receiver and the words INLANDS UND AUSLANDSGESPRACHE. International phones generally accept 10 pfennig, DM1, and DM5 coins, but it's much easier to make international calls from the post office and pay when you're done. Either way, DM5 will give you about two minutes of conversation to the United States (though rates vary from town to town). You can make collect and phone card calls through **AT&T Direct** (tel. 0130–0010) and **Sprint** (tel. 0130–0013). For the plain old **international operator,** dial 00118; for a local operator, dial 01188.

MAIL

➤ **SENDING MAIL** • Buy stamps from a local *Postamt* (post office) and mail your letters from any street-side postal box. Sending an airmail letter to North America costs DM1.40 and takes about five days; postcards cost DM2. Letters to EU countries run DM1, postcards 80 pfennig.

➤ **RECEIVING MAIL** • You can receive mail at any German post office free of charge. Simply have the letter marked with your name, the address of the post office ("Postamt," city name, zip code), and the words POSTLAGERNDE SENDUNG.

LANGUAGE Germans speak a variety of accents and dialects that vary between regions and even cities. In the north, High German (the German spoken on TV and the radio) dominates, but in the south, east, and far north you'll encounter all sorts of hard-to-understand pronunciations.

PEOPLE OF COLOR Use common sense to avoid potentially dangerous situations. Larger cities tend to be more cosmopolitan and more tolerant. Prosperous and touristed areas in general are pretty safe, but as economic conditions worsen, color prejudice seems to increase. If a confrontation arises, make it understood that you are a foreign tourist traveling through Germany. In most cases, you'll be left alone. If you're out after dark in unfamiliar areas, definitely grab a cab if you can afford it; when taking public transportation, sit close to the driver.

GAY AND LESBIAN TRAVELERS Homophobia is pretty much in check in western Germany. Smooching in public may inspire hostile looks and comment, but homosexuals are generally left alone. In large towns you'll find plenty of gay and lesbian bars, even a few "alternative" cafés and resource centers. In eastern Germany, views of gender roles are more "traditional," so expect fewer facilities and somewhat negative attitudes.

DISABLED TRAVELERS Most public transportation in Germany is accessible to the physically disabled. All trains and most public buses in the west are outfitted to accommodate passengers in wheelchairs, and the system in the former East Germany is beginning to catch up. Many hostels and some hotels and pensions can accommodate disabled travelers, but always phone ahead to check.

Frankfurt

When you tell people you're going to Frankfurt, whose main claim to fame is its airport, they usually reply, "Why?" Frankfurt is definitely not the easiest city to befriend; it's an industrial and commercial center, the drug and crime capital of Hessen, and the host of American military headquarters in Germany. But if you stay for a couple of days, it just might grow on you. Frankfurt claims an extremely diverse citizenship—from the junkie to the rushed corporate banker to the teenage techno head to the student anarchist. You may not be able to find enough tourist sights to fill a single day, but you can find tons of lively, crowded pubs and *Apfelwein* (apple wine) taverns in the Sachsenhausen district and cellars with good jazz bands almost anywhere in the city. Frankfurt is *the* German center of techno music, and discos here stay alive until 6 AM.

BASICS

➤ **VISITOR INFORMATION** • Tourist Information **Römer.** *Römerberg 27, tel. 069/2123–8708. Next to Römer in Römerberg Sq. Open weekdays 9–6, weekends 9:30–6.*

➤ **AMERICAN EXPRESS** • *Kaiserstr. 8, tel. 069/720016. 10-min walk from Hauptbahnhof. Open weekdays 9:30–5:30, Sat. 9–noon.*

➤ **CHANGING MONEY** • Your best bet are banks, which charge only 1% commission to change traveler's checks. Post offices, on the other hand, charge DM3 per check. To change money in the evenings, go to the airport or train station.

➤ **CONSULATES** • **Australia.** *Gutleutstr. 85, tel. 069/273–9090. From Hauptbahnhof turn right on Baseler Str., left on Gutleutstr.*

United Kingdom. *Bockenheimer Landstr. 42, tel. 069/170–0020.*

United States. *Siesmayerstr. 21, tel. 069/75360. Bus 35 from Konstablerwache to Palmgarten/Siesmayerstr.*

➤ **PHONES AND MAIL** • Post offices at the Hauptbahnhof and the airport are open 24 hours a day. The **main post office** near the center has poste restante services. *Zeil 108/110, tel. 069/909010. Open weekdays 8–6, Sat. 8–noon. Postal code: 60313.*

COMING AND GOING

➤ **BY TRAIN** • Frankfurt's **Hauptbahnhof** (tel. 069/19419) is the main terminal of the Deutsche Bundesbahn (German Federal Railway), so you'll have no problem getting into and out of town. Frankfurt has connections to Munich (3½ hrs), Hamburg (3½ hrs), Berlin (6½ hrs), and almost anywhere in Europe.

➤ **BY BUS** • **Deutsche Touring** sends buses to 200 European cities from the south side of the Hauptbahnhof. *Am Römerhof 17, tel. 069/79030.*

➤ **BY MITFAHRGELEGENHEIT** • **Mitfahrzentrale.** *Baseler Str. 7, on Baselerpl., tel. 069/236444 or 069/236–445. Open weekdays 8–6:30, Sat. 8–2.*

➤ **BY PLANE** • All major European cities and many U.S. cities have direct flights to **Flughafen Frankfurt,** Europe's second-busiest airport. The S-Bahn is the easiest way to reach downtown Frankfurt: S-Bahn 15 runs to the Hauptbahnhof every 10 minutes, and S-Bahn 14 goes to Hauptwache Square every 20 minutes. A taxi ride from the airport into the city center costs about DM35.

GETTING AROUND There are four main districts in Frankfurt: downtown, Sachsenhausen, Westend, and Bockenheim. **Downtown** lies on the north bank of the Main River, between Untermain Brücke on the west and Obermainbrücke on the east. From downtown you can cross the Eiserner Steg, a pedestrian bridge, to reach **Sachsenhausen,** a mostly pedestrian neighborhood with pubs and cobblestone streets. The **Westend,** Frankfurt's financial district,

Frankfurt

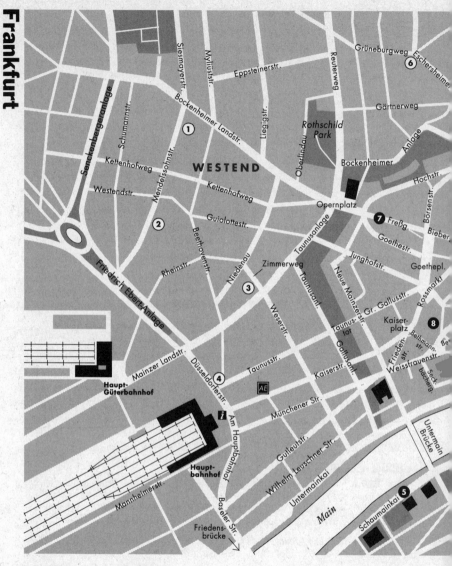

WESTEND

Rothschild Park

Haupt-Güterbahnhof

Haupt-bahnhof

Main

Untermain Brücke

Friedens-brücke

Sights ●

Dom St.
Bartholomäus, **10**

Freßgasse, **7**

Goethehaus und
Goethemuseum, **8**

Museumsufer, **5**

Römerberg, **9**

Zoologischer
Garten, **11**

Lodging ○

Haus der
Jugend, **12**

Hotel Adler, **4**

Hotel Atlas, **3**

Pension Backer, **1**

Pension Bruns, **2**

Pension Uebe, **6**

Waldhotel Hensels
Felsenkeller, **13**

Frankfurt

is northwest of downtown and north of the Hauptbahnhof. **Bockenheim,** primarily a student and low-income area, is northwest of Westend.

Frankfurt's public transportation system is complex but efficient. Short-trip tickets cost DM2, DM2.60 during rush hours (weekdays 6:30 AM–8:30 AM and 3:30 PM–6:30 PM). Day passes are DM5, three-day passes DM12. The U-Bahn and S-Bahn close at midnight and open around 5 AM. For a **taxi,** call 069/545011 or 069/250–001.

WHERE TO SLEEP Frankfurt's various trade fairs and the wealthy businesspeople they bring make inexpensive accommodation an oxymoron. If the hostel's booked, try **Campingplatz Niederräder** (Ufer 2, tel. 069/673846) or the cheap hotels in the red-light district near the Hauptbahnhof. Otherwise, **Hotel Adler** (Nidda Str. 65, 4th Floor, tel. 069/233455) almost always has a couple of musty doubles (DM105), and it's just five minutes from the Hauptbahnhof.

Hotel Atlas. Clean doubles cost DM80. Cranky management speaks a bit of French, no English. Seven rooms, shared baths. *Zimmerweg 1, tel. 069/723946. Walk up Mainzer Landstr., left on Zimmerweg.*

Pension Backer. Best deal in town excluding the hostel. Short walk to Palmengarten in safe residential neighborhood. Rooms over street are noisy. Singles DM40, doubles DM60, triples DM80. *Mendelssohnstr. 92, tel. 069/747992 or 069/747900. From Hauptbahnhof walk up Friedrich-Ebert-Anlage, turn right on Wilhelm Hauffstr., which turns into Mendelssohnstr. at Bettinapl.*

Pension Bruns. Doubles (DM75) and triples (DM105) in large, stoic building in former Jewish quarter. Some rooms have hardwood floors. *Mendelssohnstr. 42, tel. 069/748896. U6 or U7 to Westend, walk northwest on Bockenheimer Landstr., left on Mendelssohnstr.*

Pension Uebe. Good place to meet locals, mostly businessmen and apartment seekers. Small refrigerator in each room. Near Holzhausen Park and the Palmengarten. Singles DM55–DM85, doubles DM90–DM130. *Grüneburgweg 3, tel. 069/591209. U1, U2, or U3 to Grüneburgweg. Wheelchair access.*

Waldhotel Hensels Felsenkeller. Off the beaten track, south of the river in Oberrad district. Twenty basic but clean doubles cost DM95. *Buchrainstr. 95, tel. 069/652086.*

➤ **HOSTEL • Haus der Jugend (HI).** Clean, convenient, and Frankfurt's only true deal. In Sachsenhausen, near major sights and apple wine taverns. Midnight curfew not strict. Dorm beds DM20–DM24, doubles DM35 per person, singles DM50. *Deutschherrnufer 12, tel. 069/619058. Bus 46 from Hauptbahnhof to Frankensteiner Pl. Wheelchair access. Rooms and reception closed daily 9–1.*

FOOD This city is the home of the frankfurter, a smoked beef or beef-and-pork sausage. Another local specialty is *Grüne Soße* (green sauce with eggs or potatoes). Vegetarians can rely on pasta or falafels. Head over to **Freßgasse,** near Opernplatz, and take your pick from cafés, restaurants, and delis. To find inexpensive traditional German food and apple wine, visit Sachsenhausen; look for pine wreaths above the door to indicate that apple wine is on tap. To seek out black-clad hipsters or lower-income Frankfurters, head for the energetic student area **Bockenheim.** Cafés in the area are steeped in local flavor: try **Stattcafé** (Grempstr. 21) for an artsy atmosphere or **Café au Lait** (Am Weingarten 12, tel. 069/701039), where you can get breakfast until 5 PM.

Apfelwein Klaus. On small side street off Freßgasse. On sunny days munch outside on spare ribs and sauerkraut (DM15) or one of a dozen salads (DM8–DM12). *Meisengasse 10, tel. 069/282846. U-Bahn or S-Bahn to Hauptwache.*

Klaane Sachsenhauser. Locals have been eating typical Frankfurt cuisine in the large beer garden here since 1886. A definite must. *Neuer Wall 11, tel. 069/615983. Wheelchair access. Dinner only; closed Sun.*

Pizza Pedro. Large portions, low prices, and nearly perfect wood-baked pizza. Cheese pizza DM5, spaghetti DM8. *Paradiesgaße 38, Sachsenhausen, tel. 069/611576. Bus 36 from Konstablerwache to Elisabethenstr.*

Saladin. Extensive salad bar (DM2.50 per 100 g) and hot meals like tofu paprika goulash (DM10). *Adalbertstr. 6, in Bockenheim, tel. 069/779005. U6 or U7 to Bockenheimer Warte. Wheelchair access. Closed Sun.*

WORTH SEEING Most of Frankfurt's attractions are on the north bank of the Main between the Untermain Brücke and the Alte Brücke. What remains of Frankfurt's historical buildings largely lies in and around **Römerberg,** the square that was the center of city life for centuries. The Gothic three-building **Römer** (City Hall) has overlooked the markets and fairs held on the square since 1405. **Freßgasse** (Gobble Lane) is a posh, tree-lined pedestrian zone that stretches along Große Bockenheimer Straße between Hauptwache and the Alte Oper and is full of specialty cheese shops, bakeries, and outdoor cafés. The **Museumsufer,** a street with Frankfurt's seven best museums, is on the river's south bank.

Dom St. Bartholomäus. The Dom is Frankfurt's biggest church and was the coronation site for countless Holy Roman emperors. It's got plenty of standard Gothic cathedral features, including frescoes and gravestones, but the 300-foot red sandstone tower is what really sets it apart. *Römerberg Sq. U4 from Hauptbahnhof to Römer. Open Mon.–Thurs. 2–6.*

Goethehaus und Goethemuseum. The birthplace and childhood home of Johann Wolfgang von Goethe, famed writer, poet, and theorist, will mean a lot more to you if you're familiar with his work—he writes about the house in his autobiography, *Fact and Fiction. Großer Hirschgraben 23–25, tel. 069/282824. U-Bahn or S-Bahn to Hauptwache. Admission: DM4, DM2.50 students. Open Mon.–Sat. 9–5:30, Sun. 10–1.*

Museumsufer is the name locals have assigned the string of seven museums on the riverside street **Schaumainkai.** All are open Tuesday and Thursday–Sunday 10–5, Wednesday 10–8. A sure fire pleaser is the **Deutsches Filmmuseum** (No. 41, tel. 069/2123–8830); a theater on the ground floor shows famous and not-so-famous films from all over (DM3, DM1.50 students). The **Deutsches Postmuseum** (No. 53, tel. 069/60600) colorfully exhibits the history of communications. The whopper of the row is **Städel** (No. 63, tel. 069/605–0980), with an impressive collection of paintings, sculptures, drawings, and prints by such hot shots as Rembrandt, Monet, Braque, and Picasso.

The Frankfurt Flohmarkt (flea market) is among the best in Germany. It lines the Main River in Sachsenhausen every Saturday 8–2.

Zoologischer Garten. Frankfurt's zoo is one of Europe's oldest (1858) and best. The open-air enclosures leave nothing but a moat between you and the animals. *Alfred-Brehmpl., tel. 069/2123–3731. U6 or U7 to Zoo station. Admission: DM9.50, DM4.50 students. Open Mar. 16–Sept., daily 8–7; shorter hrs off-season.*

AFTER DARK At night Apfelwein taverns, restaurants, and discos transform Sachsenhausen into Party Central, though some locals prefer the nightlife in the city center. Frankfurt is the techno-pop center of all Germany, and the tons of techno discos in town prove it. Wherever you go, beer will run about DM3–DM6, and the action probably won't start until at least 11 PM. The monthly magazine *Prinz* (available in any kiosk for DM3.50), has a column in the back called *Freies Theater* that tells where and when free comedy shows, dance performances, and plays will be held in Frankfurt and outlying areas for that month.

The candlelit cellar bar **Blaubart** (Kaiserhofstr. 18, off Freßgasse, tel. 069/282229) hosts a lively, young Frankfurter clientele. Afternoons, **Club Voltaire** (Kleine Hochstr. 5, off Freßgasse, tel. 069/292408) hosts a small crowd of politically active intellectuals listening to loud music. The café serves appetizers as well as DM5 beers. The predominantly gay **Lilliput** (Sandhofpassage, tel. 069/285727) has a smug atmosphere and intimate tables for two on the patio. When you're ready to hit the discos, try **Cooky's** (Am Salzhaus 4, tel. 069/287662), where live bands jam on Monday night and DJs spin good vibes the rest of the week, or **Plastik** (Seilerstr. 34, tel. 069/285055), which has "Gay Night" every Sunday. For the best jazz in town, head to **Kleine Bockenheimer Straße,** fondly called Jazzgasse (Jazz Alley); the small **Jazzkeller** (Kleine Bockenheimer Str. 18A, tel. 069/288537) hits maximum capacity most nights.

NEAR FRANKFURT

FULDA This Baroque city, beautifully set in the Fulda River valley, has long had great impact on the Catholic world. Beginning in the 10th century, the church abbots started schmoozing their way up the Catholic ladder until they finally reached the rung of prince-bishop. To celebrate this triumph they built themselves the **Stadtschloß** (Schloßstr. 1), Fulda's overblown castle. Today, the Baroque structure mainly houses municipal offices—including the tourist office at entrance D-2—and the **Schloßmuseum** (entrance D-1), which shows off some rooms decorated in 17th-century fashion. The tiny, gridded windows of the **Michaelskirche,** across the Pauluspromenade from the northern exit of the Schloßgarten, make it look more like a stone prison than a church. An eerie circle of pillars delineate the pulpit area; downstairs is a series of tiny crypts that will make claustrophobics queasy. Practically speaking, trains run regularly to Fulda from Munich (3 hrs) and Frankfurt (1½ hrs). Once in town, you can cover the center and all the sights in a snap.

➤ **WHERE TO SLEEP** • The **HI hostel** (Schirmannstr. 31, tel. 0661/73389), a 10-minute bus ride from town (Bus 12; no Sun. service), has small rooms that need a cleaning. Bed and breakfast costs DM20–DM24. The homey hotel **Zum Kronhof** (Kronhof 2, tel. 0661/74147) feels like a garden with so many plants around. Clean doubles are DM60, singles DM30; take Bus 10 to Am Kronhof. **Pension "Gambrinushalle"** (Peterstor 14, tel. 0661/72862) has mammoth doubles for DM80. From the Hauptbahnhof, follow Bahnhofstraße to Rabanusstraße, turn right and right again on Peterstor.

MARBURG Since 1527, university students have been the driving force of Marburg. They didn't always have tattoos and purple hair, but they've always added energy and life to the city. On the western bank of the Lahn River, the well-preserved **Oberstadt** makes up the bulk of the city. This attractive mess of steep, winding cobblestone passageways is lined with half-timbered houses, old buildings with painted posts and buttresses, and bunches of pubs and cafés. Below the Oberstadt and to the north lies the earliest Gothic church in Germany, the **Elisabethkirche** (cnr. of Elisabethstr. and Deutschhausstr.; admission DM2). The huge stone edifice contains coffins, altars, and colorful stained-glass windows.

You can climb through the Oberstadt to reach **Landgrafenschloß,** an enormous castle that overlooks the entire city—or you can take Bus 16 from Marktplatz. The highlight is the castle's free **Museum of Cultural History** (tel. 06421/282355). For city maps and accommodation advice, stop back in town at the **tourist office** (Neue Kasseler Str. 1, tel. 06421/201249; open weekdays 8–12:30 and 2–5, Sat. 2–5). Marburg has direct train connections to Frankfurt (1 hr) and Heidelberg (2 hrs). The Hauptbahnhof is in the northern part of the city.

Day Tripping

Fulda is conveniently stuck between the Rhön Nature Park and the Vogelsberg. The nature park, which covers 750 square km, contains small villages, nature trails, and beautiful landscapes. Use the nearby city of Gersfeld as your base; it's got a few attractions of its own, including a 120-acre deer park and a few castles. The Vogelsberg is a region west of Fulda characterized by low, rolling hills, forests, meadow lands, and small villages. Two of these villages, Lauterbach and Alsfeld, are easy to reach from Fulda and make good day trips.

➤ **WHERE TO SLEEP** • **Campingplatz Lahnaue** (An der B 3A, behind hostel, tel. 06421/21331), on the east bank of the Lahn River, attracts some seedy characters but is cheap (DM5 per person). **Haus Müller** (Deutschhausstr. 29, tel. 06421/65659; doubles DM90) looks more like a museum of 18th-century furniture than a hotel; call ahead because it fills up fast. From the station take Bus 1, 2, 3, 4, or 5 to Deutschhausstraße. The staff at the local **youth hostel** (Jahnstr. 1, tel. 06421/23461; beds DM22–DM26) cops a serious attitude, but the facilities are all right. From the station take Bus 4 to Erlenring, turn right down Erlenring, then right again on Sommerbadstraße and on Jahnstraße.

Baden-Württemberg

Baden-Württemberg embraces such diverse landscapes as the **Neckar Valley** in the north; the **Bodensee,** or Lake Konstanz, in the south; the **Black Forest** in the east; and the underrated **Schwäbische Alb** in the heart of the *Land* (state). In stark contrast to these scenic splendors are such cities as **Mannheim** and **Stuttgart,** home to many of the cutting edge, high-technology firms that are at the center of the lean, mean, well-oiled German industrial machine. Striking a balance between these two environments are the two riverside university towns of **Tübingen,** home of Germany's oldest institution of higher learning, and **Heidelberg,** renowned for its romantic atmosphere and enormous castle. Rounding out the picture of the province is the wide variety of Romanesque, Renaissance, and especially Gothic and Baroque architecture, spared by the bombing raids that shook much of Baden-Württemberg during World War II.

The Black Forest

The steep hills and deep valleys of the **Schwarzwald** (Black Forest) stretch some 165 km from Karlsruhe to the Rhine to the Swiss border. For nature lovers, the forest has superlative outdoor activities—more than 20,000 marked hiking, biking, and cross-country trails—but only if you steer clear of the region's schlocky and heavily touristed villages. The residents of the Black Forest are some of the most colorful characters in Germany: They speak a dialect even fellow Germans have difficulty understanding, and many of them still live in the sloping, thatched homes characteristic of the Schwarzwald. These are the folks who gave the world cuckoo clocks, some of the wackiest traditional clothing on the planet, and many of the fairy tales made famous by the Brothers Grimm. Train travel within the forest is spectacular, although many towns are served only by bus—and that, often slowly and infrequently.

FREIBURG IM BREISGAU

The largest and most accessible city in the southern Black Forest, Freiburg makes a perfect base for exploring the surrounding villages and hills. The city was blown to bits in a World War II bombing raid but has since reconstructed many of its most impressive buildings, preserving the historical atmosphere of the Altstadt (Old Town). Narrow streams, known as Bächle, run through the city's cobblestone streets and add to the old-fashioned feel. Thanks to the large

Pretzels and Soggy Noodles

Perhaps the most stereotypical of all German foods, the pretzel, was first created in Baden-Württemberg. For heartier appetites, the regional "Spätzle" are thick noodles made with eggs, flour, water, and salt and boiled to a sticky, soggy perfection. Also common are "Maultaschen," a ravioli-like pasta usually filled with onions, spinach, and some form of mystery meat, and often roasted in an egg sauce.

student population, the town is packed with talented street musicians, many of whom attend the local music school, and loads of cafés.

VISITOR INFORMATION *Rotteckring 14, 2 blocks from Hauptbahnhof, tel. 0761/368–9090. Open May–Oct., Mon.–Sat. 9–9, Sun. 10–2; Nov.–Apr., weekdays 9–6, Sat. 9–3, Sun. 10–noon.*

COMING AND GOING Freiburg's **Hauptbahnhof** services Basel (DM15, 45 min), Frankfurt (DM64, 2¼ hrs), and Hamburg (DM195, 11–12 hrs). Buses to most of the small towns in the Black Forest leave from the **Omnibusbahnhof** (tel. 0761/19419), next to the train station. The local **Mitfahrzentrale** (Belfortstr. 55, tel. 0761/19444) is in the center of town. To reach the center from the station, walk up Eisenbahnstraße, Freiburg's major east–west boulevard, to its intersection with Kaiser-Joseph-Straße, the largest north–south street. Rides to most parts of the city on the **bus** or **S-Bahn** cost DM2.50. Public transportation stops running at 1 AM; for a **taxi** call 0761/31111.

WHERE TO SLEEP Aside from the characterless **HI hostel** (Kartäuserstr. 151, tel. 0761/67656), where beds run DM18.50–DM23.50, the cheapest option is **Camping Hirzberg** (Kartäuserstr. 99, tel. 0761/35054), which charges DM3.50 per tent and DM6 per person. For either, take S-Bahn 1 to Messplatz. **Hotel Hirshen-Dionysos** (Hirschstr. 2, tel. 0761/29353) offers clean doubles for DM64–DM75 in a beautiful neighborhood south of the center; take S-Bahn 4 to Klosterplatz. The small **Hotel Schemmer** (Eschholzstr. 63, tel. 0761/272424) has simple, clean doubles for DM75.

FOOD Just outside the Martinstor, in the **Freiburger Markthalle,** more than a dozen food stands serve Chinese, Indian, Italian, Greek, and even Afghan food, usually for less than DM10. **Ristorante Roma** (Kaiser-Joseph-Str. 225, tel. 0761/280077), on the other side of the Martinstor, serves good pizzas (DM7–DM17) and pastas (DM9–DM14) in an elegant but down-to-earth courtyard. For traditional German fare like schnitzel (DM11), try **Schwabentorle** (Oberlinden 23, beside Schwabentor, tel. 0761/34041).

WORTH SEEING The **Münster** cathedral, dominated by its 380-foot tower, has been Freiburg's main landmark for over 700 years. Climb the tower for a valve over the city and a close-up of the cathedral's intricate spire. The dark interior of the cathedral contains brilliant stained-glass windows, some dating to the 13th century, and 10 richly decorated side chapels. On **Münsterplatz** surrounding the cathedral, a daily outdoor **market** offers the best in fresh produce, Black Forest meats and cheeses, flowers, and local handicrafts; the market is widely regarded as the finest in southwestern Germany.

Freiburg's numerous city-run **museums** are all free, with the exception of the mediocre **Augustiner Museum** (Auginstinerpl., tel. 0761/216–3300; admission DM4, DM2 students). Housed in an old Baroque monastery between the Schwabentor and the Martinstor, it has a collection of 14th- to 20th-century paintings, sculpture, glassware, and furniture, mostly by artists from the upper Rhine region. Across the street from Augustinerplatz are the **Museum für Völkerkunde** (Museum of Ethnology, tel. 0761/216–3342) and the yawner **Museum für Naturkunde** (Natural History Museum, Gerberau 32, tel. 0761/216–3325). The **Museum für Ur-und Frühgeschichte** (Museum of Prehistory and Early History, Rotteckring 5, tel. 0761/216–3311) has a ho-hum collection of archaeological artifacts from the area, but its location in the gorgeous neo-Gothic Colombi Palace makes it worth a visit. Guarding the southeast corner of the city, the 13th-century **Schwabentor** gate houses Freiburg's smallest and quirkiest museum, the **Zinnfigurenklause,** or Tin Figure Collection (tel. 0761/24321), a moderately interesting and free way to spend a half hour.

AFTER DARK A number of bars, discos, and cafés grace the streets of the university quarter in the southwest corner of the Old City. **Circus** (Kaiser-Joseph-Str. 248, tel. 0761/36536) is Freiburg's newest hip disco, while **Schlappen** (Löwenstr. 2, tel. 0761/33494) is the most popular bar among students. **Freiburger Jazzhaus** (Schnewlinstr., tel. 0761/34973) features live blues, folk, Latin, rock, or jazz nearly every night of the week; get listings and tickets (DM10–DM40) at the tourist office, and while you're there grab a copy of *Aktuell* for theater and classical-music listings.

➤ **TITISEE** • A small lake sealed off from the rest of the world by a series of pine-covered hills, **Titisee** possesses the type of mystical natural beauty that can lure you into a dreamy never-never land. Unfortunately, never-never land has a problem with tourists. To get away from the battling rowboats and overcrowded beaches, follow one of the several excellent hiking and biking trails that circle the lake; pick up trail maps at the **tourist office** (Seestr. and Strandbadstr., tel. 07651/8101–8107) in the Kurhaus (the big building with all the flags). Rent three-speed clunkers from the train station for DM12 per day (DM8 with rail pass) or mountain bikes from **Sporthaus** (tel. 07651/7494), about 60 meters down Strandbadstraße from the tourist office, for DM25 per day. Trains travel twice per hour along the beautiful stretch from Freiburg to Titisee (40 min, DM8.40). For great summer hiking or winter skiing, take the train from Titisee to **Mt. Feldberg,** the Black Forest's tallest peak at 4,882 feet. Feldberg's **hostel** (Passhöhe 14, tel. 07676/221) lies within walking distance of the ski lifts (DM5) and hiking trails and charges DM17.50–DM24.50.

TRIBERG

Deep, thickly forested valleys surround the town of Triberg, offering some of the best hiking and biking in southwest Germany. Built on a steep hillside, the town itself offers enough attractions to draw busloads of tourists. The biggest draw is Germany's highest **waterfall,** which drops 540 feet in seven rocky steps. You pay DM2.50 (DM1 students) to view the cascade and can reach it via a path at the top of the town's main drag, Hauptstraße. The **tourist office** (Lusienstr. 10, tel. 07722/953230) is in the Kurhaus, two blocks from the entrance to the waterfall.

The **Schwarzwaldmuseum** (Wallfahrtstr. 4, tel. 07722/4434), one block from the waterfall, has a quirky collection of Black Forest culture: The museum has hundreds of cuckoo clocks (including the world's largest), models of artisans' workshops, and a room designed to look like a mining shaft, full of minerals from the surrounding hills.

WHERE TO SLEEP AND EAT Triberg's **hostel** (Rohrbacher Str. 35, tel. 07722/4110) is a steep 20-minute hike up Friedrichstraße. Beds are DM17.50–DM22. **Krone** (Schulstr. 37, tel. 07722/4524), in the center of town, has DM80 doubles with creaky but comfortable beds and a restaurant serving hearty Black Forest meals. For pizzas (DM8–DM12) or pasta (DM8–DM15), head to **Pinnochio** (Hauptstr. 64, tel. 07722/4424), also near the top of the hill.

BADEN-BADEN

Although Euro-Yuppies, tourists, and hypochondriacs taking advantage of Germany's liberal health-care system have replaced the aristocrats who once had the run of Baden-Baden, not much has changed in Baden-Baden for the past hundred years or so. As it was in the late 1800s, the **Friedrichsbad** (Römerpl. 1, tel. 07221/275920) is the most luxurious bath complex in town. Go instead to **Caracalla-Therme** (Römerpl. 11, tel. 07221/275940), a more mod-

Black Death

Just as the plague once rampaged through the human population of Europe, today Waldsterben (Forest Death) afflicts the trees of Germany's Black Forest. Symptoms of the disease include premature loss of leaves and undersize trunks. The causes of the illness, first reported in 1976 and said to affect two-thirds of the trees in the forest, are less clear. Some scientists believe the villain is nitrogen oxide emitted by cars. Such fears have led to a growing number of signs along Black Forest roads reading AUTOS TOTEN WALDER (CARS ARE KILLING FORESTS).

ern bathhouse down the street; three hours in the thermal baths here—bathing attire required—cost DM18.

Unless you're at least 21 and dressed to the nines, your only chance of seeing the inside of Baden-Baden's elegant **casino** is on one of the tours (DM3) that leave every half hour between 9:30 AM and 11:30 AM. The **Trinkhalle,** a columned 19th-century building next to the casino, has a striking entryway with 14 frescoes depicting scenes from local legends. Stretching south from the casino is **Lichtentaler Allee,** a pleasant promenade lined with rare and exotic trees; here the **Kunsthalle** museum (Lichtentaler Allee 8A, tel. 07221/23250) features rotating exhibitions of art from around the world. The **tourist office** (Augustapl. 8, 2 blocks south of Leopoldspl., tel. 07221/275200) has current listings.

COMING AND GOING The **train station** is about 4 km northwest of the center. Bus 1 runs from the station to **Leopoldsplatz,** the town's central square, which lies directly between the clutch of sights centered around Friedrichsbad and those near the casino.

WHERE TO SLEEP AND EAT You'll pay a pretty penny for most accommodations in this town unless you stay at the spotless, modern **HI hostel** (Hardbergstr. 34, tel. 07228/2427; beds DM17–DM22), up in the hills between the train station and the city center; take Bus 1 from the station. **Hotel Löhr** (Alderstr. 2, tel. 07221/26204), in the center of town, has comfy doubles for DM90. The hotel's reception desk is at Café Lohr, on Augustaplatz. During the day, **Hatip's** (Gernsbacherstr. 18, tel. 07221/22364) serves kebabs (DM6) and a host of excellent Middle Eastern vegetarian dishes; at night, the same joint serves more beer (DM3) than pita sandwiches.

Heidelberg

Heidelberg has been celebrated by virtually the entire German Romantic movement and by scores of poets, writers, and composers, including Goethe, Mark Twain, and Robert Schumann. This city surrounded by mountains, forests, vineyards, and the Neckar River is also home to the oldest university in Germany. All of this ensures two distinct interpretations of Heidelberg's personality: heaven for the nature lover and a bouncing student scene for the partyer. The city was spared destruction during World War II, and the old town is a proud Baroque achievement on Gothic foundations.

BASICS Tourist office. *In front of Hauptbahnhof, tel. 06221/21341. Open Mar.–Oct., Mon.–Sat. 9–7, Sun. 10–6; Nov.–Feb., Mon.–Sat. 9–7.*

American Express. *Friedrich-Ebert-Anlage 16, near Bismarckpl., tel. 06221/29001. Open weekdays 9–5:30, Sat. 9–noon.*

Main post office. *Belfort Str., near station, tel. 06221/551. Postal code: 69115.*

COMING AND GOING Frequent rail service joins Heidelberg with Frankfurt, Stuttgart, Mannheim, and Karlsruhe. The **Hauptbahnhof** (tel. 06221/27156 or 06221/525345) is about 3 km west of the city center. The **Mitfahrgelegenheit** office (Kurfürstenanlage 57, tel. 06221/19444) is open weekdays 9–6:30, Sat. 10–2, Sun. 11–2.

GETTING AROUND Navigating Heidelberg is quick and easy. The Neckar River runs along the northern edge of the **Altstadt,** which is bisected by the 3-km pedestrian walkway **Hauptstraße.** Most of the major attractions—such as the Baroque Rathaus—as well as many restaurants, pubs, and shops lie on or near Hauptstraße and especially near **Marktplatz.** From the Hauptbahnhof, hop on S1 to reach the western end of Hauptstraße or Bus 33 to reach the eastern end. Single rides on any **bus** or **S-Bahn** within Heidelberg cost DM2.40, a day ticket DM7. For a **taxi,** call 06221/37676.

WHERE TO SLEEP Trying to find a cheap room in Heidelberg—especially during the summer—is a royal pain in the ass. In dire straits, the **Mitwohnzentrale** (Zwingerstr. 14–16, 2 blocks south of Marktpl., tel. 06221/19445) may be able to find you a room in a hotel or private home in the greater Heidelberg area. If everything below is packed, try **Hotel Weißer**

Bock (Große Mantelgasse 24, bet. Universitätpl. and Neckar River, tel. 06221/22231; doubles DM80–DM100), or consider staying in Mannheim or another nearby town.

Astoria. A splurge near the center. Jovial proprietors, gorgeous ivy-covered building in tranquil neighborhood. Doubles DM100. *Rahmengasse 30, bet. Ladenburger Str. and Schröderstr., tel. 06221/402929. S1 from Busbahnhof to 1st stop after Theodor-Heuss Brücke.*

Hotel Elite. Great deal for groups of three or four: DM95 for two people in two double beds, but only DM10 for each additional person. Beautiful, spacious rooms four blocks south of Bismarckplatz. *Bunsenstr. 15, tel. 06221/25734. Bus 21 from Hauptbahnhof to Hans-Böckler Str., turn right on Bunsenstr.*

Hotel Jeske. The cheapest place in town, in the heart of the Altstadt. No reservations accepted; phone as soon as you arrive. Doubles, triples, or quads DM22 per person. *Mittelbadgasse 2, off Marktpl., tel. 06221/23733. Bus 33 from Hauptbahnhof to Kornmarkt. Closed late Nov.–early Jan.*

➤ **HOSTEL • Jugendherberge Heidelberg (HI).** If you can score a room here, you'll get a clean, cheap night's sleep. One of the few hostels in Germany with a bar and disco. Bed and breakfast DM18.50–DM23.50. *Tiergarten Str. 5, tel. 06221/412066. Bus 33 from Hauptbahnhof to Sportzentrum Nord. After 8 PM on weekends, S1 to Chirurgisches Klinik, then Bus 33 to Sportzentrum Nord. 11:30 PM curfew, lockout 9–1, wheelchair access.*

➤ **CAMPGROUNDS • Camping Haide** (bet. Ziegelhausen and Kleingemünd, tel. 06223/2111) and **Camping Neckertal** (tel. 06221/802506) are across the Neckar River from each other, about 5 km east of the city center. Both have clean, safe sites (DM7 per person, DM6 per tent) and showers. Take Bus 35 to the orthopedic clinic.

FOOD Hundreds of restaurants serving all kinds of food blanket the area on and around Hauptstraße, most of them expensive. For cheaper food, head for one of the many supermarkets—try **Nanz** (Hauptstr. 116)—in the center of town. **Kowa's Vegetarischem Restaurant** (Kurfürstenanlage 9, near Landhauserstr., tel. 06221/22814) can treat you to a tranquil vegetarian meal for under DM20. For late-night munchies, **Da-Elio** (Friedrich-Ebert-Anlage 2, south of Bismarckpl., tel. 06221/12805) serves pizza (DM10) and pasta (from DM10) until 3 AM.

Gino's Mexico Grill. Cafeteria-style restaurant serving nearly authentic Mexican dishes (DM6–DM15). *Hauptstr. 113A, west of Universitätpl., tel. 06221/28586. Wheelchair access.*

Goldener Stern. No-frills Greek restaurant. A favorite among locals for souvlakia (DM12) and moussaka (DM14). *Lauerstr. 16, on Neckar River, tel. 06221/23937. No lunch.*

Indian Palace. Excellent, traditional Indian dishes like eggplant *bharta* (DM17.50) and chicken *masala* (DM19). *Kettengasse 11, bet. Marktpl. and Universitätpl., tel. 06221/10710.*

Zum Sepp'l. Wooden walls and tables of this famous tavern covered with ancient graffiti. Expect large crowds. Traditional German dishes DM8–DM25. *Hauptstr. 213, east of Karlspl., tel. 06221/23085. Wheelchair access.*

WORTH SEEING **Heidelberger Schloß.** Sitting on a ridge above Heidelberg, the grandiose, well-preserved ruins of the Schloß date from the late 15th century, though most of the complex was built in the Renaissance and Baroque styles of the 16th and 17th centuries. To reach the Schloß either walk up one of the two steep paths that begin south of the Kornmarkt or ride up the Bergbahn funicular (DM4.50 round-trip). To get inside you have to join a tour, included in the admission price. In the east-wing basement of the Schloß is the excellent **Deutsches Apothekenmuseum** (German Pharmaceutical Museum; admission DM3), which contains instruments used by alchemists from the 16th to 19th centuries. *Tel. 06221/53840. Admission: DM5, DM2.50 students. Open Apr.–Oct., daily 9–5; Nov.–Mar., daily 9–4.*

Kurpfälzisches Museum. Heidelberg's leading museum packs paintings, sculptures, furniture, and historical engravings into a Baroque palace. *Hauptstr. 97, tel. 06221/583402. Admission: DM4, DM2 students. Open Tues. and Thurs.–Sun. 10–5, Wed. 10–9.*

AFTER DARK On weekends most partying Heidelbergers head toward the rowdy establishments on **Unterestraße,** a small four-block street between the Neckar and the more touristy Hauptstraße. Right before the south entrance to the Alte Brücke, **Bistro zur Alten Brücke** (Obere Neckarstr. 2, tel. 06221/20201) draws young locals with a Mexican theme, a bar, and a disco. **Sonderbar** (Unterestr. 13, tel. 06221/25200; closed Sun.) is small, sweaty, smoky, and crowded with fans of heavy-duty rock and roll. In a converted warehouse near the Hauptbahnhof, **Zigarillo** (Bergheimer Str. 139, west of Mittermaierstr., tel. 06221/160333; cover DM5; closed Sun.), Heidelberg's largest disco, plays nonstop hip-hop for a youngish crowd. The **Schwimmbad Music Club** (Tiergartenstr. 13, near hostel, tel. 06221/470201) hosts "underground" bands who play everything from funk to Subpop grunge.

Stuttgart

Stuttgart's star began to rise when Gottlieb Daimler invented the gas-powered engine in a nearby suburb in 1883. Although World War II leveled the city, leaving it devoid of historical interest, the capital of Baden-Württemberg has bounced back as one of Germany's top industrial and technological centers. In turn, the city has used its wealth to become a center for graphic and performing arts. What Stuttgart lacks in historical monuments it compensates for with a host of excellent museums, galleries, and theaters.

BASICS **Tourist Informazion.** Go to the *Jugendinformation* (information for youth) desk to get special tips on cheap places to eat and sleep and the scoop on clubs and bars. *Königstr. 1A, tel. 0711/222–8240. Open May–Oct., Mon.–Sat. 8:30 AM–10 PM, Sun. and holidays 11–6; Nov.–Apr., Mon.–Sat. 8:30 AM–9 PM, Sun. and holidays 1–6.*

American Express. *Lautenschlagerstr. 3, tel. 0711/208–9128. Open weekdays 9–5:30, Sat. 9–noon.*

COMING AND GOING Stuttgart's **Hauptbahnhof** (tel. 0711/19419) is one of Germany's main rail hubs and has regular train connections to every major city in the country. The nearby **Busbahnhof** has service to nearby towns only. Or, you could always arrange a ride through **Mitfahrzentrale** (Lerchenstr. 65, tel. 0711/636–8036).

GETTING AROUND When you come out of the underground passage of the Hauptbahnhof you'll find yourself nearly in Stuttgart's center. Ahead of you and on your right lies the city's thriving business and financial district. Ahead of you and on your left lies the commercial center whose main artery, **Königstraße,** runs into the city's main square, the **Schloßplatz.** Directly behind you, the bulk of the long, skinny **Schloßgarten** stretches northeast.

WHERE TO SLEEP Aside from the hostel, cheap lodgings in the center of Stuttgart don't exist. If you want to delve into the city's nightlife, try to find a hotel since things don't get shaking until about 11, a half hour before the hostel's curfew. Two aesthetically unappealing but clean and cheap options are **Gästehaus Garni Eckel** (Vorsteigstr. 10, tel. 0711/290995; doubles DM70–DM85) and **Hotel-Restaurant Lamm** (Karl-Schurz-Str. 7, tel. 0711/267328; doubles DM60–DM72). For city-style camping, hit **Cannstatter Wasen** (Mercedesstr. 40, tel. 0711/556696; DM5.50 per person, DM5.50 per tent), along the Neckar River 15 minutes east of the center.

Jugendgästehaus Stuttgart. Impeccable rooms, pleasant atmosphere, and an unbeatable location. Singles DM35–DM45, doubles from DM60. *Richard-Wagner-Str. 2, tel. 0711/241132. U15 or U16 toward Heumaden to Bubenbad. Laundry facilities.*

Schwarzwaldheim. Big ol' rooms, recently redone, get snatched up fast. Doubles DM80. *Fritz-Elsas-Str. 20, at Theodor-Heuss-Str., tel. 0711/296988. S1 or S6 to Stadtmitte.*

➤ **HOSTEL** • **Jugendherberge Stuttgart (HI)**. A characterless hostel in the hills east of town. Interesting crowd, though. Beds DM17.50–DM22.50. *Haußmannstr. 27, tel. 0711/241583. U15 or U16 to Eugenspl., walk down Haußmannstr. and up stairs on right. 11:30 PM curfew, lockout 9–noon.*

FOOD For something quick and cheap go directly to **Schulstraße**, which runs between Königstraße and Marktplatz. Here you'll find wurst, schnitzel, burgers, sandwiches, pasta, and seafood in a smattering of fast-food restaurants. **Le Buffet Restaurant** (Königstr. 27), in the basement of Hertie Department Store, serves regional specialties cheap (about DM7). Stuttgart has tons of cafés to choose from, but to mingle with Stuttgart's ultra-hip Yuppie crowd, try **Osho's** (Eberhardstr. 31, tel. 0711/241789). For the multicultural thing head for **Café Merlin** (Augustenstr. 72, tel. 0711/618541), which features vegetarian snacks and occasional live bands.

Iden. Yummy, cafeteria-style vegetarian food. Full-on salad bar (DM2 per 100 g), hot vegetarian dishes (DM6–DM12), and fresh juices (DM3). *Eberhardstr. 1, in Schwäben-Zentrum, tel. 0711/235989. Wheelchair access. Closed Sat. dinner, Sun.*

Litfass. Student hangout features *Schwäbische* (Swabian) and Turkish dishes to a reggae beat. Food served until 4 AM. Weekends bring local bands—reggae, funk, blues, and more. *Eberhardstr. 1, near Marktpl., tel. 0711/243031.*

WORTH SEEING Stuttgart has a wide range of specialty galleries and museums, most of which are free. In the suburbs, the **Mercedes-Benz Museum** (Mercedesstr. 136, tel. 0711/172–2578) traces the history of the automobile line as well as the development of the engine for ships and planes; take S-Bahn 1 to Neckarstadion. If you prefer drinking to driving, take U-Bahn 1, 3, or 6 or S-Bahn 1, 2, or 3 to Vaihingen and hit the **Schwäbisches Brauereimuseum** (Robert-Koch-Str. 12, tel. 0711/737–0201). It traces the history of beer from Mesopotamian times to the present. The **Hegel-Haus museum** (Eberhardstr. 53, near Rathaus, tel. 0711/216–6733) traces the life of Stuttgart's most famous native philosopher through manuscripts, letters, and pictures. Finally, don't miss the impressive **Staatsgalerie** (Konrad-Adenauer-Str. 30–32, tel. 0711/212–5050; admission free; open Tues.–Sun. 10–5, Tues. and Thurs. until 8), one of Germany's finest art museums. The newer, postmodern gallery houses 20th-century creations by such artists as Dalí, Kandinsky, Klee, and Picasso.

The center of the city's action is the spacious **Schloßplatz** (Castle Square), featuring the enormous Baroque **Neue Schloß** in the middle of the bustling commercial district. South of the Schloßplatz, the **Altes Schloß** (Old Castle) matches a drab exterior with a beautiful courtyard. The adjacent **Landesmuseum** (admission free), featuring unusual displays of astronomical and timekeeping devices.

AFTER DARK Most of Stuttgart's bars and clubs are clumped around the southern end of Königstraße. As for clubs, **Cinderella** (Tübingerstr. 17, tel. 01711/640–6000; closed Mon. and Wed.) blares funk and hip-hop; Fridays feature music solely by black artists. The lively **King's Club** (Calwer Str. 21, at Lange Str., tel. 0711/226–1607) plays techno-pop hits from the glorious '80s for a predominantly gay clientele; Sundays are for women only. If live jazz is your thing, go to the smoky **Roger's Kiste** (Hauptstätterstr. 35, tel. 0711/233148). **Der Bräu in Tü 8** (Tübingerstr. 8–10, tel. 0711/295949), Stuttgart's only microbrewery, serves homemade Pils (DM3) and Weizener (DM4.50) to a young crowd.

NEAR STUTTGART

TÜBINGEN Tübingen, resting on a stretch of the Neckar River lined with weeping willows, has enough beautiful old buildings to take you back in time. That said, the city is immersed in the life of the university, and the dress and speech of liberal students who crowd the winding, often steep cobblestone streets will jolt you quickly back to the 20th century. Add a thriving nightlife, outdoor adventures, and students (who comprise a third of Tübingen's population of 75,000), and you've got the perfect recipe for one of the most inviting university towns in Germany. The "Most Popular Bar in Town" award goes to **Marktschenke** (Am Markt

11, tel. 07071/22035), where the noisy crowds spill onto the Marktplatz. **Tangente-Night** (Pfleghof 10, tel. 07071/23007) pours Schwäben Brau pilseners and potent Klosterbrau Weizens until 3 AM every night. Tübingen's most interesting "official" attraction is the well-preserved **Bebenhausen Kloister** (tel. 07071/200–2664; admission DM3.50, DM2 students), creating a vivid picture of former monastic life in the hills about 5 km north of Tübingen's center; take Bus 7955 or 7600 to Waldhorn.

➤ **VISITOR INFORMATION** • *An der Neckarbrücke, bet. station and Altstadt, tel. 07071/35011. Open Mar.–Oct., Mon.–Sat. 9–7, Sun. 10–6; Nov.–Dec., Mon.–Sat. 9–7, Sun. 10–3.*

➤ **COMING AND GOING** • The **Mitfahrzentrale** (Münzgasse 12, tel. 07071/26789) is in a copy shop about five blocks west of Marktplatz. From the **Hauptbahnhof** (tel. 07071/19419), walk to the right to Karlstraße and head left across the bridge. To your left is the old section of town, where most of the action is; 2 km ahead lies the university where you can sit in on a few classes, if the school of life isn't doing it for you.

➤ **WHERE TO SLEEP** • Alongside the Neckar and a five-minute walk to the Altstadt, the **HI hostel** (Gartenstr. 22/2, tel. 07071/23002) has creaky beds for DM18–DM22 along with lockers and laundry facilities downstairs. Catch Bus 11 (DM2.20) and asked to be dropped at the Jugendherberge. On the north bank of the river west of the Altstadt is **Neckar Camping** (Rappenberghalde 61, tel. 07071/43145), which charges DM7 per person, DM5 per tent.

The Bodensee

Over 80 km in length and 13 km in width, the Bodensee, or Lake Konstanz, is the largest lake in the German-speaking world. Forming a natural border between Germany, Austria, and Switzerland, the lake offers warm weather, cool waters, busy resorts, and ancient cities encircled by gently sloping green hills. You can swim, boat, windsurf, water-ski, or scuba dive in the lake, or hike and bike around it. Of course, all of this comes with a price tag, which you can slash by calling ahead and reserving a spot at one of the hostels or campgrounds.

Ships are the coolest way to travel around the lake. **Weiße Flotte** ferries (tel. 07531/281389) join most nearby towns; flash an InterRail or EurailPass for 50% off regular ticket prices. Otherwise, pick up a rail line from the island of **Lindau** in the eastern end of the Bodensee to **Radolfzell,** where a second line completes the route around the German section of the lake. Regular buses fill in the gaps between trains.

KONSTANZ

Divided by the Rhine as it exits the western end of the Bodensee, Konstanz is divided into two parts: the large medieval Altstadt, on the otherwise Swiss shore of the lake, and a number of scenic grassy beaches on the long, narrow peninsula opposite. Between the main bridge connecting the two sides of town runs **Seestraße,** a romantic tree-filled promenade. Konstanz's central monument, the 11th-century **Münster** cathedral, sits on the north side of the Altstadt and is topped by a spire that affords excellent views of the city and the entire Bodensee area. The largest and most popular beach in Konstanz, **Freibad Horn,** is located at the tip of the same peninsula where most of the city sits. A shack north of the beach rents Windsurfers for DM10 per hour or DM35 per day. A younger crowd of scantily clad sun worshipers perform their rituals at a smaller, quieter beach on the university campus. If you can afford to fork out DM29 (DM23.60 students), consider the three-hour cruise down the Rhine to Schaffhausen, Switzerland, from where you can walk another 4 km to the Rheinfall, Europe's tallest waterfall; contact the ferry company **Weiße Flotte** (Hafenstr. 6, tel. 07531/281398). For city maps, stop by the **tourist office** (Konzilstr. 5, beside Hauptbahnhof, tel. 07531/28476).

COMING AND GOING A few **trains** run each day to cities like Frankfurt (4½ hrs) and Stuttgart (3 hrs), where you can connect to the rest of the towns on the German side of the lake. In the other direction, regular rail service connects Konstanz to most major cities in

Switzerland. To hitch up with a car headed in your direction contact the **Mitfahrzentrale** (Münzgasse 22, tel. 07531/21444).

WHERE TO SLEEP Konstanz's cheapest beds are in the **Otto-Moericke-Turm Youth Hostel** (Allmanshohe 18, tel. 07531/32260; beds DM16.50–DM23.50), housed in a decaying 10-story tower whose top-floor common room has an unbeatable view of the city; take Bus 4 and ask for the Jugendherberge. Quieter and closer to the beach—but 20 minutes south of the center—is the **HI Kreuzlingen Hostel** (Promenadestr. 7, tel. 0041/72/752663; beds 18 Swiss francs) in the Swiss town bordering Konstanz. Take Bus 8 to Helvetiaplatz, go a half block down Hauptstraße, turn left on Hafenstraße and left again on Promenadestraße after about 10 minutes. **Campingplatz Bruderhofer** (Fohrenbühlweg 50, tel. 07531/31388; DM5.50 per person, DM6 per tent) has 180 tightly packed sites; take Bus 5 to Falk.

Munich

Munich (München in German), Germany's third-largest city, has been a center of political and economic activity since its founding in 1158, after greedy Duke Henry the Lion redirected the profitable salt trade by destroying a strategic bridge and replacing it with a new one near Munich. The art-loving Wittelsbachs, who ruled Bavaria for almost 750 years, generously funded art museums, classical musicians, and literary academies, creating a potent cultural legacy. Even today, Munich draws an inordinate number of artists, musicians, and students to its ancient streets and hallowed halls.

Every year Munich hosts the 16-day-long Oktoberfest, a drunken festival devoted entirely to beer, which Münchners aptly refer to as "liquid bread."

Munich offers a huge array of high-quality culture, including opera, ballet, four symphony orchestras, and the world's most comprehensive museums of science and technology. But it also has a huge industry entirely devoted to beer—including beer halls, beer-stein shops, six major breweries, beer-brewing monasteries, and enormous beerfests. And just when you're getting too cultured, it'll dump you into the nearest beer garden. For the sober-minded, there's always the nearby, postcard-perfect Bavarian Alps (*see below*), a mecca for hikers and nature types.

BASICS

➤ **VISITOR INFORMATION** • **Fremdenverkehrsamt.** For 24-hour information about museums and galleries in English, call 089/239172. Arrive early if you want a private room, which the staff reserves for a DM3 fee. *Opposite track 11 in Hauptbahnhof, tel. 089/239–1256. Open Mon.–Sat. 8 AM–10 PM, Sun. 11–7.*

Central Fremdenverkehrsamt. *Sendlingerstr. 1, around cnr. from Marienpl., tel. 089/23911.*

➤ **AMERICAN EXPRESS** • *Promenadepl. 6, tel. 089/290900. Open weekdays 9–5:30, Sat. 9–noon.*

➤ **CONSULATES** • **Canada.** *Tal 29, tel. 089/290650. Open Mon.–Thurs. 9–noon and 2–5, Fri. 9–1:30.*

United Kingdom. *Bürkleinstr. 10, tel. 089/211090.*

United States. *Königinstr. 5, tel. 089/28880. Open weekdays 8 AM–11:30 PM.*

➤ **MAIL** • For poste restante address letters to: name, Post Office München 32, Poste Restante, München 80074. *Bahnhofpl. 1, tel. 089/5454–2732 or 089/5454–2733. Open 24 hrs.*

➤ **MEDICAL AID** • There are **pharmacies** at Neuhauser Straße 8 (tel. 089/260–3021), Neuhauser Straße 53 (tel.089/226901), and Schützen Straße 12 (tel. 089/595423).

COMING AND GOING

➤ **BY PLANE** • The **Franz Josef Strauss Airport** is 28 km northeast of the city and is served by most major airlines. For **Lufthansa,** call 089/977–2544. For general flight information call 089/9752–1313. S-Bahn 8 links the airport with Munich's Hauptbahnhof.

➢ **BY TRAIN** • From Munich's **Hauptbahnhof,** west of the city center, destinations include Vienna (9/day, DM83), Paris (8/day, DM171), and Berlin (30/day, DM130). The Hauptbahnhof is the main hub for all local public transport: U-Bahn lines 1, 2, 4, and 5 run beneath the station. For train info and reservations, try the chaotic **Reisezentrum** office across from Track 26. Or ring 089/19419 for info in English. The **Ostbahnhof** (East Train Station) sometimes serves as a train departure point, but it's mainly just an S-Bahn stop.

➢ **BY BUS** • **Europabus,** which also operates under the name **Touring** (in the Hauptbahnhof, tel. 089/5918–2425), offers service throughout Europe, excluding Austria and Switzerland. Destinations include: Berlin (DM66), Paris (DM100), and Prague (DM57). If you have a EurailPass or a German DB rail pass, you can ride free on Europabus's Romantic Road service, which begins in Füssen and ends in Frankfurt, with stops in Munich.

➢ **BY MITFAHRGELEGENHEIT** • **Mitfahrzentrale.** Call two to seven days in advance for info about possible rides. *Lämmerstr. 4, opposite north entrance of Hauptbahnhof, tel. 089/594561.*

Frauenmitfahrzentrale. This agency matches female drivers with female passengers. *Klenzestr. 57B, tel. 089/201–6510.*

GETTING AROUND Downtown Munich—the *Stadtzentrum* to locals—is easy to explore on foot, and sights outside the city center can be reached on Munich's excellent subway system. The Hauptbahnhof sits on the western border of the center, its front entrance facing the beginning of the main pedestrian zone, which changes names three times: from Schützenstraße to Neuhauserstraße to Kaufingerstraße. Following this crowded shopping venue leads you to the busy Karlsplatz (also known as Stachus) and on to **Marienplatz,** the heart of the city. North of the center are the **university district** and lively **Schwabing,** once a flourishing artists' quarter and now full of yuppies and outdoor cafés. The main strip cutting through the area is Ludwigstraße, which turns into Leopoldstraße past the university. The **Isar River** cuts through the city, forming camping, barbecue, and nude-sunbathing strips along its way. Cross the river at the Ludwigsbrücke to reach the heart of **Haidhausen,** a peaceful right-bank district with international and alternative restaurants, cafés, bars, and crowds, all pretty much undiscovered by tourists. If you need a **cab,** call 089/21610.

➢ **BY U-BAHN AND S-BAHN** • Together, the U-Bahn and S-Bahn cover the city well; tickets for all public transportation cost DM2.50 for two hours, as long as you travel only in one direction and stay within one zone (zones are indicated on maps at all stops). A book of 12 tickets costs DM14; cross off two tickets for each zone you pass through. A day pass costs DM10.

➢ **BY BIKE** • You can rent bikes for DM5 per hour or DM25 per day from **Radius Touristik** (Hauptbahnhof, tel. 089/596113), at the **Englischer Garten** (entrance at Veterinärstr. and Königinstr., tel. 089/282500; open 10–7 in good weather), or at some S-Bahn stations. Pick up a copy of *Radl-Touren,* a booklet with suggested biking tours, at the tourist office.

WHERE TO SLEEP The area around the Hauptbahnhof—an amalgamation of sex shops, electronics stores, and hotels—is a convenient base for exploring the city, but is also one of the seediest parts of town. Both the university district and Schwabing are great for young people and nightlife; in the latter neighborhood, the 10 comfortable rooms of **Pension am Kaiserplatz** (Kaiserpl. 12, tel. 089/349190; doubles DM75) are super-cheap and near some good nightlife, but phone reservations usually are not accepted. In any area, expect to pay DM40–DM50 for a single or DM75–DM100 for a double, sometimes including breakfast and/or showers. To save yourself a headache, reserve in advance for summer, or arrive early at the tourist office (*see* Visitor Information, *above*) to book a private room.

➢ **NEAR THE HAUPTBAHNHOF** • **Pension Augsburg.** Cheap, plain pension three minutes from station. Three-flight climb to reception. Doubles from DM70. *Schillerstr. 18, tel. 089/597673.*

Pension Hungaria. In mellow neighborhood north of Hauptbahnhof. Sunny rooms at reasonable rates: doubles DM80–DM85. *Brienner Str. 42, near Augustenstr., tel. 089/521558. Exit Hauptbahnhof to Dachauerstr., turn right on Augustenstr.*

Pension Luna. Large rooms with carpet and snazzy furniture. Doubles DM90, including breakfast and shower. *Landwehrstr. 5, tel. 089/597833. From Hauptbahnhof turn right on Schillerstr., left on Landwehrstr.*

Pension Schiller. Small pension run by pleasant proprietress right by the Augsburg. Spacious rooms. Doubles DM75 or DM70 for stays over three nights. *Schillerstr. 11, tel. 089/592435.*

➤ **CITY CENTER • Hotel Atlanta.** The management actually likes backpackers. Shower or bath in every room, all-you-can-eat breakfast buffet included. Doubles DM80–DM160. *Sendlingerstr. 58, tel. 089/263605. U1 or U2 to Sendlinger Tor, exit at Sendlingerstr., pass through old arch.*

Hotel-Pension Beck. Sleek rooms, prime location. Checkout at 10:30, with some exceptions for late nights at the Hofbräuhaus. Doubles DM90–DM120. *Thierschstr. 36, tel. 089/225768. Tram 19, 20, or 27 from Hauptbahnhof to Maxmonument (on Maximilianstr.).*

Pension Diana. Newly renovated pension off main pedestrian drag. Doubles DM100. *Altheimer Eck 15, tel. 089/260–3107. From Hauptbahnhof, turn right off Neuhauser onto Eisenmannstr., left at Altheimer Eck.*

Pension Theresia. Simple, unassuming pension, and easy to find. Doubles from DM80. *Luisenstr. 51, tel. 089/521250. U2 to Theresienstr., exit at SO AUGUSTENSTR., walk straight, turn right on Luisenstr.*

➤ **HOSTELS • CVJM (YMCA) Jugendgästehaus.** Prices lowest when you stay more than three nights. Adjoining restaurant serves dinner and free breakfast. Singles DM45, doubles DM40 per person. *Landwehrstr. 13, tel. 089/552–1410. From Hauptbahnhof, turn right on Schillerstr., left on Landwehrstr. 12:30 AM curfew.*

DJH Jugendherberge (HI). Easy walk to Hauptbahnhof, but noisy. Brace yourself for 7 AM wake-up call. Building A is nicer than B or C, if you have a choice. Lock your stuff in safety boxes. Reservations required, three-night max stay. Beds DM20. *Wendel-Dietrich-Str. 20, tel. 089/131156 or 089/167–8745. 1 AM curfew, lockout 8:30–noon.*

Jugendherberge Pullach (HI). Castle-turned-hostel is worth a try if you can't get a place in one of the more central hostels. Only people under 27 are accommodated. Beds DM15, sheets DM4.50. *Burgweg 4–6, tel. 089/793–0643. S7 to Pullach, then climb 10 min to castle. 11:30 curfew.*

Marienherberge. Women only. Safe, clean, and cheap, though in sleazy part of town. Beds DM25, singles DM31. *Goethestr. 9, tel. 089/555805 or 089/555891. Exit train station at Bayerstr. Midnight curfew, laundry facilities, kitchen.*

Youth Hostel Thalkirchen. Under 27 only. Beds DM25, singles DM35, doubles DM30 per person, including bed and breakfast. *Miesingstr. 4, tel. 089/723–6550. U1 or U2 to Sendlinger Tor, then U3 to Thalkirchen.*

➤ **CAMPGROUNDS • Camping München-Thalkirchen.** Munich's most central and crowded campground, 4 km from center. Sites DM5.50 per person, DM5.50 per tent. *Zentralländstr. 49, tel. 089/723–1707. U3 to Thalkirchen (Tierpark), then Bus 57 to last stop. Closed Nov.–early Mar.*

Kapuziner Hölzl. Enthusiasts call this oversize circus tent "Germany's Biggest Slumber Party." A spot with blankets and mats, plus a hot shower, just DM6 per night. *Franz-Schrank-Str., tel. 089/141–4300. U1 to Rotkreuzpl., then Tram 12 to Botanischer Garten. Lockout 9–5. Closed Sept.–June.*

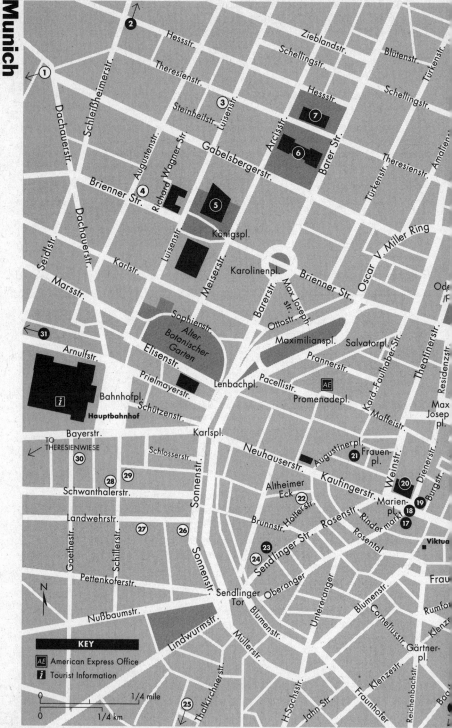

Hessstr.

Zieblandstr.

Schellingstr.

Blütenstr.

Türkenstr.

Theresienstr.

Schellingstr.

Hessstr.

Steinheilstr.

Luisenstr.

Arcisstr.

Theresienstr.

Türkenstr.

Amalien

Gabelsbergerstr.

Barer Str.

Augustenstr.

Richard Wagner Str.

Brienner Str.

Königspl.

Luisenstr.

Meiserstr.

Karolinenpl.

Oscar v. Miller Ring

Barerstr.

Brienner Str.

Ode

Dachauerstr.

Schleißheimerstr.

Seidlstr.

Karlstr.

Dachauerstr.

Marsstr.

Sophienstr.

Alter
Botanischer
Garten

Elisenstr.

Lenbachpl.

Max Joseph str.

Ottostr.

Maximilianspl.

Salvatorpl.

Prannerstr.

Pacellistr.

Promenadepl.

Kard.-Faulhaber-Str.

Maffeistr.

Theatinerstr.

Residenzstr.

Max
Josep
pl.

Arnulfstr.

Prielmayerstr.

Bahnhofpl.

Schützenstr.

Hauptbahnhof

i

Bayerstr.

TO
THERESIENWIESE

Schwanthalerstr.

Landwehrstr.

Goethestr.

Schillerstr.

Pettenkoferstr.

Nußbaumstr.

Schlosserstr.

Sonnenstr.

Karlspl.

Neuhauserstr.

Augustinerpl.

Frauen-
pl.

Kaufingerstr.

Weinstr.

Dienerstr.

Burgstr.

Marien-
pl.

Altheimer
Eck

Brunnstr.

Hotterstr.

Rosenstr.

Rindermarkt

Rosental

Sendlinger Str.

Sendlinger
Tor

Oberanger

Blumenstr.

Müllerstr.

Untereranger

Lindwurmstr.

Thalkirchnerstr.

H.-Sachsstr.

Jahn Str.

Fraunhofer

Reichenbachstr.

Klenzestr.

Corneliusstr.

Gärtner-
pl.

Blumenstr.

Rumfo

Frau

Viktua

Viktua

N

KEY

AE American Express Office

i Tourist Information

0   1/4 mile

0   1/4 km

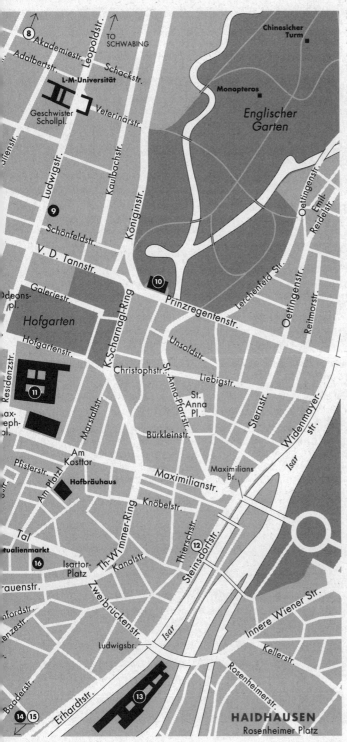

Sights ●

Alte Pinakothek, **6**

Altes Rathaus, **19**

Asamkirche, **23**

BMW Museum, **2**

Deutsches
Museum, **13**

Frauenkirche, **21**

Glyptothek, **5**

Haus der Kunst, **10**

Ludwigskirche, **9**

Marienplatz, **18**

Neue Pinakothek, **7**

Neues Rathaus, **20**

Peterskirche, **17**

Residenz, **11**

Schloß
Nymphenburg, **31**

Tierpark
Hellabrunn, **14**

Z.A.M., **16**

Lodging ○

CVJM Jugendgäste-
haus, **27**

DJH
Jugendherberge
(HI), **1**

Hotel Atlanta, **24**

Hotel-Pension
Beck, **12**

Jugendherberge
Pullach, **15**

Marienherberge, **30**

Pension am
Kaiserplatz, **8**

Pension
Augsburg, **28**

Pension Diana, **22**

Pension Hungaria, **4**

Pension Luna, **26**

Pension Schiller, **29**

Pension Theresia, **3**

Youth Hostel
Thalkirchen, **25**

FOOD Munich is the place to dabble in Bavarian specialties; some of the best are bratwurst (grilled or fried pork sausages), *Leberkäs* (warm slabs of ground beef, bacon, and pork served with sweet mustard), *Obatzta* (cheese mixed with chopped onions, egg yolk, paprika, and other spices), *Radi* (thinly sliced white radish, dipped in salt and often eaten as a snack in a beer garden), and *Dampfnudeln* (sweet dumplings in vanilla sauce).

Some of the best budget eating options include butcher shops for premade sandwiches (DM3–DM5.50) and sometimes salad bars; university cafeterias—try the ones at Leopoldstraße 13 and Arcisstraße 17—where a meal costs DM2.70–DM4; and chain restaurants, especially Bella Italia, Café Rischart, Münchner Suppenküche, and Wienerwald. All are open daily 10 AM–1 AM. The colorful **Viktualienmarkt,** Munich's best-known open-air food market, is held Monday–Saturday on the square where public executions took place during the Middle Ages. If you like beer with your food, the university area has lots of smoky, relatively cheap student pubs. The best is **Gaststätte Engelsburg** (Türkenstr. 51), with pizzas and Bavarian food for DM9–DM15.

➤ **CITY CENTER • Fraunhofer.** Lively, untouristy restaurant with adjoining theater. Earthy intellectuals socialize and drink over hearty meals (DM8–DM12) both vegetarian and porky. *Fraunhoferstr. 9, tel. 089/266460. No lunch.*

Straubinger Hof. Inexpensive, crowded Bavarian restaurant next to Viktualienmarkt. Filling meals for under DM10. *Blumenstr. 5, tel. 089/260–8444. Closed Sun.*

Zum Franziskaner. Expensive but excellent pastas and vegetarian dishes (DM12–DM16) and wursts (DM7–DM13). *Residenzstr. 9, opposite Residenz palace, tel. 089/231–8120.*

➤ **HAIDHAUSEN • El Español.** Splurge on fish dishes (DM19–DM32) or snack on tapas (Spanish hors d'oeuvres, starting at DM3 apiece). Live serenades some nights 9–10. *Pariser Str. 46, tel. 089/488496. No lunch.*

Haidhausen Augustiner. Restaurant-bar with huge menu and killer daily specials of the salad and pasta variety. *Wörthstr. 34. tel. 089/480–2594.*

Kytaro. Munich's best-known Greek restaurant isn't cheap. Lots of smoke, occasional live bands. Lamb dishes DM15–DM20. *Innere Wiener Str. 36, tel. 089/480–1176. No lunch.*

➤ **CAFES •** Many of Munich's cafés double as bars and evening hangouts, especially on Leopoldstraße (*see* After Dark, *below*). **Baader Café** (Baaderstr. 47, tel. 089/201–0638) swings at night and may be the only place in Munich where you can get a real BLT (DM7). Supposedly, the Communists who briefly took power in Munich in the 1920s loved **Café Größenwahn** (Lothringerstr. 11, tel. 089/448–5035). **Café Im Stadtmuseum** (St.-Jakobspl. 1, tel. 089/266949) attracts lots of students and artsy types.

Beer Is Good for What Ales You

In Bavaria, beer is cheaper than water, is consumed by the liter, and is often brewed by monks and nuns. It's also protected by the world's most ancient food-purity law, which hasn't changed since 1516. According to the decree, issued by Duke Wilhelm IV, only the purest ingredients—water, hops, yeast, and barley—are acceptable for the fine art of beer brewing. The only exception is made for the delicious, light "Weißbier," in which wheat is substituted for barley. When ordering the standard pale beer, ask for a "Helles"; for dark beer, "Dunkles". And don't forget to try the tasty beer-and-lemonade concoction called "Radler". And just so you know, a "Maß", equivalent to about one U.S. quart, is the standard measure of beer in Bavaria.

➤ **BEER GARDENS** • To keep their kegs cool during hot summers, brewers used to store them under shady chestnut trees. This practice evolved into the beer garden, where everyone shares long tables and laps up liters during dragging summer days. At most gardens, you can bring your own snacks or buy a pre-prepared meal. When the weather permits, gardens stay open from 9 or 10 AM to 10 or 11 PM.

Munich's infamous **Hofbräuhaus** (Am Platzl 9, tel. 089/221676) doesn't need much explanation: "American Frat Boys Take Over Local Beer Pub" is how most locals see it, and if you're hoping to run into some fellow backpacker you last saw in the Greek Islands or Amsterdam, welcome. That said, you haven't "done" Munich without coming here to down at least one mammoth stein. More authentic is **Max Emanuel Bräuerei** (Adalbertstr. 33, tel. 089/271–5158), in the university district. It has meals starting at DM8.50, plus the hottest, freshest, plumpest pretzels around (DM2). About the cheapest beer you'll find in Munich is at **Viktualienmarkt Biergarten;** squeeze in with the locals in the center of the Viktualienmarkt. Although farther from the center and pretty expensive, **Waldwirtschaft Großhesselohe** (George-Kalb-Str. 3, tel. 089/795088) features live jazz on weekends and is beautifully situated on the bank of the Isar.

WORTH SEEING Altes Rathaus. In the eastern corner of Marienplatz, the Old Town Hall was destroyed in World War II but reconstructed in the 1950s according to the original 15th-century Gothic design. In its tower is the **Spielzeugmuseum** (Toy Museum, tel. 089/29400; admission DM4; open daily 10–5:30), exhibiting 200 years of European and American toys; too bad you can't play with any of them.

Frauenkirche. Construction of this late-Gothic brick church—which has become Munich's most famous cathedral—took only 20 years (1468–1488). The towers, added 75 years later, give good views and are worth the climb. *Frauenpl. Admission to tower: DM4, DM2 students. Open Apr.–Oct., Mon.–Sat. 10–5.*

Marienplatz. Bordering Munich's main square on the north is the **Neues Rathaus,** a neo-Gothic building constructed between 1867 and 1908. It's probably best known for the **Glockenspiel,** Europe's fourth-largest carillon. Every day at 11 AM and noon (also at 5 and 9, May–Oct.), tourists flock to see the mechanical figures spinning to folk-music chimes. For DM2, tower enthusiasts can make the 281-foot climb. *Open May–Oct., weekdays 9–7, weekends 10–7.*

Residenz. For more than six centuries the Residenz served as Munich's royal palace—that is, until the last Bavarian king, Ludwig III, abdicated in 1918, after which the palace was transformed into a museum. Catch the morning or afternoon tour, or guide yourself through the lavish rooms yourself. *Entrance at Max-Joseph-Pl. 3, tel. 089/290671. U3, U4, U5, or U6 to Odeonspl., or walk north on Dienerstr. from Marienpl. Admission: DM4, DM2.50 students. Open Tues.–Sun. 10–4:30.*

Schloß Nymphenburg. The Schloß was conceived in 1663 as a small summer villa by Prince Ferdinand Maria to placate his homesick Italian wife, Henriette. The opulent group of digs you see today includes the biggest Baroque palace in Germany. Check out Ludwig I's **Schönheiten Galerie** (Gallery of Beauties), which has 36 portraits, all painted by Joseph Stieler between 1827 and 1850. Afterwards, you could spend the whole day wandering the beautiful 500-acre **Nymphenburg Park,** lined with classically French gravel paths and low, excessively trimmed hedges. The **Amalienburg,** an 18th-century hunting lodge designed by Cuvilliés, is one of the finest examples of the Rococo style. *Tel. 089/179080. U1 to Rotkreuzpl., then Tram 12 to Schloß. Admission: DM6, DM5 students. Open Apr.–Sept., Tues.–Sun. 9–12:30 and 1:30–5; shorter hrs off-season. Wheelchair access.*

Tierpark Hellabrunn. Extending over 90 acres, Munich's world-famous zoo has enjoyed tremendous success in breeding endangered species. *Siebenbrunnerstr. 6. U3 to Thalkirchen. Admission: DM6. Open Apr.–Sept., daily 8–6; Oct.–Mar., daily 9–5.*

➤ **CHURCHES AND CHAPELS** • **Asamkirche.** This church, named for the two brothers who designed it, is modest on the outside, but open the door and you enter a Baroque, fresco-filled vision of paradise on earth. *Sendlingerstr. 62. Take U1, U2, U3, or U6 to Sendlinger Tor.*

Ludwigskirche. This curious neo-Byzantine/early Renaissance parish church's claim to fame is its mammoth fresco of the Last Judgment, second in size only to Michelangelo's version in the Sistine Chapel. *Ludwigstr. 22.*

Peterskirche. Labor up the 300 stairs in the 303-foot tower for a view of the city that extends as far as the Alps on a clear day. *Rindermarkt. Admission: DM2.50, DM1.50 students. Open Mon.–Sat. 9–6, Sun., holidays 10–6.*

➤ **MUSEUMS AND GALLERIES** • Many of Munich's museums are closed Monday but open late one or two nights each week, and most offer student discounts with the ISIC card. State-run museums are free on Sunday. The ultracool, high-tech **BMW Museum** (Petuelring 130, tel. 089/3895–3306) uses videos, slides, and its gorgeous collection of cars, engines, and cycles to chronicle the development of Bayeriches Motoren Werke (Bavarian Motor Works). Book ahead for a tour, given weekdays at 9:30 and 1:15. Together, the **Glyptothek** (Königspl. 3, tel. 089/286100; admission DM5, DM1 students) and the **State Collection of Antiquities** comprise Germany's largest collection of classical art. The **Münchner Stadtmuseum** (Munich City Museum, St.-Jakobs-Pl. 1, tel. 089/233–2370; admission DM5, DM2.50 students), a group of museums housed together in a Gothic arsenal, traces the history of Munich through a unique collection of diverse artifacts. The **Staatliche Graphische Sammlung** (Studiensaal Meiserstr. 10, tel. 089/559–1490) has 300,000 Western drawings and graphics from the 14th through 20th centuries, including works by Dürer and Rembrandt. The **Zentrum für Aussergewöhnliche Museen** (Westenriderstr. 26, tel. 089/290–4121; admission DM8, DM5 students) includes the world's first museums devoted to the pedal car, the chamber pot, the corkscrew, the lock, and the Easter Bunny.

Alte Pinakothek. Ranking among the top six picture galleries in the world, the Alte Pinakothek houses some 800 works from the dominant European schools of the 14th–18th centuries. It's particularly respected for its Flemish Baroque collection—more than 80 Rubenses and 40 van Eycks. *Barer Str. 27, tel. 089/2380–5215. U2 to Königspl. Admission: DM6, DM1 students. Open Tues.–Sun. 9:15–4:30, Tues. and Thurs. also 7–9.*

Deutsches Museum. This museum of science and technology is the largest of its kind in the world. Among the 16,000 items on display are the first Mercedes-Benz, the original airplanes of the Wright brothers, and tons of hands-on gadgets. *Museuminsel 1, tel. 089/21791. Tram 18 to Deutsches Museum. Admission: DM8, DM3 students, DM2 extra for planetarium. Open daily 9–5.*

Museum of Erotic Art. Displays include erotic scrolls, cartoons, stamps, postcards, and a collection of eroticized everyday objects. The collection of aphrodisiacs includes powdered rhino horn, which supposedly costs DM40,000 per kilogram. *Odeonspl. 8, 2nd Floor, tel. 089/228–3544. U4 to Odeonspl. Admission: DM8, DM6 students. Open Tues.–Sun. 11–7.*

Neue Pinakothek. Across the street from the Alte Pinakothek (*see above*), this gallery features European art of the 18th–20th centuries. Highlights include the collection of French impressionism and the rooms for social realism and German impressionism. *Barer Str. 29, entrance on Theresienstr., tel. 089/2380–5195. U2 to Theresienstr. Admission: DM6, DM1 students, free Sun. Open Tues.–Sun. 9:15–4:30, Tues. also 7–9.*

Haus der Kunst. This pillared, neoclassical building houses the *Staatsgalerie Moderner Kunst* (State Gallery of Modern Art) in its west wing. The gallery, which displays works representing all the major art movements of the 20th century, is ranked among the top 10 modern-art galleries in the world. *Prinzregentenstr. 1, tel. 089/292710. U4 or U5 to Lehel. Admission: DM3.50, free Sun. Open Tues.–Sun. 9:15–4:30, Thurs. also 7–9.*

AFTER DARK Pick up a free copy of *München Life,* available at many hotels, for comprehensive listings of theater, music, and film venues. If you want to find a really good beer hall or bar, cruise the very cool and somewhat expensive strip **Occamstraße,** in Schwabing. **Tomate** (Siegesstr. 19) and **Schwabinger Podium** (Wagner Str. 1), opposite one another, pack in a mishmash of Germans and Americans; beers start at about DM5.50.

➢ **CINEMA** • Look for the designations "OF" and "OmU," which mean "original language" and "original language with subtitles," respectively. Otherwise, **Cinema** (Nymphenburgerstr. 31, tel. 089/555255; U1 to Stiglmaierpl.), **Türkendolch** (Türkenstr. 74, tel. 089/271–8844), and **Neues Arena Filmtheater** (Hans-Sachs-Str. 7, tel. 089/260–3265) show some films in English.

➢ **DANCING** • If you're feeling especially fashionable, try the disco **Babalu** (Leopoldstr. 19), the utterly pretentious **Park-Café** (Sophienstr. 7), **P-1** (Prinzregentenstr. 1), or the immensely popular café and jazz bar **Nachtcafé** (Maximianspl. 5). For these clubs, your best chance of gaining admission is to arrive well-dressed with a good-looking partner. More mellow—and young—is **Far Out** (Am Karlstor 2). The Latin dance parties and Irish theme parties at **Max Emanuel Bräuerei** (Adalbertstr. 33) are a blast every night, and the DM8 cover includes a drink.

➢ **JAZZ AND ROCK** • Jazz gigs are popular but expensive, though **Shamrock** (Trautenwolfstr. 6, tel. 089/331081) and **The Dubliner** (Candidpl. 9, tel. 089/655676) pack 'em in with live music—usually Irish bands—for free. Come to the intimate Munich favorite **Allotria** (Oskar von Miller Ring 3 at Gabelsberger, tel. 089/285858; cover from DM8) to hear great jazz and funky fusion bands. The small **Novak's Schwabinger Brettl** (Occamstr. 11, tel. 089/347289; cover DM5) features great blues bands. If you're a jazz junkie, you'll dig **Unterfahrt** (Kirchenstr. 96, tel. 089/448–2794). The best deal is the jam session every Sunday at 9 PM for DM5.

➢ **GAY AND LESBIAN CLUBS** • A large number of gay and lesbian bars, cafés, and clubs are concentrated between Isartor and Sendlingertor, particularly around Gärtnerplatz and on Hans-Sachs-Straße. Friday and Saturday nights are gay at **Alcatraz** (Thalkirchnerstr. 2, tel. 089/260–8403); during the week it's theme nights ('70s, subterranean, etc.) and mostly straight. **Club New York** (Sonnenstr. 25, tel. 089/591056; cover DM13) admits men only and has great dance music and decor. The women-only **Nümfe** café (Nymphenburgerstr. 182) is a good resource for lesbians and serves food at fair prices.

➢ **CLASSICAL MUSIC** • Consult the *Monatsprogramm* for detailed listings of all concerts and theater. Students with I.D. cards can get deals on first-rate operas and symphonies by getting in line an hour before the show. Or try **Studiosus-Reisen** (Amalienstr. 73, tel. 089/280768) for discounted tickets. As for venues, the **Bayerische Staatsoper Nationaltheater** (Max-Joseph-Pl., tel. 089/221316) features ballet and opera; the **Staatstheater am Gärtnerplatz** (Gärtnerpl. 3, tel. 089/201–6767) offers opera, as well as musicals and operettas. Ballet and musicals play at the **Deutsches Theater** (Schwanthalerstr. 13, tel. 089/514–4360). Top-notch classical concerts take place in one of three halls in the **Gasteig Cultural Center** (Rosenheimerstr. 5, tel. 089/480980). The favorite place to see a variety of theater is **Münchner Kammerspiele-Schauspielhaus** (Maximilianstr. 26, tel. 089/2372–1268).

Drinking on the Cheap

Many breweries, such as Löwenbräu (Nymphenburgerstr. 2, tel. 089/52000) and Paulaner-Salvator (Hochstr. 75, tel. 089/4800–5307) offer free guided tours that end with free steins of frothy cold beer. Most of the breweries, however, close in August. From the middle of September to the first week of October, during Munich's world-famous Oktoberfest, it's easy to drink your fill for free.

NEAR MUNICH

DACHAU Although the 1,200-year-old town of Dachau attracted hordes of painters and artists from the mid-19th century until World War I, most people remember it as the site of Germany's first **concentration camp.** Opened in 1933, the camp greeted more than 206,000 political dissidents, Jews, clergy, and other "enemies" of the Nazis with the promise that "Arbeit Macht Frei" (Work Brings Freedom). The camp's watchtowers and walls remain, and the gas chambers, disguised as showers, are also original. The chambers were never actually used, but more than 32,000 prisoners died here before American soldiers captured the camp in 1945. Through photographs, letters, and official documents, the **museum** (open Tues.–Sun. 9–5) chronicles the rise of the Third Reich and the vicious working and living conditions endured by the camp's prisoners. The **tourist center** (Konrad-Adenauer-Str. 3, tel. 08131/84566) is in the center of town. To reach the camp from Munich, take S-Bahn 2 toward Petershausen to Dachau (about 20 min). From here, take Bus 722 to Gedenkstätte, the camp memorial, or Bus 710 to Dachau's city center, filled with restaurants and beer halls.

Bavaria  Sprawled across some 70,200 square km, Bavaria's diverse, romantic landscape beckons to outdoorsy folks, history freaks, and those who still believe in fairy tales. Its four main cities—Nürnberg (in the northern region known as Franconia), Augsburg (in the western region of Bavarian Swabia), Regensburg (in East Bavaria), and Munich (*see above*)—are also historic and cultural giants, making a trip to Bavaria diverse, educational, and potentially very, very long. Bavaria was ruled by the royal Wittelsbach Dynasty for seven centuries, beginning in 1180 as a duchy presented to Otto von Wittelsbach by the emperor Barbarossa, and ending in the turbulent post–World War I period with the forced abdication of the last Wittelsbach monarch, King Ludwig III. Although the Prussian military and political strategist Otto von Bismarck yanked the land from Ludwig, incorporating it into his Confederation of Northern German States, Bavaria held steadfastly to its distinct traditions and dialect. Even to this day, Bavarians persist in calling it the Free State of Bavaria.

Northerners—the so-called Prussians—consider Bavarians too provincial and loud, whereas Bavarians describe northerners as stuffy and boring. Northerners will sternly remind you that Bavaria is *not* Germany in a nutshell. But nobody can deny that the most common images of the country—lederhosen, brass bands, beer gardens, castles, and Oktoberfest—originated in this state. Its contradictions make it the ideal place to look for all that you expect, hope for, and dread from Germany: It's got the scenery, the castles, the lingering legacy of Nazism, the Alps, beer (boy, does it have beer), and history. The one bummer is that Bavarian youth hostels rarely accommodate people 27 and older.

Augsburg

Augsburg is about history—touring the staunch city gates or a craftperson's centuries-old workshop, or just wandering the town's cobbled streets. Augsburg was founded in 15 BC by Drusus and Tiberius, stepsons of the Roman Emperor Augustus, and it is the oldest city in Bavaria. During the 16th century its ambitious merchant families sought out markets as far away as South America. The most famous of these well-to-do clans were the Fuggers, under whose patronage Augsburg flourished. Today a healthy student population and loads of cultural events keep Augsburg from getting stale. Despite business and industrial districts, the old town manages to preserve an honest Renaissance flavor, making it a popular destination on the Romantic Road (*see below*).

VISITOR INFORMATION The **tourist office** (Bahnhofstr. 7, tel. 0821/502070) near the train station is open weekdays 9–6, Saturday 9–1. A better bet is the **Tourist Center** (tel. 0821/502–0724; open weekdays 9–6, Sat. 10–6, Sun. 10–1) across from the Rathaus; it stocks the invaluable *Radwegskarte,* a map of bicycle routes, plus the English-language pamphlet *See and Enjoy,* which lists open hours and walking tours.

COMING AND GOING From Augsburg there are frequent trains to Munich (40 min, DM15) and Regensburg (2½ hrs, DM46). To reach the center from the Hauptbahnhof, head east down Bahnhofstraße and veer left onto Anna Straße. You'll soon reach the heart of the city, Rathausplatz. Maximilianstraße cuts north–south through the center of town, and barely anything worth a look is not far off it. Walking around is a cinch, but if you prefer to pedal, the station rents **bikes** for DM8 per day. Hook up with a car pool to other German and European cities through **Mitfahrzentrale Augsburg** (Branderstr. 36, tel. 0821/414655 or 0821/418529).

WHERE TO SLEEP Rooms in decently located hotels and guest houses start at DM35 (singles) and DM65 (doubles). Try **Jakoberhof** (Jakoberstr. 39–41, tel. 0821/510030; doubles DM65–DM125), a simple but comfy guest house near the Fuggerei. **Lenzhalde** (Theilottstr. 2, tel. 0821/520745; doubles DM75) is just behind the train station, while **Hotel-Pension Georgsrast** (Georgenstr. 39, tel. 0821/502610; doubles DM100–DM110) is past the Dom at the northern end of the city center. Campers should head for **Campingplatz Augusta** (tel. 0821/714121), in the direction of Neuburg at Autobahnsee, or **Campingplatz Ludwigshof** (tel. 08207/1077; closed Nov.–Mar.), near the district of Mühlhausen.

Augsburg's busy **HI hostel**—a three-minute walk from the Dom—is the cheapest and easiest place to crash. Only hostelers under 27 are accommodated. Beds DM16, sheets DM5. *Beim Pfaffenkeller 3, tel. 0821/33909. Tram 2 to Stadtwerke, walk toward Dom and turn right on Inneres Pfaffengäßchen. Closed Dec. 20–Jan. 20.*

FOOD Street stands line Rathausplatz and nearby Maximilianstraße. For fresh produce, meats, and cheeses, check out the **Stadtmarkt,** open weekdays 7–6, Saturday 7–noon. Enter the market from Fuggerstraße, Annastraße, or Ernst Reuter Platz.

König von Flandern. Get free, fresh homemade bread with every ⅓ liter of home-brewed beer (DM4). Small food menu but friendly price. Ramble left down the road outside to join Augsburg's night café scene. *Karolinenstr. 12, tel. 0821/158050.*

Nuova Italia. Cheap Italian food and mellow student clientele. Slices DM3.50, pastas DM7 and up. *Maximilianstr. 17, tel. 0821/152881.*

WORTH SEEING Augsburg may be a large city, but its historic Altstadt is reasonably compact and easily covered on foot. East of the tourist office is the 14th-century **St. Annakirche** (Anna Str.), Augsburg's most important Protestant church (Martin Luther once lectured in Room 5). Near the northern end of Anna Straße, **Rathausplatz** marks the historic heart of Augsburg. The square is dominated by the **Perlachturm** tower (admission DM2; open Apr.–Oct., daily 10–6), worth the climb for a good view of the city center. For a quick tour of Augsburg's medieval fortifications, head south along Maximilianstraße from Rathausplatz until you find the Obere Graben River. There you'll see the ancient city wall, and if you follow the river south you'll soon stumble upon **Rotes Tor** (Red Gate), Augsburg's most impressive medieval gate.

Brechthaus. This modest house marks the birthplace of playwright Bertolt Brecht, a dramatic genius who grew up in Augsburg before moving on to Munich, New York, and finally Los Angeles. *Auf dem Rain 7, 3 blocks northwest of Rathauspl. Admission: DM2, DM1 students. Open Tues.–Sun. 10–5.*

Dom St. Maria. The western part of this domineering cathedral comprises a Romanesque basilica originally built in the 11th century. The Dom's real draw, however, is the art inside: Besides five fantastic altarpieces by Hans Holbein the Elder, there's a stunning cycle of stained glass that dates from the 11th century. *Open Mon.–Sat. 9–6, Sun. noon–6.*

Fuggerei. The Fuggerei, a 10-minute walk east of the city center, is the world's oldest social-housing scheme. This tranquil complex was originally built in 1519 by the Fugger family to accommodate the city's poor, and it continues to serve that purpose. As long as you're a native of Augsburg, Catholic, and destitute by no means of your own (i.e., no heroin fiends), one of these simple but comfortable homes can be yours for the low price of "one Rheinish Guilder," valued today at around DM1.72 annually. You can see an original apartment in the **Fuggerei Museum.** *Admission: DM2. Open Mar.–Oct., daily 9–6.*

AFTER DARK Once the sun sets, cruise down **Maximilianstraße** for a taste of Augsburg's lively café scene. **Café Max** (Maximilianstr. 67, tel. 0821/154700) and **Peaches** (Maximilianstr. 73, tel. 0821/312258) are especially popular. Augsburg's student pubs are concentrated around the alleys and streets behind the Rathaus. Heilig-Kreuz-Straße is another good place to check out; there you'll find the **Thorbräukeller** (Wertachbrucker-Tor-Str. 9, tel. 0821/510880), a beer garden favored by locals, and **Bodega** (Heilig-Kreuz-Str. 18, tel. 0821/37115), a Spanish bar west of the Dom.

Regensburg

Although it's actually on the Danube, Regensburg gets its name from the nearby Regen River. The Romans first established a fortress here in AD 179; at that time Haidplatz, west of the center, was used for tournaments. The fortress's northern gate, **Porta Praetoria** (on Under den Schwiböggen), is still standing. In subsequent centuries Regensburg became the first capital of Bavaria, a center of Christianity, a free Imperial City, the seat of the Imperial Diets, and a major hub of trade. Mostly spared by wartime bombings, Regensburg has managed to preserve no less than 1,400 historical monuments, making a walk around the city a visceral plunge into history. If you only have a day here, take a long walk and skip the museums entirely. Pick up a map from the helpful **tourist office** (Altes Rathaus, tel. 0941/507–4410; open weekdays 8:30–6, Sat. 9–4, Sun. 9–noon). Practically speaking, Regensburg's **Hauptbahnhof** sits just south of the center and shoos frequent trains to Munich (DM32) and Nürnberg (DM23).

WHERE TO SLEEP The few cheap hotels in town are very busy, so call ahead. Some reception desks are closed on Sunday or the whole weekend; you can't check in on these days, but you can stay through the weekend if you've already checked in during the week. Confusing, isn't it?

Diözesanzentrum Obermünster. Plain but immaculate rooms in former monastery near St. Emmeram Basilica. Singles from DM40, doubles from DM75. *Obermünsterpl. 7, tel. 0941/56810. Reception open Oct.–July, weekdays 7–6; Aug.–Sept., Mon.–Thurs. 7–4:30, Fri. 7–4.*

Hotel-Restaurant Peterhof. Despite old, seedy-looking facade, rooms are in decent shape and the adjoining restaurant is a good value. Between train station and city center. Singles DM50, doubles DM75. *Fröhliche-Turken-Str. 12, tel. 0941/57514 or 0941/58874.*

➢ **HOSTEL** • **Jugendherberge Regensburg.** On an island in the Danube, a short bus ride or a 30-minute walk from the train station. Bike rental DM5 per day. *Wöhrdstr. 60, tel. 0941/57402. Bus 17 from station to Eisstadion. Or walk down Maximilianstr., cross Danube at Eiserne Brucke, and turn right at Werftstr., left at Am Wiriterhafen, and right on Wöhrdstr. 11:30 curfew.*

FOOD Fruits and veggies fill the stalls at **Donaumarkt** (near Hunnenpl.) every Saturday 6–noon. Earlier risers can catch the **Alter Kornmarkt,** in a plaza by the same name near the cathedral, which has an equally rich selection of fruits and vegetables, open daily 5 AM–8 AM. If you're sick of meat, head for **Antagon** (Rote-Hahnen-Gaße 2, tel. 0941/54661), a vegetarian bar/restaurant that stays open until 1 AM. The **Hofbräuhaus** (Waaggäßchenl., tel. 0941/51280; closed Sun.) is best for inexpensive snacks like wurst (DM5) and beer (from DM3).

WORTH SEEING Altes Rathaus. Visit the interior of the old town hall on a guided tour (DM1.50 students) of the **Reichstag Museum.** You'll see the Imperial Hall, where the country's decision makers congregated up until 1506, and some gruesomely creative torture devices. *Admission: DM3, DM1.50 students. Tours Mon.–Sat. 9:30–noon and 2–4, Sun. and holidays 10–noon; English-language tour in summer at 3:15.*

Museum Ostdeutsche Galerie. This gallery in the Stadtpark has a unique collection of 19th- and 20th-century eastern German art, plus changing exhibits. *Dr.-Johann-Maier-Str. 5, tel. 0941/22031. Admission: DM2.50, DM1 students. Open Tues.–Thurs. and Sat. 10–4, Fri. and Sun. 10–1.*

Schloß der Fürsten von Thurn und Taxis. This converted palace is the home of the Thurn and Taxis princes, a family (currently believed to be the richest in Germany) that came to Regensburg in the 16th century. Parts of the palace are open to the public, including the **Meios Museum,** one of Europe's largest collections of sleds, coaches, and harnesses. *Obermünsterstr. Admission: DM2.50.*

St. Peter's Cathedral. This church is widely considered Bavaria's most outstanding example of Gothic architecture. Built over a period of six centuries, it chronicles the development of German Gothic architecture; check out the different tower styles and colors of stone used. The Domspatzen, the famous boys' choir, performs Sunday mass at 9 AM. *Domplatz. Admission: DM2.50.*

AFTER DARK Start your night at Regensburg's largest beer garden, **Kneitinger Keller** (Galgenbergstr. 18, tel. 0941/76680), or the **Spitalgarten** (St.-Katharinenpl. 1, tel. 0941/84774), which overlooks the Danube from across the Steinerne Bridge. The chic discos **Scala** (Gesandtenstr. 6, tel. 0941/52293; cover DM3–DM7; open Wed. and Sat.) and **Sudhaus** (Untere Bachgasse 8, tel. 0941/51946), which usually has gay night on Thursdays, are by far the most popular. The crowded pub **Irish Harp** (Brückstr. 1, tel. 0941/57268) has live music; also try Keplerstraße for some solid bars.

Passau

With its Italian-influenced architecture and sublime location at the confluence at three major rivers, Passau far exceeds the typical quaintness of Bavarian towns—you might even call it beautiful. Although the town is small enough to see in a day, Passau is one of the few towns in Bavaria with the attractive appeal of a Venice or Budapest. The forest-green Danube, flowing from the Black Forest; the milky-green Inn, flowing down from the Swiss Alps; and the dark, murky Ilz, rising from the Bavarian Forest, gave Passau its nickname, Dreiflußstadt (Three River City).

VISITOR INFORMATION *Rathauspl. 3, tel. 0851/33421. Open Apr.–Oct., weekdays 8:30–6, weekends and holidays 10–2; Nov.–Mar., weekdays 8:30–5.*

COMING AND GOING Passau has frequent train and bus connections to Munich, Regensburg, and the Bavarian Forest. For **train information** call 0851/55001. You can also cruise to a number of cities in Austria from Passau: A trip to Linz, for example, costs DM35. Check the tourist office or kiosks along the river for schedules.

WHERE TO SLEEP You may have a hard time finding budget accommodations near Passau's center unless you snag a room at the cheap and central guest house, **Gasthof Zum Hirschen** (Im Ort 6, tel. 0851/362–3812; doubles from DM55). Passau's **HI hostel,** in a 13th-century castle, is a pain to reach, but at least you get a great view. Beds DM16, sheets DM5. *Veste Oberhaus 125, tel. 0851/41351. Bus 1, 2, or 3 to Ilzbrücke, or cross the Danube at Luifpoldbrücke and hike up. 11:30 curfew.*

FOOD Passau's the kind of place that inspires you to dangle your legs over the Danube with a friend as you pass a cheap bottle of wine, munch on sandwiches, and talk deep; try **Kleine Passauer Markthalle** on Ludwigstraße for all your picnic needs. Otherwise, **Pizzeria Angelina** (Brunngaße 2 off Ludwigstr., tel. 0851/33203) offers students and other cashless souls hefty, delicious pizzas and pasta dishes for only DM6–DM7. Overlooking the Inn River, **Café Innsteg** (Innstr. 15, tel. 0851/51257) doubles as a student pub at night and is ideal for an inexpensive meal, or just a beer. It's by the Fünferlsteg bridge to Innstadt.

WORTH SEEING The Gothic **Rathaus** (off Schrottgaße; admission DM1; open Easter–Oct., weekdays 10–noon and 1:30–4, weekends and holidays 10–4) was a private home until locals usurped it during an uprising in 1298. In the building's tower, Bavaria's largest **Glockenspiel** chimes daily at 10:30, 2, 7:25, and 9. It plays an extended concert every Saturday at 3:30 PM. West along the peninsula is **St. Stephan's Dom,** a church originally built in the 8th century, later converted to a Gothic cathedral, and finally rebuilt in its present Baroque style after two fires razed the city in the 17th century. Inside looms a 231-register, 17,388-pipe organ, the largest in the world; don't miss the weekday noon concerts (DM3).

Bavarian Alps

Stretching from the Bodensee in the west to Berchtesgaden in the east, the Bavarian Alps encompass famous castles, lakes, and mountains galore. Pictures of this area have graced the covers of many a tourist brochure, spreading pastoral Alpine scenes and country kitsch worldwide. Spring through fall, few non-German tourists hang out here, and the cozy towns are much cheaper, friendlier, and relaxing than nearby Munich. Sightseeing takes the backseat here to outdoor stuff like hiking, swimming, and skiing, but be warned that the weather is totally unpredictable; on a single hike you may encounter sun and fog and rain and other meteorological aberrations we haven't even thought of. Trains from Munich can get you to most of the main Alpine towns, but between towns you may have to use **RVO buses,** which accept EurailPass; InterRail holders get a 50% discount.

HOHENSCHWANGAU AND NEUSCHWANSTEIN

The **Hohenschwangau palace** (admission DM8, DM5 students; open Apr.–Oct., daily 8:30–5:30; Nov.–Mar., daily 10–4) is where Bavaria's famous king, Ludwig II, spent most of his childhood. Hohenschwangau was built by the knights of Schwangau in the 12th century, in a heavy Romanesque style, and both the exterior and the interior are worth a look. But if you really want to be dazzled, walk 20 minutes northeast; you won't be able to miss King Ludwig's so-called Fairy-tale Castle, **Neuschwanstein** (admission DM8, DM5 students; open Apr.–Sept., daily 8:30–5:30; Oct.–Mar., daily 10–4). Set atop a hill in the middle of a small forest, Neuschwanstein looks like something straight out of a storybook. It has towers and gates and battlements and courtyards and gables and spires and lookouts and spiral stairways and just about everything a proper castle should have. And that's because Neuschwanstein isn't simply *a* castle, it's *the* castle. Even Walt Disney used Neuschwanstein as a model for the castle in *Sleeping Beauty,* and later as a model for the Disneyland castle in his theme parks. The castle grounds are also spellbinding; spend some time rambling through the surrounding forest, and be sure to cross **Marienbrücke,** a giddy span that covers a deep, narrow gorge. From this vantage point, there are mind-numbing views of the Upper Bavarian plain beyond.

BASICS The easiest way to get to the two castles is from **Füssen,** a town within 5 km of each. From there, you can walk or take one of a number of buses. To give yourself enough time (especially at Neuschwanstein, where the lines can be heinous), stay at Füssen's **HI hostel** (Mariahilferstr. 15, tel. 08362/7754; under 26 only; beds DM18, including breakfast; closed Nov. 1–Dec. 15).

GARMISCH-PARTENKIRCHEN

Part of a larger region known as Werdenfelser Land, Garmisch-Partenkirchen sits gloating at the foot of the craggy Wetterstein mountains and at the juncture of the Partnach and Loisach rivers. Despite five casinos, the biggest high around here, in price and altitude, is **Zugspitze,** Germany's tallest mountain (9,781 feet). There are lots of ways to get up here, none of them cheaper than DM50. You can make the ascent on a 75-minute cogwheel train or by a 10-minute cable car leaving from **Lake Eibsee.** During winter, the round-trip costs only DM48 and includes a lift ticket.

If heights freak you out, wander through the cavelike passageways of **Partnachklamm gorge** (admission DM2), carved over thousands of years by the Partnach River. In winter, ice formations dangle from the gorge's walls. The best way to get here is to catch the local bus to the **Olympic Ski Stadium.** From the stadium it's a 35-minute hike to the gorge. To avoid getting lost, pick up a map at the **tourist office** (Richard Strauss Pl., tel. 08821/1806; open Mon.–Sat. 8–6, Sun. 10–noon).

COMING AND GOING Hourly **trains** (tel. 08821/52521) connect Garmisch-Partenkirchen with Munich (1½ hrs, DM15), while **RVO buses** (tel. 08821/51822) connect it to other Alpine villages. The train station acts as a dividing line between the two parts of town. On the western side is **Marienplatz,** the heart of Garmisch; on the east is **Ludwigstraße,** Partenkirchen's main strip. Since the two halves together become an extra-large Alpine town, you should use buses to get around. The tourist office *Kurkarte* (visitor card) gets you on free.

WHERE TO SLEEP Catch Bus 5, 6, or 7 to Burgrain to reach the **hostel** (Jochstr. 10, tel. 08821/2980, beds DM16), 4 km outside town. If the tourist office is closed when you arrive, 24-hour screens outside the office (and in the train station) list available accommodations. **Campingplatz Zugspitze** (Bundestr. 24, tel. 08821/3180, DM7 per person, DM10 per site) is at the foot of the Zugspitze, between Grainau and Garmisch-Partenkirchen.

OBERAMMERGAU

The first things you'll notice in Oberammergau are the wood-crammed shops everywhere; this tiny town is a world-renowned center of wood carving. From shop to shop you won't find much diversity of product or price (always steep), but you will find a flawless mastery of the local art. For DM2.50, down-and-out travelers can skip the shops and view an impressive collection of wood-carved crafts at the local history museum, **Heimatmuseum** (Dorfstr. 8, tel. 08822/32256; open Tues.–Sun. 2–6, Sat. only in off-season).

Still more distinguished than its wood carving is Oberammergau's **Passion Play,** which was first performed in 1634 and has been staged once a decade since 1680 with only a few interruptions. While you wait for the year 2000 to roll around you can check out the open-air **Passionspielhaus** (Passionweise; admission DM4, DM2.50 students; open daily 9:30–noon and 1:30–4:30, closed Mon. off-season), with an intriguing backstage museum devoted to the play's history.

BASICS The **tourist office** (Eugen-Papststr. 9A, tel. 08822/1021 or 08822/4771; open weekdays 8:30–6, Sat. 8:30–noon and 2–6, Sun. and holidays 2–6) can find you a private room for a DM1 fee. The **HI hostel** (Malensteinweg 10, tel. 08822/4114; beds DM15), is a 30-minute walk from the center: From the train station take Raisachweg south along the Ammer River, hang a right at König-Ludwig-Straße, and turn left on Malensteinweg.

MITTENWALD

If you have only a day or two in the Bavarian Alps, spend it in Mittenwald. Sandwiched between the Karwendel and Wetterstein mountains, this romantic, lively town epitomizes every Alpine village cliché you've ever heard—it's got everything from snow-capped peaks to breathtaking views to lederhosen-clad villagers. Best of all, most tourists overlook this cheery place in favor of its more famous neighbor, Garmisch-Partenkirchen, 20 km away. If you arrive to town late, the 24-hour computer screen by the **tourist office** (Dammkarstr. 3, tel. 08823/33981; open weekdays 9–noon and 2–5, Sat. 10–noon) lists available lodging options.

WHERE TO SLEEP Since the **hostel** (Buckelwiesen 7, tel. 08823/1701) is inaccessible by bus and a one-hour hike on the Tonihof-Buckelwiesen trail, call to see if any of the eight rooms are available at the centrally located and incredibly cheap **Haus Antonia** (In der Wasserwiese 14, tel. 08823/5749; singles DM20–DM30; doubles DM35). The family-owned **Gasthof Horsteiner** (Schibbacherweg 2, tel. 08823/1382; DM40 per person), about a 15-minute walk from town, offers cheery rooms, some with fantastic views of the mountains.

WORTH SEEING Mittenwald is known as the "Village of a Thousand Violins," thanks to Mathias Klotz, who introduced violin making to the town. The **Geigenbau-und Heimatmuseum mit Schauwerkstatt** (Ballehhaugasse 3, tel. 08823/2511) violin museum isn't nearly as exciting as seeing violin making in action at the museum's **workshop** (open weekdays until 11:45 AM). Next to the museum sits the 18th-century church of **Sts. Peter and Paul**, famous for its Baroque tower decorated with frescoes. West of the church extends the oldest part of town, **Im Gries,** which is fantastic walking territory, as is **Obermarkt,** one of the main streets lined with fruit stands and other markets.

Around town, awesome views and hiking opportunities abound; you can reach the **Karwendel summit** (7,867 feet)—boasting Germany's longest downhill ski run (6 km)—via the cable car that leaves from Alpenkorpstraße 1 (tel. 08832/8480; DM25 round-trip). Or take the chair lift up Kranzberg (tel. 08823/1553) for only DM6.50. Hikes to Leutaschklamm gorge and waterfall or to the tiny Lautersee lake aren't too strenuous.

Nürnberg

Nürnberg has a sordid association with Hitler and the post–World War II war trials, but sights and history aside, Nürnberg's Altstadt is what really merits a visit. The core of the old town, through which the winding Pegnitz River flows, dates from at least 1040, making it one of the oldest in southern Germany. Nürnberg still has its 14th-century city walls, and restored half-timbered homes and flamboyantly embellished facades are peppered throughout the old town—reminders of the city's prosperity during the Middle Ages, when Nürnberg sat at the meeting point of a dozen important trade routes. Kaiserburg castle, a sprawling complex of towers and walled-in fortresses that define the city's northern skyline, is another reminder of Nürnberg's past glories.

BASICS There's a tourist office in the **Hauptbahnhof** (tel. 0911/233632) and one on the **Hauptmarkt** (Am Hauptmarkt, tel. 0911/233635), which suffers from long lines. At the **American Express** office (Adlerstr. 2, tel. 0911/232397) in the Altstadt, you can get or cash traveler's checks (no commission), exchange currency (2% commission), and pick up mail. All the above offices are closed Sunday.

COMING AND GOING The **Hauptbahnhof** is conveniently located at the Altstadt's southeast corner; to reach the old town take the underground passage to Königstraße and continue northwest (Königstraße eventually funnels onto Lorenzerz Platz and, after a few name changes, the Hauptmarkt). To get to the **Mitfahr-Zentrale** office (Strauchstr. 1, tel. 0911/19444) from the train station, walk east through Allersberger Unterführung (it's a tunnel), then south on Allersberger Straße to Strauchstraße.

WHERE TO SLEEP Nürnberg has an excellent **HI hostel** (Burg 2, tel. 0911/221024; wheelchair access; beds DM25), housed in a castle high above the city. Unfortunately, that's about all for budget-minded wanderers. If the hostel is full (as it often is during summer), head to either tourist office (*see* Basics, *above*) and book yourself into a private room for a DM3 fee.

FOOD If you're hungry but pressed for cash, head for the university district, nestled on the Pegnitz River's southern bank a few blocks east of Museumsbrücke. You'll also find a good selection of studentish bars here. **Bratwurstglöcklein** (Handwerkerhof, tel. 0911/227625; closed Sun.), in the touristy crafts village opposite the train station, has main courses under DM12.50, and during summer, you can sit in the pleasant beer garden outside. **Zur Schranke** (Beim Tiergärtnertor 3, tel. 0911/225474; closed Sun.), is an ancient beer tavern that probably has the cheapest menu—mainly wieners and cabbage—in all Nürnberg. It's beside the Altstadt wall near Kaiserburg.

WORTH SEEING Besides the castle **Kaiserburg** (admission DM4), which looms imposingly at the northern end of Burgstraße, Nürnberg's main attraction is its colorful open-air square, the **Hauptmarkt.** During summer it overflows with street vendors and musicians; in winter, it hosts all kinds of events associated with Christkindlmarkt, an enormous pre-Christmas fair that runs from November 27 through Christmas Eve. If you're in the neighborhood, consider visiting on December 10, when Nürnberg hosts its annual candlelight Christmas march through the old town.

Albrecht-Dürer-Haus. Just west of the castle is this striking late-medieval house, formerly home to one of Germany's most talented painters and wood-carvers, Albrecht Dürer. He was born here in 1471 and returned in 1509 to live out the rest of his days. *Albrecht-Dürer-Str. 39, tel. 0911/231–2271. Admission: DM3, DM1.50 students. Open Tues.–Sun. 10–5, Wed. 10–9, shorter hrs off-season.*

Bakeries all over town sell Nürnberg's famous Lebkuchen, a delicious, sweet-smelling gingerbread cake.

Lorenzer Platz. This open-air square a few blocks south of the Haupmarkt is dominated by the medieval **St. Lorenzkirche**, lauded as Nürnberg's most beautiful church. Also on the square are the **Tugendbrunnen** (Fountain of Virtues), a popular spot for a summer's day water fight, and the lavish **Nassauer Haus** (Lorenzer Platz 6), Nürnberg's oldest dwelling house. Nürnberg claims to be the toy capital of the world, and **Spielzeugmuseum** (Karlstr. 13, tel. 0911/231364; admission DM5, DM2.50 students; open Tues.–Sun. 10–5), dedicated exclusively to toys and amusing doohickeys, documents the evolution of all sorts of imaginative diversions.

NEAR NURNBERG

BAYREUTH Depending on your perspective, Bayreuth is blessed or plagued with an annual **Richard Wagner Festival.** During this hoity-toity summer fete, the town's abuzz with 19th-century opera junkies who reserved their overpriced tickets (DM150–DM300) years in advance. The influx of high-culture fiends means it becomes impossible to find a place to crash. All this can be blamed on Wagner, who designed Bayreuth's vast opera house, the **Festspielhaus** (Auf dem Grünen Hugel, tel. 0921/20221; admission DM2). It's open to visitors when there are no performances going on, so call before planning a trip. Wagner's former home, **Haus Wahnfried** (Richard-Wagner-Str. 48, tel. 0921/757–2811; admission DM4, DM1.50 students; open daily 9–5) is now a museum with period furniture, Wagner-oriented displays, and dozens of contextual exhibits.

➤ **BASICS** • The **Gästedienst des Fremdenverkehrsvereins** doubles as a travel agency and tourist information center. Staffers at the information desk provide city maps and brochures, and make private room reservations for a DM3 fee. *Luitpoldpl. 9, tel. 0921/8850.*

➤ **WHERE TO SLEEP** • Don't bother in July or August unless you've booked months in advance. The rest of the year, Bayreuth's **hostel** (Universitätsstr. 28, tel. 0921/25262; Bus 11 to Kreuzstein; under 27 only; beds DM12) and a very few pensions are fairly priced and located within a reasonable walk of the Altstadt. A guest house in the center of the Altstadt, **Gasthof Vogel** (Friedrichstr. 13, tel. 0921/68268; doubles DM65) has its own beer garden.

BAMBERG Simply put, Bamberg is stunning. What started as a minor farming village in the late 2nd century AD was transformed into an elegant seat of power under the guidance of native son Heinrich II, an 11th-century Holy Roman emperor. He's responsible for Bamberg's impressive **Dom**, or Imperial Cathedral, considered one of the most important medieval relics in all Germany. Bamberg's old town looks like it just stepped from the pages of some medieval chronicle. Cobbled lanes meander in and out of narrow alleyways, while colorful and rickety half-timbered houses stand guard along ancient sandstone bridges. There are enough "official" sights to keep you occupied for at least a day in Bamberg, but this town was made for walking, and during summer you should stick around for the night. Bamberg's beer halls grow respectably bacchanal during the semitouristy summer season, and there are plenty of nooks along the river where you can pass time with a friend and a bottle.

➤ **COMING AND GOING** • Bamberg is well connected with the German rail network and an easy hop from Nürnberg (hourly, DM12.60), 63 km south. The staff at the **tourist office** (Geyerswörthstr. 3, tel. 0951/871161) arranges bus tours to nearby areas and books city hotels and guest houses for free. Pick up *Herzlich Willkommen in Bamberg,* a free city map that lists all the town's pensions, restaurants, and pubs.

➤ **WHERE TO SLEEP** • **Zum Gabelman** (Keßlerstr. 14, off Grüner Markt, tel. 0951/26676; doubles DM55) is a five-minute walk from Grüner Markt and the Alstadt's pubs and eateries. At **Hotel Garni Graupner** (Lange Str. 5, off Grüner Markt, tel. 0951/980400) doubles start at DM80. The **Fässla** (Obere Königstr. 21, tel. 0951/22998 or 0951/126516; closed Sun.) is a joint beer tavern and guest house. It isn't near any major sights but is only three blocks southwest of the train station. Doubles cost DM95, singles DM50, and most come equipped with a shower, TV, and radio. Wherever you stay, reserve ahead on summer weekends.

Bamberg's hostel and campground are a few kilometers from the Altstadt. **Jugendherberge Wolfsschlucht** (Oberer Leinritt 70, tel. 0951/56002; beds DM18) is set in a large mansion within a stone's throw of the Regnitz River. Take Bus 18 (service stops at 8 PM) from ZOB's Promenadestraße depot to Am Regnitzufer and walk north on Oberer Leinritt. Roughly 5 km south of the city center, **Campingplatz Insel** (Am Camping Pl. 1, tel. 0951/56320, DM10 per tent plus DM6 per person) is a beautiful and popular spot along the Regnitz River. Take Bus 18 from ZOB's Promenadestraße depot to Bug, then walk south along Hauptstraße, where you'll find the camping site well-posted.

➤ **FOOD** • Bamberg is associated with a few culinary oddities. One is *Rauchbier,* or smoked beer, a deep amber brew whose unique smoky taste comes from being filtered through charred beechwood logs. Another local specialty is *Leberkäs,* a spiced-liver sandwich available at Imbiß stands on Maxplatz and the streets immediately south and east; the dirt-cheap **Fischer** (Franz-Ludwig-Str. 5B) has a few varieties of Leberkäs. For a first-rate meal, try **Greifenklau** (Laurenziplatz 20, tel. 0951/53219), a small wiener-and-cabbage inn perched just above the old town. From Domplatz, walk south to Unter Kaulberg (which turns into Laurenziplatz) and turn right.

➤ **WORTH SEEING** • The DM2.50 admission to the cathedral museum **Diözesanmuseum** (Domplatz; open Apr.–Sept., daily 9–noon and 1:30–5, shorter hrs off-season), with its eclectic mix of church relics, random pieces of silver and jewels, and line drawings of the Dom floor plan, also buys free entrance to the adjoining **Neue Residenz,** a sprawling Baroque palace that was once home to princes and electors of the Holy Roman Empire. Domplatz's final attraction is **Alte Hofhaltung** (admission DM2; open Tues.–Sun. 9–5, shorter hrs off-season), a tired-looking, half-timbered Gothic palace. During June and July open-air concerts occasionally liven up the place. Call 0951/25256 for advance tickets, generally DM6–DM15.

The Romantic Road

The Romantic Road (Romantische Straße)—the most rewarding of Germany's tourist routes—winds its way through lush countryside, providing a thematic link to towns that might otherwise go unnoticed. It runs primarily from **Würzburg,** 90 km northwest of Nürnberg, to **Nördlingen,** about 80 km southwest of Nürnberg. So long as you don't mind sharing its cobbled streets with a crowd of camera-wielding tourists, Würzburg makes a good day trip from Nürnberg and a convenient base for longer excursions along the Romantische Straße. And from Würzburg you can also catch a bus to the justifiably popular town, **Rothenburg-ob-der-Tauber,** one of Europe's best-preserved medieval citadels.

Since renting a car is probably out of the question, your only option may be the Romantische Straße Bus. This is free to all EurailPass and InterRail holders, and to anyone with a Deutsche Bahn (DB) rail pass. Service runs only between April 10 and September 26; there are two buses daily in each direction between Frankfurt and Füssen, and Frankfurt and Munich. Along the way, buses stop at Romantische Straße destinations like Würzburg, Rothenburg-ob-der-Tauber, Dinkelsbühl, Nördlingen, and Augsburg.

WURZBURG

Würzburg is one of the Romantische Straße's major hubs; hourly trains connect Würzburg to Nürnberg (DM34) and Frankfurt (DM36); it's also a main starting point for regional buses. The town has a beautiful setting on the banks of the Main River, which passes through the town center and is crossed by three stoically weathered stone bridges. Würzburg's two main sights are **Festung Marienberg** (Marienberg Fortress) and the Baroque **Residenz** palace. The former sits atop a small hill on the western edge of town, dominating Würzburg's steeple-pricked skyline. It was under continuous construction between 1200 and 1600, and for over 450 years it provided sturdy sanctuary to the town's powerful prince-bishops. The Residenz, a short walk away on the eastern edge of the old town, was the rulers' actual residence and is considered one of Europe's most impressive architectural monuments. You could conceivably cover Würzburg in a few high-pace hours, but consider sticking around for a while to poke around in the many alcoves along the river and the pedestrian-only central market.

The town has three tourist offices: the main **tourist office** (Pavilion am Hauptbahnhof, tel. 0931/36436) is located just outside the train station; another **tourist office** (Haus zum Falken, Am Markt, tel. 0931/37398) is on the central market square; and the smaller office, **Fremdenverkehrsamt** (Am Congress Centrum, tel. 0931/37335), sits overlooking the Main River near Friedensbrücke. They all organize guided city tours and book private rooms (DM30–DM45) for a DM4 fee. They're also all closed Sunday.

WHERE TO SLEEP During summer, especially during June's **Mozart Festival,** crowds are a real problem. Würzburg's youth hostel, **Jugendgästehaus Würzburg** (Burkaderstr. 44, tel. 0931/42590; beds DM25), has an excellent location, below Festung Marienberg on the Main's west bank. It's also one of the few hostels to attract a more upscale clientele. That's because there aren't that many beds in town, and certainly not many priced under DM100. From the train station, take Tram 5 in the direction of Heuchelhof and alight at Ludwigsbrücke. From here head north along the Main (keep the river on your right) and follow the signs.

To pitch a tent in the great outdoors, head to **Campinplatz Kalte Quelle** (Winterhäuser Str. 160, tel. 0931/65598) or **Campingplatz Estenfeld** (Maidbronner Str. 38, Estenfeld, tel. 09305/228). Both are in the suburbs about 6 km from Würzburg and charge DM16–DM20 for a tent and two people. During summer, buses run one to three times a day to each campground.

FOOD Würzburg's central market, Am Markt, and the adjacent streets boast the usual high concentration of Imbiß stands, cafés, and tourist-geared beer halls. There's a cluster of cheapish food stands and greasy hole-in-the-walls around the train station and in the maze of streets around Sanderstraße and Münzstraße. **Bürgerspital** (Theaterstr. 19, tel. 0931/13861) is a popular drinking hall where glasses of sweet white Franconian wine cost under DM5—a pittance for this excellent, locally brewed elixir.

ROTHENBURG-OB-DER-TAUBER

Rothenburg is rightly considered the most evocative Romantische Straße destination—a jumble of gingerbread architecture and cobbled hillside streets set against a backdrop of towers, turrets, and staunch medieval walls. Rothenburg-ob-der-Tauber, which literally means "the red castle on the Tauber," is best known for its compact and walled-in old town, along the eastern bank of the Tauber River. Preserved inside the city wall is Bavaria's most impressive medieval citadel, without a single modern building. Sadly, on crowded summer days this striking, historic town does feel like a superficial tourist trap.

Rothenburg is best reached by train from Nürnberg (1½ hrs) or Würzburg (2 hrs). You can tour Rothenberg in three to four hours, but it does make a good base for exploring lesser-known Romantische Straße sights like Feuchtwangen and Dinkelsbühl. From here you can also take walks through forests and along rivers. Ask at the **tourist office** (Marktpl., tel. 09861/40492) for its detailed walking guide. If you want an insightful overview of the city, join a guided walking tour sponsored by the tourist office.

WHERE TO SLEEP The cheapest options are private rooms (DM25–DM35), which you can book through the tourist office, and the youth hostel, **Jugendherberge Rothenburg** (Mühlacker 1, tel. 09861/4510; beds DM18; closed Dec. 15–Jan. 2). The hostel is divided into two distinct sections, the 93-bed Roßmühle house, and the more spartan 90-bed Spitalhof annex. They're around the corner from one another at the southern end of the old town. From Marktplatz walk south along Obere Schmiedgaße and turn right into the large courtyard just before passing through the city wall. Campers should head straight for Detwang, a small historic village 1¼ km northwest of Rothenburg (cross the Tauber and follow the road signs). In Detwang, both **Tauber-Romantik** (tel. 09861/33226) and **Tauber-Idyll** (tel. 09861/33256) charge DM5 per tent and DM2 per camper.

Berlin
When you speak of Berlin you're really speaking of two very different cities. For years West Berlin was the lone bastion of capitalism in Communist Eastern Europe, an isolated stump of a city surrounded by Soviet soldiers. Especially after the erection of the Wall in 1961, while East Berlin was slowly overcome by the Communist cement-and-steel aesthetic, West Berlin was transformed into a city of neon boutiques, swank cafés, and all the trappings of a Westernized (i.e., Americanized) megacity.

All this changed on the night of Friday, November 9, 1989. As the world watched in utter disbelief, East Germans began smashing through the Wall, unhindered. East Germans packed a lifetime into their sputtery Trabants and headed west. West Berliners were thrilled to see so many Easterners in their half of the city, but they weren't quite sure what to do with them all. Troubling questions soon arose: Can West Berliners support 1.2 million East Berlin immigrants? Let them browse and gawk at the wonders of the West, but aren't they going home soon?

At the root of it all was the fact that East Berliners were needy wards of a now-defunct state. Erich Honecker—the GDR's head bad guy—and his henchmen had resigned; the Stasi, the hated secret police, had been disbanded; and seemingly overnight the Soviets had withdrawn. For a while the GDR was a country without a real government, and East Germans naturally looked to the "other" Germany for help. But after 30 years of division, two distinct kinds of Berliners had evolved—one brash and cynical and completely comfortable sipping $5 espressos in swank cafés, one sullen and accustomed to long lines. If this was to change, West Berliners soon realized, they would have to sacrifice more than just a little.

Although the Wall no longer exists, Berlin remains tangibly divided between cement apartment blocks and prim shopping avenues—by 45 years of distinct and generally incompatible development. The German Bundestag's June 1991 decision to move the capital from Bonn to Berlin will certainly help homogenize the two halves. But lawmakers have given the government until 2003 to complete the move, so it will take at least a decade before Berlin once again becomes the center of a united Germany; perhaps a generation or two before the words "east" and "west" become unnecessary as prefaces to the word "Berliner."

One of the positive aspects of Berlin's 45-year-long division is the city's funky approach to culture, both high and low. During the Cold War, people were drawn to Berlin by cheap rents, by the city's nightlife, and by a sense of urgency that was missing in other German cities. Berliners knew that at any moment Cold War politics might thrust their city into the middle of World War III. And if West Berlin was considered slightly absurd and hedonistic, that's because in many ways it was. What else can you expect from a walled-in city that was most often viewed as an issue rather than a place?

In unified Berlin, just getting around the city—which is larger than some European countries—is a challenge. To see all the "sights" is almost impossible. That's because Berlin's unmistakable character comes from its many diverse and sprawling districts. The Kurfürstendamm—Berlin's most famous shopping avenue, universally called the Ku'damm—represent the city's refined side. Other districts, like Kreuzberg, Schöneberg, and East Berlin's Prenzlauer Berg, reveal Berlin as a city where artists and punks huddle in vacant lots and tenements, as a city where immigrant factory workers, Turkish bazaars, and sputtering Trabant cars form a unique urban vignette.

BASICS

➤ **VISITOR INFORMATION** • Although they're in German, the magazines *Zitty, Tip, Berlin Programm,* and *Stadtbuch 4,* each priced around DM4, list all the major happenings in Berlin—and it doesn't take a genius to decipher dates, times, and addresses. Look for them at tourist offices or a local newsstand.

Berlin's most useful information service is the state-run **Verkehrsamt Berlin** (Berlin Tourist Information). For a DM5 fee they'll book a room for you—the easiest way to find a place in sprawling Berlin. The main office is in West Berlin's very central **Europa Center** (Breitscheid-pl., off the Ku'damm, tel. 030/262–6031). Other locations are Tegel Airport (tel. 030/4101–3145), Zoo Station (tel. 030/313–9063; closed Sun.), and East Berlin's Haupt-bahnhof (tel. 030/279–5209; open daily 8–8). Unless noted otherwise, all are open Mon-day–Saturday 8 AM–10:30 PM, Sunday 9–9.

Berlin Gay Association in East Berlin has complete listings of gay/lesbian events. *Friedrichstr. 14A. U-Bahn to Friedrichstr. Open weekdays 9–4.*

Jewish Community Center offers information and advice to Jewish visitors as well as excellent kosher meals (*see* Food, *below*). *Fasanenstr. 79, tel. 030/884–2030. Walk west on Ku'damm to Fasanenstr. Open weekdays 8:30—noon.*

➤ **AMERICAN EXPRESS** • Two branches exchange money, cash traveler's checks, and, if you have an AmEx card, hold mail. *Kurfürstendamm 11, 2nd Floor, across from Kaiser-Wil-helm Memorial Church, tel. 030/882–7575. Friedrichstr. 172, near Frankreichstr., tel. 030/238–4102. Both open weekdays 9–5:30, Sat. 9–noon.*

➤ **CHANGING MONEY** • If you can, avoid changing money in Berlin. Not one exchange place stays open 24 hours and, as a general rule, all charge heavy commissions (3%–5%). If you're desperate, most luxury hotels have bureaux de change in their lobbies. For conve-nience, try an American Express office (*see above*) or **Berliner Bank** (Ku'damm 24; open weekdays 9:30–6:30, Sat. 9:30–1:30), which charges a flat rate of DM10 per exchange, so pool your money with a friend.

➤ **EMBASSIES** • Many embassies are soon expected to relocate here from Bonn. Until then, the foreign consulates listed below can deal with the most delicate of problems.

Australia. *Uhlandstr. 181–183, tel. 030/800–0880.*

Canada. *Friedrichstr. 95, tel. 030/261–1161.*

United Kingdom. *Unter den Linden 32–34, tel. 030/220–2431.*

The Berlin Wall

Throughout the 1950s the German Democratic Republic (GDR) grew increasingly embarrassed that nearly 20,000 East Germans were crossing into West Berlin every month, never to return. To stem the flow, the government decided to seal the border completely. So at 1 AM on August 13, 1961, more than 25,000 GDR workers wiped the sleep from their eyes and set about raising a mortar and cement barrier—the Berlin Wall—along the entire length of the border, demolishing houses and bisecting streets whenever necessary.

KEY

AE American Express Office

i Tourist Information

Tiergarten

River Spree

Friedrichstr. Bahnhof

Pariser Platz

Unter den Linden

TIERGARTEN

Str. des 17 Juni

Tiergartenstr.

Paulstr.

Lüneburgerstr.

John-Foster-Dulles Allee

Moltkestr.

Entlastungsstr.

Otto Grotewohlstr.

Friedrichstr.

Karl-Liebknecht-Str.

Rathausstr.

Marx-Engels-pl.

Gendarmen-markt

Leipzigerstr.

Wallstr.

FORMER LOCATION OF BERLIN WALL

Wilhelmstr.

Stresemannstr.

Möckernstr.

Schönebergerstr.

Lindenstr.

Ritterstr.

Oranienstr.

Prinzenstr.

KREUZBERG

Lützowstr.

Potsdamerstr.

Bülowstr.

Yorckstr.

Gitschinerstr.

Paul-Lincke-Ufer

Urban str.

Gneisenaustr.

Baerwaldstr.

Monumentenstr.

Kreuzbergstr.

Victoriapark

Kolonnenstr.

Dudenstr.

Mehringdamm

Columbiadamm

Volkspark Hasenheide

Zentralflughafen Berlin-Tempelhof

Hauptstr.

Westangente

N

0   1/2 mile

0   3/4 km

AE

23 24 25 26 27 28 29 30 31 32 33 34 35 36 37 38 39 40 41 42

United States. *West Berlin: Clayallee 170, tel. 030/832–4087.*

➤ **EMERGENCIES** • **Police** (tel. 110); **ambulance** (tel. 112); info on **late-night pharmacies** (tel. 1141 in West Berlin or 160 in East Berlin); **24-hour medical hot line** (tel. 310031 in West Berlin or 1259 in East Berlin).

➤ **PHONES AND MAIL** • The reunification of Berlin's phone system is nearly complete, and the new phone code for all parts of the city is 030 (drop the first 0 if calling from abroad). Service from East Berlin, however, is still sometimes poor. Berlin's main **post office** is inside Bahnhof Zoologischer Garten (tel. 030/313–9799). Open 24 hours, it's the place to come for stamps, and to send mail, a telegram, or even a fax. Poste restante service costs DM3 per letter. Letters should be addressed: Poste restante, Postamt Bahnhof Zoo, D–10612 Berlin. Also inside are dozens of international phone boxes.

COMING AND GOING

➤ **BY TRAIN** • Berlin has four major train stations. If you're coming from western Germany, odds are you'll end up at the central **Bahnhof Zoologischer Garten** (Zoo Station), the city's busiest hub. In East Berlin, **Lichtenberg** handles the bulk of traffic to the former GDR as well as destinations in many East European countries. All stations are served by Berlin's extensive subway network. Pick up a train timetable (DM3), with all Berlin departures, at any ticket window. For German-language information, dial 030/19419 daily between 8 AM and 7 PM. Berlin's larger train stations all have luggage lockers for around DM2–DM3 per half-day. Some popular destinations from Berlin include: Munich (7 hrs, DM146), Amsterdam (8½ hrs, DM150), Prague (4½ hrs, DM52), and Vienna (10 hrs, DM104).

➤ **BY BUS** • **Zentralen Omnibus-Bahnhof** (ZOB), Berlin's main bus depot, is a grimy pit, even if it does service most major German cities. *Masurenallee at Meßedamm, tel. 030/302–5294. Bus 149 from Zoo Station to Meßedamm.*

➤ **BY PLANE** • Unified Berlin has two major airports, West Berlin's **Flughafen Tegel** (tel. 030/411011) and East Berlin's **Flughafen Schönefeld** (tel. 030/67870). Blue airport Buses 9 and 109 zip between Zoo Station and Tegel Airport (35 min, DM5). Both S9 and S10 make the 24-km trip to Schönefeld Airport trip from Alexanderplatz, but note that U6, confusingly marked "Tegel," does *not* go to the airport.

➤ **BY MITFAHRZENTRALEN** • *Zoo station, tel. 030/310331. Open daily 8 AM–9 PM.*

GETTING AROUND
Even before reunification, West Berlin was a confusing, sprawling city that took some getting used to. Rejoined with its eastern half, Berlin has now become the largest city in Europe, so prepare to be overwhelmed. Unified Berlin changes its street names like most people change their underwear, so you'll also need a detailed map, preferably the easy-to-fold *Falk Plan* (DM8–DM10), available at tourist offices and newsstands.

Bahnhof Zoologischer Garten (Zoo Station) is usually considered the center of town. It's not only within easy walking distance of the Tiergarten, the Ku'damm, and Schöneberg, but it also handles six subway lines. Outside on Hardenbergplatz, a subway information booth stocks maps, sells tickets, and consoles overwhelmed travelers. Most West Berlin bus routes run past Zoo Station. In East Berlin, the busiest bus hub is **Alexanderplatz.**

The subway operates 4 AM–1 AM, although on weekends the U1 and U9 run all night.

➤ **BY U-BAHN AND S-BAHN** • The complex subway system courses through all major sections of the city. Berlin has two types of subway: The **U-Bahn** is concentrated in central Berlin whereas the **S-Bahn** is more far-reaching and runs above ground once outside the center. Along with the city's 150 bus routes, you can get within walking distance of virtually any point in town. One ticket costs DM3.20 and gives unlimited access to every bus and subway for two hours. A pack of four tickets costs DM11. A better deal is the Berlin Ticket (DM12), valid for 24 hours. Better yet is the six-day **Berlin Pass** (DM30), good for travel between Monday and Saturday. Purchase tickets from a bus driver or from machines at subway stations. The Berlin Ticket and Pass, however, can be purchased only at the main offices of **Berliner Verkehrsbetriebe (BVG),** which also carry route maps. By the way, if you're caught riding the subway without a stamped ticket, you'll be slapped with a DM40 fine. Call 030/75660 for further BVG info. *Kleistpark U-Bahn station, open Mon.–Sat. 9–6. Hardenbergpl., in front of Zoo Station, open Mon.–Sat. 9–6, Sun. 10–4.*

➤ **BY BUS** • Standard operating hours for buses are 6 AM–1 AM daily. Buses marked with an "N" run all night ("N" bus stops are recognizable by the green and yellow tabs atop the streetside stands). From Zoo Station, the most useful lines are 146 (Kantstraße–Savignyplatz–Wilmersdorf), 119 (Ku'damm–Charlottenburg), and 129 (Joachimstalerstraße–Rathaus Schöneberg).

➤ **BY BICYCLE** • Because many locals commute on bikes, paths are everywhere and many street corners have signal lights especially for cyclists. In the center of town, the redbrick strips on sidewalks mean cyclists can legally ride among pedestrians. At **Rent-a-Bike** (Möckenstr. 92, tel. 030/216–9177; U-Bahn Yorckstr.; open weekdays 10–6, Sat. 10–2), you can hire a bike for DM20–DM25 per day; you'll have to leave your passport or up to DM150 for a deposit. If you're headed for Grunewald, there's a rental stand (tel. 030/811–5829) in the Grunewald S-Bahn station; 18-speeds fetch DM20 a day.

WHERE TO SLEEP Cheap lodging in Berlin is hard to come by. **Charlottenburg,** within walking distance of Zoo Station and the Ku'damm, has the best selection of budget hotels, and you'll find many pensions on Kantstraße, near Savignyplatz. The only drawback of staying in this area is that you'll have to take a bus or the subway for after-dark excitement. The colorful **Kreuzberg** district, bordered by what remains of the Wall on the eastern extreme of West Berlin, is 15–20 minutes from the city center by subway. It's the sort of self-contained neighborhood that's popular with punks, drunks, and poets—an ideal spot if raucous nightlife is more important than proximity to Berlin's museums. **Wilmersdorf,** a quiet, residential neighborhood in West Berlin (bordered by the Ku'damm in the north and Schöneberg in the east), has a few reasonably priced pensions, but you'll have to spend about 20 minutes on the U-Bahn in order to reach livelier areas.

If you're confused or arrive late, your best bet is to head for the **Bahnhofsmission** (*see* Hostels, *below*) or one of Berlin's tourist offices. For a DM3–DM5 fee, the latter arrange accommodation in a pension, hostel, or private room (DM30–DM50 per night). If you plan to stay in Berlin for an extended period of time and want to rent on a monthly or weekly basis, contact one of the city's **Mitwohnzentrale** (apartment-share offices): Sybelstr. 53, tel. 030/324–3031, fax 030/324–9977; Ku'damm Eck, 3rd Floor, Kurfürstendamm 227–228, tel. 030/883051; Holsteinischestr. 55, tel. 030/861–8222; or Mehringdamm 72, tel. 030/786–6002.

➤ **CHARLOTTENBURG** • **Hotel Charlottenburger Hof.** Friendly pension in the heart of Charlottenburg, just around the corner from bus and subway lines at Bahnhof Charlottenburg (S3 and U7). Wide selection of shops, eateries, and dive bars nearby. Doubles DM140–DM170, breakfast DM5–DM8. *Stuttgarter Pl. 14, tel. 030/329070.*

Hotelpension Bialas. Surprisingly elegant: Most rooms have bay windows and plush red-velvet furniture. Some have sinks. Doubles DM90, DM150 w/shower. *Carmerstr. 16, tel. 030/312–5025. From Zoo Station walk west down Hardenbergstr., left at Steinpl.*

Pension Alexis. Small and quiet, family-oriented, only 10-minutes by foot from Zoo Station. Doubles from DM90, including breakfast. *Carmerstr. 15, tel. 030/312–5144. From Zoo Station walk west down Hardenbergstr., left at Steinpl.*

Pension Knesebeck. Family-run pension in a quiet, middle-class neighborhood, 10 minutes by foot from Zoo Station. Spacious doubles DM120–DM150, including breakfast. *Knesebecksstr. 86, tel. 030/317255.*

Pension Peters. Near shops, cafés, and a few Yuppie bars. Rooms are big and clean, like a small and snazzy generic hotel. Doubles DM120–DM140, breakfast DM1. *Kantstr. 146, tel. 030/312–2278. 8 rooms, 4 w/bath.*

GERMANY

Pension Viola Nova. Modern by Berlin standards. Sunny, spotless rooms contrast with the building's tired exterior. Doubles DM110–DM140, breakfast DM9.50. *Kantstr. 146, tel. 030/316457. 9 rooms, none w/bath.*

➤ **KREUZBERG** • **Hotel Transit.** Large, upscale pension near Kreuzberg Hill and Viktoria-park. Rooms have TVs and safes. Laundry DM8 per load. Doubles DM95. *Hagelbergerstr. 53–54, tel. 030/785–5051. U7 to Yorckstr.*

Pension Kreuzberg. On a quiet, tree-lined street but still close to some great clubs. Each spacious double (from DM90) has its own bath. *Großbeerenstr. 64, tel. 030/251–1362. U6 or U7 to Mehringdamm; walk west on Yorckstr. to Großbeerenstr.*

Pension Süd-West. Pleasantly run-down pension in heart of West Kreuzberg, within reach of bars and cafés. Rooms small and damp, some street noise. Doubles from DM90. *Yorckstr. 80A, tel. 030/785–8033. U7 to Mehringdamm, then walk west on Yorckstr.*

➤ **WILMERSDORF** • **Hotelpension Elton.** A family-run hostel on a quiet side street. Rooms are well kept, but not the communal bathroom. Doubles DM70–DM95. *Pariser Str. 9, tel. 030/883–6155. From Zoo Station, Bus 249 to Pariser Str.*

Hotelpension von Oertzen. On a noisy street, but one of the cheapest pensions in Berlin. Doubles DM75–DM80, breakfast DM8. *Lietzenburgerstr. 76, tel. 030/883–3964. From Zoo Station, Bus 249 to Lietzenburgerstr.*

Hotelpension Pariser Eck. On a safe and quiet side street only a few minutes south of Ku'damm. Doubles DM100–DM130. *Pariserstr. 19, tel. 030/881–2145. From Zoo Station, Bus 249 to Pariserstr.*

Pension Iris. Medium-size pension about five minutes from Zoo Station at northernmost tip of Wilmersdorf. Friendly staff, large and comfy rooms. Doubles DM110. *Uhlandstr. 33, tel. 030/881–5770. U9 south to Uhlandstr.*

➤ **HOSTELS** • Despite curfews and daytime lockouts, Berlin's many hostels fill up fast during the summer, probably because they cost DM20–DM30 per bed, about half of what you'll pay for a pension. On the downside, many of Berlin's hostels are old and worn, so expect a minimum of comfort and sometimes dismal facilities. Most Berlin hostels require an HI or DJH membership card.

Bahnhofmission. Nonaffiliated hostel provides beds for travelers whose trains arrive late at night. Show your train ticket at all-hours front desk; mandatory 6 AM checkout and one night maximum stay. Space in a windowless, four-bed dorm runs DM15, including a meager breakfast. *Zoo Station, tel. 030/313–8088. Wheelchair access.*

Gästehaus der Fürst-Donnersmarck-Stiftung. A 45-minute subway ride from the city center. Features ramps and wheelchair-accessible bathrooms. DM25 per person. *Wildkanzelweg 28, tel. 030/40690. From either Tegel Station (U6) or Frohnau Station (S1), Bus 125 to Am Pilz, then northeast to Wildkanzelweg. Reservations advised in summer. Wheelchair access.*

Jugendgästehaus am Wannsee (HI). Large hostel near Wannsee lake on the outskirts of Berlin, a 20-minute bus or subway ride into town. Reservations imperative in summer. Space in a sprawling dorm room runs DM25, including breakfast. *Badeweg 1, tel. 030/803–2034. S3 or S5 to Nikolaßee and walk west on Spanische Alle. Midnight curfew, check-in after 3 PM. DM20 key deposit.*

Jugendgästehaus am Zoo. One of Berlin's best nonaffiliated hostels, in the heart of the city and a five-minute walk from Zoo Station. Bed in spacious four- to six-bunk dorm rooms: DM35. *Hardenbergstr. 9A, tel. 030/312–9410. Midnight curfew.*

Jugendgästehaus Berlin (HI). Prime location in the middle of town near Tiergarten. Call and reserve the minute you arrive. Beds DM27. *Kluckstr. 3, tel. 030/261–1097. From Ku'damm's Gedächtniskirche, Bus 129 to Kluckstr. Closed 9–noon, midnight curfew, luggage storage. DM10 key deposit. To book more than 2 weeks in advance, call 030/261–1098.*

Jugendherberge Ernst Reuter (HI). Helpful staff, comfy facilities, but far from town center—about 5 km north of Tegel Airport. DM21, DM18 if you're under 25, breakfast included. *Hermsdorfer Damm 48, tel. 030/404–1610. From Tegel Station (U6), Bus 125 to Hermsdorfer Damm and Dohnensteig. Flexible 11 PM curfew, check-in after 3 PM. DM20 key deposit.*

➤ **STUDENT HOUSING** • Accommodation generally entails a two- to four-bed dorm room with communal cooking and bathroom facilities. Most high-rise dorms are in the middle of student quarters. The two student hotels listed below charge DM37 per person in a double, DM33 in a quad. Both are open year-round and require a DM20 key deposit. For general information and availability, contact the student hotels directly or try Verkehrsamt Berlin (*see* Visitor Information, *above*).

Studentenhotel Berlin. The most centrally located student hotel, one block from John F. Kennedy Platz and a 10-minute walk from the Ku'damm. *Meiningerstr. 10, tel. 030/781–1878 or 030/781–2290. From Zoo Station, Bus 146 to Rathaus Schöneberg.*

Touristenhaus Grünau. In East Berlin close to Schönefeld Airport, about an hour from the city center. *Dahmestr. 6, tel. 030/681–4422. S8 to Grünau, then Tram 86 toward Köpenick for 2 stops.*

➤ **CAMPGROUNDS** • All campsites cost DM7 per night plus DM3.50–DM7 per person. Showers are DM1. To reserve a spot, contact any tourist office.

Campsite Haselhorst. Not that picturesque but best location near Spandau Citadel and Haselhorst U-Bahn. Restaurant and bar on site. *Pulvermühlenweg, tel. 030/334–5955. U7 to Haselhorst, then north on Daumstr. to Pulvermühlenweg.*

Kladow Camping. In a forest by a small lake, about 50 minutes by bus from city center. The most rural and peaceful campground and also the largest and best known. On-site bar, restaurant, and food shop. *Krampnitzer Weg 111, tel. 030/365–2797. From Zoo Station, Bus 149 to Wilhelmstr. and Heerstr., switch to Bus 135 and disembark at Krampnitzer Weg. Wheelchair access.*

FOOD Berlin's best selection of restaurants is in Charlottenburg, which boasts hundreds of cheap student dives as well as upscale eateries. If you're in the mood to follow your nose rather than a guidebook, take U9 to Savignyplatz, with its host of ethnic Imbisses, beer halls, and cafés. Schöneberg is another good district for ethnic eateries, particularly Indian. The Kreuzberg is famed for its Turkish street stands and offbeat cafés. Despite unification, you'll be dependent on East Berlin's rather bland and characterless tourist restaurants, a legacy of Communism that may not be exorcised for a few more years.

➤ **CHARLOTTENBURG** • **Bella Italia.** Large portions at ultralow prices. Pizza (DM6.50–DM18), pasta (DM7–DM10), and salads (under DM12). *Pestalozzistr. 84, tel. 030/312–3549. From Savignypl., west on Kantstr., right on Bleibtreustr., left on Pestalozzistr.*

Einhorn. Mainly vegetarian Imbiß serves everything from broccoli quiche (DM9) to lasagna (DM7.40). Portions aren't huge but the food is tasty. Closes at 6:30 PM. *Mommsenstr. 2. S-Bahn to Savignypl. and walk south on Bleibtreustr.*

Fromme Helene. Friendly and lively with an eclectic menu. Try *Trinkkeller* (DM13.50), a mix of stir-fried meat basted in Egyptian spices, or Thai-spiced tofu lasagna (DM9.50). *Bleibtreustr. 51, tel. 030/313–3278. Wheelchair access. No lunch.*

Jewish Community Center. Well-prepared kosher meals such as matzo brei, chicken soup, and brisket, all under DM15. *Fasanenstr. 79, tel. 030/884–2030. Wheelchair access. Closed Sun.*

La Piazza. Italian and German meals at bargain prices. House specialty is a salami, mushroom, and green pepper pizza (DM8). On a summer night, sit outside with a bottle of cheap red wine (from DM15). *Savignypl. 13, tel. 030/312–3990.*

Taj Mahal. Small Indian restaurant with top-rate food ranging from curried vegetables (DM8) to lamb *saag* (lamb with spinach; DM10). *Grolmanstr. 12. From Savignypl., southeast on Grolmanstr.*

➢ **EAST BERLIN** • **Arkade.** Elegant digs with a small indoor-outdoor café in front and an open-grill dining room in back. For dinner, choose steak or grilled poultry from DM20; soup and salads from DM15. *Französische Str. 25, tel. 030/208–0273. 1 block west of Marx-Engels-Pl. Closed Sun.*

Telecafé. Outer ring of tables atop Fernsehturm television and radio tower rotates 360°. For lunch there are omelets (DM7) and sandwiches (DM9). Dinner includes sausage-and-potato combinations from DM15; make reservations in summer. One bummer: It costs DM5 to enter the tower. *Alexanderpl., top floor of Fernsehturm tower, tel. 030/24040.*

Zur Letzen Instanz. Berlin's oldest restaurant, established in 1525, with a dark, old-fashioned interior and excellent food. Try beer-batter knockwurst (DM12), or goulash-style soups for around DM15. Reservations a must in summer. *Waisenstr. 14–16, off Stralauerstr., tel. 030/212–5528. U2 to Klosterstr. and walk west on Stralauerstr.*

➢ **KREUZBERG** • Eateries here come and go at a dizzying pace, mostly because they're operated on a shoestring budget or housed in the remnants of a burned-out shop or crumbling warehouse.

Café am Ufer. Trashy alternative bar doubles as a co-op café, with a limited selection of sandwiches, soups, salads, and desserts priced under DM10. Tremendous weekend brunches—eggs, cereal, cheese, and fruit—for around DM12. *Paul-Lincke-Ufer 43–44, no phone.*

Ristorante-Pizzeria Diomira. Sit outside at a sidewalk table or indoors in its dark, smoky, soothing dining room. Try spaghetti carbonara (with Parmesan and bacon; DM8) or spaghetti *amatriciana* (with spicy tomatoes and garlic; DM8.50). *Stresemannstr. 60, tel. 030/262–3183. S-Bahn to Anhalter Bahnhof and exit onto Stresemannstr. Wheelchair access.*

Spots. Soups and salads for under DM8, beer DM4. Small eating area is usually bombarded with distorted guitar music. *Prinzenstr. 50, tel. 030/445–8781. U1 to Kotbusser Tor and walk west on Gitschinerstr. No lunch.*

Thürnagel. Friendly café with a good selection of mostly vegetarian meals, from tofu omelets (DM8) to vegetable stir-fries (DM10 and up). *Gneisenaustr. 56, tel. 030/691–4800. U7 to Gneisenaustr. Closed Sun.*

➢ **SCHONEBERG** • **Café Strada.** Typical coffeehouse decor (subdued lights and literary knickknacks) complements a small menu of sandwiches and soups. Potent coffee starts at DM3. *Potsdamer Str. 129, tel. 030/223–9004.*

Extra Dry. A Wilmersdorf café that serves women only and is a good place to come for information on women-oriented events. Only nonalcoholic drinks and snacks like sandwiches and soups, most priced under DM8. *Mommsenstr. 34., no phone. Bus 149 from Zoo Station to Wilmersdorferstr. and walk south to Mommsenstr.*

Habibi. On Winterfeldplatz, this is the place to come for falafel (from DM5). It stays open late to catch the last bar-hoppers. All food served to go. *Goltzstr. 24, no phone. U4 to Nollendorfpl.*

Rani Indischer Imbiß. On Winterfeldplatz and popular. Try the chicken sabzi (DM9.50) or the Indian vegetarian plate (DM6.50), both cooked fresh and served in large portions. No sit-down seating. *Goltzstr. 34, no phone. U4 to Nollendorfpl.*

WORTH SEEING

➢ **WEST BERLIN** • **Brandenburg Gate.** Those who watched the Berlin Wall crumble in 1989 will recognize Brandenburger Tor (Brandenburg Gate), perhaps the most vivid symbol of German reunification. When the Wall was built in 1961, ostensibly as an "antifascist protection barrier," West Berliners watched in horror as their beloved city was divided and this historic gate was hidden behind a 10-foot-tall barrier. On November 9, 1989, after thousands of East Germans began smashing the Wall, the Brandenburg Gate was swamped with celebrants. Since 1989, the gate and plaza have been transformed into an open-air flea market, a place where East Berliners come to peddle postcards. Though this plays well with foreigners, it evokes a certain bitterness among Germans. *Str. des 17 Juni at Otto-Grotewohl-Str. Nearest S-Bahn is East Berlin's Bahnhof Friedrichstr.*

Checkpoint Charlie. Between 1961 and 1990, Checkpoint Charlie (Kochstr. and Friedrichstr.) was the most (in)famous crossing point between East and West Berlin. The checkpoint itself, a wooden guard hut, was removed shortly after the Wall came down in 1989. Remaining are a grim, skeletal watchtower and a somber memorial slab dedicated to those killed in escape attempts. Although the checkpoint has been dismantled, you can trace its history at the nearby **Haus am Checkpoint Charlie.** This small museum has hundreds of Cold War–era photographs and a fascinating exhibit on some ingenious escape attempts. *Friedrichstr. 44, tel. 030/251–1031. U6 to Kochstr. or U2 to Stradtmitte. Admission: DM7.50, DM4.50 students. Open daily 9 AM–10 PM.*

Dahlem Museums. The West Berlin suburb of Dahlem, 15 minutes by subway from the city center, is a quiet enclave of tree-lined streets and sleepy pubs. It's worth the trip just to escape the grimy bustle of Berlin proper, yet the suburb is best known for the Dahlem Museums. Housed inside the gigantic gallery are eight world-class museums, each with a dizzying collection of Western art. It would take at least two full days to see everything, so concentrate instead on the main galleries: the **Gemäldegalerie** (Arnimallee 23–27, tel. 030/832–6095), Germany's foremost picture gallery, with an extensive collection of European paintings from the 13th through 18th centuries; the **Kupferstichkabinett** (Arnimallee 25–27, tel. 030/832–6095), the Drawing and Print Collection, which features works by Dürer and Rembrandt; the **Museum für Völkerkunde** (Fabeckstr. 20, tel. 030/83011), an ethnographic museum; and the **Skulpturengalerie** (Sculpture Garden), in the same building, which houses Byzantine and European sculpture from the 3rd through 18th centuries. All are free and open Tuesday–Friday 9–5, weekends 10–5. From Zoo Station, take U1 to Wittenbergplatz, switch to U2, and alight at Dahlem-Dorf Station. Walk south on Fabeckstraße and enter at either Arnimallee 23 or Lansstraße 8.

Grunewald. A 32-square-km expanse of horse trails, bike paths, beaches, and trees on the western edge of town, this is Berlin's most popular weekend retreat. If you're in the mood to walk, follow the signs to **Jagdschloß Grunewald** (Am Grunewaldsee, tel. 030/813–3597), a 16th-century royal hunting lodge that now houses a privately owned art gallery. Another popular excursion is to **Pfaueninsel** (Peacock Island; admission DM2), set in a wide arm of the Havel River. The island is noted for its lush gardens—home to hundreds of wild peacocks—and its white marble **castle** (Zehlendorf, tel. 030/805–3042; admission DM3). Because the Grunewald is too large to cover in a single day, if you want nothing more than beach and water take S1, S3, or S5 to Nikolaisee Station and follow the signs to Großer Wannsee; it's about a 20-minute walk. A more traditional starting point is Wannsee Station (S-Bahn), a five-minute walk from some good hiking trails.

Kreuzberg. This is one of Berlin's liveliest quarters, home to an odd mix of progressive youth, Turkish immigrants, and factory workers. Kreuzberg has sizable gay/lesbian and student communities, not to mention untold hordes of dropouts and junkies. "Squat houses" cater to those living on the edge, while offbeat cafés attract self-proclaimed bohemians and the art crowd. This mélange can be annoying at times, especially when you stumble upon a bar that takes itself too seriously. But for the most part, Kreuzberg is the place to come for a nontraditional look at Berlin. It's also *the* place for cheap dive bars and basement cafés. The district is divided into two distinct sections: semiconservative West Kreuzberg, the area around Viktoriapark; and the wilder, grungier East Kreuzberg, the area around Kottbußer Tor and Skalitzerstraße. For the former take U7 or U6 to Mehringdamm Station; for the latter take U1 or U8 to Kottbußer Tor Station.

Kulturforum. The Kulturforum (Cultural Forum), near the Tiergarten, is a series of first-rate museums and galleries. The finest attraction is the **Neue Nationalgalerie,** with a permanent collection that leans heavily toward the impressionists, from Manet and Monet to Renoir and

Pissarro. *Potsdamerstr. 50, tel. 030/2666. U2 to Potsdamer Pl. and walk west. Admission free. Open Tues.–Fri. 9–5, weekends 10–5.*

Kurfürstendamm. West Berlin's most famous thoroughfare stretches for 3½ km, connecting Schöneberg in the east with Grunewald in the west. Its liveliest section is just south of Zoo Station and the Tiergarten, near Europa Center. On **Breitscheidplatz,** immediately opposite Europa Center, you can find people carousing and browsing at all hours of the day—a crowd evenly divided between wealthy Berliners and junkies looking to score. The Ku'damm's most famous landmark is **Kaiser Wilhelm Gedächtniskirche,** opposite Europa Center on Breitscheidplatz. The church (1895) was all but destroyed during World War II, and it has been left in a war-scarred state to serve as a memorial. *Breitscheidpl. Admission free. Open Tues.–Sat. 10–6, Sun. 11–6.*

Reichstag. Just north of Brandenburg Gate, the imposing Reichstag (Imperial Parliament) looms into view. This bulky Renaissance-style structure was built in 1894 to house the Prussian Parliament, and performed the same function for the short-lived Weimar Republic (1919–1933). On February 28, 1933, as Germany struggled with a broken economy and the Weimar Republic's warring ideologues, the Reichstag burned down under mysterious circumstances. No one's sure who actually set the fire, but the Nazis swiftly and vociferously blamed the Communists. The Nazis then suspended the constitution, and outlawed all opposition parties. Currently, the Reichstag's west wing is home to a fascinating exhibit entitled "Questions on German History." Sometime before the end of the century, the Reichstag will once again house the Bundestag (German Parliament), though it will take some time to move everything from Bonn to Berlin. *Pl. der Republik 21, tel. 030/39770. Bus 100 from Zoo Station. Admission free. Open Tues.–Sun. 10–5.*

Schloß Charlottenburg. Friedrich I, the flamboyant Prussian monarch, built the Charlottenburg Palace at the end of the 17th century for his wife, Queen Sophie Charlotte. The palace, on the outskirts of Berlin, became the city residence for all Prussian rulers, and the complex evolved under the direction of each new ruler. Visits to the royal apartments are by guided tour only; tours leave every hour on the hour from 9 to 4. Also on the grounds, you'll find the 18th-century **Belvedere House,** a teahouse that overlooks the Spree River and contains a small collection of Berlin porcelain, the **Schinkel Pavillion,** which houses paintings by Caspar David Friedrich, and some fin de siècle furniture. *Schloß Charlottenburg: Luisenpl. 19, tel. 030/320911. U-Bahn to Sophie-Charlotte-Pl. Admission: DM8, includes guided tour; palace grounds free. Open Tues., Wed., Fri.–Sun. 9–5, Thurs. 10–5; grounds open daily sunrise–sunset.*

Schöneberg. This district, which lies directly south of the Tiergarten, has a reputation for wild nightlife. At the heart of it all lies **Nollendorfplatz,** the focus of the quarter's gay and lesbian scene. If the Kreuzberg seems a bit too wild, odds are you'll find a more middle-of-the-road option for boozing and dancing here. By day, head east from the square down Bülowstraße. In the defunct U-Bahn station look for the **Nollendorf Market,** offering an odd mix of fresh produce, electronic goods, and high-quality "junk." The market operates Thursday through Monday from sunrise to sunset. Farther west is the **Bülowstraße Bazar,** where you'll find an equally bizarre mix of track suits and bootleg music. South of Nollendorfplatz stands the imperial **Rathaus Schöneberg,** which housed the West Berlin Senate until 1989. On June 26, 1963, John F. Kennedy visited the site to present West Berlin with a document supporting the city's struggle for freedom, signed by more than 17 million Americans. At the end of his famous speech against communism, Kennedy concluded: "All free men, wherever they live, are citizens of Berlin. And, therefore, as a free man, I take pride in the words 'Ich bin ein Berliner.'" Unfortunately, no one had told Kennedy that "ein Berliner" actually refers to a jelly-filled doughnut.

Tiergarten. The Tiergarten runs from Brandenburg Gate in the east to Zoo Station in the west—a peaceful expanse of forest and lake in the otherwise urban city center. Its main feature is the sprawling 1½-km-long **Straße des 17 Juni,** which connects West Berlin's Bismarkstraße with East Berlin's stately Unter den Linden. Much of the Tiergarten is undeveloped and attracts few tourists. The most interesting sections are the area surrounding Brandenburg Gate and the zoo, at the southwest corner of the park.

Zoologischer Garten. This zoo inside the Tiergarten boasts the world's largest variety of animals—over 11,000 creatures. It's also worth the extra money to check out the massive aquarium complex. *Entrances at Hardenbergpl. and Budapester Str., tel. 030/254010. U- and S-Bahn Zoologischer Garten. Zoo admission: DM9, DM7.50 students. Combined aquarium and zoo admission: DM13.50, DM11.50 students. Open daily 9–dusk.*

➤ **EAST BERLIN** • Until recently, East Berlin was regarded with a mix of dread and awe. Much of this was due to the Berlin Wall, which insulated the city from the West. Although East Berlin is still plagued by the Communist legacy of cement and pollution, it also contains excellent museums and a good number of stately, majestic avenues. Prior to World War II, in fact, Berlin's center was in the east. Jazz and cabaret dominated the club scene, while Erwin Piscator and Bertolt Brecht made their mark in theater. This was the heyday of the progressive Weimar Republic. Back then, the Ku'damm was mostly residential, and streets like Unter den Linden and Friedrichstraße, East Berlin's main thoroughfares, were the unchallenged hot spots of raucous nightlife. East Berlin also had the city's largest university, staffed in the 1920s by the likes of Albert Einstein.

Alexanderplatz. Named after Russian Czar Alexander I, this square is one of East Berlin's main landmarks. It's easy to find, thanks to the **Fernsehturm** TV tower, rising nearly 1,200 feet above the square; it also houses the Telecafé restaurant (*see* Food, *above*). From the top-floor observation deck (elevator DM5; open daily 9 AM–midnight) you get a striking 360° view of Berlin. Back on the ground, the rest of Alexanderplatz is dominated by ugly high rises, fast-food stands, and the Kaufhof department store. Near Karl-Liebknecht-Straße, look for the **Berliner Markthalle,** an informal produce market that's often stocked with boxes of fresh cherries and strawberries.

Friedrichstraße. Friedrichstraße has pockets of 1920s architecture intermixed with the cement and steel of the Communist era, and a few stylish bars. Concentrate your energy on its more scenic southern leg. Here you'll find one of the finest squares in all Europe, the **Platz der Akademie** (Johannes-Dieckmann-Str., 1 block west of Friedrichstr.). Its main feature is the 18th-century **Deutscher Dom** (admission free; open daily 9–5), with its broad steps and massive cupola. On the opposite side of the square is the neoclassic **Schauspielhaus,** one of the greatest works by Berlin architect Karl Schinkel. Nowadays it's home to the Berlin Symphony Orchestra.

Marx-Engels-Platz. Prior to World War II, Marx-Engels-Platz housed the 15th-century Berliner Schloß, a lavish Baroque palace and imperial residence. Allied bombing, however, reduced the complex to rubble. The postwar government wrecked what little remained, clearing space for the gruesomely modern **Palast der Republik.** This once housed the GDR's parliament, the Volkskammer; today it stands empty. Just north of the Palast der Republik is the 19th-century **Berliner Dom** (tel. 030/242–4277; open Mon.–Sat. 9–7:30, Sun. 11:15–5), one of Berlin's most impressive cathedrals. At the square's west end, the **Karl-Liebknecht-Brücke** leads west across the Spree River. The bridge was designed by Schinkel and is lined with classical statues, many of which sported spray-painted mustaches and pubic hair following December 1989. Just beyond is **Neue Wache,** the very first of Schinkel's Berlin creations. It's a modest structure, built in 1818 in the style of a Roman temple. Prior to World War II it was used as a military arsenal, though it later became one of East Berlin's most famous war memorials. An eternal flame burns inside its intimate, pillared hallway, which also houses the tomb of an unknown soldier, killed during World War II.

Museumsinsel. A short walk north of Marx-Engels-Platz and bordered by the Spree River on either side, Museumsinsel (Museum Island) houses four major museums. Admission to each is DM5. **Alte Museum** (Lustgarten, tel. 030/203550; open Wed.–Sun. 10–6) features a vast collection of postwar East German art. Another exhibit includes etchings by Dürer, Cranach, and Rembrandt. The **Nationalgalerie** (Bodestr., tel. 030/667–9033; open Wed.–Sun. 10–6) contains Berlin's largest collection of 18th-, 19th-, and 20th-century paintings. In the don't-miss category is the **Pergamonmuseum** (Am Kupfergraben; open daily 10–6), with one of the world's best collections of Hellenic, Egyptian, and Middle Eastern art. The museum is named for its principal display, the Pergamon altar. This dazzling 2nd-century-BC Greek temple was moved block by block from a mountaintop in Turkey. Equally remarkable in the Asia Minor section is the Ishtar Gate, which dates from the 6th-century-BC reign of Nebuchadnezzar II.

Nikolaiviertel. The Nikolaiviertel quarter, bordered by Alexanderplatz to the north and the Spree River to the south, is a replica of an entire prewar neighborhood, including exact copies of the quarter's famous historical buildings. Today's Nikolaiviertel does indeed feel pleasantly old and refined, dominated by fin de siècle facades and ornate Baroque-style apartments. The district is dominated by **Nikolaikirche** (admission DM2; open Tues.–Fri. 9–5, weekends 9–6), a 13th-century church that has been reconstructed. Just south is Berlin's most lavish Rococo house, the **Ephraim Palace** (Poststr. 16, no phone; open Tues.–Fri. 9–5, weekends 10–6), originally built in 1764 for Veitel Ephraim, court jeweler to Friedrich II. Veitel was Jewish, so in 1933 the Nazis razed the structure and plundered its collection of rare stones. Pieces of the original Rococo facade were discovered following the war and later incorporated into the reconstruction you see today.

Prenzlauer Berg. Roughly 1 km northeast of Alexanderplatz is this drab working-class quarter, filled with faceless apartment buildings. It's also the social hub of East Berlin, a twin to West Berlin's Kreuzberg district. Like the latter, Prenzlauer Berg nurtures a large gay and lesbian community as well as a fairly wild club scene. Take U2 to Senefelderplatz or Dimitroffstraße. They both empty onto **Schönhauser Allee,** the district's main artery. It's a quiet shopping street lined with old-fashioned prewar buildings. Just north of Senefelderplatz Station is **Jüdischer Friedhof** (Schönhauser Allee 23; open Mon.–Thurs. 8–4), wherein lie the haunting, ivy-covered graves of some 20,000 Jews. Continue north on Schönhauser Allee to Wörtherstraße, then turn right. Two blocks ahead is the graceful **Käthe-Kollwitz-Platz,** named in honor of the famous German artist. The square is centered around a Parisian-style park; in the middle stands Kollwitz's sculpture *The Mother.* Leading north from the square is one of East Berlin's most remarkable streets, **Husemannstraße,** lined with colorful Baroque buildings and shops.

Unter den Linden. The 1.2-km-long Unter den Linden is a sweeping, grand avenue that stretches from Brandenburg Gate in the west to Marx-Engels-Platz in the east. On it you'll find fin de siècle mansions and numerous historic buildings—the sort of imperial architecture that gives eastern Berlin a stately feel. The best way to appreciate Unter den Linden is on foot, roughly a two-hour undertaking. The traditional starting point is **Pariser Platz,** just east of Brandenburg Gate. Continuing east, you'll pass a collection of bulky, worn buildings that once housed GDR ministries. The **Altes Palais,** former palace of Emperor Wilhelm I, is closed to the public, but its staunch facade is definitely photo-worthy. Across from the palace, in the middle of the street, is an equestrian sculpture (1851) of Friedrich II. The sculptor, Rauch, took a few liberties by incorporating the heads of Gotthold Lessing and Immanuel Kant, two of the emperor's harshest critics, on the horse's rear end, right below the tail. Across from this is the 18th-century **Humboldt University,** recognizable by the statues of Wilhelm and Alexander von Humboldt, the university's founders. The area just southeast of the university is known as **Bebelplatz,** a pleasant square bordered by lime trees. Bebelplatz marks the site of the 1933 *Bücherverbrennung* (book burning), a propaganda event orchestrated by Hitler. Thrown into the fire were works considered too "dangerous" for public consumption; banned authors included Thomas Mann, Hegel, Benjamin Franklin, and Dostoyevsky. Flanking the square is Berlin's main opera house, the **Deutsche Staatsoper** (Unter den Linden 7, tel. 030/200–4762; S-Bahn Friedrichstr.; box office open weekdays noon–5:45).

AFTER DARK Berlin's nightlife has always been notorious. Post–World War I despair was transformed into giddy recklessness, and an era of cabaret, jazz, and expressionist theater was born. Following World War II, West Berlin's isolation and the influx of Western money continued to foster a flamboyant, almost reckless approach to life. While Communism transformed East Berlin into a cement wasteland, areas like the Ku'damm and Schöneberg in West Berlin developed into swank playgrounds. With unification, Berlin has regained some of its former diversity.

Internationale Filmfestspiele, Berlin's International Film Festival in February, rivals those in Cannes and Venice. It features new works from an international troop of filmmakers as well as remastered classics. Cinemas all over Berlin are co-opted for the event, and admission runs anywhere from DM6 to DM50. For tickets and more information, contact Filmfestspiele Berlin (Budapesterstr. 50, tel. 030/254890).

➤ **BARS** • Berlin supposedly has more bars per square kilometer than any other city in the world, but the city's bars are notoriously short-lived, especially those in Kreuzberg and Prenzlauer Berg. The main strip in Kreuzberg is **Oranienstraße,** noted for its Turkish watering holes and offbeat cafés. German Yuppies tend to gather at Charlottenburg's **Savignyplatz,** while **Martin-Luther Straße** in Schöneberg attracts an odd mix of artists, long-haired dropouts, and well-dressed business types. The main drag in Prenzlauer Berg is **Schönhauser Allee** and the adjacent **Kollwitz Platz,** frequented by artsy East Berliners. Bars usually open around 6 or 7 at the latest and close by 2.

Anderes Ufer. Artistic types in a quiet atmosphere. Crowd is predominantly gay/lesbian, but straights are welcome. Some nights feature live folk and blues, usually free. Beer and wine start at DM8. *Hauptstr. 157. U7 to Kleistpark.*

Die Zwei. Women-only (but not necessarily lesbian-only) bar plays varied music to its diverse crowd. Beer from DM6, sandwiches and pastries DM5. *At Martin-Lutherstr. and Motzstr. U4 to Viktoria-Luise-Pl., then walk northeast on Motzstr.*

Flip-Flop. One of Berlin's best-known gay bars, where tourists and locals drink and socialize. Beers DM5–DM8; mixed drinks start at around DM10. *Kulmerstr. 20A. S1 to Göschenstr., then walk west to Kulmerstr.*

Klo. Klo is slang for bathroom, and this theme is carried out all the way: large beers (DM11) come in bedpans, flush noises blast over the sound system, and scrub brushes dangle from the ceiling. *Leibniz Str. 57, no phone. Bus 149 from Zoo Station to Leibniz Str.*

Rost. Popular with the local theater crowd but with a surprisingly relaxed atmosphere. DM5 beer is cheap for the area. *Knesebeckstr. 29, just south of Savignyplatz, tel. 030/881–9501.*

➤ **DANCE CLUBS** • **Abraxas.** Where Charlottenburg locals come for Latin, Caribbean funk, and jazz. Cover around DM5, cocktails DM12. *Kantstr. 134, tel. 030/312–9493.*

Cha-Cha. A style-conscious dance club where DJ spins Top 40 and hip-hop records until the wee hours. Drinks DM6–DM8. *Nürnberger Str. 50, tel. 030/214–2976. From Breitscheidpl. east on Tauentzienstr., right at Nürnberger Str. Cover: DM5. Closed Mon.*

Lip Stick. Popular lesbian club open to women only on Monday, Friday, and Saturday. Other days, the crowd is mostly, but not exclusively, gay. Cover DM5. *Richard-Wagner-Pl. 5, tel. 030/342–8126. U-Bahn to Richard-Wagner-Pl. Closed Wed.*

Trash. Black walls, black lights, and a stylish Kreuzberg grunge crowd. Music includes New Wave favorites and some rap. Beer DM9. *Oranienstr. 40–41, no phone. U8 to Moritzpl. Closed Mon.*

Wu-Wu. Gay male nightclub in Schöneberg plays an assorted mix of tunes. Cover DM5 weekends, free weekdays, drinks from DM4. *Kleiststr. 4, tel. 030/213–6392. From Europa Center, east on the Ku'damm until it becomes Kleistr.*

➤ **ROCK** • **Club 29.** East Berlin's premiere rock club features alternative, independent, and just plain strange local bands. *Rosa-Luxembourg-Str. 29, tel. 030/282–4920. From Alexanderpl., north on Karl-Liebknecht-Str. and left on Belvederestr.*

Franz-Club. Popular with a university-age crowd, this relaxed, unpretentious bar has live jazz and rock most nights. It's in East Berlin's Prenzlauer Berg, within easy reach of the district's other bars. *Schönhauser Allee 36–39, tel. 030/448–5567. U-Bahn Schönhauser Allee.*

➤ **JAZZ** • The **Jazz in the Garten** festival brings local and international talent to the Neue Nationalgalerie (*see* Worth Seeing, *above*) four Fridays in June. Many of the sessions are held outside in the gallery's lush gardens and it's all free. **Jazz in July** is Berlin's premiere jazz event, attracting big-name stars from the States and Britain. It's sponsored by the Quasimo-do Club (*see below*), which is the festival's main venue. Tickets, generally priced between DM10 and DM25, should be purchased well in advance.

Blues Cafe. Seedy and intimate, Blues Cafe features local talent and the occasional big-name act. It's the place to come if you enjoy the dive jazz scene but aren't interested in flawless music. *Körnerstr. 11A, off Potsdammer Pl., tel. 030/261–3698.*

Flöz. Bohemian, dark, and smoky. Local and big-name bands play pre-1950s jazz, Dixieland, and swing. *Naßauische Str. 37., tel. 030/861–1000. U2 to Hohenzollernpl.*

Jazz for Fun. Hear new, local jazz talent or bring an instrument for Thursday night's open jam session. Cover charges up to DM8. *Kurfürsten Str. 10., tel. 030/262–4556. U-Bahn to Kurfürsrsten Str.*

Quasimodo. Largely responsible for Berlin's recent jazz renaissance. Even though it's world famous, it's also surprisingly untouristy. Cover DM10–DM25. *Kantstr. 12A, tel. 030/312–8086.*

➤ **CLASSICAL** • **Deutsche Oper Berlin.** West Berlin's German Opera hosts a wide range of ballet and music year-round. Best of all, student tickets start around DM15, regular tickets at DM25. *Bismarckstr. 35, tel. 030/341–0249. U-Bahn to Deutsche Oper.*

Philharmonic. Home to the world-famous Berlin Philharmonic and the lesser-known Berlin Radio Symphony Orchestra. Tickets are expensive (DM20–DM40) and often hard to come by; stop by the box office A.S.A.P. *Matthäikirchstr. 1, tel. 030/805–1418. S1 or S2 to Potsdamerpl., then walk northwest on Bellevue Str.*

Urania. A forum for smaller orchestras and chamber groups, Urania also has the cheapest seats in town, priced from DM10 for students. *An der Urania 17, tel. 030/242–7182. From Gedächtniskirche, Bus 129 east to An der Urania.*

NEAR BERLIN

POTSDAM No matter how short your stay in Berlin, make time for a quick visit to Potsdam, the capital of Brandenburg. The town's historic quarters are intensely beautiful and give a good sense of what Berlin might have looked like, but for World War II. On the plush side there's Friedrich the Great's palace, **Sanssouci** (French for "without a care"). It's an appropriate name for this elegant summer residence. The palaces and parks of the **Neuer Garten** are another big attraction; this is where Truman, Attlee, and Stalin signed the 1945 Potsdam Agreement divvying up Germany. Potsdam drips with history, both ancient and modern, so don't come expecting another typical Berlin suburb.

From Platz der Einheit, near the tourist office, the pedestrians-only Brandenburgerstraße meanders north through the **Baroque Quarter,** noted for its colorful facades. Avoid the touristy "market" streets and head instead for the network of lanes that fan outward from the larger shopping avenues. These run through quiet residential areas, passing a few tree-lined parks on the way. On **Alter Markt,** Potsdam's central market square, check out the classical **Nikolaikirche** (1837) and the colorful facade of the former city hall. Also notice the **Rathaus** (1753), recognizable by the gilded figure of Atlas atop the tower. Three blocks north of Alter Markt is **Holländisches Viertel,** the Dutch Quarter. It was commissioned in 1732 by Friedrich Wilhelm I, who hoped to induce Dutch artisans to settle in the city. Few Dutch ever came, but the quarter's gabled, redbrick homes give the district a distinctive, very un-German feel. Continue north past **Nauener Tor,** an 18th-century city gate, to the **Alexandrowka** district, with its dense jumble of wood houses built in 19th-century Russian style.

➤ **COMING AND GOING** • Potsdam's only 30 minutes by subway from Berlin's Zoo Station; take S-Bahn to Potsdam Stadt Station (DM3). You can easily walk around Potsdam in four hours, although it has an excellent youth hostel if you get stuck, and Potsdam's **tourist office** (Friedrich-Ebert Str. 5, tel. 0331/21100) can book you into a private room (DM20–DM40) for a DM5 fee.

➤ **WHERE TO SLEEP** • **Jugendherberge Potsdam** (Eisenhardtstr. 5, tel. 0331/225125) has cozy four- to five-person rooms and a self-service kitchen. Beds cost DM15 per person; add DM5 for breakfast and DM7 for dinner. Take Bus 604, 609, or 650 from Potsdam Hauptbahnhof north to Eisenhardt Straße.

BRANDENBURG Since reunification Brandenburg has become a popular day trip for all sorts of Berliners, and not just because of the newly upgraded train line that connects the two cities in under an hour. In terms of scenery and historical grace, Brandenburg is one of the region's finest Baroque cities. Modern industry blankets a large section of its working-class suburbs, and the city did suffer some World War II damages. But within the historic city center you'll find a pleasant mix of half-timber houses, old-style shop fronts, and relaxed, open-air squares. Brandenburg is nearly cut in half by the winding **Havel River,** so much of the town is given over to bridges, canals, and riverside walking paths. Brandenburg is divided into the Altstadt and Neustadt, with the **Dominsel** (Cathedral Island) marking the spot of the city's original 10th-century settlement, right in between. For detailed city maps, stop by the helpful **tourist office** (Plauer Str. 4, near Neustadt Markt, tel. 03381/23743; open weekdays 9–5, Sat. 9–1).

➤ **WHERE TO SLEEP AND EAT** • Brandenburg has no reasonably priced hotels—not one. Your only hope is the tourist office's list of private rooms (from DM30) or the **hostel** (Hevellerstr. 7, tel. 03381/521040; beds DM15). For food, try Hauptstraße for nice-ish cafés and bargain-priced street stands. Locals like to eat at the town's **Ratskeller** (Altstädtischer Mark 10, tel. 03381/24051), where a beer and wiener fetches at least DM10. Health nuts will enjoy Brandenburg's youth club, the **Jugendklubhaus Philipp Müller** (Steinstr. 42; closed Sun.), which doubles as a vegetarian café. Food isn't always available, but it's cheap when it is (meals under DM10).

Eastern Germany

Because Brandenburg and Saxony-Anhalt lie in what used to be East Germany, both regions still bare the scars of their decades-long tenure under the Red Army, and both are still plagued by the foul legacy that has come to define Cold War–era Communism—industry and cement. Since reunification some effort has been made to "beautify" or at least demolish and rebuild the most painful reminders of the past. Yet reunification itself has brought its own Pandora's Box of troubles. As former East Germans struggle with their new economy and supposed capitalist perspective, unemployment in these regions remains despairingly high, and skinheads and neo-Nazis scrawl swastikas and anti-Semitic sentiments on walls all over. To appreciate these regions you need to prepare for the troublesome dichotomy of modern Germany: unspoiled countryside tempered by forests thinning from acid rain; industry and pollution balanced against farmland and nature.

Thuringia, on the other hand, can be quite a surprise if you expect eastern Germany to be all cement, steel, and gloom. Although formerly part of the GDR, it remains one of the country's most picture-perfect *Länder* (states), with a dizzying array of rolling pastureland, lazy farm villages, forested mountains, forbidding castles, and lush, flamboyantly Baroque palaces. The highlights here are **Erfurt** and **Weimar** in the west, **Leipzig** in the north, and the **Thüringer Wald** in the south. If you're bound for the Czech Republic or Poland, definitely consider a stop in **Dresden.**

A major reason to visit this area is to soak up some history; if you can see past the ugly architecture of some of these towns, you might enjoy happening upon Nietzsche's or Bach's regular hangouts. Cyclists can also have a ball in these areas because the distances are not vast and the scenery—at least once you escape into the countryside—falls somewhere between rural idyllic and sylvan nirvana. Most train stations in the area rent bikes for about DM15–DM20 per day.

Dresden

In 1694 the king of Poland, August II, came to rule Dresden. He and his son, Friedrich August II, took Dresden under their royal wings, luring leading Bavarian and Italian architects to build or renovate galleries, opera houses, and theaters. The result was a breathtaking city, from gilded architecture to riverside walks. During World War II, Dresden was ruthlessly bombed by the Allies and left a gutted, smoldering ruin. Since reunification, money from western Germany has been pouring in to help this bastion of culture clean up its act. Nowadays, Dresden's restored beauty is rivaled only by the art and music traditions it nurtures: The city's music halls—which long ago convinced the likes of Carl Weber, Richard Wagner, and Richard Strauss to set up shop here—pour awesome music into the streets on balmy summer nights. On the downside, Dresden can be uncomfortably crowded in summer, so consider booking ahead.

BASICS

➤ **VISITOR INFORMATION** • *Prager Str. 10–11, tel. 0351/495–5025. Open Apr.–Sept., weekdays 8–8, Sat. 8–6, Sun. 8–2; Oct.–Mar., weekdays 9–6, weekends 9–noon.*

➤ **AMERICAN EXPRESS** • *Große Meißner Str. 15, tel. 0351/566–2865. Tram 5 from Hauptbahnhof to Neustädter Markt. Open weekdays 9–5:30, Sat. 9–noon.*

COMING AND GOING Trains leave the **Hauptbahnhof,** which also houses the bus station, every hour or so for Berlin (DM27) and Leipzig (DM18). For ride-share services try **Studentische Mitfahrzentrale** (Nürnberger Str. 57, tel. 0351/463–6060) or **Reisezentrum** (Friedrich-Engels Str. 10, fel. 0351/51216).

GETTING AROUND The sight-cramped Altstadt is easy to spot—by the jumble of towers and spires—and easy to explore on foot. Buses and trams are also efficient for short jaunts in town. The Hauptbahnhof and its network of tracks form the southern border of the city center; outside the train station, the pedestrian-only Prager Straße leads straight to the open-air **Altmarkt.** The **Neumarkt,** another elegant open-air square, is a few hundred yards north. Farther north is the Elbe River, which divides the old town on the south bank from the new town on the north bank.

WHERE TO SLEEP From the Hauptbahnhof take the S-Bahn to Bahnhof Neustadt, walk east along Antonstraße past Alberplatz, and keep your eyes peeled for the comfy **Hotel Stadt Rendsburg** (Kamenzer Str. 1, tel. 0351/51551; doubles DM115). Otherwise, book ahead for **Jugendherberge Rudi-Arndt** (Hübnerstr. 11, tel. 0351/471–0667; beds DM18, DM21 over 26), which has a choice spot in a safe, quiet neighborhood near the Hauptbahnhof. Dres-

Punting in the Spreewald

The Slavic Serbs wandered into the Spreewald, a marshland about 100 km southeast of Berlin, in the 5th century AD and have since remained in isolated pockets, preserving their ethnic identity even though more than one German ruler has vehemently sought their extinction. Today the Serbs are free to practice their traditions, speak their language, and form their own schools. In the Spreewald—the town of Lübbenau makes a good base—you'll notice many street signs in both German and Serbian. The best way to see this area is by punt, the local version of a gondola, and if you do take such a tour (about DM50 per group for 3–4 hrs), chances are good your guide will be a Serb.

den's other youth hostel, **Jugendherberge Oberloschwitz** (Sierksstr. 33, tel. 0351/33672; beds DM22–DM25), is on top of a steep hill far from downtown but is definitely worth the effort; from Bahnhof Neustadt, take Tram 6 toward Bahnhof Niedersedlitz and get off at Schillerplatz, where you catch the Swebebahn shuttle to the hostel). Call first—it may be full or closed for the weekend. The only campground, **Wostra Strandbad** (Wilhelm-Weitling-Str., tel. 0351/223–1903), is unscenic and 10 km outside town; from the Hauptbahnhof, take Tram 9 toward Kleinzschachwitz to the last stop, walk two blocks, and turn right onto Wilhelm-Weitling-Straße.

FOOD In good weather Dresden moves its drinking and dining outside, especially to the sidewalk tables of colorful shopping streets like **Münzgasse.** Try **Kleppereck** (Münzgasse at Terraßengasse) for its top-rate, topping-heavy pizzas: The veggie pie is a steal at DM7.50.

Pizza & Pasta. Small, no-frills Italian joint with good food, low prices, and exasperatingly lazy staff. Individual pies from DM5. *Bautzner Str. 9, tel. 0351/55870. 1 block east of Alaunstr. and Albertpl. Closed Sun.*

Kügelgen-Haus. Popular spot with grill, coffee bar, restaurant, and historic beer cellar. Traditional German meats and stews, or steak, burgers, and salads, all DM15–DM25. *Hauptstr. 11–13, tel. 0351/52791. Closed Mon.*

WORTH SEEING Despite the best efforts of Allied bombers and Communist city planners, the colonnaded **Altmarkt** retains much of its elegant pre–World War II grace, including the lush Baroque **Kreuzkirche** on the square's east side. If you only have one day in Dresden, focus on this square and the surrounding Altstadt.

Brühlsche Terraße, a tree-lined promenade overlooking the Elbe between Carolbrücke and Augustusbrücke, gives sweeping views of the new town and serves as the entrance to the excellent **Albertinum** museum. The collection includes Flemish and Dutch art, works by German Renaissance genius Dürer, and big-name French impressionists and expressionists. *Am Neumarkt, tel. 0351/484–0119. Admission: DM5, DM2.50 students. Open Fri.–Wed. 10–6.*

Neumarkt. Despite its name, Neumarkt is the heart of historic Dresden. The **Frauenkirche** was considered Germany's greatest Baroque cathedral until it was ravaged by a 1945 firestorm; the ragged walls remain as a war memorial. At the northwest corner of Neumarkt is the 16th-century **Johanneum,** whose dazzling outer wall is a giant jigsaw puzzle made of 25,000 hand-painted tiles. The work was done in 1904–1907 by Wilhelm Walther and depicts more than 100 members of the royal Saxon house of Wettin.

Semperoper. This famous but tragedy-prone opera house is in its third incarnation; earlier buildings fell victim to fire and bombings. The site has seen the premieres of Wagner's operas *Der Fliegende Holländer* and *Tannhäuser,* and Strauss' *Salome* and *Elektra.* Student and rush tickets sometimes go on sale the night of a performance; ask the folks at the Sofienstraße box office for an *Ermäßigung* (reduced ticket) or *Stehplatz* (standing-room ticket; DM5). *Theaterpl. 2, a few blocks northeast of Neumarkt, tel. 0351/484–2491 for box office.*

Zwinger. On the south side of Theaterplatz stands the Zwinger palace complex, one of the world's finest Baroque masterpieces. The bulk of the palace, originally designed by Matthäus Pöppelmann under the direction of King Friedrich August I, was built onto a section of Dresden's centuries-old fortifications. Today the palace is home to several museums. The best

Sleeping in the Suburbs

Radebeul, a small suburb 10 km northeast of Dresden, has three things going for it: easy access by S-Bahn (Radebeul-Weintraube station), hills covered with villas and vineyards, and a pleasant hostel (Weinstraubenstr. 12, tel. 0351/74786; beds DM18–DM21) in case everything in Dresden is booked.

include the **Sempergalerie** (admission DM3), which holds the world-renowned **Gemälderie Alte Meister** (Gallery of Old Masters; admission DM3.50), including but not at all limited to familiar Italian Renaissance paintings. *Theaterpl., tel. 0351/484–0119.*

AFTER DARK The Altstadt is for nose-in-the-air cultural events, the Neustadt for down-and-dirty nightlife. At **Tonne** (Tzschirnerpl. 3, tel. 0351/495–1354), the jazz bands vary as widely as the cover charge (DM7–DM15). For dancing, local hipsters hit **Sachs Music Hall** (Stephensonstr. 6, tel. 0351/223–8742). Or, nurse a half-liter stein among natives at **Die 100** (Alaunstr. 100, off Albertpl., no phone). Music festivals run throughout the summer; get tickets (DM10–DM60) in the **Schauspielhaus** across from the Zwinger. The **Schinkelwache** (Sofienstr., tel. 0351/484–2352 or 0351/484–2353) sells tickets for seasonal events throughout the city.

NEAR DRESDEN

It would be a shame to visit Dresden without making at least one day trip, especially if you're the outdoorsy type. Just south of Dresden lies **Sächsische Schweiz**, Saxony's "Little Switzerland." The low-lying Elbsandstein Mountains extend roughly from the outskirts of Dresden to the Czech Republic border, some 40 km southeast, offering great hikes, expansive views, and impressive sunsets. From the small, beer-hall-saturated village of **Pirna,** 18 km southeast of Dresden, you can rent a bike and strike out into Mother Nature, then stay at Pirna's **hostel** (Birkwitzer Str. 51, tel. 03501/2388; beds DM14, DM17 over 26). To reach Pirna either take the S-Bahn from Dresden, or take a **Weiße Flotte** (tel. 0351/502–2611) ferry from Dresden's Terraßenufer, on the Elbe two blocks north of Neumarkt.

MEIßEN Porcelain is to Meißen what stone and mortar are to other towns; ever since local alchemists cooked up the recipe for porcelain, the village's civic buildings have been drenched in the stuff. Check out the bells of the **Frauenkirche** (Marktpl.), for instance, or the decorative figures in **Nikolaikirche** (Stadtpark). Otherwise, the main reason to come is to tour Meißen's porcelain factories, such as the hilltop castle **Albrechtsburg** (Dompl.; admission DM5, DM3 students; open weekdays 10–6, weekends 10–8). The workshops were closed ages ago, but the castle tour (DM4) does a good job of explaining the how and why of porcelain. To see porcelain makers in action, go back down the hill and across town to the **Staatliche Porzellan-Manufaktur** (Talstr. 9; open Tues.–Sun. 10–4), which has a work station and museum. Meißen, a half-hour northwest of Dresden on the S-Bahn or train, is a definite day trip. But if an afternoon in the run-down pub **Weinschänke Vincenz Richter** (An der Frauenkirche, tel. 03521/453285; closed Mon.) somehow becomes a groggy evening, stumble to Meißen's **hostel** (Wilsdruffer Str. 28, in Altstadt off Poststr., tel. 03521/453065; beds DM12, DM15 over 26).

Leipzig

Like Berlin, Leipzig has long cultivated a progressive, almost libertine identity. Even during the GDR era, Leipzig's 15,000 or so students were vociferous critics of the Communist government, and more than once the army had to be called in to quell student-led riots. During the 1970s and 1980s this "screw-you" attitude drew thousands of disillusioned artists and dropouts to Leipzig. Even now that Germany is unified, Leipzig produces a bevy of grunge and metal bands, and its café society—at least in the student quarters—echoes what you'll find in Berlin's Kreuzberg and Prenzlauer Berg districts. In contrast to graceful Dresden, the architectural theme in Leipzig is concrete; you won't find many colorful lanes or squares. But for those who find Berlin overwhelming, Leipzig offers many of the same diversions without the suburban sprawl.

VISITOR INFORMATION **Leipzig-Information** is so big it has an information desk to direct you to the proper information desk. *Sachsenpl. 1, southwest of Hauptbahnhof, tel. 0341/79590. Open weekdays 9–7, weekends 9:30–2.*

COMING AND GOING Nearly all of Leipzig's sights are concentrated in its extremely small center, bordered by the Hauptbahnhof to the north and the university (Augustuspl.) to the south. You'll only need the **tram** or **bus** (DM1) to reach an out-of-the-way pension or private room, and even that will be a short ride. If you need a **taxi,** call 0341/7411 or 0341/594171.

Leipzig's **Hauptbahnhof** (Pl. der Republik, tel. 0341/7240) is the largest in Europe and one of the most elegant. Trains zip hourly to Berlin (DM25) and Dresden (DM18), five times a day to Frankfurt (DM56). For ride sharing, contact **Mitfahr-und Wohnzentrale** (Rudolf-Breitscheid-Str. 39, around cnr. from Hauptbahnhof, tel. 0341/211–4222) or the student-run **Mitfahrzentrale** (Augustuspl. 9, at the university, tel. 0341/719–2097).

WHERE TO SLEEP Most people at **Campingplatz Am Auensee** (Gustav-Esche-Str. 5, tel. 0341/212–3031), across the lake from the Jugendherberge Am Auensee (*see below*), are young backpackers who couldn't find a spot in town. Luckily the campground is in top form and open year-round. No tent? No problem. They rent 'em for DM3, and bungalows go for DM90 plus DM4 per person.

Jugendherberge Am Auensee. Long ride (30 min) from city center, but short walk to tree-lined shore of Auensee. Four- to eight-bunk rooms are packed in summer. Beds DM14–DM17. *Gustav-Esche-Str. 4, tel. 0341/57189. From Hauptbahnhof Tram 10 or 28 to Rathaus Wahren; walk to Linkelstr. and turn left on Am Hirtenhaus.*

Jugendherberge Leipzig-Großdeuben. Usually the last Leipzig hostel to fill up, 10 km south of city center. Flexible midnight curfew. Beds DM15, DM18 over 26. *Hauptstr. 23, tel. 034299/484 or 034299/651. From Hauptbahnhof, S-Bahn to Bahnhof Gaschwitz, then follow signs for 15 min.*

Jugendherberge Leipzig-Centrum. If you're planning a trip to Leipzig, make reservations for this great hostel RIGHT NOW. Twenty-minute walk west of center. Mostly German-filled in summer. Beds DM18, DM21 over 26, including breakfast. *Käthe-Kollwitz-Str. 62–66, tel. 0341/470530. From Hauptbahnhof, Tram 1 or 2 to Käthe-Kollwitz-Str. 1 AM curfew.*

FOOD Cafés and Imbiß stands are scattered throughout the city center. To scout out your own, head for Katharinenstraße, near Am Markt, or the narrow side streets surrounding Augustusplatz and the university. For something more substantial, try **Paulaner** (Klostergasse 3, tel. 0341/273366; closed Mon.), a small, intimate tavern that serves locals simple, satisfying grub for around DM12. At the university, **Stadtpfeiffer** (Augustuspl. 8, tel. 0341/286494; closed Sun.) has a posh indoor dining room for opera-goers and outdoor seating for grungy backpackers. Crisp salads start at DM5. Goethe liked the restaurant **Auerbachs Keller** (Grimmaische Str. 2–4, off Mädlerpassage, tel. 0341/216100) so much, he worked it into his *Faust.* Nowadays a full meal runs DM25.

WORTH SEEING Just a few blocks east of the city center, the **Grassimuseum complex** (Johannespl. 5; admission DM4, DM2 students) houses the **Geographical Museum** (open Tues.–Fri. 10–3, Sun. 9–1), where you'll find lots of maps and models of Saxony, most of which answer questions like "What is a rock?" and "How are maps made?" The adjoining **Musical Instrument Museum** (enter from Täubchenweg 2; open Tues.–Thurs. 3–6, Fri. and Sun. 10–1, Sat. 10–3) has antique instruments, music boxes, and original scores by J. S. Bach and Wagner.

Am Markt. Parts of this stunning central market square were severely damaged during World War II, but thanks to detailed restoration the square retains a centuries-old look. One side is taken up by the 16th-century **Altes Rathaus,** best known for its off-center tower and brilliant blue clock; inside, Leipzig's past is well-documented in the **Stadtgeschichtliches Museum** (Markt 1, tel. 0341/70921; admission DM3). Fanning out from the square are small streets crammed with dozens of elegant glass-roof shopping arcades; the finest is **Mädlerpassage,** on Grimmaischestraße.

Augustusplatz. Bordered by university buildings and dorms, Augustusplatz is the place to hang out with Leipzig's 15,000 students. Across from the university is the glass-and-concrete **Neues Gewandhaus** (Augustuspl. 8, tel. 0341/71320), home to Leipzig's symphony orchestra. Try for DM7 student rush tickets at the box office. If opera's your thing, the **Opernhaus** (Augustuspl. 12, tel. 0341/71680), on the square's north side, hosts top-rate performances.

Museum der Bildenden Künste. Don't cringe—the Museum of Plastic Arts is one of Leipzig's best, with an extensive collection of works by German and Dutch painters and a sizable holding of 20th-century sculpture. *Georgi-Dimitroff-Pl. 1, tel. 0341/216990. Admission: DM5, DM2.50 students. Open Tues., Thurs.–Sun. 9–5 and Wed. 1–9:30.*

Nikolaikirche. In the last months of 1989 thousands of East Germans gathered here every Monday to protest for political reform, and their peaceful pressure helped pull down the Iron Curtain. The church interior is infinitely more impressive than the bland outside suggests. *Nikolaikirchof 3, tel. 0341/200952. Open Mon.–Sat. 10–6.*

Thomaskirche. J. S. Bach was choirmaster of Thomaskirche for nearly 27 years, during which time he wrote dozens of cantatas for the church's famous boys' choir, the Thomaner Knabenchor. The choir performs free on Friday at 6 and Saturday at 3. One of Bach's friends lived across the street in what is now the **Bosehaus** (Thomaskirchof 16, tel. 0341/7866; admission DM2; open Tues.–Sun. 9–5), a Bach museum with an excellent display of period musical instruments. *Thomaskirchof 18, tel. 0341/287103.*

AFTER DARK Leipzig's club-and-bar scene doesn't have the diversity or temper of its counterpart in Berlin, but thanks to the university there are places in Leipzig where you can drink your fill among metal heads and punks, poets and prophets. Since many clubs are run—generally illegally—by student co-ops, the hip watering holes come and go. Your best bet is to scout the streets south of Augustusplatz and west of Nürnbergstraße. Also try **Moritzbastei** (Universitätstr. 9, tel. 0341/292932; cover DM2–DM8), a dungeonlike basement bar and café south of the university.

NEAR LEIPZIG

If the Bach-mania of Leipzig drives you to it, you can visit the tiny town of **Köthen,** 100 km north of Leipzig, where Johann composed the Brandenburg Concerti. No Bach sights here, but the narrow, medieval streets make a fun afternoon's diversion. If Köthen flips your lid, there's another tiny town that would love to exploit you and your cultural self. **Zwickau,** 100 km south of Leipzig, claims birthrights of Robert Schumann and flaunts them at the **Robert-Schumann-Haus** (Hauptmarkt 5, tel. 0375/25269; admission DM3; open Tues.–Sat. 10–5), which reminds you of a garage sale until you remember that the guy who owned the junk was famous. Zwickau's other baby is the Trabant car, affectionately termed "Trabi," a sputtery, clanky machine with the mechanical complexity of a wind-up clock. During the GDR era it was one of the only cars available to the public, and out of either loyalty or insanity some masochists continue to drive them.

Erfurt

Although it's the cultural and political core of the state of Thuringia and one of the most visited towns in eastern Germany, Erfurt is not your typical tourist trap. Sure, its streets are crammed with luxury hotels and expensive restaurants, but Erfurt still looks and feels like a medieval market town, from its winding network of cobblestone alleys to the spires that crowd its skyline. Unfortunately, the city has also been strongly influenced by the Communist era—it was heavily industrialized in the 1960s and is just now coming to grips with its sprawling working-class ghettos. Still, in many senses it's the highlight of eastern Germany.

VISITOR INFORMATION *Bahnhofstr. 37, tel. 0361/562–6267. Open weekdays 10–6, Sat. 10–1.*

COMING AND GOING The sleazy **Hauptbahnhof** (tel. 0361/24822) is not the best introduction to Erfurt; hurry straight down Bahnhofstraße to the historic city center. Trains arrive from Berlin (3/day, DM41), Dresden (8/day, DM36), and Frankfurt (8/day, DM55). The local **Mitfahrzentrale** doesn't have an office—you have to call 0361/25048 and leave a phone number where you can be reached.

WHERE TO SLEEP AND EAT Besides the **HI hostel** (Hochheimer Str. 12, tel. 0361/26705; Bus 5 toward Steiger Str. to last stop; beds DM18, DM21 over 26), private rooms through the tourist office are the only budget option in Erfurt. In a pinch, try **Hotel Bürgerhof** (Bahnhofstr. 35, tel. 0361/642–1307; doubles DM75), a short walk up from the train station. As for food, Erfurt's Altstadt is moderately stocked with Imbisses and cheapish cafés, but the restaurants in the area are expensive and usually tourist-oriented. An exception is the **Cafe zur Krämerbrücke** (Krämerbrücke 17, tel. 0361/24630), which serves traditional Thüringian cuisine in the thickly romantic atmosphere of a stately, 14th-century house. **Feuerkugel** (Michaelisstr. 4, at Krämerbrücke, tel. 0361/646–3197; closed Sun.) balances beer-hall ambience with hearty meals.

WORTH SEEING Three main squares constitute the heart of Erfurt's Altstadt, 1 km north of the train station. **Domplatz,** a vast open-air square atop a hill, perches at the Aldstadt's northwest extreme. From here Marktstraße leads west to **Fischmarkt,** another pedestrianized square. Here, the 16th-century **Zum Roten Ochsen Haus** (7 Fischmarkt, tel. 0361/642–2188; open Wed.–Sun. 10–6, Thurs. 10–10) houses an excellent modern-art gallery. The third and arguably least attractive of Erfurt's main squares, **Anger Platz,** is nonetheless home to the **Kaufmannskirche** (Anger Pl. 18), an 11th-century Friesian church famed for its lush Renaissance interior. On the square's southern side, the **Anger Museum** (at Bahnhofstr., tel. 0361/23311; admission DM3, DM1.50 students; open Tues.–Sun. 10–5, Wed. 10–8) houses a first-rate collection of medieval relics—coins, tools, jewelry, and a huge 14th-century crossbow—along with a hodgepodge of 19th- and 20th-century landscape paintings.

Domplatz. The name is synonymous for a vast plaza and its two adjacent churches, all on the western fringe of town at the foot of Marktstraße. The **Dom St. Mary** was founded in AD 752, but the best thing about it is the 14th-century stained glass inside. The 13th-century **Severikirche** is architecturally unique in its five equal-height naves. Its most impressive features are its carved-stone portal and, inside, the sarcophagus of St. Severus.

Luther to the Pope: Drop Dead

Martin Luther went to the town of Wittenberg in 1508 to teach theology and philosophy at Wittenberg University, whereupon Martin became disillusioned with the Catholic Church, largely because of its habit of granting absolution to slimeballs whose only redeeming quality was a bulging coffer. To show his annoyance, he jotted down a list of personal gripes. Once he got rolling, Luther didn't stop until he reached 95 individual complaints, at which point he nailed them all to the Schloßkirche's door in 1517. Needless to say, Rome was none to happy with recreant Martin Luther. In 1520 the pope thus issued a papal bull condemning "the errors of Martin Luther." Like a hippie with a draft card, Luther burned the bull and kept on preaching his new brand of religion. Today you can see the actual door where Luther nailed his Theses in Wittenberg, about an hour north of Leipzig. But before you hop the next train, be forewarned that the door is the only reason to visit an otherwise excruciatingly dull and overtouristed town.

Krämerbrücke. Walls of half-timbered houses and an incredible collection of Baroque-era houses make the Krämerbrücke (Merchant Bridge), east of Fischmarkt, one of the most beautiful shopping streets in Europe. It's also a big daytime tourist attraction, so walk instead along the shallow creek below the bridge for an undistracted view of the ornate buildings.

Museum für Thüringer Volkskunde. The Thuringian Folklore Museum portrays the history of Thuringia's impoverished masses. Tours are in German, but the guides use some impressive body language in their exuberant efforts to show you how regular Thüringen folks lived and died. *Juri-Gagarin-Ring 140A, tel. 0361/642–1765. From Hauptbahnhof, follow Bahnhofstr., turn right and continue on Juri-Gagarin-Ring for 1½ km. Admission: DM3. Open Tues.–Sun. 10–5, Wed. 10–8. Wheelchair access.*

NEAR ERFURT

EISENACH Eisenach is a small, very provincial town that's most famous for its hillside castle, the 12th-century **Wartburg,** which is considered the stylistic epitome of a traditional German castle. The best exhibits inside are those dedicated to Martin Luther, who hid out here from 1521 to 1522. It costs DM1 to enter the castle courtyard and climb the **South Tower,** from where you can look down on Eisenach or over the tourists below. The hillside castle is only 3 km from Eisenach's center, but it takes some effort to hike to the summit. Another option is the **Wartburg Trolley** (DM3), a bus which leaves from its Mariental Straße depot every 20 minutes. You can also take Bus 3 (DM2) from the Hauptbahnhof. *Tel. 03691/77072. Admission with tour: DM10, DM6 students. Apr.–Oct., daily tours 8:30–4:30, courtyard open until 6; Nov.–Mar., daily tours 9–3:30, courtyard open until 5.*

Back in Eisenach, the **Altstadt** isn't as impressive as Erfurt's, but it is still wonderfully Baroque—a mix of colorful 17th-century facades and cobbled streets. The city seems to specialize in fan-club museums. The best of them is the **Bachhaus** (Frauenplan 21, tel. 03691/3714; admission DM5; open Mon. noon–5:45, Tues.–Sun. 9–5:45), which re-creates Bach's musical career in exacting detail. Less interesting but more authentic is the **Lutherhaus** (Lutherpl. 8, tel. 03691/4983; admission DM3, DM1.50 students; open May–Sept., daily 9–1 and 2–5, shorter hrs off-season); the displays suck but Luther actually lived here for a few years. The **tourist office** (Bahnhofstr. 3–5, 2 blocks west of Hauptbahnhof, tel. 03691/4895) can fill you in on other Eisenach sights.

➢ **WHERE TO SLEEP AND EAT** • Eisenach's excellent **hostel** (Mariental 24, tel. 03691/203613; beds DM15, DM19 over 26) is a 3½-km walk from the train station and has a 10 PM curfew. If you get to town late, take a DM10 taxi to the hostel or head to the nearby tourist office and book a private room. The majority of Eisenach's restaurants are high-priced and touristy, so stick with the small food stalls and wurst shops throughout the city center. The **Bäckerei Liebefrau** (Lutherstr. 7) has excellent Thüringen pastries for only DM1.50.

Weimar

Erfurt may be the historic heart of Thuringia, but Weimar has always been the seat of literature and the arts. In its heyday the city was home to the likes of Goethe, Schiller, Nietzsche, Bach, and Liszt. Gropius formed his Bauhaus school of art and architecture here in 1919, and on any given day you could find people like Ludwig Mies van der Rohe and Paul Klee wandering its streets. Meanwhile, the German National Assembly met here in 1919 to declare the founding of Germany's first-ever republic—the short-lived Weimar Republic (1919–1933). This constitutionally based government, which drew its support from a polemical coalition of socialists, communists, and capitalists (and anyone else who could produce a manifesto) did little to stem the rise of fascism and Hitler's Nazis. During its short tenure, however, it nurtured a progressive, dynamic culture that many consider the golden age of 20th-century Germany.

VISITOR INFORMATION **Touristbüro.** *Markstr. 10, near the Rathaus, tel. 03643/202173. Open weekdays 9–7, Sat. 9–4, Sun. 10–4.*

COMING AND GOING Weimar's **Hauptbahnhof** (Baudert Pl. and Carl-August-Allee, tel. 03643/3330) is 1½ km north of the city center, which you can reach by taking Bus 3, 5, or 6 or Tram 4, 5, or 8 to Theaterplatz or Goetheplatz. Destinations include Berlin (3/day, DM38), Eisenach (9/day, DM11), and Frankfurt (3/day, DM51).

WHERE TO SLEEP AND EAT The tourist office arranges private rooms in family homes, or try one of Weimar's three youth hostels. **Jugendherberge Am Poseckschen Garten** (Humboldtstr. 17, tel. 03643/64021; beds DM16) is an independent hostel 10 minutes from the center on Bus 6. Two blocks south of the Hauptbahnhof, **Jugendherberge Germania** (Carl-August-Allee 13, tel. 03643/202076; beds DM18.50) is clean and efficient, though kind of noisy. The best features of **Jugendherberge Maxim Gorki** (Windmühlenstr., Am Wilden Graben 12, tel. 03643/3471; beds DM18) are the washing machines and the beautiful graveyard nearby. Take Tram 5 or 8 to Am Wilden Graben.

Many of the restaurants and cafés on Schillerstraße, in the center, are pseudo-German eateries aimed at tourists, so try the area near **Herderplatz,** where you'll find a handful of quiet, smoky beer halls that serve cheap pub grub. A good one is **Probierstube** (Eisfeld 4, tel. 03643/202131), one block west of Herderplatz. Another budget option is **C-Keller-Galerie** (Am Markt, tel. 03643/61984), a joint art gallery and café where students do the cooking. **Cafe Scenario** (Carl-August-Allee, tel. 03643/419640; closed Sun.), near the Hauptbahnhof, offers top-rate pizza from DM7 and vegetable-and-seafood pastas from DM6.

WORTH SEEING Weimar's **Marktplatz** dates from 1400, the year the city received its first charter. The square is appealing mainly because of its rows of gorgeous buildings. Next to the Markt, the cobblestone **Theaterplatz** is the largest square in Weimar and the site of the neoclassical **Deutsches Nationaltheater** (tel. 03643/7550) and the Weimar-centric **Kunsthalle** (tel. 03643/61831; open Tues.–Sun. 10–6, Thurs. until 8), home to plenty of Bauhaus and Gropius works. **Burgplatz,** by the Ilm River on the east end of town, is home to the vast **Weimar Castle** (tel. 03643/62041; admission DM5, DM3 students; open Tues.–Sun. 10–6). Inside are two worthwhile museums: The **Kunstsammlungen** has a collection of 20,000 paintings, sculptures, and drawings by famous masters, while the small **Castle Museum** has a collection of maps and illustrations that document the castle's evolution. Nearby, don't miss the main hall of the **Central Library** (Burgpl., tel. 03643/65433; open Mon.–Sat. 10–4), a Renaissance-era building that was later transformed into a masterpiece of Rococo design. Just north of Bergplatz, the quiet **Herderplatz** houses the 18th-century **Stadtkirche** (open daily 10–4), a Baroque cathedral that contains Lucas Cranach's *Winged Altar* triptych—a painting familiar to anyone who's ever taken an art history course. On many summer weekends Herderplatz is the site of a crafts bazaar and barbecue.

Goethe, one of Germany's most renowned poets and thinkers, lived in Weimar in the three-story **Goethehaus** (Am Frauenplan, tel. 03643/545300; admission DM5, DM3 students; open Tues.–Sun. 9–5) from 1782 until his death, in 1832. Even if you've never heard of Goethe, the monument's interior decor—from the oak-carved furniture to the pewter gaslights and wood cutlery—is worth a stop. The attractive **Liszthaus** (Marienstr.; admission DM2.50, DM1 students; open Tues.–Sun. 9–noon and 1–5) was pianist and composer Franz Liszt's final abode.

NEAR WEIMAR

BUCHENWALD Whether you call Buchenwald a death camp or a detention center, the fact of the matter is that at least 65,000 human beings were murdered here between 1937 and 1945. Very little has been physically altered since the camp was liberated in 1945: The barbed wire remains, as do the gun posts and administrative buildings. The only things missing are the prisoner cell blocks, which once covered a ½-square-km area; today only the charred foundation remains. At the north end of the compound you'll find a small **museum,** with multilingual displays and a fascinating collection of scale-model re-creations. About 100 yards south of the museum is another exhibit, housed in what remains of the camp's original "medical-research" facilities. These eventually lead into the **oven chambers,** where the majority of Buchenwald's victims were incinerated. A movie theater adjacent to the

Buchenwald tourist center shows an excellent 30-minute **film** (free) about the camp every hour and about four times a day in English. From here you can also join a free tour of the camp. Buchenwald lies 3 km north of Weimar and is easily reached by bus (DM6) from Goetheplatz Monday–Saturday, every hour on the hour 8–5, less frequently on Sunday. *Tel. 03643/430200. Admission free. Open May–Sept., Tues.–Sun. 9:30–5:45; Oct.–Apr., Tues.–Sun. 8:45–4:45.*

Buchenwald's clock has read 3:15 since April 11, 1945, in commemoration of the camp's liberation.

Thüringer Wald

The Thüringer Wald (Thüringian Forest), with its tranquil woods, rugged trails, and sleepy Alpine villages, is one of eastern Germany's treasured retreats. Sickly cement-and-steel towns encircle the forest, yet once you breach its border there's nothing but trees, lakes, and spiny peaks—an ideal setting for extended hikes. Serious hikers should consider the 168-km-long **Rennsteig** (Border Way), a mountaintop trail that extends from Eisenach through Bavaria (and ultimately all the way to Budapest, Hungary). The Rennsteig can be accessed from Eisenach, Friedrichroda, and Oberhof. The Erfurt–Almenau–Arnstadt train also stops at an unstaffed depot named Rennsteig; from here, follow the signs ¼ km to the trail, which is marked with a white "R" painted on tree trunks. Youth hostels along the route include **Brotterode** (tel. 036840/32125), 12 km east of Bad Leibenstein, and **Schnellbach** (tel. 03675/7462), 15 km southeast of Brotterode.

Of all the towns in the area surrounding the Thüringer Wald, don't miss **Ilmenau.** Not only is it well connected by train with Erfurt, Arnstadt, and Meiningen, it also has a hostel and dozens of cafés and restaurants. Best of all for hikers, Ilmenau is within easy reach of Thüringer Wald hiking trails. In the town center is the **Goethe-Gedenkstätte im Amtshaus** (Am Markt, tel. 03677/2667), where Goethe lived for a few years; the only original pieces in his re-created living room and study are his diary and some personal letters. Goethe's most lasting legacy around here is the **Goethe-Wanderweg,** also known as **Auf Goethes Spuren** (In the Footsteps of Goethe). This rigorous 18-km trail follows the path established by Goethe during his many summer ramblings and is a great way to experience the Thüringer Wald without having to rough it under the stars in a soggy sleeping bag. You'll find the trailhead on Waldstraße, 100 yards south of the tourist office on the far side of the train tracks; from there, just look for a posted "G" from time to time to be sure you're on track. Along the route, you can recover from the altitude at the expensive **Schöffenhaus** restaurant (no lunch), and the medium-price **Gasthaus Auerhahn** (closed Mon.). Get maps from Ilmenau's **tourist office** (Lindenstr. 12, tel. 03677/2358; open weekdays 9–6, Sat. 9–noon).

WHERE TO SLEEP Although Ilmenau has a good hostel, try one of the city's two luxurious pensions, both priced at about DM35–DM40 per person: **Zum Elephant** (Markstr. 16, tel. 03677/2441) or **Villa Silvana** (Waldstr. 14, tel. 03677/4881). The **HI hostel** (Waldstr. 22, tel. 03677/2358; beds DM10, DM14 over 26) is in an old, worn building. Turn right from the tourist office, cross the train tracks, and veer right onto Waldstraße.

Northern Germany

Hamburg

Hamburg is a port city through and through. Founded in 810 by Charlemagne, it has been an international trading post since the Middle Ages, and for hundreds of years it was Europe's leading port. Today, although it has fallen to third-largest port in Europe—it's still the biggest in Germany—Hamburg is again a city of enormous style, verve, and elegance. Hand in hand with this elegance comes a thriving consumer culture, and Hamburgers (no pun) are known for making money any old way they can. You'll see a lot of gray-suited commerce types earning money the old-fashioned way, and another segment of the population making its moolah in even older fashion. Prostitution, pornography, sex shows—basically anything you can do with human genitalia—have given Hamburg a reputation as a sort of Teutonic Sodom; Hamburg's **Reeperbahn** has the dubious distinction of being one of the most famous sex streets in the world. But Hamburg offers more traditional tourist attractions as well, including some beautiful (and wealthy) neighborhoods, excellent museums, a lively university district, and a happening nightlife.

Hamburg has over 2,400 bridges—more than London, Amsterdam, and Venice combined.

BASICS

➤ **VISITOR INFORMATION** • The main tourist offices are in the **train station** (tel. 040/3005–1230), at **Hanse-Viertel** (Poststr. entrance, tel. 040/3005–1220), at the **airport** (tel. 040/3005–1240), and at the **harbor** (St.-Pauli Landungsbrücken, bet. bridges 4 and 5, tel. 040/3005–1200). All locations sell the **Hamburg-CARD,** which gives free access to public transport, entrance to 11 museums, and discounts up to 30% on city tours. A one-day card costs DM9.50, a three-day card DM17.50.

➤ **AMERICAN EXPRESS** • *Rathausmarkt 5, tel. 040/331141. Open weekdays 9–5:30, Sat. 9–noon.*

➤ **CONSULATES** • **United Kingdom.** *Harvestehuder Weg 8A, tel. 040/446071. Open weekdays 9–noon and 2–4.*

United States. *Alsterufer 27–28, tel. 040/411710. Open weekdays 9–noon.*

➤ **MAIL** • The **Hauptpost,** across from the Hauptbahnhof, does not exchange money, strangely enough. *Hühnerposten 12, tel. 040/23950. Open weekdays 8–6, Sat. 8–noon.*

COMING AND GOING Most trains leave from the **Hauptbahnhof** (tel. 040/19419) in central Hamburg, an easy walk to the main sights. The **Altona** station (Max-Brauer-Allee, tel. 040/39181), west of downtown, handles trains heading north. For Mitfahrzentrale try **Karl Mai** (Stephanspl. 6, tel. 040/4140–2611), the women-only **Frauen-mitfahrzentrale** (Rutschbahn 3, tel. 040/457800), or **Altona-Mitfahr-Zentrale** (Altona train station, Lobuschstr. 22, tel. 040/19440).

GETTING AROUND Most major sights and interesting neighborhoods are sandwiched in the walkable downtown area between the Elbe River and two lakes, the **Binnenalster** and **Aussenalster** (collectively just called the Alster); the Neustadt is just below the lakes, the Altstadt below that. The **St. Pauli/Reeperbahn** area, including Hamburg's famous red-light district, is west of downtown near the harbor. The **university district** sits north of the city center and west of the Aussenalster.

HVV, Hamburg's public-transportation system, operates an extensive network of buses, as well as the U-Bahn and S-Bahn. A **Tageskarte** (day pass) costs DM6.50 and covers the whole system except night buses and first-class S-Bahn; the **Hamburg-CARD** (*see* Visitor Information, *above*) is also a good deal. One-way tickets (DM2.20–DM3.40) for the U-Bahn, S-Bahn, and buses are available at the orange ticket-dispensing machines located in U-Bahn and S-Bahn stations and at most bus stops. For a **taxi,** call 040/211211 or 040/441011.

WHERE TO SLEEP Because of its proximity to the Hauptbahnhof and ZOB, **St. Georg** is the most convenient area in which to spend the night. It has a prominent drug and prostitution scene but is safe enough if you keep your wits about you, look like you have a purpose, and don't get offended if someone asks how much you cost an hour. In St. Georg, the street **Bremer Reihe** is loaded with cheap lodgings. **St. Pauli,** within spittin' distance of the Reeperbahn, is also pretty safe and has plenty of cheap hotels. If you want to stay near the offbeat neighborhood **Schanzenviertel,** try **Hotel Sternschanze** (Schanzenstr. 101, tel. 040/433389; doubles DM75). Hamburg also has a whole slew of Mitwohnzentrale agencies that find rooms—from DM30 and up—in private houses and apartments. The Mitwohnzentrale at Schulterblatt 112 (tel. 040/19445) charges a DM8 commission (per person per night). Just tell them your price range and the area of town you prefer.

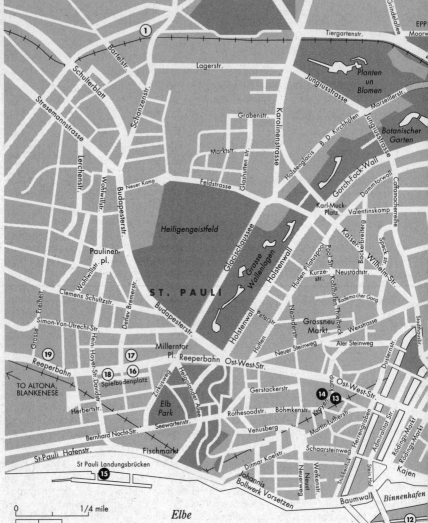

TO ALTONA,
BLANKENESE

ST. PAULI

Planten un Blomen

Botanischer Garten

Heiligengeistfeld

Elb Park

St Pauli Landungsbrücken

Elbe

Binnenhafen

0 ———— 1/4 mile
0 ———— 1/4 km

Sights ●

Abwasser-und-
Sielmuseum, **15**

Deichtorhallen, **8**

Krameramts-
Wohnungen, **13**

Kuntshalle, **4**

Michaeliskirche, **14**

Museum für Kunst
und Gewerbe, **7**

Museum für
Völkerkunde, **2**

Rathaus, **11**

Speicherstadt, **10**

Lodging ○

Auto-Hotel "Am
Hafen", **16**

Hamburg "Auf dem
Stintfang" (HI), **12**

Hotel Alt
Nürnberg, **6**

Hotel Florida, **18**

Hotel Inter-Rast, **19**

Hotel
Sternschanze, **1**

Jugendgästehaus
Hamburg "Horner
Rennbahn", **9**

Kieler Hof, **5**

Wedina, **3**

Weller's Hotel, **17**

Hamburg

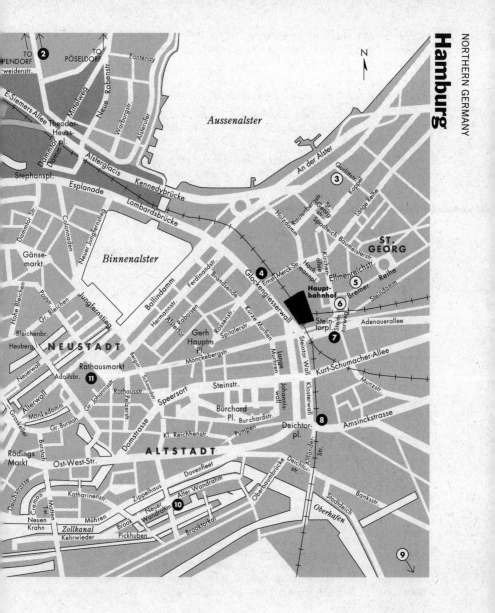

TO PENDORF

TO PÖSELDORF

Fontenay

Aussenalster

N

E-Siemers Allee

weidenstr.

Neue

Rabenstr.

Warburgstr.

Alsterufer

Mittelweg

Theodor-
Heuss-
pl.

Dammtor-
Damm

Alsterglacis

Kennedybrücke

Stephanspl.

Esplanade

Lombardsbrücke

Dammtor Str.

Colonnaden

Neuer Jungfernstieg

Binnenalster

An der Alster

Gurlitstr.

Rautenbergstr.

St.
Georg
str.

Spadreich

Baumeisterstr.

Holzdamm

Kirchen-
allee

Lange Reihe

Koppel

ST.
GEORG

Gänse-
markt.

Hohe Bleichen

Postr.

Gr. Bleichen

Jungfernstieg

Ballindamm

Hermannstr.

Ferdinandstr.

Brandsende

Alster Raboisen

Glockengiesserwall

Ernst Merck-Str.

Hohe

mannpl.

Kirchen-
allee

Ellmenreichstr.

Bremer
Reihe

Hauptbahnhof

Steindamm

Adenaueralle

Bleichenbr.

Heuberg

NEUSTADT

Gr. Bleichen

Neuerwall

Adolfsbr.

Rathausmarkt

Gerh
Hauptm
Pl.

Mönckebergstr.

Rossenstr.

Kurze Mühren

Spitalerstr.

Lange
Mühren

Steinter

Steintor-
pl.

Kurt-Schumacher-Allee

Munzstr.

Alterwall

Graskeller

Mönkedamm

Gr. Burstah

Rathausstr.

Pelzerstr.

Bergstr.

Schmiedstr.

Domstrasse

Speersort

Steinstr.

Johannis-
wall

Steintor Wall

Klosterwall

Amsinckstrasse

Rödings
Markt

Burstah

Ost-West-Str.

Deichstrasse

Cremon

Kl. Reichenstr.

Burchard
Pl.

Burchardstr.

Pumpen

ALTSTADT

Deichtor-
pl.

Deichtor-
str.

Katharinenstr.

Dovenfleet

Oberbaumbrücke

Stadtdeich

Banksstr.

Neuen
Krahn

Mühren

Zippelhaus

Neuer
Wandrahm

Alter Wandrahm

Brook

Oberhafen

Zollkanal

Kehrwieder

Pickhuben

Brooktorkai

Mattentw.

Hool

Steinter Wall

Hinter-
str.

2

3

4

5

6

7

8

9

10

11

➢ **ST. PAULI** • **Auto-Hotel "Am Hafen."** Adjacent to a bar where the managers tend to bleary regulars. Doubles start at an astonishing DM65 per night. *Spielbudenplatz 11, next to gas station, tel. 040/316631. U3 to St. Pauli.*

Hotel Florida. Respectable sorta place, with airy doubles for DM90, including breakfast. Reception desk doubles as a bar. *Spielbudenpl. 22, tel. 040/314393. U3 to St. Pauli.*

Hotel Inter-Rast. Noisy but fun 420-bed hotel at the end of Reeperbahn on Große Freiheit. Doubles DM85, including breakfast. *Reeperbahn 154–166, tel. 040/311591. S-Bahn to Reeperbahn.*

Weller's Hotel. The friendly proprietor actually likes foreigners. Lots of creaky old stairs lead to the standard DM85 doubles. *Reeperbahn 36, tel. 040/314838. U3 to St. Pauli or S-Bahn to Reeperbahn.*

➢ **ST. GEORG** • **Hotel Alt Nürnberg.** Neat hotel with beautiful reception area and basic rooms upstairs. Doubles from DM150, with breakfast. *Steintorweb 15, tel. 040/246023. Closed Dec. 25–Jan. 1.*

Kieler Hof. Tidy rooms with wood beds and fresh white linen; bathrooms have a potent lemony smell. Doubles (DM90 with breakfast) with showers and toilets in hall. *Bremer Reihe 15, tel. 040/243024.*

Wedina. A friendly Swiss man runs this ultramodern hotel and the *Gästehaus* (guest house) across the street. Doubles from DM175, with breakfast. *Gurlittstr. 23, off Lange Reihe, tel. 040/243011.*

➢ **HOSTELS** • **Hamburg "Auf dem Stintfang" (HI).** Great location overlooking the harbor but almost always full; call ahead or come before 6 PM. Beds DM17–DM21. *Alfred-Wegener-Weg 5, tel. 040/313488. U3 to St.-Pauli Landungsbr. 350 beds. 1 AM curfew.*

Jugendgästehaus Hamburg "Horner Rennbahn." Quick trip from downtown on public transit. High-quality, modern rooms for a correspondingly high price: DM26–DM32, including bed linen and breakfast. Call ahead or come early. *Rennbahnstr. 100, tel. 040/651–1671. U3 toward Mümmelmannsberg to Horner Rennbahn, then 10-min walk. 1 AM curfew, lockout 9–1. Swimming pool, wheelchair access. Closed Feb.*

➢ **CAMPGROUND** • **Zeltdorf.** In the leafy Hamburg Volkspark, a nice escape from the hectic pace of downtown. Table tennis, volleyball, badminton, and northern Germany's biggest pool. Beds DM19, including breakfast; blanket rental DM20. *Sylvesterallee 3, tel. 040/831–9939. S3 or S21 to Eidelstedt or Stellingen from downtown, then walk 15 min. 500 sites. Showers. Closed Sept.–Apr.*

FOOD Around the **Schanzenviertel** (especially on **Schulterblatt**) and on **Reeperbahn** you'll find a hefty number of ethnic restaurants (especially Turkish, Greek, and Italian) offering delicious, if not downright cheap, meals. The streets around the **university** will see you right when it comes to cheap eats; wander down **Grindelallee.** Downtown has mostly expensive restaurants; an exception is **Gestern & Heute Treff** (Kaiser-Wilhelm-Str. 55, tel. 040/344998), open 24 hours a day(!) for things like pizza (DM12) and rump steak (DM12–DM18).

The most celebrated—and tangy—local dish is probably *Aalsuppe* (eel soup). Smoked eel, called *Rächeraal,* is a particularly fatty Hamburg specialty. Other specialties to try are *Birnen, Bohnen, und Speck* (pears, beans, and bacon) and the sailor's favorite, *Labskaus,* a pickled meat, beetroot, and potato dish. Wash it all down with the local drink, *Alsterwasser,* a mix of beer and clear lemon soda.

➢ **INNENSTADT** • **Bon Appetit.** Busy stand-up café behind Mönckebergstraße, near the Hauptbahnhof and main tourist attractions. Try *Bauernfrühstück* (Farmer's Breakfast; DM7.90) or a meat-and-potatoes dish (from DM10). *Rathausstr. 4, tel. 040/324570. No dinner.*

Daniel Wischer. On pedestrian-only Spitalerstraße. Expect to share tables during busy lunch hour. Chow on greasy fish and chips (DM7) or salads (from DM4). *Spitalerstr. 12, tel. 040/382343. Closes at 7:30 PM.*

➤ **ST. PAULI** • **Billard-Salon.** Lit only by old-fashioned light globes—very atmospheric. Jam-packed after 7 PM. Try the special, *Rahmgulasch* (DM14), a cream-based goulash. *Spielbudenpl. 27, tel. 040/315815.*

Medusa. Modern, family-run Italian restaurant featuring lasagna, tortellini, or fettuccine (DM12 each). *Spielbudenpl. 21, tel. 040/313503. No lunch.*

➤ **ST. GEORG** • **Cafe Gnosa.** Check out the gay scene and get some fantastic meals. Daily dishes from DM9.50. Vegetarian *Auflauf* casserole (DM9.50) is a mixture of zucchini, cauliflower, carrots, and cheese. *Lange Reihe 93, tel. 040/243034.*

Max & Consorten. Conversation buzzes through smoke and music—perfect for a quick beer (DM5) or cheap meal. The DM8 Farmer's Breakfast fills you up any time of day. *Spadenteich 7, tel. 040/245617.*

➤ **SCHANZENVIERTEL** • **Noodle's.** Newly redecorated, clean restaurant serving noodles and pasta. A great find. Try the tortellini with broccoli and mushrooms (DM9). *Schanzenstr. 2–4, tel. 040/439–2840. Wheelchair access.*

Taverna Olympisches Feuer. Kitschy Greek restaurant in the heart of Schanzenviertel. *Kalamares* (squid) and a side salad cost DM10. *Schulterblatt 63, tel. 040/435597.*

WORTH SEEING The tourist office organizes a variety of tours (DM22–DM30) of the city and harbor, with English commentary. If you plan to pack a lot of sightseeing into a day, the Hamburg-CARD (*see* Visitor Information, *above*) is a great deal.

Hamburg's **Hafen** (harbor), a case study in modernity and efficiency, is also the focal point of the city's oldest and liveliest area. Check out the enormous, Gothic-influenced brick **Speicherstadt warehouses;** warehouses usually don't elicit many oohs and aahs, but you've got to admit these are some mighty fine storage sheds. West of Hamburg, **Altona** was an autonomous city for almost 300 years and today is home to the waterfront **Fischmarkt,** Hamburg's famous Sunday-morning market (and we mean early morning; it loses steam around 9:30 AM). To get a dose of old Hamburg, spend some time on **Deichstraße,** which has been a peaceful residential street for the past 600 or so years.

Kunsthalle. Three thousand paintings, 400 sculptures, and coin and medal collections present a remarkably diverse picture of European artistic life from the 14th century to the present. *Glockengießerwall, near Hauptbahnhof, tel. 040/2486–2612. Admission: DM3, DM.70 students. Open Tues.–Sun. 10–6, Thurs. 10–9.*

Michaeliskirche. Hamburg's most famous and best-loved landmark, the Baroque St. Michael's Church (fondly nicknamed "Michel"), stands just off Ost-West-Straße. Its copper-covered spire makes a distinct mark on Hamburg's already stately skyline. The **Krameramts-Wohnungen** (Krayenkamp 10–11), a cluster of tiny old courtyard houses in the shadow of the Michel, house galleries and a museum that replicates the setup of a typical house in the 15th century. *Krayenkamp 4C, tel. 040/376780. S1, S2, or S3 to Stadthausbrücke. Open daily 9–5:30.*

Neuengamme. The concentration camp in Neuengamme, in operation between 1938 and 1945, saw the internment of more than 100,000 victims of the National Socialists. Today a museum chronicles the horrors that occurred here, with reconstructions of "daily camp life" accompanied by documents and photographs. *Jean-Dolidier-Weg 39, tel. 040/723–1031. S2 or S21 toward Bergedorf to last station, then bus No. 227 toward Neuengamme to J-Dolidier-Weg. Admission free. Open Tues.–Sun. 10–5.*

Rathaus. The town hall presides impressively over the city-state of Hamburg in neo-Renaissance, Nordic hugeness. When neither city council nor state government is in session, you can tour (DM1) the Rathaus's innards. Especially opulent and rather tragic is the intricately carved **Orphans' Room,** created through the labors of 80 orphans aged eight to 14. *Rathausmarkt, tel.*

040/3681–2470. U3 to Rathaus or S-Bahn to Jungfernstieg. Tours Mon.–Thurs. 10:15–3:15, Fri.–Sun. 10:15–1:15.

Reeperbahn/St. Pauli. On its labels, St. Pauli beer shows a buxom prostitute toting frothing mugs of beer, and that about sums up the popular image of the St. Pauli district. In truth, most of St. Pauli is residential, but everyone seems to remember more vividly the Reeperbahn and its seamy side streets, which beckon those who will pay to have sex, to watch someone else have sex, or to watch someone else pretend to have sex. The Reeperbahn is known as "the wickedest mile in the world," but it's really the side streets—like Herbertstraße, which is off-limits to women and children—that rate highest on the slimy porno scale.

➤ **MUSEUMS AND GALLERIES** • Built in the form of a real sewer, the one-room **Abwasser und Sielmuseum** (St.-Pauli Landungsbrücken 49, near bridge 9, tel. 040/3807–3341) is home to a variety of collectibles that were found in Hamburg's 5,000-km sewage network. Call ahead, or stop by and ask for Mr. Rees. Built in 1876 as a museum and school, the **Museum für Kunst und Gewerbe** (Steintorpl. 1, near Hauptbahnhof, tel. 040/2486–2630; admission DM5, DM3 students; open Tues.–Sun. 10–6) now contains an impressive collection of handicrafts from all over the world. One of the largest ethnological museums in Germany, the **Museum für Völkerkunde** (Rothenbaum-Ch. 64, tel. 040/4419–5524; admission DM5, DM3 students; open Tues.–Sun. 10–5) has extensive and well-presented displays on Africa and South America.

AFTER DARK Most of Hamburg's pubs and discos are clustered around St. Pauli, Gänsemärkt downtown, and Große Neumarkt near S-Bahn station Stadthausbrücke; also take a look around Altona and the Schanzenviertel. Buy either *Prinz* (DM4) or *Szene Hamburg* (DM4.50) for good listings of pubs and discos; *Gay Express* (DM6) covers the gay scene.

Spitalerstraße, the pedestrian zone near the Hauptbahnhof, usually has a mix of musicians, from Peruvian folk musicians to rockers to violinists to accordion players. The **Freiluft Kino auf dem Rathausmarkt** shows movies on a big screen in front of the Rathaus at night. Admission is free, and there are usually a few films in English with German subtitles. The movies are shown on weekends in July and August. Germany's biggest fair, the **Frühlingsdom** (Spring Dom), takes place from late March through late April and again in July (when it's renamed the **Hummelfest**) at the Heiligengeistfeld, near the Reeperbahn.

➤ **BARS** • Peanut shells litter the floor of **Schramme** (Schrammsweg 10, tel. 040/477828), a small pub in Eppendorf. A truly mixed crowd gathers at **September** (Feldstr. 60, tel. 040/437611) for a truly mixed program of music and *gemütlich* surroundings. An international crowd meets in **Shamrock** (Feldstr. 40, tel. 040/439–7678), Hamburg's leading Irish pub. For consistently good jazz, check out **Cotton-Club** (Alter Steinweg 10, tel. 040/34378), Hamburg's oldest jazz club.

➤ **DISCOS** • **Madhouse** (Valentinskamp 46A, tel. 040/344193; cover DM6–DM12, women free) is super-popular and always crowded. Dark and cavernous, **Kaiserkeller** (Gr. Freiheit 36, tel. 040/319–3649) is much the same. **Knust** (Brandstwiete 2, tel. 040/324933; cover DM5) specializes in *Engtanzfeten* ("tight dance parties")—that's right, they play only slow music.

➤ **GAY AND LESBIAN** • Hamburg has a wild and very open gay and lesbian scene; some good bets include **Adagio** (Max-Brauer-Allee 114, tel. 040/382409), a lesbian café, **Spundloch** (Paulinenstr. 19, tel. 040/310798), Hamburg's oldest gay disco, and **Tom's Saloon** (Pulverteich 17, no phone), an all-men's pub where leather predominates.

The North Coast

The two regions of Germany's northern coast—**Schleswig-Holstein** and **Mecklenburg-Vorpommern**—are governed by the stormy moods of an ever-changing sea. Schleswig-Holstein joins Germany with Denmark and has been passed back and forth between the two for centuries, leaving behind much Danish influence. Prior to 1989 Mecklenburg-Vorpommern was part of the GDR. In a scenario repeated throughout East Germany, the region was partly industrialized and partly left to rot, leaving quite a mess for unified Germany to clean up.

The Hanseatic League, a powerful block that dominated trade on the Baltic from the 13th to 17th centuries, helped shape—if not create—most of the port and harbor towns on the north coast, leaving behind medieval churches and half-timber houses. But remote fishing villages and the coast's hidden coves and white-sand beaches are the area's real treasures. Many Baltic Coast aficionados consider **Rügen Island** a don't-miss attraction because of its incredible mix of attractions: famous chalk cliffs; fields of barley, wheat, and rapeseed; lighthouses at Kap Arkona and Hiddensee; scattered thatched-roof cottages; bathing resorts; Stone Age megalithic graves; and endless sandy beaches. Tourist offices all over the island can help you find campgrounds and private rooms, but it is easiest to stay in **Stralsund,** which connects to the island via frequent buses and trains. **Jugendherberge Stralsund** (Am Kütertor 1, tel. 03831/292160) is housed in a city gate dating to 1293 and charges DM13.50–DM16 per person.

LUBECK

With more historical monuments (more than 1,000) than any other German city, the small Schleswig-Holstein port of Lübeck is a museum in itself. Coursing through the town are manmade canals fed by the Trave River. The Hanseatic League princes who created this water system are responsible for Lübeck's tangible historical flavor and for its continued dominance of the region's oceanic trade. Marktplatz's most notable feature is the green-glazed **Rathaus** (town hall), dating from 1240 and built in a mishmash of styles that has left it with Romanesque arches, Gothic windows, and a Renaissance roof. Interesting tours of the Rathaus (DM3, DM1 students) are given weekdays 11–3.

By far the most impressive Dom is **Marienkirche** (Marienkirchhof), set atop a hill at the spiritual heart of the city, but the best *view* of town just might be from the nearby **Petrikirche** (Schmiedestr.; admission DM1), another of Lübeck's Gothic landmarks. Just off the square is **Jakobikirche** (Breitestr. 45; open Mon.–Sat. 9–6, Sun. noon–5) and its celebrated pews—they're adorned with grotesquely laughing faces carved *underneath* the pews. A bit farther down Breitestraße is **Heiligen-Geist-Hospital** (Am Koberg, tel. 0451/222040), a 13th-century hospital whose surrounding lanes and courtyards make it feel like a medieval

The ancient core of Lübeck is protected by UNESCO as a World Heritage Site.

city within a city. For help navigating Lübeck's crooked streets, the **Touristinformation Hauptbahnhof** (tel. 0451/72300; open weekdays 9–6, weekends 10–2), located in the train station, stocks city maps; it also books rooms for a DM5 fee.

COMING AND GOING From the **Hauptbahnhof** (Am Bahnhof, tel. 0451/19419) walk toward Holstentor and into the Altstadt. Train destinations from Lübeck include Hamburg (40 min, DM16). Lübeck's sights are all within walking distance of one another, but you can rent bikes at **Leihcycle** (Schwartauer Allee 39, in the backyard, tel. 0451/42660) for DM5 per day.

WHERE TO SLEEP The Altstadt has a good selection of budget pensions. Otherwise, Lübeck has two hostels: A 10-minute walk from the Hauptbahnhof, **CVJM-Haus** (Große Petersgrube 11, tel. 0451/78982) has doubles and 10-bed dorm rooms for DM15 per person. Or try the centrally located **Jugendgästehaus** (Mengstr. 33, tel. 0451/70399; reception closed noon–1 and 6–7). The DM25 price includes a buffet breakfast.

FOOD The Altstadt is jam-packed with food stands and semi-elegant restaurants. At **Tipasa** (Schlumacherstr. 14, tel. 0451/74811), **Hieronymus** (Fleischhauerstr. 81, tel. 0451/151117), and **Schmidts** (Dr. Julius Leber-Str. 60, tel. 0451/76182), three smart-looking student cafés, you'll find local students nursing beers and munching on fresh gourmet pizzas (about DM8). For pubs, head to **Engelsgrubestraße** (from Holstentor, turn left on An der Untertrave and right on Engelsgrube).

SCHWERIN

Schwerin, the modern capital of Mecklenburg-Vorpommern, is a very un-Baltic sort of town. It's nearly 35 km from the coast and was mostly ignored by Hanseatic League merchants. Still, the town is surrounded by seven largish lakes that give it a pleasant watery feel, and in the 19th century it was transformed into a posh lakeside retreat. Today Schwerin's riverside promenades and stunning castle draw tourists from near and far and convince many of them that this town is the highlight of the Baltic region.

On a small island on the edge of the Schwerin See, mounted by 15 turrets and surrounded by a lush expanse of well-kept gardens, stands the town's famous **Schloß Schwerin** (Lennestr.; admission DM3; open Tues.–Sun. 10–5). This opulent fairy-tale castle was built by the Mecklenburg royal family in 1857 in a mishmash of Renaissance, Baroque, and Gothic styles. Inside its 80 rooms you'll find gads of pristine antiques, silk tapestries, carved wood floors, and ornately decorated, plaster-inlaid walls.

The **Alte Garten,** Schwerin's impressive central square, is opposite the Schloß. Cheap student tickets are usually available for most shows at the majestic **Staatstheater,** on the square; check the notice board outside or the **tourist office** (Am Markt 11, tel. 0385/812314) for schedules. The **Staatliches Museum Schwerin** (tel. 0385/57581; admission free; open Tues.–Sun. 9–4), next to the theater, houses a solid collection of Flemish and Dutch masters as well as works by 19th-century German artists like Max Liebermann and Lovis Corinth.

COMING AND GOING Schwerin's train station, west of Pfaffenteich lake, has daily connections to Berlin (10/day, DM31), Hamburg (5/day, DM29), and Lübeck (8/day, DM14.80). To reach the Altstadt, follow Herbert-Warnke-Straße to Pfaffenteich lake, turn right, and go straight. The bus station is in the Altstadt by the Schloß.

WHERE TO SLEEP Inexpensive accommodations are so hard to come by that the mosquito-infested **youth hostel** (Waldschulenweg 3, tel. 0385/213005; beds DM15–DM20) is the unfortunate first choice; from the train station take Bus 15 to the last stop. Otherwise, stop by the tourist office for their woefully short list of budget accommodations in town.

Rhineland

Düsseldorf

Düsseldorfers are considered snobby because of their wealth: The annual income of Düsseldorfers is 25% higher than that of the average German, which explains why most major banking firms have their main offices here. On the other hand, the city is often written off as a dumping ground for partying blue-collar workers from Ruhrgebiet, the big industrial area north of the city. Yet Düsseldorf has nothing to be ashamed of: It contains a preserved medieval vil-

That Ain't German

After spending some time on the northern coast you'll notice that not everyone speaks the same High German you learned in school. That's because "Plattdeutsch" (Low German, literally "flat" German), a dialect common in Schleswig-Holstein, Hamburg, and Mecklenburg-Vorpommern, is still spoken in small villages and especially by the older generation—which is why southerners view Platt as the language of farmers and country bumpkins. Budding linguists should also note that the English word "shit" comes not from High German's "Scheiße" but from Platt's "Schiet."

lage and a ruined fort, excellent modern-art museums, a wealth of bars and nightclubs, and a renovated castle, to boot.

BASICS The **tourist office** (Konrad-Adenauer-Pl. 12, tel. 0211/17020), across and to the right from the Hauptbahnhof, reserves rooms for DM5. Nearby is the useful **American Express** (Heinrich-Heine-Allee 14, across from Opera, tel. 0211/822035) and the potentially useful **U.K. Consulate** (Yorckstraße 19, tel. 0211/94480).

COMING AND GOING Trains leave the **Hauptbahnhof** four times hourly for Köln (with a break between 1:30–5 AM) and hourly for Frankfurt, Hannover, and Amsterdam. Many S-Bahn lines originate at the Hauptbahnhof and serve almost every major city within an hour of Düsseldorf. S-Bahn tickets for these shorter trips are cheaper than train fare, but you can't use EurailPass.

WHERE TO SLEEP Conventions and trade fairs in Düsseldorf bring droves that fill hotels and raise—sometimes by 100%—the price of rooms. You might want to call the tourist office to make sure there's no *Messe* (convention or trade fair) when you plan to visit, and then you'll have much better luck finding cheap lodging within a five- or 10-minute walk of the train station. **Christlicher Verein Junger Menschen** (Graf-Adolf-Str. 102, tel. 0211/360764; doubles DM90), a German YMCA, has no curfew, so young people cruise in and out at all times. It's down the street and to the left from the Hauptbahnhof. The airy rooms of **Domo** (Scheurenstr. 4, tel. 0211/374001; doubles DM100–DM250) and **Komet** (Bismarckstr. 93, tel. 0211/178790; doubles DM100–DM120) are also within a couple of blocks of the Hauptbahnhof.

➢ **HOSTEL** • **Jugendherberge und Jugendgästehaus Düsseldorf (HI).** The curfew is 1 AM, but one of the hapless receptionists gets up every hour until 6 AM to let latecomers in. Crowded, bunk-filled rooms and hammocklike beds (DM20–DM24). Rooms in the adjacent **Jugendgästehaus** (DM26.50 per person) are newer and quieter. *Düsseldorf Str. 1, tel. 0211/557310. From Hauptbahnhof Bus 835 to Jugendherberge (15 min). Laundry.*

FOOD If the Altstadt is the heart of Düsseldorf, pumping all day and beating furiously at night, then *Alt Bier* is the blood that courses through the sector's veins—and taps. The rich, sweet brew is available in beer halls everywhere in the old town. If you're just looking for some fruit, cheese, meat, or bread, head for the open-air **market** on Karlsplatz, open weekdays 8–6 and Saturday 8–2.

Hausbrauerei zum Schlüssel (Bolkerstr. 43, tel. 0211/326155) offers a large kettle brimming with brew in the back and a large selection of traditional delicacies (DM9–DM15). Entirely different from traditional brew houses, **Zur Uel** (Ratinger Str. 16, tel. 0211/325369) teems with university-age eaters and drinkers who seem a little frayed and on edge. The food—mostly salads, soups, and pastas (DM9–DM14)—is basic, and the portions generous. Chicken with rice or noodles (DM6.50) is fantastic at **Bambus Garden** (Weseler Str. 35, tel. 0211/615228), especially if it's past 1:30 AM.

WORTH SEEING Bordered by the serene **Hofgarten Park** to the north and east and by the Rhine to the west, the Altstadt and its maze of small alleys is home to more than 200 bars and restaurants. If you forget the next day where you were the previous night, go to the top of the 770-foot **Rheinturm** (Stromstr. 20), and glance down at the sprawling city. The Altstadt is only about 12 blocks long and five blocks wide, but you'll need a walking map from the tourist office (*see* Basics, *above*) to avoid becoming utterly lost.

The best parts of **Schloß Benrath**, an 80-room castle, are the flowers, tree-canopied footpaths, and reflecting pools behind the Schloß. The park is a great place to relax or take a stroll. *Benrather Schloßallee 104, tel. 0211/899–7271. U717 (Richtung Benrath) to Schloß Benrath. Admission: DM5, DM2.50 students. Tours every ½ hr Tues.–Fri. 11–4, weekends 10–4.*

Kunstsammlung Nordrhein-Westfalen. This modern-art museum has works by Pablo Picasso and Marc Chagall and one of the finest Paul Klee collections anywhere. *Grabbepl. 5, tel. 0211/133961. Admission: DM8, DM5 students. Open Tues.–Sun. 10–6.*

Köln

Before becoming Europeans, Germans, or Rhinelanders, the people of this large and diverse city were Kölners. Locals hypothesize that the legacy of Italian blood in Köln, colonized by the Romans almost 2,000 years ago, makes it a little more jovial and lighthearted than the rest of Germany. You might expect that a town with so much munic-

An overwhelming number of Kölners celebrate their birthdays in November, ostensibly because nine months earlier, the city's Lent carnival is most intense.

ipal pride would frown on tourists, but instead, everyone wants to show you why the place is so great—the wealth of art museums and galleries, Roman ruins, and Köln's megalithic Dom. Köln also has (at least according to locals) more bars than any other German city, plus a gay and lesbian scene unmatched outside of Berlin and Munich. Another excuse to let loose is Köln's **carnival,** which officially starts at the 11th minute of the 11th day of the 11th month. But the real debauchees arrive at the end of February with Rose Monday (the last Monday before Lent), when the parades and processions march down Köln's streets, and costumed revelers scream, dance, kiss, and drink with beer-based passion.

VISITOR INFORMATION **American Express.** *Burgmauerstr. 14, across from Dom, tel. 0221/257-7484. Open weekdays 9–5:30, Sat. 9–noon.*

The **tourist office** is across the street from the Dom. City maps are free, but other brochures cost bucks. You can book a room here for a DM3 fee. *Unter Fettenhennen 19, tel. 0221/221-3345. Open May–Oct., Mon.–Sat. 8 AM–10:30 PM, Sun. 9 AM–10:30 PM; Nov.–Apr., Mon.–Sat. 8 AM–9 PM, Sun. 9:30–7.*

COMING AND GOING The trip to Düsseldorf takes about 30 minutes, and trains leave every 15 minutes. Other direct connections from Köln include Berlin (DM119), Paris (DM94), and Amsterdam (DM56.80). Köln is the northernmost German point on the Rhine for **Köln-Düsseldorfer ships** (tel. 0221/208–8318), a fleet of passenger liners that go as far south as Mainz. EurailPass holders get free passage; otherwise, the trip costs DM72 from Köln to Koblenz and another DM72 from Koblenz to Mainz. Yet another understaffed public-service office, the **Citynet Mitfahrzentrale** (Saarstr. 22, tel. 0221/19444) can get you to any major city in Germany with a day or two's notice. From U-Bahn Eifelplatz walk north on Am Duffenbach and turn left on Saarstraße.

GETTING AROUND To see Köln properly, you're going to have to ride some public transportation, because only the Altstadt, the museums and sights directly around the Dom, and major *Fußgängerzonen* (pedestrian zones) such as **Hohe Straße** and **Schildergasse** are accessible by foot. Luckily, Köln has an incredibly extensive subway/streetcar system. Almost all of the subway lines, which become streetcar lines outside the city center, pass underneath the Hauptbahnhof (follow the blue-and-white "U" signs).

WHERE TO SLEEP Throughout the year the city is flooded with fashion-industry representatives, so call *way* ahead. If none of the hotels listed below can accommodate you, try one of the many cheap hotels on Brandenburger Straße.

Hotel Berg. Five-minute walk from Hauptbahnhof. Singles DM55, DM80 with shower. Doubles DM80, DM140 with shower. *Brandenburger Str. 6, tel. 0221/121124. Exit rear of Hauptbahnhof onto Johannisstr. (parallel to Rhine), turn left on Brandenburger Str.*

Hotel Garni Im Kupferkessel. Spiral staircase leads to the kitchen, where all the guests breakfast together. One block west of elegant fountains and ponds lining Kaiser-Wilhelm-Ring. Singles DM50–DM75, doubles DM100. *Probsteigasse 6, tel. 0221/135338. Exit front of Hauptbahnhof and follow Dompropst-Ketzer-Str. (it becomes Gereonsstr. and then Christophstr.), turn right on Probsteigasse (15 min total by foot).*

Pension Jansen and **Pension Kirchener.** Two pensions in the same building, above an apartment; you get a key to come and go as you please. Rooms are comfortable but small. Singles at both cost DM40–DM50, doubles DM80–DM100. *Richard-Wagner-Str. 18, tel.*

0221/251875 for Jansen, 0221/252977 for Kirchener. From Dom take U9, U12, U16, or U18 to Neumarkt, then Tram 1 (direction Junkersdorf) 2 stops to Moltkestr., then double back down Richard-Wagner-Str. Reservations advised.

➤ **HOSTELS** • **Jugendgästehaus Köln-Riehl.** The biggest youth hostel in Germany. Clean, functional, and efficient, like any good production-line factory, and within 15 minutes of the Hauptbahnhof. Beds DM28.50, including breakfast. *An der Schanz 14, tel. 0221/767081. U16 or U18 from Hauptbahnhof to Boltensternstr., then walk 100 yds in same direction as train. Dinner DM7.50.*

Jugendherberge Köln-Deutz. A little smaller and cheaper, it's also a little dirtier and louder than its counterpart above. Beds DM23–DM25, lunch and dinner DM8.50 each. *Siegesstr. 5A, tel. 0221/814711. U9 from Hauptbahnhof to Deutz-Kalker Str., turn 180° and head down Deutzer Freiheit, then turn right on tiny Neuhöfferstr., left on Siegesstr. Laundry.*

➤ **CAMPGROUND** • **Campingplatz Poll.** This manicured field next to the Rhine is easy to get to, but it's not for nature lovers: The river banks are industrial, and car campers predominate. DM4–DM8 per tent, DM6 per person. *Marienburg, tel. 0221/831966. U16 from Hauptbahnhof to Marienburg, then cross Rodenkirchener Bridge.*

FOOD You won't find a lot of typical pig-and-potato German fare in Köln, but you will find lots of southern-Mediterranean restaurants, especially Greek, Turkish, and Italian. If you're just looking for some bread, cheese, and vegetables, a stroll along **Hohe Straße** and **Schildergasse** will provide everything at cut-rate prices. If you do only one thing in town besides see the Dom, sample some Kölsch beer, brewed by more than 40 different houses and served everywhere.

Remember that when Kölners toast, they clink glass bottoms—not tops.

Osho's. A tiny eatery with stand-up tables and fresh vegetarian food. Enchiladas (DM6), pizzas (DM3.50), and sandwiches (DM4) are served fast and hot. **Petit Prince** downstairs features live music to complement the **One World** disco upstairs. *Hohenzollernring 90, north of Friesenpl., tel. 0221/574–0726. U5 from Hauptbahnhof to Friesenpl. Open until 5 AM.*

Sansone. Arguably the best pasta in town. Elegant, yet surprisingly affordable (pasta DM12.50–DM16.50). *Händelstr. 47, behind Holiday Inn on Rudolfpl., tel. 0221/252949. Tram 1 (direction Junkersdorf) from Neumarkt to Rudolfspl. Closed Sun.*

Stadtgarten. Beer garden packs as many as 500 smiling, rowdy drinkers in warm weather. Inside, setting switches from gravel and benches to dark wood and avant-garde art; some night's there's a live band. Food ranges from pizza (DM4–DM7) to sausage plates (DM12). *Venloer Str. 40, tel. 0221/516037. U5 from Hauptbahnhof to Friesenpl.*

WORTH SEEING Studying a map of Köln will show you that the Rhine and Hohenzollernring, part of a curving street that connects Rudolfplatz and Friesenplatz, form something resembling a half moon. The west side of the "moon" runs along what was the medieval city wall, completed in about 1200. A walk from the Dom to Friesenplatz or Rudolfplatz, whether on a sightseeing or a beer-drinking tour, is a good way to explore the inner city.

Dom. Even if you hate the whole idea of churchgoing, this sand castle–looking church on Domvorplatz should inspire some awe. Climb the 509 steps of the **Südturm** (south tower) for a great view of the Rhine. More spectacular, however, is the **Glockenstube** (400 steps up), where the Dom's nine bells are housed, including the Petriglocke—the world's heaviest working bell. The **Diozesan Museum,** across the plaza, houses art and rings and scepters and funny hats and all sorts of strange things.

Römisch-Germanisches Museum. A tribute to and a documentation of Roman life, with an authentic mosaic floor (AD 220) and the tomb of the Roman soldier Poblicius (AD 40). *Roncallipl. 4, behind Dom, tel. 0221/221–2304. Admission: DM5, DM2.50 students. Open Tues.–Sun. 10–5.*

Wallraf-Richartz-Museum and **Museum Ludwig.** In the same building right behind the Dom, these two museums form the core of Köln's art scene. The collections span the middle ages through the Renaissance. Museum Ludwig also has a massive collection of 20th-century art. *Bischofsgartenstr. 1, behind Dom, tel. 0221/221-2372 for Wallraf Richartz, 0221/221-2370 for Ludwig. Admission: DM8, DM4 students. Open Tues.-Thurs. 10-8, Fri.-Sun. 10-5.*

AFTER DARK **Biermuseum** (Buttermarkt 39, tel. 0221/257-7802), along the Rhine south of the Dom, is always crowded, and the drinking is relatively serious. **Hallmacken-Reuthur** (Brüsseler Pl. 9, tel. 0221/517970) embraces the cheesy art deco of the late '60s and early '70s. **E-Werk** (Schanzen Str. 28, tel. 0221/621091; closed Sun.-Thurs.), in an industrial sector outside the city on the east side of the Rhine, is a gigantic warehouse with two floors and multiple bars. From the Dom, take U16 or U18 to Wienerpatz, then follow Clevischer Ring or Genovevastraße, turn right on Keupstraße, left on Schanzenstraße.

Outside that of Berlin and Munich, Köln's gay nightlife is probably the most thriving in Germany: Many bars, discos, and some saunas cater mostly or exclusively to gays and lesbians. **Gloria** (Apostelnstr. 11, tel. 0221/254433), a café and disco based in an old movie theater, is loaded with well-dressed dancers and drinkers, mostly men. **Yocoto** (Kaiser-Wilhelm-Ring 30-32, tel. 0221/132262), north of Friesenplatz, is the home of the young, elegant crowd. Friday through Sunday it's open until 4:30 AM. One of the oldest gay meeting spots in Köln is **Treff am Gürzenich** (Gürzenichstr. 28, tel. 0221/237739). On Tuesday night the disco at Osho's (*see* Food, *above*) becomes the **Pink Triangle,** a lesbian-and-gay disco.

NEAR KOLN

AACHEN Aachen, connected twice hourly by train with Köln (50 min), is also known as **Bad Aachen** because of its supposedly rejuvenating hot springs (*Bad* means baths), and as **Aix-la-Chapelle** because of Charlemagne's 8th-century, 16-sided chapel that now supports the rest of the city's cathedral. Aachen is also called "Rome North" because Charlemagne really dug this town and the 32 Holy Roman emperors who followed him were crowned in Aachen's **Dom.** The golden shrine in the cathedral contains Charlemagne's remains; pieces of his skull are on display in the **Domschatzkammer** (Cathedral Treasury). Across from the Dom, on **Katsch Hof** plaza (which has a fruit-and-vegetable market daily until 1 PM), note the regal **Rathaus,** graced by the statues of 50 Holy Roman emperors, many of whom received their titles in Aachen.

The hot springs drew the Romans here, so when in Rome North, do as the Romans did: Take a bath. The area south of the Hauptbahnhof is filled with natural springs appropriately called **Kurgebiet** (Cure Territory), but the more affordable spas are farther uptown. At the **Kurbad Quellenhof** (Monheimsallee 52, tel. 0241/180-2922) you can take a two-hour hot-spring bath for DM15.

➤ **WHERE TO SLEEP** • Hotel **Rösener** (Theaterstr. 62, tel. 0241/407215), a few blocks from the Hauptbahnhof, has doubles for DM80. **Hotel Weiss** (Adalbertsteinweg 67, tel. 0241/505007) is a little farther and a fraction more expensive (doubles DM90). To get to the **youth hostel** (Maria-Theresia-Allee 260, tel. 0241/71101; beds DM18, DM21 over 26), exit the Hauptbahnhof, turn left on Lagerhausstraße, go past the tiny gate-tower Marschier-tor, pick up Bus 2 at the corner of Lagerhausstraße and Karmeliterstraße, and ride two stops.

BONN The decision to switch the capital of Germany from Bonn back to Berlin was made in 1991, but the move will take at least 10 years because a zillion bureaucrats, along with their families and files, need to be transplanted. As Bonn's prominence wanes, its only claim to fame will likely be as the birthplace of Ludwig van Beethoven. Your first stop on the Beethoven tour should be **Münsterplatz,** which is centered around a stoic statue of the composer. Next you should visit **Beethoven Geburtshaus** (Bonngasse 20, tel. 0228/635188; admission DM5, DM2 students; open Apr.-Sept., Mon.-Sat. 10-5, Sun. 10-1, shorter hrs off-season), the house in which the master was born. The tour is tough on the non-German speaker, but the limited English material is enough to give you an idea of the raw intensity with which Ludwig lived his life. Every three years Bonn hosts a **Beethoven Festival** in April and September; you're in luck, because it's slated for 1995.

➢ **VISITOR INFORMATION** • The English-speaking staff will book a room for you for DM3. They also offer a bus tour (DM16) that leaves at 10 and 2, if you're into that kind of thing. *Münsterstr. 20, tel. 0228/773466. Follow* STADTMITTE *signs from Hauptbahnhof onto Poststr., left on Münsterstr. Open Mon.–Sat. 8–9, Sun. 9:30–12:30.*

➢ **WHERE TO SLEEP** • Bonn's hotels never sell out; the many diplomatic visitors don't look for budget accommodations and Germans don't vacation here. All the following prices include breakfast. Both hostels have a 1 AM curfew and charge DM26.20. **Jugendgästehaus Bonn-Venusberg** (Haager Weg 42, tel. 0228/289970), poised at the edge of the lush Kottenforst, should be the poster child for *Better Youth Hostels and Gardens.* Take Bus 621 from Platform B1 to Jugendherberge (about 15 min). **Jugendgästehaus Bonn–Bad Godesberg** (Horionstr. 60, tel. 0228/317516), your second-best option, is sharply dressed and sterile. Take U63 to Bad Godesberg Hauptbahnhof, then Bus 615 to Jugendherberge. **Virneburg** (Sandkaule 3A, tel. 0228/636366) is dumpy but has a nice owner and nice prices: doubles DM70, DM890 with shower. Take U62, U64, or U66 toward Bad Honnef, Obertassel, or Siegburg to Bertha-von-Stuttner Platz. **Hotel Eschweiler** (Bonngasse 7, tel. 0228/631760; doubles DM85–DM105) has an unbeatable location, some 20 yards from Marktplatz.

➢ **FOOD** • Not all plazas in Bonn are as big as **Münsterplatz** or **Marktplatz,** but all have cafés. If you're just looking for fruit, cheese, bread, and a nice wall to lean against, head to Marktplatz, which has a market that's open weekdays until 6. **University Mensa** (Nassestr. 11, off Kaiserstr., tel. 0228/737030), a cafeteria in the student union, serves lunch and dinner, each for less than DM3. Come to **Hähnchen** (Münsterpl. 11, tel. 0228/652039) if you're looking for a local crowd and local eats (DM6–DM15).

➢ **WORTH SEEING** • From Marktplatz follow Stockenstraße to Regina Weg to reach **Kurfürstliches Schloß,** a castle turned university administration building. Behind are the **Hofgarten** and **Stadtgarten,** two parks filled with students, sunbathers, punks, bums, and lots of trash.

To reach the following government buildings and museums, take U16 or U63 south toward Rheinallee/Bad Godesberg and get off at Heussallee/Bundeshaus. From the Heussallee/Bundeshaus station walk to the Rhine, and you'll find the **Bundeshaus,** Germany's senate, and the **Bundestag,** the parliament building (both on Görresstrasse). Tours begin every hour at Hermann-Ehlers-Straße. 29. Bring a passport. *Tel. 0228/162152. Admission free. Open weekdays 9–4, weekends 10–4.*

Months after the decision was made to move the country's capital to Berlin, Bonn opened two of the most spectacular modern-art museums in Germany, **Kunst und Ausstellungshalle** (Friedrich-Ebert-Allee 4, tel. 0228/917–1200; admission DM8, DM4 students; open Tues.–Sun. 10–7) and **Kunstmuseum Bonn** (Friedrich-Ebert-Allee 2, tel. 0228/776262; admission DM5, DM3 students; open Tues.–Sun. 10–7).

MAINZ Mainz is the business center of the lower Rhine and the state capital of Rhineland-Palatinate. Although the city was bombed heavily during the war, the town center has been rebuilt in its old medieval style; it's now a pedestrian shopping zone graced with plazas and fountains. The city's most important role, perhaps, is as gateway to the most spectacular, castle-studded stretch of the Rhine, between Mainz and Koblenz.

Mainz's most famous son, Johannes Gutenberg (1390–1468), invented movable type. The free and central **Gutenberg Museum** (Liebfrauenpl. 5, tel. 06131/122640) does its best to glamorize the potentially boring history of publishing. Dominating the Marktplatz in the center of the Altstadt, **Martinsdom** is a mammoth Romanesque cathedral, begun in the 10th century. The famous Jewish surrealist Marc Chagall designed the stained-glass windows of the otherwise ordinary **Stephanskirche** (Stefanspl.), in the heart of the old town. You can get to Mainz by train, but it's an excellent place to start a boat tour. The ferry line **KD** (tel. 0221/20880) sails 22 ships between Mainz and Köln and several operators offer short "castle tours." KD boats leave from the docks in front of the Rathaus (Rheinstr.).

➤ **WHERE TO SLEEP** • The miserable local youth hostel, **Jugendgästehaus** (Am Fort Weisenau, tel. 06131/85332; bed and breakfast DM25), should be used only in an emergency. Try instead the **Terminus Hotel** (Alicestr. 4, tel. 06131/229876) or **Pfeil Continental** (Bahnhofstr. 15, tel. 06131/232179), which have decent doubles for DM120–DM150. **Campingplatz Maarave** (tel. 06134/4383; DM6 per person, DM6 per tent) is on a plain splotch of grass on the east bank of the Rhine. Take Bus 13 (about 25 min) from Bahnhofsplatz to Brückenkopf Kastel. The English-speaking staff at the **tourist office** (Bahnhofstr. 15, tel. 06131/286210) charges DM5 for hotel reservations.

GREAT BRITAIN AND 10
NORTHERN IRELAND

It may appear that the British tourism industry really doesn't want your business. Prices are more expensive than in most of Europe (especially for transportation), the often-dreary weather can dim your spirits, and *the food*—well, it lives up to everything you've heard about it. Jeez, even your EurailPass isn't good here. Okay, enough with the rancor—although, owing to how expensive a trip here can be, it's usually necessary to state Britain's frustrations before its advantages.

There's certainly enough to recommend coming to Britain, and after spending three weeks in foreign-language purgatory it can be great to speak English again. What most people don't expect in Britain is how much there is to explore beyond London and first-rate towns like York, Bath, and, in Scotland, Edinburgh. If you want to, you could walk the entire length of the island from Stonehenge to Inverness along hiking and walking paths, staying at quiet hostels nearly every night. Sure you'll need a couple free months and a lot of waterproof gear, but it is *possible.* And possibilities are what makes the British Isles fun; while occasionally it seems difficult to escape the crowds in Italy and France, you can be in deepest, folksiest Wales within three hours from London. If you have the time to explore Scotland, you may want to stay on its rural islands for the rest of your life.

Most discussions of British history mark 1066, the date of William the Conqueror's invasion, as the beginning of the proper history of the isles. But between the Celts, Vikings, Saxons, and Normans—not to mention later immigrations from every corner of Empire—it's hard to claim common heritage for the residents of these two big (and thousands of little) islands. Sadly, centuries-old dialects and regional languages are dying fast, owing partly to the BBC's standardization of the English language. Many communities lament the loss of the folkways that made their ancestors proud.

Since the 18th century, Britain has often been referred to as "a nation of shopkeepers." Margaret Thatcher, herself the daughter of a greengrocer, went a long way toward fulfilling this bourgeois vision of Britain during her decade-long tenure as prime minister. Under her iron hand and the more timid touch of John Major, Britain's middle class has come into its own, the number of property owners has soared, and business has found a friend in government. Not everyone is pleased by the results, however, and a culture of anti-Tory criticism has sprung up, led by the grieving pallbearers of the English experiment with socialism. Many of Britain's most talented artists form part of this counterculture, which feels that, under the Conservatives, Britain has abandoned the poor and created a middle class of fat, dumb, and happy consumers.

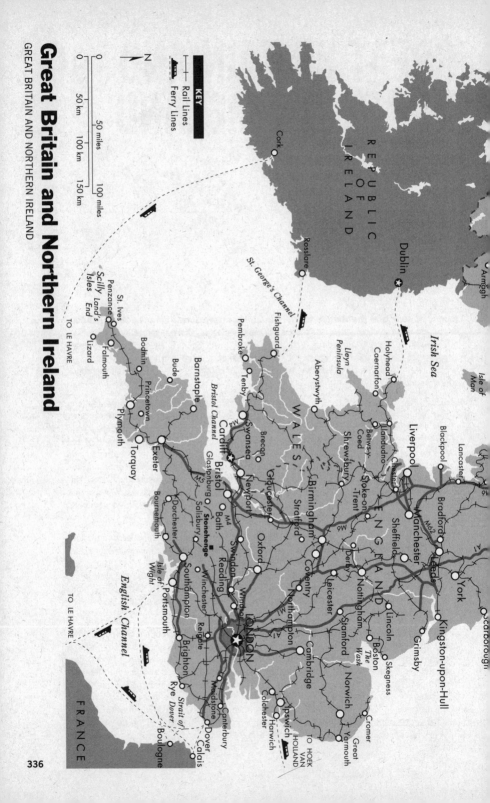

Great Britain and Northern Ireland

GREAT BRITAIN AND NORTHERN IRELAND

KEY

Rail Lines

Ferry Lines

N

| 0 | | | 50 miles | | 100 miles |
| 0 | 50 km | 100 km | 150 km |

REPUBLIC OF IRELAND

Armagh

Cork

Rosslare

St. George's Channel

Dublin

Irish Sea

Isle of Man

Holyhead

Caernarfon

Lleyn Peninsula

Llandudno

Betws-y-Coed

Chester

Blackpool

Lancaster

Liverpool

Manchester

Bradford

Leeds

York

Scarborough

Kingston-upon-Hull

Grimsby

Skegness

The Wash

Boston

Lincoln

Sheffield

Stoke-on-Trent

Derby

Nottingham

Stamford

Shrewsbury

Aberystwyth

Pembroke

Tenby

Fishguard

W A L E S

Brecon

Swansea

Cardiff

Newport

Gloucester

Birmingham

Stratford

Coventry

Leicester

E N G L A N D

Cambridge

Norwich

Cromer

Great Yarmouth

Ipswich

Harwich

Colchester

TO HOEK VAN HOLLAND

Bristol Channel

Glastonbury

Bristol

Bath

Stonehenge

Swindon

Oxford

Reading

Windsor

LONDON

Northampton

Barnstaple

Bude

Bodmin

Princetown

Plymouth

Exeter

Torquay

Bournemouth

Dorchester

Salisbury

Winchester

Southampton

Isle of Wight

Portsmouth

Brighton

Reigate

Maidstone

Canterbury

Rye

Dover

Strait of Dover

Calais

Boulogne

F R A N C E

English Channel

TO LE HAVRE

TO LE HAVRE

St. Ives

Penzance

Scilly Isles

Land's End

Falmouth

Lizard

336

Great Britain and Northern Ireland

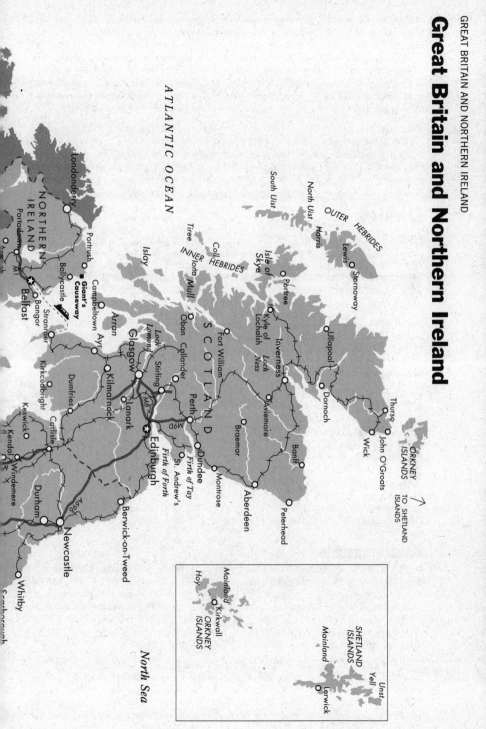

ATLANTIC OCEAN

OUTER HEBRIDES
South Uist
North Uist
Harris
Lewis
○Stornoway

Tiree
INNER HEBRIDES
Coll
Iona
Mull
Islay

Isle of
Skye
○Portree
Kyle of
Lochalsh
Loch
Ness
Inverness
Ullapool○
Dornoch○
Thurso○
Wick○
John O'Groats○
ORKNEY
ISLANDS
TO SHETLAND
ISLANDS

NORTHERN
IRELAND
Londonderry○
Portrush○
Ballycastle■
Giant's
Causeway
■Belfast
Bangor○
Stranraer
Campbeltown○
Arran
Ayr○

S C O T L A N D
Oban○
Loch
Lomond
Callander○
Fort William○
Aviemore○
Braemar○
Banff○
Peterhead○

Glasgow○
Stirling○
Perth○
Kilmarnock○
Lanark○
M8
M90
A90
Dundee○
St. Andrew's
Firth of Tay
Montrose○
Aberdeen○

Kirkcudbright
Dumfries○
Carlisle○
Edinburgh★
Firth of Forth
Berwick-on-Tweed○

Keswick○
Kendal○
Windermere○
Durham○
A696
Newcastle
Whitby○

North Sea

Mainland
Hoy
Kirkwall○
ORKNEY
ISLANDS

SHETLAND
ISLANDS
Mainland
Yell
Unst
Lerwick○

Movies like *My Beautiful Launderette* have helped focus attention on the untraditional, non-white face of Britain. The empire has come home to roost, and in recent decades Britain has gone from a largely homogeneous society to one of the world's most diverse. For a country that once espoused a belief that "wogs begin at Calais" ("wog" is a derogatory term for blacks or dark-skinned people), the influx of hundreds of thousands of Indians, Pakistanis, and West Indians has clearly changed the national character. Certainly, the process of acculturation has been difficult—witness the Brixton and Toxteth race riots of the '80s and the continued instances of "Paki-bashing," in which skinheads attack Pakistani immigrants.

Nowadays, the threat to "Britishness" comes from none other than Europe itself. Britons are divided by the European Union's attempt to forge a United States of Europe: They like the idea of lower prices, larger markets, and employment that the EU (formerly the European Community) offers, but they hate the idea of giving up their sovereignty to get them. Despite the recent opening of the Channel Tunnel, Britain is not growing any closer to its neighbors.

Basics

MONEY £1 = $1.53 and $1 = 65 pence. The unit of currency in Great Britain is the pound, broken into 100 pence. In the United Kingdom and Northern Ireland, pound (nick-named the "quid") notes (not "bills") come in colorfully designed denominations of £5, £10, £20, and £50. Scottish banks still print £1 notes (the Bank of England stopped in 1988). Coins are available in denominations of 1p, 2p, 5p, 10p, 20p, 50p, and £1. The one-shilling coin is worth 5p, and the two-shilling coin is worth 10p.

British ATMs can usually access an American checking account (although savings accounts are another thing). Major bank chains like National Westminster and Barclay's are usually linked to the Plus, Star, or Internet chains. Make sure you have a four-digit security code; if yours is longer, ask your bank about changing it. If your credit card has an access code, you can draw money off it at Barclay's (Visa) and National Westminster (MasterCard).

➢ **HOW MUCH IT WILL COST** • You will be astounded by how expensive Britain is, even relative to other European countries. Even if you stay in hostels and eat only pub grub and cheap Indian food, be prepared to drop $40–$50 a day. Lodging will be your greatest expense. Expect to pay around £8–£12 for a bed in a hostel, £12–£15 per person in a bed-and-breakfast (B&B) (although prices vary widely), and £20 and up for a hotel. The only blessing is that campsites can cost as little as £2. Foodwise, you can subsist quite easily on £10 a day, if you don't mind fish-and-chips or pub grub. Although trains are often the most convenient form of transportation, they are hideously expensive. Local transportation is expensive, too; it costs 90p just to go one stop on the Underground in London. As for tipping, leave about 10% for restaurant service (unless the menu or check indicates that service is included), 10% for taxi drivers, and nothing for pub bartenders unless you *really* like the service.

COMING AND GOING

➢ **BY PLANE** • London has two enormous airports, **Heathrow** and **Gatwick,** that are burdened with the majority of England's international traffic; upstart **Stansted Airport,** halfway between London and Cambridge on the M11, recently opened as a more pleasant alternative. Manchester, Edinburgh, Glasgow, and Belfast have airports serving some international destinations, primarily on the European continent. Although **British Airways** (tel. 0181/897–4000) is considered the national airline, international carriers like Delta, United, Virgin, American, and Air France fly to Britain from the Continent and America.

➢ **BY FERRY** • Ferries aren't always the most pleasant way of getting around, but they are the cheapest means of coming from France, Belgium, and the Netherlands. Ferries arrive at **Dover** and **Portsmouth** from Calais, Boulogne, and Le Havre; the standard round-trip fare is £44, but can drop by £20 if you return in less than five days. Holland, northern Germany, and Scandinavia are best accessed from the East Anglia town of **Harwich** by ferries bound for Hoek van Holland (Hook of Holland). The Welsh port of **Holyhead** is the best town to catch ferries to Dublin (about £19 each way), although there's also service from the Welsh port of **Fishguard** to the Irish port of Rosslare, and from **Stranraer** (Scotland) to Belfast (Northern Ireland).

GETTING AROUND

➤ **BY TRAIN** • Despite Britain's shifty allegiance to a unified Europe it *still* does not accept EurailPass. Nonetheless, most budget travelers get around Britain by train. **British Rail** operates all British trains except for a handful of short-distance private rail lines in remote areas. The backbone of the rail system is the InterCity network, which links Britain's major cities via high-speed rail. InterCity train service and service to towns within London's commuter belt are extremely frequent. However, as you get farther out into the countryside, off the InterCity routes, service drops off dramatically, and it's important to plan your itinerary carefully. This is particularly true on Sundays, especially in remote areas of northern and western England, Scotland, and Wales. The *British Rail Passenger Timetable* (£6), issued every May and October, contains details of all BritRail services; pick one up at any major train station.

If you plan to do a lot of traveling, it's probably worth investing in a **BritRail Pass,** since full-price tickets (especially one-way) are absurdly expensive. Remember that most rail passes *cannot* be purchased in the United Kingdom—you must get them *before* you leave home. Passes allow unlimited travel over the entire British Rail Network, which encompasses almost all lines you're likely to need. An adult **second-class pass** costs $219 for eight days, $339 for 15 days, $425 for 22 days, and $495 for one month. If you're 16–25 years old, consider a **BritRail Youth Pass.** It allows unlimited second-class travel in the following increments: $179 for eight days, $269 for 15 days, $339 for 22 days, and $395 for one month. Passes are available from most travel agents or from the **BritRail Travel Information Office** (1500 Broadway, New York, NY 10036, tel. 800/677–8585).

If you want to explore a specific part of Britain in greater detail, the series of **Regional Rail Rover** unlimited travel tickets offers excellent value. They cost between £26.50 and £64 (depending on the size of the area covered) for a second-class, seven-day pass (there's also a 14-day pass) and can be bought at main stations and BritRail travel agents. For travelers under 26, the **Young Person's Railcard** (around £10–£20) is good for one-third off most train tickets—an investment that will pay you back immediately.

➤ **BY BUS** • Buses take much longer than trains, but tickets are often half as expensive. Although many regional, long-distance bus companies exist, **National Express** (Caledonian Express in Scotland) has the most comprehensive coverage of towns and cities in England, Wales, and Scotland. The **Tourist Trail Pass** allows unlimited bus travel in England, Scotland, and Wales, with discount fares for ages 5–15 (youth), ages 16–23 (students), and ages 65 and up (senior citizens)—so students over 23 must pay the adult fare. It may be cheaper to buy one ahead of time in the United States if you're afraid of the exchange rate's getting

The Slow Coach

To beat the high cost of bus travel in Britain, consider spending £69 on The Slow Coach, a new around-Britain bus service for travelers of all ages. Four coaches a week run a clockwise circuit from London to Windsor to Bath to Stratford to the Lake District to Edinburgh to York to Cambridge and back again to London. Coaches stop at YHA and SYHA hostels in the above destinations, and you can board and get off any time you like. Best of all, tickets are valid for two months and are completely transferable—in other words, any unused portion of your ticket can be given or sold to other travelers. Buy tickets from YHA and SYHA hostels en route, or contact The Slow Coach (71 Bradenstoke, Wiltshire SN15 4EL, England, tel. 01249/891959) for more info.

worse during your trip; in America, the **British Travel Associates** (tel. 703/298–2232) sell tickets over the phone and can quote you the latest price in dollars. In Britain, you can get a ticket at any National Express office or at the Heathrow or Gatwick bus stations. A five-day pass is £65, an eight-day pass £90, a 30-day pass £190. You'll get a 30% discount on these passes with the **National Express Discount Coach Card** (£6), available to students age 16–25 and senior citizens over age 60. It's available at any National Express office.

WHERE TO SLEEP Unless you want overpriced, antiseptic privacy, don't bother staying at any hotels in Britain; B&Bs, hostels—both HI and privately owned—and campgrounds will help salvage your budget. Bed-and-breakfasts, which cost £10–£15 per person at the low end, are usually private homes that owners open to the public. In general, expect to share bathrooms, although many rooms have their own washbasin. Breakfast—anything from soggy toast to the full splendor of bacon, sausage, eggs, tomato, and cereal—is included in the rates. There are far more B&Bs in Britain than any other type of accommodation, and you're likely to spend at least a few nights in them.

➤ **HOSTELS** • Hostels in Great Britain vary in quality and are priced according to their level of modernization. Students between the ages of 18 and 26 with an ISIC card (see Student and Teacher ID cards, in Chapter 1) are given a £1 discount on their accommodation. All hostels have basic kitchen facilities and serve their own meals (breakfast £2.40, dinner £3.75). Most hostels carry a guide to all of Britain's hostels, including prices, dates open, and directions. Various hostel associations in the British Isles provide extremely useful information; their detailed pamphlets can help you reserve a bed well ahead of your departure date. For information, write or call **Youth Hostel Association of England and Wales (YHA)** (Trevelyan House, 8 St. Stephen's Hill, St. Albans, Herts AL1 2DY, England, tel. 01727/855215), **Scotland Youth Hostel Association (SYHA)** (7 Glebe Crescent, Stirling FK8 2JE, Scotland, tel. 01786/451181), or **Youth Hostel Association of Northern Ireland (YHANI)** (56 Bradbury Pl., Belfast BT7 1RU, Northern Ireland, tel. 01232/324733).

➤ **CAMPGROUNDS** • Facilities at campgrounds vary dramatically: Primitive campsites may offer nothing but the ground itself, while resort-style campgrounds offer showers, laundry facilities, bars, and amusement arcades. If you're planning to camp, keep the following in mind: (1) You're likely to get wet no matter where you are, (2) campgrounds in rural areas are often poorly served by public transportation, and (3) many campgrounds are closed except during summer months. For more information of Britain's more than 2,000 campsites, contact the British Tourist Authority for their free pamphlet, "Caravan and Camping Parks."

FOOD Probably the most compelling reason why Britain conquered half the world is that they wanted some decent food. For this reason alone, Britain is no longer the culinary wasteland it was just two decades ago. In larger cities, the best food is ethnic: Indian, Thai, Pakistani, Chinese. In smaller towns and villages, you may do best eating a hearty, traditional pub meal—usually pies and puddings filled with meat. The English subsist on bangers (sausages) and mash, cottage pie, Cornish pasties (a type of savory pie), and fish-and-chips. One of the best ways to avoid greasy (or microwaved) meals is to eat at vegetarian restaurants, since they not only serve fresh and cheap meals but also serve as meeting places and bulletin boards for the alternative community.

If you're like most Britons, you'll spend a considerable amount of time in pubs. The beer of choice among Britons is bitter, a lightly carbonated beer with an amber color that gets its bitterness from hops. Real ale, served from wooden kegs, is flatter than regular bitters. Stouts, like Guinness, are a meal in themselves and something of an acquired taste—they have a burned flavor and look like used motor oil. Lagers, most familiar to American drinkers, are light-colored and heavily carbonated.

BUSINESS HOURS Business hours are strictly regulated in England, thanks to the church. Standard business hours are Monday–Saturday 9–5:30. Some shops observe an early closing day once a week, often Wednesday or Thursday. In many small villages, many also close for lunch. Pubs are open Monday–Saturday 11–11, Sunday noon–3 and 7–11, or they're open 10–2 and 5–11 every day. Most banks open 9:30–3:30; some have extended hours on

Thursday evenings, and a few are open on Saturday mornings. Every other type of business is *supposed* to be closed on Sunday, but not every business follows suit.

FESTIVALS AND HOLIDAYS From mid-August to early September, the **Edinburgh International Festival,** one of the world's largest arts festivals, features exhibits, plays, concerts, film, and more. Plan early for these events—the crowds are overwhelming. In general, most annual events, such as festivals and races, take place in the spring and summer. The following are public holidays in Great Britain and Northern Ireland: January 1, January 2, Good Friday, Easter Sunday, Easter Monday (in Scotland, the Monday after Easter is *not* a holiday), December 25 and 26 (Boxing Day). Additionally, the first Monday in May, the last Monday in May, and the last Monday in August (in Scotland, it's the first Monday in August) are bank holidays.

EMERGENCIES In the event of serious injury, dial **999** for the fire brigade, police, or ambulance. England has socialized medicine, and, happily, travelers can take advantage of this. Remember, your ISIC card comes with some medical insurance!

PHONES **Country Code: 44.** British Telecom (BT) and Mercury are the only two major phone companies operating in England, Scotland, and Wales. Mercury phones (you'll probably see these only in London) require the purchase of a plastic card that contains a fixed number of units, each valued at 10p, from vending machines or magazine stands. BT pay phones are easy to find throughout the United Kingdom; the ones with a red stripe around them accept standard English coins, and phones with a green stripe require credit card-size "phone cards," available at newsstands, train and bus stations, information offices, and a number of other locations. Warning: BT is reorganizing area codes throughout the entire British Isles. We've updated as many numbers as possible, but some changes won't kick in until well into 1995. BT says they won't charge you for calling defunct numbers, and they promise to play a recording informing you of the correct new area code.

Local calls cost 10p. Public phones return any unused coins, but they don't make change, so think twice about using a £1 coin for a local call. A three- or four-minute local call costs around 40p–50p. To dial long-distance within the U.K., lift the receiver, dial the area code (including the "0") and number, and get ready to pay through the nose. If you're calling the U.K. from abroad, drop the "0" from all area codes. To dial another country direct from the U.K., first dial 00, then dial the country code, then the area code and phone number. Calls to Northern Ireland from England, Scotland, or Wales can be dialed without the international codes. To dial direct or collect using American carriers, dial **AT&T** (tel. 01800/890011), **MCI** (tel. 01800/890222), or **Sprint** (tel. 01800/877800). To place an incredibly expensive collect call using BT, dial 155. Directory assistance is 192.

MAIL Nearly every city, town, village or cluster of houses in the middle of nowhere has a post office—be it inside the butcher shop, liquor store ("off-license"), or chemist. Stamps may be bought at some grocery stores, at stamp machines, or after waiting in long lines at the post office. Rates from the United Kingdom are 39p for an international airmail letter, 34p for an international aerogramme, and 33p for an international postcard.

London

As great a city as London is, few people fall madly in love with it on first sight. Even after a few weeks people can remain noncommittal. Maybe it's the dreary weather, maybe it's London's unshakable association with Dickensian squalor, or maybe it's simply that the fabled British reserve just doesn't see the need to celebrate itself. Even Monet's famous paintings of the Houses of Parliament portray a riverside enshrouded in fog, Joseph Conrad's city of "empty streets and boulevards, big houses tightly shut, and a disquieting sense of turpitude."

Modern London is what you might expect from a city that once stood as headquarters for an empire spanning the globe. There's the maze of wide streets, cavernous palaces, and stately architecture, to be sure, but on almost any street you'll see them surrounded by the thriving immigrant populations and neighborhoods that increasingly define—and redefine—London's contemporary cultural scene. Try not to get sucked into the tour-package version of the city that narrowly focuses on traditional and royal London—a Disneyesque montage of busbied sentries, Beefeaters, pageants, and pomp and circumstance. Maybe these ceremonies held significance a few years ago, but they ring increasingly hollow today. The mystique that once shrouded the royal family has been torn asunder, and revealed is a dysfunctional family symbolic of the nation's troubled present.

You can get a better sense of local London (an amalgam of dozens of once-separate villages) by stepping away from the West End, The City, and the Thames. During these outings into multiethnic neighborhoods like Camden, Brixton, and the East End, you can't help notice just how different the London experience is for its 8 million residents, particularly in the current recession. London displays incredible disparities of wealth, class, and status. This fractious, always interesting brew helps keep London at the forefront of music, art, and fashion: London's clubs and music halls can stand up to any city's; museums display the works of outcast artists; intimate fringe drama thrives at theaters throughout the city; and enfants terribles occasionally storm august bodies like the National Theatre with radical staging. This is the London that counts, the London that can suck you in and keep you coming back for more.

BASICS

VISITOR INFORMATION The **London Tourist Information Centre** provides details about London, including information on Underground and bus tickets, theater, concert and tour bookings, and accommodations. It also provides information on the rest of Britain. *Victoria Station, tel. 0171/730–3488. Tube: Victoria. Open Mon.–Sat. 8–7, Sun. 8–5.*

Other information centers are located in **Harrods** (Brompton Rd.; Tube: Knightsbridge), **Selfridges** (Oxford St.; Tube: Marble Arch), **Heathrow Airport** (Terminals 1, 2, and 3), and **Gatwick** (International Arrivals Concourse).

The **British Travel Centre** provides details about travel, accommodations, and entertainment for the whole of Britain. *12 Regent St.. Open weekdays 9–6:30, Sat. 9–5, Sun. 10–4.*

AMERICAN EXPRESS *Main office: 6 Haymarket, SW1, tel. 0171/930–4411. Tube: Piccadilly Circus. Open weekdays 9–5, Sat. 9–6 (until noon for mail and cardholder services), Sun. 10–6 (currency exchange only).*

Other American Express locations (with shorter hours and fewer services) include 4–12 Lower Regent Street (tel. 0171/839–2682); 78 Brompton Road (tel. 0171/584–6182); 54 Cannon Street (tel. 0171/248–2671); 134 Southampton Row (tel. 0171/837–4416); 89 Mount Street (tel. 0171/499–4436); and 147 Victoria Street (tel. 0171/828–7411).

BUCKET SHOPS If you're looking for discount flights or cheap train, ferry, and bus tickets, you may want to scout the discounted fares advertised in the *Evening Standard* and *Time Out*—they're often cheaper than what travel agencies will quote you. The places with the most consistent low-cost fares are **Campus Travel** (within the YHA headquarters, 14 Southampton St., tel. 0171/836–3343; Tube: Covent Garden; and 52 Grosvenor Gardens, tel. 0171/730–3402; Tube: Victoria) and **Council Travel** (28A Poland St., off Oxford St., tel. 0171/437–3337; Tube: Oxford Circus; closed Sun.).

STA Travel arranges cheap tickets around the world, as well as ISIC cards and rail passes. *2 locations: 86 Old Brompton Rd., tel. 0171/581–4131. Tube: South Kensington. 117 Euston Rd., tel. 0171/465–0484. Tube: Euston Station.*

CHANGING MONEY Although you will find currency exchanges everywhere in London, anyone who uses these money changers is simply flushing money down the toilet—they offer exchange rates 10%–15% worse than banks. **Thomas Cook**, which has travel offices all over town, and **American Express** (*see above*) are the only exceptions, charging bank rates for their respective checks.

EMBASSIES Australia. *Australia House, The Strand, tel. 0171/887–5107. Tube: Aldwych. Open weekdays 10–4.*

Canada. *38 Grosvenor St., tel. 0171/258–6600. Tube: Bond St. Open weekdays 8:45–3.*

New Zealand. *80 Haymarket, tel. 0171/930–8422. Tube: Charing Cross or Piccadilly Circus. Open weekdays 10–noon and 2–4.*

United States. *24 Grosvenor Sq., tel. 0171/499–9000. Tube: Marble Arch or Bond St. Open Mon. and Wed.–Fri. 8:30–noon and 2–4, Tues. 8:30–noon.*

EMERGENCIES The general emergency number for **ambulance, police,** and **fire** is 999. The **Rape Crisis Line** (tel. 0171/837–1600) provides 24-hour emergency and nonemergency counseling. If you need immediate medical attention, you'll find hospitals all over town; one that accepts late-night walk-ins is **University College Hospital** (Gower St., tel. 0171/387–9300; Tube: Euston Sq.), in northwest Bloomsbury, just north of the West End. The most common pharmacy chain is **Boots,** which has stores all over London.

LUGGAGE STORAGE If you're coming from Heathrow or Gatwick airport, the best place to store luggage is in **Victoria Station** (*see* Coming and Going by Train, *below*). It costs £2.50–£3 per piece per day for a maximum of 28 days.

PHONES AND MAIL London has two new area codes: 0171 for inner London, and 0181 for outer London. The central **post office** (King Edward St., across from St. Paul's tube station, tel. 0171/239–5047) will hold mail addressed to you, marked POSTE RESTANTE, for up to one month.

COMING AND GOING

BY PLANE **Heathrow International Airport** handles the majority of international flights to the United Kingdom. There are tourist information counters (tel. 0181/730–3488) in Terminals 1, 2, and 3, along with banks and accommodations services. **Gatwick** (tel. 01293/535353) used to handle mainly charter flights, but it has been upgraded and now accommodates a steady stream of regular flights from the United States. It doesn't take any longer to reach London by train from Gatwick than from Heathrow, but it costs £8 instead of £1–£3. **Stansted** (tel. 01279/680500), London's third airport, opened in March 1991 to help alleviate some of the overcrowding at Heathrow. It serves mainly European destinations, plus American Airlines flights to Chicago and AirTransit flights to Toronto and Vancouver.

Getting in and out of London from Heathrow is a piece of cake. Probably the easiest—and cheapest—option is via the Underground's Piccadilly Line, which makes a loop through the airport before heading back through the center of London. The 45-minute ride into London costs £2.60. British Rail's **Gatwick Express** (tel. 0171/928–5100) is your best bet for getting from Gatwick to Victoria Station in central London. The 40-minute ride costs £8. Look for Gatwick Express signs in the luggage collection areas. Coming from Stansted, catch the **Stansted Express** to Liverpool Street Station. Trains run every 30 minutes and cost £8.50–£17 round-trip, depending on the time of day.

BY TRAIN London has eight major train stations (as well as a bunch of smaller ones), each serving a specific part of the country. All eight stations have tourist information booths (most close at 6 PM), rip-off currency exchanges, and luggage storage (£1–£5 per day). They are also all served by tube, so it's easy to get around after you arrive in London. Some round-trip Super Saver fares from London are available Sunday–Thursday after 9:30 AM: Birmingham (£23), Liverpool (£32), Manchester (£32), Edinburgh (£59), and Glasgow (£59). The **British Travel Centre** (*see* Visitor Information, *above*) can provide you with full train schedules, ticket prices, and other information.

Charing Cross (tel. 0171/928–5100) serves southeast England, including Canterbury and Dover. **Euston** (tel. 0171/387–7070) delivers folks to the West Midlands, north Wales, northwest England, and northwest and western Scotland. Trains to Birmingham and Glasgow leave from Euston. **King's Cross** (tel. 0171/278–2477) serves Yorkshire, northeast England, and eastern Scotland (Edinburgh included). Trains depart from **Liverpool Street** (tel. 0171/928–5100) for Cambridge, East Anglia, and Essex. **Paddington** (tel. 0171/

262–6767) sends trains to South Wales, the West Country, and Cornwall, including Bath, Stratford, and Oxford. **St. Pancras** (tel. 0171/837–5483) is the station for trains heading north to the East Midlands and South Yorkshire, and such cities as Nottingham and Sheffield. **Victoria** (tel. 0171/387–7070) serves southern England, including Gatwick Airport, Brighton, and Canterbury. Train service for virtually all Europe-bound ferries leaves from Victoria or **Waterloo** (tel. 0171/928–5100), which also serves the southwest of England. Destination ports include Sheerness-on-Sea for ferries heading to Holland, and Ramsgate, Dover, and Folkestone Harbor for those going to France and Belgium.

BY BUS The main terminal for all long-distance bus companies is recently renovated **Victoria Coach Station** (Buckingham Palace Rd. and Elizabeth St., tel. 0171/730–0202), just southwest of Victoria Station. You can save 30%–50% by buying a Standby Economy Return bus ticket (which lets you stay awhile in your destination) instead of a British Rail Super Saver fare. Sample Standby Economy fares include Birmingham (£10.50), Glasgow (£30), and Liverpool and Manchester (£18). Tickets on **National Express** (tel. 0171/730–0202) buses can be booked at Victoria Coach Station, or at one of their branch offices at 52 Grosvenor Gardens or 13 Regent Street. If you're 16–23 or a full-time student, £5 will buy you a Discount Coach Card, good for a year and offering 30% discounts on virtually all National Express and Caledonia Express fares anywhere in mainland Britain.

HITCHING If you're catching a ferry to the Continent from **Dover,** take BritRail to Blackheath and get a ride from someone heading down Rochester Way, on the A2. For **Cambridge,** get off at Redbridge tube station and try your luck at the M11 junction with Eastern Avenue. If you're going to the **West Country** or **South Wales,** take the tube to Hammersmith and get someone to pick you up at Great West Road on the A4 at Hammersmith Flyover. For **Oxford** and the **Midlands,** take the tube to North Acton and snag a ride at Gypsy Corner, the intersection of Western Avenue and Horn Lane. Also check out the **ride boards** at the University of London's Union (Malet St.; Tube: Euston Sq.) and at University College of London Union (Gordon St.; Tube: Euston Sq.). Riders are usually expected to help pay for gas.

GETTING AROUND

Fares for both buses and the Underground are based on zones. London Regional Transport (LRT) has divided London into six concentric rings, labeled Zones 1–6. With few exceptions, everything you want to see will be within Zones 1 and 2. The best deal for getting around London is the **Travelcard,** available at the "Tickets and Assistance" windows of most tube stations and at some newsstands. It's good for unlimited travel on both buses and the Underground for periods ranging from one day to a week, a month, or even a year. Your best bet is to get a Travelcard for Zones 1 and 2 (£2.60 for a day, £12 for a week); you'll need a passport-type photo if you're buying a Travelcard for a week or more. When you board an LRT bus, just show your pass to the driver or conductor. On the Underground, feed your pass into the horizontal slot at the front of the turnstiles leading into the tube station. For more bus and tube information call 0171/222–1234.

BY UNDERGROUND London is served by 11 different Underground lines, each color-coded, as well as by Docklands Light Railway (DLR) and Network Southeast. Fortunately, most visitors need concern themselves only with the Circle, District, Central, Piccadilly, and Victoria lines. Trains are reliable; waiting more than 10 minutes for a train is unusual. Fares are 90p–£2.40 one-way, depending on distance. Keep your ticket once you board a train; you'll need it at the exit. The Underground is fairly safe, probably because it closes at midnight. If you plan to party late, it pays to figure out the Night Owl buses (see below) in advance.

BY BUS Riding on the top deck of one of London's red double-deckers has a lot more sentimental appeal than riding the tube, and offers considerably better views of the city. As with the tube, bus fares are based on zones: One-way fares start at 50p in Zone 1. Grab a transit map (like the "Central London Bus Guide," available free at information counters in larger tube stations) to figure out the myriad bus network. Unlike the tube, buses run all night. From 11 PM to 5 AM, **Night Owl** buses add the prefix "N" to their route numbers, although they don't come as often nor operate on as many routes as day buses.

BY TAXI Black hackney cabs are the most reliable and least likely to rip you off. Fares start at £1 and go up 20p every 313.5 yards or 64 seconds but are higher on weekends and evenings. Minicabs (run by private companies) usually don't have meters—agree on a price with the driver before stepping in. Most companies charge extra if you call them for a special pickup. **Radio Taxis** (tel. 0171/272–0272) is open 24 hours, uses black cabs only, and charges a 60p–£2 supplement for pickup.

WHERE TO SLEEP

London entirely deserves its reputation as an expensive city, and lodging is no exception. In summer, your best bet is likely to be a dorm bed in a hostel for £10–£16 per night. For those who want the privacy of a single or double room, a number of undistinguished Motel 6–ish places in the Earl's Court and South Kensington areas charge £12–£15 per person a night, or £70–£110 weekly; similar hotels near Victoria Station are slightly more expensive. Hard-core penny-pinchers can camp in two places on the outskirts of London (about 45 minutes from town by bus or tube) for £4–£5 nightly. The **Tourist Information Centre Accommodations Service,** at Heathrow Airport and Victoria Station, can steer you toward cheap lodgings, but they're better suited to helping regular tourists than backpackers.

EARL'S COURT AND SOUTH KENSINGTON These neighborhoods have London's highest density of inexpensive lodgings, and a number of museums are in South Kensington.

Kingsway Hotel House. Dreary Route 66 motel decor, largely unknown to budget travelers. Rooms are a bargain for London: singles £15, doubles £25. *11 Eardley Crescent, tel. 0171/373–6847. Tube: Earl's Court.*

Curzon House Hotel. Popular with budget travelers, with front rooms facing the green courtyard of a parish church. Dorm beds £13, doubles £34–£38. *58 Courtfield Gardens, tel. 0171/581–2116. Tube: Gloucester Rd. AE, MC, V.*

BLOOMSBURY Just north of Soho is this neighborhood with a large number of private hostels and B&Bs. The British Museum, the University of London, and dozens of bookstores contribute to the quiet, academic atmosphere.

Maree Hotel. Family-run hotel near the British Museum. Simple, clean, fairly modern. Singles £22, doubles £32, triples £40, quads £42–£50. *25–27 Gower St., tel. 0171/636–4868. Tube: Goodge St.*

Central Club. Terrific location, and guests have access to pool and gym. Singles £31.25, doubles £60, triples and quads £18 per person. *16–22 Great Russell St., tel. 0171/636–7512. Tube: Tottenham Court Rd. MC, V.*

Langland Hotel. A run-of-the-mill establishment, in a bustling area near the British Museum. Rooms in the back are much quieter. Singles £28, doubles £40, triples £16.50 per person. *29–31 Gower St., tel. 0171/636–5801. Tube: Goodge St. AE, MC, V.*

St. Margaret's. Spacious rooms, towering ceilings, and prime location by Russell Square on a tree-lined Georgian street. Singles £36.50, doubles £48.50–£62. *24 Bedford Pl., tel. 0171/636–4277. Tube: Russell Sq.*

BAYSWATER AND NOTTING HILL GATE **Lords Hotel.** Really basic and a bit shabby, although some rooms have balconies. Singles £24, doubles £35. *20–22 Leinster Sq., tel. 0171/229–8877. Tube: Bayswater. AE, MC, V.*

Norfolk Court. Less than a minute from the Paddington tube stop. Some second-floor rooms have French windows and balconies overlooking the square, but bedrooms are basic. Singles £25, doubles £36. *20 Norfolk Sq., tel. 0171/723–4963. Tube: Paddington. AE, MC, V.*

The Gate Hotel. At the top of Portobello Road. Tiny B&B with reasonably sized rooms equipped with refrigerators, TVs, and phones. Singles £33, doubles £44–£55. *6 Portobello Rd., tel. 0171/221–2403. Tube: Notting Hill Gate. Small surcharge for AE, MC, V.*

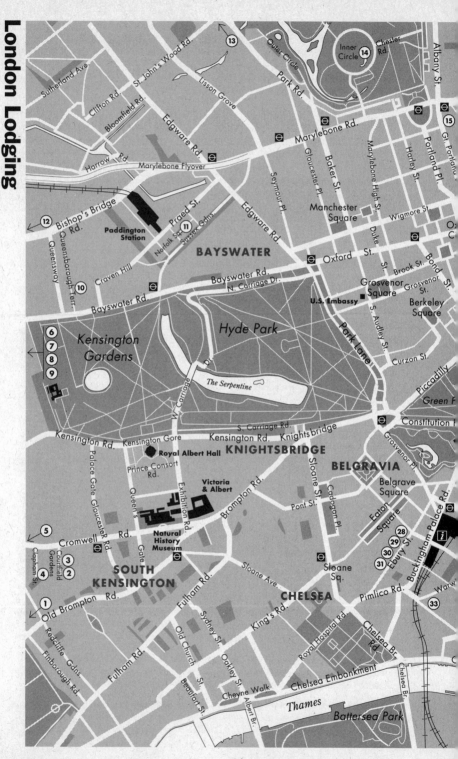

13

Inner
Circle 14   Chester
Rd.

15

Sutherland Ave

Clifton Rd.

Bloomfield Rd.

St. John's Wood Rd.

Lisson Grove

Park Rd.

Outer Circle

Albany St.

Gr. Portland

Portland Pl.

Harley St.

Marylebone Rd.

Edgware Rd.

Harrow Rd.

Marylebone Flyover

Praed St.

12   Bishop's Bridge Rd.

Queensborough Terr.

Queensway

10

Craven Hill

Bayswater Rd.

11   Norfolk Sq.   Sussex Gdns.

Seymour Pl.

Edgware Rd.

Gloucester Pl.

Baker St.

Marylebone High St.

Wigmore St.

Manchester
Square

Duke St.

Brook St.

Bond St.

Grosvenor
Square   Grosvenor
St.

Berkeley
Square

**Paddington
Station**

BAYSWATER

Bayswater Rd.

Bayswater Rd.
N. Carriage Dr.

Oxford   St.

U.S. Embassy

S. Audley St.

6
7
8
9

**Kensington
Gardens**

Hyde Park

The Serpentine

W. Carriage Dr.

Park Lane

Curzon St.

Piccadilly

Green P

Kensington Rd.   Kensington Gore

S. Carriage Rd.

Kensington Rd.   Knightsbridge

Constitution

Palace Gate

Gloucester Rd.

Royal Albert Hall

Prince Consort
Rd.

KNIGHTSBRIDGE

Sloane St.

Cadogan Pl.

Grosvenor Pl.

BELGRAVIA

Belgrave
Square

5

Cromwell

Courtfield
Gardens

Clapham St.

3
2

**Victoria
& Victoria
& Albert**

Queen's

Exhibition Rd.

**Natural
History
Museum**

Gore

Brompton Rd.

Pont St.

Eaton
Square

Buckingham Palace Rd.

28
29
30
31   Ebury St.

i

4

1   Old Brompton Rd.

**SOUTH
KENSINGTON**

Fulham Rd.

Sloane Ave.

Sloane
Sq.

CHELSEA

Pimlico Rd.

33

Redcliffe Gdns

Finborough Rd.

Fulham Rd.

Old Church St.

Sydney St.

King's Rd.

Oakley St.

Royal Hospital Rd.

Chelsea Br. Rd.

Chelsea Br.

Warw

Beaufort St.

Cheyne Walk

Chelsea Embankment

Chelsea Br.

Thames

Battersea Park

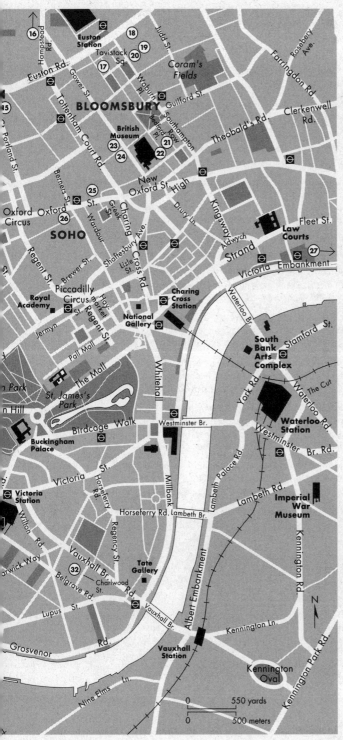

Anne Elizabeth House, **4**

Campbell House, **17**

Central Club, **25**

Chesham House Hotel, **28**

City of London Hostel (HI), **27**

Collin House, **30**

Commonwealth Hall, **18**

Connaught House, **20**

Curzon House Hotel, **2**

Earl's Court (HI), **5**

Ebury House, **29**

Fieldcourt House, **3**

The Gate Hotel, **9**

Hampstead Heath (HI), **13**

Highgate Village (HI), **16**

Holland House (HI), **7**

Holland Park Independent Hostel, **8**

Hughes Parry Hall, **19**

International Students House, **15**

Kingsway Hotel House, **1**

Langland Hotel, **23**

Lord's Hotel, **12**

Maree Hotel, **24**

Melita House Hotel, **32**

Museum Inn Hostel, **22**

Norfolk Court, **11**

Oxford Street (HI), **26**

Pyms Hotel, **31**

Quest Hostel, **10**

Regents College, **14**

St. Margaret's, **21**

Vicarage, **6**

Windermere Hotel, **33**

Vicarage. Run by the same family for nearly 30 years. Beautifully decorated, quiet, and overlooking a garden square near Kensington's main shopping streets. Singles £30, doubles £54. *10 Vicarage Gate, tel. 0171/229–4030. Tube: Kensington High St.*

VICTORIA **Chesham House Hotel.** In a row of terrace houses near Victoria. Simple, clean rooms with TVs. Doubles £43, including full breakfast. *64–66 Ebury St., tel. 0171/730–8513. Tube: Victoria Station. AE, MC, V.*

Collin House. Spotless rooms with sinks and cushy divan beds. Great location between Victoria and Sloane Square. Singles £34, doubles £48. *104 Ebury St., tel. 0171/730–8031. Tube: Victoria Station.*

Ebury House. Homey, expertly managed B&B. All rooms have TVs. Singles £40, doubles £50—including a great breakfast. *102 Ebury St., tel. 0171/730–1350. Tube: Victoria Station.*

Melita House Hotel. On a quiet street near Victoria. Strictly garage-sale furniture, but the small rooms are clean and have TVs. Singles £24–£32, doubles £36–£45. *33 Charlwood St., off Belgrave Rd., tel. 0171/828–0471. Tube: Pimlico. AE, MC, V.*

Pyms Hotel. Between Sloane Square and Victoria, and noted for its cleanliness. Singles £40, doubles £50–£65. *118 Ebury St., tel. 0171/730–4986. Tube: Victoria Station. AE, MC, V.*

Windermere Hotel. A two-minute walk from Victoria. White-stucco house with lots of amenities, including TVs in rooms. Evening meals available. Singles £44–£49, doubles £52–£67. *142–144 Warwick Way, tel. 0171/834–5163. Tube: Victoria Station. AE, MC, V.*

HOSTELS Besides the private hostels, there are seven HI hostels in central London (some are more central than others) and a number out in the boonies. These tend to be clean to the point of sterility, much like the bland breakfasts and dinners.

Anne Elizabeth House. Situated in "Little Australia." No-frills, dorm-style accommodations in singles (£18), doubles (£31), and triples (£40). A kitchen, TV room, and laundry on-site. *30 Collingham Pl., tel. 0171/370–4821. Tube: Gloucester Rd. or Earl's Court.*

City of London Hostel (HI). Great location in the middle of town. It's got zip for character, though, and attracts few backpackers. Singles, doubles, and dorms £16–£19.30 per person. *136 Carter La., tel. 0171/236–4965. Tube: Blackfriars. Walk north on Blackfriars Bridgeway for 2 blocks, turn right on Carter La. MC, V.*

Earl's Court (HI). They really pack 'em in at this joint—rooms are often stuffed with more than a dozen folks. On-site money exchange and laundry. Beds £16.10. *38 Bolton Gardens, tel. 0171/373–7083. Tube: Earl's Court. Walk south on Earl's Court, left on Bolton Gardens.*

Fieldcourt House. Friendly private hostel that's sometimes besieged by Euro teens. Dorm beds £10, singles £16, doubles £26. *32 Courtfield Gardens, tel. 0171/373–0153. Tube: Earl's Court. Walk 2 blocks south on Earl's Court Rd., turn left onto Barkston Gardens.*

Hampstead Heath (HI). The best big hostel in London. Set on beautiful grounds right on Hampstead Heath. Single, double, triple, and quad rooms all £13.90 per person. *4 Wellgarth Rd., tel. 0181/458–9054. Tube: Golders Green. Walk southeast on North End Rd., turn left on Wellgarth Rd. Laundry, currency exchange. MC, V.*

Highgate Village (HI). A serious uphill trek from Archway tube station is rewarded with a bed in an attractive Georgian house. Near Highgate Cemetery. Reserve in advance. Beds £11.40. *84 Highgate West Hill, tel. 0181/340–1831. Tube: Archway. Walk north up Highgate Hill, left on South Grove. MC, V.*

Holland House (HI). A haven of the young and weird. A fair walk from the tube but right in the middle of a huge park. Singles, doubles, and dorms £18.10 per person. *Holland Walk, tel. 0171/937–0748. Tube: Kensington High Street. Turn left as you exit station, walk down Holland Park Ave., cross street, and turn right on Holland Walk. Laundry, kitchen. AE, MC, V.*

Holland Park Independent Hostel. Friendly, relaxed, Edwardian-style house in a leafy, upscale neighborhood. Most dorms have four beds (£8 per person). *31 Holland Park Gardens, tel. 0171/602–3369. Tube: Holland Park. Kitchen.*

Museum Inn Hostel. A great base for exploring Bloomsbury, the West End, and the British Museum (across the street). Doubles £36, dorm beds £14. *27 Montague St., tel. 0171/580–5360. Tube: Tottenham Court Rd. Walk north 1 block on Tottenham Court Rd., turn right, and walk 3 blocks on Great Russell St., turn left on Montague Rd. Kitchen. MC, V.*

Oxford Street Hostel (HI). In deepest, darkest Soho. Convenient for exploring the West End and Whitehall—stagger home from the pubs without having to deal with the tube. Beds £16.70. *14 Noel St., tel. 0171/734–1618. Tube: Oxford Circus. Walk east on Oxford St., right on Poland St. MC, V.*

Quest Hostel. Near the happening Queensway tourist strip. The bummer: Many of the rooms don't have windows. Dorm beds £10.50, doubles £30. *45 Queensborough Terr., tel. 0171/229–7782. Tube: Bayswater. Turn right as you exit station onto Queensway, left onto Bayswater Rd., and left on Queensborough Terr. Kitchen. MC, V.*

STUDENT HOUSING Many college residency halls try to squeeze a few extra pounds out of their rooms by throwing open their doors during vacations—usually late June through early September and also around Easter. Most student housing is in northwest Bloomsbury, an easy 10-minute walk from the West End. Reservations are a must.

Campbell House. Quiet, clean, and in central Bloomsbury. Singles £14.50, doubles £25.50. *5–10 Taviton St., tel. 0171/388–0060 or 0171/380–7079. Tube: Euston Sq. Walk east on Euston Rd., turn right on Gordon St., left on Endsleigh Gardens, then right on Taviton St. Kitchen, laundry.*

Commonwealth Hall. Very central, with 400 comfortable single rooms and excellent amenities (like tennis courts). Singles £18.50. *1–12 Cartwright Gardens (address not marked on building), tel. 0171/387–0311. Tube: King's Cross. Walk west on Euston Rd., turn left on Mabledon Pl. Laundry, kitchen.*

Connaught House. Newly refurbished dorm overlooking a pleasant square. Singles £22.50, doubles £32. *36–45 Tavistock Sq., tel. 0171/387–6181. Tube: Euston Sq. Walk south on Evershelt St. Laundry, kitchen, TV.*

Hughes Parry Hall. High-rise dorm with basic, clean singles for £18.50 (with breakfast) and one of the better university pubs in the area. *19–26 Cartwright Gardens, tel. 0171/387–1477. Tube: King's Cross. Walk west on Euston Rd., turn left on Mabledon Pl. Laundry.*

International Students House. Huge dorm/condo offering basic, inexpensive rooms. Dorm beds £12, singles £22.70, doubles £56. *229 Great Portland St., tel. 0171/631–3223. Tube: Great Portland St. Laundry.*

Regents College. Opens in early May, before most other dorms. In the middle of Regent's Park. Singles £25, doubles £36, triples £39. The college has its own café, bar, cafeteria, tennis courts, and gym. *Inner Circle, Regent's Park, tel. 0171/487–7483. Tube: Baker St.*

CAMPGROUNDS Camping in London is a weird enough idea to be interesting, and if you don't mind a longish (½-hour or more) commute, it's practical. God knows, it's cheap enough. Both sites are inside bus/tube Zones 1 and 2—great for Travelcard holders.

Hackney Camping. Huge, empty park on the outskirts of London—ideal for cheap sleep in a little enclosed grove. Staffed largely by young French punkers. Bring your own tent. £4 per person. *Millfields Rd., tel. 0181/985–7656. Bus 22A from Liverpool St. tube station. Get* off at Millfields and Mandeville Sts., cross the bridge. Showers, toilets, luggage storage, snack bar. Open June 18–Aug. 24.

Tent City. Sleep in one of 450 cots in 14 large tents spread on Wormwood Scrubs in west London. Choose between men's, women's, and mixed tents, or pitch your own for the same daily price of £5. *Old Oak Common La., tel. 0181/743–5708. Tube: East Acton. Walk northeast on Erconwald St., turn left on Wolfstan St.* Showers, toilets, luggage storage, snack bar. Open June–Sept. 6.

FOOD

The dining scene in London is incredibly varied and, yes, expensive. Most cheapo grub is £4.50–£7, and a decent, tasty meal usually costs £9–£14, not including VAT and the service charge (50p–£1) that some restaurants add to the bill. The good news is London's endless variety of ethnic restaurants—a reminder of the days when England's empire stretched across the globe. Chinese and Vietnamese restaurants proliferate on Gerrard and Lisle streets (Tube: Piccadilly Circus or Leicester Sq.), Bengali on Brick Lane (Tube: Aldgate East), and Indian on Drummond Street (Tube: Euston Sq.). The largest concentrations of restaurants are in Soho and Covent Garden. If you want to head off the beaten tourist track, **Smokey Joe's Diner** (131 Wandsworth High St., tel. 0181/871–1785; Tube: East Putney) is an orgasmic Afro-Caribbean barbecue joint worth the schlepp out to Wandsworth. Ribs and chicken are £4.25, Smokey's legendary jerk chicken £4.75.

SOHO, PICCADILLY, COVENT GARDEN

➤ **UNDER £5 • Centrale.** Italian home cooking in a hole-in-the-wall with dark wooden booths, red tablecloths—the whole bit. Heaping plates of pasta £2–£3.50. *16 Moor St., tel. 0171/437–5513. Tube: Leicester Sq.*

Cranks. Part of a chain of pleasant, homey veggie restaurants. Vegetarian quiche £2, nut roast £2. *17–19 Great Newport St., tel. 0171/836–5226. Tube: Leicester Sq.*

Food for Thought. Vegetarian place frequented by Covent Garden hipsters. Spinach cauliflower quiche £2. *31 Neal St., tel. 0171/836–9072. Tube: Covent Garden. Closed Sun. night.*

Govinda's. Friendly Hare Krishna restaurant serving tasty vegetarian grub at rock-bottom prices. Lasagna £3.50, bean hotpot £1.80. Free (yes, free) "Sunday feast" at around 5 PM. *10 Soho St., tel. 0171/437–3662. Tube: Tottenham Court Rd. Open Mon.–Sat. 11–8:30, Sun. 5 PM–6 PM.*

Nusadua. Surprisingly inexpensive but elegant Indonesian restaurant. Try creative dishes like *gulai ayam* (coconut chicken; £4) or *sambal sontag* (squid with chili peppers; £4.50). *11–12 Dean St., tel. 0171/437–3559. Tube: Tottenham Court Rd. Open weekdays noon–2:30 and 6–11:30, Sat. 6–11:30.*

Rabin's Nosh Bar. Good kosher food, including soups (kneidal for £2.45), sandwiches, and bagels (with salt beef, £2.10). *39 Great Windmill St., tel. 0171/434–9913. Tube: Piccadilly Circus. Closed Sun.*

The Stockpot. The affordable menu changes twice daily. Items like stuffed squash (£2.65) and lamb cutlets with potatoes (£3.95) served in biggish portions. *40 Panton St., tel. 0171/287–1066. Tube: Piccadilly Circus. Other locations: 273 King's Rd. (Sloane Sq.); 6 Basil St. (Knightsbridge); 17 Old Compton St., near Cambridge Circus.*

➤ **UNDER £10 • Arts Theatre Café.** Untrendy, mellow Italian joint in the basement of the Arts Theatre. Dishes £5–£8.50. *6–7 Great Newport St., tel. 0171/497–8014. Tube: Leicester Sq. Open weekdays noon–11 PM, Sat. 6–11 PM.*

Calabash. Lively, cheerful African restaurant with terrific food. Try some ground-nut stew (£6.25) with your Nigerian beer (£2). *38 King St., Africa Centre, tel. 0171/836–1976. Tube: Covent Garden. Open weekdays 12:30–3 and 6–11:30, Sat. 6–11:30.*

Harry's Bar. Serves one of the only late-night breakfasts (£5) in Soho from 7:30 AM to 6 AM. Part of the annoying Eurochain targeting Americans abroad; a real scene in the wee hours. *19 Kingly St., tel. 0171/434–0309. Tube: Piccadilly Circus.*

Neal's Yard Dining Room. No-smoking "world food" café that opens onto a courtyard of health-food stores and juice bars. Indonesian salad £5, Egyptian falafel £3.25. *14 Neal's Yard, tel. 0171/379–0298. Tube: Covent Garden. Open Mon.–Sat. noon–8.*

New World. Schlocky atmosphere, but great fun: choose dim sum dishes from neat little carts that continually roll past your table. For £10 you'll leave stuffed to the gills. *1 Gerrard Pl., tel. 0171/734–0677. Tube: Leicester Sq.*

CHELSEA Chelsea is loaded with semicheap grazing holes—many faceless, some terrific. You won't do too much damage to your budget if you stick to the restaurants at the top of King's Road.

Ambrosiana Creperie/Creperie l'Entrecote. Hep place serving sweet and savory crepes. Pears and cinnamon (£3.50) do nicely for a late breakfast; salami, ratatouille, and cheese (£5.30) for a fine lunch or dinner. *194 Fulham Rd., tel. 0171/351–0070. Tube: South Kensington.*

Chelsea Kitchen. The original owners of the Stockpot (*see above*) bring their unique brand of low-cost meals to Chelsea. Get stuffed on some curried chicken (£2.50) or goulash (£2.90). *98 King's Rd., tel. 0171/589–1330. Tube: Sloane Sq.*

KNIGHTSBRIDGE, BAYSWATER, NOTTING HILL GATE Knightsbridge is a ritzy area, featuring restaurants priced way beyond budget range. Bayswater, on the other hand, is Knightsbridge's complete opposite: a neighborhood full of kebab joints, chippies, and delis. Notting Hill Gate has a high concentration of ethnic restaurants: Marble Arch is the place to go for Middle Eastern eateries, particularly on Edgware Road.

➤ **UNDER £5 • Café Creperie.** A daily crunch of office workers comes to sample all types of crêpes. Chicken and ratatouille crepe £4.65, pears Helene £4.35. *26 James St., tel. 0171/935–8480. Tube: Bond St.*

La Barraca. Friendly tapas bar with outdoor café atmosphere—though "outside" is noisy Kensington Church Street. Calamari £3.90, chicken garlic £3.65. *215 Kensington Church St., tel. 0171/229–9359. Tube: Notting Hill Gate. Closed Sun.*

Great London Takeaways

- *Gossip Corner Café/Puccini Café. Cheap sandwiches to accompany people-watching on Leicester Square. 35 Newport Ct., tel. 0171/734–2835. Tube: Leicester Sq.*

- *Taffgoods. Jewish deli that's just a little cheaper than Rabin's Nosh Bar. Bagel with cream cheese and lox (90p). 128 Wardour St., tel. 0171/437–3286. Tube: Piccadilly Circus.*

- *Abohammad Restaurant. The only kebab takeout on Queensway that doesn't use a disgusting meatloaf for its "shawarma" (gyro, £3). 102 Queensway, tel. 0171/727–0830. Tube: Queensway or Bayswater.*

- *Maxwell's. A serious blast of grease at one of London's premier fish-and-chip stands. 264 Old Brompton Rd., tel. 0171/373–5130. Tube: Earl's Court.*

Churchill Arms. An excellent Thai restaurant in a small enclosed garden patio behind a pub. Definitely try the *pad khing* (chicken with mushrooms; £4). *119 Kensington Church St., tel. 0171/727–4242. Tube: Notting Hill Gate. Open Mon.–Sat. noon–2:30 and 6–9:30, Sun. 6–9:30.*

Khan's. Great Indian food meets chintzy, cane-chair decor. For lunch try the chicken *shahi* (mild curry; £2.85). *13–15 Westbourne Grove, tel. 0171/727–5420. Tube: Queensway or Bayswater.*

Maison Sagne. Parisian fin de siècle decor, with white tile floor and antique light fixtures. Asparagus omelet £3.75, chicken and mushroom *vol au vent* (in puff pastry) £4. *105 Marylebone High St., tel. 0171/935–6240. Tube: Bond St. Open weekdays 9–5, Sat. 9–1.*

Malaysia Dining Hall. *The* place for cheap eats. Intended for (and mostly patronized by) Malaysian students, but everyone is welcome. Set meal of excellent, spicy Malaysian food only £1.70. *46 Bryanston Sq., tel. 0171/723–9484. Tube: Marble Arch. Open daily 8:30 AM–9 PM.*

➤ **UNDER £10** • **Geales.** Some of the best fancy fish-and-chips in London—it's not hypergreasy either. Haddock £4.50. *2 Farmer's Rd., tel. 0171/727–7969. Tube: Notting Hill Gate. Closed Sun. and Mon.*

Luba's Bistro. This Russian restaurant suffers from an overabundance of peasant art, but the food is good and the helpings large. Ten percent discount before 8 PM. *6 Yeoman's Row, tel. 0171/589–2950. Tube: Knightsbridge. Closed Sun.*

Scandies. Sidewalk eatery miraculously *not* on a noisy thoroughfare. The menu changes every two weeks; expect specialties like flaked pink trout salad (£4.50) and spicy lamb casserole (£7). *4 Kynance Pl., tel. 0171/589–3659. Tube: Gloucester Rd. Open weekdays noon–3 and 5:30–10:30, weekends noon–3 and 6:30–10:30.*

BLOOMSBURY The area around Drummond Street is the best place in London to sample authentic Indian food.

Chutney's. On everybody's short list for best Indian restaurant in town. The £4 buffet (Mon.–Sat. noon–2:30, Sun. noon–10:30) is perhaps *the* culinary steal in London. *124 Drummond St., tel. 0171/388–0604. Tube: Euston Sq.*

Indian YMCA. YMCA dining hall catering to its Indian student lodgers, but nonresidents are welcome. Breakfast £2.60, lunch and dinner £4. *41 Fitzroy Sq., tel. 0171/387–0411. Tube: Warren St. Open weekdays 8–9:15, 12:30–1:45, and 7–8; weekends 8:30–9:30, 12:30–1:30, and 7–8.*

Wagamama. Popular Japanese-style ramen bar. Healthy, abundant, and cheap. Try beet chili ramen and a jug of saki for under £10. *4 Streatham St., off Bloomsbury St., tel. 0171/323–9223. Tube: Tottenham Court Rd. Closed Sun.*

CAFES **Costa Coffee Shop.** One of the best and cheapest cappuccinos in town, right next to Victoria Station. *324 Vauxhall Bridge Rd., tel. 0171/828–5215. Tube: Victoria Station.*

First Out. Gay and lesbian café serving vegetarian food and a wide range of cakes and desserts. *52 St. Giles High St., tel. 0171/240–8042. Tube: Tottenham Court Rd.*

Monmouth Coffee Shop. Sit in teeny wooden cubicles in the womblike cove at the back of this small coffee bean store. Coffee 80p, cakes around £1.25. *27 Monmouth St., tel. 0171/836–5272. Tube: Leicester Sq. Open weekdays 9:30–6:30.*

Patisserie Valerie. Rocket-fuel espresso (85p) and insanely delicious pastries and sweets (six for £1.25) provide the morning ritual for young Londoners. *44 Old Compton St., tel. 0171/437–3466. Tube: Piccadilly Circus or Tottenham Court Rd.*

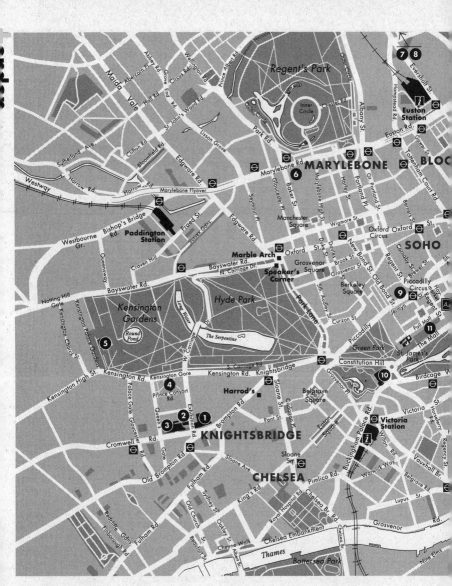

WORTH SEEING

Like any great city, London can't be done entirely in a couple of days, or even in a cou
weeks. As the fountainhead of English-speaking culture for a sizable chunk of this millen
London offers layers upon layers of sights, from royal bastions to literary landmarks to
ishing ethnic neighborhoods. Happily, the city's most famous sights, including Parlia
Westminster Abbey, and many of the palaces, are all within walking distance of one an
Still, a street map like *London A to Z* (sold at every newsstand) is an invaluable investm
you're staying more than a few days.

If you *must* see the city in half a day, a huge mass of tour companies are begging fo
money. **London Transport** (tel. 0171/222–1234) offers sightseeing tours on its double-d
buses. Ninety-minute tours run every half-hour from 10 to 5 from Marble Arch, Victori
tion, and Piccadilly Circus. Buy your ticket from the driver (£8) or from the London T
Information Centre at Victoria Station. If it's a sunny day, a boat along the Thames off
interesting perspective on the city. Tour boats leave April–October from **Westminster Pie**
0171/930–4097), **Charing Cross Pier** (Victoria Embankment, tel. 0171/839–3312)
Tower Pier (tel. 0171/488–0344). The best of the walking tours is **London Walk**
0171/624–3978), with funny, interesting guides and reasonably good rates (£4, £3 stud

BIG BEN AND VICTORIA TOWER Probably the most enduring symbol of Londo
Britain, Big Ben is actually the name of the 13-ton bell, not the clock tower (officially n
St. Stephen's Tower). At the other end of the complex is the 336-foot-high **Victoria T**
reputedly the largest square tower in the world. It's also probably the most expens
maintain—it's just undergone a £7.5 million restoration. A Union Jack flies from the
Victoria Tower and a light shines atop Big Ben whenever Parliament is in session.

BRITISH MUSEUM Anybody trying to write about the British Museum better have a
pail of superlatives close at hand—let's start with most, biggest, earliest, and finest.
the golden hoard of 2½ centuries of empire, and the sheer magnitude overwhelms.
astonishing collection, full of goodies of world historical importance: The Rosetta Ston
Elgin Marbles, the Dead Sea Scrolls, the Magna Carta, the Lindow Bog Man—hell, tha
begins the list. One visit won't be enough to see it all. The Library Reading Room is h
cally important in its own right; Marx wrote *Das Kapital* in it. *Great Russell St*
0171/6361555. Tube: Tottenham Court Rd. Admission free. Open Mon.–Sat. 10–5
2:30–6.

BUCKINGHAM PALACE A flag bearing the Royal Standard flies above Buckingham
whenever the queen is at home (usually on weekdays) in her London residence. Geo
(the tea-taxing king that the United States revolted against) bought Buckingham House
was then known, from the duke of Buckingham for a mere £28,000 in 1762. George I
ascended the throne in 1820, decided that Buckingham Palace looked far too middl
and set about remodeling with a vengeance. Following the 1992 fire at Windsor Cast
queen has opened Buckingham Palace to visitors for the first time to pay for repairs
castle without dipping into public funds. The plan is to keep the palace open every su
for the next five years—with a staggering £8 per person entrance fee.

Changing of the Guard

The biggest tourist show in town, the Changing of the Guard—the ritual in whic
diers guarding the queen hand over their duties to the next watch—starts da
11:30 AM in summer (even-numbered days only Nov.–Mar.), but if you're not the
10:30, forget about a decent frontal view of the pomp and circumstance. Latec
can still get good views from the side along Constitution Hill, the thoroughfare le
to Hyde Park corner.

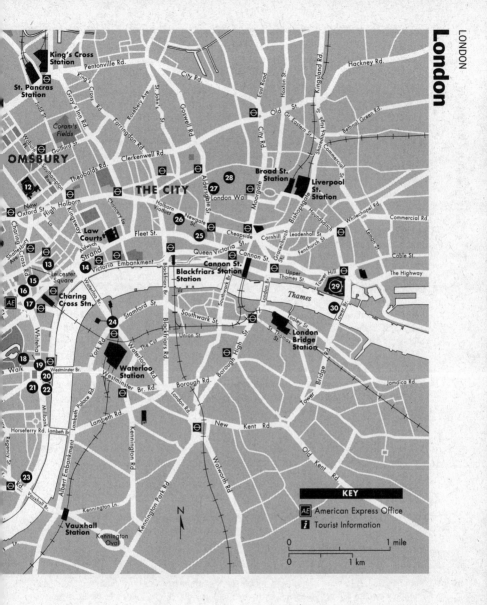

King's Cross Station

St. Pancras Station

Pentonville Rd.

City Rd.

Hackney Rd.

Coram's Fields

OMSBURY

Clerkenwell Rd.

THE CITY

London Wall

Broad St. Station

Liverpool St. Station

12

New Oxford St.

High Holborn

28

27

Commercial Rd.

26

Newgate St.

Cheapside

Cornhill

Leadenhall St.

Fenchurch St.

Law Courts

25

Fleet St.

Queen Victoria St.

Cannon St.

Cable St.

The Highway

14

Strand

Victoria Embankment

Cannon St. Station

13

15

Leicester Square

Blackfriars Station

Thames

Upper Thames St.

Tower Hill

29

16

17

Charing Cross Stn.

24

Stamford St.

Southwark St.

London Bridge

30

18

19

Stamford St.

Union St.

St. Thomas St.

London Bridge Station

Tooley St.

Jamaica Rd.

20

21

22

Waterloo Station

Borough Rd.

Borough High St.

Lambeth Rd.

Landon Rd.

New   Kent   Rd.

Old Kent Rd.

23

Horseferry Rd.

Lambeth Br.

Kennington Rd.

Walworth Rd.

Vauxhall Station

Kennington Ln.

Kennington Oval

Kennington Park Rd.

N

KEY

AE American Express Office

i Tourist Information

0   1 mile

0   1 km

The **Royal Mews** is the palace's royal stable, complete with horsies, liveried servants, and gilded carriages. If you visit when both the nearby Queen's Gallery (filled with dull Royal portraits) and the Royal Mews are open, you can cop a slightly cheaper combined ticket for £5. *Buckingham Palace Rd., tel. 0171/930–4832. Admission: £3. Open Apr.–Sept., Tues.–Thurs. noon–4; Oct.–Mar., Wed. noon–4.*

HOUSES OF PARLIAMENT The empire may be dead, but it's still fascinating to explore the seat of all that power (understanding, of course, that imperialism is bad, bad, bad). From this site, Britain stumbled its way to an empire that stretched around the globe, simultaneously establishing one of the most copied forms of democratic government in the world. Until the English Civil War (1642–1648), when the Parliamentarians rebelled against Charles I, Parliament was very much at the beck and call of the monarch; today Parliament is the main ruling body. The more important chamber is the **House of Commons,** consisting of nearly 650 elected members who argue and pass laws. The **House of Lords,** the "upper" body of Parliament, is composed of British lords (who either inherit the title or are elevated to that rank by the queen) and has little remaining power. Periodically, left-wingers call for an overhaul of the Lords, asserting that its members should not serve purely on the basis of birth or title. They have a good point.

Sitting in on a session of Parliament is one of the best cheap thrills in London. Getting in to the Strangers' Galleries is tough unless you get one of the few tickets available at your country's embassy; if you don't have a ticket, you will probably get in after 4:15 for an evening session—look for the light shining at the top of Big Ben to see if Parliament is sitting. The most exciting sessions are the prime minister's **Question Time** on Tuesdays and Thursdays from 3:15–3:30, when the opposition leader has free rein to savage the PM. Line up at St. Stephen's Entrance (on the left for the Commons, on the right for Lords). Admission is free. *Tel. 0171/219–4272. Tube: Westminster. Strangers' Galleries: Commons, open Mon.–Thurs. 2:30–late, Fri. 9:30–3; Lords, open Mon.–Wed. 2:30–late, Thurs. 3:30–late, Fri. 11 AM–late.*

HYDE PARK AND KENSINGTON GARDENS Contiguous Hyde Park and Kensington Gardens together form a 634-acre park—the biggest in London. It's not that different from other large urban parks throughout the world; it's crowded (especially on weekends), but a great no-hassle way to find a little greenery. Small boats cruise on the **Serpentine,** a long, thin lake that arcs through the middle of the two parks. You can rent a rowboat at the boat house for a few quid. Don't miss **Speaker's Corner** in the northeast corner of Hyde Park, where spielers spiel, hecklers heckle, and free speech dovetails into street theater. It really hits full swing by about 2 or 3 PM on weekends, with Bible-thumpers hogging the spotlight. *Kensington Gardens, tel. 0171/402–6075. Tube: Lancaster Gate or South Kensington. Admission free. Open daily 10–6.*

NATIONAL GALLERY AND NATIONAL PORTRAIT GALLERY After Great Britain got rich in the 19th century, it felt compelled to prove it wasn't boorish, amassing a huge haul of Renaissance Italian paintings, as well as works by Dutch, Flemish, German, English, and French masters. The collection reads like a *Who's Who* of Western art: Tintoretto, da Vinci, Monet, Caravaggio, Michelangelo, Titian, Rembrandt, and others. The last few rooms of the National Gallery offer a tantalizing nibble of the impressionists and post-impressionists, including a room full of Picassos. Terrific free lectures, films, and guided tours are available. *Trafalgar Sq., tel. 0171/839–3526. Tube: Charing Cross. Admission free. Open Mon.–Sat. 10–6, Sun. 2–6.*

Next door is the **National Portrait Gallery** with faces, faces, faces. Painted faces, sculpted faces, drawn faces, photographed faces—five floors of the visages of those who made British history and influenced British culture, including the only authentic portrait of Shakespeare made in his lifetime. *St. Martin's Pl., tel. 0171/306–0055. Tube: Charing Cross. Admission free. Open weekdays 10–5, Sat. 10–6, Sun. 2–6.*

ST. PAUL'S CATHEDRAL The structure you see now, the third in a series of cathedrals erected on this site, was built by Christopher Wren between 1675 and 1710, shortly after London's Great Fire. The dome towers 218 feet above the ground, and miraculously escaped major damage during World War II, when the rest of the city was reduced to blazing rubble. Chuck and Di married in St. Paul's in 1981. The interior of the dome's base is encircled by the **Whispering Gallery**—whisper into the wall and you'll be heard clearly 100 feet away on the other side of the gallery. Climb up the staircase to the **Stone Gallery,** outside the dome, or to the **Golden Gallery,** at the top of the dome, for some killer views of London. Inside, the **crypt** is full of famous dead people, including military demigods Nelson and Wellington. *Tel. 0171/2482705. Tube: St. Paul's. Admission: £2.50, £2 students; to galleries: £2.50, £2 students; to crypt, ambulatory, and American chapel, free. Open daily 9:30–6, galleries open Mon.–Sat. 9:30–4:30.*

TATE GALLERY Known for the impressive variety of great works, the Tate Gallery houses Monets, Dalís, and Kandinskys alongside an entire wing of oils and watercolors by British artist J.M.W. Turner. Twentieth-century masterpieces by Picasso, Ernst, Johns, and Hockney round out the collection. One warning: The Tate is extremely crowded on Sundays. *Millbank, tel. 0171/821–1313. Tube: Pimlico. Admission free, except for some special exhibits. Open Mon.–Sat. 10–5:50, Sun. 2–5:50.*

TOWER BRIDGE The instantly recognizable twin pillars of the Tower Bridge, a short walk from the Tower of London, house exhibitions on the bridge's history and engineering, as well as the history of London's bridges from Roman times onward. The two gangways across the top of the towers afford views second only to those from St. Paul's. *Tel. 0171/407–0922. Tube: Tower Hill. Admission: £4. Open Apr.–Oct., daily 10–6:30 (last admission at 5:45); shorter hrs off-season.*

TOWER OF LONDON Besides serving as the residence of every British sovereign from William the Conqueror in the 11th century to Henry VIII in the 16th century, the Tower of London has performed a variety of other roles as fortress, jewel safe, armory, zoo, and garrison. It's probably most famous, though, as a prison and place of execution for some of England's most influential people, including Sir Walter Raleigh and Sir Thomas More. With its winding staircases, tunnels, bridges, and narrow passages, the Tower is much more than its name implies—20 towers make up the fortress (the largest in medieval Europe), which covers 18 prime acres on the banks of the Thames. The **Crown Jewels,** housed in the **Jewel House** north of the White Tower, are the star attraction. The Royal Sceptre boasts the biggest cut diamond in the world, the 530-carat Star of Africa cut from the Cullinan diamond. Because shiny objects tend to attract huge crowds, it's best to visit immediately after the Tower opens or just before it closes—and head straight to the jewels.

Southwest of the White Tower is the **Bloody Tower,** where in the 15th century the Little Princes—Edward V and his little brother—were murdered, probably by the henchmen of Richard III or Henry VII. Sir Walter Raleigh's prison cell (where he wrote the modestly titled *History of the World*) is reconstructed as well. Free tours of the Tower of London, led by the Yeoman Warders ("Beefeaters"), leave from the **Byword Tower** in the southwest of the complex every 45 minutes, but you must pay the admission fee first. *Tel. 0171/709–0756. Tube: Tower Hill. Admission: £6.70, £5.10 students. Open Mar.–Oct., Mon.–Sat. 9:30–6, Sun. 10–6; Nov.–Feb., Mon.–Sat. 9:30–4.*

WESTMINSTER ABBEY Britain's monarchs have been crowned (and buried) here since William the Conqueror assumed the English throne on Christmas Day, 1066. Among the deceased sovereigns buried here are Edward the Confessor; Elizabeth I; Mary, queen of Scots; Richard II; and Henry VII. Just inside the western entrance to the abbey is a memorial to Winston Churchill. Nearby is the **Tomb of the Unknown Warrior,** commemorating an anonymous British soldier killed in World War I. **Poet's Corner,** in the south transept, houses the remains (or, more likely, memorial plaques) of nearly all the greats of English literature, including Chaucer, Shakespeare, Ben Jonson, Browning, and Tennyson. *Tel. 0171/222–5152. Tube: Westminster. Admission: £3, £1.50 students; free Wed. 6–7:45 PM. Nave and the Cloisters always free. Open weekdays 9–4, Sat. 9–2 and 3:45–5.*

NEIGHBORHOODS

➤ **THE CITY** • Taking up more than a square mile in east London, the City is London's equivalent of Wall Street: It's home to the stock exchange, the Bank of England, Lloyd's, and a host of large companies. The City rests on the original Celtic settlement, which the Romans built as Londinium; vestiges of this ancient heritage pop up occasionally in the City, but most of the buildings are ugly modern blobs. Until a decade ago, **Fleet Street,** which runs eastward from The Strand, was synonymous with newspapers and journalists. Most of Britain's major papers had their offices here, and the Fleet Street pubs were the lairs of hoary old journalists and whispered scoops. The newspapers are all gone now, scattered to cheaper neighborhoods with lower overheads, more computers, and fewer unions. Even so, "Fleet Street" remains the general term for the British press.

You can't beat the drama (it's all for real) or the price (it's free) of watching a trial at the **Old Bailey** (Old Bailey at Ludgate Hill; Tube: St. Paul's; closed weekends), officially known as Central Criminal Court. Just line up outside and scan the offering of trials—they're posted on a sort of legal menu du jour at the Newgate Street entrance. The juiciest trials happen in Courts 1–3, the old courts; Oscar Wilde was tried for homosexuality here in 1895. He lost and was sent to Reading Gaol.

A large complex of residential towers and cultural venues built between 1959 and 1981 in an ill-fated attempt to resurrect central London as a living city instead of merely a place of work, the **Barbican Centre** (tel. 0171/638–4141; Tube: Barbican) is an ugly amalgam of concrete blocks. Nevertheless, the Barbican has evolved into one of the city's principal cultural institutions and houses the **Museum of London** (tel. 0171/600–3699; Tube: St. Paul's; admission £3, £1.50 students; closed Mon.), an extremely thorough and eminently inviting look at the history of the city, from the early Stone Age to the present day. The **Barbican Hall** (*see* After Dark, *below*) hosts a variety of musical performances.

➤ **COVENT GARDEN** • Just east of Soho lies Covent Garden, a nest of narrow streets, arcades, and pedestrian malls. The area's pubs and restaurants are expensive, but this is one of the best places in London to come for free entertainment—musicians, buskers, jugglers, and comics regularly perform in the streets and squares. The original Covent Garden was a plot of land used to grow fruit and veggies for the 13th-century Abbey of St. Peter at Westminster. In the 18th century, it evolved into London's principal produce market, a bustling maze of stalls and shops selling everything from tulips to taters. The original **Central Market building** has been completely renovated and filled with boutiques and trendy restaurants.

East of the market is Bow Street, famous for the **Royal Opera House,** home to the Royal Ballet and the Royal Opera Company (*see* After Dark, *below*). Opposite the Opera House stands the **Bow Street Magistrates' Court,** established in 1749 by Henry Fielding, who was a magistrate as well as a brilliant novelist (of *Tom Jones* and others). Fielding employed a group of detectives known as the "Bow Street Runners," and paid them with fines levied by the court.

Cheap Deals in Camden Town

Probably the most bohemian and diverse neighborhood in London, Camden becomes a serious mob scene on the weekend when tens of thousands of people flock to dig the Camden markets, particularly Camden Lock (Tube: Camden Town), the funky granddaddy of London flea markets. Get your bootlegs, incense, Doc Martens, leather jackets, silver jewelry, and used clothes right here. Camden High Street is the heart of the district, with the prerequisite cafés and record stores. From the Camden tube station walk north up Camden Hight Street.

It would be another 80 years before Home Secretary Sir Robert "Bobby" Peel would officially employ policemen, called "bobbies" after his name.

➤ **KENSINGTON AND KNIGHTSBRIDGE** • An official royal residence bitter over the breakup of its most famous residents (Chuck and Di), **Kensington Palace** (Kensington Gardens, tel. 0171/937–9561; admission £3.90, £2.85 students) is open to the public—at least, little bits of it are. Check out the Court Dress Collection, with clothes worn to regal soirées from 1750 until today, including the wedding dress of Princess Diana. Also open for visitors are the state apartments of Queen Mary II and William III, which were later redecorated by Georges I and II.

A major-league concert venue, the **Royal Albert Hall** (tel. 0171/589–8212) comes into its own during the summer, when it hosts the Promenade Concerts (*see* After Dark, *below*). The interior, a huge amphitheater done up in wine-red and gold, marks the height of Victorian imperial architecture. Known as the V&A, the **Victoria and Albert Museum** (Cromwell Rd. at the corner of Exhibition Rd., tel. 0171/938–8500; admission free) features 12 acres of strange and eclectic "ornamental art." The Art and Design galleries exhibit everything from Renaissance Italian sculpture to Muslim carpets.

The six-floor **Science Museum** (Exhibition Rd., tel. 0171/938–8000; admission £4, £2.10 students, free after 4:30) alternates dry displays with a few engaging techno-displays, like the holograms in the optics section. The **Natural History Museum** (Cromwell Rd., tel. 0171/938–9123; admission £4.50, £2.20 students; free weekdays 4:30–6, weekends 5–6) does what you'd expect: displays fossils, has stuffed animals from every corner of the earth, and offers excellent interactive exhibits.

➤ **MARYLEBONE AND REGENT'S PARK** • Boring and crowded Marylebone has a few redeeming features, including a few pleasant cafés along **Marylebone High Street** and the area's proximity to Regent's Park. For reasons unknown, people have been flocking to **Madame Tussaud's Wax Museum** (Marylebone Rd., tel. 0171/935–6861) for eons. Where's the thrill of paying £7.40 to look at a wax reproduction of dead people, especially when the likeness is often so crappy? The **Planetarium** (same building as Tussaud's; admission £4, combined ticket with wax museum £9.40) is less hokey, but no better than similar displays elsewhere.

Developed in the early 19th century by the prince regent as an elite residential development for his aristocratic buddies, **Regent's Park** today contains the beautiful and amazingly varied **Queen Mary Gardens** and the **London Zoo** (tel. 0171/722–3333; Tube: Baker St.; admission £6), the world's oldest and Britain's largest.

➤ **MAYFAIR** • Mayfair is an ultraritzy residential neighborhood defined by its beautiful 18th-century deep-red-brick apartment blocks. The May Fair, the market that gave its name to the neighborhood, moved here in 1686 from the Haymarket and was famed for its ribald entertainment; later, the area became a popular haunt of prostitutes. Today, **Shepherd's Market** is a charming nest of pedestrian-only alleys loaded with cafés, wine bars, pubs, and expensive restaurants. Perpendicular to Oxford Street, **Bond Street** may be the most expensive shopping street in London. The street is divided into New Bond and Old Bond, but prices are very, very modern wherever you go. Running parallel to Bond Street is **Cork Street,** the center of London's art trade, with a number of contemporary galleries between Burlington Gardens and Clifford Street open to the public. **Piccadilly Circus** strikes tourists as the most Americanized center of contemporary London: neon lights, enormous billboards, and fast-food joints. The **Royal Academy of Arts** (tel. 0171/439–7438; admission £5, £3.40 students) is the oldest institution in London devoted to the fine arts, with rotating exhibits throughout the year.

➤ **SOHO** • Long one of the leading bohemian neighborhoods of London, Soho today is an amalgam of hip clothing stores, hair salons, sex shops, and trendy cafés with patrons practicing their sneers. The area has an international flavor that many of central London's neighborhoods lack. Greeks fleeing Turkish rule were probably the first foreigners to settle the area en masse, soon followed by French refugees escaping religious persecution; today, Soho displays more Italian and Chinese influences. Soho's **Chinatown** crowds around Gerrard and Lisle streets in the area between Leicester Square and Shaftesbury Avenue. **Leicester Square** is often compared to New York's Times Square (maybe because stands in both squares sell cheap theater tickets), but it isn't as big, as bright, or as sleazy.

➤ **THE SOUTH BANK** • Many visitors never venture across the Thames unless they're heading to Waterloo Station, and judging from the South Bank's industrial color (a result of rebuilding after World War II bombs flattened the area), that's no great loss. Still, a few museums and art institutions offer relief. A sprawling, multitier monument to poured concrete, the **South Bank Arts Centre** (Tube: Waterloo) takes its role as cultural beacon seriously and is as progressive a complex as you could hope for from any quasi-official institution. Thick brochures listing the month's attractions at the center are available in the lobbies of most hotels. In addition to housing the **National Theatre,** the **National Film Theatre,** and the **Royal Festival Hall** (*see* After Dark, *below*), the center also has the **Hayward Gallery** (Belvedere Rd., tel. 0171/928–3144; admission £5, £3.50 students), which is known for assembling thorough retrospectives of modern artists such as Magritte and Jasper Johns. Also in the center is the **Museum of the Moving Image** (MOMI) (tel. 0171/401–2636; admission £5.50, £4.70 students), an impressive though semikitschy TV and film museum.

Started in 1759 by Princess Augusta, **Kew Gardens** (tel. 0181/940–1171; Tube: Kew Gardens; admission £3, £1.70 students) is the mother of all botanical gardens. People with Zones 1 and 2 Travelcards need to pay an extra 60p each way, but it's worth it—Kew is colossal and absolutely amazing. Wild patches, hyperformal patches, lakes, ponds, half a dozen architecturally startling greenhouses, and paths abound. The **Princess of Wales Conservatory,** a modernist structure with a lushly re-created tropical jungle (complete with artificially steamy atmosphere), is first-rate.

➤ **ST. JAMES'S** • When Whitehall Palace burned down in 1698, all of London turned its eyes and its attention to St. James's Palace (closed to the public), the new royal residence. In the 18th and 19th centuries, the area around the new palace became *the* place to live, and many of the estates surrounding the palace disappeared in a building frenzy, as mansions were built, streets were laid out, and expensive shops sprung up. Today St. James's is one of London's most elegant and fashionable addresses.

The red-tarmac **Mall** cuts a 115-foot-wide swath all the way from Trafalgar Square to Buckingham Palace. It was laid out in 1904, largely because it was felt that the British monarchy should have a processional route in keeping with its imperial status. **Admiralty Arch** (built in 1911), a triumphal arch bordering Trafalgar Square, marks the start of the Mall; it continues past St. James's Park and **Carlton House Terrace,** a stately 1,000-foot-long facade of white stucco arches that is home of the **Institute of Contemporary Arts** (The Mall, tel. 0171/930–3647; admission £1.50), with lectures, films, and rotating exhibits of photography, paintings, and architectural drawings. The Mall ends in front of Buckingham Palace at the **Queen Victoria Memorial,** an irritatingly didactic monument to the glory of Victorian ideals.

➤ **THE STRAND AND EMBANKMENT** • The Strand, which turns into Fleet Street about a half-mile from Charing Cross, is smelly, noisy, and dirty—a lot of cars in a boring concrete canyon with crowded sidewalks. The Embankment is one of those civic projects so beloved by the Victorians: Constructed between 1868 and 1874 by Sir Joseph Bazalgette, who designed London's sewers, it runs from Westminster to the City and helped prevent flooding (a job now handled by the Thames Barrier).

Somerset House, constructed between 1776 and 1786 by William Chambers, is home to Inland Revenue (the British equivalent of the IRS) and the **Courtauld Institute** (The Strand, tel. 0171/873–2526; Tube: Temple; admission £3, £1.50 students), a gallery housing a collection of oils from the 15th to 20th centuries. The impressionists and post impressionists are the best represented; Manet's enormously important *Bar at the Folies-Bergère* hangs here, and the collection of Cézannes is the best in London.

➤ **WHITEHALL** • Whitehall is both a street and a vast, faceless bureaucracy. Whitehall the street runs from Trafalgar to Parliament Square through the heart of tourist London. Whitehall the bureaucracy can't be so easily defined. Essentially, the term applies to the central British government, whose ministries fill many of the buildings off Whitehall and around Carlton Terrace. The long, low **Horse Guards** building (constructed 1745–1755) is the backdrop for a smaller version of Buckingham Palace's Changing of the Guard: At 11 each day (10 on Sun.), a mounted contingent of the Household Cavalry clops its way down the Mall from Hyde Park Barracks to Whitehall, arriving here 30 minutes later to relieve the soldiers standing in sentry boxes facing the Banqueting House.

Churchill, the Cabinet, and the Chiefs of Staff coordinated Britain's war effort from the **Cabinet War Rooms** (King Charles St., tel. 0171/930–6961; admission £3.80, £2.80 students), a fortified basement in a civil-service building. An audiotape tour guides you through rooms reconstructed to look as they did at the close of World War II.

AFTER DARK

The constellation of talent that appears nightly in London's theaters and clubs is unrivaled in the English-speaking world; it's all there for you, if you're willing to spend a little. A pint of beer runs £1.80, movie tickets are £6–£7, and clubs charge covers of £6 and up, up, up. Clubs, first-run cinemas, jazz joints, and big-name theaters are concentrated around Soho and Covent Garden, but you'll find hip, alternative clubs and theaters all over London. For the latest entertainment options, check out *The Evening Standard, Time Out, What's On,* or the music weeklies *Melody Maker* and *N.M.E.*

PUBS AND WINE BARS Most pubs are open Monday–Saturday 11–11 and Sunday noon–3 and 7–10:30. Most pubs are affiliated with particular breweries and are beholden to sell the beers of that specific brewery only. Independently owned pubs, called "freehouses," are free to offer whatever they like and usually have a more extensive selection.

Black Lion. Cavernous Hammersmith pub with a primitive bowling alley and backyard garden. It's just 100 yards from a romantic path along the Thames. *2 S. Black Lion Ln. Tube: Stamford Brook.*

Blue Anchor. Airy bar along the Thames; packed on weekends. *13 Lower Mall., tel. 0181/748–5774. Tube: Stamford Brook.*

Chelsea Potter. The most happening of the million pubs on the King's Road drag. *119 King's Rd., tel. 0171/352–9479. Tube: Sloane Sq.*

Cittie of York. Intimate pub in the City, popular with bankers but still worth checking out for what is reputedly the longest bar in the world. *22 High Holborn, tel. 0171/242–7670. Tube: Chancery La.*

Coopers Arms. Newspapers, overhead fans, and Persian carpets make this a mellow Chelsea hangout. *87 Flood St., tel. 0171/376–3120. Tube: Sloane Sq.*

London's Cheap Thrills

Perhaps the best—and most popular—places to sunbathe in London are the city's voluminous cemeteries. The gay tanning stronghold is Brompton Cemetery (Tube: Earl's Court). Marx's final resting place, Highgate Cemetery (Tube: Archway), charges £1 to enter—although many people hop the fence along Waterloo Park to the west of Archway station. London's many flea markets—some more touristy than others—are gratis. Try Portobello Road (Tube: Ladbroke Grove or Notting Hill Gate), a funky market with bongos, dancing, and dozens of buskers.

Colherne. Popular gay pub, near sunbathing hot spot Brompton Cemetery. *Old Brompton Rd. Tube: Earl's Court.*

De Hems. The Dutch maintain a strong presence here; try an Oranjeboom on tap. Usually overflowing onto the sidewalks by 9 PM. *11 Macclesfield St., tel. 0171/437–2494. Tube: Piccadilly Circus.*

French House. The unofficial Resistance headquarters during World War II maintains a vaguely French aura. Great wine selection—easily the best, as well as one of the cheapest, of any London pub. *49 Dean St., tel. 0171/437–2477. Tube: Leicester Sq.*

Holly Bush. A cozy watering hole perched on a hill above the crowds of Hampstead High Street. On a cold night, warm up to the crackling fire. *Holly Mt. Tube: Hampstead.*

King's Head. Head downstairs to the "Dive Bar" for great tunes and the hippest people-watching in London without paying a cover. *Gerrard St., tel. 0171/437–5858. Tube: Leicester Sq.*

Mitre. Candles on the tables and subdued lighting make this quiet pub far more bohemian than "laddish." *Upper St. Tube: Angel.*

Prince Albert. The most jumpin' pub on Bayswater's main drag. Free live music some weekends—a rarity in London. *Queensway, tel. 0171/228–0923. Tube: Queensway. Walk north on Queensway.*

Sun. The largest selection of "real ales" (aged in wooden casks) in England. Student hangout for the nearby University of London. *63 Lamb's Conduit St., tel. 0171/405–8278. Tube: Russell Sq.*

CLUBBING Clubs are everywhere in London; most play a mix of house/techno, old R&B, '70s funk/disco, and the occasional indie platter. Check the listings in *Time Out* for something that strikes your fancy or simply wander the streets of Soho or Camden Town. Most clubs have a cover charge of at least £6 or £7. Look for flyers; they'll usually get you in at less than half the price.

The Fridge. Brixton's major dance venue is a three-ring circus, with multimedia displays, live performances, and go-go dancers. Tuesday and Saturday nights are best. Cover £3–£6. *Town Hall Parade, Brixton Hill, tel. 0171/326–5100. Tube: Brixton. Open Mon., Tues., Thurs.–Sat., and first Wed. of each month.*

Gossips. The platters tend to be older, esoteric, and eminently danceable at this basement club featuring tons of dark, sculpted corners. Cover £4–£6. *69 Dean St., tel. 0171/434–4480. Tube: Leicester Sq.*

Heaven. This massive gay club gets busy on weekends, although on Mondays and Thursdays a mixed crowd comes to dance. Cover £2–£8. *The Arches, Villiers St., tel. 0171/839–3852. Tube: Charing Cross.*

Paradise. Head to Islington's most happening rave club after a crawl through the nearby pubs. Play pool in the game room or head to one of the two dance floors. Cover £10. *1 Parkfield St., tel. 0171/354–9993. Tube: Angel.*

Wag Club. Hip-hop, contemporary R&B, and funk (with smoke-machine effects) packs this trendy club near Piccadilly. Cover £5–£8. *33 Wardour St., tel. 0171/437–5534. Tube: Piccadilly Circus. Closed Sun.*

MUSIC

➤ **ROCK AND REGGAE** • **Hammersmith Odeon.** Well-known bands perform for reasonable prices at this venerable London institution. *Queen Caroline St., across Beadon and King Sts., tel. 0181/7484081. Tube: Hammersmith.*

Marquee. Its glory days were in the '60s (during The Who's mod period), but it maintains a good reputation in its newer, slightly larger pad. Music includes indie, Gothic, and metal. *105 Charing Cross Rd., tel. 0171/437–6603. Tube: Leicester Sq.*

University of London Union. Popular local bands get top billing in the university's Manning Hall. It's everything you wanted and so much more—hot and crowded, with cheap beer and great bands. *Malet St., tel. 0171/580–9551. Tube: Goodge St.*

➤ **JAZZ • Altar Club.** This amazing once-a-week club occupies the corner of a local parish church in south London. The stone and high ceiling give a rich sound, and the BYOB makes it cheap. Cover £3. *St. Peter's Heritage Centre, Kennington La., entrance on Tyers St. Tube: Vauxhall. Open Fri. night only*

Bass Clef. This small, happening club does '70s funk on Monday; the rest of the week they alternate live jazz, Latin, and African music. Cover £4–£8. *35 Coronet St., tel. 0171/729–2476. Tube: Old St.*

100 Club. This club has evolved over 15 years from a seminal punk club to a jazz joint. Fortunately, it's still a dive. *100 Oxford St., tel. 0171/636–0933. Tube: Oxford Circus.*

Ronnie Scott's. The leading venue for jazz in London—if they're the best, they'll play here. Status is, unfortunately, reflected in the £12 cover; students pay £6 Monday–Thursday. *47 Frith St., tel. 0171/439–0747. Tube: Tottenham Court Rd.*

CLASSICAL MUSIC AND OPERA Expect to pay £5–£15 for regular symphony recitals, and even more for big-name conductors and events. If you don't have tickets, try going about a half-hour before the performance—you may be able to pick up returns. For eight weeks from July to September, the Royal Albert Hall hosts the **Promenade Concerts** (tel. 0171/589–8212). If you stand in the long lines, you can get SRO gallery and arena tickets for £2–£3; otherwise, tickets are £4–£16. The classiest venue for opera in London is the **Royal Opera House** (Bow St., Covent Garden, tel. 0171/240–1066), although the £5 upper-gallery seats are lousy. The Opera House is also the home of the world-famous **Royal Ballet.** The famous London Symphony Orchestra plays at the **Barbican Centre.** Although the emphasis is on classical music, everything from brass bands to jazz and world music is performed. Tickets cost £5–£25; ask about student standby tickets.

Royal Festival Hall. The South Bank Arts Centre is home to the London Philharmonic Orchestra. Tickets £7–£28; student tickets available 2 hours before show. *Tel. 0171/928–8800. Tube: Waterloo.*

St. John's Smith Square. With its excellent acoustics, this beautiful Baroque church has rapidly become one of the leading venues for classical music in London. Tickets £3–£10. *Smith Sq., tel. 0171/222–1061. Tube: Westminster.*

THEATER Theater in London falls into two types: The West End (London's equivalent of Broadway) and the fringe. The principal West End theaters are centered around Shaftesbury Avenue in Soho, the Haymarket in St. James, and around Covent Garden. Half-price, same-day tickets are sold from the **Society of West End Theatres' ticket kiosk** (open Mon.–Sat. noon–2 for matinees, 2:30–6:30 for evening shows) in Leicester Square, but lines are always long. Tickets run from £6 for nosebleed seats in the gallery to £20 and more for the dress circle. Fringe shows are much cheaper. Royal Shakespeare Company productions come to **The Barbican** (tel. 0171/638–4141) regularly. The **National Theatre** (South Bank Arts Centre, tel. 0171/928–2252; Tube: Waterloo; tickets £7.50, £5.50 students 45 min before the show) puts on anything from cutting-edge stuff to imaginative interpretations of old standbys. The **Shaftesbury Theatre** (Shaftesbury Ave., tel. 0171/379–5399; Tube: Tottenham Court Rd.; admission £7.50–£20, £5 standbys 30 min before performance) is a regal old building that serves up the best innovative new drama.

NEAR LONDON

WINDSOR Windsor, west of central London along the Thames, is one of London's most ancient boroughs. The 11th-century, dirt-and-wood fort built here by William the Conqueror was later rebuilt in stone by Henry II; the brawny complex eventually evolved into **Windsor Castle.** Before the 1992 fire, the queen spent most of her weekends here, and the entire castle closed whenever she rolled into town. These days, it's open more often than not, but call 01753/831118 for the latest opening times and to complain about the staggering £8 castle admission fee. The principal structure of the Lower Ward is the 15th-century **St. George's Chapel,** where many of England's kings and queens are buried. The Middle Ward is where you'll find the **state apartments** (admission £1.50), the **Gallery** (admission £1.50), and **Queen Mary's Dolls' House** (admission £1.50). The Dolls' House, measuring 8 by 5 feet, is a fully functional marvel of miniature engineering—teeny faucets even exude rivulets of water. Hours vary, but these places tend to open 10:30–5 in summer, until 3 or so in winter. The **Changing of the Guard** takes place daily at 11 AM in summer, every second day in winter. BritRail service from Paddington (£4.80 round-trip) runs every half-hour to Windsor. National Express offers bus service from Victoria Coach Station every half-hour.

The South

The South, cradling the megalopolis of London, is the most affluent region in England and seems the last place in Britain to get word of any revolution in fashion, music, food, or mind-altering substances. The scenery in the South is consistently impressive, and if the sights get you down, flee the towns and take long walks through the forests, or go for long bike rides through the placid countryside.

Canterbury

The path between London and Canterbury has long been one of the most beaten in Europe; unlike the modern BritRail traveler, though, medieval pilgrims had to hoof it to visit the shrine of the martyr Thomas à Becket. The sights within the town—essentially the cathedral and the crooked medieval streets—can be seen fairly easily as a day trip from London, although the town makes a perfect pre-London stop for those who've just crossed the English Channel. The **Tourist Information Centre** (34 St. Margaret's St., tel. 01227/766567) book beds for a 10% surcharge.

COMING AND GOING Trains leave London's Victoria Station for **Canterbury East** (£15 round-trip) every half-hour on weekdays and hourly on weekends. (A second station, Canterbury West, serves mostly local destinations in Kent.) The **bus station's** entrance is on the corner of St. George's Lane and St. George's Place. Buses leave about every two hours for London's Victoria Coach Station (£8 one-way).

WHERE TO SLEEP A gob of B&Bs line New Dover, London, and Whitstable roads; most have only a couple rooms, so call ahead before showing up. Two pleasant, small B&Bs are the **Dar Anne** (65 London Rd., tel. 01227/761513; doubles £22) and **Linden's Guest House** (38B St. Dunstan's St., tel. 01227/462339; doubles £32). The **HI Canterbury Hostel** (54 New Dover Rd., tel. 01227/462911) has beds for £8.40 (£5.60 under 18) and is usually full during summer; reserve ahead. To reach the hostel from East Station, turn right, walk about ⅓ mile, and turn right on St. George's Place, which becomes New Dover Road.

FOOD The main food drag is High Street, but cheaper places can be found just off High Street along the smaller lanes and alleys. **Borough Food Unlimited** (17–18 The Borough, tel. 01227/458368) serves cheap, healthy sandwiches like vegetarian falafel (£1.50) and chicken salad in a pita (£2). **Sugarloaf** (41 St. Peter's St., tel. 01227/456402) has a small patio out back and serves killer Cornish pastries (£1) and sandwiches. Each of the four colleges of the **University of Kent** (tel. 01027/764000) has its own bar; Keynes College's bar is the most fun, with a sociable, outgoing crowd. Take any bus heading up St. Dunstan's Street and ask the driver for the university.

WORTH SEEING The small size and high density of the town makes it easy to see all the sights in one day on foot. The hub of English Catholicism, **Canterbury Cathedral** (cnr. of Sun and St. Margaret's Sts.; admission free) is a wonder of Norman and Gothic architecture. Thomas à Becket, the French priest who disagreed with King Henry II's meddling in the church's business, was murdered in 1170 in the church's northwest transept by four of

Henry's knights. Becket's assassins probably entered by the door from the cloisters. The dazzling cathedral entrance was built to commemorate Henry V's victory at Agincourt.

Animatronics wizards have created Chuck E. Cheese's medieval England at **The Canterbury Tales** (St. Margaret's St., tel. 01227/454888; admission £4.25, £3.50 students). Excerpts from the tales are illustrated by moving plywood cutouts with "authentic smells" like smoke and horseshit. The stories are funny, but it's cheaper to buy the book. The popular **Canterbury Heritage Museum** (Stour St., tel. 01227/452747; admission £1.40, £1 students; closed Nov.–May) exhibits a somewhat boring collection of local artifacts left by pilgrims at Canterbury.

Dover

Dover's role in the English tourism industry is unique: It's the English city closest to the European continent and is visited largely because of its ferry port. The surroundings—the steep white chalk hills above the frigid waters of the Channel—made the town an ideal fortress in the past, a role that was tested in this century by relentless German bombings during World War II. The **tourist office** (Townwall St., tel. 01304/205108) gives out a free pamphlet called "White Cliffs Trails," showing the best walks—make this your first priority. Dover is experiencing chilling economic times because of the recent opening of the Eurotunnel and the decrease of ferry traffic, making it an understandably depressing place to stay long. Because many people have time to kill while awaiting boats, a bunch of cheesy exhibits vie for tourist dollars; the best is the **Old Town Gaol** (Biggin St., tel. 01304/201066; admission £3), a Victorian prison offering vivid images of torture, confinement, and lunacy. Another worthwhile stop is impressive **Dover Castle** (Castle Hill Rd., tel. 01304/201628; admission £4.50, £3.50 students), overlooking the coast with some first-rate views. Don't miss the 45-minute tour of **Hellfire Corner,** a maze of tunnels dug in the cliffs beneath the castle, complete with an eerie, subterranean World War II–era command post.

COMING AND GOING Ferries leave regularly for Calais, France (90 min), from Dover Marine Train station with **Sealink Stena Line** (tel. 01233/647047), and for Calais, Boulogne, and Ostend from the Eastern Docks with **P&O** (tel. 01304/203388). The standard round-trip fare for all destinations is £48, but if you plan on returning in less than five days, fares can be as low as £24. Call the tourist office for schedules. **Hoverspeed** and **SeaCat** (tel. 01304/240241) shorten the journey via Hovercraft from either dock. Prices are competitive with ferries: £23 one-way or £38 for a five-day round-trip. Hovercrafts leave every hour. From London's Victoria Coach Station, National Express coaches regularly run to Dover's station on **Pencester Road** (£10 one-way). Trains to London's Victoria and Charing Cross Stations leave at least once an hour from Dover's **Priory Station** (£15 one-way).

WHERE TO SLEEP AND EAT Be sure to see the room before money changes hands; some Dover B&Bs are lousy. **Clare House** (167 Folkestone Rd., tel. 01304/204553) is a well-kept family home with extra-soft mattresses (doubles £22), and **Linden Guest House** (231 Folkestone Rd., tel. 01304/205449) has immaculate facilities (doubles £32). Dover's youth hostel, the **HI Charlton House** (306 London Rd., tel. 01304/201314; beds £10.60, £7.80 under 18) is expensive, rude, and out of the way. From Priory Station, turn left onto St. Martin's Hill, then left onto Priory Road. Follow the numerous signs straight up. Most restaurants in town will make you want to scurry to local supermarkets, although **Topo Gigio** (1-2 King St., tel. 01304/201048) serves plates of tasty Italian food for less than £5.

NEAR DOVER

RYE At the mouth of the River Rother lies the ancient village of Rye, most of which is surrounded by small waterways. If you're sick of the hustle and bustle of tourist-laden towns, come to this small, sedate fishing village that once had the notorious reputation of being one of England's main smuggling centers. The **tourist information office** (Strand Quay, tel. 01797/226696; open daily 9–5:30) is inside The Heritage Centre, a building that houses the model of Rye and a small museum. They also have a book-a-bed-ahead service for a 10% surcharge.

The Old English word for "small passageways" is "twittens," and Rye is full of them. One interesting walk is near the corner of East and Market streets, close to the entrance to the Rye Art Gallery Stormont Studio on Ockman Lane. At the corner of Tower Street and Hilder's Street, you can see **Land Gate,** which guarded the only entrance into town by land when Rye was a peninsula. **Ypres Tower and the Gun Garden** is a good picnic spot with a view of the Flatlands South to the ocean inlet. The tower also houses the **Rye Museum** (4 Church Sq., tel. 01797/226728; admission £1.50, £1 students), which showcases a collection of semi-interesting relics.

➤ **COMING AND GOING** • No National Express coaches come into Rye. The only way in or out is by car or train, or through one of the private bus companies. BritRail's **Marsh Link** (tel. 01732/770111) runs from Ashford to Hastings (stopping at every one-horse town on the way), but train service ends around 9 PM on Sunday, so plan ahead. A one-way ticket to Brighton costs £8.90, Dover £7.60, and London £13.30. Private bus companies serving the area include **Eastbourne Buses** (tel. 01323/416416), **Fuggles** (tel. 01580/240522), and **Hastings Buses** (tel. 01424/226949).

➤ **WHERE TO SLEEP** • Besides Rye's B&Bs, there's a hostel in nearby Hastings (15 km from Rye), the **HI Guestling Hall** (Rye Rd., Hastings, tel. 01424/812373; beds £6.90; closed Sun. and Sept.–Apr.), 5 km from the nearest train station and up a steep hill. From Rye, take Bus 11 or 12, get off at White Hart, then backtrack about 300 meters.

Brighton

From its crowded beaches (not especially nice, but beaches nonetheless) to its tidy pedestrian lanes and Victorian architecture, Brighton draws an international crowd of all types and preferences. It can de a decadent and wild place, especially if you crave nightlife gay or straight. However, the place does have a sick, post-party feel, particularly on a sunny day when crowds of drunk, pasty Britons turn Brighton into an oceanside pleasure dome.

In 1985, the IRA nearly changed the course of British history by exploding a bomb in the beachfront Grand Hotel, barely missing Thatcher and her entire cabinet.

Looking just like the Taj Mahal, the **Royal Pavillion** (corner of North St. and Old Steine, tel. 01273/603005; admission £3.60, £2.70 students) was completed by John Nash in 1822. The interior is extravagantly decorated in Indian and Chinese styles, and during the summer the lawn becomes a venue for musical performances. The **Brighton Museum and Art Gallery** (Church St. at Marlborough Pl., tel. 01273/603005; admission free; closed Wed.) contains diverse exhibits of armor, Art Deco glass, archaeological finds, and the Closet of Curiosities, which houses a "real" mermaid's skeleton. Gaudy, beloved **Palace Pier** (tel. 01273/609361) has the requisite boardwalk video games, bumper cars, and slot machines. At night, a seedier crowd emerges, but the pier is still relatively safe. Brighton's most interesting and expensive shops—as well as its best night-clubs—are in the **Lanes,** a pocket of narrow streets near the ocean. The **North Lanes** are a cheaper alternative shopping area with several good restaurants and vintage-clothing stores.

BASICS The **Tourist Information Centre** (10 Bartholomew Sq., tel. 01273/23755), across from the town hall, offers a book-a-bed-ahead service, maps, and jillions of leaflets. **American Express** (Edward St., tel. 01273/693555) offers the usual services for cardholders.

COMING AND GOING Trains leave London's Victoria Station hourly (£16 one-way) for Brighton's rail station (tel. 01273/206755). National Express Bus 64 leaves for London every 1½–2 hours from the station across from Marlborough House (£9 one-way).

WHERE TO SLEEP The cheapest places are found along a few streets on the east side of town, such as Madeira Place, Charlotte Street, and Upper Rock Gardens. **Chester Court** (7 Charlotte St., tel. 01273/621750; wheelchair access), near the seafront, is one of the best;

doubles are around £35. The clean but inconvenient **HI Patcham Place** (London Rd., tel. 01273/556196) has beds for £10.60 (£7.80 under 18) but is more than 5 km from town on busy London Road; from Brighton Station, turn left on the major road at the bottom of the hill and keep walking. The laid-back alternative—for £9 per night—is the independent **Brighton Backpackers Hostel** (75 Middle St., tel. 01273/777717), only a half-block from the waterfront. It sports a bar, laundry, and open kitchen, and has very affordable weekly rates (£45 in summer). From Brighton station, walk to King's Road at West Street, turn left, then left on Middle Street.

FOOD Preston Street and The Lanes have restaurants aplenty and no shortage of kebab shops, chippies, and tandoori takeouts that are open until 2 AM or later. **Minna's Egyptian/Lebanese Wholefood** (34 St. James' St., tel. 01273/672274) is the only restaurant in Brighton that gives students a 10% discount. Inside a building decorated with paintings of pharaohs' sarcophagi, munch on falafels (£1.50) or shish kebabs (£2.75).

AFTER DARK Brighton is home to Britain's largest gay population outside of London, and travelers of any sexual orientation can enjoy a very hedonistic weekend here. The hub of Brighton's nightlife is, unquestionably, the clubs. Pick up the free monthly guide to nightlife, *Buzz*, at the tourist office. **The Smugglers** (10 Ship St., tel. 01273/28439) packs in an international crowd on weekends. Considered the cheapest bar in Brighton, **The Basement** (Grand Parade, tel. 01273/643190) is accessible to ISIC cardholders only and hosts a '70s disco every Saturday. **The Underground Club** (77 West St., tel. 01273/27701) features alternative music several nights each week.

Winchester

Winchester is like a historian's playground; it's old, stoic, and a pleasure to walk through. The first king of England, Egbert—yes, Egbert—was crowned here in AD 827, and even William the Conqueror thought it prudent to restage his crowning here after the "official" ceremony in London—evidence of how deep and important history is in England's self-acclaimed "ancient capital." The longer you spend in Winchester, the less you'll want to leave. Dozens of walking and hiking trails crisscross the nearby fields, streams and rivers flow through town, and centuries-old bells stir the air on Sunday mornings. The **South Downs Way**, the most well-traveled long-distance footpath in Britain, has been extended westward to Winchester, and the **tourist office** (Broadway, tel. 01962/840500) is one of England's best-stocked. Winchester's **train station** (Station Rd., tel. 01703/229393 for info) is on a direct BritRail line from London. The **bus station** (tel. 01329/230023 for National Express info) is on Broadway at the west end of town. Buy your ticket from the tourist office or the driver.

WHERE TO SLEEP Lodging is sparse and very expensive in Winchester, so reserve ahead at the hostel or plan to make Winchester a day trip from London. Many B&Bs are southwest of the cathedral, especially along Christchurch Road and its side streets. Even though **Shawlands** (46 Kilham La., tel. 01962/861166) is 1.5 km southwest of the town center, staying in this large, modern house (£16 per person) is worth the short ride on Bus 66. The **HI Old Mill Hostel** (1 Water La., tel. 01962/853723) is a tourist attraction by day, hostel by night. It's an 18th-century mill on an island in the middle of River Itchen, and it's extraordinary; definitely one of Britain's best. Book way ahead because it's also very small (38 beds; £6.90 per person). The hostel is closed on an erratic schedule in spring and fall. From the tourist office, turn right on Broadway and cross the bridge.

WORTH SEEING The majority of Winchester's glorious sights are clustered within a half-mile radius of **Winchester Cathedral** (tel. 01962/853137; £2 donation requested), England's center of religion until Canterbury's rise to power in the 13th century. With its magnificent stained-glass windows and sky-high ceilings, the Norman cathedral, originally built in 1079, is one of the airiest medieval churches in Europe. Look for Jane Austen's tomb south of the nave. The church's **library** (admission £1.50, 50p students) houses the illuminated 12th-century Winchester Bible, as well as a copy of Bede's 8th-century *Historia Ecclesiastica*. The **Great Hall** (Upper High St. at Castle Hill, tel. 01962/846476; admission free; closed winter weekdays), allegedly King Arthur's headquarters, was the seat of government until the Norman Invasion of 1066. It was the site of crucial historical events, like Parliament's first meeting (in 1246) and Sir Walter Raleigh's trial for treason (in 1603), but most visitors come to see the painted wooden disc purported to be King Arthur's Round Table.

The West Country

England's southwestern counties, known collectively as the West Country, form a happy mishmash of thatched-roof houses, fishing villages, artists' colonies, and national parks. Extensive coastal paths ring the Cornish coast while England's warmest waters lap the shore of the surfing enclaves of Penzance and Newquay. It's a shame that many visitors don't spend much time here beyond a visit to Bath—there's no shortage of worthwhile diversions nearby.

Bath

Nearly 2,000 years ago, Romans built an intricate series of baths and pools and named it Aquae Sulis. The British aristocracy updated the custom when Queen Anne's visits in 1702 and 1703 established the "Bath season," giving birth to the town's modern name. Throughout the 18th century, the small medieval village witnessed a building boom, with Georgian row houses curving through the city like scalloped paper cutouts. These days, Bath is nearly equal to Stratford as a tourist draw, so lodging and food are expensive. If you want to stay over, the efficient **Tourist Information Center** (11–13 Bath St., tel. 01225/462831) books rooms. **American Express** (5 Bridge St., tel. 01225/444767) offers regular cardmember services.

COMING AND GOING BritRail (tel. 0117/9294255) heads from London's Paddington Station to Bath's **Spa Station** (£25 round-trip). **National Express** (Minerva St., tel. 01225/464446) runs coaches to London for £17.50 round-trip.

WHERE TO SLEEP Bath's **YMCA** (Broad St. Pl., tel. 01225/460471) is in the center of town; singles are £12, doubles £22, dorm beds £9.50. The **HI Bathwick Hill Hostel** (tel. 01225/465674; beds £5.60–£8.40) is the cheapest lodging option. Take Bus 18 from the train station to avoid walking up the steep hill. **The Georgian Guest House** (34 Henrietta St., tel. 01225/424103) charges £16 per person and is probably the only B&B in the city center that will leave you with dinner money. The cozy **Joanna House** (5 Pulteney Ave., tel. 01225/335246) is near the train station and has similar rates.

For that picture-perfect moment, bring your camera to Pulteney Bridge, designed by Robert Adam in 1770 and lined with poky shops.

FOOD The town's cheap eats center around the Theatre Royal, Sawclose, and Kingsmead Square areas. **Scoffs** (Kingsmead Sq., tel. 01225/462483) is a whole-food bakery and café with vegetarian dishes for £1–£4. **The Canary Restaurant** (3 Queen St., tel. 01225/424846) serves pasta and vegetarian dishes (about £5) to chamber-music accompaniment.

WORTH SEEING Unfortunately, you can't get wet at the **Roman bath** network (Abbey Churchyard, tel. 01225/461111; admission £4), but you can tour the well-preserved, sulfurous-smelling Roman baths. Sample some vile-tasting mineral water at the **Pump Room,** above the baths. The elegant **Assembly Rooms,** built in 1771 and still used for social events, houses the **Museum of Costume** (Bennett St., tel. 01225/461111; admission £2.50), a prestigious collection that covers more than 400 years of fashion. A £5 combination ticket allows entrance to the museum and the baths. The **Royal Crescent,** built by John Wood the Younger, is typical of Bath's 18th-century Georgian architecture. Inside, check out **No. 1 Royal Crescent** (tel. 01225/428126; admission £3, £2.50 students), a museum decorated in Georgian style. A church has stood on the site of **Bath Abbey** (High St.; £1 donation requested) for 1,200 years, although the present building is from the late 15th century.

Relax after sightseeing in any of Bath's 11 parks; the 57-acre **Royal Victoria Park,** next to the Royal Crescent, has botanical gardens and an aviary.

THE WEST COUNTRY

NEAR BATH

GLASTONBURY Glastonbury is England's hippie capital and spiritual center, where the Christian mixes with the Druidic, the ancient with New Age. The chalice used during the Last Supper is reputedly buried in the hill next to **Glastonbury Tor,** a tall upcropping of land once used as a Druid congress, and the town itself is aligned most auspiciously on ley lines (invisible lines of spiritual energy that supposedly run across England). Interspersed with the healing establishments and aromatherapy dens, there's a real town with the usual assortment of English small-town characters. **Glastonbury Abbey** (tel. 01458/832267) as it stands (or crumbles) today was started by the Normans, but an early church on the site is said to have been visited by Jesus. **The Glastonbury Tribunal** (High St., tel. 01458/832949) is a well-preserved medieval town house that was once the seat of adjudication in Glastonbury. Call the **Tourist Information Office** (inside the Glastonbury Tribunal, tel. 01458/832954) for info. Buses leave from Bath nearly every hour (£4.50), though you have to change in Wells.

The annual Glastonbury Festival, held the last weekend in June, features England's best bands, 100,000 groupies, mind-alternating substances, and a three-ring circus.

Salisbury

Salisbury is dwarfed by hype from nearby Stonehenge—you can't walk two blocks without seeing leaflets and posters pointing you there. But if you overlook all the 'henge-mania, you'll find Salisbury's Tudor buildings and walkable city center worth a gander themselves. **Salisbury Cathedral** (The Close, tel. 01722/328726; admission £2, £1 students) remains, as recorded in 1401, "so great a church to the glory of God that those who come after us will think us mad even to have attempted it." The spire and tower, supported by stone columns bending underneath, weigh 6,400 tons. Don't miss the octagonal Chapter House (admission 30p), containing one of the original copies of the Magna Carta. Across the lawn from the main entrance is the **Salisbury and South Wiltshire Museum** (65 The Close, tel. 01722/332151), home to prehistoric, Roman, and Saxon archaeological exhibits and displays on local history. The **Tourist Information Office** (Fish Row, tel. 01722/334956) has the scoop on Salisbury.

COMING AND GOING BritRail (tel. 01256/464966) serves Salisbury directly from London Waterloo (£25 round-trip) via Basingstoke. Much cheaper are **National Express** (tel. 01329/230023) buses from London (£13 round-trip).

WHERE TO SLEEP AND EAT Pick up a list of B&Bs from the tourist office; most proprietors don't advertise and only display handwritten cards taped in a window. Just east of the town center is comfortable **Milford Hill Hostel** (Milford Hill, tel. 01722/327572), charging £8.40 (£5.60 under 18), slightly higher in July and August. **The Bacon Sandwich Café** (129–131 South Western Rd., next to the rail station, tel. 01722/339655) is the place for meat lovers; try the huge mega breakfast (£3.50).

OUTDOOR ACTIVITIES Following quiet country lanes and passing through small towns, the **Wiltshire Cycleway** covers the entire county, the Vale of Pewsey, and the Wylye Valley. The shortest loop is from Salisbury to Horningsham (120 km), and the longest is the County Route (270 km). Tourist information has free maps. For a £25 deposit and £7.50 per day or £45 per week, you can get your mitts on a mountain bike at **Hayball Co.** (25–30 Winchester St., tel. 01722/411378).

NEAR SALISBURY

STONEHENGE This neolithic monument has been blamed on everything from Druids to UFOs, but all anyone knows for sure is that it's been around since 1500 BC and has long been used for religious and astronomical purposes. The stones are clearly in no danger of

369

being crushed by a dwarf, but they don't look nearly as tall as 18 feet. The chain barrier around the monument was installed in 1978, as a defense against graffiti and the destruction of the stones by human traffic. Ironically, these days you can get a better view of Stonehenge from some points of the A344 highway than from the paid area (admission £1.90). Still, the stones do have a mystical quality early in the morning, when the sun peaks over the horizon. **Wilts & Dorset** (tel. 01722/336855) buses leave every hour from the bus and train station in Salisbury. Explorer tickets (£3.90) are available on the bus and are valid for 24 hours.

Exeter

When Nazis thumbed through a *Baedeker's* travel guide during World War II and found this southwestern cathedral city, they set about destroying it through several devastating air raids. These "Baedeker raids" were designed to hit England's jewel cities and erode citizen morale. But despite the damage, Exeter still has plenty to boast about, including its cathedral, university, and proximity to Dartmoor National Park. **St. Peter's Cathedral** (tel. 01392/55573; £1 donation requested) is one of the finest examples of English Gothic architecture, with the longest unbroken Gothic vault of any building in Europe. Among other treasures in the **Royal Albert Memorial Museum** (Queen St., tel. 01392/265858; admission free; closed Sun. and Mon.), you'll find a stuffed tiger shot in Nepal in 1911 by King George V. The annual **Exeter Festival** (tel. 01392/265200) in July gets everyone revved up with street theater, art exhibits, and concerts. The **Tourist Information Center** (Paris St., tel. 01392/265700), opposite the bus station, has festival info and sells maps and guides to Dartmoor National Park.

COMING AND GOING Trains from London's Paddington station to Exeter's **St. David's Station** (tel. 01392/72281) cost £34 round-trip. You can buy train tickets from the BritRail travel centre (tel. 01392/433551) in Exeter's station. National Express (tel. 01392/56231) runs buses eight times a day to London (£26.50 round-trip). From Exeter's rail station, take bus N or make the 20-minute walk up St. David's hill to the city center.

WHERE TO SLEEP **Exeter HI Youth Hostel** (47–49 Countess Wear Rd., tel. 01392/873329; beds £5–£8) is in the suburbs, amid thatched-roof houses and a contingent of sheep. Take Bus K or T from High Street and get off at the Countess Wear Post Office and follow the signs. July through September, **Exeter University** (New North Rd., tel. 01392/211500) offers private dorm rooms (furnished with tea and goodies to welcome you), access to sports facilities, and huge breakfast for £10. Otherwise, scads of budget B&Bs are only five minutes from the train station on St. David's Hill; try **Highbury B&B** (89 St. David's Hill, tel. 01392/70549; £11 per person), which has big comfortable rooms and an easygoing proprietor.

FOOD High Street and its extensions have cheap fast-food fare as well as pubs and expensive hotel restaurants. **Coolings Wine Bar** (11 Gandy St., tel. 01392/434184) is an atmospheric bistro with the historic **Host and Chalice pub** downstairs. For £3.65, you get lasagna with vegetables and sautéed potatoes or beef in Guinness. **The Gallery Café and Centre Bar** (Gandy St., tel. 01392/421111) is part of the Exeter and Devon Arts Centre. The café's lunch menu features lamb and basil casserole and vegetable-filled pancakes, all for £1–£4. **Harley's of Exeter** (in the City Arcade, off Fore St.) is a good greasy spoon with a full English breakfast for £2.40.

NEAR EXETER

DARTMOOR NATIONAL PARK This 30-km-wide patch of land between Exeter and Plymouth preserves England's most extensive prehistoric ruins—from stone monuments to burial mounds to hut circles, all dating back to around 4000 BC. Near the town of Haytor is **Hound Tor,** a geological phenomenon that from certain angles looks like a hunter and a pack of hounds bounding over the moor. For real wilderness, head for the north moor, which contains the highest peaks in the park. Farmland predominates in the west, and the northeast corner is a mix of high moor and more farms. Hikers should remember that Dartmoor gets 2½ times more rain than nearby Exeter; if you don't want to chance it, call the **weather forecast service** (tel. 01898/141203). The park's two most central information centers are in **Princetown** (tel. 0182289/414; open daily) and **Postbridge** (B3212 parking lot, tel. 01822/88272; closed weekdays Nov.–Mar.).

➤ **COMING AND GOING** • The train will get you only as far as Exeter and Plymouth, from which buses run scattershot service into the park proper. The free "Dartmoor Bus Services" guide, available at all tourist offices in and around the park, is indispensable for planning treks into the park's deepest reaches. To make life a bit easier, a dozen private bus companies cover the towns and villages ringing the park. However, only one route, the **Transmoor Link Bus 82,** goes straight through the park, from Exeter through Plymouth; contact the bus carrier **Western National** (Plymouth, tel. 01752/222666) for more info. An Explorer ticket (£4 daily) covers the whole route.

➤ **WHERE TO SLEEP** • The cheaper B&Bs in the park cost about £12 per person. **Bellever Youth Hostel** (2 km from Postbridge, tel. 01822/88227; closed Nov.–Mar.) shares a farmyard with the Forestry Commission; beds are £7.50 (£5 under 18). Princetown's **The Plume of Feathers Inn** (tel. 01822/89240) has bunks for £3.50–£4.50 and shares the grounds with a campsite (£2 per person), pub, and country inn. Reserve ahead on summer weekends. Most campgrounds in the park are closed from the end of November until February. Near Exeter is **Clifford Bridge Park** (Clifford, near Drewsteignton, tel. 01647/24226), charging £9.75 per twosome with a tent.

The Cornwall Coast

With Land's End pulling like some inexorable magnet, visitors cling like metal shavings to the pretty coves and beaches of Cornwall, England's westernmost—and warmest—county. Despite summer crowds, you can still find sleepy fishing villages, study Iron Age quoits, play on sandy beaches, and unearth the region's treasures like a modern-day pirate. Falmouth and Penzance are good bases for exploring the south, where the summer landscape is lush and beaches are mild. In the north, the landscape is more austere and dramatic, although Newquay serves as the nation's surfing capital.

With its harbor and dockyards, **Falmouth** has long been famous in maritime circles and rests comfortably below Tudor-era **Pendennis Castle** (tel. 01326/316594). The town has a number of beaches, including popular Gyllyngvase Beach and pebbly Castle Beach at Pendennis Headland. Falmouth is a great base for exploring the lush and lovely **Lizard Peninsula**, the southernmost point of mainland Britain. The **South West Coastal Path** winds along the Lizard shore, meandering through past some of England's rarest and most beautiful flora and fauna. The best cliff walks are around **Mullion Cove**. To reach Lizard from Falmouth, take Bus 2 to Helston and transfer onto Bus 320 to Lizard.

The bloody smuggling history of **Penzance** is common knowledge throughout Cornwall—apparently in the old days everyone was in on it, luring ships to its rocky shoals. Today, Penzance is a great place to explore, thanks to its seaside promenade and quiet town center. The **Maritime Museum** (19 Chapel St., tel. 01736/68890; admission £1.50) is a tiny space devoted to rusty anchors, ancient navigational charts, and scale-model displays of schooners and turn-of-the-century British warships. Because of its location and proximity to public transportation, Penzance makes a good base for most of Cornwall. The Penzance **tourist office** (Station Rd., tel. 01736/62207) has info on the town and surrounding areas.

The afternoon sun glitters off the roofs of cars in the parking lot before you see it glance off the sea beyond. Such is **Land's End**, the westernmost point in England. A tacky Disneyesque playground occupies most of the site, charging £5 to enter. WARNING: It's not worth the journey. That same cannot be said of **St. Ives**, which has fewer visitors and a far superior vista: The water is deep aqua, and the yellow lichen covering the town's rooftops looks like magic gold dust. The tiny town gets crammed with people seeking sand, sun, and surf—especially in July and August, so consider May and September if possible. The **tourist office** (Guildhall, tel. 01736/796297) has a long list of galleries to explore, including the excellent **Barbara Hep-**

worth **Museum** (Barnoon Hill, tel. 01736/796226; admission £2.50, £1.50 students), the home and studio of Cornwall's premier 20th-century sculptor. Strolling and bathing are popular at **Porthmeor** and **Porthminster** beaches, bordering the town. And while some people hate **Newquay**, clucking over the way it's been ruined by commercialism, others thrive on the prime surf and crowds. The busy **information office** (Marcus Hill, tel. 01637/871345) is across the street from the bus station.

COMING AND GOING BritRail's express tracks to Cornwall end at Penzance, with smaller lines branching off to Newquay, Falmouth, and St. Ives; trains make the brief run from Penzance to St. Ives eight times daily. The **Cornish Rail Rover** pass (£30 per week) and the **Flexi Rover** (£20 for 3 days out of 7) are good deals if you plan to stay awhile. **National Express** (tel. 01872/40404) has daily direct service from London's Victoria Coach Station to Falmouth and Penzance. The private carrier **Western National** (tel. 01736/69469) covers all of Cornwall by bus.

WHERE TO SLEEP

➤ **FALMOUTH** • B&Bs line Melvill and Avenue roads, three minutes from the Falmouth Docks station. The **HI Pendennis Castle Youth Hostel** (tel. 01326/311435), a 20-minute walk from town, has beds in an old military barracks for £8.40. On a rainy night, listen to the wind howl. From Falmouth's station, follow the road to Castle Street, climb the hill to the left, and follow the signs to the castle and hostel. By taxi, the trip costs £2.

➤ **NEWQUAY** • The independent **Backpackers Travellers Hostel** (Beachfield Ave., tel. 01637/874668; beds £6.50) is friendly, funky, crowded, and the cheapest option in town. From East Street, turn right on Beachfield toward Towan Beach.

➤ **PENZANCE** • The **HI Penzance Youth Hostel** (Alverton, tel. 01736/62666; beds £6.20–£9.80) is a terrifically refurbished 18th-century mansion. Take Bus A, B, 5, or 10B from the station to the Pirate Inn and walk from there. The impeccably clean **Penzance YMCA** (The Orchard, tel. 01736/65016) is a coed facility with beds for £6.30. Call ahead for space. For a hearty breakfast and teatime chitchat, try **Lynwood Guest House** (41 Morrab Rd., tel. 01736/65871; £12 per person), a comfy B&B with TVs and coffee makers in every room.

➤ **ST. IVES** • You can find a B&B in St. Ives for as little as £10. Tregenna Terrace, Carthew Terrace, Channel View, and Bedford Road have many options, including the **Horizon Guest House** (Carthew Terr., tel. 01736/798069), with rooms from £12 to £15 per person. The only campsite near town is **Ayr Holiday Park** (tel. 01736/795855; £8 per twosome with tent), a 15-minute walk from the town on Higher Ayr Street.

East Anglia

The growth of East Anglia, northeast of London, has mirrored the growth of the textile industry over the past millennium, and textile money built many of the cathedrals and so-called "wool churches" in the region. Most towns have experienced enormous population growth but fortunately haven't become polluted and depressed urban nightmares like some of the Midlands' larger cities. On the downside, because East Anglia is still predominantly a rural region, the public transportation system is primitive. Most towns are linked to long-distance walking paths that have been used since medieval times by merchants. If you're into pensive walks, look for **Peddar's Way,** which runs diagonally across Norfolk (in the northeast), and **Weaver's Way,** a 95-km walking path along the Norfolk Coast.

Cambridge

Even the most jaded high-school dropout won't be able to resist the lure of the stone walls, massive libraries, and robed fellows that Cambridge serves up unblinkingly. Known more for its background in the sciences than the arts (although the register of literary alumni includes Lord Byron and Virginia Woolf, among many others), Cambridge just keeps cranking out the world's greatest scientists, from Isaac Newton to Stephen Hawking. The university shares an endless (and tiresome) antagonistic tradition with Oxford University, but the town still has plenty of life left: Modern-day, progressive-thinking students swarm the streets with their three-speed Pee Wee Herman bikes; tourists swarm the tea shops; sunbathers pack the banks of the River Cam; and occasionally some studying gets done.

BASICS **Visitor Center.** The staff leads guided walking tours daily. *Wheeler St., behind Guildhall, tel. 01223/322640. Open Mon., Tues., Thurs., Fri. 9–6; Wed. 9:30–6; Sat. 9–5; Sun. 10:30–3:30.*

American Express. *25 Sidney St., tel. 01223/351636. Open Mon., Tues., Thurs., Fri. 9–5:30; Wed. 9:30–5:30; Sat. 9–5.*

COMING AND GOING The **train station** (Station St., tel. 01223/311999) is a 30-minute walk from the city center—walk down Station Road, turn right onto Hills Road, and continue straight; or you can grab a Cityrail Link bus at the station. Trains leave hourly for London (£16 round-trip). The **bus station** (tel. 01223/355554) is at the end of Drummer Street. Buses to London are £8.50 round-trip. Buy tickets on board; the driver often gives special fares the station's office doesn't list.

WHERE TO SLEEP A slew of B&Bs and the youth hostel are about three blocks from the train station; walk down Station Road, hang the first right on Tenison Avenue, and continue for a block or two. For a £3 fee, the tourist office can also book you a room.

Aaron Guest House. Lovely setting facing the park and river, with the atmosphere of an English country house. Doubles £35, four person rooms £42–£46. *71 Chesterton Rd., tel. 01223/314723. Bus 5 or 3 from train station.*

Carpenter's Arms Backpackers' Accommodations. Low cost and color TV in each room make this a popular place, but the 14 dorm-style beds (£10 per person) fill up fast. *182–186 Victoria Rd., tel. 01223/351814. From bus station, walk down Emmanuel St. to St. Andrews St., make a right and persevere through the city to Victoria Rd.*

Tenison Towers. The best Cambridge B&B, within easy walking distance of the train station. Spankin' clean, affordable, and bright yellow. Doubles £28, four-person rooms £44. *148 Tenison Rd., tel. 01223/566511.*

➤ **HOSTEL** • **Cambridge HI.** Surprisingly convenient, three blocks from the train station, with clean beds, powerful showers, and an international crowd. Book ahead. Beds £12 (£8.80 under 18). *97 Tenison Rd., tel. 01223/354601.*

➤ **CAMPGROUND** • **Toad Acre Caravan Park.** Well-equipped and bordered by apple trees. Sites £4–£5.50 per person. *Mills La., tel. 01954/780939. Bus 155 or 157 from Cambridge (1 per hr) to Longstanton.*

FOOD If you're in a rush, the pedestrian zone has plenty of small, greasy stands and take-away restaurants hidden in tiny passageways such as Rose Crescent. Every day but Sunday head to the open-air **market** in the middle of town on Market Hill (not really a hill), featuring a good selection of fruits and vegetables. **Peppercorns** (48 Hills Rd., tel. 01223/69583; closed Sun.) is Cambridge's perfect picnic supplier, serving big fat sandwiches for £1. Over-looking Downing College, **Tattie's** (26-28 Regent St., tel. 01223/358478; closed Sun.) serves baked potatoes (£3) with a variety of funky toppings. **Brown's** (23 Trumpington St., tel. 01223/461655) is a slightly more upscale place (with glass-enclosed patio) with specials like steak and mushroom pie (£7). A terrific basement vegetarian restaurant with only 10 tables, **King's Pantry** (9 King's Parade, tel. 01223/321551) serves a three-course lunch with soup, main course, and dessert for £9 (£6 students).

WORTH SEEING Cambridge University has no exact center but is based in the many residential colleges scattered around the town. The granddaddy of all colleges is **Peterhouse,** with some structures dating from the 13th century, when a disgruntled monk from Oxford's Merton College decided to begin a little school of his own. King Henry VI founded **King's College** in 1441 and five years later began constructing its greatest monument, **King's College**

Chapel (tel. 01223/350411). Completed in 1536, the 289-foot-long Gothic structure features the world's longest expanse of fan-vaulted ceiling (the spiderweb style branches supporting the arches). Rubens's *Adoration of the Magi* hangs behind the altar, and on Christmas Eve a festival of carols performed in the chapel is broadcast worldwide.

Trinity College, the largest and richest of Cambridge's colleges, counts among its graduates Lord Byron and Isaac Newton. The impressive **library** (tel. 01223/338488; closed Sun.), designed entirely by Christopher Wren down to the bookshelves and reading desks, contains an astonishing display of valuable books. Other colleges worth a long visit include **St. John's, Emmanuel, Magdalene,** and **Christ's**; the list is hard to whittle down. The grounds of most colleges close during final exams, from the fourth week of May until mid-June.

The rivalry between Oxford and Cambridge manifests itself most strongly at two annual sporting events: The Boat Race, where each university's rowing eights race down the Thames near Putney, and the rugby match, played before a sellout crowd at Twickenham in London.

The **Fitzwilliam Museum** (Trumpington St., tel. 01223/332900; admission free; closed Mon.) houses a decent permanent collection of art—paintings and prints from the Renaissance (Leonardo da Vinci included) through impressionism. **The University Botanic Garden** (Bateman St., tel. 01223/336265; admission £1, free Wed.) is the perfect place to kill time while waiting for a train; among its many delights are a glass igloo and flowers, flowers, flowers.

AFTER DARK The **Anchor** (Silver St., tel. 01223/353554) is a haven for international students, with an outdoor deck right on the River Cam and jazz on Tuesday nights. Smoky and run-down, **The Burleigh Arms** (9–11 New Market Rd., tel. 01223/316881) is the one full-time gay bar in Cambridge. The crowd is mostly—but not exclusively—male. **Clown's** (52 King St., tel. 01223/355711) is a smoky coffee bar with powerful espressos. Great rock bands come through Cambridge regularly. Look for flyers or pick up the *Varsity* to see who's playing. **The Junction** (Clifton Rd., near the train station, tel. 01223/412600) is a music fan's version of one-stop shopping—it's a dance floor, jazz joint, and rock club in one building.

NEAR CAMBRIDGE

NORWICH The wool and weaving trade once supplied Norwich's wealth, and local merchants built so many churches (30, to be exact) that subsequent city planners have allowed businesses to take them over instead of knocking them down—look for the latest camping equipment displayed in a church window. Norwich is also home to a more politically and culturally progressive populace than the rest of England, thanks to a large Green movement and the nearby University of East Anglia. Construction on remarkably tall **Norwich Cathedral** (tel. 01603/764383) began in 1096; it remains one of England's great cathedrals. **Norwich Castle** (Castle Meadows, tel. 01603/223624; admission £1.80) dates back to the 12th century and witnessed some gruesome torture in its prison and dungeon. The **tourist office** (tel. 01603/666071) is in the marketplace in the center of town.

➤ **COMING AND GOING** • Norwich's **train station** (Thorpe Rd., tel. 01603/632055) serves as a major hub for the East Anglia region but is inconveniently located a bit out of town. Trains to Cambridge cost £12.50 round-trip. The **Surrey Street Bus Station** (Surrey St., tel. 01603/660551) is much closer to the center.

➤ **WHERE TO SLEEP AND EAT** • The **HI Norwich Youth Hostel** (112 Turner Rd., tel. 01603/627647; beds £6–£8) is inconveniently out of walking distance from town; before 6:30 PM take Bus 19 or 20, after 6:30 take Bus 37 or 38. The clean, cheap, women-only **YWCA** (61 Bethel St., tel. 01603/625982; doubles £8) and the nearby, coed **YMCA** (48 St. Giles St., tel. 01603/620269; dorm bed £8.50, doubles £25) are extremely well located in the center of town. **The Treehouse** (14 Dove St., tel. 01603/763258), a co-op vegetarian restaurant, changes its menu daily and has flyers on town happenings.

The Heart of England

The Heart of England is a swath of agricul-tural central England featuring more popular sights than any area beside London. Its accessibility from London makes it easy to visit on a short tour of England, and while that means it's crowded with tour buses and tea shops, there's still plenty of reasons to go. Right in the middle of the area is **Birmingham,** England's second-largest city and a big transportation hub. Most visitors skip the town, but it's not a bad place to get stuck for a day. Despite being the birthplace of William Shakespeare, **Stratford-upon-Avon** is hardly worth the effort. Aim instead for **Oxford.**

Oxford

Home of the first English-language university in the world, the city of Oxford once was just a place where cattle herders led their flocks over the shallow waters at the wide junction of the Thames and Cherwell rivers. Oxford is not nearly as small and idyllic as Cambridge—heavy industry on the outskirts sometimes gives the town a dreary pallor. As in Cambridge, Oxford has a history of "town vs. gown" tensions between the city and the university, although most of the hostility seems buried beneath the town's studious veneer.

The congested center of Oxford is known as Carfax, where many roads meet, student masses congregate, and bikes and buses battle for space.

BASICS Don't expect much help from the presumptuous **tourist office** (St. Aldate's St., tel. 01865/726871). Just steps away is a friendlier branch of **American Express** (99 St. Aldate's St., tel. 01865/790099; closed Sun.). **STA Travel** (36 George St., tel. 01856/792800) sells ISIC cards and plane and bus tickets.

COMING AND GOING Direct BritRail service to **Oxford Train Station** (Botley Rd., tel. 01865/722333) from London's Paddington Station costs £8.25 round-trip. Oxford's **bus station** (Gloucester Green, tel. 01865/711312) is connected frequently to London's Victoria Coach Station (round-trips £7, £5.50 students).

WHERE TO SLEEP Heaps of B&Bs are within a short bus ride of the train station along Iffley, Woodstock, and Cowley roads. Prices skyrocket from early May to late June, thanks to the Mummies and Daddies flooding in at the end of term.

Brenal Guest House. Well-lit, well-kept rooms with firm beds. The huge breakfasts will keep you full until dinner. Doubles £30–£36. *307 Iffley Rd., tel. 01865/721561. From Carfax, take Bus 3 or 42 toward Rose Hill and alight at Addison Crescent.*

Woodstock Guest House. Carefully preserved Victorian house near central Oxford. Singles £25, doubles £40. *103–105 Woodstock Rd., tel. 01865/52579. From Carfax, walk up St. Giles Rd., veer left on Woodstock Rd.*

➤ **HOSTEL • HI Oxford.** Large, fun hostel on a quiet street away from the city center. Often crowded—try to reserve a few days ahead. It doesn't get any cheaper in Oxford: beds £8.70, slightly higher June–August. *32 Jack Straws La., tel. 01865/62997. Bus 73 to John Radcliffe Hospital; walk up Staunton Rd. Closed end of Dec.–Jan.*

FOOD Kebab vans—providing the cheapest meals in Oxford—stake out their territory in Carfax, charging £3 or less. Hidden on a little side street inside the Museum of Modern Art, **Café MOMA** (30 Pembroke St., tel. 01865/722733; closed Sun. and Mon.) serves quiche and soup (each £1.50) and *strong* coffee. Across from the bus station, **Harvey's** (89 Gloucester Green, tel. 01865/793693; closed Sun.) serves all kinds of sandwiches—try the ham, mozzarella, and pesto sandwich for £2.60—to go. **Café CoCo** (23 Cowley Rd., tel. 01865/200232) is worth visiting for its interior design and worth staying in to sample a pizza; try the no-cheese Mediterranean (£4.60).

WORTH SEEING The 29 undergraduate colleges, six graduate colleges, five permanent halls, and All Souls College that make up the university are scattered around town. Many colleges charge a small admission fee to roaming visitors—how annoying. **Oxford Student Tours,** run by students, gives insights into the university for £2.50 (£2 students). Tours leave daily from the tourist office.

A handful of literary big shots (including Lewis Carroll and John Locke) did time at **Christ Church College,** which has an 800-year-old chapel (admission £2.50, £1 students)—one of the smallest, most ornate cathedrals in the country. Pretty **Magdalen** (pronounced "maudlin") **College** opened its doors to undergrads in 1458 and signals the beginning of spring every May 1 at 6 AM with a college choir performing at the top of **Magdalen Tower** (admission £1.50, 50p students). As the first college built after the bloody St. Scholastica's Day Riot in AD 1215, **New College** (full name: St. Mary College of Winchester in Oxenford) incorporated new design features—such as the first enclosed quad—to protect gownies in the event of another riot. **University College** is best known for expelling Percy Bysshe Shelley after he wrote *The Necessity of Atheism.*

During orientation, Oxford students are issued a phonebook-size code of conduct, featuring some arcane—and bizarre—rules. For instance, if students come to an exam in a flawless suit of armor on a white horse, they automatically pass.

The Ashmolean Museum of Art and Archaeology (Beaumont St., tel. 01865/278000; admission free; closed Mon.), Britain's oldest public museum, boasts masterworks ranging from drawings by Michelangelo to Bronze Age weapons to the death mask of Oliver Cromwell. The **Museum of the History of Science** (Broad St., tel. 01865/277239; admission free; closed weekends) has artifacts like Einstein's blackboard. The **Pitt Rivers and University museums** (Parks Rd., tel. 01865/272950; closed Mon.), one of the greatest natural-history complexes in the world, share a building 20 minutes north of the town center. The best exhibits are of bugs—live bees in one case, African beetles in another, rare butterflies in a another, and so on. Musicians shouldn't miss the adjacent **Balfour Building** (60 Banbury Rd.), where old musical instruments and original sheet music are on display.

Punting—propelling a flat, long boat with a giant, metal-tipped stick—is one of the great Oxford experiences. Just head down to the river to hire one: Boats cost £6–£7 per hour (plus deposit) at Folly and Magdalen bridges.

AFTER DARK *What's On In Oxford,* available at the tourist office, is an invaluable free guide to clubbing in Oxford. The **Old Fire Station** (Gloucester Green, tel. 01865/794494) is an arts center with a restaurant, theater, bar, and art museum. The biggest "activity" pub in Oxford, **The Head of the River** (St. Aldate's St., tel. 01865/721600) has barbecues, snooker playoffs, mechanical bucking bronco contests, and even bungee-jumping on summer Saturday nights. Tiny, low-ceilinged **Turf Tavern and Gardens** (Bath Pl., tel. 01865/243235) is one of England's coziest pubs, serving appropriately named Headbanger cider.

Stratford-upon-Avon

William Shakespeare was born and died here—so what? The real question is whether you want to spend time in a town that has no cafés, no movie theaters, and nothing to do at night other than see a (usually sold-out) play. Inevitably, people who care deeply about Shakespeare's work will be disappointed by the commercialization going on in the Bard's name. Apart from a few Elizabethan buildings in the historic center, the town has been developed in modern style, with brand-name stores all over; even the Shakespeare sights have been reconstructed and restored repeatedly. The best thing about Stratford is the Royal Shakespeare Company stages, but you can easily catch a production in London or a number of other major British cities.

BASICS The standard-grade **American Express** (Bridgefoot, tel. 01789/415856) shares an office with the overcrowded **tourist office** (tel. 01789/293127). Head instead to the helpful headquarters of **Guide Friday** (4 Rother St., tel. 01789/294466), an office for a local bus-tour company that carries much of the same info and has shorter lines.

COMING AND GOING Stratford is easily accessible by public transportation—buses and trains come regularly from Birmingham, London, and most other major cities. To reach Stratford's **rail station** (Alcester Rd., tel. 01789/204444 or 01203/555211) from London's Paddington Station (£24 round-trip), take the train north to Royal Leamington Spa and change to the Stratford line. Buses leave from the corner of Guild Street and Warwick Road; buy tickets on board. Buses to London (£13 round-trip) leave throughout the day.

WHERE TO SLEEP Since nearly every tourist over the age of 40 is hypnotically drawn to Stratford, the town has no shortage of B&Bs; the hard part is finding cheap ones. Concentrated pockets of B&Bs are on Grove Road and Evesham Road, near the train station, and on Shipston Road, across the river from the center of town. **The Glenavon** (6 Chestnut Walk, tel. 01789/292588) has small rooms (doubles £30) convenient to the train station. The **HI Youth Hostel** (tel. 01789/297093; beds £8.40–£11.50) is about 3 km outside Stratford in the village of Alveston; from Stratford, catch Bus 18 at 37 Wood Street. Clean rooms and especially helpful management make this one of the best hostels in England. **Elms Camp** (Tiddington Rd., tel. 01789/292312; £2.50 per person; closed Dec.–Mar.) is cheap and close to town; catch Bus 18 to Tiddington.

FOOD Pretty much the only cheap meals in Stratford are at pubs and greasy fast-food stands. A noteworthy exception is **Café Natural** (Greenhill St., tel. 01789/415741; closed Sun.), a vegetarian restaurant with simple dishes like quiche (£3.15) and stuffed potatoes (£1.10) for lunch. **The Vintner Café and Wine Bar** (5 Sheep St., tel. 01789/297259) is one of the few cool hangouts in town; chow on lasagna (£5) and the vegetarian dish of the day (£5.25).

WORTH SEEING Be prepared for oxygen deprivation at these phenomenally crowded shrines to the immortal Shakespeare. Also know that you can buy an **all-inclusive ticket** (£7.50) to the major sights listed below from the tourist office or from any of the sights themselves. Shuffle through **Shakespeare's Birthplace** (Henley St., tel. 01789/204016; admission £2.50), heavily restored from its original state and displaying Bard-related paraphernalia. Adjacent to the house is the **Shakespeare Centre** (Henley St., tel. 01789/204016), with an exhibit of costumes used in BBC productions of Shakespeare's plays. Shakespeare kicked the bucket at **Nash's House** (Chapel St., tel. 01789/292325; admission £1.70) in 1616 at the age of 52. The museum within depicts Stratford life in the 16th and 17th centuries, but the adjacent garden is much more interesting. One of the least-visited sights on the Shakespeare trail, **Hall's Croft** (Old Town, tel. 01789/292107; admission £1.70) was the home of Shakespeare's daughter, Susanna, and her husband, Dr. John Hall. Of the 17th-century antiques on display, Dr. Hall's medical instruments are the coolest. **Mary Arden's House** (tel. 01789/293455; admission £3), outside Stratford in the burg of Wilmcote, is said to be the home of Shakespeare's mother, although it's probably not authentic. Preferable is the delightful 15-minute walk from Stratford to **Anne Hathaway's Cottage** (tel. 01789/292100; admission £2.10) in Shottery. The home of Shakespeare's wife (pre-marriage, of course) today hosts a fine collection of Tudor furniture.

AFTER DARK The **Royal Shakespeare Company** (Southern La., tel. 01789/295623) holds performances on its two main stages Monday–Saturday at 7:30 PM, with additional matinees on Thursday and Saturday at 1:30 PM; in any given week, about five or six different plays—not all of which are by Shakespeare—are performed. If you don't mind standing during a performance, you can buy tickets for as little as £5; balcony seats are £6–£8 and day-of-performance standby tickets are £8–£10. **Tours** of both theaters (admission £3.50, £2.50 students) are conducted Monday–Wednesday and Friday at 1:30 and 5:30, Sundays at 12:30, 1:30, 2:30, and 3:30.

Birmingham

How is it that Birmingham is the second-largest city in England yet doesn't even rank in the top 10 in visitors? While the sights aren't jaw-droppingly amazing, the nightlife is swingin' enough for at least a week of loaded nights, the bus system is extensive and efficient, and the two universities keep the cultural scene sharp. So while Birmingham is not exactly visitor-friendly, it has adapted beyond its original mission as the epicenter of England's industrial production. The downtown area around the convention center has been redeveloped into a pedestrians-only area. Unfortunately, many wonderful Victorian buildings in the downtown area were knocked down in the '50s and '60s. A few treasures of the time remain, like the fabulous Victoria Law Courts, but much of the city is dominated by blocky buildings.

BASICS The **main tourist office** (City Arcade, tel. 0121/643–2514; open Mon.–Sat. 9–5:30) is about 50 meters from the AmEx office right near New Street Station. Stop in for concert and theater tickets, and to book a room. A second **tourist office** (Central Library, Chamberlain Sq., tel. 0121/236–4622; open weekdays 9–8, Sat. 9–5) sells theater tickets but does not book rooms.

American Express. *Martineau Sq., off Union St. near Corporation St., tel. 0121/233–2141. Open weekdays 8:30–5:30, Sat. 9–5.*

COMING AND GOING Getting in and out of Birmingham is simple; the main rail station is in the center of town, and the coach station isn't far away. Although there are three rail stations, **New Street Station** is the biggest and most useful. That said, some InterCity trains do come into **Moor Street Station**; the two stations are close together and signs are posted everywhere to guide you between them. The **Snow Hill Station** near St. Philip's Cathedral is the station you need if you're heading to Stratford-upon-Avon. Call 0121/643–2711 for train information. The **Digbeth Coach Station** (tel. 0121/643–5611) is a few blocks away from the New Street Rail Station via Bull Ring and Digbeth roads. National Express coach service runs often to London (£13) and Manchester (£12).

WHERE TO SLEEP Look for the hideous, bright-blue BUDGET ACCOMMODATION sign in front of **Edgbaston Hotel** (323 Hagley Rd., Edgbaston, tel. 0121/455–9606), a bit tacky and noisy but reasonable. Doubles are £28 (£38 with bath). **Woodville House** (39 Portland Rd., Edgbaston, tel. 0121/454–0274) is probably the best B&B in town and is just a short trek from the city center via Bus 128 or 129. Rooms cost £12.50 for students, £15 for adults.

➤ **HOSTEL • Birmingham HI.** Open only from the first week of July through the second week of September. Convenient to happenin' night spots and the town's main bus and rail stations. Beds £9 per person. *Cambrian Halls, Brindley Dr., off Cambridge St., tel. 0121/233–3044. Bus 3, 10, 21, 22, 23, or 29 from the rail or coach stations. 11 PM curfew, lockout 10–5, kitchen, laundry.*

➤ **STUDENT HOUSING • Maple Bank Holiday Flats.** Single-sex residence halls for the low price of £5.70 per person. Each apartment has a kitchen, sitting room, and four bedrooms. *The Estate Office, Maple Bank, Church Rd., Edgbaston B15 3SZ, tel. 0121/454–6022. Bus 1 from New St. Station. Reservations required. Open mid-July–mid-Sept.*

FOOD Birmingham is known for its cheap Balti—an Indian specialty of pan-fried vegetables cooked in curry—restaurants on Stoney Lane and Lady Pool Road in Sparkbrook, just southeast of the city center (take Bus 12 from the city center).

Fatboy's Diner. A 1950s neon diner that stays open late (but not 24 hrs) and does its best to imitate its American models. Gorge on burgers (£5), dogs (£3.25), and soda (£1.25). *66 Broad St., tel. 0121/633–0464. Open daily noon–midnight.*

King Balti's. First-rate Balti specials plus the largest nan bread you've ever seen. Full meals from £5. *230 Ladypool Rd., tel. 0121/449–1170. Open daily 5–10.*

The Warehouse Cafe. A completely vegan restaurant with cheap meals like sweet-potato salad (£3) and black-eyed bean and mushroom curry (£3). On the second floor of Friends of the Earth building. *54 Allison St., Digbeth, tel. 0121/633–0261. Open Mon.–Thurs. noon–7, Fri. and Sat. noon–9.*

WORTH SEEING In addition to visiting the places below, you could spend a couple of worthwhile hours browsing the enormous **Birmingham Museum and Art Gallery** (Chamberlain Sq., tel. 0121/235–2834), which houses an eclectic collection of insects, sarcophagi, and watercolors. Take a break in the museum's smartly decorated **Edwardian Tea Room.**

Barber Institute of Fine Arts. The University of Birmingham's Barber Institute may be the finest small art museum in England. The gallery includes works by canonical artists like Rembrandt, Hals, and Bellini, but the real strength is the 19th- and 20th-century collection. *University of Birmingham, off Edgbaston Park Rd., near the university's East Gate, tel. 0121/472–0962. Bus 61, 62, or 63 from the city center, get off at Edgbaston Park Rd., cross the street, and walk up the small hill toward the university. Admission free. Open Mon.–Sat. 10–5, Sun. 2–5.*

Cadbury World. This shrine to chocolate about 6 km south of Birmingham tells the story of chocolate's origins (the Aztecs liked to drink it) before moving through the factory, where visitors must don paper hats while viewing the chocolatiers at work. More interesting than the factory tour is the town of **Bournville,** a community created especially for Cadbury workers in the late 1870s. *Linden Rd., Bournville, tel. 0121/451–4180. Take train from New St. Station to the Bournville Station (a 10-min ride) and follow signs. Admission: £4.75. Open Tues.–Sat. 10–5:30, Sun. noon–6, shorter hrs off-season.*

Victoria Law Courts. If you want to see the English legal system in action and don't mind being frisked, waltz right into the Victoria Law Courts and sit in on some hearings. Just about every type of local criminal—from car-jackers to murderers—passes through the 25 courts on any given day. *Corporation St., tel. 0121/236–9751. From New St. Station, turn right on New St., left on Corporation St., continue past Old Sq., and look for it on the left. Admission free. Open weekdays 8–6.*

AFTER DARK For an abbreviated but useful roundup of the town's cultural calendar, pick up the small brochure called "Birmingham What's On Where" at the tourist office. Hipper, more underground papers can provide the latest alternative hangouts; look for *City X* (free) around town. If you're looking for good live theater, the **Crescent Theatre** (Cumberland St., off Broad St., tel. 0121/643–5858; tickets £4–£5) performs an intriguing selection of plays. If you enjoy fine music, Birmingham is the home of Simon Rattle and the **City of Birmingham Symphony Orchestra.** The Convention Centre has plenty of concerts, but availability of tickets depends on the event, and the price for seats can run as high as £20. Call 01839/222888 for ticket info.

Bobby Brown's The Club (52 Gas St., off Broad St. across from the convention center, tel. 0121/643–2573; cover £1–£5) is one of those rare places that look tiny but are actually huge: The building is a wildly expansive converted warehouse with tons of intimate nooks and crannies. **Ronnie Scott's** (Broad St., across from the convention center, tel. 0121/643–4525), an offshoot of the pioneering London jazz club of the same name, hosts outstanding jazz performers every night but Sunday. **The Hummingbird** (Dale End, tel. 0121/236–4236) usually has live reggae and soul.

The North

Londoners consider the North anything just beyond the city limits, but most English define the region as beginning just above the Midlands. The area contains the sprawling cities of the industrial Northwest; the bountiful walking and hiking paths of Yorkshire; the wending pastoral landscape of the Lake District; and coal-mining Northumbria near the Scottish border. BritRail's main London–Edinburgh line runs through towns like York and Durham but skips the Lakelands and the northwest, although they're easily accessible on other rail lines.

Manchester

Despite giving the world Morrissey and Ian Curtis, Manchester is not the world's most depressing place. Sure it can be dirty and grimy, but it's also as ethnically diverse as any city in Britain, has one of the largest gay and lesbian communities in the country, and fosters an overpowering music scene. The students at Manchester University—the largest university in Europe—play a large part in Manchester's social scene and contribute to the city's progressive image. That image dates back a long way: England's suffragette movement was born here, as were Britain's first labor unions, not to mention the world's first computer.

Despite its aesthetic shortcomings, Manchester does have many worthwhile neighborhoods within easy reach of the city center. Right along Charlotte Street near Chorlton Bus Station is Chinatown, an honest-to-goodness Chinese neighborhood with busy markets and restaurants. Behind the bus station is Manchester's Gay Village, the largest gay-and-lesbian hangout north of London. Down Oxford Road past the university is Rusholme, a large Indian community; farther southwest is Hulme, home to a large Afro-Caribbean community.

BASICS Manchester's less-than-helpful **tourist office** (Lloyd St., tel. 0161/234–3157) is just off Albert Square near the town hall; from Victoria Station, walk south on Blackfriars Street, cross the River Irwell, keep straight on St. Mary's Gate, and turn right on Cross Street; the office is ½ km dead ahead. Along the way you'll also pass **American Express** (10–12 St. Mary's Gate, tel. 0161/833–0121; closed Sun.). If you need a cheap air ticket or an ISIC card, stop by student-run **Campus Travel** (Univ. of Manchester, Oxford Rd., tel. 0161/274–3105; closed Sun.). Manchester is a big city, so consider buying *The Manchester A–Z Street Plan* (£1.25) at a local newsstand.

COMING AND GOING There are several train stations in town: the main one is **Piccadilly Station** (London Rd., tel. 0161/832–8353), serving London's Euston Station (£32 round-trip) and the south. Manchester's **Victoria Station** (New Bridge St., tel. 0161/832–8353) serves the north and west, including Liverpool (£6.60 round-trip). Bus 4 shuttles between the two stations every 10 minutes. National Express buses leave regularly from **Chorlton Street Coach Station** (Chorlton St., tel. 0161/2283881) for London (£21.50) and all other major cities.

WHERE TO SLEEP Manchester has no youth hostel, no affordable YMCA, and no campsites nearby; this is a problem of nearly catastrophic dimensions. The cheapest option, 5 km from town in Chorlton (via Bus 85), is the wonderful, pet-filled **Linnea Lodge Guest House** (27 Alness Rd., tel. 0161/226–7415), with £12 singles, £20 doubles. In the center of town, **Rembrandt** (33 Sackville St., tel. 0161/236–1311), a joint pub and B&B, has reasonable doubles (£25). In summer, the University of Manchester Residence Halls sometimes open cheap rooms (£6–£10); try calling **St. Gabriel's Hall** (tel. 0161/224–7061) or **Woolton Hall** (tel. 0161/224–7244) during school vacations.

FOOD If you're looking for some late-night grub, head to the Rusholme area (take any 40's bus) and hang out with the students at the take-out tandoori shops; try the dynamic **Tandoori Kitchen** (131–133 Wilmslow Rd., tel. 0161/224–2329). **Annie Kenney's Vegetarian Café** (60 Nelson St., tel. 0161/274–3525; closed weekends), named for one of England's leading sufragettes, has yummy vegetarian deals like quiche and salad (£2).

WORTH SEEING Most of Manchester's (usually free) museums are really quite good and lie within a mile of Manchester University along Oxford Road. The **City Art Galleries** (Mosley St., tel. 0161/236–5244) reflect Manchester's diversity: The galleries display a traditional collection of British art by Gainsborough alongside progressive multimedia exhibits by artists such as the late Derek Jarman. The **Manchester Jewish Museum** (190 Cheetham Hill Rd., tel. 0161/832–7353; admission £1, 50p students), housed in a converted Spanish and Portuguese synagogue dating from 1874, stresses the community's oral history and re-creates its rooms and schools. The **Pankhurst Centre** (60–62 Nelson St., tel. 0161/273–5673) celebrates the history of Manchester's suffrage movement in the home of two of its leaders, Sylvia and Christabel Pankhurst.

AFTER DARK Manchester's nightlife is endless. Grab a copy of *City Life* or pick up alternative local magazines at restaurants like the **Cornerhouse Cafe** (70 Oxford St. at Whitworth St., tel. 0161/228–2463), which also doubles as a great cinema with nonmainstream flicks. **The Lass O'Gowrie** microbrewery (36 Charles St., off Oxford Rd., tel. 0161/273–6932) has great beer and a mellow atmosphere. **The Hacienda** (13 Whitworth St. W, by Princess Pkwy., tel. 0161/236–5051) launched The Smiths, Joy Division, The Fall, and many major local bands.

NEAR MANCHESTER

SHREWSBURY Shrewsbury (pronounced "Shrose-bur-ee") is one of England's most important medieval cities, filled with 16th-century half-timbered houses, narrow passageways, odd street names (Milk Street, Fish Street), and a multitude of bridal shops (with the appropriate number of churches to match). Besides also having a wonderful local castle, Shrewsbury is the perfect stopover between Wales and Manchester or Liverpool. The River Severn cradles the city in a horseshoe shape, and many of the streets within the "island" are now reserved for pedestrians only. Unlike many other towns in central England, Shrewsbury has not yet been milked by industry; the town has always been wealthy, and its citizens keep things in beautiful shape.

A good way to experience the town's natural character is to walk the **Frankwell Riverside Trail,** which wraps around the town parallel with the river. Otherwise, spend some time in **Quarry Park,** a huge green expanse south of the city center; from the tourist center, turn left on Swan Hill, make a right on Murivance, and look for the big park on the left. When you've sniffed one flower too many, cross the Porthill Bridge and head to **The Boathouse Inn** (Porthill, tel. 01743/62965), a pub with a perfect beer garden right on the river. The town's main draw is **Shrewsbury Castle** (Castle Forgate, next to train station; admission £1.50), begun in the 11th century as a place from which the Normans could keep an eye on Wales. Don't miss **Laura's Tower,** which offers a tremendous 180° view of Shropshire; on a clear day, you can see Wales. For maps and the like, head to the **tourist office** (The Music Hall, The Square, tel. 01743/350761; open Mon.–Sat. 9:30–6:30, Sun. 10–4).

➢ **COMING AND GOING** • There's no direct service from London to Shrewsbury's **train station** (Castle Foregate, tel. 01743/364041); take the train from London Euston and change at Birmingham or Wolverhampton. Trains to Birmingham (£7.30 round-trip), Manchester (£6.80 round-trip), and Cardiff (£23 round-trip) run about once an hour all day.

➢ **WHERE TO SLEEP** • There is a string of B&Bs on Abbey Foregate, across the River Severn from the center of town (take the English Bridge east across the river). Make sure you look at the rooms before dishing out money because many rooms face super-noisy Abbey Foregate. In a pinch try the friendly **Berwyn House** (14 Holywell St., tel. 01743/354858; £12 per person). The local **youth hostel** is a short but worthwhile walk from town. The rooms in this converted Victorian are supremely comfy. Beds £5–£7.50. *Abbey Foregate, SY2 6LZ, tel. 01743/360179. Minibus 8 from the train station to the hostel (42p). Open Apr.–mid-Sept., daily; mid-Feb.–Mar. and mid-Sept.–Oct., Mon.–Sat.; Nov.–mid-Dec., Fri. and Sat.*

Liverpool

At first glance, Liverpool suffers from the same problems as every other industrial northern city: high unemployment, unsafe streets, and depressing modern architecture. Like the rest of the northwest, Liverpool reached its zenith in the 18th and 19th centuries when it became Britain's major port for products of the Industrial Revolution as well as for immigrants heading to the New World. In World War II, Liverpool suffered serious damage when the Germans bombed the city in an attempt to interrupt convoys ferrying material from the United States. Since then Liverpool has been struggling, with little to cheer about in recent years except their soccer club and those fabulous Beatles. Corny as it may sound, the humor of the people keeps Liverpool from becoming just another industrial casualty.

COMING AND GOING **Lime Street Station** (Lime St., tel. 0151/709–9696) sends trains to Manchester (£6.60 round-trip) and London's Euston Station (£32 round-trip). The **bus station** (Brownlow Hill, opposite the Adelphi Hotel, tel. 0151/709–6481) serves most destinations, including London (£21.50) and Manchester (£4.75).

WHERE TO SLEEP If you arrive late, your best bet is the row of reasonable B&Bs on Lord Nelson Street near the train station, although you should expect to spend at least £15 for a bed. The non-HI, rowdy **Embassie Youth Hostel** (1 Falkner Square, tel. 0151/707–1089; £7.50 per person) is cheap but *very* noisy. From Lime Street Station, turn left on Lime Street/Renshaw Street, veer left on Leece/Hardman/Myrtle streets, cross over Hope Street, turn right at the stoplights and right again at Falkner Square. The **YMCA** (56–60 Mount Pleasant, tel. 0151/709–9516) is depressing and stale but does have doubles for £21.50. Three doors up is the women-only **YWCA** (tel. 0151/709–7791), with beds for £10–£12 per night. To see about cheap **dorm rooms** in the summer, call the university accommodations office (tel. 0151/794–6444).

FOOD The Indian and Middle Eastern restaurants on Renshaw Street and the Chinese eateries in Chinatown (along Nelson St.) are your best bets for affordable meals. **Blue Berrys Brasserie** (cnr. of Parker St. and Church St., tel. 0151/709–4975) serves cheap, hearty vegetarian food to a mostly student crowd. **Everyman Bistro** (9–11 Hope St., tel. 0151/708–9545) may not have any windows, but this basement cafeteria below the Everyman Theater serves cheap, tasty meals from £4. **Quo Vadis** (80 Bold St., tel. 0151/708–6855) is a spiffy, upbeat Italian restaurant with dishes for less than £7.

WORTH SEEING The **Merseyside Welcome Centre** (Clayton Square Shopping Centre, tel. 0151/709–3631), near the train station, and **The Atlantic Pavilion** (tel. 0151/708–8854) along yuppified **Albert Dock** both sell maps (£1) that cover every conceivable Beatles site. Cheesy but fun **Ticket to Ride** tours (£5, 2 hrs) depart daily at 2:20 from Albert Dock and 2:30 from the Welcome Centre. Cheesy and less fun is the "interactive" **Beatles Story** (Albert Dock, tel. 0151/709–1963; admission £3.95, £2.50 students), which doesn't tell you much you didn't already know via cardboard cutouts and re-creations of haunts like the Cavern Club. Nearby on Albert Dock is the **Tate Gallery** (tel. 0151/709–0507), an extension of the famous museum that regularly borrows exhibits from the collection in London.

AFTER DARK Nightlife in Liverpool is a big deal. Call the **Student Entertainment Office** (tel. 0151/794–4143) or stop by the university on Mount Pleasant to hear about the latest student goings-on; the Student Union bulletin board also posts info. As for clubs, **The Baa Baa** (43–45 Fleet St., tel. 0151/707–0610) serves £1 bottles of beer Monday–Wednesday and until 8 Thursday–Saturday. Live funk-and-soul DJs keep the place packed. **The Academy** (Parr St., tel. 0151/709–7023; open Fri., Sat., and last Thurs. of the month 10–2) is for the mostly under-25 set and holds huge Saturday raves. Right next to Merseyrail's Central Station, the **Midland Pub** (tel. 0151/709–2090) and the neighboring **Central Pub** (Ranelagh St., tel. 0151/709–1218) are loud but low-key places to drink. **Rosie O'Gradys** (Wood St., tel. 0151/709–6395) has cobblestone floors and a full bar, plus Irish folk and blues that run into the wee hours.

CHESTER One of England's four great medieval cities, Chester is known for its Tudor buildings, with their black-timber beams and whitewashed exteriors. The city is built on the site of a 1st-century AD Roman fortress called Deva, but it owes much of its later prosperity to its setting on the banks of the River Dee. Chester was an important port from the 12th century through to the 17th century, when the Dee silted up and Liverpool usurped the city's position. Today, Chester makes a good stopover for travelers heading to Wales; it's also a ferry port for ships to Ireland.

Near the cathedral, the **Town Hall Tourist Information Centre** (Northgate St., tel. 01244/318356) has tons of info on Chester and nearby Wales. You can also get info at the **Chester Visitor Centre** (Vicars La., tel. 01244/351609). Chester's best attraction are its fully intact **city walls,** parts of which date back to Roman times. Only the northern half of the town's **Roman Amphitheater** (across from the Chester Visitor Centre) has been excavated, but archaeologists believe it's the largest of its type in Britain. **The Grosvenor Museum** (Grosvenor St., tel. 01244/321616) displays Chester's trove of Roman artifacts. Lining Watergate, Eastgate, and Northgate/Bridge streets are the town's famous medieval **Rows,** a two-tier row of shops. Construction began on **Chester Cathedral** (St. Werburgh St., tel. 01244/324756) in the 13th century and continued through the 19th century. The most interesting feature is probably the carvings in the 14th-century Baltic Oak choir stalls. Practically speaking, there's regular service to Chester's **train station** (Station Rd., tel. 01244/340170) from nearby Liverpool (£4.30 round-trip), and buses operate from Chester's **Delamere Street Bus Station** (Delamere St., tel. 01244/381515).

➤ **WHERE TO SLEEP** • The renovated **HI Chester Youth Hostel** (40 Hough Green, tel. 01244/680056; beds £7.80–£10.50; closed Dec.) is one of those "comfort-improved" hostels with lots of niceties; take Bus 7 or 16 from the Town Hall. The **Bridge Guest House** (18–20 Crewe St., tel. 01244/340438; doubles £26) is near the train station and has spanking-new rooms and facilities.

Peak District National Park

The Peak District, a hiker's paradise of rolling hills, brooding moors, and limestone cliffs, is England's most popular and accessible national park—all only one hour from Manchester. You won't find any "peaks"—the highest point is only 2,100 feet. However, you will find more than 6,500 km of beautiful walking trails. The northern portion is known as the **Dark Peak,** an area of rugged moors and looming escarpments. To the south, **White Peak** is a bucolic region of rolling hills, crumbling stone walls, and tiny villages sheltered in swales and valleys. To get a look at the difficulty and length of the hikes, buy the *Peak District Tourist Map* (£4.25) at tourist offices in the following villages: Bakewell (tel. 01629/813227), Castleton (tel. 01433/620679), Edale (tel. 01433/670207), and Fairholmes (tel. 01433/650953). The **Pennine Way,** all 450 km of it, starts in Edale and offers amazing views along largely uninhabited territory. There are 17 hostels along the trail between Edale and the trail's end in Kirk Yetholm, Scotland.

Besides wilderness, the Peaks District is also full of charming villages. You can buy self-guided tours (20p) of many such block-long outposts at local information centers. Among them, **Bakewell** is an appealing village on the banks of the River Wye and the best spot from which to explore the White Peak area of the park (many hiking trails begin here). Nearby **Chatsworth House** (tel. 01246/582204; admission £5; closed Nov.–Mar.), home to the duke and duchess of Devonshire, has a remarkable collection of paintings plus some spectacular gardens; take Bus 170 from Bakewell to Edensor village and walk the remaining 15 minutes to Chatsworth. **Buxton** also makes a good base; it's a wonderful mixture of a country village and a cultural center, with an opera house, plenty of pubs, and a gorgeous park called the Pavilion Gardens. **Castleton** and the nearby village of Edale are both excellent places from which to explore the northern Peaks. Castleton's main claim to fame is magnificent **Peveril Castle** (tel.

01433/620613; admission £1.20), founded in 1066 by one of William the Conqueror's knights.

COMING AND GOING Surrounded as it is by major cities, the Peak District is very accessible, especially by bus. The major entry towns to the Peaks are Bakewell and Matlock in the east, Ashbourne in the south, Buxton (on the London–Manchester train line) in the west, and Glossop in the north. For train info contact the **Manchester Travel Centre** (tel. 0161/228–7811). The most direct route into (and through) the Peaks is the **Trans-Peak Bus** (tel. 01298/23098), also known as the R1. It runs from Manchester through the Peaks (Buxton, Bakewell, Matlock, and other villages) to Nottingham.

WHERE TO SLEEP There are 19 youth hostels in the Peaks; many are on major walking trails and are easier to reach on foot than by public transportation. Almost every hostel charges £6 for members under 18 and £8 for members 18 and older. You must be a member to stay at hostels in the region—except the one in Crowden-in-Longdendale. Among the Peaks' hostels, here are some of the best: The super-quiet **Bakewell** (Fly Hill, tel. 01629/812313; closed Sun. and Nov.–Mar.); **Castleton** (Castleton Hall, tel. 01433/62023; closed mid-Dec.–Jan.), wonderfully located at the base of Peveril Castle; **Edale** (Rowland Cote, tel. 01433/670302; closed mid-Dec.–early Jan.); the primo, clean **Matlock** (40 Bank Rd., tel. 01629/582983; closed Dec. 24–Jan. 2); and **Buxton** (Harpur Hill Rd., tel. 01298/22287).

Lincoln

Lincoln is fraught with history—medieval monuments seem to tumble down the steep lanes leading to the River Witham, and everywhere are reminders of the Romans and the Danes, former inhabitants of this site. As you approach Lincoln by train, the first feature visible over the mounds of rusting scrap metal is imposing **Lincoln Cathedral** (Exchequer Gate, tel. 01522/544544) high atop Steep Hill. The massive, triple-tower Gothic structure is one of the most impressive in Europe. An earthquake in 1185 destroyed most of the original Norman building, but the 13th-century restoration is nothing to sneeze at. Stop by the cheeky 15-inch gargoyle perched on a pillar in the rear of the cathedral—no one, not even the priests, claims to know its origin. The sight of William the Conqueror's impenetrable **Lincoln Castle** (Castle Hill, tel. 01522/511068; admission £2, £1.20 students) next to the gargantuan cathedral informed ancient serfs who was boss. Just west of the castle lies the **Lawn** (tel. 01522/560306), a former lunatic asylum that now boasts a 5,000-square-foot greenhouse filled with tropical plants, an archaeological display, and a shopping center. Lincoln's **tourist office** (9 Castle Hill, tel. 01522/529828) has informative pamphlets on this A-1 town.

COMING AND GOING London's King's Cross Station sends trains regularly to Lincoln's **Central Station** (St. Mary's St., tel. 01302/340222); a round-trip ticket costs £31. Directly across the street is Lincoln's **bus station** (Melville St., tel. 01522/534444).

WHERE TO SLEEP Many B&Bs line West Parade, Carholme, and Yarborough roads. The **HI Lincoln Youth Hostel** (77 South Park, tel. 01522/522076) is a killer place right in the middle of town. Beds cost £5 (under 18) and £7.50 (18 and over). One bummer is that it's closed most Sundays and Mondays in spring and fall. To reach it from the train station, turn right out of the main entrance, then right again over Pelham Bridge; after the first roundabout turn right at South Park (not South Park Ave.). On the B&B front, the **Lincoln Lodge** (7 Carline Rd., tel. 01522/529726; £11–£13 per person) is on a quiet street just beyond the city center. Both English and veggie breakfasts are available, and the proprietors can arrange horseback treks.

FOOD Enormously popular **Brown's Pie Shop** (33 Steep Hill, tel. 01522/527330) has sweets and meat-filled savouries. **Broadgate Fish** (41 Broadgate, tel. 01522/524623) may be the best chippy in Lincoln, and the grease-spattered interior proudly proclaims that the food—fish-and-chips from £2—is not approved by any heart association. The grooviest pub in town is the **Cornhill Vaults** (The Cornhill Exchange, tel. 01522/535113), a Roman wine cellar that has been converted into an underground pub decorated with freakish caricatures of regular patrons.

York

York's capricious medieval streets, teeming with pubs and people, lead you everywhere you wanted to be but didn't know it—to a shop-lined cobblestone snickleway, a museum, or a post-card-perfect garden. York's museums display a vaunted stock of art, but it can be more fun just to wander the medieval streets or walk along the stone walls that surround the old town; the wall is 3 km around, but the views of the town and the brooding Yorkshire landscape make every step worthwhile. On a busy day, it may seem that York has a zillion visitors. But as heavily beaten paths go, York ranks with the best in Britain. Even if schlepping from one museum to another bores you, the pleasure of drinking a pint in a perfectly preserved 17th-century pub makes a visit to York worthwhile.

BASICS As well as the **main tourist office** (De Grey Rooms, Exhibition Sq., tel. 01904/621756), there is a perpetually crowded train-station branch (tel. 01904/643700) and an office next to the bus depot (6 Rougier St., tel. 01904/620557); all change money for a £2.50 commission. **American Express** (6 Stonegate, York YO1 2AS, tel. 01904/611727) works its magic in the center of town.

COMING AND GOING Trains run from **York Station** (tel. 01904/642155), just outside the city walls, to London's King's Cross about twice an hour (£45 round-trip). Buses converge on Rougier Street, between the train station and Lendal Bridge; buy tickets directly from the bus driver. Call **National Express** (tel. 01532/460011) for info; their buses to London are £31 round-trip.

WHERE TO SLEEP A B&B bonanza lines Bootham and its side streets just north of the city walls. If you don't book ahead, you may end up looking farther out in The Mount area, along Scarcroft and Southlands roads. **Maxwell's Hotel** (54 Walmgate, tel. 01904/624048) isn't beautiful, but it's smack in the city center, with dorm beds for £9, singles and doubles for £18 per person. Another good B&B is **Queen Anne's Guest House** (24 Queen Anne's Rd., tel. 01904/629389; £13 per person), a 10-minute walk from the Minster. On the camping front, **Post Office Camping Park** (Mill La., tel. 01904/706288; closed Nov.–Mar.), 6 km from town along the river, has reasonably quiet sites for £3.50 per person. Take a bus heading to Acaster Malbis from central York.

➤ **HOSTELS** • The **HI York Hostel** (Water End, tel. 01904/653147; closed Dec.), an easy 20-minute ride from the city on Bus 8 or 19, is one of England's best, although it's not cheap (beds £9–£12.40). The extra-friendly staff compensate for less-than-luxurious lodging at York's centrally located **Youth Hotel** (11–13 Bishophill Senior, tel. 01904/625904). Dorm beds are £8–£12 per person and private doubles are around £12 per person.

FOOD Serving vegetarian and vegan lunches (about £3), **Gillygate Wholefood Bakery and Cafe** (Miller's Yard, tel. 01904/610676; closed Sun.) is a great place to meet alternative lads and lasses. They also serve a fabulous dinner on Friday and Saturday nights—try the Moroccan couscous for £5. The "Get Stuffed" menu at **McMillans Cafe and Bar** (1 Rougier St., tel. 01904/625438) features obscenely huge portions of Yorkshire pudding (£2–£3).

WORTH SEEING If you're planning on seeing more than three sights, buy a £1 **York Visitor Card,** which gets you a discount at many attractions. If you're a kitsch hound, the **Jorvik Viking Centre** (Coppergate, tel. 01904/643211; admission £3.50) displays a few Viking artifacts but is really a tedious sight-and-sound odyssey into the past. In other words, save your money.

York Minster. Austere, imposing, and glorious, York Minster is the largest medieval cathedral in northern Europe. The exterior, crowned by Gothic spires and supported by amazing flying buttresses, makes the Minster famous, but the wealth of stained glass in the interior makes it wondrous. Don't miss the 15th-century **Great East Window,** the world's largest expanse of medieval stained glass. You can compare and contrast the constructions of Roman, Norman, and medieval engineers in **The Foundations** (admission £1.50), underneath the Minster: models and ruins show you the way it was in Ye Olde Days. The **central tower** (admission £1.50) offers tip-top views of York for those who don't mind the 200-plus stairs. Try to catch the choral evensong held weekdays at 5 PM, weekends at 4 PM. *Tel. 01904/624426. Admission to Minster free. Open Mon.–Sat. 10–dusk, Sun. 1–dusk.*

Clifford's Tower. This crumbling beauty is a fine place from which to appreciate the magnitude of the nearby Minster. In 1190, a group of York's merchants attempted to run the local Jewish population out of town, leading the Jews to hole up in the tower and commit group suicide rather than die at the hands of the mob. *Tower St., tel. 01904/646940. Admission £1.20, 90p students. Open daily 10–6, shorter hrs off-season.*

The Shambles. One of York's most picturesque streets, The Shambles once served as butchers' row, replete with open sewers. Today, its leaning homes and cobblestone streets brim with buskers, peddlers, and shoppers. Shops on the street are open Monday–Saturday 9–5. To get here from the Minster, follow Low Petergate down Colliergate.

➤ **MUSEUMS AND GALLERIES** • The **National Railway Museum** (Leeman Rd., tel. 01904/621261; admission £4, £2.60 students) traces 200 years of train history. The **York City Art Gallery** (Exhibition Sq., tel. 01904/623839; admission free) houses an undistinguished collection of paintings from the 14th to 18th centuries. The nearby **King's Manor Gallery** (Exhibition Sq., tel. 01904/433371; admission free) has an ever-changing display of experimental art and sculpture. Call for the latest exhibition info. The **Yorkshire Museum** (Museum St., tel. 01904/629745; admission £3, £1.75 students) contains local archaeological artifacts and 10 acres of botanical gardens.

AFTER DARK There's a scad of pubs around Stonegate, where the crowds in summer usually flow out onto the streets. Less publike is **Oscar's Wine Bar & Bistro** (8A Little Stonegate, tel. 01904/652002), where cheap beer and live jazz draw large crowds of students. York's oldest pub, **Ye Olde Starre Inn** (40 Stonegate, tel. 01904/623063), opened in 1644 and still rates well with locals. The **York Arms** (26 High Petergate, near York Minster, tel. 01904/62458) serves breakfast, lunch, and dinner to a mainly—but not exclusively—gay crowd and has an ideal location inside one of York's 18th-century coffeehouses.

NEAR YORK

NORTH YORK MOORS NATIONAL PARK About 45 km north of York, the North York Moors contain some of the most varied and dramatic landscape in England. Throughout the park are wind-worn plateaus cut by steep gorges, sloping valleys carved from stone by ancient lakes, and lots of hilly moors—an experienced walker's paradise. The less avid trekker may find the inevitable rain, fog, mist, and bogs a distinct drawback. The essential *North York Moors Tourist Map* shows all the park footpaths. "Waymark Walk" pamphlets (30p each) cover more than 40 trails that crisscross the park. The **Cleveland Way**, Britain's second-longest footpath, meanders for 174 km in a loop along the outskirts, but there are good walks from nearly every village within the park.

Pickering, right on the A169 (the main north–south highway through the moors) is a good base for exploring the park. Pickering's **tourist office** (Eastgate Car Park, tel. 01751/73791) has a heap of info on park walks. The dramatic cliffs above coastal **Whitby** offer an amazing backdrop to the town's narrow cobblestone streets. Sitting on a tall headland above Whitby's beach, **Whitby Abbey** (admission £1.30, £1 students) has a majestic silhouette. The stone three-tier choir and the north transept survive, brooding over the lively harbor and town. **St. Mary's Church,** a humble structure made frightening by the tilting gravestones in front, shares the cliff top.

➤ **COMING AND GOING** • Transportation from York to the North York Moors is fast and frequent by bus—don't even bother with trains. Pickering and Whitby are the best launching pads for trips into the moors, since bus connections to these towns are particularly good. The bus carrier **Yorkshire Coastliner** (tel. 01653/692556) runs from York to Pickering every hour; some continue to Whitby. The free *Moors Connection* bus schedule, available at Whitby's **tourist office** (Langborne Rd., tel. 01947/602674), is essential.

➤ **WHERE TO SLEEP** • **Pickering** has several cheap sleeps: **Bennett Guest House** (4 Westgate, tel. 01751/76776; £12.50 per person), **Ryecroft House** (87 Ruffa La., tel. 01751/73240; £10 per person), and **White Lodge** (54 Eastgate, tel. 01751/73897; £13.50 per person). In **Whitby**, rows of B&Bs line Belle Vue Terrace and Skinner Street; most cost £11–£15 per person and are within a 10-minute walk of the beach. Several campgrounds lie just outside of town. **Whitby Holiday Park** (Saltwick Bay, tel. 01947/602664) is on the Cleveland Way, about a mile south of Whitby near Whitby Abbey. If you're tired of roughing it, check into Whitby's **Montien Guest House** (3 Belle Vue Terr., tel. 01947/600413; £12 per person). Next to Whitby Abbey at the top of 199 steps, the **Whitby Youth Hostel** (East Cliff, tel. 01947/602878; beds £6.30) offers incredible views of the abbey and the town, although even during summer it's closed Sundays and Mondays.

The Lake District

Lying in England's northwest corner, Lake District National Park boasts some of the country's most beautiful scenery and most varied features—at least by English topographical standards. The area is divided into the heavily visited villages around **Lake Windermere** and **Coniston Water** in the south and the less-explored, open areas to the north. Maybe you'll get some artistic/philosophical inspiration from this pastoral land—heck, it worked for Wordsworth, Thomas De Quincey, John Ruskin, and Beatrix Potter, all of whom once lived in this then-undiscovered Eden. Modern-day philosophers and hikers should make for **Lancaster** or **Kendal** in the south or **Carlisle** in the north; these are the major points of entry to the Lake District. From here, it's easy to reach **Windermere**, a scenic but heavily touristed outpost, or one of a dozen smaller villages that serve as trailheads for a variety of hikes.

The larger tourist offices stock heaps of useful info, including *Lakeland by Bus* (a free comprehensive bus schedule) and the *A–Z Visitors Map of the Lake District* (£2.95). Campers can buy *The Caravan and Tent Guide* (95p) and should pick up the free leaflet listing the region's camping barns. Paul Buttle's *The 12 Best Walks in the Lake District* really does list the area's best walks and is a good buy at £2. There are about 30 (and growing) youth hostels scattered about—the Southern Lakes are particularly well-supplied. Reservations are always a good idea in summer and fall. In winter and spring, you'll be limited by sparse public transportation, closed tourist offices and hostels, and, of course, wet weather.

COMING AND GOING Trains from London's Euston Station; (£44 round-trip) and Manchester (£16 round-trip) arrive daily at Windermere, and a few continue on to Keswick, the main hub of the northern lakes. Trains also join Windermere with Kendal and Oxenholme; from the latter you can rejoin BritRail's InterCity network. Once you reach these towns, it's best to use buses to navigate the area. Local buses converge about 5 km north of Windermere in Ambleside, making Ambleside a good spot to base yourself. An **Explorer Ticket** (£5) buys a day of bus travel on all local lines and is *absolutely* worth the price if you're going to more than two towns. You can buy the pass on any bus. Make sure you get *Lakeland By Bus* (free), a comprehensive schedule of bus lines. **Mountain Goat Tours** (tel. 015394/45161), a private bus line, runs a service from York to Keswick, Grasmere, Ambleside, or Windermere (£24 round-trip, £16 students).

SOUTHERN LAKES

WINDERMERE AND BOWNESS Overcommercialized Windermere and nearby Bowness are best appreciated as stopovers to grab some food and equipment before moving on, although you may want to check out Bowness's **World of Beatrix Potter** (Crag Brow, tel. 015394/88444), an exhibit re-creating the furry characters and cuddly scenes of Beatrix Potter's *The Tale of Peter Rabbit*. Windermere's **tourist office** (Victoria St., tel. 015394/46499) has so much information that you'll definitely need the assistance of the excitable people behind the counter. The 5-km round-trip climb from Windermere's tourist office to **Orrest Head** is the simplest hike in the area and offers a fine panorama of the lake and villages along the shore.

➢ **WHERE TO SLEEP** • In Windermere, the **HI Windermere Hostel** (Bridge La., tel. 015394/43543; closed Nov.–Dec.) has gorgeous views, but the 60p bus ride (Bus 555 to Troutbeck Bridge) and the ½-km uphill walk are serious bummers. For a splurge, consider the B&Bs that line Beech, Birch, Oak, and Broad streets off Crescent Road. **The Haven** (Birch St., tel. 015394/44017) is near the train station and charges £13 per person. Nearby Bowness doesn't have a hostel, only a slew of semi-expensive B&Bs on Lake Road (the main road from Windermere).

AMBLESIDE Equally busy but less corrupted than Windermere, Ambleside makes an excellent base for touring the Southern Lakes. Most Lakeland buses make connections in Ambleside, and cheap accommodations abound; get the lowdown from Ambleside's helpful **tourist office** (Church St., tel. 015394/32582). Ambleside has some of the region's best hikes, and some surprisingly difficult ones considering that you're in England. The best are highlighted in the guide *Walks Around Ambleside* (£3), available at the tourist office. The 10-km circular walk from Ambleside north to **Loughrigg Tarn** goes right by Wordsworth's home in **Rydal.** Near Loughrigg Fell, you'll get a breathtaking 360° view of Lake Windermere, Rydal Water, and Ambleside. **The Langdale Pikes,** offering some incredible views from its high ridge, is accessed from Ambleside via steep paths through rocky crags. The loop stretches 8 km and ascends nearly 900 meters; the trailhead is at the New Dungeon Ghyll Hotel, on the B5343 (take Bus 516 from Ambleside to the hotel).

➢ **WHERE TO SLEEP** • Some cheap B&Bs surround Ambleside's tourist office at Church Street and Compston Road. Try **Shirland's** (Compston Rd., tel. 015394/32999), where beds are £9 and bed and breakfast goes for £12.50 per person. From the bus stop, go right on Kelsick Road and turn right on Compston Road.

Ambleside Youth Hostel. Packed with amenities that beat every other hostel in the Lakelands. From the King Street bus stops near the tourist information office, catch a hostel shuttle bus (every 20 min, 50p). *Waterhead, tel. 015394/32304. 11 PM curfew, lockout 10–5, reception open after 1 PM. Closed Wed. Sept.–Dec.*

Tarn Foot Farm. Pitch a tent for £1.50 on the outskirts of Ambleside. Cold-water taps and pit toilets. *Tel. 015394/32596. From Ambleside, take Bus 505 or 506 to Skelwith Bridge, walk up steep Oolstep Rd., turn right at main road and make first left.*

GRASMERE A ghost town in the winter, Grasmere changes into a hive of poetry students in summer. This is Wordsworthland, the Great Romantic's home from 1799 to 1808. Although the serenity and lushness of the area inspired some of Wordsworth's worthiest works, you won't be wandering lonely as a cloud through his former haunts. Join the crowds on pilgrimage to the **Dove Cottage and Wordsworth Museum** (tel. 015394/35544; admission £3.70), Wordsworth's homestead during his "Great Decade" of composition (1799–1808). **Rydal Mount** (tel. 015394/33002; admission £2), between Grasmere and Ambleside on the A591, was Wordsworth's home from 1813 through 1850 and is still privately owned by the Wordsworth family. Take Bus 555 from Grasmere and get off at Rydal Church. Unless you're staying at one of the town's two youth **hostels** (Butharlyp How, tel. 015394/35316; Thorney How, tel. 015394/35591), Grasmere makes a better day trip than overnight stay. Pick up info on hiking in the area from the **Grasmere National Park Information Centre** (Redbank Rd., tel. 015394/35245).

NORTHERN LAKES

The northern Lake District's largest town is **Keswick,** which also has the biggest and most convenient **information center** (Market Sq., tel. 017687/72645). For park-specific information, check out the **Keswick Discovery Centre** (31 Lake Rd., tel. 017687/72803; open Apr.–Oct.). If you don't like climbing, the long but easy hike from Keswick to **Seatoller** (14 km) along Derwentwater's east shore will reward you with a view of Borrowdale Valley, one of the most beautiful spots in the Lake District. Dreamlike settings of green glens, rivulets, and pastures make this a pleasant, peaceful stroll. The cheaper B&Bs in Keswick cluster around the corner of Southey and Blencathra streets. The mellow **HI Keswick Hostel** (Station Rd., tel. 017687/72484; closed Jan.–mid-Feb.) is your best bet, as long as you book ahead.

The highest peaks in England, **Scafell Pike, Scafell, Great Gable,** and **Green Gable** are climbers' delights that are best accessed best from **Seathwaite** (a short walk from the town of Seatoller, accessible on Bus 79). This largely volcanic area west of the major villages has a stark character that brings out serious hikers. **Ullswater** is the area's largest lake north of Lake Windermere and fortunately has yet to be destroyed by the crowds. Bus 108 connects the area's major villages. For directions to waterfalls in the area, pick up the handy *Walks to Lakeland Waterfalls* (50p).

Durham

Despite its long mining history and its location midway between the industrial cities of Darlington and Newcastle, Durham remains one of England's most arrestingly beautiful cities. Situated on a promontory created by an almost circular loop in the River Wear, the city has an idyllic quality. **Durham Cathedral** (Palace Green, tel. 0191/386–2367) is probably the finest piece of Norman architecture in Britain. The detailed, impressive exterior influenced many subsequent Gothic structures, and the cathedral's choir features the earliest use of rib vaulting in Western architecture. **Durham Castle** (Palace Green, tel. 0191/374–3800; admission £1.40), on the town's highest hill, served as the palace of Durham's prince-bishops for 800 years until around 1830, when it became University College of Durham. Hours are infrequent during the academic year. The **tourist office** (Market Pl., tel. 0191/384–3720) books rooms for a 10% deposit.

COMING AND GOING Durham's **train station** (North Rd., tel. 0191/232–6262) is on BritRail's main north–south line, three hours north of London (£56 round-trip) and two hours south of Edinburgh (£25.50 round-trip). Durham's **North Road Station** (North Rd., tel. 0191/384–3323) sends frequent buses to London (£25 round-trip) and Edinburgh (£21 round-trip).

WHERE TO SLEEP Most of the town's cheap B&Bs are on Claypath/Gilesgate and its side streets, a 10-minute walk northeast of the city center. The **Durham Youth Hostel** (Providence Row, tel. 0191/384–2217; open July–early Sept.) has beds for £6.30 (£4.20 under 18). The nearest year-round hostel is in Newcastle (*see below*). **Mrs. Mary Hill** (3 Mayorswell Close, tel. 0191/384–1112; £13.50 per person) runs an immaculate B&B within easy striking distance of the town center. Another cheap possibility is staying at the colleges that rent rooms during the summer break, from July to September. The tourist office can supply you with a free list of the colleges, which you must call yourself. If you can, try to score a spot in **University College** (tel. 0191/374–3863; £17 per person), which is actually housed within the medieval stones of Durham Castle.

➤ **CAMPGROUND** • **Grange Camping & Caravan.** Beautiful, quiet campground 3 km from town via Bus 220 from Durham's North Road Station (ask to be dropped at the Grange Pub). Tents £3 per person. *Meadow La., Carrville, tel. 0191/382–4778.*

FOOD You'll have no trouble finding a bakery on one of Durham's cobblestone streets; the town's pies, puddings, and pastries are excellent. Wash down a £3¹lasagna with a smooth cappuccino (90p) at the centrally located **Vennel's Courtyard Cafe** (Saddler's Yard, tel. 0191/386–0484). For first-rate pizza and pasta (meals from £4), try **Pizzeria Venezia** (4 Framwelgate Bridge, tel. 0191/384–6777), off North Road within a stone's throw of the bus station. After dark, hit the **The Swan** (Old Elvet Bridge, tel. 0191/384–0242), a student hangout near Market Square.

NEAR DURHAM

NEWCASTLE-UPON-TYNE There's nothing subtle about Newcastle, a lively industrial city of angry rock bands and fuck-you fashion statements. If you've been trying to decide what to do with your hair, Newcastle residents will offer you a wealth of wacky examples—let it go wild . . . shave it off . . . or dye it lime green. Oh, and if your really want to blend in, don't forget your Doc Martens. Newcastle's hard-working, hard-playing residents enjoy a varied nightlife, and the campuses of Newcastle Polytechnic and the University of Newcastle keep the city young—you can't miss the youth movement if you take a walk on the Quayside along the River Tyne. As the last big city before the Scottish border, Newcastle serves as the major transportation hub for the region and is a frequent stop on the Edinburgh–London rail line.

➤ **COMING AND GOING** • Trains to Durham, York, and London depart every 30 minutes from Newcastle's **Central Station** (Neville St., tel. 0191/232–6262), and trains to Edinburgh depart every hour. **National Express** runs to London and Edinburgh every two hours and to York twice a day.

➤ **WHERE TO SLEEP** • Defiantly sporting a '60s theme with square burnt-orange sofas and Formica tables is the **Newcastle Youth Hostel** (107 Jesmond Rd., tel. 0191/281–2570; beds £4.20–£6.30; closed Dec.–Jan.), conveniently located near the Jesmond metro stop. Newcastle's **YWCA** (Jesmond House, Clayton Rd., tel. 0191/281–1233; £14.20 per person) has a few rooms available in the summer.

➤ **AFTER DARK** • Every second building in the city center is a pub, or so it seems. **Luckies Corner Bar** (14 St. Mary's, tel. 0191/232–3893) is packed with students from the time the doors open until they close. Underground and indie folk will feel at home at the **Riverside** (57–59 Melbourne St., tel. 0191/261–4386).

HADRIAN'S WALL A 118-km-long fortification spanning England at its narrowest point, Hadrian's Wall is Britain's most important Roman monument. The emperor Hadrian began construction of the wall in AD 122 to help the Roman legions control the various warring tribes in the area. The ravages of time—as well as a series of wars between the English and Scots over the territory—have left the wall in a shambles. Nevertheless, sizable ruins of forts and long stretches of a reduced wall give a sense of its original magnitude. In its heyday, the wall stood 15 feet high and was 9 feet thick; a ditch about 30 feet wide and 10 feet deep lay in front of the wall.

Carlisle and **Hexham** are the two main points for exploring the wall. BritRail runs east–west between Carlisle and Newcastle, with trains stopping in Hexham, Bardon Mill, and Haltwhistle. The trip takes about an hour. Although the rail line runs parallel to the wall, you can't see much of it from the train. Another transportation option is Bus 685 (which runs closer to the wall) from Newcastle to Carlisle, stopping in Hexham, Bardon Mill, Haltwhistle, and Greenhead. For the most spectacular views of the wall, make the 4-km walk from **Steel Rigg** to **Housesteads Roman Fort,** beginning near the tiny village of Once Brewed (4 km northwest of Bardon Mills). BritRail and Bus 685 from Newcastle and Carlisle stop in Bardon Mill. From there, you have to either walk or take a cab to Once Brewed, which is only a 10-minute walk from the wall. The Once Brewed **hostel** (Military Rd., Bardon Mill, tel. 01434/344360; beds £7.40–£9.90; closed Dec.–Jan.) is characterless, but whaddya want fer nothing? Other accommodations include the **Acomb Youth Hostel** (Acomb, 3 km from Hexham, tel. 01434/602864; beds £3.40–£5.10), which is closed Monday March–June and September–October and open only on weekends November–February. From the Hexham Bus Station, catch Bus 880 to Acomb.

Wales

Most visitors flock to England or Scotland when traveling in Britain, ignoring Wales, one of the best off-the-beaten-track destinations in Europe. There's lots of undiscovered territory here, although the coastal resorts cram in crowds of British tourists and busy **Mt. Snowdon** is being loved to death. If you want more breathing room, pick your way among the moorland sheep droppings at **Brecon Beacons National Park** or enjoy the seascapes along the **Pembrokeshire**

Coast Path. In a country that still reveres Owain Glyndŷr, a revolutionary who fought to wrest Wales from English control, it's no surprise to find a strong sense of patriotism bordering on Anglophobia, especially in the north. South Wales, which has been industrialized and increasingly anglicized for the past few centuries, maintains Welsh traditions less staunchly, but no matter where you go in Wales, you'll find friendly people—and bilingual signs to remind you that this is *not* England.

BritRail basically covers only the top and bottom edges of Wales. From London, trains depart Paddington Station for Cardiff in the south and from Euston Station to Bangor and Holyhead in the north. Once you're in Wales, regional railways take over. The **Freedom of Wales Rover** ticket (£35) gives you a week of unlimited rail travel; buy them at BritRail travel centers. **National Express buses** (tel. 0171/730–0202) depart from London's Victoria Coach Station for several points in Wales. Once you arrive in Wales, you can hook up with one of the many regional bus services.

Cardiff

Despite its Welsh street signs, Cardiff feels like just another British town filled with modern buildings and souvenir shops. It was an important port for the iron and steel trade during the industrial revolution and has been the Welsh capital since 1955, but the city lacks the full urban bustle of Britain's other capital cities. It is not particularly quaint—journeys into the nearby countryside will bring you much closer to Welsh folklore.

BASICS Cardiff Central Station conveniently houses the town's **Tourist Information Center** (tel. 01222/227281). Very Near Cardiff Castle lies **American Express** (3 Queen St., tel. 01222/668858).

COMING AND GOING Hourly trains run to well-located **Cardiff Central Station** (tel. 01222/228000) from London's Paddington Station (£32 round-trip). The next-door **bus station** (Wood St., tel. 01222/344751) sends frequent buses to London's Victoria Coach Station (£24 round-trip). To see the sights just beyond the city center (like the Welsh Folk Museum), take orange-colored **Cardiff Buses (Bws Caerdydd)** from the stop outside the train station. Rides cost 52p weekdays 9:15 AM–3:45 PM and 65p all other times.

WHERE TO SLEEP AND EAT The best shot for an affordable B&B is along Cathedral Road; take Bus 32 or 62 from the train station. The private baths and a friendly atmosphere elevate the **Georgian Hotel** (179 Cathedral Rd., tel. 01222/232594) above the others; rooms are £15–£18 per person. The bargain rates make up for the dreary rooms at **Rosanna House** (175 Cathedral Rd., tel. 01222/229780; £11 per person). The **HI Cardiff Hostel** (Wedal Rd., tel. 01222/462303; closed Dec.) is fine but requires a 30-minute bus ride. Beds are £8.70 (£5.80 under 18). Take Bus 78, 80, or 82 from the train station. On the food front, many small eateries and stands line **St. Mary's** and **High** streets. The super-yummy **Celtic Cauldron** (47–48 Castle Arcade, tel. 01222/387185; closed Sun.) offers traditional Welsh lunches for less than £5. If you want to carbo-load for tomorrow's hike, head to **Bella Pasta** (6 High St., tel. 01222/399466), right near the castle. All-you-can-eat pasta is £2.95, pizzas around £5. There's a 20% student discount on Mondays and Tuesdays.

Speaking the Language of Cymru

The Welsh revere their native language, and while everyone speaks English, signs in "Cymru" (Wales) are in English and Welsh. You'll hear Welsh spoken on Radio Cymru and on televsion programs on Channel 4 Wales. Of all Welsh constructions—from "dydd" to "bws" to "fawr" and "ystr"—the most unfamiliar sound may be the "ll," as in Lloyd. To pronounce this, put your tongue on the ridge behind your upper teeth as if pronouncing the "l" in hello and blow some hot air.

WORTH SEEING Cardiff's main sights are within 20 minutes or so of each other in the city center. In the mid-19th century, the third marquess of Bute, faced with a draughty old castle on her hands and a pile of pounds in her pocket, went all out to renovate **Cardiff Castle** (Castle St., tel. 01222/822083; admission to grounds £2.10, £3.15 with guided tour). William Burges, an architect obsessed with whimsical flights of fancy, redesigned the castle's interior. The huge **National Museum of Wales** (Cathays Park, tel. 01222/397951; admission £2; closed Mon.) has paintings and sculpture by Rodin, Cézanne, Rembrandt, and Welsh artists Richard Wilson and Augustus John. **Llandaff Cathedral** (High St., tel. 01222/561545), about 3 km northwest of Cardiff in Llandaff, was pounded by bombs in World War II but has since been beautifully restored. Take Bus 33 or 62 if you don't want to walk 40 minutes.

AFTER DARK Pick up the free *What's On Wales* at the tourist information center for the latest entertainment info. **The Philharmonic** (76 St. Mary's St., tel. 01222/230678) overflows with students drinking, dancing, and chatting it up. **The Four Bars Inn** (Castle St., tel. 01222/374962) and **Sam's Bar** (St. Mary's St., tel. 01222/345189) feature live rock; cover varies with the lineup. Classic and artsy films play at the **Chapter Arts Centre** (Market Rd., tel. 01222/399666).

NEAR CARDIFF

CAERPHILLY Caerphilly is Wales's largest fortress and possibly its most impressive, with 30 acres of grounds that lord over the tiny village of Caerphilly and the surrounding patchwork of farms. The original 13th-century Norman fortress was largely destroyed over the years; some walls have toppled while others lean haphazardly, adding to the eerie stillness of the place. Exhibits inside trace the history of this 700-year-old ruin. To reach the castle, catch a bus or train from Cardiff Central Station; the trip takes 30 minutes and costs about £3 round-trip. *Tel. 01222/883143. Admission: £2, £1.50 students.*

Brecon Beacons National Park

If you want to see some of Wales's most awe-inspiring scenery—sheep-flecked hillsides, horses trekking through the snow in winter—you shouldn't miss Brecon Beacons National Park, even if you're only in Wales for a couple of days. Arm yourself with trail maps at park centers and flip through the innumerable choices of hikes and long walks. The **Waterfall Region**, accessible from the town of Merthyr Tydfil, has a number of spectacular falls, including the park's tallest, 90-foot-high **Nant Lech**.

The town of **Brecon** is the largest within the park and makes an excellent place to stock up on groceries, rent equipment, and clue into the region's best walks. The town itself is also worth a short visit to stroll the riverside promenade. Pick up info about the town at **Brecon Tourist Information Centre** (Cattle Market Car Park, tel. 01874/622485), which shares an office with the **National Park Centre.** One of the best park paths follows the **Monmouthshire and Brecon Canal** from Brecon through Abergavenny to Pontypool, 60 km away. Many people cover the easy 35-km Abergavenny–Brecon leg over two days, staying at a B&B or campsite near Llangynidir.

COMING AND GOING You can reach Abergavenny, on the eastern edge of the park, from both London and Cardiff. You cannot go directly to the town of Brecon without hopping on a bus at some point, usually from Cardiff (£4 round-trip). The other option is to catch an hourly train from Cardiff to Merthyr Tydfil (£3.10 round-trip) and then hop on Bus 43 to Brecon from the station.

WHERE TO SLEEP In Brecon, look for B&Bs in the Llan Faes area, along Orchard, Church, and St. David's streets. The **Flag and Castle Guest House** (11 Orchard St., tel. 01874/625860) is in a 250-year-old home that was once a coaching inn; singles are £15, doubles £28. The **HI Ty'n-y-Caeau Hostel** (tel. 0187486/270; beds £4.20–£6.30; closed Nov.–mid-Feb.) is near the Monmouthshire-Brecon Canal, 4 km from Brecon. Counting sheep will take on new meaning at the rural **HI Llwyn-y-Celyn Hostel** (tel. 01874/624261; beds

£4.20–£6.30; closed late Nov.–early Mar.), 17 km from Brecon. Ask the bus driver to let you off at the entrance.

Within the park, campsites are everywhere, and rates run £2.50–£5 per person. While it's against the rules to camp randomly in the park, people do it anyway. Most hostels are more convenient to hiking trails than to towns; that should give you an idea of what an earthly paradise the park sometimes seems. The **HI Capel-y-Ffin Hostel** (tel. 01873/890650) is north of Abergavenny near secondhand-bookstore capital Hay-on-Wye. The **HI Ystradfellte Hostel** (tel. 01639/720301; closed Dec.–Feb.) places you near the waterfall region near Myrthr Tydfil. The **HI Llanddeusant Hostel** (tel. 01550/4619) is the park's westernmost hostel.

Pembrokeshire Coast and National Park

This dramatic corner of Wales, bounded by the 270-km **Pembrokeshire Coast Path**, encompasses both wild coast and popular resort towns cluttered with ice-cream huts. There's still a lot of untouched coastal wilderness here, especially in the "North Pembs," where smaller communities keep their rural roots. The free *Coast to Coast* newspaper, available at tourist information centers and newsstands, is crammed with useful information on the region.

The affable coastal town of **Tenby** makes for a good base. Women aren't allowed in the Cistercian monastery on nearby **Caldey Island**, but they can attend mass with the monks in the abbey church. The rest of the island is a neat place to explore, with cliffs, sandy beaches, and an old priory church. Tenby's busy **Tourist Information Centre** (North Beach, tel. 01834/842402) is open late by British standards—until 9 PM in July and August.

A tiny town named after the patron saint of Wales, **St. David's** is the home of the oldest and perhaps the most beautiful **cathedral** (£1 donation required) in Wales. Behind the cathedral are the 14th-century ruins of **Bishop's Palace**. Nearby is **St. Nun's Well**, where St. David was born. The town is convenient to good stretches of the Pembrokeshire Coast Path; youth hostels and towns are all within a day's walk of each other, making it easy to plan a hiking tour of the area. The **Tourist Information Centre** (City Hall, tel. 01437/720392; open Easter–Oct.), also a national park center, can help map out your next hike.

COMING AND GOING The regional railway swooshes from Cardiff through Tenby (£14 round-trip) on its way across the southern coast, but most of this area is best seen by bus. Most of these pass through the region's most central town, Haverfordwest; Bus 358 and 359 run hourly from Haverfordwest to Tenby. Bus 340 heads north from Haverfordwest to St. David's, stopping in the town of Solva. The tourist offices carry schedules of all the region's buses.

WHERE TO SLEEP

➤ **TENBY** • As you head south from High Street onto St. Julian's Street, you'll find **Caldey Vue Guest House** (St. Julian's St., tel. 01834/842126) and **Ocean Hotel** (The Croft, tel. 01834/842476). Both have rooms with ocean views for £15 per person. The nearest campsite is **Meadow Farm** (Northcliffe, tel. 01834/844829; £2.50 per person), a 15-minute walk uphill from town. On the coast at Skrinkle Haven, about 20 minutes south of town along the Tenby–Pembroke bus line, is the **HI Manorbier Hostel** (tel. 01834/871803), with beds for £7.50.

➤ **ST. DAVID'S** • The **HI St. David's Hostel** (tel. 01437/720345; beds £5.10–£6.30) is a 3.5-km walk from town toward the sea. Anyone in town can point you to this happy hostel; you may even be offered a ride if you're lucky. Some travelers rough it by sleeping on the beach, although authorities discourage it.

Aberystwyth

Home of the first university in Wales, Aberystwyth is small and casual, mingling the permissive ambience of a Victorian seafront town with the rarefied air of higher learning. Geographically, Aberystwyth is the bridge between north and south Wales. The seafront heats up in the evening as pubs draw rowdy crowds of students, and the gay scene in town is the most open in Wales. The free **National Library of Wales** (Penglais Hill, tel. 01970/623816; closed Sun.) houses many of Wales's important documents and rare books. Since 1896, the **Electric Cliff Railway** (Cliff Terr., tel. 01970/617642; admission £1.85) has been hauling visitors to the top of Constitution Hill to the free camera obscura observatory. The popular—and free—**Ceredigion Museum** (Terrace Rd., tel. 01970/617911) displays mining and seafaring artifacts. The **information** office (Terrace Rd., tel. 01970/612125) is a five-minute walk from the train station.

COMING AND GOING From London's Euston Station, trains travel to Aberystwyth via Shrewsbury (£44 round-trip). Bus 701 makes two runs a day from Cardiff (£8.80). Local lines connect the town with the rest of Wales.

WHERE TO SLEEP Walk down South Road to Marine Terrace and the side streets behind the castle and look for the unobtrusive B&B signs. The sea's around the corner and the castle's just up the street from **Linkenma** (Custom House St., tel. 01970/617480), a homey B&B charging £14 per person. **Sunnymead Guest House** (34 Bridge St., tel. 01970/617273) is curious, yellow, friendly, and asks £13 per person. The **HI Borth Hostel** (Morlais, tel. 01970/871498) is one train stop away from Aberystwyth, with beds for £7.50 (£5 under 18). The nearest campground is **Aberystwyth Holiday Village** (tel. 01970/624211; sites £4 per person), about a 15-minute walk from town along Penparcau Road on the A487.

FOOD Try Pier Street or line up with Aberystwythians at the produce shops and bakeries on Chalybeate Street, east of Great Darkgate Street. Whole-food lovers should come to eclectic **YGraig** (34 Pier St., tel. 01970/611606) and check out antinuke stickers written in Welsh while munching a healthy meal. **Eastgate Fish** (36A Eastgate St., tel. 01970/615321) is a clean, busy fish-and-chips joint where all things fried cost under £5.

AFTER DARK At **The Coopers** on north parade, you'll find Welsh-speaking students casually downing pints. **The Angel** on High Street by Market Hall is known as a "hippie" hangout, featuring leftover decorations from the '60s. New Zealanders, rugby players, and students mingle one block away at **The Black Lion** on Bridge Street.

Lleyn Peninsula

The lightly traveled Lleyn Peninsula juts out of North Wales toward the Irish Sea, separating Caernarfon and Ceridigion bays. Fields and farms dominate the landscape inland, while sandy beaches attract the cognoscenti to the coast. Some 102 km of the peninsula's coastline have been designated "Heritage Coast," meaning they won't be built up any further.

PORTHMADOG

The center of action on the peninsula, Porthmadog (port-MAD-ick) served as the primary port for the North Wales slate trade until the Cambrian Railway arrived in 1867. But the town definitely doesn't feel abandoned: In summer, the town's main street is clogged with cars and tour buses heading to nearby Blackrock Sands beach. The city serves as the crossroads of the peninsula and Snowdonia, making it a good place to base yourself. By far the easiest way to get to the town is coming from the south via the Aberystwyth rail line; buses also head here from all over northern Wales. The Porthmadog **information office** (High St., tel. 01766/512981) is a 10-minute walk from the train station. Near the Ffestiniog Railway, stay at the nifty **Skelern B&B** (35 Madog St., tel. 01766/512843), with rooms for £13 per person. Campers should head for the sites at **Tyddyn Adi Camping Site** (tel. 01766/512923; sites £4–£5), 4 km from Porthmadog and near the beach.

PORTMEIRION

Portmeirion is not so much a town as a sort of high-flown theme park. The town, designed by architect Sir Clough Williams-Ellis in 1925 to be in harmony with its natural surroundings, is perched on the edge of beautiful seaside cliffs. The pastel-colored buildings blend with the vegetation, which include some rare species that grow only in the sheltered Portmeirion coastal area. There are no budget accommodations in town, so if you insist on spending the night, you'll have to shell out big bucks for the ritzy **Hotel Portmeirion** (tel. 01766/770228). Admission to the hotel and surrounding village is a hefty £2.90, but that's because it's not so much a "village" as a displaced segment of Disneyland. Television fanatics may recognize the town as the setting for the trippy 1960s BBC show *The Prisoner,* and a gift shop has some funky *Prisoner*esque memorabilia. You can't tour the home of Number 6, but it's still kinda creepy just walking in the mysterious Village. You can reach Portmeirion by bus from Porthmadog, a 9-km trip.

CAERNARFON

The Welsh weren't too crazy about Edward I, who took the throne in 1272, so he built some fortresses to protect his men from the people of Cymru. **Caernarfon Castle** (tel. 01286/677617; admission £2.50) is one of the results. The battlements offer great views of the Menai Strait, while the displays inside clue you into castle lore. Down Pool Street is the **Segontium Roman Fort** (Beddgelert Rd., tel. 01286/675625), where a Roman governor lodged garrisons of soldiers when he invaded Britain in AD 383. Today you can see artifacts on display in the museum. The **tourist office** (Castle Ditch, tel. 01286/672232; closed Wed.) sells maps for nearby Snowdonia, including a macabre little guide about airplane crashes in the park. The only way into town is via bus; No. 701 comes from the south, with stops in Porthmadog, while a zillion others head east from Bangor.

Most B&Bs are clustered on Church Street and along North and St. David's roads. Two minutes from the castle is **Tegfan** (4 Church St., tel. 01286/673703; £12–£16 per person), a B&B with thick carpets and British bric-a-brac. **Bryn-y-Mor** (North Rd., tel. 01286/677600) and **Marianfa** (St. David's Rd., tel. 01286/675589) are also good deals, charging about £13 per person. The campsites along Llanberis Road, including **Cadnant Valley Caravans** (tel. 01286/673196), a 10-minute walk from town, cost about £3.50 per person. There are several decent restaurants along Hole-in-the-Wall Street. **Real Food and Treasures** (Hole-in-the-Wall St., tel. 01286/66430) is a homey café serving vegetarian meals. **The Bakestone** (26 Hole-in-the-Wall St., tel. 01286/675846) has pastas for under £6 at lunch, under £11 at dinner.

Snowdonia Forest and National Park

Snowdonia National Park is one of the most beloved patches of land in Wales. The southern section near Dolgellau features glowering **Cader Idris**; craggy **Mt. Snowdon** is in the northwest; the northeast near **Betws-y-Coed** has fir and larch forests; sail-flecked **Llyn Tegid** (Bala Lake) defines the east; and castles and seascapes run along the coast south of Porthmadog. Unfortunately, everyone and their dog vacations here, making Snowdonia something of a Welsh Yellowstone Park. This isn't always a drawback; facilities include wheelchair-accessible trails in **Dolgellau** and descriptive signs in Braille at the **Garth Falls Walk** at the west end of Betwys-y-Coed. Most people, though, head straight to Mt. Snowdon, which has six main paths to the summit. Park offices have 20p leaflets describing each of them.

The most popular path, the 8-km round-trip **Llanberis Path**, is often crowded with families. It starts in Llanberis and parallels the railway up to Pen-y-Pass. **Miners' Track** is another easy trail crossing the northeast section of Llyn Llydaw Lake, where King Arthur supposedly threw his sword, Excalibur, after he was mortally wounded while slaying the giant Rhita Fawr at the summit of Mt. Snowdon. The **Snowdon Ranger Path** is the shortest trail, but it does have a few steep spots. **Pitt's Head Track** meets **Rhyd Ddu Path** from the south, forming one faint trail that climbs up the face of Llechog and offers some spectacular views. Equally intriguing is the **Horseshoe Path** to the summit—if you want to try it, talk to a park ranger first and get briefed on (and maybe dissuaded from) this demanding trail. Before any excursion, contact **Mountain-call Snowdonia** (tel. 01891/500449) for weather conditions.

In an attempt to reduce erosion and to keep hikers safe, Mt. Snowdon's bridleways are closed to bicycles daily 10–5. The roads are always fair game, though. The best cycling route is the 34-km haul up **Llanberis Pass** to Pen-y-Gwrd. The **Llanberis Mountain Bike Centre** (tel. 01286/870052) rents mountain bikes for £3 per hour or £15 per day and supplies helmets and a printed guide with suggested routes. In Betws-y-Coed, **Beics Betws** (behind the post office off the A5, tel. 01690/710766) rents bikes for £2.50 per hour, £14 per day.

COMING AND GOING BritRail (tel. 01341/280562) has two lines running into Snowdonia National Park, hitting Betws-y-coed and Blaenau Ffestiniog. Betws-y-Coed is a good base from which to explore the eastern park. **Buses** will be your best bet, however, especially for getting you to Llanberis. Companies that serve the Snowdonia area include **Crosville** (Caernarfon, tel. 01286/672556) and **Ieuan Williams** (Llanberis, tel. 01286/870484).

GETTING AROUND

➤ **BY SHERPA** • The **Snowdon Sherpa** is the most convenient and environmentally safe way to get to your trails. The buses bring you to the base of the six main paths up Mt. Snowdon and run to the major towns, as well as to the youth hostels in the northwest part of the park. The buses operate from May through early October. Easy pickup points are at Betws-y-Coed, Llandudno Junction, Caernarfon, Bangor, Llanrwst, and Porthmadog. The national park also offers a **Sherpa Bus Walk,** which gives you a chance to combine Sherpa service with two short, guided walks at Beddgelert and on Snowdon, all in one day. The Bus Walk operates every Wednesday from the end of July to the end of August and costs £4.

➤ **BY LITTLE TRAINS** • Go to Snowdonia and take your pick of six "little" railways. The **Ffestiniog Railway** (tel. 01766/512340 in Porthmadog, 01766/831654 in Blaenau Ffestiniog, or 01766/514114 for 24-hr timetable info) is a 22-km track linking Blaenau Ffestiniog with Porthmadog and southbound BritRail trains along the coast. The cost is £6.40–£10.80 round-trip, depending on time of departure and whether it's a diesel or steam train. If you want to go hiking at any point in between, you can request stops and pay less for the partial journey. Some but not all of the trains accommodate wheelchairs. Other little trains include **Bala Lake Railway** (tel. 016784/666), which chugs along the southeast side of narrow Bala Lake; **Llanberis Lake Railway** (tel. 01286/870549), which covers part of the northwest perimeter of Llyn Padarn; **Talyllyn Railway** (tel. 01654/710472), connecting the coastal town of Tywyn with the village of Abergynolwyn; and **Fairbourne and Barmouth Steam Railway** (tel. 01341/250362), offering first-rate views of the Mawddach Estuary and Cader Idris. Most trains cost about £19–£26, but you can buy the **Narrow Gauge Wanderer Ticket** for unlimited travel on Wales's little trains (except the Snowdon Mountain Railway). The ticket is issued by Ffestiniog Railway and costs £20 for four days in seven, £27 for eight days in a 15-day period.

The other handy train is the **Snowdon Mountain Railway** (tel. 01286/870223), which carries passengers up the mountain. Weather and the number of passengers dictate when and how often the trains run. During the summer, trains run every half-hour from 8:30 AM to 6:30 PM. The round-trip fare is £12.

WHERE TO SLEEP Plenty of youth hostels dot the park; ask at the tourist office for the closest ones. If you're looking for atmosphere, try the **Snowdon Ranger Youth Hostel** (Rhyd Ddu, Caernarfon, tel. 01268/650391; beds £5–£7.50), next to Lake Cwellyn with its own beach and a 5-km orienteering course. The hostel in **Capel Curig** (Plas Curig, Betws-y-Coed, tel. 016904/225; beds £6–£8) is 8 km from Pen-y-Pass, but the Snowdon Sherpa stops at the front door. Book ahead for **King's Youth Hostel** (King's, Penmaenpool, tel. 01341/422392; beds £6–£7.50), 6 km from Dolgellau in a wooded, peaceful valley. Take Bws Gwynedd 28 to Dolgellau and then follow the signs on foot for an hour.

LLANBERIS

At the foot of Mt. Snowdon, Llanberis is well-rehearsed in the art of dealing with Snowdonia fun seekers. The town is small, but there's nothing particularly provincial about it. Its two lakes, Padarn and Peris, and its position as the lower terminus of the Snowdon Mountain Railway, attract hordes of hikers. Come here to stock up on food and outdoor gear. The town is only 11 km from Caernarfon and 15 km from Bangor and is easily accessible by bus from these cities.

Llanberis is the town closest to Mt. Snowdon, so it's not surprising that its **Tourist Information Centre** (tel. 01286/870765), inside the **Museum of the North,** gives more comprehensive information about Snowdonia than any other. The museum's "Power of Wales" exhibition is worth a gander, and nearby copper and slate mines are open for tours; there are crafts centers nearby, too, all of which combine to make Llanberis an interesting town, even on a rainy day.

WHERE TO SLEEP AND EAT You'll be in the thick of things at the **Llanberis Youth Hostel** (Llwyn Celin, Llanberis, tel. 01286/870280; beds £5–£7.50), only a short distance from the Llanberis Path up Mt. Snowdon. In town, a friendly proprietor and simple inviting rooms make the **Beech Bank Guest House** (2 High St., tel. 01286/870414; £12.50 per person) one of the better options in the High Street cluster of B&Bs. The great views from **Idan House** (12 High St., tel. 01286/870673; £12 per person) are cause to overlook the somewhat drab rooms. **Pete's Eats** (40 High St., tel. 0286/870358) is a smoky, funky, place filled with hikers and bikers. Pore over hiking maps while slurping a bowl of soup (£1.25) or munching on a vegan special (£4).

BALA

As you walk down the town trail—a walking trail devised by city fathers to cover the significant and historic aspects of the town—you can see the old Bala of knitters, whiskey-distillers, printers, and cattle drivers. At times, the 20th century seems like a veneer; the Henblas Garage on High Street, for instance, has its old-fashioned gas pumps on the sidewalk (you can fill 'er up from the parking lane). Today, Bala is best known for its 8-km long lake, the largest inland lake in Wales. It's a mecca for those into canoeing, sailing, and windsurfing. Powerboats are forbidden, making it one of the best sailing lakes in Britain.

Instead of the rolling, mountainous terrain found in most of Snowdonia, the area around Bala is more open, less austere, with hints of wide, green valleys.

The friendly staff at Bala's **Tourist Information Centre** (High St., tel. 01678/520367) will tell you whatever you need to know. The foyer is papered with fliers advertising everything from music to laundry services to church hours. Other than by car, your only way into this town at the eastern edge of Snowdonia is by Bus 94, which runs back and forth between the west coast and the English border, starting at Barmouth with stops at Dolgellau, Bala, Llangollen, and Wrexham.

WHERE TO SLEEP The **Bala Youth Hostel** (Plas Rhiwaedog, Rhos-y-Gwaliau, Bala, tel. 01678/520215; beds £4.60–£6.90) is 3 km southeast of town in the hamlet of Rhos-y-Gwaliau—an hour's walk from the bus stop in Bala. Abraham Lincoln's great-grandmother Sarah once lived at a B&B called **Fferm Fron-Goch** (Fferm Fron-Goch, tel. 01678/520483; £13–£15 per person), about 5 km northeast of Bala toward Fron-Goch. Now a young Welsh family inhabits this 17th-century farmhouse, which lies tucked in beautiful countryside. A very friendly and very Welsh Mrs. Jones runs the **Traian Bed and Breakfast** (95 Tegid St., tel. 01678/520059; £12–£14 per person), a short walk from Bala Lake.

BETWS-Y-COED

The Lledr, Llugwy, and Conwy rivers converge at Betws-y-Coed, tumbling over rocky outcroppings and through the tall trees of the Gwydir forest. Its shops and restaurants are upscale and expensive, but at least nothing is tacky enough to compete with the natural landscape. Several major walking trails and bike routes cross the area. The busy **tourist office** (Royal Oak Stables, tel. 01690/710426) can steer you in the right direction.

WHERE TO SLEEP AND EAT Lodging is expensive here; your best bet is to hop on the train to the Pont-y-Pant stop and bed down amid trees, fields, and sheep at the **Lledr Valley Youth Hostel** (tel. 01690/6202; beds £4.60–£6.90; closed Nov. and Jan.–Feb.). Ask the BritRail ticket taker to let you off at Pont-y-Pant, then walk left up the lane, cross the bridge, turn left onto the main road, and walk about 15 minutes.

The town's restaurants and cafés tend to be pricey. **Dil's Diner** (next to the train station, tel. 01690/710346) is one of the cheapest places, with typically British food and breakfast (£3.60) until noon. **Bodyline Health Foods** on the main street has groceries and a bakery.

Scotland

When you cross the border from northern England into southern Scotland, you might not notice right away that you've gone from one country to another. The Scots, however, will be sure to remind you, especially if you make the mistake of calling them English. To set the record straight, England and Scotland were two separate countries until 1603, when James VI of Scotland, son of Mary, queen of Scots, succeeded the childless Elizabeth I of England to become King James I of both England and Scotland. Not all Scots supported the union of the kingdoms, especially since the English tried to supress Scotland's powerful—and fiercely independent—Highland clans. As a result, the tenuous bonds between the two countries broke down and led to a civil war, during which Scotland was conquered by Oliver Cromwell. When the monarchy was restored, the two countries were once again ruled by the same king but remained separate kingdoms. During the Glorious Revolution of 1688, James VII was hurried out of town, allowing William of Orange to take the crown, but with the understanding that he would allow the English parliament to take more control of affairs than his absolutist predecessor. This increased the friction between the two countries. To keep a lid on the rebellious Scots, on May 1, 1707, the two parliaments merged into one, giving birth to the United Kingdom of Great Britain.

The Highlands are Scotland's last bastion of Celtic language, which faces extinction in the face of English television and radio.

Despite the constitutional union of the two countries, Scotland continues to maintain its own traditions. Scots parade their heritage proudly, especially in the historic, utterly beautiful cities of **Edinburgh** and **St. Andrews.** Festivals in the Highlands celebrate traditional Scottish ways of life, including the Gaelic language, which sadly has all but disappeared. The omnipresence of kilts and kitsch shops might have you wondering if all this is a show staged for tourists, and the busking bagpipers will probably get on your nerves at some point. In this case, head for the Scottish hinterland, where a crowd is a farmer and his sheep.

Geographically, Scotland is divided into three primary regions. The **Uplands** along the southern border are much like northern England, with rolling moors interrupted by rivers; the fertile **Lowlands** are spread around the Firths of Forth and Clyde; and the rugged **Highlands,** covering much of the west and north of the country, are punctuated with mountains and deep lochs—a drop-dead panorama that in itself justifies a trip to Scotland.

Edinburgh

Edinburgh (pronounced Eddin-burra) is Scotland's center of government as well as its undisputed leader in art and culture. The city's location on the north edge on the Firth of Forth and its weathered stone architecture make it one of Europe's most stunning cities. Let's repeat that: Edinburgh is utterly and truly gorgeous, so kick yourself if you somehow miss this one-of-a-kind town. The city's main appeal lies in walking around, an infinitely pleasurable pursuit as you crane to ponder Edinburgh Castle high on the hill. On misty, gloomy days, several free or cheap galleries and museums will keep you warm. On balmy afternoons, the hills surrounding the city, notably Arthur's Seat and Calton Hill, offer beautiful views of Edinburgh and the sur-

Edinburgh

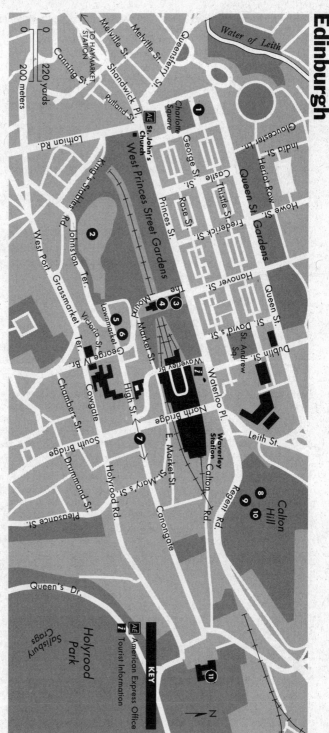

Water of Leith

TO HAYMARKET
STATION

AE St. John's
Church

0   0
220 yards
0
200 meters

Queensferry St.
Melville St.
Melville St.
Shandwick Pl.
Rutland St.
Canning St.
Lothian Rd.
King's Stables Rd.
West Port
West Princes Street Gardens
Johnston Ter.
Grassmarket
Victoria St.
George IV Br.
Lawnmarket
Chambers St.
Cowgate
South Bridge
Drummond St.
Pleasance St.
Holyrood Rd.
Canongate
Charlotte
Square
George St.
Castle St.
Thistle St.
Rose St.
Frederick St.
Princes St.
The Mound
Market St.
High St.
North Bridge
E. Market St.
S. Mary's St.
Queen St.
Hanover St.
Heriot Row
Howe St.
India St.
Gloucester Ln.
Queen St. Gardens
St. David's St.
St. Andrew
Sq.
Dublin St.
Waterloo Pl.
Leith St.
Calton Rd.
Regent Rd.
Calton
Hill
Leith St.

Waverley Br.
Waverley
Station

Queen's Dr.
Salisbury Crags
Holyrood Park

KEY
AE American Express Office
ℹ Tourist Information

N

399

rounding countryside, as well as a chance to escape the hordes of summer. Almost unbelievably, crowds double during Edinburgh's famous International Arts Festival, held from mid-August through the first week of September.

BASICS

➤ **VISITOR INFORMATION** • The **Edinburgh Information Centre,** on top of the Waverley Train Station/Shopping Complex, changes money and charges £3 to book rooms. *3 Princes St., tel. 0131/557–1700. Open mid-June–Sept., Mon.–Sat. 9–8, Sun. 11–8; shorter hrs off-season.*

American Express. *139 Princes St., across from St. John's Church, tel. 0131/225–7881. Open weekdays 9–5:30, Sat. 9–4.*

The **Edinburgh Travel Centre** has budget travel and student discount information. *2 locations: Edinburgh University, Potterrow Union, Bristol Sq., tel. 0131/668–2221; 196 Rose St, tel. 0131/226–2019.*

➤ **MAIL** • You can receive poste restante mail at the main post office, a half-block east of the train station. *2–4 Waterloo Pl., Edinburgh EH1 1AL, tel. 0131/550–8253.*

➤ **MEDICAL AID** • The **Royal Infirmary of Edinburgh** is open 24 hours; you won't be charged for consultation for minor medical problems. *1 Lauriston Pl., tel. 0131/229–2477. Go south on George IV Bridge to Lauriston.*

COMING AND GOING

➤ **BY TRAIN** • Edinburgh's main rail station, **Waverley Station**, lies at the east end of Princes Street. Trains to cities throughout Scotland and England, including London's King's Cross Station (4–6 hrs, £59 round-trip), serve this busy hub. For train information, call 0131/556–2451. Trains from **Haymarket Station** (Haymarket Sq., tel. 0131/556–2451), in the West End of Edinburgh, travel to points west and north, including Glasgow (50 min, £6.80 one-way). A taxi from Waverly to Haymarket Station should cost £3–£4.

➤ **BY BUS** • Long-distance coaches arrive at **St. Andrews Square** (tel. 0131/654–0707), near Waverly Station 1½ blocks north of Princes Street, and at **Waverley Market** at the east end of Princes Street. The bus is the cheapest way to reach Edinburgh from London, but the trip takes nine hours. **Scottish CityLink** (tel. 0131/654–0707) charges £31 one-way and £39 round-trip. If you have a **Scottish CityLink Student Card** (£7), subtract 33% from this and all CityLink fares. **Caledonian Express** (tel. 01738/33481) also has inexpensive fares; a round-trip ticket to London booked a week in advance runs £25.

GETTING AROUND Edinburgh is a compact, walkable city. The **Princes Street Gardens,** which run east–west along the southern edge of Princes Street, roughly divide Edinburgh into two areas: the winding, nonsensical streets of **Old Town** to the south and the orderly, Georgian architecture of **New Town** to the north. Buses to every part of the city run along Princes Street. Maroon and white **LRT** buses and green **SMT** (tel. 0131/556–8464) buses provide extensive service. Fares range from 50p to £1.10 for short rides. **One-day passes** are £2; **Ridacards,** good for two or more days, cost about £1.75 per day. These and other passes are available at the **LRT office** (tel. 0131/220–4111) on the corner of Waverley and Market streets.

Graveyards and Ale

No matter what part of town you're in, two facts about Edinburgh should draw your attention: the number of graveyards and the number of pubs. If you ever wanted to fall down dead drunk, you're in the right place. Sunny days at the graveyard at Grey Friars Kirk create just the right atmosphere for a relaxing lunch on benches set among the tombstones. Right behind St. John's Church, at the West End of Princes Street, you'll find wooden tables actually set up over graves.

WHERE TO SLEEP Hostels are the cheapest choice in Edinburgh, although the many B&Bs and private houses provide a reasonable alternative. The accommodations service in Waverley Station books rooms for a small fee. Edinburgh's SYHA hostels accept fax bookings from other hostels; ask for the "Book-A-Bed Ahead" service (70p). Telephone bookings can also be made less than one week in advance between 5 PM and 10 PM, excluding the day of arrival. If you don't have a reservation, a good place to look is **Minto Street,** south of the east end of Princes Street; take Bus 3, 7, 8, 18, 31, 69, or 80 from the shop side of Princes Street. You can also try **Pilrig Street,** northeast of the city center; take Bus 7, 10, 11, 14, 16, 17, 22, 25, or 87, also from the shop side of Princes Street.

Balmoral Guest House. The proprietors pamper guests silly. Substantial breakfast (including vegetarian choices) included. Book ahead. Doubles £30. *32 Pilrig St., 2 km northeast of Waverley Station, tel. 0131/ 554–1857.*

Beresford Hotel. A slightly expensive but clean family-run hotel that's rarely full. Doubles, all with shared bath, are £37. *32 Coates Gardens, just past Haymarket Station, tel. 0131/337–0850. Bus 2, 26, or 31 from Princes St.*

Crion Guest House. Newly refurbished, family-run home about 1¹/₂ km from the train station. Doubles £30. Reserve at least two weeks in advance. *33 Minto St., tel. 0131/667–2708. From the East End of Princes St., take Bus 3, 31, or 69.*

➤ **HOSTELS • Christian Alliance.** Sedate place in the very safe West End. For females, married couples, and children only. Singles £10–£15.50. *14 Coates Crescent, tel. 0131/225–3608. Bus 3, 4, 12, 22, or 26 from Princes St. (garden side). Laundry.*

HI Bruntsfield Hostel. Next to a beautiful green park 2 km uphill from Waverley Station. On the sterile side and a little oppressive. Uncarpeted rooms with high ceilings make for one cold Scottish night. Beds £7.25. *7–8 Bruntsfield Crescent, tel. 0131/447–2994. Bus 11, 15, 16, or 17 from Princes St. (garden side). Laundry, kitchen.*

HI Eglinton Hostel. Well-run hostel in the West End, near shops and pubs. Common rooms and kitchen remain open during the 10–2 lockout. Beds £9.25. *18 Eglinton Crescent, tel. 0131/337–1120. Bus 3, 4, 12, 13, 22, or 44 from Princes St. (garden side) to Palmerston Pl. Laundry, kitchen.*

High Street Hostel. In the middle of the Royal Mile, just off High Street. Friendly and informal—try this hostel first. Free walking tours of the area. Beds £8.50. *8 Blackfriars, tel. 0131/557–3984. From east end of Princes St., walk up North Bridge Rd., turn left on High St., right on Blackfriars.*

➤ **CAMPGROUND • Silverknowes Carvan Park.** The lack of sheltered space means North Sea winds may chill your bones or take your tent on an unexpected journey to Glasgow. *Marine Dr., tel. 0131/312–6874. Bus 14 from North Bridge. Closed Oct.–Apr.*

FOOD Most restaurants in Edinburgh are out of budget range, but the city has lots of take-out stands selling baked potatoes and bakeries hawking inexpensive rolls, scones, and sandwiches. An inexpensive lunch at a pub or café usually runs £4–£5. Italian, Pakistani, and Chinese restaurants are usually cheaper than traditional British food.

➤ **UNDER £5 • Angelo's.** Everthing baked by Angelo himself. Whole-grain bread with garlic and olive oil (80p) is nearly a meal in itself. Only £1 to sit at the counter with a cup of tea and a scone. In the Tollcross area of Old Town. *20 Brougham Pl., tel. 0131/228–4239.*

The Cornerstone Café. Dine among the dead at this café, which once served as the catacombs for St. John's Church. Bulletin board has info about alternative cultural events. Entire meals for less than £3. *Corner of Lothian Road and Princes St., under St. John's Church, tel. 0131/229–0212. Closed Sun.*

Khushi Tandoori Restaurant. Eat in or get food to go at this small Pakistani restaurant. Spicy "Punjabi-style" food with lots of veggie options. *32 C. Broughton St., tel. 0131/556–8092. Closed Tues.*

Maggie Dickson's. Student-overrun pub on Grassmarket Square. The lunchtime soup-and-sandwich special is a steal at £2.50. Free pizza Monday at 12:30 AM. Spicy bean burger and chips £3.10. *Grassmarket Sq., Old Town, tel. 0131/225–6601.*

Sandwiches. Several kinds of bagels populate the windows, and curried chicken and rice costs a mere £3.50. Outdoor tables set out on a pedestrian lane parallel to Princes Street. *127 Rose St., a block north of Princes St., tel. 0131/220–6171.*

➤ **UNDER £10** • **Pierre Victoire.** Culture vultures come here after a night of avant-garde films at the nearby Filmhouse. Simple but divine French cuisine. The best bargain is the fixed-price lunch (£6). *10 Victoria St., tel. 0131/225–1721.*

WORTH SEEING Edinburgh's foremost feature is its medieval castle, which broods authoritatively over the city from the crags of an ancient volcano. Many parts of **Old Town** date to the 16th century, and the area's streets, "wynds" (winding, narrow walkways), and "closes" (stone arched walkways) spill from the ramparts of Edinburgh Castle with absolutely no thought for coherent city planning. The more orderly gridded streets of **New Town** offer a perfect example of what the Enlightenment did for urban planning.

Calton Hill. The cylindrical tower, **Nelson's Monument** (admission £1), wasn't built so much to honor naval hero Admiral Nelson as to serve as a reminder to the sons of Edinburgh that they are to die for their country when duty requires it. The nearby **National Monument,** a half-completed Greco-Roman colonnade, wasn't left that way for aesthetic reasons: funding ran out and it was never finished. Also unfinished is the **City Observatory**; once built, there was no more money for a telescope. Despite its motley collection of monuments, the hill is worth climbing for its views of the city.

Edinburgh Castle. The castle has a few fine attractions inside, but the real reason to spend £4 are the mind-bending views—of Edinburgh and the entire Firth of Forth—from the castle's towering ramparts. Most of the battlements date to the 14th and 16th centuries, but the oldest building, **St. Margaret's Chapel,** dates to the 11th or 12th century (no one's sure which). The **Scottish Regalia** (the jeweled crown, scepter, and sword of Scotland) sparkle in the castle's **crown room.** Red-coated, bearskin-hatted Scots Guardmen near the entrance are well-trained for their main duties—posing sternly for pictures and firing a cannon daily at 1 PM. *Top of the Royal Mile, tel. 0131/225–7534. Admission: £4. Open Mon.–Sat. 9:30–6, Sun. 11–6; shorter hrs off-season.*

The Georgian House. Enthusiastically tended by some of the city's diehard history buffs, the interior of this 18th-century home has been carefully reconstructed to reflect the life of a middle-class couple who lived here shortly after the New Town was built. *7 Charlotte Sq., tel. 0131/225–2160. Admission: £3, £1.50 students. Open Easter–Oct., Mon.–Sat. 10–4:30, Sun. 2–4:30.*

The Mound. Bisecting Princes Street Gardens, this walkway between the Old Town and New Town contains two of Edinburgh's best galleries. The **Royal Scottish Academy** (tel. 0131/225–6671; admission £1.20, 60p students) features an annual exhibit of both established and avant-garde Scottish artists. The **National Gallery of Scotland** (tel. 0131/556–8921; admission free) sits right behind the academy and houses the national collection of Scottish art as well as works by Continental greats like Velásquez, El Greco, Rembrandt, Degas, Monet, and van Gogh. *Both open Mon–Sat. 10–5, Sun. 2–5.*

The Royal Mile. Also referred to as Castlehill, Lawnmarket, High Street, and Canongate as it heads down the hill from the castle, the main street of Old Town stretches from Edinburgh Castle to Holyrood Palace. Pubs, shops, pubs, historic attractions, and pubs line its cobblestone length. Since so many 16th- to 18th-century city-dwellers wanted to live as close to the castle's walls as possible, many five- and six-story buildings went up in this prime real-estate area; **Gladstone's Land** (tel. 0131/226–5856; admission £2.40, £1.20 students; closed Nov.–Mar.) is a six-story tenement on Lawnmarket that reflects typical decor of a 17th-century merchant's house. **Lady Stair's House** (tel. 0131/225–2424; closed Sun.), another 17th-century building, now houses free exhibits on Scotland's literary greats—Sir

Walter Scott, Robert Louis Stevenson, and Robert Burns among them. The 16th-century **Holyrood Palace** (tel. 0131/556–7371; admission £3), at the east end of the Royal Mile, is still used by the queen when she visits Edinburgh, so it's only accessible by guided tour.

AFTER DARK Edinburgh has a lot of things to do after the sun sets, from its well-known "pub crawls" to the pas de deux of Europe's finest ballet companies. *The List,* available at any newsstand for £1, is indispensable for finding out what's going on. Old Town, especially High Street and the area around the University of Edinburgh, features a good selection of music clubs and theaters. New Town is best known for its Rose Street pubs. Festivalwise, Scotland is best known for its huge **International Arts Festival** (tel. 0131/226–4001), which runs from mid-August to the first week of September every year. The **Fringe Festival** (tel. 0131/226–5257), held during the same three weeks, is everything its stodgy older brother is not: experimental, alternative, and generally inexpensive.

➢ **PUBS** • **Greyfriars Bobby** (34 Candlemaker Row, tel. 0131/225–3147) is an upbeat pub named after Scotland's most loyal terrier—he guarded his master to the grave. At the traditional **Royal Archer** (1 High St., tel. 0131/556–6338), the friendly bartenders will patiently explain the difference between their brands of local Scottish brews. For live music, head to **Royal Oak** (1 Infirmary St., tel. 0131/557–2976), *the* pub for traditional Scottish folk music. A harder-edged, leather-and-Doc-Martens crowd gathers at **Sneaky Pete's** (73 Lower Cowgate, tel. 0131/225–1757) for live grunge.

NEAR EDINBURGH

ST. ANDREWS According to legend, St. Andrews was founded in the 4th century by St. Regulus, who was shipwrecked here while toting the relics (a few bones and whatnot) of St. Andrew. Another version of the legend has these relics arriving around the 8th century when the Culdees, a strict Christian sect, founded a settlement here. Either way, St. Andrews emerged as the religious center of Scotland by the 12th century; the strong religious influence ultimately gave rise to **St. Andrews University,** the oldest university in Scotland, founded by Bishop Henry Wardlaw in 1412. But some visitors heed a higher call than academia—namely golfers hoping to tee off on golf's holiest of shrines, St. Andrews's **Old Course.** You must be a bona fide golfer to set a cleated foot on this sanctum sanctorum: You will need a current official handicap certificate and/or a letter of introduction from your home golf club, and reservations should be made up to a year in advance for summer play. These people are serious. Of course, if the ritual of golf makes you cringe, then St. Andrews is all about long rocky shores and the brooding ruins of a 13th-century castle.

Although **St. Andrews Cathedral** (at the end of North and South Sts.) was once a magnificent building, structural faults caused the 13th-century monument to collapse twice; it wasn't sturdy enough to withstand the wicked weather that blows in from the North Sea. Today, only the twin spires of the east and west ends remain, but they and the grounds are still impressive. Also still intact is **St. Rule's Tower** (admission £1.50), built between 1127 and 1244 to honor

A Brief History of Gowf

Like most games that involve hitting a ball with a stick, golf evolved during the Middle Ages and found its way to Scotland, where it came to be known as both "gowf" and "goff." The first written reference to the sport appeared in 1457, when James II of Scotland decreed that both golf and soccer should be banned because they distracted his subjects from their archery practice. The world's first golfing clubs were the Honourable Company of Edinburgh Golfers (1744) and the Royal and Ancient of St. Andrews (1754). The first golf balls, called "featheries," were made of leather and stuffed with boiled feathers.

the founder of St. Andrews. The on-site museum helps visitors interpret the remains. Directly north of the cathedral stand the ruins of **St. Andrews Castle** (The Scores; admission £2), strategically situated upon a rocky cliff that is now home to hundreds of seagulls. Although St. Andrews isn't a big town, the folks at the **tourist office** (70 Market St., tel. 01334/72021) have maps and will book you a room for free.

➤ **COMING AND GOING** • From Edinburgh, **ScotRail** only goes as far as Leuchars (£6 one-way), about 13 km north of town. From Leuchars, catch Bus 94 or 95 (£1.30 one-way) to the St. Andrews **bus station** (City Rd., tel. 01334/74238). Or you can hop on a **Fife Scottish** (tel. 0131/556–8464 or 01592/261461) express bus from Edinburgh; Bus X59 makes the trip in 90 minutes (£4 one-way). Upon arrival, get off at Blackfriar's Chapel—a ruin on South Street—*before* the bus continues to the station, three blocks beyond.

➤ **WHERE TO SLEEP** • The tourist office books rooms at local B&Bs in the £15–£18 range. For a few pounds less, you can usually book into B&Bs outside the city center. Among them, **Pennington's Bunkhouse** (West Pitkierie, tel. 01333/310768; beds £6), 17 km from St. Andrews on the B9131 just outside of Anstruther, occupies a peaceful 13th-century farm. The friendly wardens will gladly pick you up from Anstruther, although Bus 61 from St. Andrews (£2 one-way) can drop you directly at the door. In St. Andrews itself, you'll get a yummy fried breakfast at the homey **Cleveden House** (3 Murray Pl., tel. 01334/74212; £20 per person). Five minutes from the town center on foot is **Lorimer Guest House** (19 Murray Park, tel. 01334/76599; £15–£22 per person).

➤ **FOOD** • Usually packed with a trendy crowd, **Ziggy's** (6 Murray Pl., tel. 01334/73686) is sort of a Scottish Hard Rock Cafe that specializes in burgers and chicken. Lunch is the best value at £2. University students pull late-night study sessions at **The All-Night Bakery** (Abbey St., 1 block from the Cathedral off South St.), probably Scotland's only all-night anything. **The Victoria Cafe** (St. Mary's Pl., west end of Market St.), on the upper floor of an old Victorian hotel, has good pub grub. A raucous crowd at **Ma Belle's** (The Scores) enjoys the best selection of beers in town.

Glasgow

This sprawling industrial and technological center on the banks of the River Clyde has little of the architectural interest of Edinburgh and is often dismissed as just another large city. But Glasgow does have a vitality that makes Edinburgh seem stodgy in contrast. Home to two large universities, several good museums, beautiful parks, a thriving downtown area and a good night scene, Glasgow is representative of modern Scotland. The city was once considered the country's urban dumping ground, but extremely successful city planning in the last decade has brought many companies to town and rebuilt some of the more dilapidated areas. Highlights of any trip to Glasgow include one of the few medieval cathedrals to avoid destruction during the Reformation, a Victorian cemetery, and several buildings by the 19th-century architect Charles Rennie Mackintosh.

BASICS A 10-minute walk from Central Station, the **Information Office** (35 St. Vincent Pl., tel. 0141/204–4400) books rooms and sells maps and tickets for local events. Across from Central Station is **American Express** (15 Hope St., tel. 0141/221–4366). The central **post office** (1–5 George Sq., tel. 0141/242–4260) will hold mail marked POSTE RESTANTE. The postal code is G2 1AB. For a cheap flight or info on rail and ferry passes, stop by **Campus Travel** (11 George St., tel. 0141/321–8808).

COMING AND GOING

➤ **BY TRAIN** • **Central Station,** between Hope and Union streets, handles southwest Scotland and England, with many direct trains to London (£58 one-way). **Queen Street Station,** at the corner of West George and Queen streets, serves all northern destinations. Both stations are in the center of town, only a few blocks from one another and connected Monday–Saturday by a frequent shuttle bus (40p). Both also have dozens of daily trains to Edinburgh (£5.50 one-way). For rail info in Glasgow, dial 0141/204–2844 .

➢ **BY BUS** • **Buchanan Bus Station** (corner of N. Hanover St. and Killermont St., tel. 0141/332–9191), two blocks north of Queen Street Station, is the central depot for all destinations in Scotland and England. Express bus service to and from London (9 hrs) costs around £40.

GETTING AROUND The free *Visitors Transport Guide,* available at the tourist office, makes sense of Glasgow's complicated public transit system. So, too, does the **Strathclyde Transport Travel Centre** (St. Enoch Square, tel. 0141/226–4826). Most of Glasgow's bus routes are covered by orange-and-white buses, but some private companies use the same stops and charge about the same fares. Either way, most trips around the city cost about 70p. Don't bother with Glasgow's **Underground** (tel. 0141/226–4826); it connects the center with the suburbs south of the River Clyde but does not serve ScotRail depots. A taxi across town shouldn't cost more than £6; call **Black Cabs** (tel. 0141/332–7070 or 0141/332–6666).

WHERE TO SLEEP You can book a B&B through the tourist office or at the small kiosk inside the Buchanan Bus Station. **Kelvingrove Hotel** (944 Sauchiehall St., tel. 0141/339–5011; doubles £38) has a good location near Kelvingrove Park and the museums. If you're in a real bind, the **University of Strathclyde Campus Village** (Weaver St., tel. 0141/553–4148; beds £8) almost always has a spartan room to rent during summer.

➢ **HOSTELS** • **Glasgow Backpackers Hostel.** In the University of Glasgow's Kelvin Lodge dorm, with spacious rooms, a large kitchen, two lounges, a super staff, and a kick-back atmosphere. Beds £7. *28 Park Circus, tel. 0141/332–5412. Bus 44 or 59 from Central Station to Woodlands Rd., left on Lyndedoch to Woodlands Terr., right on Park Circus. Closed Sept. 24–July 3.*

HI Glasgow Hostel. Fine if empty, a nightmare when large student groups arrive. Set in the lovely Kelvingrove Park—an excellent base for exploring Glasgow. Beds £9.25. *7 Park Terr., tel. 0141/332–3004. Bus 44 or 59 from Central Station to Park Terr. stop on Woodlands Rd.*

FOOD Glasgow has the best variety of restaurants in Scotland, with choices ranging from Caribbean to 1950s American soda fountain. You can have a cheap and filling café or pub meal along Byres Road and the Hillhead area flanking the northern side of Glasgow University. If you prefer a more standard bar meal, you can stick to the deep-fried haddock at the **Exchequer Pub** (59 Dumbarton Rd., between River Kelvin bridge and Byres Rd., tel. 0141/334–3301). A mixed clientele scarfs down meals (£6–£8) at the pleasantly scuffed wooden tables at **Bon Parisian Restaurant** (184 Dumbarton Rd., tel. 0141/337–1416). Brightly colored murals cover exposed brick and dried chilies and herbs hang from the walls of **Junkanoo** (111 Hope St., tel. 0141/248–7102), a dark and funky Caribbean restaurant that serves lunch specials for around £5.

WORTH SEEING If you have an affinity for modern cities, you'll probably enjoy Glasgow. The city's sights are spread out, so you'll spend a lot of time walking or taking the bus from one place to another. The heaviest concentration of sights is around the city center and the Kelvingrove Park area.

Glasgow Cathedral. One of the few Scottish cathedrals to escape destruction during the Reformation, the small, dark, and weathered structure is everything you could want from a 12th-century cathedral. From Queen Street it's a 15-minute walk. Behind the cathedral is the hilltop **Necropolis,** *the* place to be buried in Victorian Glasgow. Families used to compete for the highest plot and the most elaborate monument to underscore their social positions. *East end of Cathedral St., tel. 0141/552–8819. Admission free. Open Mon.–Sat. 9:30–7, Sun. 2–5.*

Glasgow School of Art. Architects and designers come from all over the world to admire the masterpiece of Glasgow-born architect Charles Rennie Mackintosh. Since it's a working school of art, visitor access is sometimes limited. *167 Renfrew St., corner of Scott St., tel. 0141/332–9797.*

Glasgow University. The main building on campus is an enormous, dark Gothic structure with a 300-foot-high tower that dominates the skyline above Kelvingrove Park. The university has produced some of Scotland's leading thinkers, including Adam Smith, the famed economist, and James Watt, who made substantial improvements on the steam engine and coined the term "horsepower." The **Hunterian Museum** (tel. 0141/330–4221) and the more interesting **Hunterian Art Gallery** (tel. 0141/330–5431) are on University Avenue, in the center of campus. The gallery houses prints and drawings by Reynolds, Rodin, Rembrandt, and Tintoretto, as well as a major collection of paintings by James McNeill Whistler. *Admission free. Both open weekdays 9:30–5, Sat. 9:30–1.*

Kelvingrove Art Gallery and Museum. The architectural plans of this huge turn-of-the-century building were mistakenly turned around and the error wasn't discovered until its massive foundation had already been laid. The museum had to be built back to front, and the architect was so distraught over this folly that he committed suicide. The collection inside includes 17th-century Dutch art, French impressionists, Scottish art, and Egyptian artifacts. *West end of Sauchiehall St., Kelvingrove Park, tel. 0141/357–3929. Admission free. Open Mon.–Sat. 10–5, Sun. 2–5.*

Pollock County Park. This large park is about 5 km southwest of the city center, off Paisley Road. Within the park, you'll find the **Burrell Collection** (tel. 0141/649–7151), once the private collection of Sir William Burrell and his wife and which they donated to the city in 1944. Glasgow's finest art collection, it consists of a hodgepodge of 8,000 pieces ranging from an ancient Assyrian iron bridle to Rodin bronzes. *Take train from Central Station to Pollokshaws West Station. Admission free. Open Mon.–Sat. 10–5, Sun. 2–5.*

AFTER DARK *The List* (£1), published biweekly, lists every public event in Glasgow and Edinburgh, from opera to thrash bands to museum exhibits; buy it at any newsstand. Small and smoke-filled, **Halt Bar** (106 Woodlands Rd.), a casual but hip pub, gets packed with young locals. Loud live music nearly every night makes shouting at the top of your lungs the only means of conversation. **Uisge Beatha** (232–246 Woodlands Rd., tel. 0141/332–0473) is pronounced something like "oos'-ka-va'-hah," and is Gaelic for "water of life." The plain concrete exterior and discreet green neon sign don't do justice to the warmth inside. **Volcano** (Benalder St., near corner of Dumbarton and Byres Rd.) is a hot spot featuring different mood grooves throughout the week in its dark, minimalist interior. Cover is £2–£4. **Bennet's Discotheque** (90 Glassford St., tel. 0141/552–5761) is the most popular gay and mixed club in town; covers are £4–£8.

Central Highlands

The accessible towns of **Perth** and **Stirling** are the gateway to the Central Highlands, which stretch north of Glasgow along the jagged western coast. The slopes of the region's lochs and hills are forested with shaggy birch, oak, and pinewoods—some of the most rugged and spectacular land in Scotland. The tops of the hills are high but not too wild for most travelers to tackle. Ben Lawers, near Killin, is the ninth-highest peak in Scotland, and the moor of Rannoch is as bleak and empty a stretch as can be seen anywhere in the north.

STIRLING

Stirling is a smaller, less-crowded version of Edinburgh. Stirling's castle, built on a steep-sided rock, dominates the landscape, and the building's Esplanade offers views of the surrounding valley-plain of the Forth River. It's as impressive as Edinburgh's castle, but instead of finding Edinburgh's ragged crowds, you'll find picnic tables set inside the castle's walls, inviting you to linger and enjoy the views of the tree-covered hills and cultivated fields of the Forth Valley. If you've got wanderlust, Stirling makes a good base for trekking in the Central Highlands. Ask the helpful folks at the **Stirling and Trossachs Tourist Board** (Dumbarton Rd., tel. 01786/475019) for a free map of the city.

COMING AND GOING Trains from Stirling travel to Edinburgh (£3.70) and Glasgow (£3.20). **Buses** are a bit cheaper and not much slower. Check at the **bus station** (Goosecroft Rd., tel. 01786/473763) for information on local lines serving the area; a round-trip bus to Glasgow costs £4.

WHERE TO SLEEP AND EAT Book way ahead if you hope to get a room in the popular **Firgrove Guest House** (13 Clifford Rd., tel. 01786/475805), where Mrs. Rodgers rents out a few rooms of her large house for £36 a double. For £9.25 per night, you can stay in the newly opened **HI hostel** (St. John St., tel. 01786/473442), a 10-minute walk uphill from the train station on the way to the castle. There are plenty of places for a bite to eat around the pedestrian streets in the commercial center of town and along Murray Place and Barnton Street, north of the city center. **Café Nouveau** (17 Barton St., tel. 01786/450423) serves a variety of main courses and filled baked potatoes for lunch and early dinners in cheerful surroundings for less than £5. For good pub lunches and dinners for about £5, head to the **Golden Lion** (8–10 King St., tel. 01786/475351).

WORTH SEEING Just below the southwestern ramparts of the castle lies the curious, geometrically shaped **King's Knot,** known locally as the "Cup 'n Saucer," which was originally a terraced garden built by William III. Now it serves as a grassy park for letting children run themselves to exhaustion. Next to the castle are several buildings dating back to the 16th century. The unfinished house of **Mar's Wark** stands on Castle Hill Wynd in front of the **Church of the Holy Rude** and its adjoining cemetery. The cemetery contains an intriguing monument: a deteriorating glassed-in shrine of a marble angel standing over two young marble girls who have lost their marble heads. Along **Broad Street,** which was once the center of trade for old Stirling, is the 18th-century **Tolbooth,** the former town hall, with a traditional Scottish steeple and gilded weathercock. For centuries, the Burgh court handed down sentences here; the jail was next door.

THE TROSSACHS AND BREADALBANE

The Trossachs are technically a short gorge linking scenic Loch Katerine with the much smaller Loch Achray to the east, but generally speaking the Trossachs and the Breadalbane highlands encompass the rugged mountains and lochs to the east of Loch Lomond all the way north to Killin on Loch Tay. Hiking, biking, and fishing in the Scottish wilderness are the main attractions of this area. Transportation into this region is easiest if you have a car, but buses can get you into most areas from either Glasgow or Edinburgh, each less than 90 minutes away.

The gateway to the Trossachs, **Callander** is easily accessible from Stirling, 27 km away, by Midland Bluebird bus. Callander is scenic but not spectacular; for jaw-dropping beauty, head northeast to **Bracklinn,** an attractive town that boasts one of the region's many waterfalls. Bracklin's **Dunmar Guest House** (Ancaster Rd., tel. 01877/31199; £13.50–£17 per person) is a pleasant place on a quiet back road.

Killin, a small, woodsy town at the foot of Loch Tay, has an alpine feel. Dozens of wooded paths lead from Killin through the hills and above the loch. Ask at the **tourist office** (Main St., tel. 01567/820254) for suggestions. The white-water rapids of the **Falls of Dochart** are at the west end of the village. Across the River Dochart are the ruins of **Finlarig Castle,** built by Black Duncan of the Cowl, an infamous chieftan of the Campbell clan. The castle's beheading pit is its most hair-raising feature. Bluebird buses make the 62-km trip from Stirling once or twice every weekday. The **Fairview House** (Main St., tel. 01567/820667; £14 per person) is a small family-run guest house in the middle of a good walking area.

LOCH LOMOND

Many hikers are attracted to the "bonny, bonny banks of Loch Lomond" and the hills rising above its banks. The southern end of the loch is wide and island-studded; the north side is more enclosed. The thick-skinned swim, waterski, and windsurf in the loch's cold, peat-darkened waters, and all types take advantage of the many hiking trails around the loch. One great trail is the 153-km **West Highland Way,** which winds along the eastern side of the Loch from Milngavie north to Glen Nevis.

COMING AND GOING Trains from Glasgow travel to **Balloch** (£2.20), at the south end of the loch, and to **Tarbet** (£6) and **Ardlui** (£7.80) in the north. Balloch isn't especially interesting and doesn't offer much for backpackers. Less expensive CityLink buses go from Glasgow's Buchanan Street Station up the eastern side of the loch toward Oban and Fort William, and they will drop you off at the Loch Lomond and Inverbeg Bay youth hostels (*see* Where to Sleep, *below*). From Inverberg, you can catch a ferry (about three times daily in summer) to Rowardennan, at the base of the popular trail up Ben Lomond. Call the Rowardennan youth hostel for information on ferry schedules.

WHERE TO SLEEP Several hostels in the area are perfect for hikers. The **HI Rowardennan Hostel** (tel. 0136087/259; closed Nov.–Feb.) is a primo place with a great view of the loch. If you don't have a car, take the ferry from Inverbeg Bay. The best hostel in the area is the **HI Loch Lomond Hostel** (tel. 0138985/226; closed Nov.–Mar. 6), 4 km north of Balloch on the A82. It occupies a former duke's hunting lodge and has a superb view of the loch. CityLink buses from Glasgow's Buchanan Street Station to Oban or Fort William will drop you off in front of the hostel.

The Southern Islands

If the craggy desolation of the Highlands seems a little daunting, head for the islands that loom off the Kintyre Peninsula. In particular, Arran and Mull both have lush landscapes and coastal villages that are pleasant even when the weather isn't. They're also popular spots for Scots to sail, fish, and hike. Best of all, the islands are close enough to the mainland to make them an easy, inexpensive, and quick vacation within a vacation.

ARRAN

Many Scots (especially Glaswegians) become misty-eyed when you speak of Arran, the island that reminds them of childhood vacations. In fact, the island looks as if it were trapped in the 1950s, with its old-fasioned cafés and boarding houses. The real appeal is the rugged terrain that attracts Scottish hiking enthusiasts. On the ferry over, you'll see many fellow travelers in their hiking boots, ready to tackle **Goat Fell,** an impressive peak (2,868 ft) that gives the island one of the most distinctive profiles in Scotland. There are no goats on Goat Fell; the name comes from the words Gaoth Bheinn, meaning windy mountain.

Brodick, the largest township on the island, is really no more than a village that snuggles up to Brodick Bay. The **Arran Tourist Information Office** (tel. 01770/302140) is at the pier. In Brodick, you'll find the **Isle of Arran Heritage Museum** (Rosaburn, tel. 01770/302636; admission £1), which documents the history of the island from antiquity to the present. **Brodick Castle** (tel. 01770/302202; admission £3.50), 3 km north of Brodick pier, is decorated with opulent furniture and paintings, but the rhododendrons outside are the real draw in warm weather.

COMING AND GOING Trains make the one-hour trip from Glasgow's Central Station to **Ardrossan** about five times a day (£3.10). From here, pick up a ferry to Arran; the trip to Brodick, on the east coast of the island, takes just under an hour. Buses on the island follow the A841 around the coast to Arran's many charming hamlets. For solitude and better hiking, head to the interior.

WHERE TO SLEEP The highest concentration of hotels is in Brodick, and they're often expensive. Check with the tourist office for a list. **The Allandale Guest House** (tel. 01770/302278), just a few minutes from the ferry terminal, is a comfy guest house open March–October. Singles start at £19, doubles at £38. The **Arran Hotel** (Shore Rd., tel. 01770/302265; £22–£28 per person), in an Edwardian building facing the Firth of Clyde, is a step above most budget places, with an indoor swimming pool and a whirlpool. You can camp in Brodick at **Glenrosa Farm** (tel. 01770/302380) for £1.50 per person.

MULL

It's possible to spend a long weekend on Mull and not meet a single resident who was born north of Manchester. Mull *does* have an indigenous population, but it's so popular with retired English military men that people often refer to it as the Officers' Mess. But don't despair: Lava cliffs line the remote southern coast, a 40-million-year-old fossil tree stands guard on a rugged stretch of coast known as the Burg, and **Ben More,** the only island *munro* (a Scottish mountain over 3,000 feet) outside Skye, looms in the interior.

Most visitors arrive by sailing from Oban, on the Kintyre peninsula, to Craignure on **Caledonian MacBrayne ferries** (Ferry Terminal, tel. 01631/62285), a £3 excursion. Once you're on the island, **Bowman's Coaches** will get you from the dock and tote you over to Fionnphort (£1.30) or Tobermory (£1.30). Hitching on the island is easy.

CRAIGNURE Mull's most interesting castle, **Torosay** (3 km southeast of Craignure, tel. 0168/02421; admission £3.50, £2.75 students), is a 30-minute walk from Craignure on the A849. If you're still recovering from your trek up Ben Lomond, catch the steam-and-diesel train that takes 20 minutes to chug from Craignure's pier to the castle grounds. Along the way, you'll get a glimpse of the dramatic mountains and coast that make this island so spectacular. The Scottish baronial palace is a friendly place; visitors have virtually free run of the building and are even allowed to plop down in the castle's armchairs for a bit. The **Pennygate Lodge** (Craignure, tel. 016802/333; £15 per person) is the cheapest place to stay in Craignure and has a view of the Sound of Mull.

TOBERMORY Tobermory's brightly painted houses give the town a Mediterranean look despite its location on the northeastern edge of this windswept island. The **Mull Museum** (Main St.) documents the town's fishing history and other aspects of Mull's past. And, if you couldn't get a tee time in St. Andrews, you can play a round at the **Western Isles Gold Course,** where the game is secondary to the spectacular view of Sound of Mull. For more info, talk to the **tourist office** (The Pier, tel. 01688/2182). The **Staffa Cottages Guest House** (tel. 01688/2464), a few minutes from the harbor, has pleasant rooms for £16–£18 per person, doubles only. The **HI hostel** (Main St., tel. 01688/2481; closed Oct.–Mar. 17) lacks plush facilities but does have a knockout view of the bay for the low, low price of £3.85 per person.

IONA

Christianity was brought to Scotland in 397 by St. Ninian, but it wasn't until St. Columba founded a church here in the 6th century that the word spread among the northerners. The island survived repeated Norse sackings and finally fell into disuse around the Reformation. Restoration work began at the turn of this century. In 1938, the **Iona Community** (tel. 0168/17404), a spiritual center that holds workshops on Christianity for the thousands who make pilgrimages here, was founded at the abbey. Although the island is very small, it has an ability to absorb hordes of visitors without losing its sense of tranquillity. You can walk the sandy beaches of the northern shore, explore the religious buildings near the abbey, and visit the wild and boggy southern tip of the island. **Caledonian MacBrayne** ferries (tel. 01475/37607) leave from Mull's port town of Fionnphort frequently for the four-minute trip to Iona.

The Northern Highlands and Isles

Many travelers headed for the north of Scotland make it only as far as Fort William or Inverness. Although they are both pleasant enough, they lack the drama of the rest of the region and are best used as entrances to the rural hinterlands—Fort William to the Inner and Outer Hebrides, and Inverness to the western and northern Highlands.

Population is sparse among the mountains and moorlands here, and, not surprisingly, public transportation is spotty. Still, you'll find a number of southerners who have moved here to escape the rat race and bask (or shiver) in the natural beauty. Venture to the Isle of Skye, famous for its misty Cuillin mountains, or the Outer Hebrides, featuring some of Scotland's finest beaches, and you, too, might feel like staying in the Northern Highlands, at least until winter sets in.

FORT WILLIAM

Fort William has almost enough interesting sights to compensate for its less-than-picturesque setting. But the main reason to visit is to stock up for a trip to the western Highlands. The **West Highland Museum** (Cameron Sq., tel. 01397/702169; admission £1), a few doors down from the tourist office, explores the theme of the 1745 Jacobite rebellion, with a "secret" portrait of Prince Charles Edward Stuart that is only recognizable when viewed in a mirror. The **Scottish Crafts and Whisky Center** (135–139 High St., tel. 01397/704406) has artifacts produced in the Highlands, from haggis to kilt socks. Helpful folks staff the **tourist office** on Cameron Square (tel. 01397/703781), a five-minute walk from the train station.

If you're ready for some exercise, head east toward **Ben Nevis.** A heavily traveled path goes from Fort William to the peak. The round-trip takes about 3–5 leisurely hours. Ask at the tourist office for info about less-touristed paths, but don't attempt anything without a map, plenty of food and water, and rain gear.

COMING AND GOING About four daily trains travel from Glasgow to Fort William (£19.50) before heading north to Mallaig. Scottish Citylink buses make the same journey about five times a day for £9.70. From Fort William, take Highland Omnibuses around the area.

WHERE TO SLEEP AND EAT Fort William has more B&Bs than just about any other town this far north. The **Ben View Guest House** (Belford Rd., tel. 01397/702966) is a red stone building overlooking Ben Nevis with rooms starting at £14 per person. The **HI Glen Nevis Youth Hostel** (Glen Nevis Rd., tel. 01397/702336; closed Nov.) is conveniently situated at the head of the trail up Ben Nevis. Picnic packers can find some reasonable deals at the **Presto supermarket** at the north end of High Street.

INVERNESS

Another of Scotland's major shipping ports, Inverness, on the Moray Firth, is best known as the town from which to embark on a search for Scotland's beloved beast, the Loch Ness Monster. Inverness itself is relatively small, but it is the last substantial town as you head north into the sparsely populated regions of northernmost Scotland. The city center isn't particularly interesting; the real beauty of the town lies in the miles of trails along the quietly dark waters of the Caledonian Canal leading to Loch Ness. B&B bookings (£1), information on travel to the Hebrides, and Loch Ness tours can be arranged at the **tourist information office** (23 Church St., tel. 01463/234353).

COMING AND GOING The train station on Academy Street has several daily trains to Glasgow (£23) and the Kyle of Lochalsh for the Isle of Skye (£11). **Scottish CityLink** buses follow the same routes from the depot a few blocks from the train station, on Academy Street.

WHERE TO SLEEP Inverness's student hotel and youth hostel are pleasant enough, so you probably won't need to pay the steep prices charged by B&Bs, which are easily booked through the tourist office. The relaxed, international **Inverness Student Hotel** (8 Culduthel Rd., tel. 01463/236556; beds £7.90) overlooking the River Ness (ask for a room with a view) is reason enough to make the journey to Inverness. From the bus or rail station, take Queensgate or Union Street to Church Street, turn left toward the tourist office, left on Bridge Street, then right on Castle Street, up the hill. Across the street, the **HI Inverness Hostel** (1 Old Edinburgh Rd., tel. 01463/231771; closed Jan. 5–Jan. 29) is a distant second choice.

LOCH NESS

This most famous of Scottish lochs, 40 km long and 1 1/2 km wide, is supposedly inhabited by the Loch Ness monster, a shy beast that makes occasional appearances to observers when they least expect it. Whether or not Nessie lurks in the depths, plenty of camera-toting, sonar-wielding, submarine-traveling scientists and curiosity-seekers haunt the loch looking for a glimpse of the elusive monster, even despite the recent brouhaha about a forged photo, a death-bed admission of guilt, and a very upset tourist board. **Urquhart Castle** (3.5 km southeast of Drumnadrochit, tel. 0131/2443101; admission £2) gives you the best views over the deep, ice-cold loch; this plundered fortess, begun in the 13th century and destroyed in the 17th to prevent the Jacobites (followers of James II) from using it, stands on a promontory overlooking the loch. If you're tired of scanning the water's surface and want to see Nessie, head to Drumnadrochit's **Official Loch Ness Monster Exhibition** (A82, tel. 01456/450573; admission £4, £3 students). You'll see photographs, the unexplained sonar contacts, and the earnest testimony of eyewitnesses. You'll also see the forged photo that made international headlines when the photographer admitted it was a fake in 1994. Buses make the 20-minute trip between Inverness and Drumnadrochit along the A82. Boats also leave from Inverness and glide along the loch.

ISLE OF SKYE

Seventy-two km long and 40 km across at its widest point, the Isle of Skye is the largest of the Inner Hebrides. It's also the most popular, thanks to the ease of the five-minute crossing from the mainland. Rugged mountain peaks, forested glens, and dramatic waterfalls pack the dense interior, rural villages dot the coast, and the formidable peaks of the Cuillins rise in the center. Some of the best climbing in Britain can be found in the **Cuillin Hills**—mountains, really—that will challenge both beginners and experts. To the north are **Macleod's Tables,** two flat-topped hills that are popular with hikers, and the dramatic **Trotternish Peninsula** hanging off the northern tip. For less rugged exploring, head to the **Sleat Peninsula** on the southeast edge of the island. The lush vegetation is a dramatic contrast to the rocky terrain of the north.

Ferries arrive at the island from the Kyle of Lochalsh on the mainland, which is accessible by four daily trains from Inverness (£9.70). Scottish CityLink buses also make the five-hour trip to the Kyle of Lochalsh from Glasgow a few times daily. The free ferry trip (£5 for cars) from the Kyle of Lochalsh to Kyleakin takes five minutes. Buses on the island are inconvenient and absurdly expensive. The most reliable service is along the coast from Kyleakin through Broadford and Luib to Portree, the island's main town. Ask at the Kyleakin tourist office for bus schedules.

KYLEAKIN Ferries from the mainland land at this not-too-interesting village. The town's only real sight is the remants of the 12th-century **Castle Maol,** which overlooks the town. Its **HI hostel** (tel. 01599/4585; beds £6.50) is just a few minutes from the ferry dock. The more interesting **Skye Backpackers Guesthouse** (tel. 01599/4510; beds £9) is just a few minutes farther. The **Dunringell Hotel** (tel. 01599/4180; £15 per person), in a tranquil country house on the main road from Kyleakin to Broadford, has some of the cheapest rooms in town and is less than 2 km from the ferry landing.

PORTREE The only serious town on Skye, Portree welcomes visitors with brightly painted houses, a beautiful setting on a small and sheltered bay, frequent buses to the rest of the island, and festivals of all kinds during the summer months. Nearby places of interest include **The Storr** mountains, featuring **The Old Man of Storr,** a black monolith reaching 150 feet high. Farther on the A855 is **Quiraing,** with its spectacular lava formations. The **Springfield Guest House** (tel. 01478/612505) has some of the cheapest rooms in town, with singles and doubles from £15 per person. For more info, contact the **tourist office** (Mealle House, tel. 01478/612137).

Northern Ireland

Northern Ireland is small—about two-thirds the size of New Jersey—and is often lumped together with the Irish Republic, its neighbor to the south. The two countries share more than just a similar climate and heritage. Both are dominated by rolling pastureland, ragged stone fences, and isolated farm villages. Irish traditions of hospitality and artful conversation prevail on both sides of the border, and no matter if you're in Dublin or Derry, asking for a "pint of plain" is simply a more complicated way of saying "Guinness, please."

The similarities, however, generally stop here. Northern Ireland, unlike the Republic, is administered and governed by England. When Ireland gained its independence in 1921, England was left with a sticky problem. Roughly 85% of the north was Protestant, but the newly created Republic of Ireland was emphatically Catholic. The Protestants rightly feared they would be treated ruthlessly by the new countrywide Catholic majority. The solution was the creation of Northern Ireland on June 22, 1921, a resolution that brought with it a Pandora's box of problems.

For a small country, Northern Ireland receives more than its fair share of international press coverage—mostly along the lines of "the IRA claimed responsibility today for a bombing that has left three dead and dozens wounded." The participants in the country's violence are mainly the reborn IRA (Irish Republican Army), the RUC (Royal Ulster Constabulary, the province's police force), and numerous political-religious factions—most notably the UDA (Ulster Defense Association)—that are commited to maintaining the country's union to Britain or destroying it. These conflicts are unlikely to affect you directly as a traveler, but you should be prepared for some unsettling side effects. Heavily armed soldiers roam many a city street, and military checkpoints are a common hassle in even the most seemingly deserted countryside. Northern Ireland does have a gloomy edge to it, but if you can see past the violence, it remains a beautiful country.

COMING AND GOING The most convenient way to travel to Northern Ireland from the United Kingdom is by ferry. From Larne Harbour, a short train ride from Belfast, the **Isle of Man Steam Packet Co.** (tel. 01232/351009) offers biweekly direct service to the Isle of Man; tickets are £21 one-way. Also from Larne Harbour, **Sealink** (tel. 01574/273616) sails eight times daily to Stranraer; **P&O Ferries** (tel. 01574/274321) offers daily service to Cairnryan, Scotland. More conveniently, **Sea Cat** (tel. 01232/312002) leaves from Donegal Quay in Belfast to Stranraer, Scotland. Ferries generally cost £116–£174 per car and £32–£36 per foot passenger. InterRail holders receive 30% discounts on some ferries (except for Seacat). **Trains** from the Republic of Ireland originate in Dublin. The trip to Belfast takes $2\frac{1}{2}$ hours and costs £11.

GETTING AROUND Eurail and InterRail passes are good here, but there are a number of other options. The **Runabout** ticket costs £35 and is good for seven consecutive days of unlimited train travel in Northern Ireland only. The **Freedom of Northern Ireland** ticket costs £25 and is good for seven consecutive days of unlimited travel on all Northern Irish buses. All passes are available from any bus or rail depot in Northern Ireland. The principal bus company is the state-owned **Ulsterbus** (Belfast, tel. 01232/333000); some Ulsterbus routes give a discount with EurailPass or InterRail.

Belfast

Northern Ireland's capital, buffered by green water on one side and by heath-strewn hills on the other, has been called everything from a well-armed wasteland to "Little Beirut." In Belfast, armored troop carriers roam apartment-block ghettos while 19-year-old soldiers carrying machine guns move silently along busy shopping streets. Despite the presence of some 7,000 soldiers, thousands of residents have been wounded and killed here as a result of the Catholic–Protestant Troubles (known here simply as "the Troubles"). Despite Belfast's obvious dangers, the 25-year-old Troubles shouldn't stop you from visiting. Shouting "God Save the

Queen" in the wrong pub is certainly unwise, but as long as you don't mind the occasional security-related inconvenience—like being frisked at a train station—Belfast is a fascinating place to visit.

BASICS To get to the **Northern Irish Tourist Information Center** (59 North St., tel. 01232/246609) from Donegall Square, walk north on Donegall Place and turn right onto North Street. The local **American Express** desk is hidden inside Hamilton Travel (10 College St., tel. 01232/322455), directly across from the Fountain Centre Mall. The **General Post Office** (Castle Pl., tel. 01232/323740) is two blocks north of Donegall Square, just off Donegall Place.

COMING AND GOING Belfast has two main rail stations, **Belfast Central** (East Bridge St., tel. 01232/230310), 1 km east of the city center, and the smaller **York Gate Station** (York Rd., tel. 01232/741700), 2 km north of the center, as well as a handful of suburban depots convenient for intra-Belfast travel. Trains leave frequently for Dublin (£13) and Derry (£5.90).

Ulsterbus (tel. 01232/333000), Northern Ireland's national bus company, has two city center terminals, **Europa Buscentre** (Glengall St., tel. 01232/320011) and **Oxford Street Station.** (Oxford St., tel. 01232/320011). The first primarily serves Counties Tyrone, Fermanagh, Down, and all Irish-republic destinations; the latter, County Antrim and the area immediately surrounding Belfast.

➤ **BY PLANE** • Belfast has two principal airports. **Belfast International Airport** (Crumlin, tel. 018494/22888), 30 km northwest of town, offers service to a handful of international destinations. Airport shuttle buses (£3.50) leave every 30 minutes from the Europa Buscentre. **Belfast City Airport** (Syndenham, tel. 01232/457745), for U.K. flights only, is 6 km outside town. Take Bus 21 from Donegall Square (£1) or a train from Central Station to Sydenham Halt (£1).

GETTING AROUND Belfast's principal sights are grouped around **Donegall Square.** The easiest way to get around is via the free **Rail-Link shuttle bus** (tel. 01232/246485), which connects Belfast Central with Donegall Square, Fisherwick Place (near Ulsterbus's Europa station), Donegall Place, and the York Road depot. Outside each station and along the streets are well-marked "Rail-Link" shuttle stops, serviced every 15 minutes or so Monday–Saturday. **City buses** charge 65p–£1.10, depending on distance. Tickets can be purchased on board or at newsstands. Most buses pass through Donegall Square, where you can pick up bus maps at the **Citybus Kiosk** (tel. 01232/246485).

WHERE TO SLEEP Belfast's sleeping scene is grim. There's no campground within reach, and the only hostel is the institutional **HI Belfast Ardmore** (11 Saintfield Rd., tel. 01232/647865; beds £7.20), 5 km south of the city center. From Donegall Square, take Bus 84, 79, or 38 and ask the driver to stop at the hostel. A better bet during school vacations are the dorms at the **Queen's Elms Student Hall** (78 Malone Rd., tel. 01232/381608; beds £11.20, £8.25 students), within walking distance of Shaftesbury Square. From Donegal Square, take Bus 71 and tell the driver where you're headed. The best budget B&B is **Marine House** (30 Eglantine Ave., tel. 01232/662828). If it's full, try the **Eglantine Guest House** (21 Eglantine Ave., tel. 01232/667585) next door. Both charge £15 per person.

FOOD Belfast's city center is a culinary black hole, although **Kelly's Cellars** (3 Bank St., off Royal Ave., tel. 01232/324835) and the **Deer's Head** (1–4 Lower Garfield St., tel. 01232/239163) are renowned for their home-style pub grub. There are lots more options around the **Golden Mile,** a triangular area bordered by Howard Street, Great Victoria Street, Bedford Street, and Dublin Road. Do as the locals do at **Crown Liquor Saloon** (46 Great Victoria St., tel. 01232/249467) and call for a "pint of Guinness, bowl of stew, please," but also try the steak-and-kidney pie (95p). Botanic Avenue and Bradbury Place are two student areas peppered with good restaurants. The **Empire** (42 Botanic Ave., tel. 01232/328110) is a lively student pub with a daily pizza-and-pint special (£3) during the school year.

WORTH SEEING At first glance, Belfast is a frustrating city to explore. RUC checkpoints and the gloomy suspicion felt on the street make exploring the city a less-than-exuberant experience. Many parts of town have become "no go" for tourists, especially the Falls and Shankill districts, where most of the Catholic-Protestant violence occurs. Though unescorted forays are not recommended, ask one of the black cabs, usually driven by Belfast Catholics, who line up along Donegall Square East for a guided tour of the Catholic **Falls** area. Besides Falls Road itself, the highlight of this area is **Milltown Cemetery,** the IRA's principal burial ground. Note the IRA–Native American mural, a reference to the worldwide struggle against imperialism. With a little pleading you may get the cabbie to cross the lines into Shankill for a look at the Protestant side of the coin. Fares for these informal tours are determined by your ability to barter; an hour can cost £6–£15. If you're sticking to the city center, pick up the *Belfast Civic Trail* (free), a series of five detailed, self-guided walking tours distributed by the tourist office.

Belfast's city center is dominated by its Renaissance-style **City Hall** (Donegall Sq.), built between 1898 and 1906. Its most impressive feature is the 173-foot-high **Great Dome.** Although walk-in visitors are not allowed, guides conduct tours daily at 10:30 AM in the summer. The excellent **Old Museum Arts Centre** (7 College Sq. N., tel. 01232/235053) helped put Belfast on the world art map; although it doesn't have a permanent collection, the OMAC showcases some of the best Irish and international modern art and performances. Admission varies with each event.

AFTER DARK The area between Shaftesbury Square and Queen's University is endowed with lively student pubs, theaters, and late-night coffeehouses. Try **Lavery's Gin House** (12 Bradbury Pl., off Shaftesbury Sq., tel. 01232/327159), a pub with lots of grimy charm. The warehouse-size **Empire** (42 Botanic Ave., tel. 01232/228110) serves international beers and hosts local musicians. **Eglantine** (32 Malone Rd., tel. 01232/381994) and **Botanic Inn** (29 Malone Rd., tel. 01232/660460), known locally as the "Egg" and "Bot," are popular with students.

The Causeway Coast

The Causeway Coast, stretching 80 km along Northern Ireland's Atlantic coast, is understandably the most visited region in the north. Many budget travelers head first for **Ballycastle**, a small but lively beach town that boasts a good hostel and a brazen pub scene. From here, you're also within easy reach of **Bushmills**, home of the world's oldest licensed distillery. Three km west are the gutted remains of **Dunluce Castle**, an impressive 16th-century fortress that clings stubbornly to the jagged edge of a rocky headland, 110 precarious feet above the rough Atlantic.

PORTRUSH

On the tip of Ramore Peninsula, Portrush is one of Northern Ireland's most-touristed seaside resorts—a hodgepodge of beach, video arcades, and smarmy tourist restaurants. Its most infamous attraction is **Waterworld** (The Harbour, tel. 01265/822001; admission £3.25; closed Oct.–Apr.), a massive complex of indoor swimming pools, diving boards, water slides, saunas, and shirtless preteens. Just north of Waterworld is a pristine beach and cliff-top overlook, but when the weather's grim, you'll be stuck sipping coffee in a pricey café. The **tourist office** (Dunluce Center, tel. 01265/823333; closed wekdays Oct.–Apr.) is in the center of town.

COMING AND GOING Portrush's **train station** (tel. 01265/822395) is a five-minute walk from Portrush's center. Trains travel to Belfast (£5.90) and Londonderry (£4.50). Portrush is also well connected by bus to most of the Causeway Coast; the unstaffed depot is near the roundabout on Dunluce Avenue, a block east of the rail station.

WHERE TO SLEEP AND EAT Portrush has two good B&Bs, both with views of the beach: **The Clarence** (7 Bath Terr., tel. 01265/823575), a Georgian flat on Portrush's eastern edge, and **The Rest-A-While** (6 Bath Terr., tel. 01265/822827), a brightly colored Georgian relic next door. Both have rooms starting at £12 per person. For a reasonable meal of chips and burgers, try **Shirley's Diner** (26 Causeway St., tel. 01265/823581) or the **Singing Kettle Café** (5 Atlantic Ave., tel. 01265/823068). Both offer grub for less than £5.

DUNLUCE CASTLE

Dunluce Castle, halfway between Portrush and the Giant's Causeway, is one of Northern Ireland's most evocative ruins. Built by the MacDonnell clan in AD 1550, it perches on the edge of a ragged cliff with a commanding view of the Atlantic coast. Most of its towers and battlements were destroyed centuries ago, and over the years cliff erosion has played havoc with what's left of this 2-acre complex. Still, Dunluce's surviving patchwork of walls and round towers remains intensely beautiful, especially at sunset or on a foggy, gray day. Guarding the castle entrance is a **visitor center** (no phone) where the £1 admission to the castle is collected. Underneath Dunluce is a sea cave, accessible only by water in good weather—definitely worth the £1 fee. Inquire at the visitor center for current schedules.

Dunluce's only drawback is its location. Although Ulsterbus's Causeway Coast express drives right past it, the castle is not serviced by public transportation. Unless you have a car, you'll need to hike or hitch the 5 km from Portrush to Dunluce along the A2 highway. Fortunately, this road is quite scenic once you escape Portrush's condominium suburbs. From Dunluce, it's also quite easy to hitch or walk the remaining 4-km stretch to Bushmills, where you can catch a Portrush- or Causeway-bound Ulsterbus.

BUSHMILLS DISTILLERY

Bushmills, the oldest licensed distillery in the world, was first granted a charter in 1608, although historical records refer to a distillery here as early as 1276. Today, Bushmills is one of the busiest and most-respected distillers in Ireland, even more so after its recent low-key merger with the republic's own distillery, Jameson of County Cork. Bushmills's greatest appeal to the whiskey drinker, however, is its free guided tours, topped off with a complimentary shot of *uisce beatha,* the "water of life." To reach the distillery, take any Causeway Coast Ulsterbus between Ballycastle and Portrush; all stop in the center of Bushmills Town. From here, follow the signs to the distillery gate. *Tel. 012657/31521. Admission free. Open Oct.–June, Mon.–Thurs. 9–noon and 1:30–3:30, Fri. 9–11:45; July–Sept., Mon.–Thurs. 9–noon and 1:30–3:30, Fri. 9–3, Sat. 10–3. Tours leave every 15 min; last tour leaves 30 min before closing. Reservations not required.*

THE GIANT'S CAUSEWAY

Spanning the coast for $3^1/_2$ km, the Giant's Causeway and its 40,000 basalt columns are truly impressive. Geologists say these interlocking six- and seven-sided basalt blocks, ranging from 4 inches to 6 feet long, were formed by cooling lava 2 million years ago. Others claim the causeway was built by the mythic Irish figure Finn MacCool, who constructed the causeway to do battle with the Scotland's heroic warrior Bennandonnar. Buses from Portrush (£2.60 round-trip) arrive at the front gate of the **visitor center** (44 Causeway Rd., tel. 012657/31855). Watch their good audiovisual show (£1) on the site's history and ask about nearby hiking trails.

BALLYCASTLE

Although Ballycastle's independent youth hostel draws crowds of backpackers and cyclists, tourists have largely ignored the place—making it easier to appreciate Ballycastle's oceanfront promenade and the beautifully aged shops that line Castle and Diamond streets. Or head straight to the pub; summer nights there's bound to be some traditional music at either **House of McDonnell** (Castle St., tel. 012657/62975) or **Diamond Bar** (The Diamond, tel. 012657/62142).

The **tourist office** (Sheskburn House, 7 Mary St., tel. 012657/62024) is near the beach and docks; to reach the town center, turn left onto Mary Street and continue straight up Quay Road. Trains don't service Ballycastle, so you'll need to catch a bus from Belfast (£9 return) or Portrush (£5 return). The unstaffed **bus depot** is behind the Diamond on the west end of town. If you're staying at the hostel, a closer stop is near the intersection of Quay Road and Mary Street, opposite the Marine Hotel. From here, it's a short walk to the excellent **Castle Hostel** (62 Quay Rd., tel. 012657/62337), a 15-bed house (£5 per night) near the beach and pier, a 15-minute walk from the town's best pubs and chippers. Bummer.

Londonderry

Londonderry, known simply as Derry in the republic, is one of Northern Ireland's most underrated towns. Although factories and tenements line the banks of the River Foyle, good examples of Georgian and Victorian architecture rub shoulders with a handful of old-style pubs in the city center, which is encircled by 20-foot-tall walls from the 17th century. The **tourist office** (8 Bishop St., tel. 01504/369501) gives out free maps.

COMING AND GOING The **train station** (Duke St., tel. 01504/42228) is across the River Foyle from the city center. Destinations from Derry include Portrush (£4.50), Belfast (£7), and Dublin (£15.50). Local Bus 7 leaves from Craigavon Bridge, two blocks south of the train station, and makes the short hop across the river to the **Ulsterbus station** (Foyle St., tel. 01504/262261); catch a bus to Belfast (£5.30), Portrush (£4.75), or Dublin (£10).

WHERE TO SLEEP AND EAT HI **Oakgrove Manor** (4–6 Magazine St., tel. 01504/372273) has beds for £7. The **Florence Guesthouse** (16 Northland Rd., tel. 01504/268093; beds £12) is a homey five-room B&B near the hostel. The local **YMCA** (51 Glenshane Rd., tel. 01504/301662), on the east side of the River Foyle, has beds for £6. From Ulsterbus's Foyle Street depot, take Bus 8 to Glenshane Road. Derry's walled city center bristles with mid-range and upscale restaurants, mostly around Shipquay Street and the Diamond. One of the best cheap restaurants is **Malibu** (6 Bishop St., tel. 01504/371784), next to the tourist office, serving bargain burgers and sandwiches, as well as breakfast (£2.15) all day. Another good bet is the **Glue Pot** (34 Shipquay St., tel. 01504/367463), a family-run place with soup-and-sandwich combos for less than £4.

WORTH SEEING Most of Derry's attractions are within its well-preserved city walls, which stretch from Foyle and Magazine streets in the north to Artillery and Market streets in the south. The tourist office organizes city walks on weekdays during the summer (£1.50). One block north of the Diamond, **O'Doherty Tower** (Magazine St. Gate, tel. 01504/365151) was built in 1615 with funds from the City of London. The tower offers an audiovisual presentation on Derry's history as well as a part-folk, part-civic museum. To the south, the **Derry Craft Village** (Shipquay St.) is a novel shopping experience that combines retail shops, workshops, and residential apartments in an 18th-century setting, complete with crafts demonstrations and costumes. The **Railway Heritage Center** (Foyle St. Station, tel. 01504/265234) has mothballed locomotives, antique signal levers, and lots of railroad paraphernalia. Back inside the city walls is **St. Columb's Cathedral** (off Bishop St., tel. 01504/262746; admission 50p), a regal Protestant complex built in 1633. Notice the colorful procession of banners in the nave, a reminder of Londonderry's pro-British stance. If you want a glimpse of Derry's ugly underside, consider a trip to the **Fountain** district, a fiercely Protestant enclave sporting pro-British graffiti, burned-out buildings, and a profusion of barbed wire; it sprawls between Bishop Street Gate and the river.

AFTER DARK Derry's two best pubs are the **Strand Tavern** (Strand Rd., tel. 01504/266446) and the **Metro** (3 Bank Pl., tel. 01504/267401). The Strand is good for pub grub and low-key conversation, while the Metro has the looks of a quiet country bar.

GREECE

By Dawn MacKeen and Oliver Schwaner-Albright

One of the best things you could do when you arrive in Greece is take off your watch. Sevice is slow, schedules are often not met, and businesses open and close on a whim. If you don't resign yourself to the Greeks' sense of time, you just may go crazy. Time is not money here, and deadlines are not important—what is important is living life event by event, not minute by minute.

Greeks are heir to two distinct cultures. The modern culture of this Balkan state has been influenced by hundreds of years of Ottoman occupation and infighting with Albanians and Bulgarians, but it is the ancient Greece of Plato's philosopher king that has formed the foreign perception of the country. When Greeks were pushing for independence from the Ottoman Empire in the early 19th century, England, France, and Russia offered military, financial, and emotional support as the Greeks reclaimed the traditions of the city-states that thrived 2,000 years before. They put huge effort into educating the Greeks about an ancient past with which they had lost touch. The Greeks were amazed by the affection that the western world felt toward their forgotten culture, and they took advantage of the open hearts and open pocketbooks of other European nations.

Since gaining autonomy in 1829, Greece has endured western-appointed kings, invasions galore, and struggles between political parties. PASOK, a socialist labor party, operates in rhythm with the Greek way of life. It supports the common person, attempts to lower taxes, and loosens regulations. The New Democratic Party, on the other hand, advocates long-term economic improvements to help Greece catch up with other European nations. For the past couple of decades, the Greek people's support has oscillated between the two parties. In 1993, they opted for PASOK, electing an ailing Andreas Papandreou prime minister. How long he and his lenient party can preside over the weakest national treasury in the European Union (formerly the European Community), nobody knows.

For the time being, however, the traveler can revel in the Greek dreamworld of extended siestas and parties till dawn, often unaware of the tensions beneath the surface. The country as a whole and the Pelopónnisos in particular recall a time of gods and centaurs and ancient wonders—and you'll have to admit it's pretty cool to see where the first Olympics were held and where the oracle of Delphi once gave advice to the likes of Oedipus and Agamemnon. Northern Greece is less visited than the islands and the area around Athens, but it has just as many wonders, including Mt. Olympus and the eerie Metéora monasteries.

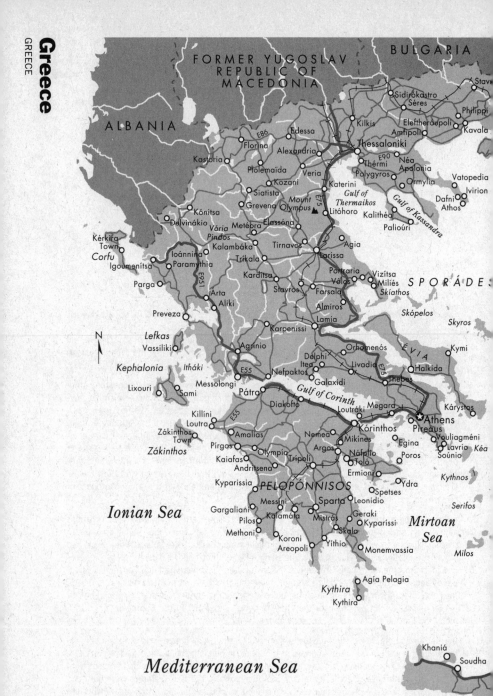

FORMER YUGOSLAV
REPUBLIC OF
MACEDONIA

BULGARIA

ALBANIA

Stav

Sidirókastro
Séres

Philippi

Kilkis
Eleftheroúpoli
Amfípoli
Kavala

E86
Florina
Edessa
Thessaloníki
Alexandria
Kastoria
Thérmi
E90
Néa
Apolonia
Ptolemaïda
Polygyros
Vatopedia
Veria
Ormylia
Ivirion
Kozáni
Katerini
Dafni
Siatista
Gulf of
Thermaikos
Athos
Kónitsa
Grevena
Mount
Dalvinákio
Olympus
Litóhoro
Gulf of Kassandra
Vória
Elassóna
Kalithéa
Metéora
Pindos
Palioúri
Kérkira
Kalambáka
Town
Corfu
Ioánnina
Trikala
Tirnavos
Agia
Igoumenitsa
Paramythia
Larissa
SPORÁDES
Karditsa
Parga
Portaria
E951
Vizítsa
Arta
Vólos
Miliés
Aliki
Stavros
Farsala
Skíathos
Preveza
Almiros
Skópelos
Lefkas
Karpenissi
Lamia
Skyros
Vassiliki
Agrinio
Kephalonia
Itháki
Orhomenós
ÉVIA
Kymi
Délphi
Itéa
Livadiá
Lixouri
E55
Nefpaktos
Halkida
Messolongi
Galaxidi
E75
Thebes
Sami
Pátra
Thebes
Kárystos
Gulf of Corinth
Diakofto
Megara
Athens
Killíni
Loutráki
Piraeus
Loutra
Kórinthos
Vouliagméni
Zákinthos
Amalías
Nemea
Mikines
Egina
Lavrio
Kéa
Town
Pírgos
Argos
Poros
Soúnio
Zákinthos
Olympia
Náfplio
Kaiafas
Tripoli
Toló
Kythnos
Andritsena
Ermioni
Kyparissia
Ýdra
Serifos
PELOPÓNNISOS
Spetses
Messini
Sparta
Leonidio
Gargaliani
Kalamáta
Mistrás
Geraki
Mirtoan
Pilos
Kyparissi
Sea
Methoni
Skala
Koroni
Yithio
Milos
Areopoli
Monemvassía

Ionian Sea

Agía Pelagia
Kythira
Kythira

Mediterranean Sea

Khaniá
Soudha

CRETE

N

0 ———— 100 miles
0 ———— 300 km

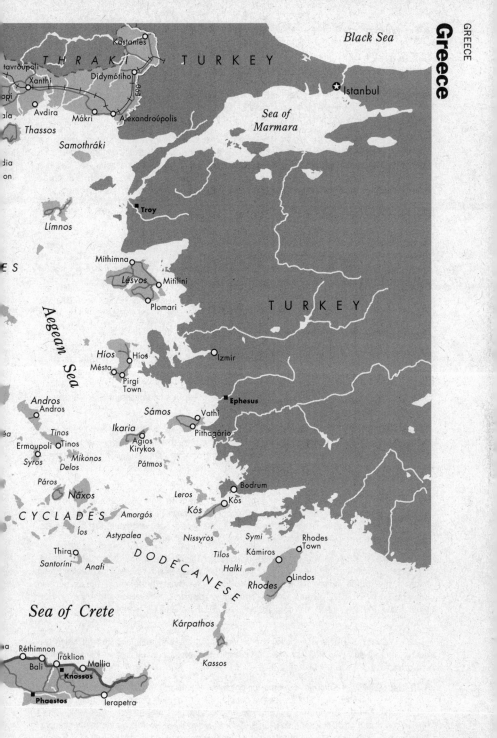

Black Sea

Istanbul

Sea of
Marmara

T U R K E Y

THRAKI

Kastaniés

tavroúpoli

Xanthi

Didymótiho

opi

Avdira

Mákri

Alexandroúpolis

ala

Thassos

Samothráki

dia

on

Límnos

Troy

Míthimna

Lésvos

Mitilíni

Plomari

ES

Aegean Sea

Híos

Híos

Mésta

Izmir

Pirgí
Town

Ephesus

Andros

Sámos

Vathí

Andros

Ikaria

Pithagório

éa

Tinos

Agios
Kirýkos

Ermoúpoli

Tinos

Pátmos

Syros

Míkonos

Delos

Páros

Náxos

Bodrum

Leros

C Y C L A D E S

Amorgós

Kós

Kós

Íos

Astypalea

Thira

Nissyros

Symi

Rhodes
Town

Santoríni

Anafi

Tilos

Kámiros

D O D E C A N E S E

Halki

Lindos

Rhodes

Sea of Crete

Kárpathos

a

Réthimnon

Iráklion

Bali

Mallia

Knossos

Kassos

Phaestos

Ierapetra

419

Basics

MONEY $1 = 225 drachmas and 100 drachmas = 45¢. The best exchange rates are, surprisingly, at ATMs, which take Visa, MasterCard, American Express, Cirrus, and Plus cards. Other than that, your credit cards will be pretty useless, since hardly any budget hotels or restaurants accept them. The best option for changing your traveler's checks into drachmas is a bank, normally open Monday–Thursday 8–2 and Friday 8–1:30; post office rates are comparable to those at banks.

➤ **HOW MUCH IT WILL COST** • Prices in Greece have been floating upward ever since the country's initiation into the EU, making the fabled inexpensive Greek vacation more of a myth with every passing year. Prices differ dramatically from season to season. You can live on about $30 a day from September through most of June; in July and August, tack on an extra $10 a day, a little more on the islands, a little less if you stay in hostels and camp.

COMING AND GOING The ferry is the only way to get all the way to Greece using your EurailPass, though you still have to pay a supplement in high season.

➤ **BY BUS** • You can bus it directly into Greece through Albania, Bulgaria, and Turkey. Private coaches and buses run by the **Hellenic State Railways** (1–3 Karolou, Athens, tel. 01/52–40–601) make the trip. Prices vary greatly, so ask at any budget travel agency for specifics.

➤ **BY PLANE** • Planes are the most expensive but least tedious way to get here. **Olympic Airlines** soars directly to Athens from Rome (2½ hrs, 53,700dr, 45,600dr students), Paris (2½ hrs, 78,000dr, 66,000dr students), and London (2 hrs, 81,100dr, 68,400dr students).

➤ **BY FERRY** • Frequent ferries travel from Italy to Greece. In summer, at least seven ferries a day sail from Brindisi and about two each from Bari, Ancona, and Trieste; all go to Corfu (Kérkira) and/or Igoumenítsa and Pátra. A number of companies run ferries, but Eurail-Passes are accepted only on ferries from Brindisi, and only on Adriatica and Hellenic Mediterranean Lines. Ferries to and from Turkey land frequently on eastern Grecian islands, but both Turkey and Greece levy huge port taxes.

GETTING AROUND Scooting around Greece on a **motorbike** is liberating, especially since many beaches and small villages aren't accessible by bus. It is not, however, terribly safe—roads are rocky, bikes are often rattly, and helmets are a rare commodity. The cheapest one-person scooters go for around 1,300dr per day; sturdier two-person scooters cost about 4,000dr per day.

➤ **BY BUS** • The national bus system, **KTEL,** is efficient and comprehensive. In large towns, it's a good idea to buy tickets in advance in case they sell out. In smaller towns, ask a local where the bus stop is (sometimes a sign, sometimes a tree) and when the buses pass. Then flag one down, climb on, and tell the driver your destination.

➤ **BY TRAIN** • Greek rail is wretched. It's cheaper than the bus, but it's also slow, crowded, dirty, and useful only for trips along the eastern coast. Make reservations to avoid long hours in the station waiting for openings. The brand-new **Innercity** trains are more expensive but worth it if you value cleanliness and efficiency. You can get tickets at stations or at **Hellenic State Railways** (1–3 Karolou, Athens, tel. 01/52–40–601), which handles all train routes.

➤ **BY FERRY** • Huge, slow boats connect most islands and mainland coastal cities frequently during summer and less often off-season. **Hydrofoils** are twice as quick and double the price.

WHERE TO SLEEP **Dhomatia** (rooms) or **pansiyons** (pensions) are the best places to sack out at night, and they start at $15 for two people. They're usually clean and run out of someone's home, and the proprietors are often willing to bargain. **Hotel** quality varies widely from one region to the next, but doubles generally start around $15. **Hostels** are normally cheaper, but lockouts and curfews force guests into a schedule contrary to that of the rest of the country. A clean **campground**, usually charging about a buck for a site plus $4 or so per person, is usually only a short bus ride away. Pitching a tent on public ground is officially prohibited but usually tolerated, particularly in untouristed coves or forested areas. Finally, ask at reception desks about **rooftop** spaces, which are generally not advertised but cost around $4 when available. Lodging reviews in this chapter are based on high-season rates. Hotels always post high- and low-season rates on the rooms' doors, but proprietors often fiddle around with prices, so the rates listed here may be a a little more than, a little less than, or on occasion, not even in the same ballpark as the actual prices.

FOOD The waiters are slow, the bread is often stale, and the national menu is short, but a meal at a Greek restaurant is a damn good time. Lunch is generally served 1–3, dinner between 9 and 11 PM. Budget travelers spend most dining time in tavernas, casual, inexpensive restaurants where the food is usually at least as good as that at more formal places. Sunday meals everywhere carry a 10% surcharge. A gratuity is included in the bill; just round up a couple hundred drachmas. For daytime snacks, street stalls sell gyros (sliced pork roasted on a spit) or souvlaki (skewered cubes of meat), both sometimes served in pita bread with tomatoes and a cucumber sauce. Other big-time Greek specialties are moussaka (layered eggplant and ground meat, topped with white sauce and cheese) and *tsatsiki* (yogurt, cucumber, and garlic dip). The Greeks wash it all down with *ouzo* (anise liquor served diluted with water). Frappés (Nescafé, sugar, and cream whipped up with ice) are the drink of choice in summer. Grocery stores are common, but they aren't much cheaper than inexpensive restaurants.

VISITOR INFORMATION The national tourist organization, **EOT,** has helpful offices in nearly every town; some book rooms for travelers.

PHONES **Country code: 30.** The national phone company is **OTE.** Most towns have at least one OTE office for metered, collect, and calling-card calls. Telecard phone booths are steadily covering the cities and moving into smaller towns—buy cards at OTE offices and some news kiosks. Press the *i* button on telecard phones for instructions in English. Metered phones at travel agencies and hotels are much more expensive than phones at OTE offices. From any phone, dial 00800–1311 for AT&T USA Direct; for MCI's Call USA, dial 00800–1211. To call outside Greece, dial 00, then the country code and number. To the United States it's $2.50 for the first minute, $1.40 for each additional minute.

The Greek ΑΒΓs

Many proper names in this chapter are just the transliterated version of the Greek name, so if you come upon signs written in the Greek alphabet, don't panic. Just use this list to figure out what you're looking at:

Greek	Roman	Greek	Roman	Greek	Roman
A, α	**a**	I, ι	**i**	P, ρ	**r**
B, β	**v**	K, κ	**k**	Σ, σ, ς	**s**
Γ, γ	**g or y**	Λ, λ	**l**	T, τ	**t**
Δ, δ	**dh or d**	M, μ	**m**	Y, υ	**i**
E, ε	**e**	N, ν	**n**	Φ, φ	**f**
Z, ζ	**z**	Ξ, ξ	**x or ks**	X, χ	**h or ch**
H, η	**i**	O, o	**o**	Ψ, ψ	**ps**
Θ, θ	**th**	Π, π	**p**	Ω, ω	**o**

MAIL The Greek mail system may get your postcards (120dr to the United States) home within a week or may leave them in limbo for months. **Post offices** are normally open weekdays 7:30–2, though larger towns have extended evening hours. They all theoretically hold poste restante for a month, though rural post offices may not know what to do with it. Mailboxes are big yellow contraptions with a picture of Hermes inside a horn.

EMERGENCIES Dial 100 for the police, 166 for a medical emergency; the call takes 10dr from pay phones. If your pocket has been picked, contact the **tourist police,** present in most towns. They're there specifically to help you and are much friendlier than the regular police.

STAYING HEALTHY Tap water is generally safe, but bottled water is cheap and readily available. Watch out for cheap alcoholic drinks on the more touristed islands, where many clubs use grain alcohol instead of tequila or vodka. For nonemergency medical problems, you can try a **pharmacy,** indicated with a green cross; pharmacists have near-doctor status and prescribe medicine. Just hope you don't get into a major accident in Greece: Medical supplies are low and treatments old-fashioned.

LANGUAGE When you first hear a Greek conversation, you might think an argument is taking place. Greek is a passionate language, involving hand gestures, facial expressions, and loud exclamations. Most Greeks also speak English, though they may resent having to do so. German comes in handy here as well.

CULTURE When visiting a church, cover your legs or hope this is one of the many Greek churches that will lend you a skirt. When using your fingers to designate numbers, keep your palm pointed toward you—an outward palm is an offensive gesture—and extend your thumb to indicate one. Women traveling solo may face some unpleasant challenges. Greek men aren't likely to be dangerous, but women travelers are likely to be propositioned, leered at, and grabbed on at least a few occasions.

Athens

Athens (Athínai in Greek), the political and intellectual center of ancient Greece, is the accidental (some say unfortunate) capital of modern Greece. Overpopulated, polluted, and ugly, Athens is a difficult city to love, although its concentration of culture makes it an impossible place to ignore. The city was designated the capital of the Greek nation-state because Western European powers were enamored with the idea of turning the ancient home of Socrates and Pericles into the seat of a modern democratic government. The foreign powers ignored the fact that the population of Athens had diminished to less than 10,000 and remade the village into a modern version of the ancient city. Dutch designers reintroduced Greek architecture to the Greeks through the neoclassical **University, Art Academy,** and **National Library** and **Royal Palace** (now the Parliament Building). Modern Athens is therefore a confusing place, a vast sprawl of concrete apartment buildings, narrow streets, imposing governmental offices, and the occasional stunningly beautiful ruin. The uncontrolled growth has turned the capital into a borderline unlivable place, prompting the government to expand the aged Metro system, create much-needed parks, and curb the freeway-style traffic.

Most people who pass through are thoroughly annoyed by what Athens has become. Many neighborhood shops close during July and August, as Athenians turn from their smog-filled city in favor of island beaches. The businesses that stay open conduct their business in the early morning, closing their doors during the afternoon when the unshaded streets seem something like hell on earth. The city comes back to life at night, when the cool breezes and darker sky erase recent memories of the heat and filth of the day.

BASICS

VISITOR INFORMATION The EOT operates two offices in central Athens, both near Platía Sindagma. *2 Karageorgio Servias, tel. 1/32–22–545. Open weekdays 8–6:30, Sat. 9–2, Sun. 9–1. 1 Ermou, tel. 1/32–52–267. Open weekdays 8–6:30, Sat. 8–2.*

AMERICAN EXPRESS The office is open on Saturday for mail pickup only. *2 Ermou, Box 332, Athens 10225, tel. 01/32–44–975. Open weekdays 8:30–4, Sat. 8–1:30.*

CHANGING MONEY Banks are gathered on Stadiou near Platía Sindagma. The national bank at 2 Karageorgio Servias has a 24-hour currency-exchange machine with good rates. The rates of the black marketeers near Platía Sindagma aren't worth the risk.

EMBASSIES AND CONSULATES **Australia.** *37 Dim Soutsou, tel. 01/64–47–303. Open weekdays 9–3.*

Canada. *4 Genadiou, tel. 01/72–54–011. Open weekdays 8:30–3.*

New Zealand Vice-Consul. *9 Semitelou, tel. 01/77–10–112.*

United Kingdom. *1 Ploutarchou, tel. 01/72–36–211. Open weekdays 9–3.*

United States. *91 Vasilissis Sofias, tel. 01/72–12–951. Open weekdays 9–3.*

EMERGENCIES To contact the **tourist police,** dial 171.

PHONES AND MAIL Two OTE phone offices operate in the city center, one at the southeast corner of Platía Omónia and the second at 15 Stadiou, at the corner of Lada; both are open 24 hours.

The central post office on Platía Sindagma at the corner of Mitropoleos (postal code 10300) is more efficient than the one just southeast of Platía Omónia at 100 Eolou (postal code 10200). Both are open weekdays 7:30–8, Saturday 7:30–2; the Platía Sindagma office is also open Sunday 9–1:30.

COMING AND GOING

BY TRAIN Two train stations serve Athens; both are northwest of Platía Omónia and they're connected to each other by an iron bridge over the tracks. Daily trains from the grand old Victorian **Pelopónnisos station** head to Pátra (5 hrs, 2,300dr), Kórinthos (2½ hrs, 1,300dr), and Kalamáta (11½ hrs, 4,200dr). Daily trains from the hectic **Laríssis station** travel to Larissa (6 hrs, 2,500dr), Vólos (7 hrs, 2,700dr), and Thessaloníki (8 hrs, 3,500dr). Take Trolleybus 1 from Laríssis station to reach Platía Sindagma or Platía Omónia.

BY BUS A KTEL station at **100 Kifissou** services most of Greece, with daily connections to Kórinthos (1½ hrs, 1,200dr), Arta (6 hrs, 4,600dr), Ioánnina (7½ hrs, 5,600dr), and Olympía (5½ hrs, 5,300dr). Buses leave from **260 Liossion** to Delphi (3 hrs, 2,300dr), Vólos (5 hrs, 4,100dr), and Larissa (5½ hrs, 4,500dr). To reach the station at 100 Kifissou, take Bus 51 from the corner of Zinonous and Menandrou three blocks east of Platía Omónia. For the 260 Liossion station, take Bus 24 from Platía Sindagma. Pick up buses to places south of Athens, including Soúnio (3 hrs, 2,000dr), at **Platía Egiptou.**

BY FERRY Ferries ship out from Piraeus for spots all over the Aegean and eastern Mediterranean; some of the most popular destinations are Crete (11 hrs, 3,200dr), Náxos (7 hrs, 2,400dr), Thíra (10 hrs, 3,100dr), and Míkonos (6 hrs, 2,300dr). From the center of Athens you can reach Piraeus by Metro, which terminates near the docks for the Aegean Islands, the Dodecanese, and Crete; from Platía Omónia on Bus 49, which terminates near the docks for the Saronic Gulf islands; or from Platía Sindagma on Bus 40, which stops at the docks for departures abroad.

BY PLANE Athens's Ellinikón Airport is 9 km southeast of town. All international flights use the east terminal; domestic flights use the west. **Express buses** link the airport to the center of Athens every half-hour during the day (160dr) and every hour from 12:30 AM to 5:30 AM (200dr). Buses also connect Ellinikón with Piraeus (*see* By Ferry, *above*) about every hour 5 AM–12:20 AM for 160dr.

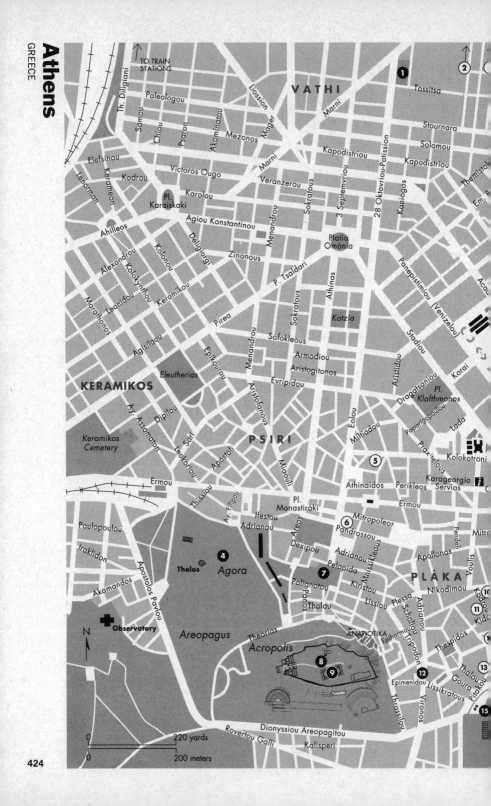

TO TRAIN
STATIONS

Th. Diligiani

Paleologou

Samou

Chiou

Psaron

Akominatou

Mezonos

Liossion

Mager

Marni

VATHI

Tossitsa

Stournara

Solomou

Kapodistriou

Kapodistriou

Themistok

Em.

Acac

Elefsinou

Keramæon

Lenorman

Kodrou

Victoros Ougo

Karolou

Pl.
Karaiskaki

Ahilleos

Agiou Konstantinou

Marni

Veranzerou

Sokratous

3 Septemvriou

28 Oktovriou-Patission

Kaniogos

Panepistimiou (Venizelou)

Alexandrou

Kolokynthou

Kolonou

Deligiorgi

Zinonous

Platia
Omónia

P. Tsaldari

Athinas

Marathonos

Leonidou

Keramikou

Pirea

Menandrou

Sokratous

Sofokleous

Kotzia

Stadiou

Aristidou

Korai

Agisilaou

Epikourou

Armodiou

Aristogitonos

Pl.
Klafthmonos

Dragatsaniou

Papariopoulou

Loda

KERAMIKOS

Eleutherias

Evripidou

Eolou

Miltiadou

Praxitelous

Kolokotroni

Keramikos
Cemetery

Dipilou

Sari

Aristofanous

Miaouli

PSIRI

Athinaidos

Perikleos

Karageorgio
Servias

Ermou

Apostoli

Thissiou

Pl.
Monastiraki

Ay. Filipou

Ifestou

Areos

Mitropoleos

Pandrossou

Ermou

Poulopoutou

Iraklidon

Ay. Assomaton

Leokoriou

Adrianou

Dexipou

Adrianou

Minisikleous

Apollonos

Pendeli

Mitro

Tholos

4

Agora

Potignotou

Pelopida

Kiristou

Lissiou

Flessa

Scholiou

Nikodimou

Adrianou

PLÁKA

Voulis

Akamandos

Apostolos Pavlou

7

Panos

Tholou

Kiristou

Thalou

Kiala

Observatory

N

Areopagus

Theorias

Acropolis

ANAFIOTIKA

Epimenidou

Tripodon

Vironos

Lissikratous

12

Thespidos

Gouta

Pitaka

13

N

8

9

Dionyssiou Areopagitou

Rovertou Galli

Kalisperi

Thrassilou

15

0   220 yards

0   200 meters

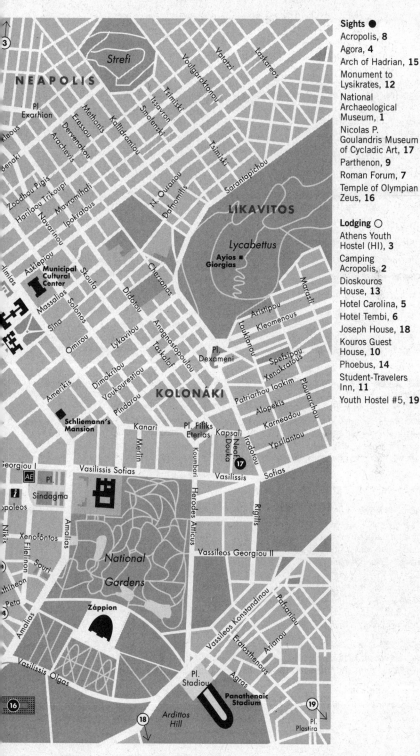

GETTING AROUND

Athens will have one of the most comprehensive public transportation systems in Europe when the new **Metro** is completed (supposedly in 1996); until then, all she has is a tangled mess of holes and shouting. The current Metro consists of a single line, running from Kifisia in the north to Piraeus in the south. Tickets cost 75dr–100dr and can be bought from the vending machines outside stations. An untamed orchestra of mopeds, taxis, and buses runs through the streets between 8 and 3; the rest of the day, traffic moves more smoothly.

From urban centers to coastal villages, Greece looks like one massive abandoned construction site. Even though many of the buildings stand half finished, the Greeks insist on fully occupying the unfinished structures, hanging laundry from the beams of third-floors-to-be and selling ice cream under tangled bars waiting to become a high-rise.

Even without the new Metro, Athens is accessible on foot and by trolleybus, bus, and taxi, all of which are cheap. The city is laid out on a grid, except for the rambling streets of the **Pláka,** Athens's oldest continually inhabited area. The Pláka spreads southwest from Platía Sindagma to the Acropolis. Just above Platía Sindagma is the wealthy residential neighborhood of **Kolonáki,** home to all the fancy boutiques.

BY BUS Athens operates three different bus systems, all of which take the same 75dr ticket. The white kiosks near stations aren't always open, and only select newsstands sell tickets, so stock up when you get a chance. **Yellow trolley-buses,** serving the central district, are crowded; routes are marked on the EOT city map, and most lines pass through Platía Sindagma, Platía Omónia, or both. **Blue buses** make many more stops and move more slowly through the city as they head out to the suburbs. Their routes are virtually impossible to figure out—all you have to go by is a metal sign at each stop naming the final destination. **Green buses** run from the center straight out to the suburbs with very few stops.

BY TAXI Athens has some of the cheapest taxis in Europe, provided the driver charges legally: a 200dr flat rate plus 50dr for every km within the city. If you radio a taxi, you pay 300dr extra; from the airport, 200dr extra. Outside the city, the price jumps to 100dr per km, and after midnight rates double. Don't just accept a quoted price from the driver as you get in—go by the book or you could get screwed. Sometimes an already taken taxi will stop for more riders; just shout the name of the neighborhood you want, jump in, and when you get out tack on 200dr to the cost of the distance you traveled.

WHERE TO SLEEP

The hotels here aren't great, but they'll do for a night or two. Most budget travelers turn to the touristy **Pláka** (*see* Getting Around, *above*) though some stay closer to **Platía Omónia,** a grungier area that can get loud and sleazy at night. Another option is to get out of the center into the petit-bourgeois neighborhoods of **Mets** and **Pangrati,** on the hills south of the National Gardens. Lodging near the train stations is pretty grim; **Joy's Hotel** (25 Fernon, tel. 01/52–48–931; doubles 5,500dr) caters to young, tired travelers. If you're headed for the islands, you may as well stay near the ferry docks at Piraeus: **Hotel Acropole** (7 Gounari, tel. 01/41–73–313; doubles 4,000dr) is clean, if you don't count the dirt under the beds. Don't crash in public unless you want to get to know the Athens police better. The exception is the Athens airport, which is well known among the destitute.

PLAKA **Dioskouros House.** Large, ghostly 19th-century neoclassic building on a quiet street. Vacant front desk adds to the somber mood; use the reception at nearby Adams Hotel. No rooms with bath. Doubles 4,500dr. *6 Pitakou, tel. 01/32–25–301 or 01/32–46–582.*

Kouros Guest House. Narrow building with simple rooms. Friendly, family-run place. Doubles 6,000dr. *11 Kodrou, tel. 01/32–27–431.*

Phoebus. Creaky neoclassic building with creaky proprietor. Kinda grungy, but the nicest option in the area. Large rooms, all with private bath. Doubles 8,000dr. *12 Peta, tel. 01/32–20–142.*

Student-Travelers Inn. Huge and heavily populated by mellow kids. Staff is sour and uninterested. Doubles 4,500dr, dorm beds 1,800dr. *16 Kidathineon, tel. 01/32–44–808.*

SOUTH OF PLATIA OMONIA **Hotel Carolina.** Incredibly clean—they must import their air from the islands. Popular with budget travelers who can afford to pay a little more for a little more. Doubles 7,500dr. *55 Kolokotroni, tel. 01/32–28–148.*

Hotel Tembi. Dilapidated building in the middle of Athens's garment district. Hectic neighborhood by day, but rooms quiet down at night. Doubles 4,300dr. *29 Eolou, tel. 01/32–13–175.*

SOUTH OF THE NATIONAL GARDENS **Joseph House.** Sarcastic management. Shabby lobby attracts local colorful characters as well as travelers for random afternoon conversations. Not always clean. Doubles 3,500dr, dorm beds 1,700dr. *13 Markou Moussourou, tel. 01/92–31–204. From Pl. Sindagma, Trolleybus 2, 4, or 11 to Panathenaic Stadium; walk west along Vassileos Konstandinou, which becomes Arditou; turn south on Markou Moussourou (2nd street); hotel is 2 blocks down. Kitchen facilities.*

HOSTELS **Athens Youth Hostel (HI).** Spacious rooms in large old building. Lobby graced by creative fluorescent light fixtures. Quiet neighborhood, near a vast number of cheesy nightclubs. *57 Kipselis, tel. 01/82–25–860. From Pl. Sindagma, Trolleybus 2, 4, or 9 north to Kipselis. Lockout 10–1:30, luggage storage.*

Youth Hostel #5. Not near anything worthwhile—residents wouldn't have it any other way. Well kept and quiet. Dorm beds 1,800dr, doubles 4,000dr. *75 Damareos, tel. 01/75–19–530. From Pl. Sindagma, Trolleybus 2 to Pangrati, walk southeast 1 block to Damareos.*

CAMPGROUNDS **Camping Acropolis.** Far north of town, near a highway. Unfiltered pool, expensive snack bar. Pay 1,300dr per person. *Tel. 01/80–75–253 or 01/80–75–804. From Pl. Omónia, Blue Bus 528 to Nea Kifissia, walk west, and cross highway.*

FOOD

The one major difference between dining in Athens and dining in the rest of Greece is that in Athens the traffic is louder and the views of the Acropolis are better. Otherwise, the feta is still white, the waiters are still lethargic, and the bill is still illegible. Avoid the most-traveled streets of the Pláka, where waiters jump out and pressure passersby. The rest of the city offers slightly less expensive meals that aren't as forcedly "authentic."

PLAKA **To Eden.** *The* vegetarian restaurant of Greece. Cheese- and nut-stuffed eggplant (1,200dr) would please even post-hippie California intelligentsia. *12 Lissiou, at Mnissikleous, tel. 01/32–48–858.*

To Kafeneio. Intentionally mismatched couches and chairs inside; outside tables spill along an alley. Post-college cats hang out and coolly size each other up. Starters sampler (1,900dr) can be a meal for two. *1 Epiharmou, tel. 01/32–46–916.*

Vakzos. Large garden has a partial but gratifying view of the Parthenon. Extensive menu plays off traditional Greek food. Lemon chicken (1,100dr) does the melting-in-the-mouth bit. *12 Thrassilou, at bottom of Acropolis hill, tel. 01/45–46–270.*

SOUTH OF THE NATIONAL GARDENS **Manessis Taverna.** Locally popular Greek restaurant dares to use spices other than salt and pepper. Chicken kebab with rice (1,300dr) is glorious. *3 Markou Moussourou, just southwest of Panathenaic Stadium, tel. 01/92–27–684.*

Oinomageireion. The world's grumpiest man serves vast amounts of cheap food. Meat and potatoes 700dr. On the corner of quiet neighborhood platía. *2 Pagkrati, on Pl. Varnava south of Panathenaic Stadium, tel. 01/70–11–101.*

NORTH OF THE NATIONAL GARDENS **Taverna Fillipoy.** Cheap, solid food in Athens's wealthiest district. Busiest between 1 and 5 PM. Old, formal waiters are conspicuously out of place in this century. *19 Xenokratous, tel. 01/72–16–390.*

Lefka. Garden lined with gigantic retsina-filled barrels. The employees don't give a damn what you do as long as they have a chance to eat their dinner. Salad, meat, potatoes, and wine for two comes in under 3,300dr. *121 Mavromihali, tel. 01/36–14– 038.*

CAFES AND OUZERI The distinction between cafés and *ouzeri* (ouzo bars), a muddled line throughout Greece, is almost nonexistent in Athens. Both serve slender glasses of the anise-based national drink along with beer, wine, frappés, and Greek coffees. Pub-like in its music and the flittering laughter of its patrons, **Cafe Pláka** (cnr. of Flessa and Tripodon) serves milkshakes and fruit juices. One of the few reasonably priced places in the Pláka, **Cafe Kuros** (cnr. of Vironos and Lissikratous) appeals to locals who disdain the generic Coca-Cola cafés on Kidathineon. Set up against the stands of the Panathenaic Stadium, **Kallimarmaron** (southern end of Pl. Stadiou) is popular with tanned tourists in the afternoon, but it becomes markedly more romantic once the air-conditioned megabuses have left. One of many cafés in the fashion-oriented district of Kolonáki, **Cafe Brasil** (cnr. of Taskalof and Pl. Filiks Eterias) is lazy during the afternoon but turns into a downright scene at night.

WORTH SEEING

The center of Athens is littered with splendidly decrepit monuments to the golden age of the city and its subsequent decline under Christian Rome. Marking the boundary between ancient Athens and the then-modern Roman addition, the AD 131 **Arch of Hadrian** (cnr. of Amalias and Vasilissis Olgas) is all that remains of the old city walls. Athens has benefited from the government's concentration of power and culture in the capital, and it houses a disproportionate number of national historic and artistic treasures. Since the expansive urban sprawl of Athens is a recent development, most sights are centralized in the older parts of the city. A pet project of the first queen of modern Greece, the **National Gardens** provide a shady reprieve from the relentless bustle of downtown Athens.

ACROPOLIS Towering over a modern city of 12 million much as it stood over the ancient capital of 50,000, the Acropolis (literally "high city") continues to be Athens's most spectacular, photogenic, and visited attraction despite hundreds of years of renovations, bombings, and artistic lootings. The buildings, constructed under the direction of Pericles during the city's golden age in the 5th century BC, were designed to be as visually harmonious as they were enormous, and they stand today in a perfect balance of stubborn immortality and elegant fragmentation. The entrance into the Acropolis is through the monumental **Propylaia,** a gateway that combines the Doric and Ionic orders. Flanking the Propylaia is the relatively small temple of **Athena Nike,** one of the first structures on mainland Greece to use the slender Ionic order exclusively. The **Erechtheion,** the most complicated Acropolis building, has a combination of two temples and three stylistically and structurally distinct colonnades. Facing the Parthenon is the **Porch of the Maidens,** where reproductions of six graceful caryatids (columns carved into a female form) support a stone architrave; the originals are in England and the Acropolis Museum. The **Parthenon,** the largest Acropolis temple, is considered a perfect example of the Doric order; the careful proportioning of height to width to breadth and column to open space create a sense of balance that belies the structure's massive size. *Admission: 1,500dr, 750dr students. Open weekdays 8–6:45, weekends 8:30–2:45.*

According to Greek myth, at the founding of the city-state of Athens, Poseidon and Athena presented gifts to the citizens in a competition to win their devotion. Poseidon's saltwater spring wasn't as enchanting as Athena's olive tree, so the Greeks named the city after the goddess and dedicated the Parthenon to her.

On-site is the **Acropolis Museum,** an excellent collection of carvings and pottery, including many of ancient Greece's best-known reliefs and freestanding statues. *Tel. 01/32–36–665. Admission: 1,500dr, 750dr students. Open Mon. 11–6:30, Tues.– Fri. 8–6:30, weekends 8:30–2:30.*

AGORA The economic, social, and political center of Athens, the ancient Agora was the site of Socrates's discourses and excellent deals on figs. Founded in the 6th century BC, the Agora passed through several stages of glory and decline before the Roman occupation of Athens, finally falling into disuse once the Christian empire eliminated the philosophy academies that had once sprouted on the site. The present-day site is a motley collection of ruined classical, Byzantine, and Turkish foundations. Dominating one side of the site is the too-perfect 1950s reconstruction of the **Stoa of Attalus,** originally built in the 2nd century BC. Facing the Panathenian Way, this long, arcaded building houses the Agora's undistinguished museum. On the opposite side of the Agora, the reconstructed 5th-century-BC **Thession** sits atop a tiny hill with many of its columns and friezes fully intact. *Admission to Agora: 800dr, 400dr students; admission to museum: 800dr, 400dr students. Open Tues.–Sun. 8:30–2:45.*

MONUMENT TO LYSIKRATES Almost entirely intact despite years of abuse, this proud cylindrical monument is the oldest known building (335 BC) to use the Corinthian column on an exterior. Originally built to support a victorious athlete's tripod, the hollow monument was the poet Lord Byron's study when he stayed at the then-connected Capuchin Convent. Today it sits amid ruined foundations in the center of a café-rimmed platía. *Cnr. of Vironos and Lissikratous.*

NATIONAL ARCHAEOLOGICAL MUSEUM This museum possesses one of the world's premier collections of ancient Greek art. The rooms of stelae (carved-relief grave markers), kouri (idealized statues of young boys), amphorae (decorated terra-cotta vases for wine or oils), and friezes are almost overwhelming. *44 28 Oktovriou-Patission. Admission: 1,500dr, 750dr students. Open Mon. 12:30–7, Tues.–Fri. 8–7, weekends 8:30–3.*

NICHOLAS P. GOULANDRIS MUSEUM OF CYCLADIC ART From 2600 to 1000 BC, the Cycladic Islands were home to the artists who produced the first known life-size statues of the female body in addition to countless fertility statuettes. The museum's collection of this generally misunderstood and undervalued ancient Greek art is the world's finest gathering of the smooth marble sculptures. *4 Neofitou Douka. Admission: 250dr. Open weekdays 10–4, Sat. 10–2:45.*

ROMAN FORUM Surprisingly undervisited, the Roman Forum, just east of the Agora, is a small, well-preserved collection of columns and monuments still undergoing gradual excavation. The hollow 1st-century **Tower of the Winds** is surrounded by the foundations of the Agora. The one fully standing structure on-site is a 16th-century **Turkish mosque** that has been used as a school, a bakery, and barracks. Next to the site entrance are the foundations and hole-filled benches of a Roman-built public toilet. *Admission: 400dr, 200dr students. Open Tues.–Sun. 8:30–2:45.*

TEMPLE OF OLYMPIAN ZEUS Vying with the Acropolis for distinction as the best-lit archaeological site at night, this temple was the largest in Greece when it was built in the 2nd century BC. Only 15 of the original 114 massive Corinthian columns are still intact, so you don't need to venture onto the site to appreciate the temple's power, which lies in the sheer size of what remains. *Cnr. of Vasilissis Olgas and Amalias. Admission: 400dr, 200dr students. Open Tues.–Sun. 8:30–3.*

CHEAP THRILLS

The tassle-top-hatted and stony-faced **Evzónes** watching over the President's House (just east of the National Gardens) spend their days acting out a changing of the guard that falls somewhere between discipline and comedy.

Built on the foundations of an ancient Roman arena south of the National Gardens, the shallow **Panathenaic Stadium** was refurbished to host the first modern Olympic Games, held in 1896. The track is filled with runners hip to becoming Olympic athletes, the stands with potential fans.

Athens's **flea market,** an unfortunate collection of poorly made pipe fittings most of the week, blooms into pandemonium on Sunday mornings, when local artisans and antique-book dealers join the Tupperware-mongers and polyester T-shirt dealers. The market is centered around Platía Monastiráki, across from the front entrance to the ancient Agora.

FESTIVAL The **Athens Festival** is best known for its staging of ancient Greek plays in the theaters in which they were first performed, but a broad spectrum of music, dance, and drama is represented. Make it a point to see some of the shows, because even the worst ballet performances are rendered gorgeous when staged in a ruined amphitheater. The performances begin in early June and last until mid-September. Tickets (1,200dr–10,000dr) can be purchased in advance or the day of a performance; schedules are available at the tourist office. Call 01/32–21–459 for more information.

AFTER DARK

BARS The loud bars collected northeast of the center around Platía Mavili, notably **Bronx** and **Loras,** are filled with black-clad college kids who sullenly contemplate life and which disco to hit later on. Less angst-filled are the stylized bars scattered over **Platía Exahrion,** in the heart of a neighborhood famed for its hyperintellectual bookstores and lazy anarchists. A dozen bars move outside onto the platía in summer; look for **Neon.**

DANCING Epic taxi rides to the decadant outdoor dance factories on the waterfront can be the most expensive event of the evening, though the clubs don't help the situation with their cover charges. With nods to New York hip hop, **Loft** (cnr. of Ermou and Assomaton in winter, taxi to Ellinikón in summer; cover 1,500dr) draws the ridiculously idle and attractive youth of Athens to bizarre theme nights. Slightly more erotic is **Sodoma** (3 Zoodhou Pigis in winter, taxi to Neraida in summer; cover 3,000dr), a Grecian heaven for leather lovers both gay and straight. Located in the city center all year, **GOA** (Xenofóntos; cover 2,000dr) brings in a steady stream of young travelers; the Europop is always danceable, if sometimes outdated. Also in the center, **Odyssia** (116 Ermou; cover 1,500dr) is a lesbian club where the occasional innocuous guy will be allowed to buy drinks for scores of beautiful and uninterested women.

CINEMAS The audience is drunk and the films are often stopped for intermission, but Athens's outdoor summer cinema/cafés are a kick. Films are always shown in the original language with Greek subtitles, with two screenings nightly at 9 and 11 (seats 1,000dr). In the heart of the Pláka, **Cine Paris** (22 Kidathineon) caters to a mainstream crowd, while **Cine Refresh** (Pl. Dexameni, Kolonáki) sometimes offers first-run European art films.

Near Athens

APOLLO COAST

The Apollo Coast has become an overtouristed purgatory for sunbathers, but it can be a Garden of Eden compared to the even more polluted and overpopulated center of Athens. The coast stretches from Pireaus to Soúnio; the first 27 km are accessible by Athens city buses. **Vouliagméni** offers the best combination of space and sea: From the Záppion gardens (east of the Acropolis), take Bus 115 (1 hr, 75dr). Tickets can be difficult to find on the coast; buy your return ticket while still in Athens.

DELPHI

The most famous and most consulted of the ancient Greek oracles, dating back to at least the 2nd century BC, Delphi was centered around a cave where a priestess would receive divine visions, perhaps inspired by hallucinogenic vapors seeping through a crevice in the earth. Questions presented to her received strange and garbled answers, which were then translated into verse by the priests. Today, the Delphi **museum** houses restructured pediments in addition to the famous bronze statue *The Charioteer,* and the site features reerected columns and buildings, including the **Sanctuary of Athena** and the **Temple of Apollo.** The highway to modern Delphi cuts through the middle of the site; be sure to explore both sides. *Tel. 0265/82313. Admission: 1,500dr. Open weekdays 8–7, weekends 8:30–3; museum not open until noon Mon.*

KTEL buses serve Delphi from Athens's Liossion station (3 hrs, 2,500dr). The bus stops at the site, but on your way back you should walk the 2 km from the ruins to the "bus station" (a table in a taverna) on the opposite side of modern Delphi to be assured of a seat on the bus.

TEMPLE OF POSEIDON

In a fit of ego, the poet Lord Byron carved his name on one of this temple's columns; the thousands of less illustrious visitors who've followed his lead haven't been able to detract from the beauty of the structure and its idyllic position on a rocky point overlooking the Aegean. From these rocks, King Aegeus, spying the mistakenly unfurled black sails that were to have been used only if his son Theseus had been slain by the Minotaur of Crete, threw himself into the water. No archaeological site offers gourmet food, but the kiosk and café at this site are exceptionally rotten—bring supplies from Athens. Orange KTEL buses (2 hrs, 1,000dr) leave for Soúnio from Platía Egiptou. *Admission: 800dr, 400dr students. Open Mon.–Sat. 9–sunset.*

The Islands
Gorgeous groups of islands encircling the Greek mainland lure visitors to big-name party resorts like Míkonos and lesser-known getaways like Lésvos. The islands offer everything from a hedonistic scene of sun and fun to secluded spots ovelooking the tranquil Aegean Sea, though the latter may be distressingly difficult to find at times. During the summer, hordes of vacationing Americans and Europeans fill up many of the islands' hotels, driving prices up and making a private patch of sand a hot commodity.

Ionian Islands

The Ionian Islands' proximity to Italy and Europe and their sheltered position on the East–West trade routes originally made them prosperous. Now they take in dollars from tourists who come to visit the clear, blue beaches, the wealth of archaeological sites, and the almost tropical foliage of these rainy islands.

CORFU

Corfu (Kérkira in Greek) has been ruled by many different powers, including the Byzantine Empire, the Normans, and the Venetians, but it has been firmly Greek since it was ceded to the country by the British in 1864. Modern-day would-be colonizers content themselves by staking out little sections of the island; at different times you'll feel surrounded by the Americans, Australians, and Germans attracted to Corfu's woodsy interior, diving cliffs, romantic architecture, sleepy coastal towns, and raging seaside villages. **Kérkira Town** is good for a day of sightseeing, but you should really head out to find your personal niche on this huge island. You might want to start with some of the best **beaches** you'll ever see, including the northwestern **Paleokastritsa,** where you can rent a boat (1,500dr) to visit nearby caves; the northern beach resorts of **Sidari, Roda,** and **Kassiopi**; and the long sandy stretch of **Glifada,** halfway down the western coast.

BASICS The **tourist office** (no phone) is on the Spianáda in Kérkira Town. Greek Skies Travel (20A Kapodistriou, Box 24, 49100, tel. 0661/30883; open daily 9–2 and 5:30–8), also on the Spianáda, is the **American Express** agent.

COMING AND GOING Boats shuttle between Corfu and Pátra (10 hrs, 3,500dr); Igoumenítsa (2 hrs, 700dr); Ancona, Italy (24 hrs, 13,600dr); Bari, Italy (6 hrs, 9,000dr); and Brindisi, Italy (8 hrs, 9,500dr). Eurailers and InterRailers get free trips on **Adriatica** (tel. 0661/38089) and **Hellenic Mediterranean Lines** (tel. 0661/39747); a 2,500dr supplement is imposed during high season. All passengers have to pay a 1,500dr port tax for all trips.

GETTING AROUND In Kérkira Town, visitors spend most time wandering through the old alleys between the **Spianáda (Esplanade)** and **Platía Sanrocco. Green buses** (tel. 0661/30627) serve distant locations like Athens (9 hrs, 6,300dr); **blue buses** (tel. 0661/31595) serve nearby villages and the city itself. Both stations are by Platía Sanrocco.

WHERE TO SLEEP AND EAT Seaside resorts dot the entire coastline, but most rooms are expensive, charging 6,000dr–8,000dr per double. Rooms in Kérkira Town are more reasonable: **Hotel Europa** (tel. 0661/39304) has comfortably furnished doubles from 3,000dr. From the Pátra port, cross the street, go right on Venizeloi, and follow the signs. Reservations are recommended. A huge **HI hostel** (on the road to Kondokáli, tel. 0661/91202; beds 1,000dr) is in a woodsy area 4½ km outside town. On the west side of the island, in Agios Gordios, perches the legendary **Pink Palace** (½ hr west of Kérkira Town, tel. 0661/483104; beds 3,000dr including meals), a haven for North Americans where every drunken night echoes the one before. Still, the beach this place overlooks is worth visiting on its own. A half-hour north of Kérkira Town, **Ipsos** is a touristy town with a terrific beach and nightlife; ask around for the student-filled hotels. Shady campsites sit across from the beach at nearby **Kérkira Camping Ipsos** (tel. 0661/93579; 500dr per tent, 500dr per person).

Kérkira Town's restaurants are generally tourist traps, but at **Kostakis** (end of Spianáda, Kérkira Town, tel. 0661/37547) you can get a delicious, piping-hot roasted chicken plate for 1,100dr. Otherwise, stock up on food at the huge **marketplace** on Markora before heading out of Town.

WORTH SEEING As you approach the island by boat you can't miss the crumbling **Old Venetian Fortress,** perched dangerously on the very edge of the island. By the Spaniáda, the 16th-century **New Venetian Fortress** (admission 200dr; open weekdays 8 AM–9 PM, Sat. 9–6, Sun. 10–7) is more intact; in fact, it's currently in use by the Greek navy. The inside is boring, but the view from the inside is worth the admission. Off the Spianáda is the elegant, colonnaded **Palace of St. Michael and St. George** (Agios Spirídhonos), built for the British High Commissioner in 1823 and used by the Greek monarchy. The former state rooms are open to the public and display Byzantine finds from the island. The **Archaeological Museum** (Vraila, at the waterfront, tel. 0661/30680; admission 400dr, 200dr students) has an impressive gorgon (an ugly demigod) pediment from the Doric Temple of Artemis.

CHEAP THRILLS Musical tunes vibrate at the Spianáda summer Sunday nights at 8:30 PM, when brass bands blast everything from classical to jazz. When the sun sets, people from all over the island head to the hilltop village **Pélekas** to watch the collage of colors.

ITHAKI

No wonder Odysseus, king of Itháki (Ithaca in English), yearned for home so badly throughout Homer's *Odyssey*. This island is composed of 13 adorable villages and a capital town that has few tourists, little noise, and tiny, unscathed coves. Set above the main town of Vathí, also known as **Itháki Town,** is the illuminated **Cave of the Nymphs** (admission 300dr; open daily 9–7), where Odysseus supposedly hid treasures acquired during his journeys. One kilometer from the village of **Stavrós** is a hill known as **Pelikáta,** where Mycenean ruins have been unearthed, spurring claims that this was the site of Odysseus's palace. The best beaches near

Vathí are between Kióni and Frikes; jump on the bus and when you see something that looks good, jump off. **Polyctor Tours** (main platía on the waterfront, tel. 0674/33120) has tourist info.

COMING AND GOING Daily ferries come into Vathí from Pátra (5 hrs, 2,300dr). Most buses leave from in front of the pharmacy off the main platía, but you should ask the pharmacy owners to be sure. The one bus route ultimately reaches Kióni (50 min, 500dr).

WHERE TO SLEEP AND EAT Most rooms in Vathí have high standards and higher prices. **Vlassopoiloi's** (tel. 0674/32119; doubles 3,000dr) has clean rooms with antique furniture and a killer view. From the port, head along the waterfront, take a right past the town hall, go up the stairs, and look for a sign advertising rooms. Local restaurants are good, if distressingly similar; cheery **O'Nikos** (off the main platía, tel. 0674/33039) serves especially delicious seafood. Calamari is 800dr.

ZAKINTHOS

Zákinthos's weather, foliage, and insects all make you feel like you're in the tropics. The only breaks in the greenery are high rocky cliffs digging into the sea. The reconstruction of **Zákinthos Town** following an earthquake in the 1950s was only marginally successful—head instead for the beach villages around the coast, all accessible by bus. The down-to-earth village **Vassilikó** is near the island's best beaches, including **Pórto Róma** and the turtle-occupied **Yérakas,** and is speckled with signs advertising rooms for rent.

Travel agencies in Zákinthos Town run boat tours, showing off such wonders as the fantastic colors of the **blue caves** on the island's northern tip and a cove that has become the permanent home to a beached ship. Tours that stop at the sights and beaches cost about 5,000dr; those that just cruise by the sights are only about 3,000dr.

COMING AND GOING Boats come into the Zákintbos Town port (tel. 0623/92100) daily from Killíni (1½ hrs, 870dr). **Buses** (Eleitherioi at Filita, tel. 0695/22656) get ferried across to Athens (6 hrs, 4,600dr) and Pátra (3 hrs, 2,000dr).

WHERE TO SLEEP AND EAT Cheap rooms are common in the small villages but scarce in Zákinthos Town, where you should stick to the generic rooms at the **Hotel Dhiethnes** (Agioi Lazaroi, tel. 0695/22286; doubles 4,000dr). From the port, go right down the waterfront, turn left on Laskareos, and go right on Agioi Lazaroi. Locals munch on traditional Greek dishes (around 800dr) at **Restaurant Zohios** (Rizospaston, near National Bank, tel. 0695/27575).

Pelopónnisos

Pelopónnisos isn't actually an island, but it may as well be. Almost completely surrounded by water, the peninsula is tenuously linked to the rest of Greece by a narrow isthmus. This rugged area has nourished kingdoms and empires over the past few thousand years, and traces of these lost realms remain, though you'll have to pull yourself away from the rocky shores and sandy beaches to get a glimpse of them.

KORINTHOS

The pillars and stones of the archaeological site of **Ancient Kórinthos** mark what was once the capital of the Greek city-state. The **Agora** still contains several small temples. In the 6th century BC, 38 columns defined the **Temple of Apollo**; today, seven remain. A **museum** right next to the Temple of Apollo houses terra-cotta sphinxes, mosaics, and statues from the excavated areas—definitely a good investment. *Tel. 0741/31480. Admission to site and museum: 1,000dr, 500dr students. Open weekdays 8–7, weekends 8:45–3.*

Hanging 575 meters over Ancient Kórinthos is **Acrokórinth,** a huge rock topped by monuments from the Byzantine, Venetian, and Turkish eras. Its fortress is supposedly the largest and oldest in the Pelopónnisos.

Seven kilometers away, **Modern Kórinthos** is best used as a base for exploring Ancient Kórinthos, though as modern Pelopónnisos cities go it's not bad, thanks to a central park with fountains and birds. Central hotels like the character-filled **Hotel Belle-Vue** (41 Damaskinou, near the waterfront, tel. 0741/22088; doubles from 3,000dr) and the more upscale **Hotel Apollon** (2 Damaskinou, at Pirinis, tel. 0741/22587; doubles 4,000dr) might even tempt travelers to stay here a while, even though most people visit Kórinthos as a day trip from Athens. The **tourist police** (51 Ermou, up the street from main bus station, tel. 0241/23282) have brochures and maps.

COMING AND GOING Modern Kórinthos's **train station** (Dhimokratias, tel. 0741/22523) sends daily trains to Athens (2 hrs, 800dr), Pátra (2½ hrs, 1,000dr), and Olympia (5 hrs, 1,800dr). The station at Ermou and Koliatsou (tel. 0741/24481) handles most **buses,** including those to Athens (1½ hrs, 1,200dr), Loutráki (20 min, 200dr), and Ancient Kórinthos (15 min, 160dr).

MIKINES

Once upon a time, Mikínes (Mycenae in English) was one of the mightiest powers in the Mediterranean, ruling most of the turf from the plains of Argos to the Saronic Gulf, including Crete. After 1300 BC, however, the city began to decline—probably because of some combination of drought, earthquake, invasion, and economic collapse—and after 1100 BC, there is no further trace of Mycenaean culture. The **Lion Gate,** whose discovery in 1841 ignited a Mycenaean-awareness craze, remains one of the best-known ruins at this ancient site. The **Treasury of Atreus,** or Tomb of Agamemnon, is the largest of the renowned beehive tombs at Ancient Mikínes. *Tel. 0751/76585. Admission: 1,000dr, 500dr students. Open daily 8–7; shorter hrs off-season.*

Modern Mikínes lacks the power, grandeur, and influence that grandpappy Ancient Mikínes possessed, but it's a convenient, if generic, base for exploring the ruins 2 km away. The hotels, all of which hug the main road, are a bit more expensive than those in other Pelopónnisos towns, and the **hostel** (main road, tel. 0751/76224; beds 1,000dr) is depressingly dingy. Check in at the restaurant Ifigenia. Famous anthropologist Heinrich Schliemann zonked out in the welcoming rooms of **La Belle Helene** (main road at bus stop, tel. 0751/76225; doubles 4,500dr) after long days of excavation. Nearby, **Dassis Tours** (tel. 0751/76123) provides tourist info. At **Restaurant Mycinaiko** (main road, bet. La Belle Helene and hostel, tel. 0751/76245) students get 20% off the tasty food.

COMING AND GOING Most buses from Athens (2 hrs, 1600dr) and Kórinthos (1 hr, 550dr) stop in **Fichtia.** From here, it's a 1½-km walk to the ruins at Mikínes, but with luck you could catch the bus (160dr) from Argos zipping through Fichtia on its way to the site.

SPARTA AND MISTRAS

Military discipline was the forte of ancient Sparta; wee Spartan boys were reputedly fed pigs' blood as formula. By looking at ancient Sparta today, you'd think they spent more time building their muscles than building architectural wonders; little is left of the ancient city, and modern Sparta is nothing to cheer about either. The only reason you'd really want to come here is because you're on your way to or from Mistrás, just 6 km away. But while you're passing through, take a look at the skeletal remains of **Acropolio** and the 1st- or 2nd-century hillside **theater,** whose marble was taken away and used in the construction of Mistrás. Sparta's **Archaeological Museum** (Likourgou, tel. 0731/285751; admission 400dr, 200dr students; open Tues.–Sat. 8:30–3, Sun. 8:30–2:30) is also a good investment. Highlights are the 2nd-century frescoes and a whole room dedicated to prehistoric finds from Laconia. The local **tourist office** (town hall, main platía, tel. 0731/24859) provides info for both Sparta and Mistrás.

Byzantine Mistrás, which for some time after the 13th-century Fourth Crusade was the spiritual center of the Greek Orthodox Church, is one of the best archaeological sites in the Pelopónnisos. It's comprised of two levels and a 13th-century castle peering over it all. You could take the bus up to the top and work your way down, but invest three hours and a little more effort and you can follow a path up the right side and down the left that will show you the best of the monasteries, churches, and palaces. *Tel. 0731/93377. Admission: 1,000dr, 500dr students. Open daily 8–7; shorter hrs off-season.*

The tiny, attractive town of modern Mistrás exists mainly to facilitate visits to Byzantine Mistrás, 2 km to the north. Station yourself in the huge, plush, colorful rooms at **Christina Vahavioloy's** (main road before bus stop, tel. 0731/93432; doubles 3,500dr), the best budget pension in town. To stay nearer the archaeological site, try the shaded and sociable **Camping Mistrás** (tel. 0731/22724; 400dr per tent, 800dr per person), served by the bus to Sparta.

COMING AND GOING Daily buses connect Sparta to Athens (4 hrs, 2,850dr), Kórinthos (2½ hrs, 1,800dr), Yíthio (1 hr, 600dr) and the Pírgos Dhiroú caves (2 hrs, 1,100dr). Buses leave from the corner of Likourgou and Leonidou in Sparta almost hourly for the 6-km trip to Mistrás (10 min, 160dr). You can also catch a bus to Mistrás from Athens (4 hrs, 2,900dr) or Kórinthos (2½ hrs, 1,800dr).

YITHIO

Helen and Paris spent their first passionate night together just off Yíthio, on the islet of **Marathonisi:** Romantic allure, pure and plentiful beaches, and a healthy balance of tourists and locals make the area perfect for a honeymoon. There aren't many sights, but this is the best base for exploration of the Mani Peninsula and the Pírgos Dhiroú Caves. The beaches near the campgrounds are especially appealing and are popular with backpackers. **Rozakis Shipping and Travel Agency** (waterfront, tel. 0733/22650) deals out transport tickets and local information.

COMING AND GOING Boats from Kastélli, Crete (5 hrs, 3,300dr) and Pireaus (10 hrs, 8,400dr) come and go once a week. Daily **buses** (tel. 0733/22228) shuttle back and forth from Athens (4½ hrs, 3,400dr) and Kórinthos (3½ hrs, 2,400dr).

WHERE TO SLEEP Lodging here is no problem, thanks to plenty of rooms to let along the waterfront. The plush doubles with bath at **Pension Koutsouris** (tel. 0733/22321) are a steal at 4,000dr for *Berkeley Guides* readers. Reserve ahead—*way* ahead if you want the one single room (*Berkeley Guides* readers 3,000dr). From the main platía, make a right at Kodak Express and another right on Moretti Street. Beachfront **Meltemi Camping** (tel. 0733/22833; 650dr per person, 650dr per tent) has a pool and a bar. It's a 3-km walk or bus ride from Yíthio on the road to Areopolis.

NEAR YITHIO Take a 45-minute boat ride through the eerie **Pírgos Dhiroú Caves** 40 km from Yíthio and watch the stalagtites and stalagmites change color and shape as the trip progresses. After the boat ride, explore on foot the Alepótripa cave and its prehistoric fossils. Buses (30 min, 500dr) leave Yíthio for the caves a few times a day. *Admission: 1,400dr. Open June–Sept., daily 8–6; shorter hrs off-season.*

OLYMPIA

The first Olympic Games took place around the 8th century BC, when a 200-meter race across the stadium at Olympia (Olympia in Greek) was recorded. Soon the games were in full swing, taking place every four years, involving at first all the Greek city-states and, before long, athletes from as far away as Sicily and Asia Minor. In AD 393, the Roman emperor Theodosius discontinued the games, calling them counterproductive to Christianity. The **Temple of Zeus,** one of the Seven Wonders of the Ancient World, is in the middle of the **Altis,** a sacred precinct where the games were originally held. On the far end of the site is the ancient **stadium,** which could at one time house up to 20,000 spectators. Most of the site is demolished, but enough of the stadium is maintained for even the unimaginative to picture crowds and athletes. If you have only a day or two in the Pelopónnisos, make Olympia a priority. *Tel. 0624/22517. Admission: 1,000dr, 500dr students. Open weekdays 7:30–7, weekends 8:30–3.*

Across the street from the site is a new and impressive **Archaeological Museum.** Inside the museum are the massive pediments of the Temple of Zeus. *Tel. 0627/22742. Admission 1,000dr, 500dr students. Open Mon. 12:30–7, Tues.–Fri. 8–7, weekends 8:30–3.*

COMING AND GOING In modern Olympia, the **EOT** (main street, tel. 0624/23100) also serves as the local bus station (tel. 0624/23100), with service to Athens (6 hrs, 4,300dr), Kórinthos (4½ hrs, 3,300dr), and Pátra via Pírgos (40 min, 300dr).

WHERE TO SLEEP AND EAT Olympia's **HI hostel** (18 Kondyli, tel. 0624/22580; beds 1,000dr) has basic bunks in cramped rooms. To reach the spacious, spotless 4,000dr doubles at **Hotel Praxiteles** (7 Spiliopoylou, tel. 0624/22592) from the bus stop, follow the main street to the post office and make two rights. The restaurant on the ground floor of the hotel is good for a peaceful meal.

PATRA

Pátra (Patras in English) has just enough sights to keep you occupied for an hour or two between ferries; multilevel, commercial buildings unabashedly line the waterway, offering that last candy bar or wilted salad before you head for more interesting places. To escape the ruckus of the port, walk from Platía Trion Simahon, the main platía, up Agiou Nikolaou to the end. Climb the decrepit stairs and wander around the Venetian **Kástro.** If you're dressed right (no shorts), you could make a pilgrimage to the church **Agios Andreas,** where the head of St. Andrew rests peacefully amid gold.

BASICS The **EOT** (international ferry port, tel. 061/653358; open weekdays 7 AM–9:30 PM, weekends 2–9:30) will point you to the specific ferry company you need. The **American Express office** (48 Othonos Amalias St., tel. 061/220993; open Mon.–Sat. 8:30 AM–9:30 PM, Sun. 11–7) is near the train station.

COMING AND GOING Ferries run daily to and from Ancona, Italy (32 hrs, 16,400dr); Bari, Italy (17 hrs, 9,500dr); and Brindisi, Italy (18 hrs, 8,500dr), sometimes with a stop in Corfu (10 hrs, 3,500dr). Tack on a 1,500dr port tax to all prices. Eurailers and InterRailers pay only a 3,500dr supplement (plus port tax) if they come from Brindisi on **Adriatica** (tel. 061/421995) or **Hellenic Mediterranean Lines** (tel. 061/623572). Both are headquartered across from Gate 6, between the train station and the international ferry port.

The main **bus** terminal (Gate 6, tel. 061/222271) serves Athens (3 hrs, 2,800dr), Kórinthos (1¼ hr, 1,700dr), and nearby villages. The other station (catercorner from train station, tel. 061/277556) serves Zákinthos (13 hrs, 1,000dr) and Delphi (3½ hrs, 1,800dr). **Trains** (tel. 061/277441) arrive from Athens (3 hrs, 2,600dr), Kórinthos (2 hrs, 1,700dr), and Pírgos (2 hrs, 1,700dr).

WHERE TO SLEEP Hotels here are expensive and depressing, but if you get stranded overnight, there's a hospitable little **HI hostel** (68 Iroon Politechniou St., tel. 061/42-72-78; beds 1,300dr, roof space 1,000dr) in an old mansion on the waterfront. **Pension Nicos** (3 Patreos and 121 Agiou Andreou, tel. 061/623757; doubles 4,000dr) has sparkling rooms and a rooftop bar.

Cyclades

Of course the islands of the Cyclades have brilliant beaches and clear blue seas, but they are probably better known as party central. Tourists pack the islands in the summer, broiling themselves on the beaches in the afternoon, partying at discos and clubs all night long, and sleeping through the morning.

MIKONOS

"If you want to see Greek culture and traditions, go to another island. Míkonos is an island for the tourists," say locals. Certainly Míkonos's tourist industry lures hordes of English-speaking workers with drachma signs in their eyes, but the unmatchable contrast created by identical white buildings jutting out of the rocky hillsides against the clear blue water keeps the visitors coming. To toast your buns in the sun like everyone else, catch a bus to the scenic beach at **Ayios Stéfanos** or walk 2 km from the northern bus station to the less appealing beach at **Toúrlos**. **Super-Paradise** is a gay nudist beach a short boat ride away from **Paradise Beach,** a backpackers' haven accessible on the Platis Yialos bus (160dr).

Greek mythology attributes the rockiness of Míkonos to the fact that this is where Hercules buried all the giants he slaughtered.

After a full day of lolling on the sand, catch the sunset at the northern end of town, where Byzantine windmills decorate the landscape, then throw yourself into Greek dancing at the **Famous Mykonos Dance Bar.** From the Delos Port, go up to the Scandinavian Bar and take a right, a quick left, and a right at Scarpa Taverna. **Scandinavian Bar** is a cheesy little spot full of tourists, but it has the cheapest drinks in town (400dr). Check out **Pierro's Bar** (tel. 0289/22177) for a wild gay scene.

BASICS Get **information** about the island from Sea and Sky Travel (at the port, tel. 0289/22853; open daily 8 AM–11 PM). Delia Travel Ltd. (at the port, tel. 0289/22322; open daily 9–9) is the **American Express** agent.

COMING AND GOING Ferries (tel. 0289/22218) shoot from the port north of Míkonos Town to Páros (2 hrs, 1,100dr), Náxos (2½ hrs, 1,000dr), Íos (4 hrs, 2,200dr), and Santoríni (7 hrs, 2,300dr) daily. Thessaloníki, Rhodes, and Crete are serviced several times a week. To get to either of the two **bus stations** (tel. 0289/23360), head right from the port on Ayiou Stefanou.

WHERE TO SLEEP AND EAT Rooms on Míkonos cost almost double what they are on other islands. **Hotel Drafaki** (5 min up Airport Rd. from southern bus station, tel. 0289/22116; doubles around 6,000dr) has basic rooms. If you phone the proprietor, he'll come pick you up. The **campground** (tel. 0289/22852; 400dr per person, 200dr per tent, bungalows 1,500dr; closed Nov.–Mar.) at Paradise Beach (*see above*) has a restaurant and bar and a shuttle to the port.

The streets in Míkonos Town were intentionally built in a maze formation to confuse the only foreigners visiting at the time—pirates.

At **Niko's Taverna** (straight up from the Delos port, tel. 0289/24320), stuffed grape leaves cost 450dr. Petros, a locally famous pelican who wanders around town, often stops by. A down-to-earth spot in the midst of fancy restaurants, **Jiacomo de Latto** (tel. 0289/23235) serves an extremely tasty gyro (250dr). Go straight up from the Delos port, turn right at the Scandinavian Bar, and make a quick left.

PAROS

The waterfront in **Paríkia,** Páros's main town, is lined with cafés, moped-rental shops, cafés, hotels, and cafés. Behind this thin slice of town is an island that has remained largely undeveloped. During the off-season, both Paríkia and the village of **Náoussa** are relatively affordable and quiet, but in peak season, Paríkia mirrors neighbor Míkonos with high prices and tourist glitz; it even has its own Hard Rock Cafe.

Civilization in Páros began as early as 4000 BC, but the **Church of a Hundred Doors** (near the port; open daily 8–1 and 4–8), dates back merely to the Byzantine Empire. Hop a bus in Paríkia for the 4-km jaunt to the **Valley of the Butterflies,** where millions of butterflies hang out on the lush greenery every summer. **Golden Beach** is one of the more attractive beaches on the island and is easily accessible by bus from Paríkia. After skipping around in the sun all day, head south of the port to **Evino's Bar** (tel. 0284/21303), where you can listen to classical music and jazz while sipping wine (500dr) at sunset. Walk five minutes farther to **Slammer Bar** for groovy tunes. If you continue on and make a left, you'll hit more of the trendy bars. A **tourist office** operates out of a windmill at the port (tel. 0284/22079).

COMING AND GOING Jump on one of the many daily **ferries** (tel. 0284/21240) to Paríkia from Pireaus (6 hrs, 2,700dr), Íos (2½ hrs, 1,900dr), or Santoríni (3½ hrs, 2,000dr). Ferries also connect Páros to Crete (8 hrs, 3,400dr) and Míkonos (2 hrs, 1,100dr). The **bus station** is north of the port (tel. 0284/21133).

WHERE TO SLEEP AND EAT In the off-season, you won't have a problem finding a place for around 3,000dr in one of the hotels and pensions near the Church of a Hundred Doors (*see above*): Make a right at the church and a quick left and head straight up the road for three minutes. In this area, the **Pension Evagelistria** (tel. 0284/21482; doubles 5,500dr) has dimly lit rooms and a shared living room and patio area. Grandma and grandpa run **Roubini's Rooms** (tel. 0284/23734; doubles 7,500dr), carefully tending the huge rooms and garden. From the port, walk north and turn right at Taverna Katerina or call Mr. Roubini to pick you up. **Koula Camping** (north of the port, tel. 0284/22081; sites 800dr) has sites on the beach under olive trees haunted by swarms of bees. At **Scouna** (north of the port, tel. 0284/23408), all the vegetables and meats come from the owners' farm. Dine for a few drachmas on the beach with ivy creeping up the wooden beams around you.

NAXOS

Fertile land, colorful buildings covered with chipped paint, and warm locals who still welcome tourists set Náxos apart from the other Greek islands. Soon you'll start to feel like a real live person, not passenger #5689 from the four-o'clock ferry. Endless glasses of Náxian wine don't hurt the island's appeal, either.

In addition to the wines, you'll find cheeses, potatoes, and olive oil produced on the island— agriculture alone could support Náxos's economy. In tiny Náxos Town, the relatively deserted **Kastro** district, centered around the **Venetian Castle,** used to be inhabited by Venetian nobles who held the island for 300 years starting in the 13th century. An **Archaeological Museum** (in the Kastro, tel. 0285/22725; admission 400dr, 200dr students, free Sun.; closed Mon.) holds findings from Mycenaean settlements, Cycladic goods from the 3rd millenium BC, and a marble funerary lion from the 4th century BC. The excellent **tourist office** (at the waterfront by bus station, tel. 0285/24525) can tell you more. To get to the discos and the closest beach, **Agios Giórgios,** go south of the port and veer toward the water when the road splits.

COMING AND GOING Daily **ferries** chug between Náxos and Pireaus (7 hrs, 2,700dr), Íos (1½ hrs, 1,600dr), Santoríni (3 hrs, 1,500dr), Míkonos (2 hrs, 1,000dr), and Páros (1 hr, 900dr). **Buses** (at the port, tel. 0285/22291) run frequently all over the island. If you rent a scooter, be wary of the extremely rocky roads. **Mike's Bikes** (tel. 0285/22883), near Agios Giórgios, rents mountain bikes for about 1,500dr a day.

WHERE TO SLEEP AND EAT The cheap, moldy-smelling **Hotel Dionyssos** (tel. 0285/24525; beds 1,000dr), in the old market area near the Kastro, has dimly lit doubles and dorm-style beds. Look for the signs. At **Hotel Savvas** (south of the port, tel. 0285/22213; doubles 9,000dr), the clean rooms have a winter-resort ambience reminiscent of a Swiss Miss commercial. **Náxos Camping** (tel. 0285/23500) is near everything and sends a minivan to meet the ferries.

Oniro's (north of the port, in Kastro district, tel. 0285/23846), whose rooftop patio offers a view of the Aegean, is a little pricey but recommended as *the* restaurant by Náxians. On the waterfront, the untouristy **Restaurant Good Heart** (south of the port, tel. 0285/22537) serves Greek specialties to locals. Look for the sign that says KALIKAPDIA; the GOOD HEART sign is easy to miss.

IOS

Imagine the nightlife of Tijuana coupled with the beaches of Hawaii, and you've got a pretty good grip on Íos. To keep up with the schedule here, be prepared to party all night, sleep until noon, and then stumble down to the nearest beach. Íos can cure you of homesickness—hell, after a couple of days here you'll never want to see another drunken English speaker in your life—and it's also one of the cheapest islands in the Aegean. The 2-km road to the sprawling white **Milopótamos Beach** would almost be picturesque if it weren't for the graffitied discotheque signs, empty beer bottles, and loitering backpackers. The secluded cove of **Kolitzani Beach** is an accessible nude beach: Follow the pathway next to the Red Lion Club off the main road in Íos Town. For more ideas, contact **Acteon Travel Agencies** (by port bus stop, tel. 0286/91343).

All the lively bars are in Íos Town, including **Pegasus Rock Club** (tel. 0286/91012), which purports to be the only real rock club on the island. **Disco 69** offers Top-40 dance tunes and cheap drinks. The **Blue Melon** is mellow with pool tables, Foosball, music, and beers in a candlelit setting. When the bars close, the action shifts to the clubs on the way to Milopótamos Beach. **The Highway Club** blares techno and disco to a nasty crowd.

COMING AND GOING Daily **ferries** motor to Íos from Santoríni (1½ hrs, 1,100dr), Páros (2 hrs, 2,100dr), Míkonos (4 hrs, 2,400dr), and Pireaus (8 hrs, 4,000dr deck class). Boats also arrive from Iráklion, Crete (10 hrs, 3,200dr) several times a week. The activity on Íos is all within a 45-minute walk, with Íos Town in the center and Yialós Port and Milopótamos Beach on either side. A **bus** traveling along the main road connects all three for 140dr; wave your arms if you want it to stop for you.

WHERE TO SLEEP AND EAT The easiest place to stay is in Íos Town or near Milopótamos Beach; pensions line the main road and are clustered behind the village bus stop. Try the island's best shot at a hostel, **Mrs. Panidou's Rooms** (on a little road next to the big church, tel. 0286/91364; beds 1,000dr), for single-sex rooms next door to party central; look for the ROOMS TO LET sign. A great basic place is **Vicky's Rooms** (halfway between the village and beach, next to Café Ostria; doubles 2,000dr). The resort-campground **Far Out Camping** (Milopótamos Beach, tel. 0286/91560; 250dr per tent, 500dr per person) has a swimming pool, volleyball and basketball courts, and hot showers.

It's easier to find food at night than during the day, but try **Mare Monte** (by the port beach, tel. 0286/91585; open daily 8 AM–3 AM) for tasty, inexpensive grub. On Milopótamos Beach, **Far Out Café** is a bamboo-covered refuge with good sandwiches from 250dr. At **Mario's** (main road, halfway between the village and beach, tel. 0286/91130), the Greek cook takes the utmost pride in his run-of-the-mill Italian concoctions.

SANTORINI

Around 1500 BC, a volcanic eruption scorched the earth of Santoríni (Thíra in Greek), scarring the island with splotches of black and red—the oddly colored beaches of today. The explosion caused massive tidal waves, sinking other islands; many believe the volcano of Santoríni caused the disappearance of the Aegean city of Atlantis, and today every other street corner in Santoríni's main town of **Firá** is home to an Atlantis Tavern or Atlantis Dry Cleaners or Atlantis Paperclip Shoppe. The cost of living here is high, thanks to a worldwide passion for the black-sand beaches, but don't pass Santoríni up. The backpacking crowd has adopted **Périssa Beach,** where there's a good hostel and a hang-loose attitude. But crowd quality aside, the **red beach** is the island's coolest, based purely on natural merit. It's at the base of the red and black cliffs, near the Akrotíri archaeological site (*see below*).

BASICS Pelikan Travel (Theotokopoulou, tel. 0286/22220; open daily 8 AM–10 PM) has useful **visitor information.** X-Ray Kilo Travel & Shipping Agency (main square, tel. 0286/22624; open daily 8 AM–10 PM) is the **American Express** agent.

COMING AND GOING The daily **ferries** (tel. 0286/22239) that make rounds in the Cycladic Islands are ultimately heading to Santoríni, so boats from Íos (1½ hrs, 1,100dr), Náxos (4 hrs, 2,000dr), Páros (5 hrs, 2,200dr), and Míkonos (7 hrs, 2,400dr) come into port every day. Overcrowded **buses** service most of the island. The central stop is on the main square, **Theotokopoulu;** other stops are at Périssa Beach (40 min, 300dr), Akrotíri (30 min, 280dr), and the main port (30 min, 260dr). Taking **donkeys** up and down hills is popular in Santoríni, but it's a costly means of transportation.

WHERE TO SLEEP AND EAT There are two main areas for cheap lodging: one up from the Firá bus stop and to the right, the other up and to the left. If you value a view, try **Stathis** (north of cable cars, tel. 0286/22835; doubles 3,500dr), a pension next to all the expensive hotels hanging off Firá's cliff. Or stay at the nice **HI Kamares hostel**; walk straight up from Theotokopoulu, past Pelikan Travel, until you see the signs. **Santorini Camping** (tel. 0286/22944; 700dr per person) is a great, shady spot to pitch a tent and features a saltwater pool and a view of the sea. From Theotokopoulu, walk straight up, go right at Pelikan Travel, and left at the main street; walk until you see signs.

Fruit stands and bakeries crowd the main square. Steer clear of the overpriced eateries on or near the cliff. For traditional Greek cuisine, try the town favorite, **Nicolas Taverna:** Above Theotokopoulu, make a left at Pelikan Travel and a right on the first street. At lunchtime, hit **Ovelistirio** (tel. 0286/22832), where almost everything costs 250dr. Above Theotokopoulu, make a left at Pelikan Travel; the stand is the second store from the corner.

WORTH SEEING In 1930, archaeologist Spyros Marinatos discovered an ancient Minoan village under all the rubble and ash that is Santoríni. Just outside the village of **Akrotíri**, his team unearthed utensils, furniture, houses, streets, and even a water supply system, all of which had been preserved by the volcanic ash. They're still excavating here, so there aren't any displays per se, but it offers a fascinating look at the excavation process and some of the pottery and walls that have been unearthed. *From Theotokopoulu, take bus (25 min, 280dr) to Akrotíri. Admission: 1,000dr, 500dr students, Sun. free. Open Tues.–Sun. 8:30–3.*

At the turn of the century, German archaeologists discovered a posteruption village, **Ancient Thíra,** that dated to the 9th century BC. Phoenicians, Dorians, Romans, and Byzantines all settled here at one time or another, leaving behind government buildings, public baths, theaters, and sanctuaries. The best way to get here is by renting a car or scooter and riding to Kamari and up the mountain. Otherwise, take the bus (20 min, 160dr) from Theotokopoulu to Kamari and start the long, hot hike, best tackled in the morning. Admission to the site is free.

Crete

The large island of Crete (Kríti in Greek) holds a special place in history. Here you can see remnants of the ancient Minoan civilization in Iráklion and Venetian buildings in Réthimnon. The island is also especially rugged; the blue-gray mountains, split with deep gorges, spread across the interior and creep up to the coastline. Although it's far from untouristed, the island is large and diverse enough for you to find an outcropping of wildflowers or stretch of warm sea that you can call your own.

IRAKLION

Until Crete was incorporated into Greece in 1913, Greeks had very little to do with this metropolis: Arabs built it in 824, Venetians took over from 1210 to 1669, and Turks controlled it until it became an independent state in 1898. Traces of these civilizations remain; bits and pieces of the old Venetian fortress walls even peek out from between modern buildings. For a view of it all, climb high above the city to the **Tomb of Kazantzakis,** resting spot of the author of *Zorba the Greek.* On his tomb is inscribed: "I fear nothing. I hope for nothing. I am free."

People in this full-fledged city move at a faster pace than on the other islands, and big, dirty-gray buildings project fiercely into the sky. But while Iráklion may not be a visual dessert, it does pack a historical punch. If you visit only a few museums in Greece, make the **Archaeo-**

logical Museum (off Pl. Eleftherías; open Mon. 12:30–7, Tues.–Sun. 8–7) one of them. Just about every interesting Minoan find from Crete winds up here sooner or later.

BASICS The main **tourist office** (1 Xanthoudidou, tel. 081/228–203; open weekdays 8:30–2:30) is uphill from the port. Try **Poulios Travel** (35 Sof. Venizelou at Handakos, tel. 081/128–4496; open daily 8:30 AM–9 PM) for information on flights, ferries, and sights. Customers get free luggage storage. Adamis Tours (23 25th Avgoustou, Box 1031, 71202; open Mon.–Sat. 8–2:30) is the **American Express** agent.

COMING AND GOING Most **ferries** to Crete land at Iráklion. Overnight ferries from Pireaus (12 hrs, 4,500dr deck class) arrive daily, and boats from Santoríni (4 hrs, 2,200dr), Páros (12 hrs, 4,000dr), and Rhodes (11 hrs, 4,600dr) come in several times per week. You can walk to the central spots in Iráklion, but if you want to explore the outskirts of the city, take the **bus** (tel. 081/245–020 or 081/221–765); the stations are east of the main port.

WHERE TO SLEEP AND EAT During the off-season, hotels here are a tad more costly than on nearby islands, but the prices don't shoot up as much come high season. Of the two local **HI hostels**, the more appealing one is at 5 L. Vironos (off 25th Avgoustou, tel. 081/286–281; beds 700dr) and run by the cutest little grandma you've ever seen. A very shady man runs the other one (24 Handakos, off Sof. Venizelou, tel. 081/280–858; beds 800dr); stay with him only as a last resort. A better choice is **Christakos Pension** (12 Eigenikoi, tel. 081/284–126; doubles 3,000dr), in the nest of pensions off Handakos. After you're settled, try some 500dr fresh fish at **Ippokampos** (Sof. Venizelou and Mitsotakis, tel. 081/280–240; closed weekends).

NEAR IRAKLION If you have even a tinge of interest in history, go to the awe-inspiring Minoan **Palace of Knossos.** As Kazantzakis summed it up, "in Knossos one's heart beats with a different rhythm, one's mind is flooded with questions." The Palace of Knossos supposedly stood for 200 years before an earthquake shook it down around 1900 BC. The Cretans quickly rebuilt, but the place was doomed; a series of natural disasters knocked it down again and again until the volcanic explosion of Santoríni finally did it in for good. The remaining faded red pillars and dusty beige walls of the palace are haunted by mystery: Was this the site of a labyrinth, where the legendary Minotaur feasted on young Athenians, or simply a symbol of Minoan prosperity? According to historians, Knossos is the site of the first Greek city-state and the earliest Greek religion and art, dating back to Neolithic times. Inside the gates of the palace, be sure to visit the **Queen's Suite** and her bathroom, complete with flushable toilet. In fact, the entire drainage system of the palace was remarkably advanced, with pipes running all underneath the building. Other highlights are the **Throne Room** off the courtyard and the **theater** in the northwestern corner of the palace. *Tel. 081/231940. From terminal on Sof. Venizelou, take Bus 2 to Knossos (20 min, 170dr). Admission: 1,000dr, 500dr students, Sun. free. Open weekdays 8–7, weekends 8:30–3.*

BALI

Five rocky coves, a handful of buildings, and locals who love foreigners make up this treasure 47 km west of Iráklion. Crete's best-kept secret has been leaked a bit to vacationing Europeans, but it remains one of the quaintest towns in the country. In this tiny town caught between mountains and the coast, the sounds of water and boats rocking in the small port replace disco tunes and rattling scooters. Even residents of Iráklion will sigh if you mention Bali.

Stay in **Nadia's Rooms** (next to Autoplan Car Rental, tel. 0834/94202; doubles 3,000dr), marked only with big red letters reading RENT ROOMS. **Chrisanthis** (off main road 3 min before port; doubles 3,000dr) has cheap rooms and a waterfront patio. **Panorama Restaurant** (tel. 0834/94217; open daily 7 AM–midnight) sits above the small port and serves a mean Greek salad for 500dr. Buses traveling between Iráklion and Réthimnon stop in Bali. From either town, the trip takes about 45 minutes and costs about 800 dr.

RETHIMNON

A Venetian fortress rests on a hill above the city, cobblestone alleyways squirm their way through Turkish and Venetian houses, and old men sit outside cafés playing backgammon while sipping cups of Greek coffee. This is old Réthimnon. But glued to this old town is a new one of high-rise hotels, pricey restaurants, currency-exchange offices, and tourists. Réthimnon is one of the most touristed spots on Crete, and Bermudas-clad couples do their best to detract from the town's appeal. Happily, they only half succeed.

The most obvious sight in town is the **Venetian Fortezza** (tel. 0831/28101; admission 200dr, 100dr students; open daily 8–8)—obvious both because everyone's talking about it and because you can see it from almost anywhere in town. The 16th-century complex includes the ruins of officers' houses, barracks, and a mosque. To get here, take the dirt path at the waterfront all the way up. Directly across from the fortress is an **Archaeological Museum** (tel. 0831/20668; admission 400dr, 200dr students, Sun. free), which displays a collection of ancient coins. To escape the heat, check out the tree-filled **Public Garden,** right behind the old town. Also, take a stroll to the town's **Venetian Harbor,** north of the port and near the fortress, which is packed solid with atmospheric but expensive little cafés and shops. For nightlife, the harbor shares top billing with the waterfront by the main port. The **tourist office** (western waterfront, tel. 0831/24143) gives out accommodations lists, maps, and sea turtle protection information.

COMING AND GOING **Ferries** (tel. 0831/22276) arrive daily from Pireaus (10 hrs, 4,100dr). Daily **buses** (tel. 0831/22212) from Iráklion (1½ hrs, 1,200dr) and Khanía (1 hr, 1,000dr) come into the main terminal on Dimokratias Street.

WHERE TO SLEEP AND EAT Most hotels in Réthimnon are comfortable and expensive. The most reasonable rates are in the old town, and private homes near the castle often rent out a few rooms. The tidy **HI hostel** (41 Tombazi, tel. 0831/22848; beds 800dr) is your best choice, with a restaurant, a garden, and laundry basins. From the bus station, go north on Dimokratias, left on Kountouri, and right on Tombazi. **Camping Elizabeth** (on the beach east of town, tel. 0831/28694; 1,000dr per person, 900dr to rent a tent) is beautifully wooded. From the main bus terminal, take the bus to Misseria and tell the bus driver to stop at the university. Walk straight up, and at the fork go left. Then take your first left, then your first right. **La Bamba Hotel** (tel. 0831/23364; doubles 4,000dr) offers nice, safe rooms in the center of the waterfront near the huge, trendy **Dolphin Disco** dance club.

Mary's Restaurant (31 George Papadzeou, tel. 0831/23262) is a small hangout for local students, and Mary really knows what she's doing in that kitchen. There's no sign; just go east on the waterfront, turn right on George Papadzeou, and ask for Mary. **Birais** (63 Sof. Venizelou, tel. 0831/27415) is more costly, but the food's worth every cent. Chicken with curry is 850dr.

KHANIA

Khanía has a will to survive. The city that today booms with the second-highest population in Crete has been struggling for years to keep its buildings and character intact. Burned to bits in 1266, rebuilt by Venetians in 1336, besieged by the Turks in 1645—this kind of history could easily have left three scorched stones, a pillar or two, and a modern sign denoting what used to be here. But somehow Khanía has stuck through it all, even managing to hold on to that comfortable small-town feel that makes it hard to leave. In fact, nothing seems to faze the old town now, not even the hordes of tourists or truckloads of military men swaggering about. The **Archaeological Museum** (Halidon, tel. 0821/20334; admission 400dr, students 200dr, Sun. free) in the old Venetian Church of San Francesco has an okay collection of statues, coins, and frescoes from the neolithic to Roman eras. The **EOT** (40 Kriari St., 4th floor of Agricultural Bank, tel. 0281/89240) is open weekdays 8–2:30.

Starting at Xyloskala, 44 km south of Khanía, the 17-km **Samarian Gorge** descends in a steep curve to the Libyan Sea and is one of the island's premier attractions. Talk to the EOT about buses to the mouth of the gorge so you can make the spectacular six-hour downhill hike.

COMING AND GOING From Pireaus, you can take a **ferry** (10 hrs, 3,800dr) to **Soudha** (tel. 0821/28888), the nearest port to Khanía. From there, jump on a blue bus (tel. 0821/23024; 170dr) to Khanía's marketplace. Or bus it all the way, on a green bus (tel. 0821/93306) from Iráklion (3½ hrs, 2,200dr) or Réthimnon (1 hr, 1,000dr).

WHERE TO SLEEP AND EAT The rooms above **Cosy Cafe** (next to cathedral, off Halidon, tel. 0821/41213; doubles 3,000dr) have sterile beds on wooden floors. For better rooms, jump back in history and stay in the former **Santa Maria de la Coer Monastery** (18 Agion Markoy, tel. 0821/54776; doubles 4,000dr), which rents spacious rooms with stone walls. From Halidon at the waterfront, make a right by Olympic Airways.

When you're low on cash, grab some souvlaki (250dr) at **Oveliztirio** (Halidon, 2 blocks from waterfront, tel. 0821/43923; open daily 8 AM–4 AM); the awning reads SOUVLAKI FAST FOOD. Or grub at **Tamam** (S. Zambeliu St., off Halidon; closed lunch), in a former Turkish bathhouse. Pasta with bacon costs 700dr. Feeling domestic? Buy cheeses, bread, and fruit at the **marketplace** (open daily 8–2, Tues. and Fri. also·6–9 PM) where the buses from Soudha arrive.

Dodecanese

At the eastern edge of the Aegean, hugging the west coast of Turkey, the Dodecanese (Twelve Islands) are some of the hottest tourist spots in Greece. Rhodes and Kos, two of the most popular, unfold in fertile splendor and are creased with streams.

RHODES

The fairy-tale town of Rhodes (Ródhas in Greek), capital of the island by the same name, is dominated by the looming **Palace of the Grand Masters** (tel. 0241/23359; admission 800dr, 400dr students; open Tues.–Sun. 8:30–3), a fortified castle built by crusaders in the 14th century. The crusaders kept control until the Ottomans showed up in 1522, adding a library, several mosques, and **Turkish baths** (tel. 0241/27739; admission 500dr, 150dr Wed. and Sat.; open Mon.–Sat. 7–7) that you can dip your dusty backpacking self into; from the port, take Knight's Road and make a left on Menekleous. In 1912, the Italians noodled their way in, ousted the Turks, and later rebuilt the then-decrepit palace as a summer getaway for Benito Mussolini.

Even with all the turnover, Rhodes has held onto some of its ancient Greek sites. As you enter Mandhráki Harbor, you'll spot two ancient columns with bronze deer standing on them. The columns mark the spot where one of the Seven Wonders of the Ancient World, the **Colossus of Rhodes,** a massive bronze statue of the sun god Helios, supposedly stood until an earthquake leveled the city in 227 BC. Greek and Roman finds that were later uncovered are now housed in the **Archaeological Museum** (near the palace, tel. 0241/27674; admission 600dr, 300dr students, Sun. free; open Tues.–Sun. 8:30–3). For more information, visit the **tourist office** (tel. 0241/35945) on Rimini Square.

An hour away by bus on either side of Rhodes Town are two ancient towns. Definitely make the trip east to **Líndhos** to see the **Acropolis of Ancient Líndhos** (tel. 0244/31258; admission 800dr, 400dr students; open Tues.–Sun. 8:30–3). Inside is a Temple of Apollo, the site of an ancient music school and an ancient stadium. In the opposite direction and also worth the trip is the ancient town **Kamiros** (tel. 0246/41435; admission 400dr; open Tues.–Sun. 8:30–3), showcasing ruins of a Doric temple, a monastery, and a proto-Christian catacomb. To reach either site, catch a bus (tel. 0241/27706; 30 min, 600dr) from Rimini Square.

Head down to the **Valley of the Butterflies** between June 20 and September to find millions of winged creatures in a valley of waterfalls and foliage. Catch a bus (tel. 0241/26300; 40 min, 700dr) behind the marketplace in town. Admission to the valley is free at the beginning and end of the season; there's a small fee when the swarms are present.

COMING AND GOING Plenty of daily **ferries** (tel. 0241/22220) hit Rhodes, including those from Pireaus (18 hrs, 5,900dr) by way of Kos (4 hrs, 2,500dr) or Pátmos (10 hrs, 3,900dr) and from Marmaris, Turkey (1½ hrs, 5,000dr plus 4,000dr port tax). Boats come less frequently from Páros (17 hrs, 4,500dr), Iráklion (11 hrs, 4,400dr), Sámos (13 hrs, 4,600dr), and Lésvos (19 hrs, 5,700dr). In Rhodes Town, Socrates Street leads from the port into the heart of town.

WHERE TO SLEEP AND EAT Most of the island's cheap accommodations are in Rhodes Town. For pensions, check around Avenue of the Knights, the main drag. **Steve Kefalas' Pension** (60 Omirou St., tel. 0241/24357; beds 1,500dr), complete with rooftop patio and laundry machine, is one of your best bets for a home-style, hostel-like situation. From the port, take Socrates Street to a left on Pithagora and a right on Omirou. **Lia's Boarding House** (66 Pithagora, on side street off Pithagora about 3 houses from the corner, tel. 0241/26209) has clean, drachma-saving singles (1,500dr) and doubles (2,000dr). **Sunlight Hotel** (32 Ipodamou, tel. 0241/21435; doubles 3,500dr) is the best deal in town for nicer, airy rooms. Follow Socrates from the port and go left on Ipodamou to the reception in Stavros Bar—ask for a room in the building around the garden.

When your stomach starts grumbling, don't fall victim to the touristy cafés and restaurants on Socrates Street or Avenue of the Knights. Head instead for **Makedonía** (off Pithagora, tel. 0241/23996), a family-operated place that serves some of the best Greek dishes on Rhodes to a crowd of locals. From the port, follow Socrates Street to a left on Pithagora. **Diafani's** (3 Arionos Sq., opposite Turkish baths, tel. 0241/26053) charges a little more for delicious Greek specialties (moussaka 1,000dr) but offers a garden atmosphere. From the port, take Socrates Street and hang a left on Menekleous Street.

KOS

Kos native Hippocrates, father of Western medicine, must have immunized the island against foreign infections; despite the obscene number of tourists clotting Kos Town, the rest of the island remains uncrowded, if you don't count the zillions of bleating goats who live on this oasis of jutting mountainous cliffs and relatively unscathed beaches. Reminders of Hippocrates cover the whole island, starting right near the port (across from the castle) where the **Plane Tree of Hippocrates,** supposedly the oldest tree in Europe, stands—well, sort of stands, with the help of metal supports.

In the evening, music blasts and drinks are slammed as Kos turns into an upscale version of Íos. A whole section of town near the Agora, smack at the waterfront, is lined with bars.

The **Archaeological Museum** (Pl. Eleftherias, tel. 0242/28326; admission 400dr, 200 dr students; open Tues.–Sun. 8:30–3) holds Hellenistic and Roman sculpture by Koan artists, including a 4th-century BC statue of Hippocrates. From the port, walk west down the waterfront and make a left on A. Ioannidi across from the marketplace. Toward the port, the **Castle** (admission 400dr, 200dr students; open Tues.–Sun. 8:30–3) dates back to around 1450, when the knights in charge of the island were apparently feeling constructive. The best thing to do here is walk around the walls for a bird's-eye view of town.

Muscle aches after all that walking? Use your last bit of strength to go to **Thermi,** where hot water trickles from rocks down into the sea. The 49°C (120°F) sulfurous water, whose odor has all the allure of rotten eggs, is supposedly good for arthritis, rheumatism, and skin ailments. Take the bus to Agios Fokás and walk the remaining 5 km, or bike the whole thing. The route to Thermi takes you past secluded stretches of sand, but the most beautiful beach on Kos is **Paradise Beach**; from the station at the back of town, take a green bus headed for Kéfalos. **Tourist info** is available west of the port at Travel Agency Koulias (tel. 0242/26985).

The **Asclepion,** 4 km southwest of Kos Town, was the renowned medical school where Hippocrates's legacy was carried on. He planned the school but died in 377 BC before it was built later that century, when it was dedicated to Asclepius, the god of medicine. On your way in, take a peek at the Roman baths at the front of the building. *Tel. 0242/28763. From the water-front, take the bus (120dr). Admission: 600dr, 300dr students. Open Tues.– Sun. 8:30–3.*

COMING AND GOING **Ferries** (port tel. 0242/26594) from Pireaus (14 hrs, 5,400dr), Rhodes (3½ hrs, 2,500dr), and Pátmos (3½ hrs, 2,100dr) dock daily. Boats also connect with Sámos (8 hrs, 2,600dr) several times a week and Iráklion (18 hrs, 3,600dr) once a week. The best way to cover Kos Town is by pedaling. Rent bikes for 300dr per day at **Moto Holidays:** Walk west from the port and left on Alexandry. If you're hooked on **buses,** catch a blue one (on waterfront west of castle, tel. 0242/26276; tickets 120dr–200dr) to get around town or a green one (off Grigoriou, at back of town, tel. 0242/22292) to other parts of the island.

WHERE TO SLEEP AND EAT Hotels on Kos are ridiculously expensive, but **Pension Alexis** (9 Irodotou, at Omirou, tel. 0242/28798), complete with outdoor patio, is a saving grace. An airy double costs 4,500dr. Head west from the port down the waterfront and make a left on Alexandrou and a right on Irodotou. **Kos Camping** (across from beach, tel. 0242/23910; 900dr per person; closed mid-Oct.–mid-May) is a nice escape 2½ km outside town. Take the bus headed for Agios Fokás and ask for the campground; a shuttle also meets the ferry.

Grab home-cooked spaghetti (400dr) with the locals at **Antones Taverna** (tel. 0242/25645); from the port, go west on the waterfront and turn left on Alexandrou then right on Theofrastou. **Angelos Taverna** (13 Psarron, tel. 0242/23979) is more touristy but has great food. Try the tasty fried lamb chops (700dr). From the port, go right down the waterfront, left on Alexandrou, right on Irodotou, and left on Psarron.

PATMOS

The island of Pátmos seems as spiritual and as peaceful as it must have been when St. John reputedly lived here. A religious mystique hangs over the island, infusing it with a sense of calm that other islands in the Dodecanese cannot approach. The natural beauty and calm water of Pátmos, called the Jerusalem of the Aegean, heals your body and soul, revitalizing you for the rest of your trip.

While here, make your pilgramage up to the village of Hóra to see the **cave** and the surrounding **Monastery of the Apocalypse** (open Mon., Wed., Fri., and Sat., 8–2, Tues. and Thurs. 8–2 and 4–6, Sun. 8–1 and 4–6). According to tradition, St. John wrote the text of Revelations in the cave. A bit further up the hill in Hóra is the **Monastery of St. John the Theologian** (same hours as the cave), built to commemorate St. John in the 11th century. Be sure to see the 13th-century murals in the chapel of the Madonna. Inside the monastery, the **treasury** and **library** (tel. 0247/31398; admission 500dr) display relics, elaborately embroidered vestments, illuminated manuscripts, and codices containing parts of the Gospel of St. Mark and the Book of Job. To get to Hóra from the main town of Skála, take a bus (10 min, 120dr) or walk half an hour.

VISITOR INFORMATION The tourist office offers maps, bus and ferry schedules, brochures, and spiritual counseling (just kidding). *Right off the main platía, tel. 0247/31666. Open weekdays 8–3.*

COMING AND GOING **Ferries** (at the port, tel. 0247/31231) from Piraeus (10 hrs, 4,295dr), Kos (3½ hrs, 2,015dr) and Rhodes (10 hrs, 3,981dr) arrive daily. Boats go to Sámos (3 hrs, 1,650dr) three times a week and to other islands in the Northeast Aegean a little less frequently. To get around the island, pick up a **bus** at the port.

WHERE TO SLEEP AND EAT A mob of residents will meet you at the port telling you about rooms they have to let. For only 3,000dr per bathless double you can stay at **Irini Gril-li's** (tel. 0247/31852) rooms, which are clean and well tended. To get here, walk north of the port along the water, and make a left on the third alleyway after Hotel Chris. Look for the ROOMS TO LET sign. **Stefanos Camping** (at Méloi Beach, tel. 0247/31821; 900dr per person; closed mid-Oct.–mid-Apr.) is a good spot to pitch your tent while gazing at Méloi Beach.

Cooking facilities and laundry basins are provided. Walk north of the port along the water for about 1,500 meters to the campground.

At **Grigoris Grill and Fish Tavern** (tel. 0247/31515; open daily 6 PM–midnight) you can eat *pastítsio* (pasta cooked with meat; 750dr) and sip a soda (200dr) while outside on the waterfront. The restaurant is slightly south of the port, where the waterfront and the paved road to Hóra meet.

Northeast Aegean

The islands of the northeast Aegean aren't easy to categorize—about the only thing they share is their proximity to Turkey. Seductive Sámos was home to some of Greece's greatest thinkers; Híos is known for its interesting buildings, decorated with geometric patterns; and Lésvos was the birthplace of a number of important artists and writers who were inspired by the island's beauty.

SAMOS

You couldn't find a much more impressive list of natives than those of Sámos: Pythagoras, Epicurus, Aristarchus (the first in history to place the sun at the center of our solar system), and Aesop are the brightest stars. To top it all off, Antony and Cleopatra hung out here for a time, and the tyrant Polycrates, who stormed through the Aegean snatching all the loot he could, stashed his goodies at his home in Sámos. Along the way, he ordered the construction of the **Temple of Heraion** (tel. 0273/91577; admission 500dr, 300dr students; open Tues.– Sun. 9–2:30). Now in ruins outside the small coastal town of **Pithagório,** this temple where the Sámians worshipped their patron goddess, Hera. To get here from **Vathí,** the island's main town, take the bus to the Heraion stop (30 min, 350dr). Polycrates's slaves also created an amazing 1-km-long underground aqueduct, known as the **Efpalinion tunnel** (tel. 0273/61400; admission free; open Tues., Wed., Fri., and Sun. 9:30–2, Thurs. 11:30–2, Sat. 10–2). The tunnel's builders had only primitive tools and no means for measuring, so they simply dug through the ground toward each other every day until, 15 years after they had begun, they met in the middle. Today you can walk 1,000 feet into the slippery, dimly lit tunnel near the Pithagório bus stop. Wear good shoes and bring a flashlight.

Sámos native Pythagoras was the first to note the mathematical relations in music and the beauty of proportions— ideas that prompted the development of classical architecture.

Tsamadou Beach, 8 km from Vathí and served by bus, is one of the most beautiful beaches anywhere and attracts nude sunbathers in droves. Beaches near the island's main towns are often pretty grungy, but **Psilí Ammos,** just 5 km south of Vathí, is clean. For more info on the island, contact the **EOT** (up from the Music Cafe at the Vathí waterfront, tel. 0273/28530) or the **Pithagório Tourist Office** (toward water from Pithagório bus stop, tel. 0273/61389).

COMING AND GOING Most **ferries** dock at Vathí. Daily connections link Sámos with Pireaus (12 hrs, 4,100dr), and several boats a week go to Páros (6 hrs, 3,00dr), Híos (5 hrs, 1,800dr), and Kos (8 hrs, 2,600dr). Daily boats also cross over to Kuşadaşı, Turkey (1½ hrs, 4,500dr plus 4,000dr port tax). The main **bus station** (tel. 0273/27262) is in Vathí on Lekath, which leads right into town.

WHERE TO SLEEP AND EAT Hotels are costly in Pithagório and pretty cheap in Vathí, though aesthetically Pithagório is more rewarding. In Vathí, turn to **Pension Ionia** (5 Kalomíri, tel. 0273/28782; doubles from 2,000dr) for a clean, no-frills room; from the port, walk along the waterfront and make one left on Etamapali and another on Kalomíri. But go to Pithagório's **Pension Arokaria** (tel. 0273/61287; doubles from 3,000dr) when you're feeling homesick: The old proprietor is sympathetic to poor student travelers and will set you up in a homey room. From the bus stop, walk toward the water and make a right on Metamorfoseos.

Sámos is definitely lacking in the food department. In Vathí, **Alekos** (tel. 0273/27965) serves local culinary delights; from the waterfront, turn up at Music Cafe. In Pithagório, try **Manolis Barbeque** (tel. 0273/61470), a self-service restaurant with an eating area on the water and souvlaki for 240dr; from the Pithagório bus stop, make a left at the water.

HIOS

Until now, Greece has probably made you feel pretty important, between store owners beckoning you into their stores and hotel proprietors offering you the family jewels if you'll stay for a night. In Híos, all that changes. Locals go about their daily business without giving you a second glance, and you fend for yourself. The island itself is gorgeous and, outside Híos Town, largely untouched. As well as pure beaches, there are small towns in which you actually see Greeks in action. **Pirgí Town** is Híos's most interesting community architecturally—all the houses have *ksistá* (geometric designs) covering their facades. Beaches to check out are the black pebble beach of **Emborió**, near Pirgí Town, and **Nagós**, near the beautiful coastal town of **Kardhámila**.

The most impressive thing to see on the island is the **Monastery of Néa Moní** (tel. 0271/27507; open daily 8–1 and 4–sunset). On this site, an image of the Virgin Mary supposedly prophesied that Constantine Monomarchus would one day become emperor of Byzantium. Constantine promised that if the prophecy came true, he would build a monastery. Six months later the throne was his and the monastery was built with the icon inside. Buses from Híos run here twice a week; otherwise rent a scooter. Near the monastery is **Anávatos**, an ancient town on a plateau that has been eerily deserted ever since hundreds of residents, when faced with Turkish occupation in 1822, opted for death and jumped off the cliff.

COMING AND GOING Daily **ferries** (at the port, tel. 0271/44434) arrive from Pireaus (8 hrs, 3,600dr) and Lésvos (3 hrs, 2,400dr). Other connections include Sámos (4 hrs, 1,900dr), Kos (12 hrs, 4,000dr), Rhodes (16 hrs, 5,600dr), and Thessaloníki (16 hrs, 6,000dr) at least once a week. Híos is one of Greece's largest islands, so make use of the thorough **bus system**, stemming from the garden in the middle of Híos Town; local buses leave from the front of the garden (closer to the water), long-distance buses from the back.

WHERE TO SLEEP Staying in Híos is costly. The central, homey **Savvas Rooms to Let** (34 Rodokouraki, tel. 0271/41721; doubles from 3,000dr) is the best deal; otherwise, try **Rooms with a View** (7 Rodokouraki, tel. 0271/20364; doubles 3,500dr) across the street.

LESVOS

The poetry of Lésvos's most noteworthy citizen, Sappho, resonates through wooded regions, sandy beaches, rocky mountains, and petrified forests. The poet's influence here is indicative of the island's general reverence for women. Rarely will you see so many statues of women or hear of so many female leaders of the people. The island is huge—you could easily spend a glorious week exploring its beaches, villages, petrified and living forests, and hiking trails.

Lésvos's capital, **Mitilíni**, is jammed with buildings, cars, and fast-paced people. For info on the island and city, go to the **tourist office** (tel. 0251/42513) up the street to the left of the port. Rooms in Mitilíni are costly and scarce, but you can crash in cozy 3,300dr doubles at **Salina's Garden** (tel. 0251/42073). Follow the waterfront toward the big semicircle of cafés, go right on Lochagou Georgiou Voutsika, right again on the long shopping alleyway, which becomes Ermou, and follow the signs. The freshest food in town is at **Yapotabepna** (tel. 0251/23818), right on the water. The grilled souvlaki plate costs 1,000dr.

Míthimna, on the northernmost coast, is Lésvos's touristy resort, where cobblestone streets, small shops, and rooms to let cluster around an old castle. At the **tourist office** (tel. 0253/71347) on the main road, you'll usually find a number of women with rooms to let. Otherwise, pitch a tent at **Camping Míthimna** (tel. 0253/71079; 600dr per person; closed Nov.–Apr.) or just pitch a tent in a secluded spot; freelance camping is tolerated over most of the island.

Sporádes

This small cluster of islands off the coast of central Greece is just a short hop from the mainland. Maybe that explains why the islands are completely overrun by visitors in the high season. The Cyclades aren't the only Greek islands that serve up a cup of culture and a gallon of hedonism to visitors looking for that perfect tan.

SKIATHOS

The 3,900 residents of the island are eclipsed by the 50,000 visitors who come here each year for clear blue waters and scores of beaches; the gyro stands and suntan lotion shops of the uninteresting neon **Skíathos Town** cater to the tourist trade. The island's most popular beach is **Koukounariés**; take a bus (220dr) from the shelter on the north end of the waterfront in Skíathos Town. A short, marked walk from Koukounariés is **Banana Beach,** slightly quieter and nuder than its neighbor. The relatively unpopulated beach at the microtown of **Agia Eléni,** one bus stop before Koukounariés, is one of Skíathos's nicest. Surrounding all these beaches are hundreds of sandy inlets accessible only by climbing and swimming; try to find an unpopulated one since the nude sunbathers on them are like territorial dogs. After dark, a cluster of bars plays music to a hang-loose crowd by the waterfront. The riotous disco **La Piscine** has outdoor café tables and an Olympic-size pool hosting naked, drunken Brits. **Cafe Santan** offers live music after midnight to the mellow; walk inland on Papadiamados, and turn right at the post office.

BASICS The volunteers at the ferry dock kiosk are enthusiastic but know almost nothing about the island. Papadiamántis Street hosts the **post office, OTE,** several **banks,** and the tourist **police** (tel. 0427/231–72). Mare Nostrum Holidays (21 Papadiamántis St., Box 16, 37002 Skíathos, tel. 0472/214–63) is the **American Express** agent.

COMING AND GOING Skíathos is regularly served by **ferries** and hydrofoils from Vólos (3½ hrs, 2,000dr), Agios Konstandinos (3 hrs, 2,500dr), and Skópelos (30 min, 700dr).

WHERE TO SLEEP AND EAT Hotels abound; unfortunately, competition has done little to lower their cost. Rooms to let are worse—doubles run around 5,000dr. The best **campground** by far is on Aselinós Beach, far from town and near the sea; sites go for 1,200dr plus 250dr per person. Above a secluded inlet on the water is **Tarsanas** (tel. 0427/21251; closed lunch), a taverna worth the steep, five-minute hike through the old town's beautiful streets: Follow the path above Jimmy's Bar up the stairs, down an incline, and under bougainvillea to the blue menu stand; the taverna is next to Plakes, a rocky vista point.

SKOPELOS

The approach to **Skópelos Town** by sea is almost cinematic—the whitewashed village and tree-lined bay slowly reveal themselves from around a rocky hill. The town's narrow streets are populated by stores and cafés that range from tastefully expensive to self-consciously funky; even the OTE looks like it should be selling potpourri and sandalwood soap instead of phone cards. **Glóssa,** a town midway up the mountain from Loutráki, refuses to be dominated by tourism and is an attractive place to spend quieter moments on Skópelos. Ask M. Satmataki, the proprietor of Glóssa's only taverna, **T'Agnanti** (on path into town, tel. 0424/33070), to call for a room. Otherwise, accommodations on Skópelos are difficult to find; the rooms offered as you step off the ferry are cheap but require a long hike up the hill. **Club 52, Labikas,** and several other small indoor discos are concentrated one block from the waterfront, bordering Old Skópelos. The scene at each club changes nightly—geriatric one night, juvenile the next—so try a few before you choose one. The music played at the bar **Glaros** is a welcome break from discotechno.

COMING AND GOING Skópelos is served daily by **ferries** from Vólos (4 hrs, 2,400dr) and Skíathos (30 min, 700dr). The one road running the length of the island is served by overburdened buses that hit all the major towns and terminate at the uninteresting town of **Loutráki.**

Northern Greece

Northern Greece is less visited than the south, and at first glance it's easy to see why. Travelers often pass through the transport hubs of Vólos or Alexandroúpolis and figure they have seen enough. You can be sure, though, if they had seen the monasteries at Metéora, built on the heights of rock pinnacles rising more than 545.5 meters, they wouldn't have been so quick to move on. The north may not have as many miles of drop-dead-gorgeous coastline as the south, but the sparsely populated mountains and valleys make up for it if you brought your hiking boots as well as your bathing suit.

Ipiros

Stretching along the Ionian Sea south from the Albanian border, the region of Ipiros has always maintained a sense of autonomy—the mountain ranges that flank it kept the foreign powers that have controlled the rest of Greece at bay. But when Ali Pasha, the wayward and flamboyant Ottoman governor sent to Ipiros by Turkey, tried to take advantage of this isolation and set up his own mini-empire, he angered the Turkish goverment back home and was assassinated in 1822. The Turks started keeping a closer eye on the region until it finally went back to Greece in 1913.

IOANNINA

Idyllically situated at the foot of the Píndos Mountains on the shores of Lake Ioaninon, Ioánnina is one of Greece's most beautiful cities, retaining much of the Ottoman flavor it developed while acting as the capital of Ali Pasha's empire despite fires, wars, earthquakes, and the Greek distaste for all things Turkish. The majority of Ioánnina's sights are relics of Ali Pasha's life and exploits. **Vrelli's Wax Museum** (admission free; open daily 8–7:30), accessible by Bus 2, graphically re-creates dramatic battle scenes using enough lolling tongues and severed arms to scar an impressionable imagination for life. The **citadel walls** Ali Pasha built still encircle part of the town; within the walls a boring folklore museum is housed in the more interesting **Aslan Pashi Jami Mosque.** Go to the opposite end of the walls to explore the inner citadel; bring a flashlight.

The city is best seen at sunset while crossing the lake; ferries (120dr) leave from the café side of the citadel to cross to **Nissí,** a small island whose narrow cobblestone streets and several monasteries hid Ali Pasha before his assassination at the monastery **Pandelímonos.** Of the monasteries, **Ayíou Nikoláou Filanthropinón** has the most dramatic and best-preserved frescoes, though the other four are also worth a visit. Beyond the sights, quiet Ioánnina is the perfect base from which to explore the northern reaches of the Píndos Mountains. One of the jolliest **OTE** offices in Greece (southeast cnr of Pl. Pirrou, tel. 0651/25086) can tell you how.

COMING AND GOING Buses heading south and west, including to Pátra (4 hrs, 2,300dr), leave from the station at 28 Vizaniou; buses to everywhere else, including Athens (7½ hrs, 5,600dr) and Thessaloníki (6 hrs, 4,600dr) leave from the station at 4 Zossimadon.

WHERE TO SLEEP AND EAT The best budget accommodations are on Nissí, where the exceptionally clean pension **Varvara Vas Varaka** (tel. 0651/81596) offers 3,100dr doubles in a tiny house on a lakefront platía. Good deals in the center are the modest hotels **Paris** and **Agari** (16 Tsirigoti, tel. 0651/20541; doubles 2,000dr), which share a reception desk. From the citadel, walk into town along Averof past the bazaar, turn right onto Anexartisias, walk one block, and veer left onto Tsirigoti. On Níssí, several dockside restaurants serve murky little creatures brought up from Lake Ioaninon. On Ioánnina's central platía, the signless café **G. Matsoikes** doubles as a restaurant, serving a great pork cutlet in wine sauce for 1,000dr. But the best meal in Ipiros is at **Allottino** (21 Pirsinella, tel 0651/25695 or 0651/22522), a modern fresco-covered taverna. It's worth the long walk: From the citadel, walk into town along Averof and turn left past the city administrative offices onto Pirsinella.

NEAR IOANNINA Second only to Delphi in sacredness to the ancient Greeks, the oracle of Zeus at **Dodoní** was established in the second millenia BC, when either a woman or a bird (the modern translation is a bit muddy) arrived from Egypt and discovered a sacred oak tree in a valley southwest of Ioánnina. A temple was built, and people came to worship Zeus and listen to the prophecies revealed by the rustling leaves of the oak. The amphitheater is still almost entirely intact, providing a stunning view of the mountains across the valley. The site is not frequently visited, so you can enjoy an almost private exploration. *Tel. 0652/82287. Admission: 400dr, 200dr students. From Ioánnina, catch bus (6:30 AM or 4:30 PM) at 28 Vizaniou. Open weekdays 8–7, weekends 8:30–3.*

VORIA PINDOS

The northernmost stretch of the Píndos Mountains, the Vória Píndos is home to Greece's second-highest peak and a cluster of villages known as the **Zágoria**. The village of **Monodéndri** is at the trailhead of the **Víkos Gorge**, a dramatic icy waterway slicing through limestone cliffs. Trail 03 runs along the gorge 13 km from Monodéndri to the village of **Megálo Pápingo**, home to many excellent 18th-century mansions. **Mikró Pápingo**, farther along the path at the base of a rock cliff, is just large enough to have several tavernas and three hotels, the best of which is **Exarhou** (tel. 0653/41130; doubles 3,800dr). **Bus service** to the Píndos and Zágoria from Ioánnina's Zossimadon station (1½ hrs, 950dr) is meager; plan ahead.

Thessalía

A fairly mundane stretch of farmland bounded by the mountains of Ipiros to the west and the Aegean Sea to the east, Thessalía is usually passed through rather than visited, and with reason: The region's main towns of Lamia, Vólos, and Larissa are unpleasant concrete cities. The magnificent monasteries of the Metéora and the historic villages of the Pílio, however, are spectacular cultural enclaves where nature plays an active role and are absolutely worth a visit.

VOLOS

Rarely will you find so much nothing concentrated in one city: no culture, no charm, no hints of faded glory, no promise of glory to come. Vólos performs its job as a transportation and distribution center efficiently and with little grace. Even potentially poetic touches like the orange trees along city streets fail miserably: The oranges drop and rot, creating a moldy, insect-ridden mess.

Unfortunately, if you want to explore the Pílion Peninsula, you'll probably find yourself here for at least one night in one of the plenty of cheap hotels that line the waterfront behind the ferry dock. One of the most pleasant is **Pension Roussas** (1 Tzaanou, tel. 0421/21732; doubles 3,500dr), down the waterfront from the docks. Vólos is home to a grand selection of overpriced seafood restaurants scattered along the length of the waterfront. A decent option is the grill **Vangelis** (4 K. Kártali, 1 block north of flying dolphin dock). The train station, bus station, ferry docks, and **tourist office** (in park, tel. 0421/23500 or 0421/37417) are all within 2 km of each other along Girgoriou Lambaraki; Bus 2 connects them. You can get here by train from Athens (8 hrs, 2,700dr) or Thessaloníki (4 hrs, 1,700dr).

THE PILION MOUNTAINS

The low Pílion mountain range, mythical home of centaurs, stretches from Vólos along a lush, slender peninsula. Once you rise past the olive trees that skirt the mountains, the air is filled with the sound of running water. Water springs magically from fountains and crevices, flowing along cobblestone paths and across roads. The EOT has named the two Pílion villages of Makrinítsa and Vizítsa landmark settlements, dedicating any tourist dollars that come in to the towns' upkeep. All access to the Pílion is by KTEL bus from Vólos; once in the mountains it's difficult to get around, but several buses make daily sweeps through the peninsula's northern tip.

Only a few minutes from Vólos by bus, **Makrinítsa** is the most popular destination in the Pílion. Visitors come to admire its meticulously maintained Byzantine church, steep winding paths, and flagstone square but wind up staying in more touristy but cheaper **Portaria,** a 20-minute walk away. The Portaria hotel **Alkestis** (behind the platía, tel. 0421/99178 or 0421/99529; doubles 5,000dr) has simple rooms and a beautiful overgrown garden. Several tavernas congregate just below the road to Makrinítsa; **O. Baggeles** has reasonable prices.

The rest of the Pílion has only a fraction of Makrinítsa and Portaria's tourists. Lately, successful painters and writers have been quietly buying homes in **Miliés,** turning the town into something of a yuppie artist colony. New York–trained actor Nikiforos Naneris recently opened a local taverna to get away from the stress of cities: **Tsitsiravo** (terra-cotta building on main road, tel. 0422/8624) is home to possibly the greatest Greek salad ever. **O Palios Strathmos** (tel. 0421/86425; doubles 9,000dr) offers beautiful rooms in a house next to the old train station. **Mihalis Pappas** (tel. 0423/86207; doubles 4,000dr) prefers that you stay at least three days in his modest private rooms, but he's willing to compromise.

Twenty-five minutes farther down the road, **Vizítsa,** like Makrinítsa, reflects its EOT-canonized status in room and meal prices. The luscious calm can be almost overwhelming—a mule passing by may be the most exciting event in a Vizítsa afternoon.

METEORA

Jutting out from the edge of the Píndos Mountains, the profoundly surreal gray cliffs and tiny buildings of the Metéora could have been created only by a combination of nature and spirituality. The inaccessibility of the monasteries (until recently, you could only reach them by scaling the rock face or being pulled up in a net) allowed the monks of the Metéora to practice their religion unhindered by Greek politics. The monasteries themselves are organic-looking structures, collections of stone and timber that seem to have sprouted from the land. After inspiring the faithful between the 13th and 16th centuries, the monasteries began a gradual deterioration that only recently has been stopped by the fascination and money of

If the rocks were a little redder and the monks ran a little faster, the Metéora would look like a misplaced backdrop from a Road Runner cartoon.

visitors. Today six are in operation, all catering shamelessly to the tourist trade. But the elegant frescoes, impressive structures, and breathtaking views are worth the 300dr admission and crowds of videotaping tourists.

You could visit all six monasteries in a full day of ambitious walking, but if time is limited, head straight up to **Méga Metéron** (open Wed.–Mon. 9–1 and 3:20–6), west of the others. The largest and most distinguished of the monasteries, this has traditionally also been the best funded, as reflected in the frescoes of its chapel and the idols and manuscripts displayed in its library. Looming above the road between the other monasteries is **Roussánou** (open daily 9–1 and 3–6), which occupies one of the most dramatic sites in the Metéora. If you want to visit any of the monasteries, you must wear suitable clothing: Men must wear long pants, women must wear dresses cut below the knee, and nobody can expose shoulders.

COMING AND GOING Five km down the road from the Metéora, the town of **Kalambáka** is served by frequent trains from Vólos (4½ hrs, 1,140dr), Thessaloníki (6½ hrs, 2,050dr), and Athens (7½ hrs, 2,500dr) and by KTEL buses from Ioánnina (3 hrs, 1,920dr) and Athens via Tríkala (6 hrs, 3,400dr). From here, find a taxi (500dr) or walk up to **Kastráki,** where accommodations are situated at the foot of the Metéora.

WHERE TO SLEEP AND EAT Along the road to Kastráki there are many modest hotels and rooms to let. **Hotel Kastráki** (tel. 0432/22286; doubles 4,000dr) has doting managers and a perfect location at the start of the road to the Metéora. Plenty of campgrounds cover the area; the incredible location of **Camping the Cave** (tel. 0432/24–802; 900dr plus 200dr per person), at the absolute base of the rocks, compensates for the somewhat cramped sites.

Makedonía

Makedonía, a rarely visited area in the north of Greece, is a region of legend and history, full of architectural treasures and remnants of the reign of Alexander the Great. Although the legend-enshrouded Mt. Olympus is perhaps the best reason to come here, the large city of Thessaloníki ensures that the region has a least a little cosmopolitan flair.

THESSALONIKI

Thessaloníki has always been a second city, playing a supporting role to Pélla in ancient times, Constantinople during the Byzantine Empire, Istanbul after the Ottoman Empire, and Athens in the modern era. Rather than wallow in this eternal bridesmaid status, Thessaloníki has excelled as a cultural and intellectual center. Here Aristotle taught young Alexander the Great in the 4th century BC, St. Paul wrote his epistles in the 1st century AD, and Jews fleeing persecution from their native Spain were given refuge and protection by the Ottoman sultan in 1492.

The city wears its urbanity with a distinctly domestic flavor, denying visitors who expect either a jet-set stomping ground or a sweaty provincial port town. Thessaloníki is charming, tasteful, expensive, and not wholly accessible to tourists. The shops, cafés, platías, and architecture are stylized almost to a fault, and the Armani suits and 1,200dr coffees provide a startling contrast to the ruins of the city walls and the spirited bartering of the city's bazaar.

BASICS The **tourist office** (Pl. Aristotelous 8, at Mitropoleos, tel. 031/271888) is open weekdays 8–8. The **American Express** office (Tsimiski 19, Box 54110, tel. 031/126–9984; open Mon.–Thurs. 8–2, Fri. 8–1:30) has the usual services. Pick up poste restante mail at the **central post office** (Tsimiski 45, tel. 031/264208; postal code 54101).

COMING AND GOING Thessaloníki is home to one of Greece's largest and nicest **train stations** (Monastiriou St.), 3 km west of the city center. It serves Athens (11 hrs, 3,440dr) and Alexandroúpolis (8 hrs, 2,620dr) and has international service to Sofia (about 10 hrs, 3,500dr) and Istanbul (about 17 hrs, 5,500dr). Take Bus 10 or 31 into town.

KTEL has decided **bus service** to Thessaloníki should be as fragmented as possible, though a central station was under construction at press time. To Athens (8 hrs, 5,100dr), Péla (1 hr, 700dr), and Alexandroúpolis (6 hrs, 4,100dr), buses will *probably* leave from 22 Anagenisseos, two blocks south of the train station—check at the tourist office to be sure. For service to Halkidikí, buses leave from 68 Karakassi (tel. 031/924445); from the center, take Bus 31, get off at the corner of Egnatia Odos and Karakassi, and walk two blocks north on Karakassi.

GETTING AROUND The focus of the lower city is the waterside Platía Aristotelous, the center of shopping, banking, and socializing. The city is large and hilly, but **buses** cover it all; board single-length buses in the front and buy a ticket from the vending machine behind the driver, or board caterpillar buses through the rear door and pay the seated conductor the 75dr fare. No **taxi** fare in town should run above 700dr.

WHERE TO SLEEP Budget hotels on **Komnínon Street,** two blocks west of Platía Aristotelous by the waterfront, are run-down but beautifully located; those on **Egnatia Street** around Venizelou Street tend to be cleaner but louder during the day. If all else fails, the train station is a relatively safe place to crash— try the rubber mats by baggage claim.

Hotel Luxembourg (6 Komnínon St., tel. 031/278449; doubles 3,500dr), a Greek interpretation of a Beaux Arts building, fits in well with the surrounding sophisticated neighborhood cafés. From Platía Aristotelous, go 2 blocks west on Mitropoleos Street and turn toward the waterfront on Komnínon Street. **Hotel Continental** (doubles 3,750dr) across the street is the Luxembourg's twin. A service-obsessed manager keeps the rooms at **Hotel Atlas** (40 Egnatia St., tel. 031/537046; doubles 4,000dr) excessively clean. From Platía Aristotelous, go north on Aristotelous Street and west on Egnatia Street. The only thing the **HI Youth Hostel Thessaloníki** (44 Svolou St., tel. 031/225946; beds 1,300dr) has going for it is its location. From Platía Aristotelous, go north on Aristotelous Street, then east on Ermou, which becomes Svolou.

FOOD Thessaloníki's cuisine is exquisite, and you pay dearly for it. Horrifically expensive tavernas and restaurants fill the streets by the waterfront—walk up toward the old town for better deals. **Ta Adeltia** (9 Arianou St., tel. 031/266432) is a small taverna whose outdoor tables spill along the entire block. Greek salads are 750dr. Local businesspeople gather for

Makedonía: It's Greek to Them

Makedonía is not just a geographic region; it's also the subject of a bitter dispute about the importance of a name. In the 4th century BC, under the charge of King Philip II, Makedonía defeated a coalition of Greek armies and succeeded in bringing the city-states of Greece under its control. Alexander the Great soon expanded his father's empire to include most of the eastern Mediterranean. At this time, the Hellenistic period, Makedonía was inhabited almost solely by Greeks, but over the next few centuries the Greeks were joined by heirs to other cultures: Slavs, Turks, and Bulgars, to name just a few. After World War I, however, more Greeks settled here by the thousands. What was once a collage of ethnicities has become an overwhelmingly Greek region, and the population looks back to the good old days of Philip and Alexander as the source of their cultural heritage, all but ignoring the past two millennia of cultural diversity. The slogan MACEDONIA IS ONE AND ONLY AND IT IS GREEK stamped on telecards, the omnipresent bumperstickers proclaiming MAKEDONIA IS GREEK, and the minting of a 100dr coin with Alexander on the front and a Makedonian sun on the back all express this sense of regional nationalism.

When the Yugoslav Republic dissolved in 1991, a small and newly independent region bordering Greece took "Macedonia" as its name and the Makedonían sun as its flag. Hundreds of thousands of insulted Greeks demonstrated in Thessaloníki over the issue of the name and symbol, as the international community belittled threats by Greece to withdraw from the United Nations if the new republic (which Greeks refer to as "Skopje") was recognized as Macedonia. Despite Greece's diplomatic maneuvers, the new republic has been recognized by the United Nations as the Former Yugoslavic Republic of Macedonia, and has been allowed to keep its flag—a settlement that is scarcely satisfactory to any of the involved parties.

lunch at the modest **Moeseki Taverna** (192 Slefkidon, tel. 031/238498). A **bazaar** (weekdays 7–4) operates two blocks north of Platía Aristotelous, offering fruit, cheese, bread, and olives.

WORTH SEEING Thessaloníki isn't exactly filled with sights, but it does have a couple of worthwhile tourist stops. A better-than-usual **Folklife Museum** (68 V. Olgas, tel. 031/830–591) displays costumes and cultural artifacts from the last 250 years. The elaborate interior of the city's oldest church, **Panayía Ahiropíitos,** is also worth a look.

The stunning spoils from the 1978 excavations of the royal tombs of ancient Makedonía are displayed in the **Archaeological Museum.** The finds were vital in reconstructing the history of Makedonía and documenting the origin of the symbol of the Makedonían sun (found on the cover of the gold box that held Philip II's bones). The quality of the found objects and the sheer opulence of the gold pointed conclusively to a glorious regional history. *In park, cnr. of Tsimiski St. and Angelaki St., tel. 031/830538. Admission: 1,000dr, 500dr students. Open Mon. 12:30–7, Tues.–Fri. 8–7, weekends 8:30–3.*

The facade and setting of the **White Tower,** which once marked where the city walls met the waterfront, are more attractive than the exhibits inside, though the museum does have a modest collection of ancient and Christian art. The six floors of the tower wind up to a tiny café and a terrace with a view of Thessaloníki and the sea. *Pavlou Mela St., east of Pl. Aristotelous. Admission: 500dr, 300dr students. Open Mon. 12:30–7, Tues.–Fri. 8–7, weekends 8:30–3*

AFTER DARK Thessaloníki is at its best after the sun sets, when the entire city pours onto the streets and into the cafés down Gounari Street and along the waterfront to Platía Aristotelous. The cafés on Nikis Street are some of the trendiest and most expensive in Greece. In winter, bars and discos congregate on Kormoula and Margariti streets; during summer, many relocate onto the airport road, 10 km outside town; any taxi driver will know where to go (1,500dr ride). The most popular of the outdoor clubs among university students is the smokey **Summer Buzios** (cover 1,000dr–2,000dr). **Milos,** a café, restaurant, gallery, blues club, bar, and theater all rolled into one, is housed in a complex of buildings centered around an old converted wheat mill. It tends to draw a diverse mix of people who come to do their own thing. Any taxi driver should be able to bring you here, just outside town on the road to Athens, for about 400dr. **Egli** (3 Agios Nikolaou St., next to Agios Dimitirou, tel. 031/54633) is another multifaceted nightspot, with a gallery, bar, restaurant, theater, and outdoor cinema housed in a 17th-century bath.

MT. OLYMPUS

Mt. Olympus (Oros Olimbos in Greek) dramatically ascends from greenery to rock to cloud, with no bothersome rolling hills to muddle the effect. **Mytikas,** the mountain's highest peak at about 2870 meters, is accessible to an inexperienced but enthusiastic climber during the warmer months—the winter climb requires some equipment and more knowledge.

The most popular way to climb Mt. Olympus is by a succession of two- to three-hour hikes broken up by stays in refuges. The initial leg, from Litóhoro to the itsy-bitsy village of **Prionia,** can be an 18-km hike along a gorge or an equally adventurous taxi ride (2,500dr) along a skinny gravel road. From Prionia, the E4 trail leads from the 1,100-meter mark to the 2,100-meter **Refuge A** (tel. 0352/81800; beds 1,500dr; closed Nov.–Apr.), where you can stock up on water, overpriced food, and sleep; call ahead during summer. Camping in the national park is not allowed, but at the refuge campers can pitch a tent on the terrace for 700dr. From here, it's a 2½-hour hike along cliffs to the peak of Mytikas. For longer, more dramatic routes to higher-altitude refuges, check with the EOOS (Greek Climbing Society) office in Litóhoro.

LITOHORO A breezy little village at the bottom of Mt. Olympus, Litóhoro is a pleasant base from which to explore the mountain despite the buses and backpackers who tromp through the platía year-round. The Greek climbing club **EOOS** (tel. 0352/81944; open weekdays 8:30–2:30) operates an office below the platía where you can get maps and information on the mountain and national park; the office will also radio up the mountain to reserve you a bed at a refuge. Housing in Litóhoro is limited, but **Mirto** (below platía, tel. 0352/81398 or 0352/81498) and **Enipeas** (on platía, tel. 0352/81328) offer acceptable doubles at about 4,000dr. The 10 PM curfew, 9 AM checkout, and unfriendly staff sour the savings at the **HI hostel** (above platía, tel. 0352/81311; beds 950dr, sheets 400dr). Litóhoro's worst-kept dining secret is **To Pazari** (Ikosioktó Oktovriou, 2 min from platía, tel. 0352/81429), whose fried calamari (800dr) outshines the wurst and spaghetti offered by other restaurants on the platía. Several markets sell fruit, snacks, and water for the march up the hill. Litóhoro is served by many indirect trains and buses; the only direct buses come from Kateríni in the north (30 min, 330dr) and Larissa in the south (1 hr, 970dr).

Thraki

The region of Thraki, comprising the far northeast corner of the country, has been a part of Greece only since 1922, when it was formally ceded by Turkey. Despite years of attempted repatriation of the Turks and Bulgarians who have settled here, the region contains one of Greece's most diverse religious and cultural populations. This mixing of peoples causes its

The Ancient and the Restless

Look up at or down from Mt. Olympus and you'll understand why people settled at its foot and dreamt up the 12 Greek gods believed to live in the folds of the mountain; early Greeks blamed natural disasters on their personality clashes. Here's a short rundown on each of them:

Zeus is the Big Daddy, king of the gods and frequent lover (and sometimes rapist) of goddesses, nymphs, and mortals. His symbol and favorite weapon is the lightning bolt. Hera is his official wife and the divine symbol of motherhood. She spends a lot of time taking revenge on everyone Zeus sleeps with. Demeter, Zeus's sister, is the goddess of the earth. When Hades (god of the underworld) kidnapped her daughter Persephone, Demeter instantly forbade all trees to bear fruit and all grain to grow, until life on earth was threatened with extinction. Demeter relented only when Hades agreed to let Persephone back above ground for part of the year; thus we have seasons. Another frustrated guy is the god of fire and iron, Hephaestos, whose wife Aphrodite is the goddess of love, flirting and teasing and sleeping with any immortal she can get her hands on. Twins Apollo and Artemis, illegitimate children of Zeus, are both great hunters, though each also has an individual role: Apollo is the sun god, Artemis a virgin goddess who hangs out with attending nymphs in the woods and punishes any man who sees her naked. One of Zeus's few legitimate children, Ares, is the god of war and a pretty unlikable fellow since he likes a fight for the fight's sake. His female counterpart, Athena, was born by springing from her father Zeus's head, fully armed. However, she is also the goddess of wisdom and, unlike Ares, fights for good causes only. Perhaps the most popular of the Greek gods is Dionysus, the god of wine and partying—his followers often performed orgiastic rituals in their worship. And finally, the guy who maintains open communication among all the others—godly skirmishes can result in centuries of the silent treatment—is Hermes, the messenger god of golden-sandal fame.

share of problems and resentments, and the borders with Turkey and Bulgaria, though certainly passable on train or bus, are heavily militarized and have a highly charged atmosphere.

SAMOTHRAKI

Rising 1601 meters from the surface of the Aegean, the peak of Mt. Fengári on the island of Samothráki provided the perfect vantage point for Poseidon to watch over the siege of Troy. Far more accessible than the peak, though, are the ruins of the **Sanctuary of the Great Gods,** one of the most mysterious and revered sites of ancient Greece. The sanctuary was the center of religious worship in Thraki and the north Aegean until Roman times, when the rise of Christianity caused the fall of the cult. A map at the entrance shows the excavated **site** (admission 400dr) in clearly labeled English, and five re-erected Doric pillars give you an idea of the sanctuary's original size. French archaeologists liberated the famed Nike of Samothrace statue from the top of the amphitheater, bringing it to the Louvre and sportingly sending a plaster copy to the site's **museum** (admission 400dr), which is otherwise devoted to actual finds from the sanctuary. A nearly abandoned dirt road leads from Hora (also called Samothráki Town) through the town of Paleopóli to the sanctuary; the site and museum are open Tuesday–Sunday 8:30–3. Other than mountains and ruins, the sparsely visited island is home to a quiet landscape of forests, goats, pebble beaches, and German hippies.

Samothráki's single road fails in its attempt to circumnavigate the island—only half is accessible by car. Along the road is the port town of **Kamariótissa,** a dullish collection of houses and cafés. To the south, the road eventually leads to **Pahía Ammos,** the island's only beach of note; to the north, it hooks up with **Thérma,** home of hot springs, package tour buses, and a hippie colony that has managed to stretch the '60s into its fourth decade. A road cuts from Kamariótissa to the village of Samothráki, nestled up on the slope of Mt. Fengári. Public buses, headquartered just north of the ferry dock, travel all paved roads. The only moped rentals are right off the dock. They're expensive—4,000dr per day—but this is a fun and practical island to scoot around, especially since the bus isn't too efficient.

COMING AND GOING The easiest way to get here is from the boring transportation hub of **Alexandroúpolis;** seven daily buses (16 hrs, 10,000dr) run to Alexandroúpolis's bus station (38 Evroy St.) from Athens. From there, catch the **ferry** to Samothráki (3 hrs, 1,800dr). The boat leaves once daily, twice on Thursday and Saturday.

WHERE TO SLEEP AND EAT Though Kamariótissa offers some rooms to let, a far more interesting option is staying in **Hora,** a mountain village some 8 km up the mountain from Kamariótissa. Hora has a few rooms to let, two tavernas, several cafés, and the beautiful ruins of a medieval fortification crowning the village. Hora can be reached by bus from the ferry dock.

HUNGARY

12

By Mary Bahr and Karyn Krause

Visitors to Eastern Europe may want to start their travels in Hungary. The culture shock is far less pronounced here than in some other Eastern European countries, in part because Hungary is comparatively unscarred by the legacy of Communism. Even during the height of the Cold War, Hungary attempted a kinder, gentler totalitarianism, which encouraged certain types of private enterprise and rejected the collectivization of the land. This "goulash communism," as it came to be called, wasn't freedom, but it sure wasn't Romania.

If you really concentrate, you can pick up a few Hungarian words, but don't even try to figure out general grammar rules—just relax and enjoy a language that sounds like someone speaking with a mouthful of marbles from the bottom of a stream bed.

As Hungarian Communism differed from the other Eastern European models, so Hungarians as a people differ from other East Europeans. Whereas most of this part of the world is Slavic, the 10.5 million Hungarians are Magyars, descendants of an Asian race that arrived in Europe in the 9th century. Hungarians' closest relatives are the Finns, the Estonians, and the Vogul and Ostiak peoples of Siberia. The most obvious reminder of this unusual genealogy is the language, a tongue so unlike any other in Europe that even its closest relative, Finnish, is less similar to it than Italian is to German. Their language gives the Hungarians a sense of national identity—and national isolation—that helps insulate them from the tensions that have ripped apart more ethnically diverse Eastern European nations.

When the Eastern European economy collapsed in the late 1980s, it dragged the Hungarian Communist party down with it. Hardline leaders were removed in May 1988, a multiparty system was introduced in October 1989, and Hungary's first free elections in more than 40 years were held in 1990. Free elections don't automatically put food on the table, however, and like the rest of Eastern Europe, Hungary remains beset by economic problems, including rampant unemployment and inflation. On the bright side, foreign investment is pouring hard currency into the economy, and the country has been tagged for membership in the European Union. For travelers, Hungary provides the opportunity to witness a society in transition to democratic capitalism. What will emerge from the clash of Eastern heritage and Western aspirations remains to be seen.

Hungary

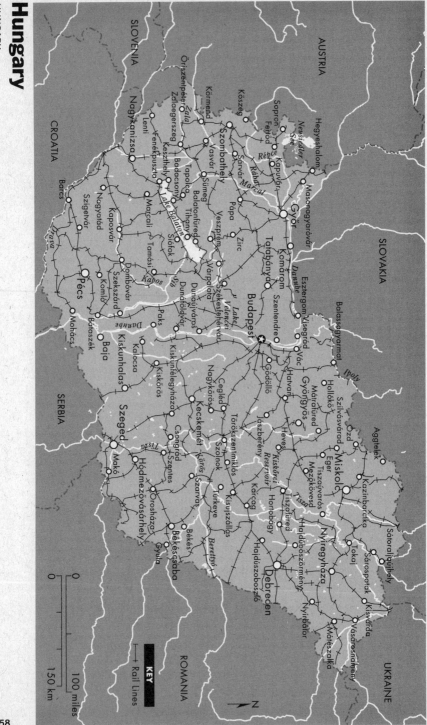

SLOVENIA

AUSTRIA

SLOVAKIA

CROATIA

UKRAINE

SERBIA

ROMANIA

Nagykanizsa
Lenti
Őriszentpéter
Zalaegerszeg
Zala
Körmend
Fenékpuszta
Keszthely
Zdaegerszeg
Badacsony
Tapolca
Sümeg
Vasvár
Szombathely
Kőszeg
Sopron
Fertőd
Hegyeshalom
Neusiedler See
Répce
Kapuvár
Rábca
Marcal
Mosonmagyaróvár
Győr
Komárom
Tatabánya
Esztergom
Visegrád
Vác
Balassagyarmat
Ipoly
Pápa
Veszprém
Zirc
Székesfehérvár
Velencei
Budapest
Szentendre
Gödöllő
Hatvan
Gyöngyös
Jászberény
Mátrafüred
Hollókő
Szilvásvárad
Eger
Mezőkövesd
Ózd
Aggtelek
Miskolc
Kazincbarcika
Sátoraljaújhely
Tokaj
Sárospatak
Kisvárda
Vásárosnamény
Mátészalka
Nyírbátor
Debrecen
Hajdúszoboszló
Hajdúböszörmény
Nyíregyháza
Tiszafüred
Hortobágy
Tiszavasvári
Tiszaújváros
Kisköre Reservoir
Karcag
Kisújszállás
Szolnok
Törökszentmiklós
Jászberény
Heves
Kecskemét
Nagykőrös
Cegléd
Kiskunfélegyháza
Kiskőrös
Kiskunhalas
Kalocsa
Baja
Bátaszék
Mohács
Szekszárd
Komló
Pécs
Szigetvár
Barcs
Kaposvár
Nagyatád
Marcali
Tamási
Dombóvár
Kapos
Siófok
Balatonfüred
Tihany
Lake Balaton
Várpalota
Dunaújváros
Dunaföldvár
Paks
Danube
Csongrád
Szentes
Szeged
Makó
Hódmezővásárhely
Orosháza
Békéscsaba
Gyula
Békés
Szarvas
Körös
Berettyó
Tisza
Túrkeve
Maros
Komárom
Danube
Rába
Sárvár
Tata

N

KEY
—— Rail Lines

0   100 miles
0   150 km

Basics

MONEY $1 = 102 forints and 100 forints = 98¢. Traveler's checks are accepted in larger cities and some Lake Balaton resorts but are impractical for everyday use—usually only big banks and exchange offices know what to do with them. Try not to change too much money at one time, because it's not always easy to change forints back into hard currency. Officially, you're allowed to change back 50% (up to US$100) of the original amount when you leave, but only if you have the exchange receipts.

➤ **HOW MUCH IT WILL COST** • Hungary is no longer dirt cheap. Overall, you'll find it about on a par with the Czech Republic and slightly more expensive than other East European countries. You can probably get by on $35 a day, most of which will be spent on lodging. Hotels are expensive ($15–$100), but livable youth hostels ($6–$15) abound, private homes ($8–$25) are an option, and food is still a bargain. Be warned that areas like Lake Balaton raise prices during July and August. If you have an ISIC card, always show it and say "Diak" (dee-yahk), meaning "student"—you may get a 50% discount on domestic bus and train rides.

VISA AND ENTRY REQUIREMENTS Travelers with a valid U.S., Canadian, or British passport do not need visas to visit for less than 30 days. Australians and New Zealanders need visas and should contact the Hungarian Consulate in Australia (Suite 405, Edgecliff Center, 203–233 New South Head Rd., Edgecliff NSW 2027, Sydney, tel. 2/328–7859).

COMING AND GOING EurailPasses, European East passes, and InterRail passes are valid throughout Hungary. **Trains** run frequently between Vienna and Budapest; the fastest, an early morning Eurocity express from Vienna's Sudbahnhof to Budapest's Déli Station, makes the journey in just under three hours. From Prague, the trip is 8½ hours; from Istanbul, 30½ hours. Budapest's **Ferihegy Airport** (see Coming and Going, in Budapest, below) is about 22 km southeast of the city. For same-day flight information in English, call 1/157–7155. **Malév Hungarian Airlines** (tel. 800/223–6884 in New York) flies nonstop from Budapest to New York and most European capitals. **Delta** also flies between Budapest and New York, and **British Air** offers nonstop service from Budapest to London.

GETTING AROUND You can travel to all major cities in Hungary on **trains,** which are usually less crowded and more comfortable than buses. Hungary's train network is like a wheel, with Budapest as its hub. If the town you're traveling to is on the gyorsvonat (express train) route, definitely go express; személyvonat (local trains) are sometimes painfully slow. A 100-km trip costs about $4; a one-way trip from Budapest to Debrecen or Pécs (both about 220 km from Budapest) costs about $10. People under 26 can get a discount train pass for seven or 10 days of unlimited travel, but it's worth it only if you plan to spend lots of time on the train. Always buy your ticket before you board, or you'll pay an additional $4.

WHERE TO SLEEP A **panzió** (pension) is cheaper than a hotel and usually has a homey atmosphere and a kitchen. But you can't get much homier than one of your cheapest options—a room in a private house. **Private rooms** are usually booked through tourist offices, or you can walk around looking for signs that say SZOBA KIADO (room to rent) or ZIMMER FREI. Even cheaper are **hostels** ($6–$15), located in all major Hungarian cities. For a list of all of them, contact **Hungarian Youth Hostels Association** (1535 Budapest, Konkoly Thege Miklos út 21, Csilleberc, tel. 1/156–2857, fax 1/175–9327). In July and August, cheap **student dorms** are open to travelers and are a place to meet young people; ask at local tourist offices or hunt down the nearest university. **Camping** can be the cheapest, most scenic way to go. If you don't have a tent, look for one of the many campgrounds that let bungalows. A detailed brochure called "Camping" is free at tourist offices. For more information, contact the Hungarian Camping and Caravaning Club, or **MCCC** (Budapest VIII, Ullöi út 6, tel. 1/133–6536), or call **Tourinform** (tel. 1/117–9800) in Budapest.

FOOD Food is cheap; a full meal in a decent restaurant, including wine or beer, costs $6–$7. Dishes tend to be very heavy on the grease—with lots of sour cream and deep-fried and breaded meats—and woefully short on anything but the soggiest of vegetables. One exception is *gulyás* (goulash), a soup or stew with meat, potatoes, small noodles, and plenty of paprika (most things you eat will be red with paprika). It's hearty enough to be eaten as a main course but not so loaded with cholesterol as to significantly shorten your life. Budapest offers several vegetarian restaurants, but elsewhere the pickings are slim.

If you want to keep your food, keep your utensils crossed: One American living in Budapest "lost many dinners" before someone informed her that putting silverware down parallel on the plate is a signal for the server to take it away.

BUSINESS HOURS Food markets are usually open weekdays 7 AM to 6 or 8 PM and Saturday 7–1. Most other stores are open weekdays 10–6 and Saturday 9–1. Museum hours are generally Tuesday–Sunday 10–6. "Nonstops" (24-hour convenience stores) are opening all over the country, but some use the term loosely to mean the store keeps longer hours (e.g., 5 AM–midnight).

VISITOR INFORMATION The variable service of **IBUSZ**, Hungary's national tourist office, ranges from Budapest's 24-hour "Accommodation Office" to minor operations in the countryside that open only when the people in charge feel so inspired. IBUSZ can usually give you info about private rooms, exchange your money, and load you up with maps and brochures. **Tourinform** and **Cooptourist** provide roughly the same services, but their offices are not as numerous. The many **Express** youth-and-student travel offices are good resources for travel info.

PHONES AND MAIL **Country code: 36.** Hungary's phone lines are old and often unreliable. Give the party you're calling your phone number, as you'll quite likely be disconnected. Blue public phones are coin-operated and silver ones take phone cards, available at post offices, Telefon centers, and shops displaying a sticker that reads PHONE CARDS SOLD HERE. For long-distance calls within Hungary, wait for the tone, dial 06 and wait for the tone, then dial the area code and number. For international calls, dial 00 and wait for the strange tone, then dial the country code, area code, and number. To reach an AT&T operator, dial 00, wait for a tone, then dial either 360–111 or 8000–1111. For direct access to the United Kingdom, dial 364–411 after the tone; for Canada it's 361–1111; for Australia 366–111.

Sending a postcard by airmail costs 30 Ft, and letters are 50 Ft. Your card must have a blue LEGI-POSTA sticker or have "Airmail" printed on it, or it will go by boat and your loved ones will think you've been abducted by the Moonies. Airmail letters usually arrive within in one or two weeks.

Budapest
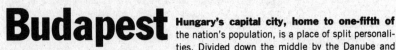

Hungary's capital city, home to one-fifth of the nation's population, is a place of split personalities. Divided down the middle by the Danube and laced together by seven bridges are two distinct cities: Buda's peaceful, historic hills climb westward, and the smoggy urban flatlands of Pest sprawl to the east. A mix of fiery pride, bleak pragmatism, and gay unconcern have sustained the city and its people through a rocky history. Budapest was totally destroyed by the Mongols in 1241, captured by the Turks in 1541, and nearly destroyed again by the Soviets in the 20th century. In its present incarnation as the most Western of Eastern Europe's capitals, it continues to resist easy characterization. Though the economy remained semicapitalist, even after the Soviets took power in 1956, you'll notice a faint legacy of Turkish occupation and a still-clearing Communist grogginess. From a Western perspective, Budapest is a vacation bargain and an excellent place to launch a trip into Eastern Europe: user-friendly enough to be comforting, disorienting enough to be exotic.

BASICS

VISITOR INFORMATION You'll see small, independent tourist agencies on almost every corner in Budapest, but most cater to the well-heeled. If you're a student or under 26, **Express** offers the best travel bargains. Of their four offices, **Express–Semmelweis utca** has the best range of services. The staff changes money, sells train tickets at student rates, and arranges hostel accommodations. *Semmelweis u. 4, tel. 1/176–634. Metro: Astoria. Open Mon.–Wed. 8:30–4:30, Thurs. 8:30–5, Fri. 8:30–3.*

IBUSZ has offices at more than a dozen locations throughout the city, including branches at the train stations and one at the airport. Most are open until at least 7 PM. For the most comprehensive services, go to the **24-hour office** on Petőfi tér. *Petőfi tér 3, behind Duna Intercontinental, tel. 1/118–5707.*

The patient staff at **More than Ways Travel Agency** (Váci u. 12, near Vörösmarty tér) deals mostly with youth hostels but prides itself on helping travelers find everything they need. Reservations are handled at the **Hostel Diáksportszálló** office (Dózsa György út 152, tel. 1/129–8644).

AMERICAN EXPRESS This full-service office (with 24-hour ATM) will bend over backward for its cardholders, cashing personal checks and arranging lodging and travel. *Deák Ferenc u. 10, tel. 1/267–2022. Open weekdays 9–6, Sat. 9–noon.*

CHANGING MONEY For a hefty commission the 24-hour **IBUSZ** at Petőfi tér changes traveler's checks into hard currency or forints and provides Visa cash advances. **Hungarian Foreign Trade Bank Ltd.** (Szent István tér 11, tel. 1/169–0922, Metro: Arany János; open Mon.–Thurs. 9–2, Fri. 9–1) cashes traveler's checks (6% commission) and gives cash advances on credit cards.

EMBASSIES **Australia.** *Délibáb u. 30, tel. 1/153–4233. Open weekdays 9–noon.*

Canada. *II. Budakeszi út 32, tel. 1/176–7688. Open Mon.–Thurs. 9–11 AM.*

United Kingdom. New Zealand citizens may also use this embassy. *V. Harmincad u. 6, tel. 1/226–2888. Open weekdays 8:30–11:30 and noon–2.*

United States. *V. Szabadság tér 12, tel. 1/112–6450 or 1/132–8933. Open weekdays 8:30–1 and 2–4.*

PHONES AND MAIL The **main post office** has international pay phones and is open Saturday, but it's always packed. *V. Petőfi Sándor u. 13–19. Metro: Ferenciek tere. Open weekdays 8–8, Sat. 8–3.*

COMING AND GOING

BY TRAIN Budapest has three main train stations. **Keleti Station** in eastern Pest (Baross tér, tel. 1/113–6835) runs express trains to Sopron (3 hrs) and to most international destinations. From **Nyugati Station** (tel. 1/149–0115), just north of downtown Pest, trains run to a small number of domestic and international destinations. **Déli Station** in Buda (tel. 1/155–8657) serves mostly southern points.

BY BUS Buses from **Erzsébet tér Station** (Erzsébet tér, tel. 1/117–2966 for domestic info, 1/117–2562 for international info, Metro: Deák tér), in the center of town, go to major Western cities and many domestic stops. LRI airport shuttles also depart from here every half hour. **Árpád híd Station** (tel. 1/129–1682), north of downtown Pest, is the terminal for buses to the Danube Bend. **Népstadion Station** (tel. 1/252–4496) in eastern Pest serves northern Hungary.

BY PLANE Hungary's only airport, **Ferihegy,** lies 22 km southeast of town. Terminal 2 is served by Lufthansa, Malév, and Air France; all other airlines use Terminal 1. The **LRI minibus** ($2.50) runs between the two terminals and Erzsébet tér bus station regularly. For more info, *see* Coming and Going, in Hungary Basics, *above.*

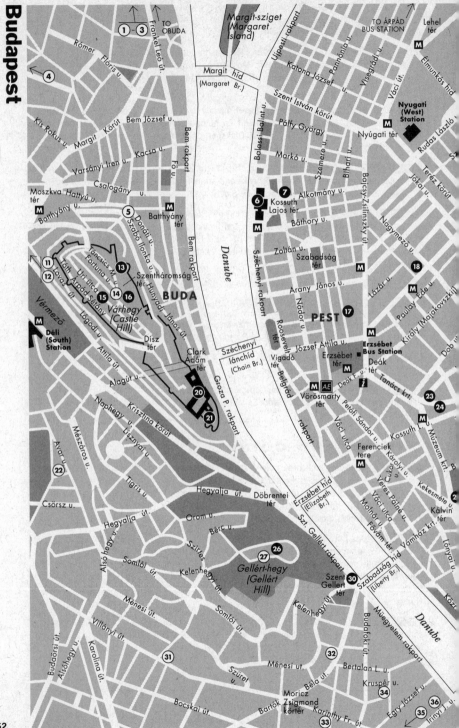

Budapest

TO OBUDA

TO ÁRPÁD
BUS STATION

Margit-sziget
(Margaret
Island)

Lehel
tér

Frankel Leó út

Újpesti-rakpart

Élmunkás tér

Römer

Flóris u.

Katona József

Pannónia u.

Váci út

Szent István körút

Nyugati
(West)
Station

Margit híd
(Margaret Br.)

Balassi Bálint u.

Nyugati tér

Rudas László

Kis Rókus u.

Bem József u.

Pálfy György

Terész körút

Margit Körút

Bem rakpart

Szenere u.

Bihari u.

Jókai u.

Varsányi Iren u.

Kacsa u.

Markó u.

Bajcsy-Zsilinszky út

Csalogány

Fö u.

Nagymezö u.

Moszkva
tér

Hattyú u.

Batthyány u.

Alkotmány u.

Báthory u.

Moszkva
Hattyú

Batthyány
tér

Kossuth
Lajos tér

Donáti u.

Szabó Ilonka u.

Zoltán u.

Szabadság
tér

Lázár u.

Táncsics M. u.

Fortuna u.

Szentháromság
tér

Arany János u.

Paulay Ede u.

Király (Majakovszki)

Úri utca

Hunyadi J.

BUDA

Nádor u.

PEST

Tóth Árpád sétány

Lovas út

Hovas út

Várhegy
(Castle
Hill)

János u.

Roosevelt

József Attila u.

Erzsébet
Bus Station

Dob u.

Vérmezö

Dísz
tér

Erzsébet
tér

Deák
tér

Tanács krt.

Déli
(South)
Station

Clark
Ádám
tér

Széchenyi
lánchíd
(Chain Br.)

Vigadó

Vörösmarty
tér

Tógodi u.

Attila út

Alagút u.

Gróza P. rakpart

Belgrád

Petöfi Sándor u.

Kossuth L.

Múzeum krt.

Krisztina Körút

Naphegy

Liszányi u.

Váci utca

Ferenciek
tere

Károlyi u.

Kekesméte u.

Mészáros u.

Tigris u.

Hegyalja út

Döbrentei
tér

Erzsébet híd
(Elizabeth
Br.)

Veres Pálne u.

Kálvín tér

Avar u.

Csörsz u.

Hegyalja út

Orom u.

Bérc u.

Szt. Gellért rakpart

Váci utca

Fövám tér

Vámház krt.

Lónyai u.

Alsó hegy u.

Somlói út

Kelenhegyi u.

Gellért-hegy
(Gellért
Hill)

Szent
Gellért
tér

Szabadság híd
(Liberty Br.)

Danube

Budaörsi út

Alsóhegy út

Karolina út

Ménesi út

Villányi út

Szüret

Somlói út

Kelenhegyi

Müegyetem rakpart

Budafoki út

Egry József u.

Irinyi J. u.

Bocskai út

Szüret

Béla u.

Ménesi út

Bertalan L. u.

Kruspér u.

Moricz
Zsigmond
körtér

Bartók Zsigmond

Karinthy Fr. út

Danube

462

Sights ●

Budapesti Történeti Múzeum, **21**

Castle Hill Labyrinth, **15**

Citadella Szabadsá Szobor, **26**

Gellért Hotel and Baths, **30**

Halászbástya, **13**

Magyar Nemzeti Galéria, **20**

Magyar Nemzeti Múzeum, **28**

Mátyás templom, **16**

Nagy Zsinagog, **24**

Néprajzi Múzeum, **7**

Operaház, **18**

Országház, **6**

Szent István Bazilika, **17**

Szépművészeti Múzeum, **9**

Zsidá Múzeum, **23**

Lodging ○

Aquincum Panzió, **3**

Bárczy, **10**

Camping Hárs-hegy, **11**

Diáksportszálló, **8**

Dominik Panzió, **19**

Donáti, **5**

Express Hotel, **22**

Felvinci, **4**

Hotel Citadella, **27**

Hotel Kulturinnov, **14**

Hotel Lidó, **2**

Hotel Metropol, **25**

KEK, **31**

Landler, **32**

Rómaifürdő Camping, **1**

Rózsa, **33**

Schönhertz, **35**

Selye Janos, **29**

Universitas, **36**

Vásárhelyi, **34**

Zugligeti Niche Camping, **12**

GETTING AROUND

The fastest way to get around town is on the **Metro,** which branches out into all parts of Pest but has only three stops in Buda. Three color-coded lines run 4:30 AM–11 PM; all meet at Deák tér, smack in the center of town. Reliable *villamos* (trams) and **buses** also serve the city. Buy tickets (25 Ft) good for all forms of mass transit or an unlimited day pass ($2.50) at *pénztárs* (ticket booths) in Metro stations, open daily 6 AM–7 PM. You can also stock up on tickets at most *hirlaps* (newsstands) and shops.

The number in Roman numerals in front of many addresses denotes one of Budapest's 22 districts. District I, in Buda, includes Buda Castle and its environs. Across the river on the Pest side, District V contains Váci utca, Vörösmarty tér, and most of the banking and business neighborhoods.

WHERE TO SLEEP

With the recent boom in youth hostels, no one should have a problem finding a bed in Budapest. Since single rooms are almost impossible to come by, hostel beds are definitely the best option for solo travelers. Reservations aren't needed for hostels, although they're a good idea at hotels. Cheap hotels are in short supply, but private accommodations and summer dorm rooms are great deals. **Budapest Tourist** has the largest number of **private rooms** ($10–$15) at their disposal—about 5,000 throughout the city. They have several outlets in Budapest and have shorter lines and a better selection than the crowded IBUSZ office (*see* Visitor Information, *above*). *Déli Station, tel. 1/115–4296. Open weekdays 8:30–5, Sat. 8–1 (May–Sept., Sat. 8–2). Keleti station, Baross tér 3, next to Grand Hotel Hungaria, tel. 1/133–6587. Open weekdays 8–8, Sat. 8–5 (May–Sept., Sat. 8–8), Sun. 2–8.*

BUDA **Hotel Citadella** (Citadella sétány, tel. 1/165–5794; dorm beds $5, quads w/shower $34) is a great find for anyone who wants to sleep on top of the world in a hunting lodge. Take Tram 6 from Nyugati Station to Móricz Zsigmond körtér, catch Bus 27 on Villányi út to the last stop, and follow the cobblestones. The cheap **Express Hotel** (Beethoven u. 7–9, tel. 1/175–3082) gives discounts to HI members. The interior is just run-down enough to merit rock-bottom prices (doubles $18). Take Tram 2 from Déli Station, walk up Böszörményí út two blocks, and turn left on Beethoven utca. The elegant turn-of-the-century **Hotel Kulturinnov** (Szentháromság tér 6, around cnr. from Hilton, tel. 1/155–0122) is definitely worth the price (doubles $60)—it's spotless and right next to Mátyás templom on Várhegy (Castle Hill).

PEST Pest's accommodations are generally shabbier than Buda's, but they're closer to nightlife and sights. The less expensive hotels are along seedy Rákóczi út near the Keleti train station and on Ferenc körút (off Petőfi bridge to the south). Some of the hostels have nicer locations, near City Park or the Danube. The clean, bright **Dominik Panzió** (Cházár A. u. 3, tel. 1/122–7655; doubles $25) sits next to a brick church on a residential street near Keleti Station. Take Bus 7 for two stops from Keleti Metro. Centrally located on one of the busiest streets in a red-light district, the well-worn **Hotel Metropol** (Rákóczi út 58, tel. 1/142–1175, Metro: Blaha L. tér) has doubles for less than $45.

OBUDA Along the northwestern bank of the Danube is the suburb of Obuda (District III). Hotels here are easily reached on the HEV train from Batthyány tér Metro and are no more than 25 minutes from the city center. **Hotel Lidó** (Nánási u. 67, tel. 1/188–6865) is a squat resort where you can rent canoes or play tennis. In summer, motorboat shuttles give rides to the center of town. Rooms ($25 per double) are nondescript, but they do the trick. Take the HEV to Rómaifürdő, walk east on Rozgonyi Piroska utca, and turn right on Nánási utca. Near an ancient Roman military camp, modern, clean **Aquincum Panzió** (Szentendrei út 105, tel. 1/250–2394) has doubles for less than $30. Take the HEV to Köles utca, walk through the underpass, turn left, and walk half a block.

HOSTELS The stiff competition among youth hostels is good news for budget travelers in search of cheap, central beds and a lively atmosphere. Hostels have no age limits or membership requirements, and bedding is free. Reception is open 24 hours, and there are no curfews, but you usually have to check out by 9 AM. Most hostels open in July and August only, but several operate year-round. Book ahead through the various companies or just look for a representative in the appropriate T-shirt at the train station when you arrive. Express and IBUSZ can also book you with certain companies. Hostels are listed by the corporations that run them; More than Ways (*see* Visitor Information, in Basics, *above*) has the biggest selection.

➤ **CITY CENTER HOSTELS BUDAPEST** • **Bárczy.** In a decent neighborhood near Városliget (City Park) and sights; bed in triple or quad (w/shower) $6.25 w/HI card, $7 without. *VII. Damjanich u. 41–43, tel. 1/121–3526. From Keleti Station, take Bus 20 or 30 away from center 2 stops, turn left on Damjanich u. Open July–Aug. 25.*

Schönhertz. Giant blue-and-white Technical University dorm along Buda's busiest street, west of Petőfi bridge. Beds $7 w/HI card, $7.75 without. Incredible amenities include a nightly disco. *XI. Irinyi J. u. 42, tel. 1/166–5460. Take Tram 4 over Petőfi bridge from Nyugati Station; dorm is on left. Laundry, pool tables, restaurant/bar, money exchange. Open July–Aug. 25.*

➤ **MORE THAN WAYS TRAVEL AGENCY** • In addition to offering the most accommodations, they have free shuttles to and from hostels and train stations, bus tours in five languages, day trips, and Danube-boat disco parties. Even if you're not staying at one of their hostels, chat with the warm staff at any reception desk or hostel bar, or at the slick underground office at Váci utca 12, near Vörösmarty tér. The main headquarters is at Diáksportszálló.

Diáksportszálló. Loose and lively place open year-round. It's not clean or quiet, but "never full" policy means there's always space for one more. Beds $4–$7 per night in smallish rooms. *XIII. Dózsa György út 152, across from Volga Hotel, tel. 1/140–8585. Metro: Dósza György.*

Donáti. Year-round hostel near Batthyány tér and Várhegy. Older building with crowded dorms at $5.50 per night. *I. Donáti u. 46, tel. 1/201–1971. Metro to Batthyány tér, walk 3 blocks up Batthyány u., turn left on Donáti u.*

Felvinci. Eclectically decorated hostel in the hills above Moszkva tér is a real hike, but beds in cluttered, bunk-style rooms are just $5. *II. Felvinci út 8, tel. 1/135–4983. From Moszkva tér Metro, take Bus 49 2 stops, walk up Garas u., left on Felvinci út. Open mid-June–late Aug.*

KEK. Relaxing and quiet hostel in a tree-lined neighborhood beside Gellért-hegy in Buda. Two-to-a-room beds $9, $12.50 w/shower. *XI. Szüret u. 2–18, tel. 1/185–2369. Bus 7 or Tram 6 to Móricz Zs. körtér, then Bus 27 for 2 stops. Open July and Aug.*

Selye Janos. Prime location near Kálvin tér in Pest. Courtyard, great kitchen facilities, washing machines, and bar with pool table. Beds $8.25–$10. *VIII. Ullői út 22, tel. 1/219–0326. Metro to Kálvin tér, exit at Ullői út, 2 blocks on left. Open July 5–Aug. 23.*

Universitas. Mammoth Technical University dorm adjacent to infamous black-market cafeteria in Buda. It's really noisy, so passionate romps won't be noticed. Doubles w/sinks $8–$9. *XI. Irinyi J. u. 9–11, tel. 1/181–2313. Tram 4 or 6 to 1st stop after Petőfi bridge on right. Open July and Aug.*

➤ **UNIVERSUM LTD.** • All three of this company's summer-only hostels are in the flat, accessible Buda neighborhood between the Gellért Hotel and Petőfi bridge. None is distinctive, but you'll find lots of cheap beds, and pets are allowed. To book directly, write, call, or fax them. *H-1014 Budapest, Uri u. 4, tel. 1/156–8726, fax 1/156–8726.*

Landler. Location a few blocks from Gellért Hotel can't be beat, but toilets and hot water are unpredictable. Beds $6–$8. *XI. Bartók Béla u. 17, tel. 1/185–1444. Tram 47 or 49 from Kálvin tér Metro to Bertalán Lajos u. Open July and Aug.*

Rózsa. Small hostel near pizzeria and mongo supermarket. Beds in doubles $7.50. *XI. Bercsényi u. 28–30, tel. 1/166–6677. From Móricz Zs. körtér, walk 2 blocks on Karinthy Ferenc út, turn right on Bercsényi u. Laundry, kitchen facilities.*

Vásárhelyi. High volume of guests makes receptionists short-tempered. Beds $8 in double, $6.80 in quad. *XI. Kruspér u. 2–4, tel. 1/185–3794, fax 1/185–2217. Tram 47 or 49 or Bus 7 down Bartók Béla u. to Bertalán Lajos u.; walk 2 blocks down Bertalán Lajos u., turn right on Budafoki út, left on Kruspér u.*

CAMPGROUNDS **Camping Hárs-hegy.** A 10-minute bus ride from Moszkva tér, on a tree-covered hillside in the shadow of a tall hotel. Clean kitchen and bathrooms, washing machine, snack bar, recreation area. Tents $3.25 plus $3.25 per person; two-bed bungalows $13. *Hárshegyi út 5–7, tel. 1/115–1482. Bus 22 from Moszkva tér to Helyközi Megállóhely stop. Open Easter–Oct. AE, MC.*

Rómaifürdő Camping. City's largest campground is unexpectedly mellow, with excellent outdoor pool/park. In Obuda, 20 minutes on HEV from Batthyány tér Metro. Tents $3.50 plus $4 per person, but students get a 10% discount. Double bungalow $12. *Szentendrei út 189, tel. 1/188–7167. Opposite Rómaifürdő HEV. Kitchen, restaurant, money exchange.*

Zugligeti Niche Camping. Close to city center in gorgeous valley in Buda Hills. Superclean bathrooms, 24-hour snack bar. Polite English-speaking staff provides maps and arranges tours. Tents $2.50 plus $3 per person. *Zugligeti út 101, tel. 1/156–8641. Bus 158 from Moszkva tér Metro to last stop. Closed late Oct.–Mar.*

FOOD

Even the most finicky eater won't go hungry in Budapest. You can snack your way through the city at *Lángos* stands, which sell deep-fried potato-puff pancakes; *goffri* stands, which feature waffles; and *pékaru* stands, which offer pastries and small sandwiches. Produce vendors operate from small street stands and huge open-air markets like the **Fény utca vegetable market,** one block north of Moszkva tér, or the massive **Skála** (VII, Klauzál tér 11; open weekdays 7–8, Sat. 7–3), two blocks south of Blaha Lujza tér. The **Central Market** (Központi Vásár Csarnok, Metro: Kálvin tér; open Mon. 6–4, Tues.–Fri. 6–6, Sat. 6–2), on the Danube in the 18th-century Customs House, is a banquet of things to see, smell, and taste. Cafés and bakeries number in the thousands, but without a doubt Budapest's most famous café is **Gerbeaud Cukrászda** (Vörösmarty tér 7, tel. 1/118–6823; open daily 4 AM–10 PM), overlooking a busy street. It's been baking its renowned Dobos pastry (chocolate-cream cake with a hardened caramel top) since 1858.

In addition to American fast food and Chinese restaurants, Budapest offers a New York–style bagel shop and an authentic Mexican restaurant. So much for paprika chicken and goulash.

BUDA For a fresh pizza ($1.80–$2.50) named after a Commie leader, come to **Marxim** (Kisrókus u. 23, tel. 1/115–5036; open Mon.–Thurs. noon–1 AM, Fri.–Sat. noon–2 AM), two blocks down Margit körút from the Moszkva tér Metro stop. The loud music draws a lively crowd.

➢ **UNDER $5 • Malomtó Etterem.** Best-kept secret in Buda, tucked away in industrial area north of Margit körút. Friendly waiters serve light fare: teriyaki turkey breast ($4.20), game dishes, and salad bar ($1.75). Run-down entrance, but interior is open and airy. Outdoor patio in back. *Frankel L. út 48, tel. 1/135–0315. Make 1st right off Margit körút at Margit híd stop (Tram 4 or 6), 5-min walk along Frankel L. út.*

Tabáni Kakas Vendéglő. Good Hungarian food in cozy restaurant lit with candles. Specialties include turkey Kiev ($4) and chicken-liver stew over gnocchi ($3.50). *I. Attila út 27, tel. 1/175–7165. Bus 78 across Erzsébet bridge 2 stops.*

Technical University Cafeteria. If you're really hungry, low on cash, and don't feel like dealing with waiters, this cafeteria is for you. *Goldmann György tér, at Egry József u. Tram 4 or 6 across Petőfi bridge from Boráros tér to 1st stop, just beyond underpass. Closed weekends. No dinner.*

➤ **UNDER $10** • **Fairyland Chinese Restaurant.** Best Chinese cuisine in Budapest. Scrumptious food in generous portions outshines blaring red-and-gold decor. Try fabulous veggie monk's dish ($3.25). English menu. *Margit körút 4, tel. 1/201–6339. Tram 4 or 6 two stops beyond Margit híd, restaurant on left.*

PEST Fast-food joints have taken over Pest, but the restaurants listed below won't cost you much more, and your food won't be thrown at you wrapped in yellow paper. If you have money to dish out, head to pricey **Acapulco** for the kind of excellent Mexican food that makes homesick Americans cry. Toss back margaritas ($4.50) or a Corona ($3.75) with chips and salsa in the lively cantina, or eat a full-blown chicken-fajitas dinner ($9) in the colorful restaurant. *VII. Erzsébet krt. 39, tel. 1/122–6014. Metro: Blaha L. tér. AE.*

➤ **UNDER $5** • **Bohémtanya Vendéglő.** Efficient service and cheap food attract a talkative student crowd. House special is a stuffed pork chop ($3.25). English menu. *VI. Paulay Ede u. 6, off Bajcsy-Zsilinszky út, tel. 1/122–1453.*

Csendes Etterem. "The Quiet Restaurant." Local favorite, with dim lighting and blues music; great place to enjoy wine and conversation. Turkey with mushroom sauce $2.75, Bolognese pork chops $3. English menu. *V. Múzeum krt. 13, tel. 1/117–3704. Múzeum exit at Astoria Metro; walk 1 block, turn right at side street.*

Finóm Falatok Vendéglö. Flashy mirrored sign gives away this popular basement restaurant. Try the famous *somlói galuska* (sponge cake with whipped cream and chocolate) for $1. *VII. Dob u. 50, tel. 1/268–0382. On side street, 1 block from Erzsébet krt. No Sun. dinner; closed Sun. June–Sept.*

Kanári Salátabár. Locals-only hole-in-the-wall above an ice-cream counter and arcade. Nothing's in English, but you can load a big plate with salad for less than $2. Come with favorite Hungarian dish in mind, as kitchen prepares your request (within reason). *Pannonia u. 3, no tel. Behind Vigszinhaz off St. István krt. between Margit bridge and Nyugati Metro.*

Nagyi Palacsintázója. Huge selection of hot crepes: 10 jams, more than 15 meats and veggies, and another 15 dessert combos. It's open 24 hours. *I. Hattyú u. 16, tel. 1/201–8605. Near Moszkva tér, off Széna tér across from gas station.*

New York Bagels. Manhattan-style boiled versions, plus an assortment of lox, spreads, and schmears. Check out the traveler-oriented bulletin board. It's open 24 hours. *IX. Ferenc körút 20, tel. 1/215–7880. 3 blocks south of Ferenc krt. Metro.*

Semiramis. Excellent Middle Eastern fare in a loft. Gyros, hummus, and other tasty spreads are all less than $4. *V. Alkotmány u. 20, off Bajcsy-Zsilinsky út at Nyugati Metro, tel. 1/111–7627. Closed Sun.*

Vegetárium Etterem. Creative vegetarian eatery serves veggie tempura ($3.75) and paprika mushrooms over saffron rice ($3.50). Save room for a delicious muffin. Sake, beer, and organic wine available. Live guitar after 7. *V. Cukor u. 3, tel. 1/138–3710. Ferenciek tér Metro, church side; look for red apple. AE, MC, V.*

WORTH SEEING

Budapest presents almost unlimited sightseeing opportunities; what you'll find below is a greatest-hits package. Many small galleries and temporary exhibits are listed in the periodicals *Budapest Week* and *Budapest Sun.* If you crave more guidance, grab a copy of András Török's witty, detailed *Budapest, A Critical Guide.* All these publications are available at newsstands.

VARHEGY Várhegy (Castle Hill) is the historic center and tourist mecca of Buda. There are three easy ways to get there: by Vár minibus from Moszkva tér, on Bus 16 from Deák tér to Disz tér, or by cable car from the base of Széchenyi lánchíd (the bridge with the lions).

➤ **MATYAS TEMPLOM** • The distinctly painted, 13th-century Matthias Church on Várhegy was originally the Church of the Blessed Virgin, but the 15th-century king Matthias Corvinus, who was married here twice, had other ideas. Weekly organ recitals in the Baroque building are a popular evening event. *Szentháromság tér 2, next to Hilton Hotel, tel. 1/155–5657. Admission free. Open daily 6 AM–8 PM.*

The equestrian statue of General András Hadik stands at the intersection of Szentháromság utca and Uri utca, near the Hilton. It's a tradition for medical students to shine the testicles of the horse for good luck on the night before exams.

Just off of Szentháromság tér sits Budapest's oldest dessert shop, **Ruszwurm Cukrászda** (Szentháromság u. 7, tel. 1/175–5284). The building has housed a bakery for 500 years, which is as good an excuse as any to try one of their yummy pastries. Behind the Hilton is a huge, turn-of-the-century wall called **Halászbástya** (Fisherman's Bastion). A crowded 328-foot promenade with stunning views of the Országház (Parliament) across the Danube stretches along the wall.

➤ **BUDAPESTI TORTENETI MUZEUM** • The Budapest History Museum, in the southern wing (Building E) of the **Királyi Palota** (Royal Palace), displays palace artifacts from the Romanesque, Gothic, and Renaissance periods. This is the best destination for anyone interested in the city's past. It's worth shelling out 100 forints for the English guidebook. *Szent György tér 2, tel. 1/175–7533. Admission: 40 Ft, 20 Ft students, free Wed. Open Tues.–Sun. 10–6; closes earlier in winter.*

➤ **MAGYAR NEMZETI GALERIA** • Also in the Királyi Palota (Wings B, C, and D in the main building, entrance facing the Danube) is the prestigious Hungarian National Gallery, displaying the work of the country's finest painters from the 15th to 19th centuries. Of particular interest are the Hungarian Impressionists, notably Pál Szinyei Merse and Kosztka Tivadar Csontváry. *Tel. 1/175–533. Admission: 40 Ft, students free, free Sat. Open Tues.–Sun. 10–6.*

➤ **CASTLE HILL LABYRINTH** • The Catacombs Restaurant and Wine Bar operates this wax museum housed in the miles of underground caverns, originally used for storage, that run beneath Várhegy. You see wax replicas of Hungarian heroes from pagan times to the 19th century. Half-hour tours begin every 15 minutes and are available in English. Have a glass of wine or beer in the cellar bar beforehand. *Uri u. 9, tel. 1/175–6858. Admission: $1.90, $1.70 students. Open daily 10–6.*

GELLERT-HEGY At the base of the Buda Hills, where Szabadság híd (Liberty Bridge) meets the posh Gellért Hotel, lies Gellért Hill. Here, tree-lined walkways lead up to the **Citadella** (citadel), built so the Imperial armies could keep an eye on the city after the failed Hungarian Revolution of 1849. Now stone walls enclose a mini-village with shops, an expensive restaurant, and a cheap student hotel. From almost anywhere in the city you can spot the hill's main sight, the **Szabadság Szobor** (Liberation Monument). The Hungarian Statue of Liberty (holding a palm leaf, not a torch) was erected in 1947 to commemorate the Soviet victory over Nazi Germany. Bus 27 from Móricz Zsigmond körtér circumvents the half-hour hike up the hill.

SZENT ISTVAN BAZILIKA St. Stephen's Basilica (1905), Budapest's largest church, holds as many as 8,500 people. No doubt the massive structure would have pleased St. Stephen, Hungary's first king, who made Christianity the national religion. A statue of the man himself is behind the main altar, and his mummified right hand is displayed in a small room off the nave. It's worth the dizzying climb up the **cupola tower** to see the view on clear days. *Szent István tér. Metro: Arany János u. Basilica admission: 30 Ft, 10 Ft students. Tower admission: 100 Ft, 50 Ft students. Open daily 9–5.*

ORSZAGHAZ The huge, neo-Gothic parliament building is the most visible symbol on Budapest's left bank. It was designed by Hungarian architect Imre Steindl and took 1,000 workers 17 years (1885–1902) to build. The exterior and interior reflect the tastes of the time—grandiose but delicate. The outside is lined with 90 statues; inside are 691 rooms, 10 courtyards, and 29 staircases. Unfortunately, the parliament is not open to individual visitors, so join a tour set up by IBUSZ (tel. 1/118–5707), Budapest Tourist (tel. 1/117–3555), or Omnibusz Travel (tel. 1/117–2369). To reach the building, take waterfront Tram 2, or take Metro M2 to Kossuth tér station. Opposite the Országház, the **Néprajzi Múzeum,** or Ethnographic Museum (Kossuth Lajos tér 12, tel. 1/132–6340; admission 50 Ft, students free; open Tues.–Sun. 10–6), occupies a grand, neo-Renaissance palace worth a visit in itself. An amazing exhibit on peasant life includes a model of their living quarters.

NAGY ZSINAGOGA When the building isn't undergoing restoration, nearly 3,000 worshipers can fit into the Byzantine-Moorish Great Synagogue (1859). The 141-foot onion dome is visible from blocks away. In the garden behind the synagogue, a **Holocaust Memorial** stands over a mass grave. Next door, the **Zsidá Múzeum** (Jewish Museum) has a moving collection of such devotional objects as medieval Torahs and prayer books, and a powerful display on concentration camps and the deportation of Hungarian Jews. *Dohány u. 4. Metro: Deák tér. Admission free (donation advised). Open May–Oct., Mon. and Thurs. 2–6, Tues., Wed., Fri., and Sun. 10–1.*

MAGYAR NEMZETI MUZEUM The National Museum walks you through time from the distant past to the 19th century. The biggest attractions are the royal crown and the crown jewels, which were smuggled to the United States after World War II and returned by President Carter in 1978. The crown, reputedly given to St. Stephen by the pope in about AD 1000 (making it nearly the oldest royal crown around), has been stolen a number of times; the cross was bent during one such escapade. *Múzeum krt. 14–16, tel. 1/138–2122. Metro: Kálvin tér. Admission: 30 Ft, 10 Ft students. Open Tues.–Sun. 10–5:45.*

VAROSLIGET City Park, 1 square km of greenery in Pest, is home to a zoo, a circus, and an **amusement park** (Allatkerti krt. 14–15; open Apr.–Sept.). The row of statues of Hungarian heroes in **Hősök tere,** the gateway to the park, was erected in 1896 as part of the millennial celebration of Magyar settlement. For a crash course in Hungarian architecture, check out **Vajdahunyad Castle** on the lake. Also built for the 1896 celebration, the complex includes Renaissance, Baroque, Transitional, Gothic, and Romanesque sections. Few people know that all of Hungarian history was shifted forward a year so the building could be completed; the Magyars really came to the area in 895.

Also in the park is the **Szécheny Bath** (Allatkerti krt. 11), one of the largest of its kind in Europe. Built in 1909, it's a popular spot for fierce water-chess competitions, played on boards made of cork. Nearby, the **Petöfi Csarnok Recreation Center** has a great flea market, nightlife, and several museums, including the **Museum of Flight and Space** (tel. 1/142–4767; admission 20 Ft, students free; open Tues.–Sun. 10–6), with everything from old fighter planes to turbojets, hang gliders, and helicopters. You can also go for a canoe ride on the lake or get a beer in one of the tented beer gardens. To reach the park, take the Metro to Hösök tere.

➤ **SZEPMUVESZETI MUZEUM •** Flanking one side of Hősök tere at the entrance to Varosliget, Budapest's world-famous Fine Arts Museum has the largest collection of Spanish masters outside Spain. The Modern Gallery features all the French biggies—Monet, Renoir, Cézanne, Gauguin, you name it. In 1983, the great art robbery of the century took place here, when two skilled thieves made off with seven Old Masters (later recovered and returned). *Dózsa György út 41, tel. 1/142–9759. Metro: Hösök tere. Admission: 50 Ft, students free, free Sat. Open Tues.–Sun. 10–5:30.*

MARGIT-SZIGET Margaret Island in the Danube is a popular recreation spot, especially on weekends, when it fills up with families. You can rent *sétacikli* carts—altered bikes that seat up to four people—to cruise along the island's many paths. The popular **Palatinus Strand** (admission 140 Ft, 52 Ft after 4; open May–Sept., daily 8–7), at the northwest end of the island, has many pools and a water slide. To get there, take Bus 26. **Margit hid,** the main bridge linking the island to Buda and Pest, is four blocks from Nyugati Metro station. The bridge brings back painful memories for Budapest's older residents: During rush hour in November 1944, the Germans blew it up, killing hundreds.

CHEAP THRILLS

Budapest, known as the "City of Baths," harbors 123 **natural hot springs,** whose medicinal properties attract thousands of people looking for relief from stiff necks, arthritis, and chronic back pain. One of the most popular is the art-nouveau bathhouse adjoining the grand **Gellért Hotel,** whose spacious lobby is itself worth a visit. Two swimming pools, two saunas, a mud bath, and a thermal spa are open to men and women on different days. During the 10-minute massage ($2), attendants wearing only their skivvies soap you up, pummel you, and hose you down. Don't forget to tip. *Kelenhegyi út 4, tel. 1/166–6166. Admission to spa: $2.50. Admission to pool: $3.75. Open May–Sept., Mon.–Sat. 6:30 AM–7 PM, Sun. 6:30–1; shorter hrs Oct.–Apr.*

Set aside a few hours to visit the **Ecseri Flea Market,** a ways from the city center but a great place to pick up interesting souvenirs. The old and the new—from expensive Italian leather jackets to family heirlooms—are jumbled together. Be prepared to bargain, and don't buy anything from the first vendor, since you're likely to find something similar two tables down. Watch out for kids with quick fingers. *XIX. Nagykörösi út 156. Metro: Határ út; then Bus 54 to Nagykörösi út; get off at 1st footbridge that crosses road. Open weekdays 8–4, Sat. 8–3.*

AFTER DARK

In addition to inexpensive, internationally renowned opera, symphony, ballet, choral music, jazz, and folk dance, Budapest has a lively club scene—everything from slick, see-and-be-seen nightspots to dark, smoky standbys featuring local bands. Cover charges and tickets at the most exclusive discos are a third of what you'd pay for the same thing in Paris or New York. Check *Budapest Week* and *Budapest Sun* for up-to-the-minute listings of cultural events and clubs before you set off. Between 11:30 PM and 5 AM, when most other public transportation shuts down, the 6E night bus runs from Moszkva tér around the Nagykörút to Móricz Zsigmond körtér. It can get you to and from almost all of the happening areas.

We don't list bars separately, but there are plenty of lively ones clustered around the nightclubs—especially along Szent István körút between Margit bridge and Nyugati Station, and on the side streets around the Opera and Oktogon. Also look between Kálvin tér and Jozsef körút, along Bartók Béla in Buda, and around Moszkva tér.

Budapest's exquisite **Operaház** (Opera House), completed in 1884, is the home of high-quality, affordable performances. Even if you're not interested in the music, it's worth the meager $2–$5 ticket price just to view the polished marble stairs, plush red carpeting, crystal chandeliers, and magnificent frescoed ceiling of the 1,289-seat main hall. *Andrássy út 22. Open Tues.–Sat. 10–2 and 2:30–7, Sun. 10–1.*

CLUBS **Black and White Jazz Pizzeria.** Modern, black-and-white-tile underground spot features well-respected jazz and blues bands every night (8–midnight). *VII. Akácfa u. 13, 1 block from Rákóczi út, tel. 1/122–7645. Metro: Blaha L. tér. Open Mon.–Sat. 11 AM–2 AM, Sun. 6 PM–2 AM.*

Fortuna. Hip disco with Big Apple–style doorman who may hustle you past the waiting line if you meet his standards. Crowded but more fun than pretentious—once you get in. Mixed hetero and low-key gay crowd. *I. Hess András tér 4, on Várhegy across from Hilton, tel. 1/175–2401. Cover: $5.25. Open Wed., Fri., and Sat. 8 PM–4 AM.*

Franklin Trocadero. Salsa and Latin jazz have come to Budapest. This airy, split-level club has dancing downstairs, billiards upstairs. *VI. Szent István krt. 15, bet. Nyugati Metro and Margit bridge, tel. 1/111–4691. Cover changes nightly.*

Jazz Cafe. Cozy local favorite with mellow jazz and two pool tables. Live music 8–10 nightly. *V. Balassi Bálint u. 25, off Szent István krt., tel. 1/132–4377. Metro to Nyugati, or Tram 4 or 6 to Jaszai Mari tér near Margit bridge.*

Picasso Point. Upstairs area, with modern artwork and live jazz or folk 8–10 nightly, is reminiscent of a San Francisco coffeehouse: intellectual, slightly snobby, but hip just the same. Cellar is newly redone for dancing, heavier drinking, and pool. *VI. Hajós u. 31, tel. 1/132–4750. Metro: Opera or Arany János. (Hajós u. runs between Andrássy út and Bajcsy-Zsilinsky út.)*

Sancho American-Mexican Pub. Lively rock and Latin dance club doubles as a cheap Mexican restaurant. *VII. Dohány u. 20, no phone. Metro: Astoria. (Dohány u. is off of Károly krt., parallel to Rákóczi út.)*

Tilos Az A. Smoky, bohemian hangout has kept students, artists, and wanderers warm and hydrated till dawn for years. Check out live music down in the cave. *VII. Mikszáth Kálmán tér 2, tel. 1/118–0684. Metro to Kálvin tér, then walk 2 blocks up Baross u., turn left on Szentkirály u.*

OUTDOOR ACTIVITIES

Rising above the smog of the Budapest flatlands, the **Buda Hegyek** (Buda Hills) are a great outdoor retreat. Hiking trails cut through forests thick with beech and oak, and you'll see a few breathtaking views as you walk. The most popular scenic overlook is accessible by bus or on the **János-hegy chairlift.** The *Budaihegység* map shows the well-marked hiking trails in this protected conservation area. Other outdoor fun includes a **railway** that circles a scenic forested area and two **caves** some 90 feet below ground. *Chairlift: Zugligeti út 97, tel. 1/176–3764. Bus 158 from Moszkva tér to Zugligeti Niche. Admission: 100 Ft. Open summer, Tues.–Sun. 9–6; winter, Tues.–Sun. 9:30–4. Railway: Starts at Budapest Hotel (take Tram 56 from Moszkva tér to 2nd stop).*

Danube Bend

For a break from Budapest's urban pace and pollution, escape north along the Danube River, where the riverbanks provide fertile soil for crops and opportunities for hiking and horseback riding. Budapest's urbanites flock to the Bend for vacations, and transportation couldn't be easier: **Trains** go from Budapest's Nyugati railway station to Visegrád ($1.60 one-way) and Esztergom (1½ hrs, $3 one-way), and the **HEV suburban railway** runs every 10 minutes between Budapest's Batthyány tér and Szentendre (40 min, 50 Ft). **Buses** (75¢–$2) leave from Budapest's Árpád hid Station for villages along the west and east banks of the Danube, and as if that weren't enough, scenic **ferries** ($1–$3) leave from Budapest's Vigadó tér and Batthyány tér (red Metro line) for towns along the Bend. Many day-trippers go by boat and return by train to save time. Students can buy ferry tickets at a 50% discount.

Szentendre

The most popular day trip from Budapest is to the colorful, Baroque village of Szentendre (St. Andrew). Walking along cobblestone roads lined with trees and Serbian brick houses, you quickly realize why artists have thrived here for more than a century. The village's art galleries, museums, and restaurants can be enjoyed in one afternoon (for transportation info, *see above*). **IBUSZ** (Bogdányi u. 11, tel. 26/313–596; open summer, weekdays 9–12:30 and 1–5, Sat. 9–12:30 and 1–6; winter, weekdays 8:30–4) arranges private rooms (doubles $17), exchanges cash and traveler's checks, and rents bikes. Maps are also sold at IBUSZ, but those at **Dunatours** (Bogdányi u. 1, off Fő tér, tel. 26/311–311) are better.

WHERE TO SLEEP AND EAT Private accommodations arranged through the tourist offices are only slightly cheaper than low-end hotels. Do everything you can to get a room at the delightful **Villa Apollo** (Méhész út 3, tel. 26/10–909; doubles $17), where the English-speaking owners serve breakfast (included) in a garden or airy dining area. To reach the hotel from the HEV station, take a northbound bus to the third stop, turn right, and walk half a block. The cheaper, grimy **hostel** (Szabadkai u. 9, tel. 26/312–788) is barely bearable at $7.25 for a bed in a double and $4 per extra bed. To get here from the HEV station, walk through the ABC complex, turn left on Dózsa György út, go left on Vasúti villasor út, turn left and go five blocks on Szabadkai utca, and cross the tracks. Take any northbound bus to reach **Pap-sziget Campground** (tel. 26/310–697; closed Oct.–Apr.), which has a pool and restaurant. You'll pay $7 per tent, $12.50 for a dorm bed, and $28 for a triple bungalow; reservations can be made at the reception desk of the pricey **Danubius Hotel** (Ady Endre u. 28, tel. 26/312–511).

Food's no problem, with the variety of restaurants in this village, but only **Vidám Szerzetesek** is known for its first-rate kitchen. The so-called "Jolly Monks" restaurant attracts an international clientele. Try the house specialty, Joy of Monks, a beef dish with onion, potatoes, and paprika served on rice ($5.50). *Bogdányi út 3–5, off Fő tér, tel. 26/310–544. Weekend reservations advised.*

WORTH SEEING Browse through Szentendre's museums, which include several devoted to great Hungarian artists. One of the most popular museums in the country is the open-air **Szabadtéri Néprajzi Múzeum** (Szabadforrás út; admission 60 Ft; open Apr.–Oct., Tues.–Sun. 9–5), which re-creates 18th- and 19th-century village life and will eventually contain 300 buildings representing each region of the country. From the HEV station, take any bus (20 Ft) from Stand 6 or 8, and get off when you see spires on the right (5 km). The **Kovács Margit Múzeum** (Vastagh György u. 1, bet. Görög u. and Futó u. below Fő tér; admission 60 Ft; open Tues.–Sun. 10–6) explores the life and work of the famous ceramist Margit Kovács.

The museums and churches on **Templomdomb** (Church Hill) are within walking distance of each other, and admission is free to students. Most houses of worship are usually closed, but the impressive **Greek Church** (Fő tér and Görög u.; admission 20 Ft; open summer, Tues.–Sun. 10–5, winter, weekends 10–5) is an exception. It holds a cherished piece of Rococo art: an 18th-century iconostasis (the screen that stands before the sanctuary).

Visegrád

Placid, enchanting Visegrád sits on the most gorgeous stretch of the Danube Bend, about 23 km north of Szentendre. Visegrád was Hungary's capital during the 14th century, under the Angevin dynasty, and the stone remnants of the town's heyday still tower above the town, in the form of the 13th-century **citadel** (admission 30 Ft; open daily 9–6). Just a short walk away (follow the signs), the **Nagy Villám Hill lookout tower** offers spectacular views of the entire Danube Bend. At the foot of the hill is the 350-room **royal palace** (Fő u. 27–29), which reached the pinnacle of its splendor in the 16th century, only to be left in ruins after a Turk siege in 1543 and dynamited in 1702. Parts of the grounds and courtyard have been reproduced. Midway up the hill, the massive **Salamon torony** (Solomon's Tower) can be spotted from kilometers away. Inside, the **Mátyás Király Múzeum** (King Matthias Museum), open Tuesday–Sunday 10–5, displays royal artifacts. A well-marked hiking trail (3½ km one-way) leads from the edge of town to **Pilisszentlásló,** a nature reserve in which bears, bison, and wild boars roam freely.

Walking among the ruins of what was once the royal palace, impressionable types are guaranteed to feel the ambition of kings and the decay of empires rising from the ground.

Svada (Rév u. 6, tel. 26/328–160), a small tourist office a few doors up from the ABC market, sells maps and arranges private rooms (doubles $19). The ugly **Hotel Eötvös** (Fő u. 117, north of Nagy L. u., tel. 26/328–165; doubles $20) is partially redeemed by new paint, new carpets, and sparkling bathrooms. Don't let the gloomy reception scare you away from inexpensive

Hotel Salamon (Salamon-torony u. 5, tel. 26/328–278), just below the tower; doubles ($15) are light and clean. Beware, though: The second-floor disco cranks music until 4 AM on Friday and Saturday. **Sirály Restaurant** (Rév u. 15, tel. 26/328–376), across Highway 11 from the ferry station, is a great place to enjoy venison goulash ($3.50). For info on transportation to Visegrád, *see* the introduction to the Danube Bend, *above.*

Esztergom

Follow the Danube to the Slovakian border and you'll reach Esztergom, the religious capital of Hungary. The star attraction among the restored 12th-century **palace ruins** on Várhegy (Castle Hill) is the room where some believe King István I, founder of Hungary, was brought into the world. In addition to uniting the Magyar tribes, István established Christianity as the national religion and built the country's first cathedral here. The ruins also contain a Gothic chapel and the frescoed Hall of Virtues (admission 30 Ft, 10 Ft students; open Tues.–Sun. 9–5). Esztergom's 19th-century **basilica,** the largest in the country, stands on Várhegy next to the palace ruins. In its courtyard, you may see street musicians in tights, who will put you in a Renaissance mood for viewing the Italian frescoes, the marble **Bakócz chapel,** and the largest altarpiece in the world. The **treasury** houses a valuable collection of relics dating back 1,000 years. It's worth waiting behind hordes of school kids to make the steep climb to the top of the **cupola.** *Szent István tér 1. Treasury admission: 20 Ft. Cupola admission: 30 Ft, 10 Ft students. Open daily 8–5.*

As you walk toward the basilica, watch for signs with arrows directing you to other sights, including the **Keresztény Múzeum,** or Christian Museum (Berényi Zsigmond u. 2, near Pázmany Péter u.; open Tues.–Sun. 10–5:30), which contains priceless medieval and Renaissance paintings. In the center of town, beautifully designed Baroque buildings surround Széchenyi tér. A block away, a large **food market** and several travel agencies are clustered around busy Rákóczi tér. Lőrinc utca, off Rákóczi tér, leads down to the Kis-Duna (Little Danube) and the bridge to **Primate Island,** where you can sunbathe and picnic. For info on transportation to Esztergom, *see* the introduction to the Danube Bend, *above.*

WHERE TO SLEEP AND EAT As in most Hungarian villages, private rooms abound; check with the helpful **IBUSZ** staff (Lőrinc u., near Rákóczi tér, tel. 33/312–552; open weekdays 7:30–4, Sat. 7:30–11:30). Smack in the center of the town on the river, **Platán Panzió** (Kis-Duna sétány 11, off Rákóczi tér, tel. 33/311–355) has a poorly marked entrance and the cheapest doubles in town ($17). The homey **Alabárdos Panzió** (Bajcsy-Zs. u. 49, tel. 33/311–147) offers large rooms (doubles $30–$35, quads $60) and an excellent view of the basilica from upstairs. If the caretaker isn't in the panzió, you can find him working in the superb adjoining **restaurant** or in the garden.

Northern Hungary

Don't make the foolish mistake of skipping northern Hungary just because it doesn't get a lot of press. Be one of the enlightened few to appreciate the region's winsome towns and peaceful wheat, corn, potato, and sunflower fields. Opportunities for recreation abound: Three mountain ranges provide ample hiking and biking trails, as well as many caves for spelunking enthusiasts. Historic sites include the Eger castle and the renowned village of Hollókő, where residents dress in traditional costumes. The temperate, hilly region produces excellent wines, including Eger's Bull's Blood.

Hollókő

Hollókő has attracted swarms of tourists since it was added to UNESCO's world cultural heritage list in 1988, but if you catch it on an off day, it's pretty mellow. Villagers dress in the folk costumes of Nógrád County and welcome photo-snapping visitors to their wood homes. Looming above the village are the ruins of 13th-century **Hollókő Castle,** whose expansive views make it one of the most inspiring picnic spots in the country. It's accessible on a dirt road from the parking lot by the cemetery. The only way to reach Hollókő is on a three-hour bus trip from Budapest's Népstadion Station via Balassagyarmat and Szécsény.

The **tourist office** (Kossuth út 68) provides maps and brochures, changes money, and arranges stays in private rooms (singles $8, doubles $13). But don't bother with rooms when there's the beautiful new **Panorama Camping és Panzió.** Everything about this place, from the view to the sparkling-clean bathrooms, is awesome. Doubles are $18, luxurious four-person bungalows $25, and tents $1.25 plus $1.25 per person. You can write ahead for reservations. *Sport út 3176. Follow signs from Kossuth út 1 block from bus stop. 9 rooms with bath. Laundry, restaurant.*

According to local legend, Hollókő (Raven Stone) got its name when a count went out of town and his mother-in-law ordered a troop of ravens to move his castle to a new hill. The overworked birds might disagree, but you'll think the move was worth the effort when you see the stunning view.

Eger

Pastel Rococo buildings and outdoor cafés line the narrow, banner-hung streets of Eger, a student town ideally situated between the Mátra Mountains and the cave-riddled, volcanic Bükk range. Here you'll find the famous cellars of the Bull's Blood (Egri Bikavér) label—a hair-raising, cheek-warming red wine. Baroque churches, a Turkish minaret, friendly bars, cheap lodging, thermal baths, and a small stream on the east side of town conspire to make this "City of Wine and Grape" the great charmer of Heves County.

A patient, English-speaking staff member at **Egertourist** (Bajcsy-Zsilinszky Endre u. 9, tel. 36/311–724; open May–Oct., weekdays 8–7, Sat. 8–2; Nov.–Apr., weekdays 8–4) can change money; arrange a private room (doubles $13), apartment ($17–$24), or motel; and help with visits to the Bükk Mountains. **IBUSZ** (Bajcsy-Zsilinszky Endre u., follow signs in square, tel. 36/311–451; open weekdays 8–noon and 1–4) has similar services and can arrange tours and horseback-riding trips. Or flip through the brochures at **Tourinform** (Dobó tér, follow green "i" signs; open daily 8–8).

COMING AND GOING Trains run daily from Budapest's Keleti Station (2 hrs) to Eger's **train station** (Allomáss tér 1, tel. 36/314–264). To reach the town center, walk up Vasút utca, turn right onto Deák Ferenc út, and head for the basilica. Buses make the trip from Budapest's Népstadion Station to Eger (3 hrs). The **bus station** (Pyrker tér) is in the center of town behind the basilica.

WHERE TO SLEEP AND EAT The bottom-of-the-barrel bargains are at college dorms. Rooms at **Berzeviczy Gizella Kollégium** (Leányka u. 2, tel. 36/312–399) go for $7–$11 per double. To get there, walk past the castle entrance at Dózsa György tér, and continue up Var utca past the railroad tracks. The rooms at the **GMSZ** dorm (Rákóczi Ferenc u. 2, tel. 36/311–211) are the best-kept secret in Eger. Beds go for a mere $4 per person, and the dorm is five minutes from the center (take Szécheny István utca). If you're willing to pay a bit more, try **Vénusz Panzió** (Pacsirta u. 49, tel. 36/311–421; doubles $28), which has a sauna and Jacuzzi. It's 10 minutes from the center: Follow Deák Ferenc út south, then turn right on Arpád utca and left on Pacsirta utca. At mealtime, **Jóbarát Etterem** (Bródy Sándor u. 3, off Széchenyi út, tel. 36/310–496) serves Hungarian favorites ($1.50–$2) to a local clientele. If you crave Greek fare, stop in for souvlaki ($3.50) at **Gyros** (Széchenyi út 10).

WORTH SEEING Two statues in the center of town on Dobó István tér commemorate the Hungarian army's historic defeat of Turkish forces in 1552. Also here is the 1771 **Minorite Church** (open daily 9:30–5:30), one of the finest examples of Baroque architecture in Central Europe. Reduced to ruins when the Turks occupied the city, **Eger Castle** (Dózsa György tér; admission 60 Ft, 30 Ft students) is now interesting primarily for its casemates (artillery vaults) in a labyrinth of underground tunnels that has been only partially excavated. You can arrange an English tour for $1. The castle **museum** (open Tues.–Sun. 9–5) displays ancient weapons, coins, and utensils from the excavations.

Built in 1776 by the archbishop of Eger, the impressive **Eszterházy Károly Teacher Training College** was one of the first post-secondary schools in Hungary. Visit the examination room, where frescoes on the ceiling represent the faculties of law, medicine, theology, and the arts. The library holds one of the most valuable book collections in the country, including the first Latin edition of Dante's *Divine Comedy*. The ceiling fresco is a trompe l'oeil affair that makes the room look higher than it really is. On the ninth floor an amazing view of the city is reflected through the lens of a camera obscura. *Szabadság tér, opposite basilica. Admission: 20 Ft. Library open Tues.–Fri. 9–2, weekends 9:30–1.*

As a reminder that Turkey once occupied this town, a **minaret** stands more than 100 feet tall at the corner of Knézich Károly utca and Torony utca. The muezzin would climb the spiral steps to the top of the minaret several times a day to call the faithful to prayer. The imposing 19th-century **Nagy templom** (basilica) on Szabadság tér (admission free; open daily 7 AM–8 PM) is Hungary's second-largest cathedral.

CHEAP THRILLS Pass an afternoon sampling regional wines for 10 Ft per glass in **Szépasszony völgy** (Valley of the Beautiful Women), a 20-minute walk from the center of town. The valley's name is misleading: Wine cellars, not women, line its dirt roads. Dozens of little stone doors set into the valley walls lead to cellars, each with its own twist on the regional favorites. Legend has it that if you manage to stick a coin into the mildew of the cool cellar walls, you will return someday. *Walk 1 block on Deák Ferenc út away from basilica; turn right on Telekesy István to Király u., which becomes Szépasszony völgy u.*

NEAR EGER

SZILVASVARAD An hour north of Eger in the Bükk Mountains, this village is a base for hiking and mountain biking. Regional map *No. 7A Bükk* details the extensive trails. The most traversed route is the 4-km hike along a stream through **Szalajka Valley.** The path begins at the end of Egri út near the equestrian stadium. Hiking up past the modest **Veil Waterfall,** you'll find the upper terminus of the **cog railway** (40 Ft one-way, 25 Ft students) in a large meadow; the lower terminus is by the trailhead. For a real huff-and-puff climb, follow the signs above the meadow (labeled BARLANG) to **Istállóskői Cave,** where tools were found that date from the Ice Age. Bus 11 makes the one-hour trip ($2) from Eger to Szilvásvárad; the train ($2.25) will get you there a bit quicker. If you want to stay overnight, contact Judith Mihályné (Egri út 22), the village-appointed agent for the **pensions.** Ask for an "*Olcsó szoba*" (cheap room), and hold firm to your price (about $20 is reasonable).

Tokaj

Spread against the volcanic backdrop of Kopasy Hill, sleepy Tokaj is the pearl of the Hegyalja wine-producing region. Wine cellars dot the hillside along Rákóczi utca, the town's main road. Signs direct you to Europe's largest cellar, **Rákóczi** (Kossuth tér), where Ferenc Rákóczi II, the Hungarian hero whose name graces many a street, was chosen to lead the War of Independence against the Habsburg Empire (1703–1711). Wines cost about 30 Ft per glass; don't forget to sample *Tokaji aszú,* a sweet dessert wine. Tokaj is three hours by train from Budapest (transfer at Szerencs).

WHERE TO SLEEP AND EAT The large **Tisza Camping** ($2.50 per tent, $1.50 per person, bungalows $8–$15; closed late Sept.–Apr.) is crowded with young people. The bathrooms are pretty dirty, and there's no hot water, but the thickly wooded waterfront setting is a plus. If you'd prefer a room, look for ZIMMER FREI signs indicating private rooms for rent (doubles around $25), or try the newly remodeled **Makk–Marci Panzió** (Liget köz 1, tel. 41/352–336; doubles $23), where the bathtubs really sparkle. Reservations are essential in summer. The restaurant downstairs serves decent pizza ($1.50), spaghetti ($1.20–$1.50), and onion soup (50 Ft). Another good restaurant choice is **Dreher Söröző** (Kossuth tér 17; open daily 10–10), where you can eat chicken with mushrooms ($2.25) and watch young locals play pool.

Lake Balaton

Balaton is Central Europe's largest lake, and its shore towns keep vacationers coming back. Quite frankly, the lake is not all it's cracked up to be: It's crowded, overdeveloped, and expensive. The resorts on the southern shore, especially Siófok, lure the largest crowds with their warm, shallow waters and glitzy nightlife, but they're really the least attractive part of the lake. The more subdued northern shore is rich in volcanic soil (which makes good wine) and history (which makes good sightseeing), and northern towns such as Balatonfüred have class. Between the lake and Budapest, Székesfehérvár is a handy, historic hub. An efficient system of trains and buses moves tourists around the lake. The most scenic (if slowest) way to travel, though, is on MAHART ferries, which serve 22 towns around the lake from mid-June to mid-October.

*Everywhere you look,
brochures swoon about the
"Hungarian Sea" and the
"Nation's Playground"—but
it's wise to realize that the lake
is just a lake, not an ocean. The
wind occasionally whips up a
wave or two, but nobody's
going to hang ten here.*

Siófok

Less than two hours from Budapest, Balaton's main hub for transport, commerce, and recreation makes a good starting point for a journey around the lake. Some might complain about its flagrant commercialization, but as Oscar Wilde said, "Nothing succeeds like excess." People pack the beaches by day and the discos by night. You can sneak onto the beach by entering any of the restaurants and continuing past the patio, or, if you're honest, fork over a $1.50 beach charge. The two streets you need to know run parallel to each other: Petőfi sétány goes along the beach by the large hotels, and Fő utca, a few blocks inland, runs next to the train tracks, through the main square (Szabadság tér), and across the Sió River. The **train and bus stations** are next to each other on Fő utca. Trains run daily from Budapest's Déli Station (2 hrs, $5).

A generous staff at **Tourinform** (Fő u. 41, tel. 84/310–117), west of the train station in a huge water tower, can help with all of your needs. Buy a map ($1.50) and a transportation schedule (60 Ft) here. **Cooptourist** (Mikes K. u., tel. 84/310–279) has rooms to rent. Go to the main **IBUSZ** office (Fő u. 174, west of train station, tel. 84/311–107) for money exchange, private rooms, and general info—the beachside location handles only hotel reservations.

WHERE TO SLEEP AND EAT The key to a low-budget excursion to Siófok is to come anytime but high season (July–Aug.), when hotel prices start as high as $60 per double. Look for cheap private rooms away from the beach, or ask at one of the tourist offices. Otherwise, **Hotel Dolce Vita** (Siraly u. 8, tel. 84/311–336; beds $7; closed Oct.–June) is worth the 25-minute trek from town for its immaculate rooms and restaurant. The sunny building is 100 yards from a free stretch of grassy waterfront. Head west on Fő utca, cross the river, and then turn right on Vitorlás utca, left on Erkel Ferenc utca, and right on Siraly utca. **Csárdás** (Fő u. 105, tel. 84/310–642) is a little pricey, but good service and excellent food make it worth the extra forints.

AFTER DARK Save your energy for night, when Siófok turns into disco central. The favorites are **Siótour** (Petőfi sétány at Táncsics u.), **Paradiso** (cnr. Petőfi sétány and Mártírok útja), **Matroz** (next door to Paradiso), and **Flört** (Mártírok útja, south of Fő u.). Discos are open 9 PM–4 AM.

NEAR SIOFOK

KESZTHELY Keszthely is the second-most-touristed town on Lake Balaton, but unlike Siófok it's not completely characterless; buildings from the last century lend the town some distinction. Kossuth Lajos utca, the main street, runs past **Festetics Palace** (Kastély u. 1, tel. 83/312–190; admission $3, 50 Ft students; open daily 9–5), built in 1745 and renovated with a lovely garden and a fascinating room of mirrors. In high season (June–Aug.), tourists descend like devouring locusts on the town. **Trains** run from Siófok, as do **ferries** (tel.

84/310–061 for info). If you need a room, knock on any door marked ZIMMER FREI, or seek a dorm bed at the stark **Pannon University of Agriculture** (Festetics György u. 7, tel. 83/311-290; beds $5; closed Sept.–May). This place has stinky bathrooms—bring your own TP.

BADACSONY A combination of excellent wine and striking rock formations may sound dangerous, but they're what make Badacsony so attractive. Great hiking and 700-foot basalt columns draw outdoorsy types, who usually mix well with snooty wine connoisseurs. The flat-topped **Badacsony Hill** has good hiking trails; a map in the parking lot of Kisfaludy Ház restaurant has details. A die-hard party crowd hangs out at the beach, and every other structure is a *borozó* (wine bar) or *söröző* (beer hall). To sample some of Hungary's best wines, knock on the front door of any vineyard/cellar you see (many line Római út, southwest of town). Most private cellars welcome wine tasters and charge less than $2 per liter. **IBUSZ** (II Capitano shopping center on pier, tel. 87/331–292) can arrange a private room and help with visitor info. Trains run regularly from towns around the lake.

Balatonfüred

Füred (natives drop the prefix), the most aristocratic Balaton resort, hosts sailing regattas and has first-class hotels, curative mineral springs, and a world-famous hospital for cardiology. This sports haven is easily the most beautiful of the Balaton towns. The beaches are sandy and shallow, and you can avoid the high prices. **IBUSZ** (Petőfi Sándor u. 4A, tel. 86/342–327), on the main drag near the dock, has visitor info, and the helpful staff will find you a room. The **train** and **bus stations** are off Horváth Mihály utca. Trains and **ferries** (50 Ft) run frequently from towns around the lake. If you miss your train, head next door to a wine warehouse. The staff at **Badacsonyi Pincegazdaság**, open weekdays 7:30–3, will let you taste some of the finest wines in the region for about 75¢–$1 per ½ liter.

WHERE TO SLEEP AND EAT If you can spare a few forints, **Hotel Blaha Lujza** (Blaha L. u. 4, across from Balatontourist, tel. 86/342–603) is the best of the cheap hotels. Rooms (singles $20, doubles $30, breakfast included) are spotless and bright, and the best **restaurant** in town is here. **Kertészeti Szakközépiskola** (Hősök tere 1, Balatonarács, tel. 86/342–651; beds $6), just outside Füred, has wonderful summer dorm rooms. Take Bus 4/4A from Füred to Balatonarács. The wheelchair-accessible **FICC Rallying Camping** (Széchenyi u. 24, tel. 86/343–823) is the mother of all campgrounds, a great place to meet people, do laundry, or sunbathe in the buff. You'll pay $7 for one person and a tent, $9 for two people. From the ferry dock, walk 2 km west, or take Bus 1 or 2.

Tihany

The little town of Tihany (pronounced "tee-hahn") dominates a 5½–km peninsula that hosts many of Balaton's more discriminating summer visitors. If you arrive by **ferry** from Balatonfüred (May–Sept. only, 50 Ft), you'll get a great view of the town and its stately **Apátsági templom** (Benedictine church). This twin-tower structure, a descendant of an abbey built in 1055, is one of the finest monuments to the Baroque in a country that eventually overdosed on the style. Next door in the **Tihany Múzeum,** check out the impressive lapidarium in the basement, which displays stone carvings, capitals, statues, pillars, and tombstones from as early as the 2nd century AD. *Batthyány u. Abbey admission: 20 Ft. Open Mon.–Sat. 10–6. Museum tel. 86/348–405. Admission: 30 Ft. Open Mar.–Oct., Tues.–Sun. 10–6.*

Hiking trails lead from the abbey. Walking along Pisky sétány toward the Echo Restaurant, you can descend to the ferry dock or follow the marked trail to **Csúcs Hill;** the two-hour hike to the peak is worth it for the lovely views. For a less strenuous 40-minute walk, take the long way down to **Belső-tó** (Inner Lake)—go north from the downtown area on Kossuth Lajos u. and follow the trail marks on the right. **Buses** leave Balatonfüred's station hourly for Tihany ($1.25) via Tihany-rév.

If a quiet night by the lake appeals to you, see if **Balaton-tourist** (Kossuth Lajos u. 20, tel. 86/348–519) can fix you up with a room. Expect to pay $15–$18 for a single or a double. Rooms can be scarce, so also try **Tihany Tourist** (Kossuth u. 11, tel. 86/348–481), which has an English-speaking staff. The restaurant **Kakas Csárda** (Batthyány 1, tel. 86/348–541), north of the post office, has an English menu and meals for around $5.

Székesfehérvár

The mouthful that is Székesfehérvár—say "SAKE-esh-feh-hare-var," meaning "Seat of the White Castle"—may be Hungary's oldest settlement. Archaeological digs have found remains from the Copper Age, which was long before King István I made the town capital of Christian Hungary. As you enter the old town, you pass by the **Garden of Ruins** (Koronázó tér), containing the remains of the 11th-century royal **basilica** (admission free; open Apr.–Oct., Tues.–Sun. 9–5), where for more than 500 years Hungarian kings were buried. The **city hall** dominates the main square, Szabadság tér. Nearby is the **cathedral** (Arany János u.), founded in 1235, then rebuilt in the mid-18th century. Two blocks from the square, the well-preserved Baroque **Fekete Sas Patkiamúzeum** (Black Eagle Pharmacy), open Tuesday–Sunday 10–6, started as a Jesuit-run pharmacy in the mid-18th century and stayed in business until 1971. Don't miss the **King Stephen Museum** (Fő u. 6; open daily 10–6) and its Roman artifacts—here you can also pick up information in English about free days at the town's other museums.

An important transport hub, Székesfehérvár is served by frequent trains from Budapest, one hour away. To reach the old city from the **train station,** walk north on József Attila utca, then turn left on Rákóczi utca (20 min), or take Bus 32 to Rákóczi utca. The **bus station** (Piac tér, tel. 22/315–056) is one block southwest of downtown.

Albatours (Szabadság tér 6, tel. 22/312–494) is hands down the best tourist office in town. It's centrally located, and the staff speaks a little English. They can provide brochures and town maps, book private rooms ($10–$15), and arrange your stay in the cheap **hostel** (Jókai u. 2; beds $4; open Mar.–Oct.) near the office. There's also one inexpensive hotel, **Rév Szálló** (József Attila u. 42, tel. 22/314–441), which has single, double, and triple rooms, each for $15. From the train station, walk north on József Attila utca or take Bus 32. The restaurant **Korzo Söözö** (Fő u. 2) has a lively crowd and affordable, hearty food.

Transdanubia

The Danube divides Hungary into eastern and western regions that differ substantially in character and history. The western region, known as Transdanubia (Dunántúl in Hungarian), is characterized by mountains and hills, tracts of flat, open countryside, and magnificent sunflower fields. The region gracefully bears signs of Roman occupation and 150 years of Turkish rule. The Austrian influence, too, is more visible here than elsewhere in Hungary, as evidenced by a dumbfounding number of Baroque buildings. Architecturally striking Sopron is heavily touristed, but medieval Kőszeg and the hills around Pécs remain unspoiled.

Just minutes away from busy towns, fat, sunburned men in their underwear work their gardens and wave when a train goes by; and people leave homegrown vegetables and flowers on the street with a box for passersby to pay on the honor system.

Győr

Called the "City of Balconies" for its gracious railed windows and the "City of Rivers" for the three that meet here, Győr (pronounced "dyur") mixes well-preserved Baroque architecture and depressing industrial complexes. Fortunately, most factories lie south of the charming town center. Narrow streets lead up to the historical **Káptalan-domb** (Chapter Hill), where the town's oldest church, the **Episcopal cathedral,** sits imposingly on 11th-century foundations. An adjoining **Gothic chapel** (admission 40 Ft) houses a medieval masterpiece, the gilded bust of King St. Ladislas, rumored to contain part of the saint's skull. Across the square from the cathedral, the **Püspökvár** (Bishop's Palace) has an interesting hilltop garden from which you can view graffiti in several languages on the walls below. The impressive **Ark of the Covenant Monument,** at the southern tip of the hill, was built in apology by Charles III after Habsburg soldiers knocked the Host from a priest's hands.

Fine Baroque houses line the eastern side of Bécsi kapu tér. The main feature of the square is an 18th-century Italianate-Baroque **Carmelite church.** A chapel within houses a statue of St. Mary reputed to prevent the waters of the Rába River from overflowing. Also on the square are 16th-century fortifications built to repel the Turks. Szechenyi tér, an unadulterated Baroque square in the heart of Győr, is home to a **Jesuit church,** the **Patika Múzeum** (Pharmacy Museum), and the **Xantus János Múzeum,** worth a look for its furniture replicas.

COMING AND GOING   Exactly halfway between Budapest and Vienna, Győr is an important transport hub. Trains travel to Budapest (2 hrs), Sopron (1 hr), and Vienna. The **main train station** (Révai Miklós u.) is 10 minutes south of the historic center. The **bus station** is connected to the train station by a nifty underground passage. Trains are faster, but take the bus to nearby Pannonhalma abbey (*see* Near Győr, *below*); it will drop you much closer than the train.

WHERE TO SLEEP AND EAT   The helpful multilingual agents at **IBUSZ** (Szent István út 29–31, 2 blocks northeast of train station; open Mon.–Thurs. 8–4, Fri. 8–3:30) arrange rooms and change money. Don't take a room in the unappealing southern part of town. The safe dorms of the **Technical School (KTMF)** (Hédarvái u. 3, tel. 96/329–722) sleep three people per room. Beds are $3; haggle if you're asked to pay for the whole room ($10). From Kossuth Bridge, turn left on Kálóczy tér to the KTMF parking lot; the dorm is to the west. **Hotel Aranupart** (Aldozat u. 12, tel. 96/326–033) looks like a convalescent hospital, but you won't pay more than $5 for a dorm bed, $15 for a single. From the station, take Bus 11. The inviting, central **Teátrum Panzió** (Schweidel u. 7, tel. 96/310–640), overlooking the town theater, has $35 doubles. From the train station, walk north on Aradi Vértanúk utca, turn right on Arany János utca, and cross Czuczor Gergely. The former wine cellar **Szúrkebarát Pinceborozó** (Arany János u. 20, tel. 96/311–548) offers affordable cold meals.

NEAR GYOR

PANNONHALMA ABBEY   As you head south from Győr, you can see the giant Pannonhalma abbey (Vár 1, tel. 96/370–191; admission $5; open Tues.–Sun. 9–4) looming in the distance. Perched high in the Sokorói Hills, the 1,000-year-old Benedictine abbey commands a superb view. During the Middle Ages it was an important ecclesiastic center and wielded considerable political power. A library of more than 300,000 volumes holds priceless medieval documents. Unfortunately, you have to take a guided tour that tends to be rushed. Saturday-afternoon organ recitals are held once a month in summer. The abbey is 21 km from Győr; buses (½ hr, $1) leave from Platform 11 of Győr's station.

Sopron

Having escaped the Mongol and Turkish invasions, Sopron has kept its Renaissance and Baroque buildings beautifully intact. Well-preserved architecture, a festive air, and frequent connections to Budapest's Déli Station (3 hrs), Vienna (1 hr), and Győr (1½ hrs) make this one of the most visited (and expensive) towns in Hungary. The 200-foot tall tŰztorony (fire tower), the symbol of Sopron, embraces a range of styles, with medieval foundations, a Renaissance balcony, and a Baroque spire. From an observation platform (admission $1; open Tues.–Sun.), you can look out over the forested Lővér foothills. At the base of the tower is the **Loyalty Gate;** local legend has it that if an adulterous woman walks through, its bells will ring (unfaithful men can slip right by, though). The gate commemorates Sopron's vote to remain Hungarian rather than turn Austrian.

Below the gate is Sopron's main square, Fő tér. **Fabricus House** (Fő tér 6; admission 50 Ft) has a fine Renaissance courtyard leading to an archaeological museum. In the Gothic cellar you can see Roman statues that were unearthed beneath the square. **Stornoház** (Fő tér 8; admission 50 Ft), built by Italian chimney sweeps, is an impressive Renaissance palace complete with corner turrets and a collection of period furniture. In the center of the square stands the Baroque **Holy Trinity Column,** built by survivors of the plague in the early 17th century.

The **Bencés templom** (Templom u.), or Goat Church, acquired its unusual name from a grateful goatherd who paid for its construction with gold unearthed by his animal. The church's early Gothic interior was the site of five national assemblies and three coronations in the 17th century. Sopron's Jews were expelled in 1526, but one of the town's original **synagogues** (Uj u. 22, tel. 99/311–463; admission 50 Ft; open Wed.–Mon. 9–5) has been converted to a museum of Judaica, complete with a stone *mikva* (ritual bath).

WHERE TO SLEEP AND EAT IBUSZ (Várkerület 41, tel. 99/312–455), the most helpful tourist office in town, can arrange private rooms ($9–$30). The best deal if you're traveling in summer is a bungalow at **Lövér Camping** (Pócsi-domb, tel. 99/311–715; closed late Oct.–early Apr.), in beautiful woods on the outskirts of town. If you bathe in insect repellent and bring earplugs, you'll enjoy the simple $8 bungalows or $3 tent sites. Take Bus 12 from the train station to the end of the line (10 min, 50¢). You can splurge at **Hotel Palatinus** (Uj u. 23, 2 blocks south of Fő tér, tel. 99/311–395; doubles $50), in the heart of the inner town; the interior is clean and modern, and the managers are friendly. Breakfast is included in the room rate.

Locals mingle with tourists at wheelchair-accessible **Deák Etterem** (Erzsébet u. 20, 2 blocks north of station; closed Sun.). Outstanding meals (under $5) are enhanced by the restaurant's pleasant, dark interior. For big appetites and little budgets, **Onkiszolgáló Etterem** (Széchenyi tér 7; no dinner) is food heaven. It will remind you of your grade-school cafeteria, but the food is hearty and authentic. If you can eat more than $5 worth, you should be on TV.

NEAR SOPRON

FERTOD Fertőd can be reached in 30 minutes by bus from Sopron (less than $1 one-way). The main attraction here is the magnificent Baroque **Fertőd palace,** built in 1720 by the Esterházy family. The palace's large French park and hall of mirrors inevitably invite comparisons with Versailles. Badly damaged in World War II, the palace has been painstakingly restored. Music lovers will enjoy the occasional concerts held here, as well as the exhibit on Haydn. You can stay overnight in the palace ($15 per room), but tour groups tend to fill the place. Call ahead for reservations. *Bartók Béla út 2, tel. 99/370–971. Open May–Sept., Tues.–Sun. 8–noon and 1–5; Oct.–Apr., Tues.–Sun. 8–noon and 1–4.*

Kőszeg

This fortress town lies in the easternmost foothills of the Alps at an elevation of 267 meters, a strategically desirable position in a country of lowlands. Kőszeg (meaning "stone top") was designed with an eye for defensibility, a strategy put to the test in 1532, when a valiant resistance against 200,000 Turks kept the invaders from pillaging Vienna. The fortress, **Jurisics-vár** (Rájnis u. 9; admission 40 Ft; open Tues.–Sun. 10–5), now resembles a slightly organized pile of rocks. Still, the tower affords a spectacular view, and the history museum inside is engaging. In the center of town, **Jurisics tér** is packed with historical buildings: a red-striped town hall, an 18th-century well, a pharmacy museum, and two churches. The Catholic **Szent Jákobtemplom** (St. James Church) is a magnificent Gothic structure; it's next to the Baroque, Protestant **Szent Imre-templom** (St. Emerich's Church).

The staff at **Kőszeg Tourist** speaks a little English and compensates for vocabulary deficiencies with good-humored helpfulness. The office changes money, arranges lodging, and provides local and international maps. *Rákóczi Ferenc u. 19, tel. 94/361–258, fax 94/361–259. From* *train station, cross bridge and walk northwest up Rákóczi Ferenc u. 10 min. Open weekdays 9–4.*

COMING AND GOING To reach Kőszeg from Budapest, take a train to Szombathely (3½ hrs) and transfer to Kőszeg (30 min, $1). The **train station** (Vasutállomas u., tel. 94/360–053) is in a beautiful wooded area about 10 minutes south of the town center; head north along Rákóczi Ferenc utca or grab any local bus (preferably Bus 1) to reach town. The **bus station** (Liszt Ferenc u., off Kossuth u.) is one block southeast of the town center.

WHERE TO SLEEP AND EAT The tourist office *(see above)* can arrange a private room for $12–$18. The popular **Hotel Strucc** (Várkör u. 124, at Rákóczi u., tel. 94/360–323) has housed visitors for more than 300 years. A friendly English-speaking clerk will set you up in a spotless room, and you can have breakfast in the hotel restaurant. Doubles are less than $25. Originally a church, the deluxe **Hotel Park** youth hostel (Felszabadulás tér, tel. 94/360–366) has great amenities: tennis courts, a restaurant, and free laundry service. A double room with no shower costs $15 ($13.50 with HI card). From Fő tér, follow Várkör utca west, then walk north to Hunyadi utca and follow that ¾ km west. **Bécsikapu Söröző** (Rájnis u. 5, off Jurisics tér near castle, tel. 94/360–854 or 94/360–297), one of the best restaurants in Transdanubia, serves a great venison with potato doughnut ($5). It's also one of the few places where an English menu doesn't mean inflated prices.

Pécs

Pécs (pronounced *"paytch"*), southern Transdanubia's most interesting destination, reflects a rich 2,000-year history. Many of the town's buildings—including two mosques, a synagogue, and several cathedrals—have recently undergone restoration, adding to the pleasant atmosphere created by the warm climate, red-tile roofs, rambling streets, and lush vineyards. Pécs has long served as an outpost of art and learning; Hungary's first university was established here, but nothing remains of it today. The town has produced several noteworthy artists, including humanist poet Jánus Pannonia and the Zsolnay family, whose ceramics are widely admired. Entertainment here tends to be refined, with more than a dozen museums and many art galleries to visit, along with excellent ballet and symphony performances at the national theater.

Although summer is the busiest travel time, the **Express** office shortens its hours after the school year. The exchange rate here tends to be good, though, and the office has private rooms and hostel information. *Bajcsy-Zsilinszky u. 6, tel. 72/413–407. Open Mon.–Wed. 8–noon and 12:30–3:30, Thurs. 8–noon and 12:30–4:30, Fri. 8–noon and 12:30–1:30.*

COMING AND GOING Trains run regularly from Budapest's Déli Station (3 hrs, $10). Pécs's **train station** is south of town. To reach the town center, follow Jokai utca north to Széchenyi tér, or take Bus 36 or 37. The **bus station** (Nagy Lajos Király u., tel. 72/415–215) has frequent service to surrounding villages, but you should take the train for longer jaunts, as it's faster and cheaper.

WHERE TO SLEEP AND EAT **Fönix Hotel** (Hunyadi J. u., off Széchenyi tér, tel. 72/311–680; singles $25, doubles $35) has clean rooms with wood interiors, cable TV, refrigerators, showers, and breakfast. **Szént Mor Kollegium** (Vasvári P. u., at Egyetem u., tel. 72/311–199; beds $6; closed Sept.–June) offers cheap, clean, quiet rooms. From the train station, walk north on Jókai utca, turn right on Nagy L. K. útca past the bus station, walk around the bend on Rákóczi út, and turn right on Egyetem utca. **Szalay László Kivalo College** (Universitas u. 2, tel. 72/311–966; closed Sept.–June) accommodates guests for $15 per triple, a good deal if you can share the room—otherwise you get stuck for the empty beds. Follow directions to Szént Mor Kollegium, but turn right off Rákóczi út onto Vargha D. utca and left on Universitas utca.

If you've heard rumors about Hungary's great food but haven't tasted the proof, Pécs's eateries should convince you. **Fiáker Vendéglö** (Felsőmalon u. 7, tel. 72/327–859) may be the best budget restaurant in a 100-mile radius. Toothsome entrées go for less than $5, and a few veggie options (most deep-fried) are available. Foreign and Hungarian students flock to the pricey **Barbakán Borozó** (Klimó G. u. 18, tel. 72/324–930; no lunch), built into the old town wall in a former catacomb. Dinners ($5–$7) are large, but save room for the *palacsinta,* dessert pancakes with chestnut-and-chocolate sauce. From Széchenyi tér, walk west on Ferencesek utca to Kórház tér, then north on Klimó G. utca.

WORTH SEEING If you like museums, Pécs is your town; the central Káptalan utca is accurately dubbed "Museum Street" by locals. The impressive **Csontváry Museum** (Jánus Pannonius u. 11–13, off Káptalan u.; admission 50 Ft, students free; open Apr.–Sept., Tues.–Sun. 10–5:45, Oct.–Mar., Tues.–Sun. 10–5) exhibits the work of pharmacist turned expressionist painter Mihály Tivadar Csontváry Kosztka (1853–1919). You won't need your 3-D glasses to be optically astonished by the works of Victor Vasarely, founder of op art, at the **Vasarely Museum** (Káptalan u. 3, tel. 72/324–822; admission 50 Ft, students free; open Tues.–Sun. 9–5).

Pécs's central square, Széchenyi tér, is crowned by the 16th-century **Gazi Khassim Pasha Inner City Parish Church** (Rákóczi út 2; admission 35 Ft; open Thurs.–Tues. 10–1 and 2–6), the largest and finest relic of Turkish architecture in Hungary. When the Turks occupied Pécs from 1543 to 1686, they destroyed St. Bartholomew's Church and recycled its stone to build this mosque. Muslim and Christian elements are combined not only in its name but also on top of its dome, where a cross shares space with a gilded crescent. Near the entry, a *mihrab* (prayer niche) faces east toward Mecca, and the walls are inscribed with quotes from the Koran; but Christian statuary and frescoes are displayed beneath the Turkish arcades.

Don't be put off by the austere exterior of Pécs's four-tower **cathedral** (Dóm tér; admission 40 Ft, 20 Ft students; open Tues.–Sat. 10–4). Inside, no stone has been left unpainted, and the frescoes and mosaics practically explode with color. Built by Hungary's patron saint and first king, István, the building still has some of its original parts, including an 11th-century crypt with walls dating way back to the 4th century. The 18th-century **Bishop's Palace** next door has a great collection of Gobelin tapestries. A metal sculpture of composer Franz Liszt leans over a balcony from which he once gave a piano concert.

The huge **synagogue** (Kossuth tér, 3 blocks south of Széchenyi tér off Irgalmasok u.; admission 35 Ft, 25 Ft students; open May–Oct., Sun.–Fri. 9–1 and 1:30–5) used to fill up with the town's large Jewish population, but today the congregation barely takes up a fraction of the place—a sad reminder of the Nazi era, as are the names of Holocaust victims inscribed in the entryway.

Great Plain
Like, say, Nebraska, the Great Plain (Nagyalföld in Hungarian) doesn't get much attention as a fun vacation spot. When asked what he thought of the region, one local said, "I call it the Big Nothing." Still, there's more to this flat area than wasteland, Magyar longhorns, herds of sheep, wild boars, and a stray cowboy or two. You'll find sprawling farms, villages of one-story houses, and several important cities. Because the Great Plain is one of the last outposts on the usual travel itinerary, much of it remains unspoiled by tourism, and residents genuinely welcome outsiders.

Kecskemét
Only an hour by train from Budapest ($9), Kecskemét is a popular destination for those interested in a brief glimpse of the Great Plain. It's a small town that's big on architecture and agriculture. A quick spin around Szabadság tér, the main square, reveals diverse architectural styles, and a visit to any café or bar offers a chance to sample regional wines and the famous *barack pálinka* (apricot brandy). To reach the main square from the **train and bus stations,** walk through the park and turn west on Rákóczi út.

The turreted and tiled **town hall,** built in 1893 in the colorful Hungarian Art Nouveau style, stands in Kossuth tér. Every hour, bells play selections by Mozart, Kodály, Handel, Beethoven, and other composers. At the northern end of Szabadság tér, the **Cifra palota** (Ornamental Palace) is another classic example of Hungarian Art Nouveau. Decorated with brightly colored majolica tiles, the palace houses the **Kecskemét Gallery** (Rákóczi u. 1; open Tues.–Sun. 10–6), which exhibits works by Farkas István and other great Hungarian artists.

For tourist info and private rooms (doubles $12–$15), try **Co-op tourist** (Két templom köz 9, off Kossuth tér, tel. 76/481–472) or **IBUSZ** (Széchenyi tér 1–3, tel. 76/322–955). **Caissa Pension** (Gyenes tér 18, tel. 76/481–685; singles $15, doubles $18), an unassuming fifth-floor hotel, has gorgeous contemporary rooms and common areas that overlook the park. The pension hosts ongoing chess tournaments and draws a truly interesting crowd; and the owner helps you find a room if his are full. From Szabadság tér, walk north on Luther Kös and through Jokai tér to Gyenes tér. Park your hungry carcass at **Italia** (Hornyik János u. 4, south off Jokai tér, tel. 76/328–327; open daily 11:30–11) to enjoy home-baked, thick-crusted pizza ($2–$3.50), Italian chicken ($2.50), and pasta specialties. **Három Gúnár Fogado** (Batthyánny u. 2, south off Kossuth tér via Katona tér; open daily 6:30 AM–11 PM) features goose special-ties ($4–$6.50) and meat dishes ($4), though you can get vegetarian strudel ($2) if you don't eat meat.

Szeged

The main tourist attraction here is the **Open-Air Theater Festival,** which livens up the streets July 20–August 20. Tickets for classic Hungarian plays, ballets, and other performances are $6–$14. But the festival is not all there is to Szeged: The town contains one of Hungary's most beautiful squares, **Dóm tér,** and one of its largest churches, the towering, neo-Romanesque **Votive Church** (Dóm tér), built in the 1920s. Szeged's 15 universities make it a young town, with the grooviest crop of jazz/blues clubs on the plain, including **Mojo Club** (Alföldi u. 1, tel. 62/321–525; open daily until 2 AM), a haven of low lights, funky wood tables, and tapestry-covered couches.

Szeged Tourist (Klauzál tér 7, south of Széchenyi tér, tel. 62/321–800; open July–Aug., week-days 8:30–1 and 1:30–6, Sat. 9–1, Sept.–June, weekdays 8:30–1 and 1:30–5) will change money and arrange private rooms (about $12), but the hostel, **Eötvös Lóránd Kollégium** (Tisza Lajos krt. 103, across from Aradi Vértanuk tere on Tram 1 route; beds $7), is the best deal in town. **Alabárdos** (Oskola u. 13, off Roosevelt tér east of Széchenyi tér, tel. 62/312–914) is Szeged's best restaurant, with meals for less than $10. Trains run regularly from Budapest (2½ hrs, $9) and Kecskemét (1 hr, $5) to Szeged's **train station** (Indóház tér 2, tel. 62/310–906). From here, take Tram 1 to reach the center.

Debrecen

A perennial runner-up to Budapest, the capital of the Great Plain is surprisingly interesting and hard to leave off your itinerary. The second-largest city in Hungary, it has an urban downtown, a pleasant park enthusiastically named the **Great Forest,** an attractive university campus, and a first-rate thermal spa. The noteworthy **Reformed College** (tel. 52/314–744; admission 25 Ft; open Tues.–Sat. 9–5, Sun. 9–1) was founded in 1538, two years after Calvinism first appeared in Debrecen. Climbing the stairs to the oratory, you pass frescoes depicting student life and famous moments in Hungarian history. The building houses a historical museum with exhibits on the college's history and religious art. One block northwest, the **Déri Museum** (Déri tér, tel. 52/317–577; admission 30 Ft, 15 Ft students; open Tues.–Sun. 10–6) displays the fascinat-ing collection of a wealthy Hungarian silk manufacturer, which runs the gamut from Egyptian archaeology to modern Hungarian art.

The most popular attraction in Debrecen doesn't have much of a past. A full day of splashing around in the excellent thermal baths, **Nagyerdei Gyógyfürdő** (Nagyerdei krt. 9–11, tel. 52/316–000; open daily 8–6:30) costs $2. You can choose between indoor baths (first tram stop in the Great Forest) and outdoor pools (next tram stop in front of Hotel Termál).

Kölcsey Cultural Center (Hunyadi u. 1–3, behind Déri Museum, tel. 52/313–977) offers tours and concerts and organizes loads of cultural events throughout the year. The English-speaking manager, Ilona Fülöp, is a great source of information. She moonlights as a private guide and arranges cheap rooms in school dorms in summer. Call or fax her at home (tel. and fax 52/322–902) if you're interested.

COMING AND GOING Trains run frequently from Budapest (3½ hours, $9) to the Debrecen **train station** (Piac u.). The center of town is about a 20-minute walk down the main thoroughfare, or you can jump on Tram 1 (20 Ft), Debrecen's only tram line, which travels up Piac utca to the university and then returns to the train station. Debrecen's **bus station** (tel. 52/313–999) is on the corner of Széchenyi utca and Nyugati utca. To get to the center, head east on Széchenyi utca to Piac utca, at which point you'll be four blocks south of Kálvin tér.

WHERE TO SLEEP AND EAT If you plan to see the famous Virág (Flower) Carnival on August 20, reserve well in advance. Private rooms can be arranged at the tourist offices and through Ilona Fülöp of the Kölcsey Cultural Center (*see above*). **Hotel Fönix** (Barna u. 17, tel. 52/313–355), five minutes from the train station, has decent singles ($9) and doubles ($16), but the best deals are the cramped quads ($20). At the central **Kölcsey Tanitóképző Főiskola Kollégium** (Blaháné u. 13, tel. 52/310–166; closed late Aug.–early June), you get a bed in a double for a measly $3 per person. To get there, walk south on Piac utca, turn left on Csapó utca and right on Liszt F. utca to Blaháné utca. You don't have to enroll in the Hungarian-language summer course at **Kossuth Lajos University** (Egyetem tér 1, tel. 52/316–666; closed Sept.–May) to stay in a dorm. Just take the tram from the station to the campus in the Great Forest and get set up with a room ($12–$16).

Vegetarians should plant their tent pegs at **Déri-téri Etterem** (Perényi u. 1, near Déri Museum, tel. 52/311–819; closed Sun.). The vegetarian menu has more than 20 options ($1.50–$3.50). **Gilbert Pizzeria** (Kálvin tér 5, tel. 52/333–681; closed late Aug.) makes some of Hungary's best pizza ($2.50). From the outside, **Malom Söröző** (Nádor u. 9, off Fúredi u., tel. 52/317–307) looks like a Laundromat, but it's actually a well-kept local secret, with outstanding meals for less than $5.

IRELAND

By Scott McNeely

An island has the natural barrier of the sea to protect it from enemies, but the history of Ireland really is the history of its many conquerors, be it Viking raiders or British landlords. The first documented invaders were the Celts, a Continental tribe of warriors who arrived sometime during the 6th century BC and quickly dominated the island. Their arrival was the beginning of ancient Ireland's Golden Age, a time of druidic learning and bardic poetry—a time when burly warriors roamed the land in search of honor, glory, and heads (head-hunting was a common Celtic practice). Ireland's next wave of conquerors were the Christians, who appeared in the 4th century AD in search of converts and solitude. Over the next eight centuries, while continental Europe languished in the so-called Dark Ages, Ireland became a beacon of enlightenment, evidenced today by the number of churches and convents that still dot the countryside. (Some say Christianity has left a deep scar on the country—perhaps this explains why divorce is still illegal, and why all forms of contraception were banned until the mid-1980s.)

With the decay of Christianity and the rise of Viking rule in Ireland, it was English-born Pope Adrian VI who, in 1170, boldly granted King Henry II (a fellow Englishman, no less) total dominion over Ireland—the sort of presumptuous move that, to many Irish, tells the whole tangled story of English-Irish relations. By the time the last of Ireland's Gaelic kings—the O'Neills and O'Donnells—had their lands confiscated by the British in 1603, Ireland had become a servile colony where English nobles lorded over an adopted homeland. Following Henry VIII's conversion to Protestantism, Ireland was further divided not only along political lines but also along religious ones. The religious schism became even more acute in the aftermath of the English Civil War, when the pro-Catholic Charles I was deposed by the vigorously Protestant Oliver Cromwell. Cromwell came to Ireland in 1649, intent on further alienating the already bitter Irish Catholics with his Act of Settlement (1652). It mandated that all Catholics had to pack their bags and move into a small splotch of land west of the River Shannon—"to Hell or Connaught," as the saying goes.

Another traumatic episode in Irish history was the Great Famine of the 1840s and '50s. Throughout the 19th century, Irish peasants worked for absentee British landlords and either paid exorbitant rents (for pitiable plots of land) or simply starved. The system was hardly equitable, but somehow the bulk of Ireland survived the lean years prior to 1845. Within a year, however, a potato blight ruined crops throughout the country. By 1857, the population of Ireland had dwindled from 8 million to 3 million. Starvation was largely to blame for the horrific decline, although this period also marks the first large-scale emigration to America, Australia, and Canada—a draining and disruptive phenomenon that continues to haunt Ireland. (In 1848, nearly 250,000 people emigrated; today the number hovers around 30,000.)

ATLANTIC OCEAN

North Channel

Malin
Head

Fanad
Head

Tory Island

**Giant's
Causeway**

Portrush

Coleraine

TO
CAIRNRYAN,
STANRAER

Aranmore
Island

Letterkenny

Londonderry

DERRY

Larne

Gweebarra
Bay

DONEGAL

**NORTHERN
IRELAND
(Great Britain)**

ANTRIM

TO
LIVERPOOL

Glencolumbkille

Donegal

Omagh

Belfast

Kilcar

Killybegs

TYRONE

Lough
Neagh

Lisburn

Donegal
Bay

Lower
Lough Erne
FERMANAGH

Armagh
City

DOWN

Newcastle

Belmullet

Killala
Bay

Sligo Bay

Upper
Lough Erne

ARMAGH

Newry

Killala

SLIGO

Sligo Town

Monaghan
Town

Bangor

Lough
Conn

LEITRIM

MONAGHAN

Dundalk

Irish Sea

Achill
Island
Clare Island

MAYO

Castlebar

ROSCOMMON

Cavan

CAVAN

Drogheda

Westport

Lough
Mask

WESTMEATH

MEATH

TO
LIVERPOOL,
HOLYHEAD,
DOUGLAS

Inishbofin

Lough
Corrib

Mullingar

Clifden

GALWAY

Galway
City

Athlone

REPUBLIC OF IRELAND

Dublin

DUBLIN

Rossaveal

Galway Bay

OFFALY

Bray

TO
HOLYHEAD

Aran
Islands

Doolin

Portlaoise

KILDARE

Dun
Laoghaire

**Cliffs of
Moher**

CLARE

Rosecrea

Glendalough

WICKLOW

Wicklow
Town

Ennis

LAOISE

Arklow

Kilkee

Limerick
City

Rock of
Cashel

CARLOW

Shannon

KILKENNY

Kilkenny
Town

WEXFORD

Listowel

LIMERICK

Cashel

Wexford
Town

Mouth of
the Shannon

TIPPERARY

Clonmel

Waterford
City

Tralee

Mallow

CLONMEL

Rosslare
Harbour

Dingle
Peninsula

KERRY

Killarney

WATERFORD

TO
FISHGUARD,
LE HAVRE,
CHERBOURG

Dingle

Blasket
Islands

Dingle Bay

CORK

Tramore

Valencia
Island

Iveragh
Peninsula

Cahirciveen

Kenmare

Blarney

Cork
City

Youghal

Skellig
Rocks

Kenmare Bay

Cobh

Beara Peninsula

Bantry Bay

Bantry

Clonakilty

St. George's Channel

Mizen Head

Cape
Clear

N

486

TO
ROSCOFF,
LE HAVRE

The other great victim of the famine was Irish culture. Whole areas of the island were depopulated, and many villages simply ceased to exist. As the soul of a centuries-old way of life slipped into oblivion, the English language became a de facto replacement for Irish. Although some effort has been made to preserve the ancient Gaelic language, these days fewer than 20,000 people are estimated to speak Gaelic with any degree of fluency. In the worst cases, Irish is spoken strictly for the benefit of tourists and their video cameras.

Thanks to a booming tourism industry, Ireland is often reduced to embarrassing clichés (i.e., leprechauns and druids). In reality, this brooding, storm-battered island is more about fluffy sheep and stone-strewn fields. About biting wit, the subtle twist of a phrase, and chats over tea and biscuits. About Guinness, traditional music, and stumbling along an empty road in the pitch black, guided only by the distant glow of a pub and its tendrils of peat smoke.

Basics

MONEY £1 = $1.46 and $1 = 68p. The Irish currency is technically known as the punt, but nearly everyone calls it the pound. Bills come in denominations of £5, £10, £20, £50, and (rarely seen) £100. Coins come in denominations of 1p (worthless), 2p (equally worthless), 5p, 10p, 20p (good for pay phones), 50p, and £1. Also remember that Irish and English pounds are *not* interchangeable. Exchanging money in Ireland is rarely a problem, and nearly every backwater town has a Bank of Ireland or Allied Irish branch. In general, Irish banks are open weekdays 10–12:30 and 1:30–3. For weekend exchanges, try gift shops (which extort large commissions) or post offices.

COMING AND GOING

➤ **BY FERRY** • Ireland is an island, so you'll probably arrive on a ferry. The country has three principal ferry ports, two in Dublin (one at the docks and one in nearby Dún Laoghaire) and one in Rosslare Harbor, near Wexford in County Cork. The shortest crossing (3–4 hours) is from Holyhead, in Wales, to Dublin.

The other principal service is from Le Havre or Cherbourg, in France, to Cork—a 24-hour journey. Most ferries to the Republic are free (or substantially reduced) to InterRail and EurailPass holders. **B&I** (tel. 01/874–3293) and **Sealink** (tel. 01/280–8844) are the main carriers. Both have offices in Dublin and Cork.

➤ **BY PLANE** • Ireland has two principal airports, Dublin International and Shannon International (near Limerick in southwest Ireland). All international flights originating in the United States must land and clear customs in Shannon. From here, you can catch any one of a dozen daily connections to Dublin. There's talk, however, of opening the Dublin airport to flights from North America; ask your travel agent. Ireland's major carriers are **Aer Lingus** (tel. 01/844–4777) and **Ryanair** (tel. 01/844–4411).

GETTING AROUND Ireland's trains and express buses (which serve major cities) are free to all InterRail and EurailPass holders. If you don't have one of these—and if you're under 26 with a valid ISIC student card—definitely purchase the invaluable **Travelsave Stamp** (£7). This stamp will reduce all rail fares by about 50% and bus fares by about 30%; all ferries by 25%–30%. Both the stamp and ISIC cards are available from USIT, Ireland's excellent student-run travel organization (with offices in Dublin, Cork, and Galway). Another pass you might consider is the new **Irish Rover RailPass,** valid on all trains in both the Republic and Northern Ireland; it's valid for five days in a 15-day period and costs £80. If you're planning to ride lots of buses consider the bus-and-rail **Emerald Card,** which costs £105 for 8 days in a 15-day period and £180 for 15 days in a 30-day period. Irish Rail's **Rambler** ticket is good for 8 out of 15 consecutive days, costs around £60, and is good for free travel on all Irish Republic trains. Bus Eireann's **Rambler** ticket is also valid 8 out of 15 consecutive days, costs £60, and is valid for free travel on all Irish buses. The above passes can be bought at any Irish Rail or Bus Eireann depot, or in advance from CIEE (in U.S. tel. 800/243–8687).

➤ **BY BUS** • **Bus Eireann,** Ireland's national bus service, provides cheap, comfortable service to nearly every town in Ireland. Bus fares are generally £2–£5 cheaper than the equivalent train fare, and since Ireland's rail network only covers the large hubs, you'll probably end up taking a bus at least once. InterRail and EurailPass holders also note: You can ride Bus Eireann's Expressway buses, which travel between Ireland's largest towns, for free. Expressway routes are listed in yellow in the Bus Eireann timetable (£1), available at any depot or at its Dublin office.

➤ **BY TRAIN** • Ireland's rail network is quick and efficient. Trains generally run between 5 AM and midnight. Reservations are a good idea on the popular Dublin–Galway and Dublin–Cork routes, especially on summer weekends. Irish trains are operated by **Iarnród Eireann** (Irish Rail), the state-owned rail company.

➤ **BY BIKE** • Ireland is a cyclist's paradise. The roads are flat and uncrowded, the scenery phenomenal, and the distance from one village to the next is never more than 25 km. On the downside, foul weather and rough-paved roads are all too common, so rain gear and spare parts are a must. You can rent bikes from Raleigh Rent-A-Bike shops, which are scattered throughout Ireland. The going rate is £7 per day or £30 per week, plus a refundable deposit of £40. For a list of Raleigh Rent-A-Bike dealers, contact any Bord Fáilte tourist desk.

➤ **HITCHING** • Hitching in Ireland is very safe. The Irish are stereotyped as friendly, chatty sorts who willingly pick up hitchhikers for a chance to gab. Of course, you should always be careful and never accept a ride with anyone who gives you the creeps. If you're traveling between large cities, head to the appropriate highway and stake your claim either well before or well after a roundabout.

WHERE TO SLEEP Without exception, Irish hotels charge a scandalous £40–£60 per person for a night's accommodation, so get used to sleeping in hostels or, for a few extra pounds, in a cozy B&B. The only other option is to camp. There are hundreds of campgrounds in Ireland, and you'll typically pay £3–£5 per tent space plus an additional 20p–£1 per person. Many are only open April–September, sometimes through October, and during summer the majority are also quite crowded. Reservations are advised whenever possible.

Youth hostels offer the cheapest beds in Ireland—generally between £4 and £8 per person, per night. There are two principal youth hostel associations in Ireland. **An Oige,** the "official" association, is affiliated with Hostelling International (HI). If you have an HI card, you do not need a separate An Oige pass. If not, you must purchase a membership card (£7.50) from An Oige's Dublin office or from a member hostel. Almost all An Oige hostels have 11 or 11:30 PM curfews, daytime bedroom lockouts, and check-in between 8–11 AM and 3-ish–8 PM only. Unless you bring your own sleep sheet or sleeping bag, you must rent one (60p–£2.50). A better bet are hostels overseen by the **Independent Hostel Owners (IHO),** a friendly organization that boasts nearly 90 hostels throughout Ireland. There's no IHO membership card to buy, IHO hostels don't have curfews or daytime lockouts, and you can check in at any time of day. Many also have camping facilities.

VISITOR INFORMATION **Bord Fáilte,** the Irish Tourist Board, can book you into a room and fill your pockets with maps, brochures, and pamphlets. They also publish the *Ireland Accommodation Guide* (£4), a massive 215-page listing of every board-approved hostel, B&B, and campsite in the country. Offices are scattered throughout the country.

MAIL The Irish mail service is known as **An Post.** Post offices and smaller substations (generally housed in the back of shops or news agents) are located in every block-long town in Ireland. Look for the snot-green AN POST sign. All offices sell stamps—52p per letter and 38p per postcard for international destinations, 32p per letter and 28p per postcard for domestic and EU destinations—and offer telegram service for a standard rate of 15p per word. Larger offices are usually open Monday–Saturday 9–5:30.

PHONES Country Code: 353. Within Ireland, the cost of a three-minute local call is 20p. If you're having any trouble, dial 10 (free) to speak with an Irish operator. For free directory assistance, dial 190. To place collect and credit-card calls to the United States, dial **AT&T** (tel. 800/550–000), **MCI** (tel. 800/551–001), or **Sprint** (tel. 800/552–001) from any coin box. The call is usually free. If you're calling Ireland from abroad, don't forget to drop the "0" from all area codes.

Dublin

In his celebrated work *Ulysses*, James Joyce provided a detailed map of turn-of-the-century Dublin. Except for a few name and street changes, much of Joyce's Dublin remains intact. The dirty lanes are still here, the soot-covered flats, the dockside slums and smoky pubs. Many of the people, too, seem to be from a distant era: Portly grandmums complaining about the price of tea in Bewley's Café, gruff pub flies soaking themselves in stout, triple-checking the horse sheet between cordial hellos and handshakes. As writers like Joyce, Yeats, and O'Casey discovered long ago, Dublin's greatest asset is the scruffy Dubliner.

The capital of modern Ireland, Dublin was first settled by Celtic traders in the 2nd century AD. They christened it *Baile Átha Cliath,* or City of the Hurdles, a name that is still used by Gaelic speakers. Dublin's convenient location by the River Liffey, however, meant that it was only a matter of time before the Vikings got wind of the settlement and descended en masse in their dreaded longboats; by AD 850, Dublin, known back then as *Dubh Linn* (Black Pool), was firmly under Viking control. Judging by the Norse gold and jewelry found here, Dublin was definitely one of the most important conquests ever made by the Vikings.

As political ties were strengthened between Ireland and England in the Middle Ages, Dublin was thoroughly refashioned. Under the guidance of the English—who provided the money, artisans, and urban planners—the city grew into a modern capital. Over time, the English influence also led to the creation of Trinity College (1591) and to the city's still-surviving Victorian and Georgian architecture. But despite their English flavor, places like Merrion Square and northside Dublin appear uniquely Irish, if only because they're hemmed in by the grimy tenements of working-class Dublin. In the capital, the unemployment rate hovers around 15% (around 40% in some parts of the city), so don't be surprised to see beggars and ragged drunks, even horse-drawn carts pulling loads of trash or coal. The tourist board does its best to suppress such images of Ireland's "cosmopolitan capital," but in an odd way both poverty and the constant play between the ancient and modern are at the heart of Dublin's appeal.

BASICS

AMERICAN EXPRESS *116 Grafton St., directly across from Trinity College, tel. 01/677–2874. Open weekdays 9–5, Sat. 9–1.*

BUCKET SHOPS USIT. Besides offering currency exchange and heaps of information on budget travel in Ireland, this neon-colored student agency can book you on any rail, plane, boat, or rickshaw tour imaginable. ISIC cardholders under 26 can also pick up the invaluable **Travelsave Stamp** (£7.50). Arrive early to avoid hour-long lines. *19 Aston Quay, west of O'Connell Bridge, tel. 01/679–8833. Open weekdays 9–4, Sat. 11–4.*

PHONES AND MAIL Towering over O'Connell Street, two blocks north of the River Liffey, is the majestic **General Post Office** (GPO). For currency exchange, walk inside, turn left, and follow the signs. *1 Princess St., at O'Connell St., tel. 01/872–8888. Open Mon.–Sat. 8–8, Sun. 10:30–6:30.*

VISITOR INFORMATION Bord Fáilte has three offices in Dublin. Stop in to book a room, get train and bus schedules, or to purchase their excellent walking tour pamphlets (£1 each). *14 Upper O'Connell St., tel. 01/874–7733. Open July–end of Aug., Mon.–Sat. 8:30–8, Sun. 10:30–2; shorter hrs off-season. Baggot St. Bridge, facing Grand Canal, tel. 01/676–5871. Open Mon.–Sat. 10–4:30. Dublin Airport, Main Terminal, tel. 01/844–5387. Open June–Sept., daily 8 AM–10:30 PM; shorter hrs off-season.*

KEY

AE American Express Office

i Tourist Information

Phoenix Park

Berkeley St.

Eccles St.

North Circular Rd.

Belvidere Pl.

Wellington St.

Blessington St.

Upper Gardiner St.

② ③

Mountjoy Square

Great Charles St.

Phibsborough Rd.

Royal Canal Bank

Lower Dorset St.

Temple St.

Hill St.

Summerhill

① Western Way

Mountjoy

Upper Dorset St.

Great Denmark St.

N. Great George's St.

Marlborough St.

Sean McDern

Upper Dominick St.

④

⑤

Lower Dominick St.

Parnell Square

Railway St.

Gardiner St.

Constitution Hill

Coleraine St.

Parnell Sq. W.

Parnell St.

Fa

Lower Grangegorman

Upper Grangegorman

N. Brunswick St.

Parnell St.

O'Connell St.

Earl St. N.

Talbot St.

⑥

⑦

King St.

Henry St.

Abbey Theater

Busáras Bus Station

Beresford St.

Green St.

Arran St.

Capel St.

Mary St.

Prince's St. N.

⑧

Sackville Pl.

Lower Abbey St.

C

Custom

Smithfield

⑨

Bow St.

Church St.

Mary's La.

Liffey St.

Jervis St.

Abbey St.

Upper Abbey St.

i

Middle Abbey St.

O'Connell

Eden Quay

Butt Br.

George's G

Mary's Abbey

Strand St. Great

Lotts

Bachelor's Walk

Burgh Quay

Tara St. Station

Arran Quay

Inns Quay

Ormond Quay

Grafton

Ormond Quay

River Liffey

Poolbeg

Usher's Quay

Whitworth Br.

Merchant's Quay

Wood Quay

Essex Quay

Wellington Quay

Temple Bar

Aston Quay

Fleet St.

Doller St.

Townsend St.

⑩ TO HEUSTON STATION

St. Augustine St.

Cook St.

Winetavern St.

⑫

⑬

TEMPLE BAR

Dame St.

College Green

Bank of Ireland

Anglesea St.

Fownes St.

Copea St.

Westmoreland

College St.

Pearse St.

⑪ W. Thomas St.

Oliver Bond

High St.

St. Nicholas St.

Bride St.

Lord Edward St.

Castle St.

City Hall

Castle

Exchequer St.

Suffolk St.

AE

⑭

Trinity College

Nassau St.

Leinster St.

Line

St. Francis St.

Patrick St.

St. Patrick's Close

Ship St. Great

Golden La.

S. Great George's St.

Drury St.

William St. S.

Clarendon St.

Wicklow St.

Duke St.

Anne St.

Molesworth St.

Frederick La. S

⑳

㉑ Upper Merri

The Coomb

New Row

⑮

St. Patrick's Park

Bride St.

Lower Kevin St.

Aungier St.

Camden St.

Mercer St.

Cliffe St.

York St.

⑯

Dawson St.

St. Stephen's Green N.

St. Stephen's Green E.

Kildare St.

Mill St.

Camden Row

Lower Bride St.

Heytesbury St.

Pleasants St.

ST. STEPHEN'S GREEN

St. Stephen's Green S.

N

Lower Clanbrassil St.

Charlotte St.

Grantham St.

University College

Harcourt

Upper Hatch St.

Lower Hatch St.

Lower Leeson St.

Earlsfort Ter.

Pembroke St.

Victoria St.

Harrington St.

Harcourt Rd.

Adelaide Rd.

S. Richmond St.

S. Circular Rd.

Lennox St.

Charlemont St.

⑰

0   250 yards

0   250 meters

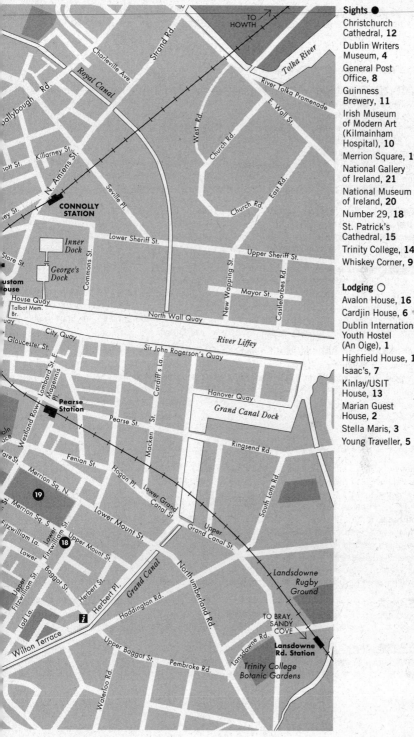

Sights ●

Christchurch Cathedral, **12**

Dublin Writers Museum, **4**

General Post Office, **8**

Guinness Brewery, **11**

Irish Museum of Modern Art (Kilmainham Hospital), **10**

Merrion Square, **19**

National Gallery of Ireland, **21**

National Museum of Ireland, **20**

Number 29, **18**

St. Patrick's Cathedral, **15**

Trinity College, **14**

Whiskey Corner, **9**

Lodging ○

Avalon House, **16**

Cardjin House, **6**

Dublin International Youth Hostel (An Oige), **1**

Highfield House, **17**

Isaac's, **7**

Kinlay/USIT House, **13**

Marian Guest House, **2**

Stella Maris, **3**

Young Traveller, **5**

An Oige provides maps and listings of its hostels and issues membership cards (£7.50) on the spot (not necessary if you already have an HI card). *61 Mountjoy St., tel. 01/836–3111. Open weekdays 10–5:30.*

COMING AND GOING

BY TRAIN Dublin has two train stations, **Heuston** (tel. 01/703–2131 weekdays 7:30 AM–10 PM) and **Connolly** (tel. 01/703–2358 weekdays 7:30 AM–9:15 PM), located across town from one another but connected by frequent shuttle bus (£1). Buses leave for Heuston from outside USIT's downtown office; from Heuston Station, take any bus labeled AN LÁR (city center). Connolly Station is a block from the Busáras bus depot. A number of hostels are within an easy walk of Connolly, or you can take any bus marked AN LÁR for Trinity College and O'Connell Street. **Iarnród Eireann** (Irish Rail, 35 Lower Abbey St., tel. 01/836–6222; open Mon.–Sat. 9–6, Sun. 10–6) provides info on all domestic passenger routes and DART (Dublin Area Rapid Transport) trains.

BY BUS **Busáras** (pronounced bus-R-us), Bus Eireann's only Dublin depot, is around the corner from the Connolly rail station. Splurge on Bus Eireann's incredibly helpful, novel-size timetable (50p). *Store St., tel. 01/366–111. Information desk open Mon.–Sat. 9–5:30 year-round, Sun. 9:30–5 summer only.*

BY PLANE Dublin Airport (tel. 01/844–4900) is 11 km north of town. Daily flights to and from Britain and the Continent are offered by the Irish carriers **Aer Lingus** (41 Upper O'Connell St., tel. 01/705–6705) and **Ryanair** (3 Dawson St., tel. 01/677–4422). Between 8:10 AM and 9 PM express buses (£2.50) run directly between the airport and Busáras's city-center depot. You can save some money by taking Bus 41 (95p) to the airport from Eden Quay (immediately east of O'Connell Bridge, facing the River Liffey).

BY FERRY Both **B&I** (16 Westmoreland St., tel. 01/874–3293 or 01/660–6666) and **Sealink** (15 Westmoreland Row, tel. 01/280–8844) offer regular car and passenger service between Dublin and Wales (Holyhead). B&I (£19 one-way, bikes free) sails directly into Dublin Harbor. Sealink (£18 one-way, bikes free) docks in Dún Laoghaire, 4 km south of the city center. Make reservations in summer. A taxi from Dún Laoghaire to the city center should cost no more than £6.

GETTING AROUND

Though far from picture-postcard perfect, Dublin's **northside** (which once sheltered the likes of James Joyce and Brendan Behan) is the place to soak up the pure, unadulterated city. Be doubly warned that O'Connell Street, the northside's main artery, is inordinately long (about 3 km), and that this part of town has a well-deserved reputation for being dangerous at night. Dublin's **southside,** with its smart shopping avenues and rowdy pubs, is the place to be. **Trinity College** and the adjacent **Bank of Ireland,** a block south of the River Liffey from O'Connell Bridge, are the area's most famous landmarks. Any bus labeled CITY CENTER or VIA AN LÁR will eventually deposit you here. Dublin's meager excuse for a subway is the DART (Dublin Area Rapid Transport), an aboveground train that connects central Dublin with the suburbs. DART trains run daily between 6:30 AM and 11 PM. Single fares range between 50p and £1.10.

BY BUS Buses run between 6 AM and 11:30 PM. Fares range between 55p and 95p, and most drivers give change. **Bus Atha Cliath** (Dublin Bus, 59 Upper O'Connell St., tel. 01/873–4222; open weekdays 9–5:30) stocks maps and timetables.

BY TAXI There's no shortage of taxis in Dublin, but at £1.20 per mile you'll do better to explore the city center on foot. If you don't see any cabs, try **Blue Cabs** (tel. 01/676–1111), available 24 hours a day. Tipping is optional.

WHERE TO SLEEP

If everything seems booked solid, Bord Fáilte makes B&B reservations for a £1 fee. Another option between late June and early October are student dorms. For the same price as a hostel you'll get a private or semiprivate room, clean sheets, and modern conveniences. Try the **Trinity College dorms** in Rathmines (Dartry Rd., tel. 01/497–1772; Bus 14 or 14A from city center), 3 km north of the city center. **University College Dublin** has dorms in nearby Belfield (UCD Village, tel. 01/269–7696); take Bus 10 (46A on weekends) from the city center.

HOSTELS **Avalon House.** Elegant Georgian relic with cheap dorm beds (£7, breakfast included), private rooms (£12.50 per person), and luxurious singles (£17.50). Crowds during summer. *55 Aungier St., tel. 01/475–0001. Bus 16, 16A, 19, or 22 to front door. Laundry, wheelchair accessible. Reception open 24 hrs. No curfew. MC, V.*

Cardjin House. Shoe-box-size hostel squeezes 50 beds into small dorm rooms. Coffee shop downstairs. Strict bedroom lockout 10 AM–4:30 PM. Breakfast included in £6 fee. *15 Talbot St., tel. 01/878–8484 or 01/874–1720 after 6 PM. Talbot St. ends next to train station and passes 1 block north of bus depot. Showers 50p.*

Dublin International Youth Hostel (An Oige). One of Dublin's finest hostels, housed in a 19th-century convent. Centrally located and first to fill up in summer. Spacious dorm rooms cost £9; add 50p if you don't have An Oige/HI card. *61 Mountjoy St., tel. 01/830–1766. From bus station walk north on Lower Gardiner St. MC, V.*

Isaac's. Offbeat northside safe house caters to good-natured degenerates and international students. Large and semi-institutional dorm rooms (beds £6, doubles £11.25/person). *2 Frenchman's La., around corner from bus station, tel. 01/874–9321. Bedroom lockout 11 AM–5 PM.*

Kinlay/USIT House. In heart of southside Dublin, like something from a Dickens novel with red masonry, wrought-iron fixtures, tall windows. Musty but comfy dorms (£7.50/person) and doubles (£12.50/person), both including breakfast. *2–12 Lord Edward St., tel. 01/679–6644. From Trinity College, walk west down Dame St. or take Bus 49, 50, or 77 to front door. Luggage storage, kitchen facilities. MC, V.*

Young Traveller. Kinda grungy, kinda crowded, and always noisy northside hostel with a small café. Space in four- to six-bed dorms costs £6.50–£8. Be careful walking alone in neighborhood after dark (take a taxi). *St. Mary's Pl., tel. 01/830–5000. Walk north on O'Connell St. to end, turn left on Parnell St., right on Parnell Sq. Reception open daily 7 AM–11 PM. MC, V.*

B&BS **Highfield House.** Quiet suburban living in a prim, grandmotherly home (£17/person). Buses 13, 14, and 14A run regularly to city center. *1 Highfield Rd., Rathgar, tel. 01/497–7068.*

Marian Guest House. Clean, quiet home run by friendly woman who'll talk your ear off. £13/person. Check out 10 AM. *21 Upper Gardiner St., tel. 01/874–4129. MC, V.*

Stella Maris. High ceilings and dark oak staircase grace this beautiful old house. Airy and bright rooms cost £15/person. The only problem? A daily queue outside the single shower. *13 Upper Gardiner St., tel. 01/874–0835.*

FOOD

Dublin is hardly known for its exotic dining scene, so get used to the basics: sandwiches, bags of greasy chips, eggs and rashers (a sort of bacon), Cadbury chocolate, and Guinness. Besides the hard-to-miss **McDonald's** (on Grafton Street) and **Beshoff's** (fast-food fish, opposite Trinity College), a common sight in Dublin are chippers—grungy holes-in-the-wall that charge £2–£4 for such delicacies as burgers, chips, sausage rolls, and plates of eggs and beans. Considering the high price of food in Dublin, chippers and tea shops are manna from heaven.

➤ **UNDER £5** • **Alpha Cafe.** No-frills food served by two grandmotherly women. Hearty dishes like eggs and beans, roast and potatoes, for under £4. Hard to find (two floors above no-name shop). 37 Wicklow St., 1 block off Grafton St., tel. 01/710–362. Open generally 11–6.

The Cellary. Hole-in-the-wall café with excellent homemade vegetarian meals (£3) and moody jazz decor; this former dockside warehouse is now one of Dublin's trendiest eateries. *1 Lower Fownes St., tel. 01/671–0362. Closed Mon.*

Munchies. The ultimate sandwich shop: Thick slabs of freshly baked bread filled with your choice of meat (tandoori chicken, tuna, roast turkey; about £2.50) and various side salads. *3 locations: 146a Lower Baggot St.; 17 Harcourt Rd.; 2 S. William St. All closed Sun.*

To blend in with the locals, eat only when faint, scorn all fruits and vegetables, and drink plenty of stout.

Rock Garden. Doubles as a bar, live-music venue, and trendy Temple Bar eatery. Munch on burgers, so-called "Mexican" food, and an excellent Sunday brunch. *3a Crown Alley, tel. 01/679–9114. Open daily.*

Wed Wose Café. Cramped sandwich shop popular with hangover-suffering locals. "Mega Breakfast" is served all day and is best deal in town: eggs, bacon, sausages, black pudding, beans, toast, and coffee for £3.50. *18 Exchequer St., off Great George's St., no phone. Closed Sun.*

The Well Fed Café. Dublin's most famous vegetarian stronghold, with rotating selection of bland but wholesome meat-free and vegan entrées (lasagnas and casseroles from £2). Convenient location in Temple Bar district. *6 Crow St., tel. 01/677–2234. Open Mon. 10–4:30, Tues.–Sat. 10–8:30.*

➤ **UNDER £10** • **Elephant & Castle.** One of Dublin's most accessible upscale restaurants, in the heart of Temple Bar district. Filled daily with wealthy business people and ragged students. Try the huge, delicious hamburgers (£6) or Chinese chicken salad (£6.50). *18 Temple Bar, tel. 01/679–3121. Open daily.*

Little Lisbon. Yummy Portuguese food in lively, arty setting. The food ain't overly spicy (or overly daring), but you can bring your own wine. *Dame St., opposite Central Bank, tel. 01/671–1274. Open daily 12:30–2 and 6–midnight.*

Taj Mahal. Dublin's best curry (£4–£6) and tandoori (£5) dishes. A bit pricy, but portions large enough for two. *17 Lincoln Pl., southeast side of Trinity College, tel. 01/676–0568. Closed Sun.*

COFFEEHOUSES Dubliners spend a good deal of the day at one of three **Bewley's Cafés,** the city's oldest (founded in 1847) and most famous coffeehouse chain. Pastries, sandwiches, eggs and beans served all day. *3 locations: 78 Grafton St., tel. 01/677–6761; 13 S. Great George's St., tel. 01/679–2078, closed Sun.; 12 Westmoreland St., tel. 01/677–6761.*

Don't leave Dublin without lingering over coffee and a book at the **Winding Stair Café and Bookshop,** in a three-story warehouse overlooking the River Liffey near pedestrian-only Ha'penny Bridge. *40 Ormond Quay, tel. 01/733–292. Open Mon. 1–6, Tues.–Sat. 10:30–6.*

WORTH SEEING

Follow the River Liffey west from O'Connell Bridge for a good overview of Dublin, or try one of the self-guided walking tours published by Bord Fáilte (*see* Visitor Information, *above*). **Bus Eireann's** (tel. 01/873–4222) three-hour bus tour also covers the main sights (£10 per person). Another option is **City Cycle Tours** (1a Temple La., Temple Bar, no phone), which organizes guided cycling treks through central Dublin for £12, including a six-speed bike and helmet. In summer groups depart Monday–Saturday at 10:30 AM, 2:30 PM, and 7 PM. Reserve in person at least 30 minutes before departure.

CHRISTCHURCH CATHEDRAL Christchurch, the Church of Ireland's flagship, is also Dublin's oldest standing monument, founded in 1038 by the mead-swilling Sitric, king of the Dublin Norseman. Check out the lavishly detailed fenestration and gallery-level carvings. The crypt, which is nearly as large as the church itself, contains some fine religious relics including the tabernacle of James II. *Christchurch Pl., tel. 01/677–8099. Admission: 50p. Open daily 10–5.*

DUBLIN WRITERS MUSEUM Rare manuscripts, personal memorabilia, and a rich collection of portraits and publicity posters commemorate Ireland's most famous writers. Ireland's three Nobel Prize winners (Shaw, Yeats, Beckett) are especially well represented, along with the likes of Wilde, O'Casey, Behan, Swift, Joyce, Synge, and O'Brien. *18–19 Parnell Sq. N, tel. 01/872–2077. Walk north up O'Connell St. to Parnell Sq. Admission: £2.25, students £1.50. Open Mon.–Sat. 10–5, Sun. 1–5.*

It's said that of the 10 million pints of Guinness produced daily, some 6 million are consumed in Ireland alone.

GUINNESS BREWERY Located in the heart of the Liberties—the Fairfield Market section of Dublin—the Guinness Brewery is the most popular tourist destination in town: Expect noisy crowds of Americans in summer. The brewery itself is off-limits, but the part-museum, part-gift-shop **Hop Store** (lined with vats, barley roasters, and a display of Guinness memorabilia) is open year-round. After a brief tour, enjoy a free glass of what's generally considered the best Guinness in the world, poured straight from the adjoining factory. Afterward, spend some time walking the perimeter of the 65-acre brewery, which has changed little since first opened by Arthur Guinness in 1759. *Crane St., tel. 01/453–6700. From Trinity College, walk due west down Dame St., Lord Edward St., High St., and Thomas St.; turn left at Crane St. Admission: £2. Open weekdays 10–4:30.*

IRISH MUSEUM OF MODERN ART (KILMAINHAM HOSPITAL) The Royal Hospital of Kilmainham, built in 1684 to house retired soldiers in style, is itself one of the best examples of aristocratic, 17th-century Dublin architecture. Inside is an excellent collection of works by Rembrandt, Dürer, Manet, and Hogarth, along with temporary exhibits. *Corner of Steven's La. and James's St., tel. 01/671–8666. Walk west along Liffey and turn left on Military Rd. (at Heuston Station); or take Bus 79, 90 or 24. Admission free. Open Tues.–Sat. 10–5:30, Sun. noon–5:30.*

NATIONAL GALLERY OF IRELAND This museum is a must, with a permanent collection of more than 3,000 paintings, watercolors, sculptures, and etchings (both international and Irish). Admission is free, and there's a top-rate café on-site. *Merrion Sq. W, tel. 01/661–5133. Bus 7, 10, or 48A. Open Mon.–Sat. 10–6 (Thurs. until 9), Sun. 2–5.*

NATIONAL MUSEUM OF IRELAND Whenever a work crew unearths the stray Viking tool or Celtic broach, it gets shipped here for display. *Kildare St. and Merrion Row, on northside of St. Stephen's Green, tel. 01/661–8811. Admission free. Open Tues.–Sat. 10–5, Sun. 2–5.*

NUMBER 29 Everything in this exquisite Georgian town house has been meticulously refurbished according to the designs and tastes of the period. Hand-painted trunks and porcelain dolls are strewn about the attic; hairbrushes and jewelry sit expectantly on lace-covered dressers. *29 Lower Fitzwilliam St., opposite Merrion Sq., tel. 01/676–5831. Admission free. Open Tues.–Sat. 10–5, Sun. 2–5.*

ST. PATRICK'S CATHEDRAL St. Patrick's is the oldest and most prominent Christian landmark in Ireland. Jonathan Swift (1667–1745), poet, author, witticist, and dean of St. Patrick's between 1713 and 1745, is generously remembered with monuments and plaques. Sunday services (8:30 and 11:15 AM) are worth a nondenominational visit. *Patrick's Close, tel. 01/475–4817. Open weekdays 9–6, Sat. 9–4, Sun. 10–4:30.*

TRINITY COLLEGE The oldest university in Ireland, Trinity College was established in 1592 by a grant from Queen Elizabeth I of England. Historically, Trinity was Dublin's most prominent pro-Brit enclave; as recently as 1966, Irish Catholics faced excommunication for attending classes here, even though Trinity itself opened its doors to all creeds (and to women) at the turn of the century. These days nearly 70% of its students are Catholic.

Trinity has nurtured an impressive list of graduates over the years, including Dracula creator Bram Stoker, writer Jonathan Swift, and Nobel Prize–winner Samuel Beckett. For a good overview, don't miss the **Guided Tour of Trinity** (£1.50) with Joseph, resident fop and wit. His hourly tours (May–Sept., daily 10–3) are notoriously wry and patronizing. Meet under the main arches and keep your eyes peeled for the gentleman sporting tweed and a cravat.

In Trinity Library's **Long Room** (tel. 01/677–2941; admission £2.75, £2.25 students) look for the *Book of Kells,* considered the most striking manuscript ever produced in the Anglo-Saxon world. This 682-page gospel was obsessively illustrated by monks with a penchant for iconographic doodling and frantic spirals. Equally impressive is the smaller and older *Book of Durrow,* essentially a 7th-century coloring book punctuated now and again with religious verse. Also on display are Beckett, Joyce, and Wilde manuscripts.

WHISKEY CORNER Housed in a former distiller's warehouse, this small northside museum offers a detailed look at how Irish whiskey is made. The best feature of the compulsory guided tour is—you guessed it—the tasting at the end, when you're free to sample five Irish whiskeys at your leisure. *Bow St., tel. 01/872–5566. Admission: £1.50. Tours weekdays at 3:30 PM. Reservations advised.*

> *The only bad thing about Irish pubs is that they close—at 11 PM in winter, at 11:30 PM in summer. When the barman shouts "last call" around 10:55, he means it.*

AFTER DARK

Whether you're up for a staggering pub crawl or a quiet chat over a pint of plain, head to any one of Dublin's 1,000 public houses. If your head is still throbbing from last night's singalong, stagger to the theater or to any one of a dozen music pubs in the city center. If you're stuck for inspiration, pick up the excellent weekly magazine *In Dublin* (£1.50).

PUBS As a general rule, the area between Grafton and Great St. George's streets is a gold mine for untouristy student pubs. Another good bet is the Temple Bar district, sandwiched between Dame Street and the River Liffey.

An Béal Bocht. The name was inspired by the Flann O'Brien play *An Béal Bocht* ("The Poor Mouth"). It's a long walk from the city center and virtually undiscovered by tourists. Some nights there's theater or live music. *58 Charlemont St., 2 bridges west from Baggot St. Bridge.*

The Brazen Head. Dublin's oldest pub (built in 1688) served as the headquarters for the United Irishmen during the late-18th century. Loaded with character and friendly drunks, the Brazen Head has live, untouristy traditional music nightly. *20 Lower Bridge St.*

Foggy Dew. Smart-looking but tiny pub on edge of Temple Bar district. It's jammed on weekend nights—come early. *1 Fownes St., off Dame St.*

Kenney's. During the day this old-style pub is quiet and smoky. At night, traditional musicians keep it noisy and smoky. *31 Westland Row, 1 block from Pearse St. DART.*

McDaid's. Most nights you'll hear jazz, blues, or Irish folk music in the upstairs lounge of this popular student pub. *3 Harry St., off Grafton St. and across from Bruxelles.*

Mulligan's of Poolbeg Street. Drunken journalists, locals, and students flock here for what is argued to be "the Best Pint of Guinness on Earth." *Poolbeg St. Take the first left off Pearse St. onto Poolbeg St.*

Stag's Head. No visit to Dublin is complete without lunch (£3–£4) at the Stag's Head, the city's most impeccably well-preserved pub. On weekend nights it's packed with Trinity students. *1 Dame Ct., parallel to and 1 block south of Dame St.*

Toner's. Epitome of a good pub. Built in the early 1800s and still retains its original furnishings and flavor. Cheap grub available daily. *139 Lower Baggot St.*

MUSIC Dublin's music scene is excellent. Bands range from U2 sound-alikes to moody blues. Grab a copy of *In Dublin* magazine for current listings or take a walk down Grafton Street and keep your ears open. In addition to the **Underground** (Dame St.) and the **International Bar** (Wicklow St.), a number of city-center pubs double as independent music venues (covers £2–£5): Try the **Baggot Inn** (143 Baggot St.), filled on weekends with slackers of all ages; the northside club **Slattery's** (Capel St.); or **The Waterfront** (Sir John Rogerson's Quay), Dublin's trendiest dance club. The **Rock Garden** (3a Crown Alley) in Temple Bar hosts big-name and local bands, plus discos and miniraves (cover £2–£5).

THEATER Dublin's theater scene is impressive, even by New York and London standards. Especially popular (at least with tourists) are the Irish classics staged every summer. Most theaters offer sizable student discounts (I.D. card required). If you're in the mood for low-key entertainment with some good-natured song and dance thrown in, the **Olympia Theater's** (74 Dame St., tel. 01/677–8962) "Midnight at the Olympia" program on Friday and Saturday nights is an excellent choice. Shows start and end late and cost around £6. The following are some of Dublin's better known theaters: **Abbey Theater and Peacock Theatre** (Lower Abbey St., tel. 01/878–7222), **Project Arts Centre** (6 Essex St., tel. 01/671–2321), and **Riverbank Theatre** (Merchant's Quay, tel. 01/677–3370).

NEAR DUBLIN

GLENDALOUGH First the good news: Glendalough is one of Ireland's premier monastic sites, nestled in the rugged Wicklow mountains among trees, trees, trees, and acres of heather. Glendalough flourished as a monastic center from around AD 400 until 1398, when English soldiers plundered the site, leaving it in the ruins you see today. Highlights include **St. Kevin's Cell,** a hive-shaped rock pile by the Upper Lake; the perfectly preserved, 108-foot-tall **Round Tower,** built in the 11th or 12th century; the well-preserved shell of **St. Mary's Church;** and the impressive graveyard.

Now the bad news: Glendalough has been ruthlessly exploited by the tourist board, making it one of the most visited sights in eastern Ireland. To make the most of Glendalough, you'll need to arrive early and/or spend the night. Most everyone goes home around 6 PM, when the parking lot and **visitor center** (tel. 0404/45325; admission £1) close for the evening.

➤ **COMING AND GOING** • USIT (*see* Dublin Bucket Shops, *above*) organizes full-day bus excursions to Glendalough for around £10 per person. A cheaper option is **St. Kevin's** bus service (tel. 01/874–555; £8 round-trip), which departs daily at 11:30 AM from in front of the Royal College of Surgeons on St. Stephen's Green in Dublin.

➤ **WHERE TO SLEEP** • Glendalough's best hostel is the IHO **Old Mill Hostel,** in an old farmhouse within sight of the ruins. *Rathdrum Rd., tel. 0404/45156. From visitor center, turn right onto main road and keep straight; look for and follow hand-painted HOSTEL sign. No curfew or lockout. £5.90 per night, tent spaces £3.*

Southeast Ireland

With few typically Irish attractions (romantic coastlines, wild bogs, etc.), the southeast is one of the least touristed parts of the country. One of the main reasons for coming, in fact, is strictly practical. Rosslare Harbour, near Wexford, is one of only three ferry ports in the country and is perhaps the most convenient hub for EurailPass and InterRail travelers headed for the Continent (traveling to the United Kingdom, however, requires passage from Dublin).

Kilkenny

Kilkenny is called "Ireland's Medieval Capital," no doubt because it's a well-preserved, 900-year-old Norman citadel with a spooky castle and brawny city wall. Kilkenny also boasts a lively pub and traditional music scene, which merit a visit by themselves. In August, the **Kilkenny Arts Week** showcases Irish film, theater, and music; for schedules call the Arts Council (tel. 056/63663) or the **tourist office** (Rose Inn St., tel. 056/21755), which is opposite Kilkenny Castle in the city center. From the joint **bus and train station** (Upper John St., tel. 056/22024), buses travel daily to Dublin, Waterford, Cork, and Galway. Kilkenny is also on Irish Rail's Dublin (Heuston Station)–Waterford line.

WHERE TO SLEEP AND EAT The only hostel in town is the large, high-ceilinged **IHO Kilkenny Tourist Hostel** (35 Parliament St., tel. 056/63541; beds £5.50; closed Dec. 21–Jan.), in the city center. From the train and bus station, turn left onto John Street, cross River Nore, and head right onto Kieran or High streets (both eventually turn into Parliament Street). The walk takes 15–20 minutes. The nearest campground is 60 km away, so the only other choices are a B&B in town or An Oige's impressive **Foulksrath Castle Hostel** (tel. 056/67674; beds £3.50–£4.50; closed Nov.–Feb.), 13 km north of Kilkenny in the small village of Jenkinstown. Call the hostel for travel details. Most of Kilkenny's B&Bs are on the Waterford Road; one of the best is **Beaupre House** (Waterford Rd., tel. 056/21417), a family-run establishment with large, airy rooms (£13/person).

Two doors from the hostel, the dark, romantic **Italian Connection** (38 Parliament St., tel. 056/64225) serves tasty pizzas (from £3.25) and fettuccine (£4.50). For cheap pastries and soup-and-salad lunches, try the **Castle Café** (no phone) inside Kilkenny Castle.

WORTH SEEING In summer, both the tourist office and **Tynan Walking Tours** (tel. 056/61348) organize guided walks of Kilkenny (£4 per person). If you'd rather tour alone, pick up Joseph O'Carroll's *Historic Kilkenny* (£2), available from the tourist office.

Kilkenny Castle. The castle has served (since 1391) as the seat of the earls and dukes of Ormond, one of the more powerful clans in Irish history. Sadly, only one room is currently open for viewing: the Long Room, a refined hall with a nicely carved ceiling. *The Parade, opposite tourist office, tel. 056/21450. Admission: £1, 40p students.*

Rothe House. This Tudor-era home was built in 1594 by merchant and beer brewer John Rothe; until renovations are completed, it serves as the County Kilkenny museum with a collection of Bronze Age artifacts, smithy tools, and 16- and 17th-century coins. *Parliament St., tel. 056/22893. Admission: £1.50. Open Apr.–Oct., Mon.–Sat. 10:30–5, Sun. 3–5; Nov.–Mar., weekends 3–5.*

St. Canice's Cathedral. Kilkenny's most famous cathedral is also the second-tallest (212 feet) in Ireland. St. Canice's was founded in 1197 and later used to store volumes of the Irish Annals and other one-of-a-kind manuscripts. The cathedral's interior has been blandly restored, and the complex's biggest attraction is the adjacent 102-foot-tall Round Tower (closed), built in 847 by King O'Carroll of Ossory. *Coach Rd., at northern foot of Parliament St., no phone.*

AFTER DARK If you're looking for drunken conversation, browse the pubs along John, High, and Parliament streets. If historical pubs turn you on, try the beautifully worn, Victorian-era **Marble City Bar** (High St., tel. 056/21984) or **Kyteler's Inn** (Kieran St., tel. 056/21064), the oldest in town. For traditional music in summer, try **Caisleán Ui Cuain** (High St., opposite Kilkenny Castle, tel. 056/51702).

Rosslare Harbour

If you're traveling to Ireland from the Continent, chances are you'll end up on a boat bound for Rosslare Harbour. Ireland's three principal ferry companies—Sealink, B&I Line, and Irish Ferries—have small information kiosks in the terminal building, adjacent to the full-service **tourist office** (tel. 053/33622). You can purchase tickets at the terminal, but in summer reserve space in advance (contact the companies' Cork or Dublin offices) to avoid sellouts and cancellations. Reservations are also a must if you're traveling by car or motorcycle because on-board parking space is at a premium. All ferries will transport your bicycle for free.

From Rosslare, **B&I Line** (tel. 053/33311 or 01/606–666 for 24-hr information) makes the 4½-hour crossing to Pembroke, Wales, at 8:30 AM and 8:30 PM; the return voyage leaves Wales at 2:45 AM and 2:15 PM. Rates for pedestrian passengers are £18–£25. **Sealink** (tel. 053/33115 or 01/280–8844) sails at 9 AM and 9:40 PM to Fishguard, Wales, with returns at 3:15 AM and 3 PM. Pedestrian passengers pay £18–£24. **Irish Ferries** (tel. 053/33158 or 01/661–0511) make the 20-hour crossing to Cherbourg and Le Havre, France, once daily and charge pedestrian passengers £65–£112. Bring your own food and potent potables if your ferry departs after 11 PM, when the terminal's shops close.

BASICS From Rosslare's **train station** (tel. 053/33114), adjacent to the ferry terminal, there are frequent trains to Dublin's Connolly Station (£11 one-way). For all other destinations, change at Rosslare Strand. Bus Eireann's **bus depot** adjoins the rail station. Destinations from Rosslare include Dublin (£8 one-way) and Cork (£12 one-way).

Rosslare is one of the dullest places in Ireland, so spend as little time here as possible. If you're stuck, there's an 82-bed An Oige **youth hostel** (Goulding St., tel. 053/33399; beds £5–£6.50) directly opposite the ferry terminal, at the top of the hillside stairway.

Cashel

Cashel owes its fame to the surrounding **Rock of Cashel,** a ragged outcrop of limestone that, over the centuries, has been endowed with churches, towers, and carved crosses by successive troops of religious orders. To generations of devout peasants, the rock must have inspired awe, but today's tourist coaches give it a theme-park feel. Still, the Rock of Cashel does give a comprehensive, breathtaking overview of Irish religious architecture: Set atop the limestone hill are a completely restored Romanesque church, a mostly complete round tower, a buttressed medieval cathedral, the 15th-century Hall of Vicars, and the remnants of two priories. *Admission free. Open Apr.–mid-Sept., daily 9–6; mid-Sept.–Mar., Mon.–Sat. 10–5, Sun. noon–5.*

Most tourist buses arrive after noon, so come as early as possible. Guided tours (£2) are organized every hour during summer by the **tourist office** (Town Hall, Main St., tel. 062/61333). Cashel's unstaffed **bus stop** is located outside O'Reilly's shop, on Main Street. From Cashel, Bus Eireann's serves Dublin (£9 one-way), Cork (£4.40 one-way), and Cahir (£1.80 one-way). The closest train station is in Cahir, with trains to Tralee, Killarney, Waterford, and Rosslare Harbour.

WHERE TO SLEEP The drab **Abbey House** (1 Dominic St., tel. 062/61104) is open year-round and has the cheapest rooms in town (£13 per person). A better bet is the IHO **Lisakyle Hostel** (tel. 052/41963; beds £5–£6.50, tent space £3), 18 km south in the village of Cahir. The hostel is actually 1½ km outside Cahir, but free transportation is provided from its office in Cahir, housed in M. Condon's Shop (Church St.) across from the post office.

Southwest Ireland

The southwest, which encompasses all of County Kerry and much of County Cork, is by far the most touristed part of Ireland. Its principal attraction is Killarney, a largish market town that attracts an upscale breed of tourists—mostly retired Americans who happily pay £90 for "real" Irish sweaters. Killarney is still the best base for exploring the adjacent Ring of Kerry, a 180-km coastal loop that encircles the rugged Iveragh Peninsula. Cyclists are the real winners in this part of Ireland: They not only avoid the tourist crunch, but can also get into the remotest stretches of the equally spectacular Dingle Peninsula, where rural pubs and traditional music soften the roughest of roads.

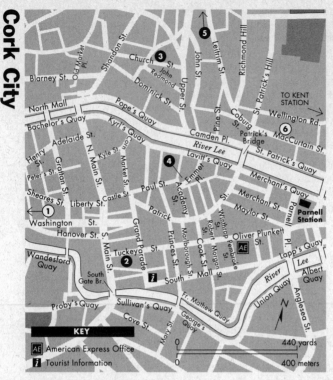

Sights ●
Bishop Lucey
Park, **2**
Crawford Art
Gallery, **4**
Murphy's Brewery, **5**
Shandon Church
and Steeple, **3**

Lodging ○
Campus House, **1**
Isaac's, **6**

KEY

AE American Express Office

i Tourist Information

0 — 440 yards
0 — 400 meters

Cork

Even though Cork is Ireland's second-largest city, Dubliners consider this town of 175,000 small and provincial. For them, a trip to Cork is a trip to the country, a place to come for hurling, Gaelic football, and locally televised plowing contests. Throughout Ireland, Cork is (in)famous for burly farmers and a concoction named Murphy's, a locally brewed stout that locals actually prefer to Guinness.

In the words of one Dubliner, Corkonians speak with a blunt, guttural lilt that "reeks of the farm and field."

Cork has few "don't miss" attractions, but that's not the point. It has a formidable pub scene and some of the country's best traditional music. It has a respected and progressive university—University College Cork (UCC). It has art galleries and offbeat cafés. And, like Galway, it nurtures an active community of artists, musicians, and poets. This is best seen along Cork's South Mall, or along the lanes that fan northward from Patrick Street—areas that mark the historic and modern heart of Cork. Numerous bridges and quays make Cork confusing at first, but they also add character to this ancient port town.

BASICS

➤ **VISITOR INFORMATION** • Brittany Ferries has a small information desk next door to the **Bord Fáilte** tourist office. *42 Grand Parade, 1 block from Washington St., tel. 021/273–251. Open July–Aug., daily 9–7; shorter hrs off-season.*

The student-run **USIT,** with two Cork locations, has the best rail, bus, and plane prices in town. *10–11 Market Parade, tel. 021/270–900. UCC Travel, Boole Library, tel. 021/273–901.*

➤ **AMERICAN EXPRESS** • Heffernan's Travel, Pembroke St., tel. 021/271–081. Opposite General Post Office.

➤ **MAIL** • The **General Post Office** (tel. 021/272–000) is on the corner of Oliver Plunkett and Pembroke streets.

COMING AND GOING Cork's **Kent Station** (Lower Glanmire Rd., tel. 021/506–766) is on the north side of the River Lee, 1 km east of the city center. To reach the bus terminal, turn left out of Kent Station and walk west on Lower Glanmire Road, keeping the river on your left. At Mac Curtain Street, turn left and cross the river. Rail destinations from here include Dublin (3 hrs, £31.50, £20 on Tues. and Wed. mornings), Killarney (1¼ hrs, £12.50), and Limerick (2 hrs, £12.50). All local and Bus Eireann buses depart from **Parnell Station** (Parnell Pl., tel. 021/508–188 or 021/506–066), on the south side of the River Lee. Principal destinations include Belfast (10 hrs, £17), Dublin (4½ hrs, £12), and Galway (4 hrs, £13).

Cork's ferry port is in **Ringaskiddy** (tel. 021/378–401), a desolate industrial complex 16 km south. Frequent buses shuttle passengers from the bus station to the ferry port (45 min, £3). **Brittany Ferries** (42 Grand Parade, tel. 021/277–801) sail twice weekly for Roscoff, France (£49–£70 one-way). **Swansea-Cork Ferries** (55 Grand Parade, tel. 021/271–166) sails daily in summer to Swansea, Wales (£18–£26). **Irish Ferries** (Bridge St., tel. 021/504–333) sails haphazardly to Le Havre, France (£66–£112). Always ask for student discounts.

WHERE TO SLEEP Cork is never short of cheap beds, but reservations are imperative during the insanely crowded October Jazz Festival. Cork's B&Bs are mainly clustered around the train station on Lower Glanmire Road and near the UCC campus on Western Road. To reach Western Road, take Bus 8 from Parnell Station past Cork University; a barrage of B&Bs will confront you on all sides. Turn right from the train station for the small but comfortable **Kent House** (47 Lower Granmire Rd., tel. 021/504–260; £13 per person), **Oakland House** (51 Lower Granmire Rd., tel. 021/500–578; £12.50 per person), and **Tara House** (52 Lower Granmire Rd., tel. 021/500–294; £15 per person).

➤ **HOSTELS** • Cork has six reasonably good hostels. If those below are filled, try **Cork City Independent Hostel** (100 Lower Granmire Rd., tel. 021/509–089; singles and dorm beds £5), opposite the train station; the impersonal **HI Cork International Youth Hostel** (1–2 Redclyffe, Western Rd., tel. 021/543–289; beds £4.50–£5.90, £1.25 extra for nonmembers); the large, upscale **Kinlay House/USIT** (Bob Walk, Shandon, tel. 021/508–966; singles £15, doubles £21, dorm beds £7); or the relaxed **Sheila's Hostel** (Belgrave Pl., Wellington Rd., tel. 021/505–562; singles £9, doubles £15, dorm beds £5.50).

Campus House. Smallest and most relaxed hostel in town, popular with cyclists and friendly vagabonds. No curfew, no lockout. Twenty-minute walk from city center. Beds £5.50. *3 Woodland View, Western Rd., tel. 021/343–531. Bus 8 from Parnell Station to Cork University (on Western Rd.). Sheets 50p.*

Isaac's. Cork's finest hostel, in a stately four-story Georgian town house. All rooms with polished oak floors, bay windows, and firm beds. Singles £18.50, doubles £13.50 per person, dorm beds £5.50. *48 Mac Curtain St., tel. 021/500–011. From train station, turn left and continue straight for ½ km.*

➤ **CAMPGROUND** • **Cork Camping Park.** Sites 2½ km southwest of UCC are nothing special, but cost only £4 plus 75p per person. *Togher Rd., tel. 021/961–866. Bus 14 from Parnell Station. Closed Oct.–mid-Apr., except during Oct. Jazz Festival.*

FOOD For breakfast and afternoon snacks, snag an outdoor table at the **Gingerbread House** (French Church St., off Oliver Plunkett St., tel. 021/276–411), famous for its cappuccinos and buttery croissants. Cork's slackers and long-haired hippies tend to gather at **The Other Place** (7–8 Augustine St., off Grand Parade, tel. 021/317–660), where they sip coffee and fill up on cheap (£1–£2) vegetarian salads and soups. **Paddy Giribaldis** (8 Carey's La., tel. 021/277–915) is a dark-oak-and-classical-music sort of place—perfect for romantic meals and meaningful post-dinner chat. Try the thick cheeseburgers (£3.75) and homemade pizzas (£3.95).

New Maharajah. The best and cheapest Indian food in Cork. Set-lunch menu (appetizer, tandoori dish, dessert) is a steal at £5.50. Dinner prices slightly higher. *19 Cook St., off Patrick St., tel. 021/276–576. Open Mon.–Sat. 5–10.*

Quay Co-op. Part whole-food store, part gritty café, and one of Cork's hippest hangouts. Breakfast on coffee and the newspaper, lunch on sandwiches and salads with a veggie twist. *24 Sullivan's Quay, 1 block south and across river from tourist office, tel. 021/967–660. Open Mon. and Tues. 10–6, Wed.–Sat. 10–10:30.*

Triskel Arts Café. Vaguely vegetarian entrées, soups, and sandwiches. Inside Triskel Arts Center. *Tobin St., beside Christchurch, tel. 021/965–011. Open weekdays 10:30–5:30, Sat. 11–5.*

WORTH SEEING **Bishop Lucey Park,** one block north of the tourist office, was opened in 1985 to celebrate the 800th anniversary of the town's charter. Next to the site is the 16th-century **Christchurch,** where Edmund Spenser married the Irish Elizabeth Boyle while writing the *Fairie Queene. Grand Parade. Admission free.*

Crawford Art Gallery. This is Ireland's most active and respected provincial art gallery, with regular exhibitions of modern Irish and foreign works. *Emmet Pl., tel. 021/273–377. Admission free. Open Mon.–Sat. 10–5.*

Murphy's Brewery. Murphy's is a true Cork drink—a rich, thick, semisweet stout that's scorned by nearly everyone born without a County Cork accent. Murphy's began brewing here in 1856, but the company's purchase by Heineken in 1975 has led diehards to bemoan that the ol' familiar "hasn't been the same since." Taste for yourself in the Brewery Tap Pub across the road or on the short tour (£3). *Lady's Well, Leitrim St., tel. 021/503–371.*

Shandon Church and Steeple. This Cork landmark is on the north side of town atop a steep hill. The steeple's motley red sandstone and bleached limestone faces have become Cork's official city colors—red and white. After a treacherous climb to the top of the 170-foot-tall tower, ring Shandon's famous bells for a small fee. *Church St., off Shandon St., no phone. Admission: £1.50. Open May–Oct., Mon.–Sat. 9:30–5; Nov.–Apr., Mon.–Sat. 10–4.*

AFTER DARK One of the most popular stops in Cork is **Union Quay,** overlooking the River Lee on the south side of town opposite the South Mall. Here three excellent pubs stand side by side: **An Phoenix** (tel. 021/964–275), famed for its nightly traditional music sessions; **The Lobby** (tel. 021/311–113), a rock-and-roll pub packed with Yuppies and middle-aged slackers; and **Donkey Ears** (tel. 021/967–241), home to drunk bikers and youthful fashion slaves. **Turner's** (Parliament St., tel. 021/276–933) has drink specials daily 4–7 and free music nightly. Both of the main gay pubs in town—**Sir Henry's** (S. Main St.) and **Loafers** (Douglas St.)—are papered with gay and lesbian community information and hot-line numbers.

NEAR CORK

BLARNEY CASTLE Eight km northwest of Cork City, Blarney Castle is one of Ireland's most famous historical sites; in other words, it's plagued by herds of tourists and nearly impossible to enjoy. That said, it's hard to deny the allure of the **Blarney Stone,** set in a wall below the castle's battlements. Tradition holds that all who kiss the Blarney Stone will gain the gift of eloquence and a crafty tongue. To receive this blessing, you lean backward from the second-story parapet and stick your head through a small opening, grasping an iron rail for support. Despite the difficulty, there's generally a long line of overweight retirees waiting to scale the skeletal remains of the castle. From Cork's bus station, Bus Eireann offers 15 daily coaches (£1.70) to Blarney Square. You can also walk (1½ hrs) from Cork by following the N8 highway past the train station. *Tel. 021/385–252. Admission: £3.50, £2 students. Open summer, daily 9–6:30; winter, daily 9–sundown.*

Killarney

A constant flow of foreigners pass through Killarney, spending a few days eating in fancy restaurants, buying kitsch in crafts shops, and taking coach tours on the Ring of Kerry (*see below*). If you, too, are planning to explore the Ring by thumb, bicycle, or tourist coach, you will inevitably find yourself stranded in Killarney for at least one night. But don't despair. Hidden behind the endless rows of double-parked luxury coaches is a handful of reasonably priced crafts stores, a couple of cheapish coffee shops, and a few pubs that have somehow avoided the blight of tourism.

The **Killarney National Park** (tel. 064/31665), a pristine 26,000-acre wood whose principal entrance is 1½ km east of town, is yet another reason to visit. Much of the park straddles **Lough Leane,** a windswept lake that's littered with rocky islets. It would take days and a good map to explore the park fully, but you can easily walk the lakeshore by following any of the marked trails that converge at the park's entrance.

BASICS Besides booking B&B rooms for £1, the **tourist office** (New Town Hall, south end Main St., tel. 064/31633) arranges tours of the Ring of Kerry with the dozens of coach companies that have offices across the street.

COMING AND GOING The **train station** (tel. 064/31067) is right next to the **bus station** (tel. 064/34777); turn left from either and follow East Avenue Road as it curves past the tourist office. Four trains go daily to Dublin (£20) and Tralee (£5); change in Mallow to reach Cork (£13). Expressway bus destinations from Killarney include Cork (£8), Dublin (£14), and Galway (£13).

WHERE TO SLEEP City-center hostels fill up quickly in summer, so reserve in advance. Muckross Road has the largest selection of B&Bs; try **Innisfallen House** (Muckross Rd., tel. 064/34193; £15 per person), **Killarney House** (Muckross Rd., tel. 064/33122; £15–£18 per person), or **The Arch House** (E. Avenue Rd., 300 ft from train station, tel. 064/32184; £13 per person and up).

➤ **HOSTELS • An Súgán** (Lewis Rd., tel. 064/33104; beds £6) is the nicest hostel in town, with 18 beds spread throughout a two-story, stone cottage. Turn right from the train station, left on Park Road, then right on Lewis Road. **Four Winds** (43 New St., tel. 064/33094; beds £6) is large and generally crowded, but is bang in the middle of town and has a fire-warmed common room. Turn left from the train station and follow East Avenue Road as it curves past the tourist office, then turn left on New Street. The excellent **Peacock Hostel** (tel. 064/33557; beds £5) is in the mountains 10 km outside town—pretty but a bit isolated. Free shuttle service is provided by the peacock-adorned Land Rover that meets most arriving trains and buses.

FOOD The **Mayflower Chinese Restaurant** (Church La., College Sq., tel. 064/32212) serves sizzling hot chow meins (£4) and curries (£3–£5), along with generous portions of fried rice (£1.50). At the other end of town, **Grunts** (New St., off E. Avenue Rd., tel. 064/31890) has good soups and sandwiches for less than £2.50; also try the lasagna (£4). Next door, the **Country Kitchen** (New St., tel. 064/33778) is famed for its sausage-egg-rasher-chips-bean-and-pudding breakfasts (£2.95) and for its home-baked pies (£1.20).

AFTER DARK Most of Killarney's pubs are unabashedly devoted to the tourist trade, excluding **Taylor's** (New St., tel. 064/32385), which is a sitting room–size pub popular with drunks and unemployable locals. **O'Connor's** (High St., tel. 064/31345) is a worn 1960s pub that mixes large crowds of tourists with frequent traditional music. In summer, a sure bet for nightly traditional music is the **Fáilte Bar** (College St., tel. 064/33404).

Ring of Kerry

The Ring of Kerry is one of Ireland's most famous—and heavily visited—attractions. The circular, 180-km Ring can be accessed at any number of places, although Killarney (*see above*) is the most practical starting point. On sunny days, the two-lane highway that handles the bulk of traffic is choked with rental cars, tourist coaches, and cyclists all engaged in the vain struggle to find the real, rural Ireland. But there are parts of the Ring that are still rural and unexplored, especially the sparsely developed Ballaghisheen Pass and the stretch of coast between Valentia Island and Bolus Head.

As long as you don't mind sharing the road, you will encounter some incredibly stunning coastal and mountain views. To do the Ring justice, you'll need a minimum of two days—and a sturdy bicycle. Allow some time for detours on winding back roads, or to do the 36-km **Skellig Loop,** a scenic circuit ignored by most luxury coaches. Most people prefer to tackle the Ring in a counterclockwise direction, starting from Killarney, then pausing for a night in Glenbeigh, Caherciveen (also spelled Cahersiveen), Valentia Island, Ballinskelligs, Waterville, or Kenmare.

GETTING AROUND Hostels spaced every 20 km or so and the mostly flat terrain mean that even wimps can tackle the Ring by bike. If you're short on time, one of the best and cheapest ways to see the Ring is on Bus Eireann's **Ring of Kerry Service** (tel. 064/34777), which departs Killarney twice daily in summer, stopping at Killorglin, Glenbeigh, Caherciveen, and Waterville before returning to Killarney. A day trip around the loop costs £9, but you can't get off the bus; for £12, you can stop at any town along the way, provided you complete the circuit within three days. Other options are private coach tours arranged by a dozen or so private companies in Killarney—the going rate is about £15 for a full-day tour. Ask the tourist office to recommend a private carrier.

WHERE TO SLEEP

➤ **GLENBEIGH** • The **Hillside House Hostel** (Killorglin Rd., tel. 066/68228; beds £4) is a quiet two-story farmhouse with views of the surrounding mountains.

➤ **CAHERCIVEEN** • The **HI Sive Hostel** (15 East End, tel. 066/72717; beds £5.50, tent sites £3), three blocks from Caherciveen's small square, arranges day trips to the Skellig Islands.

➤ **VALENTIA ISLAND** • The **HI Ring Lyne Hostel** (Chapeltown, tel. 066/76103; beds £5, tent sites £3) is an immensely comfortable hostel within a stone's throw of Chapeltown's pubs and chippers. More intimate is the **Royal Pier Hostel** (Knightstown, tel. 066/76144; singles £6.50, dorm beds £5, tent sites £3), housed in a brooding manor house.

➤ **WATERVILLE** • Peter's Place (tel. 066/74608; beds £5, tent sites £2.50), 900 feet west of town, is the quieter of the two HI hostels here. The **HI Waterville Leisure House** (tel. 066/74400; beds £5–£6) is generally packed with families and school groups. The best B&B is **Clifford's** (Main St., tel. 066/74283; £13/person; closed Nov.–Feb.).

➤ **KENMARE** • Kenmare's **HI Fáilte Hostel** (Henry St., tel. 064/41083; singles £7.50, dorm beds £5.50) is in a beautifully restored town house with a pleasant courtyard. If it's full, try the centrally located **Kenmare Private Hostel** (Main St., tel. 064/41260; beds £5.50). Kenmare's cheapest B&B is **Ardmore House** (Killarney Rd., tel. 064/41406; £13.50/person; closed Dec.–Feb.).

The Dingle Peninsula

The Dingle Peninsula stretches for 50 km between Tralee in the east and Slea Head in the west. Its small size makes it one of Ireland's most accessible summer retreats, especially for cyclists and hitchhikers who don't have time to cover the larger Mizen, Beara, or Ring of Kerry circuits. Despite its size, the Dingle Peninsula is diverse and brazenly scenic, encompassing the rugged Slieve Mish Mountains in the east, the Brandon Mountains in the west, and smooth, rolling hills on either side.

Dingle Town is a small fishing village that makes an excellent base for exploring the surrounding peninsula. Although many expect Dingle to be undeveloped, it's actually a haven for pricey seafood restaurants and a handful of luxury hotels. Still, it has the peninsula's only **tourist office** (Main St., tel. 066/51188) and **Moriarty Bikes** (Main St., tel. 066/51316), which rents bikes by the week (£20).

From Dingle, an excellent walk or cycle is to **Ventry,** a small outcrop of pubs and newsagents 3 km west. The town's most famous landmark is undoubtedly **Paidí O Seá's** pub (tel. 066/5546). If you keep to the R559 coast road from Ventry, you'll soon end up on the 35-km **Slea Head Loop,** an incredible circuit that skirts the foot of Mt. Eagle (1,692 feet) and eventually curves north past Dunmore Head and Dunquin. This road is treacherous for cyclists, but the views of the coast and Blasket Islands are unforgettable. **Dunquin** itself is nothing more than a collection of sheep fields and isolated, peat-smoke-spouting cottages. Except for the hostel, the only reasons to stop is for lunch at **Kruger's Pub** (tel. 066/56127) or to catch the **Blasket Island Ferry** (Dunquin Pier, tel. 066/59876). After the 20-minute ferry ride (£6), spend the day exploring Blasket Island, where you'll find the ruins of a few 15th- and 16th-century monasteries and dozens of good hiking trails. Depending on the weather, the ferry will collect you two–three hours later.

COMING AND GOING   The town of Tralee makes a good springboard from which to explore the Dingle Peninsula. Although Irish Rail does not serve the Dingle Peninsula (the last train tracks were dismantled in the 1960s), it does have daily service to Tralee from Killarney (£6), Cork (£16), and Dublin (£18). From Tralee, Bus Eireann offers year-round Expressway service to Dingle (£5.70, £7.90 round-trip); buses drop passengers in the center of town. During summer, there's also local bus service to Dingle and Dunquin (£5.20, £8 round-trip).

WHERE TO SLEEP   Dingle has the largest selection of cheap accommodations, including three hostels. The two best, the **Rainbow** (The Wood, no phone; beds £5, tent sites £3) and the **Westlodge** (The Wood, no phone; beds £4.30, tent sites £2), are in the countryside west of Dingle. For either, walk west from town along the waterfront and follow the signs. For a more central location, try **Dyke Gate House** (Dyke Gate St., tel. 066/51549; £13/person), a snug five-room B&B in the heart of town.

Dunquin's **HI hostel** (Bally Ferriter, tel. 066/56145; beds £4.50–£5.90) has a superb location, overlooking the coast and Blasket Islands, but inside it's pretty spartan. If you're traveling the Slea Head Loop, 7 km south of Dunquin, it's hard to miss the brightly painted and teddy-bear-themed **Slea Head House** (tel. 066/56234; £12/person), a luxurious B&B perched on the edge of a cliff with fantastic views of the ocean.

Western Ireland

The west embodies all the stereotypes generally associated with Ireland— thatched cottages, sheep, rugged seascapes, misty bogland, and fire-lit country pubs, all processed through a filter of Guinness and traditional music. Fortunately, these characterizations hold more truth than many cynics might expect, which helps to explain why the west is the second-most touristed part of the country. But even with the heavy influx of summertime travelers, a few areas—notably the Burren, Doolin, and the Aran Islands—balance accessibility with an authentic take on rural Ireland.

Doolin and the Cliffs of Moher

Although this small village boasts a larger population of sheep than people, Doolin is *the* place for traditional music. Its three pubs—O'Connor's, McGanns, and McDermotts—host top-rate music sessions nightly throughout the year. Happily, the three pubs also habitually thwart the puritanical 11:30 PM closing time by bolting the doors and drawing the curtains. Best of all, with just one long, uncluttered road, getting lost in Doolin is more of an accomplishment than a concern.

Doolin's other main draw is its proximity to both the Aran Islands (*see below*), visible off the coast, and the Cliffs of Moher. **Doolin Ferries** (Doolin Pier, tel. 065/74455 or 065/74189) make the 30-minute trip to the islands of Inisheer and Inishmore (£18 round-trip). For a stunning ocean view of the Cliffs of Moher, the trawler *Jean Marie* (Doolin Pier, tel. 065/74390) totes passengers below the cliffs for £7.50, £5 for students. Still, the best way to see the Cliffs of Moher is by hiking the 4-km-long **Burren Way** from Doolin. This rugged dirt trail (walk past the Doolin Hostel over the riverbed and continue straight) keeps entirely to the coast, giving great views of the sea and clusters of ancient thatched cottages. At some points, the only thing separating you from the ocean, 700 feet below, is a patch of slippery heather that may or may not offer a last-chance handhold. For other walks and a good rundown of the area's history, pick up Martin Breen's *Doolin Guide & Map* (£1.50) in shops and at the tourist desk.

BASICS You can exchange money or buy maps at the **tourist desk** in Doolin Hostel, which also serves as the local Raleigh Rent-A-Bike outlet and Bus Eireann depot. Express buses run once a day Thursday–Sunday between Doolin and Dublin. Other destinations include Ennis, Lisdoonvarna, and Galway (June 8–Sept. 26 only). Buses leave for the Cliffs of Moher (80p) daily at 8:30 AM, with an additional bus at 5 PM in the summer.

WHERE TO SLEEP Of Doolin's three hostels, the **Aille River** (on the road bet. Fisherstreet and Roadford, tel. 065/74260; beds £4.50; closed Jan.–mid-Mar.) is the most comfortable. Across the road, the **Rainbow Hostel** (tel. 065/74415; beds £5) has slightly cramped and damp bedrooms, but there's a cozy common room and farmyard facilities for camping (£3 per person). At the other end of town, the bright white **Doolin Hostel** (tel. 065/74006; beds £6) is large and rather characterless.

Galway

Ireland's third-largest city is a progressive student town with a flair for the hip and offbeat. The small city center has the atmosphere of a bustling market town, especially in the chaos of streets that lead from the River Corrib to Eyre Square, the city's main social hub. Galway is also western Ireland's most prominent music and arts center. Because of its close proximity to the surrounding *Gaeltacht* (communities where Irish is still commonly spoken), Galway's music scene is happily and predominantly traditional. Lacking large numbers of historic sites, Galway seems to cherish its traditional music pubs with a vengeance, recognizing their importance to the town's cultural (and tourist) appeal. Civic pride also stems from the city's famed academic institution, the University College Galway (UCG), a center of Irish language and Celtic studies. The **Galway Arts Festival** (tel. 091/67277), held the last week in July, showcases Irish and international drama in a dozen city center venues. Book a bed in advance and get to the pub early if you want a seat.

BASICS The **tourist office** (Victoria Pl., 1 block east of Eyre Sq., tel. 091/63081; open Mon.–Sat. 9–6) arranges city tours and can book your ferry passage to the Aran Islands. Student-run **USIT** (New Science Bldg., UCG, tel. 091/24601; open weekdays 10–5) works miracles in finding cheap transport tickets. The local **AmEx** travel desk is inside the John Ryan Travel Agency (1 Williamsgate St., just off Eyre Sq., tel. 091/61587).

The Burren

The Burren, a limestone escarpment that hugs the coast from Black Head in the north to the Cliffs of Moher in the south, ranks as one of Ireland's fiercest landscapes. No matter which direction you approach from, rolling green hills give way to jagged shelves of rough and porous rock. Even on a sunny day, the Burren seems stuck in mourning, silent except for the pound of the surf and the cry of a scavenging gull. Surveying the region for Oliver Cromwell in 1650, General J. Ludlow wrote that the Burren "is a country where there is not water enough to drown a man, wood enough to hang one, nor earth enough to bury him." If you're cycling in the area, don't miss the IHO Bridge Hostel (Fanore, tel. 065/76134; beds £5), on the coast road south of Galway.

COMING AND GOING **Ceannt Station** (tel. 091/62000), on the corner of Eyre Square, doubles as the rail and bus depot. Galway is served four times a day by train from Dublin (£14, £8.50 students), but for any other destination you'll have to change in Athlone. Bus Eireann Expressway buses make daily hauls to Dublin (£11), Donegal (£12), Sligo (£9), and Cork (£13). To reach the hostels and pubs from the station, turn left at Eyre Square, right at the corner of Victoria Place, and left at the corner onto Williamsgate Street.

WHERE TO SLEEP Although Galway has eight hostels, reservations are recommended in July and August. What **Corrib Villa** (4 Waterside, tel. 091/62892; beds £5.90) lacks in modernity, it makes up for in character. Take Williamsgate Street from Eyre Square, turn right on Eglinton Street, and follow it to the end. **Woodquay Hostel** (Woodquay, tel. 091/62618; beds £5.90, £6.90 June–Sept.), Galway's newest and most comfortable hostel, is a 10-minute walk from Eyre Square. From the fountain side of the square, walk down Rosemary Avenue, turn left on Eyre Street, and right on Woodquay. Farther out is the luxurious **Stella Maris Holiday Hostel** (151 Upper Salthill Rd., tel. 091/21950 or 091/26974; doubles £6.50 per person, dorm beds £5.50). It overlooks the ocean in Salthill, a small resort 3 km west of Eyre Square (take Bus 1 to Salthill).

FOOD Galway has an abundance of cheap restaurants and cafés, most of which are located south of Eyre Square between Abbeygate Street and the River Corrib. If you want to browse, take a walk down Shop and Guard streets. **Fat Freddy's** (Quay St., tel. 091/67279; open daily 10–10) does good pizzas and pastas in the £4–£6 range and is about the only cheapish sit-down place that's open on Sundays. Unpretentious **Food for Thought** (Lower Abbeygate St., no phone) serves homemade soups, sandwiches, and veggie casseroles for less than £2, as well as one of the punchiest cups of coffee in Ireland. Come to **The Town House** (1 Market St., off Abbeygate St., tel. 091/66515) for candlelit, upscale dining in a beautifully decorated, 16th-century villa. Lunch is £4–£8, dinner £5–£10. More down to earth is the **Hungry Grass** (15 Cross St., off High St., tel. 091/63717), where Irish stew and sandwiches cost less than £5.

WORTH SEEING Your first glimpse of Galway is likely to be **Eyre Square,** opposite the bus and train station. Formerly a green where livestock and produce were sold, it's not much to look at today (although the park in its center is a fine place for an afternoon snooze). From Eyre Square's southwest corner, Galway's main shopping artery (called Williamsgate, Williams Street, Shop Street, High Street, and Quay Street at different points) leads to the River Corrib. Walk toward the river on this multinamed artery, turn right on Abbeygate and left on Market Street to reach **Nora Barnacle House** (Bowling Green, Market St., no phone; admission £1), birthplace of James Joyce's wife. Joyce and Nora Barnacle first met in Dublin on June 16, 1904, a date known to most Joyce fans as Bloomsday. Inside the house is a mediocre collection of photographs and letters and a small gift shop.

AFTER DARK There are dozens of good pubs scattered throughout Galway's eminently crawlable city center. For traditional music, **Taaffes** (19 Shop St., tel. 091/64066) and the **King's Head** (15 High St., tel. 091/66630) are musts, though a recent deluge of green-sweater-wearing folks threatens the authenticity of their summer sessions. During the summer season, two underpublicized old-style music pubs are **An Púcán** (11 Forster St., tel. 091/61528) and the **Crane Bar** (2 Sea Rd., tel. 091/67419). The **Lisheen Bar** (Bridge St., tel. 091/64361) and **Sally Long's** (33 Upper Abbeygate St., tel. 091/65756) are dependably good for jazz and folk.

The Druid Theater Company (tel. 091/68660) has built up an international reputation with their revivals of Anglo-Irish classics and a slew of Irish-language plays. More touristy, but no less entertaining, the Irish-language theater **An Taibhdhearc** (tel. 091/62024) is famous for its bilingual productions of lesser-known Irish plays. Inquire at the tourist office for performance info.

The Aran Islands

No one knows for certain when the Aran Islands—Inishmore, Inishmaan, and Inisheer—were first inhabited, but judging from their Bronze and Iron Age forts, 3000 BC is a safe guess. Why nomads would be attracted to these barren islets remains a greater mystery, not the least because fresh water and farmable land were (and still are) scarce commodities. During this century there has been a renewed interest in the islands' monastic settlements, and in the locals' traditional lifestyle—blame playwright J. M. Synge and his book *The Aran Islands* (1907) for that. Within the past decade or so, the islands have also become popular with day-trippers from Galway and Doolin. The reality, however, is that in order to let the harsh beauty of the islands sink in, you must spend the night on one.

COMING AND GOING **Aran Ferries** (Eyre Sq. tourist office, Galway, tel. 091/68903) and **Island Ferries** (Victoria Pl., directly opposite tourist office, tel. 091/61767) offer nearly identical service (£15–£18) to Inishmore from both Galway (70-min crossing) and Rossaveal (1-hr coach ride, 20-min crossing). To reach Inisheer, bypassing Inishmore, you'll have to leave from Doolin (*see* Doolin and the Cliffs of Moher, *above*).

INISHMORE

Inishmore is both the largest and the most popular Aran Island. Most people only visit for the day, content to see the island from the window of a minibus before catching the last ferry back to Galway. Once these folks clear out, Inishmore's fierce, brooding beauty is disturbed only by the noise of sheep and the incessant rush of the wind. Even if you only have a few hours to explore Inishmore, spend £5 on a rental bike (available next to the ferry dock) and head straight for **Dún Aengus**, a 4,000-year-old stone fort perched on the edge of a 300-foot cliff, reached after a 20-minute walk up a stone-strewn hill. Repeat: Do not leave without visiting Dún Aengus; it's on the far side of the island, 6 km from the port (follow the weathered signs). At the southern end of the island, **Black Fort** (*Dubh Cathair*) is Inishmore's other archaeological treasure, built around 1000 BC into a cleft of razor-sharp rocks.

Around sunset locals peddle their squeaky bikes down the long road to **Kilronan,** the island's port and largest village. A few pubs grace this block-long harborfront settlement, along with a chipper, grocery store, and **tourist office** (tel. 099/61263; open late-May–mid-Sept., Mon.–Sun. 10–1 and 2–6). Half a mile west of Kilronan's ferry port, the first-rate **Mainistir House** (tel. 099/61169; beds £5.50, £7 in summer) is built onto a rocky plateau overlooking Galway Bay. Minibuses (free) often meet incoming ferries in summer to shuttle backpackers to the hostel. **Clai Bán** (tel. 099/61111; £12/person; closed Oct.–mid-Mar.) is one of the nicest B&Bs on Inishmore, an easy five-minute, well-marked walk from Kilronan's center.

INISHEER

Inisheer may be the smallest island in the Aran chain, but its proximity to Doolin (10 km) means it's often packed with day-trippers—a problem compounded by the fact that the two roads here make it difficult for tourists to blend in. On the plus side, Inisheer's relative prosperity means you'll find a hostel, a cheapish hotel, numerous B&Bs, pubs, and restaurants near the ferry dock. You'll want to check out the ruins of **O'Brien Castle,** set inside a stone ring fort that's clearly visible from the pier. The castle was ruined and abandoned in 1585, but it still casts an impressive shadow over the surrounding fields. A stone's throw to the south is **Teampall Chaomháin** (St. Kevin's Church), one of Inisheer's finest ruins, surrounded by thorny brambles and a stark graveyard.

At sunset, you'll find most people ambling slowly toward the pier-side village and its pubs. One hundred yards from the pier, the hostel **Radharc na Mara** (tel. 099/75024; beds £5.50) doesn't look like much, but its cozy common room has a blazing peat fire whenever the weather is gray. Nearby, the **Ostan Inis Oír** (tel. 099/75020) offers hotel-style accommodations (£15/person) to well-heeled tourists mid-April–September. Gluttons should plan to eat at least one meal at the **Fisherman's Cottage** (tel. 099/75073), which boasts an all-you-can-eat seafood buffet (£8).

Northwest Ireland

Even among the Irish, northwestern Ireland is considered rugged and wildly gorgeous. No matter where you're headed, a common denominator is the landscape—harsh and satisfyingly empty, dotted with tiny villages and quiet rural pubs. It's said that in this part of Ireland sheep outnumber people by roughly 100 to 1. Thankfully, sheep also outnumber tourists by a large margin. While this isn't as true of Sligo or Donegal Town, the region's largest villages, few tourist buses will attempt the jagged 450-km coastline. It's not surprising, then, that the region presents some transportation challenges. Talk to **McGeehan Coaches** (tel. 075/46150) or **Lough Swilly Buses** (tel. 074/22400) about routes ignored by the national bus company.

Sligo

Considering its location, straddling the mouth of Lough Gill, Sligo ought to be a picturesque and thoroughly enjoyable market town. Over the past 20 years, however, Sligo has fallen victim to its own prosperity. Companies from Dublin and the Continent continue to refashion the small city center with bleakly modern shopping malls, and family-run shops have been replaced with fast-food restaurants. In other words, Sligo is little more than a functional stopover on the way to somewhere else, preferably County Donegal and its wonderful coastline. If you've got a few hours to kill, don't miss **Hargadon's** (4-5 O'Connell St., tel. 071/70933), Sligo's most famous pub—a dark place filled with sepia photographs and antique whiskey jugs.

The **tourist office** (Temple St., tel. 071/61201) sells a useful *Walking Tour of Sligo* (£1), which covers the town's architecture and history in meticulous detail. Sligo's **County Museum, Municipal Art Gallery,** and **Yeats Museum** are all housed in the local library (Stephen St., tel. 071/42212; admission free; open Mon.–Sat. 10–12:30 and 2:30–4:30). The art gallery has a small collection of Irish and Anglo-Irish canvases. Inside the Yeats Museum, there's a comprehensive collection of Yeats's writings from 1889 to 1936 and Yeats's 1923 Nobel Prize medal. And, if you haven't had enough of Yeats yet, the **Yeats Memorial Building** (Hyde Bridge and O'Connell St.) houses a Yeats gallery (admission free; open Mon.–Sat. 10–5) and the headquarters of the **Yeats Society** (tel. 071/42693). During the Yeats Summer School in August, the society organizes lectures and theatrical performances. Across the street is a sculpture of the poet, draped in a flowing coat overlaid with poetic excerpts.

COMING AND GOING Trains and buses both stop at **McDiarmada Station** (Lord Edward St., tel. 071/60066), a 10-minute walk from the city center. Almost all trains, even those to nearby Galway or Belfast, go through Dublin, so take the bus unless you're Dublin-bound. Bus Eireann destinations from Sligo include Belfast (4/day), Cork (3/day), Donegal Town (5/day), and Galway (5/day).

WHERE TO SLEEP The only time accommodations can be a problem is during August, when the Yeats Summer School draws poets and Yeats fans from around the world. The **IHO White House** (Markievicz Rd., tel. 071/45160; beds £5), overlooking the river in the heart of the city center, is the best of Sligo's three hostels. From the station walk downhill, turn left, and follow Lord Edward Street until you cross the river; the hostel will be on your left. Opposite the train station is the damp, bland **Yeats Country** hostel (Lord Edward St., tel. 071/60241), where £6 buys a bed but not much else. If you want your own room, try one of the city center B&Bs. The **Central House** (Upper John St., off O'Connell St., tel. 071/62014; £13/person) and **Harbour View House** (Quay St., off Wine St.; £12/person) offer standard private rooms and lovely fried breakfasts.

Donegal Town

Donegal Town is a small outcrop of pubs and shops overlooking the River Eske. The entire village can be walked in 10 minutes, and nearly everything of interest is centered around the **Diamond,** a former marketplace that's now used as a parking lot. The town was founded in AD 1200 by the O'Donnell clan; in 1474, Red Hugh O'Donnell commissioned a castle (now destroyed) and the **Donegal Monastery,** located on the riverbank south of the Diamond. The ivy-covered ruins are impressive considering that the complex was ransacked by the English three times between 1593 and 1607.

Donegal may sound like a pretty dull town, but it's still a popular stop with guided tours and day-trippers from Sligo. If you're just passing through, stay in one of Donegal's hostels and hunker down in **Charlie's Star Bar** (Main St.) or **McGroarty's** (the Diamond, tel. 073/22519), both of which have live traditional music most summer nights. The **tourist office** (Quay St., tel. 073/21148) has the usual selection of maps; it's on the N15/Sligo Road.

COMING AND GOING All Bus Eireann coaches arrive and depart from the Diamond; pick up schedules from the tourist office. Express destinations from Donegal Town include Sligo (£3), Galway (£8), and Dublin (£15). Slower local service buses go to Kilcar for less than £4.

WHERE TO SLEEP Donegal's best youth hostel is a five-minute walk from the Diamond. The **HI Peter Feely's** (Bridge End, tel. 073/22805; beds £5; closed Dec. 24–Jan. 2) attracts a mixed bag of cyclists, families, and backpackers. Mr. Feely will also rent campers a patch of grass for £3.50. If it's booked, take any Bus Eireann bus toward Killybegs for the 5-km bus ride out to the peaceful, beachside **Ball Hill Hostel** (tel. 073/21174; beds £5.50). Back in town, B&Bs are easy to come by. Both the **Riverside House** (tel. 073/21083; £12.50/person) and the **Castle View** (tel. 073/22100; £12.50/person) provide spacious rooms on Waterloo Place, just off Bridge Street near the hostel.

NEAR DONEGAL TOWN

KILCAR AND SLIEVE LEAGUE The village of **Kilcar** would probably be forgotten were it not for the nearby **IHO Derrylahan Hostel** (Carrick Rd., tel. 073/38079; £5/person, £3 tent space). The hostel is 3 km north of Kilcar on the road to Carrick; if you call from either town, one of the staff will come get you. From the hostel, you're within hiking distance of both **Slieve League** (1,917 ft) and the **Bunglass Cliffs,** the highest overhanging sea cliffs in the country. Forget the hyperbole and hype—these two natural wonders are simply the most intense and beautiful places on earth. To access the mountain, hitch or hike from the hostel to Carrick, walk 1 km south on the road to Teelin, then follow the signs for Bunglass. The hike is fairly easy, and the views are nothing short of incredible. From Bunglass, follow the few signs to Slieve League's summit (be extra careful on windy and rainy days). Once you reach the summit, take a well-anchored peep over the edge: 2,000 feet below, the ocean moves in slow motion, soundless. On the way down, head south for Cappagh and finally Teelin (follow the occasional sign), where you can chow and recuperate at the **Rusty Mackerel Pub** (tel. 073/39101). The entire circuit from Carrick to Slieve League to Teelin takes five hours of medium-paced hiking, slightly more when heavy fog calls for vigilance.

ITALY 14

The fact that the Italian peninsula juts into the Mediterranean Sea in the shape of a boot is a nifty geographical coincidence. In character as well as form, Italy seems at first glance like the high-heeled boot that treads loftily upon cobblestone, emphasizing style over substance—or at least style and splendor over efficiency. Italians have been stereotyped as a group of well-dressed pasta aficionados with a taste for fine wine and fine art, but the truth of the Italian nature is far more complex.

Italy in the mid-1990s is asking itself just what sort of a country it is, and, at times, whether it is really a country at all. Its history of cultural achievements stretches back for centuries, but Italy as a nation is young and still unsure of itself—it is, after all, nearly 100 years younger than the United States. When the political unit we now call Italy was patched together, painfully and controversially, in the mid-19th century, the statesman Massimo d'Azeglio remarked: "We have made Italy; now we must make the Italians." Many are beginning to wonder if that process has finally failed—or if it ever got started in the first place. In the end, it may be impossible to unify the disparate regions in this land of geographical extremes that stretches from the chilly mountains of central Europe to a south that resembles North Africa more than Austria or Switzerland.

Some Italians sense a tension between their country's antiquity and its modernity, between its role as the storehouse of a massive chunk of the Western cultural tradition and its position as a modern industrial society. Early in this century, the radical writer Filippo Tommaso Marinetti advocated blowing up the museums and giving Venice a helpful shove on its way down into its lagoon, and the number of tourists streaming through Italy's museums and churches has grown even more unwieldy since then. Much of Italy's current self-questioning has to do with this very difficulty: Should the country accept, or even exploit, its role as cultural theme park to the Western world, or should it resolve clashes between past, present, and future in favor of the future? When a factory's pollution endangers an ancient monument, do you close the factory or bulldoze the monument? How do you bring the information superhighway to a country where it can take six months to get a phone line installed?

Most of the traveling multitudes who flock to Italy each year find little time to ponder such questions in their haste to enjoy the country's social and cultural life. The time-honored reasons for visiting Italy are still as compelling as ever: If the view of Florence from Fiesole, the Ligurian coastline, or two minutes on the Grand Canal fail to move you, you're probably comatose. Italy will envelop and even drown you in its unbelievable artistic heritage; in the elegance of its cars, furniture, and clothing; and in the richness and seemingly infinite variety of its cooking—but what a way to go.

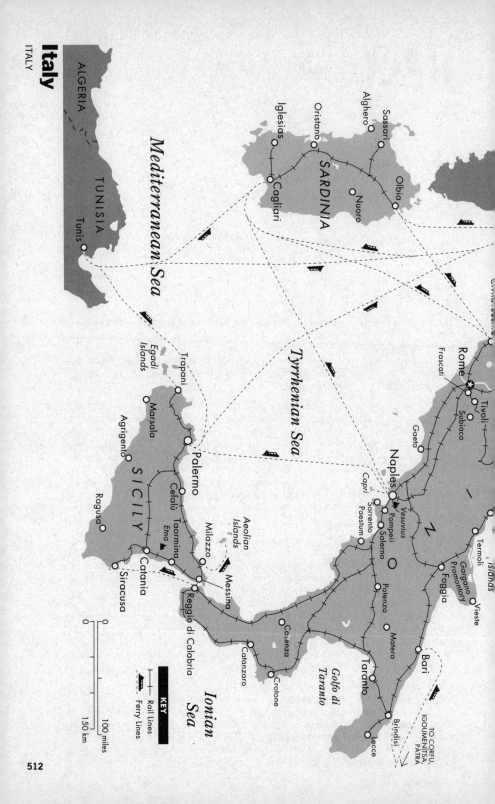

ALGERIA

TUNISIA

Tunis

Mediterranean Sea

Iglesias

Oristano

Alghero

Sassari

SARDINIA

Cagliari

Nuoro

Olbia

Egadi
Islands

Trapani

Marsala

Agrigento

Ragusa

S I C I L Y

Palermo

Cefalù

Etna

Taormina

Catania

Siracusa

Milazzo

Aeolian
Islands

Messina

Reggio di Calabria

Tyrrhenian Sea

Rome

Frascati

Tivoli

Subiaco

Gaeta

Naples

Vesuvius

Capri

Sorrento

Paestum

Pompeii

Salerno

I

N

Z

O

Termoli

Gargano
Promontory

Foggia

Vieste

Potenza

Matera

Bari

Taranto

*Golfo di
Taranto*

Cosenza

Catanzaro

Crotone

Brindisi

Lecce

*Ionian
Sea*

TO CORFU,
IGOUMENITSA,
PATRA

KEY

Rail Lines

Ferry Lines

0   100 miles

0   150 km

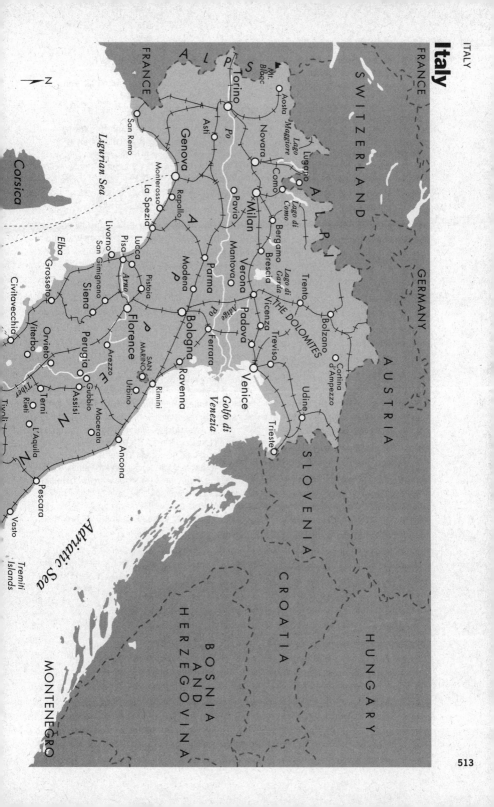

Basics

MONEY $1 = 1540 lire and 1000 lire = 65¢. The best place to change money in Italy is usually the bank (Banca Antoniana is great if you can find one); banks often have the best rates and charge little commission. Most banks in Italy now have ATM machines. Many will work with foreign bank and credit cards, although your PIN code must be four digits or fewer.

➤ **HOW MUCH IT WILL COST** • In general, Italy is cheaper than most of Western and northern Europe but more expensive than Eastern Europe and Spain. Northern Italy is generally more expensive than the south. A train trip from Florence to Rome costs only about L20,000; a bed in a hostel L15,000–L20,000; a budget double hotel room L45,000–L80,000; and an inexpensive three-course meal L20,000–L30,000. If you're careful, you can travel on $40–$50 or so a day, less if you're really frugal.

Venice may be known as the Most Serene Republic, but it's also the Most Expensive City in Italy. Expect to spend at least 20% more here than you would elsewhere in the country.

GETTING AROUND Clean, affordable, and mostly on time, trains are generally the way to go. Buses are sometimes a little bit cheaper, and they may be the only way to get to some remote towns. Flying from one city to another is not worth the expense.

➤ **BY TRAIN** • The fastest Italian trains are **Intercity (IC)** and *rapido* trains. You pay a *supplemento* (extra charge) of up to 50% of the trip's usual cost for IC and rapido service, although the supplement is waived for EurailPass holders. *Espresso* trains make a few more stops and are usually a little slower, but they don't require a supplement. *Diretto* trains make even more stops, and the *locale* is slow as molasses, stopping in every little podunk station along the way.

EurailPasses are good on almost all Italian trains, but fares are so affordable that you might not need one. If you will be in Italy for any length of time without a EurailPass, consider getting one of the Italy-specific discount passes, available at train stations throughout the country. The **Italy Flexi Railcard** costs $116 for four days second-class travel within nine days; $164 for eight days of travel within 21 days; and $210 for 12 days of travel within 30 days. The **Italian Rail Pass** or **BTLC** gives you unlimited travel for eight days ($152), 15 days ($190), 21 days ($220), or 30 days ($264), all in second class. The **Italian Kilometric Ticket** is valid for up to two months and can be used by up to five people to travel a total of 3,000 km. Since 3,000 km is a mighty long way, you'll have a hard time using it up unless you're traveling with at least a few companions. This pass costs $156 for second-class travel, plus $10 per person. The **Cartaverde** for youths under 26 and the **Cartargento** for travelers over 60 save you 20%–30% on all train trips. Both cost about L40,000 and are good for three years. With these last two cards, the discount is not available June 26–August 14 and December 18–28.

➤ **BY BUS** • Towns in the hills and mountains are likely to be served by bus only. Buy bus tickets either at *tabacchi* (tobacco shops), at bars in front of the town bus stop, at the bus station (if there is one), or on the bus. If you buy a ticket before you board, you're expected to punch the ticket on the bus. Occasionally conductors will check tickets and fine those who haven't punched theirs.

WHERE TO SLEEP Hotels in Italy are classified by the government in categories ranging from one to five stars. Most hotels reviewed in this book are one- and two-star establishments costing L40,000–L80,000 per double. One-star hotels vary from gross to charming, with most falling into the "clean but generic" category. Two-star facilities are usually a little nicer and have more rooms with private bath. The words *albergo, pensione,* and *locanda* all basically mean hotel and are interchangeable for the purpose of budget travelers.

Hostels, which usually charge L15,000–L20,000 per night, are an especially good deal for solo travelers. The **Associazione Italiana Alberghi per la Gioventù** (Via Cavour 44, 00184 Rome, tel. 06/487–1152, fax 06/474–1256), the official Italian hostel organization, puts out a complete guide to HI hostels in the country. Independent hostels, sometimes run by religious organizations, offer alternatives to expensive hotels and full hostels, but they are often open only to women and have a score of rules to follow.

The Alps and other mountain groups are scattered with huts called **rifugi.** While some rifugi are always open and free, most cost about as much as a hostel. Inquire about space in your prospective rifugio before you trudge up a mountain only to find that no beds are available. Tourist boards in the towns at the base of the mountains will provide you with a list of rifugi and usually call them for you. **Club Alpino Italiano** (Via Ugo Foscolo 3, 20122 Milan, tel. 02/7202–3085) owns hundreds of these huts and publishes an annual guide with information on access, prices, and equipment.

Campgrounds near cities are often big, ugly affairs—a large piece of roadside dirt with tents. You can save money by camping instead of staying in a hotel (sites usually cost L7000–L15,000), but be prepared for long bus rides in and out of town. **Federazione Italiana del Campeggio,** a.k.a. "Federcampeggio" (Calenzano, 50041 Florence, tel. 055/882391), issues a free, complete list of campgrounds and a map.

FOOD Regions like Emilia-Romagna, Tuscany, and Sicily are particularly famous for their food, but every part of Italy cooks local specialties and classic Italian fare that will leave you mumbling "gnocchi, funghi" for months to come.

Eating *panini* (sandwiches) from a bar or food assembled from the market will probably cost less than L5000. A cup of espresso in your average bar should cost L800–L1200, and a cappuccino about L500 more. Most universities have a *mensa* (dining hall) where you can eat a big, decent meal for around L5000 if you have a student ID.

When eating at a sit-down restaurant, the best way to keep costs down is by not ordering a full three-course meal. You can always just get *primi piatti,* or *primi* (first courses), usually pastas and risottos, and skip the more expensive meat course (*secondo*), despite your waitperson's expectant solicitations. Bread is usually included in the *coperto* (cover charge) of around L2000. The price of desserts, cappuccino, and after-dinner drinks may rudely surprise you. It's almost always cheaper to go to a bar or a gelateria (ice-cream shop) for dessert and coffee.

Lunch is served roughly 1–3, dinner 8–10, sometimes a little later. Most restaurants serve the same menu for lunch and dinner, so lunch isn't really any cheaper. The waiters, though, are less likely to sneer at you for not ordering a secondo at lunch than at dinner.

BUSINESS HOURS Business hours in Italy will inevitably irritate and confound you. The average business is open weekdays or Monday–Saturday, from around 9 in the morning to about 7:30 at night. Many businesses, especially in the south, shut down for a few hours between noon and 4—right when you wanted to go out and buy/eat/see something. Everything closes on Sundays. Banks, open weekdays 9–noon and around 3:30–4:15, have the most absurd hours of all.

FESTIVALS AND HOLIDAYS Businesses throughout Italy close for the following dates: January 1 (New Year's Day), January 6 (Epiphany), Easter Monday, April 25 (Liberation Day), May 1 (Labor Day), August 15 (Assumption of the Virgin), November 1 (All Saints' Day), December 8 (Immaculate Conception), December 25 (Christmas Day), and December 26 (St. Stephen's Day). In addition, many cities and towns celebrate the day of their patron saint, and, around August 15, it seems every Italian closes up shop for at least a few weeks during *ferragosto,* the traditional Italian August holiday.

Two of the biggest celebrations in this festival-happy country are Il Palio in Siena (July 2 and August 16), a fiercely competitive bareback horse race dating back to the Middle Ages, and **Venice's** Carnivale, celebrated in late February or early March.

VISITOR INFORMATION Even the dinkiest town will usually have a tourist office, often run by the **Azienda di Promozione Turismo** (**APT**) or **Ente Provinciale per il Turismo** (**EPT**). Usually you'll find at least one employee who speaks some English. **Informagiovani** offices provide the usual tourist office fare with a slant toward students; pick up their useful magazine *Informagiovani.*

PHONES **Country Code: 39.** The best place to make a long-distance call is from a booth in a phone office labeled SIP, ASST, or TELECOM. Here operators will assign you a booth, help you place your call, and collect payment when you're done. In some towns, you can use an AT&T or similar phone card to charge your call. At these offices you can also buy *schede*—phone cards in denominations of L5000 and L10,000. These cards can be used in about half the pay phones you'll see; the other half accept coins. To use a pay phone for a local call, deposit L200 or insert a phone card and dial. To use a credit card or call collect from a pay phone, deposit L200, which you get back when you finish the call. To call collect, dial 170 to get an English-speaking operator or call AT&T USA Direct at 172–1011 or MCI at 172–1022. For directory assistance, dial 12.

One Berkeley Guides writer decided that SIP (the official Italian pay phones) stood for Sucky Italian Phones; possibly half the pay phones in Italy are out of order.

MAIL Italian mail is slow and unreliable. Letters to the United States take about 10 days to arrive. Postcards are low priority and take longer than letters. Stamps are available at post offices and tabacchi everywhere. Stamps cost L1250 for an average letter, L1100 for a postcard. The Italian words for poste restante are *fermo posta,* though having your mail held at the nearest American Express office is a more reliable option than having it held at the post office.

EMERGENCIES For the *polizia* (local constables), dial **112**; for the *carabinieri* (federal police), call **113.**

LANGUAGE Italians will be receptive to your attempts to speak the language, even if you can only manage a few words. While most people working in the tourist industry speak English, the average person on the street probably does not.

WOMEN TRAVELERS Italian men can be very obnoxious, but attention is usually limited to the verbal realm. Women travelers should respond to unwanted male attention by ignoring it—this may be a big enough blow to their ego that they'll give up. If you speak Italian, shouting a hearty string of curses might make you feel better, if not make the culprit feel worse.

GAY AND LESBIAN TRAVELERS Italy is a Catholic country with a strong dose of machismo, and obvious displays of homosexual affection could get you in big trouble, in some places with the police. Be subtle in small towns and in the south, and live it up in Bologna, Milan, Florence, and Rome, where the gay scenes are booming. Bologna is the headquarters of the national gay organization called **ARCI-Gay** (P. di Porta Saragozza 2, Box 691, 40100 Bologna, tel. 051/436700). Their organization for lesbians, **ARCI-Co-ordinamento Donne** (Via F. Carrara 24, Rome, tel. 06/35791), is in Rome.

Venice and the Veneto

For hundreds of years, the cities of the Veneto came when Venice whistled. But the Veneto, the stretch of land that sprawls east–west between Venice and Verona and reaches far north to the Dolomites, is actually much more than just a suburb of The Canaled One. While the Venetian Republic was busy becoming a maritime bully, the rest of the Veneto cities were forming civic centers, a university, and discrete personalities. Today the region is expensive both to live and to travel in. Residents are notoriously closed to outsiders, but it doesn't deflect the annual flood of travelers who come to ponder Palladian villas, peaceful green hill towns, and paintings by locals Titian and Giorgione. The extensive hostel network, the allure of Venice, and the all-around cultural wallop the Veneto packs make it one of the most tourist-trodden provinces in Italy.

Venice

Pink palazzi, green canals, the blue(ish) Adriatic Sea, yellow signs everywhere pointing to Piazza San Marco, and far too many red-faced tourists swirl together to form Venice—no wonder the city's artists were into color over form. Venice (Venezia in Italian) is simultaneously a smelly stew of tourists and the most enchantingly beautiful place you've ever seen. Built on 100-something islands crisscrossed by palazzo-lined canals, Venice was a burgeoning port town, dominated at first by the Byzantine Empire. You can see the Byzantine thumbprint everywhere, especially in the onion-shaped domes and opulent gold mosaics in the Basilica di San Marco. Venice hit its peak in the 13th–15th centuries, when rich merchants commissioned scores of ostentatious Venetian-Gothic palazzi, visible today along the Grand Canal. The city is now largely dependent on tourism, and you're just going to have to adjust to paying L30,000 or more per person to sleep, and not much less for an edible dinner.

BASICS

VISITOR INFORMATION APT has a small office in the train station (tel. 041/719078; open weekdays 9–noon and 3–6, Sat. 8–2). Buy the Rolling Venice pass (*see box, below*) for L5000 here. The **main office** on Piazza San Marco is less hectic. The bilingual guide *Un Ospite di Venezia* lists everything that's going on. *Main office: San Marco 71/G, tel. 041/522–6356. At the end of Procuratie Nuove on P. San Marco. Open Mon.–Sat. 8:30–7.*

AMERICAN EXPRESS *San Marco 1471, on Salizzada San Moisè, tel. 041/520–0844. Down the street starting just behind the Museo Correr. Open weekdays 9–5:30, Sat. 9–12:30; financial services available Mon.–Sat. 8–8.*

CHANGING MONEY Change your money in Padova or in Mestre, because the rates here are a travesty. Banks cluster around Salizzada San Moisè and Via 22 Marzo in the San Marco area and in Campo San Bartolomeo near the Ponte Rialto.

CONSULATE United Kingdom. *Dorsoduro 1051, near the Accademia, tel. 041/522–7207.*

PHONES AND MAIL Make calls and buy *schede* (phone cards) at the **SIP kiosk** in the main post office or the **SIP office** on Piazzale Roma. You can make long-distance calls and pay afterward at the **Iritel/SIP** office in the train station. The **main post office** (San Marco 5554, on Salizzada del Fontego dei Tedeschi, tel. 041/528–9317) is just past the Ponte Rialto.

COMING AND GOING

BY TRAIN The **Venezia–Santa Lucia** train station (tel. 041/715555) is in Venice proper; don't get off at Venezia-Mestre. Trains go to Milan ($3^1/2$ hrs, L18,700); Rome (5 hrs, L40,200); Padova (30 min, L3200); and Florence (3 hrs, L18,700).

Like a Rolling Venetian

If you're between the ages of 14 and 29, the best way to save money in Venice is to buy a Rolling Venice card from the APT office in the train station. Cardholders get discounts on food, hotels, sights, and shopping. The information that comes with the card is itself worth the card's L5000 price: a decent map marking all the places that give discounts; a book of cheap alternative things to do here; and a booklet of useful phone numbers and names of bars. Bring a passport-size photo when you buy the card.

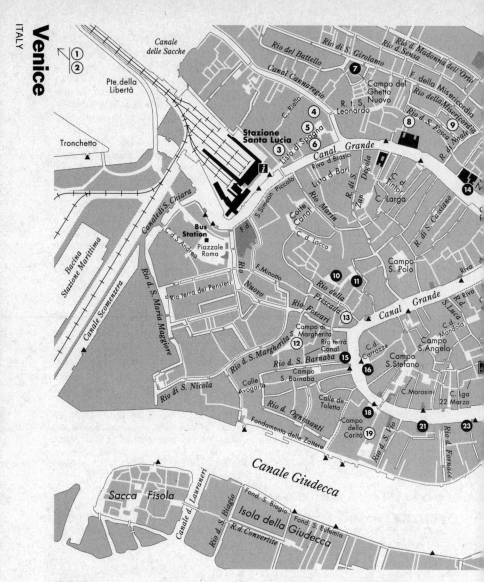

Canale
delle Sacche

Pte.della
Libertà

Canale di S. Girolamo
Rio del Battello
Rio di S. Girolamo
Rio d. Madonna dell'Orti
Rio d.Sensa

Canal Cannaregio

7

Campo del
Ghetto
Nuovo

F. della Misericordia
Rio della Misericordia

R. t. S.
Leonardo

C. Riello

4

8

Rio d. S. Fosca

9

R. di S. Noale

Tronchetto

**Stazione
Santa Lucia**

5

3

6

Lista di Spagna

Canal Grande

Riva di Biasio

Lista di Bari

R. di Noale

Zan Degola

C. d.
Fintor

C. Larga

14

Canali S. Chiara

C. d. S. Andrea

**Bus
Station**

Piazzale
Roma

Rio d. S. Simeon Piccolo

F. d. S. Simeon Piccolo

Corte
Canal

C. d. Lacca

Rio Marin

R. di S. Cassiano

Bacino
Stazione Marittima

Canale Scomenzera

Rio d. S. Maria Maggiore

Rio terra dei Pensieri

Rio Nuovo

F.Minotto

Rio della
Frescada

Rio Foscari

10

11

Campo
S. Polo

Riva

Canal Grande

13

R. d. Riva

S. Luca

Rio d. S. Margherita

Campo di
S. Margherita

Rio terrà
Canal

12

C. d.
Mandala

Campo
S. Angelo

Rio di S. Nicola

Calle
Avogaria

Rio d. S. Barnaba

15

Campo
S. Barnaba

C. d.
Carrozze

16

Campo
S. Stefano

C. Morosini

C. lga
22 Marzo

Calle de
Toletta

18

Campo
della
Carità

19

R. d. S. Vio

21

23

Rio d. Forncice

Fondamenta delle Zattere

Canale Giudecca

Sacca   Fisola

Canale d. Lauraneri

Rio d. S. Biagio

Fond. S. Biagio

Isola della Fond. S. Eufemia **Giudecca**

R.d.Convertite

Sights ●

Basilica di
San Marco, **28**

Ca' d'Oro, **14**

Ca' Rezzonico, **15**

Campanile di
San Marco, **27**

Chiesa Santa Maria
della Salute, **23**

Collezione Peggy
Guggenheim, **21**

I Frari, **11**

Gallerie
dell'Accademia, **18**

Museo Correr, **24**

Museo Ebraico, **7**

Palazzo Ducale, **29**

Palazzo Grassi, **16**

Piazza
San Marco, **26**

Ponte Rialto, **20**

San Giorgio
Maggiore, **36**

Santi Giovanni e
Paolo, **30**

Scuola di San
Giorgio degli
Schiavoni, **34**

Scuola Grande di
San Rocco, **10**

Lodging ○

Albergo Rossi, **5**

Alloggi Trattoria
Nuova, **6**

Antico Capon, **12**

Archie's House, **8**

Albergo Bernardi-
Semenzato, **17**

Camping Jolly delle
Querche, **1**

Camping Marco
Polo, **2**

Caneva, **22**

Casa Bettina, **33**

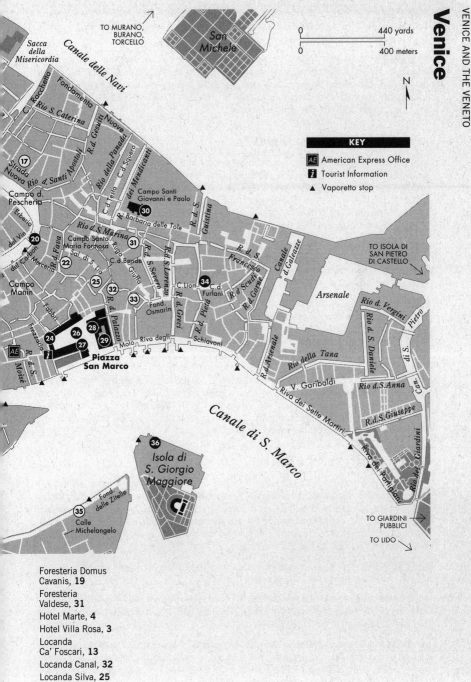

TO MURANO,
BURANO,
TORCELLO

Sacca
della
Misericordia

San
Michele

Canale delle Navi

0   440 yards

0   400 meters

N

KEY

AE   American Express Office

i   Tourist Information

▲   Vaporetto stop

C. Racchetta
Fondamenta Nuove
Rio S. Caterina
R.d. Gesuiti
Rio della Panada
C.d.Squero
dei Mendicanti

Strada
Nuova
17

Rio d. Santi Apostoli

Campo d.
Pescheria

Campo Santi
Giovanni e Paolo

30

R. Barbaria delle Tole

Giustina

Rio d.S. Marina
Rugo
C.d.Fava

Elberia
del Vin
20

Campo Santa
Maria Formosa
Sal. di S. Lio
31

R.d.S.
Francesco

Canale
d. Galeazze

TO ISOLA DI
SAN PIETRO
DI CASTELLO

del Caban
Merceria
22
C.d.Bonde
R.d. S.Severo
R.d.S.Lorenzo

Campo
Manin
25
32
33
C.Lion
34
C.d.
Furlani
R.d.Scudi
R.d.Gorne

Arsenale

Rio d. Vergini

Fabbri
Frezzeria
24
26
28
29
R.d. Palazzo
Molo
Riva degli
Schiavoni
R.d. Pietà
R.d. Greci
Fond.
Osmarin

Rio d. S. Daniele
R.d.S

R.d. S.
Moisè
AE
i
27
**Piazza
San Marco**

R.d. Arsenale

Rio della Tana

V. Garibaldi

Rio d.S.Anna

Can. di S. Pietro

Canale di S. Marco

Riva dei Sette Martiri

R.d.S. Giuseppe

36

Isola di
S. Giorgio
Maggiore

Rio dei Partigiani

Rio dei Giardini

TO GIARDINI
PUBBLICI

Fond.
delle Zitelle

35

Calle
Michelangelo

TO LIDO

BY BUS ACTV (Piazzale Roma, tel. 041/528–7886) buses run to cities on the mainland. Take Bus 2, 4, 7, or 12 to Mestre (L1000). Buses for Padova leave every half-hour (L4000), but the train is cheaper and faster.

BY PLANE **Marco Polo Airport** (tel. 041/260–9260) is a half-hour north of Venice, on the mainland. It's international but small, with mostly intra-European flights. **ACTV** Bus 5 runs hourly from the airport to Piazzale Roma (Venice's parking lot) and back. It only costs L1000, but you have to schlepp your luggage on your lap. The **ATVO** bus runs hourly to and fro as well; pay L5000 to have a place for your stuff.

GETTING AROUND

Venice's narrow alleys and close-quartered buildings make it difficult to get your bearings. A good map is essential (try the yellow *Rialto* one, sold everywhere for L3000). The train station and bus station are on the northwest end of the city; **San Marco** is south/central. The **Grand Canal** (the big one you see as you walk out of the station) makes a big backwards "S," slicing the city in two. The city is divided into six *sestieri* (neighborhoods): **Castello, Cannaregio, San Marco, Dorsoduro, Santa Croce,** and **San Polo.**

Just to screw with your mind, addresses usually don't include a street name but contain the name of the sestiere and a seemingly random number. You'll have to navigate by finding major landmarks. The yellow signs all over town pointing you to San Marco and the Rialto are also great navigational tools.

BY VAPORETTO The *vaporetto* (water bus) is the only way to get to the hostel on Giudecca, or to any of the other islands. **Vaporetto 1** (L2200) docks at every stop along the Grand Canal; **2** (L3300) makes fewer stops. The **5** (L2200) circles the main island in both directions: **5 destra** (right) runs from the station to the Fondamente Nuove, cuts through the Arsenale, chugs down the Canale Giudecca (stopping at the hostel), and travels back to the station. The **5** *sinistra* (left) goes the other way around and is by far the faster way to get to the hostel. Vaporetto **82** also runs down the Giudecca Canal (L2200) from the main vaporetto dock at San Zaccharia on Riva degli Schiavoni. You'll be fined L30,000 if you're caught riding a vaporetto without a ticket, but many take the risk. If you don't have a ticket, buy one from the conductor *before* any ticket-punching commences; there's a L500 charge for buying on the boat. Vaporetti schedules are posted at all the stops.

WHERE TO SLEEP

You'll need a miracle to find a cheap place to stay in Venice during the summer if you don't have reservations. Most budget hotels are in Cannaregio (along the Lista di Spagna), scattered through Castello, and in Dorsoduro (near the university). Most budget hotels will run you L25,000–L45,000 per person; breakfast is usually included. If you're willing to stay outside the city limits, the best option is to commute from the hostel in Padova, but you have to leave Venice early to get back by the 11 PM curfew.

CANNAREGIO This neighborhood near the station isn't the most scenic part of town, but it's full of cool bars and chock-full of hotels.

➢ **UNDER L50,000 • Alloggi Trattoria Nuova.** Rooms are dark and ugly, but clean. Register and get key at trattoria down the street. Doubles L45,000. *Trattoria: Cannaregio 189, on Lista di Spagna, tel. 041/716005. AE, MC, V.*

➢ **UNDER L60,000 • Albergo Bernardi-Semenzato (dipendenza).** The *dipendenza* (annex) of this otherwise unremarkable hotel is in an old palazzo with some canal and garden views. Double with breakfast L55,000. *Cannaregio 4363–4366, on Calle dell'Oca off Strada Nuova, tel. 041/522-7257. Luggage storage. MC, V.*

Tintoretto. Good location, nice managers, and homey rooms. Somewhat noisy doubles L59,000. *Cannaregio 2316–2317, on Campiello della Chiesa off Strada Nuova, tel. 041/721872. MC, V.*

➢ **UNDER 70,000 • Albergo Rossi.** Impeccably clean rooms are a bit noisy. Doubles L67,000. *Cannaregio 30121, on Calle delle Procuratie off Lista di Spagna, tel. 041/715164. AE, V.*

Hotel Marte. Comfortable in an antiseptic, chain-motel way. If full, they'll send you to similarly priced **Biasin** across the canal. Doubles L60,000. *Cannaregio 388, tel. 041/716351. From Lista di Spagna, turn right just before Ponte delle Guglie. AE.*

Hotel Villa Rosa. Small, clean rooms in a quiet location. Doubles L60,000. *Cannaregio 389, on Calle della Misericordia, tel. 041/716569. Wheelchair access. MC, V.*

DORSODURO The presence of the university means you'll find students and several casual cafés in this neighborhood.

➢ **UNDER L70,000 • Antico Capon.** Cool campo views, uncool noise. Passable doubles run L60,000. *Dorsoduro 3004/B, Campo Santa Margherita, tel. 041/528–5292.*

➢ **UNDER L80,000 • Locanda Ca' Foscari.** Friendly, English-speaking manager, good location. Spacious, pleasant doubles L70,000. *Dorsoduro 3887/B–3888, on Calle della Frescada, tel. 041/522–5817. From I Frari, go down Scalater San Rocco (off Salizzada San Rocco), and turn left on Crosera San Pantalon; Calle Frescada is at the end.*

CASTELLO The edge of Castello that's closest to San Marco is predictably expensive, but you'll find some pretty good deals a bit deeper into the district.

➢ **UNDER L40,000 • Casa Bettina.** Large rooms with wood floors go for L39,000, L47,000 with bath. *Castello 4388, on Campo San Giovanni Novo, tel. 041/523–9084.*

➢ **UNDER L60,000 • Caneva.** Airy rooms, but unhelpful staff. One of the cheapest places you'll find in such a central location. Doubles L50,000. *Castello 5515, on Ramo della Fava, tel. 041/522–8118. From Campo San Bartolomeo, take Calle Stagnieri and walk past Campo della Fava; Ramo della Fava is on the right.*

➢ **UNDER L70,000 • Locanda Canal.** Clean, good-size rooms with rickety furniture. Ask for a key if you want to stay out past midnight. Doubles L66,000. *Castello 4422/C, on Fondamenta Remedio next to Locanda Silva (see below); tel. 041/523–4538.*

Locanda Silva. Popular with Italian travelers. Some rooms have canal views. Small, comfortable doubles L65,000. *Castello 4423, on Fondamenta Remedio, tel. 041/522–7643. From Campo Santa Maria Formosa, walk behind the church to Campiello Querini, veer right to Fondamenta Remedio. 2 AM curfew.*

HOSTELS Venice only has one HI hostel, but both APT offices give out lists of private and nun-run hostels—most called *foresterie*—that are cheap but heavy on rules and regulations.

Archie's House. This 14th-century palazzo was bombed in World Wars I and II, and looks it. Doubles L23,000 per person, dorm beds L21,000; prices go down the longer you stay. *Cannaregio 1814/B, on Rio Terrà del Cristo, tel. 041/720884. Hot showers L1500; cold showers free. Check in before 2 PM or after 8:30 PM.*

Foresteria Domus Cavanis. Great location between the Accademia and the Zattere. Nicer than most, but run by a stern woman. Doubles L70,000, L50,000 with ISIC card. Students get 10% off the second night, 20% the third. *Rio Terrà Foscarini 912, down the main street from the Accademia, tel. 041/528–7374. Midnight curfew. Closed Sept.–June 9.*

Foresteria Valdese. Basic dorms L24,000 the first night, L20,000 thereafter. One large room with kitchen (L28,000 per person) great for groups of three to six. *Dorsoduro 5170, tel. 041/528–6797. From Campo Santa Maria Formosa, walk down Calle Lunga Santa Maria Formosa to the end, and cross the bridge to the Protestant church; it's on the right. Lockout 1–6.*

Ostello della Gioventù Venezia (HI). Get your butt here early in the morning to grab a spot. Beds L19,000, including breakfast. HI members only; they'll sell you a card for L30,000. *Giudecca 86, tel. 041/523–8211. Take vaporetto to Zitelle/Ostello stop and turn right. Luggage storage. Lockout 9–6.*

CAMPGROUNDS If you're expecting unspoiled beaches, you're out of luck. **Camping Jolly delle Querche** (Via A. Di Marchi 7, Marghera, tel. 041/920312; closed Nov.–Jan. 2), a well-equipped site in ugly surroundings, costs L7500 per person the first night, with reductions after that. Bungalows start at L12,000. From Piazzale Roma, take Bus 6 (L1000), get off at Piazza Foscori, and follow the signs. Similar to Jolly but without the bungalows, **Camping Marco Polo** (Via Triestina 167, Tessera, tel. 041/541–6003; closed Nov.–Jan 2) is a good place to stay if you're flying into Venice. Prices are the same as at Jolly. Take Bus 5 from the airport or Piazzale Roma.

FOOD

It's just not fair that the pigeons eat better than you do, but there's not much you can do about it. Food in Venice is expensive. Whatever you do, stay away from the extortionate restaurants in San Marco, unless you go to the wine bar **Vino, Vino** (San Marco 2007/A, on Calle del Sartor di Veste, tel. 041/523–7027), which has creative and delicious primi for L6000. If you're really scrimping, put together a meal of your own at the morning market on the San Polo side of the Rialto Bridge. When you're ready to splurge, try some of the city's famous seafood, like *polenta alla seppia nera* (polenta with squid in ink) and *spaghetti alle vongole* (spaghetti with clams). The Rolling Venice card gets you a discount of 10%–20% (and sometimes a free drink, too) at many of the restaurants reviewed below; ask about it or you might miss out.

CANNAREGIO Avoid eating near the station and head out toward Strada Nuova.

➤ **UNDER L10,000 • Iguana.** Venice's only Mexican place serves drinks all day and a rice-and-bean fix at lunch and dinner. Chimichangas L6000. *Cannaregio 2515, on Fondamenta della Misericordia, tel. 041/716722. Closed Tues.*

Trattoria Casa Mia. Wide range of pizzas (L6000–L10,000), tasty primi (L6500–L11,000), and great *contorni* (vegetable side dishes). *Cannaregio 4430, off Strada Nuova on Calle dell'Oca, tel. 041/528–5590. Closed Tues.*

➤ **UNDER L20,000 • Ristorante l'Arca di Noè.** Venice's coolest vegetarian restaurant. Primi (L8000–L12,000) include tagliatelle with seitan (wheat gluten) ragù. *Cannaregio 5401, on Calle Larga Giacinto Gallina, tel. 041/523–8153. On Castello border, near Chiesa Santi Giovanni e Paolo. Open weekdays 9–3 and 5–11, Sat. 5–11.*

DORSODURO Look for cheap food near the university and the Accademia and cool cafés on Campo Santa Margherita.

➤ **UNDER L10,000 • Crepizza.** Specializes in crepes and pizza (get it?). Popular with young Venetians. Pizzas L5000–L9000. *Dorsoduro 3757–3761, on Calle San Pantalon, tel. 041/522–9189. Closed Tues.*

We All Scream for . . . Gelato?

Il Doge (Campo Santa Margherita; closed Mon.), touted by many as the best gelateria in Venice, serves two big scoops for L2000. Try any of the fresh fruit flavors, the pistachio, or the "stracciatella" (chocolate chip). Dissenters favor Nico (on the Zattere; closed Thurs.), with outdoor seating on the waterfront and a specialty called "gianduotti," an immense hunk of dairy involving pralines and whipped cream.

CASTELLO As long as you stay away from the back side of Piazza San Marco, you'll do okay in Castello. Via Garibaldi has lots of little places with reasonable fixed-price menus of varying quality.

➢ **UNDER L15,000** • **Trattoria alla Fonte.** Pizzas and standard primi are cheap and good. Try *gnocchi ai quattro formaggi* (gnocchi with four cheeses; L8000). *Castello 3820, in Campo Bandiera e Moro, tel. 041/523–8698. Closed Wed.*

➢ **UNDER L25,000** • **Osteria al Mascaron.** Great food, amazing wine, cool owners, and a handwritten menu with art-nouveau doodles. Huge primi L9000–L12,000, fish dishes L19,000–L22,000. *Castello 5225, on Calle Lunga off Campo Santa Maria Formosa, tel. 041/522–5995. Closed Sun.*

SAN POLO AND SANTA CROCE Tourists rarely make their way here to the local restaurants, *pasticcerias* (pastry shops), and cafés—perhaps they just get lost in the winding streets on their way.

➢ **UNDER L6,000** • **Mensa Universitaria.** A full meal costs L5000. You can't get in without youth ID (an ISIC card or a Rolling Venice pass works), and priority is given to Italian students. Look for the line of hungry students waiting outside. *San Polo 2480, on Calle Magazen, tel. 041/520–4496. From I Frari, cross the bridge, turn left on Fondamenta dei Frari and left on Rio Terrà San Tomà. Closed Sun. evening and Aug.*

➢ **UNDER L15,000** • **Alle Ocche.** The best pizzeria in Venice serves big pizzas in a small restaurant. *Santa Croce 1552, on Calle del Tintor off Campo San Giacomo dell'Orio, tel. 041/524–1161. Closed Sun.*

Trattoria Donna Onesta. Seafood antipasti (L6000–L10,000) come in an incredible variety. Pasta dishes L5000–L7000. *San Polo 3922, on Calle della Madonna, tel. 041/522–9586. Closed Sun.*

➢ **UNDER L20,000** • **Osteria la Zucca.** Interesting, delicious food and a low-key atmosphere. Primi of various pastas and polentas run L9000; secondi of meat or fish cost L13,000–L24,000. *Santa Croce 1762, off Campo San Giacomo dell'Orio, tel. 041/524–1570. Closed Sun.*

WORTH SEEING

Dazzling architecture, narrow shady streets, and art as colorful as the peeling paint on the buildings—there's a hell of a lot to see in Venice. The museum-happy can buy one bargain ticket (L16,000) that gets you into the Palazzo Ducale, the Museo Correr, Ca' Rezzonico, the glass museum on Murano, and other sights. The Rolling Venice card gets you a discount on most entrance fees; always ask.

SAN MARCO The center of cultural life in Venice, the sestiere of San Marco is dominated by the tourist-clogged Piazza San Marco and its spectacular basilica, but it's also home to some slightly less hyped attractions. Operas are still performed at **Teatro La Fenice** (down Salizzada San Moisè/Via 22 Marzo, tel. 041/521–0161), and the **Palazzo Grassi** (San Marco 3231, in Campo San Samuele, tel. 041/523–1680) contains the best displayed and most impressive temporary exhibits in the city. Ask at the tourist office about the current show if you don't see one of the posters all over the town.

After visiting the Basilica di San Marco, catch Vaporetto 1 or 5 from San Zaccharia to Isola di San Giorgio Maggiore to see the beautiful, island-bound Church of San Giorgio Maggiore. The bare white Palladian walls are the best antidote in Venice for Byzantine overload.

➢ **PIAZZA SAN MARCO** • The doges' backyard since the 9th century, the piazza has historically been the seat of the municipal government in Venice. The piazza's huge **Basilica di San Marco** (open Mon.–Sat. 9:45–5, Sun. 2–5) was constructed in 1094 after the original was burned down in an uprising against the new doge. The builders of the church were obviously smitten with

Byzantine architecture: Onion domes and gold mosaics abound. The interior is a confusing and wonderful jambalaya of Byzantine, Gothic, and Renaissance styles.

The doges' private home and the seat of courts, prisons, and political intrigues, the pink-checkered **Palazzo Ducale** (tel. 041/522–4951; admission L8000, L4000 students; open daily 9–7), next to the basilica, is a perfect example of Venetian Gothic architecture. Inside, the rooms are covered with paintings by Tintoretto, Veronese, Tiepolo, Titian, and other Venetian masters. From the Great Council Hall, walk down to the Ponte dei Sospiri (Bridge of Sighs), which leads to part of the prisons.

The two long buildings stretching out from the basilica, the Procuratie, were the offices of the procurators, who tended to the more mundane aspects of running the city. The **Procuratie Vecchie** starts at the **Torre dell'Orologio**, where bronze "Moors" strike the hour on the roof; the **Procuratie Nuove** stands opposite. The 325-foot-high **Campanile di San Marco** was erected in 912 as a watchtower and lighthouse. In 1902, the whole tower toppled over for no reason. An exact replica was rebuilt in 10 years. The view from the breezy belfry is the tower's best feature (elevator admission L4000; open daily 9–7:45).

During the Risorgimento, those who backed Italy conspired in Caffè Florian, on the Procuratorie Vecchie, while supporters of Austria plotted in Quadri, on the Procuratorie Nuove. Now they seem to plot together to ream tourists, charging L8500 for caffè when the bands are playing.

DORSODURO The seat of the university and two of Venice's greatest museums (*see below*), Dorsoduro is also a mellow residential district. Fantastically festooned **Chiesa Santa Maria della Salute**, at the tip of Dorsoduro, was designed by Longhena to honor the Virgin. The main draw of the church is its sacristy, where some of the few Titians left in Venice are housed.

➤ **GALLERIE DELL'ACCADEMIA** • You may *think* you're sick of Venetian art, but this awesome collection of the city's best from the 14th to the 18th centuries should not be missed. The gallery contains *The Tempest,* by Giorgione, and Veronese's enormous *Feast in the House of Levi,* which takes up a whole wall. *Dorsoduro, Campo della Carità (a.k.a. Campo dell'Accademia), foot of Ponte dell'Accademia, tel. 041/522–2247. Admission: L8000. Open June–Sept., Mon.–Sat. 9–7:15, Sun. 9–1; Oct.–May, Mon.–Sat. 9–2, Sun. 9–1.*

➤ **COLLEZIONE PEGGY GUGGENHEIM** • It's fortunate for us that heiress Peggy Guggenheim—who moved to Venice, bought a palazzo, and stuffed it with art by her friends and favorites—had good taste. She left Venice with the best collection of 20th-century art in Italy, including works by Pollock, Klee, De Chirico, Picasso, Man Ray, Giacometti, and Kandinsky. Be warned: The place is both staffed by and crawling with Americans. *Dorsoduro 701, on Fondamenta Venier dei Leoni, tel. 041/520–6288. Admission: L7000, L4000 students, free Sat. 6 PM–9 PM. Open Sun.–Mon. and Wed.–Fri. 11 AM–6 PM, Sat. 11 AM–9 PM.*

CANNAREGIO This neighborhood of extremes covers both the salty area around the Misericordia and Fondamente Nuove and the upscale **Strada Nuova,** a commercial street lined with shops and gelaterias. Cannaregio also holds the Jewish ghetto and several thousand churches within its northern bulge.

➤ **CA' D'ORO** • Called the "House of Gold" because the facade once had gilded carvings, this Gothic palazzo is no longer golden, but it's still an amazing example of Venetian-Gothic architecture. Inside, the Galleria Giorgio Franchetti displays. *St. Sebastian* by Mantegna and *Venus* by Titian. *Cannaregio 3932, just off Strada Nuova, tel. 041/522–2349. Admission: L4000. Open daily 9–2.*

➤ **GHETTO EBREO** • Many Jews were attracted to Venice during the Middle Ages and the early Renaissance because of its relatively liberal policy toward immigrants of any faith. The situation abruptly changed, however, in 1516, when all the Jews in Venice were shunted to this one small area, forced to wear identifying clothing, and denied equal economic opportunity; as you walk under the *sottoportego* (underpass) leading to the ghetto, you pass the grooves where bars were placed to keep the residents in at night. The **Museo Ebraico** (admission L4000, L3000 students) houses a small collection of Torah screens and the like; more interesting is the museum's hourly tour (L10,000, L8000 students) of three synagogues still used by the tiny but active Jewish community. *Cannaregio, Campo del Ghetto Nuovo 2902/B, tel. 041/715359. Off Fondamenta di Cannaregio. Open June–Sept., Sun.–Thurs. 10–7; Oct.–May, Sun.–Thurs. 10–4. Closed Jewish holidays.*

CASTELLO Castello extends from behind the Basilica di San Marco, up to the mammoth Gothic church of **Santi Giovanni e Paolo,** and down past the Arsenale and the gardens to the tip of the city. Curvilinear **Chiesa Santa Maria Formosa** and its palazzo-lined campo of the same name occupy an appealing little residential area here.

➤ **SCUOLA DI SAN GIORGIO DEGLI SCHIAVONI** • Once a guild for Venice's large Slavic community, the Scuola di San Giorgio degli Schiavoni houses paintings by Carpaccio that juxtapose portraits of noblemen with scenes from the Bible. The building itself has barely been touched since the 1600s. *Castello 3259, on Calle dei Furlani, tel. 041/522–8828. Admission: L5000. Open Apr.–Oct., Tues.–Sat. 9:30–12:30 and 3:30–7:30, Sun. 11:00–12:30; Nov.–Mar., Tues.–Sat. 10–12:30 and 3:30–6, Sun. 11–12:30.*

Every summer, Venice puts on the Bienniale, a world-class extravaganza of international contemporary art or architecture (they alternate each year). Dozens of pavilions displaying avant-garde works from various countries are set up in the Giardini Pubblici in Castello. It's L18,000 to get in, and very worth it.

SAN POLO AND SANTA CROCE Most of this area near the center of Venice, almost surrounded by a curve of the Grand Canal, is full of quiet streets and tiny canals. The neighborhood around the little church of **San Giacomo dell'Orio** is strictly local—mostly older Venetians having a *granita* (crushed-ice drink) before continuing their daily shopping. The bulky brick frame of the church **I Frari** (Campo dei Frari) is incongruous with the delicate art inside. *The Assumption* altarpiece, one of the biggest and best Titians in Venice, depicts a crowd of angels heaving the Holy One's mother up to heaven. Traditionally the link between the commercial heart of the city and San Marco, the **Ponte Rialto** is now full of souvenir sellers and gawking tourists. The bridge was built by Antonio da Ponte (whose name means "of the bridge") after he beat out both Sansovino and Palladio in a 1551 competition to design a marble bridge.

➤ **SCUOLA GRANDE DI SAN ROCCO** • Tintoretto was a busy, busy guy: His paintings are plastered all over Venice, but this former guild building contains some of his best work. Some of the most interesting paintings are in the Mary cycle on the ground floor. *San Polo 3052, tel. 041/523–4684. On Campo San Rocco, just before I Frari. Admission: L7000, L4000 students. Open Mar. 28–Nov. 2, daily 9–5:30; shorter hrs off-season.*

AFTER DARK

Venice's nightlife is notoriously low-key. If you want to go clubbing in summer, you have to go to Mestre or the Lido, but if you're looking to get quietly tipsy and hang out, you'll have plenty of options. **The Irish Pub** (Cannaregio 3847, on Corte dei Pali Gia Testori off Strada Nuova, tel. 041/523–9930; closed Wed.) serves Guinness for L6000 a pint. **Paradiso Perduto** (Cannaregio 2540, on Fondamenta della Misericordia, tel. 041/720581) will immediately become home base for traveling hipsters. The food and drinks are excellent and affordable, although drink prices go up when bands play (about once a week). Paradiso Perduto is closed Wednesdays, a week in January, and a week in August.

NEAR VENICE

Murano is most famous for its production of glassware and really has little else to offer. From the vaporetto stop, walk over the bridge to the Fondamenta Venier to get good deals on glass goods, but expect salespeople to grab you by the arm and try to steer you into their shop. Pay

L5000 admission at the Museo Vetrario Antica di Murano (Fondamenta Giustinian 8, tel. 041/739586; closed Mon.) to see a nifty exhibit of glass through the ages.

"The lace island" probably isn't a compelling enough description of **Burano** to make you want to visit, but this old fishing community is immensely pretty and tranquil, with low, brilliantly painted houses. Deserted, swampy **Torcello** was once the most populated island in the lagoon—about 200,000 people lived here in its heyday. One of the only remnants left is the Cattedrale di Torcello, a.k.a. Santa Maria Assunta (follow the path from the vaporetto stop, tel. 041/730084; admission L1500). The church was built in the 7th century, and the building's interior has astonishing 11th- and 12th-century mosaics.

The tragic elegance of the **Lido** in Thomas Mann's *Death in Venice* is now the tragic scuzz of too many people, too much pollution, and not enough sand. If looking at water all day has made you desperate for a swim, the Lido's free public beach (down Viale Santa Maria Elisabetta from the vaporetto stop) is fine.

COMING AND GOING Vaporetto 12 goes from Venice's Fondamente Nuove to Murano, Burano, Torcello, and Treporti on the Lido. Tickets are L5000 *andata* (going) and L3500 *ritorno* (return). Vaporetto 5 stops at Fondamente Nuove and goes to San Michele and Murano (L2200); Vaporetti 1, 2, 82, and 6 (each L2200) all stop at Punta Santa Maria Elisabetta on the Lido.

Padova

Most people use Padova (Padua) as a place to stay while visiting Venice—they see the beautifully Giottoed Cappella degli Scrovegni, and then skedaddle. If you come in August, when Padova is hotter than hell, this reaction might be justified. Otherwise, take some time and stay a while. A city of both high-rises and history, it's definitely not beautiful, but it's cheaper, more convenient, and a little more mellow than other Veneto towns. Cheap food, bizarre theme bars, and English-language bookstores are everywhere. The **APT** tourist office (open Mon.–Sat. 9:20–2:45 and 3:15–7:20, Sun. 9–noon) is in the train station.

COMING AND GOING The large **train station** (Piazzale Stazione Ferrovia, tel. 049/875–1800) has frequent trains to Venice (30 min, L3200) and Milan (2 hrs 50 min, L17,000). The **ATP** bus station (Via Trieste 42, tel. 049/820–6811) has buses to small towns in the Veneto. To get to the bus station from the train station, walk up Corso del Popolo and turn left on Via Trieste. Corso del Popolo runs from the train station to the center of town.

WHERE TO SLEEP AND EAT Most cheap hotels lie southeast of the university. Tiny, spotless doubles at **Al Santo** (Via del Santo 147, ½ block north of basilica, tel. 049/857–2131) cost L60,000. **Turismo** (Via Santa Chiara 49, tel. 049/651276) has good-size doubles for L45,000. At the hostel, **Ostello Città di Padova** (Via Aleardi 30, tel. 049/875–2219), L16,000 gets you a bed and breakfast. The price goes down to L14,000 if you stay three or more nights. From the station, take ACAP Bus 3, 8, or 18 to Prato della Valle, turn left on Via Cavalletto, and follow the signs. "Holiday houses" pop up July–September; try **Antonianum** (Via Donatello 24, tel. 049/651444), which has doubles with bath for about L40,000.

Your food budget goes pretty far in Padova. One money-stretcher is the daily open-air market in twin piazze Erbe and Frutte. The **Mensa Universitaria** (Via San Francesco 12, tel. 049/660903; open 11:45–2 and 6:45–9) has good, filling meals for L7000. From Palazzo Bò, walk east on Via San Francesco. **Trattoria al Pero** (Via Santa Lucia 38, 1 block north of P. dei Signori, tel. 049/875–8794; closed Sat. and Aug.) serves typical Veneto food at low prices. After dinner, head to **Lucifer Young** (Via Altinate 89, tel. 049/875–2251), an imaginative bar based on Dante's *Inferno*. To get here, walk down Corso del Popolo, and turn left on Via Altinate, just after Piazza Garibaldi.

WORTH SEEING The APT office (*see above*) sells an all-inclusive ticket to Padova's sights for L19,000. Padova's claim to fame is the **Capella degli Scrovegni** (P. Eremitani, tel. 049/875–0905; closed Mon. Jan.–Feb.). Giotto's famous frescoes that adorn the interior of this tiny chapel look like brilliant, illuminated manuscripts painted on walls instead of parchment. The admission ticket (L10,000, L7000 students) also gets you into the other museums in the Eremitani complex. Other notable sights include the Gothic **Basilica di San Antonio** (P. del Santo; open daily 6:30 AM–7 PM; summer 6:30 AM–7:45 PM), whose multiroom interior with confessionals for speakers of five languages is an imposing minimall for the pious. Check out Donatello's statues on the main altar and the equestrian monument, *Gattamelata,* outside. **Caffe Pedrocchi** (Piazzetta Pedrocchi; open daily 7 AM–11 PM), the most elaborate place in Padova to sip coffee, was a Risorgimento haven for students and intellectuals. On February 8, 1848, it was the seat of a nationalist insurrection.

Verona

Beautiful Verona is one of those places to which time has been very kind. It hit its first peak in the 1st century BC, when the Romans used it as a pit stop on the trade route to the rest of Europe. In the Middle Ages, the Scaglieri clan built the city up as a prestigious family domain, and in the 15th century, Venice came west and sucked the city into its empire. Instead of challenging Venice's power, the Veronese decided to turn all its aspirations inward, building up its cultural cache (Shakespeare placed Romeo, Juliet, and a couple of gentlemen here) and restoring the Roman ruins. Tourism is very big here, and most of the residents are wealthy, status-conscious, and a little snide. But unlike Venice, Verona feels like some of the people in the streets might actually *live* here.

BASICS Two blocks south of Piazza Brà, the Fabretto Viaggi e Turismo (C. Porto Nuovo 11; open weekdays 8:30–12:30 and 3–7, Sat. 9–noon), the **American Express** agent, changes traveler's checks. **APT** has tourist offices on Piazza Brà (Via Leoncino 61, tel. 045/592828; open Mon.–Sat. 8–8) and Piazza delle Erbe (tel. 045/800–0065; open Mon.–Sat. 9–7:30). Ask for the *Informagiovani* magazine, which lists cheap hotels and restaurants and has an excellent map.

COMING AND GOING The main station is **Verona Porta Nuova** (P. XXV Aprile, tel. 045/590688). Trains run to Milan (1 hr 45 min, L10,500), Venice (2 hrs, L8800), Rome (5 hrs via Bologna, L36,900), and Florence (2 hrs 45 min via Bologna, L15,400). Buses leave the **APT** station (P. XXV Aprile, tel. 045/800–4129) for the less-visited towns of the region. From either station, walk down Corso Porta Nuova to Piazza Brà at the center of town.

WHERE TO SLEEP AND EAT The center has a few budget hotels, but if you're not allergic to curfews or teenage travelers, stay in the hostel. **HI Ostello della Gioventù Villa Francescati** (Salita Fontana del Ferro 15, tel. 045/590360), a 16th-century villa adorned with frescoes, lets beds for L14,000; camping in the garden costs about 7000. From the center of town, cross Ponte Nuovo, go right on Lungadige Re Teodorico, turn left on Ponte Pignolo, and follow the signs. Call in advance to sunny, central **Locanda Catullo** (Via Valerio Catullo 1, tel. 045/800–2786; doubles L44,000). Walk up Via Mazzini from Piazza Brà and turn left at Via Valerio Catullo. **Volto Cittadella** (Via Volto Cittadella 8, tel. 045/800–0077) has clean, somewhat noisy doubles for L36,000–L42,000. Walk down Corso Porto Nuova from Piazza Brà, and turn left at Via Volto Cittadella.

A Shrine for Star-Crossed Lovers

Avoid the touristy houses and tombs of Romeo and Juliet. They're architecturally boring and totally spurious; the Cappuletti (Capulet) and Montecchi (Montague) families did live in Verona, but the protagonists are fictitious. If you must see a testament to teenage love, save your money and look at the entrance of the Casa di Giulietta (Juliet's House; Via Cappello 23, tel. 045/803–4303), covered with layers of graffiti written by modern-day lovebirds.

Cross the river into the Veronetta (university) district and you'll find better food at better prices than in the center. The vegetarian restaurant **Il Grillo Parlante** (Vicolo Seghe San Tommaso 10, off P. Isolo, tel. 045/591156; closed Thurs. dinner and Sun.) serves filling secondi (L7000–L7500) and spinach croquettes (L7500) to an alternative crowd. **Trattoria dal Ropeton** (Via San Giovanni 46, tel. 045/803–0040; closed Tues.) serves delicious pasta (around L7000) and meaty secondi (L12,000) to locals. From the hostel, walk down Salita Fontana del Ferro and turn left on San Giovanni.

WORTH SEEING The center is jammed with Austrian, Venetian, and Roman buildings, all within easy walking distance of each other. Most of Verona's sights are free the first Sunday of every month and closed Mondays. Roman arches mark the entrance to piazze Brà and Dante and the beginning of Corso Porta Borsari. The cavernous, pink 1st-century-AD **Arena** (admission L6000, L1500 students), smack in the middle of Piazza Brà, is a testament to both the ingenuity of the Romans and the meticulous upkeep of Verona by its inhabitants. Rock stars occasionally play at the arena, but it's famous for **opera,** which is definitely worth the cost of the ticket. For prices, call 045/590089 or 045/807–7111. The opera season is late June–August. Walk to the end of Via Roma from Piazza Brà to reach the seriously fortified **Castelvecchio** (C. Cavour 2, tel. 045/594734; admission L5000, L1500 students), next to a dramatic bridge crossing the Adige River. The museum inside features works by Titian, Veronese, Tintoretto, Pisanello, and Rubens, as well as a startling number of breast-feeding Madonnas.

The candy-cane, Romanesque-Gothic **duomo** (cathedral) on Piazza Duomo was built on an ancient spa site, where paleochristian architectural remnants have been found. A fresco by Titian, *The Assumption,* is in the first chapel on the left. Beautiful, Romanesque **San Zeno Maggiore** (P. San Zeno) has bronze doors with scenes from the Bible and Andrea Mantegna's glorious triptych, *Madonna and Saints,* on the high altar. The arch-lined 12th-century cloister of the adjoining Benedictine abbey is thick with atmosphere.

Northeastern Italy

Many travelers to northern Italy don't seem to be aware that the country stretches east and north of Venice. Perhaps that's because the provinces of Trentino–Alto Adige (north of the Veneto) and Friuli–Venezia Giulia (northeast of Venice) are the least "Italian" of the country's regions, and, before the 20th century, neither was even part of Italy. Trentino–Alto Adige was part of Austria's South Tirol region for centuries, and the inhabitants prefer speaking German over Italian and eating schnitzel over pasta. In Friuli, the *friuliani* speak their own bizarre language, and the inhabitants of Trieste in Venezia Giulia have Slavic roots as well as a history of Austrian domination.

Trento

The breezy, frescoed town of Trento is the last northern outpost of "real" Italy before you hit Alto Adige's Italo-Germanic towns. In the 16th century, Trento hosted the famous Counter-Reformation showdown, the Council of Trent. The 18-year-long council did wonders for the city, and most of the palazzi, porticoes, and frescoes date from this era. Mellow Trento is the bus hub for the surrounding mountains and a good place to relax (and shower) in between tackling the **Parco Naturale Paneveggio,** the Brenta mountain range, and the nearby Monte Bondone (*see* Near Trento, *below*). The **APT** (Via Alfieri 4, tel. 0461/983880), across Piazza Dante from the station, provides oodles of helpful info on the city and Monte Bondone. For a map of the province and a list of *rifugi* (hiking shelters), walk 15 minutes to **APT Trentino** (C. III Novembre 132, tel. 0461/980000).

COMING AND GOING The **Stazione di Trento** (P. Dante, tel. 0461/234545) sends trains to Venice (1½ hrs, L12,100) and Munich (4 hrs 20 min, L53,200). To the right of the train station is the **bus station** (Via Pozzo 6, tel. 0461/983627). Buses run to Paneveggio (3 hrs, L8800) and Molveno (1½ hrs, L4600). The electric **Ferrovia Trento–Malè** train (Via Secondo da Trento 7, tel. 0461/822725) runs to Malè (1 hr 10 min, L5500) and other mountain destinations. To get to the Ferrovia Trento-Malè from Stazione di Trento, turn left onto Via Dogana, veer left around the curve to Via Segantini, and walk straight ahead; it's at the end of the street and to the left.

WHERE TO SLEEP AND EAT Trento is short on budget hotels; ask the APT for a list. The proprietors of the **Albergo Posta** (Via Roccabruno 2, just behind post office, tel. 0461/984709; doubles L52,000) are nice, but the large, clean rooms don't get much sun. The **HI Ostello Giovane Europa** (Via Manzoni 17, tel. 0461/234567) was closed for repairs at press time but should reopen soon. Most rooms are doubles or quads with bath. From the train station, turn left on Dogana, right on Via Romagnosi, and left on Via Manzoni. It's worth the 15-minute train ride south on the Verona line to reach **Ostello Città di Rovereto** (Viale delle Scuole 16, Rovereto, tel. 0464/433707). Rooms have two to six beds, bath, and some have a terrace. Some of the best food in Italy is served at lunch and dinner (L12,000 each). From the Rovereto train station, cross the street through Piazza Corsi and take the street on your right that starts with stairs; continue and turn left on Viale delle Scuole.

Wurst and strudel sneak onto Trento's menus, but the best bet is to stick with Italian dishes; highly recommended is *strangolapreti* (strangle the priests), a Trento specialty of green gnocchi, Gorgonzola, tomatoes, and basil. The home of the best salad bar for miles is **Al Giulia** (Via Gazzoletti 15, tel. 0461/984752; open daily 11:30–3), in an alley behind Banco di Roma on the left end of Piazza Dante. The cheapest full meal is at **Trattoria al Volt** (Via Santa Croce 16, tel. 0461/983776); primi are L5000–L6000 and secondi a mere L7000 (roasted chicken is a highlight).

WORTH SEEING The **Castello di Buonconsiglio** (Via Bernardo Clesio 5, tel. 0461/233770) is really two buildings: the **Castelvecchio,** a 14th-century hunk o' stone renovated in the 15th century to give it that trendy Venetian Gothic look; and the **Magno Palazzo,** a Renaissance palace commissioned by prince-bishop Bernardo Clesio in the 16th century. The result is a huge maze that's sure to get you lost. The real reason to visit the complex (and pay the L10,000 admission) is the **Aquila Tower,** which houses the wonderful Gothic fresco *Cycle of the Months,* which details everyday life of both the plebes and aristocrats. From the train station, turn right on Via Pozzo and left on Via Roma; follow it to the end and turn left on Via Bernardo Clesio. The **duomo** (P. Duomo), site of most of the meetings of the Council of Trent, is a dark, gloomy cathedral. Left of the nave, a superb fresco tells the legend of San Giuliano Ospitaliere, a sort of cross between Oedipus and Othello.

NEAR TRENTO

Trento's very own overgrown pet rock, **Monte Bondone,** hovers over the Adige River and rates as the locals' preferred site of picnics, ski trips, and afternoon strolls. Three towns are carved into the side of Monte Bondone: **Sardagna, Vaneze,** and **Vason**. All three have excellent hiking in summer and skiing in winter and are accessible by a short bus ride from Trento's bus station.

Italia Irredenta

The typical Italian street name of "Trento e Trieste" dates from the Irredentist movement of the early 20th century, when Italy attempted to regain control of certain areas—including Trento and Trieste—that were inhabited mostly by Italians but were ruled by the Austrians. The regions, called Italia irredenta, or unredeemed Italy, were, depending on your interpretation, either seized from the Austrians or returned to Mamma Italy with the 1919 Treaty of Versailles.

DOLOMITI DI BRENTA The Brenta Dolomites are a forbidding series of craggy peaks that look like giant stalagmites. Many of the trails that crisscross the range include metal ladders placed in rock (as prominently featured in Sylvester Stallone's *Cliffhanger,* in which the Dolomites stood in for the Rockies); you'll need a lot of alpine know-how (if not climbing equipment) to get through, as well as the *Kompass Wanderkarte* map (L8000), available in bookstores and some tourist offices. In winter, skiers pack this area; the best slopes are on **Monte Paganella,** accessible by chair lift from Andalo, a stop on the Trento–Molveno rail line. Inquire at the **Skipass Paganella-Brenta** office (Via Paganella, tel. 0461/585869) in Andalo about equipment.

The resort town of **Molveno,** 1½ hours from Trento by bus (L4600), is the best base for hiking in the Brenta Dolomites. The **APT** (P. Marconi 7, tel. 0461/586924; open Mon.–Sat. 8:30–12:30 and 3–6:30, Sun. 9–noon) doesn't have much hiking info but can help you find a room in one of the overpriced Molveno hotels. Try **Gani Camping** (Via Lungolago, tel. 0461/586169), a building with large, bland rooms for L66,000 a double. RV rest home **Camping Spiagga Lago di Molveno** (Via Lungolago 27, tel. 0461/586978) costs a whopping L5500–L8500 per person and L8000–L13,000 per tent, depending on the season.

Trieste

Squashed between the Adriatic and Slovenia in the eastern corner of Italy, Friuli–Venezia Giulia's biggest city lies within sight of Slovenia's shadowy hills across the water, and Slavic languages are often heard in the streets. Most of the city's older architecture was smashed by the Austrians who thought neoclassic was the apex of taste. Those of us who beg to differ won't get a thrill from walking around the city, but **Capitoline Hill,** overlooking the city, and the modern annex of **Museo Revoltella** (Via XXIV Maggio 4, at P. Venezia, tel. 040/361675), designed by the wacky architect Carlo Scarpa, are worth a look. Sun-crazed locals crowd the rocky shores in the summer, the nearby **Carso** mountains beg to be hiked, and **Aquilea,** an unbelievably well-preserved Roman ghost town, is a short bus ride away. Stop at the **APT** (in the train station, tel. 040/420182; open Mon.–Sat. 9–2 and 3–8) for brochures and a decent city map.

COMING AND GOING **Stazione Centrale** (P. Libertà 8, tel. 040/418207) runs trains to Venice (2 hrs, L12,100) and Udine (1½ hrs, L6500). From the adjacent **bus station, SAITA** buses (tel. 040/425001) run to Aquilea, Grado, and Udine. To reach the center from either station, veer right down Corso Cavour to Piazza Unità d'Italia.

WHERE TO SLEEP AND EAT Trieste doesn't have much in the way of cheap lodging, aside from the beachfront **Ostello Tergeste** (Viale Miramare 331, tel. 040/224102), where L17,000 gets you a bunk and breakfast. To get here, take Bus 36 catercorner from the train station; the last bus runs at 10 PM. Central **Locanda San Nicolò** (Via San Nicolò 2, tel. 040/366532) charges L38,000 for dark doubles, plus L2000 for a shower. From the station, walk down Corso Cavour and turn right at Piazza Tommaseo to Via San Nicolò. James Joyce's old stomping ground, **Osteria da Libere** (Via Risorta 9; closed Wed.), attracts a mix of local oldsters, hip intellectuals, and sailors who stumble in and get drunk on the excellent vat wine. A meal of soup, bread, and wine is only L3500; heartier meals are L8000.

Milan and Lombardy

Lombardy is probably Italy's most modern and efficient region, and its prompt trains and buses make getting around a breeze. Unfortunately, these same polluting trains and buses are packed with eager tourists—Italians and foreigners alike—who've come to enjoy the cultural, gastronomic, and scenic attractions. Having been conquered at one time or another by every yahoo with an army this side of Jerusalem, the people of Lombardy retain a deep fear of outsiders. To travelers—especially haggard backpackers—the regional attitude comes across as snobbishness or indifference. But with all the apparent drawbacks, there's still a reason to visit the region: Amid the chaff of pollution, attitude, and high prices, there remains the natural beauty of the lakes and the architectural beauty of high-cultured Milan, Mantova, and Bergamo.

Milan

In no way will Milan (Milano) satisfy your yearnings for the laid-back, beautiful, and charmingly disorganized Italy; it's faster, more serious, and annoyingly expensive. It also lacks the aesthetic appeal of other Italian cities, thanks largely to the fact that it's been ravaged three times by war—in AD 539, 1157, and 1944. Still, Milan does have the cultural buzz (and amenities) of an international metropolis. It has loads of classical and contemporary art, and a fantastically unique duomo. It also offers excellent shopping and people-watching, a glitzy nightlife, and one of the few gay scenes in Italy. On the down side, Milan is a real bummer if you're dirt poor or pollution sensitive.

BASICS

VISITOR INFORMATION The two main **APT** tourist offices are at the **Stazione Centrale** (tel. 02/669–0532; open Mon.–Sat. 8–7, Sun. 9–12:30 and 1:30–6) and in the **Palazzo del Turismo** (Via Marconi 1, tel. 02/809662; open Mon.–Sat. 8–8, Sun. 9–12:30 and 1:30–5) on Piazza del Duomo. For more information, particularly regarding the arts, **Comune di Milano** (Galeria Vittorio Emanuele, at P. Scala, tel. 02/878363; open Mon.–Sat. 8–8) gives out *Guida ai Serviza della Città*, an invaluable source book for all city services.

AMERICAN EXPRESS *Via Brera 3, 2 blocks behind La Scala Opera, tel. 02/876674. Mailing address: Via Brera 3, 20121 Milano. Open Mon.–Thurs. 9–5:30, Fri. 9–5.*

CHANGING MONEY You can change cash and traveler's checks for a 1%–2% fee at the information office in the Stazione Centrale. Or look for **Banca Commerciale** (there's a branch in front of Stazione Centrale), which does not charge a commission.

CONSULATES **Australia.** *Via Borgogna 2, tel. 02/7601–3330. Open weekdays 9–noon and 2–4:30.*

Canada. *Via Vittor Pisani 19, tel. 02/669–7451, 02/6698–0600 in an emergency. Open weekdays 9–12:30 and 1:30–5:15.*

United Kingdom. *Via San Paolo 7, tel. 02/869–3442. Open weekdays 9:15–12:15 and 2:30–4:30.*

United States. *Via P. Amedeo 2/10, tel. 02/2900–1841. Open weekdays 9–1.*

PHONES AND MAIL For collect or cash calls, go to the **Iritel** office (open daily 8–7:45) at Stazione Centrale or the **main post office** (Via Cordusio 4, tel. 02/869–2069; open weekdays 8:15–7:50, Sat. 8:15–5:50), at the Cordusio Metro stop.

COMING AND GOING

Stazione Centrale (tel. 02/67500), on Metro lines 2 and 3 a few km northeast of downtown, handles trains to Venice (4–5 hrs, L18,700), Florence (3 hrs, L30,000), and Rome (5–7 hrs, L60,000). Long-distance and international buses depart from outside the **Autostradale** office (P. Castello, tel. 02/801161; open daily 6:30 AM–7 PM).

Linate Airport (tel. 02/738–0233), about 10 km from the city, and **Malpensa Airport** (tel. 02/4009–9111), 45 km from downtown, both handle domestic and international flights. Frequent **STAM** buses (tel. 02/6698–4509) connect Linate (10 min, L4000) and Malpensa (45 min, L10,000) with Stazione Centrale. Look for signs marked AEROPORTI DI MILANO to the right outside the train station.

GETTING AROUND

Three concentric thoroughfares encircle **Piazza del Duomo,** the center of town. The area that lies within the innermost circle, the **Cerchia dei Navigli,** holds the majority of Milan's attractions. Tickets good for the Metro, buses, and trams cost L1200. You can also buy 11-ticket packs (L11,000) or one-day (L3800) or two-day (L6600) passes in the Cadorna, Romolo, S. Donato, and Centrale Metro stations. Offices in the Duomo Metro station and Stazione Centrale provide maps and information about all public transportation.

WHERE TO SLEEP

The best area for cheap lodging is the somewhat seedy Città Studi district around the university, east of the central train station, but the city's center has a handful of more convenient, affordable rooms.

Hotel Cesare Correnti. Well-lit hotel in center has singles for L35,000, doubles L50,000–L55,000. *Via Cesare Correnti 14, 2nd floor, tel. 02/805–7609. 5-min walk from duomo.*

Hotel Pedrotti. Central and cheap: Singles are L25,000, doubles L40,000. The manager sometimes enforces a three-night minimum stay. *Via San Tommaso 6, 3rd floor, tel. 02/864–6971. Off Via Dante. Reservations advised. Reception closed Sun.*

Hotel Ullrich. Clean, friendly, cheap, and central. Small singles about L35,000, doubles L50,000. *C. Italia 6, tel. 02/8645–0156. 5-min walk from duomo.*

HOSTEL **Piero Rotta Hostel.** On the outskirts of town. Beds L20,000. *Via Martino Bassi 2, tel. 02/3926–7095. 5-min walk from Lotto Metro. Pay phone, luggage storage, hot showers L1000. 12:30 AM curfew, lockout 9 AM–5 PM. Closed Dec. 24–Jan. 12.*

FOOD

Milan does not cater to budget-minded diners, and only in the Navigli quarter will you find vaguely cheap eats. Most restaurants are closed on Sundays and many close in August. Strapped travelers head to the supermarkets **Esselunga** (Viale Piave 38/40, tel. 02/204–7871) and **Standa** (C. Buenos Aires 37, tel. 02/204–9297).

For a quick, cheap lunch, latterie (milk and cheese stores) with TAVOLA CALDA signs serve simple local dishes. One of the best is Latteria Unione (Via Unione 6, bet. San Satiro and the Duomo).

A beer bar across from San Lorenzo church, **Birreria San Lorenzo** (C. di Porta Ticinese 14, tel. 02/837–8508; closed Wed.) serves good sandwiches (about L7000 each) and stays open until 2 AM. Also across from San Lorenzo, **Trattoria Artisti** (C. di Porta Ticinese 16, tel. 02/8940–1105) has primi for L7000 and hearty secondi for L7000–L12,000. **Il Moro** (Via Laura Ciceri Visconti 8, tel. 02/5518–8128) serves exotic pizzas topped with curry and shrimp or kiwi and banana. You'll pay L12,000 for pizza and a beer. From the city center, take Bus 84 to the Via Pistrucci–Imperator Tito stop. You can sample Milan's thriving café scene at **Bar Magenta** (Via Carducci 13, at Via Magenta), near Santa Maria delle Grazie, where cocktails are served until 2 AM.

WORTH SEEING

Most of Milan's main attractions are clustered within the city's innermost ring; other sights are easily accessible by public transportation. At the impressive glass-arched **Galleria Vittorio Emanuele** shopping mall, next to the duomo, you can people-watch, sip an overpriced caffè, or stand on Taurus's testicles in the central mosaic for good luck.

CASTELLO SFORZESCO This brawny brick castle was built by the Sforza and Visconti clans in 1450. Bramante designed the castle's *rochetta* (fortress) and bridge, and Leonardo da Vinci decorated the interior. The castello currently houses a variety of museums; most memorable is the **Pinacoteca** (picture gallery). The castle's **Museo d'Arte** is worth a look for Michelangelo's haunting, unfinished sculpture, the *Rondanini Pietà. P. Castello, tel. 02/6236. Metro: Cairoli or Cadorna. Admission free. Open Tues.–Sun. 9:30–12:15 and 2:30–5:15.*

DUOMO Construction began on this ornate creature in 1386 and was not finished until 1897 (as late as 1958 workers were still tying up loose ends). The many hands that worked on the mammoth duomo created an odd but incredible mix of Gothic and Baroque styles. The vast interior is colored by stained-glass windows, and the central crucifix hangs from a suspension device designed by Leonardo da Vinci. *P. del Duomo. Metro: Duomo. Admission free. Open daily 7–7.*

THE LAST SUPPER To the left of the Santa Maria delle Grazie church is the former refectory of a Dominican monastery that holds Leonardo da Vinci's *Last Supper.* The embattled fresco has suffered innumerable attacks: Napoléon's troops used the wall for target practice, and in August 1943, a bomb nearly destroyed the church. If you can overlook the scaffolding, the fresco still has an odd transfixing power. *P. Santa Maria delle Grazie, tel. 02/498–7588. Metro: Cadurno. Admission: L6000. Open Tues.–Sun. 8:15 AM–1:45 PM.*

MUSEO DI SCIENZA E TECNICA Housed in a former Benedictine monastery, this is one of the world's foremost museums of science and technology. The Leonardo Gallery has a collection of models based on designs by da Vinci. *Via San Vittore 21, tel. 02/4801–0040. Metro: S. Ambrogio. Admission: L6000.*

PINACOTECA BRERA Milan's most important museum has 38 rooms housing such masterpieces as Lorenzetti's *Madonna and Child,* Piero della Francesca's *Urbino Altarpiece,* Raphael's *Marriage of the Virgin,* Mantegna's *Dead Christ,* Giovanni Bellini's *Pietà,* and Caravaggio's *Supper at Emmaus. Via Brera 28, tel. 02/808387. Metro: Lanza. Admission: L8000. Open Tues.–Sat. 9–5:30, Sun. 9–12:45.*

Make an effort to see something at La Scala (P. della Scala, tel. 02/805–3418), a sacred pilgrimage site for opera buffs and Verdi lovers. The opera season runs December–May, and discount tickets on the day of the performance cost as little as L10,000.

AFTER DARK

Like many big cities, Milan has a hopping but expensive nightlife. The newspapers *Il Corriere della Sera* and *La Repubblica* regularly list cultural events and club schedules. For information on Milan's gay scene, visit the bookstore **Babele** (Via Sanmartini 21, tel. 02/669–2986). **Nuova Idea** (Via de Castiesa 30, tel. 02/689–2753) is Italy's largest gay disco, where you can boogie on the main floor or get involved in an intricate tango on the couples' floor. **Portnoy Caffè Letterario** (Via de Amicis at C. di Porta Ticinese, tel. 02/837–8656) pairs coffee with nightly poetry readings and poetry-related lectures. **Capolinea** (Via Lodovico Il Moro 119, tel. 02/470524) is the preeminent jazz club in Milan.

NEAR MILAN

BERGAMO On a day trip, you can skip over charmless Bergamo Bassa (Lower Bergamo) and head straight up to majestically beautiful Bergamo Alta (Upper Bergamo), where the town's main attractions lie. Bernard Berenson, Le Corbusier, and Frank Lloyd Wright thought that Bergamo Alta's **Piazza Vecchia** was one of Italy's loveliest squares. It marks the heart of the upper city and is a gathering place for both locals and tourists. Piazza Duomo features both the frothily decorated **duomo** and the impressive pink-and-white marble **Capella Colleoni,** designed by Giovanni Antonio Amadeo. **Accademia Carrara** (P. dell'Accademia, tel. 035/399426; closed Tues.) contains an excellent collection of Italian paintings. **APT** (Vicolo Aguila Nera 2, off P. Vecchia, tel. 035/232730) has more info on sights. If you want to stay the night, **Ostello di Bergamo** (Via Galileo Ferraris 1, tel. 035/342349; closed Nov. 14–Feb. 16) charges L16,000 for a bed and breakfast. They were under restoration at press time. To get here, take Bus 14 from Porta Nuova. Trains run hourly between Milan and Bergamo's **train station** (P. Marconi, tel. 035/247624); the one-hour trip costs L4300.

Mantova

A city rich in art, history, and political intrigue, Mantova (Mantua in English) alternates between being gloomily gothic and outrageously decadent. The Gonzaga family ruled the city from the early 14th to the early 18th century, and they oversaw the creation and (often ostentatious) decoration of everything from the Palazzo Ducale, Palazzo Te, and the duomo to the churches of Sant'Andrea and San Sebastiano. Too much wealth and flamboyance in too small an area has left the city both enchanted and overwhelmed, which is why Mantova is one of the most fascinating towns in the region. **APT** (P. Mantegna 6, tel. 0376/350681) has the usual info and changes cash and traveler's checks for a 1% commission. The **Centro Prenotozione Alberghiera** (Via Accademia 46, tel. 0376/365401) arranges private accommodations.

COMING AND GOING Mantova's small **train station** (P. Don Leoni) sends trains to Milan (2 hrs, L12,000) and Verona (45 min, L3200). All long-distance buses depart from the **Autostazione** (Piazzale le Mondadori, tel. 0376/327237), two blocks east of the train station. From the train station, the center of town is a 10-minute hike east.

WHERE TO SLEEP Mantova has few budget lodgings, so it's best to make reservations. The hostel **Sparafucile Ostello per la Gioventù** (Strada Legnaghese, tel. 0376/372465; beds L14,000; closed Oct. 16–Mar.) has a daytime lockout and an 11 PM curfew. Take Bus 2M, 6, or 9 from Piazza Cavalotti to get here. At charming **Rinascita** (Via Concezione 4, tel. 0376/320607), singles cost L25,000, doubles L40,000; from the station, take Via Alberto Pitentino to Via Portazzolo, then go two blocks east. Grim **ABC Moderno** (P. Don Leoni 25, tel. 0376/322329), across from the station, has L35,000 singles and L55,000 doubles.

FOOD The **open-air market** on Piazza Erbe sells all sorts of picnic food; Thursday morning is the best time to visit. Try **Ristorante Fast-Food Il Punto** (Via Solferino 36, tel. 0376/327552) for cheap and filling sandwiches, burgers, pizza, and pasta. **Ai Garibaldini** (Via S. Longino 7, tel. 0376/328263; closed Wed.) is a bit expensive but serves a delicious variety of Mantovan dishes. Come to **Leoncino Rosso** (Via Giustiziati 33, behind P. Erbe, tel. 0376/323277) for fish and a selection of roasted meats (L7000–L10,000). At night, this is a good place for low-key carousing.

WORTH SEEING Prepare to be overwhelmed by architecture that ranges from severe and heavy-handed to frothy, eccentric, and over-the-top. In one afternoon, you can experience the facade of Leon Battista Alberti's poorly renovated **San Sebastiano** (Via N. Sauro), with ziggurratlike stairs that discourage rather than invite entry, and, just beyond the town walls, Giulio Romano's **Palazzo Te** (Viale Te, tel. 0376/632–3266; admission L10,000; open Tues.–Sun. 10–6), a Mannerist pleasure palace that does not skimp on decorative details. The town's 11th-century **duomo** (P. Sordello) has a distinctive carved ceiling and parallel lines of Corinthian columns. The Gonzaga family's **Palazzo Ducale** (P. Sordello, tel. 0376/320283; admission L10,000; open Sun.–Mon. 9–1, Tues.–Sat. 9–1 and 2:30–4, until 5 in summer) is a 500-room extravaganza—a sprawling complex of living quarters, courts, meeting halls,

The Lakes

"The Lakes" of northern Italy are a vast region that is spread over the middle third of the borderlands and into Switzerland. North of Milan, things are uniformly green and watery, but each of the lakes has a distinct personality: among them are Lago di Garda, the so-called party lake; Como and Maggiore, the ritzier lakes; and Orta, the small, serene lake. All are well-connected by rail to Milan, and all feature prime hiking (though Garda is best for water sports). Lake Garda is also the best outpost for weary backpackers, because of the Benacus Youth Hostel (P. Cavour 10, tel. 0464/554911; beds L14,000; closed Nov.–Feb.) in Riva del Garda. Frequent daily trains run from Milan to Garda's train station.

and excellent artwork by Mantegna, Pisanello, Titian, Rubens, and Correggio. Alberti's austerely arched **Chiesa Sant'Andrea** (P. Mantegna) holds court painter Andrea Mantegna's tomb and burial chapel and, in the crypt, a reliquary containing the supposed blood of Christ.

The Italian Riviera

The Italian Riviera of the flashy '60s postcard—absurdly long yachts and women in gold-plated bikinis—is today a hazy delusion for people in expensive sunglasses. Maybe it's the word "Riviera," calling up visions of the chichi French coast, that sends the imagination running wild. Luxurious bliss does exist here, but only for those who don't carry their own luggage. The rest of us have to settle for blue ocean, a profusion of flowers, hot focaccia, and hostel beds. **Finale Ligure** to the west and **Santa Margherita Ligure** in the east both beckon the budget traveler, although Cinque Terre's cliff-clinging seaside villages are the best destination for adventurous backpackers. Genova, the fascinating but weathered sailing town in the center of the Riviera, doesn't attract many except as a transportation hub, but it deserves more attention and careful exploration.

Genova

The central town of the Italian Riviera is a composite of extremes. The people seem to mimic the geographic highs and lows of mountains and sea as they vacillate between wild gesticulation and melancholy reserve. Visibly, Genova (Genoa in English) has come down in the world since its Renaissance glory days of commerce and conquest. Though the city is soiled from neglect, you don't have to look hard to see its former splendor—artistic spoils procured from the Crusades, the colonial era, and foreign occupation are everywhere. The best way to understand Genova is to surrender to its mood swings: Get lost in back alleys, feast on regional cooking, and take in the view from high on a hill.

BASICS The **exchange bureaus** in the two major train stations, Stazione Principe (P. Acquaverde, tel. 010/284081) and Stazione Brignole (P. Verdi, tel. 010/562956), offer the best rates and charge no commission. Make long-distance calls at the **Iritel** office (Via XX Settembre 136/A). The **post office** (Via d'Annunzia 34, tel. 010/591762) is open Monday–Saturday 8:15–7:40. The postal code is 16100. You'll find one **EPT** visitor information office on Via Roma (tel. 010/541541; open weekdays 8–1:30 and 2–5, Sat. 8–1:30) and one at Stazione Principe (tel. 010/262633; open Mon.–Sat. 8–8).

COMING AND GOING Genova has two main train stations, **Stazione Principe** (P. Acquaverde, tel. 010/262455) and **Stazione Brignole** (P. Verdi, tel. 010/586350). Both stations are on the same line, but sometimes trains scheduled to pass through both will only stop at one, so ask the conductor when you board. Trains run to Milan (2 hrs, L11,200) from both stations and to Rome (6 hrs, L33,000) from Brignole. The **Tigullio** bus line (tel. 010/313851) runs frequently from Piazza Vittoria (near Stazione Brignole), linking Genova with other towns on the Riviera. **Tirrenia Navigazione** (Stazione Marittima, Ponte Colombo, tel. 010/258041) offers ferry service to Sicily. Schedules and prices vary drastically from season to season.

GETTING AROUND Stazione Principe is on the west end of town, Stazione Brignole on the east; in between lies the maze-like **centro storico** (old town), where most of the interesting sights are. City bus tickets are sold at any tabaccheria and at the train stations. One ticket (L1000) is good for 90 minutes. Bus 33 travels between the train stations; Buses 37 and 41 will take you into the town center from Stazione Principe. A series of *funicolari* (trams) and *ascensori* (elevators) help truck you up and down the hills.

WHERE TO SLEEP The best area for affordable lodging is near Stazione Brignole. **Albergo Carletto** (Via Colombo 16/4, off P. Verdi, tel. 010/588412) has spacious, quiet doubles (L55,000–L75,000). **Albergo Fiume** (Via Fiume 9r, across from Stazione Brignole, tel.

010/59691) lets charming doubles for L55,000. The inconvenient but heavenly **Ostello per la Gioventù** (Via Costanzi 120, tel. 010/242–2457) charges L13,000 (including breakfast) for a dorm bed or L20,000 per person for a family room with bath. Take Bus 40 from Stazione Brignole to the top of the hill. If you want to camp, the excellent **Villa Doria** (Via Vespucci 25, tel. 010/680613) in the Pegli suburb costs L6000 per person, or you can stay in a bungalow for L50,000–L100,000 (two–six people). Take the local train to Pegli, then take Bus 93.

FOOD Don't leave Genova without indulging in a little *pesto* (the Genovese sauce made of basil, olive oil, and pine nuts), either over *trennette* (a potato-based pasta similar to gnocchi) or on a pizza with pungent *stracchino* cheese. **Caffè degli Specchi** (Salita Pollaioli 43r, off P. Matteotti, tel. 010/281293) serves sandwiches (L4000–L6000) downstairs and has a sit-down restaurant upstairs, where you can get a plate of cold specialties (L9000) that includes *la farinata*, a torte made from garbanzo beans. At **Trattoria da Maria** (Vico Testadoro 14r, off Via XXV Aprile, tel. 010/581080), you eat at big tables side by side with everyone from loony ex-sailors to chic businessmen. A full meal including wine costs L12,000. Just down from the hostel, **La Rosa del Parco** (Via Costanza 40, tel. 010/2425375) serves pasta, pizza *al forno* (cooked in a wood-burning oven), meat, and fresh fish. After dinner, head to **Polena** (Vico del Filo 21r, off P. San Lorenzo, tel. 010/207400), a local beer bar where people bring their own instruments and play while Massimo, the owner, supplies them with English beer on tap.

Stay away from Genova's centro storico after dark—with your lost look and fanny pack screaming "mug me"—unless you know exactly where you're going or are with locals.

WORTH SEEING The **centro storico,** extending west from Piazza de Ferrari to Piazza Caricamento, south to Piazza Sarzano, and north to Piazza Nunziata, is where you find most of the good stuff. The **Porta Soprana,** an entrance to the district off Piazza Dante, leads to a maze of convents and monasteries and to Piazza Sarzano. It's next to Casa Colombo (in fact, Christopher Columbus's father was the gatekeeper of the Porta Soprana). You'll see traces of the city's former Baroque splendor on the palace-packed **Via Garibaldi,** though the buildings suffer from centuries of sooty neglect. **Palazzo Bianco** (Via Garibaldi 11; admission L4000; open Tues.–Sat. 9–7, Sun. 9–noon) is not so bianco anymore, but it houses a collection of outstanding paintings by Ligurian, Dutch, and Flemish masters.

The **Cattedrale San Lorenzo** (Via San Lorenzo, off P. Matteotti), built in 1118, meshes Romanesque, medieval, and Renaissance architecture, even integrating the remains of a World War II naval shell. The Gothic **Museo di Sant'Agostino** (P. Sarzano 21; admission L4000, free Sun.; closed Mon.), once a church, is now a beautiful architecture and sculpture museum. The collection includes 15th-century panels that are part of Giovanni Pisano's famous funerary monument. In the Palazzo Spinola's **Galleria Nazionale della Liguria** (Via Pellicceria 1, tel. 010/294661; admission L4000), notice the detailed old maps lining the stairway walls. You can also check out some great works by Van Dyck here. The richly adorned **Doria Apartments,** home of the powerful Doria family during the Renaissance, and the **Chiesa San Matteo** circumscribe Piazza San Matteo. Summaries of glorious Dorian achievements are ever-so-modestly inscribed on the exterior of the church.

Cinque Terre

Cinque Terre, a conglomeration of five tiny villages (Monterosso, Vernazza, Corniglia, Manarola, and Riomaggiore), is the Cinderella of the Italian Riviera. In their rugged humility, the five old fishing towns seem to mock the caked-on artifice of neighboring resorts. Multicolored architecture emerges almost seamlessly from cliffs, and rocky mountains rise precipitously to gravity-defying olive groves. **Monterosso** is the biggest, least attractive, and most expensive of the towns; **Vernazza, Corniglia,** and **Riomaggiore** are far more appealing. Trains run from Genova about six times daily to the five towns (1 hr 45 min, L6500). Train service between the towns is frequent, but the best way to see the vineyards, olive groves, and sea is to travel on foot. The **Visitor Associazione Turistica Pro Loco** (Via Fegina 38, tel. 0187/817506), just outside the Monterosso train station, has a map of the scenic footpaths as well as lots of info about hotels and boat rides.

WHERE TO SLEEP AND EAT *Camere affite* (private rooms for rent) abound here, especially in little Riomaggiore; look for signs posted on homes or ask the first matronly person you encounter. Call ahead to stay at the rooms managed by **Edda Silvestri** (Via Sant'Antonio 96, Riomaggiore, tel. 0187/920020; doubles L50,000). In Vernazza, **Pensione Barbara** (P. Marconi 23, tel. 0187/812201; closed winter) has swell doubles overlooking the port for L55,000; call ahead. At **Ostello Mamma Rosa** (Piazzale Unità 2, Riomaggiore, tel. 0187/920050; beds L20,000), men and women of all ages sleep in the same rooms, and HI membership is not required.

For snacks or picnic fixings, locals go to the popular **Focacceria il Frantoio** (Via Gioberti 1, tel. 0187/818333) in Monterosso. **Bar Trattoria la Grotta** (Via Colombo 123, Riomaggiore, tel. 0187/920187) is a family-run trattoria, actually in a grotto, specializing in typical Ligurian food like *spaghetti allo scoglio,* a seafood pasta (L9000). For the closest thing to an all-night diner, try **Caffè Cagliari** (Via Roma 13, tel. 0187/817164).

Bologna and Emilia-Romagna

The green, rain-fed, Po-enriched plains of Emilia-Romagna reach from the Adriatic Sea halfway across the country, and from the ridge of the Apennines up to the Via Emilia, the old Roman road. Emilia-Romagna is composed of two distinct provinces with very different histories. Emilia, stretching from Bologna to Piacenza, is a wealthy area and the indisputable food capital of the country. To the east, Romagna, as its name implies, preserves Roman traditions, monuments, and cuisine. As the region with the highest standard of living in Italy, Emilia-Romagna can get expensive, tempting the traveler into its own luxurious way of life. It's hard to resist indulging in the area's world-renowned music, exquisite food, and fine wine. Aside from Bologna, capital of Emilia and the old Communist Party, and Parma, a continual art and food fest, in Emilia-Romagna you'll find mosaic-filled **Ravenna; Modena** and **Ferrara,** which display the spoils of both modern wealth and a rich artistic and architectural past; and **Rimini,** Italy's pleasure zone, home to color coordinated beach clubs and scandalous all-night dance clubs.

Bologna

Though rooted in a rigid scholastic tradition, Bologna, home to Europe's oldest university, is by no means the self-flagellating ascetic of the academic world. Rather, it boasts a history of indulgence that is hinted at by the tasteless postcard that reduces the city's essence to three Ts: "Torre, tortellini, e tette" (towers, tortellini, and tits). But this type of adolescent humor is at once muted by the city's perfectly porticoed Renaissance sophistication, soberly majestic red rooftops, medieval towers, and radically symmetrical layout. But this seat of seminal wisdom has loosened up enough to encompass the country's most active communist and radical student organizations, as well as a thriving gay community. The plethora of students make eating cheap and easy and nightlife a blast.

When the Renaissance dawned in Italy, Emilia-Romagna's towns developed into court cities, glorified by their often eccentric and generally tyrannical dukes and lords: the Estes in Ferrara, the Pepolis and Bentivoglios in Bologna, the Malatestas in Rimini, and the Farnese in Parma.

BASICS The **post office** at Palazzo Comunale (Via Oleari 3, off Via Ugo Bassi, tel. 051/223598) is open weekdays 8:15–6:30, Saturday 8:15–12:20. To make an international phone call, head to **Iritel** (P. Otto Agosto 24, no phone), open daily 7 AM–10:30 PM. The **IAT** booth at the train station (tel. 051/246541) will book accommodations, but it isn't as well equipped as main office at Piazza Maggiore 6 (tel. 051/239660; open Mon.–Sat. 9–7, Sun. 9–1.)

COMING AND GOING Bologna's **train station** (P. della Medaglie d'Oro, tel. 050/246490) is a major rail hub. Trains depart frequently to Rome (4½ hrs, L33,000), Florence (50 min, L7200), and Milan (1 hr 40 min, L15,400).

Bologna is walkable. Its Renaissance walls are pierced by 12 *porte* (entrances), usually connected to streets that one way or another will get you to Piazza Maggiore, in the middle of the centro storico. The conspicuous medieval towers in Piazza Ravegnana are visible from just about anywhere.

ATC buses cover the city. Offices at the train and **bus station** (P. XX Settembre 1, tel. 051/248374) post schedules and sell tickets daily 6 AM–8 PM. The ticket and information booth on Via Marconi at Via delle Lame (open 6:45 AM–7:15 PM) is much more convenient. A L1300 bus ticket is good for an hour.

WHERE TO SLEEP Unless you stay at the hostel or campgrounds, accommodations are expensive. Be sure to call ahead, especially in August, because a lot of places shut down for a few weeks every year. Run by a fastidious plant lover, **Albergo Panorama** (Via Livraghi 1, tel. 051/221802) has spacious doubles with a view for L65,000. From the station, take Bus 25 to Via Ugo Bassi; Via Livraghi is between Via Cesare Battisti and Via della Zecca. Clean and central **Albergo Apollo** (Via Drapperie 5, tel. 051/223955; closed Aug.) has so-so doubles for L66,000. From the station, take Bus 25 to Piazza Maggiore, walk down Via Rizzoli, and turn right on Via Drapperie. Smack in the center of Via Ugo Bassi, **Albergo Centrale** (Via della Zecca 2, tel. 051/225114) has air-conditioned, newly remodeled doubles without bath for L72,000. From the station, take Bus 25 to Via Ugo Bassi.

Villa-turned-HI hostel, **Ostello per la Gioventù** (Via Viadagola 14, San Sisto, tel. 051/519202; closed Dec. 20–Jan. 19) has beds for L16,000, breakfast included. A satellite **HI hostel** (Via Viadagola 5, tel. 015/501810) accommodates the overflow. To get to the main hostel from the train station, walk a block to Via dei Mille/Via Irnerio and take Bus 93, 20B, or 301 to Località San Sisto. Grassy **Camping Città di Bologna** (Via Romita 12/4a, tel. 051/325016) costs L7000–L9000 per night. From the train station, take Bus 25, 11, or 30, ask the driver where to get off, and follow the signs.

FOOD A good place to look for food is trattoria-lined **Via Pratello,** at the end of Via Ugo Bassi away from the towers, or the area near **Via delle Belle Arti,** between Via dell'Indipendenza and Via Zamboni around the university. To pick up your own supplies, head to the **Mercato delle Erbe** (Via Ugo Bassi 2; open Mon.–Wed. and Fri. 7:15–1 and 5–7, Sat. 7:15–1). The **Irnerio Mensa** (P. Vittorio Puntoni 1, tel. 051/246115; closed Mon.), officially restricted to those bearing student IDs, serves a full, tasty meal for L5000. Tucked away in a residential neighborhood, **Da Vito Trattoria** (Via Musolesi 9, tel. 051/349809; closed Wed. and 3 wks in Aug.) serves pastas for around L7000. Try the delicious *tagliatelle spek e funghi* (pasta with a meat and mushroom sauce). Share a delicious *crostini* (toasted bread with a variety of toppings) platter at **Osteria del Montesino** (Via del Pratello 74/B, tel. 051/523426; closed Mon.). After 10 PM, it's a great place for a late-night snack and a beer.

WORTH SEEING Although it may not boast a *David* or a *Mona Lisa,* the city as a whole is exceptionally beautiful. To catch a glimpse of Bologna's red rooftopped splendor, climb up the city's most conspicuous point of reference, the **Torre degli Asinelli** (P. di Porta Ravegnana). The physically fit can try the arduous but rewarding climb 9–7 daily for L3000. Museums are generally open 9–1 or 2 and 3:30–7.

Dominating central **Piazza Maggiore,** the massive **Basilica di San Petronio** was designed by Antonio di Vincenzo. Jacopo della Quercia carved the *Madonna and Child* and the main doors depicting scenes from the Old and New Testaments. Note the Gothic arches, Parmigianino's *San Rocco,* the frescoes by Giovanni da Modena, and the sadly unfinished exterior (funds ran out). Across the square, Giambologna's **Fontana del Nettuno**'s erotic putti and breast-clenching sirens spurt water aplenty for the crowds.

Santo Stefano (Via Santo Stefano 24, tel. 051/223256), a complex of three adjoining churches (there were originally seven) dating from the 9th to 13th centuries, is probably the most interesting architectural attraction in Bologna. The Romanesque **Crucifix Church** retains a medieval Lombard style; the **Holy Sepulcher Church,** containing St. Petronio's remains, is thought to have been a pagan temple in the 1st century AD; **the Church of Santi Vitale e Agricola** is the oldest church in the group, built from bits and pieces of Roman artifacts. Amid the churches is **Pilate's Courtyard,** with its sepulchers and *St. Peter's Cock,* a stone rooster whose presence is a reminder of St. Peter's denial of Christ.

Gelateria Ugo (Via San Felice 24, tel. 051/263849; open Mar.–Oct.) makes the most unbelievable ice-cream sandwich—a single or double scoop stuffed between hot, sweet, raisin focaccia bread and topped with whipped cream (L4000).

Inside **Palazzo Ghisilardi-Fava,** the **Museo Civico Medievale** (Via Manzoni 4, tel. 051/228912; admission L5000, L2500 students; closed Tues.) houses a fabulous collection of 13th- to 14th-century sepulchers depicting masters with their sleeping or otherwise distracted students, along with medieval and Renaissance ceramic, glass, and bronze instruments. The **Pinacoteca Nazionale** (Via delle Belle Arti 56, tel. 051/243249; admission L6000) has a collection of paintings from the Byzantine to Baroque eras. Huge canvases by Guido Reni include the impressive *Pietà dei Santi Petronio, Domenico, Carlo Borromeo, Francesco d'Assisi, e Procolo* and the dramatic *Crosifissione.*

AFTER DARK Like in any other college town, what's hot and what's not is in a constant state of flux. Pick up a copy of *Anteprima* (L2000) for listings of live music and theater. For information on gay and lesbian entertainment, call **Centro di Documentazione il Cassero** (tel. 051/431143).

In summer, the city hosts **Bologna Sogna,** a series of events ranging from classical concerts and live jazz to DJs spinning dance music in parks and on hillsides. Near Via San Vitale, the bar **Vicolo Bolognetti** (in a piazza off the alleyway Vicolo Bolognetti) is one of Bologna Sogna's only regular venues. **Circolo della Musica di Bologna** (Via Galliera 11, tel. 051/227032) has free classical music concerts throughout summer. Piazza Maggiore often holds free rock and alternative concerts in summer, and students can almost always be found hanging out in Piazza Verdi, near the university. **Osteria del Moretto** (Via San Mamolo 5, across from Chiesa San Francesco, tel. 051/580284) is as close to a pub as you're going to find in Italy. Wine, beer, and guitar music attract people of all ages.

Parma

In spacious Parma, filled with parks and piazze, flawlessly dressed locals leisurely pedal their bicycles over the cobblestones. The city, an hour west of Bologna, boasts the highest standard of living in Italy and manifests its style in everything it does. In between mouthfuls of the country's finest prosciutto, parmigiano cheese, and tortelli, catch a look at work by native Mannerist painters Corregio and Parmigianino (their work is *everywhere*). Frequent trains run to Parma every hour on their way to Milan (1½ hrs, L10,500), Bologna (1 hr, L10,000), and other major destinations. The station is a five-minute ride on Bus 9 or 15-minute walk down Via Verdi from the center. Parma's **visitor information** office (P. Duomo 5, tel. 0521/234735; open weekdays 9–12:30 and 3–5, Sat. 9–12:30) has more info on sights and transportation.

The Romanesque **duomo** (P. Duomo, tel. 0521/235886), built in the mid-11th century, contains Correggio's innovative *Ascension of the Virgin*; the duomo's octagonal, pink marble **baptistry** (admission L3000, L500 students) is next door. The **Palazzo della Pilotta** (tel.

0521/233309), an unfinished cluster of brick fortresses that dominates the banks of the River Parma, holds the lavishly frescoed **Teatro Farnese** (admission L4000; open daily 9–7:30), as well as the **Galleria Nazionale** (open daily 9–1:45), another showcase for Correggio and Parmigianino. The gallery's L10,000 admission price includes a look at the Teatro. The ethereal, 16th-century church of **Santa Maria della Steccata** (Via Garibaldi, bet. Via Dante and Piazzale della Steccata, tel. 0521/234937) houses the tombs of the Farnese dukes and a pair of organ doors by Parmigianino. Its cupola is frescoed by Bernardo Gatti in the tradition of Correggio's perspective realism.

WHERE TO SLEEP AND EAT There are a couple of affordable hotels within spitting distance of the train station and a couple more in the heart of town, near Piazza Garibaldi. The **Albergo Croce di Malta** (Borgo Palmia 8, tel. 0521/235643; desk closed Sun.) has shiny, spacious doubles for L55,000; from Piazza Garibaldi, follow Via Farini for a block and turn right on Borgo Palmia. The **Albergo Moderno** (Via A. Cecchi 4, tel. 0521/772647), a few doors down from the train station, has clean and attractive doubles for L58,300. The 16th-century Farnese citadel becomes the **HI Ostello Cittadella** (Via Passo Buole, tel. 0521/581546) May through September. Gritty, dorm-style beds cost L13,000. From the station, take Bus 9.

The production center of parmigiano and prosciutto, Parma loves its food. There's a permanent **outdoor market** in Piazza Ghiaia, just south of the Palazzo della Pilotta. Stop by the **Salumeria Specialità di Parma** (Strada Farini 9/C, tel. 0521/233591) to pick up some of the city's finest meat, cheese, pasta, and wine in Parma's oldest shop. The second-floor **Mensa Università** (Vicolo Grossardi 4, tel. 0523/213638; closed mid-July–mid-Sept.), west of the river, serves a full meal for only L8000 with a student ID, L11,000 without. At **Melrose** (Borgo Mameli 9/A, in the Piazzale della Steccata, tel. 0523/238875), try *pizza Ischia* (L10,000) with clams, mussels, and squid, or the *gnocchi alle vongole* (potato dumplings with clams; L13,000).

Florence

Michelangelo's *David* **and Botticelli's** *Primavera* may be Florence's most famous works of art, but the city's attitude toward visitors is best represented in Donatello's *St. George*: Valiant but cautious, the saint surveys an approaching dragon with a slightly worried eye. Like the wary Florentines, you may be put off by the massive onslaught of tourists that descends on the city each summer, but don't let them scare you away. Florence contains the most phenomenal array of Renaissance art and architecture you'll ever see, most of it commissioned by the Medici, first family of the Florentine Renaissance, in the 15th and 16th centuries. The streets are relatively clean and safe, major sights lie within a few blocks of each other, food and accommodations are surprisingly affordable for a tourist-oriented city, and nearby hill towns like Siena and San Gimignano make great day trips.

BASICS

VISITOR INFORMATION The best **visitor center** (Via Cavour 1r, tel. 055/276–0382) is beside the Palazzo Medici-Riccardi, about two blocks north of the Duomo. A second office is just off Piazza della Signoria (Chiasso Baroncelli 17r, tel. 055/230–2124), and a third is beside the train station (P. della Stazione, tel. 055/212245) near the Track 16 exit. **ARCI Gay** (Via del Leone 5r–11r, tel. 055/239–8722), the local gay resource center, has information on gay clubs and meeting places.

AMERICAN EXPRESS *Via Dante Alighieri 22r, tel. 055/50981. From Duomo, south on Via de' Calzaiuoli, then left on Via dei Tavolini, which becomes Via Dante Alighieri. Open weekdays 9–5:30, Sat. 9–12:30.*

BUCKET SHOPS CTS (Centro Turistico Studentesco Giovanile). *Via de' Ginori 25r, tel. 055/289721. From Duomo, north on Borgo San Lorenzo, which becomes Via de' Ginori. Open weekdays 9–12:45 and 2:30–5:45, Sat. 9–12:45.*

CHANGING MONEY Banks have the best rates, but they usually charge a commission of L5000 and change money only in the morning. **Thomas Cook** (Lungarno Acciaioli 6r, ½ block west of Ponte Vecchio on north side of Arno, tel. 055/289781) changes Thomas Cook or MasterCard checks at decent rates with no commission, but charges a L4000 commission on all other checks. The money exchange at the train station charges no commission but has poor rates.

ENGLISH BOOKS AND NEWSPAPERS Florence is one of the rare European cities that has good English bookstores. **The Paperback Exchange** (Via Fiesolana 31r, tel. 055/247–8154) and **After Dark** (Via del Moro 86r, tel. 055/294203) have the best selections.

PHONES AND MAIL For international calls, the **SIP** office in the train station (open daily 8:30–8), has a bank of quiet, private phone booths at which you pay after your call is finished. The **main post office** (Via Pellicceria, off P. della Repubblica, tel. 055/213384) has operator-assisted phone booths weekdays 8 AM–11:30 PM and takes care of mail needs weekdays 8:15–7, Saturday 8:15–12:30.

COMING AND GOING

BY TRAIN The huge **Stazione Santa Maria Novella** (P. della Stazione, tel. 055/288785) has luggage storage (by Track 16, L1500 per bag per day), information counters (open daily 7 AM–8 PM), a money exchange, a reservations desk for international trains and couchette booking (open 7 AM–8:30 PM), and an office that books hotel rooms for a small fee (open daily 9–9). Trains go to Rome (2 hrs, L22,000), Milan (3 hrs, L22,000), and Venice (3 hrs, change in Bologna, L18,700), as well as to Pisa's airport (1 hr, L6500).

BY BUS If you want to explore hilly areas where trains don't go, you'll have to deal with buses. The most comprehensive bus company is **SITA** (Via Santa Caterina da Siena 15r, tel. 055/483651 weekdays, 055/211487 weekends), with service to Siena (1 hr 15 min, L9000) and San Gimignano (1½ hrs, switch at Poggibonsi, L8100). To reach the SITA station, which is open daily 6 AM–8:30 PM, exit the train station by Track 5, cross Via Luigi Alamanni, go left, and then make a right on Via Santa Caterina da Siena.

GETTING AROUND

You'll need a detailed map to navigate Florence's twisting alleys; the best one is the ubiquitous "One, Three, Five . . . Days in Florence," available free at the tourist office and many hotels. To make things difficult, the city uses two different numbering systems for addresses on each street: blue numbers for residences and hotels, red ones (denoted here by an "r" after the number) for businesses.

In the center of town, it's almost always faster to walk than to wait for the bus, even if you're crossing the river to the Oltrarno. To explore suburban attractions or reach the hostel or campgrounds, you'll need to take a bus. A L1100 ticket good for an hour can be purchased at tabacchi or machines. The city bus line, **ATAF** (tel. 055/580528), gives out free route maps from a booth outside the train station on the Track 16 side. Most buses stop near the train station. Buses stop running around midnight or 1 AM.

WHERE TO SLEEP

No one would mistake Florence's budget hotels for charming country villas, but at least the city offers a host of affordable choices, especially around the train station. March–June and September–October are high season in Florence; during July and August, many hotels lower their prices to winter rates. Arrive in town early in the morning if you haven't reserved, because empty spaces disappear fast.

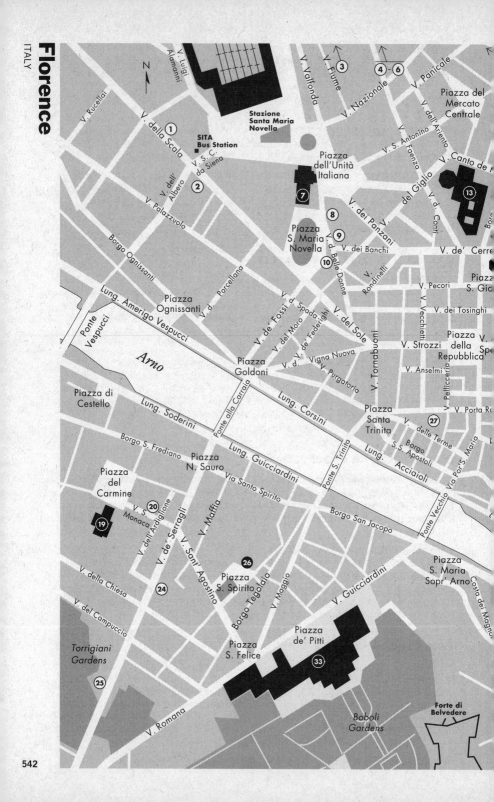

N

V. Luigi Alamanni

V. Rucellai

V. della Scala

①

V. dell'Albero

②

V. Palazzuolo

Borgo Ognissanti

Lung. Amerigo Vespucci

Piazza Ognissanti

V. d. Porcellana

V. S. C. da Siena

SITA Bus Station

Stazione Santa Maria Novella

Piazza dell'Unità Italiana

⑦

Piazza S. Maria Novella

⑧

⑨

⑩

V. dei Panzani

V. dei Banchi

V. d. Belle Donne

V. Valfonda

V. Fiume

③

④ – ⑥

V. Nazionale

V. Panicale

Piazza del Mercato Centrale

V. S. Antonino

V. Faenza

V. dell'Ariento

del Giglio

V. d. Conti

⑬

Borg

V. Canto de

V. de' Cerre

Piazza S. Gio

V. Rondinelli

V. Pecori

V. dei Tosinghi

V. Vecchietti

Piazza della Repubblica

V. Strozzi

V. de Spe

V. Anselmi

V. Pellicceria

Piazza Santa Trinita

V. Porta Re

㉗

V. delle Terme

Borgo S.S. Apostoli

Lung. Acciaioli

Via Por S. Maria

Via Por S. Maria

Costa del Magno

V. de' Fossi

d. Spada

V. del Moro

V. de' Federighi

V. del Sole

V. d. Vigna Nuova

V. Purgatorio

V. Tornabuoni

Piazza Goldoni

Arno

Ponte Vespucci

Piazza di Cestello

Lung. Soderini

Lung. Corsini

Ponte alla Carraia

Borgo S. Frediano

Piazza N. Sauro

Via Santo Spirito

Lung. Guicciardini

Ponte S. Trinita

Piazza del Carmine

⑲

V. S. Monaca

⑳

V. dell'Ardiglione

V. de' Serragli

V. Sant'Agostino

V. Maffia

V. della Chiesa

㉔

V. del Campuccio

Piazza S. Spirito

㉖

Borgo Tegolaio

V. Maggio

Borgo San Jacopo

Ponte Vecchio

Piazza S. Maria Sopr' Arno

Piazza S. Felice

Piazza de' Pitti

㉝

Torrigiani Gardens

㉕

V. Romana

Boboli Gardens

Forte di Belvedere

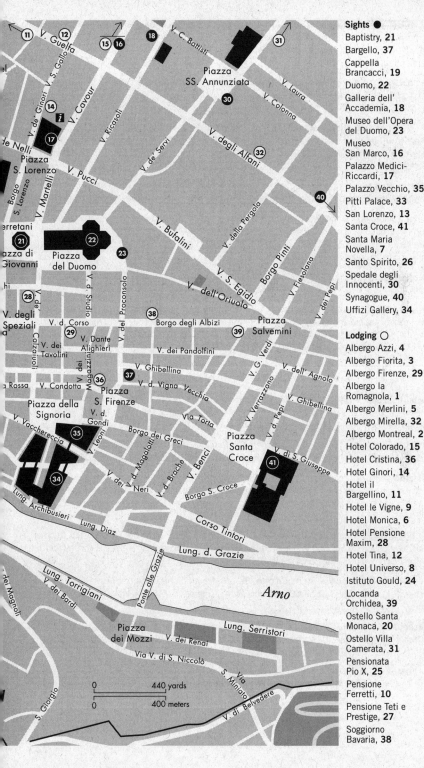

Sights ●

Baptistry, **21**

Bargello, **37**

Cappella Brancacci, **19**

Duomo, **22**

Galleria dell' Accademia, **18**

Museo dell'Opera del Duomo, **23**

Museo San Marco, **16**

Palazzo Medici-Riccardi, **17**

Palazzo Vecchio, **35**

Pitti Palace, **33**

San Lorenzo, **13**

Santa Croce, **41**

Santa Maria Novella, **7**

Santo Spirito, **26**

Spedale degli Innocenti, **30**

Synagogue, **40**

Uffizi Gallery, **34**

Lodging ○

Albergo Azzi, **4**

Albergo Fiorita, **3**

Albergo Firenze, **29**

Albergo la Romagnola, **1**

Albergo Merlini, **5**

Albergo Mirella, **32**

Albergo Montreal, **2**

Hotel Colorado, **15**

Hotel Cristina, **36**

Hotel Ginori, **14**

Hotel il Bargellino, **11**

Hotel le Vigne, **9**

Hotel Monica, **6**

Hotel Pensione Maxim, **28**

Hotel Tina, **12**

Hotel Universo, **8**

Istituto Gould, **24**

Locanda Orchidea, **39**

Ostello Santa Monaca, **20**

Ostello Villa Camerata, **31**

Pensionata Pio X, **25**

Pensione Ferretti, **10**

Pensione Teti e Prestige, **27**

Soggiorno Bavaria, **38**

NEAR THE STATION On a map, this area seems far from the major sights, but the Duomo is no more than a 10-minute walk and the train station is considerably closer. Dozens of cheap hotels line **Via Faenza, Via Fiume,** and **Via Nazionale,** many on different floors of the same building.

➤ **UNDER L50,000** • **Albergo Montreal.** Young, mellow managers charge L44,000 and up for bright doubles, L30,000 for singles without bath. *Via della Scala 43, tel. 055/238-2331. 1:30 AM curfew.*

➤ **UNDER L60,000** • **Albergo la Romagnola/Soggiorno Gigliola.** With 40 rooms, it's less likely to fill by noon than smaller places nearby. Dark but comfy doubles start at L54,000, singles at L36,000. Terrifically helpful staff. *Via della Scala 40, tel. 055/211597. Midnight curfew.*

Albergo Merlini. Great view of hills surrounding Florence. Tastefully decorated doubles with comfy beds start at L55,000; singles go for L35,000. *Via Faenza 56, tel. 055/212848.*

Hotel il Bargellino. Appealing Italian decor gives it the air of a bed-and-breakfast. Meticulously tended doubles around L55,000, singles L35,000. Some rooms have sunny terraces. *Via Guelfa 87, tel. 055/238-2658. Exit station at Track 16 and turn left, right on Via Cennini, left on Via Faenza, right on Via Guelfa.*

Pensione Ferretti. Quiet rooms in quirky building have some character. Doubles L50,000; for L5000 more, you get breakfast. *Via delle Belle Donne 17, tel. 055/238-1328.*

➤ **UNDER L70,000** • **Albergo Azzi.** Bright young staff makes visitors feel welcome. Solo backpackers share triples and quads for only L23,000 per night (L27,000 with breakfast). Terrific doubles start at L64,000, singles about L40,000. *Via Faenza 56, tel. 055/213806. 12:30 AM curfew (keys available for returning late). MC, V.*

Albergo Fiorita. Airy top-floor inn one block from train station. Cheerful doubles start at L65,000, singles are L45,000. *Via Fiume 20, tel. 055/283183.*

Hotel le Vigne. Wood-paneled lobby is a surprise after the decrepit exterior. Dark, quiet doubles with cushy beds start at L65,000; singles are L50,000. *P. Santa Maria Novella 24, at Via delle Belle Donne, tel. 055/294449. AE, MC, V.*

Hotel Monica. Pastel colors give a southern California feel. View from outdoor terraces. Clean, bright doubles without bath L60,000, singles L45,000. *Via Faenza 66, tel. 055/283804.*

Hotel Universo. Upscale hotel on Piazza Santa Maria Novella drops its rates in July, August, and December–February to L50,000 per double without bath, L40,000 per single. Other months you pay L60,000 for either. Some rooms have views. *P. Santa Maria Novella 20, tel. 055/281951. AE, MC, V.*

THE CENTER Prices fluctuate wildly in the heart of tourist Florence, between the Duomo and Santa Croce. This area is a bit of a haul from the train station, but it's a good place to settle down if you plan to stay a while.

➤ **UNDER L60,000** • **Hotel Cristina.** Terrific location one block from the Uffizi. Large, generic Euro-doubles L55,000 without bath, singles L36,000. *Via Condotta 4, tel. 055/214484. 12:30 AM curfew.*

Locanda Orchidea. English-speaking proprietors go out of their way to help you. Small, comfortable singles L35,000, doubles L55,000, triples L80,000, quads L100,000. *Borgo degli Albizi 11, tel. 055/248-0346. Closed Aug. 1–15.*

➤ **UNDER L70,000** • **Albergo Firenze.** American-style hotel lacks charm, but rooms are clean. Doubles L66,000 (L77,000 with bath), breakfast included. *P. Donati 4, off Via del Corso, tel. 055/214203. Wheelchair access.*

Pensione Teti e Prestige. Sunny, clean top-floor rooms two minutes from the Mercato Nuovo. Doubles L60,000, singles L40,000. Request a room with a view. *Via Porta Rossa 5, tel. 055/239–8435.*

Soggiorno Bavaria. Recently renovated inn atop an old palazzo. Enormous, sunny rooms with views on top floor; downstairs rooms are smaller and darker. Doubles L55,000–L85,000. *Borgo degli Albizi 26, tel. 055/234–0313.*

➤ **UNDER L85,000 • Hotel Pensione Maxim.** Lime-green decor is a bit odd, but hotel is incredibly well located one block south of Duomo. Students and young wayfarers flow in and out. Prices drop nearly 30% July–August and November–February; you pay 5% more with credit card. Doubles L74,000 in high season, L55,000 in low. *Via de' Calzaiuoli 11, tel. 055/217474. AE, MC, V.*

PIAZZA SAN MARCO AND THE UNIVERSITY QUARTER Very busy **Via Cavour** has some good upper-floor inns near the student restaurants and cafés, and quieter options are one block west on **Via de' Ginori** and **Via San Gallo.** Prepare for a long walk from the station, or take Bus 7 to Piazza San Marco.

➤ **UNDER L60,000 • Albergo Mirella.** Inch for inch, the cheapest rooms in Florence. Enormous, pleasant doubles L50,000, singles L35,000. Perfect location for checking out student cafés on Via degli Alfani. *Via degli Alfani 36, tel. 055/247–8170.*

Hotel Colorado. Small, friendly pensione two blocks north of Piazza San Marco. Sunny, clean doubles about L50,000, singles L30,000. *Via Cavour 66, tel. 055/217310. From P. San Marco, 2 blocks north on Via Cavour.*

➤ **UNDER L70,000 • Hotel Ginori.** Deservedly popular with students, and much more inviting than cheap alberghi nearby. Modern, streamlined doubles (L60,000) are immaculate. *Via de' Ginori 24, tel. 055/218615.*

Hotel Tina. Happy-go-lucky manager keeps hundreds of magazines for guests to peruse. Perfectly maintained doubles start at L60,000, breakfast included. *Via San Gallo 31, tel. 055/483519.*

HOSTELS Florence's hostels are a great bargain, but you have to arrive early and wait in long lines if you don't reserve ahead. If you can't get into the HI hostel or Istituto Gould, **Ostello Santa Monaca** (Via Santa Monaca 6, off Via de' Serragli, tel. 055/268338) charges L17,000 for a dorm bed and L2500 for sheets. You can't reserve ahead; put your name on the sign-up sheet at 9:30 AM and return between 4 and 5:30 to check in officially. **Pensionata Pio X** (Via de' Serragli 106, tel. 055/225044) costs L18,000 per person, L20,000 if you only stay one night. Rooms are large and clean, and the management is great, but they don't take reservations unless you're in a big group.

Istituto Gould. Glorious hostel has room for only 70 people, so reserve ahead or show up early. Thoroughly scrubbed doubles with big windows start at L50,000, triples and quads at L21,000 per person. *Via de' Serragli 49, tel. 055/212576. Office open weekdays 9–1 and 3–7, Sat. 9–1.*

Ostello Villa Camerata (HI). Excellent megahostel far from town in a villa surrounded by green acres. Reserve by writing or faxing, or through computers at hostels in Rome, Naples, and Venice. Check-in begins at 2 PM (3 in winter). Beds L18,000 with HI card (L5000 more without), breakfast included. *Viale Augusto Righi 4, tel. 055/601451, fax 055/600315. Exit train station at Track 5 and take Bus 17B, which stops outside hostel gates. Midnight curfew, lockout 9–2 (winter 9–3).*

CAMPGROUNDS Campgrounds are hot in summer, and wall-to-wall people detract from the great outdoors, but this is still the cheapest way to sleep. From July to mid-September, the city opens a free campsite to accommodate tourists: **Camping Villa Favard** (Via Rocca Tedalda; closed daily 10:30 AM–7 PM), basically a covered space to lay out a sleeping bag. To get here, take Bus 14 from the train station; it's probably not a good idea to come alone. For info, call the Comune di Firenze (tel. 055/284015). Tremendous views of the city redeem the scorching-hot **Camping Italiani e Stranieri** (Viale Michelangelo 80, tel. 055/681–1977; L6000 per person, L7000 per tent; closed Nov.–mid-Mar.). Arrive early to grab a shady site. Exit the train station at Track 5 and take Bus 13 to the stop after Piazzale Michelangelo. The office is open 6 AM–midnight, and you can check in after 10 AM. **Camping Villa Camerata,** adjoining the HI hostel (*see above*), charges L5500 per person, L7000 per tent. To reserve a space, contact the hostel.

FOOD

The tourist menus posted everywhere are both a blessing and a curse: They allow you to eat a lot without paying the service charge and standard L2000 cover fee, but they often feature the dregs of the menu. Still, if you're eating solely for sustenance, they're the way to go. Don't leave without treating yourself to some local specialties, though. Rich Tuscan soups are delicious and affordable—the thicker the better. *Pasta e fagioli* (pasta with beans) is a favorite among residents, as is the huge, undercooked *bistecca alla fiorentina* (Florentine steak), for the staunchest carnivores only.

To stock up on fresh fruit, vegetables, meats, breads, and pasta, head to the Mercato Centrale (open Mon.–Sat. 7–2), just north of the church of San Lorenzo behind the leather and souvenir stands. Vegetarians should bypass the graphic butcher displays on the first floor and head straight upstairs to the produce section.

NEAR THE STATION The good news is that you can find a decent meal near Stazione Santa Maria Novella for less than L15,000. The bad news is that in recent years every tourist and their mother has figured that out, and any claims to authentic local cuisine are fading fast.

➤ **UNDER L15,000** • **Trattoria da Giorgio** and **Trattoria il Contadino.** Two decent joints across the street from each other serve similar food at similar prices: pasta, meat, vegetable, and unlimited bread, water, and wine for L14,000. *Giorgio: Via Palazzuolo 100r, no phone; open daily 11–3 and 6–10. Contadino: Via Palazzuolo 69r–71r, tel. 055/238–2673; open Mon.–Sat. 11–3 and 7–midnight.*

Trattoria il Biribisso. Restaurant/pizzeria popular with locals offers L14,000 fixed-price menu. Try unusual dishes like *farfalle con salmone* (bow-tie pasta with smoked salmon). *Via dell'Albero 28r, tel. 055/288670. Open Mon.–Sat. noon–3 and 7 PM–1 AM.*

➤ **UNDER L25,000** • **Il Latini.** Everything is delicious, from chopped-liver *crostini* (toasts), to thick, rich soups (about L6000), to savory roast meats (about L15,000). Abundant assortment of primi costs L9000 per person. Arrive before 7:30 to avoid waiting in line for a hungry eternity. *Via dei Palchetti 6r, tel. 055/210916. From P. Santa Maria Novella, take Via de' Fossi, turn left on Via della Spada, right on Via de' Federighi, left on Via dei Palchetti. Wheelchair access. Open Tues.–Sun. 12:30–3 and 7:30–midnight. Closed mid-July–Aug.*

THE CENTER The city center is home to horrendously expensive tourist traps, terrific little take-out stands, and everything in between. Near Santa Croce, you'll find tantalizing options on **Via dei Neri** and the streets branching off to the north.

➤ **UNDER L15,000** • **Antico Noè.** Florence's best sandwich counter has fresh turkey and roast-beef sandwiches (L3500 each) with mouth-watering accoutrements. *Volta di San Piero 6r, tel. 055/234–0838. From Duomo, east on Via dell'Oriuolo, take covered passageway on right. Open Sun.–Fri. 10–10. Closed Aug.*

CarLie's Bakery. American bakery serves chocolate-chip cookies (L1200) and brownies (L1750). Great English-language bulletin board lists apartments for rent and people looking for conversation partners. *Via delle Brache 12r–14r, tel. 055/215137. Wheelchair access. Open Tues.–Sun. 9–1 and 3:30–8. Closed mid-July–Aug.*

Il Nilo. Cheap take-out counter, popular with North African immigrants, has great veal shawarma and falafel (L3500 each) and a fine selection of bottled beers (L3000 each). *Volta di San Piero 9r, tel. 055/234–4467. Across from Antico Noè (see above). Open Mon.–Sat. 10–10.*

➤ **UNDER L25,000 • Trattoria I'Che C'è C'è.** Serves everything from staggeringly large bowls of *ribollita* (thick bean soup; L6000) to the costly bistecca alla fiorentina (L25,000 and up). One of the best trattorias near the Palazzo Vecchio, despite its touristy look. *Via de' Magalotti 11r, tel. 055/216589. Open Tues.–Sun. 11–3 and 7–midnight.*

PIAZZA SAN MARCO AND THE UNIVERSITY QUARTER In the small area bordered by Piazza San Marco, Piazza Santissima Annunziata, and **Via degli Alfani,** neighborhood joints cater to the university population. Northwest toward Piazza della Indipendenza, along **Via Guelfa** and **Via XXVII Aprile,** narrow side streets offer solid, reasonably priced restaurants.

➤ **UNDER L15,000 • Betty Boop.** It looks like Pee Wee's playhouse, but surprisingly good salads go for only L5000, and tasty pastas are about the same price. In summer, it closes before dinner. *Via degli Alfani 26r, west of Via della Pergola, tel. 055/234–6786. Wheelchair access. Closed Sun.*

Da Cose Buone. Florence's best American-style breakfast (L9000). At night, this place serves crepes, pizza, and pasta (about L7000 each) and has a bar full of beers. *Via San Zanobi 63r, tel. 055/473184. From San Lorenzo, north on Via dell'Ariento, right on Via Panicale. Wheelchair access. Open Mon.–Sat. 7:30 AM–1 AM.*

Rosticceria Alfio e Beppo. Take-out counter offers satisfying lasagna, tortellini (L4000 per serving), roast chicken, and rice salad. *Via Cavour 118r, below P. San Marco, tel. 055/213059. Wheelchair access. Open daily 8 AM–9 PM, closed Sat. Sept.–June.*

Almanacco (Via delle Ruote 30r, tel. 055/475030) is one of Florence's few all-vegetarian restaurants. You have to pay a L10,000 membership fee to eat here, but if you're in town for a while, it may be worth it.

THE OLTRARNO You'll have no problem eating well south of the Arno. Just one block away from the river, **Borgo San Jacopo/Via Santo Spirito/Borgo San Frediano** (one long street that changes names) is packed with good restaurants.

➤ **UNDER L15,000 • I Tarocchi.** Thin-crust pizzas, including the *margherita dei Tarocchi* (fresh tomato and mozzarella; L8000), make the trek worthwhile. *Via de' Renai 12r–14r, tel. 055/234–3912. Cross Ponte alle Grazie and make second left. Wheelchair access. Open Tues.–Sat. noon–3 and 7:30–1.*

➤ **UNDER L25,000 • Trattoria la Casalinga.** Very large and very crowded. Memorable pastas about L7000, secondi about L8000. Look for unusual daily specials like fried chicken breast (L7800). *Via dei Michelozzi 9r, tel. 055/218624. From Santo Spirito church (facing piazza), turn left. Open Mon.–Sat. noon–3 and 7–midnight.*

Gelaterias

Inevitably, the local gelato shops will suck you in and force you to eat soft Italian ice cream until you suffer from giddy brain freeze. The most famous, most popular, and most expensive gelateria is Vivoli (Via Isola delle Stinche 7, off Via Torta from P. Santa Croce, tel. 055/292334), where the skimpy servings (L3000 and up) come in cups and the rich alcoholic flavors pack a punch. Quantity isn't a problem at l'Angolo del Gelato (Via della Scala 2r, at P. Santa Maria Novella, tel. 055/210526), which has great fruit flavors. A massive cone or cup will run you L2000.

WORTH SEEING

Although Florence is compact, it's impossible to see it all in one or two days. Your best bet is to hit the major museums—the Uffizi, Pitti Palace, and Accademia—an hour or two before closing, when the crowds thin out. Spend mornings in the city's voluminous churches or smaller museums. Museum hours can change drastically from season to season, so pick up a schedule, updated every few months, from the tourist office. Avoid the city on Monday, when most museums are closed. Florentine sights are insanely expensive. Churches are the only places that let you in free, and even then you pay to enter the cloister, chapels, tower, or dome. Student ID is practically useless; state and city museums, which harbor most of the major attractions, don't accept them. A cumulative ticket (L10,000) gives you access to all city-run museums, but the only ones worth visiting are the Palazzo Vecchio and the cloisters of Santa Maria Novella.

PIAZZA DEL DUOMO The **Duomo** (officially Santa Maria del Fiore) has been Florence's greatest church since its construction in the 15th century. **ARS,** a student organization, gives free guided tours of the cathedral several times daily mid-July–mid-August in seven languages, including English. Architect Filippo Brunelleschi had to design his own tools to produce its huge dome, an engineering breakthrough that actually consists of two domes connected by an elaborate system of ribs and supports. Climb the dome (admission L5000; open Mon.–Sat. 10–5) or Giotto's **campanile** (admission L5000; open Apr.–Oct., daily 8:30–7, Nov.–Mar., daily 9–4:30) for a supreme view of Florence.

After the dazzling exterior of green, white, and pink marble, the Duomo's massive interior (open daily 10–5:30) disappoints. Paolo Uccello created the weird clock above the entrance, which counts down the hours from the last sunset to the next, and the portrait of John Hawkwood (1436) near the entrance on the right, which approaches its subject from two geometric angles. The cathedral's best works, though, have been removed to the **Museo dell'Opera del Duomo** (P. del Duomo 9, behind Duomo, tel. 055/230–2885; admission L5000; open summer, Mon.–Sat. 9–7:30, shorter hrs in winter). Here you'll find Michelangelo's *Pietà*, Donatello's harrowing *Mary Magdalene,* and some of Ghiberti's panels from the baptistry doors. The museum also contains perhaps the greatest celebration of youth created in the Renaissance, Luca della Robbia's *Cantoria* (Choir Stall).

The Pietà was a source of frustration to Michelangelo. The 80-year-old genius hacked off Christ's left arm and leg in a fit of anger over his failure to achieve perfection. A student reattached the arm, but the back leg is still missing.

Just opposite the Duomo's facade, the **baptistry** (admission free; open Mon.–Sat. 1:30–6, Sun. 9–1) is the city's oldest standing building, constructed in the 6th or 7th century AD. Inside you'll find a medieval mosaic with Jesus in the center surrounded by the usual array of biblical scenes. The baptistry's eastern doors (facing the Duomo) are the most famous sculptural panels in Renaissance art. Ghiberti beat out Donatello and Brunelleschi for the chance to make the bronze doors; his 10 panels survey the Old Testament with a depth and emotion unprecedented in this medium. The panels now on the baptistry doors are copies—some originals are in the cathedral museum (*see above*) and some are being restored.

PIAZZA DELLA SIGNORIA The public spaces the Medici designed were excuses to celebrate the family's power, and nowhere is that more clear than in Florence's principal open square, Piazza della Signoria. The Medici dominated the square: They lived in the Palazzo Vecchio and funded the Loggia della Signoria and the Palazzo degli Uffizi (now the Uffizi Gallery). The **Palazzo Vecchio** (tel. 055/276–8965; admission L8000; open weekdays 9–7, Sun. 8–1), a slab of rusticated brickwork at the piazza's southeast corner, was the city hall in medieval times and is so again today. The exterior is an irregularly shaped combination of palazzo and crenellated castle; inside are a wide variety of artworks, including Michelangelo's *Victory* sculpture, Mannerist art by Vasari and Bronzino, and statues by Giambologna. The **Loggia della Signoria,** a porch on the square's south side, contains Cellini's bronze *Perseus* (carrying Medusa's head) and Giambologna's twisted *Rape of the Sabines,* both masterpieces of the 16th century.

➢ **UFFIZI GALLERY** • Vasari was commissioned by the Medici family in 1560 to design the Uffizi as an office for local government, but the top floor was reserved for the family's amazing art collection, which was donated to the city of Florence in 1737. Key works include Piero della Francesca's coolly detailed portraits of Federico da Montefeltro and his wife Battista Sforza; Paolo Uccello's *Battle of San Romano* (1456), with wild perspective effects like dramatically foreshortened horse legs; Botticelli's *Birth of Venus, Primavera,* and *Adoration of the Magi; The Annunciation,* for which Leonardo da Vinci painted the angel (and perhaps more); and Michelangelo's only non-fresco painting, *The Holy Family. Tel. 055/23885. Admission: L10,000. Open Tues.–Sat. 9–7, Sun. 9–1.*

➢ **BARGELLO** • Florence's police headquarters and jail during the Renaissance, the Bargello is now Italy's foremost museum of Renaissance sculpture. On the ground floor are some of Michelangelo's early works, several small bronze statues of Perseus by Cellini (studies for the Loggia della Signoria), and a few of Giambologna's major works. Upstairs, look for Donatello's effete bronze *David,* his guarded, watchful *St. George,* and Verrochio's skirted version of *David. Via del Proconsolo 4, tel. 055/210801. Admission: L6000. Open Tues.–Sun. 9–2.*

PIAZZA SANTA MARIA NOVELLA It may look a little seedy, but this piazza is the best free grassy space in the center of Florence. It's surrounded by a wonderful church, outdoor cafés and restaurants, and the city's cheapest gelateria (*see box,* Gelaterias, *above*). A complex facade enlivens the church of **Santa Maria Novella** (tel. 055/210113; open daily 7–11:30 and 3:30–6). The circles and scrolls on the upper level, designed by Alberti, were purely ornamental additions to a more somber Gothic lower level. The interior of the church features the black-and-white striped marble characteristic of the early Renaissance. Massaccio's tremendous fresco *Trinity* (1428), important for its strict geometric patterning, dominates the left-hand wall along the nave. The **Strozzi Chapel** holds Filippino Lippi's melodramatic frescoes, with Roman ruins in the background. You can check out Paolo Uccello's frescoes in the adjoining **cloister** (tel. 055/282187; admission L4000; open Mon.–Thurs., Sat. 9–2, Sun. 9–1).

PIAZZA SAN LORENZO Standing literally and figuratively in the shadow of the Duomo, **San Lorenzo** (tel. 055/216634; open Mon.–Sat. 8–noon and 3:30–5:30, Sun. 3:30–5:30) is one of the city's most elaborate churches. The Medici wished to equal the Duomo in beauty and prestige, but because the exterior designed by Michelangelo was never built, it's lonely and unimpressive from the outside. Brunelleschi's interior, however, is sumptuous, with monumental pillars and arches forming a Latin cross. On the right side of the transept is the **Sagrestia Vecchia** (Old Sacristy), which features sculpture by Donatello (who's buried here).

The church cloisters, upstairs off the left aisle, contain the **Biblioteca Laurenziana** (tel. 055/210760; open Mon.–Sat. 9–1), the only place in Florence where you can see Michelangelo's work for free. The artist's famous convex staircase, a pun on the Renaissance exactitude of architects like Brunelleschi, pushes out for no other reason than because it looks cool. Medici ostentation is apparent in the **Cappelle Medici** (admission L9000; open Tues.–Sat. 9–2, Sun. 9–1), a set of chapels accessible from the back end of the church. The **Cappella dei Principi,** built to house the family's remains, is a dizzying mess of green, black, and pink marble. Escape to Michelangelo's much more subtle **Sagrestia Nuova** (New Sacristy), with the sculpted tombs of two minor members of the Medici clan. The unusual, slippery poses of the figures on the tombs confirm the artist's total mastery of the male form (but his women look like men with silicone implants).

The area around San Lorenzo is congested, but not with churchgoers: Shoppers crowd dozens of leather stands near the church, and the city's premier food market, the **Mercato Centrale,** is just a block away. The nearby **Palazzo Medici-Riccardi** (Via Cavour 1, tel. 055/276–0340; open Mon., Tues., Thurs.–Sat. 9–1 and 3–6, Sun. 9–1), former Medici headquarters, ushered in a new age of Florentine civic architecture with its solemn but unimposing rusticated brick facade. The second-floor **chapel** holds the exquisite *Procession of the Magi* by Benozzo Gozzoli (1460). Unfortunately, the cost to enter the small chapel is L6000, and the frescoes, though delightful, are all you get.

PIAZZA SAN MARCO AND PIAZZA SANTISSIMA ANNUNZIATA These two neighboring squares north of the duomo are hangouts for local students (the university is nearby). In Piazza San Marco, the **Museo San Marco** (tel. 055/210741; admission L6000; open Tues.–Sat. 9–2, Sun. 9–1) was once the city's Dominican convent. Here the devout Renaissance painter Fra Angelico spent years as a friar. A gallery contains his oil paintings and altarpieces, including two *Depositions* and a *Last Judgment*. In the Sala Capitolare is his wall-size *Crucifixion*, and at the top of the stairs you'll find his most famous *Annunciation*, with sparkling colors projected onto a geometrically perfect space. On the same floor are 44 monks' cells, each with its own small fresco by Fra Angelico and his students.

Piazza Santissima Annunziata contains the **Spedale degli Innocenti** (Foundling Hospital), whose portico, designed by Brunelleschi, is considered by some the first manifestation of true Renaissance style in architecture. Begun in 1419 by the master, it was completed in 1445 by Francesco della Luna. The simple columns topped by perfect half-circle arches seem standard today, but they mark the beginning of Brunelleschi's infatuation with perfect mathematical equilibrium. Andrea della Robbia sculpted the 10 tondi (circular paintings) between the arches.

Michelangelo succeeded incomparably in painting, sculpture, and architecture, and he's just the tip of the iceberg in Florentine art. Spend a little time here and you'll get to know the work of architect-sculptor Filippo Brunelleschi, painter-architect Giotto, painter-historian Giorgio Vasari, and a firmament of others.

➤ **GALLERIA DELL'ACCADEMIA** • The L10,000 entrance fee is steep to see essentially one statue, but Michelangelo's *David* almost justifies it. The artist began the work in 1501 from a single block of marble. The statue is considerably larger than life, and its proportions increase the higher you look: The head seems slightly large for the body, and the hands are enormous. The surrounding gallery holds a series of *Slaves* by Michelangelo from the 1520s, figures that just barely emerge from solid stone. *Via Ricasoli 60, tel. 055/214375. Admission: L10,000. Open summer, Tues.–Sat. 9–7, Sun. 9–2; winter, Tues.–Sat. 9–2, Sun. 9–1.*

PIAZZA SANTA CROCE Piazza Santa Croce marks the southeastern edge of the Florentine tourist triangle. Here the city's main Franciscan church, the late-13th-century **Santa Croce** (tel. 055/244619; open summer, Mon.–Sat. 8–6:30, Sun. 8–12:30 and 3–6:30, winter, Mon.–Sat. 8–12:30 and 3–6:30, Sun. 3–6), holds the tombs of Michelangelo, Galileo, Ghiberti, and Machiavelli, as well as monuments to Dante, Leonardo da Vinci, and Raphael (the last three are buried elsewhere). Giotto's fresco cycles of St. Francis in the **Cappella Bardi** near the altar, and his *John the Baptist* in the adjacent **Cappella Peruzzi**, helped prod painting out of stiff medieval conventions and into more imaginative and psychologically complex compositions.

On the right-hand side of the facade is the entrance to the cloisters, containing the church **museum** and Brunelleschi's justly famous **Cappella Pazzi** (combined admission L3000; open summer, Thurs.–Tues. 10–12:30 and 2:30–6:30, shorter hrs in winter). The chapel, with its squat dome, was begun in the 1430s and completed almost 40 years later. Luca della Robbia and friends did the terra-cotta tondi of the apostles, as well as the evangels above the door. The museum boasts Donatello's massive bronze *San Ludovico d'Angio* (1423), Domenico Veneziano's ravaged *John the Baptist and St. Francis,* and Cimabue's *Crucifixion,* which was heavily damaged by a 1966 flood.

Built in the 1870s in Moorish/Byzantine style, Florence's enormous **synagogue** (Via Farini 4, tel. 055/245252; admission L5000, L4000 students; open Mon.–Thurs. 11–1 and 2–5, Fri. 11–1), a few blocks north of Santa Croce, is both wonderful and garish. Ornate, hand-painted arabesques cover the walls, and Turkish-style domes decorate the exterior. Upstairs, a small, worthwhile **museum** depicts the history of Florence's Jewish population.

THE OLTRARNO On the way to the south side of the Arno, cross the **Ponte Vecchio**, Florence's oldest bridge, rebuilt in the 14th century from a wooden structure dating to Roman times. In the late 16th century, Ferdinando I installed jewelry merchants on the bridge, and today the tradition continues. From the Ponte Vecchio, a street leads to the massive **Pitti Palace**, designed as a home for businessman Luca Pitti but bought by the Medici in 1549. If you don't watch yourself, you could spend more than L20,000 visiting the palace's museums and gardens. The most substantial museum, the **Galleria Palatina** (tel. 055/210323; admission L8000; open summer, Tues.–Sat. 9–7, Sun. 9–2, shorter hrs in winter), has works by Rubens, Caravaggio (look for his tooth-pulling scene in the first room), Titian, Raphael, and Van Dyck. Outside, the luxurious **Boboli Gardens** (tel. 055/213440; open summer, Tues.–Sun. 9–7:30, closes 1 hr before sunset in winter) were built by the Medici as an idyllic retreat. When the park was made into free public space in the last century, Florentines visited regularly. Unfortunately, the city recently imposed a L5000 entrance fee, and now almost all visitors are tourists.

You wouldn't guess it from the unadorned yellow exterior, but the nearby church of **Santo Spirito** (P. Santo Spirito, tel. 055/210030; open daily 8–noon and 4–6), another of Brunelleschi's mathematically precise projects, was one of the most ambitious creations to come out of the Renaissance. Unfortunately, Brunelleschi died before completing the church, and the original design was modified to a more traditional style. In the right transept is Filippino Lippi's *Madonna and Child with Saints,* and off the left aisle of the nave sits a harmonious sacristy designed by Giuliano da Sangallo.

Perhaps the most moving fresco cycle in Florence is the one in the tiny **Cappella Brancacci** (P. del Carmine, behind church of Santa Maria del Carmine, tel. 055/238–2195; admission L5000; open Mon., Wed.–Sat. 10–5, Sun. 1–5). Though important contributions to the cycle were made by Masolino and Filippino Lippi, the cycle is best known for Massaccio's brilliant frescoes *Expulsion from Eden* and *The Tribute Money.* The Adam and Eve expulsion scene is perhaps the most wrenching artistic image of the Renaissance, and Massaccio, who died at the age of 27, painted it in less than a month.

AFTER DARK

The Italian-language *Firenze Spettacolo* (L2500), available at local newsstands, lists films, discos, music, and cultural goings-on. Also look for *Quir,* a bilingual (Italian/English) gay magazine listing local events that's available at English bookstores (*see* Basics, *above*). For a bar, try **The Fiddler's Elbow** (P. Santa Maria Novella 7r, no phone), open nightly in summer. Beers aren't cheap (L6000 a pint), but you can drink them on an outdoor patio or on Piazza Santa Maria Novella. On Piazza Santo Spirito, wasted youths and foreign students sit on the church steps, while more alert types frequent popular cafés with outdoor tables. **Cabiria Café** (P. Santo Spirito, tel. 055/215732) is the hippest place in town, busy all afternoon and evening. In the student area near Piazza San Marco, try the happening **Cardillac Caffè** (Via degli Alfani 57r, tel. 055/234–4455), which hosts gay and lesbian night every Thursday beginning at 10.

Admission to discos costs around L15,000–L20,000, but discount passes are handed out on Piazza del Duomo, Piazza della Repubblica, and Via de' Calzaiuoli. Two of the better discos are the cavernous **Yab Yum** (Via Sassetti 5r, tel. 055/282018), closed in summer, and the gay/straight **055** (Via Verdi 57, tel. 055/244004). Gay discos come and go, and the scene is much more accommodating for gay men than for lesbians. **Crisco Club** (Via Sant'Egidio 42r, tel. 055/248–0580), a men-only disco closed Tuesday, is popular with locals, who disappear into the dark rooms downstairs. Friday night, **Flamingo** (Via de' Pandolfini 26r, near P. Salvemini, tel. 055/234–0210) is the city's lesbian hot spot; other nights, it's men only. The club closes July–August.

The only screen in town that shows English-language films full-time is **Cinema Astro** (P. San Simone, across from Gelateria Vivoli, no phone; closed mid-July–mid-Aug.). American hits from six months ago are interspersed with frequent showings of the unavoidable *Room with a View.*

Near Florence

Travel into the Tuscan countryside surrounding Florence and you'll swear you're in a Renaissance painting. That makes sense, since the most important developments in Renaissance art took place here. What's surprising is that Tuscan cities have changed so little in 500 years; they've retained their unique architecture and their focus on agriculture instead of industry. Tourists come to Tuscany's medieval cities and tiny hill towns in droves, and prices rise accordingly during high season. Getting around is no problem: The main towns are connected by rail, and buses shuttle you up to the hill towns, where you'll find some of the most beautiful scenery this side of an E. M. Forster novel.

PISA

The name Pisa is instantly recognized worldwide, not because of the city's former status as a major maritime republic, but because of an engineering mistake. Most visitors stop in Pisa only long enough to catch a glimpse of the famous Leaning Tower between connecting trains. Many of Pisa's secondary sights are lousy, it's true, but the city does have some redeeming qualities: Lodging is much more affordable than in nearby Siena and Florence, the university gives Pisa a youthful character, and many parts of town are free of tourist crowds and merchants hawking Leaning Tower ashtrays. If possible, arrive in the late afternoon, when the main drag quiets down. The **visitor information office** at the train station (tel. 050/42291; open summer, Mon.–Sat. 9:30–1 and 3:30–7, shorter hrs in winter) runs out of maps early in the day but will gladly point you in the right direction. A better office (tel. 050/560464) is just north of the Leaning Tower on Piazza del Duomo.

COMING AND GOING Trains to Florence (1 hr, L6500) leave hourly, as do trains to Siena (1 hr, transfer at Empoli, L8800). Most city buses (L900 for an hour ticket) stop in front of the train station. Bus 1 runs to the duomo, baptistry, and Leaning Tower. Pisa's **Galileo Galilei Airport** (Piazzale d'Ascanio, tel. 050/500707) is 1 km from the train station. If you're headed to Florence from a European country, you may fly through here. The train from Florence continues past Pisa's central station to the airport, or you can catch Bus 7 from the central station.

WHERE TO SLEEP AND EAT At **Albergo di Stefano** (Via Sant'Appollonia 35, tel. 050/553559), large, clean doubles (some with an outdoor terrace) go for only L35,000. From Piazza del Duomo, walk east past the tower, veer left on Via San Giuseppe, and go right on Via Sant'Appollonia. The well-located **Albergo Gronchi** (P. Arivescovado 1, tel. 050/561823) has big, comfortable doubles with dirty floors for L44,000. **Ostello Madonna dell'Acqua** (Via Pietrasantina 15, tel. 050/890622), a church-run hostel, charges only L17,000 for a bed but is tainted by the stench of a nearby sewer. Bus 3 will take you here; the reception doesn't open until evening, but unfortunately the bus stops running around 7:30 PM. The best food deal in town is the extraordinarily cheap **Mensa Universitaria** (Via Martiri, near Palazzo dei Cavalieri, tel. 050/599395; closed mid-July–mid-Sept.). Buy tickets downstairs; students get a full meal for L6000.

Fiesole: A Suburb with a View

Fiesole, a 20-minute ride on Bus 7 from Florence's train station, has an ancient Roman theater, an excellent museum of Etruscan ruins, and a magnificent view of Florence to boot. If you have a couple hours to spare, it's definitely worth the journey up the olive-groved hill to get a different angle on the local scene. In summer, the town is home to the spectacular Estate Fiesolana festival (tel. 055/597277), a music, dance, theater, and film series that many consider the region's richest cultural event.

WORTH SEEING The **Leaning Tower** on Campo dei Miracoli is one of the world's most famous buildings because of its amazing tilt, about a 13-foot discrepancy between top and bottom. Work began on the tower in 1173, but the soil under the site began to shift, a problem that a succession of frustrated architects tried unsuccessfully to correct over the next 150 years. A wondrous belfry by Tomasso di Andrea da Pontedera crowns the tower, which has been closed for the past five years. The black-and-white striping on the nearby **duomo** is perhaps the church's most famous trait, although time has eroded the black marble. Inside, have a look at Giovanni Pisano's eight-sided pulpit, which outdoes the pulpit built by his father, Nicola Pisano, for the circular **baptistry** (admission L5000) next door. The baptistry is known for its perfect acoustics and irregularly shaped dome. The long, low, white edifice on Piazza del Duomo is the **camposanto** (admission L5000), a cemetery that looks more mysterious from the outside than the inside; think twice before paying to enter. Legend holds that the soil here is from the hill on which Jesus was crucified.

Contrary to popular belief, Pisa isn't just a so-so town with one major sight—it's a so-so town with three major sights: the Leaning Tower, the duomo, and the baptistry.

SAN GIMIGNANO

The first thing you'll notice about San Gimignano is its skyline, marked by towers built during the city's tempestuous medieval period. This is what attracts the tour groups who clog this hill town at midday. Escape them by heading outside the city walls for a hike, and return to explore town in the late afternoon, when things quiet down and the shadows cast by the towers take on fascinating shapes. The **Torre Grossa** (admission L6000; open June–Aug., Sun.–Wed. 9–7:30, Thurs.–Sat. 9–11:30 AM, shorter hrs off-season) is the only tower you can climb, but at least it's the biggest in town. The nearby Palazzo del Popolo, built in the late 13th and early 14th centuries, houses the **Museo Civico** (P. Duomo, tel. 0577/940340; admission L6000; open same hrs as Torre Grossa), which features Taddeo di Bartolo's celebratory *Bethroned San Gimignano and His Miracles* and Memmo di Filipuccio's frescoes. A combined L10,000 ticket gets you into the museum and the tower during the afternoon. Also on Piazza Duomo, the **Duomo Collegiata** (tel. 0577/940316) has a treasure trove of well-preserved frescoes.

If you're spooked by the words "rectal," "impale," or "emasculate," avoid the **Museo di Criminologica Medievale** (Via del Castello, off P. della Cisterna, tel. 0577/942243; admission L9000, L5000 students; open daily 9–1 and 2–6), which displays medieval torture devices. Weeds are beginning to cover the stones of **La Rocca,** the town's medieval fortress, but the corner tower offers the best free view of the city. Catch current movies (L7000) dubbed in Italian here during July and August.

To reach San Gimignano, catch a bus (L2100) from Poggibonsi, about 12 km away. Poggibonsi's **train station** (tel. 0577/936462) is on the Florence–Siena line; trains from the former cost L5600, from the latter L2400. The **tourist office** (P. Duomo 1, tel. 0577/940008) has lists of homes that rent rooms for great prices. Reserve ahead for the way-above-average **San Gimignano Youth Hostel** (Via delle Fonte 1, tel. 0577/941991; beds L17,000; closed Nov.–Feb.). The rosticceria **Chiribiri** (P. della Madonna 1, tel. 0577/941948; closed Wed.) serves budget travelers lasagna with pesto (L6000) and pizza slices (L2500).

SIENA

Once Florence's main competitor for control of Tuscany, Siena stopped growing about 600 years ago, but it never stopped flourishing. Unlike many of the hill towns that surround it, Siena has aged well, retaining its traditional charm while integrating the conveniences of modern life. Fourteenth-century palazzi now house Laundromats and pastry shops, and residents still gather on the central piazza, Il Campo. The town's character is very much defined by its 17 medieval *contrade* (neighborhoods), each with its own church and symbol. For info on which ones to visit, stop by the **APT** office (P. del Campo 56, tel. 0577/280551; open Apr.–Sept., Mon.–Sat. 8:30–7:30, Oct.–Mar., Mon.–Sat. 9–12:30 and 3:30–7).

COMING AND GOING Siena's **train station** (P. Fratelli Rosselli, tel. 0577/280115) sells tickets daily 6 AM–9:30 PM. Trains from Florence (1½ hrs, L7200) run less frequently than buses, but they're cheaper. You may have to transfer at Empoli. Trains from Rome (2½ hrs, L18,700) require a switch at Chiusi. **TRA-IN/SITA** buses run hourly from Florence (1¼ hr, L9000) and San Gimignano (1 hr, L6300). The **bus station** (P. San Domenico, tel. 0577/204111) sells tickets daily 5:50 AM–8:15 PM. TRA-IN (P. Gramsci, tel. 0577/204111) also sends orange buses (not to be confused with blue long-distance buses) around the perimeter of town. A L1000 ticket is good for one hour. Buses going to the center empty at Piazza Gramsci or beside it on Viale Federico Tozzi. To get to Il Campo from here, take Via Malavolti through Piazza Matteotti to Via dei Terme.

The city's roofs and the surrounding hills are deep brown-red—a color so distinctive that a "burnt sienna" crayon has found its way into every Crayola caddie.

WHERE TO SLEEP AND EAT Hotels in Siena charge outrageous prices, and they get away with it because of the city's popularity. Lodging is sparse and prices skyrocket when the Palio (*see box, below*) comes to town on July 2 and August 16—reserve well in advance. The independent, ultra-clean **Ostello Guidoriccio** (Via Fiorentina 89, tel. 0577/52212) charges L18,000 per person, breakfast included. It's 4 km from town, an easy ride on Bus 15. A series of staircases leads to **Tre Donzelle** (Via delle Donzelle 5, tel. 0577/280358), where sizable, worn doubles without bath cost L50,000 and singles go for L30,000. From Il Campo, climb the stairs next to the tourist office, turn right on Banchi di Sotto, and go left on Via delle Donzelle. If you've always dreamed of throwing open your bedroom shutters to a postcard panorama, **Bernini** (Via della Sapienza 15, tel. 0577/289047; doubles L70,000), one block from the bus station, is for you.

For good vegetarian pizza and spectacular focaccia (about L1500 for a huge slice), come to **Forno Indipendenza** (P. Indipendenza 27, tel. 0577/280295), Siena's premier bakery. **Malborghetto Pizzeria Braceria** (Via Porta Giustizia 6, on P. del Mercato, tel. 0577/289258; closed Wed.) serves brick-ovens pizzas (L7500) and pastas (L5000–L7000). For a sit-down meal, try **Osteria dell'Artista** (Via Stalloreggi 11, tel. 0577/280306; closed Thurs.), with grilled chicken for L7000 and amazing pasta for L10,000.

WORTH SEEING The southeast corner of Piazza del Campo (known as Il Campo) is dominated by the stupendous **Palazzo Pubblico** (Town Hall). Built in the late 13th and early 14th centuries, the building features the crenellated cornices and three-part arches that define Sienese architecture. Inside, the **Town Museum** (P. del Campo, tel. 0577/292263; admission L6000, L3000 students) has frescoes and paintings by Siena's great artists Simone Martini, Lorenzetti, and Duccio. The Palazzo Pubblico's most distinctive feature is the famous **Torre del Mangia** (admission L4000), a 335-foot tower built in 1334. It offers the greatest possible view of Siena—only fair, since you'll climb more than 400 stairs to get there.

They're Not Just Horsing Around

Siena's Palio horse race takes place twice a year, on July 2 and August 16, but its spirit lives all year long. Three laps around a makeshift track in Il Campo earn participants from each contrada the respect or scorn of the town, and the event is so important to the Sienese that almost nothing is too underhanded to be against the rules. Like the Spanish bullfight, the tradition is criticized for its violence and inhumanity. Horses are repeatedly injured, and jockeys aren't above knocking the competition off their horses. But if you can stand being mobbed by a hot sea of fans for hours (the weary get carried out on stretchers), by all means catch the Palio; it's a spectacle you won't soon forget.

The marble floors of the black-and-white-striped **duomo** (P. del Duomo, tel. 0577/283048) depict an array of biblical subject matter, and the arched vaulting is covered with simulated stars. Don't miss Nicola Pisano's carved pulpit. Next door, the **Museo dell'Opera del Duomo** (admission L5000) houses Duccio's ambitious *Maestà* (1310). Donatello's famous *Feast of Herod* decorates the rear right-hand side of the font in the **baptistry** behind the cathedral. The **Pinacoteca Nazionale** (Via San Pietro 29, tel. 0577/283048; admission L8000) has a memorable collection of Madonna-and-child paintings, as well as Simone Martini's (unlabeled) *St. Augustine and His Miracles* (1324), depicting the bloody occurrences that Augustine's powers reversed.

AFTER DARK You can join locals in a *passeggiata* (stroll) through the cobblestone streets, hang out on the central piazza, or walk down Via Pantaneto, the continuation of Via Banchi di Sotto, in search of discos. **The Gallery** (Via Pantaneto 13, tel. 0577/288378) is the butt-shakin' dancetorium of choice, but **Al Cambio** (Via Pantaneto 48, tel. 0577/43183) down the street sometimes grooves when The Gallery is closed. The hours for both are unfathomable—they're open something like every 10 days from 10 PM to 3 AM. Only the socially challenged show up before midnight.

Umbria and Marche

Tuscany's quiet sister, Umbria, lies tantalizingly close to the route traveled by Baedeker-toting tourists since Victorian times, yet it has remained largely untouched. Here, in the center of Italy, olive groves and vineyards swell and dip around a wealth of extraordinary hill towns. Perugia is the provincial capital, a university town known for its cultural vivacity and its chocolate. Also worth a visit are Orvieto, built atop a volcanic outcropping; **Spoleto**, with its international arts festival; and **Gubbio**, one of Italy's best-preserved medieval cities. Marche, to the east, encompasses mountains and a long stretch of Adriatic beaches. Its main port town, **Ancona**, is a gateway to Greece and the former Yugoslavia, but the wonderful university town of Urbino is a better place to visit. Natural beauty is the area's principal attraction, but it also offers superior wines and regional ceramics. Buses are the way to travel throughout the region, since trains often leave you and your backpack with a long uphill walk to the town center.

Perugia

Perugia, the capital of Umbria, has a dramatic history to match its spectacular views. In addition to the usual barbarian conquests and medieval chaos, the town's volatile and often nasty past includes the birth of the Flagellant movement, a masochistic Christian sect that publicly whipped themselves bloody to pay for the sins of mankind. Today Perugia seems civilized enough, though half-swallowed ruins hint at past bloodshed. The town's large student population and cultural savvy have prevented it from becoming lost in its medieval past like so many Umbrian hill towns. And every year, Perugia throws the all-out, feel-good festival **Umbria Jazz**, which attracts big- and small-time soul musicians from all over and sets central Italy a'humming.

BASICS Pick up a copy of *Perugia What, Where, When* (L1000) from a newsstand as soon as you arrive—it's a gold mine of information, with a monthly calendar of special events. Perugia's **tourist office** (P. IV Novembre 3, tel. 075/572–3327) is open weekdays 8:30–1:30 and 3:30–6:30, weekends 9–1.

COMING AND GOING The main **train station** (P. Vittorio Veneto, tel. 075/500–1288) is outside the town center, below the city. Trains go from here to Rome (3 hrs, L15,400), Florence (2 hrs, L12,100), and Assisi (30 min, L2400). From the station, Bus 20, 26, 27, 28, or 29 will get you to Piazza Italia, and Bus 33 or 36 goes to Piazza Matteotti. **Long-distance buses** depart from Piazza dei Partigiani, just beyond Piazza Italia.

WHERE TO SLEEP AND EAT The cheapest lodging in town is at the hostel, **Centro Internazionale di Accoglienza per la Gioventù** (Via Bontempi 13, off P. Dante, tel. 075/572–2880; closed Dec. 15–Jan. 15). Beds cost L14,000 a night, and sheets are L1000 extra. **Camping il Rocolo** (Via della Trinità 1, tel. 075/517–8550; open June 15–Sept. 15), outside town in Colle della Trinità, costs L6500 per person and L5500 per tent in high season. Take Bus 36 from the station to Colle della Trinità, and then follow the yellow signs uphill about 1 km. Ultra-friendly **Hotel Sebastiano** (Via San Sebastiano 4, tel. 075/573–2006) provides comfortable singles (L35,000) and doubles (L45,000) without bath. From the station, take Bus CD to Piazza Fortebraccio and walk downstairs to the left of the palace. Then take Via Santa Elisabetta and turn left on Via San Sebastiano.

Perugia's claim to fame is the delicious Perugina chocolate. If you want to sample some, fill a sack at the gourmet pasticceria Sandri (C. Vannucci 32, tel. 075/572–4112).

For produce and fresh deli specialties, the **Mercato Coperto** (P. Matteotti 18/A) is open weekdays 7–1:30, Saturdays 7–1:30 and 4:30–7:30. If you have student ID, the **Mensa Universitaria** (Via A. Pascoli, just past Via Vanvitelli on the right, tel. 075/43670) serves three-course meals for around L7000. Popular **Pizzeria Medio-Evo** (Via Baldo 6, off P. Repubblica, tel. 075/572–0764; closed Wed.) makes the biggest pizzas in town for L4500–L5500.

WORTH SEEING Perugia's main street, Corso Vannucci, runs from Piazza Italia to Piazza IV Novembre, where two key monuments face each other across the **Fontana Maggiore** (1275), a fountain designed by Perugian architect Fra Bevignate and sculptors Nicolà and Giovanni Pisano. The **duomo** (P. IV Novembre, open daily 7–noon and 3–7), constructed between 1345 and 1490, houses Federigo Barocci's *Deposition* and the Virgin's wedding ring, a hunk of onyx that Mary is supposed to have worn in her earthly marriage to Joseph; it's exhibited only once a year on July 30. The enormous, white **Palazzo dei Priori** (C. Vannucci 19, tel. 075/572–0316; open Mon.–Sat. 8:45–1:45 and 3–7, Sun. 9–1) holds the **Galleria Nazionale dell'Umbria** (admission L8000), containing works by Fra Angelico, Agostino di Duccio, Taddeo di Bartolo, and Piero della Francesca. The palazzo's guildhalls are equally impressive.

The church of **San Domenico** (P. Bruno, off C. Cavour, tel. 075/573–0750) is Perugia's largest. The interior frescoes are peeling away, but the apse is brightened by one of Italy's largest stained-glass windows (75 feet tall). The **Museo Archeologico Nazionale dell'Umbria** (admission L4000; open Mon.–Sat. 9–1:30 and 2:30–6, Sun. 9–1), inside the cloister to the left of the double staircase, displays Etruscan and Roman artifacts. Beside the large church of San Francesco al Prato, now just an attractive facade, shines the **Oratorio di San Bernardino** (P. San Francesco, off Via dei Priori, tel. 075/373–3957; open daily 8–12:30 and 3:30–7). Its marvelous facade (1461) is the work of sculptor Agostino di Duccio. The sarcophagus that serves as altar is a 3rd-century Roman piece.

NEAR PERUGIA

ASSISI The legacy of St. Francis, founder of the Franciscan order of monks, permeates the rose-colored hill town of Assisi. Each year, thousands of pilgrims make the trek here to pay homage to this mendicant monk, who was the first person to receive the stigmata (wounds in his hand, feet, and side corresponding to those received by Christ on the cross). Today, Franciscan friars in simple brown habits and belts of knotted rope still stroll among the *vicoli* (alleys) that wind from one magnificent church to the next.

Churches in Assisi are particularly strict about dress codes, so cover yourself accordingly before heading out for the day.

The sloping Piazza del Comune, Assisi's main square, shelters the **tourist office** (P. del Comune 12, tel. 075/812534; open weekdays 8–2 and 3:30–6:30, Sat. 9–1 and 3:30–6:30, Sun. 9–1) and the **Pinacoteca** (Palazzo del Priori, tel. 075/812599; admission L2500; open daily 9:30–1 and 2:30–6), which displays a survey of Umbrian art. The **Tempio di Minerva,** with a classical facade and corrugated columns supporting a tympanum, and the **Roman forum** (Via Portica, turn left down small flight of steps), a museum of Roman remains under the piazza, were both closed for restoration at press time. To stop by the little **Chiesa Nuova** (tel. 075/812339) atop St. Francis's family home, take Via Arco dei Priori out of the piazza. In a city full of churches, the **Basilica di San Francesco** (tel. 075/813061) is exceptional. This celebration of Italy's patron saint is a double church—a Gothic basilica built atop a Romanesque basilica, each one remarkably beautiful and decorated floor to ceiling with some of the finest frescoes in the world. In one of the great ironies of Christianity, St. Francis, known for his commitment to poverty, was honored with this monument of unabashed grandeur.

➤ **COMING AND GOING** • **Trains** run almost hourly between here and Perugia (30 min, L2400). The ASSISI–SANTA MARIA DEGLI ANGELI bus travels between the station and town, 4 km away. Hop off at the end of the line in Piazza Matteotti.

➤ **WHERE TO SLEEP AND EAT** • **Ostello Fontemaggio** (Via Eremo delle Carceri, Fontemaggio, tel. 075/813636) is part of a compound that includes a campground (L6000 per person, L4500 per tent), a restaurant, and a hotel. Beds cost L15,000 a night, breakfast included. From Piazza Matteotti, exit town through Porta Cappuccini and follow Via Eremo delle Carceri 1 km uphill to the Fontemaggio turnoff on the right. **HI Ostello Lapace** (Via Valecchi, tel. 075/816767), near the train station, is better maintained than the hostel at Fontemaggio, but it lacks the beautiful setting. **Hotel la Rocca** (Via Porta Perlici 27, tel. 075/812284 or 075/816467) has spacious doubles, many with balconies, for L41,000 without bath. From Piazza Matteotti, take Via del Comune Vecchio to Via Porta Perlici.

Assisi's culinary specialties include such expensive delicacies as truffles and porcini mushrooms, as well as pecorino cheese. **Ristorante Spadini** (Via Sant'Agnesi 6, off Via Mazzini, tel. 075/813005; closed Mon.) cooks up regional specialties, and unpretentious **Hostaria Agnese** (P. del Comune 38; closed Mon.) serves pizza (L5500–L7000) and beer under a portico.

ORVIETO Stunning Orvieto sits atop a plateau of tufa stone that was shoved up from the valley floor by volcanic movements. A subterranean network of wine caves and Roman wells provides insight into the city's Etruscan inhabitants of yore, but the medieval town—especially the flamboyant **duomo**—is Orvieto's primary attraction. Narrow streets in the center of the plateau are full of shops selling the city's famous exports: ceramics and wine. Come to the **tourist office** (P. Duomo 24, tel. 0763/41772; open weekdays 8–2 and 4–7, Sat. 10–1 and 3–8, Sun. 9–7) to find out what you can see—most of Orvieto is currently hidden behind scaffolding.

Orvieto lies on the Rome–Florence rail line. To get to Perugia (2 hrs, L8800), you have to switch trains in Terontola. A **funicular** (L1000) carries you between the train station and Piazza Cahen, at the eastern edge of the city plateau. You'll find a couple budget hotels in Orvieto Scalo, the area near the train station. In the centro storico, **Hotel Duomo** (Via di Maurizio 7, tel. 0763/41887), down a flight of steps from Piazza Duomo, has doubles for L45,000 without bath, L64,000 with.

Urbino

Urbino resembles an enchanted kingdom more than just aesthetically; it's about as easy to reach as Shangri-La, Narnia, or Oz.

You may never have even heard of it, but Urbino is held by many to be the ideal Renaissance city. The concept of absolute harmony is a local preoccupation, exemplified in the popular obsession with the mysterious painting *Città Ideal* (Ideal City), which hangs in Urbino's Galleria Nazionale. Not only spatially, but historically, artistically, and demographically, lively little Urbino feels almost as perfect as the city in the painting. Isolated in the hills, it flourishes with a respected university and summer programs that attract students from all over the world. The alleys and arch-covered passages that knit Urbino together are thought by many locals to be the town's most important sights, but the sublime Renaissance **Palazzo Ducale** (P. Duca Federico, tel. 0722/2760) is certainly more prominent. The palace is open Monday 9–2,

Tuesday–Sunday 9–7; admission is L8000. The **tourist office** (P. Duca Federico 35, tel. 0722/2441) can direct you to other sights.

To reach Urbino, you have to come from Pesaro, either on one of the frequent buses (50 min, L5500) or by car. You can reach Pesaro on a train from Rome (6 hrs, L23,700), Bologna (L10,500), or Ancona (50 min, L4300). From Pesaro, buses arrive at Urbino's Borgo Mercatale, beneath the Palazzo Ducale. The **Bar Europa** in the piazza has a schedule, and there's usually a driver you can ask for information. The tourist office has a long list of rooms available in private homes; **Albergo Italia** (C. Garibaldi 32, off P. della Repubblica, tel. 0722/2701) has doubles without bath for L48,000.

Rome

Although modern-day pilgrims may arrive with a backpack and a EurailPass instead of gifts for the pope or emperor, Rome (Roma) is the same as it ever was: overwhelming and awe-inspiring. Since its conception in 753 BC—supposedly by the twins Romulus and Remus, who were abandoned on the banks of the Tiber River and suckled by a she-wolf (the symbol of Rome) to maturity—Rome has changed and expanded, but it has never taken time to clean up its 2,500 years worth of historical scraps. Centuries of political and religious influence lie on top of, below, and in between one another as a backdrop to the hustle, dirt, and noise that comes with a modern population of 6 million. The irony of Rome, however, is that even lacking a modern city center, everything fits smoothly enough—from the traffic-clogged streets to the high-fashion cafés and crumbling Roman ruins. Practically speaking, there's no right amount of time to spend in Rome—you could do it in a day, a week, or a lifetime.

Besides all the must-see's and do's, Rome has a small-town charm that's often overlooked. On most summer evenings, hues of gold and copper bathe Rome's piazze and narrow alleyways, casting shadows over matriarchs and pudgy old gentlemen who've been having the same conversations for 25 years. Cafés and restaurants are often frequented by an unmistakable local crowd that gathers for a lazy afternoon meal, only to return around 10 PM for dinner and more gossip. Rome is certainly overrun with Vespas and Armani slacks, but at any given moment you can probably find a priest or nun within two blocks of where you're standing.

BASICS

VISITOR INFORMATION **EPT,** Rome's semihelpful tourist organization, has a wealth of brochures, maps of Rome, events schedules, public transportation info, and lists of restaurants and lodgings. English is spoken, and all services are free. Look for the small branch opposite Track 2 in **Stazione Termini** (tel. 06/487–1270), or trek to the **main office** (Via Parigi 5, tel. 06/488–3748) three blocks northwest of the station. Both are open Monday–Saturday 8:30–7.

Enjoy Rome, 3½ blocks from Stazione Termini, is a good stop for maps, accommodations, information, updated event schedules, and friendly advice in English. *Via Varese 39, tel. 06/445–1843. Open weekdays 8:30–1 and 3:30–6, Sat. 8:30–1.*

AMERICAN EXPRESS *P. di Spagna 38, tel. 06/67641. Open weekdays 9–5:30, Sat. 9–12:30.*

CHANGING MONEY For instant gratification, go to the sketchy-looking office in **Stazione Termini** (on the south side of EPT tourist office) with the cardboard NO COMMISSION sign in the window. The **main post office** (*see* Mail, *below*) has the highest rates around and only charges a 1% commission; money transactions take place at windows 25–28.

CONSULATES AND EMBASSIES **Australia.** *C. Trieste 25/B, tel. 06/852721. Open weekdays 9–noon and 1:30–4.*

Canada. *Via Zara 30, tel. 06/440–3028. Open weekdays 8:30–3.*

New Zealand. *Via Zara 28, tel. 06/440–2928. Open weekdays 8:30–12:45 and 1:45–5.*

United Kingdom. *Via XX Settembre 80/A, tel. 06/482–5441. Open weekdays 9:30–12:30 and 2–4.*

United States. *Via Vittorio Veneto 121, tel. 06/46741. Open weekdays 8:30–noon and 2–4.*

EMERGENCIES The general emergency number for **first-aid** or **police** is 113. For **fire,** call 115; for an **ambulance,** dial 5510. If you have to file the all-too-routine theft report, an English speaker is usually on staff at the **main police station** (Via San Vitale 15, just north of Via Nazionale, tel. 06/4686).

ENGLISH BOOKS AND NEWSPAPERS *Metropolitan* (L1500) and *Wanted in Rome* (L1000), available at most newsstands, are biweekly English publications with listings of current events and classifieds. The closet-size **Altempo Ritrovato** (103 P. Farnese, tel. 06/6880–3749; open Tues.–Sun. 10–8) is Rome's largest women's book store. Five blocks south of Stazione Termini, **Economy Book and Video Center** (136 Via Torino, 1 block south of Via Nazionale, tel. 06/474–6877; open Mon. 3–7, Tues.–Sat. 9:30–7:30) has new and used English-langauge books and English movies and VCRs.

MAIL Post offices are conveniently positioned all over Rome; they all sell stamps and send mail on its way weekdays 8:30–7:30, Saturdays 8:30–11:30. The **main post office** (P. San Silvestro, tel. 06/65643 or 06/6771), a block east of Via del Corso, handles stamp sales at windows 22–24; currency exchange is at windows 25–28.

MEDICAL AID **Rome American Hospital** (Via Emilio Longoni 69, tel. 06/22551) has English-speaking doctors and dentists on hand. All pharmacies post listings of late-night branches. The 24-hour **Farmacia Piram Omeopatia** (Via Nazionale 228, tel. 06/488–0754) and **Internazionale Piazza Barberini** (P. Barberini 49, tel. 06/482–5456) are centrally located.

PHONES Long-distance calls can be placed at several ASST and SIP phone centers in central Rome and near transportation hubs—Fiumicino has one, Termini two. The main **ASST** office, next to the central post office on Piazza San Silvestro, is open daily 8 AM–11:30 PM; the office on Via Porta Angelica, near St. Peter's Basilica, opens at 8:30 Monday–Saturday and closes weekdays around 9 PM, Saturdays by 2 PM.

COMING AND GOING

BY TRAIN Rome's principal rail depot is Stazione Termini, a gargantuan complex right in the thick of things. Other Rome stations include **Ostiense,** with daily service to Genova, Naples, Palermo, and Nice. Rome's **Trastevere** station is useful only if you're forced to sleep in the suburbs.

Trains from **Stazione Termini** (P. dei Cinquecento, tel. 06/4775) serve major Italian and European cities and many points in between. Budget accommodations and public transportation are right outside. The main lobby has snazzy multilingual computers that list train departures, price, and duration. A **cassa di cambio** (open daily 7–7) is in the glass-enclosed gallery at the front of the station, near a special window that exclusively serves EurailPass holders.

Stazione Termini has a multitude of shops and restaurants, and **24-hour luggage storage** near Track 1 and 22. Downstairs, an **albergo diurno** (day hotel) charges L10,000 for showers; towels are included, but not soap (L500) or shampoo (L1200). The **waiting room** near Track 1 is a safe place to kick back since it's inside the ticketed area. If theft befalls you, go to the 24-hour **police booth** at Track 1.

BY BUS Rome does not have a central bus terminal. Instead, blue **ACOTRAL** buses leave from different points around town. Get service and sales details from ticket agents and tourist offices, or by calling ACOTRAL directly (tel. 06/57531 or 06/591–5551).

Between Piazza dei Cinquecento and Piazza della Repubblica, **private buses** from a dozen different companies leave for destinations throughout Italy. Most charge more than ACOTRAL, but that's because most offer plush seats and air-conditioning. Buy tickets at the stuffy, no-name agency at the corner of Via Nazionale and Piazza della Repubblica. It's open intermittently 7 AM–11:30 PM, and they accept AmEx.

GETTING AROUND

"All roads lead to Rome," where they leave you confused, disoriented, and befuddled. Luckily, Rome has gobs of landmarks to orient yourself by. First and foremost, the **Tiber River** runs north–south through the city, making a big bend that cradles the centro storico to the east and the Vatican to the west. Brown-and-white signs are posted throughout the center, directing pedestrians to major sights along the most direct routes.

BY METRO Rome's subway system is sorely limited. The red **Line A** runs between Ottaviano and Anagnina, hitting most of Rome's major piazze—among them Repubblica, Barberini, and Spagna. The blue **Line B** runs between Laurentina and Rebibbia and is useful for reaching the Colosseum and the Ostiense train station (at the Piramide stop). The only point where the two lines intersect is Stazione Termini. Line A operates daily 5:30 AM–11 PM. On weekdays, Line B runs 5:30 AM–9:30 PM; on weekends, until 11:30 PM. Tickets cost L1000.

BY BUS Stops for Rome's trusty orange buses are marked by yellow or green posts and labeled FERMATA. Most stops list bus numbers, the main destinations along each route, and lines with night service (marked with an *N* or by a black circle). Bus tickets (L1200) are valid for 90 minutes of unlimited travel and are sold at coffee bars and newspaper kiosks displaying the ATAC emblem.

BY BIKE **I Bike Rome** (Via Vittorio Veneto 156, tel. 06/322–5240) rents bikes by the hour for L5000, tandems for L12,000, and mountain bikes for L7000; full-day renters get substantial discounts. It's open weekdays 9–1 and 3–7, weekends 9–8. **Bicimania** (P. San Sonnino at Viale di Trastevere, tel. 06/780–7755) has five-speed bikes for L5000 per hour, L16,000 per day. They're open daily 9 AM–12:30 AM (until 8 PM Oct.–Nov.).

WHERE TO SLEEP

If you're not too picky, a clean double in a no-nonsense pensione can be had for L45,000–L60,000. In the L60,000–L90,000 range, you'll get ambience, a private bath, and a somewhat central address. Definitely find the energy to make reservations in August and September. If you don't mind some dirt and noise, try the streets around Stazione Termini. Pensions in the centro storico are convenient to major sights and priced accordingly.

NEAR STAZIONE TERMINI To reach the pensiones and hotels on **Via Palestro** from the station, walk north on Via Marsala, turn right on Via Vicenza, then left on Via Palestro. To reach the hotels and pensiones on **Via Principe Amedeo,** walk southwest on Via Cavour and turn left. To reach **Via del Viminale,** walk northwest through Piazza dei Cinquecento (in front of the station) and turn left.

➢ **UNDER L60,000 • Home Michele.** Above Hotel Marini (*see below*), with plush doubles from L50,000. Most rooms are away from the street and its din. One shared bathroom, one shared cat. *Via Palestro 35, tel. 06/444–1204.*

Hotel Gexim. Sun streams in wide windows to spotlight the Gexim's tile floors and large rooms. The management is young and friendly, the communal showers big and spotless. Doubles L55,000, singles L40,000. *Via Palestro 34, tel. 06/446–0211.*

Hotel Marini. Within spittin' distance of station and run by a friendly matriarch. Doubles (L50,000) are small but comfy. *Via Palestro 35, tel. 06/444–0058.*

Hotel Papa Germano. Papa Germano is listed in scores of travel books, so reservations are a must. Clean, renovated rooms sport twin beds and pastel wallpaper. Doubles L55,000. *Via Calatafimi 14/A, tel. 06/486919. MC, V.*

Hotel Pensione Rosa. She runs around cleaning all the time, and he hangs out by the phone at the front desk; together they run a clean, no-nonsense pensione. Basic doubles L50,000. *Via Palestro 87, tel. 06/491065.*

Pensione Virginia. Small pensione on a quiet street with sunny doubles from L50,000. All rooms have either a sink or shower. *Via Montebello 94, tel. 06/488–1786.*

➤ **UNDER L80,000 • Hotel Cervia.** Twenty-three rooms means vacancies are common. Helpful *ragazzi* (kids) look after the joint and hang in the TV room. Singles L35,000, doubles L75,000. *Via Palestro 55, tel. 06/491057. 1 AM curfew in winter, 2 AM in summer.*

Hotel Pensione Corallo. Top-floor rooms are bathed in sunlight; some even have small terraces. The 1 AM curfew is not absolute if you ask politely for an extension. Doubles L65,000. *Via Palestro 44, tel. 06/445–6340.*

➤ **UNDER L90,000 • Hotel Akragas.** Healthy green plants oxygenate the common spaces, which include a social room and large dining area with an espresso bar and TV. Doubles L82,000–L95,000. *Via Viminale 8, tel. 06/482–3307 or 06/487–2536. AE, MC, V.*

CENTRO STORICO **Albergo Abruzzi.** It's dreary and reeks of mothballs, but it's within feet of the Pantheon. All rooms have sinks; some have front-row views of the piazza. Doubles L82,000. *P. della Rotonda 69, tel. 06/679–2021.*

Panda. Convenient to public transportation and passeggiata life. Steep stairwell brings you to clean, functional rooms. Doubles L85,000. *Via della Croce 35, tel. 06/678–0179. Take Metro Line A to P. di Spagna and walk 2 blocks south on Via della Croce. AE.*

Pensione Mimosa. Rooms range from medium to huge, and all have sinks. Guests are welcome to use two living rooms, the fridge, and any of tables in the sunny meal room. Doubles L90,000. *Via Santa Chiara 61, tel. 06/6880–1753. From Stazione Termini, take Bus 64, 65, 70, 75, 170, or 492 to Largo di Torre Argentina, then walk 3 blocks north and turn left on Via Santa Chiara.*

WEST OF THE TIBER Metro Line A serves Ottaviano and the Vatican area, while a score of buses travel Viale di Trastevere.

Giuggioli Hotel. The same lovely woman has run things for 40 years, and her stately antiques have accumulated in the high-ceilinged rooms. Doubles L75,000. *Via Germanico 198, tel. 06/324–2113. From Lepanto Metro station, walk 1 block west on Via degli Scipioni and turn left on Via Paolo Emilio.*

Hotel Pensione Manara. Most rooms have windows overlooking an outdoor market. Plain rooms are in demand because of the ideal location. Doubles L58,000. *Via Luciano Manara 25/A, tel. 06/581–4713.*

Pensione Esty. Right on traffic-plagued Viale di Trastevere. Convenient enough, but the street din can get out of hand. Doubles L58,000. *Viale di Trastevere 108, tel. 06/589–1201. Just past Viale Aurelio Saffi on Viale di Trastevere, turn up driveway and enter first doorway on left, marked SCALA A.*

HOSTELS **Fraternus Domus.** Run by Catholic nuns, which means everything is clean and orderly. Hearty four-course lunch or dinner costs L15,000, wine included. Major drawback is the 11 PM curfew. Beds L40,000. *Via Monte Brianzo 62, tel. 06/654–2727. Metro Line A to Spagna, then walk southwest on Via Condotti.*

Hotel Pensione Sandy. Five blocks southwest of Stazione Termini and run by the same friendly owners of Pensione Ottaviano (*see below*). The big difference is there's no common room or elevator here. Beds L15,000–L20,000. *Via Cavour 136, tel. 06/488–4585.*

Ostello del Foro Italico. A flat rate of L18,000 includes sheets, hot showers, and breakfast. Hostel cards are required and can be issued on the spot for L30,000. *Viale delle Olimpiadi 61, tel. 06/323–6267. From Stazione Termini, take Bus 32 1 stop past Via Maresciallo Giardino*

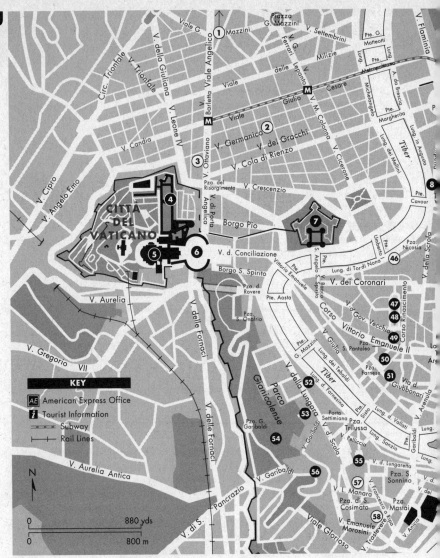

KEY

AE American Express Office

ℹ Tourist Information

⎯⎯⎯ Subway

⊢⊢⊢ Rail Lines

N

| 0 | 880 yds |
| 0 | 800 m |

(it's on the river), walk 1 long block and turn left. Midnight curfew, lockout 9 AM–2 PM. Max stay 3 days.

Pensione Alessandro. Private hostel just north of Stazione Termini. Feel free to use the dining room, TV, fridge, and showers. Bunk beds in sunny dorm L15,000–L20,000. *Via Vicenza 42, tel. 06/446–1958.*

Pensione Ottaviano. You're only a block from the Vatican, with many transportation options close at hand. Beds in sunny rooms L20,000. *Via Ottaviano 6, tel. 06/3973–8138 or 06/3973–7253. Metro Line A to Ottaviano, then walk 3 blocks south.*

FOOD

The main concentrations of cheap eats are around **Stazione Termini, Trevi Fountain, Piazza Navona,** and on the **Campo dei Fiori.** If you're staying near the Vatican, head south to Trastevere and its cafés, espresso bars, and trattorias; Viale di Trastevere is the district's main drag. For those on a really tight budget, open-air markets are plentiful around Stazione Termini, Campo dei Fiori, and just west of Piazza Navona.

Spots with the word *Romanesca* in the name usually specialize in traditional Roman cuisine. Highlights here include *saltimbocca* (veal rolls flavored with sage), *abbacchio* (spring lamb), and *filetti di baccala* (salted cod filets). *Carciofi* (artichokes) come fried or marinated. Yummy *supplì* (fried rice balls filled with mozzarella) are favored appetizers at food stands.

NEAR STAZIONE TERMINI Stazione Termini is surrounded by cheap trattorias and beer halls. A good place to start looking south of the station is **Via Manin**; north of the station try **Via Milazzo.** There's another cluster of taverns and restaurants in the streets surrounding **Piazzale Tiburtino;** to reach it from Stazione Termini, walk seven or so blocks southeast on Via Giovanni Giolitti, turn left on Via Santa Bibiana, go through the tunnel, and walk across busy Viale Pretoriano.

➤ **UNDER L10,000 • Bar Miss Roma.** The owners lure dinner crowds with affordable pizza and pasta, though the best deal is the self-service antipasti bar (L6000). Panini start from L2000, hamburgers from L3500. *Via Palestro 65, tel. 06/4455–4385. Open Mon.–Sat. 7 AM–11 PM.*

Formula Uno. Hectic waiters charge around a large, brightly lit mess of tables, dealing out two-fisted mugs of beer (L3500) and pizza from the wood-burning oven (L6000–L8000). *Via degli Equi 13, tel. 06/445–3866. From Piazzale Tiburtino, take Via Tiburtina to Via degli Equi. Open Mon.–Sat. 6:30 PM–12:30 AM.*

La Pappardella. Around 8:30 PM the promise of a cheap, hearty dinner packs 'em into Pappardella's vine-covered courtyard. Try cannelloni stuffed with herbed ricotta (L6000) or ricotta and spinach ravioli (L6000). *Via degli Equi 56, tel. 06/446–9349. From Piazzale Tiburtino, follow Via Tiburtina to Via degli Equi. Open daily 12:30–2:30 and 7:30–midnight. Closed Mon. off-season.*

➤ **UNDER L15,000 • Aduliss.** Billed as a restaurant but more like a social club for Rome's African, Turkish, and Middle Eastern immigrants. Kick back while Pop Aduliss cooks up piles of Ethiopian food. Gargantuan plate of curried potatoes, lentils, and spiced beef with injera bread goes for L15,000. *Via Milazzo 1/E, tel. 06/445–1695. Open Thurs.–Tues. noon–1 AM.*

Trattoria La Suburra. Dig into saltimbocca for L13,000 or *trippa alla Romana* (tripe stewed with wine and herbs) for L10,000. Linguine *alla cozze* (with mussels) goes for L9000. *Via Urbana 69, next to lower level of Cavour Metro station, no phone. Open Tues.–Sun. noon–2 and 8–10.*

CENTRO STORICO Budget restaurants in the heart of Rome are grouped in three areas: between **Piazza Navona** and the Tiber River, around **Campo dei Fiori,** and along **Corso Vittorio Emanuele II** between the river and Piazza dei Chiesa.

La Buffetto. The brief menu features a variety of superthin pizzas (L5000–L9000) and crunchy calzone (L6000–L9000). Vie for seating in the street-facing front room. *Via del Governo Vecchio 114, tel. 06/686–1617. From Piazza dei Chiesa, walk west on C. Vittorio Emanuele II, turn left on Via Soro, then right on Via del G. Vecchio. Open daily 6:30 PM–1 AM.*

Cartoccio d'Abruzzi. Your proximity to Piazza Navona means first-rate gawking on warm Roman nights. For L8000, chow on generous portions of linguine *alla vongole* (with clams) or spaghetti *carbonara* (with cream, ham, and peas). *Via di Tor Sanguigna 4, tel. 06/6880–2427. From P. Navona, follow Via di Lorenesi 1 block west to Via di Tor Sanguigna. Open Tues.–Sun. 8–11:30 PM.*

Er Grottina. Budget choices include large bowls of pasta (L8000–L9000) and meat dishes like *piccatina al Marsala* (veal sautéed in Marsala wine; L9000). *Via dei Baullari 25/27, tel. 06/688036. From P. Campo dei Fiori, walk 2 blocks northeast. Open Wed.–Mon. noon–3 and 7–midnight. Closed mid-Aug.–late Aug.*

La Monte Carlo. One of Rome's more affordable wood-oven pizzerias. Super-thin pizzas come small (L5000), medium (L7500), and large (L9000). *Vicolo Savelli 11A/13, tel. 06/686–1877. From P. dei Chiesa Nuova, walk 3 blocks east on C. Vittorio Emanuele II and turn left. Open daily 6:30 PM–1 AM. Closed Mon. off-season and early Aug.*

La Nuovo Shanghai. It ain't great Chinese food, but Italians lap it up. Skip the soups (thick and bland; L5000) but not the spring rolls (L3000). Sizzling pork, shrimp, chicken, and beef (L7000 each) are the house specialties. *Via dei Giubbonari 52, off P. Campo dei Fiori, tel. 06/654–1636. Open Tues.–Sun. 7–11 PM.*

TRASTEVERE Restaurants in this neighborhood are grouped around the riverfront **Piazza Trilussa,** off Lungotevere Sanzio near Ponte Sisto, and in the streets and alleyways that lead from **Viale di Trastevere.** From Stazione Termini, take Bus 27 or 75 and, once you cross the Tiber River, get off at any point along Viale di Trastevere.

➤ **UNDER L10,000 • Il Duca.** Pictures of Rome circa 1910 and dimmed iron lanterns set a romantic, mellow tone. Foot-wide pizzas (L6000–L10,000) and crispy calzone (L8000) are slowly baked in a wood-burning oven. *Vicolo dei Cinque 54, tel. 06/581–7706. From P. Trilussa, walk 1½ blocks on Vicolo dei Cinque toward Via Pelliccia. Open Tues.–Sun. 7 PM–midnight.*

Pizzeria da Ivo. The epitome of a Roman pizzeria, complete with sidewalk tables, exhaust fumes, and a busy street scene. Beer and pizza L6000–L10,000. *Via Francesco a Ripa 157, tel. 06/581–7082. From Viale di Trastevere, walk 3 blocks north on Via Francesco a Ripa. Open daily 7 PM–1 AM.*

Popi Popi. Spiffy pizzeria with affordable pizzas and calzone (L7000–L9000), not to mention about a dozen different pastas. Beware the watery house wine (bottles from L4500). *Via delle Fratte di Trastevere 45, tel. 06/589–5167. From Viale di Trastevere, walk 2 blocks north on Via Francesco a Ripa and turn right. Open Fri.–Wed. 5 PM–2 AM.*

Torrefazione Frontoni. Fat and affordable focaccia sandwiches (from L4000) near Ponte Garibaldi. Create your own combos. *Viale di Trastevere 52, at Via Francesco a Ripa, no phone. Open Mon.–Sat. 8–2 and 5–8.*

➤ **UNDER L15,000 • Il Cial.** First-course specialties (L5000–L7000) include *polenta* (cornmeal) prepared with *fagioli* (beans) and *porcini* (a kind of mushroom). Second-course dishes (L10,000–L15,000) are mostly grilled poultry and game. Expect crowds on warm summer evenings. *Vicolo dei Cinque 21, off P. Trilussa, no phone. Open Tues.–Sun. 8:15 PM–midnight.*

WORTH SEEING

You can take the "I don't care what it is, I'm just going for the aesthetic pleasure" approach, or the more methodical "first ancient Rome, then Christian Rome, then modern Rome" angle. Somewhere in between is the more typical "see some ruins, check out a church, and drink red wine by a fountain" schedule. If you've only got three or four days to tackle Rome, your priorities should be Ancient Rome, Piazza della Repubblica, Piazza di Spagna, the centro storico, and the Vatican.

ANCIENT ROME Geographically speaking, Ancient Rome comprises most of the area southeast of Piazza Venezia. Trajan's Forum, the Roman Forum, Palatine Hill, and the Baths of Caracalla are the only sites that charge admission, but you get a darn good view from outside the gates. One warning: Do not tackle Ancient Rome in one fell swoop on hot summer days. There ain't much shade here, nor many drink stands.

Colosseum. Nothing is as symbolic of Rome as the Colosseum, built in a mere eight years and inaugurated in AD 80 with 100 consecutive days of games. The 50,000 spectators who came to watch were protected from the elements by *velarium,* the world's first awning system. Pay admission to the upper levels (L6000) to see a scale model of the Colosseum in its glory days. *P. del Colosseo, tel. 06/700–4261. Admission free. Open daily 9–1 hr before sunset (until 1 PM Wed. and Sun.).*

Palatine Hill. On the southern (i.e., Colosseum) side of the Roman Forum, follow Via Sacra all the way up to Palatine Hill, where the very first traces of Rome—a rectangular complex of huts dating back to 753 BC—were discovered. Over the next few centuries, the hill became a prime piece of real estate. The majority of ruins are from the **Imperial Palace,** consisting of the Domus Audustana (the emperor's residence), the Domus Flavia (the reception building), and the gigantic sunken stadium where races and games used to take place. *Admission: L3000. Open Mon., Wed.–Sat. 9–5, Tues. and Sun. 9–1; shorter hrs off-season.*

Roman Forum. Once a swampy marshland, the valley was drained around 100 BC and transformed into the political and social heart of the Republic, the site of processions, trials, and elections. Nowadays the Forum is mostly big chunks of disheveled marble. Bookstores sell thick guides to the forum and its surrounding ruins, but it's best just to let your mind contemplate the weathered pieces of the once-impressive whole. *Entrances on Via dei Fori Imperiali and Via di San Gregorio. Admission: L10,000. Open Mon., Wed.–Sat. 9–6, Tues. and Sun. 9–1; shorter hrs off-season.*

San Giovanni in Laterno. Originally built in the 4th century on a piece of land that Emperor Constantine donated to the newly sanctioned sect of Christians, it largely owes its present appearance to Borromini, who "modernized" it in Baroque style in the 17th century. Under the Gothic tabernacle above the altar, look for the heads (yes, the actual skulls) of St. Peter and St. Paul. *San Giovanni in Laterno. Metro Line A to San Giovanni and walk west to church. Admission free. Open daily 9–noon and 3–6.*

San Pietro in Vincoli. Two pieces compete for attention at this sparsely decorated, sickly overtouristed church: the chains that bound St. Peter during his prison stays in Jerusalem and Rome (you can't miss 'em beneath the altar), and Michelangelo's *Moses,* anatomically perfect in every sense (even doctors say so) and one of his most powerful sculptures. *P. San Pietro in Vincoli, bet. the Colosseum and Via Cavour. Open daily 7–12:30 and 3:30–6.*

Santa Maria Maggiore. One of Rome's oldest and most striking cathedrals has a legend behind it. In the 4th century, Pope Liberius had a dream that instructed him to build a great cathedral to St. Mary on Esquiline hill. Hesitant to shell out cash because of sleep-induced fancy, he shelved the project. That is, until St. Mary herself visited Liberius in his sleep, then dumped a bunch of snow (in the middle of August, mind you) on the spot where the church was destined to be built. Modern pilgrims can see a re-creation of the scene in a 13th-century exterior mosaic, which costs L3000 to view close up. *P. Santa Maria Maggiore, off Via Cavour. Open daily 9–6:30.*

Terme di Caracalla. Maybe even more than the Forum, the Baths of Caracalla give some sense of the size, scope, and engineering genius of ancient Rome's civic architecture. Some of the facilities still have their original plumbing, as well as extensive floor mosaics. *Via Terme di Caracalla. Metro Line B to Circo Massimo. Admission: L6000. Open Mon.–Sat. 9–3, Sun. 9–1.*

Trajan's Forum and Markets. After Rome gained "empire" status, the original forum just couldn't hold all the trials, discussions, and meetings that it took to run Western civilization, so Caesar built a new one. Apparently he started a trend, because over the next 200-plus years (43 BC–AD 180), four different emperors—Augustus, Domitian, Vespasian, and Trajan—followed suit. Trajan's Forum (admission L4000) was the grandest in size and scope: its basilica is equivalent in proportion to that of St. Paul's. To prevent landslides, arcaded markets were dug into the hillside, growing over the centuries into a large complex of storehouses, plazas, and alleyways. Nowadays they're known as Trajan's Markets (Via IV Novembre 94; admission L3750, L2500 students; open daily 9–1:30) and are worth a few hours' exploration.

CAMPIDOGLIO Campidoglio (Capitoline Hill) was and is the most important of Rome's original seven hills. Strategically located high above the Tiber River, "capital" hill was Rome's natural bulwark and the center of political activity during the Republic. After catching fire and falling into serious disrepair, the hill was restored by Michelangelo in 1537. He redesigned **Palazzo Senatorio** (which now houses Rome's city hall) and made architectural improvements to the Palazzo dei Conservatori and to the slightly convex **Piazza del Campidoglio.** Whatever Michelangelo did to the hilltop square worked, because the views of Rome from Piazza del Campidoglio are alone worth the trek. Also climb the stairs to the plain brick **Basilica Santa Maria in Aracoeli** (admission free; open daily 7–noon and 4–7). The interior is dark and undergoing perpetual restoration, but the views of Rome are first-rate.

Museo Capitolino. Housed in the Palazzo Nuovo (New Palace), the Capitoline Museum was designed by Michelangelo to blend stylistically with the adjacent Palazzo dei Conservatori. Stay away if you hate sculpture, because you've stepped into Rome's most comprehensive classical galleries. *P. del Campidoglio, tel. 06/6710–2071. Admission: L10,000, L5000 students. Open Tues. 9–1:30 and 5–8, Wed.–Fri. 9–1:30, Sat. 9–1:30 and 7:30–11:30, Sun. 9–1; shorter hrs off-season.*

Palazzo dei Conservatori. In the ground-floor courtyard look for the bits and pieces of what must have been an enormous statue of Constantine—the toenail alone is as big as a human hand. On the first floor are several fresco-filled rooms, including the **Salone dei Orazi e Curiazi,** with carved wooden doors and statues by Bernini. Its prize piece is the *Capitoline Wolf,* a 5th-century-BC Etruscan bronze that from time immemorial has been the symbol of Rome. Ironically, the suckling figures of Remus and Romulus were added during the Renaissance to adapt the statue to the legend of Rome's founding. Admission prices and hours are identical to those at the Museo Capitolino (*see above*). *P. del Campidoglio, tel. 06/6710–1244.*

PIAZZA DELLA REPUBBLICA AND PIAZZA BARBERINI Although the area's big boulevards, big buildings, and big price tags are not conducive to wandering, chances are you'll pass through multiple times on the way from Stazione Termini to the centro storico. Take a peek at the nearby museums, then head northwest from the square on Via Orlando and veer right onto Via Barberini. This dead-ends at Piazza Barberini, a heavily trafficked square sporting Bernini's graceful **Tritone** (Fountain of the Triton), designed in 1637 for Pope Urban VIII. From here, it's a short walk up Via delle Quattro Fontane to Palazzo Barberini.

Galleria Nazionale. This national art gallery leads you room by room from the 13th to the 18th century with works by the likes of Fra Filippo Lippi, Zucchi, Pulzone, Passarotti, Caravaggio, and Reni. *Via delle Quattro Fontane 13, tel. 06/481–4591. Admission: L6000. Open Tues.–Sat. 9–2, Sun. 9–1.*

San Carlo alle Quattro Fontane. The sumptuous Church of the Four Fountains got its name from the four fountains—each representing a season—that stand on opposite corners of the intersection. It was designed by Gianlorenzo Bernini's main rival, Borromini, and is one of the first experiments in a pure Baroque style. *Via del Quirinale at Via delle Quattro Fontane, tel. 06/767–6531. Admission free. Open daily 7–noon and 4–7.*

Santa Maria degli Angeli. Hidden on the eastern side of Piazza della Repubblica, the basilica of Mary and the Angels was designed by Michelangelo, who built the basilica atop the foundations of the 4th-century Baths of Dioclesian, the largest of Rome's ancient baths. *P. della Repubblica. Admission free. Open daily 7:30–12:30 and 4–6:30.*

Santa Maria della Concezione. Beneath the nave, built on mud brought from Jerusalem by command of Pope Urban VIII, are four chambers decorated with the remains of 4,000 Capuchin monks. A few skeletons are intact, dressed in traditional brown robes, but most have been pulled apart—bone by bone—to make ornate ceiling decorations, lamps, and archways. *Via Vittorio Veneto 27, tel. 06/462850. Donation requested. Open daily 9–noon and 3–6.*

PIAZZA DEL POPOLO Very round, very explicitly defined, and very traffic-laden, Valadier's Piazza del Popolo—the People's Square—is one of Rome's biggest. Head south from the piazza along Via Ripetta to the mammoth, partially submerged **Augusteum** (closed to the public), a brick-faced mausoleum commissioned in 28 BC by Augustus for his own use. From the mausoleum, follow your nose to the hard-to-miss **Ara Pacis** (Peace Altar), built in 13 BC to celebrate Augustus's victories in Gaul and Spain.

Santa Maria del Popolo. This church looks plain at first glance, but the artwork inside makes up for any decorative deficiency. To the left of the altar are two Caravaggio canvases depicting the martyrdom of St. Peter (left) and St. Paul (right). None other than Bernini can take credit for the plump cherubs and ghastly saints that hang from the nave's ceiling. *P. del Popolo. Admission free. Open daily 8–1:30 and 4:30–7.*

PIAZZA DI SPAGNA Piazza di Spagna may be the soul of tourist Rome, but forget the "meet you at the Spanish Steps" thing—it can take hours to find familiar faces in the dense crush. At the same time, heavy crowds mean prime people-watching. Still, the piazza's main draw is the 18th-century **Spanish Steps,** which connect ritzy shops at the bottom of the hill with ritzy hotels at the top. The reward for climbing to the top is a dizzying view of central Rome. Because the steps face west, the views are especially good around sunset. Byron, Shelley, and Keats all drew inspiration from the hues of the piazza at dusk and dawn. Keats lived at No. 26; today it's the **Keats Museum** (P. di Spagna 26; admission L5000; open Mon.–Sat. 11–1 and 3–5), with a fine collection of Romantic-era relics, including left-behind books, letters, pictures, locks of hair, and old furniture.

From the narrow end of Piazza di Spagna, take Via Propaganda Fide to Sant'Andrea delle Fratte. Veer left on Via del Nazareno, cross busy Via del Tritone to Via della Stamperia, and there you have it—the famous, 17th-century **Trevi Fountain,** one of the few in Rome that's actually more absorbing than the people crowding around it. The fountain is most alive at night, when its underwater lights are aglow and the Italian pick-up scene is most annoying.

VILLA BORGHESE Rome's largest open space is filled with playful fountains, sculptured gardens, and forests of shady pine trees. The **Pincio,** a public park above Piazza del Popolo, is better kept than the villa's somewhat overgrown interior. But that's not the point: The real attractions are Villa Borghese's art museums.

Galleria Borghese. Some of Bernini's most celebrated pieces are here, including *David,* which the artist finished at the ripe age of 18. The gallery's Raphael, Caravaggio, Titian, and Boticelli paintings are temporarily housed in **San Michele a Ripa** (Via di San Michele 22, tel. 06/58431; open weedays 9:30–1 and 4–8, Sat. 9:30–1:30), which is included in the price of admission (hold onto your ticket). *Via Raimondi, tel. 06/858577. Admission: L4000. Open Mon.–Sat. 9–1:30, Sun. 9–1.*

Galleria Nazionale d'Arte Moderna. Rome's modern-art museum, in an immense neoclassical building on the fringe of Villa Borghese, houses a brilliant collection of Italian Impressionist and Romantic art, as well as works by Klimt, Degas, Cézanne, and Zorn. *Viale delle Belle Arti 131, tel. 06/322–4151. Admission: L8000. Open Tues.–Sat. 9–2, Sun. 9–1.*

Museo di Villa Giulia. The villa of Pope Julius III, on the southwest edge of Villa Borghese, houses one of the world's most important collections of Etruscan artifacts—earthenware water jugs, terra-cotta bowls, dozens of small bronze figures, and look-alike jewelry. The highlight is the *Sarcophagus of the Sposi,* a simple but elegant device meant for married Etruscan couples. *P. di Villa Giulia 9, tel. 06/320–1951. Admission: L8000. Open daily 9 AM–2 PM (until 7 PM on Wed. and 1 PM on Sun.).*

CENTRO STORICO Rome's historic center—bordered by the mausoleum of Augustus to the north, Via del Corso to the east, and the Tiber River to the south and west—encompasses the bulk of central Rome and spans the greatest numbers of centuries. If you only spend one day in Rome, this is the place to do it. **Campo dei Fiori,** one of the area's more inviting piazze, is home to Rome's largest and oldest (since 1490) daily outdoor produce market. It's also one of the only church-free piazze in Rome—a reason in itself to visit.

Galleria Spada. The majority of the Spada's four-gallery collection is divided between 16th-century portraits and religious scenes, with a few landscapes and still lifes thrown in for good measure. Bologna's Guido Reni (1575–1642), Florence's Pietro Torrigiani (1471–1528), and Naples-born Salvator Rosa (1615–1673) are well represented. *Via dei Giubbonari, 1 block southeast of Campo dei Fiori, tel. 06/876–1344. Admission: L4000. Open Tues.–Sun. 9–2.*

Il Gesù. Excluding St. Peter's Basilica, Il Gesù is the most colorful church in Rome—every inch is covered with marble stained red, green, gold, and pink. Even the altar to St. Ignatius of Loyola (the founder of the Jesuits), lathered in silver and gold, gets a gasp from the crowd. *Via del Plebiscito. Open daily 6–12:30 and 4–7:15.*

Pantheon. Built by Marcus Agrippa in 27 BC, the Pantheon was originally a pagan temple built in honor of all—not just one—gods. In the 2nd century AD, Hadrian rebuilt the structure, and to him much of the credit is due for the Pantheon's perfect dimensions: 141 feet high by 141 feet wide, with a vast dome that seems to hover unsupported above the circle-shaped chamber. In the middle of the dome, a 30-foot-wide oculus lets in a brilliant shaft of amber light; as the day wanes, the circle of light glides slowly across the marble floor, then slowly up the far wall as afternoon turns to dusk. *P. della Rotonda, tel. 06/654–3311. Admission free. Open July–Sept., daily 9–6; Oct.–June, Mon.–Sat. 9–5, Sun. 9–1.*

Piazza Navona. You couldn't concoct a more Roman street scene: cafés and crowded tables at street level, coral- and rust-colored houses one and two floors above, most lined with flower boxes and wrought-iron balconies. In the center of the busy piazza are gushing fountains by Bernini and his pupils. The **Fountain of the Four Rivers,** the only Piazza Navona fountain done by Bernini himself, was carved from an enormous rock squared off by statues representing the four corners of the world. Before someone figured out that the adjacent church **Sant'Agnese in Agone** was designed *before* the fountain, common belief held that Bernini's fountain-figures were poised as if looking in terror at the inferior creation of Francesco Borromini, Bernini's big rival.

Santa Maria Sopra Minerva. Santa Maria's slightly pointed arches and glass rosettes qualify it as one of Rome's only Gothic churches—just barely. It was originally built above a temple dedicated to Minerva (hence the name). Check out the the frescoes by Fra Filippo Lippi, the tomb of artist Fra Angelico, and Michelangelo's statue *The Redeemer. P. delle Minerva, 1 block south of Pantheon. Admission free. Open daily 7–noon and 4–7.*

JEWISH GHETTO In 1555, Pope Paul II decided to "purify" the Christian faith by relocating Rome's Jews—about 8,000 at the time—from their homes in Trastevere to five or so undesirable acres "across the river," a triangular space marked today by Ponte Garibaldi, Ponte Fabricio, and Largo Aremula. During World War II, after Mussolini was executed and Rome was occupied by German troops, the majority of Rome's Jews were deported to concentration camps. Rome's current Jewish population is 15,000, though only about 1,000 remain in the ghetto. Among the most interesting sights are **Fontana delle Tartarughe** (Fountain of the Turtles) on Piazza Mattei and the weather-beaten, laundry-laden houses along Via Portico d'Ottavia.

Musei Ebraico. This two-room museum has decorative crowns, prayer books, holy chairs, and tapestries dating from the 17th century. One of the more haunting displays is a prayer book that literally saved its owner's life during a 1982 attack on the synagogue—bullet holes and blood stains tell the tale. One ticket admits you to the museum and adjacent **synagogue**; the latter can be toured only with a guide. *Lungotevere Cenci, on the river near Ponte Fabricio, tel. 06/687–5051. Admission: L3000. Open Mon.–Thurs. 9:30–6, Fri. and Sun. 9:30–12:30.*

JANICULUM HILL Janiculum Hill, which rises high above the Trastevere district and is bordered by the Vatican gardens to the north, is scattered with interesting tidbits from various centuries. **Via Garibaldi,** the main road leading up the hill from the Via della Lungara, was the site of a major battle between Garibaldi's troops and the French, commemorated by a simple columnar war memorial. Across from the Garibaldi war memorial, the supposed spot where St. Peter was crucified in AD 64, is marked by the late-15th-century church of **San Pietro in Montorio** (donations requested; open Tues.–Sun. 10–1 and 5–8) and its accompanying convent. If you are approaching the hill from its northern end, head up the vine-covered steps of **Via di San Onofrio**; at its northern foot lies **Chiesa di San Onofrio,** the church where the poet Tasso is buried.

TRASTEVERE Few artists or merchants load their goods off boats anymore, so Travestere's location near the Tiber River isn't as key as it once was. But the 'hood is still a meeting point for artisans, actors, and alternative thinkers—as hip and happenin' (especially at night) as it gets in Rome. The definitive heart of Trastevere is **Piazza Santa Maria in Trastevere,** surrounded by jumbled alleyways, dusty workshops, and cheap ethnic restaurants.

Galleria Nazionale d'Arte Antica. Ignore the temporary metal facade and head straight inside the flamboyant Villa Corsini, which houses the National Gallery of Ancient Art and its collection of works by Caravaggio, Reni, Maratta, Preti, Reubens, and van Dyck. *Via della Lungara 10, tel. 06/654–2323. Admission: L6000. Open Tues.–Sat. 9–2, Sun. 9–1.*

Villa Farnesina. Built in 1511 for Agostino "the Magnificent" Chigi, an obviously well-off Roman banker, the two-story Villa Farnesina is a relic of the High Renaissance. The architect, Baldassare Peruzzi, is responsible for the wall and ceiling frescoes, Raphael for the frescoes in the ground-floor chambers. *Via della Lungara 230, tel. 06/650831 or 06/654–0565. Admission free. Open Mon.–Sat. 9–1.*

You are not allowed into St. Peter's or the Vatican in shorts, sleeveless T-shirts, short skirts, or anything a Catholic priest might deem too revealing.

CITTÀ DEL VATICANO To see Città del Vaticano (Vatican City) in one day is simply impossible, a result of confusing hours and the sheer vastness of it all. If you absolutely must see everything in one go, start early at Castel Sant'Angelo, head up to Piazza San Pietro and catch one of the shuttle buses to the Vatican museums, and then finish up with St. Peter's. True art fiends should head straight for the museums, since it can take up to six hours for even the most basic tours.

Meet the Pope

You don't have to be Catholic to appreciate the pomp and ceremony of a papal audience. "Private" audiences are held for the masses every Wednesday at 11 AM in the Papal Audience Hall (10 AM if the weather is unbearably hot). Tickets are available Mondays and Tuesdays 9 AM–1 PM and Wednesdays 9 AM–10 AM through the bronze doors on the west side of Piazza San Pietro. For advance tickets, write to Prefettura della Casa Pontifica, 00120 Città della Vaticano, indicating the date you prefer and the language you speak. Another option is to stand with up to 200,000 others on Piazza San Pietro every Sunday at 11 AM, when the pope appears at the window of the Vatican Palace to bless the public.

Castel Sant'Angelo. The original structure was probably built under the orders of Hadrian in AD 135 as a mausoleum for himself and his successors. Inside, tourists gawk at the frescoed halls and views from the rooftop café. *Lungotevere Castello 50, tel. 06/687–5036. Admission: L8000, L6000 students. Open Apr.–Sept., Mon.–Sat. 9–7; Oct.–Mar., Mon. 2–7, Tues.–Sat. 9–1, Sun. 9–noon.*

St. Peter's Basilica. It's quite a shock to enter the broad, enveloping arms of **Piazza San Pietro** (St. Peter's Square), one of Bernini's unquestioned masterpieces. It took Bernini only 11 years to design and oversee the construction of this massive square, capable of holding 400,000 people within its symmetrical arms (symbolic of St. Peter embracing the people). At the end of it all looms St. Peter's, the world's most significant Christian church and an absolute must on any Roman itinerary. In AD 319, Constantine (the first Christian emperor of Rome) decided to bankroll a basilica for the newly legitimized sect of Christians. In 1506, Pope Julius II instructed Donato Bramante (1444–1514) to raze the site and completely redesign the basilica. Over the next 120 years, Italy's greatest artists and architects—including Bramante, Bernini, Raphael, Perruzi, Sangallo the Younger, and Michelangelo—contributed to the design and decoration.

The Vatican. Primary residence of popes since 1377, the Vatican comprises no fewer than nine interlocking buildings with 1,400 chapels, galleries, and private living chambers. The main entrance to the museums, on Viale Vaticano, is a long walk from Piazza San Pietro, which is why buses (L2000) shuttle visitors from the piazza to the museums' entrance. Buses run 8:45 AM–12:45 PM except on Wednesdays and Sundays (when the piazza is crowded in anticipation of a papal audience). Buy tickets at the Vatican Information Office on Piazza San Pietro. Other options are Bus 49 from Piazza Cavour to the Vatican's front door, Bus 81 to Piazza del Risorgimento and a short walk south, or Metro Line A to Ottaviano and a short walk southeast.

Once inside, four color-coded trails lead through the labyrinthine Vatican, lasting two, three, four, and six hours, respectively. Choose your poison (leaflets at the door describe each in detail) or venture through on your own. Either way, the English-language taped commentary is definitely worth the L3000 rental fee. General admission to everything in the Vatican is L12,000.

The highlight, of course, is the **Sistine Chapel**—but forget the romantic notion of wandering silently under Michelangelo's masterpiece. The chapel is always packed with neck-craning tourists, but that's because nearly every "important" Renaissance artist had a hand in its decoration—Pintoricchio, Signorelli, Botticelli, Cosimo Rosselli—even before Michelangelo, much to his dismay, was asked by Pope Julius II to paint the ceiling, a barrel-vaulted artist's nightmare. Contrary to popular belief, Michelangelo didn't actually work on his back but stood on his tiptoes. (It's said that after finishing the Sistine Chapel, Michelangelo couldn't read anything without holding it above his head.) Twenty years after completing the Sistine Chapel, Michelangelo was commissioned to paint the *Last Judgment* on the wall behind the simple altar. *Viale Vaticano, tel. 06/698–3333. Admission: L12,000, free last Sun. of month. Open Easter week and July–Sept., weekdays 8:45–5 (last admission 4 PM); Oct.–June, Mon.–Sat. 9–2 (last admission 1 PM); also last Sun. of every month 9–2. Closed Jan. 1, Jan. 6, Feb. 11, Mar. 19, Easter Sun. and Mon., May 1, June 29, Aug. 15–16, Nov. 1, Dec. 8, Dec. 25–26.*

VIA APPIA AND THE CATACOMBS Via Appia (Appian Way) is just as dirty and noisy as any other Italian street, despite its glorious title as the "Queen of Roads." All the brouhaha comes from the miles upon miles of underground cemeteries that lay buried beneath. Since burial was and still is forbidden within Rome's city limits, early Christians buried their dead in the suburbs, in Via Appia's soft tufa clay. Most of the bodies are long gone, so you'll have to make do with eerie subterranean passageways and lots of Christian graffiti—mainly variations on the fish, the Greek symbol for Christ. Although the catacombs themselves stretch for miles, there are only three official entrances: **San Callisto** (Via Appia Antica 110, tel. 06/513–6725; closed Wed.), **Domitilla** (Via Appia Antica 190, tel. 06/554–8766; closed Tues.), and **San Sebastiano** (Via Appia Antica 136, tel. 06/788–7035; closed Thurs.). Each charges L6000 and is open 8:30–noon and 2:30–5.

SHOPPING

Unless you're traveling on somebody else's credit card, be content with browsing the exclusive shops off Piazza di Spagna, especially those along nearby **Via Frattina** and **Via dei Condotti.** One thing Rome does have is junk—from priceless Renaissance antiques to modern throwaway baubles. **Via Margutta,** between Piazza di Spagna and Piazza del Popolo, is the Mecca of antiques shops, but again, nothing comes cheap. For funky boutiques and used clothing, head toward the Pantheon and Campo dei Fiori; the streets off **Corso Vittorio Emanuele II** are also packed with every sort of boutique and shop. Products of the New Age, from the groovy to the esoteric, abound in shops near Piazza Santa Maria in Trastevere. Religious articles are plentiful near the Vatican and in the Centro Storico around Piazza della Minerva.

Outdoor markets offer some of the best bargains in Rome. **Campo dei Fiori,** Rome's oldest continuous market, sets up Monday–Saturday from 6 AM until 11 PM or so. The farmers and fishermen who sell their fresh wares here love to haggle, but they do not appreciate people who buy *an* apple or *a* fish. On Sundays from 6 AM to 2 PM, the **Porta Portese flea market** sets up along Via Portuense, on the western bank of the Tiber just south of Trastevere; find your way to the river and walk to Ponte Sublicio, one bridge south of Ponte Palatino. The carnival atmosphere comes from a blend of East Europeans and Africans selling just about anything you can imagine. Keep a tight grip on your valuables.

AFTER DARK

Indispensable for anyone with an after dark agenda is *La Trova Roma,* a supplement published in Thursday's *La Repubblica* newspaper. It's in Italian, but the lists of clubs, concerts, raves, and restaurants is easy to decipher. *Wanted in Rome* and *Metropolitana,* two English-language magazines that also list concerts and clubs, are available at most newsstands.

The big bummer in Rome is the *tessera* (membership fee) charged by many clubs. Memberships last anywhere from a month to a year and cost L10,000–L20,000. Don't worry about two passport-size photos; clubs will take your money and issue a membership card on the spot. Also remember that most clubs and bars don't get interesting until 1 or 2 AM.

MUSIC AND DANCING You can either listen to an orchestra or choir in some spectacular setting, or truck out to Testaccio and its main drag, **Via Monte di Testaccio** (Bus 27 from Stazione Termini), where you can take your pick of blues, salsa, jazz or rock from the half-dozen clubs wrapped around the base of Mt. Testaccio. One warning: Testaccio is on the seedy side, and women traveling solo should consider a taxi (L10,000–L12,000).

Blatumbas Amozonas. Set in a tropically decorated, white stucco alcove, with faux jungle plants and parrots. The Venezuelan owner is among a group of talented artists that play nightly. For L10,000–L15,000 per person, he'll whip up a batch of paella if you call in advance. *P. in Piscinula 20, tel. 06/589–6421. West bank of Tiber, 1 block south of Ponte C. Fabricio. Closed Mon. and July.*

Caffè Caruso. Rhumba, mambo, and salsa with a mellow crowd of Italians and Latinos. The music is live and always danceable. The one bummer is the L20,000 tessera, valid for nine months. *Via di Monte Testaccio 36, tel. 06/574–5019.*

Circolo degli Artisti. A warehouse space with a bar and blasting hip-hop music. In summer, expect the occasional live band and performance-art piece. Tessera L15,000. *Via Lamarmora 28, tel. 06/446–4968. Metro Line A to Vittorio Emanuele, Via Lamarmora is 1 block south. Open Thurs.–Sat. 11 PM–very late.*

Club Picasso. Live or recorded? Rock, acid, reggae, or funk? The only way to find out what's playing is to call ahead or check the newspapers. No hooligans or funky backpackers, but grunge is okay if it looks intentional. Tessera L10,000. *Via Monte di Testaccio 63, tel. 06/574–2975. Open Fri.– Sat. 10 PM–4 AM.*

Folkstudio. Folkstudio's booths and intimate tables attract a relatively mellow crowd for Italy—but still no Birkenstocks or tie-dye. Most nights there are live performances by local musicians, poets, whatever. Nightly cover L10,000. *Via Frangipane 42, tel. 06/487–1063. Open nightly 7 PM–1:30 AM.*

Ombre Rosse. This Trastevere hangout is not unlike a San Francisco café, with round marble tables and a tangible intellectual feel—as if someone might burst out with a poem any minute. *P. Sant'Egidio 12, no phone. Closed Sun.*

St. Louis. Rome's favorite spot for jazz. Bands start at 10 PM, but by 9:30 things are packed. Which is to say, the 8–9:30 happy hour is not only a bargain but a good way to ensure a seat. *Via del Cardello 13, south off Via Cavour, tel. 06/474–5076. Metro Line B to Colosseo, then walk northwest on Via del Colosseo to Via del Cardello. Closed Mon. and Thurs.*

CLASSICAL MUSIC Rome's main venues are **Accademia di Santa Cecilia** (box office tel. 06/654–1044), **Accademia Filarmonica Romana** (Teatro Olimpico, Via Gentile da Fabriano 17, tel. 06/396–2635 or 06/320–1752), and the **Instituzione Universitaria dei Concerti** (Via Bolzano 38, tel. 06/361–0051). Fans of Baroque music should check out the **Gonfalone series** (Via del Gonfalone 32, tel. 06/687–5952), one of Europe's best productions of Baroque music. Both **Il Tempietto** (tel. 06/481–4800) and **Associazione Musicale Romana** (tel. 06/656–8441) produce concerts throughout the year. Ticket prices range from L16,000 to L45,000 depending on the location and event. Students with an ID get a 10% discount at the Instituzione Universitaria.

OPERA AND BALLET Rome's opera season runs November–May in the **Teatro dell'Opera** (Via dei Viminale, tel. 06/6759–5725 for info in English). The box office opens for limited hours (10–1 and 5–7) two days prior to the performance, and tickets run L20,000–L60,000. The **Rome Opera Ballet** also hosts performances in the Teatro dell'Opera; call the box office for schedules. If you're not an opera fan by nature, consider a midsummer's night performance in the great outdoors at the **Baths of Caracalla**—an amazing setting. Prices are the same as for regular performances and can be bought in advance at the Teatro dell'Opera box office or at the baths themselves on the day of the performance.

Near Rome

FRASCATI

Huddled on a steep hillside 40 km southeast of Rome, Frascati is like a balcony to the world, or at least to Rome's rural suburbs. If you need an excuse for a day trip, consider the sweeping views of Rome and the Alban hills and the Tyrrhenian Sea on exceptionally clear days. More to the point, there's fresh country air and barrels of smooth wine that the town of Frascati is famous for. Once you've exhausted Frascati's narrow streets and lounged on the central **Piazza San Pietro,** it's time for the obligatory *degustazione* (tasting) of the local potables. Take your pick from the cafés and trattorias fronting the piazza, or try the totally touristy, totally loud, totally fun **Cantina Gomandini** (Via Emanuele Filiberto 1, tel. 06/942–1585; open Tues.–Sun. noon–10 PM). Look for it halfway up the stairs when trekking from the train station to the city center. **AAST** (P. Marconi 1, tel. 06/942–0331; open Mon.–Sat. 9–2 and 3:30–7) has a detailed map marked with wine-tasting spots in Frascati and nearby villages, plus lodging suggestions.

COMING AND GOING Trains from Rome's Stazione Termini (hourly, L2400) drop you at Frascati's tiny one-track depot. To reach the center, climb the hillside stairs to Piazza Marconi; Piazza San Pietro is two blocks to the left, Villa Aldobrandini straight ahead along Via Catone. **Buses** leave from the Rome's Anagnina Metro station (every 20 min, L1500) and drop you in the middle of Piazza Marconi. Buy tickets for the return trip to Rome from **ACOTRAL** (P. Marconi 5) or AAST.

SUBIACO

Subiaco, 75 km east of Rome, owes its fame to St. Benedict, who established the first of his Benedictine monasteries in this remote hilltown. At one time there were 13 monasteries around Subiaco, but nowadays only two remain to give some sense of the exquisite craftsmanship that living in total peacefulness can induce. A car will make your life easy; otherwise, it's a 3-km walk from Subiaco to San Scolastica monastery, and another 30 minutes uphill to San Benedetto.

The largest of the two monasteries is **San Scolastica,** built by St. Benedict and his sister, Scolastica. With its three cloisters—one Renaissance, one Gothic, and one Cosmatesque—and an 11th-century Roman campanile, the monastery is a textbook example of hodgepodge Italian architecture. *Tel. 0774/85525. Admission free. Open daily 9–12:30 and 4–7.*

More interesting is the nearby **San Benedetto** monastery, built over the grotto where St. Benedict lived in seclusion for three years (follow the footpath that climbs uphill from San Scolastica). The most impressive features are the nine towering arches that provide support for this clifftop fortress. Wait around long enough—the stockpile of monastic home brew in the souvenir shop eases the pain of waiting—and one of the monks will fetch you for a guided tour. *Tel. 0774/85039. Admission free. Open daily 9–12:30 and 3–6.*

BASICS Bus 4 leaves hourly from Rome's Rebibbia Metro station (2 hrs, L4800), stopping at Subiaco's Piazza Roma. The monasteries are 2 km northwest along Via Papa Braschi. The **tourist office** (Via Cadorna 59, tel. 0774/822012; open Mon. 8–2, Tues.–Sat. 8–2 and 3:30–7:30, Sun. 9–noon) is 1 km southeast along Via Cavour, past Piazza San Andrea.

CIVITAVECCHIA

Founded by Emperor Trajan to enhance Rome's Mediterranean trade base, Civitavecchia does have a few Roman relics spread among the modern housing, oil storage tanks, and port paraphernalia cluttering its shore. But let's be honest: The only reason to visit this bland industrial tragedy is to catch a ferry to Sardinia. If you end up trapped here, as many are while en route to Sardinia, rest assured that food is cheap and beds are plentiful. For the usual maps and accommodation listings, stop by **AAST** (Viale Garibaldi 40–42, tel. 0766/25348; open weekdays 9–1 and 4–7, Sat. 9–12:30) inside the Turlazio travel agency about five blocks south of the docks.

COMING AND GOING **Stazione ES** (Viale delle Quattro Porte, off Viale della Vittorio, tel. 0766/24975) has frequent service to Rome (1 hr, L10,000). A taxi to the distant port should cost no more than L10,000. **ACOTRAL** buses (tel. 0766/35961) leave every 30 minutes from Viale Giulio Cesare, a few steps from Rome's Lepanto Metro station (1$^{1}/_{2}$ hrs, L4000). Buses stop at Via Cadorna, one block east of the FS ports, and at Piazza Vittorio Emanuele II, two blocks east of Tirrenia's dock.

Civitavecchia is the main Lazio port for ferries to Sardinia. **Tirrenia Lines** (tel. 0766/500580) has sparkling white ferries that leave from two adjacent docks on Lungoporto Gramsci, near Piazza Vittorio Emanuele II. **FS** (tel. 0766/23273 or 0766/25850) ferries dock at the end of Via Cadorna, where there's a small terminal laden with grimy bathrooms and a not-so-thrilling snack bar. With either company, you'll pay L15,000–L25,000 for basic passage, upward of L60,000 for a luxurious cabin. Definitely reserve in advance if you plan to make the crossing in summer.

VITERBO

The main attractions in Viterbo, 80 km northwest of Rome, are its 12th-century walls and towers and its perfectly preserved **Quartiere San Pellegrino,** a relic of the Middle Ages that should capture the imagination of any oaf. If you are coming from Porta del Carmine, cross Ponte Paradiso and step into this eerie 13th-century time capsule, complete with dark curving roads and a jumble of misshapen houses that tilt gracefully with age. Much of the area is pedestrian-only, which makes it a fine place to plant yourself on a piazza with a bottle of cheap wine. The **EPT** office (P. dei Cadotti 16, tel. 0761/346363; open Mon.–Sat. 8–2) in the northern part of the centro storico has maps and information on accommodations throughout the area.

Stazione Porta Romana is in the southwest corner of the city, about three blocks south of the centro storico's Porta Romana entrance. A second station, **Stazione Porta Fiorentina,** is north of the centro storico on Viale Trento, a short walk from the **ACOTRAL bus depot.** Within a block or so is the depressing but fairly cheap **Pensione Trieste** (Via Nazario Sauro 32, tel. 0761/341882; doubles L50,000), which sometimes has additional rooms to let about four blocks west on Viale Trieste.

Naples and Campania

Campania stacks hectic urban centers, snazzy coastal resorts, and some of the oldest ruins this side of Constantinople into a mammoth must-see sandwich. More travelers visit this region than any other in the south, and it's no wonder. The balmy climate and breathtaking vistas of the Bay of Naples and Gulf of Salerno have attracted pleasure-seekers for centuries. Greeks and Romans built luxury palaces here, and in the 17th and 18th centuries, Naples was the requisite final stop on every noble's grand tour of Europe and Italy. Today, you can visit the famed archaeological sites of **Herculaneum** and **Pompeii** (both with views of menacing Mt. Vesuvius) for a little culture, or flit from island to island in the Bay of Naples, or lie on cliffside beaches on the **Amalfi Coast.** Then, of course, there's Naples, the notorious provincial capital. Its bad reputation keeps the tourist crowds away, which is all the better for those who discover its innumerable fascinations.

Naples

From the moment you arrive at chaotic Piazza Garibaldi, Naples (Napoli in Italian) blasts you with a confounding mix of beauty, poverty, and a glorious past. It is at first (and second) look a battered city—crowded, polluted, crime-ridden, and inhospitable to the traveler. Vespas, Fiats, and city buses careen insanely around town, heeding neither traffic light nor hapless pedestrians. And petty theft—driven by ever-apparent poverty—runs rampant. But despite the problems, a feeling of community pervades, especially in the neighborhoods of Old Naples. The city has a spirit that makes urban centers of the north look positively comatose in comparison, and some of the country's finest churches and museums are here.

BASICS Naples's American Express office has recently closed; now the only one in Campania is in Sorrento (*see below*).

➤ **VISITOR INFORMATION** • Pick up the free guide *Qui Napoli* at the **EPT** office (tel. 081/268779; open Mon.–Sat. 8:15–8, Sun. 9–2) in Stazione Centrale for cultural listings and transportation info. Another **tourist office** (tel. 081/552–3328; open Mon.–Sat. 9–7, Sun. 9–2) in Piazza Gesù Nuovo specializes in information on Old Naples.

➤ **CHANGING MONEY** • If you want convenience, use the **Ufficio di Cambio** (open daily 7:15 AM–8 PM) inside the train station. For good value, though, you'll do better around Piazza Municipio in Naples's small financial district, just above the Castel Nuovo (take Bus C55 or 150 from Stazione Centrale).

➤ **EMERGENCIES** • The central **police** station (Via Medina 75, at Via Diaz, tel. 081/794–1111) is across from the main post office; their *ufficio stranieri* (foreigners' office) usually has an English speaker on staff.

➤ **PHONES AND MAIL** • The 24-hour **AAST** office in Stazione Centrale lets you make local and long-distance calls. The main **post office** (P. Matteotti, off Via Diaz, tel. 081/551–1456) is open weekdays 8 AM–7:20 PM and Saturday 8–noon. Branches in

Stazione Centrale and Galleria Umberto I have the same hours. Naples's postal code is 80100.

COMING AND GOING Frequent trains leave Naples's **Stazione Centrale** (P. Garibaldi, tel. 081/554–3188) for Rome (2 hrs 45 min, L15,400), Milan (7 hrs, L56,700), and Brindisi (6½ hrs, L27,100). The **Ferrovia Circumvesuviana** leaves from Platform 4 for Pompeii (45 min, L2500) and Sorrento (1 hr, L3900). **ACTP** (tel. 081/700–5091) runs buses to nearby towns. **Tirrenia Navigazione** (Stazione Marittima, tel. 081/720–1111) and **Caremar** (Molo Beverello, tel. 081/551–5384) run ferries and hydrofoils to Capri, Sorrento, Palermo, and elsewhere.

GETTING AROUND Naples stretches along the Bay of Naples with its back to the Vomero hills. Stazione Centrale, on Piazza Garibaldi, is in the eastern part of town. Corso Umberto I runs from the station to Piazza Bovio. Northwest of Piazza Bovio lie Piazza Dante, Piazza Gesù Nuovo, and the university district, which constitute the heart of Old Naples. Bisecting Via Roma near monument-ridden Piazza Gesù Nuovo, Spaccanapoli (literally "splitting Naples") is the spine of the old quarter; it changes names many times on its way through the center.

City bus CD (L1000) runs from the train station down Corso Umberto to Piazza Dante; CS goes to Piazza Cavour and the Museo Archeologico; and 106 and 150 roll through Piazza Municipio and Piazza del Plebescito to the Mergellina district. The **Metropolitana** is a limited but efficient subway system that begins at Stazione Centrale's Platform 4. A series of *funicolari* (cable cars) trek up and down Naples's steep hillsides, and the **tram** system runs from Stazione Centrale to the Mergellina district.

WHERE TO SLEEP Considering how divey the dives can be, you may want to shell out the extra lire for a little cleanliness and security. Budget hotels around Piazza Garibaldi are plentiful, but the area is sketchy. If you can, nab one of the few budget rooms in the Old Quarter or near the waterfront.

➤ **UNDER L45,000 • Casanova Hotel.** Good deal near Piazza Garibaldi—close to station so you can catch your morning train. Relatively quiet and secure. Clean doubles without bath L42,000. *Via Venezia 2, at C. Garibaldi, tel. 081/268287. Go diagonally right as you leave station; it's several blocks down on the right.*

Pensione Teresita. Clean rooms by the bay—some with balconies—cost L40,000 per double. *Via Santa Lucia 90, tel. 081/764–0105. Bus 140 east from Stazione Centrale. Reservations advised.*

➤ **UNDER L65,000 • Europeo Hotel.** In a small alley across from the university in central Naples. Clean doubles L60,000, including breakfast. *Via Mezzocannone 109, tel. 081/551–7254. From P. Bovio, take C. Umberto I; left on Via Mezzocannone.*

➤ **UNDER L80,000 • Le Fontane al Mare.** Luxury accommodations near the waterfront. Short walk from Villa Comunale, a beautiful park. Doubles without bath L75,000. *Via Niccolo Tommaseo 14, tel. 081/764–3470. Bus 140 or 150 from Stazione Centrale. Reservations advised. AE.*

➤ **HOSTEL • Ostello Salita della Grotta (HI).** Toward the outskirts of town. Three-day maximum stay enforced July–August. Reserve ahead in summer. HI members pay L16,000, nonmembers L21,000. *Salita della Grotta 23, tel. 081/761–2346. Take subway from station to Mergellina stop and follow signs.* 11:30 PM curfew.

FOOD Neapolitans like their architecture Baroque but their cuisine classic and simple; you'll have no trouble finding cheap, delicious food. One of the best **open-air markets** is on Via Tribunali between Piazza Dante and the duomo. A local specialty is *frutti de mare* (seafood, primarily shellfish) mixed into pasta. *Spaghetti alle vongole* (spaghetti with small, sweet tomatoes and baby clams) and *zuppa di pesce* (fish stew) are other favorites, though these can cost up to L15,000 a plate. Naples is also the birthplace of the pizza, so have a few slices while you're in town.

Pizzeria Trianon da Ciro (Via Pietro Colletta 44–46, near P. Garibaldi, tel. 081/553–9426) makes some of the best-tasting pizza in Naples (L7000–L12,000), with more than 18 topping combinations. **Trattoria Tipica da Giovanni** (Via Soprammoro a Portanolana 9–10, off C. Umberto I, tel. 081/268320; closed Sun.) serves inexpensive and authentic Neapolitan fare; seafood pastas are L6000. **Ristorante Bellini** (Via Santa Maria di Costantinopoli 80, at Via San Pietro, tel. 081/459774; closed Sun.) serves small pizzas and fried dough with cheese inside (L1500) by day, and at night breaks out with *vermicelli alle vongole* (L10,000), thin noodles with clams and lava-colored tomatoes grown in the rich Vesuvian soil. **Ristorante Ciro** (Via Cuculliana 2, tel. 081/764–6006; closed Mon.), by the water, serves the tasty rice-and-fish dish *risotto alla pescatore* (L12,000).

WORTH SEEING Naples has a numbing array of churches and museums, especially in Old Naples, near Piazza Dante and the duomo. To get a handle on them all, pick up a free itinerary from the tourist office in Piazza Gesù Nuovo (*see* Visitor Information, *above*). It delineates four different tours of medieval, Renaissance, Baroque, and Rococo churches. Naples's **duomo**, the Cathedral of San Gennaro (Via Duomo; open daily 8:30–1 and 5–7:30), was built at the end of the 13th century. It's relatively blah from the outside, but inside more than 100 granite columns line the nave, holding up a flat ceiling that peaks in a frescoed domed above the altar. The duomo's big moment comes each year when it hosts the celebration of San Gennaro, Naples's patron saint (*see box, below*).

In the middle of Piazza Gesù Nuovo, the **Guglia dell'Immacolata,** a prickly looking Spanish spire, exemplifies the Baroque style of the square. The spire faces the **Trinità Maggiore,** popularly referred to as the **Gesù Nuovo.** In 1601, this former palace was turned into a Jesuit church with a brilliant Baroque interior. Immediately to the left as you walk into the church is an unusual Christ figure sculpted out of a large block of marble and lying in a small shrine. The large, airy church of **Santa Chiara** (Via Benedetto Croce, tel. 081/552–6209; open daily 7–5), where locals come to hear morning mass, houses an interesting funerary monument to King Robert the Wise. The exquisite **cloister** (open 8:30–12:30 and 4–6) behind the church has antique tiles and columns that were painted with fanciful landscapes in the 18th century. The **Capella Sansevero** (Via de Sanctis 19, near P. San Domenico Maggiore; admission L5000; open Mon., Wed., Thurs., and Fri. 10–1 and 5–7, Tues. and Sun. 10–1) is a ghoulish Baroque church overflowing with putti, melancholic Madonna images, and bizarre frescoes. Most spectacular is the centerpiece marble sculpture, known as the Veiled Christ.

The excellent **Museo Archeologico Nazionale** includes the famous marble Farnese Bull, as well as some remarkably sophisticated mosaics and paintings from Pompeii and Herculaneum. *P. Museo, tel. 081/440166. Admission: L8000. Open Tues.–Sat. 9–2, Sun. and holidays 9–1.*

Set in a large wooded park (open daily 9 AM–1 hr before sunset), the 18th-century **Museo e Gallerie di Capodimonte** was built as a Bourbon homestead. It now houses several galleries displaying an enormous range of well-chosen paintings. *Parco di Capodimonte, tel.*

A Bloody Good Time in Naples

In the semiannual Festival of San Gennaro, Neapolitans turn to their patron saint for a little help predicting the future. Twice annually—the first Saturday in May and September 19—crowds gather at the duomo to see if two vials of San Gennaro's blood will liquefy. If they stay congealed after being withdrawn from the sacristy, Naples is in for it. In 1943, for instance, the blood didn't turn; soon afterward, Vesuvius blew its top. In 1973, it again remained congealed, and Naples suffered a severe cholera outbreak. During the festival, the entire town reaches a fever pitch, gathering early at the cathedral and praying earnestly as the archbishop raises the vials to the crowd before and (God willing) after the liquefaction.

081/744–1307. Bus 160 or 161 from P. Dante toward Vomero district. Admission: L8000. Open Tues.–Sat. 9–2, Sun. and holidays 9–1.

Brightening up Piazza del Plebescito in vacuously grand fashion, the **Palazzo Reale** is pure surface and space. The entrance is dominated by a sweeping marble stairway; upstairs, the living apartments stretch endlessly, all gilt, mirrors, and repetitious paintings. The **Biblioteca Nazionale,** in the back of the Palazzo Reale, has the oldest extant copy of Dante's *Divine Comedy. P. del Plebescito, tel. 081/413888. Admission: L6000. Open daily 9–1:30.*

This enormous **Castel Sant'Elmo** was built under the Bourbon king Robert of Anjou, who chose the site for its strategic vantage point. Ascend to the broad roof and check out the new library/archive or the astounding view. To reach the castle, take the Funicolare Centrale from Piazzetta Duca d'Aosta, opposite Galleria Umberto I on Via Toledo. *Admission free. Open Mon.–Sat. 9–8, Sun. and holidays 9–1.*

AFTER DARK Piazza **Dante** and Piazza **Bellini** are the places for hanging out at night, though nocturnal Neapolitan theatrics take place everywhere on the streets. The magazine *Qui Napoli* and the local newspaper *Il Mattino* list club events, theatrical performances, and movies and provide information about free summer concerts in Capodimonte Park. Grand opera productions at **Teatro San Carlo** (box office tel. 081/797–2111; open Tues.–Sun. 10–1 and 4:30–6:30) run December–June; economy seats go for L20,000 and L30,000.

Decorated in '50s retro-Americana, **Le Rock** (Via Bellini 9, next to P. Dante; open weekends 9 PM–2 AM) features U.S. rock and blues played by local musicians. In the Forcella area of Old Naples, **The Riot** (Via San Biagio dei Librai 39, tel. 081/552–3231; closed Mon. and Aug.) is Naples's version of an avant-garde scene. Jazz groups jam throughout the evening, while young leftist intellectuals hang out and listen.

NEAR NAPLES

POMPEII Pompeii, 45 minutes southeast of Naples, is a massive ruin—a classic ghost town where the ancients once lived high. It was a hub of commercial activity in the region until Mt. Vesuvius destroyed it all in the big eruption of AD 79. Today, tourists come in droves to see the incredibly well preserved shops and homes, the lewd pornographic mosaics, and a few of the eruption's carbonized victims—whose death screams, flailing arms, and tortured poses are cast permanently in stone.

Some highlights of the archaeological site are the **Gladiators' Barracks** (Via Stabiana), a square in which mock gladiators staged contests to warm up for the real thing, and, next to the barracks, the **Teatro Grande** and the **Teatro Piccolo.** The Teatro Grande held 5,000 ancient Pompeiians, with box seats for bigwigs. Today, it hosts weekend music performances—some by noteworthy classical groups. Northwest on Via Stabiana lie the **Stabian Baths,** Pompeii's largest bathhouse. This indoor/outdoor facility had locker rooms for men and women, a variety of hot and cold baths and steam rooms, a swimming pool, and even boxing rings. Continue northwest to reach the **Lupanare,** ancient Pompeii's red-light district, and check out the two-story brothel **Lupanar Africani et Victoris.** The **House of the Vetii** boasts a small room of well-preserved Roman paintings, but most remember it for its depictions of Priapus, who shows off with absurdly swollen pride why he is the god of fertility. Pick up a free map at the **tourist office** next to the east entrance (Via Sacra 1, tel. 081/850-7255) or at the smaller office on the west end, near Porta Marina, to find your way around. *Admission: L10,000. Open daily 9 AM–1 hr before sunset.*

At the Lupanar Africani et Victoris brothel, each prostitute's door was decorated with an illustration of the particular sexual position or act promised within.

➤ **COMING AND GOING** • Take the Circumvesuviana line from Naples to the Pompeii–Villa dei Misteri stop (45 min, L5000 round-trip), near the west entrance to the site. To reach the east entrance, take the same line to the Torre Annunziato stop, switch to the Naples–Poggiomarino line, and get off at Pompeii-Santuario. An orange local bus

(L1000) makes the run between the east and west entrances, though it's easy and often quicker to walk along Via Roma (about 2 km).

CAPRI The island of Capri has long been the life of the party in the Bay of Naples, outshining its sister islands in both glamour and scenery. Emperor Augustus spent his vacations here, and Tiberius made it a home away from home, littering the island with 12 villas, including the impressive **Villa Jovis** (Via Tiberio; admission L4000), a 45-minute walk east of Capri Town. The towns of Capri and Anacapri feel like ant farms in summer, when a zillion tourists swarm about. But the island retains enough charm to make it well worth the boat ride over. Mountains drop off suddenly into cliffs; capacious caverns like the famed **Grotta Azzurra** dot the landscape; scenic Roman, Norman, and Arab-influenced architecture abounds; and you'll even find a few rocky beaches.

➤ **VISITOR INFORMATION** • **AAST** information offices are at the main dock in Marina Grande (tel. 081/837–0634), in the center of Capri (P. Umberto I, tel. 081/837–0686), and off Piazza Vittoria in Anacapri (Via Orlandi 19/A, tel. 081/837–1524).

➤ **COMING AND GOING** • **Alilauro** (Agenzia Staiano, tel. 081/837–7577), **Caremar** (tel. 081/837–0700), and **Navigazione Libera del Golfo** (tel. 081/837–0819) are major carriers that serve Capri. Ferries run daily to Naples (1 hr 15 min, L8000) and Sorrento (50 min, L4800). Buy tickets at the windows outside the entrance to Marina Grande. Buses (L1500) run every 20 minutes between Capri's two towns, the two main ports, and some major points of interest. A funicolare connects Marina Grande with the center of Capri every 15 minutes (L3000 round-trip), and a chair lift carries view seekers up to the top of **Mt. Solaro** (the highest point on the island) from Anacapri.

Boats make trips around the island, affording a glimpse of countless caves and crannies. You'll pay L13,550 (and a L1250 surcharge on weekends and holidays) for the two boats it takes to get to the **Grotta Azzurra.** To walk to the cave from Anacapri, take Via Tuoro until it changes to Via Grotta Azzurra, or take the walkway that begins west of Chiesa San Michele. To the west of the private beaches at Marina Piccola, you'll find the **Scoglio delle Sirene** public beach. On the other side of Capri, along Via Cristobol Colombo, **Bagno di Tiberio** is a large public beach accessible by bus, with some sand scattered among the rocks.

➤ **WHERE TO SLEEP AND EAT** • Even the barest rooms are costly in swanky Capri Town. Inquire at the AAST (*see* Visitor Information, *above*) for a listing of private residences with rooms to let. **Hotel ABC** (Via Serafina 37, tel. 081/837–0683; open Apr.–Oct.), has doubles, many with views, for L53,000–L65,000; in high season, you may have to pay for breakfast as well, bringing the cost to L87,000. You'll compete with fewer crowds in Anacapri. Downtown, the two-star **Hotel Loreley** (Via Orlandi, tel. 081/837–1440; open Mar.–Oct.), offers a garden and doubles for L50,000–L90,000.

Buying food from bakeries and markets is the best way to eat cheaply, but there are a couple restaurants worth trying. From Capri Town, take Via Matermania toward Arco Naturale to find **Le Grottelle** (Arco Naturale, tel. 081/837–5719). Pastas average L10,000 and feature homegrown ingredients like lemon leaves, figs, tomatoes, and local cheeses. In Anacapri, expect to pay about L9000 for pasta at **Mamma Giovanna** (Via Boffe 3–5, tel. 081/837–2057).

Sorrento

At the tip of the Bay of Naples, Sorrento stretches across a plateau that ends abruptly at a steep tufa cliff 164 feet above the sea. At the base of the cliff lie ports and rocky beaches, where Speedo babes deep-fry in coconut oil. Sorrento's manageable size, combined with its location and transportation connections, makes it a fine base for exploring the Bay of Naples and, to the south, the Gulf of Salerno. Hotels are plentiful, cheap food is easy to track down, and you have a decent choice of late-night bars and clubs.

The narrow stretches of beach along **Marina Piccola, Marina San Francesco,** and **Marina Grande** are the most convenient and can get crowded. Prime sections are private and cost about L3500. Farther down the coast, below Via Capo, you'll find free beaches mixed in with the private ones; take the bus toward Capo di Sorrento to reach them. Sick of beach bumming? Sorrento's best museum, **Museo Correale di Terranova a Sorrento** (Via Correale 48, 2 blocks from P. Tasso, tel. 081/878–1846; admission L5000; closed Tues. and Sun. afternoon), is filled with Greek, Byzantine, and Roman statues, plus Italian art and furniture.

BASICS The **AAST** office (Via Luigi de Maio 35, tel. 081/878–1115) is open Monday–Saturday 8–8 in summer. There's an **American Express** office (tel. 081/878–4800) on Piazza Lauro.

COMING AND GOING The private trains on the **Circumvesuviana** line (tel. 081/779–2267) make frequent trips between Sorrento and Naples's Stazione Centrale (1 hr, L3900). The Sorrento station is a block inland from Corso Italia and two blocks up from Piazza Tasso. **Alilauro,** also known as **Linee Lauro** (tel. 081/807–3024 or 081/878–1430), **Caremar** (tel. 081/807–3077), and **Navigazione Libera del Golfo** (tel. 081/878–1861) send ferries and hydrofoils from Sorrento to Naples, Capri, and elsewhere.

WHERE TO SLEEP AND EAT The cheapest shelter you'll find here is the **HI Ostello Surriento** (Via Carpasso 5, tel. 081/878–1783; beds L13,000; closed Oct.–Apr.), though they might be closing soon. From the train station, go right on Corso Italia and turn left at the AGIP station. Sunny doubles at **Hotel del Corso** (C. Italia 134, tel. 081/878–1299; closed Nov.–Jan.) are L62,000. From the Circumvesuviana station, go left on Corso Italia. Reservations are a must in high season. **Villaggio Campeggio Santa Fortunata** (Via Capo 39/A–B, tel. 081/878–2405; closed Nov.–Mar.) has its own beach and costs L8000–L11,000 per person, L8000–L15,000 per site.

For cheap nutrition, seek out the delis and produce stands along car-free **Via San Cesario,** toward the bay. Corso Italia is a locus for cheap pizzerias. A **Standa** supermarket (C. Italia 221, a block left of the train station) provides basic food and sundries. Next door, **Bar Rita** has delicious pastries and thick pizza slices.

Puglia and Calabria

The *Mezzogiorno* (southern Italy) is so much the opposite of its northern counterpart that it's sometimes hard to believe they belong to the same country. The southern regions of Puglia and Calabria—the heel and toe of the boot, respectively—define the Italian backwater. Conquest, climate, and the Corleones have prevented this part of Italy from experiencing anything like the economic and cultural wealth of the north. But the south's flat plains, sloping hillsides, virgin forests, and isolated beaches are attracting travelers (and their lire) to the region in increasing numbers. Calabria is just beginning to turn tourism into a profitable industry; Puglia's strategic coastal location put it on travelers' maps long ago. The Puglian towns of Bari and Brindisi are ferry gateways to Greece, and Calabria's Reggio di Calabria is the ferry departure point for Sicily. Buses are the way to go in Calabria, where the rail lines are not as extensive as in Puglia.

Bari

Across the peninsula from Naples, the thriving business and commercial center of Bari is responsible for shuttling goods and tourists throughout the eastern Mediterranean. Most people just pass through Bari on the way to somewhere else, but if you have time, wander through the labyrinthine **old quarter,** check out the remains of St. Nicholas (as in Santa Claus) in the **Basilica di San Nicola** (P. San Nicola; open daily 9–1 and 4–7), or stop in the beautiful **Cattedrale di San Sarino** (off P. Odegitria). Even with the crime that flourishes after sundown, Bari is still a good city to base yourself in while exploring Puglia.

VISITOR INFORMATION The ubiquitous **Stop-Over in Bari** stands help young budget travelers (under the age of 30) plan stays in town. Look for their "magic bus," open daily 9–9, outside the main train station. Stop-Over's **main office** (Via Dante Alighieri 111, off P. Umberto I, tel. 080/521–4538; open summer, daily 8 AM–9 PM) is just a short walk from the train station. The **EPT** office (P. Aldo Moro 33/A, tel. 080/521–2361; open weekdays 9–1 and 4–8, Sat. 9–11), diagonally across from the train station, is less hectic than the Stop-Over booths.

Women traveling solo will have to deal with plenty of catcalls and bullshit. It's generally harmless, although women should probably not go out alone after dark.

COMING AND GOING Trains head to Milan (10 hrs, L60,000), Rome (8 hrs, L33,600), and Naples (5 hrs, L22,000) from Bari's **train station** (tel. 080/521–6801). Orange local buses and blue long-distance **SITA buses** leave from the front of the train station in Piazza Aldo Moro. SITA's office in the piazza (tel. 080/521–3714) has schedule information.

Bari's **Stazione Marittima** has cheaper and better ferry connections to Greece and the eastern Mediterranean than Brindisi, unless you're using a EurailPass or Interrail. Ferries head to Corfu (9 hrs), Igoumenítsa (12–13 hrs), and Pátra (15–20 hrs). Tickets to Corfu cost about L45,000–L55,000, to Pátra L70,000–L90,000. These rates are *posta ponte,* which means you sleep in chairs inside. Ask about student and round-trip discounts. Tickets coming from Greece may be much cheaper. To reach the ferries from the train station, take Bus 20 (L800, but free during the summer for visitors under 30).

WHERE TO SLEEP AND EAT The Stop-Over people (*see* Visitor Information, *above*) have set up a free campsite at the edge of town, in **Pineta San Francesco Park** (take Bus 3 or 5 from the station). If camping isn't your style, the main Stop-Over office can set you up in a pension or private apartment for only L30,000 for two nights—*if* you're under 30 and visit between mid-June and mid-September. Otherwise, the **HI Ostello del Levante** (Via Nicola Massaro 33, tel. 080/552–0282; beds L12,000) is in a tranquil spot on the outskirts of town. Take Bus 1 from Piazza Eroi del Mare, off Corso Cavour. **Pensione Darinka** (Via Calefati 15/A, tel. 080/235049) rents palatable doubles without bath for L40,000; go north from the station past Piazza Umberto I and take a right on Via Calefati.

If you need something quick to eat, head just off Piazza Aldo Moro to the **Gran Makador** (P. Umberto I 46–47, tel. 080/523–7605). The food isn't fantastic, but you can have a plate of pasta and a beer or coffee for around L5000. If you have more time, **Al Pescatore** (P. Federico II di Svevia 6, tel. 080/237039; closed Mon.), across from the castle, serves the best seafood in town.

The Gargano Promontory

The "spur" of Puglia, the Gargano Promontory, juts out into the sea three-quarters of the way down the Adriatic coast. Until 20 years ago, the promontory consisted mainly of small fishing towns and an unspoiled woodland interior. Ever since German and Italian vacationers "discovered" the region, though, it's been a main stop on summer tourist itineraries. If you approach from Foggia, you can breeze through a whole series of coastal towns, from Manfredonia to Vieste and Peschici. The latter two have the best beaches, and their charming old quarters have hardly been affected by the modernizing influences of tourism.

Brindisi

Think of Brindisi as the backpacker's rite of passage into the big leagues of budget travel (if you find this place hot and crowded, just wait until you get to Greece). Exchange offices, ticket agents, and café/bars have multiplied like rabbits on the strip that leads from the train station to the docks, where ferries depart for Albania, Greece, and beyond. On some lines, you can book passage in advance from other major Italian cities, thus saving you the hassle of having to fight the crowds at the ticket agents in Brindisi. It's also a good idea to bring some fresh batteries for your Walkman, a deck of cards or a book to read, a warm shirt for the crossing, and a cushion or mat to sit on while you wait . . . and wait, and wait.

BASICS The **visitor information** office (P. Dionisi II, tel. 0831/521944) is open weekdays 8:30–12:30 and 4:30–7:30, Saturday 8:30–12:30. The **American Express** office (C. Umberto 147) has competitive exchange rates and is open daily 7 AM–10 PM.

COMING AND GOING The **train station** is in Piazza Crispi, 1 km from the ferry port. Three trains leave daily for Rome (8 hrs, L43,500), more for Milan (10½ hrs, L66,600) and Bari (1½ hrs, L8800). **FSE buses** leave from the main train station for major Puglian towns. For more info, contact the **Pattimare Travel Agency** (P. Dionisi II, next to EPT office on lungomare, tel. 0831/521985).

Brindisi handles a huge volume of ferry traffic to and from Greece. Stick with the well-established ferry lines and book far in advance if you're traveling between July and August. After buying your ticket, head to the **Stazione Marittima police station** to show your passport and have your boarding pass stamped. You must arrive at your terminal at least two hours before departure. **Marlines** (C. Garibaldi 73, tel. 0831/526548) and **Pattimare** (P. Dionisi II, tel. 081/521985) send ferries to Corfu (7½ hrs), Igoumenítsa (9½ hrs), and Pátra (17½ hrs). **Adriatica Ferry Services** (C. Garibaldi 87, tel. 0831/523825) also has ferries to Greece, and Eurail and InterRail travelers pay only L10,000.

Reggio di Calabria

Whether you're traveling through Calabria to Sicily or bumming around the coast at the bottom of the boot, chances are at some point you'll pass through Reggio, Calabria's capital. With the exception of the wonderful **Museo Nazionale della Magna Grecia** (P. de Nava; admission L6000) and a few good fish restaurants, there aren't many reasons to stick around. The earthquakes that rocked the town at the turn of the century and some heavy aerial bombing during World War II leveled most of the historic buildings. If you're actually visiting and not just on your way to Sicily, the **Albergo Noel** (Via Zerbi 13, tel. 0965/330044; doubles L60,000) is a decent place to spend the night. It's on a somewhat seedy street, but it's just across from the sea and a short walk from the center of town.

COMING AND GOING You can see Sicily across the narrow channel that divides the island from the mainland. Nearby **Villa San Giovanni,** a small, unattractive town a short train ride from Reggio, is the best place to catch a ferry to the island (20 min, L5000). For information on ferries, contact the **Pro Loco** office (P. Stazione, tel. 0965/751160). All rail traffic stops at the **Stazione Centrale** (P. Garibaldi, tel. 0965/898123), which has a **tourist information** office (open Mon.–Sat. 9–noon and 4:30–6:30). Trains go regularly to Villa San Giovanni (10 min, L1600), where the ferry departs for Sicily. Several trains also leave daily for the Rome Termini Station (7 hrs, L46,800).

Sicily

Sicily (Sicilia), the largest island in the Mediterranean, was one of the great melting pots of the ancient world. Over the centuries it has been occupied by every great Mediterranean civilization—from the Phoenicians and Carthaginians to the Greeks, Romans, Arabs, French, and Spaniards. Needless to say, well-preserved Greek ruins, beautiful Arab-Norman monuments, Baroque townships, and blue-oceaned beaches are what Sicily is all about. Sicily's capital, Palermo, is an urban dervish as famous for its extensive medieval quarters as for its Mafia connections. In the east, the Ionian coast has beaches galore, volatile Mt. Etna, and the ancient ruins of Siracusa. Other Sicilian hot spots include the easy-to-reach Aeolian Islands, a sort of volcanic paradise where all grades of tourists rub themselves with medicated mud and bum on black-sand beaches

COMING AND GOING Messina, on the northernmost tip of the Ionian coast, is the main gateway to Sicily. Messina's ferry terminal, **FS Stazione Traghetti**, northeast of the train station, serves the mainland ports of Villa San Giovanni (20 min, L5000) and Reggio di Calabria (35 min, L6500). Messina's hydrofoil station, **SNAV** (C. Vittorio Emanuele), is 1 km north of the train station. Hydrofoils go to Naples (3 hrs, L135,000) and Reggio di Calabria (15 min, L5000). It's also possible to ferry from Naples to Palermo, and from Reggio to Siracusa.

Palermo

Sicily's capital is certainly noisy, chaotic, and occasionally dangerous. But it also has numerous historical and artistic attractions that show the influence of its Arab and Norman conquerors. Palermo has a deserved—but somewhat exaggerated—reputation for crime. Rather than Mafia-inspired violence, crime often takes the form of Vespa-riding bag snatchers and adept pickpockets. That said, there's no reason to be overly paranoid, and travelers who make the effort to chat with locals will be rewarded with a friendliness rarely found in large Italian cities.

BASICS Inside Stazione Centrale is a helpful **tourist office** (tel. 091/616–5914; open weekdays 8–2 and 4–8, Sat. 8–2). The local **American Express** representative is G. Ruggieri e Figli (Via Emerico Amari 40, tel. 091/587144; open weekdays 9–1 and 4–7, Sat. 9–1). From Stazione Centrale, take Bus 7 or 25 to Piazza Castelnuovo, then follow Via E. Amari toward the port.

COMING AND GOING Ferries and hydrofoils dock at Palermo's **Stazione Marittima** (Via Francesco Crispi); from Stazione Centrale, take Bus 39. Tickets for ferries to Genova and Livorno are available at **Grandi Traghetti** (Via Mariano Stabile 59, tel. 091/587939), while **Tirrenia** (Via Emerico Amari, tel. 091/602–1230) arranges passage to Naples.

Stazione Centrale (Via Roma at P. Giulio Cesare) is at the southern end of Via Roma near the medieval districts. Destinations include Agrigento (2 hrs, L10,500) and Siracusa (5 hrs, L22,000). Bus companies **Autoservizi Salemi** (Via Gregorio 44), **SAIS** (Via Paolo Balsamo 16), and **Autoservizi Segesta** (Via Balsamo 26) service long-distance destinations. Most buses stop on Via Paolo Balsamo, around the corner from the train station. Palermo's local **AMAT** buses (tel. 091/350111) serve the city.

Gelato was invented in Palermo, and it's here that you'll find some of the most interesting flavors ever concocted, including gelsomino (jasmine) and rosa (rose). Two of Palermo's best gelaterias are Bar Ventimiglia (C. Vittorio Emanuele 434), just west of Quattro Canti, and Il Golosone (P. Castelnuovo).

WHERE TO SLEEP Palermo's cheapest hotels are squashed in a square between Via Maqueda, Via Roma, Corso Vittorio Emanuele, and Stazione Centrale. If you're worried about crime, head toward Piazza Castelnuovo—take Bus 1, 6, or 15 from Stazione Centrale—and keep out of the La Kalsa district. **Albergo Italia** (Via Roma 62, tel. 091/616–5397), one of the best budget hotels in Palermo, is only a few hundred yards from Piazza Giulio Cesare. High-ceilinged doubles cost L35,000. Housed in a decayed 18th-century palace, **Albergo Orientale** (Via Maqueda 26, near the station, tel. 091/616–5727) has singles for L25,000, doubles around L40,000. Exceptional **Albergo Diana** (Via Roma 188, near C. Vittorio Emanuele, tel. 091/329959) has clean doubles for L42,000. Three or more can stay at a group rate.

FOOD Fans of seafood should try the local specialties *sarde* (sardines), *pesce spada* (swordfish), and *polpo* (octopus). At the **Hostaria Da Ciccio** (Via Firenze 6, off Via Roma, tel. 091/329143), try fried shrimp (L9000) or the excellent antipasto plate (L6000). The atmosphere at **Osteria Al Ferro di Cavallo** (Via Venezia 20, off Via Roma, tel. 091/331835) is hectic and lively. A lunch of salad, pasta, bread, meat or fish, and drink costs L7000–L12,000. **Ristorante/Pizzeria Italia** (Via dell'Orologio 54, tel. 091/589885; closed Mon.) serves 25 kinds of pizza (L5000–L8000).

WORTH SEEING Palermo's attractions are scattered among the streets and alleyways of its four medieval quarters. **Galleria Nazionale di Sicilia** (Via Alloro 4; admission L2000; open Mon.–Sat. 9–2; also Tues., Thurs., and Fri. 3–8; Sun. 9–1), near the waterfront, contains an outstanding collection of paintings and sculpture from the 11th to 17th centuries. The **Museo Internazionale delle Marionette** (Via Butera 1; admission L5000, L2000 students; open Mon.–Sat. 9–1; also Mon., Wed., and Fri. 4–7) displays thousands of puppets, marionettes, shadow figures, and scenery displays; ask about puppet shows performed here. Originally founded in 1143 by the Norman admiral George of Antioch, **La Martorana chapel** (P. Bellini 3, off Via Maqueda; open Mon.–Sat. 9:30–1 and 3:30–5:30, Sun. 8:30–1) later became part of a convent. The Baroque exterior was refurbished in 1588, but the interior still glows with gilded Byzantine mosaics.

Palazzo dei Normanni (P. Indipendenza), a former Saracen castle, was transformed into a royal palace by Sicily's 12th-century Norman king Roger de Hauteville. Today it houses the Sicilian Parliament and is closed to the public. However, the palace's **Cappella Palatina** (Palantine Chapel) remains open and is worth a tour. Its elaborate interior shines with brilliant mosaics and a honeycombed wooden ceiling. The imposing 12th-century **duomo** (C. Vittorio Emanuele) is a grab-bag of architectural styles. Inside, notice the numerous saint sculptures, the 15th-century portal, and various royal tombs. **Museo Archeological Regionale** (P. Olivella 4, off Via Roma; admission L2000; open Mon.–Sat. 9–1:30; also Tues. and Fri. 3–6, Sun. 9–12:30) is one of the best archaeological museums in Italy. The most famous exhibits are in the **Sala di Selinunte.** From Stazione Centrale take Bus 15, 34, or 37.

AFTER DARK Palermo's bars tend to be fashionable spots for socializing rather than venues for unabashed boozing. **Pub/Birreria Kovacs** (Via della Libertà 6, near P. Castelnuovo) has an outstanding range of draft beers, and **Liberty Pub** (Via N. Cozzo 20, off Via Maqueda just past Teatro Massimo) is a cool place to grab some food and a beer while contemplating Italian disco.

Taormina

Perched high above the coast on the cactus-covered slopes of Monte Tauro, exquisite Taormina boasts views of Mt. Etna and the Ionian Sea that have seduced travelers since the turn of the century. Nowadays, this resort village swells with tour-bus crowds and is uncomfortably

Creepy Cappuccini

Entombed within the Catacombe dei Cappuccini (Via Cappuccini) are more than 8,000 ghostly mummies, most displayed behind flimsy mesh screens. From the early 16th to the late 19th century, the Capuchin monks embalmed and dried cadavers, which were then dressed attractively and inserted upright into individual wall niches. The Capuchins take their job pretty seriously and have divided the mummies into well-marked sections according to their earthly occupation, gender, and social class. It's not quite as revolting as it sounds, but the squeamish could lose their lunch looking at the glass-encased mummified remains of babies and small children. Take Bus 5 or 27 from Corso Vittorio Emanuele and ask to be let off at Via Pindemonte; it's a short sign-posted walk. A donation of L1000 is recommended.

packed in summer, but Taormina's narrow streets and hidden piazze remain enchanting. A wealth of well-preserved 15th- to 19th-century architecture, often draped with brightly-hued bougainvillea, and the remains of a magnificent **Greco-Roman theater** further contribute to the town's intoxicating atmosphere. To escape from the crowds, take one of the frequent buses to **Giardini-Naxos,** home of both Greek ruins and greasy beach bodies, or to **Gole dell'Alcantara** (Alcantara Gorge) for great swimming and climbing. The medieval **Castello San Pancrazio,** perched on a cliff just above Taormina, can be reached by footpath, as can **Castelmona,** a tiny village not far from the site. In Taormina stop by **ASST** (Palazzo Corvala, at P. Vittorio Emanuele, tel. 0942/23243; open Mon.–Sat. 8–2 and 5–7) for maps and lodging options.

COMING AND GOING The **Taormina-Giardini** train station sits inconveniently below the elevated center of town. **SAIS** long-distance buses, which aren't as speedy or scenic as the train, stop at the **bus terminal** (Via Pirandello, tel. 0942/625301), five minutes downhill from Porta Messina.

WHERE TO SLEEP You're loopy if you think you can simply show up in August and find a room in Taormina. If everything is full, consider staying in a small town nearby where prices and availability are much better. At **Il Leone** (Via Bagnoli Croci 126/A, tel. 0942/23878), spacious doubles without bath cost L44,000. Rustic **Villa Liliana** (Via Dietro Cappuccini 4, tel. 0942/24373) has doubles for L50,000. **Camping San Leo** (tel. 0942/24658) charges L5000 per person; tent and bag rentals are about the same. From the train station, take any bus toward Taormina proper and ask driver to drop you at "il camping."

FOOD Restaurateurs expect tourists to arrive with bulging money belts, and they charge accordingly. **Mercato Venuto** (Via Bagnoli Croci 68) is one of the cheapest places to buy unprepared food. Just outside Porta Messina, **Trattoria Rosticepi** (Via San Pancrazio 18, tel. 0942/24149) stays open until 2 AM in summer and serves up a spicy *tagliatelle con pepe verde* (pasta with green pepper) for L6000.

Siracusa

During the millennium of Greco-Roman domination, Siracusa (Syracuse) was among the most powerful and influential cities in the Western world. Many of the temples and amphitheaters built during this ancient age have been well maintained, as have later Baroque masterworks. This combination of living history, beautiful architecture, and temperate seaside climate draws the inevitable hordes of archaeology buffs and shutterbugs, but even the crowds do not diminish the honest splendor of Sicily's most majestic Greco-Roman settlement. Around AD 1000,

Aeolian Islands

The seven Aeolian Islands (Isole Eolie) have been inhabited for more than 3,000 years, and Aeolian natives have understandably developed a fearful reverence for their temperamental, volcanic homeland. The threat of fiery ruin has neither stemmed the tide of tourists, nor stopped the outcrop of ritzy beach and health resorts. With its hoppin' nightlife, Vulcano is a fun but expensive island—a definite day trip unless you're loaded with cash. Lipari is a lot cheaper but also more crowded, so you may have to fight for bed space in summer. Of all the Aeolian Islands, Panarea is the most Grecian, with whitewashed houses and smooth black-sand beaches. On the other hand, Stromboli is the place for hiking to the calderas of active volcanoes. Ferries and hydrofoils to the islands leave most frequently from the town of Milazzo on Sicily's Tyrrhenian Coast. SNAV (hydrofoils only) and Siremar (hydrofoils and ferries) are the two largest carriers; they have offices on every island.

the Normans built medieval and Baroque buildings mostly on the island of Ortygia (which is connected to Siracusa by bridge). These structures are also worth a visit, although you should save time for remote **Noto, Ragusa,** and other small towns on Ortygia's southeastern corner. South of Siracusa you'll find great beaches, although in summer you'll probably have to pay a small access fee. **Fontane Bianche,** 18 km from town, is the sandiest and most social.

BASICS For maps, brochures, and lodging listings, head to **AAPIT** (Viale Paradiso, Parco Archeologico, tel. 0931/60510), **AAT** (Via Maestranza 33, 1 block east of P. Archimede, tel. 0931/464256; closed Mon.), or **Ufficio Informazioni** (Stazione Centrale, tel. 0931/464298).

COMING AND GOING **Stazione Centrale** (Via Francesco Crispi, tel. 0931/66640) has rail service to Catania (1½ hrs, L6500) and Palermo (5 hrs, L22,000). **AST** buses (P. delle Poste, just left of Ponte Nuovo on Ortygia, tel. 0931/462711) go to nearby towns. **SAIS** buses (Piazzale Marconi) serve Catania (1½ hrs, L6100) and Palermo (4 hrs, L22,100). Ferries dock at **Molo Zanagora** (C. Vittorio Emanuele II), on the west side of Ortygia. For ferry info, contact **Tirrenia** (Viale Mazzini 5, near the pier, tel. 0931/66956; open Mon.–Sat. 9–1 and 3–6).

WHERE TO SLEEP **Ostello della Gioventù** (Via Epipoli 45, Belvedere, tel. 0931/711118), 10 km from town, costs L20,000 a bed, including breakfast. It's a 20-minute ride from Corso Umberto on Bus 9 or 11. The only cheap hotel on Ortygia is **Hotel Gran Bretagna** (Via Savoia 21, tel. 0931/68765), where faintly charming doubles cost L65,000. **Hotel Milano** (C. Umberto 10, tel. 0931/66981) has tidy doubles for L40,000; from the station, turn left on Corso Umberto and take Bus 1, 4, 5, 8, or 10 to the end. **Camping Fontane Bianche** (Via Mazzarò 1, tel. 0931/790333; closed Oct.–May) is 18 km from town, but it has a popular

Mt. Etna

With soft ridges and gradual slopes, snowcapped Mt. Etna (Monte Etna) proves the old adage that looks can be deceiving. Etna is actually the highest (10,899 feet) and most active volcano in Europe, a temperamental lout that's erupted more than 130 times in recorded history. Despite the dangers, veteran travelers often say that Mt. Etna is the highlight of Sicily. To maximize your own experience, take a bus to the top and then hike down, exploring the moonlike landscape and eerie lava channels. Climbing the volcano is possible only between April and October, when the summit is not buried in snow. Make sure you take durable shoes and warm clothes—even if it's scorching at the beach, it'll be freezing up top. Pay attention to the omnipresent signs and to the stern recommendations of official hiking guides.

For maps and guide info, visit the town of Nicolosi and its helpful visitor center (Via Etnea 65, tel. 095/914580; open daily 8:30 AM–1 PM and, in summer only, 4–7:30 PM). AST buses run hourly from Catania to Nicolosi (45 min, L14,000), where you can catch a cable car (L40,000 round-trip) that climbs Mt. Etna to an elevation of 6,560 feet. SITA minibuses (tel. 095/911158) travel between Nicolosi and the 1,007-foot mark May–October only. Tickets cost L14,000 each way. The privately owned Ferrovia Circumetnea (FCE) railway runs a 114-km circuit around the base of Mt. Etna (rail passes are not accepted). To make the circuit from north to south, catch an FCE train in Giarre-Riposto (often shortened to Giarre), which is best reached by rail from Messina or Catania, or by bus from Taormina.

beach nearby. In summer, make reservations or at call before hopping on Bus 21 or 23 west from Corso Umberto. Sites cost L6500, tents L10,000.

Take a gander at the produce and cheese for sale in the open-air **market** just over the bridge in Ortygia. It's open daily (except Sunday) 7 AM–1 PMish. The food is basic (at best) at **Trattoria Paolina** (Via Francesco Crispi 14, Piazzale le Marconi; closed Sun.), but the portions are big and the prices rock-bottom. Friendly, chaotic **Spaghetteria do Scogghiu** (Via Gemmellaro Scinà 11, downhill from P. Archimede; closed Sun. and Mon.) is definitely *the* place to come on Ortygia. Choose from 20 different kinds of spaghetti (L6000). **Soup and Beer Pub** (Via delle Vergini 9; closed Tues.) has an excellent selection of international beers.

The disco Malibu (Via Elorina 172; cover L15,000) is Siracusa's late-night hot spot in summer. Take Bus 21 or 23 toward Fontane Bianche beach (about 20 min) and tell the driver where you're going.

WORTH SEEING On Ortygia, the **Museo Regionale d'Arte Medioevale e Moderna** (Via Capodieci 16, tel. 0931/69511; admission L2000; open Mon.–Sat. 9–2, Sun. and holidays 9–1) inside Palazzo Bellomo houses some outstanding works of medieval art, plus Sicilian ceramics, old maps, and horse-drawn carriages from the 1700s. Ortygia's **Piazza del Duomo** qualifies as one of Sicily's most impressive squares, dominated by the incredibly detailed **Palazzo Beneventano del Bosco** (currently under restoration), with an impressive courtyard and elegant winding staircase. The hard-to-miss **duomo** (open daily 8–noon) was built by the Greeks in the 5th century BC as a temple to the goddess Athena and was consecrated as a Christian basilica in 640.

Museo Archeologico (Viale Teocrito 66, tel. 0931/464022; admission L2000; open Tues.–Sun. 9–2), on the mainland, has a great collection of ancient Greek artifacts. Across from the museum, the **Santuario della Madonnina** (tel. 0931/64077; open daily 6–12:30 and 4–8:30) houses *La Madonna delle Lacrime* (Our Lady of the Tears), a small plaster plaque of the Virgin Mary that supposedly shed human tears for five days in 1953.

Sicily's best-known archaeological site, **Parco Archeologico** (admission L2000; open daily 9 AM–one hr before sunset), is composed primarily of the ruins of **Neapolis**, a large cluster of well-preserved structures originally started by Hiero II in 275 BC. Aeschylus presented works at the **Teatro Greco** (Greek Theater) here, which could hold 15,000 spectators. From Corso Gelone or Corso Umberto, take Bus 1, 4, 5, 8, or 10 west to park entrance.

Agrigento

As you approach Agrigento, you may begin to grasp why Sicily's ancient invaders were so reluctant to leave. To the south is the sun-baked Mediterranean, to the east and west ripples of hills where almond orchards and vineyards blaze with golden colors. Agrigento has a pleasant medieval center, but despite its worthwhile attractions, most people come to explore what the Greek poet Pindar called "the most beautiful city of mortals," what the Greeks called Akragas, and what today is known as the Valley of the Temples (Valle dei Templi).

COMING AND GOING Disembark at Agrigento's **Stazione Centrale** (P. Marconi), which sits immediately south of Piazzale Aldo Moro. Agrigento's long-distance **bus station** (P. Fratelli Rosselli) is just east of Piazza Vittorio Emanuele II. **SAIS** (Via Ragazzi del '99 12, tel. 0922/595620; open 5:30 AM–8 PM) offers spotty service to Catania (via Canicattì and Caltanissetta). For other companies and routes, check the schedules posted in **Bar Sprint** (Via Ragazzi del '99). The town's helpful tourist office is **AAST** (Via Atenea 123, tel. 0922/20454; open Mon.–Sat. 8–2 and 4:30–6:30), in the center of town.

WHERE TO SLEEP AND EAT Book ahead in summer. At **Hotel Bella Napoli** (P. Lena 6, tel. 0922/20435), smack in the medieval center, singles start at L25,000, doubles at L40,000, triples at L70,000. **Hotel Belvedere** (Via San Vito 20, tel. 0922/20051) has comfy singles for L30,000, doubles L50,000; from Piazza Vittorio Emanuele II, follow Via Cicerone to Via San Vito and turn right. **Camping Internazionale San Leone** (Via Lacco Ameno 4, tel.

0922/416121; closed Nov.–Mar.) sites cost L7000 per person. Tent and bag rentals cost L8000 and L5000, respectively. Take Bus 10 (or any labeled SAN LEONE) from in front of the train station.

Most of the restaurants in the center of town cater to tourists. Your best bet may be the grocery stores along Via Pirandello. **Trattoria Black Horse** (Via Celauro 8, tel. 0922/23223; closed Sun.) serves an immense plate of *calamari fritti* (fried calamari) for L12,000. **Trattoria La Forchetta** (P. San Francesco; closed Sun.) is the place to come for *penne alla siciliana* (pasta with eggplant, mozzarella, and tomato sauce; L6500) and succulent grilled swordfish (L10,000).

WORTH SEEING The most interesting attraction in the medieval quarter is the 13th-century **Chiesa Santa Maria dei Greci,** which was built by the Normans on the site of a 5th-century-BC Doric temple. Visible inside are some of the temple's original columns, as well as some ceiling paintings and partially preserved 14th-century frescoes. The **Valley of the Temples** (admission free; open daily 9–1; also Tues., Thurs., and Sat. 4–7) can be reached every 30 minutes by Buses 8, 9, 10, or 11 from in front of the train station. From the parking lot that separates the park's eastern and western sections, walk down Via dei Templi and turn left to the **Tempio di Ercole** (Temple of Hercules), the oldest temple in the valley, dating from approximately 520 BC. Follow the central path (an ancient street still marked with the ruts of Greek carts) to the **Tempio della Concordia** (Temple of Concord), one of the best-preserved Greek temples in the world. The easternmost temple in the valley, **Tempio di Giunone** (Temple of Juno), dates from 460 BC; about two-thirds of its original columns remain, and some still bear splotches of red from fire damage caused during the Carthaginian siege in 406 BC. The western half of the archaeological zone isn't as striking as its counterpart across the road.

LUXEMBOURG

By Zak Smith

Although Luxembourg is the smallest country in the European Union, it has its act together—the standard of living is one of the highest in Europe. Residents know that world headlines will never be shaped by what takes place here, but their political powerlessness has its advantages. Unlike Germany, Luxembourg faces no national struggle with its past; unlike Britain, it doesn't wrestle with its role in the European Union; unlike Greece, it has no serious conflicts with its neighbors. The Grand Duchy of Luxembourg packs dense forests and pristine countryside into its small space, and the capital city (creatively named Luxembourg City) is worth checking out. The country is usually overlooked as a travel destination—(except by a few diehard passport-stamp collectors)—but if any place exhibits "small-town charm" on a national scale, this is it.

So few outsiders speak Letzeburgesch, Luxembourg's native language, that residents have had to become multilingual. Almost everyone knows French, German, and English.

Basics

MONEY $1 = 32 Luxembourg francs and 10 Luxembourg francs = 30¢. The Luxembourg franc is locked into the same exchange rate as the Belgian franc. All Belgian currency is accepted in Luxembourg, but only Luxembourg bills are accepted in Belgium, and even those aren't always taken. Banks (and Luxembourg has plenty) offer the best exchange rates, but the American Express office in Luxembourg City is also a good bet. Banks are generally open 9–noon and 12:30–4:30.

➤ **HOW MUCH IT WILL COST** • Luxembourg is pricey, a little more expensive than Belgium. If you don't eat at too many sit-down restaurants, you can get by on $45–$50 a day, less if you sleep in a hostel and really scrimp.

GETTING AROUND   Train travel in Luxembourg is cheap because there's never far to go. Buy a **Billet Reseau** for 140LF at any train or bus station and you can travel all day on the country's buses and trains (bus service is more comprehensive). EurailPasses and the Benelux Tourrail Pass (*see* Basics, in Chapter 3) are also accepted on the trains.

WHERE TO SLEEP   Hostels provide the cheapest bed-and-breakfast deals in Luxembourg (about 350LF, 450LF for nonmembers), but don't expect the managers to arrange your social calendar, and don't expect cozy common rooms. A hotel double with breakfast goes for about

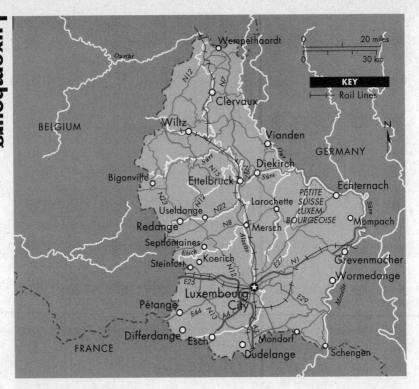

1,500LF. Not all hotels have free showers (many charge around 250LF), so ask before you sign on the dotted line.

PHONES AND MAIL **Country code: 352.** The telephones and postal service in Luxembourg are efficient and reliable. Send mail at the yellow post boxes attached to walls in every city. To reach AT&T's USA Direct line, dial 08–000–111 from any phone; for MCI, dial 08–000–112. Dial 0010 for an operator.

EMERGENCIES The central emergency number is 012.

Luxembourg City

It doesn't look too promising when you exit the train station, but La Ville de Luxembourg is one of Europe's most inviting cities. The tiny capital has a mere 75,000 inhabitants, but financial institutions from all over the world have set up camp here, bringing jobs and money and maintaining the city wonderfully. You'll find clean streets, restored historical sights, and pristine public squares edging up to the deep gorge that cuts through the city. Luxembourg City does have two big downers, though: expensive restaurants (finding a meal under 400LF is cause for celebration) and steep hills that will challenge anyone who hasn't left his or her backpack at the station. At press time, Luxembourg City was gearing up for the exhibits and festivities that will come to town when it assumes the title of Cultural Capital of Europe for 1995.

BASICS The **Office National du Tourisme** (9 pl. de la Gare, tel. 48–11–99), near the train station, has tourist info for the entire country. From July to mid-September, it's open weekdays 9–7:30, Saturday 9–noon and 2–6:30. Off-season hours are Monday–Saturday 9–noon and 2–6:30. The **city office** (pl. d'Armes, tel. 22–28–09) deals specifically with Luxembourg City. From June 15 to September 15, it's open weekdays 9–7, Saturday 9–1 and 2–7, Sunday 10–noon and 2–6. Off-season hours are Monday–Saturday 9–1 and 2–6.

Luxembourg City

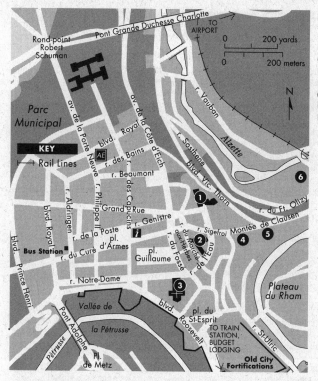

Auberge de
Jeunesse
Luxembourg (HI), **6**

Bock Casemates, **5**

Cathédrale
Notre-Dame, **3**

Eglise St-Michel, **4**

Grand Ducal
Palace, **2**

Musée National, **1**

The two main **post offices,** one near the train station (28 pl. de la Gare, tel. 47–65–47–65)
and the other in the city center (25 rue Aldringen, tel. 47–65–47–65), have phones. Also in
the center is the **American Express** office (34 av. de la Porte Neuve, tel. 22–85–55).

COMING AND GOING There's no information booth at the train station, **Gare Centrale,** but
there is an exchange office (open Mon.–Sat. 8:30 AM–9 PM, Sun. 9–9) with decent rates. The
city has surprisingly meager international rail connections, but frequent trains zip to Brussels
(3 hrs, 876LF) and less frequent ones go to Amsterdam (6 hrs, 1,824LF) and Paris (4 hrs,
1,460LF). **CFL intercity buses** (tel. 49–24–24) leave from the depot to the left as you exit
the train station. Buses are useful for getting to places like Echternach (*see below*) that
aren't on the rail lines. Bus schedules are posted outside the depot.

GETTING AROUND Luxembourg City is tiny, and if it were flat it would be easy to get
around on foot. But it isn't flat: The city is built on four high plateaus overlooking steep
gorges, at the bottom of which the dinky Pétrusse and Alzette rivers flow. You'll want to take
a bus if you have your backpack, though the strenuous walking reveals some breathtaking
views. There are two main **bus depots,** one at the Gare Centrale and the other on rue Aldringen in front of the central post office. At both locations you'll find maps detailing routes and
hours. Buses generally run 6 AM–10 PM and charge 35LF (and sometimes an extra 35LF for
large luggage). Call 44–21–96 for bus info.

WHERE TO SLEEP Almost all the city's hotels, from dirtbag dives to the poshest places,
are near the train station. A double without a private shower should run about 1,500LF. Single rooms rarely go for less than 900LF.

Axe. Not classy, but pretends to be, with wall-to-wall purple carpet and fabric everywhere.
Worth a shot if the others are full. Doubles 1,600LF, w/shower 1,900LF. *34 rue Joseph Junck,
tel. 49–09–53. From Gare Centrale, take rue Joseph Junck. AE, MC, V.*

591

Le Papillon. Narrow, creaky stairs lead to rooms painted full-on pink. Pricey restaurant downstairs. Helpful couple has run the place for 10 years. Doubles 1,500LF, w/bath 1,600LF. *9 rue Jean Origer, tel. 49–44–90. From Gare Centrale, right on av. de la Gare, left on rue Jean Origer. AE, MC, V.*

Touring. One of the best deals in town, though hotel and Italian restaurant below are run by a woman with Mussolini's disposition. Big rooms with wood floors and squishy beds. The 900LF singles are about as cheap as you'll find. Doubles 1,300LF, w/shower 1,800LF. *4 rue de Strasbourg, tel. 49–33–67. From Gare Centrale, take av. de la Liberté, left on rue de Strasbourg. AE, MC, V.*

➤ **HOSTEL • Auberge de Jeunesse Luxembourg (HI).** Nice location; the city center is a short uphill hike away. Showers, inconveniently located on bottom floor, are separated by sex but otherwise communal. Breakfast served only until 8:30. If you eat dinner (230LF) here, avoid the pizza. Singles 600LF; doubles 1,000LF; dorm beds 350LF, 420LF over 26; sheets 100LF. Nonmembers 110LF more. *2 rue du Fort Olizy, tel. 22–68–89. From Gare Centrale, Bus 9 (tell driver where you're going). Lockout 9:30–1, kitchen facilities, bike rental. Reception open 7:30–9:30 AM and 2–11 PM.*

➤ **CAMPGROUND • Camping Kockelscheuer.** The closest campground to the city, but still pretty far away. Trailers get the nicest spots—tents are crowded into an open, grassy area. Limited bus service to the city, especially on Sundays. Tent sites 100LF, plus 90LF per person. *22 rte. de Bettembourg, tel. 47–18–15. From Gare Centrale, Bus 2 toward Kockelscheuer. Laundry. Closed Nov.–Easter.*

FOOD Hope you didn't actually want to eat in Luxembourg City. Natives look dumbfounded when asked about inexpensive restaurants, though you can find some bargains on Italian food. Most restaurants are downtown near the place d'Armes and around the Gare Centrale. If you want something really cheap and quick, try **Créole** (34 pl. de la Gare, tel. 48–52–52), across the street from the train station, which has pizza slices for 75LF–95LF.

Giorgio. Portions look small but are actually very filling—it must be done with smoke and mirrors. Pizza 200LF–400LF, pasta about 300LF. Waiters sing when they're in a good mood. *11 rue du Nord, off av. de la Côte d'Eich 1 block north of Grand Rue, tel. 22–38–18. Closed Sun.*

Le Taormina. Dimly lit interior designed to look like an exterior, with roof eaves extending into the room and fake windows on the walls. Typical Luxembourg pub with a hodgepodge of Belgian, French, German, and some Italian food. Vegetarians get nothing but salads. Meals about 450LF. *28 rue Philippe II, just south of Grand Rue, tel. 22–02–72. Closed Sun.*

WORTH SEEING One of the best attractions is the **Bock Casemates** (Corniche Promenade, tel. 2–28–09), the remains of a huge complex of tunnels and fortresses built by the Austrians as a defense against the French in the mid-18th century. The casemates were used most recently as bomb shelters during the two world wars. Eleven miles of tunnels are still intact, and you can walk around some of them for 50LF (40LF students). Near the Bock Casemates, the tiny **Eglise St-Michel** (rue Sigefroi) has been around in one form or another since the 11th century, but it owes its present appearance to a restoration in 1688. The interior vaults are a good example of late Gothic architecture. Also look for a Baroque organ and an interesting altarpiece depicting the Assumption of the Virgin. On the whole, it's more worthwhile than the **Cathédrale Notre-Dame** (rue Notre-Dame), partially built in the 20th century, where the 14th-century king of Bohemia John the Blind hangs out in a crypt.

From the Eglise St-Michel, you can see the entrance to the **Musée National** (rue Wiltheim, tel. 47–87–08; admission free; open Tues.–Sun. 10–noon and 2–6). Inside are displays on ancient art, natural history, modern art, ceramics, and the military. The **Grand Ducal Palace** (rue du Marché-aux-Herbes), sections of which were built in the 16th century to serve as the town hall, was under scaffolding at press time, but its elaborate Spanish Renaissance ornamentation ought to be in fine form by the summer of 1995.

CHEAP THRILLS The Vallée de la Pétrusse is one of the most beautiful city parks in Europe, full of willows and cherry trees. Cliffs thrust up on either side, and stairways lead down to the valley floor; finding your way in and out is half the fun. For more adventure, wander north of the city to the Pont Grande Duchesse Charlotte, a huge red bridge where those afraid of heights will have a fit of vertigo and others will put their cameras to good use.

Ettelbruck

Ettelbruck proudly proclaims itself the "Gateway to the Ardennes." Maybe residents make so much noise about the designation because this town of 6,500 actually has so little to offer travelers. You have to be a big World War II fan to enjoy the **Musée Patton** (13 Grand-Rue, tel. 8–20–68), which has leftover goodies from the Battle of the Bulge. Still, the city is a bus and train hub for northern Luxembourg, so if you're exploring the country, you'll probably have to make a pit stop here. For minimal assistance, hit the **tourist information office** (tel. 8–20–68) at the train and bus station on the northern edge of town. The best thing to pick up here is a trail map (80LF), which shows some well-marked trails that run from the center. A couple of trains every hour travel from Ettelbruck to Luxembourg City (35 min, 140LF).

The biggest thrill you get in Ettelbruck may be boarding the train and pulling out of town. After all, you can only gaze at the General Patton monument for so long.

WHERE TO SLEEP AND EAT It's devoid of atmosphere, but the **HI hostel** (rue Grande-Duchesse Joséphine Charlotte, tel. 8–22–69; closed mid-Nov.–Feb.) does provide a cheap bed (300LF). A little more swanky is **Hotel Herckmans** (3 pl. de la Résistance, tel. 81–74–28; doubles 1,350LF). Eating in Ettelbruck can be a huge challenge. The hostel offers dinners for 230LF, but everything else in town (which isn't much) is overpriced. Your best bet is the cozy **Taverne Arthur** (1 rue Neuve, tel. 8–14–27), with meals for 450LF.

NEAR ETTELBRUCK

DIEKIRCH To reach the town of Diekirch, take the train or bus from Ettelbruck (5 min, 20LF one-way) or walk the 5 km, following a path along the Sûre River. Diekirch has been inhabited since before Roman times, and the remains of early civilizations can still be seen today. The oldest monument in town, **Deiwelselter,** is a dolmen (a small, Stonehenge-like monument) believed by some to be an ancient sacrificial altar of the Celts. Its uncertain origins and forest setting give it a mysterious aura. To find Deiwelselter, take hiking path D from the route de Larochette in the south of town. The **Musée Mosaïques Romaines** (pl. Guillame, tel. 80–30–23; admission 20LF) houses beautiful Roman mosaics from around the 3rd century, displaying an unexpected sensitive side of that rowdy civilization. The **Vieille Eglise St-Laurent** (pl. de la Libération), not to be confused with the modern church of the same name, was built in the 15th century. Its best feature is an old crypt, discovered in 1961, that dates from the time of the Franks and holds a collection of sarcophagi, one still containing a full skeleton.

Echternach

Although this town of 4,000 in eastern Luxembourg was largely destroyed during the 1944 Battle of the Bulge, many of its historical sights have been restored to their original splendor. The **Basilique de St-Willibrord,** which had to be rebuilt after the war, is boring, but you can visit the crypt downstairs and see the neo-Gothic tomb of the church's namesake saint. A better religious sight is the **Eglise Sts-Pierre-et-Paul,** which sits on a hill in the center of town. It's significant because parts date from the 7th century, and some remains even go back to the Roman era, when a palace stood on the site. Another Roman palace, the **Palais Romain,** is 10 minutes' walk south of town along rue de Luxembourg. It would look better if you could see the whole layout from above, since the villa's remaining walls and columns are only two feet high.

The helpful **tourist office** (Porvis de la Basilique, tel. 7–22–30), across from the basilica, sells maps of nearby hiking trails, which wind through the Petite Suisse and Basse-Sûre regions of Luxembourg. The 80LF map details hikes ranging from 3 to 12 km that pass by castles, forests, streams, and rocky cliffs.

COMING AND GOING **CFL buses** serve the town daily from Luxembourg City (1 hr, 120LF). Echternach's **train station** (tel. 72–90–09) is in the northwest corner of town, within easy walking distance of everything. Rent mountain bikes at **Irisport** (31 rte. de Luxembourg, tel. 7–20–86), three-speeds at **Activ Sports** (27 rue Ermesinde, tel. 7–21–48).

WHERE TO SLEEP AND EAT The **HI hostel** (9 rue Andre Duchscher, tel. 7–21–58; beds 300LF, 350LF for nonmembers) is in a prime location near the center of town. If you're looking to get rid of extra cash, try **Hotel Aigle Noir** (54 rue de la Gare, tel. 7–23–83; doubles 1,300LF–1,500LF), with spiffy checkerboard-tile floors. For camping, try **Camping Officiels** (rte. de Diekirch, tel. 7–22–72), near the Sûre River. Two people with a tent pay 330LF.

Rue de la Gare and the area around the place du Marché brim with restaurants. Prices are better than in Luxembourg City, but that's not saying much. Still, every town should have a restaurant like **La Coppa** (22 rue de la Gare, tel. 72–73–24), with a fun, laid-back atmosphere. The youthful employees serve up exotic cocktails and meals for less than 300LF.

Vianden

Vianden, northeast of Ettlebruck along the German border, fits fairy-tale visions of European villages, with a beautiful castle on a hill, a meandering river, lush forests, cobblestone streets, and old churches. Get info on what to see at the **tourist office** (37 rue de la Gare, tel. 8–42–57) or just go out exploring on your own—the town is small enough that finding everything of interest shouldn't be too hard. Buses run from Ettelbruck to Vianden daily (30 min, 140LF). The bus station, really just a hyped-up bus stop, lies south of town on rue de la Gare.

The big attraction here is the **Château de Vianden** (tel. 8–41–08; admission 110LF, 80LF students), visible from all over town. Restorations completed in 1983 have preserved its medieval appearance while adding facilities for exhibitions and concerts. Your entrance fee buys you a small guidebook in English with info on the entire building, including the colorfully painted chapels and the tapestried Count's Hall. Two churches worth a peek are the **Eglise des Trinitaires,** on the Grand Rue, and the **Eglise St-Nicolas,** next to the tourist office. Both have altars that look like they could have come from Paris's Notre-Dame or London's Westminster Abbey instead of a tiny town in the Ardennes.

WHERE TO SLEEP AND EAT The upbeat **HI hostel** (3 rue du Château, tel. 8–41–77; doubles 400LF per person, dorm beds 300LF) is near the château, about a 20-minute hike from the bus station. The campsite closest to town is **Camping op dëm Deich** (tel. 8–43–75), but **Camping du Moulin** (tel. 8–45–01) is a bit more back-to-nature. Both are on the Our River and charge 360LF for two people with a tent.

Most restaurants lie along rue de la Gare or the Grand Rue. At **Pension City Corner** (1 rue du Vieux Marché, tel. 8–47–97), the menu starts with sandwiches and omelets and keeps on going to fancy French food at a variety of prices. Expect to pay around 380LF for a meal, though you could get out for less if you choose carefully.

MOROCCO

By Meir Rinde

16

Moroccans love to go on and on about their hospitality—especially their practice of taking visitors under their wings, feeding them couscous, and becoming lifelong friends. And a lucky few visitors do come away completely seduced—some by the people, some by Morocco's half-modern, half-medieval society, and some simply by the landscape. But an unfortunately large contingent—particularly budget travelers eager to mix with the crowd on the street—are so plagued by hustlers that they cut short their visits and rate the trip a net loss.

The hustlers—an umbrella term that includes unofficial tour guides, self-inflicted friends, dope dealers, and assorted scam artists—are more annoying than dangerous. At worst you may be coerced into buying an overpriced carpet, or you may "accept" (i.e., finally break down and say yes to) an invitation to a local's home—and then be asked to hand over some traveler's checks in exchange for a ride back to your hotel. The real bummer is that unless you refuse even to speak, there's no way to guard against most scams.

That said, you can minimize the threat by (1) acting decisively and always knowing in advance where you want to go, (2) never admitting that you have a credit card, (3) politely refusing all requests to be shown around or escorted to a hotel, restaurant—whatever, and (4) remembering that everything a merchant says is BULLSHIT (announced prices are 5 to 10 times higher than what most will settle for).

To avoid becoming severely stressed out in Morocco, prepare for verbal abuse and constant harassment. Your life isn't in danger here; just get used to persistent hustlers who rarely take "no" for an answer.

The average monthly income in Morocco is about $75, which explains why hustlers are so eager to separate foreign tourists from their money. On the upside, if the delicate Palestinian Liberation Organization–Israeli peace accords don't fall apart, officials predict an annual 15%–20% jump in tourism plus sizable increases in trade (particularly with Israel), all of which may help jump-start the moribund Moroccan economy. Another hopeful sign is the recent cessation of hostilities in Western Sahara. Morocco's King Hassan II started the resource-draining skirmishes in 1975, largely as a propaganda maneuver. Today, with the help of a United Nations–backed peace initiative, armed encounters are becoming less common, ostensibly freeing up money for things like hospitals, schools, and roads.

King Hassan II's ancestors, the 'Alawites, have ruled as sultans of Morocco for more than 300 years. Hassan's father, Mohammed V, started calling himself "king" when the state gained independence from France and Spain in 1956. Since then, the two kings have been virtually deified. Hassan II is leader of the faith, head of the army, and the unchallenged big cheese of

PORTUGAL

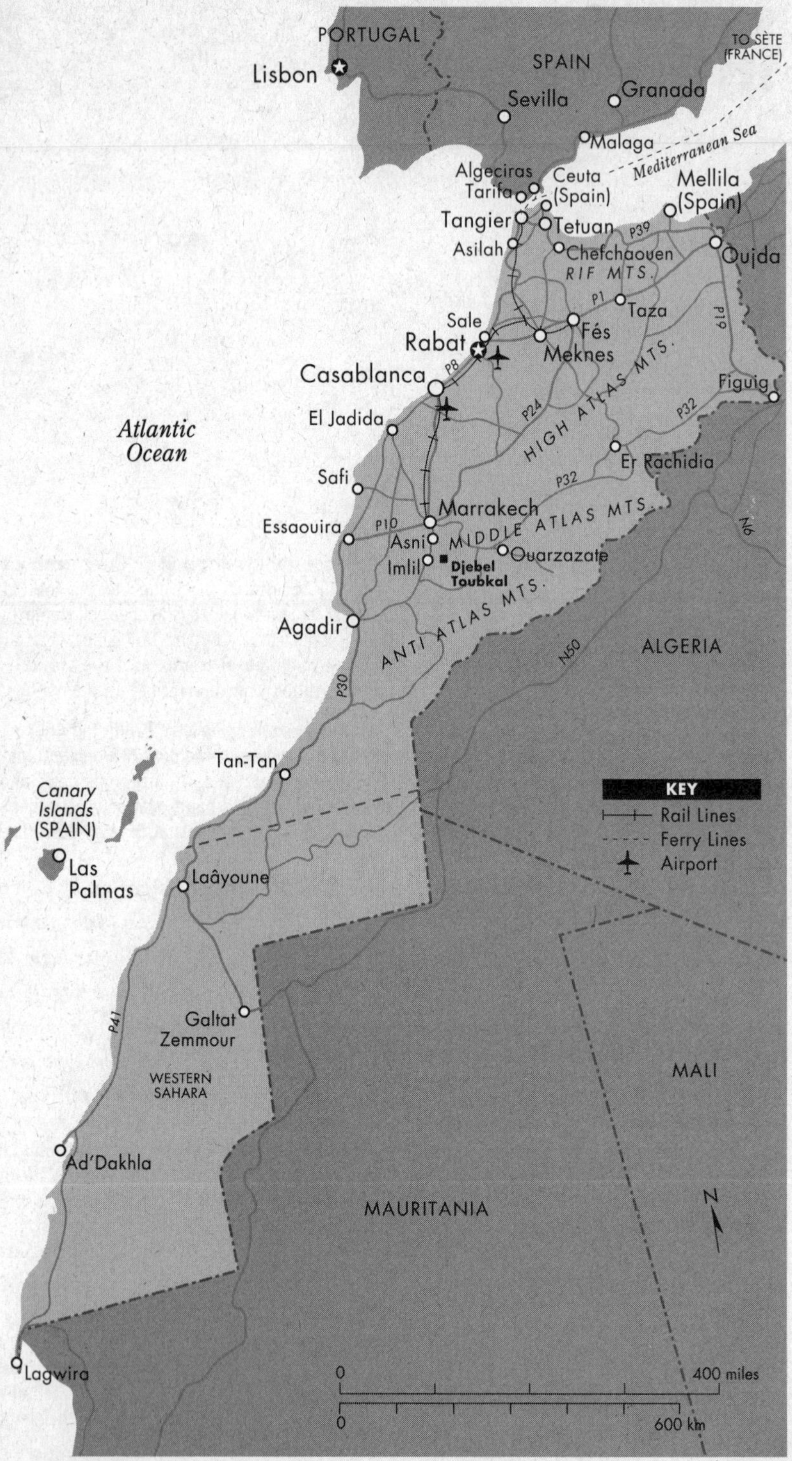

SPAIN

TO SÈTE
(FRANCE)

Lisbon

Sevilla

Granada

Malaga

Mediterranean Sea

Algeciras
Tarifa

Ceuta
(Spain)

Mellila
(Spain)

Tangier

Tetuan

P39

Oujda

Asilah

Chefchaouen

RIF MTS.

Sale

P1

Taza

Rabat

Fés

Meknes

P19

Casablanca

PB

HIGH ATLAS MTS.

Figuig

El Jadida

P24

P32

Atlantic
Ocean

Safi

Er Rachidia

P32

Essaouira

Marrakech

MIDDLE ATLAS MTS.

N6

P10

Asni

Imlil

Djebel
Toubkal

Ouarzazate

Agadir

ANTI ATLAS MTS.

N50

ALGERIA

P30

Tan-Tan

Canary
Islands
(SPAIN)

KEY

Rail Lines

Laâyoune

Ferry Lines

Las
Palmas

Airport

P41

Galtat
Zemmour

MALI

WESTERN
SAHARA

N

Ad'Dakhla

MAURITANIA

0   400 miles

0   600 km

Lagwira

government; his picture hangs in nearly every Moroccan shop and business, gazing down like a mildly benevolent Big Brother.

The 'Alawites have produced their share of palaces and monuments, but it's the earlier dynasties—especially the 13th-century Almohads and their successors, the Merenids—that are responsible for the ornate religious buildings that, together with various *medinas* (old towns) and markets, are the country's chief attractions. But Morocco isn't really about tourist sights. In many ways it's about expanding your cultural horizons—pausing for the call to prayer or greeting a pilgrim fresh from Mecca. In markets it's about smells (goats, crushed mint, sun-baked spices) and sounds (distant religious chants, bickering merchants). If you're a stress case, it's about crafty carpet dealers who will wear you down with mint tea and charm. If you're a rugged type, it's about trekking in North Africa's highest mountains or surfing on deserted beaches. If you're a burner, it's about hash, police informants, and not getting caught.

Basics

MONEY $1 = 9.22 dirhams and 1 dirham = 11¢. The dirham is divided into 100 centimes. Credit cards (Visa, MasterCard, American Express) and Eurocheque traveler's checks are accepted at upscale hotels and restaurants and at most shops, although some will charge *you* the 5%–6% transaction fee unless you're a good haggler. Credit-card fraud is increasing, so pay in cash when possible.

When exchanging currency, stick to banks. They offer the government-set rate and do not charge commissions. In some cities, exchange windows of the ubiquitous Banque Marocaine du Commerce Extérieur (BMCE) are open daily 8–8. Before leaving Morocco, try to spend all your dirhams: to reconvert them into your own currency you'll have to show original exchange receipts, and even then you can only exchange up to half of the total.

Customs officials frown on hippies, so wear a clean shirt, and tie back that long hair. Otherwise, you may experience the Moroccan version of red tape, which isn't pretty.

➤ **HOW MUCH IT WILL COST** • Compared to Europe, Morocco is dirt cheap. Per night, simple hotel doubles cost 60dh and up, hostels about 25dh, campgrounds 10dh–15dh. Be warned that lodging prices can jump drastically in July and August and around Christmas and Easter. At restaurants you'll pay 15dh–25dh for entrées of the couscous-and-veggie variety. Even without a rail pass, Morocco's trains are cheap by any standard, particularly if you don't mind traveling fourth-class with families and their livestock.

CUSTOMS AND DUTIES North Americans and Europeans (except for the Dutch and the Belgians) do not need entry visas for stays of up to 90 days. If you have a South African or Israeli stamp on your passport, you theoretically could be refused entry, but this happens only rarely. To stay longer than three months, either reset the timer by leaving Morocco for a few days and, to be safe, reenter at a different place, or inquire at a police station about a residency permit.

COMING AND GOING

➤ **BY FERRY** • From the Spanish port of **Algeciras**, the ferry to **Tangier** (2½ hrs, 2,700 pesetas) takes longer and is more expensive—but ultimately more convenient—than the ferry to the Spanish-owned port of **Ceuta** (1½ hrs, 1,700 pesetas), which further requires a local bus to the Moroccan border, a taxi to Tetuan, and another bus if you want to hook up with Morocco's train system. Another good thing about the Tangier ferry: InterRail-pass holders (but *not* EurailPass holders) receive a 30% discount. For more information on ferry companies *see* Coming and Going *in* Tangier, *below.*

➤ **BY PLANE** • From New York, **Royal Air Maroc** (RAM) (tel. 212/750–6071 or 800/344–6726) has weekly direct service to Casablanca; round-trip fares from the United States are $1,416 (economy) and $766 (APEX). From Paris, RAM flies to Morocco's major cities; from Madrid and London, RAM flies to Tangier and Casablanca.

GETTING AROUND Public transportation is cheap, so don't be afraid to spend a few extra dirhams on first-class upgrades. Trains are slightly more expensive than buses (especially on long-distance trips) but offer faster travel with much more legroom. Trains, however, travel only between Tangier and Casablanca/Rabat and from Casablanca to Fès and Marrakech. For all other routes take a bus or, for about 15% more, a *grand taxi* (collective taxi). The latter are typically privately owned Mercedes that travel between major (and not-so-major) towns for a negotiable fee; they're also downright comfortable and much faster than trains.

➤ **BY TRAIN** • Second-class is the most popular—and cheapest—way to travel on **ONCF**, the national rail company. First-class offers air-conditioning for only a few dollars more—something to consider on a sweltering July afternoon. If you prefer traveling in cattle cars, you can ask for a spot in E (économique) class. Sample second-class fares from Tangier are as follows: Marrakech 134dh, Fès 66.50dh, Casablanca 81.50dh. Note that trains denoted "*rapide*" cost one-third more but are not so rapid. Also remember that only InterRail (*not* Eurail-) passes are accepted on Moroccan trains.

➤ **BY BUS** • **CTM,** the national bus company, serves large and medium-size towns on a regular basis. Buses are relatively comfortable and fast; the best are so-called deluxe coaches that, for a few extra dollars, provide air-conditioning and badly dubbed American films. Although buses run by private lines are never air-conditioned, they are usually cheaper, are always an adventure, and can serve as a backup if your schedule doesn't match CTM's.

➤ **BY TAXI** • Six-passenger **grands taxis** are ideal for short treks between towns. Grands taxis generally follow specific routes, and for longer journeys you may have to change cars. The price is theoretically the same regardless of the number of passengers, although it's usually necessary to haggle. Check at your hotel, or check bus fares to estimate a fair price to your destination. Either way, always agree on a price *before* leaving. The smaller **petits taxis** are allowed to carry as many as three passengers on trips within a city's limits. Most rides are 5dh–10dh; ask the driver to turn on the meter or state the price in advance.

WHERE TO SLEEP Some Moroccan hotels are government-regulated (*classé,* or classified), but most are of the cheaper *nonclassé* (nonclassified) sort. The latter, typically found in a town's medina, are either great finds (sunny and clean) or utter disasters (dirt, vermin, and atrocious plumbing). Across the board, sinks and toilets in nonclassé hotels are inadequate, and hot water is rare. Nonclassé rates may rise sharply during peak periods (July, August, Christmas, and Easter). Morocco has HI-affiliated hostels in 16 cities; all are dirt cheap at 10dh–25dh per night. Campers will pay 10dh per person plus 10dh per tent to stay at the simplest kind of campground, about twice that to camp at places with swimming pools, nightclubs, and hordes of Eurokids.

FOOD Moroccans don't eat out much, so for complete meals you'll probably end up in a tourist-oriented restaurant. But don't fret: even touristy spots serve inexpensive, fairly authentic dishes. Look for *tajine,* a vegetable-and-meat stew that's sweet and spicy; *harira,* a thick, chickpea-based soup with beans and a bit of meat thrown in; *brochettes,* small pieces of skewered steak; *kefta,* balls of spicy ground meat; and grilled *poulet* (chicken), *viande* (beef), or *agneau* (lamb). The quintessential Moroccan dish is *couscous,* a bowl of steamed semolina grain, onions, beans, and other vegetables, topped with meat. Vegetarians should stick with tajine and bean soups prepared without meat—ask for your food *sans viande.* Other veggie options include salads, *leben* (a yogurt drink), and munchies like olives, almonds, dates, carefully washed fruit, and French-style bread and pastries.

The quintessential Moroccan drink is "thè à la menthe," fresh mint steeped in boiling water and served with gobs of sugar.

BUSINESS HOURS Moroccan shops, bazaars, and banks are open weekdays 9–noon and 2:30–6; many are closed on Friday afternoons. Tourist sights are open daily, except for museums (closed Tuesdays) and some religious buildings (closed Fridays for prayer).

FESTIVALS AND HOLIDAYS The most important holiday to avoid, or at least to prepare for, is the monthlong fast of **Ramadan,** when eating, drinking, and smoking are forbidden during daylight hours (at sunset, however, the country goes wild). In 1995 Ramadan begins on February 1; in 1996, January 21. Other feast-filled holidays are **Mouloud,** the birthday of the prophet Mohammed, usually celebrated in September or October, and **Aïd el Kebir** (around June), which is followed shortly by **Moharem,** the Muslim New Year. The best and biggest event of the year is Marrakech's tourist-oriented **Folklore Festival** (early June), which draws performers from around the country; make hotel reservations far in advance.

VISITOR INFORMATION Most towns have at least one tourist office, called either *Syndicat d'Initiative* or **ONMT**; some towns have both. Each offers tourist brochures with fairly useful maps and phone listings. The staffs speak French, Arabic, and often a little English and can set you up with official tour guides or refer you to hotels that supply them.

PHONES **Country code: 212.** The most convenient calls are made from **PTT** (post and telephone) offices. For direct and collect calls, write down the number, city, country, and your name, hand it in at the counter, and wait (anywhere from 10 to 45 minutes) until your name is called. In large cities, some PTT offices are open 24 hours. To call long distance from pay phones, dial 00, wait for the tone, then dial the country code. Per-minute rates are about 70dh to the United States and Canada and about 40dh to western Europe. At press time there was no AT&T, MCI, or Sprint direct-dial service from Morocco.

MAIL Post offices are open weekdays 8–noon and 3–6:30. Letter postage is about 6dh to North America and about 4.50dh to Europe; postcards are 1dh less. Travelers can receive mail at larger hotels and main post offices. For the latter, address to: last name (underlined), first name, Poste Restante, PTT Centrale, city name, Morocco.

CRIME AND PUNISHMENT The smoking of *kif* (a.k.a. hash, *chocolat, parfumé*) is widespread among Moroccans, who just offer a small bribe if the police bother to notice. However, tourists caught with drugs are in a much worse situation—a definite fine and possible jail time. If smoking is your top priority, know that many dealers double as police informers; in some cases, after you're arrested, the kif is returned to the dealer for resale to another foreign-looking stooge.

EMERGENCIES For an **ambulance,** dial 15. The emergency **police** number is 19. If you somehow land in jail or a hospital, immediately call your local consulate; the staff can arrange local assistance and contact someone back home. Most consulates and embassies are located in Casablanca and Rabat, with a few in Tangier.

LANGUAGE AND CULTURE Morocco's official languages are French and Arabic, although Spanish is widely spoken in Tangier and Tetuan. English is becoming more common, but Moroccans truly enjoy hearing Westerners grapple with their native tongue. Some handy Arabic phrases are *salaam-alaikum,* a hello that is answered with *aláykoom-saláam*; *la bés,* a less formal hello; *shókran* (thank you); *lah,* no; and *na'am* (yes). Other terms you'll hear are *medina,* an Arabic word referring to the oldest part of a town, usually composed of winding alleyways and tightly packed shops and apartments, and *ville nouvelle,* the "new city" built by the occupying colonial power (France), with wide streets, banks, commerce, and big

Up in Smoke

Hash is a fact of life in Morocco. You'll see it smoked in cafés and on the street, and at some point you'll probably be passed a pipe if you're male and sitting somewhere quiet with a large group of Moroccan men. No one will be offended if you politely decline, and no one will likely bust your butt for saying yes. Still, it's better to be safe than to wake up baked in a Moroccan jail.

hotels. Sights include the *kasbah* (fortress or castle), *bab* (gate or archway), and *medersas* (Koranic schools housing students, attached to a mosque).

Except on the beach, long pants are a good idea for women and men. Although many Moroccans drink, alcohol is forbidden to Muslims, and some medinas are officially dry. Nicer hotels and restaurants usually stock beer for foreigners, and every ville nouvelle has bars and liquor stores. Still, be sensitive about drinking around Moroccans. Also keep in mind that the left hand is used in the toilet, not for eating or shaking hands.

WOMEN TRAVELERS Western women in Morocco carry the burden of a slutty image. To avoid undo hassle, wear long pants and long sleeves. The next best thing is a long skirt. Less bundling is necessary in a city's ville nouvelle and in resort towns, and swimsuits are okay on (although not elsewhere near) the beach. If you get caught in a sticky situation, yelling in the presence of many bystanders will usually bring assistance.

STAYING HEALTHY No inoculations are required to visit Morocco. The only truly dangerous water comes from streams and still lakes or pools, which are often infected with harmful bacteria. Tap water won't kill, but it may raise hell with the uninitiated stomach. Protect yourself by drinking and brushing your teeth only with mineral water (make sure the bottle is sealed when you buy it). Either way, diarrhea is a given if you drink the water, eat at food stalls, or ingest unwashed or prepeeled fruit and vegetables. The best cure is to consume only yogurt, plenty of water, and mint tea until the dreaded "D" passes.

Moroccan summers are hot as hell, and you must drink plenty of water to avoid the headache and nausea of heatstroke. Bring your own water when traveling by train or bus; you may not find it otherwise. Morocco's pharmacies are usually well stocked. Large hotels and some tourist offices sometimes provide lists of English-speaking doctors.

Tangier  **Tangier has a lovely beach, swell views across the** Strait of Gibraltar, and a fascinating role in modern Western culture—but you may be better off catching the first train outta here. The hustlers at Tangier's train station are among Morocco's most intimidating and have a reputation for scaring travelers right out of the country. From the moment you step off the ferry, prepare to be harangued and hassled by unofficial guides and "friends" intent on showing you the medina, their favorite restaurant, or the inside of a carpet shop.

Tangier entered the European imagination in the years following 1912, when the major European powers settled all claims on this strategically important city by granting it international status—which meant everyone had a finger in the Tangier pie. Until Moroccan independence in 1956, this luxurious resort was home to shadowy financiers, a host of expatriate writers and musicians, and an unprecedented gay scene. Hints of the period remain—the United Kingdom, Germany, and France still have consulates here, and there's a small community of foreign expatriates—but it's now a resort strictly on Moroccan terms.

To reach the city from the waterfront Avenue d'Espagne, walk northwest on Zankat Salah Eddine el Ayoubi. You'll emerge onto **Grand Socco** (in places called Place de 19 Avril 1947), once Tangier's central market. On the square's east side are two arches, and to their right is a narrow crowded lane, Rue es Siaghin, which curves right toward the **Petit Socco**, once a 19th-century market and now a noisy hangout; try the terrace of Pension Fuentes (*see* Where to Sleep, *below*) for a haughty vantage point. The left-hand arch, **Bab Fahs,** opens onto Rue d'Italie. From here follow the signs up Rue de la Kasbah (you'll go through a tunnel, a small square, and then a second tunnel) to **Place de la Kasbah,** where the town's government was once centered. Head through the **Bab Hahr** gate (left of the square) for a panoramic peek at Spain's coast. On the square, hidden in the right corner, is the entrance to the old **Dar el Makhzen** (Royal Palace); it now houses a **museum** (tel. 09/93–20–97; admission 10dh), with pottery, clothing, daggers, plus a room of archaeological finds from the Roman site of Volubilis, near Meknes. **Rue des Almohades,** a popular shopping street, snakes into the medina from the Hotel Mauritania's entrance on the Petit Socco. As a rule, save your dirhams for cheaper and more authentic goods in cities farther south.

Tangier

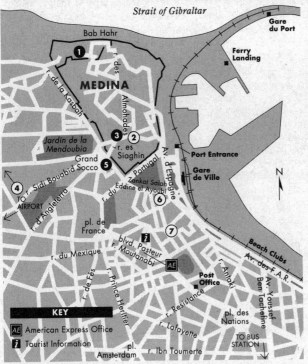

Sights ●
Grand Socco, **5**
Petit Socco, **3**
Place de la
Kasbah, **1**

Lodging ○
Camping
Miramonte, **4**
Hotel el Muniria, **7**
Pension Detroit, **6**
Pension Fuentes, **2**

BASICS

VISITOR INFORMATION The staff at **ONMT** speaks English and has city maps. *29 Blvd. Pasteur, tel. 09/93–82–39. Open weekdays 8–noon and 4–7.*

AMERICAN EXPRESS *Voyages Schwartz, 54 Blvd. Pasteur, tel. 09/93–34–59 or 09/93–34–71. Open weekdays 9–12:30 and 3–7, Sat. 9–12:30.*

CONSULATES United Kingdom. *9 Rue Amerique du Sud, tel. 09/03–58–97. Open summer, Mon.–Thurs. 9–noon and 2–5, Fri. 9–noon; fall–spring, Mon.–Thurs. 9–12:30 and 2:30–5:30, Fri. 9–noon.*

PHONES AND MAIL Central post office, *33 Blvd. Mohammed V, tel. 09/93–16–66. Open weekdays 8–7:15. Phone room around cnr. open 24 hrs.*

COMING AND GOING

Most of Tangier is walkable, but if you're foot weary or headed to the bus station, hail a blue petit taxi. Most trips cost 7dh–10dh.

BY TRAIN Tangier's main train station, the **Gare de Ville** (Av. d'Espagne, tel. 09/93–45–70), is by the port entrance. Destinations include Meknes (5 hrs, 55.50dh), Fès (6 hrs, 66.50dh), Rabat (5½ hrs, 62.50dh), and Marrakech (9 hrs, 134dh).

BY BUS The **main bus station** (Sahat Al Jamia Al Arabia, tel. 09/94–66–82) is 2 km from the city center; take a petit taxi (5dh). Baggage storage is 2dh. CTM buses leave from the main bus terminal and from the CTM office (tel. 09/93–24–15) at the port entrance. From Tangier there are daily CTM buses to Fès (66dh, 77.50dh for air-conditioned trip at 6 PM), Marrakech (146dh), Casablanca (88.50dh), Rabat (67dh), and Tetuan (13dh). Private companies serve the same destinations at competitive prices; get to the station early and ask at the various windows.

601

BY FERRY When you buy a ticket in Morocco, the ferry company will give you a departure form. Fill it out and take it to the police desk. They'll inspect your form and passport, after which you're allowed to go through customs. When planning your trip, remember that Morocco sets its clocks two hours behind Spain in summer and one hour behind Spain from fall through spring. All arrivals and departures are listed in local Moroccan times.

The 2½-hour trip between Tangier and Algeciras (Spain) costs 200dh on the **Transmediterranea** and **Limadet** ferry lines. Both companies have 12 departures daily in summer, six daily in winter. In Tangier you can buy ferry tickets from Limadet (13 Rue du Prince Moulay Abdallah, tel. 09/93–36–25), from any travel agency on Boulevard Pasteur or Avenue d'Espagne, and at the port entrance. InterRail holders receive a 30% discount. If you're pressed for time, Transmediterranea's hydrofoil to Algeciras is quicker (50 min, 196dh); there are two daily departures in summer (at 10 AM and 3:30 PM) and one daily the rest of the year (at 3:30 PM). There is no hydrofoil service in January.

Transtour (4 Rue el Jabha al Outania, tel. 09/93–40–04) has ferries to Tarifa (Spain) once daily (55 min, 196dh). Catamarans to Gibraltar (1½ hrs, 220dh) are a more adventurous option; they leave Friday at 8:30 AM (return 6:30 PM) and Sunday at 4 PM (return Monday at 8:30 AM). Buy tickets at Transtour or any agency.

Comanov ferries (43 Av. Abou el Alla el Maari, tel. 09/93–26–49) make the 36-hour trip to Sète (France) twice weekly at 6 PM. A bed in a basic cabin is 1,760dh (1,230dh for students and those under 26). Comanov does not operate during the first half of February.

WHERE TO SLEEP

Lodging is tight in July and August, and reservations are an excellent idea. You'll find a bunch of cheap pensions in the Petit Socco and on Zankat Salah Eddine el Ayoubi.

Pension Detroit. Super-cheap and right off Avenue d'Espagne by the port. Usually booked in late summer, so call ahead. Doubles 45dh. *130 Zankat Salah Eddine el Ayoubi, around cnr. from Hotel Valencia, tel. 09/93–48–38. Hot shower 5dh.*

Pension Fuentes. On the Petit Socco in the medina's heart. Noisiest, liveliest pension on the square, with a large café. Basic, boring doubles 80dh–100dh. *Petit Socco 9, tel. 09/93–46–69. Hot shower 5dh.*

Hotel El Muniria. Between Avenue d'Espagne and Boulevard Pasteur. Slightly rickety, but friendly atmosphere. Bill Burroughs wrote *Naked Lunch* here; British owner J. C. Sutcliffe is a Tangerine centerpiece. Doubles with (hot) shower 120dh. *Rue Magellan, tel. 09/93–53–37. From Av. d'Espagne, walk up Rue Magellan.*

CAMPGROUND Camping Miramonte. Small, shaded camping area 3 km west of kasbah, near a small beach. 15dh per person, 10dh per tent. If you don't have a tent, there's also an overpriced hotel (rooms 120dh–150dh). *Rte. Marshan, tel. 09/93–71–33. Bus 12/21 from stop on Rue Sidi Bouabid, 1 block west of Grand Socco. Get off at Café Fleur de la Montagne and walk toward sea. Restaurant, supply shop; swimming pool 50dh per day.*

▶ FOOD

The streets south and west of the Grand Socco are packed with fruit and vegetable markets. For cheap restaurants, look in the alleys on the east side of the Petit Socco and on Rue Mexique, behind the RAM office on Place de France. A couple of must-see cafés are **Café de Paris** (1 Pl. de France, tel. 09/93–84–44), a hotbed of political intrigue during World War II, and **Restaurant Detroit** (1 Rue Riad Sultan, tel. 09/93–80–80), which has good views of the bay.

Restaurant Dallas. Clean, quiet, and near Boulevard Pasteur. Emphasis on seafood in menu and decor. Solid fish plates 25dh, tajine 15dh. *16 Rue Moutanabi, 1 block south of Blvd. Pasteur, tel. 09/93–99–09.*

Restaurant La Marsa. *The* place for pizza (served noon–3 and 6 PM–11 pm only), whether it's plain cheese (23dh) or the topping-heavy house special (42dh). Despite tablecloths and uniformed waiters, this place is a comfortable spot to linger with a friend. *92 Av. d'Espagne, tel. 09/93–19–28.*

NEAR TANGIER

CEUTA Ceuta is a Spanish-owned military town with some duty-free shopping thrown in. Most travelers pass through only on their way from Spain to Morocco—if that describes you, don't bother to linger. If you're Morocco-bound, take the bus marked CENTRO (75 pesetas) from Ceuta's ferry terminal to Plaza de la Constitución. Get some dirhams from a nearby exchange bank, then take Bus 7 (60 pesetas) to the *frontera* (border), about 10 minutes away in Fnidek. At the border, ignore all those who want to fill out your *débarquement* form for a hefty tip. Pick up the form yourself from a customs window, then wait in line (sometimes an hour or more during late summer and holidays). Once you're through, take a grand taxi (6 people maximum; 2dh–4dh) to a nearby bus stop, where you can connect with a bus to Tetuan or Tangier. However, it's quicker and certainly more comfortable to take a grand taxi straight to Tetuan (15dh). The **Patronato Municipal de Turismo** (Alcalde J. Victori Goñalons, tel. 956/51–40–92), on the main plaza, has ferry schedules and a list of Ceuta's hotels and restaurants.

If you stay in Ceuta, the **Residencia de la Juventud** youth hostel (27 Pl. Rafael Gibert, near Plaza de la Constitución, tel. 956/51–51–48; dorm beds 1,600 pesetas; HI card required) is up some stairs next to a mediocre Chinese restaurant. The hostel is open July and August only.

ASILAH This mellow beach town is an easy one-hour bus, train, or taxi ride from Tangier—well worth the effort if Tangier's hustlers are getting you down. Asilah follows a pattern often repeated farther south: plentiful sand, plentiful seafood, and a Portuguese medina that dates from the 16th century (when Portugal controlled Morocco's western coast). Walking through the medina from an entrance off **Avenue Hassan II** (Asilah's main drag), you'll reach a terrace overlooking the sea. Nearby is **Palais de Raisuli,** built in 1908 by its namesake, a legendary bandit who ruled the Berber tribes of the western Rif mountains. The palace is only open in August, when it hosts an annual festival of art and music (and when lodging in town is impossible to find). Asilah has a few Berber carpet shops with decent prices, but your dirhams are better spent on a donkey trek to nearby **Paradise Beach,** a mellow spot where local burners like to smoke hash and watch the sunset. Ask at the Hotel Asilah (*see below*) for info on guides, and don't pay more than 20dh per person.

➢ **BASICS** • If you arrive at the **train station** (tel. 09/91–73–27), either take a shuttle (5dh) to the Central Plaza Mohammed V, or walk south for about 2 km, turning right at the first street that splits from the highway (look for the RABAT sign). Everything in Asilah is grouped around the main plaza: the bus station is a few blocks north; the medina, restaurants, and beaches a few blocks west. Caveat Emptor: On the train from Fès, hustlers may try to lure you to Asilah. Get off only if *you* want to, and don't accept invitations to stay with locals. That said, Asilah is a pretty mellow place.

The centrally located **Hotel Asilah** (79 Av. Hassan II, tel. 09/91–72–86; doubles with hot shower 100dh) has simple, clean rooms; ask for one on the terrace. As for food, chow on fresh fish, clams, squid, and swordfish in one of the restaurants along Avenue Hassan II. If you can afford a bit more style, try **El Espigón** (Rue Yacoub el Mansour, tel. 09/91–71–57); it's by the beach north of the medina, at the end of the tiled promenade.

TETUAN Tetuan has awe-inspiring views of the coast and Rif mountains, which means it's a popular summertime resort among Moroccans. This university town also has a distinct Spanish feeling, and for good reason: It served as capital of the Spanish Protectorate from 1913 to 1956. To tour the wide-laned, white-and-blue-walled medina, follow the road next to the Royal Palace, then enter through **Bab el Rouah** (Gate of the Wind). Turn left at the first fork and follow the main lane (as straight as you can) to the T-shape intersection, then bear right. A little farther on is the entrance to a large cemetery (closed Friday). Climb the hill inside for good views over Tetuan.

If you turn right at that first fork, you'll pass through the souks before reaching a fish-and-poultry market, where plucked chickens hang in neat rows. Spend some time savoring the pungent aroma of dead fowl, then exit the medina by heading east through the Bab Okla city gate (on your right).

➤ **BASICS** • The **tourist office** (30 Blvd. Mohammed V, tel. 09/96–44–07) arranges official guides for 50dh–100dh per half-day. Tetuan is 1½ hours from Tangier, and by far the easiest way to get here is by bus (the closest train station is near Asilah). From Tetuan's bus depot, **CTM** (tel. 09/96–16–88) serves Ceuta (7.50dh), Tangier (13dh), Chaouen (17dh), and Fès (5dh). **Supratours/ONCF** (18 Rue Achra Mai, tel. 09/96–75–59) sells combined tickets that include bus fare (to the train station near Asilah) and train fare to your final destination—perhaps the best bet for those headed to or from Casablanca (180.50dh). From Tetuan's bus station, turn left and walk about four blocks to reach Place de Moulay el Mehdia.

Tetuan is filled with hustlers, so don't let a local recommend a hotel, and don't stay too close to the medina. A good budget choice is **Hotel Principe** (20 Rue Youssef Ibn Tachfine, tel. 09/96–27–95), well located on the path between the bus station and Place de Moulay el Mehdia. Good-size singles cost 50dh, doubles 91dh.

Fès

In Fès the streets are thick with donkeys, narrow shops, and smells that range from pungent to putrid to just plain mysterious. In a raw way, this is Morocco at its best—a place where dead chickens and spices, street merchants and hustlers, form a street scene you won't soon forget. Still, as the quintessential Moroccan city, Fès offers a complex web of pleasures and traps; hustlers are a problem *everywhere* you go, and even hotels and tourist offices display signs that warn: "Beware unofficial guides." Heed the advice and take no one at face value.

Morocco's most confusing medina is Fès el Bali, an exhilarating, daunting place to explore. Hustlers here come in two varieties: troublesome and persistent.

It's said that the opulence of 14th-century Fès was rivaled in the Islamic world only by that of Cairo; the same could probably be said of Fès's religious and academic traditions. The Kairaouine Mosque, one of the world's oldest universities (AD 859), educated generations of Fassis (Fès residents), not to mention Christians and Muslims from all over the world. As the Christian conquest of Spain gained momentum, Fès attained further prestige and influence in North Africa; after the fall in 1492 of Granada (the last Muslim kingdom on the European continent), persecuted Jews and Muslims fled here from southern Spain, and Fès was left heir to almost 800 years of Andalusian culture.

Noticeably, these accomplishments are set mostly in the past tense, signalling Fès's slow but sure decline. This reached a critical point in 1980, when UNESCO announced a $500 million plan to save Fès el Bali, the oldest part of the city. The plan called for the relocation of one-third of the medina's 290,000 inhabitants, and the population today stands at about 200,000.

BASICS

VISITOR INFORMATION Stop by the multilingual **Syndicat d'Initiative** for free maps and to hire friendly official guides (30dh/half-day, 50dh/full day). *Pl. Mohammed V, no tel. Open weekdays 8–noon and 4–7, Sat. 9–noon.*

ONMT has good maps but does not arrange guides. *Pl. de la Resistance, tel. 05/62–34–60. Open weekdays 8–3.*

PHONES AND MAIL The **main post office,** in the ville nouvelle, is at the corner of Avenue Hassan II and Boulevard Mohammed V. The phone annex, open daily 8:30 AM–9 PM, has a separate entrance on Boulevard Mohammed V. *Dial 16 for info. Post office open weekdays 8–noon and 4–7.*

COMING AND GOING

BY TRAIN The **Gare de Fès** (Av. des Almohades, tel. 05/62–50–01) is on the ville nouvelle's western edge—a long walk from Fès el Bali (Old Fès) and the main medina sights. Take a taxi (10dh–15dh) to your hotel or Bus 10 (1.60dh) from the station to Place des Alaouites (in Fès el Jdid) or Bab el Mahrouk (in Fès el Bali). From Fès, trains head to Meknes (15dh), Rabat (62dh), Casablanca (87dh), and Tangier (88dh). The slowpoke train to Marrakech (11–12 hrs, 153.50dh) travels via the coast—a long, tedious journey.

BY BUS From the **CTM station** (Blvd. Mohammed V, tel. 05/62–20–41), two blocks south of the tourist office, long-distance buses head to Rabat (47.50dh), Casablanca (69dh), Tangier (77.50dh), and Marrakech (110dh). Bus 9 from the tourist office serves Fès el Bali and the medina. Fès's private bus companies depart from Place Baghdadi, outside Bab Boujeloud.

GETTING AROUND

Fès el Bali (Old Fès) is the dense network of tiny streets northeast of the train station; this is where you'll find the medina, best accessed via the Bab Boujeloud gate. Fès el Jdid (New Fès), is split by the oft-crammed market street Grande Rue de Fès el Jdid. The train station is in the ville nouvelle, which starts at Place de la Resistance and continues down the broad Avenue Hassan II. Taxis are best for trekking between the ville nouvelle and the medina.

BY BUS All buses within the city cost 1.60dh. The most useful is Bus 9, which stops near the Syndicat d'Initiative and the youth hostel (if you ask the driver). Bus 10 stops at the train station, at Bab el Mahrouk (near Bab Boujeloud), and near the Merenid Tombs.

WHERE TO SLEEP

Most cheap hotels are just inside Bab Boujeloud in Fès el Bali; expect small rooms, odd smells, and poor lighting. If you want to pay substantially less than 30dh per person, the only place worth considering is Fès's phenomenal youth hostel.

➤ **UNDER 75DH • Hotel Cascade.** Right inside Bab Boujeloud; terrace has view of the busy gateway. Rooms are musty but adequate, with stench-filled showers that occasionally run hot. Doubles 60dh. *Bab Boujeloud, tel. 05/63–54–68.*

Hotel du Commerce. The best choice in Fès el Jdid, opposite the Royal Palace. Very clean, comfy rooms; some share a large terrace. Expect noise from nearby market. Doubles 60dh. *Pl. des Alaouites.*

Hotel du Jardin Public. Sixty meters outside Bab Boujeloud, down a short alley. Rooms are clean but a bit cramped and dark. Friendly managers and reliable plumbing mean this place is often full. Doubles 60dh. *153 Kasbah Boujeloud, tel. 05/63–30–86. Free hot showers (except in summer).*

Hotel Erraha. Just outside Bab Boujeloud. Large rooms and firm beds. Hold your nose in the toilet. Doubles 50dh. *Kasbah Boujeloud, tel. 05/63–32–26. Free cold showers.*

➤ **UNDER 150DH • Hotel Kairouan.** Between the train station and the ville nouvelle's Place de la Resistance, in a quiet neighborhood with a few nearby restaurants. Hot water—no problem. Doubles 103dh, 121dh with bath. *84 Rue Soudan, tel. 05/62–35–90. From Pl. de la Resistance turn right on Rue d'Angleterre, walk 2 blocks farther and turn right again.*

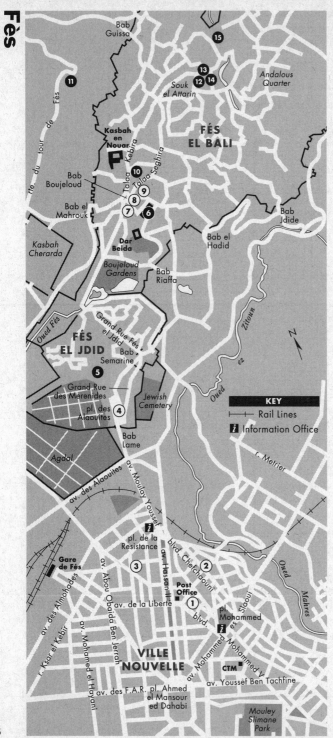

Fès

MOROCCO

Sights ●

Attarine
Medersa, **12**

Bou Inania
Medersa, **10**

Dar Batha
Museum, **6**

Kairaouine
Mosque, **13**

Merenid Tombs, **11**

Royal Palace, **5**

Seffarine
Medersa, **14**

Tanneries, **15**

Lodging ○

Hotel Cascade, **9**

Hotel du
Commerce, **4**

Hotel du Jardin
Public, **7**

Hotel Erraha, **8**

Hotel Kairouan, **3**

Hotel Olympic, **1**

Youth Hostel, **2**

KEY

├─┤ Rail Lines

𝒊 Information Office

Bab Guissa

(15)

Andalous Quarter

(13)
(12) (14)

Souk el Attarin

FÈS EL BALI

(11)

rte. du tour de Fès

Kasbah en Nouar

Talaa Kebira

Talaa Seghira

Bab Boujeloud

(10)

(9)
(8)
(7) (6)

Bab el Mahrouk

Bab Jdide

Kasbah Cherarda

Dar Beida

Boujeloud Gardens

Bab el Hadid

Bab Riaffa

Oued Fès

FÈS EL JDID

Grand Rue Fès el Jdid

Bab Semarine

Zitoun

(5)

Grand Rue des Merenides

Jewish Cemetery

pl. des Alaouïtes (4)

Oued ez

Bab Lame

N

Agdal

av. des Alaouïtes

av. Mouley Youssef

r. Metrier

KEY

├─┤ Rail Lines

𝒊 Information Office

blvd. Chefchaouni

Oued

Mahres

𝒊

pl. de la Resistance

Gare de Fès

(3)

(2)

av. Abou Obaïda Ben Jerrah

av. Hassan II

Post Office

(1)

r. Ksar el Kebir

av. des Almohades

av. de la Liberté

blvd.

pl. Mohammed

𝒊

av. Mohamed el Hayani

av. Mohammed V

av. Mohammed V

VILLE NOUVELLE

CTM ■

av. des F.A.R. pl. Ahmed el Mansour ed Dahabi

av. Youssef Ben Tachfine

Mouley Slimane Park

Hotel Olympic. Centrally located in the ville nouvelle. Comfortable rooms with small balconies. Scads of hot water. Doubles 135dh, 175dh with bath. *Blvd. Mohammed V at Rue 3, tel. 05/62–45–29. Restaurant, bar.*

HOSTEL **HI Association des Auberges de Jeunes de Fès.** In ville nouvelle, an easy 1-km trek from train station. Friendly, experienced manager gives the lowdown on hustlers. Expect bunk beds, cold showers, and a kitchen. HI members receive priority and pay 15dh; non-HI members pay 17.50dh. *18 Rue Adbeslam Seghrini, tel. 05/62–40–85. Bus 9 from tourist office (1.60dh; ask driver to stop) or taxi from train station (pay no more than 15dh). Reception open 8–9, noon–3, and 6–10. 10 PM curfew.*

CAMPGROUND **Diamant Vert.** Tons of trees and space in the Ain Chkef forest 5 km southwest of town. Campers get free use of water park; loud music makes that corner of site noisy. Take Bus 17 (20 min, 1.70dh) from Avenue de la Liberté (stop is near post office). 20dh per person, 15dh per tent. *Tel. 05/60–83–68. Free hot showers, restaurant.*

FOOD

In the medina there's a good selection of restaurants near Bab Boujeloud. In Fès el Jdid look for similar places at the southern end of Grande Rue de Fès el Jdid. If cleanliness is a serious concern, try the restaurants along Boulevard Mohammed V in the ville nouvelle.

Al Khozama Fast Food. Ville-nouvelle restaurant with wide selection—tajine, fish, and couscous (25dh–35dh) as well as French dishes like mushroom crêpes (35dh). Sit by a noisy TV or choke on traffic fumes outside. *23 Av. Mohammed es Slaoui, ½ block west of Blvd. Mohammed V, tel. 05/62–23–77.*

Restaurant Bouayad. A touristy, ville nouvelle–style eatery in Fès el Bali. It's spacious, cool, and dependable: 40dh for tajine, couscous, or pastilla. *26 Bab Boujeloud, tel. 05/63–62–78.*

Restaurant du Centre. Paper tablecloths for your doodling pleasure. Eat with Moroccans in this dark, no-nonsense place with first-rate chicken tajine (30dh). Fixed-price meals start at 45dh. *105 Blvd. Mohammed V, tel. 05/62–28–28.*

WORTH SEEING

If you're courageous enough to explore the medina without a guide, Talaa Kebira is one of two main streets that run northeast from Bab Boujeloud through the heart of Fès el Bali. The only "official" sight in Fès el Jdid is the mammoth Dar el Makhzen (Royal Palace). It's closed to the public, but you get a decent view from Place des Alaouites. The ville nouvelle, although comfortable and busy, doesn't offer any noteworthy sights.

TALAA KEBIRA AND BOU INANIA MEDERSA Enter Bab Boujeloud and push past the swarm of unofficial guides lying in wait, then take the first left onto **Talaa Kebira,** which leads through the medina toward Kairaouine Mosque. Walking this cramped, aromatic lane is what Fès el Bali is all about: Dodging donkeys and vulturous merchants, you pass scores of stalls laden with mint, mountains of olives, and exotic fruits. One hundred meters from your

---

The Steamy Truth about Hammams

The scarcity of hot water in Fès is tolerable because "cold" water is generally tepid. Nonetheless, hammams (bathhouses) are still the best place to bathe; bring a suit or extra pair of underwear, soap, shampoo, and towel. Admission is rarely more than 10dh, a few dirham more for a massage. Hours are noon–8 PM for women, 8 AM–noon and 8 PM–1 AM for men. Non-Muslims may not be admitted on Thursdays and Fridays. In Fès el Bali there's a hammam by Bab Boujeloud, on the first street to your right.

entry point, on the right, is the **Bou Inania Medersa** (admission 10dh; open daily 9–6), the largest and most beautiful of the Koranic schools built in Fès by the 14th-century Merenid dynasty. Medersas were chiefly dorms for poor students who studied at nearby mosques, and their construction was at once an act of charity, a proof of religious devotion, and a monument to the builder, in this case Sultan Abou Inan (1351–58). The medersa's walls are incredibly dense in their decoration; also notice the cedar ceilings, the ablution fountain in the courtyard, and the oratory (no admittance). Students once lived in the small, bare rooms upstairs, which are sometimes open for a peek.

KAIRAOUINE MOSQUE AND AROUND Talaa Kebira eventually becomes **Rue ech Cherabliyin** (Slipper Makers' Street). Shortly thereafter look for Cherabliyin Mosque on your left and Fès's central market, the **Souk el Attarin** (Spice Sellers' Market), on your right. The giant **Kairaouine Mosque** is ahead on your right, at the street's end. Founded in AD 859 and enlarged under the Almoravid and Merenid dynasties, the mosque has long been one of Islam's chief intellectual centers, drawing students from Europe and beyond. The university was moved to the ville nouvelle in 1947, and Kairaouine is now used exclusively for prayer; non-Muslims aren't allowed in, but tour groups continually cluster at the main door to gawk. The mosque is hard to find despite its size: The encircling street is narrow and looks like any other medina lane, densely packed with people and animals.

The concept of zero was reputedly invented at Kairaouine Mosque.

It's harder to miss the large bronze door of **Attarine Medersa** (admission 10dh; open Sat.–Thurs. 9–noon and 3–6), across Souk el Attarin from the mosque. This smaller, slightly older structure rivals the workmanship of Bou Inania, especially with Attarine's complicated floor tiling, patterned with stars and other celestial shapes. At Attarine, non-Muslims may enter the oratory, which is not used for prayer (the roof, if open, offers an enlightening view of Karaouine Mosque). Circumnavigate the mosque until you reach the small **Place Seffarine**, where brass workers share stalls, then head down a tiny lane on the square's southeast side to **Seffarine Medersa** (admission 10dh; open Sat.–Thurs. 9–noon and 3–6), the oldest of Fès's Koranic schools (AD 1280). Every guided tour of the neighborhood also visits the **tanneries** near Oued Fès (Fès River), accessed by an unmarked lane on Place Seffarine's northeast corner. If you're lost, follow the stench of cow, sheep, goat, and camel skins that have been laid out to dry before being dyed. For many, these medieval tanneries are an intense, stick-with-you-forever experience: especially memorable is the network of round dye pits, some bright yellow and blue, some murky brown and blood red, some filled with pigeon shit and slithery entrails.

CHEAP THRILLS

Late one afternoon, hot and sweaty, climb the hill above the medina for an inspiring view. Your first stop should be the posh **Hotel Les Merenides,** where you can sit on the terrace sipping a real beer (this is a Europeanized, air-conditioned hotel, so let loose). Your next stop should be the nearby **Merenid Tombs,** a few pieces of ancient defenses that overlook Fès's ocher walls

---

Necessary Evils

Guides are an unfortunate necessity in Fès el Bali: necessary because the medina is so labyrinthine and confusing; unfortunate because, well, they cost money. Official guides booked through the tourist office make peanuts from the half-day fee (30dh)—the real money comes from commissions, which is why you'll spend most of the day trekking from carpet warehouse to pottery store to engraving shop. Be firm, and refuse to enter shops if you do not want to buy. A hit-or-miss option are unofficial guides (some are greedy bloodsuckers, some friendly students with kind hearts). Most congregate around Bab Boujeloud and charge 30dh for a half-day tour.

and white rooftops. From Bab Boujeloud walk through the bus station square and turn right, exiting through Bab el Mahrouk. Follow the road to your right and climb the hill.

Rabat

A stop in "Raba," as the capital is known, provides an easy break from the rigors—and the excitement—of traveling in Morocco. Due to the royal presence (Rabat is the king's primary residence), it's a showcase city without much in the way of character. Rabat's true appeal lies in its (relatively) laid-back demeanor, which means you can talk to people on the street without the constant worry of being hustled. For some stress-prone backpackers, this is enough to recommend a short stay in Morocco's fourth-largest city.

Once a launching point for the Muslim conquest of Spain and then an autonomous port noted for its mercenary pirate fleets (the Salé Rovers, scourge of Spanish treasure galleons), Rabat regained prominence as the French administrative center of Morocco in 1912. After independence in 1956, Rabat was crowned capital, even though Casablanca was (and still is) the country's financial and industrial leader. Still, modern Rabat is home to most foreign embassies and to wide, calm streets where nothing much seems to happen. After a day or two of strolling about, you'll be ready to move on to the real Morocco.

BASICS

VISITOR INFORMATION **Syndicat d'Initiative.** Think twice before making the 15-minute trek for this office's few maps and brochures. *22 Rue Al Jazair, tel. 07/73–05–62. From train station, follow Av. Mohammed V south to Grand Mosque and turn left on Av. Moulay Hassan, which turns into Rue Al Jazair. Open Mon.–Thurs. 8–noon and 2:45–6:30, Fri. 8–11:30 and 3–6:30.*

EMBASSIES **Canada.** Australians should inquire here, as well. *13 Rue Jaafar Assadik (Agdal), tel. 07/77–13–75.*

United Kingdom. *17 Blvd. Tour Hassan, tel. 07/72–09–05 or 07/72–09–06. Open weekdays 8–11:30 (also 2–5 PM for British citizens).*

United States. *2 Av. de Marrakesh, tel. 07/76–22–65. Open weekdays 8:30–12:30 and 2:30–5:30.*

PHONES AND MAIL The post office is near the train station; the 24-hour poste restante and phone annex are across the street. *Av. Mohammed V at Rue Soekarno, tel. 16 for general info. Open weekdays 8:30–6:30.*

COMING AND GOING

BY TRAIN Do not get off the train at Rabat-Agdal (also called Rabat-Salé); if you're headed into Rabat proper, you want the **Rabat-Ville station,** in the center of town. You can exchange money inside the station at the BMCE booth (open weekdays 8:15–6:45, weekends and holidays 9:15–5:45). Trains head to Aéroport Mohammed V (1¼ hrs, 50dh), Fès (4 hrs, 62.50dh), Marrakech (5 hrs, 71dh), and Tangier (5 hrs, 79dh). *Av. Mohammed V, tel. 07/76–73–53.*

BY BUS The station for all buses is on the road to Casablanca, 3 km southwest of Rabat on Place Zerktouni. To reach the depot take Bus 30 (2.70dh each way) or a petit taxi (less than 10dh). From Rabat, **CTM** (tel. 07/79–51–24) serves Tangier (67dh), Fès (47.50dh), and scads of nearby villages. Grands taxis bound for Casablanca and Marrakech also depart from the Place Zerktouni terminal; prices are negotiable but usually end up 10%–15% higher than the corresponding bus fare. Between Rabat and Aéroport Mohammed V, buses (50dh) run every 90 minutes from 5 AM–6:30 PM. The stop is in front of Hotel Terminus, across the street from the train station.

WHERE TO SLEEP

Hotels along Avenue Mohammed V are safe bets. However, the real deals are in the medina, along Rue Souika and Rue des Consuls. That said, as you disappear farther into the medina, the skank quotient goes way up.

Hotel de France. A spartan, cheap hotel to your left as you enter the medina on Rue Mohammed V. No showers, and you'll have to share a hall toilet. Doubles 50dh. *46 Rue Souk Semara, tel. 07/72–34–57.*

Hotel Gaulois. A few blocks from the medina, and noticeably plush and touristy. Although not exactly a splurge, there's a bar, and hot showers around the clock. Doubles 74dh, 95dh with shower. *1 Zankat Hims, tel. 07/72–30–22. From Blvd. Hassan II, walk 1 block south on Av. Mohammed V, then turn right on Zankat Hims.*

Hotel Kasbah. With a sunny, colorful courtyard and clean rooms, this is a prime find. The clerk speaks fair English and is eager to negotiate with budget travelers. Doubles 62dh. *22 Zankat Sidi M'hamed El Ghazi, no tel. Enter medina on Rue Mohammed V and make second right at HOTEL sign.*

HOSTEL **Auberge de Jeunesse (HI).** Two minutes from the medina, with surprisingly well-kept gardens inside. On the down side, the bathrooms are grim and the showers teeth-chatteringly cold. Beds 25dh. *43 Rue Marassa, Bab el Had, tel. 07/72–57–69. From train station, turn left on Av. Mohammed V to medina, left through city wall, then right. Lockout 10–noon and 3–6.*

FOOD

La Clef. Lounge on couches and comfy pillows while you chomp on crispy, cinnamon-covered chicken pastilla (30dh); there's also a daily fixed-price menu (45dh). Before noon and after 7 PM, try the downstairs café. *On small lane off Av. Moulay Youssef, tel. 07/76–19–72. From train station, turn right, then right again at Hotel Terminus.*

Restaurant Saadi. This is culinary heaven—honest. Try the delicious *tajine de kefta* (spicy meatballs served with an egg; 60dh); it's brought simmering to your table. A complete meal starts at about 75dh. *23 Av. Allal Ben Abdallah, at Rue le Caire, tel. 07/73–10–28. 4 blocks south of medina, on first street east of Av. Mohammed V.*

Restaurant Taghazout. Chicken tajine and other standards like *harira* (bean soup with meat) go for 19.50dh. For breakfast try an omelet. *7 Rue Sebbahi, tel. 07/72–40–61. Off Rue Mohammed V, third right from medina entrance.*

WORTH SEEING

Rabat's layout is easy to grasp: Boulevard Hassan II runs east–west along the medina walls, and Avenue Mohammed V slices through the medina (where it's renamed "Rue"), intersects Boulevard Hassan II, and passes the post office and train station.

KASBAH DES OUDAIAS Originally the site of a 10th century *ribat* (a fortified camp), the kasbah became in 1146 the launching point for the newly established *jihad* (religious war) against Christian Spain. Three hundred years later the intolerant Spanish monarchy expelled most Muslims from the Iberian peninsula; some sought refuge here, leaving the kasbah and its surrounding streets with an Andalusian look. The fortress's main attraction is the impressive **Bab Oudaïa** (at the top of the outside steps), a masterpiece of Almohad architecture. From the gate, the kasbah's short main street leads to a large platform with intense views of the sea and the Bou Regreg river. The lower kasbah entrance opens onto the peaceful **Andalusian Gardens,** a **craft museum** (admission 10dh; open Wed.–Mon.) with manuscripts and Berber jewelry, and an outdoor café. Don't bother with the guides at the entrance—the kasbah is small and accessible. *From Rue Mohammed V in medina take Rue Souika almost to end; turn left on Rue des Consuls. Open daily 8 AM–sunset.*

HASSAN TOWER AND MOHAMMED V MAUSOLEUM The Almohad sultan Yacoub el Mansour celebrated his conquest of North Africa and Spain by initiating construction of the giant **Hassan Mosque,** designed to hold 20,000 people. Upon his death in AD 1199, work stopped permanently. All that remains is the 170-foot-tall minaret, staring forlornly over the city, and the structure's sand-worn support columns. Also here is the **Mohammed V Mausoleum,** resting place of the current king's father, who died in 1961. The mausoleum is an ornate Moroccan version of Napoléon's tomb in Paris, complete with stern-faced royal guards in cream-color capes. *Follow Blvd. Hassan II east to river, then look right. Open daily 8 AM–sunset.*

CHELLAH The Merenid sultan Abou el Hassan built the fortified walls of the necropolis Chellah in the early 14th century, yet the site was inhabited much earlier: There's archaeological evidence of a Phoenician settlement dating from 700 BC and the visible remains of ancient Rome's southernmost African colony. A flight of stairs to the right of the entrance lead to Merenid tombs and a mosque. But it's Chellah's lush gardens that are most enjoyable—a clear stream and tranquil views over the river Bou Regreg. *Outside Bab Zaër, at south end of Av. Yacoub el Mansour. Admission: 10dh. Open daily 8 AM–sunset.*

MUSEE ARCHEOLOGIQUE The best finds from Morocco's most important Roman site—Volubilis, near Meknes—are on display in this small but worthwhile museum. Highlights include the celebrated bronze *Guard Dog* and two marble heads named after their possible models, Cato the Younger and King Juba II of Numidia. *Zankat el Brihi. From train station walk south on Av. Yacoub el Mansour, turn left on Av. Moulay al 'Hassan, then right on Zankat el Brihi. Admission: 10dh. Open Wed.–Mon. 9–noon and 3–6.*

NEAR RABAT

CASABLANCA You idolize the Bogart-Bergman film, but so what? Casablanca is definitely not worth a special trip, and if you happen to fly into its Aéroport Mohammed V, do yourself a favor and take the bus or train directly to Rabat for a gentler introduction to Morocco. That said, if you're going to spend the night waiting for a train or bus, don't be afraid to take a quick dip in the city's Westernized, dense urban crush. The two faces of Casablanca, old and new, stare at each other across **Place Mohammed V.** This turbulent intersection is flanked on the north by the souks and food stalls of the hustler-infested medina and on the south and east by banks, hotels, and tourist shops. If the government had its way, it would like you to think Casablanca was more like **Place des Nations Unies,** a large, fountain-filled square where millions of pigeons live in harmony with a mixed crowd of locals and tourists. Smart-looking French-colonial buildings line the square, but it's hard to feel that this is the real Morocco.

➤ **BASICS** • For general information and a small guidebook packed with phone numbers and maps, stop by the friendly, English-speaking **Syndicat d'Initiative** (98 Blvd. Mohammed V, tel. 02/22–15–24; open Mon.–Sat. 9–noon and 3–6, Sun. 9–noon). Expect the usual services from **American Express** (Voyages Schwartz, 112 Av. du Prince Moulay Abdullah, tel. 02/27–80–54; open weekdays 8:30–noon and 2:30–6:30, Sat. 8:30–noon). If you're naughty, contact the **United States consulate** (8 Blvd. Moulay Youssef, tel. 02/26–45–50; open weekdays 9–12:30 and 1:30–5:30) or the **Great Britain consulate** (60 Blvd. d'Anfa, tel. 02/26–14–41; open daily 9–noon and 2–5).

➤ **COMING AND GOING** • Most international flights to Morocco land at **Aéroport Mohammed V** (tel. 02/33–91–00), 28 km southwest of Casablanca. An hourly **shuttle** (20dh, exact change required) heads to Casablanca's main bus station; or take a train (from a station below the airport) to Casablanca (25dh) or Rabat (50dh). If you're headed to Casablanca by train, stay on until you reach the centrally located **Casa Port** station (tel. 02/22–30–11); it's at the north end of Boulevard Houphouët-Boigny. From here you can catch a train to Rabat (24.50dh), Marrakech (68dh), Fès (87dh), or Tangier (103dh).

Casablanca's main bus station, **CTM Gare Routière** (23 Rue Leon l'Africain, tel. 02/31–20–61), is behind Hotel Safir on Avenue des F.A.R., a five-minute walk east of Place Mohammed V. Buses go to el Jedida (2 hrs, 17dh), Rabat (1½ hrs, 22dh), Marrakech (4 hrs, 57.50dh), and Fès (6 hrs, 69dh). Private bus lines operate from the **Dar Ben Jdia** station, off Rue de Strasbourg. A petit taxi to Dar Ben Jdia should cost less than 15dh.

➤ **WHERE TO SLEEP** • **Auberge de Jeunes (HI).** This excellent youth hostel is the cheapest option in town; dorm beds (including breakfast) are 30dh, 33dh without HI card. Clean rooms, colorful tiles, and a high ceiling make for cool, comfy lounging. *6 Pl. Admiral Philbert, tel. 02/22–05–51. From Casa Port, walk west on Blvd. des Almohades and head left up curved driveway through medina wall; hostel is on right. Reception open daily 8–10, noon–2, and 6–11.*

Hotel Mon Rêve. A good bargain among the several safe, cheap hotels near the CTM bus station. Often full. Free hot showers in hallway. Doubles 62dh. *7 Rue Colbert, ½ block west of CTM station, tel. 02/31–14–39.*

Marrakech

Marrakech commands the southern part of the country just as Fès commands the north; but while Fès contains grand Andalusian mosques, Marrakech has palm trees, desert-bound caravans, and oceans of sand. The High Atlas mountains, south of Marrakech and just out of sight, have kept the Sahara at bay for centuries. Yet in many ways Marrakech is *the* gateway to North Africa's torpid, sun-baked interior. It may not be *Lawrence of Arabia* come to life, but this crowded desert town seems to validate even the most romantic images of North Africa. With a population of nearly 2 million, it's also the largest city in Morocco after Casablanca.

BASICS

VISITOR INFORMATION ONMT in Gueliz (Marrakech's ville nouvelle) has maps and can arrange guides. *Place Abdelmoumen Ben Ali, on Av. Mohammed V at Rue de Yougoslavie, tel. 04/44–88–89. Open Mon.–Sat. 8:30–noon and 2:30–6:30.*

In Marrakech the sun beats down relentlessly and slows life to a mellow pace. Not until dusk do the souks bustle with bodies and trade.

AMERICAN EXPRESS *Voyages Schwartz, Rue Mauritania, tel. 04/43–66–00. From tourist office, walk 2 blocks south on Av. Mohammed V and turn right. Open daily 6 AM–11 PM; exchange desk open weekdays 8:30–11:30 and 2:30–4.*

PHONES AND MAIL The **main post office** (Pl. du 16 Novembre; open weekdays 8:30–noon and 4–6:30) is in Gueliz at the corner of Mohammed V and Hassan II. The phone office is open daily 7 AM–9 PM. In the medina there's a **post office** in the southwest corner of Place Djemaa el Fna, next to Place de Foucauld. The phone annex (open Mon.–Thurs. 8–noon and 4–7, Fri. 7–11:30 and 4–7) is around the corner and down a flight of stairs.

COMING AND GOING

BY TRAIN The **train station** (Av. Hassan II, tel. 04/44–77–68) is on the far side of Gueliz, five minutes from the hostel and campsite and 30 minutes from the medina. Catch Bus 3 or 8 across the street for the CTM bus station and Place Djemaa el Fna (1.20dh). Trains from Marrakech serve Casablanca (3½ hrs, 52.50dh), Tangier (9 hrs, 134dh), and Fès (9 hrs, 121.50dh).

BY BUS The **Place Mourabiton** bus station is at the medina's northwest gate (Bab Doukkala), some 20 minutes by foot from Place Djemaa el Fna. From the station, cross the street and take Bus 3 (1.70dh) to the medina; buses to the train station depart from in front of the bus depot. From Place Mourabiton, CTM (tel. 04/43–44–02) serves Casablanca (4 hrs, 57.50dh), Fès (7 hrs, 110dh), and Tangier (10 hrs, 130dh).

BY PLANE Marrakech's **airport** (Rte. de l'Aéroport, tel. 04/44–74–84) is 5 km southwest of the city, past the Menara Gardens. For most destinations, you have to change planes at Casablanca. Taxi fare to or from the medina should be 30dh–50dh. Bus 11 also makes the trip into town (2dh); to reach the unmarked stop, leave the terminal parking lot, turn left, and walk for about 10 minutes to the main road (cross the road and flag a bus). Contact **RAM** (Av. Mohammed V, tel. 04/43–62–05) for flight information; if no one answers, try the airport number.

GETTING AROUND

In the medina, everything radiates from the triangular Place Djemaa el Fna, one of Morocco's most intriguing open-air squares. It's bordered by cheap hotels to the south and souks to the north. Local buses stop on its west side, on the tree-filled Place de Foucauld. From Place Djemaa el Fna, Rue Bab Agnaou heads south to the Sa'adi Tombs and other sights, and Avenue Mohammed V, Marrakech's principal street, runs northwest into Gueliz. At Place du 16 Novembre it intersects Avenue Hassan II, which leads eventually to the train station.

BY BUS AND TAXI Bus 1 runs up and down Avenue Mohammed V, between the Place de Foucauld and Gueliz (1.60dh). Buses 3 and 8 travel between Place de Foucauld, the bus station, and the train station (1.70dh). Petits taxis are your best bet for the Agdal and Menara gardens. A trip between the medina and the train station should cost 10dh–15dh. Remember that rates increase 50% after dark.

BY CALECHE Horse-drawn carriages charge 35dh–40dh for short treks through the medina. Get ready to bargain if you're interested in a leisurely, more comprehensive tour. Carriages line up on the street between Koutoubia Minaret and Place Djemaa el Fna.

WHERE TO SLEEP

Cheap, nearly identical hotels lie just south of Place Djemaa el Fna, about 80 meters east of Hotel CTM. Another clump of cheapo hotels is on Rue de Bab Agnaou, just west of Hotel CTM. Whichever you choose, bring earplugs.

➤ **UNDER 75DH • Hotel Eddakhla.** Ambitious, eager-to-please management draws foreigners as well as Moroccans. Small kitchen, large terrace, clean sheets. Doubles 50dh. *43 Sidi Bouloukate, tel. 04/44–23–59. Follow Rue de Bab Agnaou from Pl. Djemaa el Fna; turn left at first alley, then take first right, then first left. Hot showers 5dh.*

Hotel Essaouira. A first-rate choice next to Hotel Medina. A café on the rooftop terrace gives sweeping views of Koutoubia Minaret and the Atlas mountains in the distance. Some rooms are spacious; ask to see several before choosing. About 30dh per person. *3 Derb Sidi Bouloukate, tel. 04/44–38–05. Hot showers 5dh.*

Hotel Medina. Great location and conscientious managers who mop daily. Only 10 rooms, each differently priced; doubles start at 50dh. Reserve in advance. *1 Derb Sidi Bouloukate, tel. 04/44–29–97. Walk through hotel arch, past Hotel de France; it's down first alley on right. Hot showers 5dh.*

➤ **UNDER 150DH • Hotel CTM.** Front and center on Place Djemaa el Fna. Its classified status means clean rooms and a large, mat-covered courtyard. Breakfast on the terrace costs 16dh extra. Doubles 71dh, 81dh with shower. *Pl. Djemaa el Fna, southwest corner of plaza, next to hotel arch, tel. 04/44–23–25.*

Hotel Gallia. Slightly farther south in medina. Nineteen lovely rooms, most with flowers on the desk and a toilet and bathtub. When air-conditioning is installed, it'll become classified and more expensive. Doubles 127dh. *30 Rue de la Recette, tel. 04/445–913. From Pl. Djemaa el Fna follow Rue Bab Agnaou to third alley on left; walk to end and look for sign. AE, MC, V.*

HOSTEL **HI Auberge de Jeunesse.** In Gueliz near the train station—convenient, but far from the medina sights. Good for evening arrivals and always has space. Cold showers, seatless toilets. Beds in dorms 20dh. When it's slow, HI cards are not strictly necessary. *Rue el Jahid, tel. 04/44–77–31. Turn right from train station, make first left, and walk past Tony's Bar to end, then turn right. Reception open daily 8–9, noon–2, and 6–10.*

CAMPGROUND **Camping Caravan de Marrakech.** Close to train station. Plenty of trees and a swimming pool. Often packed—call ahead about new campsites to open soon. 10dh per person. *Av. de France, tel. 04/43–66–18 or 04/43–66–17. Turn left from train station to first large intersection and turn right on Av. de France. Lukewarm showers, wheelchair access, café, market.*

FOOD

The restaurants on Rue Bani Marine, west of Place Djemaa el Fna through an arch next to the post office, are good for an oily, 25dh meal. If breakfast evokes visions of fried eggs, onions, bread, and mint tea (3.50dh), walk from Place de Foucauld along the southern wall of Koutoubia Minaret (the lane is called Rue Ibn Khaldoun); at the first square you'll notice the smell of sizzling onions wafting from a handful of food stands.

➢ **UNDER 40DH • Café Chaabia.** A good budget choice in Gueliz. Twelve dirhams buys a plate of fish, beef, or chicken; 3dh buys a spicy tomato "salad" you sop up with bread. *73 Blvd. Moulay Rachid, tel. 04/43–28–50. From train station, walk east on Av. Hassan II, 3 blocks past large Av. de France intersection, and turn left on Rue Mauretania.*

Café Toubkal. If you'd rather starve than eat at a food stand, try this quick, efficient, clean café by the hotel arch on Place Djemaa el Fna—there's no sign, so look for the red sunshade and white tables. Salad (5dh) is a good prelude to steak or brochettes with fries (25dh). *Bab Riad Zitoun, tel. 04/22–44–62.*

Chez Chegrouni. The best cheapo eatery on Place Djemaa el Fna has dirty yellow grating and ornery flies. Try the excellent chicken tajine (18dh) followed by a cup of sweetened yogurt (2dh). There is no sign. *Pl. Djemaa el Fna. Walk east from hotel arch past Café de France.*

➢ **UNDER 100DH • Hotel de Foucauld.** Tourists flock here for the thick harira, for wine and beer, and for the friendly waiters. Fixed-price meals start at 70dh. *Av. el Mouahidine, tel. 04/44–54–99. On Pl. de Foucauld, walk 250 feet south of Koutoubia Minaret.*

Restaurant Argana. The terrace offers stunning nighttime views of Place Djemaa el Fna. Chow on Frenchified Moroccan eats like lamb tajine with prunes (37.50dh). If you're feeling frisky, try the horse-meat burger. *1 Souk Jadid, on Pl. Djemaa el Fna, tel. 04/44–53–50.*

CAFES Watch the famous rosy sunsets of Gueliz at **Cafeteria le Jet de l'Eau** (Pl. de Liberte, tel. 04/44–69–54), at the intersection with the large, inoperative fountain, halfway up Avenue Mohammed V. A good choice for pastries is **Mik Mak** (Rue Moulay Ismail, tel. 04/44–14–19), a popular French-style patisserie next to Hotel Ali on Place de Foucauld. Baguettes cost 1dh, chocolate croissants 1.60dh.

WORTH SEEING

Don't bother covering Marrakech in a logical manner—the real joy is wandering aimlessly in Place Djemaa el Fna and the surrounding souks, which are extensive but manageable even without a guide. If you're pressed for time and/or not in the mood to deal with hustlers, hire an official guide from ONMT in Gueliz (*see* Visitor Information *in* Basics, *above*).

PLACE DJEMAA EL FNA By day this triangular plaza is filled with photogenic snake charmers, microphone-blaring salesmen, and trained monkeys. Chocolate sellers peddle unwrapped gobs of fly-covered goo, and itinerant merchants hawk daggers, fried fish, hash pipes, Koranic texts, and popcorn. Beggars beat their palms for money, and water carriers negotiate the thick crowds. As the sun rises higher and the heat becomes unbearable, the crowds melt away. As dusk approaches, the square is revived by fortune-tellers, drummers, guitarists, and animated storytellers. One sober piece of advice: When exploring the medina, leave your valuables behind and stay alert.

Lording it over the plaza is the 200-foot-tall **Koutoubia Minaret,** visible from nearly every approach. Construction of the tower began in about 1158 and was completed in 1190 under Yacoub el Mansour, the same Almohad sultan who commissioned Rabat's (still unfinished) Hassan Mosque. Entrance is forbidden to non-Muslims.

The name Place Djemaa el Fna means "Assembly of the Dead," recalling a time when freshly decapitated heads were displayed here as a warning to would-be thieves.

SOUKS To explore the labyrinthine network of souks north of Place Djemaa el Fna, move to the eastern side of the square and, with your back to the white GRAND TERRASSE CAFÉ DE FRANCE sign, walk straight ahead down Rue Souk Smarine, the medina's main thoroughfare. Cloth is the big seller here, with nuts, figs, and lots of schlocky tourist stuff thrown in. Farther down, the street splits in two: Souk Attarin is to the left, Souk el Kebir straight ahead. Before the split, look for the right-hand entrance to **Rahba Kedima,** a small square where medicinal and so-called magical herbs are sold. An alley at the far (north) end of the herb market opens onto the **Criée Berbère** (Berber Carpet Market), which caters mostly to tourists (prices here are only so-so).

Back at the split, continue straight on Souk el Kebir. After it turns 90° to the left, make the first right and continue straight. To the left (in the open-air square) is the entrance to **Koubba al Baroudiyin** (admission 10dh), an 11th-century mosque that, despite the many sackings of Marrakech, has survived a millennium largely intact.

More interesting by far is the nearby **Ben Youssef Medersa** (admission 10dh); from the Koubba's entrance, continue straight down the street with the grillwork on the windows. Founded in the 14th century by Abu el Hassan, the "Black Sultan" who built many of Marrakech's mosques and Koranic schools, this medersa is noted for its stunning decorative detail. Go upstairs and duck into some of the tiny rooms where students once lived; you enter via a long, dark corridor that leads to a courtyard filled with tile mosaics. An intriguing detour from here are the **tanneries** east of the medersa (go past the entrance and turn right at the first fork, then walk straight for 10 minutes). Once you're within spittin' distance, you'll be accosted by snotty little kids eager to be your guides—offer no more than 10dh.

SA'ADI TOMBS The diminutive Sa'adi cemetery is strewn with the narrow graves of 162 princes and members of the elite who were buried facing Mecca; all of the bodies were interred between 1557 and 1792 but not rediscovered until 1911. Most of the structure was built by Sultan Ahmed el Mansour, who is remembered for getting rich in the 16th-century conquest of Timbuktu. He also built the **El Badi Palace** (admission 10dh), now a ruin. You can still see the palace's pools and wander the small maze of underground prisons. *From Pl. Djemaa el Fna, walk south on Bab Agnaou and turn left through Bab Agnaou gate; tombs are straight ahead. For El Badi Palace, turn left through Bab Agnaou gate and right at first street to Pl. des Ferblantiers; walk across parking lot and through arch in wall.*

NEAR MARRAKESH

HIGH ATLAS MOUNTAINS **Djebel Toubkal,** the highest mountain (4,167 meters) in North Africa, is a popular trek from Marrakech. In terms of scenery, it's everything you imagine Morocco to be—sun beaten and rugged, surrounded by vast stretches of desert where few tourists tread. In terms of getting there, it's a definite hassle, requiring a few bumpy bus rides into the sweltering heart of the Atlas Mountains. Another word of caution: Only experienced climbers should attempt Toubkal in winter, when nighttime temperatures drop far below freezing. In spring and summer, when the area swarms with backpackers and amateur walkers, the weather turns hot and windy. If you're a serious hiker bring your own gear—tent, sturdy boots, cooking gear, food, you name it.

To reach Toubkal, head first for **Asni,** a tiny town filled with hustlers (do not to accept invitations to anyone's home or to visit "nearby" Berber villages). In Marrakech catch a grand taxi (1 hr, 15dh per person) ouside the Bab er Robb gate at the south end of Rue Bab Agnaou. It's a nail-biting trip on a narrow mountain road that overlooks a long, treacherous drop. Asni's large **HI youth hostel** (tel. 44/7713) has plenty of 15dh dorm beds; head through the market arch, turn right, and walk about 100 meters.

From Asni head as quickly as possible to **Imlil,** a good base for the Toubkal climb. By *camionette* (pick-up truck) it costs 15dh from Asni, by grand traxi around 100dh. (In the off-season you may have to wait for a passing truck or until the taxi is filled with Imlil-bound travelers.) Although the asphalt disappears halfway through the hour-long trip, the roadside waterfalls, the cows grazing by the stream below, and the cool Moroccan breeze (for once) more than make up for the bumps. Imlil's **youth hostel,** run by the Club Alpin Francais (CAF), is a low stone structure next to the main parking lot (beds 20dh, 26dh without HI card). During summer it's popular among European backpackers, even despite the squat toilets, cold showers, and lack of bedding (bring your own sleeping bag or blanket). The small kitchen has a cooking range (4dh per hour). The privately-run **Ribat Tours** and the government-operated **Bureau des Guides et des Accompagnateurs,** both across the street from the hostel, provide guides and info on Toubkal. To reach the peak itself from Imlil, first walk 5–6 hours to CAF's **Neltner Refuge** (30dh, 35dh without HI card), spend the night, and make the three-hour ascent the following morning. If you're very clear on the route, a guide is not mandatory. However, if you have *any* doubts, definitely hire one of the officially qualified guides pictured on the bulletin boards outside Asni's and Imlil's hostels. The official guide rate is 160dh per day, more if you need supplies, boots, snow equipment, or mules (75dh). A map of the region is 75dh.

THE NETHERLANDS 17

By Christine Gomez

Traditionally, travelers have come to the Netherlands in search of windmills and watery canals, looking for fields of tulips as far as the eye can see and residents shod in wooden shoes. Certainly tulips grow in abundance in some rural areas, and those windmills are still pumping water from the marshy land, but since World War II the Netherlands has developed into a more urban (albeit tiny), culturally rich, hip hangout. Today's budget travelers are usually attracted by the country's reputation for political, social, and cultural progressivism and an anything-goes social scene.

The country spends a huge chunk of its tax revenue on social-welfare programs; the gap between poor and rich is relatively small, and the government subsidizes all sorts of educational and artistic pursuits. The Netherlands gained an even greater reputation for liberalism when it passed the world's least restrictive laws on euthanasia in 1993. The country's liberal bent goes all the way back to the open-door policy of the 17th century, when religious refugees arrived here from all over Europe. The Netherlands still has one of the most ethnically diverse populations in Europe, although many members of the country's ethnic minorities—mostly Indonesians, Surinamese, Turks, and Moroccans—argue that things aren't as rosy as they seem. Job prospects are dim for many of them, forcing them to live in rapidly growing ghettos.

The Dutch are unfailingly courteous and helpful, though they may not seem like the warmest bunch at first. Perhaps the ever-increasing population density is the reason they protect their privacy so vigilantly. Although the country is only half the size of Maine, the population is up

Water, Water, Everywhere

According to a Dutch proverb, "God made the world, but the Dutch made Holland." The proverb is truer than most. Since 500 BC, inhabitants of the Netherlands have fought the sea for possession of the land. More than half of this pancake-flat country has an altitude of less than 16 feet, making it extremely vulnerable to flooding, and, up until a few centuries ago, half of the country was under water. To wage war against the water, the Dutch have built dikes along all of the major inland rivers and the entire north coast. Those famous windmills you see on postcards are primarily used to drain lakes and keep the reclaimed land (known as polders) dry.

North Sea

Wadden Islands

Schiermonnikoog

Ameland

Terschelling

Dokkum

Groningen

Delfzijl

Winschoten

Wadden Islands

A7/E22

Leeuwarden

Drachten

Assen

N41

N34

Emmen

Vlieland

Harlingen

Bolsward

A32

N371

N28/E232

Hoogeveen

Texel

Sneek

A50

Meppel

N48

N34

Den Helder

Waddenzee

IJsselmeer

Zwolle

Almelo

N36

Hengelo

Enkhuizen

Lelystad

N35

A1/E30

Enschede

Hoorn

A28/E232

Deventer

Alkmaar

A6

Winterswijk

Purmerend

Apeldoorn

Doetinchem

Zaanstad

Amsterdam

Bussum

Hoge Veluwe
National Park

Haarlem

Hilversum

Amersfoort

Arnhem

Rhine

Zandvoort

A9

A1/E14

Rijn

Utrecht

A12/E35

Rijn

Oosterbeek

GERMANY

Leiden

A12

Gouda

Tiel

A50

Nijmegen

Scheveningen

E30

E25

Lek

A27

A15/E31

Oss

The Hague

Delft

Waal

Maas

's Hertogenbosch

Veghel

Rotterdam

Dordrecht

A59

Haringvliet

Overflakkee

Grevelingen

Eindhoven

A67/E34

Schouwen
Duiveland

Steenbergen

Breda

Tilburg

Tholen

A16/E19

Weert

Roermond

Oosterschelde

Bergen op Zoom

A2/E25

Goes

Béveland

A58

Sittard

Aachen

Walcheren

Middelburg

Westerschelde

Maastricht

Vaals

Breskens

Terneuzen

Antwerp

BELGIUM

Brussels

Liège

Roermond

Schelde

KEY

├─┤ Rail Lines

---- Ferry Lines

0 ___ 40 miles

0 ___ 60 km

N

to 15 million. To get to know the Dutch better, try hanging out at any neighborhood bar (known as brown cafés here), which is more like a home away from home than an escape from it for these people. Here locals of all ages take pleasure in each other's company (an idea embodied by the Dutch word *gezellig*) and they usually don't mind if a few out-of-towners join in.

Basics

MONEY $1 = 1.85 guilder and 1 guilder = 54¢. The guilder, written as Dfl, fl, or just f, as in this book, is divided into 100 cents. Banks usually have the best exchange rates and charge about f5 commission for changing cash or traveler's checks. Most banks in the Netherlands are open weekdays 9–4. Many banks in larger cities are also open Thursday 7 PM–9 PM and Saturday morning. Train stations usually have a **De Grenswisselkantoren (GWK)** office, which offers rates and fees similar to those of banks. If you have an ISIC, the GWKs waive the commission for cash exchanges. GWK offices are generally open Monday–Saturday 8–8 and Sunday 10–4. Try to avoid changing money at tourist offices and bureaux de change.

➤ **HOW MUCH IT WILL COST** • Compared with other Western European countries, the Netherlands is fairly inexpensive. You can spend as little as $25–$30 a day if you stay in hostels and really scrimp, $35–$40 if you stay in budget hotels and eat out once in a while. Doubles in an average budget hotel will set you back about f80, but camping is usually only f7. Fast food will fill you for f5, but expect to pay f10 in a cheap restaurant, f15–f20 in a relatively nice one. Train trips come cheap; you can travel about 40 km on f6. Admission to museums rarely costs more than f5.

COMING AND GOING Most travelers arrive by **train** at Amsterdam's busy Centraal Station (tel. 020/620–22–66 for international information). Eurolines (tel. 020/694–1791 in Amsterdam) **buses** run between London and Amsterdam's Amstel Station a few times per day. One-way tickets cost f85 if you're under 26; otherwise they are f95. You can also take Eurolines from Amsterdam to Scandinavian countries and, during the high season, to other European cities. To buy tickets, call Eurolines or go to the bucket shop, Budget Bus (Rokin 10, Amsterdam, tel. 020/627–5151). Amsterdam's Schiphol Airport (*see* Coming and Going *in* Amsterdam, *below*) is a popular destination for international **flights**. Flights from the United States generally cost as much as those to Paris or Frankfurt. The Netherlands' main **ferry** ports are in the Hook of Holland, Rotterdam, and Vlissingen. Many bus companies offer **bus-ferry-bus** combinations. Hoverspeed UK (tel. 081/554–7061 in London) goes from London to Amsterdam via the Dover–Calais ferry, as does Eurolines.

GETTING AROUND Since the country is so compact, getting from one town to another should be no problem. Trains are frequent, efficient, and cheap. Most cities are on the rail lines, and the nationalized bus system, charging comparable rates, is a good alternative for getting to more remote places. For information on buses and trains call the toll-free national transportation line (tel. 06–9292). The Netherlands is prime territory for biking, also. Most major towns are clustered together, and the terrain is so flat that even the wimpiest weekend warrior can pedal from town to town. You can rent bikes all over the country for about f8–f9 a day.

All local buses, trains, and metro lines in the Netherlands use *strippenkaarts,* cards that contain two to 45 strips. The number of strips you use on a trip depends on how many zones you cross; one strip equals one zone. Most trips within a town take about two strips. To use a strippenkaart on a bus, tell the driver where you want to go, and he or she will cancel the appropriate number. On trains and metro lines you're expected to cancel them yourself at the yellow machine inside the vehicle. If you don't, and a uniformed inspector nabs you, you'll have to fork over a hefty fine, usually f60–f100 plus the price of the ticket. A 15-strip card is f10.75, a 45-strip one f31. You can buy strippenkaarts at train stations, post offices, tobacconists, and, for slightly more, from bus and train drivers. If you don't buy a card you'll pay the driver about f3–f4 for each zone you cross.

➤ **BY TRAIN** • The EurailPass and InterRail pass are good on all train trips. Even if you don't have a rail pass, you won't have to dig too deeply into your pockets for city-to-city fares. In fact the Benelux Tourrail Pass (*see* Basics in Chapter 3, Belgium) isn't really worth the cost unless you plan on traveling from one end of the country to the other every day. You don't need reservations for trains within the Netherlands—just buy your ticket and show up at the appropriate *spoor* (track). **Nederlandse Spoorwegen (NS),** the national railway, runs trains between major cities every 15 minutes and between smaller towns every half-hour.

WHERE TO SLEEP With the exception of Amsterdam, most cities in the Netherlands are short on cheap sleeps. A double room in a budget hotel starts at about f75, and a single is about three-fourths the price of a double. To reserve rooms before you leave home, contact the **Netherlands Reservation Center** (Box 404, 2260 AK Leidschendam, tel. 070/320–5000, fax 070/320–2611). Once in the country you can book a room at any tourist office (VVV) as soon as you walk into town for f3–f7 per person. The VVV is a good place to book rooms in private homes, which cost a little less than hotel rooms.

If you don't mind sacrificing privacy, you'll save a bundle by staying in any of the 45 **HI hostels,** run by Nederlandse Jeugdherberg Centrale (NJHC). Most hostels charge members f19.50–f25 for a dorm bed, including breakfast. All prices given in this chapter are for members; nonmembers pay about f5 more. For a complete list of hostels, contact the NJHC (Prof. Tulppl. 4, Amsterdam, tel. 020/551–3155). Unofficial hostels charge about the same amount as NJHC hostels, but they're often shabbier and dirtier.

FOOD Traditional Dutch food is hearty and basic; beef, chicken, fish, and a variety of cheeses are often served with potatoes and other veggies or tossed into a hearty stew. *Eetcafés* (like it sounds, it's a café where you can eat) serve this traditional food, usually at reasonable prices. Brown cafés (*see* After Dark in Amsterdam, *below*) are more like pubs; they serve alcoholic drinks and sometimes simple food. Those who want to spend as little money and as little time as possible will rely on Dutch fast food such as *patats* (french fries) served with tangy mayonnaise and *broodjes* (sandwiches on little buns). *Shoarmas,* spit-roasted lamb in pita bread, is available at takeout stands everywhere.

Look for herring stands selling their salty, slimy delicacy, usually served with chopped onion.

Perhaps the best Dutch food you'll find is really Indonesian. Indonesia was once a colony of the Netherlands, and you'll see lots of immigrants preparing their native food in restaurants here. Surinamese food, which is somewhat like Chinese and Indonesian cuisines, is also plentiful. For an Indonesian blowout, treat yourself to a *rijstaffel* (rice table; about f25), an assortment of meat, poultry, and vegetarian dishes served with peanut, curry, and chili sauces that'll leave you as content as a cow.

BUSINESS HOURS Stores, banks, post offices, and many restaurants are closed Sunday, and the Dutch are in no hurry to get the work week started: Many places don't open until late morning or early afternoon on Monday. The rest of the week, expect shops to be open about 9–5, museums 10–5. Museums are rarely open Monday.

VISITOR INFORMATION You'll find a tourist office, or VVV, in every town that has even the teeniest tourist attractions. VVVs sell maps and book rooms; some change money when the GWK (*see* Money, *above*) is closed. If you plan to visit more than three museums in the country, take a passport-size picture and f45 to the VVV and buy the Museumkaart, good for admission to all municipal and state museums. The card is good for one year.

PHONES Country code: 31. Puke-green public phone booths come in two models: those that take coins and those that take phone cards. Available at post offices and train stations, phone cards cost f5 for 20 local calls. Local calls cost 25¢ for about five minutes in a coin-op booth. Phone booths take 25¢, f1, and f2.50 coins. To call out of the country, dial 09 then the country code. The international operator's number is 06–0410. The AT&T operator is 06–022–9111; MCI is 06–022–9122.

MAIL Post offices are open weekdays 8:30–5 and often Saturday 9–noon. A few are open until 8 on Thursday. Most offer poste restante, sell postcards, and exchange money. To send mail abroad, put it in the OVERIGE slot at the post office.

CRIME AND PUNISHMENT Contrary to popular belief, marijuana is *not* legal here. It's widely tolerated by police and residents alike, but you can still get busted for having more than 30 grams. Possession of hard drugs, on the other hand, will get you busted fast and make you subject to fines and jail time. Don't even think about taking drugs across the border; young budget travelers are favorite targets of the customs officials and their drug-sniffing dogs.

EMERGENCIES The national number for the police, fire department, and ambulances is 06–11. Health care isn't free for travelers; make sure you bring your health-insurance card.

Amsterdam

Amsterdam is a city with a split personality. This cultured, museum-crowded metropolis built around a series of concentric canals is also one of the most hedonistic cities in the world. There is an incomparable romance about the canals at night, and a wealth of art and artifacts in the city's great museums, but the oldest church in the city has to compete for attention with the prostitutes in the windows across the street.

Many people come to Amsterdam because they're curious. They've heard about the pot sold in cafés, the prostitutes on display, the in-your-face gay scene—well, it's all there. If you're here for a radical party scene, stick to the Red Light District and you'll get more than an eyeful, stomach full, and head full of vices. It won't take long for you to tire of barfing German and English meatheads, sketchy drug addicts, and drug dealers muttering "Treeps? Aceed?" in your direction every five minutes.

A few blocks west, however, Amsterdam is another place entirely. Most locals stick to the Jordaan, an area west of Dam Square filled with brown cafés along beautiful canals. Party-minded residents head to Leidseplein in the southwestern part of the city to mingle with out-of-towners. The city's green parks are ideal for wandering on warm, sunny days. Vondelpark, south of the center, is a good spot to picnic or rest your dogs after an afternoon of avid museum going. Explore pocket neighborhoods scattered throughout the city and you may find some little-known Indonesian restaurant, outdoor art, or gorgeous 17th-century architecture. Then you'll understand why residents love this beautiful, crazy city with more canals than Venice.

BASICS

VISITOR INFORMATION Amsterdam's main **VVV,** just outside Centraal Station, has a good selection of maps for f3–f7.50 and books accommodations for f4. Nothing, not even a cheesy brochure, is free, and the bureau de change is a rip-off. The lines are shorter and the staff is in a better mood at the branch office in the heart of Leidseplein. *Main office, Stationspl. 10, tel. 020/626–6444. Open Easter–June and Sept., Mon.–Sat. 9 AM–11 PM, Sun. 9–9; July–Aug., daily 9 AM–11 PM; Oct.–Easter, weekdays 9–6, Sat. 9–5. Branch office, Leidsestr. 106, no tel. Open Easter–June and Sept., Mon.–Sat. 9 AM–11 PM, Sun. 9–8:30; July–Aug., daily 9 AM–11 PM; Oct.–Easter, weekdays 10:30–5, Sat. 10:30–8.*

Stinky budget travelers may feel more welcome at **Sleepin's International Centre for Youth Culture and Tourism** ('s Gravesandestr. 51, tel. 020/694–7444), housed in the Sleepin Arena (*see* Where to Sleep, *below*). The staff can give you the scoop on what's up in Amsterdam and listings of social activities at the Sleepin Arena, including films, concerts, and plays. Their free magazine, *Use-It,* includes a handy directory of local services and organizations.

AMERICAN EXPRESS The main office holds client mail and gives cardholders the best exchange rate in town, but it's perpetually crowded. Cardholders can use the cash machine outside if the office is closed. The smaller office close to Museumplein isn't as central and doesn't hold mail. *Main office, Damrak 66, 1012 CM, tel. 020/520–7777. Open weekdays*

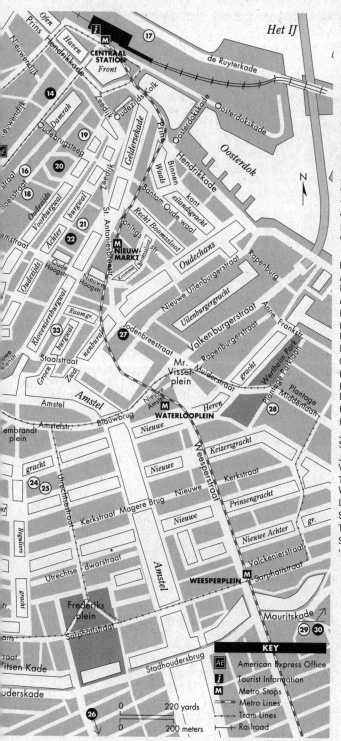

Sights

Amsterdam Historisch Museum, **15**

Anne Frankhuis, **2**

Hash Marihuana Museum, **22**

Koninklijk Paleis, **8**

Museum Amstelkring, **20**

Museum Het Rembrandthuis, **27**

Nieuwe Kerk, **9**

Rijksmuseum, **7**

Sexmuseum Venustempel, **14**

Tropenmuseum, **30**

Van Gogh Museum, **6**

Verzetsmuseum, **26**

Lodging

Anna Youth Hostel, **13**

Aspen, **4**

Bill's Residence, **3**

Bob's Youth Hostel, **10**

Eben Haëzer, **1**

Get Lucky, **25**

Hortus, **28**

Hotel Beursstraat, **16**

Hotel Brian, **11**

Hotel Winston, **18**

Jeugdherberg Stadsdoelen, **23**

Jeugdherberg Vondelpark, **5**

The Last Waterhole, **19**

Liberty Hotel, **12**

Seven Bridges, **24**

The Shelter, **21**

Sleepin Arena, **29**

't Anker, **17**

KEY

AE American Express Office

i Tourist Information

M Metro Stops

Metro Lines

Tram Lines

Railroad

0   220 yards
0   200 meters

9–5, Sat. 9–noon. Branch office, Van Baerlestr. 38, tel. 020/673–8550. Open weekdays 9–5, Sat. 10–4.

CHANGING MONEY Damrak, Leidsestraat, and Rokin overflow with rip-off bureaux de change. Don't be deceived by ads for excellent rates—many charge a whopping 10% commission. Banks offer good rates and generally charge a much smaller commission but are closed weekends. Besides American Express (*see above*), the best bureau is **GWK**. The offices at **Centraal Station** (tel. 020/627–2731) and **Schiphol Airport** (tel. 020/601–0507) are open 24 hours. The office south of Museumplein (Gabriel Metsustr. 2–6, tel. 020/627–2731) is open weekdays 9–5.

BUCKET SHOPS Young travelers in the know head to **NBBS** (Rokin 38, tel. 020/620–5071) for cheap plane and train tickets. Down the road, **Budget Bus** (Rokin 10, tel. 020/627–5151) offers great deals for transcontinental bus travel. Inside the office is an **Airhitch** desk (tel. 020/625–6597), where you can arrange cheap standby flights to the United States.

CONSULATES Consulates for Australia, Canada, and New Zealand are in The Hague (*see* Basics in The Hague, *below*).

United Kingdom. *General Koningsln., tel. 020/676–4343; visa information, tel. 020/675–8121. Open weekdays 9–noon, 2–3:30.*

United States. *Museumpl. 19, tel. 020/664–5661. Open weekdays 1:30–5:15.*

PHONES Public phone booths are plentiful on main tourist drags. For long-distance calls go to the 24-hour **Telehouse** (Raadhuisstr. 48–50, tel. 020/674–3654), west of Dam Square. Rates are lowest after 8 PM. If you're closer to Leidseplein, the **Tele Talk Centre** (Leidsestr. 101, tel. 020/620–8599) may be more convenient; it's open daily 10 AM–midnight. Avoid tourist phone centers, which gouge customers with steep rates.

MAIL The main post office, west of Dam Square off Raadhuisstraat, holds poste restante mail. Have your pen pal address mail to "Hoofdpostkantoor ptt, Singel 250, 1012 SJ Amsterdam." *Singel 250, tel. 020/555–8911. Open Mon.–Wed. and Fri. 8:30–6, Thurs. 8:30–8, Sat. 9–noon.*

COMING AND GOING

If you arrive at Schiphol Airport, frequent trains (f5) will whisk you to Centraal Station, a 15-minute ride away.

BY TRAIN Amsterdam's **Centraal Station** (tel. 020/620–2266) is a major hub for European trains as well as local buses, metros, and trams. From the station it's a five-minute walk to Dam Square (a.k.a. the Dam), Amsterdam's central square. Upon arrival you can change money at the station's GWK (open 24 hours). Just outside the station to the east is the city's main tourist office (VVV) and public-transportation office (GVB).

HITCHING Before you start hitching, consider calling the **International Lift Centre** (Nieuwezijds Voorburgwal 256, tel. 020/622–4342). For a f10 subscription fee plus a f10–f20 processing fee, they'll hook you up with drivers heading to cities all over Europe. Once you get matched, you pay the driver about 6¢ per km.

If you want to do it the old-fashioned way, here are some hints. Those bound for Haarlem or Zandvoort should take Tram 12 or Bus 15 toward Station Sloterdijk and get off at Haarlemmerweg. If you're heading east or to Scandinavian countries, take Tram 12, Bus 15, or the Metro to Amstel Station and stand on Gooiseweg. To reach Utrecht and destinations farther south, take Tram 15 to Utrechtsweg and start at the bridge. To Leiden and The Hague, take Tram 6, 16, or 24 or Bus 15 to Stadionplein and start on Amstelveensweg.

GETTING AROUND

Amsterdam can be horribly confusing at first. One canal looks like another, and street names change every few blocks. If you'll be here more than a few days, shell out some money for a big map. With your back to Centraal Station, the street that juts out of the Stationsplein is Damrak, which leads to Dam Square, a half-mile away. The four canals that form concentric semicircles around the station and the Dam are Singel, Herengracht, Keizersgracht, and Prinsengracht. The main tourist strip, Leidsestraat, cuts through the four canals. Raadhuisstraat, a main thoroughfare lined with bureaux de change, hotels, and other businesses, runs west from the Dam. The Red Light District is to the east.

The best way to conquer this mess is on foot, but trams, buses, and a Metro also cover the city. Amsterdam's official public-transportation company, **GVB** (Stationspl. 15, by the VVV, tel. 020/627–2727), distributes maps and information and sells strippenkaarts (see Getting Around the Netherlands, *above*), accepted on all trams, buses, and Metro lines. You usually don't need more than two strips per trip within the city. If you plan to use public transportation a lot, a *dagkaart* (day card) might be a better option. It offers unlimited travel within the city for f11 for a day, f13.60 for two days, and f3.20 for each additional day.

> **BY TRAM** Trams cover the city the more extensively than buses and the Metro. Trams 1, 2, and 5 cut through the city from Centraal Station along Leidsestraat to Vondelpark. Passengers are expected to cancel their strips in the yellow machines on board, but few do, and conductors rarely check. If you're caught by a uniformed inspector, though, you'll pay a f100 fine on the spot.

> **BY METRO** You can catch both Metro lines at Centraal Station, but the Nieuwmarkt stop is the only really useful one; most Metro stops are in the suburbs.

> **BY BUS** Whatever trams don't cover, buses do. The area across the canal north of the train station, where you'll find a few campgrounds, is reachable only by bus, and night buses are the only form of public transportation that runs after midnight. Routes are limited, and buses are infrequent. The GVB will give you a handout with all the night-bus information.

> **BY TAXI** If you're in a jam, call 020/677–7777. The rate is f2.60 per km, f3.25 after midnight, plus an initial charge of about f5. You'll find taxi stands at the train station and on Dam Square.

WHERE TO SLEEP

In this densely populated city, private crash space isn't cheap, but you can find plenty of beds in hostels for less than f25. The hostel scene is pretty lively. Travelers socialize and smoke joints at the private hostels, which have very late or no curfews. Official hostels are a bit more pristine, with earlier curfews and a no-drugs policy. Doubles in the cheapest budget hotels start at f75, but most cost f80–f100. The area five minutes southeast of the train station, around and including the Red Light District, is crammed with hostels and budget hotels. If you're willing to walk a little farther west toward the Jordaan or to take public transportation south toward Vondelpark, you won't have to dodge drug dealers or walk through seedy alleys to get to your hotel. If you haven't made reservations, try to arrive at Centraal Station around 10 or 11 AM and start making phone calls. The VVV will also book you a room for a f4 fee.

➤ **UNDER F80 • Bill's Residence.** A 15-minute walk from the station. Dreamy, canalside location—perfect for barhopping the Jordaan. Highly addictive cup of coffee and cake delivered to your room every morning. Doubles f75, none w/bath. *Leliegr. 18, tel. 020/ 625–5259.*

Hotel Beursstraat. Cheaper than most. Near the station, but back rooms overlook one of the seediest alleys in town. Firm beds and clean rooms, but the gaudy carpets are a major hallucination. Doubles f70. *Beursstr. 7, tel. 020/626–3701.*

➤ **UNDER F90 • Aspen.** Front rooms face a busy street, but windows are double-paned so rooms are pretty quiet. Large, clean rooms, all with phone. No lounge, so it's not the most social place. Singles f50, doubles from f80. *Raadhuisstr. 31, tel. 020/626–6714.*

Hortus. Across the street from Hortus Botanicus. Nicer, cleaner, and more spacious than more expensive hotels in the city center. Rooms in new wing are small and dark compared to those in the original building. A good 15- to 20-minute walk from the city center. Singles f60, doubles f80, breakfast included. *Plantage Parkln. 8, tel. 020/625–9996. From station, Tram 9 to Artis Zoo, walk west on Plantage Middenln., turn left on Plantage Parkln. AE, MC, V.*

Hotel Winston. Chummy front-desk person. Rooms are clean but tacky. A favorite of English rugby and soccer teams in spring and summer. Within spitting distance of the Red Light District. Breakfast in well-stocked bar is f10. Singles f60–f70, doubles f80–f90. *Warmoesstr. 123–129, tel. 020/625–3912.*

Liberty Hotel. Young staff is a welcoming bunch. Free use of kitchen, stereo, and bongs that are on display in the homey lounge. Front rooms overlook a busy canal. Singles available only in the off-season. Doubles, none with bath, f80. *Singelgr. 5, tel. 020/620–7307.*

➤ **UNDER F100 • Get Lucky.** Tiny place in a beautiful, quiet neighborhood. Coffee shop downstairs serves pot, espresso drinks, and yummy food. Front double has a fireplace and windows overlooking the canal. Doubles, none with bath, f90. *Keizersgr. 665, tel. 020/ 622–9617. From station, Tram 16, 24, or 25 to Keizersgr. and walk 1 block east.*

Hotel Brian. Rooms, some with canal views, are small and tidy. Beer in fridge is bought on the honor system—don't be a cheapskate. Doubles f90. *Singelgr. 69, tel. 020/624–4661.*

➤ **UNDER F150 • Seven Bridges.** Treat yourself without going too far overboard. Decorated with oriental rugs, wicker furniture, and marble sinks. Top-floor rooms are the smallest; first-floor room is practically palatial. Doubles f110–f170, breakfast included. *Reguliersgr. 31, tel. 020/623–1329. From station, Tram 16, 24, or 25 to Keizersgr. and walk 1 block east to Reguliersgr.*

NJHC HOSTELS **Jeugdherberg Stadsdoelen (HI).** Not quite in the Red Light District but close enough for easy access. Bar is complete with pool table and cheapest pints of beer in town until 2 AM. Beds f21.50 members. *Kloveniersburgwal 97, tel. 020/624–6832. 2 AM curfew, laundry, luggage storage f3.50, kitchen facilities, reception open 7 AM–2 PM, sheets f6.*

Jeugdherberg Vondelpark (HI). Specializes in accommodating large groups (i.e., raucous adolescents). Picturesque location next to Vondelpark and Museumplein. Worth a call if you're sick of the Red Light District. Beds f23 members, breakfast included. *Zand Pad 5, tel. 020/683–1744. From station, Tram 1, 2, or 5 to Leidsepl., and walk 5 mins southwest to Vondelpark. 2 AM curfew, lockout 10:15–3:30, luggage lockers, sheets f6.*

CHRISTIAN HOSTELS **Eben Haëzer.** Nicer part of town than The Shelter (*see below*), but the interior isn't as impressive. Beds f15, breakfast included. *Bloemstr. 179, tel. 020/642–4717. From station, Tram 13, 14, or 17 to Westermarkt, walk north on Prinsengr., turn left on Bloemstr. Midnight curfew, lockout 10–1, luggage lockers f10 deposit.*

The message board at The Shelter reads NO OBSCENE LITERATURE . . . hope you left that copy of Hustler at home.

The Shelter. Truly a haven from all the sinning and sleazing surrounding it, if that's what you're looking for. Free religious booklet when you check in. Sunny, clean rooms, nice little courtyard. Lockout is 10–1, but common rooms are always open. Substantial dinner f8.50. Beds f15, breakfast included. *Barndesteeg 21, tel. 020/625–3230. Midnight curfew weekdays, 1 AM curfew weekends, luggage lockers f1, reception open 7:30 AM–midnight.*

PRIVATE HOSTELS **Anna Youth Hostel.** Clean, co-ed dorms, with cement floors. Bathrooms are spotless. Smoking (of any kind) tolerated around the front desk but not in the rooms. Save the amiable owner, Yatsek, a headache, and go to the coffee shop across the street instead. Beds f25. *Spuistr. 6, tel. 020/620–1155. Wheelchair access. Closed late Oct.–mid-Dec. and mid-Jan.–Mar.*

Bob's Youth Hostel. You'll get a contact high just sitting in the coffee shop downstairs. Janitors kick you out at 10 AM, but after they're done you're free to take an afternoon siesta. Mixed-sex dorms and a very social crowd. Grungy showers. Cheap dinners (f5) are mere sustenance. Beds f20, including breakfast and sheets. *Nieuwezijds Voorburgwal 92, tel. 020/623–0063. 3 AM curfew, luggage lockers f10 deposit.*

The Last Waterhole. Young guns rounded up into rooms with about 12 metal bunks. Bar downstairs complete with pool table and live rock/blues every night. Close to the Red Light District and five minutes from Centraal Station. Beds f25. *Oudezijds Armsteeg 12, tel. 020/624–4814. Lockout 11–1, luggage lockers.*

Sleepin Arena. Really huge, beautiful brick complex renovated in June '93. Spankin' new mattresses, paint job, restaurant, bar. Serves as the International Centre for Youth Culture and Tourism (*see* Visitor Information in Basics, *above*)—guests get a 30% discount on all their programs. Doubles (f80) are on top floor, away from most of the ruckus. Dorm beds f17.50. *'s Gravesandestr. 51, tel. 020/694–7444. From station, Tram 9 or Bus 22 to Oosterpark or Metro to Weesperpl., at northwest cnr. of Oosterpark. Lockout noon–3, sheets f5.*

't Ancker. Cleaner than most private hostels, and there's no pot-smoking in the "family" bar. Manager Karen and her welcome-wagon staff answer any and all questions. Restaurant and bar open all day. Call ahead; rumor has it that it may close soon. Beds f30, breakfast and sheets included. *De Ruyterkade 100, tel. 020/622–9560. From rear exit of Centraal Station, turn right and walk 3 min. Luggage lockers f10 deposit, towels f5 deposit.*

CAMPGROUNDS **Vliegenbos.** Closest campground to Centraal Station, on the fringe of a quiet residential area north of the station. Popular with local youth and young international backpackers. Tent sites on grassy fields are bordered by trees and tiny cabins. Get your shower tokens (f1.50) at the reception desk. Sites f5.75 per person. *Meeuwenln. 138, tel. 020/636–8855. From station, Bus 32 or 39. Closed Oct.–Mar.*

Zeeburg. Way, way east of the city. Popular with dirty, young backpackers. Live music regularly. Late-night bar, snack bar. Showers f1.50. Sites f5 per person plus f2.50 per tent. *Zuider Ijdijk 44, tel. 020/694–4430. From station, Bus 22 to Muiderpoort Station then transfer to Bus 37; ask driver where to get off, and walk 10 min.*

FOOD

Budget travelers needn't starve in Amsterdam. If you're really scrounging, you can always head for the ubiquitous snack bars that serve patats for less than f2, burgers for f4, and falafel broodjes for f5. You can buy groceries at **Mignon** (Leidsestr. 74) and the late-night **Big Banana,** just across the street, but the **Albert Heijn** (P.C. Hooftstr. 129, near Vondelpark and Westerstr. 79–87) and **Dagmarket** (Elandsgr., north of Leidsegr. off Prinsenstr.) supermarkets are cheaper. If you don't mind shelling out some money, try any restaurant that serves Indonesian, Surinamese, or Chinese dishes. None is especially cheap; some of the better values are in the Red Light District and around Albert Cuypstraat. For more traditional hearty meals, head for any eetcafé, most of which double as brown cafés (*see* Bars, *below*).

➤ **UNDER F10** • **Toscana.** Pizzas and pasta dishes are cheaper here than they are at other joints. It gets really packed; it's the most popular pizzeria—and there are many—on this pedestrian street. Spaghetti f7.50, pizza with ham and mushrooms f8. *Haarlemmerstr. 130, tel. 020/622–0353. Open daily 5 PM–midnight.*

Velida. A step above the other snack bars in the city center. Friendly counter people have the Egyptian channel on TV—it's almost like eating in someone's kitchen. Cheeseburgers f4, *nasi goreng* (fried rice) with satay f10. *Roadhuisstr. 19, tel. 020/623–3154.*

➤ **UNDER F15** • **Egg Cream.** A vegetarian institution. Despite it's overwhelmingly high profile, locals still go back for more. Wholesome sandwiches start at f4, dinners average f12. *St. Jacobsstr. 19, off Nieuwezijds Voorburgwal, tel. 020/623–0575. Closed Tues.*

Kam Yin. Busy Surinamese/Chinese joint. Expect to wait for a table. Large portions of tasty specials, most for less than f12. Surinamese nasi with chicken f11, wonton soup f8. *Warmoesstr. 6, 2 blocks east of Damrak, tel. 020/625–3115.*

Keuken Van 1870. Began as a soup kitchen in said year. Hearty meat-and-potato Dutch meals. Dish of the day includes soup, entrée, and dessert for f10. Pork chops with veggies and potatoes f10. *Spuistr. 4, 5-min walk southwest of station, tel. 020/624–8965. Open weekdays noon–8, weekends 4–9.*

Pannekoekenhuis "Upstairs." Climb practically vertical stairs to get to the tiny dining area. One of the cheapest places to get good crepes. Show your ISIC and get 10% off. Soup f4, pancake with powdered sugar f6; savory crepes start at f10. *Grimburgwal 2, east of Rokin, tel. 020/626–5603. Closed Mon.*

➤ **UNDER F20** • **Antilliaans/Chinees Eethuis.** Order Antillean or Chinese food takeout like everyone else, or eat at the counter or one of the few tables if you prefer to sit in this dive. Huge, tasty meals—one portion is more than enough for two people. Stewed chicken with rice f15, chow mein f14. *Gouwenaarssteeg 4, in an alley off northern end of Nieuwendijk, tel. 020/626–3927.*

Bojo's. Best value in town for Indonesian food, despite proximity to tourist-infested Leidseplein. Open until 2 AM weekdays, 5:30 am Friday and Saturday—perfect for late-night munchies. Packed during dinner but empty at lunch. A filling fried-rice special f12, other entrées about f14. *Lange Leidsedwarsstr. 51, tel. 020/622–7434 or 020/626–8990. Wheelchair access.*

SMOKING COFFEE SHOPS Going to a coffee shop to smoke a little pot is almost as common as going out for a beer in Amsterdam. However, pressure from the EU may force the Netherlands to rethink its attitude toward drugs. In the meantime, coffee shops are still great places to hang and enjoy the company of other mellow fellows. To spot a "smoking" coffee shop, look for red, green, and yellow rasta colors and (more obviously) the smell of burning doobage wafting from the establishment. These are dead giveaways that marijuana in its many forms, be it grass, hash, or space cake, is sold there. Weed and hash are sold by the gram and cost anywhere from f7 to f13. Menus at each coffee shop have prices and sometimes a description of the degree of highness you can achieve with each. Most are open daily from about 10 AM to midnight or 1 AM.

The Bulldog. Tacky, glitzy, full of people trying their damnedest to impress each other. Goons at front door pretend to be discriminating. Pot is expensive, but this huge club/bar/coffee shop is still popular. *Leidsepl. 13–17, tel. 020/627–1908.*

Chocolata. Well-known for its chocolate space cakes—they need a good half-hour to take effect. Laid-back, with lots of young backpackers. *Spuistr. 51, tel. 020/622–6241.*

De Dampkring. More locals than tourists, yet convenient to Leidseplein. The pot counter looks like a fast-food express window. Microscope on hand, so patrons can inspect the density of the sparkling THC crystals. *Handboogstr. 29, no tel.*

The Other Side. Mainly gay clientele, but straights are welcome. Milk shakes served to relieve that cotton-mouth syndrome. *Reguliersdwarsstr. 6, tel. 020/625–5141.*

WORTH SEEING

Before you head off to Amsterdam's blockbuster museums, get to know the city by wandering around the Red Light District, Dam Square (*see below*), and the Jordaan (*see* Cheap Thrills, *below*). On an average day you'll see everything from sex shops to tourist traps to local student hangouts.

RED LIGHT DISTRICT The Red Light District is like a city unto itself and is totally unlike the rest of Amsterdam. If you want to witness some very intense weirdness, just cruise through the area on any weekend night. Bring a friend with you for safety and moral support. Tourists, lecherous men, drug dealers, drug addicts, and prostitutes mix strangely on Oudezijds Voorburgwal, Oudezijds Achterburgwal, and the seedy alleys in between. During the day the curtains of the houses are usually drawn; those that are open showcase unattractive, strung-out prostitutes. At night, when the number of patrons gets bigger and the competition more fierce, these women are replaced with slender, glamorous ones. Disturbingly, they're mostly Surinamese.

The big museum in this area is the Museum Amstelkring (see Museums, below), but the **Hash Marihuana Museum** (Oudezijds Achterburgwal 148, tel. 020/623–5961; admission free) hands out educational pamphlets on the benefits and uses of marijuana plants. Next door the **Sensi Seed Bank** (Oudezijds Achterburgwal 150, tel. 020/624–0386) sells everything you need to start your own garden, from books and seeds to crop-protection devices.

AROUND DAM SQUARE Dam Square is a crowded meeting place for tourists, young people selling hair wraps, and thousands of pigeons. The former royal residence **Koninklijk Paleis** (Nieuwezijds Voorburgwal 147, tel. 020/624–8698), which hovers over the square, was described by Golden Age poet Constantijn Huygens as the "eighth wonder of the world," but that's stretching it. If you're a fan of Golden Age art, the palace's chimney pieces by Ferdinand Bol and Govert Flinck—students of Rembrandt—may make up for the largely unspectacular interior. It's accessible only by guided tour (f5). **Nieuwe Kerk** (New Church) next door is a spacious, bright, 15th-century church that is used mainly for temporary exhibits. On the opposite side of the Dam, **Madame Tussaud's** (Dam 20, tel. 020/622–9239) gouges customers with a f17 entrance fee. Toward Centraal Station along Damrak is the **Sexmuseum Venustempel** (Damrak 18, tel. 020/622–8376), one big commercial cliché that tries hard to seduce thrill seekers into shelling out a f4 entrance fee. If it's cheap thrills you're after, you're better off cruising the Red Light District or spending some time in a leather/latex fetish store.

MUSEUMS

Many of the big museums are conveniently clustered on the south edge of the city around Museumplein. If you're going to more than three or so museums, take a photo of your smiling face to the VVV and buy a f45 museum card, which will get you into most museums (but not the Anne Frankhuis) free. Few museums give student discounts.

AMSTERDAM HISTORISCH MUSEUM This museum a few blocks south of the Dam is filled with paintings, artifacts, and furniture documenting the history of Amsterdam from the 13th century on. The back entrance is on Kalverstraat, a popular pilgrimage site from the 14th to 16th centuries. Apparently, in a house on this street a man receiving the last rites on his deathbed upchucked the host (that little wafer, for you non-Catholics). It was subsequently thrown on the fire but was discovered the next morning, undamaged by the flames. *Nieuwezijds Voorburgwal 357, tel. 020/523–1822. Admission: f5. Open daily 11–5.*

ANNE FRANKHUIS The lines to get in are always long in summer, and justifiably so. Here you can follow the plight of the world's most famous Jewish refugee and young diarist, Anne Frank, and see the cramped quarters where she hid. The museum's account of the Holocaust is very moving. *Prinsengr. 263, tel. 020/556–7100. Admission: f7. Open Sept.–Apr., Mon.–Sat. 9–5, Sun. 10–5; May–Aug., daily 9–7.*

MUSEUM AMSTELKRING It looks like a typical canal house from the outside, but the inside is a surprise. Although Roman Catholics were forbidden to hold public services during the Reformation, certain private house churches were tolerated. The attics of three adjoining houses were turned into a small but beautiful Baroque church nicknamed "Our Lord in the Attic." On the lower floors you walk through sumptuous 17th- and 18th-century interiors. *Oudezijds Voorburgwal 40, tel. 020/624–6604. Admission: f3.50, f2 students. Open Apr.–Oct., Mon.–Sat. 11–5, Sun. 1:30–5; shorter hrs off-season.*

MUSEUM HET REMBRANDTHUIS This was the Golden Age master's home from 1639 to 1660. The art collection is not too spectacular, but you'll be entertained by his etched self-portraits, which capture his many moods, hairdos, and hats. *Jodenbreestr. 4–6, tel. 020/624–9486. Admission: f4. Open Mon.–Sat. 10–5, Sun. 1–5.*

RIJKSMUSEUM This immense, beautiful (but graffiti-covered) building houses an extensive collection of paintings and applied art, mostly by 17th-century Dutch artists. The pièce de résistance is Rembrandt's *Nightwatch,* which dominates one room. If you can find enough space for a decent view, it's really impressive. You may have more breathing room at the less-hyped but perhaps more recognizable *Kitchen Maid* by Vermeer. The bottom floor has roughly chronological displays on Dutch history. If you don't want to pay the hefty admission fee, the exterior of the building may be worth a look-see. It's a montage of sculptures, tile work, and reliefs paying homage to the movers and shakers of Dutch art. *Stadhouderskade 42, at northern end of Museumpl., tel. 020/673–2121. Admission: f10. Open Tues.–Sat. 10–5, Sun. 1–5.*

The building housing the Rijksmuseum was created between 1876 and 1885 by architect Pierre Cuypers and Ministry of Home Affairs big cheese Victor de Stuers. They included their self-portraits in the product: Try to spot these two gargoyles emerging from the brickwork.

TROPENMUSEUM The Tropenmuseum, way southeast of the city center, has wonderful touchy-feely displays that shed light on life in tropical and subtropical cultures. The profoundly interesting temporary exhibits range from photography to studies on the impact the Western and Third worlds have on each other. Visitors are sometimes allowed to sit in on classes in the adjoining studios; African drumming is one of the most popular. *Linnaeusstr. 2, tel. 020/568–8200. Tram 6 or 10 to Oosterpark. Admission: f7.50. Open weekdays 10–5, weekends noon–5.*

VAN GOGH MUSEUM It's Van Gogh's "best of" collection—all the sunflowers, irises, and blossoming trees you could hope for and more. The first floor features a permanent collection of 19th-century painters such as Gauguin and Emile Bernard. The second floor is devoted to Van Gogh. His disturbing self-portraits are an intense send-off to the anticlimactic third floor, which is filled mostly with sketches and lithographs. Next door is the **Stedelijk Museum** (**Municipal Museum**; Paulus Potterstr. 13, tel. 020/573–2911), Amsterdam's museum of modern art. Along with some far-out work by Dutch artists, it has a Picassos, Matisses, and a random sprinkling of impressionists and postimpressionists. *Paulus Potterstr. 7, tel. 020/570–5200. Admission: f10. Open Mon.–Sat. 10–5, Sun. 1–5.*

VERZETSMUSEUM It's a bit out of the way but worth the trip. The museum is housed in a former synagogue and tells the story of resistance fighters during World War II. Here you can learn fascinating details about espionage, sabotage, and underground communication. Occasionally, volunteer tour guides, many of whom are former resistance fighters, are on hand to tell stories. *Lekstr. 3, tel. 020/644–9797. Tram 4 or 5 from station. Admission f3.50. Open Tues.–Fri. 10–5, weekends 1–5.*

CHEAP THRILLS

If you're tired of the Red Light scene or were never interested in it in the first place, head for the Jordaan area west of Dam Square. The narrow streets, the bridges over the canals, and the nighttime lights reflecting off the water make this one of the best places in the Netherlands for a romantic stroll. And you don't have to spend a dime, unless you decide to stop for a drink in one of the many brown cafés. Beers are reasonable—about f2.50 per glass.

The best picnic area in Amsterdam is way south, by Vondelpark. Markets around here tend to be cheaper than the more central ones. From June until the end of August, Vondelpark hosts free concerts Wednesday at noon and Sunday at 2. On Thursday night at 8 you can listen to classical concerts, and on Friday and Saturday nights at 9 some theater group or other is always staging a performance.

FESTIVALS Everyone gets into the act on **Koninginnedag (Queen's Day),** April 30, the former Queen Juliana's birthday. Markets, live music, and parties fill the streets, blocking all traffic. Festivities start at midnight on the 29th and continue for as long as anyone can stand, usually until about 3 AM on the first of May. Many in the gay scene celebrate Queen's Day in their own way by dressing in drag.

AFTER DARK

Most of Amsterdam's nightlife is concentrated around Leidseplein and Rembrandtsplein, which bustle seven days a week. Discos and jazz clubs can be expensive, so most locals fall back on the quieter pleasure of downing a few beers in a brown café.

BROWN CAFES We would call them bars or pubs, but they're called brown cafés here, due to the color of their walls, which are stained with nicotine by generations of cigarette smokers. Recently, "designer" cafés, painted every color but brown, have become the rage. You'll find boisterous brown cafés around Rembrantsplein and Leidseplein, but the small alleys and canal sides of the Jordaan area contain slightly more subdued bars that are popular with students day and night. Most bars are open until 1 AM during the week and until 2 AM Friday and Saturday. In addition to Cafe de Reiger (*see below*), other noteworthy cafés in the Jordaan include **De Prins** (Prinsengr. 124, tel. 020/624–9382), **Twee Prinsen** (Prinsenstr. 27, tel. 020/624–9722), and **Nieuwe Lelie** (Nieuwe Leliestr. 83, tel. 020/622–5493).

Cafe de Reiger. Good jazz and R&B playing in the background. Crowd of hip young locals here for good conversation. Classic brown interior and big wood tables lighted by candles. Dinner served 6–10. *Nieuwe Leliestr. 34, tel. 020/624–7426.*

East of Eden. Great pit stop after a visit to the Tropenmuseum, across the street. Courtyard in front is packed with young people, mostly from nearby hostels. Huge windows at front let you bask in sunlight. *Linnaeusstr. 11A, tel. 020/665–0743.*

't Gasthuys. Close to heavily trafficked Rokin, but on a quiet side street overlooking a canal. A popular student hangout when the university across the canal is in session. Reasonably priced meals. Soup with bread and garlic butter f7, beer f3. *Grimburgwal 7, tel. 020/624–8230.*

CLUBS You'll have no problem finding dance clubs; some kind of party goes on every night. Wander around Leidseplein, Rembrandtsplein, and Prinsengracht looking for the coolest crowds. **Mazzo** (114 Rozengr., tel. 020/626–7500) is as hip as it gets. Nothing matches the extravagance and liveliness of the gay scene. Gay clubs go in and out of business regularly, but Warmoesstraat, Reguliersdwarsstraat, Amstelstraat, and Kerkstraat, near Leidseplein, are sure to harbor some clubs of the moment. One successful new venture is the women-only **Clit Club** (for information, tel. 020/624–8764) which, at press time, takes place every Friday 10 PM–3 AM at the **Web Club** (Oudezijds Voorburgwal 15–17). Call the information line for the latest location. For general information on the hip gay and lesbian spots of the moment, call the **Gay and Lesbian Switchboard** (tel. 020/623–6565).

(Almost) Free Beer

Down the road past the Rijksmuseum, the now-defunct Heineken Brewery gives informative tours on Heineken history and the brewing process, although in one room you're subjected to a 10-minute onslaught of glitzy Heineken ads projected on about 50 TVs. After you've weathered this, you get munchies and all the beer you can drink in a half-hour. If you come on your birthday you get a free mug, too. Stadhouderskade 87, tel. 020/523–9239. Admission: f2. Tours Oct. 16–June 14, daily 9:30 and 11; June 15–Oct. 15, daily 9:30, 11, 1, and 2:30.

MUSIC To see major-league international artists, you'll have to travel to the east edge of the city on Tram 9 to the **Jaap Edenhal** (Radioweg 64, tel. 020/694–9894). Closer to Amsterdam's center, **Melkweg** (Lijnbaansgracht 234, tel. 020/624–8492; admission f10–f25) and **Paradiso** (Weteringschans 6–8, tel. 020/626–4521; admission f15–f30) are two popular spots that get big-name artists. To plug into the scene, look for a copy of *Time Out* at newsstands.

Alto. One of the more popular jazz clubs around Leidseplein. No cover charge on weekends. Small but jammin' and full of locals. *Korte Leidsedwarsstr. 115, tel. 020/626–3249.*

Bimhuis. Local and international hotshots play regularly at this modern jazz joint. Dutch Jazz Orchestra plays informal concerts every Wednesday. *Oudeschans 73, tel. 020/623–1361. Cover f10– f20.*

De Kroeg. Alternative, funk, hard soul, and punk. Regulars are twentysomething locals. Cover is free or f4–f10, depending on who's playing. *Lijnbaansgracht 163, tel. 020/420–0232.*

The Randstad and Around

The Dutch refer to the area encircled by the four cities of Amsterdam, The Hague, Rotterdam, and Utrecht as the Randstad (Round City); the megalopolis is also called "the West" by young, provincial Randstad wanna-bes who see it as the place to hit the big time. In addition to harboring the capital of international justice (The Hague) and the world's largest port (Rotterdam), the 10 small and medium-size cities in this small area are home to more than 25% of the country's residents—and that's not counting the tulip growers and vegetable and dairy farmers who fill in what little open land remains in the area.

Haarlem

Haarlem was once a thriving artist's colony, home to artists such as Frans Hals, Judith Leyster, and Jan Miense Molenaer, who put their works up for sale every week at the market. After the decline of the Golden Age, however, they packed up their easels and headed for Amsterdam. Now all that's left of them is in Haarlem's museums—about the only places worth visiting in this quiet town. The much-hyped Saturday and Monday outdoor market is fairly small.

The town center is surrounded by quiet residential neighborhoods, where you'll find most of the bed-and-breakfasts. If you're lucky enough to get a cheap room (usually booked through the VVV), the town is a great base for exploring Kennemerduinen National Park (*see* Near Haarlem, *below*) or nearby towns such as Zandvoort. Haarlem's **VVV** (Stationspl. 1, tel. 023/31–90–59), next to the train station, changes money for a f3 commission, books rooms for f7, and sells maps and accommodations lists.

COMING AND GOING Haarlem is 15 minutes from Amsterdam by train; a ticket is f5.25. All trains pull into **Haarlem Station NS** (Stationspl. 11, tel. 023/31–79–38), at the north end of town. **Grote Markt,** the main square, is less than 10 minutes from the station on foot. **Buses** stop at the train station on their way through the city.

WHERE TO SLEEP AND EAT The precious few budget hotels in Haarlem aren't all that cheap. The **Carillon** (Grote Markt 27, tel. 023/31–05–91; doubles from f85), just off the northern end of Grote Markt, is attached to a relaxed outdoor café. **Stads Café** (Zijlstr. 56, tel. 023/32–52–02; doubles from f75), less than five minutes west of Grote Markt, rents large rooms over the restaurant. If you want a cheaper private room (f60–f70 for a double), your best bet is to book a B&B at the VVV. The HI hostel, **Jeugdherberg Jan Gijzen** (Jan Gijzenpad 3, tel. 023/37–37–93; closed Nov.–Feb.), charges f20, but don't forget to factor in a few strips off your strippenkaart to get here. The staff is friendly, but that doesn't quite make up for the prisonlike building. Bus 2 or 6 will pick you up from the station and drop you off at the hostel's front door.

Do-it-yourselfers can shop for sustenance at the **Albert Heijn** supermarket (63 Raameest) at the end of Grote Houtstraat. **Donatello's** (Gierstr. 66, tel. 023/31–75–81) sells generous portions of pizza and pasta for f8.50, but they're open for dinner only. **De Karmeliet** (Spekstr. 6, in front of St. Bavokerk, tel. 023/31–44–26) has hearty Dutch specials from f14.

WORTH SEEING Haarlem's major sights are its museums, most of which cluster around **Grote Markt,** where vendors sell flowers, fruits, fabrics, and french fries Monday and Saturday. The colossal **Grote St. Bavokerk** (tel. 023/32–43–99; admission f2, f1.50 students; open Apr.–Aug., Mon.–Sat. 10–4; shorter hrs off-season) dominates the square. The highlight of this mostly Romanesque church is the monumental Müller organ, played by Mozart when he was a wee 10-year-old. You can discover just how much sound those 5,068 pipes can belt out during free weekly concerts mid-May–mid-October, Tuesdays at 8:15 PM; July and August, Thursdays at 3.

Three blocks south of the church is Haarlem's pride and joy, the **Frans Hals Museum** (Groot Heiligland 62, tel. 023/31–91–80; admission f6; open Mon.–Sat. 11–5, Sun. 1–5), a former almshouse that now houses a collection of late-16th- to 17th-century paintings, many by Frans Hals himself. Two blocks east of Grote Markt along the Spaarne canal is the **Teylers Museum** (Spaarne 16, tel. 023/31–90–10; admission f6.50; open Tues.–Sat. 10–5, Sun. 1–5), which touts itself as the oldest museum in the Netherlands. Although it was founded in 1778 by local rich guy Pieter Teyler van der Hulst to further the arts and sciences, today it's just an interesting hodgepodge of art, fossils, and scientific gadgets. The **Corrie ten Boomhuis** (Barteljorsstr. 19; admission free; open Tues.–Sat.) looks like an ordinary clock shop—and that's exactly the point. During World War II the ten Boom family hid Jewish refugees above their family store before being carted off by the Gestapo themselves. Wait outside the shop, and someone will let you in to see the collection of photos and documents of the family's history.

NEAR HAARLEM

NATIONAL PARK DE KENNEMERDUINEN Taking a bike ride through this park (tel. 023/25–76–53), about a 10-minute ride west of Haarlem, is one of the cooler things to do around here, both literally and figuratively. Dirt paths wind through the forest, and paved paths cut through the dunes—you can feel the air get cooler as you near the North Sea. You can rent bikes for f7.50 per day plus deposit at the train station in the room marked RIJWIELVERHUUR (tel. 023/31–70–66).

ZANDVOORT Ten minutes from Haarlem by train, this former fishing village is now a budding Atlantic City, complete with a large casino, luxury hotels, race-car track, and crowded beaches. A big gay crowd gets busy on the shores of Zandvoort, particularly at the end of the nude section about a 15-minute walk from the south end of the main boulevard. The best reason to come here is the abundance of pensions, most of which are cheaper than Haarlem's hotels. Hogeweg and Brederodestraat, south of the train station, are lined with pensions, where doubles start at f55. One of the nicer ones is **E. E. Shields** (Brederoderstr. 40, tel. 02507/1–26–37).

Zandvoort's **VVV** (Schoolpl. 1, tel. 02507/1–79–47) has a listing of pensions and also books rooms for f3.50. Trains travel frequently to Amsterdam (30 min, f11.50) and Haarlem (25 min, f8). The **NZH office,** which distributes local and regional bus information, is next to the train station.

Leiden

Leiden made its way into the history books for its role in the Eighty Years' War with Spain. On October 3, 1573, after the town had spent weeks facing starvation because of a Spanish siege, William the Silent ordered the dikes to be thrown open, flooding the Spaniards' stakeout site. The starving Dutch were finally relieved with baskets of white bread and herring. To this day, **633** you can party with the townsfolk and eat as much bread and herring as you can stand every October 3, during Leiden's biggest festival, the **Relief of Leiden Celebration.** After the Spanish troops fled the scene, Prince William set up the university to make the town a center for Protestant learning. Prestigious Leiden University is still a strong force in the town, which looks like Amsterdam's Jordaan quarter with twice the number of cafés and hundreds of clean-cut students hanging around town, acting like they have nothing better to do than cruise by in rowboats and enjoy life. Certain parts of the town are so collegiately idyllic it makes you wonder how any studying ever gets done. With some excellent museums, a great botanical garden, and beautiful canal-lined streets, this city makes a great detox site that's away from Amsterdam but not totally in the sticks.

GETTING AROUND Leiden's street pattern is utterly illogical, as is the bus map available at the NZH office. Arm yourself with a good map, and hoof it. **Haarlemmerstraat** is the main pedestrian street, lined with shops and cheap places to eat.

WHERE TO SLEEP Cheap sleeps are an endangered species in Leiden. The few pensions listed at the **VVV** start at f80 for a double. **In de Goede Hoek** (Diefsteeg 19A, tel. 071/12–10–31; doubles from f80) gets booked fast, but the friendly owner will usually refer you to another good place. **Witte** (Witte Singel 80, tel. 071/12–45–92; doubles from f84) is in a gorgeous spot across the street from the Hortus Botanicus. The privately owned **Lits-Jumeaux Youth Hotel** (Lange Scheistr. 9, tel. 071/12–84–57) is close to the station and has doubles for f60 and dorm beds for f22.50. The double rooms are right next to the heavily trafficked Langegracht; the dorms are much quieter. **Pilgrim Father** (Vestestr. 15B, tel. 071/17–06–91 or 071/14–37–23) is kind of a pit, but with dorm beds plus the use of a (grungy) kitchen for f15, few broke backpackers complain.

FOOD During lunch many locals line up for a quick fix at pastry shops and snack bars around town; Haarlemmerstraat is full of them. **Dagmarket** (Stationweg), a few steps from the train station, has cheap picnic fixings. **Annie's Verjaardag** (Hoogstr. 1A, tel. 071/12–57–37), which means "Annie's Birthday," is at the fork of the Oude Rijn and Nieuwe Rijn canals and *does* have a festive atmosphere, with an outdoor patio floating on two pontoons. Tapas are f7, and pasta dishes start at f9. Sorry, no birthday cake. **Hong Kong** (Pieterskerkchoorsteeg 26, tel. 071/13–03–83) is one of many pricey restaurants on the intimate alley off Pieterskerkplein. Go at lunchtime to get a student deal. The Bami special (Indonesian noodles with three entrées) costs f12.50 and is large enough for two. By day **Pastamania** (Hogewoerd 18, tel. 071/12–33–11) is an Italian restaurant; by night it's a bar called **Odessa.** Spaghetti bolognese is f8.50, eggplant lasagna f14.50.

After dinner the cafés along the Nieuwe Rijn canal and Rapenburg fill up with a conservative, well-dressed crowd. You'll have to elbow your way into **'t Keizertje** (Kaiserstr. 2), just off Rapenburg. **Zarrera** (Rapenburg 56) has tables on the sidewalk along the canal. If you don't feel like rubbing shoulders with so many good-looking strangers but refuse to live the life of a mole, go to **Babbel's** (Boisotkade 1), where the atmosphere is more sedate.

WORTH SEEING Practically all of Leiden's 15 museums are in the western half of the city, between Lange Mare and Witte Singel. Pick up the free handout "Leiden Museumstad" at the VVV for a complete listing. The **Rijksmuseum Van Oudheden** (National Museum of Antiquities; Rapenburg 28, tel. 071/16–31–63; admission f3.50; open Tues.–Sat. 10–5, Sun. 1–5) is divided into sections on classical, Near Eastern, Egyptian, and Dutch archaeology. The mummies on the second floor are well preserved, and the masks displayed above them give an idea of what once lay under all those bandages. Sometimes referred to as the "Mausoleum of the University" because of the number of academics buried here, the 15th-century **Pieterskerk** (St. Peter's Church; Pieterskerkpl., tel. 071/12–43–19; open daily 1:30–4) also functions as a giant exam room for university students. Of all the dead buried here, the most notable are Rembrandt's parents. Built in 1743, the **Molenmuseum De Valk** or **Windmill Museum** (Binnenvestgr. 1, tel. 071/16–53–53; admission f3; open Tues.–Sun.) is one of the last remaining corn mills in the Netherlands. Although it doesn't grind corn any longer, the blades still turn every now and then for show. The **Hortus Botanicus** (Rapenburg 73, tel. 071/22–72–49; admission f3.50; open Mon.–Sat. 9–5, Sun. 10–5) is Europe's oldest botanical garden; the first seeds were planted in 1587. Follow the red brick paths, which are lined with exotic plants visited by fuzzy bees the size of birds. The 90°F heat, the wonderfully overwhelming humidity, and the smell of damp earth make the tropical rain-forest **greenhouse** (open Apr.–Sept., weekdays 9–12:30 and 1:30–4:30, weekends 10:30–12:30 and 1:30–4; shorter hrs off season) the most sensual place in Leiden.

CHEAP THRILLS For the best view of Leiden, climb to the top of the **Burcht** (at the east end of Oude Rijn), a big, ugly, 12th-century citadel built on an artificial mound. It's a popular make-out spot for local 18-year-olds, so don't plan on a quiet evening under the stars. At the bottom of the steps is the popular **Koetshuis Café** (Burgsteeg 13, tel. 071/12–16–88), a "literary" café with outdoor seating. For the latest scoop on musical and other cultural events, check the lobby wall of the building at the base of the citadel.

The Hague

The Hague (Den Haag or 's Gravenhage in Dutch) is a worthwhile destination if you're interested in a glimpse of the royal history and political structure of the Netherlands. Home to the royal family and diplomats, the exclusive north edge of the city center is full of somber mansions, fenced-off palaces, and overpriced everything. For the most part, The Hague is a sprawling, largely unimpressive mass of identical lower-middle-class dwellings and retail stores.

One tourist brochure claims "Even in trams, people of The Hague . . . have a certain style, and all of them, of whatever class, have a feeling for the way things should be. The Hague has assigned a place for everything." Everything has its place, indeed. While the diplomats live in their mansions north of the city center, ghettos are forming to the south and west.

Economic disparities aside, most of the people here are pretty friendly toward outsiders. And, although it's no cosmopolitan giant, The Hague still manages to stage some exciting cultural events. Every July more than 60,000 people swarm to The Hague for the **North Sea Jazz Festival** (tel. 070/350–2034), a three-day whirlwind of jazz, blues, and gospel acts featuring such giants as B.B. King, Santana, and other musicians from around the world.

BASICS The staff at the **VVV** (Koningin Julianapl., tel. 070/354–6200) is adept at hardselling The Hague's attractions. In the same complex as Centraal Station, the office also handles accommodations reservations for f3.50 per person. Cash traveler's checks and pick up client mail at **American Express** (Venestr. 20, tel. 070/370–1100), in the heart of the shopping district between Grote Markt and the Binnenhof. The most convenient **post office** (Koningin Julianapl. 6, tel.070/383–9276) is across from Centraal Station.

➤ **CONSULATES • Australia.** *Carnegieln. 12, tel. 070/310–8200. Open Mon.–Thurs. 9–12:30 and 1:15–5:15, Fri. 9–12:30.*

Canada. *Sophialn. 7, tel. 070/361–4111. Open weekdays 9–1 and 2:15–3:30.*

New Zealand. *Mauritskade 25, tel. 070/346–9324. Open Mon.–Thurs. 9–12:30 and 1:30–5:30, Fri. 9–12:30 and 1:30–5.*

COMING AND GOING Trains from Amsterdam (40 min, f15) and Rotterdam (15 min, f7) arrive at Holland Spoor Station (Den Haag HS). If you're coming in from Utrecht (40 min, f15) you'll arrive at Centraal Station (CS). Trams 9 and 12 scoot between the stations regularly.

The major museums and palaces are about a 10-minute walk northeast of Centraal Station—perfect for day trippers. If, however, you plan on spending the night you'll definitely have to contend with local **buses** and **trams**. Before you step out of the station, get your strippenkaart, or you'll have to pay the driver f4.25 for even a short trip. Just around the corner from the hostel (*see* Where to Sleep and Eat, *below*), you can rent a **bike** for f9 per day at Orie (Looisduinse Hoofdstr. 679, tel. 070/397–4897). The tiny beach resort of Kijkdijn is just a 15-minute ride away.

WHERE TO SLEEP AND EAT If you don't have major bucks to spend, you can forget about 95% of the hotels in The Hague. If you really want a private room in the city, ask the tourist office to book you a room in a private home (f50–f60 per person) since the budget hotels just south of Holland Spoor Station are pretty grim. The **HI Jeugdherberg Ockenburgh** (Monsterseweg 4, tel. 070/397–0011; beds f26) is in a beautiful park, but the busloads of rowdy pubescents here guarantee you'll hear slamming doors and clunky footsteps all evening. To get to the hostel from Centraal Station, take Bus 122, 123, or 124 to Ockenburgh. The **campground** (Wijndaelerweg 25, tel. 070/325–2364) in the same park is expensive as far as campsites go—f11.50 per tent plus f6 per person.

Reasonably priced restaurants lie west of Centraal Station along Herengracht, Plein, and Grote Markt. During summer, most put tables outside so you can breathe in that city air while you eat. **Tin-On** (Herengr. 54) is one of the cheaper Chinese/Indonesian restaurants in town, with most dishes in the f10–f25 range. The eetcafé **La Perroquet** (Plein 12A, tel. 070/363–9786) has daily specials for f14–f17. **Sinbad Shoarma Grillroom** (Oude Molstr. 15, tel. 070/364–9892) is one of the few late-night restaurants in the city center. They serve shawarmas, kebabs, and the like for f7 and up from noon to 3 AM.

WORTH SEEING Most of the town's major sights encircle the Hofvijver, a cement-lined pool in the center of town. If you visit more than one of the town's museums (not including the Binnenhof) on a single day you get a f1 discount by showing a ticket from another museum. Unless otherwise noted, admission to each of the following is f4–f5. Dutch politics and power games are business as usual at the **Inner Court**, or **Binnenhof** (Binnenhof 8A, tel. 070/364–6144), the center of Dutch government for centuries. You can visit the Knight's Hall, the senate, and either the first or second chamber of parliament (when they're not in use) by guided tour only. It's a popular tour, so call to reserve a space. The **Mauritshuis** (Korte Vijverberg 8, tel. 070/346–9244; admission f7.50), a.k.a. the Royal Picture Gallery, houses a wonderful collection of 17th-century paintings, including Rembrandt's *Anatomy Lesson of Professor Tulp*. Andy Warhol's rendition of Queen Beatrix has the dubious honor of hanging in the locker area. Across the street is the **Haags Historisch Museum** (Korte Vijveburg 7, tel. 070/364–6940), which has a collection of paintings, furniture, and other relics tracing three centuries of Hague history. If you haven't seen enough 17th-century art, visit the **Museum Bredius** (Lange Vijverburg 14, tel. 070/362–0729). Once the home of art collector extraordinaire Abraham Bredius, the museum now houses his substantial collection. Paintings by lesser-known artists (with a handful of masters thrown in) and the natural lighting give a certain homeyness to the place. West of the Hofvijver is the **Rijksmuseum Gevangenpoort** (Buitenhof 33, tel. 070/346–0861), which served as a prison from 1420 to 1828. You can see the cells and torture devices by guided tour only. Tours are given weekdays at 10, noon, 1, 2, 3, and 4 and on Sunday hourly 1–4. Several blocks to the northwest, the **Haags Gemeentemuseum** (Hague Municipal Muesum; Stadhoudtersln. 41, tel. 070/338–1111; admission f7) showcases a diverse collection of delftware, rare musical instruments, and modern art, including some great Mondrians and Eschers.

Common folk aren't allowed into the three **royal palaces,** but if you make reservations at the VVV and pay f15 you can join the **Royal Tour** for a 2½-hour bus ride from palace to palace. Better yet, take a gander at the palaces yourself. The free pamphlet "An Historic Walk Around The Hague," available at the VVV, gives lengthy descriptions of **Noordeinde Palace** (Noordeinde 68), still used by Queen Beatrix; **Kneuterdijk Palace** (Kneuterdijk 20), former abode of Princess Juliana; and **Lange Voorhout Palace** (Lange Voorhout 74), where Queen Emma, the queen mother, lived until her death in 1934.

NEAR THE HAGUE

KIJKDUIN Just north of The Hague is the tiny beach resort of Kijkduin, where sunbathers suit up to soak up some sun or just loll around in the buff. It's much quieter than other resorts on this coast, but is by no means an isolated getaway. Near The Hague's hostel you can rent a bike (*see* Coming and Going in The Hague, *above*) and pedal a pleasant 10 or 15 minutes to Kijkduin. Once here, you can follow a number of bike trails through the dunes and shrubbery—watch out for wabbits.

Delft

When the Dutch East India Company started importing Chinese porcelain during the 17th century, Delft artisans put this city on the map by producing fine imitations. Soon the town had 30 or so factories producing delftware, though only one factory survives. Despite the thousands of tourists who swarm the markets to buy delftware, this pint-size city is a good place to get away from the traffic and noise of larger cities. The narrow brick roads, the canals filled with lily pads, and row after row of old canal houses make this town look like every Dutch postcard you've ever seen. The town is at its busiest on market days. On Thursday the outdoor market takes up the entire Markt square, the heart of the city; on Saturday, Brabantse Turf Markt hosts hawkers and vendors. The **VVV** (Markt 85, tel. 015/12–61–00) is a 10-minute walk north of the station. The staff books rooms for f4, but you're better off buying their f3 pamphlet, which has a complete list of hotels plus a neat little map.

COMING AND GOING   Tram 1 from The Hague (30 min, 4 strips) ends up at Delft's **train station** (tel. 015/13–19–45), at the southern end of town. Trains arrive from Amsterdam (1 hr, f16) via The Hague and Leiden.

WHERE TO SLEEP AND EAT   A lot of reasonably priced hotels are smack-dab in the center of town, but most fill early in the day. The sunny rooms at **Les Compagnons** (Markt 61, tel. 015/14–01–02; doubles from f60) are among the best. **Dalmacya** (Markt 39, tel. 015/12–37–14; doubles from f70), a few doors down, has showers and phones in all rooms. The sweet owner of **Pension de Vos** (Breestr. 5A, tel. 015/12–32–58) rents doubles in her home for f60. It's a ways from the square but only a block from the station.

Delft suffers no shortage of restaurants and eetcafés. **Markt** is packed with them (and with camcorder-toting tourists, as well). Locals tend to stay away from all that commotion and hang out in **Beestenmarkt,** which is filled with outdoor tables and shade trees. If you want to splurge a little, locals suggest **De Hollaindse Dis** (Beestenmarkt 34) for hearty meat-and-potatoes dishes (about f25). For something lighter and cheaper, mellow **Kobus Kuch** (Beestenmarkt 1, tel. 015/12–42–80) serves broodjes to local hipsters for f3.50 and up. On the nearby pedestrian shopping street, **Lunchroom Loes, Chris, and Zonon** (Brabantse Turfmarkt 61, tel. 015/14–70–14) serves creative sandwiches to the health-conscious for f6 Saturday–Thursday until 6, Friday until 9.

WORTH SEEING   Pick up a combination ticket (f3.50) at the following museums, good for admission to all of them. The **Prinsenhof Museum** (St. Agathapl. 1, tel. 015/60–23–58; open June–Aug., Tues.–Sat. 10–5, Sun.–Mon. 1–5; Sept.–May, Tues.–Sat. 10–5, Sun. 1–5), housed in Prince William the Silent's former abode, also served as the Convent of St. Agatha during the 15th century. The museum displays House of Orange portraits, as well as an intriguing account of Prince William's assassination by Balthasar Gerards in 1584—you can still see the bullet holes in the wall at the foot of the stairs. North of this museum is **Museum Huis Lambert van Meerten** (Oude Delft 199, tel. 015/60–23–58; open Tues.–Sat. 10–5, Sun. 1–5), in the former home of a prosperous Delft factory director. On display are tiles, more tiles, and artifacts from the 16th century. The most interesting thing about it is the house itself, integrating ceramic design with dark, carved wood in the Dutch Renaissance style.

Delft has two churches you might want to cruise by. Admission to each is f2.50, but at either church you can buy a combination ticket for f3.50. The **Nieuwe Kerk** (New Church; Markt, tel. 015/12–30–25; open May–Oct., Mon.–Sat. 9–5; shorter hrs off-season) isn't really *that* new— it was built in 1381. Prince William added a mausoleum in 1548, and since then all members of the House of Orange have been buried here. **Oude Kerk** (Old Church; Heilige Geestkerkhof, tel. 015/12–30–15; open Apr.–Nov., Mon.–Sat. 10–5) contains the tombs of Jan Vermeer and other Dutch notables. Check out the stained-glass windows, done by Joep Nicolas.

If you haven't had your fill of delftware yet, you can take a free tour of **De Porceleyne Fles** (Rotterdamseweg 196, tel. 015/56–92–14), the last remaining original delftware factory, and watch hand-painting demonstrations.

Rotterdam

Rotterdam's jumble of modern buildings and mass-transit lines may make you want to flee and take cover in a smaller town that is more immediately attractive. Germans bombed the town's historical center during World War II, destroying everything except the **Stadhuis** (Town Hall; Coolsingel 4, tel. 010/417–9111), possibly left intact because they could have used the documents stored there against the town's citizens. Surrounding it now are hastily constructed buildings from the '50s, but many are being torn down to make room for newer, more innovative ones. The vast empty spaces around the harbor, particularly around Noordereiland, are prime targets for ambitious architectural projects. Even the architecturally ignorant should get a charge out of the **Kijk-Kubus** (Show Cube; Overblaak 70, tel. 010/414–2285; admission f2.50), a cubic tree house open to visitors. The surrounding cube houses are all occupied, mostly by yuppies who eventually move to bigger houses.

To see what the city looked like before the bombings, take the Metro to **Delfshaven,** the city's historic quarter, where you'll find the familiar canal homes and small shops. Look for the modest wood gate on Aelbrechts-Kolk next to the Tin Factory; America-bound pilgrims passed through the gate before they set sail.

The city also has a smattering of art and historical museums, spread out south of the city center. The most impressive is the **Boymans–Van Beuningen Museum** (Mathenesserln. 18–20, tel. 010/443–1495; admission f6). In addition to works by well-known old masters and impressionists, the museum displays works by surrealists Dali and Magritte, but the temporary exhibitions are what attract crowds.

Exhibits at the **Prins Hendrik Maritime Museum** (Leuvehaven 1, tel. 010/413–2680) explain how Rotterdam became the economic capital of the Netherlands. For a better idea of the size of the transport empire here—and to get some sun and fresh air—take the 1¼-hour cruise (f12.50) around the city's docks and waterways with **Spido** (Willemspl., tel. 010/413–5400). During the summer they also offer longer trips to the Delta Expo, an array of massive dikes that prevents the country from being swallowed by the sea.

BASICS Inside Centraal Station is a small **VVV kiosk** that books rooms for f2.50, distributes a free accommodations list, and sells city maps. Rotterdam's **main VVV office** (Coolsingel 67) does the same and sells tickets for theater performances and concerts, as well. **American Express** (Meent 92, tel. 010/433–0300) offers the usual cardholder services.

COMING AND GOING Rotterdam has several train stations. The most convenient to the city center and all forms of public transportation is **Centraal Station** (tel. 010/411–7100), where you can catch frequent trains to Amsterdam (1 hr, f20), Delft (10 min, f5), and The Hague (15 min, f6.50).

Rotterdam's sprawling urban landscape is well served by tram, Metro, and bus, but most travelers will use only the Metro, which stops near all major sights. Buy your public-transportation map and strippenkaart at the city's public-transportation office, **RET** (Stationspl., in front of Centraal Station).

WHERE TO SLEEP AND EAT The best deal for a bed is at **Sleep-Inn** (Mauritsweg 29B, tel. 010/412–1420 or 010/414–3256), dorms run by students from Erasmus University. It's a 10-minute walk south of Centraal Station. From mid-June to the beginning of August you can get a bed and breakfast for f15. The sociable staff proudly claims to serve the cheapest beer in town at their bar, which is open all night. The central **HI City Hostel Rotterdam** (Rochussenstr. 107–109, tel. 010/436–5763; beds f23) doesn't have a lockout, although the Paul Anka and Elvis songs piped into every room in the early afternoon may drive you away for a while. To get here from Centraal Station, take the Metro to Beurs, transfer to a Marconiplein-bound tram, and disembark at Dijkzigt; the hostel is above the station. There are a number of mediocre budget hotels along Nieuwe Binnenweg, about a 20-minute walk from the station. **Hotel Metropole** (Nieuwe Binnenweg 13A, tel. 010/436–0319) offers singles for f35 and doubles for f65, breakfast included.

The absolute cheapest place for a sit-down meal is **De Pui** (Oostzeedijk Beneden 221, tel. 010/413–4349), a bar that serves traditional Dutch food for a measly f3.50. The catch is that you have to be there at 6:30 when they decide to serve customers dinner. **Cafe Oude Sluis** (Havenstr. 7, tel. 010/477–3068), in Delfshaven, is a café with outdoor tables overlooking the historic harbor. The daily special is f14. **Betty Beer** (Betty Bear; Blaak 329, tel. 010/412–4741) is part of a chain of local restaurants named after different bears. The restaurant serves daily specials of traditional Dutch food Monday–Thursday for f12.50–f16.

Gouda

This tiny town between Rotterdam and Utrecht gets lots of attention, mostly because of its namesake cheese. Every Thursday morning in summer you'll find Gouda cheese galore at the **cheese market** from 9:30 to 12:30. Farmers weigh their cheese at **Waag** (Markt 36), the same weigh house that has been in use since the 17th century. If you're overcome by a terrible fit of dorkiness, you can join in and have yourself weighed for f2.50. Across the Markt to the south stands the **Stadhuis** (Markt 1, tel. 01820/88475). Built in 1450, it's the oldest town hall in the Netherlands. Farther south, it's hard to miss the towering Gothic **Grote St. Janskerk** (Achter de Kerk 15, tel. 01820/12684; admission f3; open Mar.–Oct., Mon.–Sat. 9–5; shorter hrs off-season), the longest in the country. It was originally a Catholic church, but when the Reformation hit Gouda in 1572, the Protestants took possession. They kept the original stained-glass windows, which depict biblical scenes, and added a few of their own, many representing moments in Dutch history. Across the street is the **Stedelijk Museum Het Catharina Gasthuis** (Municipal Museum St. Catherine's Hospital; Achter de Kerk 14, tel. 01820/88440; admission f3.50; open Mon.–Sat. 10–5, Sun. noon–5), once the town hospital. It now houses a collection of 16th- and 17th-century paintings and reconstructed house interiors from the 17th to 19th centuries. If you missed the Verzetsmuseum in Amsterdam, here's your chance to redeem yourself. The **Zuidshollands Verzetsmuseum** (South Holland Resistance Museum; Turfmarkt 30, tel. 01820/20385; admission f3) has documents detailing antifascist actions during World War II. Everything is in Dutch, but you can ask for an English booklet.

When you say Gouda, pronounce it "how-dah" with a hard "h," as if you're prepping to hock a loogie. For some reason, hearing English speakers make hearty attempts at their town's name amuses many natives.

The **train station** (tel. 01820/94400) has frequent trains to and from Rotterdam (15 min, f6.5), Utrecht (20 min, f8), and Amsterdam (40 min, f15). The **VVV** (Markt 27, tel. 01820/13666), 10 minutes south of the station, books B&Bs for f3.50 per person.

WHERE TO SLEEP AND EAT Hotels in Gouda often don't advertise, so get a list from the VVV. The unofficial hostel/budget hotel **Herberg Het Trefpunt** (Westhaven 46, tel. 01820/12879), less than 10 minutes south of Markt, has singles for f60 and doubles for f75. The friendly management serves Italian gelato and snacks in the downstairs bar/restaurant. For cheaper private rooms, try the nearby **H't Blauwe Kruis** (Westhaven 4, tel. 01820/12677; doubles from f65) or **Pension 't Centrum** (Korte Tiendweg 24, tel. 01820/26684; doubles from f75), east of Markt.

For inexpensive Surinamese and Indonesian food, **Warung Blauwgrond** (Wijdstr. 22, south of Markt, tel. 01820/82158) is a modest restaurant/snack bar serving rice dishes for f9.50–f12.50. The friendly staff at **Cafeteria de Scherf** (Korte Groenendaal 6, tel. 01820/13623) serves everything from omelets (f6) and pancakes (f4) to Wiener schnitzel (f10.25).

Utrecht

Life in this heart-of-Holland city doesn't revolve around its prestigious university, although you might notice a subtle tension between students (who may refer to locals as "ordinary people") and locals (who may describe students as "cliquish"). The city has a couple of major sights and a smattering of tiny, eccentric museums. Travelers may best enjoy the city by rubbing shoulders with its people, and cafés around Oudegracht, Domplein, 't Wed, and Noblestraat offer plenty of opportunities for people-watching.

Utrecht's must-see sight is also the tallest and hardest to miss. The **Dom Tower** (Dompl., tel. 030/91–95–40) was the highest structure in the Netherlands until Rotterdam's Euromast assumed that title. You can go to the top after a guided tour (f3.50). Count on seeing Gouda and Rotterdam from the tower, but the day has to be especially clear to see Amsterdam. The Gothic **Domkerk** (Dompl., tel. 030/31–04–03; admission free; guided tour f2.25) next door used to be connected to the tower by a nave, which collapsed during a storm in 1674. You can still see the outline of the old nave on the square between the church and tower. **Het Catharijneconvent** (Nieuwegr. 63, tel. 030/31–72–96; admission f4; open Tues.–Fri. 10–5, weekends 11–5) tells the story of Christianity in the Netherlands. The museum's medieval-art collection is the largest in the country.

For a duck's-eye view of Utrecht, rent a canoe from **Ducky** *(Tolsteeg, tel. 030/51–52–26), down the road from Parkhotel. In your two-person canoe (f12 per hour) you can row around the beautiful park until you have the hankering to disembark at a canal-side café for a drink.*

BASICS To get to the **VVV** (Vredenburg 90, tel. 030/33-15–44) from the train station, just walk into the Hoog Catharijne mall and go to the far end of the first floor. The office sells maps, gives out an accommodations list, and charges f3.50 to book rooms.

GETTING AROUND Utrecht is a major international rail hub, with trains leaving for Budapest, Vienna, and Zurich, to name just a few destinations. To make reservations and buy international tickets, go to the **NS Reisburo** (tel. 030/33–25–55) in the train station. Utrecht also has direct lines to Amsterdam (30 min, f10), Rotterdam (35 min, f13), and Maastricht (2 hrs, f34). The train and bus stations are connected to the monstrous Hoog Catharijne shopping complex in the western part of the city center. If you plan to take a bus from Centraal Station, remember that *Staadbussen* cover only the city and *Streekbussen* go to neighboring towns.

WHERE TO SLEEP AND EAT Utrecht's cheap sleeps are outside the city center. The **HI Rhijnauwen** (Rhijnauwenseln. 14, tel. 03405/61277; beds f21.50–f24) is an old country house in the middle of peaceful countryside, a 20-minute ride from Utrecht in Bunnik. Take Streekbussen 40, 41, or 43. **Parkhotel** (Tolsteegsingel 34, tel. 030/51–67–12), across the street from a canal and park, charges f50 for a single and f75 for a double. The terrace adjoining the breakfast room is a great place to wind down. From Centraal Station take Bus 2 or 22 to Ledig Erf. The smaller **Pension van Ooyen** (Danteln. 117, tel. 030/93–81–90) is on the western outskirts of the city and charges f42 for its one single, f70 for each of the two doubles. Take Bus 8 to Everard Meijsterlaan. The closest campsite is **De Berekuil** (Ariënsln. 5, tel. 030/71–38–70; f5 per person plus f3 per tent), but it's closed November–March. To get here take Bus 57 to Blitse Rading.

Utrecht has lots of nice cellar cafés/restaurants along Oudegracht, but expect to pay more than f20 for a meal here. The collectively run **De Baas** (Lijnmarkt 8, tel. 030/31–51–85; closed lunch) nearby serves scrumptious vegetarian, fish, and meat dishes for less than f15. For something a little different, try **Mad Mick and Big Mamou** (Oudkerkhof 29, tel. 030/31–80–04), which serves tasty Cajun food that Americans may find a little tame. Gumbo is f7.50, Cajun hamburgers f8. The highly recommended student mensa **Veritas** (Kromme Nieuwe Gr. 54) serves meals for about f7 after 5 on weeknights. On Sunday evening it turns into a student disco.

AFTER DARK Nightlife doesn't get going until after 11. The Noblestraat bars just north of the Dom, such as **De Kneus** (Nobelstr. 303) and **Hef Pandje** (Nobelstr. 193), are packed with students. **De Zotte** (Noblestr. 243) is open the latest, until about 4:30 AM. Domplein and the tiny street off Oudegracht, 't Wed, have several bars with outdoor tables. You can get into the student sweatbox **Woolloomooloo** (Janskerkhof 14) only if you have an ID from your college; the ISIC doesn't work here. There's no cover, and drinks are cheap.

Elsewhere in the Netherlands

Despite the small size and relatively flat terrain of the Netherlands, the countryside is quite diverse. In the northern provinces, events such as the weekly Leeuwarden cow market and *polsstokspringen* (pole-vaulting over canals) take the place of urban entertainment. Much of the center of the country is covered in park- and forestland; an important art museum is hidden deep in the 13,000 De Hoge Veluwe nature reserve (*see* Near Arnhem, *below*). The southern border provinces are a mix of windswept peninsulas, riverside industrial areas, and gentle hills covered with half-timbered farmhouses. The oldest city in the Netherlands, Maastricht, edges up to the Belgian border.

Leeuwarden

Leeuwarden is the capital of Friesland, one of the Netherlands's northernmost provinces. The town has some pretty, historic sections, particularly around the canals and quiet streets. It's a good place to start if you plan to explore the Friesland area, known for its sprawl of woods in the southeast corner at Appelscha; the bird sanctuaries and cliffs of Gaaserland; and the prime sailing waters of Grouw.

Leeuwarden's most famous resident was Mata Hari, the World War I spy and exotic dancer. A statue immortalizes her on Korfmakersstraat, in the middle of town. You can also visit her house, now known as the **Frisian Literary Museum** (Grote Kerkstr. 28, tel. 058/12–08–34; admission free; open weekdays 9–12:30 and 1:30–5), which contains some Frisian documents and Mata Hariana. Anyone interested in exotic designs, colors, and patterns should check out the tile rooms at the **Museum Het Princessehof** (Grote Kerkstr. 9–15, tel. 058/12–74–38; admission f5; open Mon.–Sat. 10–5, Sun. 2–5), particularly those containing North African, Spanish, and Persian tiles. It's definitely not your run-of-the-mill delftware. The **Fries Museum** (Turfmarkt 24, tel. 058/12–30–01; admission f4; open Tues.–Sat. 10–5, Sun. 1–5) is an interesting regional museum where you can learn about the history of the province through archaeological finds and Frisian arts and crafts.

BASICS The Friesland-Leeuwarden **VVV** (Stationspl. 1, tel. 058/13–22–24) reserves f27.50 B&B rooms for f2.50 per person. The staff also gives out free accommodations lists and sells more complete ones for f2. On Sunday, when the office is closed, the lists are posted outside.

COMING AND GOING The **train station** (tel. 058/12–22–41) sends trains to Amsterdam (2½ hrs, f39) every half-hour. Most other trains coming from the south stop at Zwolle, which has direct service to Leeuwarden every half-hour. Buses stop in front of the station, and it's only a five-minute walk to the central shopping district around **Nieuwestad**, which runs along a canal going roughly east to west. Buses 71, 91, 92, and 97 run toward Europaplein, northwest of the center, where many of the budget B&Bs are found.

WHERE TO SLEEP AND EAT The B&Bs booked by the VVV are outside the town center, usually a 30-minute walk west or north of the station. If you prefer to stay in town, try **Hotel De Pauw** (Stationsweg 10, tel. 058/16–07–93), across the street from the station. Rooms are clean and simple, plus you get breakfast in the cozy restaurant. Singles start at f40, doubles at f77.50. For a quieter place in the center of town, check out **Hotel 't Anker** (Eewal 69–75, tel. 058/12–52–16), which offers singles for f38.50, doubles for f77.

Snack bars aplenty, most filled with surly high-school kids, line Ruiterskwartier. More mature locals frequent the slightly more expensive restaurants along Nieuwestad. The best bargain in town for a nice dinner is at **Istana Indonesia** (Grote Hoogstr. 26), open Tuesday to Saturday 4–9. With generous portions of *pepesan ikan* (fish in chili sauce) for f8 and *bami goreng* (fried noodles) for f6, this may be the cheapest Indonesian restaurant in the country. **Marten's Cafeteria** (Nieuwestad, tel. 058/13–47–47; closed Sun.) serves an egg breakfast for f4.25 and hamburgers and pancakes for less than f5.

Arnhem

What's in Arnhem isn't nearly as interesting as what lurks on the outskirts (*see* Near Arnhem, *below*). Not much is shaking here; the most action this town ever saw took place in World War II, during "Operation Market Garden," when British and Polish troops were slaughtered here trying to take control of the bridge, **John Frost Brug.** The bridge is a fairly unspectacular sight, but the area surrounding it is still undeveloped and quiet, so you can sit on the banks and envision the battle once fought here. Arnhem's other main attraction, the **Gemeentemuseum** (Utrechtseweg 87, tel. 085/51–24–31; admission free; open Tues.–Sat. 10–5, Sun. 11–5), is on the opposite end of town, west of the station. Here you can see more delftware, some Asian ceramics, and landscape paintings. Arnhem's **VVV** (Stationspl. 45, tel. 085/42–03–30) is east of the train station.

COMING AND GOING Arnhem's train station, northwest of the town center, has frequent **trains** to Amsterdam (1 hr, f24), Rotterdam (70 min, f26), and Maastricht (2 hrs, f29). City buses leave from in front of the station, regional buses from the western side.

WHERE TO SLEEP AND EAT The VVV directs everyone to **HI Alteveer** (Diepenbrockln. 27, tel. 085/42–01–14; beds f23.50–f25.50), set in a green suburb north of the city. From the station, take Bus 3 to Gemeente Ziekenhuis. The **HI De Zilverberg** (Dalweg 1, tel. 085/33–43–00; beds f22.50), west of town in the middle of the woods, is better looking, less crowded, and cheaper. You can use the kitchen after 9 PM when the staff is done with it. For something more central, try the **Hotel-Pension Parkzicht** (Apeldoornsestr. 16, tel. 085/42–06–98), which offers comfortable doubles for f75, singles for f42.50. It's a 15-minute walk east of the station. The huge **Camping De Bilderberg** (Sportln. 1, tel. 085/33–22–28; f4.25 per person plus f2.75 per tent) is open all year. To get here, take Bus 50, 80, 81, or 88 to Oosterbeek, near the Airborne Museum, and walk north on Sonnenborglaan to Sportlaan.

You won't have any problems finding cheap snack bars and french-fry stands at **Korenmarkt,** the shopping area around Jansstraat. For a reasonable sit-down dinner, **Eufraat** (Nieuwe Pl. 26, tel. 085/43–10–30), catercorner from the station, is an intimate restaurant offering pizza for f8.50 and pasta for f10 every night except Monday. **Cafe Meijers** (Beekstr. 2, tel. 085/42–38–07), on the eastern edge of the shopping district, is popular with the lunch crowd. Sandwiches start at about f3, and there are plenty of sidewalk tables.

NEAR ARNHEM

The green, forested areas outside Arnhem are great places to get a glimpse of the Netherlands's rural past and present. West of Arnhem in Oosterbeek is the **Airbourne Museum** (Utrechtseweg 232, tel. 085/33–77–10; admission f4, f2.50 students), which gives fascinating, detailed accounts of the 1944 Battle of Arnhem. The video at the beginning of the exhibition thoroughly outlines Operation Market Garden, the Allies' unsuccessful effort to capture bridges between Eindhoven and Veghel. Housed in the former divisional headquarters, the museum displays weapons, photographs, and other images of the war. North of the museum is the **Airborne Cemetery,** the peaceful resting place of casualties of the war. From Arnhem's station, take Bus 50, 80, 81, or 88. You might want to set aside an entire afternoon to get through the 45 hectares (111 acres) of the open-air museum **Nederlands Openluchtmuseum** (Schelmseweg 89, tel. 085/57–63–33; admission f11.50; open Apr.–Oct.). Several paths lead to reconstructed farmhouses, windmills, and other fixtures of 19th-century rural Dutch life. Demonstrations show you how bread and cheese were made, and the working paper mill is an interesting example of how some farmers earned a second income. Everything made during the demonstrations is sold on the spot. Take Bus 3 or 13 from Arnhem's station.

HOGE VELUWE NATIONAL PARK The Hoge Veluwe National Park is the Netherlands's largest, with more than 13,000 acres of heath, woodland, sand dunes, and grassy fields. The area is home to such furry forest creatures as deer, wild boar, foxes, and badgers, although your chances of seeing any are almost nil, since access to their stamping grounds is restricted.

Besides wildlife, the real highlight of the park is the huge (and free, once you've paid park admission) **Kröller-Müller Museum** (tel. 08382/1241; open Apr.–Oct., Tues.–Sat. 10–5, Sun. 11–5; Nov.–Mar., Tues.–Sat. 10–5, Sun. 1–5), which houses an impressive collection of modern art, with lots of works by Picasso, Braque, and Gris. The collection of Van Gogh paintings is so vast that only a fraction of the works can be shown at any one time. Behind the museum is Europe's largest **sculpture garden**, filled with works by well-known sculptors such as Rodin, Jacques Lipchitz, and Henry Moore. About 5 km north of the museum is **St. Hubertus**, a 1920s Art Deco hunting lodge designed by Hendrik Berlage, the Netherlands's "father of modern architecture." From May to November, park visitors can take a free guided tour of the interior. The rest of the year you'll have to be satisfied with walking around the beautiful garden and lake surrounding the lodge.

The best way to see all of this is by bike, and once you pay the f7.50 entrance fee you can help yourself to one of the 400 bikes in the park. Snag one at Marchantplein, near the Koperon Kop restaurant, or at the visitor center, both near the center of the park. Return the bikes there or at any park entrance. To avoid biking in circles for days, buy the *Stichting Het Nationale Parke De Hoge Veluwe* for f3, available at the **Aanschouw visitor center** (tel. 08382/1627; open Apr.–Oct., daily 9:30–5; Nov.–Mar., daily 10–4), next to the Koperon Kop restaurant. *Park office, tel. 05768/1441. Park open Apr.–Oct., daily 8 AM–sunset; Nov.–Mar., daily 8–5.*

COMING AND GOING Bus 12 from Arnhem's station stops at the visitor center hourly June–October, Tuesday–Sunday, after passing by the Kröller-Müller museum. If you stay past 5 PM, when Bus 12 stops running, ride a bike south to the Rijzen entrance and walk 15 minutes to Schaarsberglaan to catch the bus to Arnhem.

Maastricht

When you walk through the cobblestone streets of Maastricht you may get the strange feeling you're not in the Netherlands anymore. Instead of picturesque streets lined with 17th-century canal houses, you'll see hip boutiques, trendy outdoor cafés, and wide buildings made of brick and stone. Despite all this, Maastricht still gives off ancient vibes. More than 2,500 years ago the Romans set up shop here, and this little finger of land was a source of contention among the Germans, Belgians, and Dutch until the end of World War II. More recently, Maastricht was the site of the signing of the 1992 Treaty of European Union (a.k.a. the Maastricht Treaty), an important step in the formation of the EU. It's a beautiful, historic town with its fair share of museums and churches, but go elsewhere if you're looking for a concentrated taste of traditional Dutch life.

BASICS Maastricht's **VVV** (Kleine Staat 1, tel. 043/25–21–21) is a 15-minute walk from the train station. Walk straight up Stationstraat to the west, cross the bridge, and turn right when you reach the end. The staff books rooms for f2.50 per person and sells a guide (f1.75) that includes a map and complete list of hotels and pensions.

COMING AND GOING Since Maastricht is so far south, you can easily catch trains to Köln, Germany (1½ hrs, f32) and Liège, Belgium (30 mins, f12). Trains also go to Amsterdam (2½ hrs, f40) via Utrecht from the **Maastricht Station** (tel. 043/21–45–63).

Maastricht is divided by the River Maas; most of the action is on the west bank. The town's main square, **Vrijthof,** is surrounded by cafés and two churches. You can easily walk from the eastern edge of town (where the train station is) to the western edge (past the shopping district and museums) in less than 30 minutes, but you will have to bus it to the youth hostel. The **bus station** is to your left as you exit the train station.

WHERE TO SLEEP AND EAT Get a list of rooms in private homes, most of which cost f27.50–f37.50 per person, from the VVV. **Zwets** (Bredestr. 41, tel. 043/21–64–82; f32.50 per person) is just a few steps from the Vrijthof. **Hotelboot** (Maasblvd. 95, tel. 043/21–90–93; doubles f70–f80), something a little more unique, is anchored along the west bank. Rooms on the boat are small but clean. Maastricht's **HI De Dousberg** (Dousberg-weg 4, tel. 043/43–44–04; beds f25) is a massive, modern hostel that caters to conference groups. In the same building is the **Sportel,** which has nicer private accommodations with doubles for f85. Take Bus 7 from the train station.

One of the best bargain restaurants in town, frequented by lots of students, is **De Preuvery** (Kakeberg 6, tel. 043/25–09–03), about 200 yards south of the Vrijthof. It serves hearty meals for f9 and huge baguette sandwiches for f3.50 until 1:30 AM. Farther east, toward the river, is **Alexandria** (Koestr. 21, tel. 043/21–51–55), a shawarma grill that makes great pizzas for f8.

WORTH SEEING Maastricht's main sights are within a 10-minute walk of each other. To get a look at the big picture, walk along the remaining walls of this once heavily fortified city. Pick up a free "Maastricht Fortifications Walk" guide from the VVV, or just walk down to Onze Lieve Vrouwe Wal and along the walls as they turn west. The oldest part of the walls, along Maasboulevard, was built in 1229; extensions and reinforcements were added in the 16th century, during the war with Spain.

Dominating the Vrijthof square is the Romanesque church **St. Servaasbasiliek** (Vrijthof, tel. 043/21–78–78; admission f3.50), which houses the remains of St. Servatius, the first bishop of Maastricht. The church was begun in about AD 1000 and enlarged during the 14th and 15th centuries. As you enter the spacious nave, your eyes are immediately drawn to the richly colored, vaulted ceiling. Hidden in the southwest corner of the church's courtyard, "Grameer" (Grandmother) is billed as the largest bell in the Netherlands, but you'd never guess it from looking at it. Also on the Vrijthof square is the Protestant **St. Janskerk,** a smaller, somber church. Piped-in organ music adds to the solemnity. Admission is free, but pay f2 if you want to climb the tower for a view of the city. The **Onze Lieve Vrouwebasiliek** (Onze Lieve Vrouwepl., tel. 043/25–18–51; admission free) is quieter, darker, and more intimate than the two Vrijthof churches. Services are often held in front of the statue of Stella Mare (Our Beloved Lady), next to the church entrance, so be quiet as you enter. The **Bonnefanten Museum** (Dominikanerpl. 5, tel. 043/25–16–55; admission f3; open Tues.–Fri. 10–5, weekends 11–5) houses a diverse array of exhibits, including modern art, medieval paintings, and archaeological remains of the Roman occupation in the Limburg province—a strange mix, but it works well. The museum is scheduled for a big move to another location in 1995, and hours are limited, as are the displays, while the move takes place.

NORWAY

By Trisha Smith

Norway's severe, dramatic landscape has left its mark on the Norwegians; with the power of nature constantly asserting itself, they are forced to adapt or die. An old man in a youth hostel reminisced about a couple who, after World War II, went north to hike. They set out for glacier territory and were never seen again. Recently their bodies were recovered: The glacier had spit their frozen carcasses into a lake. This wild land gives rise to countless similar stories of human frailty in the face of nature, as well as a fair share of fairy tales, most involving trolls who lurk about wreaking havoc on fishermen and farmers. The steep mountains and deep valleys have kept regions isolated from each other, resulting in a number of cultural and language variations.

Norwegians learn early that their country is unusual: School lessons insist that the sun rises every day in the east and sets in the west, but they live through perpetually dark arctic winters and long summer days when the sun doesn't set at all. They meet the severe climate head-on, indulging regularly in outdoor sports from skiing (a Norwegian word) to hiking, biking, and climbing. Families regularly trek to mountain *hytter* (cabins), and many own heavy-duty hiking boots unheard of in America.

If you've come to Norway to do some trekking, you'll have plenty of elbow room. The distance from northern to southern Norway (1,752 km) is the same as the distance from southern Norway to Rome, Italy. The population density is only 13 people per square kilometer—compare that to Great Britain's 228.

Summer is the most popular time to visit Norway; days are long, hostels are open, and transportation is beefed up. But Norway in winter is a wonderland of snow-covered mountains glowing under the northern lights, and few tourists are around to get in your way. The Gulf Stream, which flows the Norwegian coast, keeps the weather surprisingly mild for such a high latitude. May and September are also great times to visit, although public transportation is sporadic.

The Norwegians' best-known ancestors were the Vikings, an unruly bunch of merchants and explorers who terrorized Europe during the 9th century and landed on the American continent long before Columbus took his first breath. By the 11th century St. Olav, a Viking king, had introduced Christianity to his red-blooded, pagan subjects; and it was shortly afterward that many of Norway's stave churches, lavishly decorated with dragon heads and icons from Viking mythology, were built. Norway has spawned a number of modern-day adventurers as well: Roald Amundsen was the first man to reach the South Pole, and Thor Heyerdal, of *Kon Tiki* fame,

200 miles

300 km

KEY
Rail Lines

*ATLANTIC
OCEAN*

*Norwegian
Sea*

Nordkapp

Honningsvåg

Vardø

Vadsø

Hammerfest

Kirkenes

Alta

Finnmark

Karasjok

Masi

Tromsø

Kautokeino

FINLAND

Lofoten Islands

Narvik

Bardu

Stamsund

Å

Vestfjorden

Bodø

Fauske

Saltdal

Arctic Circle

Mo-i-Rana

Umbukta

Sandnessjøen

Møsjøen

Brønnøysund

E6

S W E D E N

Vikna

Namsos

Steinkjer

Gulf of Bothnia

Trondheim

Meråker

Støren

Kristiansund N.

Geirangerfjord

Oppdal

Røros

Ålesund

Andalsnes

Tynset

Geiranger

Dombås

Stryn

Otta

Hellesylt

Koppang

Florø

Nordfjord

Jostedalsbreen

Jotunheimen

Rena

Balestrand

Fjærland

Lillehammer

Sognefjord

Flåm

Myrdal

Finse

*Lake
Mjøsa*

Hamar

Voss

Eidsvoll

Bergen

Geilo

Hardangerfjord

Hønefoss

⭐ Oslo

Kongsberg

Drammen

Sarpsborg

Baltic Sea

Haugesund

Larvik

Fredrikstad

Porsgrunn

Stavanger

Sandnes

Arendal

Evje

Grimstad

Skagerrak

Kattegat

Mandal

Kristiansand

sailed across the Pacific and Atlantic oceans in reconstructions of early balsa-and-reed rafts to lend credence to his migration theories.

Norway has been part of Denmark and Sweden, but the country gained its independence in 1905 and has guarded it fiercely ever since. Hitler's army invaded in 1940 and began an occupation that would last five years, but Norwegian resistance was strong throughout. By 1945 the Germans had surrendered, Norwegian Nazi leader Vidkun Quisling had been executed, and King Håkon VII's exiled Norwegian government had triumphantly returned. Modern Norway has a constitutional monarchy similar to Britain's in that the king's position is mainly symbolic; the prime minister heads the country. The current prime minister, Dr. Gro Harlem Brundtland, has been at the forefront of the world environmental movement and is one of Europe's most progressive leaders.

Basics

MONEY $1 = 6.8 kroner and 1 krone = 15¢. Post offices are convenient places to change money because most are open on Saturday. Banks are generally open weekdays 8–3 in summer, 8–3:30 in winter (often until 4 on Thursday). Both banks and post offices charge a service fee of 10kr per traveler's check, with a 20kr minimum fee, so carry large denominations. Strangely, banks and post offices give a better rate for traveler's checks than for cash.

➤ **HOW MUCH IT WILL COST** • Norway is one of Europe's most expensive countries. Hotel doubles for less than 400kr are practically nonexistent, and even a basic sit-down meal will almost assuredly cost more than 50kr. Transportation costs are high because everything is so spread out. If you insist on staying in hotels and eating out, expect to spend upward of $50 or $60 a day. If you camp rough, buy groceries, and stick to the areas covered by your EurailPass, you can see the Great White North for about $15 a day, closer to $30 if you stay in hostels. ISIC cards and hostel-membership cards pay for themselves almost overnight.

COMING AND GOING Most travelers reach Norway by **train,** riding north to Copenhagen, Denmark, crossing to Sweden, and eventually arriving in Oslo. EurailPass and the InterRail, Scanrail, and Nordturist passes (*see* Getting Around, *below*) cover the short ferry ride that carries the train across the water from Denmark to Sweden. International **ferries** connect Norway with England, Denmark, Germany, Sweden, and Iceland. Service, frequency, and price

They Don't Kill Whales for Fun

In 1993, when the Norwegians announced their decision to resume limited minke whaling in the North Atlantic, they were a little baffled by the vehement opposition of other countries. After all, the decision was based on research by the International Whaling Commission indicating that the minke-whale stock (87,000 in the North Atlantic alone) is capable of supporting a sustainable harvest. Whaling follows internationally accepted principles for the management of renewable resources: Energy consumption is low in relation to yield, and there is no pollution from fertilizers, pesticides, or other chemicals. The Norwegians point out that the whales face a greater danger from Central Europe's industrial waste and acid rain, which destroy their habitat, than from Norway's hunting, limited to 300 whales per year. They react to the condemnation with a dose of wry disgust. A popular homemade T-shirt proclaims WE KILL WHALES FOR FUN and pictures a harpooned whale with the caption ONLY 86,999 TO GO.

increase in summer. *See* the sections on Oslo, Kristiansand, Stavanger, and Bergen, *below*, for ferry specifics.

If you want to reach Norway from elsewhere in Europe and don't have a EurailPass, **flying** is a better option than you might think. Student discounts abound, especially during summer, and Oslo, and Bergen are hubs for international flights. From London you'll pay about $155 one-way to Oslo (2 hrs), from Paris $195 (2 hrs). Many flights are handled by the Scandinavian airline **SAS.**

GETTING AROUND Norway's transportation system is a complex, comprehensive web of trains, planes, ferries, and buses. It's fully detailed in the massive *Rutebok for Norge,* available in Norwegian bookstores for US$12. Most tourist offices and travel agencies keep a copy on hand, and the staff will often photocopy relevant information for you. Less hefty is the free *Rutehefte for Turister* (Tourist Timetables). It includes information on the main train, ferry, bus, and air routes. Always pick up local timetables at tourist offices to supplement these two guides. Many routes are cut back in winter, and bus service stops altogether on mountain roads closed by snow.

➤ **BY TRAIN** • EurailPass and the InterRail, Nordturist, and Scanrail passes are good for free travel on all Norwegian trains. If you plan to stay in Norway or Scandinavia for any length of time, consider buying a **Nordturist** or **Scanrail** pass. Nordturist is expensive (adult second-class 1,870kr, youth second-class 1,390kr) but allows 21 days of unlimited rail travel in Norway, Sweden, Finland, and Denmark. The Scanrail pass, available only outside Scandinavia, gives you four free days of travel in a 15-day period (US$149 second-class), nine free days of travel in a 21-day period (US$254 second-class), or one month of unlimited travel (US$374 second class). Both Nordturist and Scanrail offer many ferry and bus discounts not available to EurailPass holders.

Other discount tickets include the **Midtukebillet,** a one-way ticket that allows stopovers, and the **Minigruperbatt,** good for a 25% discount on journeys of 100 km or more made by at least two people. Norway's train system goes only as far north as Bodø, just above the Arctic Circle. Trains from Sweden, though, cross the border farther north at Narvik. Train prices fluctuate drastically; weekends are usually the most expensive travel times. Seat reservations, mandatory on certain long-distance trains and all Oslo–Bergen trains, cost 20kr.

➤ **BY BUS** • Buses career along one-lane roads and around hairpin turns, and it's hard to find one that doesn't pass through heart-stopping scenery. Buses are the only way to hop fjords and are just about the only option for land travel north of Bodø. The **Nord Norge Bussen** has regular if infrequent service from Bodø to Kirkenes on the Russian border. Various companies offer discounts to students and travelers using InterRail, Nordturist, or Scanrail passes—always ask. Eurailers get no official discounts, but try flashing your pass anyway.

➤ **BY FERRY** • Ferries stop at all ports of significance and often, in the fjords, connect roads that dead-end at the water's edge. Hydrofoils also zip around to popular destinations in the fjords and the Lofoten Islands. They're considerably faster than ferries but at least twice as expensive; students and rail-pass holders sometimes get a 50% discount. A plush alternative is the **Hurtigrute,** a coastal steamer that departs daily from Bergen on a six-day journey to Kirkenes, stopping at ports along the way. Prices are steep, but overnight travelers save a little money: You can buy a deck-class ticket and sleep in the sleeping-bag room or anywhere in the lounge. Up north, Hurtigrute tickets are comparable in price to full-fare bus tickets.

➤ **BY PLANE** • Flying is a viable travel option within Norway, given the country's huge size and expensive land-transportation system. Contact **Kilroy Travel** (*see* Oslo and Tromsø, *below*) for information on **Widerøe** flights, with a summer fare of 410kr to a limited number of destinations.

WHERE TO SLEEP Hotels are prohibitively expensive, but tourist offices in many towns book rooms in **private homes** for 100kr–200kr a night per person. Norway also maintains an excellent network of well-located **hostels,** used by people of all ages. Most serve breakfast, a hearty all-you-can-eat smörgåsbord, for 40kr–55kr. Many also have kitchens, although few provide pots, pans, and utensils. Prices range from 65kr to 150kr for a dorm bed. *Van-*

drerhjem i Norge, a valuable book available from **Norske Vandrerhjem** (Dronningensgate 26, Oslo, tel. 22/42–14–10), details every last hostel in the country, with descriptions in Norwegian. **Campgrounds** litter the countryside, although most cater to the motor-home crowd. Tent spots go for 40kr–150kr, and you often pay 10kr–15kr extra per person. Almost every campground also has cabins, starting at about 200kr for four beds (BYO sleeping bag). **Camping rough** is a Norwegian tradition enshrined in law—just make sure you're 150 meters (500 feet) from buildings and the road. **Den Norske Turistforening** (*see* Visitor Information, *below*) runs a network of mountain *hytter* (huts) in the main wilderness areas. Prices start at 70kr for members, 120kr for nonmembers.

FOOD This will be a big expense. When considering the price of a room, figure in whether breakfasts are included—these all-you-can-eat smörgåsbords can save you money for the rest of the day. Supermarkets will probably provide the bulk of your nourishment, and the kitchens in almost all budget lodgings give you a chance to whip up something warm now and then. Beer is available in supermarkets, but wine and hard liquor are sold only in government liquor stores, which usually close at about 4:30 weekdays, 1 PM Saturday. For a drink at a bar, expect to pay 25kr–42kr.

Many cafeteria-style restaurants offer a *dagens rett* (daily special) for 35kr–70kr, especially at lunch. Norway is a meat-and-potatoes kind of place, not very friendly to vegetarians, but if you eat fish you'll have lots of options. The exorbitant food prices will probably keep you from sampling local delicacies on a daily basis, but travelers able to splurge may get to try reindeer steak, cod tongues, or boiled sheep's head.

VISITOR INFORMATION Every tiny settlement with any tourist trade whatsoever has a tourist information office, often open only in summer. Be sure to pick up local guides, which list accommodations, restaurants, and often hikes. Norway's mountain-touring association, **Den Norske Turistforening (DNT)** (Stortingsgata 28, Oslo, tel. 22/83–25–50), is the best place to go for help in planning a hiking or climbing trip. A yearlong membership, which will reduce the cost of staying in DNT's rural huts (*see* Where to Sleep, *above*), starts at 150kr for those under 26, 270kr for those 26 and over.

PHONES Country code: 47. At press time, all phone numbers in Norway were in the process of being changed. Numbers in this book should correspond to the new system, but don't be surprised if a few have been altered by the time you arrive. Changes will be announced in Norwegian when you call the old number; it's a good idea to learn some Norwegian numbers so you can figure it all out.

Pay phones accept 1kr, 5kr, and 10kr coins but don't give change. Every call costs a minimum of 2kr. Phone cards (35kr), available at telephone offices in most towns, are useful for calling long-distance, but phones that accept cards are uncommon outside Oslo. Dial 095 to make direct international calls (almost futile without a phone card), 093 for an English-speaking operator, and 050–12–011 to reach an AT&T USA Direct operator.

LANGUAGE There are two official written languages in Norway: *Bokmål* (book language); and *Nynorsk* (new Norwegian), the language spoken by most residents. These days, Norwegians begin learning English when they're about 10, so most young people have a good grasp of the language. Older people, especially those in rural areas, may not be as proficient.

Oslo
What sets Oslo apart from other European cities is not so much its cultural tradition or its internationally renowned museums, as its spectacular natural beauty. What other world capital has subway service to the forest, or lakes and hiking trails within the city limits? And where else but Oslo could you get lost in the woods while making your museum rounds? But Norwegians will be quick to remind you that Oslo is as cosmopolitan as any world capital and that its burgeoning music and art scenes rival those of Copenhagen and Stockholm (for what that's worth).

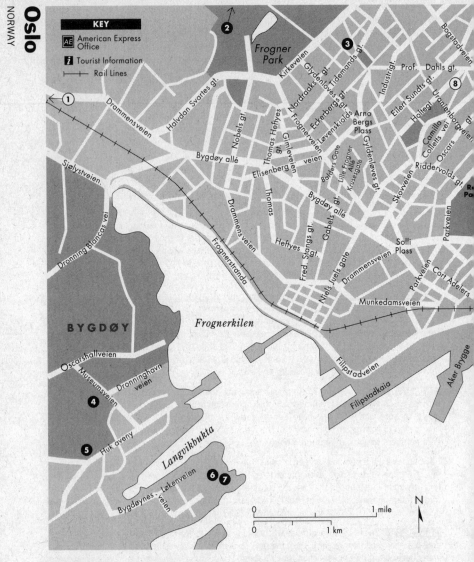

KEY

AE American Express Office

🚹 Tourist Information

├─┼─ Rail Lines

Frogner Park

BYGDØY

Frognerkilen

Langvikbukta

0 ——— 1 mile
0 ——— 1 km

N

Sights ●

Akershus Slott
and Norges
Hiemmefront-
museum, **12**
Fram-museet, **7**
Holmenkollen, **3**
Kon-Tiki Museum, **6**
Kunstindustri-
museet, **10**
Munchmuseet, **18**
Norsk
Folkemuseum, **4**

Oslo Domkirke, **15**
Teatermuseet, **11**
Vigelands Sculpture
Park, **2**
Vikingskips-
museet, **5**

Lodging ○
City Hotel, **14**
Cochs Pensjonat, **9**
Ekeberg
Camping, **19**
Ellingsen's
Pensjonat, **8**
Haraldsheim
(HI), **17**
Holtekilen
Sommerhotell
(HI), **1**

Hotel Fønix, **13**
KFUM InterRail
Point (YMCA), **16**

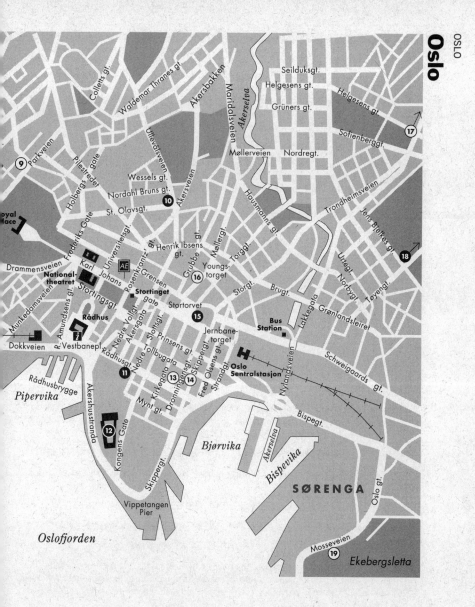

Seilduksgt.
Helgesens gt.
Helgesens gt.
Grüners gt.
Akerselva
Collets gt.
Waldemar Thranes gt.
Akersbakken
Maridalsveien
Sofienberggt.
(17)
Parkveien
(9)
Ullevalsveien
Møllerveien
Nordregt.
Trondheimsveien
Pilestredet
Holbergs gate
Wessels gt.
Akersveien
Hausmanns gt.
Jens Bjelkes gt.
Nordahl Bruns gt.
(10)
St. Olavsgt.
(18)
Drammensveien
Frederiks Gate
Universitetsgt.
Henrik Ibsens gt.
Møllergt.
Torggt.
Urtegt.
Karl
Johans
Rosenkrantz' gt.
Grensen
Gubbe
Youngs-torget
Storgt.
Brugt.
Norbygt.
Tøyengt.
National-theatret
Stortingsgt.
Stortinget
gate
Stortorvet
(16)
Grønlandsleiret
Munkedamsveien
Amundsens gt.
Rådhus
Nedre Voligt.
Akersgata
(15)
Storgt.
Lakkegata
Dokkveien
Vestbanepl.
Rådhusgt.
Nedre Slottsgt.
Prinsens gt.
Jernbane-torget
Bus
Station
Schweigaards gt.
Rådhusbrygge
Akershusstranda
(11)
Tollbugata
Skippergt.
Fred Olsens gt.
Strandgt.
Oslo
Sentralstasjon
Nylandsveien
Pipervika
Kirkegata
(13) (14)
Dronningensgt.
Kongens Gate
(12)
Mynt gt.
Bispegt.
Bjørvika
Akerselva
Bispevika
Skippergt.
SØRENGA
Vippetangen
Pier
Oslo gt.
Oslofjorden
Mosseveien
(19)
Ekebergsletta

Modern architectural monstrosities and 17th-century palaces sit side by side on cobblestone avenues, in a strange harmony that will grow on you if you stick around.

Oslo, founded by Harald Hardråde in about 1048, is the oldest Scandinavian capital. After the original city on the eastern side of the Oslo fjord was repeatedly destroyed by fire, the 17th-century Danish king Christian IV moved it to its present site and renamed it Christiania. (Its original name was reinstated in 1925.) The city sprawls around the Oslo fjord and into the surrounding woodlands, and a mind-boggling public transit network connects all the major (and minor) sights, most of them outside the city center. **Akershus** and **Nordmarka,** the wilderness areas surrounding Oslo, are full of opportunities for hiking, boating, rafting, biking, fishing, and skiing. Check with the DNT or tourist offices (*see* Visitor Information, *below*) for details, or just take Tunnelbanen (T-bane) 15 to Frognerseteren and go for a hike.

BASICS

VISITOR INFORMATION Oslo's main **Information Center** sells the Oslo Card, good for free admission to museums, unlimited travel on public transit, and discounts at shops and restaurants. Prices start at 95kr for one day. The center also distributes the *Oslo Guide* and *What's On in Oslo*, with up-to-date info on things to see. A **kiosk** at the train station (tel. 22/17-11-24) books rooms in private homes for a 20kr service charge. *Main office: Vestbaneplassen 1, tel. 22/83-00-50. Open May–Sept., weekdays 9–6, weekends 9–4, with extended hours June–Aug.; Oct.–Apr., weekdays 9–4.*

Use It has tons of information for budget travelers. Its *Streetwise* magazine is a comprehensive guide to cheap eats, sleeps, and fun in and around Oslo. The staff can also book rooms in private homes and arrange sublets for longer stays, all at no charge. *Møllergata 3, tel. 22/41-51-28 or 22/41-51-32. Open June–Aug., weekdays 7:30–6, Sat. 9–2; Sept.–May, weekdays 11–5.*

Den Norske Turistforening (DNT) is your one-stop hiking-information warehouse, with maps, brochures, and keys for Norway's extensive mountain-hytter network. *Stortingsgata 28, tel. 22/83-25-50. Open weekdays 8:30–4, Thurs. until 6.*

AMERICAN EXPRESS **Winge Reisebureau.** *Karl Johans gate 33/35, tel. 22/41-20-30.*

BUCKET SHOPS **Kilroy Travel** is *the* student travel agency in Oslo. *Nedre Slottsgate 23, tel. 22/42-01-20.*

EMBASSIES **Canada.** *Oscars gate 20, tel. 22/46-69-55. Open weekdays 8–3:30.*

United Kingdom. *Thomas Heftyes gate 8, tel. 22/55-24-00. Open weekdays 9–12:30.*

United States. *Drammensveien 18, tel. 22/44-85-50. Open weekdays 9–noon.*

EMERGENCIES For an **ambulance** or the **police** call 022; for the **fire** department call 001. For non-emergency police matters, stop by or call the **station** (Grønlandsleiret 44, tel. 22/66-90-50). A **24-hour pharmacy** called Jernbanetorgets Apotek (tel. 22/41-24-82) is across from the train station.

PHONES AND MAIL Phone cards are available at **Teleekspedisjon,** the telephone office (Kongens gate 21, tel. 22/40-55-09), or at the ubiquitous **Narvesen kiosks,** which sell newspapers and tobacco. Pick up poste restante mail at the main **post office** (Dronningensgate 15, tel. 22/33-40-71). The postal code is 0152.

COMING AND GOING

BY TRAIN Oslo is the rail hub for Norway. Trains head southwest to Stavanger (9 hrs, 380kr), west to Bergen (6 hrs, 380kr), and north to Åndalsnes (6 hrs, 320kr) and Bodø (19 hrs, 490kr). Prices rise almost 70% on weekends. **Oslo Sentralstasjon** (Jernbanetorget, tel. 22/42-19-19), also known as **Oslo S,** has 20kr luggage lockers, tourist info, a currency exchange, and a lost-luggage office (tel. 22/36–80–47). The **Norwegian National Railway (NSB)** has an office in the station. Call 22/36–65–50 for rail information. The **InterRail Center** (open summer, daily 7 AM–11 PM) in the station basement has showers and a kitchen for those with a train ticket.

BY BUS **Norway Bussekspress** (Karl Johans gate 2, tel. 22/33–01–90, or 22/17–52–90 for reservations), northeast of the train station in the Galleri Oslo, operates an extensive bus network with service to Sørlandet and the Jotunheimen Mountains. The trip to Haukeliseter in Sørlandet takes six hours and costs 292kr. Some buses give student discounts, so be sure to ask.

BY PLANE Oslo has two airports: **Fornebu,** 7 km from the city center, and **Gardermoen,** about 50 km from town. The **SAS Flybussen** connects both airports to Oslo's bus terminal. Buses head to Fornebu (20 min, 30kr) every 15 minutes from 6:45 AM to 10 PM, except on Saturday night, when they stop running at 8:30. Buses to Gardermoen (50 min, 60kr) leave the bus terminal two hours before flight departures.

BY FERRY Three ferry companies link Oslo with Germany, Denmark, and England. Call **Color Line** (Hjortneskaia, tel. 22/83–60–60), **Scandinavian Seaways** (Karl Johans gate 1, tel. 22/41–90–90), or **Stena Lines AS** (Stortingsgata 5, tel. 22/41–22–10) for the latest schedules and prices. Prices are seasonal and hover around $100 per trip. Ask about student discounts, which can save you up to 50% in the off-season. Ferries dock at Vippetangen Pier near Akershus castle; from the train station, walk or take Bus 29.

GETTING AROUND

Oslo's city center is easily navigated on foot. **Karl Johans gate,** the main street, runs east–west from the train station to the Royal Palace and the **Nationaltheatret,** a local transport hub. Beyond the city center, Oslo resembles Los Angeles in its suburban sprawl; but unlike L.A., Oslo has subways, local trains, buses, trams, and ferries that link even the most remote suburbs. To figure out which mode of transport to take, ask or use the maps at **Trafikanten** (Jernbanetorget, in front of train station, tel. 22/17–70–30). Here you can buy a card good for 24 hours of transport for 35kr. The entire network is free with the Oslo Card (*see* Visitor Information, *above*). Buy individual tickets (15kr), good for an hour's transport, from bus or tram drivers or from machines in the subway stations.

Most **buses** stop at the train station or the Nationaltheatret on Karl Johans gate. Night buses, starting at midnight, are a rip-off at 30kr. The **Tunnelbanen (T-bane)** has a hub at Stortinget in the city center, from which eight lines set out for the suburbs. The system starts up at 6 AM and runs until 12:30 AM. **Tram** hubs are Stortorvet and Jernbanetorget, in front of the train station. **Local trains** run from the train station and the Nationaltheatret.

Ferries connect the city center with the Bygdøy peninsula, the fjord islands, and outlying districts along the Oslo fjord. Ferries leave for Bygdøy from the docks outside the Rådhus, for the islands from Vippetangen Pier behind Akershus castle, and for other destinations from the Aker Brygge pier. Oslo is a great city for **biking,** and the forests offer excellent mountain trails. Bikes are allowed on the subway, so you can get a head start up the hills. **Den Rustne Eike** (Vestbaneplassen 2, next to main tourist office, tel. 22/83–72–31) rents mountain bikes starting at 65kr for three hours, but a 500kr–1,500kr deposit is required.

WHERE TO SLEEP

Cheap summer rooms in Oslo are about as easy to find as water in the Sahara. Plan ahead and be creative. For the best lodging deal in town, rent a room in a private home through Use It (*see* Visitor Information, *above*). The rooms, all less than 130kr and most about 100kr, fill up fast in high season and can be some distance from the center. The tourist information center at the train station also books rooms in private homes, but these start at 150kr (plus a 20kr fee).

➤ **UNDER 300KR** • **Ellingsen's Pensjonat.** On a tree-lined street on the central west side. Enthusiastic proprietress gives the place a homey feel. Smallish, tidy rooms. Doubles 280kr. *Holtegata 25, tel. 22/60–03–59. Tram 1 from station toward Majorstuen.*

➤ **UNDER 400KR** • **Cochs Pensjonat.** Spacious, almost antiseptic rooms behind the palace on the central west side. Most come with hot plates. A good deal if you're in a group—showerless quads are 520kr. Doubles 380kr, with shower 490kr. *Parkveien 25, tel. 22/60–48–36. Tram 7 or 11 from station toward Majorstuen.*

➤ **UNDER 500KR** • **City Hotel.** Clean, basic rooms in the center. Charming reception area furnished with antiques. Weekends are cheaper than weekdays, and you get 10% discount on weekday prices with Use It card. Double without bath 535kr weekdays, 420kr weekends; breakfast included. *Skippergate 19, tel. 22/41–36–10. Off Karl Johans gate near station. AE, MC, V.*

Hotel Fønix. Small rooms off Karl Johans gate with matching wood furniture. Breakfast (included in price) served in a regal dining room next door. Doubles 450kr, 400kr weekends. *Dronningensgate 21, tel. 22/42–59–57. Laundry. AE, MC, V.*

HOSTELS **Haraldsheim (HI).** Your basic generic hostel with a view of the Oslo fjord. Nice lawn and plush solarium, but you may get an overdose of screaming kids. Reservations essential in summer. Beds 141kr, 162kr nonmembers, breakfast included; sheets 35kr. *Haraldsheimveien 4, tel. 22/15–50–43. Tram 1 or 7 from station to Sinsen; climb hill. Lockout 10–3, laundry.*

If you have a tent, you'll never be without a place to crash in Oslo. Pitch it anywhere in the forest at least 150 meters from a dwelling, and you've got a perfectly legal, free home base.

Holtekilen Sommerhotell (HI). Far from the center but easily reached by train. Chalkboards and desks add a schoolhouse touch to rooms. Singles 240kr, 265kr nonmembers; dorm beds 140kr, 165kr nonmembers; sheets 35kr. *Michelets vei 55, Stabekk, tel. 67/53–38–53. From station, local train (toward Drammen) to Stabekk; turn right outside station and follow footpath across highway. Closed Aug. 16–May.*

KFUM InterRail Point (YMCA). The cheapest beds in town. Centrally located and hard to beat, although it's only open July–August 20. Cultural evenings on Thursday. Take a number next door at Use It when reception isn't open. Requisite 20kr membership card good at all European YMCAs. Beds 75kr. *Møllergata 1, entrance on Grubbegate, tel. 22/42–10–66. Reception open daily 8–11 and 5–midnight, kitchen facilities.*

CAMPGROUNDS If you've forgotten your tent, talk to **Den Norske Turistforening** (*see* Visitor Information, *above*) about wilderness huts.

Ekeberg Camping. Only 3 km from the center, with a fabulous view of the Oslo fjord, although many sites have a rear view of a trailer parking lot. Sites 80kr, 120kr with car. *Ekebergveien 65, tel. 22/19–85–68. Bus 24, 45, or 46 toward Ekeberg. Laundry, kitchen facilities. MC, V. Closed Sept.–May.*

FOOD

You'll find the cheapest hole-in-the-wall restaurants and small grocery stores in the immigrant areas of Grønland and Tøyen, northeast of the train station. Also look for produce markets at Jernbanetorget, Grønlands torg, and Youngstorget.

➤ **UNDER 50KR** • **Cafe Sekel.** Good for breakfast. Floral drapes and wood tables evoke the atmosphere of a country home. Friendly staff serves heaping portions. Try the starchy *pytt i panne*, with potatoes, sausage, and egg, for 35kr. Coffee 10kr. *Tollbugata 6, near Karl Johans gate, tel. 22/42–42–12.*

Punjab Sweet House. Indian specials served in a spartan atmosphere in the Grønland district. Nan, salad, dahl, and three entrées all for 30kr. Try chicken curry (33kr) or snack on samosas (10kr each). *Grønlandsleiret 24, outside Grønland T-bane, tel. 22/70–20–86.*

➤ **UNDER 75KR** • **Krishna's Cuisine Vegetarian Restaurant.** One of the city's best bargains. All-you-can-eat specials (65kr) include salad, soup, rice, pakora, and two entrées. Mouthwatering curries and Indian fare also served à la carte. *Kirkeveien 59B, tel. 22/60–62–50. Outside Majorstuen T-bane.*

Vegeta Verthus. The oldest vegetarian restaurant in Oslo. Buffet with hot entrées, pizza, and salad fixings costs 61kr for a small plate, 69kr for a large, and 98kr all-you-can-eat. Comes with your fill of bread and cheese. *Munkedamsveien 3B, near Nationaltheatret, tel. 22/83–40–20.*

WORTH SEEING

Oslo has museums up the wazoo, but you'll also have plenty of opportunities to spend time outdoors. Most museums and sights are outside the city center—get a complete list at the tourist office if you want to track down every last one.

CITY CENTER You can explore interesting dungeons and courtyards at **Akershus Slott** (tel. 22/41–25–21; admission 10kr, 5kr students), a castle built in about 1300 and converted into a Renaissance palace by Christian IV in the 17th century. This place is infamous for having housed a Nazi headquarters during World War II. The castle's resistance museum, the Norges **Hiemmefrontmuseum** (tel. 22/40–31–38; admission 15kr, 5kr students), documents the episode in an eerie collection of photographs, papers, and recordings. Also in the city center, the **Kunstindustrimuseet** (St. Olavs gate 1, tel. 22/20–35–78; admission 15kr, 10kr students; closed Mon.) displays Norwegian handicrafts, industrial designs, and royal costumes dating from the 7th century. In the old city hall, built in 1641, the **Teatermuseet** (Nedre Slottsgate 1, tel. 22/41–81–47; admission 10kr, 5kr students; open Wed. 10–3, Sun. noon–4) houses old costumes, props, and theater sets.

BYGDØY PENINSULA The peninsula has its share of museums, but they're a far cry from the usual staid collections of paintings. You can wander the forests and explore reconstructed buildings and farms dating from the Middle Ages at the **Norsk Folkemuseum** (Museumsveien 10, tel. 22/43–70–20; admission 35kr, 25kr students), an outdoor exhibit documenting the development of rural architecture. The earthen roofs, constructed with eight layers of waterproof bark, provided excellent insulation—in fact, modern alternative-building circles are returning to this style.

On the opposite side of the peninsula, the **Kon-Tiki Museum** (Bygdøynesveien 36, tel. 22/43–80–50; admission 20kr, 10kr students) displays the original *Kon Tiki* raft that Thor Heyerdal took across the Pacific in 1947. *Ra II*, the reed boat that he sailed across the Atlantic, is also on display. Roald Amundsen's vessel from his 1911 Antarctic odyssey is beached at the **Fram-museet** (Bygdøynesveien, tel. 22/43–83–70; admission 20kr, 10kr students; closed Jan.–Mar.). The reconstructed living quarters reveal the cramped conditions the explorers endured. Three Viking burial ships from the 9th century, along with the loot found inside, are on display at the **Vikingskipsmuseet** (Huk aveny 38, tel. 22/43–83–79; admission 20kr, 10kr students). You can escape the museum circuit at **Huk Beach,** behind the Vikingskipsmuseet and through the woods. Ferries to the Bygdøy peninsula leave every 30 minutes between 7:45 and 6 from the Rådhusbrygge; you can also take Bus 30 from Jernbanetorget.

When Edvard Munch's masterpiece The Scream *was stolen from the National Gallery in 1994, anti-abortionists tried to claim responsibility, hoping to strong-arm the government into televising a film that depicts abortion as murder (the group uses Munch's painting in its propaganda).*

MUNCHMUSEET Edvard Munch, Norway's most famous painter and one of the founders of expressionism, donated all the works in his possession to the Oslo city council upon his death. Only a part of the massive collection is displayed, and you'll be lucky if *The Scream*, stolen in 1994 but recovered six months later, is on exhibit. Whatever the lineup, you're sure to get your fill of women, violence, love, and death. *Tøyengata 53, tel. 22/67–37–74. T-bane or Bus 20 to Tøyen. Admission 40kr, 15kr students. Open June–mid-Sept., Mon.–Sat. 10–6, Sun. noon–6; shorter hrs off-season.*

VIGELANDS SCULPTURE PARK A vast expanse of manicured lawns frames the open-air display of Gustav Vigeland's most famous works. His fantastic parade of bronze sculptures depicting the human life cycle culminates in the obelisk, a seething mass of human forms that thrusts 65 feet into the sky. Admission is free; take the T-bane to Majorstuen or Tram 2 to Frognerpark.

Gustav wasn't the only artist in the family. His brother, Emanuel, created his own version of the life cycle, with a heavy emphasis on death and decay. Emanuel's most famous work is his own **tomb** (Grimelundsveien 8, tel. 22/14–93–42; admission free; open Sun. noon–3), located northwest of Frognerpark and the city center (take T-bane 15 to Vinderen). Frescoes covering the walls reveal his dark vision, and the acoustics of the room and the artist's ashes above the door add to the sense that the place is haunted.

HOLMENKOLLEN You get a dizzying view of Oslo from this world-famous ski jump. In summer the bottom is filled with water, and concerts and weird water-slide fests are held here. All year long you can peek into the attached ski museum, which is more interesting than you might expect. *Tel. 22/92–32–00. T-bane 15 toward Frognerseteren to Holmenkollen. Admission 50kr, 35kr students.*

CHEAP THRILLS

After enduring an arctic winter, hardy Norwegians don't seem to mind the cold waters of Oslo's inner fjord. Its islands make a relaxing summer day trip. **Hovedøya,** closest to town, is most crowded. **Langøyene,** to the south, has nude beaches and often hosts all-night beach parties. Ferries to the islands leave from Vippetangen Pier. You can also take T-bane 4 to **Sognsvann,** in the hills north of the city center, where you'll find a spectacular lake that will make you forget you're in a European capital.

Those with a morbid curiosity should explore the crypt underneath **Oslo Domkirke** (Stortorvet 1, tel. 22/41–63–00), the city's cathedral. Rotting wood coffins line the walls of two chambers, and in another rests an ornate marble tomb containing the remains of the richest man in 18th-century Oslo. To get into the crypt, go to the cathedral (open weekdays 10–3 and Saturday 10–1) and ask someone to take you downstairs.

AFTER DARK

Pick up the free *Natt & Dag* anywhere in town for the whole story on Oslo's nightlife. The city has plenty of bars and pubs; those in east Oslo are cheapest. Many bars have happy hours before 9 with half-liters for about 25kr. After 9, prices rise to about 36kr, often more in outdoor cafés. Most nightlife takes place in the streets off Karl Johans gate; just pick the blasting music that you like best. **Head On** (Rosenkranz' gate 11) attracts a mellow alternative crowd. **Café Fiasco** (in Galleri Oslo, above bus station) has cheap beer on an outdoor patio, but **Prince Edward** (on Akerselva River at Grønland) is just as cheap and has a sunnier patio. **Den Sorte Enke** (Møllergata 23) is Oslo's premier gay hangout.

Oslo's live music scene is definitely picking up, and international tours often pass through. **Rockefeller** (Torggata 16) and **Sentrum** (Arbeidersamfunnets plass 2) host touring bands. The **Center for African Culture Exchange (CAK)** (Brenneriveien 5) has an African disco, and the **Blitz** (Pilestredet 30), where Punk Rök lives on, often hosts bands in the European underground scene.

Sørlandet

In the summer Oslo's residents migrate to the southern coast to soak up some sunshine while the rest of the country suffers from incessant rain. Unfortunately, unless you have plenty of time or a car, you'll probably catch only glimpses of the spectacular Sørlandet region through a train window. The international ferry ports of Kristiansand and Stavanger are easy to reach, but there's no reason to make a special effort to see them. Your best bet for exploring Sørlandet (composed of Telemark, Aust Auger, Vest Auger, and Vestfold counties) is to pick a youth hostel or mountain hut and make your way there. **Odda,** on the Kristiansand–Voss bus line, is on the farthest inland arm of the Hardangerfjord; it's a good base for setting off into the Hardangervidda, Norway's largest mountain plateau. The **Odda Vandrerhjem** (Sørfjordheimen, Røldalsveil 33, tel. 53/64–14–11; beds 130kr) is open June through September.

Kristiansand

Despite Kristiansand's popularity with Norwegian vacationers, the town offers little of interest for budget travelers. The best beaches lie some distance away, the cutesy old town and tourist-mobbed pedestrian malls aren't worth a special trip, and unless you have a tent the likelihood of landing a place to sleep for less than 300kr is practically nil. If you do find a room, head for the beach; the **tourist information office** (Dronningensgate 2, tel. 380/2–60–65) can give you tips on the best ones and help with directions. At the north end of town the **Baneheia recreation area** has lakes, waterfalls, plenty of hiking trails, and a nice crag from which to view the city.

Kristiansand is Norway's number-one beach resort, and everyone from hormone-crazed teens to the silver-haired set basks in its sunshine on holidays.

COMING AND GOING **Trains** from Oslo (6 hrs, 320kr, 370kr weekends) stop right next to the bus and ferry terminals at the southwestern edge of town. **Color Line** (tel. 380/7–88–88) runs ferry service to Hirtshals, Denmark (4–6 hrs, about 300kr in summer, 100kr in winter). **Sørlandsruta** (tel. 380/2–43–80) runs an express bus to Voss (9–10 hrs, 413kr), a town on the Oslo–Bergen train route. The streets of Kristiansand form a grid, with the Domkirke in the center and the old town in the northeast corner. **City buses,** which converge at the bottom of Henrik Wergelands gate, cost 11kr.

WHERE TO SLEEP AND EAT The **HI Kristiansand Vandrerhjem** (Kongsgård allé 33C, tel. 380/9–53–69; beds 120kr, 140kr nonmembers; closed Sept.–May), about 1 km outside town, is almost always booked solid. If you've reserved in advance, take Bus 15 or 16 toward Lund. These buses will also take you to **Roligheden Camping** (Framnesveien, tel. 380/9–67–22) on the beach, where cabins with four beds go for 450kr.

Your best bet for a meal is the **Skipperstua Kafeteria** (Skippergaten 21, tel. 380/2–90–75), where daily specials are 43kr and coffee is always free. **Peppe's Pizza** (Gyldenløves gate 7, across from Domkirke, tel. 380/2–23–22) has large pizzas for 100kr–170kr and an outdoor patio filled with young people.

Stavanger

Despite its dubious distinction as the oil capital of Norway, prosperous Stavanger has managed to maintain a sense of history. You wouldn't want to make a special trip here; but if you find yourself in town waiting for ferry connections, it's worth taking time to explore the narrow, cobblestone streets of **Gamle (Old) Stavanger,** which has the world's only sardine canning museum, the **Norsk Hermetikkmuseum** (Øvre Strandgate 88A, tel. 51/52–60–35; admission 20kr). Stavanger is also a good base for excursions to Preikestolen (*see* Outdoor Activities, *below*) and western Sørlandet. Hook up with **Stavanger Turistforening** (Muségata 8, tel. 51/52–75–66; open weekdays 9–4) to get details on the 900 km of trails and 30 mountain huts in the area. For a complete list of stuff to do, pick up the *Stavanger Guide* at the **tourist information office**

(Stavanger Kulturhus-Sølvberget, tel. 51/89–66–00), in the center of the main shopping district.

COMING AND GOING Trains from Oslo (9 hrs, 380kr–580kr) arrive in the center of town next to the bus station, where you can catch the express bus to Bergen (7–8 hrs, 290kr). **Color Line** (Strandkaien, tel. 51/52–45–45) runs ferries from Newcastle, England (20 hrs), that continue to Bergen. Fares start at US$34 and go sky high. For a quick trip to Bergen, take the **Hurtigbåt** (4 hrs, 450kr) from the bottom of Kirkegata. Students and those with hostel cards or rail passes get substantial discounts. Call 51/52–20–90 for information. Cheaper but slower is the **Kystveien car ferry** (7 hrs, 175kr, 120kr students). Call 51/32–74–91 for schedules before you hop on Bus 169, which goes to the dock at Randaberg.

WHERE TO SLEEP AND EAT The **HI hostel** (H. Ibsensgate 21, tel. 51/87–09–77; beds 110kr) is one of Norway's nicest. You can camp lakeside next door at **Mosvangen Camping** (Tjensvoll 1, tel. 51/53–29–71; closed Oct.–May) for 55kr or rent a four-bed cabin for 325kr. Take Bus 130 from the cathedral to reach the campground. **Roglandsheimen Bed and Breakfast** (Muségata 18, tel. 51/52–01–88; dorm beds 150kr, doubles 390kr) occupies a charming old wood home. It's upstairs behind the train station and under the highway.

Near the harbor, **Skagen China Town** (Skagen 14, tel. 51/56–72–22) has daily lunch specials for 52kr–69kr, and the **Thai restaurant** across the street offers 65kr specials all day. At **Café Akvariat** (Folken, Olavs Kleiva 16, tel. 51/56–57–67), a student hangout, you get can coffee for 5kr and lasagna for 35kr.

OUTDOOR ACTIVITIES Plunging almost 2,000 feet to the turquoise waters of Lysefjord below, **Preikestolen** (Pulpit Rock) is one of the area's most popular attractions. The climb to the top takes two or three hours. For the most interesting hike, follow the red marks up the boulder fields while the tour-bus crowd takes the easy road. From Stavanger an 8:30 AM ferry runs to Tau (40 min, 25kr), where you board a connecting bus to Jørpland (35kr) that stops at the trailhead from mid-June to September. The bus returns at 4, but from June to September you can stay overnight at the **Preikestolen Youth Hostel** (tel. 51/74–72–66; beds 100kr), in a little farmhouse on the shores of a fabulous mountain lake.

Central Norway and the Fjords

The Norwegian fjords snake inland from the Russian border in the far north all the way to the country's southern tip. In spectacular inlets like Sognefjord and Geirangerfjord, vertical rock walls shoot up out of the water, jagged snowcapped peaks blot out the sky, and water tumbles down off the mountains in an endless variety of colors, from thundering turquoise to wispy white. Even the Nordfjord, a comparatively modest slice into Norway's coastline, offers stunning views of the massive Jostedalsbreen glacier.

This is troll country, home to many a magical creature. Unfortunately, it's also package tour country, so you'll have a hard time discovering the fjords' beauty in solitude. After a tough three-hour hike to the top of a mountain, it can be discouraging to look down the other side at an armada of tour buses coming up the easy road just in time to spoil your glorious view. Campgrounds are plentiful, but they're often packed with trailers. The strategically placed youth hostels are a good bet, and you'll encounter mountain hytter regularly. If you travel in a group, you'll expand your options considerably—almost every campground has four-bed cabins for 250kr–500kr. The food scene is very basic in all the fjord towns except Bergen. Most towns have cafeterias with specials for about 60kr–80kr, but for anything else prepare to play chef in the hostel kitchens.

Bergen

Eurailers who make it as far as Norway often bypass Oslo and barrel straight ahead to Bergen. This isn't a bad idea: Bergen is the gateway to Norway's gorgeous fjords, and it has managed to keep an intimate, small-town feeling despite the fact that it's the second-largest city in Norway. If you arrive between June and August, though, you may feel like a small speck of dust in the tourist cloud that swarms over the city.

Bergen was the capital of Norway for 600 years and was a vital outpost of the medieval, German-based Hanseatic merchants' league. But until the Germans built a road from here to Oslo during the Nazi occupation, Bergen was isolated from the rest of the country and had closer ties to mainland Europe. Composer Edvard Grieg is to Bergen what Mozart is to Salzburg—a local hero and source of pride. You'll find his name all over town, and it's just a matter of time until someone starts selling a Grieg fish cake. The **Bergen International Music Festival** is the town's biggest blowout, with 12 days of music, drama, and dance performances. The festival is strategically scheduled for late May and early June, when statistics say the sun will shine the most, but be prepared for rain whenever you come.

BASICS The **tourist office** changes money after hours at lousy rates. It caters more to bus-tour types than to budget travelers, but its *Bergen Guide* is indispensable. *Cnr. of Bryggen and Lodin Leppsgate, tel. 55/32–14–80. Open May–Sept., Mon.–Sat. 8:30–9, Sun. 10–7; Oct.–Apr., weekdays 9–4.*

The Bergen **DNT** office can help you arrange extended trips to the fjords and can recommend hikes in the nearby mountains. *Tverrgaten 4/6, toward town from train station, tel. 55/32–22–30. Open weekdays 10–4, Thurs. 10–6.*

The main **post office** (tel. 55/54–15–00) is in the green building with the clock on Småstrandgaten. Make long-distance calls from the **Telegraph Building** (Starvhusgaten 4, next to post office; open weekdays 8–8, Sat. 9–2).

COMING AND GOING The Oslo–Bergen train (6 hrs, 380kr, 460kr weekends, 20kr reservation required) travels from lush pine forests through the bleak, snow-covered tundra of the Hardangervidda and into the fjords. The Bergen **train station** is on Strømgaten (tel. 55/96–60–00) at the south end of town. Long-distance buses leave from the **bus station** (tel. 55/32–67–80), next to the train station on Strømgaten. Buses are most useful for trips to the Hardangerfjord area and for getting to southern Norway without returning to Oslo.

International ferries from England, Iceland, Denmark, Scotland, and the Faroe Islands dock at **Skoltegrunnskaien,** on the east side of the harbor. **Color Line** (Skuteviksboder 1/2, tel. 55/54–86–60) runs to Stavanger and on to Newcastle, England (24 hrs). Fares fluctuate drastically. From the same office as Color Line, **P&O Lines** (tel. 55/54–86–60) runs to Lerwick and Aberdeen, Scotland (about 24 hrs, fares from US$75). **Fjord Line** (Slottsgaten 1, across from Bryggens Museum, tel. 55/32–37–70) runs to Denmark (15 hrs, fares from US$30). Most ferry companies give students a reduction of up to 50% in the off-season.

Express boats to Stavanger and Hardangerfjord leave from **Munkebryggen** (west side of harbor, tel. 55/23–87–80). Boats to Sognefjord and Nordfjord sail from **Strandkai Terminal** (west side of harbor, tel. 55/32–40–15). Students and rail-pass holders get a 50% discount. The **Hurtigrute** coastal steamer leaves from **Freleneskalen,** behind the Natural History Museum.

GETTING AROUND Bergen's center is walkable, and only a few attractions will force you onto the bus. Most local buses converge on **Småstrandgaten,** behind the post office on Olav Kyres gate, and at **Torget,** the fish market. Around town you'll pay 12kr for a one-hour ride.

WHERE TO SLEEP Bergen has a good selection of cheap accommodations, but rooms fill up fast in high season. The DNT (*see* Visitor Information, *above*) operates hytter on Mt. Ulriken and Mt. Fløien. Another option is to pay the tourist office 20kr to book you a double in a private home for 260kr–310kr per night.

Nordnes-
parken ❶

Skoltegrunn-
skaien

Sjøgaten

❷

❸

Bergenhus

Bradbenken

Dreggsalm Nye Sandviksveien

Ladegårdsg.

Øvre Sandviksveien

Breistølveien

❹

❺ ❻

Bryggen

Øvregaten

Steinkjellergt.

Skanselien

Fjellveien

Vågen

Strandgaten

Haugeveien

M. Nøstegaten

Klosteret

Klostergt.

TO
STAVANGER

N

Nøstegaten

Nestegaten

C. Sundts gate

ℹ
Iepps gt.

❼

Funicular

Rosenkrantzgt.

Fløyveien

Mt. Fløien

Torget

Vetrlidsalm

Korskirke alm

Vetrlidsalm

Vågsalm Allehelgens gt.

Kong Oscars Gate

Brattlien

Lille Øvregt.

Domkirke

Funicular

Prof. Hansteens gate

Dokkeveien

Strandgt.

Jon Smørs gt.

Marke veien

Engen Vaskerelven

Neumanns gt.

Magnus Barfots gt.

Torgalmen-
ingen

Smådstrandg.

Olav Kyrres gt.

Christies Gate

Kaigaten

Domkirkegt.

Domkirkegt.

Fjellveien

Leilet

Lille
Lungegårdsvann ❽ ❾

Lungegårdsgt.

Kalfarveien

Ole Irgens vei

Train
Station

Nygårdsgaten

Fosswinckels gt.

Lars Hilles Gate

555

Weltevnens gate

Konsul Børs gate

Prof. Hansteens gate

Strømgaten

Bus
Station

J.Reins gt

H.Tanks gt

E68

0 — 250 yards

0 — 250 meters

Michael Krohns gate

Nygårdsparken

TO OSLO

❿

TO OSLO

Bergen Akvariet, **1**

Bryggens
Museum, **5**

Gamle (Old)
Bergen, **2**

Håkonshallen, **3**

Hanseatisk
Museum/Theta
Museum, **7**

Mariakirchen, **6**

Municipal Art
Museum/
Stenersen's
Collection, **8**

Rasmus Meyer's
Samlinger, **9**

Rosenkrantz-
tårnet, **4**

Troldhaugen, **10**

Fagerheim Pensjon. A bit outside town but charming and cheap. Old wood mansion with funky mix-and-match furnishings and a nice view. Singles 170kr, doubles 300kr, breakfast 40kr. *Kalvedalsveien 49A, tel. 55/31–01–72. Bus 2, 4, 7, or 11 from town center. Kitchen.*

Kloster Pensjon. Central location on the southwest side of Vågen harbor. Mountain-cabin ambience. Singles 250kr, doubles 380kr, including breakfast. *Klosteret 12, tel. 55/90–21–58. From train station head toward water on Kaigaten, which becomes Markeveien, Klostergate, then Klosteret.*

➤ **HOSTELS • Intermission.** Family-run coed dorm offers mattresses on the floor in an 18th-century wood home. Friendly staff and homey atmosphere make this the best deal in town. No-reservations policy means no groups of noisy schoolchildren. Talk to warden about staying out past the 11 PM curfew. Beds 90kr. *Kalfarveien 8, tel. 55/31–32–75. Behind train station and northeast up hill; Bus 2, 4, or 11 from town center. Lockout 11–5, laundry, kitchen. Closed mid-Aug.–mid-June.*

InterRail Point. Cheapest, most central spot in town. Mattresses on the floor in a slightly run-down old building. Bring your own sleeping bag. Beds 90kr, breakfast 25kr. *Nedre Korskirkealm 4, tel. 55/31–73–32 or 55/31–72–52. 1 street south of Torget. 1 AM curfew, lockout 11–5, kitchen, sauna. Closed Sept.–mid-June.*

Montana Vandrerhjem (HI). Massive youth hostel at the foot of Mt. Ulriken with that familiar institutional feeling. Sitting room with fireplace and TV has great views of the mountain and Bergen. Far from the center. Curfew at 11, but ask the warden if you can come in later. Beds 141kr, including breakfast; sheets 35kr. *Johan Blydtsvei 30, tel. 55/29–29–00. Bus 4 from town center along Kalfarveien. Lockout 10–4:30.*

➤ **CAMPGROUNDS •** A favorite spot for camping rough is atop Mt. Fløien, but the last funicular goes up at 11 PM.

Bergshallens Camping. The only official camping spot within the city—10 minutes by bus from the center. 40kr per tent, no cabins. *Vilh. Bjerknesvei 24, tel. 55/27–01–80. Bus 3 from town center. Closed Oct.–late June.*

FOOD Look for restaurants with a *dagens rett* (daily special)—most cafeterias have one for 45kr–70kr. Seafood is plentiful and cheaper than you'd expect. The Torget fish market sells ready-to-eat boiled shrimp, crab, and salmon *rundstykke* (open sandwiches). Also try the local specialty *schillingsbolle*, a sugar-and-cardamom bun.

Pasta Sentral. Ask anyone in town about a cheap meal, and this place comes up. Basic pasta with sauce and bread fills you for 45kr. Daily pasta special with soda is only 39kr. Another location is on Ole Bulls plass, above Maxime. *Lars Hillesgate 22A, behind bus station, tel. 55/96–00–37.*

Spisestedet Kornelia. The only vegetarian crunch-fest in town. Specials are the best deal at 45kr–60kr. Ask about student menu during the school year. *Fosswinckelsgate 18, tel. 55/32–34–32. Closed summer weekends.*

USF Kulturhuset. Former United Sardine Factory is now a culture center and café/pub run by a bunch of artists. Daily meat, fish, and pasta specials 49kr. The 55kr barbecue is sure to satisfy you. Drink your reasonably priced beer (34kr) on a tourist-free waterfront deck. *Georgarnes Werft 3, tel. 55/90–05–71.*

WORTH SEEING Bergen has almost as many museums as Oslo. For a complete list, get the *Bergen Guide* at the tourist office. Although they're fairly low-key as far as castles go, **Rosenkrantztårnet**, a 16th-century fortified tower residence, and **Håkonshallen,** the 13th-century royal home (both on northeast side of harbor, tel. 55/31–60–67; admission 10kr, 5kr students), seem to impress tourists. Likewise, the aquarium, **Bergen Akvariet** (Nordnesparken; admission 40kr), is nothing to shout about, but it's interesting to see what the region's fish look like alive instead of dead on your plate.

➢ **AROUND BRYGGEN** • The gabled wood warehouses lining Bryggen, the wharf on the northeast side of Bergen's harbor, mark the site of the original settlement. The first buildings were destroyed by fire, and the current structures date from the 18th century, but they reflect the architectural styles of the 15th century, when the Hansa merchants controlled the economy.

If 19th-century paintings are too tame for you, head to the Leprosy Museum (Kong Oscarsgate 59), open daily 11–3 in summer. The former leper hospital chronicles Norwegian doctors' struggle against the disease and exhibits some truly creepy drawings. At 15kr (6kr students), it's a must-see for the morbid and a must-miss for the squeamish.

Although it's full of schlocky shops and artists, Bryggen harbors a few interesting museums. The **Hanseatisk Museum** (tel. 55/31–41–89; admission 15kr, 8kr students) re-creates the living quarters of a Hanseatic merchant in a well-preserved wood building. Check out the intricate wall paintings. The moving **Theta Museum** (follow signs to attic of Hanseatisk Museum; admission 15kr, 5kr students) was once the headquarters of a Nazi-resistance group. The young students of the Theta group helped the Allies bomb a German ship in Trondheim before having to abandon the operation when their secret room was discovered. West of the Bryggen complex is the **Bryggens Museum** (tel. 55/31–67–10; admission 15kr), which displays archaeological finds from around Bergen, including the foundations of some 12th-century buildings unearthed when the museum was under construction. Behind the Bryggens Museum is the city's oldest building, the 12th-century **Mariakirchen** (admission 10kr; open weekdays in summer, Tues.–Fri. off-season), a church with a weird Baroque pulpit.

➢ **OTHER MUSEUMS** • You'll find a string of art museums on Rasmus Meyer's allé. The **Rasmus Meyer's Samlinger** at No. 7 and the **Municipal Art Museum** at No. 3 focus on works by Norwegian artists, and **Stenersen's Collection,** also at No. 3, houses paintings by modern artists, including Picasso, Klee, and of course Munch. All charge 15kr admission and are open Monday–Saturday 11–4 and Sunday noon–3 in summer, Tuesday–Sunday noon–3 off-season. For information, call 55/97–80–00.

Hiking Areas Along the Oslo–Bergen Rail Line

The mountains between Bergen and Oslo are filled with nooks and crannies that will take your breath away if you see them from the train, and may knock you over dead if you actually get off the train and spend the night. Geilo, a popular winter ski center, has good summer hiking and a youth hostel (tel. 32/09–03–00; beds 90kr; closed mid-Sept.–Nov. and May–mid-June). From Finse, on the perpetually snowbound Hardanger plateau, you can begin a popular trek through the Aurland Valley and end up near Flåm (see below), from which a train runs to Bergen and Oslo. The DNT operates hytter, evenly spaced throughout the valley, for the three- to five-day journey from Finse to Vassbygdi. Check on weather conditions before setting out; Finse can be snowed in until July. The youth hostel in Mjølfjell (tel. 56/51–81–11; beds 85kr; closed Sept.–mid-Feb. and May–mid-June) caters to winter skiers, but summer finds the old farmhouse fabulously deserted; it's in a secluded valley next to a raging ice-blue river. To get here, take the Bergen–Myrdal train, ask the conductor to stop at Ørnaberget, and follow the steep trail down into the valley.

You can wander around outside in **Gamle (Old) Bergen** (tel. 55/25–78–50; open mid-May–Aug., daily 11–6) for free, but you have to pay for a guided tour (25kr, 15kr students) through the 18th- and 19th-century wood houses, filled with fascinating period antiques—toys, furnishings, scary medical equipment, and even scarier beauty supplies. You can attend a Grieg concert every Sunday at 1 for 25kr. To get here from the city center, take Bus 1 or 9 and get off after the second tunnel.

Composer Edvard Grieg's home, **Troldhaugen** (tel. 55/91–17–91; admission 15kr), has been turned into a museum exhibiting mementos from his life. Grieg and his wife Nina are buried in a cliff below the house. During summer, concerts are held here on Wednesday and weekends. The house, open daily 9:30–5:30 from May to September, is 8 km south of Bergen. Catch a bus from Platform 18, 19, or 20 at the bus station (double-check with the driver), get off at Hopsbroen, turn left on Troldhaugsveien, and follow the signs for 20 minutes.

AFTER DARK Bergen is a university town, so nightlife thrives. Lots of films, concerts, performances, and parties happen at the **USF Kulturhuset** (*see* Food, *above*). A nice hangout with an international flavor is **Café Opera** (Engen 24, tel. 55/23–03–15). **Maxime** is a no-frills, rock-and-roll patio spot on Ole Bulls plass. **Garage,** on the corner of Nygårdsgaten and Christies gate, has a hipster atmosphere and often hosts bands and parties. **Nye Ugla** (Olav Kyres gate, bet. Vaskerelven and Nygårdsgaten), a working-class dive, has the cheapest beer in town—24kr until 9 and 36kr after that, except for 15 minutes before every hour, when it's only 29kr.

OUTDOOR ACTIVITIES Two of Bergen's mountains have transportation to the top for those who don't like to work for a view. **Mt. Fløien's** famous funicular (14kr one-way) leaves from a spot 500 feet from the fish market. To get to the top of **Mt. Ulriken** you can take a cable car (25kr one-way, 45kr round-trip) accessible by frequent buses from the Bryggen tourist office. Walking to the top of either peak, though, is a better way to go. Trails up Ulriken start behind Montana Vandrerhjem (*see* Where to Sleep, *above*), and the trail to Fløien starts at the center of town. At the top of both mountains, trails head into the wilderness. Pick up maps at the DNT office.

Sognefjord

Water cascades down a 1,000-meter rock face into Sognefjord, Norway's longest and deepest fjord and also its most accessible, especially if you're traveling by rail. Several towns near here have youth hostels, and hytter are everywhere. If you have a tent, fly and be free—sleep next to a rushing river or wake up beside the still fjord water. Pick up the comprehensive *Sognefjorden Guide* from local tourist offices.

The best bases for exploring the fjord are Flåm and Balestrand (*see below*), but if you must have cement beneath your feet, head to **Sogndal,** the closest thing in the area to a thriving metropolis. From here a three-hour bus ride will take you to Nigardsbreen, the most popular arm of the Jostedalsbreen glacier (*see below*), or you can head for the Jotunheimen mountains to the east. Stay at Sogndal's **hostel** (tel. 57/67–20–33; beds 80kr; closed mid-Aug.–mid-June), and talk to the **tourist office** (across from bus terminal, tel. 57/67–30–83) to rent bikes and plan day trips.

COMING AND GOING The easiest ways to approach Sognefjord are by train from Bergen to Flåm (1 hr, 50kr), by bus from Voss to Gudvangen or Vangsnes (1 hr, 50kr), or by hydrofoil from Bergen. From June to September, **Fylkesbaatane** (in Bergen, tel. 55/31–05–76) operates a daily 8 AM hydrofoil service from Bergen to Flåm with stops along the way (5 hrs, 450kr, 50% discount for students and rail-pass holders). The scenic Flåm railroad, or Flåmsbana (*see below*), also carries masses of tourists to Flåm from the town of Myrdal. Buses run to Sogndal from Otta (*see* Jotunheimen National Park, *below*) and Oslo in the east and to Balestrand from many points north. Pick up the massive *Sogn og fjordane* timetable at local tourist offices, or ask the staff to copy relevant pages.

FLÅM AND THE FLÅMSBANA

The Flåmsbana zooms from Myrdal, high in the mountains, down to Flåm. Along the ride, you'll see waterfalls spilling off the sheer valley walls and a raging sapphire river that thunders through narrow gorges. You'll be comforted to know that the train is equipped with not one, not two, but five (count 'em) sets of brakes. Hundreds of tourists pour off the 8:45 AM train from Bergen to Myrdal and cram into the railroad cars that make the journey to Flåm (50kr). If you want to lose the tourists, bag the train ride and walk the 20 km from Myrdal to Flåm (about 5 hrs). If you have a full pack with you, you can send it down on the train for 40kr.

Flåm's waterfront district is swamped with day-trippers who stream off of the Flåmsbana at noon, have lunch in the cafeteria, and sweep out of town at about 3. After they leave, Flåm is a wonderful place to spend the night beneath towering fjord walls. There's lots to do in the area, and the friendly folks at the **tourist information office** (in train station, tel. 57/63–21–06) can give you maps and transportation schedules. Don't try to get info during the midday rush, though. **Flåm Camping and Youth Hostel** (tel. 57/63–21–21; closed mid-Oct.–Apr.) sits beneath a massive peak with a view of a waterfall. Beds are 75kr, camping 45kr per tent plus 15kr per person.

BALESTRAND

Balestrand has been Sognefjord's main resort since the 19th century, and it's still extremely popular with older Brits. Nonetheless, this feels more like a town where people live than a tourist center. The village sits beneath snowy peaks that abruptly soften into rolling hills and farmland before hitting the water. The **Viking burial mounds** on the waterfront are the only real sights, although the new **Viking Center** (tel. 57/69–13–33; admission 40kr; open May–Sept., daily 10–6) in the nearby town of Dragsvik has a reconstructed Viking farm. From Dragsvik you can take a ferry to Vangsnes and then a bus to Vik, which drops you 1 km from the **Hopperstad Stave Church** (1130). It has a rare intact canopy—a small wooden roof featuring a carved bust of a monk pillaged from a French monastery by the Vikings. Ask at Balestrand's **tourist information office** (at harbor, tel. 57/69–12–55) for more details.

COMING AND GOING The **hydrofoil** from Bergen to Flåm (*see above*) stops at Balestrand twice daily; many other ferries go to Dragsvik instead of Balestrand. For a more scenic route from Bergen, take the **train** to Voss and transfer to a bus that travels through the snow-packed Vika mountains to Vangsnes, a short ferry or hydrofoil hop from Balestrand. **Buses** leave from Balestrand for Dragsvik almost every hour, although you can walk the 8 km if you have time.

WHERE TO SLEEP The **Balestrand Youth Hostel** (Kringsjå Hotel, tel. 57/69–13–03; beds 85kr; closed mid-Aug.–mid-June) has private baths and balconies with stupendous fjord views. You'll find cheap cabins at **Sjøtun Camping** (past school, south along main street, tel. 57/69–12–23)—only 75kr for two beds and 150kr for four. You can pitch a tent for 45kr plus 15kr per person.

Jostedalsbreen Glacier

Hovering over the entire inner Nordfjord and Sognefjord regions is the Jostedalsbreen glacier, the largest ice field on the European continent. In geological time, the glacier formed 5,000 years ago, is relatively young. The ice is in constant motion, crawling as much as 2 km a day in certain places. *Never, ever* climb a glacier on your own; snow often conceals crevasses that could swallow you whole. Guided tours of the blue ice, available on several arms, are absolutely worth the splurge. Prices correspond to distance and difficulty; one-hour walks start at 50kr. You can gaze at the glacier from any of 24 icy arms that ooze into the valleys. **Nigardsbreen** is the most popular (read: crowded) of Jostedal's arms, and has a new **Glacier Center** (tel.

57/68–32–50) in the town of Gjerde at the foot of the ice. It's hard to reach, but one bus leaves from Sogndal at 9 AM.

FJÆRLAND

The **Glacier Center** (tel. 57/69–32–88; admission 60kr) in Fjærland is a good place to go for glacier facts, as well as a short panoramic film and a model that re-creates the feeling of walking through a glacier tunnel. Fjærland makes an easy day trip from Balestrand: Ferries run up the fjord daily at 9 AM and 12:25 PM and connect with handy buses that transport you to the center and then to Flatbreen to stare at the glacier itself. Balestrand's tourist office arranges the whole shebang (188kr, including museum admission). For **guided walks** in the area, contact Anders Øygard at 57/69–31–18, or arrange a walk through a nearby tourist office.

The Jostedalsbreen glacier covers about 500 square km of Norway, but that figure cannot begin to describe the massive presence of this field of ice. If you want to feel its power, take a guided walk through the yawning chasms, listening to the thunder as blue ice grinds over buried rock.

BØDALSBREEN

From the rustic cluster of huts at Bødalseter you can ascend the fractured ice of Bødalsbreen or attempt the 12-hour climb to Lodalskåpa, Jostedal's highest peak (2,083 meters). Tour buses never get this far. If you're up for some adventure, call Eivind Skjerven (tel. 57/87–12–00) of **Stryn Fjell-og Breførar-lag** to arrange a walk. This ain't no stroll in the woods—even the so-called easy walk is demanding. Call Eivind a day or two in advance to arrange transportation from Stryn (*see* Nordfjord, *below*).

Nordfjord

This isn't the most interesting part of the fjord region, but cliff roads along the water make for pleasant viewing, as do the mountain peaks that shoot up and cradle the monstrous Jostedalsbreen glacier. Summer skiing, hiking, and glacier visits (*see* Jostedalsbreen Glacier, *above*) are the Nordfjord's main attractions, and the water—made conspicuously blue-green by glacial silt and crystal—is unique. Although it has little character, **Stryn** is the best base in the inner Nordfjord, with cheap lodging and bus connections to Oslo, Bergen, Balestrand, Geiranger, and Trondheim. Stryn's **tourist information office** (Perhusvegen 19, tel. 57/87–15–26) has reams of information on local activities and also rents bikes. Pick up their *Guide for Stryn* and *Nordfjord Guide.* Hydrofoils and the coastal steamer from Bergen stop at **Maloøy,** at the Nordfjord's mouth; from here, buses will bring you into the fjord.

> ## *Do-It-Yourself Fjord Recipe*
>
> **Ingredients:**
> - *1 extra-thick glacier, heavier inland than near the coast*
> - *Several river beds*
> - *1 Ice Age*
>
> *Spread glacier inland, covering river beds. Let sit for a couple of million years. Ice will gouge deep into valleys already dug by rivers. Slowly warm planet so that ice begins to melt. As ice retreats, oceans will rise and flood deep river valleys with salt water. Voilà—fjord.*

WHERE TO SLEEP Stryn's **hostel** (up the hill behind the bus station, tel. 57/87–11–06; beds 80kr; closed mid-Sept.–mid-May) has a nice view and overflows with skiers, hikers, and glacier explorers. The **campsite** (tel. 57/87–11–36) in the center of town is full of caravans, but you'll find better camping elsewhere in the region. The quiet town of **Byrkjelo,** a bit south of the Nordfjord in a spectacular valley on the bus route between Stryn and Sognefjord, also has a modest **hostel** (tel. 57/86–73–21; beds 65kr; closed mid-Sept.–mid-May).

Geirangerfjord

The narrow Geirangerfjord is one of Norway's most impressive, most visited attractions. The towns of Geiranger and Hellesylt, at opposite ends of the fjord, offer spectacular scenery and hiking. Raging rivers crash down the mountains, cutting through both towns. The towns are similar, but Geiranger has everything on a larger scale: steeper cliffs, more waterfalls, tons of hotels, heaps of tourists, and clouds of bus exhaust. **Hellesylt Tourist Information** (at dock, tel. 70/26–50–52; open June–Aug., daily 8:30–5:30) and **Geiranger Tourist Information** (at dock, tel. 70/26–31–23; open June–Aug., daily 9–6) both distribute hiking maps. Several daily ferries make the trip (70 min, 27kr) from Hellesylt to Geiranger and back, blaring a taped travelogue that babbles in seven languages, pointing out famous waterfalls and abandoned farms along the way. The spectacle seems contrived, and there's a certain urge to jump out and touch the fjord walls to make sure they're not just a fake backdrop.

COMING AND GOING Hellesylt is one hour's journey (59kr) from Stryn (*see above*), on the bus to Ålesund. You can reach Geiranger from Stryn in two hours or from Otta (*see* Jotunheimen National Park, *below*) in four. One of Norway's most scenic bus rides, the **Golden Road,** goes from Geiranger north to Åndalsnes. The Ørneveien (Eagle's Highway) from Geiranger to the top of the fjord cuts a seemingly impossible path, weaving its way up one of the fjord walls to the first of many five-minute photo stops. Just when you thought you'd choked on the last breathtaking view, the bus plunges over Trollstigen (Troll's Path), a vertical wall topped by knife-edge peaks and thundering waterfalls. A one-way journey on the Golden Road costs 102kr and takes about three hours.

WHERE TO SLEEP The only **hostel** on the fjord is at Hellesylt (up path next to waterfall, tel. 70/26–51–28 or 70/26–36–57; beds 85kr, 4-bed cabins 200kr; closed Sept.–May). It has a tremendous fjord view. In Geiranger you'll find a whopping 10 campgrounds; **Geiranger Camping** (tel. 70/26–31–20; 40kr per tent plus 10kr per person) is on the fjord, smack in the center of the town. The cheapest cabins are at **Dalen Camping** (about 4 km up road from tourist office, tel. 70/26–30–70), where four-bedders start at 150kr.

Jotunheimen National Park

Norwegians love the mountains, and the Jotunheimen range, in the center of the country, is one of the most popular year-round playgrounds. The boulder-strewn range is Europe's highest mountain chain north of the Alps, and it contains Glittertind and Galdhøpiggen, the country's highest peaks. Hostels dot the area around Jotunheimen and the nearby Rondane and Dovrefjell ranges; consult your handy *Vandrerhjem i Norge* (*see* Norway Basics, *above*) for details. **Otta,** on the Oslo–Trondheim railway, is an important transport hub, and its **tourist information office** (in train station, tel. 61/23–02–44) has timetables and maps. You can stay overnight at **Sagatun Gjestgiveri** (Ottekra 1, behind Otta Hotel, tel. 61/23–08–14; doubles 220kr) or **Killis Overnatting** (Ola Dahlsgate 35, tel. 61/23–04–92; doubles 210kr).

West of Otta the massive peaks of Jotunheimen National Park loom over Norway. Walking trails crisscross the park, with hytter at day-hike intervals. Don't even think about setting off into the mountains without the proper gear, and remember that a Norwegian "six-hour hike" often takes more like eight or nine hours. Companies offering guided activities abound. Try **Nor-UT Activity Center** (Ola Dahlsgate 8, tel. 61/23–16–00) in Otta.

Åndalsnes

For the average traveler, Åndalsnes is merely the northern gateway to the fjords. Rock-climbers, though, are hip to Åndalsnes because of nearby **Trollveggen** (Troll Wall), the highest vertical mountain wall in Europe. You can learn all about it from the ground at the **Tindemuseum** (on road to Åndalsnes Camping; open weekdays 3–6, weekends 2–6). You may not be able to tackle Trollveggen, but a steep two-hour climb to the top of **Mt. Nesaksla,** behind town, is good for a view. The **tourist information office** in Åndalsnes (across river from train station, tel. 71/22–16–22) hands out trail maps, rents bikes and cars, and books accommodations.

APPROXIMATE DATES FOR VIEWING THE MIDNIGHT SUN

• *Alta: May 21–July 23* •
Bodø: June 4–July 8 •
Nordkapp: May 14–July 30 •
Stamsund (Lofoten): May 28–July 17 • *Tromsø: May 21–July 23*

COMING AND GOING Åndalsnes, at the end of a **rail** line that splits off the main line in Dombås, is the northern jumping-off point for the western fjord region. The **bus** trip to Geiranger (3 hrs, 112kr) takes you over the practically vertical Trollstigen wall (*see* Geirangerfjord, *above*), where 11 hairpin turns twist up to the summit.

WHERE TO SLEEP AND EAT Most of the cheap lodging is in the countryside outside Åndalsnes. The **HI Setnes Youth Hostel** (cross Rauma River on E9 to Ålesund, tel. 71/22–13–82; beds 90kr; closed mid-Sept.–mid-May) is famous for its amazing 50kr breakfast. Follow the signs for 2 km from the Åndalsnes train station, or, if you're arriving by bus, ask the driver if he'll drop you off. For riverside **Åndalsnes Camping** (tel. 71/22–16–29; 40kr per tent plus 12kr per person, cabins 80kr–550kr), go toward the hostel and turn left on the road just after the bridge.

Northern Norway

A narrow but immensely long strip of land stretches between Trondheim and Kirkenes in northern Norway. Finnmark, the northernmost chunk, is by itself the size of Denmark, although its population density is more comparable to Siberia's. In the vast northern territory, you'll encounter dramatically different ways of life and a great variety of geographical features, from the craggy peaks of the Lofoten Islands to the vast, barren stretches of the Finnmarksvidda. Students dominate the university towns of Trondheim and Tromsø, but elsewhere in the region the nomadic Sami people still rely on reindeer herding and hunting for their livelihood.

A large portion of northern Norway lies above the Arctic Circle, where the sun shines nonstop for two to three months in summer and then disappears for several months in winter. Seeing the midnight sun in the north is a special experience—it's not every day that you descend a mountain at 1 AM and find your path lighted by pink-and-orange sun glow.

Budget travelers usually ignore northern, thin stretch of Norway between Trondheim and Tromsø. Most people head straight for Lofoten or Nordkapp, stopping only briefly in Bodø, the northern terminus of Norway's rail line. If you get stuck in Bodø, there's a hostel (Nordstrandveien 1, tel. 75/62–56–66; beds 95kr; closed mid-Aug.–late June) about 1 km away. Bodø's major tourist attraction is Saltstraumen, the world's largest maelstrom, where the water from two fjords churns and dashes in a narrow strait at high tide. Even at its most powerful the sight is not that impressive but if you want to see it, buses make the 33-km run from Bodø to Saltstraumen daily.

Buses bound for the far north depart from **Fauske,** about 45 minutes before the Bodø stop. The town's **hostel** (Nyvegen 6, tel. 75/64–67–06; beds 87kr; closed mid-Aug.–May) will do if you're stuck for the night. **Narvik,** to the north, is an important transit point, especially for trains from Sweden. If you're staying over, head for the **hostel** (Havnegate 3, tel. 76/94–25–98; beds 135kr; closed Christmas), about 1 km from the train station.

Trondheim

In 997 the Viking king Olav Tryggvason founded Trondheim and made it Norway's first capital. Only 33 years later, King Olav Haraldson (St. Olav to future generations) fell at the battle of Stiklestad and was buried underneath what is now Nidaros Domen (Nidaros Cathedral). Norway's kings have been crowned ever since in Trondheim's Gothic behemoth, giving the town a special place in Norwegian history and politics. Trondheim's historical significance and large university make it an interesting, lively place, and you're almost sure to stop here as you head north, since it's on the rail line between Oslo and Bodø.

BASICS Trondheim has an enthusiastic **tourist information office** (Market Sq., tel. 73/92–93–94) that rents bikes, changes money after hours, and books rooms in private homes. The **DNT** office (Munkegata 64, near wharf, tel. 73/52–38–08) hands out maps and helps plan hiking trips. You can send mail at the **main post office** (Dronningensgate 10, tel. 73/95–84–00) and the **telephone office** (Kongensgate 8 tel. 73/54–30–11).

COMING AND GOING Trondheim lies almost halfway between the beginning of the rail line in Oslo (7–8 hrs, 400kr–600kr) and the end of the line in Bodø (11 hrs, 750kr). The Inter-Rail Center in the **train station,** at the north edge of town near the Trondheimsfjord, has 10kr showers, hot plates, and couches for crashing. The **Hurtigrute** stops twice daily north of the train station. Long-distance buses originate at the **Coach Terminal** (Erling Skakkesgate 40, tel. 73/52–44–74). City buses leave from Munkegata at the corner of Dronningensgate. Most budget lodging is across the Nidelva River, which loops around town.

WHERE TO SLEEP AND EAT There's no shortage of cheap beds in Trondheim—in fact, the fierce competition for customers drives some places out of business, so call ahead. To reach the **Singsaker Sommerhotel** (Rogertsgate 1, tel. 73/52–00–92; doubles 330kr, dorm beds 120kr), a comfortable student dorm, take Bus 63 from the train station. **Traveller's Inn** (Bakke Bydelshus, Norde Berggate 2, tel. 73/51–12–58; beds 70kr; closed Sept.–June) offers sleeping-bag accommodations in bunk beds scattered around the rec room of an old church. It's spacious, clean, and friendly, but noisy. Walk straight down Sondregate from the train station, turn left on Olav Tryggvasongate, cross the bridge, turn right on Kirkegate, and look for the clock tower. **Trondheim InterRail Center and Café** (Elgesetergate 1, behind Nidaros Domen, tel. 73/89–95–23; beds 80kr; closed Sept.–June), a student-run international hangout, gives you a mattress on the floor in a popular entertainment complex. Bring your own sleeping bag.

There's no reason to bother with the sterile **HI Rosenberg Youth Hostel** (Weidemannsvei 41, tel. 73/53–04–90; beds 150kr; closed Dec. 22–Jan. 5), except that it's open almost year-round. About 10 km south of town, **Sandmoen Camping** (Heimdal, off E6, tel. 72/88–61–35; tent sites 60kr, four-bed cabins 230kr) is the closest camping spot with the best bus connections. Take Bus 44/45 from the town center.

Unless you're willing to splurge, eating out in Trondheim is less than thrilling. A mediocre all-you-can-eat pizza stuff-fest is 49kr at **Pizzakjelleren** (Fjordgate 7; open until 4 AM) or at **City Pizza Bar** next door. The **Peking Restaurant** on Bryggen has a 35kr lunch special from noon to 4. You'll find the cheapest beer (25kr) and coffee (5kr) at the **Studentsenteret AVH,** a popular student hangout on Bryggen (Kjøpmansgate 19). At night, visit **Café Ni Muser** (Bispegate, at Prinsensgate).

WORTH SEEING Trondheim is dominated by the Gothic **Nidaros Domen** on Kongsgårds-gate, erected over the grave of St. Olav, the Viking king who brought Christianity to Norway. This cathedral, Scandinavia's largest medieval building, is the site of all Norwegian coronations. Admission is 10kr, 5kr for students, and every half-hour you can twist your way up a cramped circular staircase (170 steps) to the top of the tower for 5kr. The entrance fee for Nidaros also gets you into the almost interesting **Erkebispegården** (Archbishop's Palace), Scandinavia's oldest secular building, across the courtyard.

At the **Ringve Museum of Music History** (Lade allé 60, tel. 73/92–24–11; admission 40kr, 25kr students), music students demonstrate many of the instruments on display. English tours depart at 11, 12:30, and 2:30, with an extra tour in high season and fewer in winter. The museum lies within the Ringve Botanical Garden, the northernmost in the world. To get here, take Bus 4 (toward Lade) to Fagerheim. Museum hounds should also check out the **Trøndelag Folkemuseum** (Sverresborg, tel. 73/53–14–90; admission 30kr, 10kr students), with exhibits from the turn of the century and a stave church from Haltdalen. The **Nordenfjeldske Kunstindustrimuseum** (Munkegata 5, tel. 73/52–13–11; admission 20kr, 5kr students), a decorative-arts museum, has period rooms from the Renaissance to the 1950s.

Lofoten Islands

Sawtooth, glacier-carved peaks rise out of the sea to form the Lofoten island chain, Norway's most popular budget destination next to Bergen and the fjords. Seaside fishing villages hug the shores and extend over the sea on wood boardwalks, although these days more tourists than fishermen pack the old fishing *rorbuer* (shanties). Most people stop in Stamsund and Å (*see below*), but the more ambitious also head to the islands of **Værøy** and **Røst** to watch colonies of puffins, terns, razorbills, and guillemots, as well as the rare sea eagle. **Svolvær**, an important transportation hub on the island of Austvågøy, is a soulless city in the midst of this arctic paradise, with an equally bleak **hostel** (Vågan Folkenhøgskole, tel. 76/06–81–03; beds 120kr; closed mid-Aug.–May). Svolvær's best-known attraction is a weird, two-horned rock formation called the **Svolværgeita** (Svolvær goat), where thrill seekers leap from side to side, hoping to miss the graveyard below.

COMING AND GOING Lofoten's four main islands—Moskenes, Flakstad, Vestvågøy, and Austvågøy—are connected to each other and the mainland by **bus** and a variety of ferries. The cheapest and easiest way to get to the islands is on one of several daily **ferries** from Bodø to Moskenes (4½ hrs, 89kr). The 11 AM boat is great for those who took the night train from Trondheim. A few ferries per week travel from Bodø to Værøy and Røst. Talk to the Bodø tourist information kiosk inside the train station for other bus and ferry options. More than twice as expensive but twice as fast, **express boats** run during summer from Bodø to Leknes on Vestvågøy, from Bodø to Værøy, and from Skutvik to Svolvær on Austvågøy. Students get 25%–50% off. The **Hurtigrute** makes daily stops in Stamsund on Vestvågøy and in Svolvær. The ride from Tromsø to Stamsund (19 hrs, 614kr) costs only slightly more than a full-fare bus ticket, and it's infinitely more scenic.

MOSKENES

The island of Moskenes has some of Lofoten's most picturesque (and most photographed) fishing villages. The **Moskenestraumen,** a powerful whirlpool between Værøy and the southern tip of Moskenes, moved Jules Verne and Edgar Allan Poe to literary excess. **Å,** one of the prettiest and most popular villages, is where you'll find the island's cheapest accommodations. Å's boardwalk, lined with red rorbuer, is an open-air museum full of buildings preserved since the 19th century. The **Norske Fiskemuseum** (admission 25kr, 15kr students) contains odds and ends from Lofoten's colorful past. Boat trips arranged through the tourist office skirt the whirlpool and explore caves containing ancient drawings. For more adventure, rent bikes from the youth hostel for 100kr per day and head for the fairy-tale villages of **Reine** and **Hamnøy.** The **tourist information office** (tel. 76/09–15–99) is at the ferry dock in the town of **Moskenes.** From here it's a 5-km walk or bus ride to Å.

Å has a **hostel** (tel. 76/09–11–21), with beds (95kr) inside 19th-century shanties along the sea. If it's full, try **Å-Hamna Rorbuer** (tel. 76/09–12–11), which is just as atmospheric and rents beds at the competitive price of 100kr. Hike around the lake outside town to find a camping spot.

VESTVÅGØY

From **Leknes,** Vestvågøy's boring capital, you can catch a bus to the town of **Stamsund,** one of those places where budget travelers come for a day, only to find themselves still loafing about weeks later. The main reason is the town's rustic seaside hostel, the **Stamsund Vandrerhjem Justad Rorbuer** (tel. 76/08–93–34; beds 70kr; closed Nov.–mid-Dec.), about 1 km from the business center of Stamsund (ask the bus driver to drop you off). The low-key caretaker, Roar Justad, lends rowboats and fishing lines for free, contributing to the hostel's close-knit, communal atmosphere. Many prefer to lay around on the sun-drenched dock at the hostel, but the most spectacular (and only) place to view the midnight sun is atop **Steinetinden,** a precarious two-hour climb from the hostel. A scenic bike ride (rent bikes for 70kr per day from the hostel) runs 4 km from Stamsund to Steine. If the hostel is full, try the friendly **Nordbakk Overnatting** (around bend from hostel toward town, tel. 76/08–97–43; beds 75kr), where showers and coffee are free.

Tromsø

Tromsø is the world's northernmost university city, bathed in summer by the midnight sun and in winter by the northern lights. Snow-covered mountains cradle the city, and spectacular hiking is just a bus ride away. The student population jump-starts Tromsø's nightlife, which is enhanced by more bars per capita than in any other Norwegian city.

BASICS The **tourist information office** (Storgata 61, near cathedral, tel. 77/61–00–00) is open weekdays 8:30–7 and weekends 10–5 from June to mid-August, weekdays 8:30–4 in winter. The **post office** (Strandgata 41, tel. 77/62–40–00) takes care of mail needs, and the **Telesenter** (Sjøgata 2, tel. 77/60–14–00) is the place to make phone calls. **Kilroy Travel** (Havna Hotel, Beivika Havn, tel. 77/67–58–20) is a great bucket shop.

COMING AND GOING From Bodø the **Hurtigrute** takes 24 hours and costs 701kr. From Honningsvåg it takes 19 hours and costs 614kr. **Long-distance buses** depart from near the docks. Buses run to Narvik (5 hrs, 251kr) and Fauske (10½ hrs, 502kr), access points for the railway. Buses to Alta (7 hrs, 323kr), in Finnmark, leave at 2 PM. Tromsø is the air hub for northern Norway, and **air travel** is surprisingly cheap. Special fares from Oslo hover around 750kr, and travel to selected northern destinations costs only 410kr. Book tickets through Kilroy Travel (*see* Basics, *above*). The city of Tromsø and the airport are both on the island of Tromsøya. **City buses** stop at Stortorget on Havnegata and at Fr. Langesgate on Storgata. Get schedules and routes from the tourist office.

WHERE TO SLEEP Tromsø is no mecca of cheap lodging, and the **HI Tromsø Vandrerhjem** (Elverhøy, Gitta Jønsonvei 4, tel. 77/68–53–19; closed mid-Aug.–mid-June) is a depressing monstrosity about 2 km uphill from town (take Bus 24 from Fr. Langesgate). Even the closest campground, **Tromsdalen Camping** (tel. 77/63–80–37), on the mainland 3 km from central Tromsø, is expensive, with tent sites for two people at 110kr. To get there, take Bus 36 from Stortorget. The tourist office books rooms in private homes starting at 150kr per person. This is always a hit-or-miss proposition, but certain homes are fabulously cozy; considering the options, they're probably your best bet.

Park Pensjonat (Skolegata 24, tel. 77/68–64–80; follow Fr. Langesgate and walk through park) is the cheapest hotel near the center, with singles for 260kr, doubles for 320kr, and three- to five-bed rooms for 120kr per person. **Skipperhuset Pensjonat** (Storgata 112, past Stortorget, tel. 77/68–16–60; doubles 380kr) is a central, comfortable, friendly place to crash.

FOOD The **Domus** grocery store on Stortorget is large and cheap. For a hot meal, try **Prelaten** (Sjøgata 12, tel. 77/68–20–85), a basement pub with filling specials that start at 50kr. **Paletten** (Storgata 51, tel. 77/68–05–10) has two outdoor patios and a 50kr salad bar and is probably the only place in Norway where beer prices drop (from 36kr to 30kr) at night. **Café Panorama** (Sjøgata 39, tel. 77/68–81–00) offers a 48kr lunch special between 11 and 1:30. Bars on practically every corner serve the tasty local brew, Mack Beer. Try **Middagskjelleren**

(Strandgata 22), a rustic basement bar featuring excellent folk and alternative music and 32kr Mack. The nearby **Blå Rock Cafe** (Strandgata 14/16) is a multilevel postmodern nightspot with band memorabilia on the walls. **Verthuset Skarven** (Strandtorget 1) is more upscale; crowds of people soak up the midnight sun on its outdoor patio.

WORTH SEEING Across the bridge on the mainland, the white, angular **Ishavskatedrale** (Arctic Cathedral), open Monday–Saturday 10–5 and Sunday 1–5, dominates the skyline. Admission is 5kr. The architecture is meant to mimic a snow-covered mountain, symbolizing northern Norwegian nature, culture, and faith. The cathedral contains the largest stained-glass window in Europe. During summer, organ concerts are offered every Thursday for 20kr. Take Bus 30 or 31 from Stortorget.

> *Tromsø was dubbed the "Paris of the North" by someone who had obviously never been to Paris. An observer with better perceptive powers offered the more fitting title "Gateway to the Arctic."*

You can learn about the northern lights in a 360° panoramic film at the **Northern Lights Planetarium** (in university, Breivika, tel. 77/67–60–00; admission 50kr, 40kr students). Take Bus 25 from Sjøgata. Check out arctic geology, botany, zoology, archaeology, and Sami ethnography at the **Tromsø Museum** (Folkeparken, tel. 77/64–50–00; admission 10kr, 5kr students), where the admission fee also gets you into the aquarium next door. To reach the museum, take Bus 27 from Storgata.

Finnmark

On the roof of Europe, atop the vast, windswept Finnmarksvidda, roam Europe's only nomadic indigenous people, the reindeer-hunting Sami. Most still live in traditional tents and dress in colorful costumes, although the most visible evidence of their lifestyle consists of roadside souvenir stands and tourist exhibits. The desolate expanses and treeless tundra of the Finnmarksvidda are a popular trekking destination, and you're almost guaranteed an encounter with reindeer herds, as well as helicopter-size mosquitoes—bring lots of repellent.

The region stretches from the rugged cliffs at Nordkapp (North Cape) to the lush river valleys below the Finnmarksvidda, encompassing the towering gray-slate mountains near Alta and the Russian border at Kirkenes. Travel is neither convenient nor cheap. **Buses** never run overnight, so be sure to check timetables for the night stop, often in **Alta**. There's not much to do here, but the town does have a **hostel** (Midtbakken 52, tel. 78/43–44–09; beds 100kr; closed mid-Aug.–mid-June). InterRail-pass holders get 50% off of all bus fares; international students and EurailPass holders get zippo, although you can always flash your pass and see what happens. North of Bodø, the **Hurtigrute** is a viable travel option, with fares that are often comparable to full-price bus tickets. **Flying** is also a good way to travel in Finnmark. Call **Kilroy Travel** (*see* Tromsø, *above*) for the best deals.

NORDKAPP

So you finally arrive at the edge of the continent, the tip of the Great White North, only to find what you came to escape—a great big shopping mall. Nordkapp, a rugged piece of rock jutting into the Arctic Ocean at 71°11′21″, is Europe's northernmost point (if you don't count Knivskjelloden, a peninsula to the west that reaches 71°11′48″). Nordkapp is invaded daily by an army of tourists, pushing and shoving their way through **Nordkapp Hall,** an underground exhibit center where you can view the midnight sun from inside the cliff instead of from the top of it. You're likely to be socked in by round-the-clock fog, but on a sunny evening a walk along the cliffs, which plunge more than 1,000 feet into the Arctic Ocean, is almost worth the trip and the expense. The total cost for the whole thing—the round-trip bus from nearby Honningsvåg and entrance to Nordkapp Hall—is 190kr.

The **Hurtigrute** stops in Honningsvåg (19 hrs from Bodø, 614kr), and an **express bus** runs from Bodø and Narvik to Nordkapp (2 days, 960kr). **Widerøe** flies to Honningsvåg from Tromsø for 410kr, and there's also an **express boat** from Hammerfest. During summer, regular public buses run from Honningsvåg to Nordkapp. In Honningsvåg's **hostel** (8 km toward Nordkapp at Skipsfjorden, tel. 78/47-33-77; beds 100kr; closed Sept.–May) is a spartan hut on a barren plateau with a huge luxury hotel behind it.

KARASJOK AND KAUTOKEINO

Karasjok and Kautokeino are the two major Sami settlements in Norway. Both towns explode with activity during the Sami **Easter celebration,** the best time to visit. Traditional concerts, mass weddings and confirmations, and reindeer-sledge races are all part of the fun. Karasjok, in a lush river valley below the Finnmarksvidda, is the seat of the Sami parliament. You'll find the **tourist information office** (tel. 78/46-73-60) in the Samelandssenteret (Sami Cultural Center), which also has a Sami camp exhibit, a slide show, and a gold-panning river. Kautokeino sits atop the wide-open Finnmarksvidda and is famous for its silversmiths. The **tourist information office** (tel. 78/45-65-00) in the Duodji Siida can direct you to the Kautokeino museum and help with hiking itineraries.

COMING AND GOING Karasjok is on the bus run from Alta to Kirkenes (from Alta, 5 hrs, 244kr; from Kirkenes, 5 hrs, 316kr). Kautokeino is on the **Express 2000** bus route from Hammerfest to Oslo and has daily connections to Alta. Buses run between Karasjok and Kautokeino four times weekly.

WHERE TO SLEEP AND EAT Karasjok has a **hostel** (Karasjok camping, tel. 78/46-61-35; closed Sept.–Mar.) 1 km from the tourist office, on the road to Kautokeino in the midst of a mosquito-infested forest. The reception area has a small kiosk that sells food, and you'll find plenty of cafeterias and groceries back in town. Ask at the Kautokeino tourist office about cheap *fjellstue* (mountain cabins).

POLAND 19

By Greg Magnuson and Alyson McCleve

Through 600 years of history, the streets of Kraków have seen the construction of medieval castles, Gothic and Baroque Catholic churches, and universities; they have mutely witnessed Poland conquered, partitioned, and erased from the map of Europe by countless waves of invaders; they have felt the footsteps of German knights, Napoleon's officers, Hitler's armies, and Soviet soldiers. In the spring of 1989, these same streets, witnesses to 30 generations of the Polish struggle for independence and statehood, saw the wheel of history spin in favor of the Poles. Solidarity, the workers' trade union, was given a chance to participate in the first free elections in Eastern Europe since World War II. In the streets of Kraków, protest demonstrations soon underwent metamorphoses, becoming election campaigns; a new generation of Poles discovered democracy and celebrated the birth of an autonomous Poland.

Poles are still surprised to encounter travelers who come simply to visit; you may be asked frequently if you're visiting relatives. Poland is not a place that will steamroll you with excessive natural beauty or stunning architecture; Nazis razed many of Poland's historical sights. Major points of interest in Poland include the north, which encompasses the fishing villages and resort towns along the Baltic coast; the capital city of Warsaw, which lies in the east-central part of the country; and the south, which features the beautifully preserved medieval city of Kraków and nearby Oświęcim (alias Auschwitz). The best hiking and skiing in Poland center on the mountain village Zakopane (*see* Near Kraków, *below*), in the peaks of the Tatra Mountains.

Basics

MONEY $1 = 22,000 złoty and 10,000 złoty = 45¢. The złoty rarely appears in public in denominations of less than 50. You'll get the best exchange rates at ubiquitous private exchange offices (Kantory Wimiany Walut). In most towns you can find a kantor open until 7 or 8; after 8, try the big hotels. You can exchange traveler's checks at some banks, some hotels, and Orbis offices for the official rate minus a commission, which will be heftier at Orbis.

HOW MUCH IT WILL COST Inexpensive hotels charge about $10–$30 a night for a double; hostels charge about $3–$5. You should rarely spend more than $2–$7 for a complete meal in a restaurant, and it would be hard to spend more than $5 on a train trip within the country's borders. If you forgo staying in the large government-owned hotels and don't travel via hot-air balloon or limousine, you can live for less than $35 a day.

Baltic
Sea

Łeba

Utska

Wejherowo

Gdynia

Zatoka
Gdańska

Gdańsk

Słupsk

Sławno

Koszalin

Kołobrzeg

Kościerzyna

Tczew

Miastko

Starogard
Gdański

Malbork

Karlino

Sztum

Kwidzyn

Swinoujście

Zalew
Szczeciński

Szczecinek

Chojnice

Grudziądz

Goleniów

Nowogard

Szczecinek

Jastrowie

Stargard
Szcz.

Szczecin

Pyrzyce

Kalisz
Pom.

Piła

Chodzież

Biskupin

Bydgoszcz

Toruń

Inowrocław

Włocł

Gorzów
Wlkp.

Rogoźno

Skwierzyna

Pniewy

Gniezno
Września

Krośniewice

Poznań

Rogalin

Kórnik

Świebodzin

Zielona
Góra

Jarocin

Zgier

Leszno

Kalisz

Zduńska

Krotoszyn

Sieradz

Pio

Kozuchów

Ostrów
Wlkp.

Rawicz

Szprotawa

Lubin

Kępno

Wieluń

Bolesławiec

Oleśnica

Legnica

Wrocław

Jelenia
Góra

Kluczbork

Brzeg

Wałbrzych

Opole

Lubliniec

Nysa

Gliwice

Bytom

Kudowa-Zdrój

Kłodzko

Chorzów
Katowice

Bystrzyca-Kłodzka

Międzygórze

Bielsk
Biała

GERMANY

CZECH REPUBLIC

N

0   60 miles

0   90 km

RUSSIAN
FEDERATION

LITHUANIA

Zalew Wiślany

ka
ska

Frombork
Górowo
Iławeckie
Bartoszyce

Elbląg

Pasłek

Węgorzewo
Giżycko

Suwałki

Lldzbark
Warm.

Mrągowo

Augustów

Olsztyn

Mikołajki

Ełk

Ostróda

Grajewo

Szczytno

Szczuczyn

Nowe
Miasto
Lubawskie

Nidzica

Łomża

Czarna
Białostocka

Białystok

Mława

Ostrołęka

Zambrów

Ciechanów

Ostrów
Maz.

Bielsk
Podlaski

Wkra R.

Wyszków

Siemiatycze

BELARUS

Płock

Biebrza R.

Bug R.

Kutno

Sokołów
Podl.

Łowicz

*Kampinoski
Park Narodowy*

Warsaw

Biała
Podlaska

Brest

Żyrardów

Otwock

Siedlce

Łódź

Gróiec

Mińsk
Maz.

Pilica R.

Garwolin

ierz

Tomaszów Maz.

Radzyń
Podl

Wisła R.

Kock

Włodawa

iotrków
Tryb.

Puławy

Radom

Lublin

Radomsko

Skarżysko-
Kamienna

Kazimierz
Dolny

Chełm

Bug R.

Kielce

Ostrowiec
Świętokrzyski

Krasnystaw

Częstochowa

Kraśnik

Zamość

Jędrzejów

Sandomierz

Janów

Tomaszów
Lubelski

Sosnowiec
Jaworzno

Miechów

Wisła R.

Stalowa
Wola

San R.

Leżajsk

UKRAINE

Oświęcim

Ojców

Mielec

Łańcut

Kraków

Dębica

Rzeszów

Jarosław

Wieliczka

Tarnów

Przemyśl

E462

Myślenice

Nowy
Sącz

Krosno

ka
a

Rabka

Gorlice

Sanok

Chochołów

Krynica

Ustrzyki
Dolne

Kiry
Zakopane

SLOVAKIA

Ustrzyki
Gorne

675

VISA AND ENTRY REQUIREMENTS U.S. and British citizens no longer need a visa to enter Poland for up to 90 days. Canadians *do* still need a visa to enter the country. Canadians have three visa choices: transit visas (valid for two days), single-entry visas (valid for up to 90 days), and double-entry visas (allowing two entries within 90 days). Apply for visas at Polish consulates prior to travel and allow several days for processing.

COMING AND GOING **LOT Polish Airlines** (500 5th Ave., New York, NY 10017, tel. 212/869–1078) has the cheapest student fares to Warsaw, but even those hover in the $800 range round-trip from New York. In other words, you'll probably want to take the train from another country. Warsaw and Kraków are the major travel hubs; there are seven daily trains from Berlin to Warsaw (10 hrs) but only one from Prague (12 hrs).

GETTING AROUND Buses are generally crowded and uncomfortable, and renting a car is expensive. This leaves you with the train. InterRail and EurailPasses, however, are not worth the paper they're printed on in Poland. The **Polrail Pass,** Poland's national rail pass, costs $35 (eight days)–$50 (one month), second class. The **European East Pass** covers Poland, the Czech Republic, Slovakia, Hungary, and Austria, but isn't much of a bargain given Eastern Europe's low train ticket prices. The pass costs $169 for five days' travel spread out over a 15-day period, $275 for 10 days' travel over a 30-day period. Both passes are available through Orbis (*see* Visitor Information, *below*).

The proper hitching technique is to stick your arm out and wave your wrist up and down a little. Really.

PKP is the Polish national train service. Polish trains run at three speeds: *ekspres* (express), *pośpieszny* (fast), and *osobowy* (slow); avoid slow trains at all costs. Both fast and express trains have first- and second-class cars; for long trips it's worth the few extra dollars for a seat in first class, as second class can get overcrowded. A seat reservation is required on all express trains. Stations will usually post a complete timetable, with *odjazdy* (departures) listed on the yellow posters and *przyjazdy* (arrivals) listed on the white posters. Roman numerals indicate the arrival or departure platform.

WHERE TO SLEEP You need not submit to the seductive power of expensive high-rise hotels when you have so many ugly and *cheap* alternatives to choose from. In most towns you can find a decent room for $10–$20 per night for a double. In the peak season, you can choose among hotels, rooms in private homes, university housing, and campgrounds. Many hostels are in schools, so they're only open in the summer. Many private homes hang out signs offering *pokoje* (rooms) or *noclegi* (lodging).

FOOD Food in Poland is heavy, hearty, and cheap; you can survive on a daily food budget of $5 without any hunger pangs. *Bar mleczny* (milk bars), which serve mostly meatless dishes, are an incredible budget option for hot food. In general, Polish cuisine features a wide variety of soups, pastries, and delicious starch-based (usually noodle or potato) dishes. Common varieties of soup include *barszcz* (clear beet broth), sometimes served with *uszka* (dumplings), *kartoflanka* (potato soup), and *jarzynowa* (vegetable soup). Standard main courses include the ever-present *kotlet schabowy* (pork cutlet); *bigos* (hunters' stew); and pierogi (dumplings with meat or cheese fillings). Dessert is a passion for the Poles, and sugar addicts should try *lody* (ice cream), *naleśniki* (crepes with sweet cheese or fruit), and *makowiec* (dense poppy-seed cake)—but not all at once.

BUSINESS HOURS Banks are usually open weekdays 8–5. Most post offices are open weekdays 7 AM–8 PM, Saturday 9–2, and Sunday 9–11. Stores are generally open weekdays 10–6 and Saturday 9–2. Food shops are open weekdays 8–6, with scaled-back hours on Saturday; most are closed Sunday. Tourist offices are open from 9 until anytime between 3 and 6. Museums are usually closed Monday.

VISITOR INFORMATION **Orbis,** the government tourist agency in Poland, often doubles as an American Express representative and is handy for getting cash advances on credit cards, changing traveler's checks, obtaining train info, or finding someone who speaks English. **PTTK** has general information offices and runs a number of youth hotels; they provide more information than Orbis about cheap lodging. **Almatur,** the Polish student-travel organization, can provide information on places to crash (university dorms, in particular).

PHONES **Country code: 48.** Feel free to take out your naked aggressions on Poland's non-functional telephones. Pay phones accept tokens (for sale at the post office in 3,000 zł or 5,000 zł denominations) or the more reliable phone cards (available at kiosks for 50,000 zł). For international calls, dial 901, 902, or 903 for an English-speaking operator, or go through the post office, where a clerk will make your connection and you pay at the end of the call. You can dial direct to most of Europe. If you have an AT&T calling card, dial 01/04–800–111 from Warsaw. In other parts of Poland, dial 0, wait for a tone, then dial the same number as above.

MAIL Standard airmail rates for letters to North America are 7,000 zł; postcards, 5,000 zł. For an extra 4,000 zł you can send items by airmail express, which will cut their travel time in half. Put airmail into the blue postal boxes, local mail into the green boxes, and any old mail into the red boxes.

EMERGENCIES Dial 997 for the **police**, 998 for the **fire department**, and 999 for an **ambulance**.

Warsaw

The geographical and political center of Poland since 1595, Warsaw (Warszawa) will shock the first-time visitor with its bleak, postwar architecture and thick, polluted air. As you begin to understand the amazing history of the city, though, your initial dismay will develop into appreciation and amazement. Set in the worst location possible during World War II, Warsaw was used as a pawn by two of the most brutal regimes in world history—the Nazis and the Soviets. The city was literally rebuilt from the ashes by the surviving one-third of its inhabitants starting in 1945.

Despite its devastating history, Warsaw is today a bustling urban center, with well-stocked stores and crowded outdoor markets and cafés. Warsaw's greatest charm is its generous acres of parks, but even amidst the urban drabness there are a few architectural attractions as well. A large number of prewar buildings, especially in the Stare Miasto (Old Town) were painstakingly restored or completely reconstructed from old prints and paintings. Closed to all traffic except horses and carriages, the beautiful, cobblestoned Rynek Starego Miasta (Old Town Square) is an impressive reproduction of the original marketplace. The Royal Palace, which houses a museum, is the greatest of the rebuilt monuments.

BASICS

VISITOR INFORMATION PTTK (Świętokrzyska 32, tel. 022/24–14–18; open daily 9–6) is a good resource for info on campgrounds and cheap hotels. But if you think PTTK is good, you'll love **Almatur,** which has the best maps and the scoop on student hotels and hostels. *Ul. Kopernika 23, tel. 022/26–35–12. East of Nowy Swiat, bet. al. Jerozolimskie and Świętokrzyska. Open weekdays 9–5, Sat. 10–2.*

Orbis has offices all over the city, but they aren't too helpful except for exchanging cash and occasionally traveler's checks. The following offices offer services to foreigners: *Ul. Marszałkowska 142, at ul. Królewska, tel. 022/27–36–73; Krakowskie Przedmieście 13, tel. 022/26–16–67; Swiętojanska 25–27. All open daily 11–7.*

AMERICAN EXPRESS Poland's only full-service American Express office cashes personal and traveler's checks, holds mail for its cardholders, issues traveler's checks, arranges accommodations, and provides transit information. *Krakowskie Przedmieście 11, opposite Europejski Hotel, tel. 02/635–2002. Open weekdays 9–5, Sat. 10–2.*

EMBASSIES **Australia.** *Ul. Estonska 3–5, tel. 022/17–60–81. Open weekdays 9–1.*

Canada. *Ul. Matejki 1–5, tel. 022/29–80–51. Open weekdays 8:30–1 and 2–5.*

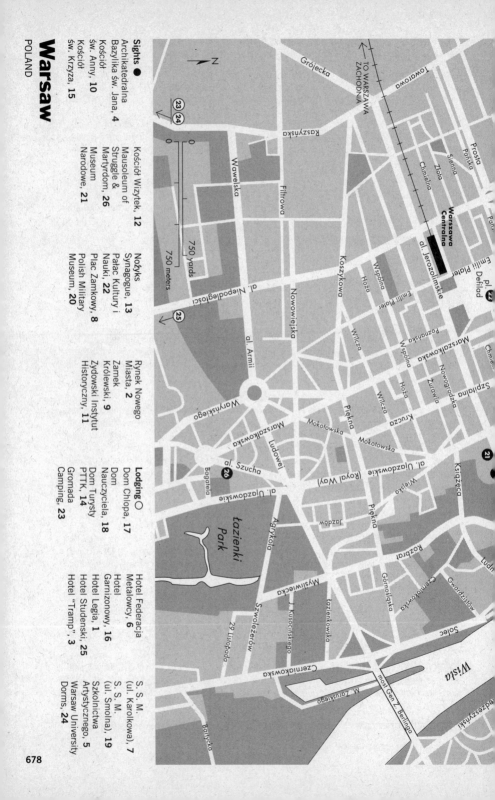

Warsaw
POLAND

Sights ●

Archikatedralna
Bazylika św. Jana, **4**
Kościół
św. Anny, **10**
Kościół
św. Krzyża, **15**

Kościół Wizytek, **12**
Mausoleum of
Struggle &
Martyrdom, **26**
Muzeum
Narodowe, **21**

Nożyks
Synagogue, **13**
Pałac Kultury i
Nauki, **22**
Plac Zamkowy, **8**
Polish Military
Museum, **20**

Rynek Nowego
Miasta, **2**
Zamek
Królewski, **9**
Żydowski Instytut
Historyczny, **11**

Lodging ○

Dom Chlopa, **17**
Dom
Nauczyciela, **18**
Dom Turysty
PTTK, **14**
Gromada
Camping, **23**

Hotel Federacja
Metalowcy, **6**
Hotel
Garnizonowy, **16**
Hotel Legia, **1**
Hotel Studenski, **25**
Hotel "Tramp", **3**

S. S. M.
(ul. Karoikowa), **7**
S. S. M.
(ul. Smolna), **19**
Szkolnictwa
Artystycznego, **5**
Warsaw University
Dorms, **24**

678

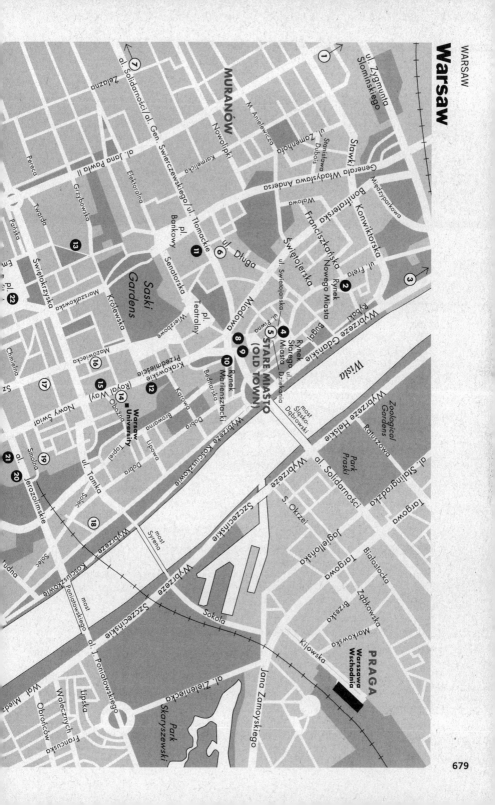

MURANÓW

ul. Zygmunta
Słomińskiego

Sławki

al. Solidarności/ al. Gen. Świerczewskiego/ ul. Tłomackie

Nowolipki

M. Anielewicza

ul. Stanisława Dubois

ul. Zamenhofa

Generała Władysława Andersa

Wołowa

Kornelicka

Żelazna

Elektoralna

Bankowy

Senatorska

pl.
Bankowy

ul. Długa

Świętojerska

Franciszkańska

Bonifraterska

Konwiktorska

Międzyparkowa

Rynek
Nowego Miasta

ul. Freta

Saski
Gardens

Wierzbowe

Marszałkowska

Królewska

Mazowiecka

pl.
Teatralny

Krakowskie
Przedmieście

Miodowa

ul. Świętojańska

ul. Piwna

Bugaj

Rynek
Starego
Miasta

ul.
Dziekania

Wybrzeże Gdańskie

Wisła

Rynek
Mariensztacki

Bednarska

Karowa

Browarna

Dobra

Lipowa

Wybrzeże Kościuszkowie

Warsaw
University

STARE MIASTO
(OLD TOWN)

Wybrzeże Gdańskie

Rybaki

most
Śląsko-
Dąbrowski

Wybrzeże Helskie

Zoological
Gardens

Radzuszowa

Park
Praski

al. Solidarności

al. Stalingradzka

Targowa

Pereca

Twarda

Grzybowska

Pańska

Świętokrzyska

pl. ...
22

Chmielna

Sz

Chmielna

17

16

15
14
Obożna

Nowy Świat

Oboźna

12

13

11

6

8
9

10

5
4
2

3

Szczecińska

s. Okrzei

Jagiellońska

Targowa

Białostocka

7

Żelazna

21

20

19

al. Smolna

ul. Tamka

Sóc

ul.
Jerozolimskie

Soec

Wybrzeże

Szczecińskie

most
Syreny

Wybrzeże

Kościuszkowie

Poniatowskiego

most
Poniatowskiego

al. J. Poniatowskiego

Sokola

Jana Zamoyskiego

Brzeska

Ząbkowska

Markowska

Kijowska

PRAGA

Warszawa
Wschodnia

18

Soec

Szczecińskie

Wybrzeże

Wał Miedz.

Obrońców

Francuska

Waleczych

Lipska

al. Zielieniecka

Park
Skaryszewski

Ludna

PRAGA

679

United Kingdom. *Al. Róz, tel. 022/28–10–01.*

United States. *Al. Ujazdowskie 29–31, tel. 022/28–30–41. Enter on ul. Piękna 12. Open weekdays 8:30–5.*

ENGLISH-LANGUAGE PUBLICATIONS For the latest Warsaw happenings, pick up the American embassy's *Yellow Pages*, the weekly *Warsaw Voice*, or the monthly comprehensive *What, Where, When* magazine, which includes a handy map. These publications, as well as same-day English newspapers, are available at the **Marriott Hotel** (al. Jerozolimskie 65–79, tel. 022/30–63–06) and other top-bracket hotels.

PHONES AND MAIL The person who devised Warsaw's phone system had a nasty sense of humor. Warsaw's area code is officially 022, but that applies only if you're dialing a six-digit number; if the number has seven digits, the area code is just 02. But if it's a six-digit number starting with the digits 28, then add a 6 so you have 628, and, since you now have a seven-digit number, the area code is 02. Got it? You can make operator-assisted long-distance calls around the clock from the **main post office** (ul. Swiętokrzyska 31–33, near ul. Jasna), which is open daily 8–8 for regular mail services.

COMING AND GOING

BY TRAIN **Warszawa Centralna** is Warsaw's main station. In the heart of the city, the station sits between the Palace of Culture, Marriott Hotel, and Holiday Inn. Unfortunately, it's also a mecca for criminals: Be on your guard in the station and on trains. Since most trains to and from Warsaw also pass through either **Warszawa Wschodnia** (ul. Kijowska, tel. 022/18–34–97), the eastern station, or **Warszawa Zachodnia** (al. Jerozolimskie 144, tel. 022/36–59–34), the western station, consider using these safer stations.

Warszawa Centralna has four levels: The first contains all the train platforms; the second contains the baggage check area, information kiosks, and exits to aleja Jerozolimskie, the main thoroughfare; the third has ticket offices for domestic trains and a timetable for all trains; and the fourth has an international ticket office. *Al. Jerozolimskie 54, tel. 022/25–99–42; international rail info, tel. 022/20–45–12; domestic rail info, tel. 022/20–03–61.*

BY BUS **Dworzec PKS Stadion** (intersection of ul. Targowa, ul. Zamoyskiego, and al. Zieleniecka, tel. 022/17–51–49) serves northeastern destinations; **Dworzec PKS Marymont** (ul. Marymoncka and ul. Zeromskiego, tel. 022/34–74–44) serves mostly local destinations; and **Centralny Dworzec PKS** (al. Jerozolimskie 144, tel. 022/23–63–94), a 10-minute ride on Bus 130 or Tram M from Warszawa Centralna, serves most long-distance express routes and local routes to the west. Tickets for all destinations can be purchased at Centralny Dworzec PKS or at ulica Puławska 43. Buses are crowded, filthy, and not air-conditioned.

BY PLANE Travelers arriving in Warsaw by air will be pleasantly surprised when they set foot in the modern **Okęcie Airport** (tel. 022/952), 6½ km south of the city center. To reach the town center, your best bet is to hop on the bus marked AIRPORT CITY, which leaves Terminal 1 every 20 minutes on weekdays and every 30 minutes on weekends from 6 AM to 11 PM. It hits the main train station, major hotels, and main drags and costs about $1.50.

GETTING AROUND

Warsaw is flat except for the ravine carved by the **Wisła River,** which runs through the city north to south. Most sights, attractions, and hotels lie west of the river. Major thoroughfares include **aleja Jerozolimskie,** which runs east–west, and **Nowy Swiat,** which runs north–south through a main shopping district, passes the university, and ends at the entrance to Old Town.

BY BUS AND TRAM Until the new subway system is completed in the distant future, you'll have to manage with the bus and tram systems that operate 5 AM–11 PM. Tickets (sold at Ruch kiosks) are accepted on both buses and trams and cost 1,200 zł each. If you have a student ID, punch only one-half of a 2,000 zł ticket. The map inside the *What, Where, When* guide (*see* English-Language Publications, *above*) shows all transit routes.

Buses with black numbers (100–299) serve the city center but often end up stuck in traffic jams. Express buses, marked with red letters, will take you all over the burbs for 2,400 zł. Accelerated buses (with red numbers or numbered from 400) make all stops in the city center but then go nonstop to the outskirts of the city for 2,400 zł. Night buses, numbered from 600, operate between 11 PM and 5 AM; purchase your ticket (4,800 zł) from the driver if your supply has run out.

WHERE TO SLEEP

Warsaw's shortage of budget hotels means you have to consider alternatives, like the town's three hostels or the bungalows at **Gromada Camping** (ul. Zwirki i Wigury 32, tel. 022/25–43–91; closed Oct.–Apr.). Next to the Skra Stadium, this crowded urban campground charges $3 per person to camp and $7 per double room ($13 per quad) in its unheated bungalows. To get here, take Bus 128 from Warszawa Centralna to the Warsaw University dorms. Another alternative is staying in a private room; **Romeo and Julia** (Emilii Plater 30, Room 15, tel. 022/29–29–93; open daily 9–7), across from the Marriott, arranges these for $15 (single) and $21 (double). Slightly cheaper is **Syrena** (ul. Krucza 16/22, tel. 02/628–7540; open daily 8–7), which arranges singles for $9 and doubles for $14.

➤ **UNDER $10** • **Hotel Legia.** Your basic Polish hotel room—clean, drab, and spartan. *Ul. Powákowska 59, tel. 02/308–3031. Bus 122 or 170 from Old Town; get off at 2nd cemetery.*

Hotel "Tramp." In Nowe Miasto. The staff is not very friendly, but rooms are decent and cheap. *Ul. Smoleńskego 16, tel. 02/614–3727.*

Szkolnictwa Artystycznego w Warzawie. The best deal in Warsaw is this music school with limited space during the school year, but ample room in summer. Excellent location in north part of Stare Miasto. Clean, well-furnished rooms and generous meals included in ridiculously low price. *Ul. Miodoa 24a, tel. 022/12–19–45.*

➤ **UNDER $15** • **Dom Nauczyciela Belfer.** A few blocks from the Wisła River. Priority given to Polish teachers, but there's plenty of space. Clean, sparse, but comfortable rooms. *Wybrzeże Kościuszkowie 31–33, on eastern division, tel. 02/625–0571. Laundry, bar, café. AE, MC, V.*

Dom Turysty PTTK. Ideal locale between Stare Miasto and the university. Recently renovated, but still a bit shabby. *Krakowskie Przedmieście 4–6, tel. 022/26–30–11. Restaurant, laundry.*

Hotel Federacja Metalowcy. Despite overall drabness, this is a bargain after maids add their sanitizing touch. A short walk from Rynek Starego Miasta. *Ul. Długa 29, tel. 022/31–40–21. From pl. Zamkowy, take al. Gen. Swierczewskiego west to ul. Długa.*

Hotel Garnizonowy. Sterile, central hotel gives priority to soldiers and does not take reservations. Entire apartments rent for about $33. *Ul. Mazowiecka 10, tel. 022/27–23–65.*

➤ **UNDER $20** • **Dom Chlopa.** Newly remodeled hotel between Nowy Swiat and Palace of Culture, near the main train station. Surprisingly cheap for the area. *Pl. Powstańców Warszawy 2, no phone.*

HOSTELS **Hotel Studenski.** In southern Warsaw. Rooms (all triples) are clean, bathrooms are *not*. First night $4, each additional night $3.50. *Ul. Smyczkowa 5–7, tel. 022/43–86–21. Take Tram 4, 36, 19, or 33 from pl. Zbawiciela. Closed Oct.–Apr.*

Szkolne Schronisko Młodziezowe (HI). It's clean, friendly, and central. Beds $1.75, $3.50 nonmembers. *Ul. Smolna 30, tel. 022/27–89–52. Near cnr. of Nowy Swiat and al. Jerozolimskie; take Bus 175 from Warszawa Centralna. 11 PM curfew. Reservations advised.*

Szkolne Schronisko Młodziezowe (HI). Lacks central location, but this place is hoppin'—it backs onto the bar Wenecja. Beds $3.75, $4.50 nonmembers. *Ul. Karolkowa 53a, tel. 022/32–88–29. Tram 5, 22, or 24 from Warszawa Centralna. 11 PM curfew.*

STUDENT HOUSING **Warsaw University Dorms.** Two mammoth dorms house more than 1,350 travelers in summer; some rooms are open year-round. Clean communal bathrooms, but bring your own toilet paper. Kitchens on each floor. Reception open 24 hours. Beds in triples $4.50. *Zwirki i Wigury 95–99, tel. 022/22–74–09 or 022/22–46–78. Take Bus 136 or 175 from Warszawa Centralna to ul. Banacha.*

FOOD

New, privately owned restaurants pop up every day in Warsaw. On the high end (about $15 per meal), tucked away in a candlelit wine cellar, **Klub-Restauracja Świętoszek** (ul. Jezuicka 6–8, 1 block south of Rynek Starego Miasta, tel. 022/31–56–34) serves up the best food in Warsaw, according to many Varsovians. Call ahead, as "klub" members have priority. On the other end of the scale, you can fill up at the food stands near Warszawa Centralna and the Palace of Culture for less than $1. And don't miss Polish ice cream: **Lody Zielonabudka** (ul. Puławska 11, tel. 22/49–89–38; open daily 10–8) has the best in town.

➤ **UNDER $5** • **Bar Hipoland.** Excellent pizza ($1.75) and cappuccino with chocolate teddy bears. Extra-thick milk shakes will clog your straw. *Al. Jerozolimskie 23–25, 1 block east of Hotel Forum, tel. 02/528–6256.*

Pizzeria Giovanni. Excellent pizza—by Polish standards. Vegetarians will fall to pieces over cheese pizza or Hawaiian pizza topped with bananas. *Ul. Krakowskie Przedmieście 37.*

Pod Gołębiami. Locals cheer their favorite soccer teams while slurping killer beetroot soup (5,000 zł) in this small, brightly lit place. English menu. *Ul. Piwna 4a, off Rynek Starego Miasta, tel. 02/635–0156. Open daily 10–10.*

Restauracja Pod Samsonem. Despite its tourist-infested location in the center of Stare Miasto, locals head here for wide variety of fish dishes or seasonal fresh veggies at way-low prices. English menu. *Ul. Freta 3–5, opposite Curie museum, tel. 022/31–17–88. Open daily 10–10.*

➤ **UNDER $10** • **El Popo-Restauracja Meksykanska.** The many Mexican dishes are a little odd but tasty. When in doubt, you can dump the great salsa over everything. *Ul. Senatorska 35, near Bielańska, tel. 022/27–23–40. Open daily noon–11.*

Nowe Miasto. Amazing vegetarian restaurant in New Town Square will make you forget you're in Poland; fresh, innovative salads and extensive wine list. Eat well for under $5, but you may want to gorge yourself here. English menu. *Rynek Nowego Miasta 13, tel. 022/31–43–79. Open daily 10 AM–midnight.*

➤ **UNDER $15** • **Gessler.** You'll be served Viennese and light Polish cuisine on the cobbled Old Town Square by lamplight. Live jazz ensemble on summer weekends. *Rynek Starego Miasta 27, tel. 022/31–03–13. Wheelchair access.*

CAFES AND BAKERIES In Poland, whipped cream is considered a basic food group. The best bakery in the city, **A. Blikle** (Nowy Swiat 35), piles whipped cream on top of your excellent pastry. If you can pronounce "*kawa z śmietanką,*" you'll get coffee with whipped cream. Cafés in Warsaw fulfill more than mere dairy fetishes, though. Many *kawiarnie* (cafés) become *winiarnie* (wineries) and even discos when the sun goes down. University students flock to Rynek Starego Miasta to get their caffeine fixes. The smoky, underground **Mannekin Café** (Rynek Starego Miasta 27; open daily noon–midnight) is an ideal place for a rendezvous with a lover, a pack of cigarettes, or that novel you're writing.

WORTH SEEING

Most of the museums and churches are located in or around the Stare Miasto (Old Town). Parks and little patches of greenery are found throughout the city, especially south of aleja Jerozolimskie and on the east bank of the Wisła River.

STARE MIASTO After the war, the city spared this area from the "brutalist" architecture in favor of restoring it to its original style. The result is a welcome respite from the rest of the city and gives a glimpse of the grandeur that characterized Warsaw's past.

➤ **AROUND PLAC ZAMKOWY** • You'll probably enter Stare Miasto through Plac Zamkowy, the plaza on the southern border of the district. You can't miss the **King Zygmunt III statue,** which perches on the towering column in the center of the plaza. This statue of the king who moved the capital from Kraków to Warsaw in the early 17th century now stands guard over the restless youths, Hare Krishnas, and Bermuda-clad tourists who lounge on its steps.

North of the Zygmunt III statue is the 14th-century **Zamek Królewski** (Royal Castle), which remained the royal residence and seat of the Polish parliament until the end of the 18th century. Blown up by the Nazis, the castle was meticulously re-created from old plans and photos. The castle now gleams as it did in its glory days, with gilt, marble, and murals. You can't see the whole castle without a tour, and the upper parts are really spectacular, so hook up with an English-speaking group. Tours start hourly from the side entrance. Get here early, as some parts close after 2:30 PM. *Pl. Zamkowy 4, north of Krakowskie Przedmieście, tel. 02/635– 3995. Admission: 10,000 zł, 5,000 zł students; free Thurs. Open Tues.–Sat. 10–5, Sun. 9–5.*

➤ **RYNEK STAREGO MIASTA** • The Rynek Starego Miasta (Old Town Square) bustled with traders and merchants in its heyday, from the 13th to the 19th centuries. Although it's now closed to traffic and no formal market is held here, the square is still as lively as ever. Artists and artisans sell their wares, and scheduled and impromptu concerts take place constantly. Traces of original Gothic architecture still remain at the **Klucznikowska Mansion** (Rynek Starego Miasta 21) and the **Mansion of the Mazovian Princes** (Rynek Starego Miasta 31). Several Renaissance mansions line the square; the **Historical Museum of Warsaw** (Rynek Starego Miasta 28; admission 10,000 zł, 5,000 zł students; open Tues. and Thurs. 11–6, Wed. and Fri. 10–3:30, weekends 10:30–4:30) is housed in several of these mansions, and its film about the devastation of Warsaw during World War II is worth a look.

➤ **ARCHIKATEDRALNA BAZYLIKA SW. JANA** • Built in the late 13th century as a mere parish church, the Cathedral of St. John underwent renovation after renovation through the centuries. From the 16th to the 18th centuries, it was often chosen as the site for the coronation of Polish kings. The renovations were all for naught—the cathedral was almost destroyed during World War I. *Ul. Kanonia 6. Vault open Mon.–Sat. 10–2 and 4–5:30, Sun. 2–5:30.*

JEWISH GHETTO For centuries, Warsaw was home to a thriving Jewish community. By 1942, 300,000 Warsaw Jews had been deported to Nazi death camps, prompting the Jewish Combat Organization (ZOB) to launch the Ghetto Uprising in April 1943. After four heroic weeks of Jewish resistance, the Nazis razed the ghetto, killing most of its inhabitants. On the site of the once-smoldering ruins stands the **Pomnik Bohaterów Getta** (Monument to the Heroes of the Warsaw Ghetto; ul. Zamenhofa). Using materials that Hitler intended for a monument to his own anticipated victory, the sculptor Natan Rappaport erected this monument in 1948, on the fifth anniversary of the uprising.

In 1939, about 380,000 Jews resided in Warsaw. Just six years later, only 300 or so remained.

The modern neighborhoods of Muranów and Mirów, which now cover what was once the ghetto, are speckled with remnants of the once-thriving Jewish community. **Nożyks Synagogue** (ul. Twarda, behind theater; open weekdays 10–3, Sat. 9–noon) is the only synagogue of the ghetto to survive World War II bombings. The **Zydowski Instytut Historyczny** (Jewish Historical Institute; al. Tłomackie 3–5, off al. Solidarności near pl. Bankowy, tel. 022/27–92–21, ext. 28; open weekdays 10–3) houses a library, a research institute, and a museum that includes photographs, memorabilia, and a model of the bunker used by the Varsovian Jews during the Ghetto Uprising.

NOWE MIASTO Although Nowe Miasto (New Town) is primarily a residential district, it contains an increasing number of restaurants and galleries, too. To commemorate a victory over the Turks in 1683, the cool, white **Kościół Sakramentek** (Church of the Sisters of the Blessed Sacrament) was built on the quiet **Rynek Nowego Miasta** (New Town Square). In the course of heavy fighting during the Warsaw Uprising, the church was destroyed, and more than 1,000 people lost their lives.

LAZIENKI PARK AND PALACE If Warsaw is not your idea of paradise, head to beautiful Lazienki Park, stretching to the east of aleja Ujazdowskie. In the late 18th century Poland's last king turned the grounds into an English-style garden. The star of the park is Lazienki Palace, or the Palace on the Lake (admission 24,000 zł, 12,000 zł students; open Tues.–Sun. 9:30–3). The palace was so faithfully reconstructed after the war that there is still no electricity—visit when it's sunny, or you won't see a thing inside.

On Sundays in summer, classical **concerts** and other performances are held at noon and 4 PM near the park entrance at the foot of the Chopin Monument or in the wooden theater of the 18th-century orangery. Also on park grounds is the **Zamek Ujadowsk Palace**, a haven for Poland's most controversial contemporary art.

MAUSOLEUM OF STRUGGLE AND MARTYRDOM Visit the cells where political prisoners were tortured before being transferred to Pawiak Prison, and the re-created Gestapo office where Hitler's portrait hangs ominously on the wall. *Al. Armii Wojska Polskiego 25, off pl. Na Rozdrozu, tel. 022/29–49–19. Admission: 5,000 zł. Open Wed. 9–5, Thurs. and Sat. 9–4, Fri. 10–4.*

MUZEUM NARODOWE The National Museum of Warsaw has an amazing collection of contemporary Polish and European paintings and Gothic icons. Also on display are the famous Canaletto paintings, used as references to facilitate the rebuilding of Warsaw after the war. Allow a good couple of hours to see the whole museum. For military buffs, the **Polish Military Museum** is next door. *Al. Jerozolimskie 3, tel. 022/21–10–31. Admission: 10,000 zł, 5,000 zł students, free Thurs. Open Tues. and Sun. 10–5; Wed., Fri., and Sat. 10–4; Thurs. noon–6.*

PALAC KULTURY I NAUKI The sinister-looking skyscraper, Pałac Kultury i Nauki (Palace of Culture and Science), donated to the city by Stalin in 1955, rises phallically over downtown Warsaw. It houses the Zoological and Technical Museums, the Polish Academy of Science, a congress hall, four cinemas, four theaters, a nightclub, a bookstore, restaurants, exhibit halls, a swimming pool, and even a casino. Varsovians joke that this is the best place to view the city, since it's the only place from which you can't see the monolith itself. *Observation deck admission: 30,000 zł, 10,000 zł students (before 3 PM). Open Mon.–Sat. 9–8, Sun. 10–8.*

Warsaw University's buildings are scattered throughout the city, a design preferred by the previous government in order to diffuse the threat posed by intellectuals. The core of the university, though, is just beyond the large gate on Krakowskie Przedmieście. This is the place to find out about lectures and musical happenings.

CHURCHES One of the few buildings that survived World War II unscathed is the **Kościół Wizytek** (Church of the Nuns of the Visitation; Krakowskie Przedmieście 34, near Rynek Nowego Miasta), the site of organ performances by Chopin. Generally this church is open to the public only during or between masses; otherwise, go to the side gate and a nun may let you in. Farther down the street, at Krakowskie Przedmieście 68, is the resplendent **Kościół św. Anny** (St. Anne's Church), founded in the mid-15th century. The Baroque and Rococo interior has recently been redecorated and regilded and is laden with sculptures, and painting. The 17th-century **Kościół św. Krzyza** (Holy Cross Church) at Krakowskie Przedmieście 1, south of Traugutta, houses the largest organ in Warsaw. If Chopin is your heartthrob, head to the second pillar to the left of the nave, where an urn holds Frederic's heart.

AFTER DARK

If you look hard enough, you'll find several places to drink, hang out, or dance till you drop. The city's student clubs are a great option for budget travelers during the school year (October–May). They offer a wide range of activities (drinking, discussion, dancing) and give discounts to people toting any kind of student ID; foreign students are warmly received. The **Riviera Remont** (ul. Waryńskiego 12, tel. 022/25–74–97; cover $6, $3 students), the best-known club in town, attracts a variety of people with its political discussions, international folk music, Zen meditation, Hare Krishna meetings, and all-night jam sessions. It's open daily as a coffee shop, on weekends as a disco, and on Thursday as a jazz club, and features rock concerts on some Fridays. Take Tram 4, 31, 46, 112, 117, or 180. Consult *Warsaw Voice* for more club info.

As summer rolls around and tourists start to fill the clubs, students flock to bars. Those named after famous beers like **Guinness Bar** (ul. Koszykowa 1) and **Heineken** (ul. Puławska 101) are most popular. To get to the latter, take express Bus A or U, or Tram 4, 31, or 36 south. For something more authentic, try **Pasieka** (ul. Freta 7–9), near the Stare Miasto. For further insight into the bar scene, pick up a copy of *Gazeta Wyborcza, Zycie Warszawy,* or *The Insider* from Ruch kiosks or a major hotel.

MUSIC In Warsaw you can hear just about every kind of music played live. The appeal of Western jazz music has given rise to a large and talented population of Polish jazz musicians; they haunt the city's several jazz clubs and participate in the citywide **Jazz Jamboree** each October. **Akwarium Jazz Club** (Emilii Plater 49, near the Palace of Culture, tel. 022/20–50–72) is *the* place for jazz, where top Polish players and foreign groups play to a jumping crowd in smoky surroundings.

Classical concerts are the craze in Warsaw, so it's best to book in advance through **Orbis** (*see* Visitor Information, *above*). Information for concerts also can be obtained through the **Warsaw Philharmonic Orchestra Office** (Sienkiewicza 10, tel. 022/26–72–81, ext. 37), or take a look in the ever-helpful *What, Where, When* guide (*see* English-Language Publications, *above*). The **Towarzystwo im. Fryderyka Chopina** (Chopin Society; Palac Ostrogskich, ul. Okólnik, tel. 022/27–95–99) organizes recitals and chamber concerts of music by Chopin and other composers. **Wielki Theater** (pl. Teatralny, tel. 022/26–32–87) stages spectacular productions of classic operas and ballets.

Near Warsaw

KAMPINOSKI PARK NARODOWY In 1959, Kampinos National Park was founded to preserve the flora and fauna of this region 30 km northwest of Warsaw. Pay a small admission fee, pick up a map from the **information center** (ul. Krasińskiego 49, tel. 022/34–25–14) at the entrance, and take to the hiking trails. If you call in advance you can arrange for an English-speaking guide to show you around (about $1.75 an hour). A hike to the northeastern section of the park will lead you to a cemetery; buried here are Nazi victims who were secretly driven to the countryside and shot. To reach the cemetery, stay on Bus 708 until its terminus, then hoof it down the northeast road. Bring water with you; insect repellent wouldn't hurt, either. A day trip to Kampinos is feasible if you get an early start and catch the last bus back (about 6 PM). Bus 708 from Warsaw's Dworzec PKS Marymont serves the park, as does an hourly PKS bus from Zachodnia train station.

WILANOW Just 10 km south of Warsaw on the Royal Road, **Wilanów** definitely merits a short visit. This small town was originally known as Villa Nova, or New Town, and dates back to 1677, when King Jan III Sobieski began to expand an existing manor to create his ideal summer residence—a project that went on for 20 years, even after his death. The end result was a magnificent **Baroque palace** that is often compared to Versailles. Tours of the palace interior are 10,000 zł, 5,000 zł for students; pay an extra 5,000 zł to walk around the grounds. The palace is open Wednesday–Monday 9:30–2:30; the park is open until dark. An easy day trip from Warsaw, Wiłanów is served by several buses; the most convenient is Bus 180 from Marszałkowska, near the Palace of Culture.

Kraków  It's fitting that Joseph Conrad spent his formative years in Kraków, the city that sits in the heart of one of the darkest moments of the 20th century. During World War II, more people died in nearby death camps than reside in the city today. Yet paradoxically, the city has remained incredibly enlightened: Warsaw may be the capital of Poland, but Kraków is the country's cultural center. Home to Eastern Europe's second-oldest university, seat of the Polish monarchy from the 11th to 15th centuries, and former diocese of Cardinal Karol Wojtyła (now Pope John Paul II), Kraków has had an indisputable influence on Polish history. Thanks to a surprise maneuver by the Soviet army, Kraków escaped destruction at the hands of Nazis during World War II and still boasts an enchanting collection of Renaissance arcades, onion-shaped domes, and Baroque spires, as well as the imposing Wawel Castle and Cathedral.

BASICS

VISITOR INFORMATION **Orbis** is based in the Hotel Cracovia. This office, the **American Express** representative, provides tourist information, changes money, and arranges tours of Kraków ($15), Auschwitz and Birkenau ($20), and the Wieliczka Salt Mine ($15). *Al. F. Focha 1, across from Błonia meadow, tel. 012/22–46–32. Take ul. Piłsudskiego west from Old Town; or Tram 15 or Bus 119. Open winter, weekdays 8–4; summer, weekdays 8–8, weekends 8–4.*

CONSULATES **United States:** *Ul. Stolarska 9, tel. 012/22–60–40. Off ul. Sienna, 1 block east of Rynek. Open daily 9–3.*

PHONES AND MAIL The central post office building contains a telephone office (open 24 hours). *Ul. Wielopole 2, 3 blocks south of stations, tel. 012/22–86–48. Open weekdays 7:30 AM–8:30 PM, Sat. 8 AM–2 PM, Sun. 9 AM–11 AM.*

COMING AND GOING

East of city center is the main train station, **Kraków Główny** (pl. Kolejowy 1, tel. 012/22–22–48). Finding your way around can be confusing, but just remember this: All tracks can be reached via an underground passageway just north of the rear of the station. Frequent express buses depart from the **bus station** (pl. Kolejowy, tel. 012/936; open daily 4 AM–11 PM) opposite the train station.

GETTING AROUND

To reach the center of town from the train station, check with the **MPK booth** off Platform 1 for local bus info, or look left as you exit the train station and grab a tram; most run along ulica Basztowa and ulica Lubicz. Or get some exercise and walk 10 minutes to Stare Miasto. Head right out of the train station and through the pedestrian underpass at the far corner of the taxi lot. Turn right out of the underpass to reach the city center.

The Planty Gardens encircle the Stare Miasto (Old Town). Buses and trams follow the ring road there, leaving the central streets and main square to pedestrians. The handy transit map, *Kraków Plan Miasta*, is sold at Ruch stands and bookstores on the Rynek. Tickets cost 4,000 zł for either the bus or tram and can be purchased at MPK or Ruch stands. Students need punch only one side of their ticket per trip, but those with large backpacks travel at the full fare. From 11 PM to 5 AM, buses run twice an hour for double the fare.

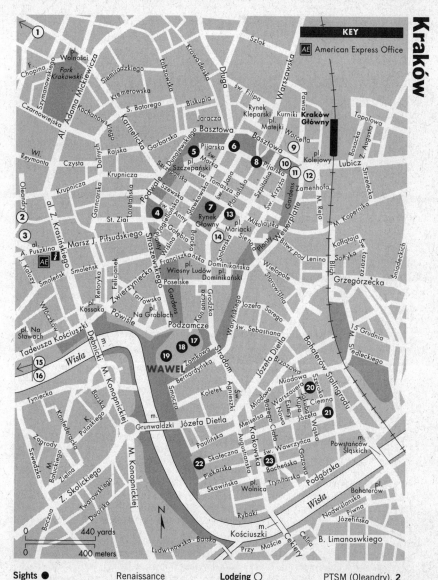

WHERE TO SLEEP

A huge flock of tourists swamps Kraków each year, and hotel space is limited. Accommodations near the stations are within easy walking distance of the main sights, but if you stay at a hostel or campground you'll need to use a bus or tram to get around. **Almatur** (Rynek 7–8, tel. 012/22–63–52; open Mon.–Thurs. 8–4:30, Fri. 8–4) provides info on student summer hotels, most of which are a good 20 minutes away. **Wawel Tourist** (ul. Pawia 8, across from stations, tel. 012/22–19–21; open weekdays 8 AM–9 PM, Sat. 1–7) arranges stays in private homes, most outside the city center. It rents singles for $5–$10, doubles for $8–$15, and triples and quads for $4–$6 per person.

➤ **UNDER $20 • Hotel Polonia.** Elegant hotel decked out with chandeliers and faux marble. Basic singles $13, doubles $19, triples $23. Rooms in front are noisier but have balconies. *Ul. Basztowa 25, tel. 012/22–16–61. Wheelchair access. Reservations advised. MC, V.*

Hotel Warszawski. Simply furnished hotel with noisy but comfy rooms that can easily accommodate more people (hint, hint). Singles $12, doubles $17, triples $19. *Ul. Pawia 6, opposite train station, tel. 012/22–06–22. Reservations advised.*

➤ **UNDER $25 • Hotel Europejski.** One of the nicest places to stay near station. Comfortable rooms; singles $14, doubles $22, triples $31. *Ul. Lubicz 5, south of station, tel. 012/22–09–11. Reservations advised. AE, MC, V.*

➤ **UNDER $40 • Pod Kopcem.** A definite splurge; a converted 19th-century Austrian fortress with hardwood floors and first-class amenities. Luxurious rooms overlook the fortress walls. Doubles $30–$39, including breakfast. *Al. Waszyngtona, near Kościuszko mound, tel. 012/22–20–55. From station walk 3 blocks west to pl. Matejki and catch Bus 100 to terminus. Reservations advised.*

HOSTELS AND STUDENT HOUSING **Hotel Studencki Zaczek.** Busy dorm where you can mingle with Polish students. Tours to Auschwitz and the Wieliczka Salt Mine arranged. Per person, singles, doubles, and triples cost $6.25–$15. Open July 7–September 24 only. *Al. 3 Maja 5, tel. 012/33–54–77. Take Tram 15 or Bus 119 from station to Hotel Cracovia, go 1 block down al. 3 Maja. Wheelchair access, kitchen, jazz club. Reservations advised.*

Letni Summer Hostel (HI). Open July 1–September 20 only. Doubles with baths and balconies $6, $12 for nonmembers. *Al. Jana Pawła II 82, tel. 012/48–02–07. Take Tram 4, 5, 10, or 44 from station.*

PTSM (Kościuszki) (HI). Above Augustine convent 10 blocks from town center. Bunk beds in quiet, clean, nonsmoking building on Wisła River. Pray a nun is downstairs to let you in. Beds $2.50, $3 nonmembers. *Ul. Kościuszki 88, tel. 012/22–19–51. From station, take Tram 1, 2, 6, or 21 to terminus or Bus 100 to convent. 10 PM curfew, lockout 10–5. Reservations advised.*

PTSM (Oleandry). Looks like it was jointly designed by Salvador Dalí and Alice Cooper. Busy hostel overrun with noisy kids. B.Y.O.T.P. (Bring Your Own Toilet Paper). Beds $3.75–$5. *Ul. Oleandry 4, tel. 012/33–88–22. Take Tram 15 from station to Hotel Cracovia, walk 1 block down al. 3 Maja to ul. Oleandry. Laundry, kitchen.*

CAMPGROUND **Camping Krak.** Northwest of town. Excellent amenities, but has all the charm of a truck stop. Pay $2.50 per person. *Ul. Radzikowskiego 99, tel. 012/37–21–22. Take Bus 130 or 173 to Motel Krak. Kitchen, wheelchair access. Closed Oct.–Apr.*

FOOD

If you can't find anything to eat in Kraków, we wash our hands of you. Snack bars and restaurants are scattered along ulica Floriańska and ulica Sienna, off the Rynek, as well as in the university district along ulica Szewska and plac Szczepański. Most restaurants close early (around 8 or 9), but the numerous cafés keep their doors open until 10 or 11. **Jama Michalika** (ul. Flo-

Just downhill from the university, the **Museu Nacional Machado de Castro** has one of Portugal's finest collections of sculpture, as well as paintings, ceramics, jewels, and furniture. Beneath the museum, Roman catacombs contain fascinating relics, including tombs for infants. *Largo Dr. José Rodrigues, tel. 039/23727. Admission: 250$, students free. Open Tues.–Sun. 10–5.*

Northern Portugal

Natives call northwestern Portugal the *Costa Verde* (Green Coast) because of its lush forests and clear mountain streams, fed by winter rains. The stunning Minho, Douro, and Tras os Montes regions, which make up the north, contrast remarkably with the flat, barren lands of central and southern Portugal. More than in other parts of the country, the people of the north are deeply suspicious of change. Visitors may garner uncomfortable stares, although most residents are actually hip to meeting foreigners and are very friendly when approached. You might even get shown around by a local or invited in for a meal. This is about as off-the-beaten-track as Portugal gets, especially in the northeast, where tourism seems nonexistent. The region is mostly rural, but you'll find a few cities, including Porto, an industrial capital that has grown world-famous producing port wine, and lively Braga, with transport links to the northern and northeastern corners of the country.

Porto

The capital of the north and the second-largest city in Portugal, Porto is unabashedly commercial. As a Portuguese proverb puts it, "Coimbra sings, Braga prays, Lisbon shows off, and Porto works." This is not a graceful city—it has few aesthetically pleasing monuments and many traffic jams, crowded sidewalks, and drug dealers. In summer, the heat can be oppressive. Just as in most big cities, you'll find striking contrasts here: The decrepit shantytown of **Cais da Ribeira** clings to the steep cliffs above Ponte Dom Luis I, while just 4 km to the west Portuguese yuppies thrive in the **Foz do Douro** beach district. Across the river, the city of Vila Nova de Gaia has been the headquarters of the port-wine trade since the late 17th century. A good place to get your bearings and escape the hubbub of downtown is the **Torre dos Clérigos** (Rua dos Clérigos, tel. 02/200–1729; admission 100$; open Thurs.–Tues. 10:30–noon and 3:30–5). After an exhausting 225 steps, you get an unparalleled view of the city, bridges, and river.

BASICS For visitor info, try the main **turismo** (Rua Clube Fenianos 25, tel. 02/312740) at the north end of Avenida dos Aliados. It's open weekdays 9–6:45, Saturday 9–3:45, and Sunday 10–12:45 in summer; hours are shorter off-season. There's a satellite office on Praça Dom João I. Porto also has an **American Express** office (Top Tours, Rua Alferes Malheiro 96, tel. 02/208–2785), open weekdays 9–12:30 and 2:30–6:30. Nearly all the banks are around Praça da Liberdade and Avenida dos Aliados. **Banco Espiritu Santo** (Av. dos Aliados 45–69, tel. 02/200–8726), which charges the lowest commission, has a 24-hour cash exchange machine.

To make a phone call, go to **Telcom Portugal** (Pr. da Liberdade), open Monday–Saturday 9–7. Send mail at the **correios** (Av. dos Aliados 320, tel. 02/208–0251), open weekdays 8–9, weekends 9–6. Porto's postal code is 4000.

COMING AND GOING Most trains stop at **Estação de Campanhã** (tel. 02/564141), a bit outside town. The trip from Lisbon (1,300$) takes four hours. Every 20–30 minutes a free shuttle train runs from the station to **Estação de São Bento** (tel. 02/200–2722), in the heart of the city. São Bento has an information office for train travel. Bus terminals are scattered throughout town; either ask at turismo for the best option or check with **Rede Expressos,** the national bus company, which has two stations. The one at Praça Filipa de Lencastre 178 (tel. 02/200–3152) serves the north and east areas of Portugal, and the one on Rua Alexandre Herculano 364 (tel. 02/200–6954) sends regional and express buses to Lisbon (3½ hrs, 1,400$) and southern Portugal.

GETTING AROUND Porto lies on a steep hillside above the Douro River. The commercial area centers around **Avenida dos Aliados,** a wide, sloping boulevard that points toward the river. At its southern end, **Praça da Liberdade** is the hub from which downtown Porto radiates. The two-tiered **Ponte Dom Luis I,** the middle of three bridges that span the Douro in Porto, leads to the town of Vila Nova de Gaia. Although Porto sprawls, most of the interesting sights are around Avenida dos Aliados and Praça da Liberdade, right near Estação de São Bento. Nearly all buses stop at Praça da Liberdade, which has bus information and ticket booths. Individual tickets cost 140$, a one-day pass 300$, a four-day tourist pass 1,340$, and a seven-day tourist pass 1,860$.

WHERE TO SLEEP Most of the good pensãoes are west of Avenida dos Aliados and Praça da Liberdade, on the other side of the square as you exit the São Bento train station. Signs reading HOSPEDEIRA indicate small, family-run places where you can usually find a double for 1,500$–2,500$.

Pensão Duas Nações. Rock-bottom. Acceptably clean and quiet, at least after sunset when activity on the praça dies down. Friendly management. Singles 1,250$, doubles 2,000$. *Pr. Guilherme Gomes Fernandes 59, tel. 02/208–1616. From Pr. da Liberdade, take Rua Clérigos to Rua Carmelitas, and turn right on Pr. Guilherme Gomes Fernandes. 2:30 AM curfew.*

Residencial Paris. Wonderful old building with a classy breakfast room. Well-tended gardens have fountains. Popular, so call ahead in summer. Central location, though the neighborhood can be sketchy at night. Singles 2,300$, doubles 3,300$. *Rua da Fábrica 27, off Pr. da Liberdade, tel. 02/321396. Wheelchair access.*

Residencial Porto Chique. Homey atmosphere and antique four-poster beds. Great neighborhood can be noisy at night, so choose a room away from the street. Very friendly manager. Singles 2,000$, doubles 2,500$–3,500$. *Rua Conde de Vizela 26, tel. 02/208–0069. From Pr. da Liberdade, take Rua Clérigos and turn right on Rua Conde de Vizela.*

➤ **HOSTELS • Pousada de Juventude do Porto (HI).** A large, soulless place far from the action of the city. Crowded in summer. Beds 1,200$, breakfast included. *Rua Rodrigues Lobo 98, tel. 02/606–5535. From Pr. da Liberdade, Bus 3, 18, 19, or 52 to Pr. Galiza, then follow signs. Midnight curfew, lockout 10:30–6, kitchen facilities.*

FOOD Workers' cafés around **Avenida dos Aliados** serve lunches for less than 500$, but the street is dead after sunset, so you'll have to look elsewhere for dinner. For a treat, take Tram 18 from Praça Guilherme Gomes Fernandes (west of Praça da Liberdade) all the way to **Avenida do Brasil,** a beachside promenade about a 15-minute ride west, and have dinner in one of the cheapish seafood restaurants. Porto is a center for *tripas* (tripe), and the adventurous can try a plate with rice for about 700$. Buy your own staples at **Mercado de Bolhão** (Rua Sá da Bandeira, at Rua Formosa), open weekdays 7–5 and Saturday 7–1.

Casa Meia Lua (Rua T. Cimo de Vila 151, 1 block south of Pr. Batalha, tel. 02/200–4124), a workers' café with a very local atmosphere, shows soap operas on a TV in back. Russian salad with sardines goes for 600$, tripas are 650$, and fried octopus with rice costs 600$. At the wheelchair-accessible **Confiteria M.L.** (Rua Mártires de Liberdade 143, 2 blocks south of Pr. da República, tel. 02/321730), a student crowd gathers on the sunny patio to eat shellfish stew and other regional specialties. Pizza is 500$, and the plate of the day goes for as little as 240$. **Restaurante Polo Norte** (Rua da Fábrica 28, off Pr. da Liberdade, tel. 02/200–0790) has an attractive stained-wood interior. Angolian chicken is grilled before your eyes for 600$, and fried cod with rice costs 800$. Finish the meal off with homemade cakes and pastries.

WORTH SEEING Igreja de São Francisco. This late-14th-century church is Gothic on the outside, but the inside was redone in the 1700s with ornate gilt carvings. For an earthier thrill, visit the museum next door. Skip the boring religious artifacts and ask to be let down to the basement, where you'll find hundreds of covers for shallow indoor graves. As the bodies decomposed, the bones were removed and placed in a holding room. You can see them from a grate in the floor if you venture in far enough. *Rua Infante D. Henrique 1, tel. 02/200–6493. Admission: 350$. Open Mon.–Sat. 9–5.*

Port Wine Cellars. A stroll across Ponte Dom Luis I (take the upper level) leads to the suburb of Vila Nova de Gaia, home of port wine. Actually, the wine is brought in from the Douro Valley and only aged and fortified here, and most *caves* (cellars) have been bought out by foreign corporations. The cellars, which advertise with large white lettering on their roofs, are within a few minutes' walk of one another. They offer tours, detailed explanations of the port-making process, and, best of all, free tasting. Avoid the big-name places along the river and head uphill for the less touristy wineries, like **Osborne** (Rua Cândido dos Reis 670, tel. 02/302648).

CHEAP THRILLS Take the tram to **Avenida do Brasil** (*see* Food, *above*), where people come to see and be seen. Students congregate here, especially after a hot summer day; and fashion designers often sponsor lavish, free parties in the beachside bars. Back in town, an **open-air cinema** shows independent releases in their original languages at Praça do Marquês de Pombal, northeast of Praça da República. In summer, bands play in the Cais da Ribeira at the river's edge, and drunken revelers carry on until things peter out around 3 AM.

Braga

An hour by train from Porto (425$) and five hours from Lisbon (1,900$), lively Braga is one of Portugal's oldest cities (it is thought to have Celtic origins). Braga became an important bishopric in the 6th century. Today it's a center of religious study, filled with churches built in the 16th century. Braga holds Portugal's most impressive Easter celebrations; during **Holy Week,** the churches are covered with flowers and hooded penitents bearing torches parade through town at midnight.

At the center of the old town is the huge **Sé** (cathedral), originally Romanesque but now representing a blend of styles. Nearby, the former **Paço dos Arcebispos** (Archbishop's Palace), parts of which date from the 14th century, houses the faculty from the university and functions as the **public library** (Largo do Paço 1, tel. 053/612234), with an impressive collection of over 250,000 volumes. At the **Palácio dos Biscainhos** (Rua dos Biscainhos 46, tel. 053/27645; admission 400$; open Tues.–Sun. 10–12:15 and 2–5), a Baroque mansion, you can tour the former archbishop's home and gardens and see rotating museum exhibits.

Turismo (Av. da Liberdade 1, tel. 053/22550) can arrange transport to nearby sights. The **train station** (tel. 053/22166) is a 15-minute walk from the center of town. The **bus station** (tel. 053/616080) sends buses to all points in northern Portugal, as well as running express lines to Porto (1 hr 15 min, 465$) and Lisbon (5 hrs, 1,650$).

WHERE TO SLEEP AND EAT Finding a cheap room in Braga can be tough; there are only five pensãoes in town. The threadbare **Francfort** (Av. Central 7, tel. 053/22648; doubles 3,000$) dates back 100 years and has touches of class to make up for its peeling paint. **Pensão Convivio** (Av. Central 128, tel. 053/22260; doubles 2,500$), above Vice Versa Café, is run by a family with dogs, cats, and birds, and has basic rooms with religious themes. **Residencial Ignacio Filho** (Rua Francisco Sanches 42, tel. 053/23849; doubles 4,000$) has tasteful antique furniture. The bright, cheery **HI Pousada de Juventude** (Rua de Santa Margarida 6, tel. 053/616163; beds 1,200$) is another good bet. To reach it from the tourist office, walk east on Avenida Central until the park turns into a rose garden and then make a left uphill.

You can buy nearly anything at the municipal mercado (Praça do Comércio 1; open Mon.–Sat.), filled with old farmers' wives chatting, spitting, and commenting on the nutty foreigners who have wandered in.

For the cheapest lunch in town, head to **Co-op Restaurant** (Av. Central 88, tel. 053/676172; lunch only, closed Sun.), over the grocery store. For under 500$, you can have a daily special such as fried fish and rice, plus a salad and a beer. A little fancier and more expensive, **Restaurante Biscainhos** (Rua dos Biscainhos 47, tel. 053/611491), across from the museum entrance of the Paço dos Arcebispos, specializes in *açorda de gambas,* a delicious thick soup with bread crumbs and prawns (1,250$). Braga's cafés are an integral part of the city's culture. There are three on Praça da República: the classy old **Café Astoria** (tel. 053/73944), with wood paneling and beveled mirrors; **Café Vianna** (tel. 053/22336), a combination of high-tech lighting and antique chairs; and the old-style **A Brasileira** (tel. 053/26865). The cafés also serve as the town's nightspots; they're open until 2 AM but close Sundays.

NEAR BRAGA

PARQUE NACIONAL DE PENEDA-GERES In the northern reaches of the country, next to the Spanish border, Portugal's largest nature park is a stunning collection of granite mountains, freshwater lagoons, and rivers and streams (including the beautiful Lima River, the least polluted in Portugal). Wild eagles watch over villages that seem untouched by the last 200 years. FAPAS, the largest ecological organization in Portugal, runs a nature school and tree farm in the park and has the formidable task of instilling conservationism in villagers who follow centuries-old grazing and farming techniques.

The park is best accessed from Braga. Daily buses run to several villages within the park, including **Lindoso,** with spectacular camping by the river, and **São João de Campo,** where an excellent and cheap hostel (tel. 053/351339) perches high on a mountain overlooking the resort town of Vilarinho das Furnas.

BOM JESUS A weekend retreat and religious theme park built by a wealthy archbishop, the pilgrimage site of Bom Jesus consists of a long Baroque staircase leading up to a neoclassical chapel. As you ascend the stairs, you encounter a series of miniature chapels, each depicting a scene from the life of Christ. Especially during Holy Week, the staircase is packed with pilgrims making the climb on their knees. On weekends, you'll see wedding processions and Portuguese picnickers trekking up. The walk can be pleasant, but for the slothful a tram (90$) makes the 300-meter climb in a startling three minutes. At the top, you get an inspiring view of the countryside all the way to the coast. For a laugh, check out the lake at the top of the hill, choked with awkward rowboats bumping into one another. Several cafés sell beer and other snacks. To get to Bom Jesus, take Bus 2 (30 min, 140$) from Braga's Praça Municipal. The site is open daily sunrise to sunset; admission is free.

ROMANIA 21

By Terence Priester

Visitors to Romania rarely arrive with any real understanding of this country; those who stay long enough to form an impression are either horrified or deeply moved. Since the 1989 revolt that marked the end of Communist dictator Nicolae Ceauşescu's reign, Romania has had one of the lowest standards of living in Europe. The unemployment rate is 30%, and prices seem to rise on a monthly basis. But what makes the country unique is the way the people accept daily difficulties of survival nearly incomprehensible to the Western traveler. After all, this is the gruff bunch that weathered 25 years of Ceauşescu's cruel tyranny. Lessons in perseverance are etched in the face of every old woman who takes your change at the rest-room door.

Locked away from the Western world for so long, many Romanians have never met a Western tourist. You'll notice that you're the center of attention. "Where are you going?" people will ask. "Are you American? I have cousins in Chicago—do you know them?" The country's tourist facilities show signs of neglect, but if you take the time to meet average residents, you'll find they take their obligation as hosts very seriously. You're likely to be invited for a meticulously prepared meal, and they'll make up for their nation's decayed infrastructure by personally taking you to see the sights.

To enjoy your time in Romania, you should be prepared to get away from the industrial cities; most of the population centers were built as cheaply and hideously as possible. The beautiful Carpathian Mountains and Moldavia's agricultural areas are well worth a look, but it's difficult to travel here unless you have a car or lots of time to kill. Fortunately, there are several beautiful towns on major rail lines in Transylvania where you can explore Dracula's old haunts and soak up some of the country's medieval Saxon history.

Basics

MONEY $1 = 1,660 lei and 100 lei = 6¢. The exchange rate of the Romanian leu (plural lei) fluctuates wildly. If you plan to stay here, it's imperative to bring American dollars in small denominations. They'll get you unstuck from sticky situations, and you must buy international train tickets in hard currency. Banks charge a 5% commission on traveler's checks; tourist offices and the few luxury hotels that accept checks take a 5%–10% bite.

➢ **HOW MUCH IT WILL COST** • Your first discovery about Romania will be that there are few things you can't afford. Even if you blow your money on fancy dinners, clothing, clubs, and discos, it's easy to spend less than $30 in an average day. The only big expense is

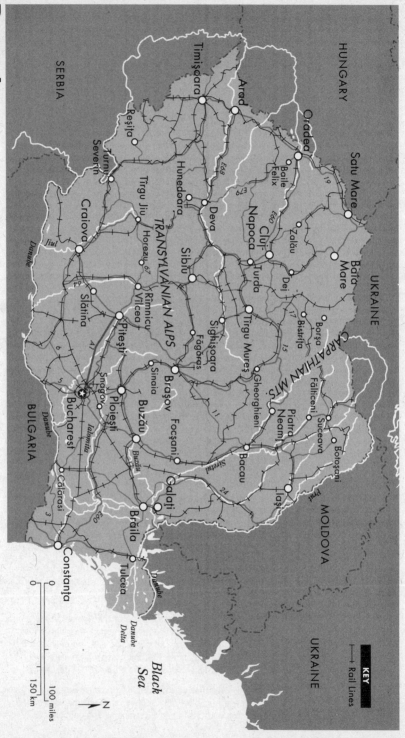

Romania

ROMANIA

HUNGARY

SERBIA

Timişoara

Arad

Oradea

Satu Mare

Reşiţa

Baia
Felix

Turnu
Severin

Tîrgu Jiu

Hunedoara

Deva

Baia
Mare

UKRAINE

Craiova

Horezu

Sibiu

Cluj
Napoca

Zalău

Dej

Turda

Tîrgu Mureş

Bistriţa

Borşa

Slatina

Rîmnicu
Vîlcea

TRANSYLVANIAN ALPS

Sighişoara

Făgăraş

Gheorghieni

Fălticeni

Suceava

CARPATHIAN MTS.

Piatra
Neamţ

Boroşani

Pieşti

Sinaia

Braşov

Snagov

Ploieşti

Buzău

Focşani

Bacău

MOLDOVA

Bucharest

Galaţi

Iaşi

BULGARIA

Călăraşi

Brăila

Constanţa

Tulcea

Danube
Delta

Black
Sea

UKRAINE

Jiul

Danube

Danube

Ialomiţa

Buzău

Siretul

Prut

KEY

Rail Lines

0

0

100 miles

150 km

N

lodging: In cities, many hotels have begun to charge higher prices to foreigners—anywhere from $10 to $40 a night.

VISAS AND ENTRY REQUIREMENTS All visitors must purchase a 60-day, single-entry visa from a Romanian consulate or at the border. You'll pay more at the border ($30–$35 instead of $15–$20), and you must pay in hard currency.

COMING AND GOING Most budget travelers arrive in Bucharest on a **train** from Budapest. The national airline, **TAROM** (in U.S., tel. 212/687–6013), flies two or three times per week from Chicago and New York to Bucharest. You can also fly TAROM from London, although you're probably better off taking **Air France** (in U.S., tel. 800/950–5000) via Paris. **Delta** (in U.S., tel. 800/241–4141) flies from major U.S. cities to Bucharest via Frankfurt.

GETTING AROUND Unless you bring a car with you (and have the parts and know-how to fix it yourself), you'll spend most of your time on trains and buses. A cross-country ride on either costs less than $10; scuzzy intercity buses are slower, more expensive, and more crowded than trains. TAROM connects many Romanian cities, but once you see the plane you may have second thoughts.

➢ **BY TRAIN** • Romanian trains do not accept InterRail or EurailPasses. There are five categories of train service: *express, rapid, accelerat, personal,* and *cursa,* in descending order of price and speed. Make reservations, since trains are often overbooked. You can buy tickets up to two days in advance at the station or through **CFR,** the national train company. After you pay, you'll be handed a scrawny piece of cardboard with illegible scribbles on it—this is your ticket. Most stations list arrivals (*sosira*) and departures (*plecari*) by the ticket windows. If you're planning overnight journeys, pack food and lots of toilet paper.

WHERE TO SLEEP Finding a place to stay in Romania is usually not a problem, but don't expect many bargains. In general, look for a private room first, a private hotel second, and a state-run hotel last. Hostels don't exist, and hotels can charge foreigners $25 for a room that would cost a Romanian $4. Check everything out first—price is no indication of quality or availability of hot water. Private rooms, usually $5–$15 a night, can be tricky to find; try inquiring at the local tourist office. Camping is by far the best budget option. Tent spaces usually run $2–$5 a night, two-person bungalows about $8 per night.

If a slimy waiter rips you off, smile, make some wild hand gestures, spit on the floor, and leave. You'll only be out a few dollars, and they'll think you have Romanian blood.

FOOD You'll be able to find food, but how much choice you get depends largely on the season. For four months in summer, produce floods the markets, but everything (including canned goods) becomes scarcer and more expensive in winter. Typical restaurant fare includes pork, pork, and pork, as well as occasional steak, chicken, omelets, cold potatoes with goat cheese, sausages, beans, and ground lamb. For liquid refreshment, try beer, wine, or *tzuicâ,* a Romanian plum brandy taken at the beginning of a meal. *Cotnari, Murfatlar* (a dessert wine), and *Tirnave* are good Romanian wines. Also keep an eye out for *syrup,* a soda made from juice concentrates and seltzer water.

BUSINESS HOURS Standard business hours are weekdays 8–4:30 and Saturday 8–1. Most museums are open Tuesday–Sunday 10–6. Restaurants and beer halls open their doors from 11 to 11 and may close on Sunday.

PHONES AND MAIL **Country code: 40.** Romania's phone system is primitive at best, non-functional at worst. You can use pay phones (with 1- and 5-leu slots) for local calls; to dial another area code or make international calls, go to the post office or phone office. Here you write down your name; the country, city, and number you wish to reach; and how long you want to talk. Give these to the operator at the front desk. English-speaking operators are rare, so learn such handy phrases as "*taxa inversa*" (collect call) and "*poftim SUA*" (USA, please). When the operator gets through—a process that can take up to two hours—your name or country and city will be called, and you'll be directed to a booth. Several cities are connected with AT&T's USA Direct service (tel. 01/800–4288), but few operators will understand what you're babbling about; your best bet is to call USA Direct toll-free from a private home.

Romania's mail service has improved vastly over the past few years. Intra-European mail takes one week, and you can't beat the 2½ weeks a letter or postcard takes to go overseas. An international stamp is 120 lei.

Bucharest

The theologians who dreamed up the idea of purgatory were having prescient visions of Bucharest (Bucuresti in Romanian), where the exhaust seems impenetrable and the buildings look like they'll crumble if you piss on them. Still, the city looks better with each passing year since the '89 revolt. Flower beds have begun to sprout here and there, the worst of the rubble has been cleared away, and some stately fin de siècle edifices and fountains have been spruced up. Bucharest is struggling to regain the reputation it earned 50 years ago as the Paris of the East, but the ambience is still that of the European Third World. You can enjoy the amenities of a comfortable life in a city that's relatively inexpensive for Western travelers, but keep in mind that the overwhelming majority of locals struggle to get enough food on the table: for them, paying 50¢ for a movie is an extravagance.

BASICS

VISITOR INFORMATION In the Gara de Nord, look for the door marked TOURIST in bold orange and green. The **tourist office** staff will answer your questions in just about any language you throw at them. Maps, brochures, and train schedules are rare, though. *Tel. 01/617–2160. Open weekdays 7:30–8, Sat. 7:30–3, Sun. 7:30–1.*

Downtown, the friendlier staff at **ONT Carpaţi S.A.** (which also serves as the American Express and TAROM airlines office) can change your money at the official rate, help with lodging, or book you on a flight to Tahiti. *B-dul. Magheru 7, tel. 01/312–2596. Open weekdays 8:30–5:30, Sat. 9:30–2.*

AMERICAN EXPRESS Romania's only AmEx office doesn't hold mail, but cardholders can get traveler's checks drawn from their checking account or card. *B-dul. Magheru 7, tel. 01/312–2596. Open weekdays 8:30–5:30, Sat. 9:30–2.*

CHANGING MONEY Tourist offices and luxury hotels charge a hefty fee to exchange your traveler's checks, and you shouldn't trust their math. The **Romanian Bank for Foreign Trade (BRCE)** is a better bet; the staff will give you dollars or lei for your checks (go for dollars). *Str. Eugen Carada 1–3, at Str. Lipscani. Open weekdays 8 AM–11:30 AM.*

EMBASSIES AND CONSULATES **Canada.** *Calea Nicolae Iorga 36, near Piaţa Romană, tel. 01/312–0365. Open weekdays 9–5.*

United Kingdom. This embassy also serves Australians. *Str. Jules Michelet 24, off B-dul. Magheru, tel. 01/312–0303. Open weekdays 9–1 and 2–5.*

U.S. Consular Section. *Str. Snagov 26, tel. 01/312–4042; in emergencies, 01/312–6386. At Str. Batiştei, near InterContinental Hotel. Open weekdays 8–noon and 1–3.*

PHONES AND MAIL Make international calls at the **PTTR** exchange (Calea Victoriei 37, 1 block north of B-dul. Kogălniceanu), open 24 hours a day. The **main post office** (Matei Millo 1D, off Calea Victoriei) is open Monday–Saturday 8–6.

COMING AND GOING

BY TRAIN **Gara de Nord** (west of downtown, bet. Calea Griviţei and B-dul. Golescu) receives 98% of Bucharest's rail traffic. If hell were a train station, this would be it. Only luck will get you information in English, and the train schedules (if you can get them) are impossible to read. Your best bet is to stop by ONT (*see* Visitor Information, *above*). For international trains, buy your ticket one day in advance from the station's ticket office (open 24 hours) or from the **CFR** office (Str. Eforiei, at Str. Brezoianu; open weekdays 9–5). A ticket to Budapest (15 hrs) is $45. For *couchette* (sleeping car) reservations, go to the CFR office at the Piaţa Unirii 2 Metro stop. Downtown hotels are a 20-minute walk or a short Metro ride east of the train station. If you arrive after 11 PM, when the Metro and buses stop, splurge on a taxi. The fare to the center of town should be no more than $3.

BY BUS Almost all intercity buses are privately owned and don't print schedules, and there's no central bus depot. Since few buses go where trains don't, you shouldn't need to deal with the convoluted bus system; but if you must, contact the tourist office at Bulevardul Magheru 7 for current information.

BY PLANE Bucharest's main airport is **Otopeni International.** In Romania, buy tickets at a tourist office or at one of the international carriers along Bulevardul Magheru. Cab rides to the airport should cost $3–$6. Bus 783 runs to Piaţa Universităţii from the airport. *Sos. Bucareşti-Ploieşti 40, tel. 01/633–6602.*

GETTING AROUND

Bucharest is a sprawling city rife with Orwellian cement apartment buildings. The city center (*centrum*) has more character than the outskirts, and it's easier to get your bearings here. The towering InterContinental Hotel in Piaţa Universităţii makes a good landmark. Most sights, lodgings, and restaurants are on Bulevardul Magheru or Calea Victoriei, which basically run parallel. Piaţa Victoriei—the locale for window shopping and financial and travel services—is just north of the centrum. Head south from Piaţa Universităţii on Bulevardul Brantianu to reach Piaţa Unirii, and go farther south for the Gypsy bazaars. West on Bulevardul Kogălniceanu are an assortment of cafés and restaurants and Cişmigiu Park. Public transportation runs 5 AM–11 PM.

BY METRO The Metro system is the best way to get to the city center from outlying regions. To ride, drop 50 lei into the slot as you enter. Transfers are free. The M2 blue line includes the central Piaţa Romană, Universităţii, and Piaţa Unirii 2 stops. Try to get on at the rear of the train; the front section is an express class, and the doors don't open at every station.

BY BUS AND TRAM Overcrowded trams and buses cover the city extensively, but service is irregular. Each stop has a sign displaying all lines that serve the stop. Trams and buses use the same ticket (30 lei), which can be purchased at most stops from kiosks marked RATB TICHETE or SI BILETE. Each ticket is good for a single ride; there are validating machines at bus entrances.

WHERE TO SLEEP

Staying with a Romanian family is the cheapest option ($5–$15 per person). The tourist office downtown (*see* Basics, *above*) can't arrange for a place to stay, but the staff will offer unofficial advice. A few reasonably cheap hotels lie near the Gara de Nord—not a great neighborhood, but convenient if you're fleeing town early the next morning. To stay downtown, take the Metro from Gara de Nord to the Universităţii stop and walk down Bulevardul Republicii toward Bulevardul Kogălniceanu; turn right for the cleaner, more expensive hotels, or left for the bizarre, colorful hotels of the Gypsy district.

Ask to see your room before you accept, or you may end up counting mice rather than sheep.

➤ **UNDER $25 • Cerna Hotel.** New, spacious rooms with matching decor, within a stone's throw of Gara de Nord. Singles $10–$19, doubles $18–$30. *B-dul. Golescu 29, tel. 01/637–4087. 80 rooms, some w/shower. Wheelchair access.*

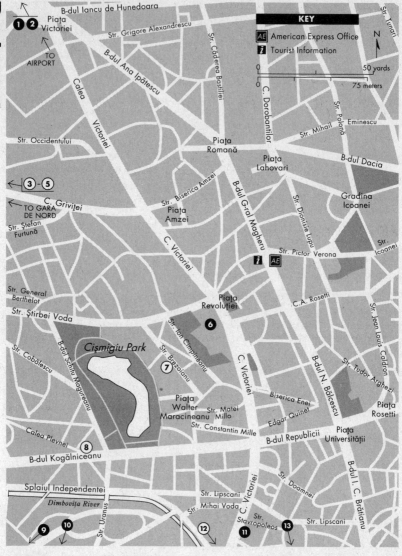

KEY

AE American Express Office

i Tourist Information

N

0 _____ 50 yards

0 _____ 75 meters

Sights ●

Herăstrău Park, **1**

Muzeul Satului, **2**

Muzeul National
de Arta, **6**

Ghencea
Cemetery, **9**

Casa Republicii, **10**

Muzeul de Istorie
Nationala, **11**

Palatul
Voievodul, **13**

Lodging ○

Hotel Bucegi, **3**

Cerna Hotel, **4**

Hotel Grivita, **5**

Hotel Opera, **7**

Hotel Venetja, **8**

Hotel Rahova, **12**

Hotel Bucegi. Good if you've lost your sense of smell and are buff enough to fend off black-market hustlers. Singles $10, doubles $20, triples and quads $22–$30. *Str. Witing 2, across from Gara de Nord, tel. 01/637–5225. 50 rooms, some w/bath.*

Hotel Grivita. Spacious rooms on a quiet street near Gara de Nord. Hotel decorator saw *Saturday Night Fever* one too many times. Singles $11, doubles $18, all without bath. *Calea Griviței 130, tel. 01/650–5380. From station, walk 3 blocks up Calea Griviței; opposite Hotel de Nord. 15 rooms.*

Hotel Rahova. Experience exotic sounds and scents at one of Bucharest's best bargains, near the flea markets and open-air bazaar of the Gypsy district. Doubles $20. *Calea Rahovei 2, tel. 01/615–2617. Metro: Piața Unirii. 20 rooms, most w/bath.*

➤ **UNDER $40 • Hotel Opera.** Mediocre rooms and decrepit bathrooms downtown. Some rooms have a nice view of the park. Singles $15–$18, doubles $30. *Str. Brezoianu 37, tel. 01/614–1075. 25 rooms, most w/bath.*

Hotel Venetja. Elegant, quiet hotel near downtown restaurants. Escape polluted air on a balcony overlooking the park. Singles $20, doubles $35. *Piața Kogălniceanu 2, tel. 01/615–9149. 10 min from Metro Eroilor. 20 rooms, all w/bath. Wheelchair access.*

FOOD

Average Romanians can't afford to eat out, so head to a beer garden or street stand to enjoy the company of locals. Or try **Spring Time** (Piața Victoriei A-6), where the best burgers and fries in town are served on a crowded outdoor patio—Bucharestians go wild for it. You can easily spend an entire day on **Bulevardul Kogălniceanu** discovering the cafés and pastry shops that attract many students and locals. Also check out the **Gypsy district,** where closet-size, unmarked kitchens serve excellent meals. At all costs, avoid the extortionate restaurants around the Gara de Nord.

➤ **UNDER $5 • Casa Capsa.** Enjoy good food (even a vegetarian meal upon request) by the light of a chandelier in an 1852 building, and imagine what Bucharest was like in its heyday. *Str. Edgard Quinett 16, off B-dul. Kogălniceanu at Calea Victoriei, tel. 01/615–5985. Open daily 12:30–5 and 7–10.*

Restaurantul Ciresica. Excellent service, beer garden, and local crowd. Portions aren't enormous, but food is good. Wiener, fries, and a large beer run about $2.50. *B-dul. Kogălniceanu 45, 1 block west of Piața Kogălniceanu. Open daily 11 AM–midnight.*

Restaurantul Pescarul. Friendly place shaped like a wine barrel. Good selection of Romanian wines. Eat fresh fish until you drop. *B-dul. Magheru 2, tel. 01/650–7244. Closed Sun.*

➤ **UNDER $10 • Bradet.** Hippest place in town; vegetarians shouldn't leave Bucharest without trying it. Stellar Lebanese cuisine and service. Hummus is recommended, as are reservations. *Str. Dr. Carol Davila 60, tel. 01/638–6014. 3 blocks southwest of Metro Eroilor, off B-dul. Eroilor. Open daily noon–midnight.*

Hanul Lui Manuc Inn. Clean, elegant Ottoman-style place hidden behind an 18th-century church in the Gypsy district. Dole out the extra lei for excellent pork, steak, fish soup, and *sarmale* (pork and rice wrapped in grape or cabbage leaves). Great Romanian beer. *Str. Iuliu Maniu 62, tel. 01/613–1415. Metro Piața Unirii, then cross river and turn right past Red Church. Open daily 7– 10 AM, noon–5 PM, and 7 PM–midnight.*

WORTH SEEING

At the turn of the century, many of Bucharest's monuments and museums were as stylish as those of Paris or Prague. Now the city's look is depressingly Communist, but you'll discover remnants of a European ambience if you set out on foot. The most interesting sights aren't on a map: peculiar back alleys, run-down 19th-century flats, overgrown gardens, and inebriated workers contemplating half-liters of beer. Tourist offices can arrange guided tours, or you can arm yourself with an up-to-date map and strike out alone from Piaţa Universităţii. **Herăstrău Park,** north of Piaţa Victoriei on Bulevardul Aviatorilor, is a good place to take a rest, rent a rowboat, or stroll on walking paths.

CASA REPUBLICII The second-largest government building in the world (after the U.S. Pentagon), the House of the Republic was Ceauşescu's most ambitious project, complete with a secret Metro stop and a vast underground bomb shelter. An unfinished "White House" wallows at the end of an atrociously decadent avenue of cement-and-marble waste. The 1,000-plus rooms are closed to the public, but you can climb through the surrounding rubble and sewage. *B-dul. Libertăţii, near Piaţa Naţiunile Unite.*

GHENCEA CEMETERY You won't win any friends by asking where the Ceauşescus are buried—visiting their graves is construed by many Romanians as paying homage to the creator of their suffering. Only a perverted curiosity could cause you to take Bus 168 from Onesti station on Bulevardul Magheru, transfer at Răzoare to Bus 226, and get off on Sebastian near this graveyard. If you go, look for the white church inside the cemetery; 10 yards in front, occupying both sides of the dirt path, are the unmarked, flower-ridden graves. He's on the left, she's on the right.

MUZEUL DE ISTORIE NATIONALA Head straight for the basement of the Museum of National History to see an incredible collection of antique jewels, gold crowns, and regal scepters, dating from pre-Dacian times to the 20th century. *Calea Victoriei 12, at Str. Stravropoleos, tel. 01/615–7055. Admission: 150 lei, 50 lei students. Open Tues.–Sun. 10–5.*

MUZEUL NATIONAL DE ARTA Many of Ceauşescu's Securitate forces took refuge inside this former palace during the '89 revolution, only to be shot and thrown from the second-story windows. These days, an exhibit of 18th- and 19th-century art, including works by Picasso, Renoir, Monet, and El Greco, lines the south wing of the National Museum of Art. Across the street are the charred remains of the **University Library,** set ablaze in '89 by the Securitate in hopes of quelling the student-led insurrection. *Str. Stirbei Vodă 1, near Calea Victoriei. Admission: 50 lei. Open Wed.–Sun. 10–5.*

MUZEUL SATULUI The open-air **Village Museum** sprawls across 20 acres and contains more than 80 replicas of Romanian peasant homes and churches. Most of the full-scale homes are inhabited by "peasants" (museum workers) in traditional dress, allowing you to see what life in 16th-century Moldavia was really like. Catch the folk performance on Sunday at 11. *Calea Soseaua Kiseleff, near Lake Herăstrău, tel. 01/617–5920. Metro: Aviatorilor. Admission: 40 lei. Open Mon. 9–5, Tues.–Sun. 11–7.*

PALATUL VOIEVODUL The stone remains of the 13th-century Princely Court are among the oldest structures in the city. A former royal palace, this is now a poor monument to the aspirations of the Wallachian princes, including Vlad Tepeş (a.k.a. Dracula), who constructed it. For a donation you'll be given a guided tour and a history of the area. *Str. Iuliu Maniu 31–33. Open daily.*

SHOPPING

The **Gypsy district,** between Strada Lipscani and the Dimbovita River, is a four-block conglomeration of artisans, craftspeople, and Muslims who've forgotten they're not in Istanbul or Marrakech. The atmosphere is something else, especially around sunset. Along Strada Lipscani— a narrow, crooked street that winds from Bulevardul Brătianu to Calea Victoriei—you'll find a big open-air bazaar that resembles those in Moroccan medinas. After exploring the Gypsy district, head to the **open-air market** in Piaţa Amzei, between Calea Victoriei and Bulevardul Magheru, where you get first crack at high-quality produce.

AFTER DARK

Most restaurants stay open until 11 or midnight, and even if they don't have a bar, you're welcome to grab a table and drink with friends. Beer runs 200 lei–700 lei for a hearty half-liter; after two or three of these you may end up joining in the chorus of a Romanian drinking song. Drink up at the smoky **Gambrinus** (B-dul. Kogălniceanu, 1 block from Cişmigiu Park), packed with old men with eye patches and knife wounds. The clean, lively **Efes Pub** (B-dul. Magheru 24) is refreshing among so many crowded and grimy older bars.

The real nightlife doesn't begin until after the restaurants close, and it often goes on until 5 AM. For mellow jazz, head to **Karioka** (B-dul. Dacia, 2 blocks east of Piaţa Romană; open daily 6 PM–4 AM), which features live jazz Thursday and Saturday. Twentysomethings mingle with middle-age businessmen at the chintzy, $3-a-head **Vox Maris Disco** (B-dul. Kogălniceanu 2–4, at Calea Victoriei, tel. 01/615–5030; open daily 10 PM–5 AM). If classical is more your speed, don't miss the symphony, which plays at the magnificent **Ateneul Român** (Str. Stirbei Voda, at Calea Victoriei, tel. 01/614–5987). Rumor has it that one of the conductors was shot when he refused to lead a performance in honor of Ceauşescu's 60th birthday. Daytime admission to the building is 100 lei, concert tickets 300 lei–400 lei.

Near Bucharest

LAKE SNAGOV

The **monastery** at Lake Snagov may or may not be the final resting place of the 15th-century prince of Wallachia Vlad Tepeş, alias Count Dracula. Legend has it that Vlad was captured by Turks, barely escaped execution, and fled to Snagov. He ordered the monastery built on one of Lake Snagov's islands for protection. To visit the count's purported grave, take a commercial boat (50 lei) from the nearby village of Snagov, or row to the island in a rented boat (150 lei). Trains from Bucharest's Gara de Nord make the 35-km trip to Snagov twice daily during summer (once a day in winter). Walk out of the train station, turn right, and follow the signs to the lake, 2 km down the road.

When Vlad Dracula became king of Wallachia, he acquired a nasty habit of impaling riffraff and criminals on pikes, earning himself the nickname Tepeş, Romanian for "the Impaler."

CONSTANTA

Constanţa, the major town on the Black Sea coast, is home to plenty of hustlers and aggressive pickpockets. Still, it attracts a large crowd during summer, primarily because it has more than just a beach. Some of Romania's best museums are here, including the **Archaeological Museum** (Piaţa Ovidiu 12; admission 200 lei; open Mon.–Sat. 10–6, Sun. 10–4), with an impressive collection of Greek busts and Roman coins. The medieval-looking town center is filled with beer patios, stately hotels, and elegant restaurants. **Bulevardul Carpaţi**, a marble-covered boardwalk, winds along the south shore, and on the west shore you'll find public beaches. The **ONT** desk at Hotel Continental (B-dul. Tomis 69, tel. 0916/15–660; open daily 10–6) can help with visitor info. **Gara Feroviăra** (Piaţa Victoriei 1, tel. 0916/16–725) is a major transport hub, with trains to and from Bucharest, Braşov, and Cluj. To reach the town center from the station, walk 30 minutes on Bulevardul Republicii or take Bus 40 or 43.

WHERE TO SLEEP AND EAT   You're going to have to shell out some cash, so you might as well head for the **Hotel Albatros** in nearby Mamaia (B-dul. Siutghiol 8, tel. 0918/31–047), probably the nicest hotel within 500 km. The stylish, comfortable doubles (less than $50) have real bathtubs and hot water, and most have bay windows and a balcony. To get here from Constanţa, take Bus 40 from the train station to the end of the line, then Bus 47 for four stops. Otherwise, you'll have to settle for the superclean but unspectacular **Hotel Tineretului** (B-dul. Tomis 20/26, tel. 0916/13–590), with singles for $25 and doubles for about $40.

Casa Cu Lei (Str. Dianei 1, off Piaţa Traian, tel. 0916/18–050) serves the town's best meal, in a dark dining room with antique tapestries and turn-of-the-century furniture. House specialties include grilled pork with garlic-and-cheese potatoes ($3). The popular **Restaurant Cazino** (B-dul. Carpati 2, tel. 0916/17–416), on the water, has outdoor seating and meals for $2–$3.50.

Transylvania

The name Transylvania (Latin for "across the forest") conjures up B movies filled with bloodthirsty vampires, Gothic castles, and the walking dead. But many of Transylvania's Dracula-related tourist attractions are pleasant, well-preserved towns in their own right, easily reached by rail on the route from Budapest to Bucharest. The ominous Bran Castle, where Count Dracula earned his reputation as "Vlad the Impaler," draws visitors to Braşov. The medieval village of Sighişoara, purported birthplace of old Vlad, hasn't changed much since he left. The Hungarian stronghold of Cluj affords a glimpse of Magyar culture, and the old fortified Saxon settlements at Sibiu, Braşov, and Sighişoara are impressive legacies of the considerable economic power once wielded by German settlers. Aside from these medieval towns, most of Transylvania remains undeveloped. Bleak industrial complexes are the exception rather than the norm, and the Carpathian Mountains are *the* place to break out your hiking and camping gear.

Braşov

Set against the lush backdrop of Mt. Tîmpa and Mt. Postăvarni, Braşov still displays an impressive system of medieval fortifications erected by Saxon merchants during the 12th century. The town is worth a visit if only to see the small alleys, squat battlements, and ornate facades of its historic center. If you speak German, try to make friends with one of the toothless old men who sit drinking in the **Parcul Central** (Central Park), spinning tall tales about Kronstadt (the city's German name). The staff at the **ONT** office (B-dul. Eroilor 9, in lobby of Hotel Aro-Palace; open weekdays 8–4) can't arrange private rooms, but they do book hotel rooms and sell maps of Braşov.

On the southern edge of the large, stylish **Piaţa Sfatului,** the impressive **Black Church** (open Mon.–Sat. 10–6:30) is a rare Protestant stronghold in the Balkans. By the time the Saxon founders got around to building the bell tower, they ran out of money, which is why it's so small. In Piaţa Unirii lie the spired **St. Nicholas's Church** and the **First Romanian School Museum,** where you can see what a 15th-century classroom looked like (they haven't changed much in 500 years). To get perspective on all of Braşov and beyond, head up the winding trail to the summit of **Mt. Tîmpa,** or take a smooth three-minute ride on the cable car ($1.50; open Tues.–Fri. 10:30–7, weekends 10–8) 200 yards southwest of Piaţa Sfatului.

COMING AND GOING Trains run from Braşov to Bucharest (3 hrs), Cluj, and other major cities. Buy international train tickets at the **CFR** office (Str. Republicii 53, tel. 09/214–2912; open Mon.–Sat. 7 AM–7:30 PM). From the smelly **train station** (B-dul. Gării, tel. 09/211–0233), take Trolley 4 to reach Parcul Central, or walk 20 minutes into town: Head southwest on Bulevardul Victoriei, and follow Strada Kogălniceanu to Bulevardul 15 Novembrei to Bulevardul Eroilor.

WHERE TO SLEEP AND EAT The budget-lodging situation is ugly: Big hotels are overpriced (from $40 a night), and the tourist office doesn't arrange rooms. If it's summer and you're willing to grovel, there's a slim chance you can rent a dorm room at the **University of Transylvania** (B-dul. Eroilor 29, tel. 09/214–1580). Otherwise, stand outside the Hotel Aro-Palace (B-dul. Eroilor 27) and look helpless; passing locals sometimes rent rooms to travelers. Be cautious—you could end up paying $5 for a space on the floor. If you're desperate and don't mind spending $35, head to the **Hotel Postăvarul** (tel. 09/214–4330), an elegant 19th-century building in the town center.

Strada Republicii has food stands, cafés, and the **Istanbul Export-Import Co.** (Str. Republicii 20), which serves kebabs and the best fresh-baked bread in town. Also check out the many snacking possibilities along Strada Mureşenilor; if the great prices don't get you, the smells will. For your sit-down dining pleasure, Piaţa Sfatului has an endless supply of restaurants. If you can get a seat at **Sirena Gustari** (Piaţa Sfatului 15, tel. 09/215–0857), endure the slow service and join the throng scarfing up hearty omelets and pizzas (both about 425 lei).

NEAR BRASOV

CASTELUL BRAN Looming in the shadow of Mt. Bucegi, 28 km southwest of Braşov, Bran Castle looks like one of those gruesome fortresses you find in a Poe story. Erected in 1377 by Braşov's Saxon merchants, the castle was intended to protect the town's stalwart citizens from bandits and Turkish raiders. Although it has become known as "Dracula's Castle" because of Vlad Tepeş's periodic raids on Braşov, his ferocious armies never conquered the fortress itself, and it's likely the count never set foot inside its well-defended walls. A guided tour of the castle, which is open Tuesday–Sunday 10:30–6, costs $1.50. Besides the weapons room, dungeon, and meeting hall, there's an excellent display of medieval torture devices in the basement. It's not usually open to visitors, but your guide may take you through if you ask politely (a $5 bill may also help). To get there from Braşov, catch the bus marked BRAN (100 lei), which runs every other hour from 10 to 4, at the intersection of Strada Mureşenilor and Bulevardul Eroilor.

Sighişoara

The medieval village of Sighişoara juxtaposes multicolored 16th-century houses and cobblestone streets with jagged mountains, lush forests, and a peaceful river. In the heart of a quiet old neighborhood sits the legendary birthplace of Vlad Tepeş, now the popular **Restaurantul Berarie** (Piaţa Muzeului 5). A faded fresco of Dracula's dad can still be seen in the upper corner of the main dining room.

Other than that, Sighişoara's main draw is its medieval **citadel**, in the hills above the modern city. The fortress has three rings of walls and 14 towers, including the Tinsmith's Tower, with variously shaped stories, and an elaborate clock tower. Built by the Saxons in 1345, the Gothic **Bergkirche** sits atop Castle Hill, next to a 14th-century cemetery. The park here is the perfect site for an afternoon lunch, and a few hiking paths meander south. To reach the church, walk to the south end of Strada Scolii and climb the **Covered Stairway** (1650). The church is open daily noon–1, but the caretaker doesn't mind if you explore the grounds on your own. The **OJT** office (Str. 1 Decembrie 10, tel. 0950/71–072; open weekdays 8–3, Sat. 9–noon) is across the river from the train station.

COMING AND GOING Sighişoara's **train station** (Str. Libertăţii 51, north of downtown, tel. 0950/71–886) is on the Cluj–Bucharest line, and all trains running between Budapest and Bucharest via Oradea stop here. Buy international tickets at the **CFR** office (Str. 1 Decembrie 2, tel. 0950/71–820) at least one day in advance. To reach downtown, turn right on Strada Libertăţii and left on Strada Gării, cross the Tiârnava Mare River at the bridge near the cemetery, and turn left on Strada Marii to Strada 1 Decembrie.

WHERE TO SLEEP At the well-kept **Hotel Steaua** (Str. 1 Decembrie 12, tel. 0950/71–594), you'll pay $23 for a double with bath. You can camp at remote **Dealul Gării** (Str. Dealul Gării 1; closed Nov.– Apr.) for almost nothing, or pay 100 lei for a double cabin. It's a short cab ride or 30-minute hike from the train station: Walk east along the train tracks, cross the first bridge, turn left, and walk up the hill.

Sibiu

Of the original seven *sedes* (seats) settled by the Saxons in Transylvania, Sibiu was for many centuries the wealthiest and most powerful. Few Romanian cities have remained as pleasant, and after a few days you may understand why some residents refer to this as the city of "mystical sadness and impossible beauty." Sibiu has two levels: the historic upper citadel and the lower citadel, a charmless wasteland. Strada N. Bălcescu runs from Piaţa Unirii to the town's main pedestrian mall, Piaţa Revoluţiei, in the upper section. Here you'll find a host of cafés, bookstores, and specialty shops. The **Prima Ardeleana S.A.** office (Piaţa Unirii 1, tel. 0924/11–788; open daily 8–5) gives visitor info and makes hotel reservations. Sibiu's **train station** (Piaţa Cării, tel. 0924/11–139) is northeast of the town center, a 10-minute walk from Piaţa Revoluţiei on Strada Magheru or a $1 cab ride. Purchase international train tickets at the **CFR** office (Str. N. Bălcescu 6, tel. 0924/10–215). Coming from Cluj, you'll change trains at Copşa Mică. For connections to Bucharest, change at Braşov.

Near Piaţa Revoluţiei sit the rich **Brukenthal Art Museum** (open Tues.–Sun. 10–4:30), a **Catholic Cathedral** with an elaborate interior, and the **Orthodox Cathedral,** a miniature of the Hagia Sophia in Istanbul. On Piaţa Mica, a collection of medieval weapons and relics is squeezed into the 14th-century **Turnul Sfatului** (City Council Tower). Piaţa Grivitei is dominated by the imposing **Evangelical Cathedral** (open weekdays 9–1), a Lutheran church rumored to shelter the tomb of Dracula's son, Mihnea the Bad. Connecting the upper and lower towns are dozens of tunnels and hidden passageways, installed to evacuate people during Turkish raids. Today most have been sealed off, but if you're feeling adventurous, ask some children to point out the tunnels still in operation. Most sights are closed Monday.

WHERE TO SLEEP AND EAT Reservations are a must for the five rooms ($7–$15) at the keen **Hotel La Podul Minciunilor** (Str. Azĭui 1, tel. 0924/17–259), a converted house decorated with antiques. From Piaţa Gării, walk up Strada 9 Mai to Strada Azĭui. **Hotel Sport** (Str. Octavian Goga 2, tel. 0924/22–472) offers spartan $5 rooms; take a taxi from the station to Strada Andrei Saguna, walk down Strada Someşului (which becomes Strada Scoala de Inot), turn left at Hotel Parc, and look for the hotel on the right, beside the stadium.

Most of Sibiu's restaurants are downtown. Hit the **Impăratul Romanilor** (Str. N. Bălcescu 4) at lunch, when the ceiling is partially drawn back to let in a little sunshine. Excellent meat and vegetarian dishes are about $2. **Dori's Bistro** (Piaţa Mica 3) has sandwiches and hamburgers for less than $1 and the best coffee in Romania for a nickel. Also check out the excellent outdoor **market** on Bulevardul Spitalelor near the Hotel Continental.

Cluj (Cluj-Napoca)

Cluj is a major educational and cultural center in the heart of Transylvania, a longtime magnet for Hungarian intellectuals escaping persecution in Budapest and Vienna. The well-preserved center consists of three sprawling piaţas amid a colorful profusion of 15th-century town houses, umbrella-filled patios, and dusty medieval alleys. Halfway between the Someşul Mic River and the overgrown **Botanical Garden** (Str. Republicii 42), you'll find the historic core: Piaţa Unirii and **St. Michael's Church** (open daily 7 AM–8 PM). The church, which overshadows all other buildings in town, is strangely situated because mid-14th-century builders wanted the sun to shine directly through the doorway on St. Michael's Day (Sept. 29). At the eastern end of the church wall sits the amazingly intact **Tailor's Tower,** built in 1456. Try to get inside, as it's worth more than a quick photo out front. For visitor info and unofficial advice about private rooms, head to **Tourism Feleacul (OJT)** (Str. Memorandumului, at Str. 30 Decembrie, 6 blocks west of Piaţa Unirii; open weekdays 8–5).

COMING AND GOING Cluj is on the Oradea–Sighişoara–Bucharest line, with four trains daily in both directions. Try to book a reservation at the **CFR** office one day in advance. The International CFR (Piaţa Unirii 9) is open weekdays 8–7, and the Domestic CFR (Piaţa Mihai

Viteazul 20) is open weekdays 8–7 and Saturday 8–1. The **train station** is at the end of Strada Horea, about 3 km north of town. Take any trolley labeled CENTRUM to Piaţa Unirii.

WHERE TO SLEEP AND EAT Three hotels charge less than $30 for a double: the 200-year-old **Hotel Astoria** (Str. Horea 3), the clean **Hotel Pax** across from the station, and the central **Hotel Vlădeasa** (Str. Gh. Doja 20). Budget travelers may want to head straight for OJT in search of private accommodations, which usually fetch $15 per night. If you've been fantasizing about a hot slice, **Pizzeria New Crolo** (Str. Victor Babeş, near Botanical Gardens) will be like manna from heaven.

Bukovina

In the northeastern corner of Romania, Bukovina is one of the country's most isolated and pristine provinces. This stunningly wild land teems with medieval-looking villages and anachronistic farming settlements. Travelers must rough it a bit; but if you don't mind sleeping under the stars and foraging for food in the occasional peasant market, you'll discover a part of the world untainted by cement, steel, and technology. Even better, you'll get the chance to explore Bukovina's painted monasteries, considered some of Romania's outstanding artistic treasures. The monasteries are remote, but you can reach a couple of them, including Putna and Moldoviţa, by train from the city of Suceava.

Suceava

Since medieval times, Suceava's lavishly adorned churches and relic-filled treasuries have tempted European fortune hunters. The wily Habsburgs invaded and conquered the town in 1775, and Suceava was part of Austria and Germany until the end of World War I. The city has never fully recovered from its chaotic past. Ceauşescu was bent on bringing his country into the industrial age at all costs, but Suceava's infrastructure was so impossibly decrepit that even the great dictator despaired of the town's rehabilitation. Its failure to modernize during the past century is one reason Suceava remains so attractive. There are a few ugly cement high-rises in the center, but for the most part, the town has escaped unharmed. You won't find much in the way of discos and nightlife, but you can spend a summer afternoon scrambling through rugged terrain in the company of trees and pensive farm animals. More important, Suceava makes a great base from which to explore Bukovina's spectacular monasteries. The friendly folks at **ONT** (Str. N. Bălcescu 2, cnr. of Piaţa 22 Decembrie, tel. 0987/11–297) will give you maps of the region, and they can also hook you up with a car and driver (250 lei per km) for a tour of four or five monasteries.

COMING AND GOING Suceava has two train stations: **Gara Suceava** (Str. N. Iorga 6, tel. 0987/13–897) and **Gara Nord** (Str. Gării 4, tel. 0987/10–036), both a couple kilometers from the city center. To get to the city center from Gara Suceava, take Trolley Bus 2, 3, or 26 for seven stops (the bus stop is across the street from the train station). From Gara Nord, take Bus 1 nine stops to the center. Express trains run to Bucharest, Cluj, and Braşov twice daily, and a slew of local accelerat trains head north to the Bukovina region five times daily.

WHERE TO SLEEP AND EAT **Hotel Suceava** (Str. N. Bălcescu 2, north side of piaţa, tel. 0987/22–497) is far and away the best place to drop your bags for a night. Hot water (7–10 and 4–7) is plentiful, beds are comfortable, and the staff may whittle a few dollars off the price if you look haggard. A decent restaurant in the lobby serves food and drink until 10 PM. Doubles, all with bath, run about $35, singles about $25. High-quality **Hotel Arcasul** (Str. Mihai Viteazu 4/6, tel. 0987/10–944) gives you a good night's sleep in one of 100 rooms, all with bath. Singles are $26, doubles $40. The restaurant here (open daily 8 AM–11 PM) serves an excellent chicken-bone soup and lamb stew. To reach the hotel from Piaţa 22 Decembrie, head west on Strada Ciprian Porumbescu. Suceava's only official campground, **Camping Suceava** (Str. Ilie Pintilie), is 4 km from the city center. For $10 per tent, $15 per bungalow, you get third-rate bathroom facilities (cold water occasionally) and a view of a sewage-processing plant. Bring your own food if you can; a good **outdoor market** on Strada

Petru Rareş stocks the standards, but it closes daily at 4. To reach the campground from either train station, take Bus 30 until you see a small sign for the campground.

WORTH SEEING The **Sfintu Ioan Cel Nou Monastery** (Monastery of St. George), built in 1522, looks a bit ragged today. Its immense exterior frescoes, beautifully composed in lush hues of purple and blood red, are badly faded. Still, the frescoes convey a sense of how capable and artistically innovative Romania's 16th-century craftspeople were. If you can't make it to any of Bukovina's monasteries, come here to get a sense of what you'll be missing. *Str. Ioan Vodă Viteazu 2, at Str. Metropolitei. From Piaţa 22 Decembrie, south on B-dul. Ana Ipătescu; left on Str. I. V. Viteazu. Admission free. Open daily 8–7.*

The immense **Parcul Cetăţii**, on the east side of the city, is one of northern Romania's most expansive and beautifully overgrown attractions, encompassing some 20 square kilometers of lush forests and meandering rivers on a large hill. The climb to the top is steep; plan on at least a 45-minute walk from Piaţa 22 Decembrie to the summit, where you'll find a medieval-looking burial ground. There are a couple of caves and abandoned silver mines on the far side of the mountain. Be warned: If you get caught in Parcul Cetăţii after sunset, you'll have one heck of a time finding your way out.

NEAR SUCEAVA

Most visitors come to Bukovina to see the monasteries, built between 1460 and 1550 to commemorate the region's growing power and to provide fortified havens for its armies. Because these armies were composed of illiterate farmers, the Moldavian princes made the monasteries dynamic educational tools, augmenting the church's traditional word-and-song service with something easier to understand—pictures and illustrations. Recognizing that Moldavia's small, dark churches could receive only a few visitors at a time, the princes had images painted on the outside of the churches, visible to all when illuminated by the early morning sun.

The Bukovine monasteries seem far beyond the reach of modern civilization, but most have small hotels and restaurants nearby. If you miss your return train to Suceava, you can arrange lodging at any point along the so-called monastery trail. Be aware, though, that most towns lack such conveniences as telephones and plumbing, and that the pace of life here is extraordinarily slow. The monasteries and their frescoes are stunning, but a three-hour visit is usually sufficient, with an additional hour for lunch and two hours' travel time. **Voroneţ Monastery,** on the cusp of a forested ridge, is the most impressive of the group, but it's tough to reach without a car. If you're up for a journey, take a bus or a train from Suceava to the village of Gura Homorului, and catch one of the unreliable buses to the monastery, 3 kilometers south of town.

MOLDOVITA MONASTERY Moldoviţa, built in 1532, is Bukovina's largest and best-preserved monastery. Its fortified walls, each 230 feet wide and 20 feet high, enclose a vast interior space disrupted only by the monastery, a tree-lined garden, and the living quarters of the nuns who maintain the site. On the monastery's exterior you'll see the famed *Siege of Constantinople,* a massive fresco cycle divided into comic-book-like panels. Styles in this series range from gruesomely realistic (see the panel of Turkish cavaliers stomping through a sea of crushed bodies) to the highly stylized and allegorical image of the infant Jesus tipping the scales of justice against the Turks.

To get to Moldoviţa, take the Suceava–Cluj train to **Vama** and transfer for Vatra Moldovitei; the train station is 1 kilometer from the monastery. Moldoviţa is not difficult to reach, but once there you'll have to spend at least a few hours in the monastery or in the small town of **Vatra Moldovitei.** A campground not far from the railway station offers tent spaces ($6) and bungalows ($16). A restaurant is 2 kilometers from the station on the road to Vama.

PUTNA MONASTERY Built in 1466, Putna is the least dramatic Bukovine monastery. Although it contains the tomb of Stefan the Great and an excellent museum of 15th-century manuscripts, the monastery has undergone so many renovations that it feels more like a modern building than one that's more than 500 years old. Part of the problem is that Putna is an active monastery, with a company of 45 monks who see to it that things are kept in good repair. There are no crumbling bell towers, no holes left in the walls from an Ottoman saber, nothing that might suggest Putna is anything other than an efficient, sterile religious enclave. To make matters worse, the exterior frescoes are in poor condition and are difficult to see.

Putna's one redeeming quality is its proximity to Suceava. Trains run four times a day, and the countryside between the two towns is beautifully unblemished. Outside the monastery are a restaurant and small hotel (doubles $16). The monastery and tourist facilities lie 2 kilometers from the station; follow the dirt road until it dead-ends. If you have the energy and time on your return trip, walk from Putna to **Gura Putnei,** and catch the train to Suceava from there. The 6-kilometer road winds through incredible countryside.

VORONET MONASTERY Perched on the cusp of a forested ridge, Voroneţ Monastery is by far Bukovina's best. Erected by Stefan the Great in 1486 (illuminated in 1546–57), Voroneţ was considered in its day to be the flagship of the monastery fleet. Its west wall contains the strikingly detailed *Last Judgment* fresco, a masterpiece that includes souls being guided to heaven by shepherds in peasant costume; sinners wearing turbans (the symbol of the condemned) and screaming for mercy as their bodies are torn apart by wild animals; and Ottoman soldiers parading through the fiery ruins of postapocalyptic earth on their way to hell. On the south wall is the *Tree of Jesse,* a biblical genealogy that includes Adam, Eve, Christ, and St. John of Suceava, whose tomb is in the monastery of Sfintu Ioan Cel Nou (*see* Suceava, *above*). Also of interest is the intense blue that's used as a background for Voroneţ's frescoes, a pigment that has not been found in any other fresco. In honor of the monastery, the color has been named Voroneţ blue. For info on how to reach Voroneţ, *see* the introduction to Near Suceava, *above*. For tips on staying in the nearby village of Gura Humorului, *see* Humor Monastery, *below*.

HUMOR MONASTERY Humor Monastery was built in 1530 by Toader Bubuoig and Petru Rareş. It was painted in 1534 by an artist named Toma, one of the few to sign his name on a Bukovine fresco (look for a soldier coming out of a Moldovan stronghold with the name Toma written on his head). Although little is known about Toma, his work at Humor speaks for itself, especially the 20 panels dedicated to St. Nicolae on the southern wall. St. Nicolae was one of the most popular saints in the Middle Ages, and it is perhaps because of this popularity that the artist allowed himself a little room for creativity when illuminating the saint's life. In particular, notice the "funny devil," as he's known by the monks, depicted not as a horrifying monster but as a fat old woman with an infectious belly laugh.

To reach Humor Monastery, take the train from Suceava to Gura Humorului, a small town 6 km south of Humor and 3 km north of Voroneţ Monastery. Buses run from Gura Humorului to Humor (and Voroneţ) six times a day, although you may want to walk. The road that leads to the monasteries runs through a beautiful stretch of forested hills and wide, sweeping valleys. It's possible to rough it at Humor, but your best bet is to look for a room at one of Gura Humorului's two hotels, the **Carpati** and the **Arinis.** Both are in the center of town, 22 yards from the train station. Both serve meals, and a double in either will run you $19.

SUCEVITA MONASTERY In true late-medieval fashion, Suceviţa Monastery (1586) is more a fortified stronghold than a religious retreat—a place in which 16th-century monks wielded lances and swords rather than prayer books and candles. Today its primary attraction is the famous *Procession of Philosophers* fresco, which depicts Aristotle, Plato, Socrates, and Pythagoras in brilliant colors and Byzantine costume. Look for the exquisitely preserved *Scale of Virtues* fresco on the north wall. It portrays Jesus on the day of judgment, casting the impure into a bubbling cauldron of liquid "deceit" while gently goading the pure into paradise. According to legend, the west wall remains bare in homage to a workman who was crushed to death in 1585. Even today, locals claim the workman's ghost appears in their dreams, warning against decorating the wall in any way. The monks have no comment about such "ridiculous superstitions."

There's a lot to see at Suceviţa, but getting there is a serious problem. It isn't anywhere near a train line (the closest one is in **Radăuti,** 20 km away), and bus service is irregular. Your best bet is to head to Radăuti (on the Suceava–Putna line) by train and look for a bus marked SUCE-

VITA. There are usually two a day. Obviously this hit-or-miss approach may not work, but it's better than waiting around in Suceava for the one weekly bus to Suceviţa, which leaves on Sunday at 6 AM from Suceava's Gara Nord and returns by 5 PM. There's also an early morning bus from Moldoviţa to Suceviţa. Rooms (doubles $24) and meals are available in the **Suceviţa Hotel,** 1 km from the monastery on the road to Radăuti, or you can rough it in the hills surrounding the monastery.

SPAIN

22

By Andrew Brandt, Pamela Harris, and Corey Nettles

An exuberant liberality characterizes the Spanish people, and the Spanish youth in particular. It is revealed in the apparent ease with which the younger generation embraces the modern, and the equanimity they display towards things that would have scandalized their parents. Though they would seem in this respect no different from youth the world over, their spirit cannot be reduced to just another attempt to define themselves by defying their parents. Rather, their liberality seems a natural response to the passing of a 39-year, highly repressive fascist dictatorship; General Francisco Franco died in 1975, leaving a nation injured, but not demoralized. Franco's regime was so much more than just a set of social, political, and economic arrangements; it penetrated every aspect of Spanish life from the language people spoke to their sexual morality.

Perhaps the most pronounced legacy of the Franco regime is a widespread sense that Spain got left behind as the rest of Western Europe modernized and enjoyed general prosperity in the decades following World War II. Spain did, however, achieve an "economic miracle" in the '60s, the *años de desarollo* (years of development). The development of tourism, especially along the coast (the Costa del Sol is Exhibit A) spawned and sustained this economic growth, though not without a high environmental and cultural cost.

Spain's relatively solid natural boundaries—water surrounds the country to the north and south and the rugged Pyrenees Mountains run along the border with France—can mask the great diversity that lies within them. Once the home to Celtiberians, Romans, Visigoths, Moors, and Jews, Spain has always preserved important regional distinctions. Even with the Christians' final defeat of the Moors in 1492 and the subsequent dominance of Catholicism, Iberia remained internally incoherent, consisting of several distinct and independent kingdoms. The Catholic nation that came to be the richest and most powerful in the world was in many ways an artificial unity, forged out of disparate kingdoms by strategic royal marriages, the expulsion of Moors and Jews, and the forceful subjection of the other kingdoms to the Crown of Castile. Seeking to strengthen this fragile unity, Franco insisted on centralization, suppressing regional languages and disparaging identities rooted in the old kingdoms. It is no wonder that Spain's integral components—Basques, Catalunyans, Gallegos, Andalucíans, Aragonese, Asturians, Leonese, Navarrese, Muricians, and even Castilians—are reasserting themselves in these more liberal times.

Bay of Biscay

El Ferrol
Ribadeo   Luarca   Gijón
La Coruña   Ribadesella   Santander   Se
           Villalba   Bil
Santiago de   Oviedo
Compostela   Lugo   Mieres   Cangas
Muros   de Onis   PICOS DE
                                                      EUROPA
Pontevedra   Ponferrada   León
Vigo   Orense   Astorga   Burgos   Logro
Tui/Túy   Soria
CANTABRIAN   Benavente   Palencia
MTS.   Valladolid
           Zamora   Tordesillas   Duero
                                                                        SIERRA DE GUADARRAMA
P O R T U G A L   Salamanca   Adanero   Segovia
                                                                  Guada
           Ciudad   Avila   El Escorial   MADRID
           Rodrigo   Tara
                    SIERRA DE GREDOS   Toledo
           Plasencia   Talavera   Aranjuez
                           Tajo   de la Reina   Alcázar
                    Guadalupe   San Jua
           Cáceres   Trujillo
                    Guadiana   Ciudad
           Mérida   Abenójar   Real   Valdepeñ
           Badajóz   Almadén
Jerez de los   Zafra
Caballeros   SIERRA   MORENA   Ubeda
Fregenal   Córdoba   Linares   Baeza
de la Sierra   Bailén   Jaén   Caz
Aroche   Guadalquivir   Baena   Guadix
           Sevilla   Ecija   Lucena   Granada
                    Carmona   SIERRA
Huelva   Sanlúcar de
Gulf of   Barrameda   Loja
Cadiz   Ronda   Antequera   Nerja
COSTA DE LA LUZ   Jerez de   Torremolinos   Málaga   Motril
           Cádiz   la Frontera   Fuengirola   COSTA DEL SOL
ATLANTIC   Estepona   Marbella
OCEAN   Algeciras   Gibraltar
                    Strait of Gibraltar
TO CANARY
ISLANDS

F R A N C E

San Sebastián
Fuenterrabia
ilbao
Roncesvalles
Vitoria
Pamplona
ANDORRA
Viella
oño
Jaca
Parque Nacional de Ordesa
P Y R E N E E S
La Seu d'Urgell
Puigcerdà
Port Bou
Tudela
Huesca
Cadaqués
Barbastro
El Pont de Suert
Vich/Vic
Girona/Gerona
La Pobla de Segur
Manresa
ria
Zaragoza
Lérida
Montserrat
COSTA BRAVA
Calatayud
Daroca
Alcañiz
Barcelona
Medinaceli
Caminreal
Sitges
Tarragona
Monreal del Campo
La Jana
Tortosa
COSTA DORADA
lalajara
Tajo
Teruel
Vinaròs

Balearic Sea

TO MENORCA →

Cuenca
Castellón de la Plana
rancón
Sagunto
Golfo de Valencia
Palma
Requena
Valencia
Mallorca
ar de an
Íucar
Gandia
Piles
Ibiza
BALEARIC ISLANDS
Albacete
eñas
Alcaraz
Benidorm
Ibiza
Hellín
COSTA BLANCA
Formentera
Alicante
Villajoyosa
Elche
Segura
Menorca
Murcia
Orihuela
Ciudadela
Mahón
azorla
Lorca
Manga del Mar Menor
ix
Cartagena
NEVADA
COSTA CALIDA
KEY

⊢—⊣ Rail Lines

Almería

Mediterranean Sea

COSTA DE ALMERIA

N

A L G E R I A

0   100 miles

0   150 km

Basics

MONEY $1 = 129 pesetas and 100 pesetas = 77¢. Traveler's checks can be exchanged in banks, *casas de cambio* (exchange offices), or El Corte Inglés, a large department store chain found in major cities throughout Spain; all three have competitive rates. Banks are usually open weekdays 9–2 and, in winter, also 9–1 on Saturdays. Major credit cards such as Visa, Mastercard, and American Express are widely accepted in Spain, although most cheap restaurants and hotels don't take them. You can also use your credit card to draw money from Spanish ATMs—check with your credit card company before you leave home.

➤ **HOW MUCH IT WILL COST** • Although the cost of traveling in Spain keeps creeping up, it's still much cheaper than traveling in many other European countries. Expect to pay around 600 ptas–700 ptas for a filling *menú del día* (menu of the day) in an inexpensive place, 2,000 ptas–2,500 ptas for a double room in a cheap pensión, and about 600 ptas for a 100-km bus ride. Frugal travelers should be okay with $30–$35 a day. Don't feel compelled to leave a tip in your basic bar or café, but in a restaurant you should leave 10%–15% for good service if it's not included in the bill.

GETTING AROUND Most towns you'll want to visit are on the rail lines, but occasionally you'll have to resort to buses, which are sometimes a bit cheaper than trains.

➤ **BY TRAIN** • The national train company **RENFE,** which operates most trains in Spain, accepts InterRail and EurailPasses, though the smaller, private companies **FEVE** (running trains mostly in the north) and **ET** (operating trains in the Basque region) do not. RENFE has many different varieties of trains. The fastest and most luxurious are the *electro, talgo,* and *TER* trains, but these can cost up to 70% more than standard trains and rail pass holders usually have to pay a *supplemento* (supplement). Ordinary trains are called *expresos* or *rápidos* and are comparable in speed and price to buses, while *semi-directos, tranvías,* and *correos* (mail trains) are the cheapest, but also the slowest—the last is so slow it appears to move backward. You can buy tickets and make reservations, recommended for *largo recorrido* (long distance) trains, at RENFE stations, travel agents displaying the RENFE logo, and RENFE offices. Buy tickets for *cercanías* (commuter trains traveling short distances) at the ticket machines in larger stations to avoid the long lines at the windows.

RENFE gives a 20% discount to students and the under-26 crowd on all their trains—always ask. The cheapest times to travel are on *días azules* (blue days), nonpeak days. Get the schedule detailing peak and nonpeak days at any RENFE station. Traveling from Barcelona to Madrid costs 4,500 ptas; Burgos to San Sebastián 2,500 ptas; and Tarragona to Valencia 1,500 ptas.

➤ **BY BUS** • If you don't have a train pass, taking the bus is often the cheapest and most convenient way to go. There is no national bus line, but instead a vast number of private bus companies. You'll have to call individual companies for information; buses often depart from different locations in a city, even when a central bus depot exists. Be aware that service is reduced—and sometimes nonexistent—on Sunday and holidays. Bus fare from Barcelona to Madrid is 2,700 ptas; Burgos to San Sebastián, 1,600 ptas; and Barcelona to Andorra, 2,100 ptas.

WHERE TO SLEEP The budget traveler in Spain isn't condemned exclusively to hostels; **fondas, casas de huéspedes, pensiónes, hostales, hospedajes,** and **hostal-residencias** all offer basic accommodations, usually with a bed, desk, sink, and a shared bathroom down the hall, often for only a little more than a hostel bed. Generally, you can get a double for 2,000 ptas–2,500 ptas. *Hoteles* (hotels), considerably more plush, charge at least 5,000 ptas for a double.

Hostels, or **albergues juveniles,** are run by the HI-affiliated REAJ. Buy a hostel card (500 ptas, 1,000 ptas for those 26 and over), which is necessary to stay in them, at REAJ offices, some travel agencies, or TIVE student travel offices, found in most large cities. Some hostels also sell them, but don't count on it. Beds cost 600 ptas–1,000 ptas for those under 26 and 800 ptas–1,700 ptas for those 26 and over. Breakfast is usually included. Unfortunately, hostels tend to be taken over by school groups in summer, and most have midnight curfews that mean you're locked in just when the nightlife is heating up. You can ask for a comprehensive guide to all the 147 hostels in Spain at larger tourist offices.

Cheapest of all are the many **campgrounds,** where you'll pay about 300 ptas–450 ptas per person. Tourist offices and bookshops carry the *Guía de Campings,* listing all the campgrounds in the country.

FOOD You can eat well and cheaply in Spain, thanks in large part to the national custom of eating *tapas* (appetizers). This kind of casual grazing is perfect for Spain's highly social lifestyle; you stand at the bar with your friends, gulp a *cerveza* (beer) and munch on little plates of delicious stuff such as *gambas al ajillo* (shrimp in garlic), *calamares* (squid), *alcachofas* (artichokes), and *jamón serrano* (smoked ham). Almost every bar and café displays a selection of tapas, usually costing 100 ptas–350 ptas, on the counter. *Raciones* are simply entrée-size servings of such food, and *pinchos* are small tapas.

Spaniards eat lunch between 1 PM and 4 PM; after lunch, all of Spain closes down for the siesta (more commonly called the *descanso*), and supper doesn't roll around until 9 PM–11 PM. The midday meal is the most substantial of the day, most commonly consisting of an appetizer, main course, bread, wine, and dessert. The menú del día offered in most restaurants is usually the best bargain for a full meal; you'll get the above dishes plus a drink and bread for 600 ptas–900 ptas. Another cheap option is the *plato combinado* (combination plate), a filling main course (usually meat, fish, or eggs) and a couple of side dishes. The classic budget staple is a filling *bocadillo* (sandwich), served in almost any bar.

Each region offers its own culinary specialties, but in general Spanish cooks make good use of garlic and olive oil, and agree that *tortilla española* (potato omelet), gazpacho (cold vegetable soup), and paella (saffron rice with meat and seafood) are excellent staple dishes. Vegetarianism hasn't really caught on here, and if you don't eat meat you're in for countless tortillas or *bocadillos con queso* (cheese sandwiches).

You'll see sangria (red wine served cold with fruit) everywhere, but this is hardly the best Spanish wine. Spain produces truly excellent, world-class wines (*vino blanco* is white and *tinto* is red), particularly the reds of La Rioja, and the sherries of Jerez in Andalucía. You can get consistently good wine for surprisingly little money, and even just the old house wine (*vino de la casa*) tends to be decent and not more than 100 ptas–200 ptas a glass.

BUSINESS HOURS The great Spanish tradition of taking an afternoon siesta or descanso is still very much alive. You should generally count on shops, museums, churches, and tourist offices being shut weekdays 1:30 PM–4:30 PM. Take a nap, take a walk, have lunch, or down a beer—many hotels, restaurants, and bars don't close. Everything will eventually reopen around 4:30, and stay open until 7:30 or 8. Stores are generally open Saturday morning, but are closed all day Sunday, and many stores close for a few weeks in late summer.

FESTIVALS AND HOLIDAYS Major festivals to plan your schedule around include Semana Santa (the entire week before Easter), Corpus Christi (early June), Carnaval (late February), Los San Fermínes (the running of the bulls in Pamplona the second week in July), and Las Fallas (March 12–19 in Valencia). Innumerable smaller festivals celebrate favorite local saints and miracles. By all means, come and join in the fun, but be aware that rooms and public transportation can become scarce commodities during festivals. Expect most businesses to be closed on national holidays such as Epiphany (Jan. 6), Good Friday, Easter Sunday and Monday, Labor Day (May 1), St. John's Day (June 24), St. James's Day (July 25), Assumption Day (Aug. 15), National Day (Oct. 1), and Christmas and New Year's days.

PHONES **Country code: 34.** Telephones in Spain are operated by **Telefónica.** Ubiquitous blue phone booths accept coins, credit cards (American Express and Diners Club only), and Telefónica cards with values of 1,000 or 2,000 ptas (buy them at post offices and tobacco shops). Since international phone calls are so expensive (555 ptas for a three-minute call to most European countries, 970 ptas to the United States, and a whopping 1,875 ptas to Australia), it's often easier to make them from a Telefónica office, where you get a booth and pay afterward (sometimes you can use a credit card). Private telephone offices, known as *locuto-*

rios, offer similar services at similar rates. To call another country direct, dial 07, wait for the tone, then dial the country code, area code, and phone number. It's quite easy to make an international collect call (*cobro revertido*) from any phone in Spain: dial 900–9900, followed by 11 (MCI), 14 (AT&T), or 13 (Sprint) for the United States, 15 for Canada, 44 for the United Kingdom, or 61 for Australia. Local calls start at 15 ptas. Dial 009 for the Spanish operator.

MAIL You can receive mail either at *correos* (post offices) or at American Express offices (traveler's check or cardholders only). Letters to be held at post offices should be marked *Lista de Correos* and include the name of the town and province. Post offices are generally open weekdays 8 AM–9 PM and Saturday 9 AM–2 PM. A letter to the United States or Canada takes about 10 days and costs 90 ptas, while it takes about five days and costs 45 ptas to get a letter to another European country. You can buy stamps at *tabacs* (tobacco shops) and some hotels, as well as the post office.

LANGUAGE AND CULTURE A constant reminder of Spain's past as a collection of disparate kingdoms and peoples is the fact there are four official languages here: Castellano (Castilian or Spanish); Gallego (Galician), a cross between Portuguese and Castilian that's spoken in the far northwest; Catalán (Catalan), the language of Catalunya and other eastern regions; and Euskera (Basque), the unrelated, exotic language spoken in Euskadi, the Basque region. Spanish is almost universally understood throughout the country, however, in no small part because of Franco's official ban on all languages other than Castilian. It's important to be aware of this history of linguistic suppression and the fierce regional pride of the different communities. Make an effort to speak the regional language and never, ever refer to either Catalan or Galician as a "dialect" of Castilian or refer to Castilian as Spanish in these regions.

Madrid

You might find Madrid disappointing at first. By European standards, it's not an especially beautiful or charming city, nor does it have a particularly compelling history. Felipe IV created this city in 1561, planting the new Spanish capital here high on a plateau and dead in the center of Spain to help him consolidate and increase his power over the country. Strategic and political considerations won out over romantic and aesthetic ones.

Madrid's centrality and political importance, though, mean that today it is the focus of Spain's political, economic, and cultural energies. Madrid has some of the greatest art museums in the world and a constant program of cultural events. But as those who have taken the time to appreciate Madrid will tell you, the real spirit of the city lies in the lifestyle of its people and the passion with which they pursue the pleasurable. In Madrid you can drink in more bars, dance in more clubs, and stay out later than you may have thought possible. Forget about grand squares, beautiful buildings, and impressive monuments—this may be the only town in the entire country where you don't feel obligated to visit a single church. Sure Madrid has them, but if you dive into the lifestyle here, you might not be awake to see them by day or be bothered to see them at all. But chances are, you won't feel as though you've missed a thing.

BASICS

VISITOR INFORMATION The municipal tourist office is conveniently located at Plaza Mayor 3. *Tel. 91/266–54–77. Metro: Sol. Open weekdays 10–2 and 4–8, Sat. 10–2.*

Most of the following national tourist offices are open weekdays about 9–7 and Saturday about 9–1. *Torre de Madrid, Pl. de España, tel. 91/541–23–25. Metro: Pl. de España; Duque de Medinaceli 2, tel. 91/429–49–51 or 91/429–44–87. Metro: Antón Martín; Chamartín train station, tel. 91/315–99–76. Metro: Chamartín; Barajas Airport, tel. 91/205–86–56.*

AMERICAN EXPRESS Here cardholders can cash traveler's checks, change money, have Am Ex cards and checks replaced, and receive poste restante mail. They also have an excellent travel agency with English-speaking employees. *Pl. de Cortes 2, tel. 91/ 322–54–40, 900/99–44–26 for traveler's-check refunds. Metro: Banco de España. From C. Alcalá, go south on Marqués Cubas. Open weekdays 9–5:30, Sat. 9–noon.*

BUCKET SHOP **TIVE.** They specialize in student and youth travel discounts. *Fernando el Católico 88, tel. 91/543–02–08 or 91/543–74–12. Metro: Moncloa. Open weekdays 9–2, Sat. 9–noon.*

CHANGING MONEY American Express offers a competitive exchange rate and charges no commission. The same holds for **El Corte Inglés** department stores, open until 9 weekdays and Saturday, 8 on Sunday. There are four throughout the city, the most central of which is at Calle Preciados 3, at the Puerta del Sol. For larger transactions, you're better off at one of the banks **Banco Central, Central Hispano,** or **Caja de Madrid,** all of which charge a small commission (250 ptas–500 ptas), but offer significantly better rates; you'll find these banks all over Madrid. The smaller cambios along **Gran Vía** and **Sol** are usurious, but some stay open all night.

EMBASSIES **Australia.** *Paseo de la Castellana 13, tel. 91/579–04–28. Open Mon.–Thurs. 9–1 and 2–4:30, Fri. 9–2.*

Canada. *C. Núñez de Balboa 35, tel. 91/431–43–00. Open weekdays 9–12:30.*

Great Britain. *C. Fernando el Santo 16, tel. 91/308–52–08. Open weekdays 8–2:30.*

Ireland. *C. Claudio Coello 73, tel. 91/576–35–00. Open weekdays 10–2.*

United States. *C. Serrano 75, tel. 91/577–40–00. Open weekdays 9–12:30 and 3–5.*

EMERGENCIES For the **police** dial 091, for the **fire department** 080, and for an **ambulance** 91/479–93–61.

PHONES AND MAIL There are two **Telefónica** offices in Madrid, one at Paseo de Recoletos 37–41 (Metro: Banco de España), the other at Gran Vía 30 (Metro: Gran Vía). Both are open Monday–Saturday 9 AM–midnight, Sunday 10 AM–midnight.

Your every postal need can be met at the **Palacio de Comunicaciones.** *Pl. de la Cibeles, tel. 91/536–01–10. Metro: Banco de España. Open weekdays 8 AM–9:30 PM or 10 PM, Sat. 8:30–2, Sun. 10–1.*

COMING AND GOING

BY TRAIN Madrid's two main train stations are **Estación de Chamartín** (Metro: Chamartín) and the newly remodeled and enlarged **Estación de Atocha** (Metro: Atocha RENFE); many trains stop at both. Some popular destinations are Barcelona (7½ hrs, 4,500 ptas), and Paris (14 hrs, 12,000 ptas). Buy tickets at either station, travel agents, or at the **RENFE office** (C. Alcalá 44, tel. 91/563–02–02, Metro: Banco de España). For general rail information in Madrid, call 91/429–02–02.

BY BUS While many private companies' buses leave from points all over the city, Madrid's main station is **Estación Sur de Autobuses** (C. Canarias 17, tel. 91/468–42–00, Metro: Palos de la Frontera). Other important points of departure include **AUTO RES** (Fernández Shaw 1, tel. 91/551–72–00, Metro: Conde de Casal) and **La Sepulvedana** (Paseo de la Florida 11, tel. 91/230–48–00, Metro: Norte).

BY PLANE **Barajas Airport** (tel. 91/305–83–43) is 16 km northeast of Madrid. Buses (tel. 91/401–99–00) run between the airport and the bus terminal at Plaza de Colón in Madrid's center from 4:45 AM to 1:00 AM, leaving every 12–30 minutes; the ride costs 300 ptas and takes about 40 minutes. Or take Bus 101 (125 ptas), which connects the airport to Metro Canillejas.

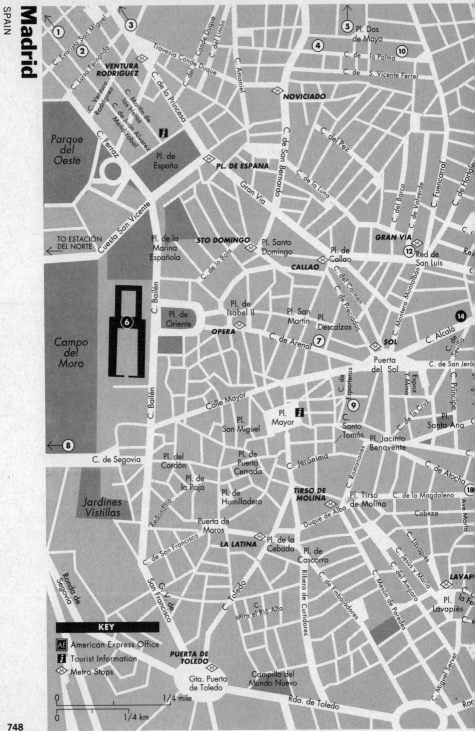

Parque
del
Oeste

VENTURA
RODRIGUEZ

C. Evaristo San Miguel

C. Luisa Fernanda

C. de la Princesa

C. Ventura Rodriguez

C. de Juan Álvarez Mendizabal

C. de los Heros

C. Martín de

C. Ferraz

Travesia Conde Duque

Conde Duque

C. del Limón

C. Amaniel

C. del Limón

NOVICIADO

Pl. Dos
de Mayo

C. de la Palma

C. de S. Vicente Ferrer

C. del Pez

C. de San Bernardo

C. de la Luna

Gran Via

GRAN VIA

C. del Barco

C. de Valverde

C. Fuencarral

C. de Hortale

TO ESTACIÓN
DEL NORTE

Cuesta San Vicente

Pl. de
España

Pl. de la
Marina
Española

STO DOMINGO

C. de la Bola

Pl. Santo
Domingo

Pl. de
Callao

CALLAO

C. del Carmen

C. de Preciados

Red de
San Luis

Rei

Pl. de
Isabel II

Pl. San
Martín

Pl.
Descalzas

C. de Arenal

OPERA

Pl. de
Oriente

C. Bailén

Campo
del
Moro

Puerta
del Sol

SOL

C. de Sevilla

C. Alcalá

C. de San Jeró

Espoz
y Mina

C. de Montera Montalbán

C. Príncipe

C. de
Esparteros

Calle Mayor

C. de la Cruz

Pl.
San Miguel

Pl.
Mayor

Santo
Tomás

Pl. Jacinto
Benavente

Pl.
Santa Ana

C. Bailén

C. de Segovia

Pl. del
Cordón

Pl. de
la Paja

Pl. de
Puerta
Cerrada

C. Jerónima

C. Romanones

C. de Atocha

Jardines
Vistillas

Redondilla

Pl. de
Humilladero

Puerta de
Moros

Duque de Alba

TIRSO DE
MOLINA

Pl. Tirso
de Molina

C. de la Magdalena

Cabeza

Ave María

Ronda de Segovia

C. de San Francisco

G. v. de San Francisco

LA LATINA

Pl. de la
Cebada

Pl. de
Cascorro

Ribera de Curtidores

C. de Embajadores

Mesón de Paredes

C. Jesús y María

C. del Amparo

C. Lavapiés

LAVAP

Pl.
Lavapiés

C.
la Fe

C. Toledo

C.
Mira el Río Alta

PUERTA DE
TOLEDO

Gta. Puerta
de Toledo

Campillo del
Mundo Nuevo

Rda. de Toledo

C. Miguel Servet

Ror

KEY

AE American Express Office

i Tourist Information

Ⓜ Metro Stops

0 ————— 1/4 mile

0 ————— 1/4 km

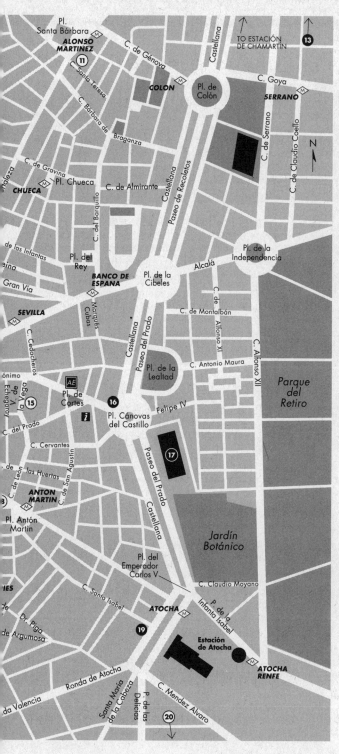

Sights ●

Centro de Arte
Reina Sofía, **19**

Museo de
la Ciudad, **13**

Museo de la Real
Academia de Bellas
Artes de San
Fernando, **14**

Museo del
Prado, **17**

Museo Thyssen-
Bornemisza, **16**

Palacio Real, **6**

Lodging ○

Albergue Juvenil
Richard Schirrmann
(HI), **8**

Albergue Juvenil
Santa Cruz de
Marcenado, (HI), **3**

La Asturiana, **5**

Gredos, **2**

Hostal Alfaro, **15**

Hostal Alicante, **7**

Hostal Castilla, **11**

Hostal Centro, **10**

Hostal Encarnita, **9**

Hostal-Residencia
Alegría, **20**

Hostal-Residencia
Conde de Alba, **1**

Hostal-Residencia
Flores, **12**

Jemasaca, **4**

Pensión Pacios, **18**

HITCHING To get out of Madrid for the price of a tank of gas, call **Nuevos Viajes** (tel. 91/308–30–98); their staff will try to hook you up with someone driving your way.

GETTING AROUND

In the very center of Madrid is **Puerta del Sol** (a.k.a. Sol), a large, roundabout intersected by major avenues and pedestrian streets. The surrounding area is the oldest part of Madrid and is bordered in the east by the city's main park, **Parque del Retiro,** and in the west by the **Manzanares River** and **Casa de Campo,** a sprawling park. To the north of Sol, **Gran Vía** is the major east–west artery. The area just north of Gran Vía is seedy but interesting, and further north things get more spread out and gentrified, especially along the **Paseo de la Castellana,** the major north–south artery. East of Paseo de la Castellana, the **Salamanca** neighborhood includes wealthy residential areas and upscale shops. South of Puerta del Sol, the traditionally working-class neighborhoods **La Latina** and **Lavapiés** stretch south of Plaza Mayor and Calle de Atocha.

Madrid has efficient Metro and bus (EMT) systems, though you can walk almost everywhere. A single ride on the Metro or the bus costs 125 ptas, and tickets valid for 10 rides are only 550 ptas—ask for a *billete de diez* (ticket of 10) for the Metro or a *bonobus* for the bus pass. A monthly pass covers both systems and costs 2,300 ptas–6,250 ptas, depending on your age and how many zones you want to cover.

BY METRO No address lies very far from one of the Metro's many stops. You can get a Metro map at any ticket window. All lines run daily from 6 AM to 1:30 AM, except line 6 to the university, which runs only weekdays 7 AM–10 PM, and not at all in August.

BY BUS The bus system is more complicated than the Metro; if you want to make the effort to stay above ground, pick up a map and a schedule at the tourist office, or, if you speak Spanish, call 91/401–99–00. Bus service begins at 5:45 AM or 7 AM, depending on the line, and ends at midnight. A few night buses (marked with an N) run all night long.

BY TAXI Although taxis are generally a pretty good deal in Madrid, surcharges for traveling to the airport (300 ptas) or at night or on Sunday (150 ptas) may make the price you pay very different from what you see on the meter. Expect to pay at least an initial fare of 150 ptas and 70 ptas per km. Hailing a cab should be no problem, but you can request one by calling **Tele-Taxi** (tel. 91/445–90–08).

WHERE TO SLEEP

The overwhelming advantage of avoiding the hostels is that you can stay out as late as you like—a serious consideration in Madrid.

SOUTH OF GRAN VIA The center of Madrid, from Gran Vía south to Calle de Atocha, holds many inexpensive hostales, pensiónes, and casas de huéspedes, and is near most main sights as well as serious nightlife action. Poke around **Sol, Plaza Mayor, Santa Ana, Tirso de Molina, Antón Martín,** and **Estación de Atocha.**

➤ **UNDER 3,000 PTAS • Hostal Encarnita.** Ideally located between Sol and Plaza Mayor. Doubles 2,600 ptas, 2,900 ptas with shower. *C. Marqués Viudo de Pontejos 7, tel. 91/531–90–55 or 91/532–98–20. Metro: Sol. From C. Mayor, turn left on C. de Esparteros, then take first left.*

Hostal-Residencia Alegría. Clean, bleak rooms near Estación de Atocha. Doubles 2,400 ptas. *Rafael de Riego 8, tel. 91/528–76–82. From station and Pl. del Emperador Carlos V, take C. de Méndez Alvaro, and turn right on Rafael de Riego.*

➤ **UNDER 4,000 PTAS • Hostal Alfaro.** Fresh-smelling place amid funky restaurants and pubs. Doubles 3,000 ptas, 3,500 ptas with shower, and one really classy double for 5,000 ptas; dingy singles 1,500 ptas. *Ventura de la Vega 16, tel. 91/429–61–73. Metro: Sol or Sevilla. AE, MC, V.*

Hostal Alicante. With flower-laden balcony windows practically overlooking Sol, it's almost posh for the area. Doubles 3,900 ptas *C. de Arenal 16, tel. 91/531–51–78. Metro: Sol.*

Hostal-Residencia Flores. Right on Gran Vía, but eight floors up, so quiet as well. A step up from other pensiónes: art in the hallway, plants in the bathroom. Doubles 3,500 ptas, 4,000 ptas with bath. *Gran Vía 30, tel. 91/522–81–52. Metro: Gran Vía.*

Pensión Pacios. Quiet, tastefully decorated rooms and impeccably clean bathrooms down the hall. Stumble home one block from Plaza Santa Ana and Calle Huertas. Doubles 3,000 ptas. *C. de Atocha 28, tel. 91/369–33–71. Metro: Antón Martín.*

NORTH OF GRAN VIA As you move from the center of Madrid north—around **Argüelles, Malasaña,** and **Plaza Santa Bárbara**—rooms become prettier, quieter, and cheaper. Consider staying around Malasaña if you're in search of the ultimate bar, near Santa Bárbara or Argüelles if you're after a good night's sleep.

➢ **UNDER 3,000 PTAS • La Asturiana.** Balconies overlook one of the most happening areas in Madrid, but the beds are mushy. Gregarious owner might lower the prices if she likes you. Doubles 2,900 ptas. *C. de Ruiz 11, tel. 91/456–11–21. From Bilbao Metro take C. Manuela Malasaña and turn left on C. de Ruiz.*

Gredos. In an old, pretty building that smells like freshly baked bread, with polished hardwood floors. Rooms range from a tiny single (1,200 ptas) to spacious, balconied doubles (2,400 ptas). Incredible value, but only 10 rooms, so reserve ahead. *C. Martín de los Heros 35, tel. 91/547–46–42. Metro: Ventura Rodríguez.*

Hostal Castilla. Less than a block from Plaza Santa Bárbara, in a calm but fun neighborhood. Rooms are cheapest in the area, and some are pretty. Third floor, no elevator. Doubles 2,000 ptas. *C. Santa Teresa 9, tel. 91/310–26–76. Metro: Alonso Martínez.*

Hostal Centro. Nicely decorated and surrounded by dozens of bars, pubs, and restaurants. Book ahead. Singles 1,500 ptas, doubles 2,500 ptas. *C. de la Palma 11, tel. 91/447–00–47. Metro: Tribunal.*

➢ **UNDER 4,000 PTAS • Hostal-Residencia Conde de Alba.** Dark halls lead into bright, white rooms with big sinks, hot water. Clotheslines hang over a sunny, quiet, courtyard. Doubles 3,000 ptas, 3,200 ptas with shower. *C. de Juan Alvarez Mendizábal 44, tel. 91/542–28–39. Metro: Argüelles.*

Jemasaca. Crumbling entrance leads into bright, plant-filled hotel. In the middle of Malasaña nightlife scene; lots of restaurants and little markets nearby. Book ahead. Singles 1,500 ptas, doubles 3,000 ptas–3,500 ptas. *C. de la Palma 61, tel. 91/532–70–11. Metro: Noviciado.*

HOSTELS **Albergue Juvenil Richard Schirrmann (HI).** A 20-minute walk from the nearest Metro. In a large park where you can jog, swim, or hang with the geese. Friendly atmosphere and no curfew, though it's a ways from nightlife. HI members only. Beds 650 ptas, 800 ptas age 26 and over, breakfast included. *Casa de Campo, tel. 91/463–56–99. From Lago Metro stop turn left and left again on first main road and walk about 20 min. Laundry, lockers, bar, library, phones.*

Albergue Juvenil Santa Cruz de Marcenado (HI). You won't find a cheaper bed in Madrid, and even if you did it probably wouldn't be as clean and well located. Only 74 beds in four- to 10-person rooms, so check in between 9 and 10 AM. Beds 650 ptas, nonmembers 950 ptas. *C. Santa Cruz 28, tel. 91/582–42–16. From Argüelles Metro take C. de la Princesa south, turn left on C. Serrano Jover, and right on C. Santa Cruz de Marcenado. 1:30 AM curfew, laundry, lockers. Closed Sun. noon–5.*

CAMPGROUND **Osuna.** Hopping bar, parties, bands, and good food. Close to beautiful El Capricho Jardín. People, cars, and tents pay 475 ptas each. Bungalows for two with bath 3,500 ptas. *Av. de Logroño, tel. 91/741–05–10. From Canillejas Metro cross pedestrian bridge, take road that cuts through the 2 parking lots, turn right just past BURGOS sign, and look for campground's BAR RESTAURANT COKE sign.*

FOOD

Madrid's tapas bars and *cervecerías* (beer bars) are everywhere, but are concentrated around Sol and Plaza Mayor, by Estación de Atocha, between the La Latina and Embajadores Metro stops, and in the students' area around the San Bernardo, Noviciado, Argüelles, and Moncloa Metro stops. Malasaña is a good place to look for ethnic restaurants. For the cheapest food, visit one of Madrid's many indoor markets. Try the one on **Plaza San Miguel** (open Mon.–Sat. 9–2 and 5:30–8:30), a few blocks west of Plaza Mayor, or **Galería Comercial** (C. Quintana at C. Mendizibal; Metro: Argüelles).

In a city where people have churros con chocolate (deep-fried dough with chocolate) and beer for breakfast, it matters less what you eat than when, where, and how you do it: Don't eat dinner before nine, linger three hours over lunch, and never eat in the streets—it's considered impolite.

➤ **UNDER 500 PTAS • Cervecería la Vega.** A great place to be Sunday afternoons after shopping at El Rastro (*see* Cheap Thrills, *below*). It's so packed that people sit on the sidewalk, eating generous portions of paella (300 ptas), drinking cheap beer (100 ptas), and playing guitar. *C. del Encomiendo 2, no tel. Metro: Lavapiés.*

Restaurante Magumar. Very good and very cheap food—the student bustle and the smell of garlic more than make up for a lack of ambience. Tapas dinner for two 950 ptas. Combination plate 450 ptas–500 ptas. Wonderful *champiñones* (mushrooms). *C. San Bernardo 61, tel. 91/532–84–55. Metro: San Bernardo. Meals served 1–8:30, tapas until midnight.*

➤ **UNDER 1,000 PTAS • La Biotika.** A vegetarian oasis for those who never want to eat another cheese sandwich. Also one of the few no-smoking establishments in Madrid. Gazpacho 400 ptas, menú del día 900 ptas. *Amor de Dios 3, no tel. Metro: Sol or Antón Martín. From Pl. Santa Ana, turn right on C. Principe, left on C. Huertas, then right. Closed 4:30–8:30.*

El Brillante. Mostly local clientele. A pictorial menu helps those who know not what *callos* (tripe) is. Roast chicken, bread, and wine 750 ptas. *C. de Atocha 122, across from station, tel. 91/468–05–48. Metro: Atocha RENFE.*

Café Bellas Artes. In the self-consciously bohemian Museo del Bellas Artes, this elegant café is well worth the 100 ptas you pay to enter the museum. Sip a café Vienés (300 ptas) on your own leather couch. Breakfast 180 ptas–500 ptas, tapas from 375 ptas. *Círculo de Bellas Artes, C. Alcalá 42, tel. 91/531–77–00. Metro: Banco de España.*

El Granero de Lavapiés. Vegetarian and macrobiotic food served amid Japanese lamp shades and '60s beads. Lots of vegetable cream soups, gazpacho, and paella. All entrées under 725 ptas. *Menú de la casa* (house menu) 950 ptas. No smoking. *C. Argumosa 10, tel. 91/467–76–11. Metro: Lavapiés. Open Sun.–Fri. 1–4.*

Peyunia Cafetería. Loud and popular Lavapiés bar/cervecería/restaurant with an interesting selection of roast chicken, ham, churros, and fresh juices. Waiters chuck the food at you, but it's part of the fun. Menú del día 850 ptas. *C. Embajadores 39, tel. 91/467–13–69. Metro: La Latina or Embajadores.*

Pizzería Mastropiero. Trendy but intimate restaurant with creative thin-crust pizzas. Slice 185 ptas, small pie from 700 ptas. *C. San Vincent Ferrer 34, no tel. Metro: Noviciado or Tribunal.*

Restaurante la Tuna. Hearty portions of Spanish food and wine served to local workers on their lunch break. *Arroz cubano,* rice with ketchup, comes with fried egg, plantain, and bread for only 300 ptas. Menú del día 750 ptas. *C. Ferdinand el Católico 68, tel. 91/243–25–24. Metro: Moncloa. Closed Mon. night.*

Restaurante Martín e Hijos. Comfortable atmosphere; students, workers, and suits all come here to enjoy tapas at the bar and the restaurant in back. Menú del día 800 ptas. *Martín de los Heros 40, tel. 91/247–67–36. Metro: Argüelles.*

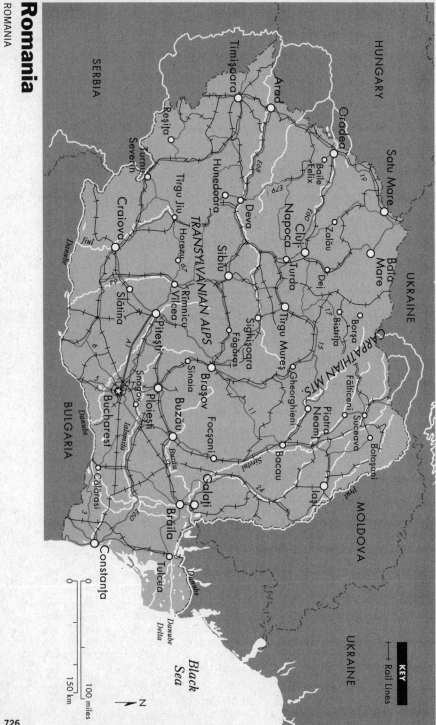

Romania

ROMANIA

HUNGARY

SERBIA

UKRAINE

BULGARIA

MOLDOVA

UKRAINE

Black Sea

Timişoara

Arad

Oradea

Satu Mare

Baia Mare

Reşiţa

Baile Felix

Zalău

Turnu Severin

Tirgu Jiu

Hunedoara

Deva

Cluj Napoca

Turda

Dej

Bistriţa

Borşa

TRANSYLVANIAN ALPS

Craiova

Sibiu

Sighişoara

Tirgu Mureş

Gheorghieni

Fălticeni

Suceava

Botoşani

Horezu

Rimnicu Vilcea

Fǎgǎras

CARPATHIAN MTS.

Piatra Neamt

Slătina

Piteşti

Sinaia

Braşov

Focşani

Bacau

Iaşi

Snagov

Ploieşti

Buzău

Galaţi

Bucharest

Brǎila

Cǎlǎraşi

Constanţa

Tulcea

Danube Delta

Danube

Jiul

Ialomiţa

Buzǎu

Siretul

Prut

Danube

E68

E79

E60

19

E60

613

17

15

24

11

A1

5

6

3

E60

KEY
Rail Lines

N

0   100 miles

0   150 km

Bay of Biscay

El Ferrol
Ribadeo   Luarca   Gijón
La Coruña   Ribadesella
Villalba   Oviedo   Santander
Santiago de   Lugo   Mieres   Cangas
Compostela   de Onís   PICOS DE
Muros   CANTABRIAN   MTS.   EUROPA   B

Pontevedra   Ponferrada   León
Vigo   Orense   Astorga   Burgos
Tui/Túy   Log

Benavente   Palencia   Sc

Tordesillas   Valladolid
Zamora   Duero

Salamanca   Adanero   Segovia   SIERRA DE GUADARRA

Ciudad   Avila   Gua
Rodrigo   El Escorial
PORTUGAL   MADRID
Plasencia   SIERRA DE GREDOS   Toledo
Tajo   Talavera   Aranjuez   Ta
Guadalupe   de la Reina
Cáceres   Trujillo   Alcáz
San J
Mérida   Guadiana   Ciudad
Abenójar   Real
Badajoz   Almadén   Valdep
Jerez de los   Zafra
Caballeros   SIERRA   MORENA   Linares
Fregenal   Bailén   Ube
de la Sierra   Córdoba   Baeza
Aroche   Jaén   C
Baena
Guadalquivir   Écija   Lucena   Gua
Sevilla   Granada
Huelva   Carmona   SIERRA
Gulf of   Sanlúcar de   Loja
Cadiz   Barrameda   Ronda   Antequera
Nerja
Cádiz   Jerez de   Torremolinos   Málaga   Motril
la Frontera   Fuengirola   COSTA   DEL   SOL
ATLANTIC   Estepona   Marbella
OCEAN   Algeciras
Gibraltar
TO CANARY   Strait of Gibraltar
ISLANDS

FRANCE

San Sebastián
Fuenterrabia
ilbao
Vitoria
Roncesvalles
Pamplona
Jaca
Huesca
Tudela
oño
Zaragoza
ría
Calatayud
Daroca
Medinaceli
Caminreal
Monreal del Campo
dalajara
Teruel
Cuenca
rancón
Sagunto
Requena
Valencia
ar de
an
Albacete
eñas
Alcaraz
Hellín
Benidorm
Villajoyosa
Alicante
Elche
Murcia
Orihuela
Lorca
Cartagena
ix
NEVADA
Almería

Parque Nacional de Ordesa
Viella
La Seu d'Urgell
PYRENEES
ANDORRA
Puigcerdà
Port Bou
Cadaqués
Barbastrò
El Pont de Suert
Vich/Vic
Girona/Gerona
La Pobla de Segur
Manresa
Lérida
Montserrat
Barcelona
Sitges
Tarragona
COSTA BRAVA
COSTA DORADA
Tortosa
La Jana
Vinaròs
Castellón de la Plana
COSTA DEL AZAHAR
Golfo de Valencia
Gandia
Piles
COSTA BLANCA

Balearic Sea

TO MENORCA →

Palma
Mallorca
Ibiza
Ibiza
Formentera
BALEARIC ISLANDS

COSTA CALIDA
Manga del Mar Menor

Mediterranean Sea

Menorca
Ciudadela
Mahón

KEY
—+— Rail Lines

COSTA DE ALMERIA

ALGERIA

N

| 0 | | 100 miles |
| 0 | | 150 km |

743

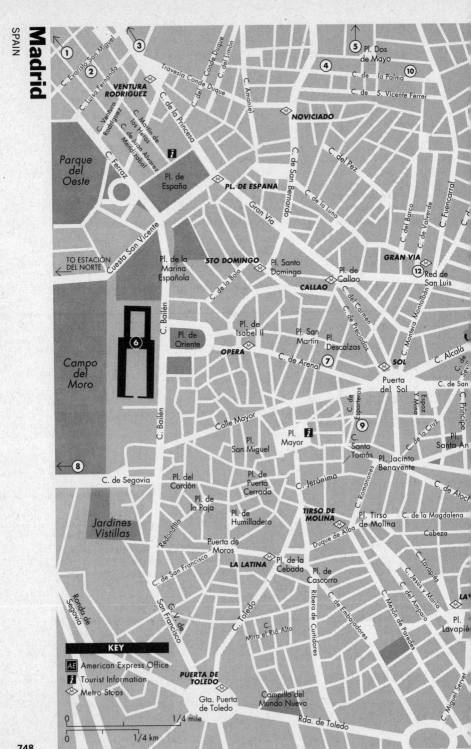

Madrid

SPAIN

Parque del Oeste

VENTURA RODRIGUEZ

C. Evaristo San Miguel
C. Luisa Fernanda
C. Ventura Rodríguez
C. Mazitin de los Heros
C. de Juan Alvarez Mendizabal
C. Ferraz

Travesía Conde Duque
C. Conde Duque
C. del Limón
C. del
C. Amaniel
C. de S. Vicente Ferrer
C. de la Palma

Pl. Dos de Mayo

NOVICIADO

C. de la Princesa

Pl. de España

PL. DE ESPANA

Gran Vía

C. de San Bernardo
C. de la Luna
C. del Pez

GRAN VIA
C. del Barco
C. de Valverde
C. Fuencarral

TO ESTACIÓN DEL NORTE

Cuesta San Vicente

Campo del Moro

C. Bailén

Pl. de la Marina Española

STO DOMINGO
C. de la Bola
Pl. Santo Domingo

Pl. de Callao
CALLAO
C. del Carmen
C. de Preciados

Red de San Luis
C. Montera
C. Maltalbán

Pl. de Oriente
Pl. de Isabel II
OPERA
C. de Arenal

Pl. San Martín
Pl. Descalzas

SOL
Puerta del Sol
C. Alcalá
C. de San
C. Principe

Calle Mayor
Pl. San Miguel
Pl. Mayor

C. de Esparteros
Espoz Y Mina
C. de la Cruz

C. Santo Tomás
Pl. Jacinto Benavente

Pl. Santa An

C. de Segovia
Pl. del Cordón
Pl. de Puerta Cerrada
C. Jerónima
C. Romanones
C. de Atoch

Jardines Vistillas
Redondilla
Pl. de la Paja
Pl. de Humilladero
TIRSO DE MOLINA
Duque de Alba
Pl. Tirso de Molina
C. de la Magdalena
Cabeza

Puerta de Moros
LA LATINA
Pl. de la Cebada
Pl. de Cascorro

Ronda de Segovia
C. de San Francisco
G. V. de San Francisco
C. Toledo
C. Mira el Río Alto
Ribera de Curtidores
C. de Embajadores
C. Mesón de Paredes
C. Jesús y María
C. del Amparo
C. Lavapiés
LA
Pl. Lavapié
C. Miguel Servet

KEY

AE American Express Office
i Tourist Information
M Metro Stops

PUERTA DE TOLEDO
Gta. Puerta de Toledo
Campillo del Mundo Nuevo
Rda. de Toledo

0 — 1/4 mile
0 — 1/4 km

748

> **UNDER 1,500 PTAS** • **Restaurante Hylogui.** An elegant place for dinner or lunch (specials 550 ptas–750 ptas). Gazpacho 550 ptas, meat and fish dishes 600 ptas–1,300 ptas. Attached to a wonderful bar where you can have a glass of wine and some appetizers for 100 ptas while watching the news. *Ventura la Vega 3, tel. 91/429–73–57. Metro: Sol or Tirso de Molina.*

WORTH SEEING

Named Culture Capital of Europe in 1992, Madrid has been the object of increasing attention in the last few years—and for good reason. The Prado, the Centro de Arte Reina Sofía, and the recently installed Museo Thyssen-Bornemisza constitute a trinity of stellar art museums.

To recover from cultural overload or frayed nerves, stop by the Parque del Retiro, where the pace of life slows down to a leisurely stroll.

CENTRO DE ARTE REINA SOFIA The focus of this first-class collection of modern art is great Spanish artists, including Picasso, Dalí, and Miró. The surrealism room is breathtaking and leads to the most shattering painting of all, Picasso's *Guernica,* painted in the month following the Franco-sponsored, German-executed bombing of that town in northern Spain. The Dalís in the next room further challenge cognitive and emotional equilibrium. *C. Santa Isabel 52, tel. 91/467–50–62. Metro: Atocha RENFE. Admission: 400 ptas, students free. Open Mon., Wed.–Sat. 10–9, Sun. 10–2:30.*

MUSEO DE LA CIUDAD With exhibits describing the culture, agriculture, history, and technology of Madrid, this museum will greatly enrich your knowledge of this city. You can learn how water from the Fuente de la Cibeles flows through ancient aqueducts to high-tech purification plants, and read about the political struggles underlying the modern system. Also essential are the drawings of old Madrid—the city has dramatically changed, but some places are still recognizable. *C. del Príncipe de Vergara 140, tel. 01/588–65–77. Metro: Cruz del Rayo. Admission free. Open Tues.–Fri. 10–2 and 4–6, weekends 10–2.*

MUSEO DE LA REAL ACADEMIA DE BELLAS ARTES DE SAN FERNANDO This fine-arts museum houses an excellent collection and doesn't demand the terrific stamina that the Prado does. It features works by El Greco, Goya, Veronese, Caravaggio, Tintoretto, and Rubens, in addition to *La Primavera* (Spring) by Giuseppe Arcimboldo and Ribera's *Ecce Homo. C. Alcalá 13, tel. 91/265–30–62. Metro: Sol or Sevilla. Admission: 200 ptas, students free. Open Tues.–Fri. 9–7, Sat.–Mon. 9–2:30.*

MUSEO DEL PRADO The Prado is dizzying. Exhibits range from the ecstatic (El Greco) to the dark and romantic (Goya) to the downright trippy (Bosch), with thousands of works by artists such as Mantegna, Raphael, Titian, Dürer, Bruegel, and Botticelli. This museum is reason enough to come to Madrid—and stay for a long while. Some masterpieces you might remember as slides in art history class include Fra Angelico's *La Anunciación* (The Anunciation); Bosch's *El Jardin de las Delicias* (The Garden of Delights), a triptych of creation, hell, and the earthly delights in between; Peter Paul Rubens's *Las Tres Gracias* (The Three Graces), sensual and ample nudes; Velázquez's *Las Meninas* (The Maids of Honor), which depicts the artist painting a most unusual royal portrait; and Goya's *El Tres de Mayo* (The Third of May), showing Napoleon's soldiers executing Spaniards. Check out Goya's *pinturas negras* (black paintings) downstairs, so different from some of the vivid works of his early years. *Paseo del Prado, tel. 91/420–28–36. Metro: Atocha RENFE, Banco de España, or Retiro. Admission: 400 ptas, students free. Open Tues.–Sat. 9–7, Sun. 9–2. Wheelchair access.*

MUSEO THYSSEN-BORNEMISZA It seems like the height of arrogance to display one's private art collection right across from the Prado, but Baron Heinreich's collection in fact warrants such placement. Like the Prado, this museum is an art history aficionado's playground. The works here span seven centuries, but the emphasis is squarely on modern and German art, including works by Hans Holbein, Max Ernst, Max Beckmann, and Paul Klee.

Paseo del Prado 8, tel. 91/420–39–44. Metro: Banco de España. Admission: 600 ptas, 350 ptas students. Open Tues.–Sun. 10–7.

PALACIO REAL Visiting the Royal Palace should be high on your list of things to do while in Madrid. Its aesthetic appeal is strong, and its political and historical importance—it was home to the Spanish monarchs from 1764 to 1931—makes it another source of Madrileño pride. Today King Juan Carlos, who lives in the far less ostentatious Zarzuela Palace outside Madrid, uses it only for official state functions. Because there are no signs or explanations inside the palace, the best way to glean a few historical tidbits is by taking one of the guided tours, offered in English and Spanish. The frequency of these tours seems entirely random and the quality varies tremendously. *C. Bailén, tel. 91/542–00–59. Metro: Opera. Admission: 350 ptas. Open Mon.–Sat. 8:30–5, Sun. 9–2.*

PARQUE DEL RETIRO This is where it's at on Sundays, when thousands of Madrileños, their dogs, and kids come here to stroll, play ball, relax, browse through stalls of books, and have a drink at one of several outdoor cafés. The heart of this formal park is the **estanque** (pond), presided over by a grand statue of Alfonso XII. The surrounding steps are often packed with people hanging out or catching the sunset. For a more dramatic view, you can float to the middle of the pond in a rowboat (400 ptas for 45 min).

PLAZA MAYOR Once the place to celebrate bullfights, the canonization of saints, and public burnings of heretics, these days one comes to Plaza Mayor (Metro: Sol) to watch tourists, pigeons, and peaceful political rallies. This spacious, arcaded plaza lies in the center of the city but is quite hidden from the main streets. Designed originally by Juan de Herrera, the architect who also built the Escorial outside Madrid, the plaza was inaugurated in 1620 during the reign of Felipe III, whose statue stands in the middle. Under the arcades that ring the square are several expensive cafés, which set up hundreds of outdoor tables in summer. Better (that is, cheaper and less touristy) cafés lie just off the plaza; look around Calle Ponteros on your way out.

CHEAP THRILLS

You can graze at outdoor food stands, get your hair wrapped by hippies, and buy tacky imported knickknacks and local street art the world over, but Madrid's famous flea market is special. **El Rastro** (Metro: La Latina) is huge—roughly framed by Calle Toledo, Calle Ribera de Curtidores, and Ronda de Toledo—and gets packed every Sunday from 10 to 3. Here, you can buy leather bags (from 2,000 ptas), secondhand Levi's (800 ptas), and even small animals.

Just as exciting as this weekend market are **La Latina** and **Lavapiés.** These traditionally working-class neighborhoods, stretching south of Plaza Mayor, are two of the oldest in Madrid. Centuries ago, before the Inquisition, this area housed Madrid's Jewish community. Today it's the most racially diverse area of Madrid, embracing immigrants from Africa, Asia, and South America. Lavapiés has recently been attracting attention from the professional classes and undergoing a bit of gentrification, but its character remains intact. If you walk through the narrow, twisting streets, you'll see that it's still an authentic and dynamic neighborhood.

Join tourists and die-hard Spaniards at a bullfight, **Los Toros.** During the main season from March to October, the bulls face the toreadors every Sunday and Thursday at 7 at the stadium **Plaza Monumental de Las Ventas** (Metro: Ventas). A cheap ticket costs about 300 ptas—you might not be able to see all the details, but then again, you might not want to. Buy tickets at the stadium; for more information call 91/356–22–00.

AFTER DARK

During the summer, the sun doesn't even set until 10:30, so Madrileños continue their after-dark activities until well after dawn. What makes the Madrid night scene so exceptional is not just the abundance of bars, pubs (bars that feature music and dancing; "clubs" here refer to a kind of nightlife better endorsed by *Playboy* than *The Berkeley Guides*), and discos, but also the passion with which people pursue these activities. For the most comprehensive and timely listings, consult the weekly *Guía del Ocio,* sold for 100 ptas at newsstands.

There is a distinct rhythm to nightlife in Madrid. Having emerged refreshed from your siesta and primping no earlier than 10, you might start by drinking and eating tapas, either at bars or cuevas (*see* Bars, *below*). This can go on until 2 or 3, and only at this point might you want to hit the discos (any earlier and they will either be empty or full of teenagers). Giants of the Madrid discotecas are **Joy Eslava** (C. de Arenal 11, tel. 91/266–37–33); **¡Oh Madrid!** (Carretera de la Coruña, tel. 91/207–86–97); and **Archy** (Marqués de Riscal 11, tel. 91/308–31–62). All charge about 1,500 ptas cover, about 2,000 ptas on weekends. Take a break at 5 to eat, return for more drinking and dancing, and then take your final leave at around 8, in time for a breakfast of churros con chocolate.

The area around Plaza Santa Ana and nearby Calle Huertas and calles Echegaray and Ventura de la Vega, ooze with small discos, many of which have no cover, and great pubs. To the north, in Malasaña, the tone is more alternative. Madrid's oldest quarter, Lavapiés is crammed with interesting bars, pubs, and discos. From Plaza Mayor, wander down Calle de Cuchilleros, making your way to Calle de Segovia, Calle Constanilla San Pedro, and Plaza la Villa. Madrid has an active and visible gay community, with bars and pubs concentrated around Plaza Chueca.

BARS *Cuevas* (caves), concentrated around Plaza Mayor, are cozy little places with low ceilings and dim lights; each serves drinks and specializes in a certain type of tapa. Go down Escaleria de las Piedras and around the corner to the right to Cava de San Miguel. Here you should see at least six such places, including **Meson de Champiñones** (17 Cava de San Miguel, tel. 91/559–67–97). Not immune to tourists, the cuevas nonetheless retain a distinctively local feel and clientele. Sangria and tapas cost about 600 ptas per person—don't forget to tip the musicians.

Casa Antonio. Pictures of bulls cover tiled walls. Look out the window to see the large cross and muraled buildings in the Plaza de Puerta Cerrada. They specialize in excellent Spanish wines; a cup costs a mere 50 ptas. *C. Latoneros 10, tel. 91/266–31–20. Metro: Sol.*

Cervecería de Santa Ana. A happening bar in an exciting neighborhood. Indoor and sidewalk seating great for scoping good-looking Madrileños and tourists. *Pl. Santa Ana 10, tel. 91/429–43–56. Metro: Sol. Open until 2, 1:30 Sun.*

Chocolatería San Gines. Your early morning stop for churros con chocolate. It looks like an ice cream parlor, only there's a full bar and techno vibrations from the disco next door. *C. de Coloreros 5, off C. de Arenal. Metro: Sol. Open Mon. 8 AM–noon, Tues.–Thurs. 4 AM–noon, Fri. and Sat. 6 PM–10 PM and 1 AM–7 AM, Sun. 6 PM–10 PM.*

La Escondida. A cool, unpretentious bar. Sit on little wooden stools in one of two cozy nooks and listen to their great jazz collection. *Pl. Puerta Cerrada 6, tel. 91/365–34–19. Metro: Sol.*

Eucalipto. One of many funky bars in this area. You can drink a *mojito,* made with mint, white rum, and lemon, as you take in the African-Caribbean music. *C. Argumosa 4, no phone. Metro: Lavapiés.*

Galeria d'Arte. Like a posh garden stuck inside a warm, artsy café. Couples make out in corners, while groups drink up before hitting Joy Eslava (*see above*) around the corner. *C. Coloreros 5, tel. 91/356–35–19. Metro: Sol. Open daily 6 PM–midnight.*

Medina Magerit. Groovy, in the original sense of the word. Sip fancy coffees and unusual teas on couches in the smoky, dim, terribly hip back room or basement. Great music, pool tables, board games, lectures, poetry readings, and theater. *Divino Pastor 21, at C. Ruiz, tel. 91/594–37–51. Metro: Bilbao. Open daily 4 PM–3 AM.*

Siglo XIX. If you don't mind the stuffed boar and the model of a woman's breasts on the wall, get a cup of wine and a pickled egg for 80 ptas at this students' bar. *C. Noviciado, near C. San Bernardo, no tel.*

PUBS AND DISCOS **No Se Lo Digas a Nadie, Nadie, Nadie.** Opened by a women's collective, this eclectic café/disco/bar features a library, drag cabaret, pool table, and two bars. Where else could you read *Mujeres y la Revolución,* get drunk, eat, write a short story, and dance all night? *Ventura de la Vega 7, tel. 91/420–29–80. Metro: Sol. Open Mon. 8:30 AM–3:30 PM, Tues.–Sat. 8:30 AM– 3:30 PM and 8 PM–3 AM.*

La Habana. Dance to salsa (they even offer classes) with one of the more racially diverse crowds in Madrid. *C. San Vicente Ferrer 23, tel. 91/531–31–13. Metro: Tribunal or Bilbao. Open 11 PM–5 AM.*

No Te Prives. A women-only club in a city where this usually implies a male strip show—not so here. *C. Ancora 23, tel. 91/530–08–03. Metro: Palos de la Frontera. Open Tues.–Sun. 9 PM–2:30 AM.*

Montera 33. Packed with hot gay guys, this underground club is divided into many rooms, '80s British music filling them all. *Montera 33, tel. 91/523–03–61. Metro: Sol.*

La Rosa. This mixed disco welcomes all types. Good dancing music from '80s hits to techno, and, of course, Madonna. *Tetuán 27, no phone. Metro: Sol.*

El Jardin de las Delicias. A beautiful pub, replete with plants, sculptures, and big windows. A venue for everything from feminist jazz to rhythm and blues, Celtic folk, and funky blues. Shows begin at midnight. Drinks from 200 ptas. *Pl. Christino Martol 5, tel. 91/559–18–14. Metro: Pl. de España. Open until 3:30 AM.*

Stella. Get drunk and bowl to music. Mixed gay and straight crowd. *Arlabán 7, tel. 91/531–01–92. Metro: Sevilla. Closed Mon. night and Thurs.–Sun. afternoon.*

Near Madrid

The beauty of the historic cities surrounding Madrid and the role they have played in their country's history rank them among Spain's most worthwhile sights. Ancient Toledo (the former capital) the great palace-monastery of El Escorial, tranquil Cuenca, and elegant Segovia all lie within a few hours of the capital. If you have the time, these small towns are all worthy of extended visits.

EL ESCORIAL

The main attraction of El Escorial, an elegant town on the slopes of the Guadarrama Mountains, is the enormous **Real Monasterio de San Lorenzo de El Escorial.** El Escorial, as the monastery is referred to, was founded by Felipe II in the 16th century both to thank God for the Spanish victory over the French on the feast day of San Lorenzo, and to honor his father's (Carlos V's) wish that a pantheon be built to house his earthly remains and those of his descendants. It's a massive complex consisting not only of a functioning monastery and church, but also a school, library, royal palace, mausoleum, and museums. *Tel. 91/890–59–05. Admission: 750 ptas, 600 ptas students. Open Tues.–Sun. 10–7; tours 10–1:30 and 4–7.*

El Escorial is organized into two zones for your viewing pleasure. Zone A houses the biggest attractions. The **Museo de Pintura,** a dramatic collection of mostly 16th- to 18th-century paintings, displays primarily religious works by artists such as Tintoretto, José Ribera, Francisco Zurbarán, and El Greco. The **Royal Apartments** contain the usual old paintings, royal beds, and royal treasures, but their elegant decor and beautiful tiles give them a distinctively Spanish character. There are two parts to the mausoleum: the **Panteón de los Reyes,** a seductively creepy room containing the sarcophagi of all but two Spanish monarchs since Carlos V, and the **Panteón de los Infantes,** where those royalty who didn't make it to king- or queenhood, or adulthood, are enshrined. The **Sala Capitular** contains paintings by Ribera, two by El Greco, and, best of all, Bosch's triptych *La Creación* (The Creation). You can take a 45-minute guided tour through Zone A. Spanish-speaking tour guides often herd around as many as 300 people, so even if you understand the language, you may not see or hear all that much; if you can get together a group of 30, they'll give a tour in English.

Zone B consists of only two parts. The altar inside the **basilica** is amazing: A crucified Jesus, cast in gold, stands on top. The gray stone of the church walls makes the painted altar, flanked by gold statues, all the more gorgeous. The last thing you will need your ticket for is the **library,** filled with rare manuscripts, codices, ancient books, and a painted ceiling: In Tibaldi's representation of the seven liberal arts, Philosophia and Theologia face off at opposite ends of the room.

VISITOR INFORMATION *C. Floridablanca 10, tel. 91/890–15–54. Open weekdays 10–2 and 3–4:45, Sat. 10–1:45.*

COMING AND GOING Eight trains leave daily from Madrid for Avila, stopping in El Escorial (1 hr, 300 ptas). The **train station** (tel. 91/890–04–13) sits at the bottom of the hill; take Bus L-1 (10 min, 65 ptas) to get to the monastery from here. Buses leave about every half hour from Madrid (C. Fernández de los Rios, at Isaac Peral, tel. 91/543–36–45, Metro: Moncloa) and stop at Bar Cesino, near the monastery. The trip takes 50 minutes (330 ptas); buy your ticket as you board.

TOLEDO

Only an hour away from Madrid, Toledo rises high above the banks of the Tagus River, which practically surrounds the city, creating a sort of natural moat. The city's labyrinthine cobblestone streets and spire-filled skyline give it a magical appeal, though the thousands of tourists cruising through Toledo in unwieldy buses that barely fit through the narrow streets make it decidedly less attractive. But it will take more than a number of smog-spewing buses to bring down this little city on a hill. Roman strategic stronghold, site of the Visigoths' court, home to Muslims and Jews, capital of Christian Spain until 1561, and one-time location of Spain's main military outpost, Toledo wears the scars of its turbulent history beautifully; buildings and artifacts remain from all these periods. After elbowing your way through the crowds, you will happily come upon Mudéjar (Spanish Muslim) architecture, tiled doorways, and an occasional Toledano.

VISITOR INFORMATION The **tourist office** (tel. 925/22–98–43; open Mon.–Sat. 9–2 and 4–6) is just outside the Puerta de Bisagra. A satellite kiosk (tel. 925/22–14–00; open Mon.–Sat. 10–6, Sun. 10–3) is in Plaza de Zocódover, the main plaza. Toledo is small but not easy to navigate. Invest in a *plano callejero* (street map), sold at newsstands for 350 ptas.

COMING AND GOING Toledo's **train station** (Paseo de la Rosa, tel. 925/22–12–72) is just east of the city's main attractions, across the Río Tajo. Several daily trains leave for Madrid (1 hr 15 min, 465 ptas). Most go to Estación de Atocha, though a couple finish at Estación Chamartín. To get to the center of town from the station, walk 20 minutes uphill or take Bus 5 or 6 (70 ptas) from just to the left of the station to Plaza Zocódover.

Buses run between Toledo's **bus station** (Av. de Castilla-La Mancha, tel. 925/21–58–50) and Madrid's Estación Sur every half hour (1 hr, 510 ptas). Toledo's bus station is about a 15-minute walk south of the center of town, or a short ride on Bus 5 or 6.

WHERE TO SLEEP There are precious few budget accommodations here, but Toledo's still worth an overnight stay. Don't count on finding a cheap room without a written reservation in the height of the tourist season.

Fonda Segovia. Nine comfortable, plain rooms with big beds. Doubles 1,900 ptas, triples 2,700 ptas. *C. Recoletos 2, tel. 925/21–11–24. From C. Real del Arrabal, go up stairs and around corner.*

Hotel San Pedro. The best value in town. Recently renovated rooms right by the cathedral look over the city or the tiled courtyard. Restaurant downstairs dishes out home-cooked meals for 600 ptas. Singles 1,600 ptas, doubles 2,600 ptas, all with private bath. *Callejón de San Pedro 2, off C. Cardenal Cisneros, tel. 925/21–47–34.*

Pensión Virgen de la Estrella. Sterile and full of religious artifacts—probably not for unmarried couples or partyers. Singles 1,500 ptas, doubles 3,000 ptas. *C. Real del Arrabal 18, tel. 925/21–12–34. Right up from Puerta de Bisagra, 5 min down from Pl. Zocódover.*

➢ **HOSTEL • San Servando (HI).** You won't live like a king or queen in this medieval castle on the outskirts of town, sharing a room with five others, locked out from 10:30 to 5:30, and turned into a pumpkin at midnight. Still, it's pleasant and has a TV room and swimming pool. Only 48 beds, so come early or reserve ahead. Beds 775 ptas, 950 ptas 26 and over. *Tel. 925/22–45–54. From train station, go right (west) on Paseo de la Rosa, left at Puente de Alcántara bridge, and uphill toward castle. Midnight curfew, laundry.*

➢ **CAMPGROUND • Circo Romano.** Blackberry trees, patio restaurant-bar, tennis courts, a huge heated pool, and only a 15-minute walk from the center of Toledo. Sites 400 ptas–450 ptas plus 450 ptas per person. *Av. Carlos III 19, tel. 925/22–04–42. From Puerta de Bisagra, facing away from Toledo, make a left and turn onto Carlos III at the traffic circle.*

FOOD "But where do Toledanos eat?" "In their homes," said the woman at the tourist office. The pickings are slim, but you don't have to spend all your money if you have your big meal during the day and tapas for dinner. **El Coralito** (Corral de Don Diego 10, off Pl. Magdalena, tel. 925/21–50–24) has pungent, garlicky *boquerones* (sardines); a bocadillo with a *copa* (small glass) of sangria costs 500 ptas. On the main road between Plaza Zocódover and Puerta de Bisagra, **Restaurante Cafetería Bisagra** (C. Real del Arrabal 14) has combination plates for 375 ptas–800 ptas and a menú del día for 700 ptas. **La Abadia** (Pl. San Nicolás 3, tel. 925/25–47–06) is a café-bar-restaurant with lots of students and good German beer. In addition to the tapas (300 ptas–400 ptas) bar, there's a restaurant in back. Inside the **Mercado Municipal** (Pl. Mayor 2; open weekdays 8:30–2 and 4:30–7:30, Sat. 8:30–2) you can buy inexpensive bread, cheese, meat, fruit, and vegetables.

WORTH SEEING Toledo's art and architecture have been deeply influenced by the large Jewish and Muslim populations, as well as by El Greco, resident of Toledo during the Renaissance.

➢ **EL ALCAZAR •** Lording over Toledo and the surrounding region, this former fortress stands as a monument to Spain's onetime military and political glory. Despite such cheesy displays as a room filled with *photocopies* of important documents and military background music, this museum offers a fascinating glimpse into Spain's history and the sources of its national pride. The Alcázar was most recently trashed during the Civil War when the Republicans attacked the Nationalists who had barricaded themselves here with 100 left-wing hostages for 72 days. You can hear the dramatic telephone conversation between Nationalist General Moscardó (whose son had been taken hostage in Madrid) and the Republican representative reenacted in about 10 different languages. *Cuesta de Carlos V, tel. 925/22–30–38. Admission: 125 ptas. Open Tues.–Sat. 9:30–1:30 and 4–6:30, Sun. 10–1:30 and 4–6:30.*

➢ **CATEDRAL •** Since construction of this monument spanned from 1226 to around 1492, the cathedral is a hodgepodge of Gothic, Renaissance, and Mudéjar styles. In the middle of the ambulatory is a dizzying example of extravagant Baroque architecture known as the Transparente, a representation of angels reaching toward heaven, sometimes magically illuminated by light through a hole in the roof. The sacristy houses a kind of miniature Prado, featuring works by El Greco, Goya, Velázquez, Titian, Rafael, Zurbarán, and Caravaggio. *Enter at C. Arco de Palacio, off Pl. del Ayuntamiento. Admission: 300 ptas. Open daily 10:30–1 and 3:30–7, until 6 in winter.*

➢ **EL GRECO'S TOLEDO •** Toledo owes its fame, in part, to El Greco, a Greek artist of the late 16th and early 17th centuries who spent most of his life here. He is known for his paintings of religious subjects and for his distorted, elongated figures. The inspired, ecstatic visions he captured here have a contemporary relevance when viewed in Toledo—his mysterious clouds seem to be the same ones that still hang over the city. One of his most famous works, *El Entierro del Conde de Orgaz* (The Burial of the Count of Orgaz), is the only painting housed in the modest **Iglesia de Santo Tomé** (C. del Angel Santo Tomé; admission 100 ptas; open daily 10–1:45 and 3:30–6:45, shorter hrs off-season). Besides lots of bleeding Jesuses on crosses and some beautiful tapestries, the 16th-century church and hospital-cum-museum **Museo de Santa Cruz de Toledo** (C. Santa Fe, tel. 925/22–10–36; admission 200 ptas; open Mon. 10–2 and 4:30–6:30, Tues.–Fri. 10–6:30, Sat. 10–6:30, Sun. 10–2) contains an outstanding collection of El Greco.

For an amazing view of Toledo, cross the Tagus River and follow the Carretera de Circunvolación upward.

➤ **JEWISH TOLEDO** • Before the Spanish Inquisition, Toledo was home to Spain's largest and most prominent Jewish community. Today, only two of an estimated 10 synagogues remain. The strangely named **Sinagoga de Santa María la Blanca** (C. de los Reyes, at C. de la Judería; admission 100 ptas; open daily 10–2) was built in 1203 and was used as a synagogue until 1405, when it became a church. Inscriptions of IHS (for Jesus Christ), combined with Mudéjar architecture make this a most un-Jewish synagogue. The other synagogue, **El Tránsito** (C. de la Judería; open Tues.–Sat. 10–1:45 and 4–5:45, Sun. 10–1:45) was completed in 1357 and endured as a synagogue until 1492, after which it served various military units and causes. Today it is but a shell of an elegant synagogue, with mosaic work, tapestries, and delicate marble etchings of biblical quotations. At press time, they were planning to open a museum of Sephardic culture here.

➤ **MUSLIM TOLEDO** • Muslims defeated the Visigoths in the 8th century, ruling Toledo (as well as most of Iberia) until Alfonso IV took it for the Christians in 1085. The Muslims then became known as Mudéjars, "subjected ones." The Mudéjar's mosques were turned into churches, and when new churches had to be built, the Muslim architects continued to build in their traditional style, using simple materials to construct multiform, luxurious complexes. The Muslim influence on Toledo's architecture can be seen in the geometric tiles framing doorways, Mudéjar arches on street corners, and in the cathedral and the monastery **San Juan de los Reyes** (C. de los Reyes, off Pl. de San Juan de los Reyes; open daily 10–2 and 3:30–7, until 6 in winter). Only one wholly Muslim building remains, the beautiful 10th-century mosque now named **El Cristo de la Luz** (Callejón San José).

SEGOVIA

With its gorgeous late-Gothic cathedral, a Roman aqueduct that stretches from the walls of the old town to the lower slopes of the Sierra de Guadarrama, and beautiful buildings decorated with sculpted, geometric shapes, it's no wonder that so many tourists flock to Segovia. But Segovia maintains its identity and integrity in spite of it all, celebrating every Sunday with music, small parades, and dancing in the streets. Plaza Mayor houses the **oficina de turismo** (Pl. Mayor 10, tel. 911/43–03–28) as well as some elegant cafés.

COMING AND GOING The **train station** (tel. 911/43–66–66) dispatches about eight iron horses a day to Madrid (2 hrs, 650 ptas). Buses from the sleazy **bus station** (tel. 911/44–30–10) roll to Madrid (1½ hrs, 685 ptas) and Salamanca (3 hrs, 1,250 ptas). Both stations are in the newer part of Segovia, and the local buses (75 ptas) that stop in front of them end up at Plaza Mayor in the *centro histórico* (historic center). Otherwise, it's a 15- to 20-minute walk.

WHERE TO SLEEP AND EAT The quality and location of Segovia's budget hotels vary widely. The cheapest and most austere hostal, **Casa Huéspedes Aragon** (Pl. Mayor 4, tel. 911/43–35–27; doubles 2,300 ptas), sits in the middle of the nicest part of town. There's a de facto curfew, as the owner likes to go to bed at midnight. A block from Plaza Mayor, **Pensión Ferri** (C. Escuerdos 10, tel. 911/43–05–44) has much better rooms and cleaner bathrooms for the same price. Though more expensive, with doubles ranging from 2,500 ptas to 4,800 ptas, **Residencia Tagore** (C. Santa Isabel 11–13, tel. 911/42–00–35), a 10-minute walk from Plaza Mayor, is perhaps the best deal in Segovia. It's a kind of budget resort, with a pool, TV room, library, restaurant, and laundry facilities.

Restaurants in the centro histórico cater to tourists and are expensive; it's unusual to see a menú del día for less than 2,000 ptas. **Cueva de San Esteban** (C. Valdelaquila 15, tel. 911/43-78-11), though, dishes out food to Segovians at more reasonable prices; a menú is 800 ptas.

WORTH SEEING The last Gothic cathedral built in Spain, Segovia's **catedral** (open daily 9-6) has a sumptuous facade and a warm, golden interior illuminated by light streaming in through 16th-century Flemish windows. Entering the cathedral's museum and cloister costs 200 ptas.

Whether because of the unusually flashy Mudéjar ceiling, the mannequins behind the armored masks and breastplates, or the electric candelabras, there's something surreal about Segovia's Alcázar.

Since the 12th century, the **Alcázar** has served as a fortress, royal palace, military school, and as the original symbol of Segovia. So when it was gutted by fire in 1862, the city took pains to reconstruct it. What the Alcázar lacks in authenticity, it compensates for by indulging romantic myths of medieval knights and castles and by offering amazing views of seemingly endless plains. *Tel. 911/43-01-76. Admission: 350 ptas. Open daily 10-7, 10-6 in winter.*

Below the Alcázar and across the Río Eresma stand a clump of churches, all worth poking into if you've not already had enough. And even if you feel you have had enough, **Iglesia de la Vera Cruz** (admission 125 ptas; open Tues.–Sun, 10:30–1:30 and 3:30–7) is fascinating. Originally designed for the crusading Knights Templar, it was built to resemble the Church of the Holy Sepulcher in Jerusalem. If you're not claustrophobic or agoraphobic, and haven't started smoking a lot, climb to the top of the Mudéjar bell tower for a view of the Alcázar and surrounding plains.

Built in 1721 for the Bourbon king Felipe V, the perfectly symmetrical **Palacio Real de la Granja** and adjoining gardens are actually worthy of the epithet mini-Versailles. They rest on the northern slopes of the Guadarrama range in the town of La Granja de San Ildefonso, 11 km southeast of Segovia. The highlight of the palace is the tremendous tapestry room. The gardens are not as well-preserved as the royal palace, but they are set in the midst of a forest, and it's worth the short trek out here if only to picnic in the gardens; about 12 buses a day leave from the bus station (80 ptas). *Tel. 911/47-00-20. Admission to palace: 500 ptas, 400 ptas students. Open mid-June–Sept., Tues.–Sun. 10-6; Oct.–mid-June, Tues.–Sat. 10-1:30 and 3-5, Sun. 10-2.*

CUENCA

Set in a wild and rocky countryside cut with dramatic gorges, Cuenca features a number of worthwhile sights as well as a dramatic landscape. As you stand at the top of the *ciudad vieja* (old city), surrounded by deep canyons and the rivers Huécar and Júcar, with ruins, grand churches, and a Mudéjar tower unfolding below, it's hard not to be overcome by the dramatic tranquility of Cuenca. This is the place to come to relax after a hectic visit to Madrid.

Plaza Mayor, the charming central square of the ciudad vieja, is dominated by the 12th-century Gothic **catedral** (open weekdays 9-2 and 4-6, Sat. 9-2 and 4-9). The songs of birds nesting in the rafters can be heard below in Gothic and Renaissance chapels and at the golden altars. Around the corner and to the left as you exit the cathedral, the **Museo Diocesano** (admission 200 ptas; open Tues.–Fri. 11-2 and 4-6, Sat. 11-2 and 4-8, Sun. 11-2) at first seems like a rug shop, only the rugs are already worn, and bear representations of Jesus motioning you to come hither. Downstairs are two paintings by El Greco. Across the street, **Museo de Cuenca** (admission 200 ptas, students free; open Mon.–Sat. 10-2 and 4-7, Sun. 10-2) traces the city's history, emphasizing Cuenca's Roman period, the Visigoth conquest, and Arab architecture. Cuenca's most unique and celebrated museum is the completely modern **Museo de Arte Abstracto Español** (admission 200 ptas; open Tues.–Fri. 11-2 and 4-6, Sat. 11-2 and 4-8,

Sun. 11–2:30), featuring the works of the remarkable generation of Spanish abstract artists who grew up in the 1950s. The museum is in Cuenca's famed **Casas Colgadas** (Hanging Houses), built on steep rocks practically projecting over the town's eastern precipice. For more info, go to the **tourist office** (C. Palmacio Garcia 8, tel. 966/22–22–31), two blocks north of the bus and train stations (*see below*).

COMING AND GOING Cuenca is connected by train with Madrid's Estación de Atocha (3 hrs, 1,075 ptas) and by bus with Madrid's Estación Sur (2½ hrs, 1,170 ptas). From Cuenca's train (tel. 966/22–07–20) and bus (tel. 966/22–11–84) stations on the south edge of town, Buses 1, 2, and 7 zip up to Plaza Mayor for 60 ptas. Otherwise, it's a 15- to 20-minute uphill walk.

WHERE TO SLEEP AND EAT The only reason to spend more than 15 minutes in the *ciudad nueva* (new city) is to save a few hundred pesetas on food and lodging. Several budget hostales have installed themselves on Calle Ramón y Cajal, which starts across the street from the tourist office and turns into Calle las Torres. In the ciudad vieja, **Posada de San José** (C. Julián Romero 4, tel. 966/21–13–00), just up the hill from the cathedral, has large, classy rooms so nice that you'll want to unpack and stay for a while. The prices of the rooms vary widely; singles are 1,650 ptas–3,600 ptas, doubles 3,200 ptas–7,000 ptas, depending on the day of the week and the season. **Pensión Real** (C. Larga 39, tel. 966/22–99–77; doubles 3,500 ptas) has four lovely rooms at the peaceful top of Cuenca.

The best place to eat in Cuenca, **Mesón-Bar Tabanqueta** (Pl. Trabuco 13, tel. 966/21–12–90) offers excellent, freshly made tapas, low prices (menú del día 900 ptas), and a crazy view of the Júcar River. Though in a student dormitory, **UIMP** (Ronda de Julián Romero, 14, tel. 966/22–09–25) is an elegant *comedor* (dining room) overlooking the Huécar, and the menú de la casa (1,000 ptas) is one of the cheapest meals on the hill.

Old Castile

The name for the dominant language of Spain, Castellano, derives from the area known as Old Castile, encompassing Castile y León and cities such as Burgos, León Logroño, and Valladolid. The name Castile, in turn, derives from the many castle fortresses (*castillos*) built here on the dry plateaus to defend against the Moors who controlled almost all of Spain over a thousand years ago. This relatively small area north of Madrid is historically and sentimentally the cradle of modern, unified Spain, and it was here that the first successful organized resistance to the Muslims was achieved.

You are in the heart of "Spanish" Spain when visiting this region, where the militaristic, almost fanatical, Catholicism that would become Spain's hallmark was forged on these high plateaus known for their dry, scorching summers and bitter winters. One of Spain's national heroes and celebrated Moor-battlers, El Cid, hails from just outside Burgos. The national saint of Spain, St. James (subsequently dubbed Santiago Matamoros, or James the Moorslayer), also figures prominently in the region's history; his tomb in Galicia remains a popular stop for pilgrims on the Camino de Santiago route. The merging of such fervent religion with so much military might has resulted in some of the most impressive cathedrals in the land, especially in León, Burgos, and Salamanca.

Salamanca

Home of Spain's first university, Salamanca is a beautiful city perfect for serious study by day and enjoyment by night. One can't help being drawn into **Plaza Mayor,** the town's elegant square. Built between 1729 and 1755 under the guidance of Salamanca's favorite architect, Alberto Churriguera, it is dominated by the **ayuntamiento** (town hall). Here, one is struck by the weight of tradition and the liveliness of the people in Salamanca. On warm nights, Tunas, groups of young men dressed in traditional costume, sing and play the music that feeds the passion of the moment on warm nights in Plaza Mayor. The plaza's arches bear medallions depicting Spanish kings and other celebrated countrymen—look for them under the café awnings.

BASICS The **Oficina Regional de Turismo** (Pl. de España 39–41, tel. 923/26–85–71; open weekdays 9:30–2 and 4:30–7, Sat. 10–2, Sun. 11–2) specializes in information on the region, the **Oficina Municipal de Turismo** (Pl. Mayor 10, tel. 923/21–83–42; open weekdays 10–1:30 and 4–6, Sat. 10–2) in info on the city. Though more expensive, the privately owned **locutorio** (Rua Mayor 39, Escalera 3; open daily 10 AM–11:15 PM) is a little more conveniently located than the **Telefónica** (Pl. Peña Primera 1; open Mon.–Sat. 9–3 and 4–11). The main post office, **Correos y Telégrafos** (Gran Vía 25, tel. 923/24–30–11; open weekdays 9–2 and 4–6, Sat. 9–2; postal code 37008), holds mail.

COMING AND GOING The **train station** (tel. 923/22–57–42) sits on the north end of town. From here you can go directly to Avila (2 hrs, 620 ptas); Madrid (4 hrs, 1,230 ptas); Barcelona (14 hrs, 6,000 ptas); and Paris (16 hrs, 11,000 ptas). Bus L1 will take you from the station to Plaza del Mercado, adjoining Plaza Mayor, or turn left as you leave the station and it's a 25-minute walk. For ticket purchase and general info, there's a **RENFE office** (Pl. de la Libertad 10, tel. 923/21–24–54; open weekdays 9–2 and 5–7) just southwest of Plaza Mayor.

In most cases, it's much faster to take the bus in and out of Salamanca. The **bus station** (Filoberto Villalobos 71, tel. 923/23–67–17) is a 25-minute walk south of Plaza Mayor. Otherwise, take Bus L4 to Plaza de España and walk for 10 minutes up Calle Toro. Buses travel to Avila (1¼ hrs, 740 ptas); Madrid (2½ hrs, 1,910 ptas); and Barcelona (13½ hrs, 5700 ptas).

GETTING AROUND Plaza Mayor is at the heart of Salamanca. The university and most other sights lie to the south, toward the Río Tormes. Gran Vía, a boulevard loaded with great bars, runs along the modern part of the city to the north. You can rent bikes for 600 ptas a day at **Alguilar de Bicicletas** (C. Peña Primera 19, bet. Pl. Mayor and Pl. de la Fuente, tel. 923/21–91–09).

WHERE TO SLEEP A popular destination for young, budget travelers, Salamanca has numerous places in which to find shelter. The best place to start looking is around Plaza Mayor and on Rua Mayor, Calle Meléndez, and their side streets.

Fonda San José. Cheap and decent rooms. Reserve in advance and you might be able to get a double for 1,600 ptas, normally 2,000 ptas. *C. Jesus 24, off Rua Mayor, tel. 923/21–27–24.*

Pensión Las Vegas. Though occupied by students during the year, this pension's bright rooms are the best deal you'll find in summer. Doubles 2000 ptas. *C. Meléndez 13, tel. 923/21–87–49.*

Pensión Madrid. Nice, clean, and allows you look out on Plaza Mayor without paying 300 ptas for a soda at a café. Singles 1,695 ptas, doubles 2,650 ptas. *C. Toro 1, tel. 923/21–42–96.*

Pensión Mary. With windowed and spacious singles for 1,300 ptas, a one-person closet for 1,000 ptas, and lovely doubles for 2,000 ptas, this is one of the best values in Salamanca. *C. Doctrinos 4–6, off C. Iscar Peyra, tel. 923/21–86–38.*

FOOD Salamanca's many colleges serve tapas at what seem like subsidized prices. **Hospedería de Anaya** (Pl. Anaya) is especially great; eat in the brick-and-mortar cellar or out on the patio. Combination plates are all under 425 ptas, and coffee is a mere 60 ptas. **Le Mans Cervecería** (C. Sánchez Barbero 13, at Rua Mayor) is the perfect place to assuage that late-night hunger. Try grilled sandwich #18 (350 ptas). Salamanca has a great **indoor market** (open weekdays 9–2) in Plaza del Mercado, right past the east arch of Plaza Mayor.

Bambu. This very popular basement bar serves good tapas. Comedor in back has a menú del día for 850 ptas. *C. del Prior 7, off west side of Pl. Mayor, tel. 923/26–00–92.*

Mesón de Cervantes. Overlooking Plaza Mayor, but its cozy atmosphere and down-to-earth prices make it anything but touristy. Combination plates under 600 ptas. Outside seating is about 200 ptas more and worth it. *Pl. Mayor 15, tel. 923/21–72–13.*

Plus Ultra. Serves elaborate *pinchos* (like tapas, but generally smaller), like the one with tuna, lemon, artichoke, mayo, anchovies, and an olive on a toothpick. Two big tapas and wine 350 ptas. Combination plates 400 ptas–600 ptas. *C. del Consejo 4, off Pl. Mayor, tel. 923/21–72–11.*

El Trigal. Serves all the vegetarian staples plus a large selection of Spanish food that you can relish without fear of lard or little pieces of chorizo. Meals 700 ptas. *C. Libreros 20, tel. 923/21–56–99.*

WORTH SEEING All over town gorgeous Plateresque buildings stand embellished with patterns both playful and profound. Plateresque architecture, popular in the 16th century, got its name from the word *platero* (silversmith), and was based on Italian Renaissance forms, with some Gothic and Moorish designs thrown in for good measure.

➤ **UNIVERSIDAD** • Though the reputation of this great university, founded in the 13th century, has declined—attributed to sacking by the French during the Spanish War of Independence, general 19th-century decadence, and Nationalist repression—its mystique persists, in no small part because of its beautiful Plateresque buildings. Somewhere on the intricate facade of the main building is a little frog on top of a skull; if you find it without help, you'll be married within a year, or do well on your exam, or something of the like. The lecture hall, **Sala de Fray Luis de León,** looks the same as it did when León coolly returned after five years of Inquisition torture with the words "as we were saying yesterday." In the **Escuelas Menores** on the other side of the patio by the same name, the **Sala de Exhibitiones** holds various exhibits, and the **Museo de la Universidad** contains the 15th-century fresco *El Cielo de Salamanca* (The Sky of Salamanca). *C. de Libreros. Admission: 200 ptas. Open weekdays 9:30–1:30 and 4–6:30, until 6 in winter; Sat. 9:30–1:30 and 4:30–6; Sun. 10–1.*

➤ **CATEDRAL** • When Salamanca's 12th-century Romanesque cathedral became too small for the town's growing population in the 16th century, the **Catedral Nueva** (New Cathedral) was added on. The Gothic facade is unbelievably grand, but the golden stone inside makes this a uniquely warm cathedral. The adjacent **Catedral Vieja** (Old Cathedral; admission 200 ptas; open Apr.–Sept., daily 10–2 and 4–8, shorter hrs off-season) is much smaller and less ornate, which makes the amazing paintings and altarpiece stand out even more. *Pl. de Anaya, next to the university.*

Check out the columns up on the balcony of the Convento de las Dueñas. They're decorated in such a way that as you walk by, children's faces turn to skulls, men become birds, and horses become dragons.

➤ **CONVENTO DE SAN ESTEBAN** • The 16th-century Plateresque west facade of this church might be the most fabulous in Salamanca. The altar inside, a Baroque masterpiece by José Churriguerra, answers the question: "What did they do with all that gold from America?" The monks of San Esteban were among the first to support Columbus. *At south end of Gran Vía, tel. 923/21–50–00. Admission: 150 ptas. Open daily 9–1 and 4–8.*

Across the street from San Esteban, you'll find the Dominican **Convento de las Dueñas,** founded in 1419. The 16th-century Plateresque cloister is a bit disconcerting; the lines and angles are uneven and it has five sides. On your way out, you can buy sweets from the nuns. *Tel. 923/21–54–42. Admission: 150 ptas. Open daily 9–1 and 4–8.*

CLERECIA The headquarters of the Pontifical University, this church combines Baroque lavishness with Herrerian austerity, making it suitable for reflecting on faith and dogma. Signs inside the building honor academics for defending the principle of the Immaculate Conception in the 17th century, and the posted curriculums prove that this remains a place of classical and religious study. It seems as though modernity has not entered these halls; walking through them, you just might get the feeling that God is in heaven, and the empire is doing well. *C. San Isidro, off Rua Mayor.*

The **Casa de las Conchas** (House of Shells), across the street, was constructed by Dr. Rodrigo Maldonado around 1500. It's embellished with hundreds of sculpted-stone shells; when he built it, he had recently been made chancellor of the Order of Santiago, whose symbol is the shell.

AFTER DARK Salamanca's nightlife hops year-round, though in summer you have to make an effort to avoid big groups of Americans. Two ways to do this are to go to pubs that play Spanish music (like **Karaoke** at C. Teresa 21) and to stay out really late. Partying Salamanca-style means hanging out in Plaza Mayor until about 1 AM, where you can collect coupons for free drinks at some of the lamer bars. **Chupatería** (Pl. de Monterrey 6) is a good place to load up on 125-ptas tequila shots before moving on. Many of Salamanca's most entertaining bars clear away chairs in the early morning to become de facto discos, like the neoclassical **Cum Laude** (C. Prior 6) and **Santa Bárbara** (C. Boraderos 4). You can start dancing earlier at the ever-popular, medieval-style **Camelot** (C. Boraderos 3) or at the medieval-cum-Polynesian **Morgana** (C. Iscar Peyra 34). **Cafe La Polémic** (Pl. de la Fuente 5) is one of several excellent bars on Plaza de la Fuente.

Burgos

This city in the valley of the Arlanzón River was once the home of the Counts of Castile, making it the Cabeza de Castile (Head of Castile) and therefore a pretty happening place. It was the center of Spain long before Madrid had any pretensions of greatness, and there is still a feeling of importance here, even though its glory days were over a good 400 years ago. Reminders of Burgos's past splendor are very much in evidence; its Gothic cathedral is truly amazing. Filled with impressive stone buildings, graceful squares, and a river with weeping willows and swaying grass on its banks, Burgos is a restful, worthwhile stop on the way north from Madrid.

BASICS There are two tourist offices just east of the cathedral up Calle Lain Calvo. The more on-the-ball one is the **Oficina de Turismo de Castilla y León** (Pl. Alonso Martínez 7, tel. 947/20–31–25; open weekdays 9–2 and 4:30–6:30, Sat. 10–1:30). The second office (C. San Carlos 1, tel. 947/20–89–60; open Mon.–Sat. 10–2 and 5–8) is just down the road from here. The **TIVE** office (Pl. San Juan, tel. 947/20–98–81; open weekdays 9–2), distributing hostel cards and advice on cheap travel, is near Iglesia de San Lesmes, in the Casa de Cultura. The **Correos** (Pl. del Conde de Castro 1, tel. 947/26–27–50; postal code 09080) faces the river at Puente de San Pablo. The **Telefónica** (C. San Lesmes 18) is just off Plaza España.

Burgos was home to one of Spain's greatest heroes, the Moor-slaying El Cid. There's a statue of El Cid in the Plaza General Primo de Rivera—he's either pointing grandly toward the sea of infidels he's about to mow down, or simply pointing the way across the bridge to the post office.

COMING AND GOING The **RENFE** station (Pl. de la Estación, tel. 947/20–35–60) is a 10-minute walk west of the town center and budget lodging. Trains zip to Madrid (4 hrs, 2,200 ptas–2,700 ptas), León (1,400 ptas), Pamplona (1,800 ptas), San Sebastián (2,500 ptas), and Barcelona (5,000 ptas). You'll find a handy RENFE office (C. Moneda 21, tel. 947/20–91–31; open weekdays 9–1 and 4:30–7:30, Sat. 9:30–1:30) off Plaza Primo de Rivera.

The **bus station** (C. Miranda 4, tel. 947/26–55–65) is centrally located just off Plaza de Vega. Buses head to Barcelona (4,450 ptas), Madrid (1,680 ptas), San Sebastián (1,600 ptas), and León (1,530 ptas).

GETTING AROUND Burgos is split in half by the lovely **Río Arlanzón.** The cathedral and surrounding old town are on the north side, and the bus and train stations are in the newer area on the south. As you exit the train station, walk straight up Conde de Guadalhorce to the river, then head right until you get to the **Puente de Santa María.** Cross it to reach the cathedral, or head right onto Plaza de Vega for cheap lodging possibilities. The only time you'll need to use the bus is to reach the hostel or the monastery of Cartuja de Miraflores (*see below*), 3½ km from the city center. Bus tickets cost 65 ptas, and most buses stop at either Plaza Primo de Rivera or Plaza España.

WHERE TO SLEEP AND EAT You should have no problems finding good, inexpensive lodging here. Check around Plaza de Vega on the south side of the river and the streets leading off to the east of Plaza Mayor (shown on some maps as Plaza José Antonio) near the cathedral. **Pensión Paloma** (C. La Paloma 39, tel. 947/27–65–74; doubles 2,400 ptas, 3,200 ptas in summer), right next to the cathedral, has large rooms with wood armoires. **Pensión Boston** (C. San Pablo 13, tel. 947/26–13–14), near the bus station, has spacious, bright rooms for 2,800 ptas. To get to the hostel **Albergue Juvenil Gil de Siloé** (Av. General Vigón, tel. 947/22–03–62), take Bus "Río Vena" from Plaza España to the stop on Calle Sagrada Familia just before Avenida General Vigón; the hostel will be a short walk to your right. There's a dandy wooded campsite about 3½ km east of town along the river at **Camping Fuentes Blancas** (tel. 947/22–10–16; 425 ptas per person, 375 ptas per tent; closed Oct.–Mar.). To get here take Bus "Fuentes Blancas" from Plaza Primo de Rivera.

The budget restaurants generally don't stray too far from the cheap hotels; the best hunting ground is in and around the squares near the cathedral, an area known as Las Llanas. A great spot for cheap bocadillos (150 ptas–275 ptas) and raciones (400 ptas–500 ptas) is **Bar Espejos** (C. Cardenal Segura 11, tel. 947/26–07–36; closed Aug.), where everyone packs in elbow-to-elbow at the bar to eat the bocadillos served up by the athletic barmen. For a treat, go to **Ristorante Prego** (C. Huerto del Rey 4, tel. 947/26–04–47), a cozy Italian place serving lots of vegetarian options. The best place for tapas is **Meson de Los Herreros** (C. San Lorenzo 20, off Pl. Mayor, tel. 947/20–24–48), where the long bar is lined with everything from the usual tortilla to the unusual innards and gizzards. For buying your own supplies, head to either **Mercado de Municipal de Abastos** (open Mon.–Sat. 7:30–3), half a block from the bus station, or **Mercado Norte** (open Mon.–Thurs. and Sat. 7:30–3, Fri. 5:30–8), just off Plaza España. In the drinking and nightlife department, join every other young person in town and go cruise around **Las Llanas,** centered around Plaza Huerto del Rey. The packed bars and discos disgorge merrymakers into the squares, and teeny-boppers flirt on the benches. The comfy couches and dim lighting of **Oliver** (C. de la Llana de Afuera 11, tel. 947/20–90–07) make it a fave spot for young couples to cuddle. Calle Fernán González, just behind the Plaza Huerto del Rey, is home to some heavier, industrial bars, if that's your thing.

WORTH SEEING Burgos's attractions derive mostly from its long history as the Cabeza de Castile and as a key pit stop along the Camino de Santiago (the religious pilgrims' route to Santiago de Compostela). For evidence of the former, pass by the impressive 15th-century stone mansion **Casa del Cordón** (C. Santander), where Columbus was patted on the back by the Catholic monarchs Ferdinand and Isabella on his return from his second American expedition. Pilgrim stops included two fine monasteries just outside town (*see below*), and Burgos's cathedral (*see below*), all housing mind-boggling displays of wealth.

➤ **CATEDRAL** • Begun in 1221, Burgos's cathedral is an absolute masterpiece of Gothic design, both inside and out. Its many chapels overflow with incredible treasures, including ornate works by Diego de Siloé. Tours show off all these treasures and include entry into the *coro* (choir), a look at the tomb of El Cid and his wife Ximena, and a museum hoarding even more goodies. Be sure to check out the highly morbid representation of the Crucifixion in the first chapel to the right of the main entrance; the Christ figure has real human hair and nails and is covered in leathery animal skin complete with grisly wounds. *Pl. de Santa María, tel. 947/20–47–12. Admission to museum and chapels: 350 ptas, 200 ptas students. Open daily 9:30–1 and 4–7.*

➤ **MONASTERIO DE LAS HUELGAS** • Founded in 1187, this was once the cream of the crop as far as convents go, housing the virginal daughters of some of Spain's wealthiest families. The treasures inside are appropriately elaborate, and the abbey boasts both a Gothic cloister containing gorgeous Mudéjar designs on the ceilings and a Romanesque cloister with lovely rose gardens and a fountain. The main church houses tombs of Castilian royalty, along with rich *retablos* (retables) and tapestries. Unfortunately, entry to the cloisters and main hall is only possible by way of an obligatory tour in rapid-fire Spanish, and the works themselves are very poorly marked. *Tel. 947/20–16–30. Take Bus "Barrio del Pilar" from Plaza Primo de Rivera or walk 20 min west along the river. Admission: 400 ptas, 150 ptas students, Wed. free. Open Mon.–Sat. 11–1:15 and 4–5:15, Sun. 11–1:15.*

➤ **CARTUJA DE MIRAFLORES** • This Gothic monastery still in use was commissioned by Isabella la Católica to house the remains of her parents, Juan II and Isabel of Portugal. The designer of the exquisitely carved, star-shaped sepulchre, Gil de Siloé, also designed the dizzying retablo, gilding it with the first gold plundered from the Americas. To get here, it's a wonderful 45-minute (3½ km) walk east along the river on Paseo de La Quinta, or you can take the Bus "Fuentas Blancas" to the campground nearby; it's about a 10-minute walk up the hill from here. *Open Mon.–Sat. 10:15–3:15 and 4–6, Sun. 11:20–12:30, 1–3, and 4–6.*

León

The midsize city of León has a dignified feel to it, perhaps a legacy of the city's former glory years as the Christian capital of Spain. Even if the city is not as powerful as it once was, the cathedral still stands as evidence of León's former greatness. The cathedral dominates the pleasantly lived-in maze of streets in the old town, while the newer part heading toward the River Bernesga to the west has the modernity and sophistication of a larger city.

The once-powerful Kingdom of León eventually succumbed to the greater might of the Kingdom of Castile, and now the two are grouped under the title Autonomy of Castile and León. Apparently, there are those who resent the regional title; graffiti on city walls demands "León Solo" (León Alone).

BASICS The **oficina de turismo** (Pl. de Regla 3, tel. 987/23–70–82; open daily 10–1 and 4–8, shorter hrs off-season) faces the cathedral. The **TIVE** office (Conde Guillén 2, tel. 987/20–09–51; open Mon.–Sat. 9–2) is just off Avenida de la República Argentina. **Nouvelles Frontieres** (C. Burgo Nuevo 14, tel. 987/26–09–90) is a travel agency specializing in cheap deals. Stamps and Lista de Correos service are available at the **post office** (Jardin de San Francisco, tel. 987/23–42–90; postal code 24080) weekdays 9–9 and Saturday 9–2. The **Telefónica** (open weekdays 9–2:30 and 4–10:30, Sat. 9–2 and 4–9) is on Calle Burgo Nuevo just past Plaza Cortes.

COMING AND GOING León is well served by bus and train. Both stations are on the west side of the Río Bernesga. From the center of town, walk straight down Avenida de Ordoño II, and cross the bridge at Avenida de Palencia to the train station; the bus station is a five-minute walk south along the river from there.

The **RENFE station** (tel. 987/27–02–02) sends trains to Madrid (5 hrs, 2,480 ptas), Burgos (2½ hrs, 1,500 ptas), Oviedo (2 hrs, 670 ptas), and Barcelona (10 hrs, 5,800 ptas). From the train station, Bus 4 will take you to Plaza de Santo Domingo, where you can catch Bus 8 to the hostel.

Several different companies operate from the **bus station** (Paseo del Ingeniero Sáenz de Miera, tel. 987/21–10–00). **ALSA** (tel. 987/20–47–52) heads to Burgos (1,600 ptas), Oviedo (900 ptas), and Sevilla (4,400 ptas). **Fernandez** (tel. 987/22–62–00) goes to Madrid (2,225 ptas) and, June–September, to Santander (1,975 ptas).

WHERE TO SLEEP Finding cheap lodging in León is not a problem. Just over the bridge heading away from the train station you'll find many hostales along Avenida de Roma and on Avenida de Ordoño II and its side streets. During the school year the large, well-kept rooms at **Hostal Espanya** (C. Carmen 3, off Av. de Ordoño II, tel. 987/26–60–14; doubles 2,200 ptas) are usually full of students, but in the summer you'll receive a warm welcome. **Hostal Oviedo** (Av. de Roma 26, tel. 987/22–22–36) is a friendly, family-run place with slightly dark but clean doubles for 2,500 ptas. If they're full, **Hostal Europa** just downstairs has rooms for the same price. Two hostels, both charging 750 ptas, 1,000 ptas for those 26 and over, lie slightly to the south of the city center. Of these, the better option is **HI Residencia Juvenil Infanta Doña Sancha** (C. Corredera 2, tel. 987/20–34–14; closed Sept.–June), a five-minute walk south of the post office off Jardín San Francisco. If you continue south down this street to the other side of the Plaza de Toros you'll come to hostel **Consejo de Europa** (Paseo Parque 2, tel. 987/20–02–06; closed Sept.–June); it's popular with groups of school children. Bus 8 from Plaza Santo Domingo swings by both hostels.

FOOD The liveliest areas for food and drink are around Plaza Mayor and Plaza San Martín and the small streets connecting them, as well as along Calle del Cid on the north side of Avenida Generalisimo Franco. **Pizzería Rocco** (Pl. San Martín, tel. 987/20–13–27; closed Mon. and Tues. lunch) is a great spot to check out the scene on the plaza from outdoor tables while enjoying salads and pastas in the 450 ptas–700 ptas range. Next door at **Bar Chivani,** the whistling proprietor will set you up with fried calamari or sardines for 200 ptas–300 ptas. After 11 PM, the streets of Plaza San Martín are flooded with young people spilling out of the many bars in the area. A happening student bar that serves up beer for 150 ptas and hosts live jazz and blues is **El Gran Café** (C. del Cid near Pl. de Omaña).

Don't miss the elaborate depiction of the Last Judgment on the facade of the cathedral, where unfortunates are depicted being eaten alive and submerged into boiling pots with gruesome detail.

WORTH SEEING The metal casts of scallop shells (the pilgrim's official symbol) embedded in the streets all over town reflect León's status as an important stop on the Camino de Santiago.

➤ **CATEDRAL** • This 13th- to 14th-century Gothic masterpiece is arguably one of the most beautiful in all of Spain, thanks chiefly to its famous stained-glass windows lining nearly every wall. The windows rival those found in the cathedrals in France, which influenced their design. Try to visit at different times of day so you can see the sun penetrating the windows of electric colors at all angles. You can enter the **cloister** and a **museum** (admission 300 ptas; open weekdays 9:30–1:30 and 4–7, Sat. 9:30–1:30), containing sculptures from the 5th to 8th centuries and a collection of ivory crucifixes, by taking a guided tour. *Pl. de la Regla. Admission to cathedral free. Open daily 8:30–2 and 4–7:30.*

➤ **BASILICA DE SAN ISIDORO AND EL PANTEON REAL** • This Romanesque church containing the remains of San Isidoro dates from the 12th century, while the impressive Pantheon of Kings contained within is one of the oldest Romanesque constructions in Spain, built between 1054 and 1063 to contain the tombs of Fernando I and Doña Sancha. A guided tour takes you into the Pantheon, well-preserved 10th-century painted ceilings, including scenes depicting the nine mysteries of the life of Christ. There's also a treasury and library containing exquisite reliquaries, coffers, and chalices, and moldy, rotting manuscripts. *Pl. de San Isidoro. Admission: 300 ptas. Open Mon.–Sat. 9–2 and 3–8, Sun. 9–2.*

➤ **MONASTERIO DE SAN MARCOS** • Originally founded in the 12th century for the Knights of St. James who protected pilgrims on the often perilous journey to Santiago, the building now boasts an ornate Plateresque facade and a Baroque relief of St. James (depicting him on horseback in Moor-slaying mode) added much later. Inside there's a **museum** with an eclectic collection of works dating from the 1st to the 17th centuries, including the famous 11th-century Cristo de Monasterio de Carrizo, an ivory crucifix with penetrating black eyes and strangely proportioned limbs. The monastery next door has been converted to a five-star *parador* (state-run hotel), one of the most expensive in all of Spain. There's a swank café adjoining the lobby if you want to have a drink and pretend you're staying here. *Pl. San Marcos. Admission: 200 ptas. Open Tues.–Sat. 10–2 and 5–7:30, Sun. 10–2.*

Andalucía

Andalucía, the province that borders Portugal on the west and the Atlantic to the south, has been enormously influenced by its neighbors across the sea in North Africa. Arabs from the south took this fertile land in the Middle Ages, and by the end of the 7th century, the Moorish caliphate of Al-Andalus was flourishing. Countless palaces and mosques sprung up in Al-Andalus, and in battle after battle the region acquired more territory. By the 12th century, though, the tide had turned and Christian knights flocked to Al-Andalus to rid the area of the enemies of Christiandom. By the 15th century, the Moors were completely removed, leaving only their tremendous architecture—bridges, castles, palaces, and mosques—as evidence that the civilization here was among the richest and most powerful anywhere. And, try as they might, the Christian conquerors never could surpass the beauty of the Moorish granite edifices of peaks and swoops and elaborate ornamentation.

Sevilla

If you stay in Sevilla long enough, you just might pick up the infectious good humor and casual attitude of its residents and never want to leave. The city's history is so rich that the departure of Christopher Columbus on his voyage in 1492 seems only a footnote, and its awe-inspiring beauty makes it a must-see city, even for visitors who hadn't planned on spending much time in Spain. The swinging nightlife in this city stems partly from the blazing heat (in midsummer it doesn't begin to cool down until midnight), and partly from the number of university students who live here.

BASICS

VISITOR INFORMATION The **oficina de turismo** is two blocks south of the cathedral. *Av. de la Constitución 21B, tel. 95/422–14–04. Open weekdays 9:30–7:30, Sat.10–2; closed Sat. off-season.*

AMERICAN EXPRESS In addition to the regular cardholder services, this office offers an Express Cash machine and a travel agency. *Viajes Alhambra, C. Teniente Coronel Seguí 6, tel. 95/422–44–35 or 95/421–29–23. 1 block north of Pl. Nueva. Open weekdays 9:30–1:30 and 4:30–8, Sat. 9:30–1.*

BUCKET SHOP **Wasteels** sells their under-26 international train tickets at the kiosk inside Santa Justa station. *Tel. 95/442–50–65. Open weekdays 9:30–2 and 5–8, Sat. 9:30–1:30; closed Sat. off-season.*

CHANGING MONEY The best rates and lowest commission charges are at the kiosk inside Santa Justa train station and at **Banco Español de Crédito** (Av. de la Constitución 30).

CONSULATES **Canada.** *Av. de la Constitución 30, 2nd floor, tel. 95/422–94–13. Open weekdays 10–2.*

Great Britain. *Pl. Nueva 8B, tel. 95/422–88–75. Open weekdays 9–2.*

United States. *Paseo de las Delicias 7, tel. 95/423–18–83 or 95/423–18–85. Open weekdays 10–1.*

PHONES AND MAIL **Telefónica.** *Pl. de la Gavidia, tel. 95/456–07–68. Open Mon.–Sat. 10–2 and 5:30–10.*

Correos. *Av. de la Constitución 32, across from cathedral, tel. 95/421–95–85. Open weekdays 8 AM–9 PM and Sat. 9–2. Postal code 41001.*

COMING AND GOING

BY TRAIN Sevilla is the rail hub for southwestern Spain, but Sevilla's **Estación de Santa Justa** (tel. 95/441–41–1) is more than 3 km from the downtown area. Take Bus 27 to Plaza de la Encarnación in the center of town. High-speed AVE trains travel to Sevilla from Madrid's Estación de Atocha (2½ hrs, 6,000 ptas). and from Córdoba (55 min, 1,700 ptas).

BY BUS Two bus stations serve Sevilla's numerous companies: Most intercity buses use the **Estación Central de Autobuses** (tel. 95/441–71–11) at Prado de San Sebastián, but those bound for Badajoz and Huelva use **Estación de Autobuses Damas** (no tel.) along the river. The major companies are Sevibus (tel. 95/453–87–00), Linesur-La Valenciana (tel. 95/411–14–19), Alsina Graells (tel. 95/441–88–11), Benisa (tel. 95/441–46–60), Los Amarillos (tel. 95/441–52–01), Leda (tel. 95/441–43–58), and Comes (tel. 95/441–68–58).

BY PLANE San Pablo International Airport (tel. 95/451–61–11), about 15 km from the city center, has regular flights to most large European airports. Iberia (tel. 95/451–06–77), Alitalia (tel. 95/425–50–50), Air France (95/456–97–00), and Lufthansa (tel. 95/425–50–50) serve the airport. There is no public transportation from the airport to town, so be prepared to pay about 1,500 ptas for a taxi.

GETTING AROUND

No doubt about it, Sevilla is a huge city. Nearly a third of Andalucía's residents call this city home. Although very large, the city is walkable, and even seems to promote pedestrianism with its dozens of tiny lanes. The heart of the city, centered around the cathedral, on **Avenida de la Constitución,** lies to the east of the Guadalquivir River.

Tussam (tel. 95/441–11–52) local buses can get you anywhere in the city for 100 ptas; a Bonobus ticket good for 10 rides is sold at tobacco shops for 595 ptas. Buses run from about 6 AM to midnight, when special night service begins. The oficina de turismo office gives out free maps that show every route in town. Most buses stop at **Plaza Nueva,** at the north end of Avenida de la Constitución and/or **Plaza Encarnación,** about seven blocks northeast of Plaza Nueva.

WHERE TO SLEEP

The only time you'll face stiff competition in finding a cheap room will be during Sevilla's popular festivals (*see below*). There are dozens of cheap pensions and hostales in the neighborhoods north and west of Plaza Nueva; most doubles here cost about 3,000 ptas.

➢ **UNDER 3,500 PTAS** • **Hostal Alvarez Quintero.** It's central, but noisy buses pass by until 11:30 PM. A French-style building with huge doors, blue and white tile everywhere, antique beds, fancy armoires. Run by a cool family. Singles 2,000 ptas, doubles 3,000 ptas. *C. Compañia 1, in Pl. de la Encarnación, tel. 95/421–16–40.*

Hostal Monreal. In a noisy neighborhood of bars and clubs. Singles 2,000 ptas, doubles 3,000 ptas. *C. Rodrigo Caro 8, tel. 95/421–41–66. 2 blocks east of Pl. del Triunfo and up the stairs.*

Hostal Nuevo Suizo. Hidden on a small side street near a main shopping district, it resembles a 19th-century French apartment building. Very clean. Singles 2,000 ptas, doubles 3,000 ptas; prices shoot up late-July through August. *C. Azofaifo 7, tel. 95/422–91–47 or 95/421–36–58.*

Hostal Regi. A big heavy door, no sign, typical tiled patio with hanging plants, small lounge area, amiable owner. Only 1,500 ptas per person. *C. Carlos Cañal 42, tel. 95/421–57–64.*

➢ **UNDER 4,000 PTAS** • **Hostal Residencia Central.** Relatively modern building. Sunny, nice-smelling rooms. Singles 2,000 ptas, doubles 4,000 ptas. *C. Zaragoza 18, tel. 95/421–76–60.*

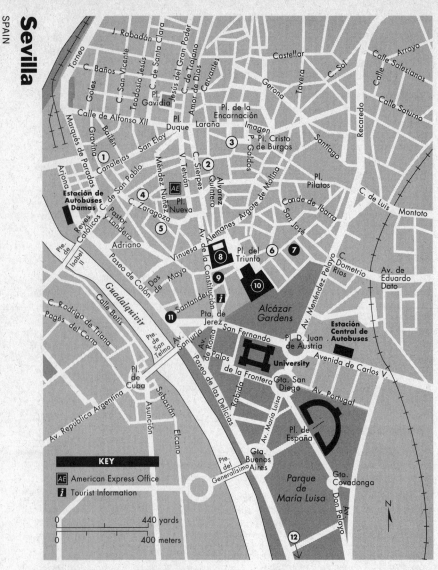

J. Rabadán
C. Baños
Torneo
Goles
C. San Vicente
Gravina
Bailén
Marqués de Paradas
Ariona
Calle de Alfonso XII
Teodosio Jesús
C. de Santa Clara
Jesús del Gran Poder
C. de Trajano
Amor de Dios
Cervantes
Castellar
Gerona
Tavera
Santiago
C. Sol
Calle Salesianas
Calle
Calle Saturno
Recaredo
Arroyo

Pl. Gavidia
San Eloy
Canalejas
Pl. Duque
Laraña
Pl. de la Encarnación
Imagen
P. Galdos
Pl. Cristo de Burgos
①
②
③
Reyes Católicos
San Pablo
C. Y Landero
Méndez Núñez
C. Sierpes
V. Tetuán
Álvarez Quintero
Argote de Molina
Pl. Pilatos
C. de Luis
Montoto

Estación de Autobuses Damas
④
C. Pastor
C. Zaragoza
AE
Pl. Nueva
⑤
Adriano
Conde de Ibarra
San José
Av. de Alemanes
Av. de la Constitución
Vinuesa
Dos de Mayo
Pl. del Triunfo
⑥ ⑦
⑧
⑨
i
⑩
Alcázar Gardens
Menéndez Pelayo
C. Dometrio Ríos
Av. de Eduardo Dato

Guadalquivir
C. Rodrigo de Triana
Calle Betis
Pagés del Corro
Pte. de Isabel II
Paseo de Colón
Santander
Pta. de Jerez
⑪
Pte. de San Telmo
Av. de Roma
Av. de Palos de la Frontera
Av. Sanjurio
San Fernando
Pl. D. Juan de Austria
Estación Central de Autobuses
University
Avenida de Carlos V.

Pl. de Cuba
Av. República Argentina
Sebastián
Asunción
Elcano
Paseo de las Delicias
Av. María Luisa
Gta. San Diego
Av. Portugal
Pl. de España
Parque de María Luisa
Gta. Covadonga
Gta. Buenos Aires
Pte. del Generalísimo
Av. Don Pelayo

N

KEY
AE American Express Office
i Tourist Information

0 ——— 440 yards
0 ——— 400 meters

⑫

Sights ●
Alcázar, **10**
Barrio de
Santa Cruz, **7**
Casa Lonja, **9**
Catedral, **8**
Torre del Oro, **11**

Lodging ○
Albergue Juvenil-
Sevilla (HI), **12**
Hostal Alvarez
Quintero, **3**
Hostal Monreal, **6**
Hostal Nuevo
Suizo, **2**
Hostal Regi, **4**
Hostal Residencia
Central, **5**
Hostal Residencia
Gala, **1**

Hostal Residencia Gala. Sparse, small rooms but good beds. Singles 2,500 ptas; doubles, most with bath, 3,500 ptas. *C. Gravina 52, tel. 95/421–45–03.*

HOSTEL **Albergue Juvenil-Sevilla (HI).** Beds in modern doubles, triples, or quadruples for 854 ptas (under 26) or 1,166 ptas (26 and over). TV lounge. *C. Isaac Peral 2, tel. 95/461–31–50. Bus 34 from Pl. Nueva towards Heliopolis.*

FOOD

Avoid the overpriced tourist traps along Avenida de la Constitución across from the cathedral—the posted prices usually don't include a 15% to 20% service charge. On the other hand, you don't have to eat the crappy fast food dished up on Avenida Reina Mercedes, near the hostel, either. Small bars, especially those away from the central shopping district, serve the best meals. Wander the streets between the cathedral and the river or on the north side of town near the Alameda de Hercules monument to find good neighborhood bars.

Bar Tobias. A bar with Sevillan design and an owner who's proud of it. Posters of bullfights won't let you forget you're eating fish for a reason. Combos of squid, omelet, and salad 700 ptas; fried eggs, potatoes, chorizo, and olives 650 ptas. C. *Arfe 26, no phone. From Pl. Nueva, go south on Av. de la Constitución, right on C. Garcia de Vinuesa, then left on C. Arfe. Closed Mon.*

Bodega Sierpes. Small café with a large selection of tapas (100 ptas–125 ptas) and cheap combo plates. Half a roasted chicken, fries, salad, bread, and drink 725 ptas. *Azofaifo 9, off C. Sierpes, tel. 95/421–3044. Closed Tues.*

Cafetería Pasaje Ateneo. Tiny, modern bar serves wine, beer, and coffee to the suit-and-power-tie crowd all day long, but after 8, the dinners start rolling out. Combination plates are great values: breaded chicken with garlicky spinach and fries 650 ptas. *Pasaje Ateneo s/n, off C. Rioja, no phone. From Pl. Nueva walk 3 blocks north on C. Velázquez Tetuán to C. Rioja, turn right, then right again mid-block. Closed Sun.*

Doña Carmen. Wood-and-tile restaurant/bar dishes up healthy-size raciones at lunch and giant tapas at dinner. Family-size tortilla with ham 750 ptas, and *urta,* fish prepared with onions, celery, peppers, and tomatoes, 800 ptas. *C. San Eloy 19, tel. 95/456–07–21. From Pl. Nueva, go north on C. Mendez Nuñez to C. San Eloy. Closed Sun.*

La Traviatta. Modern pizzeria serves vegetable pizzas (650 ptas), plain pizzas (475 ptas), and cannelloni (725 ptas). Snazzy wood and marble interior. *C. António Díaz 4, off Paseo de Colón, tel. 95/456–25–56. Wheelchair access.*

WORTH SEEING

Even after visiting the gargantuan cathedral and King Juan Carlos's pad, El Alcázar, you won't be lacking for sights to see. The **Barrio de Santa Cruz,** the old Jewish quarter, is prime wandering territory. Twisting alleyways lead to cobbled squares and pass some of Sevilla's most beautiful mansions and patios. For another outdoor excursion, visit the expansive **Parque de María Luisa,** whose gardens blend formal design and wild vegetation and whose pathways lead to unexpected courtyards.

ALCAZAR The high, fortified walls of the Alcázar belie the delicacy of the palace's interior. Though occupied by various groups since the Roman era, the current site became a Mudéjar masterwork *after* the conquest of the Christian kings. In the 14th century, Pedro the Cruel brought in Moorish artisans and sculptors from Granada, pillaged stones and capitals from elsewhere, and completely rebuilt the palace. The intricately decorated **Patio de las Doncellas** (Court of the Damsels) was the center of official functions. The most grandiose room is the **Salón de Embajadores** (Hall of the Ambassadors), featuring a cedarwood cupola of green, red, and gold. Today, the Alcázar is the official residence in Sevilla of the queen and king of Spain. Skip your way out to the immense **gardens** and dip your tootsies into the fountains.

Hope you brought your lunch. *Pl. del Triunfo, tel. 95/422–71–63. Admission: 600 ptas, students free. Open Tues.–Sat. 10:30–5, Sun. 10–1.*

CASA LONJA Designed in 1572 by the architect of El Escorial, Juan de Herrera, the Casa Lonja contains the so-called Archivo de Indias (Archive of the Indies). You can see documents related to the discovery of the New World, old maps, drawings, and the autographs of some of Europe's best-known navigators, like Magellan and Columbus. *Av. de la Constitución s/n, tel. 95/421–12–34. Admission free. Open weekdays 10–1.*

CATEDRAL The biggest and highest cathedral in Spain and the largest Gothic building in the world, Sevilla's cathedral was built on the former site of a mosque. The **Giralda** was originally built as the minaret of the great mosque that stood here, but when the Christians tore down the mosque, they couldn't bring themselves to destroy this tower so they incorporated it into their new cathedral as the bell tower. At over 100 meters high, the tower provides amazing views of the city. Though the dim interior may be disappointing, look for beautiful Virgins by Murillo and Zurbarán as well as the flamboyant mausoleum in the south aisle containing the remains of Christopher Columbus. *Av. de la Constitución s/n, tel. 95/456–33–21. Admission: 500 ptas, 150 ptas students. Open Mon.–Sat. 11–6, Sun. noon–5.*

TORRE DEL ORO Along the river near the Puente de San Telmo, the 12-sided Tower of Gold (it used to be covered with gold tiles) was built by the Moors in 1220 to defend the harbor. They used to close off the harbor by attaching a chain across the river from the base of this tower to another (no longer there) on the opposite bank. In 1248 Admiral Ramón Bonifaz succeeded in busting through the barrier, thus enabling Ferdinand III to capture the city. The tower currently houses a small Naval Museum. *Paseo de Cristóbal Colón s/n, tel. 95/422–24–19. Admission: 100 ptas. Open Tues.–Fri. 10–2, weekends 10–1.*

AFTER DARK

Check out the bar scene in the neighborhoods east and north of the cathedral. **Plaza del Salvador** is lively at night and has a casual, friendly atmosphere. Three small bars here serve cheap beer (80 ptas–100 ptas) and tapas; people gather at wooden tables or sit on nearby church steps. **Pecata Mundi Bar** (C. García de Vinuesa 31, no phone) and **Bodega Santa Cruz** (C. Rodrigo Caro 1, no phone) both have cheap beer (100 ptas–150 ptas), and the latter serves up great tapas (150 ptas–175 ptas) until 2. **Calle General Polavieja,** a block northeast of Plaza Nueva, is jam-packed with bars. **Parque de María Luisa** is home of two snazzy bars. The better one, **Alfonso** (Paseo de las Delicias, no phone), is frequented by an attractive, well-dressed crowd that buys the very expensive drinks (as much as 1,900 ptas). A different sort of scene takes place on weekends at the **university.** Students and their friends hold tailgate parties in the parking lot.

The capital of flamenco, Sevilla has a few regular flamenco clubs, patronized more by tourists than by locals. **Los Gallos** (Pl. Santa Cruz, tel. 95/421–69–81) is a small, intimate club in the heart of the Barrio de Santa Cruz that has good, fairly pure flamenco. Nightly shows at 9 and 11:30 cost 3,000 ptas, including your first drink.

FESTIVALS

Although every town celebrates **Semana Santa** (Holy Week), Sevilla's processions are the most famous in the country. Since the 16th century, Sevilla has celebrated with traditional processions organized by *codafrías* (religious brotherhoods). Crowds gather in the streets during the solemn, evening processions that take place each day of the week before Easter. Some members of the codafrías dress as penitents, wearing hoods, masks, and capes, and carrying candles; others carry huge platforms or *pasos* on their shoulders, with statues representing scenes of the Passion of Christ. Hard on the heels of Semana Santa is the **Feria de Abril** (April Fair), celebrated with six days of bullfights, parades, flamenco performances, and fireworks.

Laid-back **Jerez de la Frontera** is a cool place to hang for a couple of days tasting sherry. Jerez's six major *bodegas* (wine cellars) churn out the fortified wine by the barrel and you can go on tasting tours for about 250 ptas. The **oficina de turismo** (Alameda Cristina 7, tel. 956/33–11–50) is west of the **train station** (tel. 956/34–23–19), where frequent trains arrive from Sevilla (1¼ hrs, 575 ptas).

Córdoba

On the right bank of the Guadalquivir River, Córdoba preserves its Moorish heritage better than any other town in Andalucía. From the 8th to the 11th centuries, the Moorish emirs and caliphs held court here and the town became one of the world's greatest centers of art, culture, and learning. Córdoba is famous for its Moorish mosque, the Mezquita, which now houses a cathedral. La Judería, the old Jewish quarter that surrounds the mosque, consists of a maze of medieval streets and contains one of the few pre-expulsion Jewish synagogues that survived post-expulsion demolition or conversion to a Christian church.

BASICS You'll find two **tourist offices** within a few minutes' walk of the Mezquita: one in Plaza Juda Leví, the other near the southwest corner of the Mezquita (C. Torrijos 10, tel. 957/47–12–35). You can take free guided walking tours of the Mezquita from the second office, or from the entrance of the mosque.

➤ **PHONES AND MAIL** • **Telefónica.** *Pl. Tendillas, at C. Diego León. Open weekdays 9:30–1:55 and 5–10:55, Sat. 9:30–1:55.*

Correos. *C. José Cruz Condé 15, tel. 957/47–82–67. Open weekdays 8 AM–9 PM, Sat. 9–2. Postal code 14003.*

COMING AND GOING High-speed AVE trains connect Córdoba's **train station** (tel. 957/49–02–02) with Madrid (2½ hrs, 4,300 ptas), Málaga (2 hrs, 1,700 ptas), and Sevilla (1½ hrs, 1,700 ptas). The slower expreso trains take about 50% longer but leave more frequently, nearly every hour. The bus company **Alsina Graells** (Av. de Medina Azahara, tel. 957/23–64–74) has frequent service to Sevilla (1½ hrs, 1,000 ptas) and Málaga (3½ hrs, 1,360 ptas).

The train station is a 30-minute walk north of the historical Judería district. For 80 ptas, Bus 12 will take you to La Judería from a stop just east of Avenida del Gran Capitán on Avenida de América, about a five-minute walk from the train station.

WHERE TO SLEEP Your best bet for cheap accommodations is the hostel, but if there's no room, you'll find a number of pensions and hostales spread out in La Judería and in the narrow streets roughly parallel to Avenida de América, south of the train station. At **Hostal Mari 2** (C. Horno de Porras 6, southeast of Mezquita, tel. 957/48–60–04; 1,100 ptas per person) rooms are cheap and somewhat clean, and the staff speaks English. **Hostal Trinidad** (Corregidor Luis de la Cerda 58, southeast of Mezquita, tel. 957/48–79–05; doubles 2,500 ptas) is a small, family-run place with friendly service. The **HI Albergue Juvenil Córdoba** (Pl. Juda Leví, tel. 957/29–01–66; beds 900 ptas, 1,100 ptas 26 and over) has an antiseptic atmosphere but great features: double rooms, good showers, a backyard, and a real drinking fountain. From the northwest corner of Mezquita, go west on Calle Herreros, and left on Calle Manriquez; the hostel is in an alcove on your right.

FOOD Stay away from the extravagant spots around the Mezquita; just two blocks away, prices are much better. During daylight hours Monday–Saturday you can stock up at an **open-air market** in Plaza de la Corredera (C. Armas at Pl. Cañas).

Bodega Taberna Rafaé (C. Deanes 1, 1½ blocks north of hostel, no phone) is a tacky-yet-cool old tavern quietly tucked on the corner of two narrow lanes. Large raciones of traditional dishes such as paella (375 ptas) or *chuleta de cerdo* (pork chops) are served with fresh bread for 475 ptas. **La Montería** (El Triunfo Hotel, Corregidor Luis de la Cerda 75 , at southeast cnr. of

Mezquita, tel. 957/47–72–56) overcharges for everything save the large platos combinados (710 ptas). Choose from plates with paella, *croquetas* (croquettes), a tortilla with ham, or a grilled pork chop.

WORTH SEEING *The* sight in Córdoba is the Mezquita (Mosque), which dominates La Judería. Córdoba also has an impressive Alcázar, eighteen churches, a few museums, and a medieval Jewish **synagogue** (C. Judíos, tel. 957/29–81–33), the only one in Andalucía to survive the expulsion of the Jews in 1492, though it is no longer a place of worship. A remnant of Roman rule, the **Puente Romano** still spans the Guadalquivir. At the southern end of the Roman bridge is the **Torre de la Calahorra,** built in 1369 to guard the entrance to Córdoba; it's now a museum of the three major religions that once flourished here.

➤ **MEZQUITA** • The center of Muslim religious practice for over a thousand years, Córdoba's grand mosque once served the religious needs of one of the largest Muslim communities in the world. Abd Ar-Rahman I began construction of the mosque soon after he acquired control of nearly all of Spain in the 8th century. As the wealth and power of the emirate of Al-Andalus grew, so did the mosque; by the beginning of the 11th century, subsequent emirs had more than doubled the size of the original mosque and constructed a new mihrab, a prayer niche that is supposed to face in the direction of Mecca. Due to an error in calculation, Córdoba's mihrab faces more south than east.

In the center of the huge mosque is a Gothic cathedral, added in 1523. Although the addition of the cathedral was originally sanctioned by King Carlos V, he later regretted the construction of the **Cathedral Coro,** which obscures the mihrab, telling the local Catholic church authorities they had "destroyed something that was unique in the world." Cnr. of *C. Torrijos and C. Cardenal Herrero, tel. 957/47–05–12. Admission: 600 ptas. Open Apr.–Sept., daily 10–7, Oct.–Mar., daily 10–1:30 and 2:30–7.*

➤ **ALCAZAR DE LOS REYES CRISTIANOS** • Córdoba's Mudéjar-style royal palace contains a display of ancient archaeological finds (explained in Spanish only), a modern re-creation of a Roman bath, a few large Roman mosaics, and a large, ornate garden littered with fallen oranges. The excavation of a true Roman bath could continue into late 1995. *Pl. Campo Santo de los Mártires, tel. 958/47–20–00 ext. 210. Admission: 250 ptas, free Tues. Open Tues.–Sat. 9:30–1:30 and 5–8, until 7 in winter.*

➤ **MUSEO ARQUEOLOGICO** • When original Roman mosaics were discovered on the walls of what everyone thought was a 16th-century mansion, the whole affair was converted into a museum. The collection contains an impressive array of Roman statuary, tombstones, mosaics, and glassware, as well as a large number of Moorish artifacts. *Pl. de Jerónimo Páez 7, tel. 957/47–40–11 or 957/47–10–76. Admission: 250 ptas. Open Tues.–Sat. 10–2 and 6–8 (5–7 in winter), Sun. 10–1:30.*

Granada

If every city were as beautiful as Granada, people would never travel. They would stay at home and enjoy their own fountains, outdoor plazas and parks, and their castle on a hill against a backdrop of snowcapped mountains. Granada's importance during the Moorish period of Andalucía's history is evident in the striking Alcázar, where some of the rooms are literally covered from floor to ceiling with Muslim engravings. The city's importance to the Catholic royalty, and particularly to Ferdinand and Isabella, is equally evident in the massive cathedral and the statue dedicated to Isabella in the center of town.

BASICS Granada has both a **regional tourist office** (Pl. Mariana Pineda 10, tel. 958/22–66–88; open summer, weekdays 9:30–2 and 4:30–7, Sat. 10–1, shorter hrs off-season) and a **municipal office** (Corral del Carbón, southwest of Pl. de Isabel la Católica, tel. 958/22–59–90; open summer, Mon.–Sat. 9:30–2:30, shorter hrs off-season).

➤ **AMERICAN EXPRESS** • *Viajes Bonal, Av. de la Constitución 19, tel. 958/27–63–12. Open weekdays 9:30–2 and 5–8 (4:30–7:30 in winter), Sat. 10–1.*

➤ **PHONES AND MAIL** • **Telefónica.** *C. Reyes Católicos 54. Open weekdays 9–2 and 5–10.*

Correos. *Puerto Real 1, tel. 958/22–48–35. Open weekdays 9–9, Sat. 9–2. Postal code 18080.*

COMING AND GOING RENFE **trains** connect Granada to Madrid (6 hrs, 6,400 ptas) and Barcelona (15 hrs, 3,600 ptas). As well as the information window in the station (tel. 958/27–12–72), there is an information and ticket office by Plaza de Isabel la Católica at Calle Reyes Católicos.

There is a tiny **Enatcar bus station** (Av. Andaluces, tel. 958/28–42–51) half a block north of the train station. Buses leave daily for Madrid (5 hrs, 2,055 ptas), Valencia (9 hrs, 4,320 ptas), and Barcelona (15 hrs, 6,980 ptas). South of the train station and university campus is the gigantic **Alsina Graells bus station** (Camino de Ronda at Glorieta Arabial, tel. 958/28–42–51), which serves Andalucían cities such as Málaga (2 hrs, 1,015 ptas), Córdoba (4½ hrs, 1,600 ptas), and Sevilla (5 hrs, 2,420 ptas).

GETTING AROUND The train and bus stations are about a 20-minute walk from the center of town. **Avenida de la Constitución** leads southeast from the train station toward the center of town and feeds into **Gran Vía de Colón** (usually called Gran Vía), which continues south, past the cathedral, to **Plaza de Isabel la Católica.**

Autocares Rober (tel. 958/81–37–11) buses cover every inch of Granada. Ask for the "Esquema Lineas de Autobuses" (Bus Line Plan) at one of the tourist offices. The buses cost 85 ptas per ride, and tabacs sell a Bonobus pass that gives you 10 rides for 525 ptas. To get to the center of town from the train station, catch Bus 3, 4, 7, 8, 9, or 11 from Avenida de la Constitución at Avenida Andaluces.

WHERE TO SLEEP There are two cheap sleep areas: the small streets east of Puerta Real and the neighborhood southwest of the cathedral. Rooms closer to the Alhambra cost more, and every place, from the crappiest pensión to the nicest hotel, will charge around 3,000 ptas for a double.

Los Arraynes (C. San Diego 9, tel. 958/25–97–91; doubles 3,500 ptas) has snazzy, modern rooms with bathroom, phone, and radio. From Plaza de Isabel la Católica, go southwest on Calle Reyes Católicos, turn left on Calle de San Antón, left on Calle Nueva de la Virgen, then left again on San Diego. **Hostal Princesa** (San Matías 2, tel. 958/22–93–81; doubles 3,000 ptas) is a very clean, small pension in the city center. From Plaza de Isabel la Católica, go southwest on Calle Reyes Católicos, left on Calle Angel Gavinet, and left on Calle San Matías. The floor slopes in some places at the **Hostal Roma,** (C. Navas 1, tel. 958/22–627–7; doubles 3,000 ptas–3,500 ptas), but the beds in this funky building are really nice. From Plaza de Isabel la Católica, walk around Banco de Santander to Calle San Matías, continue five blocks, and turn right on Calle Navas.

The **HI Albergue de la Juventud** (Camino de Ronda 171, tel. 958/27–26–38) is your basic hostel in the Estadio de la Juventud sports field. From the train station, go left on Avenida de la Constitución, left at the fork, then left on Camino de Ronda.
Sierra Nevada (Av. de Madrid 107, tel. 958/15–00–62), charging about 400 ptas per person and 375 per tent, is the closest campground to town; take Bus 3 from the town center.

For great ice cream, head to Cafe Futbol (Pl. Mariana Pineda 6, tel. 958/22–64–33), where you can feast on rich chocolate ice cream while watching waiters dodge cars until 3 AM every day.

FOOD Expect to pay around 700 ptas–800 ptas for a real meal around the city center. On Saturday afternoon visit the open-air **fruit and vegetable market** in the Pescadería area behind the cathedral.

The extravagantly decorated **Casa de Wu** (C. San Juan de Dios 10, tel. 958/27–57–56) serves up great *sopa de Wan-tu* (wanton soup; 265 ptas) and *pollo con piña* (535 ptas), chicken served in a half-pineapple. **Raices Vegetarian Restaurant** (Av. Pablo Picasso 30, tel.

958/12–01–03; closed Mon.) is a groovy café on the east side of the River Darro. Try a fried tomato, roast pepper, olive, and cheese tortilla (475 ptas) or cream of vegetable soup (425 ptas). The English and Spanish menus have different prices—ask to see both.

WORTH SEEING Granada's historic neighborhoods are as interesting as the city's major sights. The old Moorish quarter, **El Albaicín,** stands on a hill across the ravine from the Alhambra. The area is an alluring maze of tiny lanes, dilapidated white houses, and immaculate private villas enclosed by high walls. The old gypsy quarter, **Sacromonte,** is up the hill north of the city center (Bus 12 runs from Gran Vía). Here you'll find dozens of *cuevas de flamencos* (flamenco caves), where tourists go to watch traditional song and dance and have a couple drinks.

➤ **ALHAMBRA** • Dozens of postcards depict this massive Moorish palace against the background of the Sierra Nevada. The Alhambra is truly an imposing sight and a time-consuming place to visit. Plan to spend at least three hours wandering the vast grounds—after you wait in the huge line to buy your ticket, that is.

The **Alcazaba** is the oldest segment of the palace grounds, and the least interesting except for its amazing view of the city from the towers of the old fortress, now in ruins. Far more impressive is the **Alcázar,** which served as the residence as well as fortress for the Spanish emirs. Several halls are decorated with tilework and sculpture similar to that in the Alcázar at Sevilla. Among the more notable chambers of the palace are the **Palacios Nazaries,** covered in Arabic script carvings, and the **Palacios de los Liones,** the ceiling of which looks like a natural formation of stalactites. *Tel. 958/22–75–27. From Pl. Nueva take C. Cuesta up the hill, go through gate, ascend dirt footpath on the left. Admission: 650 ptas, free Sun. 3–6. Open summer, daily 9–8, and 10 PM–midnight Tues., Thurs., and Sat.; in winter, daily 9–6 and Sat. 8 PM–10 PM.*

➤ **CAPILLA REAL** • Built specifically for the burial of Ferdinand and Isabella, this Gothic chapel was sacked by the army of Napoleon and no remains remain—the sarcophagi that held the Catholic monarchs lie empty in the crypt, underneath huge marble tablets in the floor. Next door, the **cathedral,** built in the 16th century in a Gothic-Renaissance fusion, is much like those in every town, and isn't nearly as interesting as the Capilla Real. *Gran Vía de Colón, tel. 958/22–29–59. Admission to crypt: 200 ptas. Open daily 10:30–1 and 4–7 (3:30–6 in winter).*

Costa del Sol

The ultrarich and tacky, the middle-class and bourgeois, and the poor-but-hip all make their way to the Sun Coast, Spain's Riviera. The Costa del Sol stretches from near Gibraltar to Almería in the east. For the most part, the beaches here are clean and the nightlife in larger towns is worthy of a few all-nighters. Smaller towns feature more fun and less crass commercialism.

MALAGA

Welcome to the capital of the Costa del Sol, an ugly port city with a decent beach and good transport connections to other coastal destinations. Towering above town, the **Alcazaba** (tel. 95/221–60–05; admission 20 ptas; closed Mon.) is a fortress begun in the 8th century, when Málaga was the principal port of the Moorish kingdom. The inner palace was built between 1057 and 1063 when the Moorish emirs took up residence here. Inside, you'll also find the **Museo Arqueológico,** notable for its Moorish art and pottery collections. Further up the hill, through the Alcazaba gardens, is the ruined **Castillo de Gibralfaro** (open daily 9–9), which consists of a seriously fractured wall that appears to have once encircled the Alcazaba. A romp around the ruins and gardens is worth it for the views of the Alcazaba and the city below.

BASICS The regional **oficina de turismo** (C. Marqués de Larios 5, at Pl. de la Constitución, tel. 95/221–34–45) is staffed by unhelpful people; you're better off going to the municipal **turismo kiosk** (Pl. de la Merced, no phone). There's an **American Express** office inside Viajes Alhambra (C. Especerías 10, tel. 95/221–37–74 or 95/222–22–99).

COMING AND GOING A 10-minute walk from the center of town, the **train station** (tel. 95/236–0202) serves Córdoba (2 hrs, 1,700 ptas), Madrid (6 hrs, 6,000 ptas), and other destinations in the south. The **bus station** is one block north and one block west of the train station. **Portillo** (tel. 95/233–0191) buses go to Ronda (2 hrs, 925 ptas), Algeciras (2½ hrs, 1,075 ptas), and Gibraltar (3 hrs, 1,650 ptas). Next to the entrance to the port is a small stop for local buses serving the nearby beach towns of Torremolinos (45 min, 105 ptas) and Fuengirola (1½ hrs, 240 ptas).

The central **Plaza de la Marina** overlooks the port. From here, the park-lined Paseo del Parque leads to the east, toward the town's beaches. From Paseo del Parque, you can catch Bus 11 to **Pedregalejo,** a fishing village/tourist town with a nice beach. If you're planning to stay in the hostel or use the local buses frequently, pick up a 10-ride Bonobus ticket for 575 ptas at tabacs; otherwise, you'll pay 95 ptas per ride.

WHERE TO SLEEP AND EAT Unless you stay at the hostel, plan to spend some money. There are some pensions across the street from the train station, but they're not as cheap as places on Alameda Principal near the intersection with Marqués de Larios, about a 10-minute walk toward town from the station. **HI Albergue Juvenil-Málaga** (Pl. Pío XII 6, tel. 952/30–85–00; beds 954 ptas, 1,166 ptas 26 and over) is in a snazzy building. From the bus or train station, take Bus 18 toward Carranque to the end of the line. More central is **Avenida** (Alameda Principal 5, tel. 95/221–77–28; doubles 2,400 ptas–3,400 ptas), which has fairly clean rooms and a refrigerator for guests' use. Across the street from the train station is **La Hispanidad** (Explanada de la Estación, tel. 95/231–11–35; doubles 3,900 ptas), which has funky trinkets decorating the interior.

Most eateries are in the center of town around Plaza de la Constitución or in the neighborhood north and east of the plaza. Most of these are expensive, but **Pitta Bar** (C. Granada 23, tel. 95/221–11–28) serves up a mean falafel for only 350 ptas. **Bar Luz Mary** (C. Mendez Nuñez 9, tel. 95/222–80–48) is another light shining in Málaga's culinary darkness, with tortillas for 150 ptas and ham-and-cheese bocadillos for 200 ptas.

MARBELLA

A fashionable seaside resort town, Marbella is a favorite travel destination of middle-age British couples. Fortunately, development has stopped short of ruining an amazing old quarter of narrow, twisting lanes. In the 9th century, Moorish rulers encircled this area with high walls and built a fortress. After its reconquest by Catholic forces four centuries later, the fortifications were refurbished and strengthened. Today, you'll find the remains of the walls and the Alcazaba in the old quarter, and a beautiful square at the center; Plaza de los Naranjos is decorated with flower beds, rows of orange trees, a large fountain, and the requisite number of café tables. The old quarter would be enough reason to visit Marbella, but most people come to Marbella for its beach. The clear blue waters of the Mediterranean draw huge crowds to the wide strip of sand and to the resorts stretching 16 km or so on either side of town.

BASICS You'll find an **oficina de turismo** in Plaza de los Naranjos (tel. 95/282–35–50), and another a block west of Parque de la Alameda (Av. Miguel Cano 1, tel. 95/277–14–42). **American Express** (Av. Arias Maldonado 2, tel. 95/282–14–94) offers all cardholder services.

COMING AND GOING There's no train station in Marbella, but **Portillos** buses (tel. 95/277–21–35 or 95/277–21–92) connect Marbella with Málaga (1½ hrs, 455 ptas), as well as other major towns in Andalucía. The old quarter is a 15-minute walk east of the bus station.

WHERE TO SLEEP AND EAT Most budget establishments are in the old quarter. If at all possible, hit up **Hostal del Pilar** (C. Mesoncillo 4, off C. Peral, tel. 95/282–99–36; doubles 2,500 ptas), which is run by a British couple who have turned the place into a funky haven for travelers, with laundry service and real English breakfasts. A little cheaper but not quite as nice is the small **Hostal Internacional** (C. Alderete 7, no phone; doubles 2,400 ptas).

Slightly better rooms in the characterless **Hostal La Estrella** (C. San Cristóbal 36, tel. 95/277–94–72; doubles 3,000 ptas) all have bathrooms with showers.

Most of the cheap restaurants in Marbella serve up greasy fast food, but there are a few diamonds among the coal. **El Bocata Loco** (Av. Duque de Ahumada, in the Marbella Center mall, no phone) whips up quick, healthy sandwiches with names like "El Zipi y Zape" for under 400 ptas. The **Restaurante Juan David** (C. Marqués de Nájera, at Pl. de Tetuán, tel. 95/286–23–56) makes huge lunches (open daily 1–4) for about 500 ptas–600 ptas. Fresh fish and plenty of it is what you'll find at **El Chambe** (C. Alonso de Bazán, ½ block east of Telefónica kiosk, no phone), where most items are under 500 ptas.

Ronda

Perched on a steep 100-meter cliff above the River Guadalevín, the small town of Ronda overlooks a valley of farms and is surrounded by a small ring of mountains. With its strategic position, Ronda was the last stronghold of the legendary Andalucían bandits and the scene of the last great rising of the Moors against Ferdinand and Isabella. El Tajo, Ronda's dramatic ravine, divides La Ciudad, the old Moorish town, from El Mercadillo, the newer town which developed after the Christian Reconquista (Reconquest). Today, young families are settling in the newer parts of town, north of the river, and tour buses roll in daily from the coast. The natural beauty of the surrounding countryside (especially upstream) and the older, cobbled streets on the south side of the river make Ronda a worthwhile diversion from the Costa del Sol itinerary.

The few run-down sights of historical interest within town are less interesting than the beauty of the surrounding countryside and the old quarter, where residents have maintained the medieval charm of their neighborhoods. The more beautiful scenery is south and east of town, around the impressive **Puente Nuevo** (New Bridge) and through the old quarter. East of the south side of the Puente Nuevo, down Calle Santo Domingo you'll find the less-crowded **Puente Arabe.** From here, a dirt trail leads south along the outer edge of the town wall to Plaza San Francisco, at the south side of the Moorish gate, **Puerta de Almocabar.** The views of El Tajo are good from the Alameda del Tajo park or Paseo de Blas Infante (behind the bullring), but the best place to watch the sunset is from Plaza del Campillo, south of Puente Nuevo at the end of Calle Tenorio. The friendly, English-speaking staff provides maps at the **tourist office** (Pl. de España 1, tel. 95/287–12–72).

COMING AND GOING   The **train station** (tel. 95/287–16–73) has regular service to Algeciras (3 hrs, 570 ptas) and Málaga (2 hrs, 740 ptas) via Bobadilla. The **bus station** (Pl. Concepción García Redondo) has several companies, including **Comes** (tel. 95/287–19–92) and **Portillo** (tel. 95/287–21–62), that will get you just about anywhere. Both stations are a five- to 10-minute walk north of the center of town. To get around the countryside, rent a mountain bike at **Bici-Serrania** (Comte Salvador Carrasco 1, next to bus station, tel. 95/287–81–88) for 200 ptas an hour, 1,500 ptas a day.

WHERE TO SLEEP AND EAT   Finding cheap lodging in Ronda shouldn't be a problem. Most hostales and pensiónes are on the streets one block to either side of Carrera Espinel, a five-block-long pedestrian shopping street. For small, bright rooms, try **Hostal Ronda Sol** (C. Almendra 11, tel. 95/287–44–97; doubles 2,300 ptas). If you can finagle one of the doubles or triples on the roof of **Hotel Virgen de los Reyes** (C. Lorenzo Borrego 13, tel. 95/287–11–40), so much the better, at 1,250 ptas per person. Ronda has a new campground, **El Sur** (Carretera de Algeciras, tel. 95/287–59–39), 2 km south of town. The uphill walk is well worth the effort. For 400 ptas, you also get use of the swimming pool and an amazing view of town. For a real splurge, rent a bungalow with a full kitchen and private bathroom (4,500 ptas–7,000 ptas for 1–6 people); there's no market at the campsite, so bring food along.

Back in town, most bars, cafés, and restaurants are within a block of the stretch of Carrera Espinel between Calle Monterejas and the bullring. For standard bar/café fare, try the **Cafetería Cuatro Caminos** (Carrera Espinel 83, tel. 95/287–69–15), which serves hefty portions of your fried fish favorites for under 500 ptas. If Chinese food's what you're craving, peek into **Peking**

(C. Los Remedios 14, tel. 95/287–65–37), serving up Spanishized Chinese dishes (pork fried rice is a specialty) for about 700 ptas. Go to **Supermarquez** (C. Molino 36, 5 blocks northwest of Carrera Espinel) for all your grocery needs.

Algeciras

The port city closest to Morocco is the armpit of Spain. Petty crime runs rampant, and although a heavy police presence is a deterrent in daytime, at night these are mean streets. Ferries and jet foils travel from here to Morocco and Ceuta, a Spanish territory on the tip of Morocco, several times daily. Ferries are much cheaper (1,625 ptas–1,700 ptas for ferries and 2,650 ptas–2700 for jet foils), but jet foils cut the journey time almost in half. Although tickets are available at the ferry port, EurailPass holders can buy discount tickets to Tangier at **Wasteels** (tel. 956/63–23–32) in the RENFE station. Regular train service on high-speed Talgo trains from Málaga (4½ hrs, 1,350 ptas) or Madrid (12 hrs, 5,300 ptas) means you don't have to arrive until in Algeciras until the day your ship leaves. The **oficina de turismo** (C. Juan de la Cierva, tel. 956/57–26–36) is between the train station and the ferry port.

It's an unappealing prospect to spend the night in Algeciras. But if you're headed to Tangier, you ought to avoid arriving there in the evening, so you might have to crash here for a night. The **HI hostel** (Barriada El Pelayo, tel. 956/67–90–60; beds 954 ptas under 26, 1,676 ptas 26 and over) is 8 km from the center of town. Take the bus toward Tarifa and ask to be let off at the albergue. **Hostal Camas** (C. José Santacana 9, tel. 956/65–57–56; doubles 2,000 ptas) is a less-than-perfect place to rest your head; from the train station, head east (toward the water) and turn left on Calle José Santacana. If you have an hour or two to kill before your ferry leaves, hit up the **Chocolatería Iñaki** (Av. Virgen del Carmen 27, tel. 956/61–23–04) for a cup of joe and rap with the owner.

Gibraltar

The British have clung tenaciously to this tiny territory for hundreds of years. The town is a haven for English speakers dying to hear familiar sounds of their language on the streets, but in general the town of Gibraltar is an example of how low a place will stoop to boost tourism profits.

Gibraltar's claim to fame is the Rock, occupied since 1404 as a Mediterranean military base. Take the cable car to the **Top of the Rock.** The cable car ticket (£4) includes admission to the only real sight on the Rock, **St. Michael's Caves**, all lit up with green lights. After touching a clammy, graffitied stalagmite, why not go pet the tailless **Barbary apes,** the "last wild primates in Europe." You can take the cable car to the top station, walk down to the caves, then toward the middle station. The apes usually hang out in the road between the caves and the middle station. Bring a camera to capture the wacky ape action.

BASICS

VISITOR INFORMATION There is an **information booth** (tel. 9567/74982; open weekdays 9–6, Sat. 10–2) just outside the Grand Casement Gates and an **information office** at the Gibraltar Museum (1820 Bomb House Ln., east of Main St., tel. 9567/74289. **American Express** (cnr. of Irish Town and Market Ln., tel. 9567/72617) operates out of Bland Travel.

CHANGING MONEY All of Gibraltar's banks are on Main Street; most exchange money weekdays about 9–4. The bank with the best rate is **Jyske Bank** (76 Main St., tel. 9567/72782).

COMING AND GOING

There is no way to get here by train. **Comes buses** make the trip from most Andalucían cities, including Algeciras (½ hr, 535 ptas round-trip) and Málaga (2½ hrs, 1,635 ptas round-trip). There is no bus station here, so for information you need to call Comes in the town you're coming from.

Gibraltar is a tiny place; the entire town is jammed between the Rock and the frontier (the border with Spain), with water to the east and west. The entrance to town at the north end is an opening in the city wall called the Grand Casement Gate, which leads into Casemates Square and **Main Street,** which runs the length of town. The Rock is at the south end of town, a 20-minute walk at most.

WHERE TO SLEEP AND EAT

There's really no reason to spend the night here; besides, lodging is very expensive. The cheapest motel in town is **Queens** (Boyd St., tel. 9567/74000), where the doubles run £33! Three people traveling together can at least get a £50 triple. If you want to stay at **Sunrise Motel** (60 Devil's Tower Rd., tel. 9567/41265; doubles £48), the second least expensive place in town, reserve the room at least a week in advance.

You could try to camp on the beach on the Rock's east side, but you might get kicked off by silly-helmeted police officers.

Gibraltar offers really expensive restaurants, moderately expensive pubs, and a bunch of crappy fast food joints. The best (and only) shop of its kind, **The Breadbin** (49 Main St., tel. 9567/44558), sells sandwiches on half-baguettes and rolls. A chicken breast sandwich costs £1.90. Stop in at **Cannon Bar** (27 Cannon Lane, tel. 9567/77288) for greasy morsels of cod and chips (£5.75) or fried eggs and potatoes (£4.75).

The Mediterranean Coast

The little-known and little-touristed stretch of coast that reaches south from Valencia nearly to Cartagena is known as the Costa Blanca (White Coast) because of its fine, powdery beaches. Although the beaches at Valencia and Alicante look like garbage dumps, the town of Gandía, halfway between the two, more than makes up for them. **Benidorm,** dominated by a truly beautiful beach and discos with names like Penelope and Star Garden, is the Costa Blanca's nighttime playground. The small, ancient village of **Villajoyosa,** 10 km south of Benidorm, is a pristine village sporting multicolored window shutters, funky old buildings, and aging fishermen.

Alicante

About 100 km south of Valencia on the Costa Blanca, Alicante is an atmospheric, slow-paced town with cheap lodging. There's not much to see or do here except visit a ruined castle on a hill, walk along a seafront esplanade while licking an ice cream cone, or hang out at an outdoor café in the old quarter. Come here to sleep off a five-day tour of every late-night club in Barcelona, and when you're ready to party some more, head to nearby Playa de San Juan (*see* Coming and Going and After Dark, *below*).

The only real attraction here is the **Castillo de Santa Bárbara** (tel. 96/526–31–31), on top of the hill at the east edge of town. An elevator on Calle Virgen del Socorro along the south face of the hill will whisk you up for 200 ptas (although if you walk up—a good 45 minutes—you can ride down for free). The castle itself is fairly fun if you're into make-believe, though it's covered with graffiti in some places. Three museums fill the castle's halls: **Museo de Armas** features copies of weapons spanning three centuries; **Museo Ceramico** has a small collection of pottery from antiquity to the present; the **Museo de Foguera** celebrates the annual midsummer bonfire festival and features sometimes-beautiful, sometimes-grotesque parade floats by local artist Pedro Soriano. The last museum costs 25 ptas, the rest are free, and all are closed Monday.

VISITOR INFORMATION **Municipal tourist office.** *C. Portugal 16, in front of bus station, tel. 96/514–92–95. Open summer, weekdays 9–9, Sat. 9–2; winter, weekdays 9–2.*

Regional tourist office. *Explanada de España 2, tel. 96/520–00–00. Open Mon.–Sat. 10–8.*

COMING AND GOING High-speed trains connect Alicante to Madrid (4 hrs, 6,400 ptas) and Valencia (2 hrs, 2,900 ptas). There's an information window at the station (tel. 96/592–02–02), but you can avoid waiting in a long line by going to the **RENFE travel office** (Explanada de España, tel. 96/521–13–03) instead.

The center of Alicante is Plaza de los Luceros, a huge roundabout a few blocks east of the train station. The old district, **Alicante Antiguo,** also referred to as **El Barrio,** is southeast of Luceros and bordered by the seafront promenade. To get to the pretty, clean beach **Playa de San Juan,** 8 km further east, catch Bus C-1 (100 ptas) from Plaza del Mar.

WHERE TO SLEEP AND EAT Most of the cheap sleeps are on calles San Francisco and San Fernando, between Avenida Doctor Gadea and Rambla Mendez Nuñez. **Hostal San Fernando** (C. San Fernando 34, tel. 96/521–36–56) has rooms with big balconies for only 2,500 ptas. Backpackers dig the cool vibes at **Hostal García** (C. de Castaños 3, tel. 96/520–58–66; doubles 3,000 ptas), where the proprietress is as laid-back as a beach chair. The modern **HI Albergue Juvenil la Florida** (Av. Orihuela 59, tel. 96/511–30–44) opens up large single, double, and triple rooms (770 ptas per person) to HI cardholders from June to August. Take Bus G from the bus station entrance to the end of the line.

Thanks to the number of wealthy tourists shoveling pesetas into the local economy, food is outrageously expensive. Dozens of cafés and restaurants line the Explanada de España. There are a few cheap tapas spots in the old town, behind the cathedral, on Calle Labradores, San Isidro, and San Pascual. Try **Café-Bar Temple** (Pl. San Isidro 6, tel. 96/521–76–30) or **Taberna Labradores** (C. San Pascual 7, no phone) for tapas selections under 250 ptas. **Doña María Pizzería** (C. San Fernando 29–31, tel. 96/520–02–13) serves filling Italian dishes for around 650 ptas.

AFTER DARK The few discos and bars in Alicante are high-tech, modern, expensive, and empty during summer. People hang out in cafés in El Barrio until around midnight or 1 before going to Playa de San Juan (*see* Coming and Going, *above*). Here **Escola Bruselas** between Avenida de la Costa Blanca and Avenida Niza is so densely packed with bars, people are drinking in the street half a block away.

Valencia

In March, people converge on Valencia for Las Fallas, a festival celebrating the rites of spring. Huge papier-mâché figures that satirize current events are torched, lighting up the sky.

Before any Roman armies ever set foot on Iberian soil, Valencianos began cultivating large, sweet oranges in the fertile soil. But oranges aren't the only orange thing in Valencia—the ground itself is a dusty, pastel color, as are the aging plaster walls of the buildings of Valencia's Ciutat Vella (Old Town). The characteristic dish of the city, paella, is cooked with dark threads of saffron until it, too, takes on the color of the western sky at sunset. The town's magnificent cathedral and its accompanying tower may not share the city's characteristic hue, but they and the hopping university district and the lively gay scene are equally important to the city. Valencia is also a great jumping-off point for trips to the Balearic Islands, but the city's filthy beaches are utterly missable.

BASICS The **regional oficina de turismo** (Av. Marqués de Sotelo, tel. 96/352–85–73; open weekdays 9–8, weekends 10–7) is at the train station; the **local oficina de turismo** (tel. 96/351– 04–17; open weekdays 8:30–2:15 and 4:15–6:15, Sat. 9:15–12:45) is at Plaza del Ayuntamiento 1.

➤ **AMERICAN EXPRESS** • *Viajes Duna. Cirilo Amorós 88, tel. 96/374–15–62. Open weekdays 9:30–2 and 5–8:30, Sat. 10–1:30.*

➤ **PHONES AND MAIL** • **Locutorio.** *Pl. del Ayuntamiento 25. Open Mon.–Sat. 9–11.*

Correos. *Pl. del Ayuntamiento 24, tel. 96/394–20–59. Open Mon.–Sat. 8 AM–10 PM. Lista de Correos open weekdays 9–8. Postal code 46004.*

➤ **CONSULATE** • **United States.** *C. de la Paz 6, tel. 96/351–69–73. Open weekdays 9–2.*

COMING AND GOING Valencia is on the main AVE line between Madrid and Barcelona. The main station, **Valencia Termino** (tel. 96/352–02–02), is in the center of town and has daily service to Alicante (2 hrs, 2,900 ptas), Tarragona (3 hrs, 3,900 ptas), and Barcelona Sants (4 hrs, 4,700 ptas).

The main **bus station** (Av. Menéndez Pidal 13, tel. 96/349–72–22) is a 30-minute walk from the center of town. **Auto Res** (tel. 96/349–22–30) has buses to Madrid (4½ hrs, 2,540 ptas); **Ubesa** (tel. 96/340–08–55) goes to Barcelona (4 hrs, 2,650 ptas); and **Bacoma** (tel. 96/347–96–08) goes to Andalucían destinations like Granada (9 hrs, 4,310 ptas) and Algeci- ras (14 hrs, 6,390 ptas). You can catch a FEVE suburban train a block west of the station entrance and take it to the center of town (Pl. Espanya) for 110 ptas.

GETTING AROUND The Ayuntamiento and adjacent plaza are at the center of town. The train station is south of the plaza, and the Ciutat Vella, where most tourist sights are located, is to the north. The city is large, but not too large to walk. You'll have to take a bus to the beaches and port, however. Local buses run by **Empresa Municipal de Transportes de Valen- cia (EMT)** (tel. 96/352–83–99) cost 75 ptas per ride. Maps are posted at nearly every stop. Every bus in the system converges on Plaza del Ayuntamiento, Calle Játiva by the train sta- tion, or on the two streets on either side of the train station. Bus 8 goes between the train and bus stations. Buses 1, 2, 19, 20, 21, 23, 31, 91, and N-1 go to the beach. Buses 1, 2, 3, 4, 19, and 30 go to the ferry port.

WHERE TO SLEEP There is no shortage of cheap beds here, but avoid the HI hostel. You can find a few cheap places on Calle de Bailén and Calle de Pelayo, next to the train station, but your best bet is to wander the streets of the old town between the Mercado and Plaza de la Virgen, if none of the following is available.

Hostal Residencia del Rincón. Their cheap rooms are only 900 ptas per person, but doubles with private bath are 2,900 ptas. Old place run by a laid-back proprietor and his cat. Try to get a room on the second or third floor, and make sure it doesn't face the street. *C. Carda 11, tel. 96/391–79–98 or 96/391–60–83. From Pl. del Ayuntamiento, walk north, follow the left fork of Av. María Cristina, then turn left onto C. Carda.*

Pensión Paris. Only detriment is the number of stairs you have to climb to get to your room. Nice beds in bright but boring rooms. Bathrooms kept spotless by a young and friendly staff. Doubles 2,800 ptas. *C. Salvá 12, tel. 96/352–67–66. From Pl. del Ayuntamiento, east on C. Barcas, left on C. Poeta Querol, right on C. Salvá.*

Pensión Universal. A five-minute walk east of Plaza del Ayuntamiento. Rooms are airy and bathrooms are scrubbed to a high gloss. Make sure your room doesn't face busy Calle Barcas. Doubles 2,800 ptas. *C. Barcas 5, tel. 96/351–53–84.*

➤ **HOSTEL** • **Albergue Juvenil-Valencia (HI).** There are so many things wrong with this place, we hardly know where to begin. Far from town center and absolutely filthy. Beds 850 ptas, sheets 250 ptas. *Av. del Puerto 69, tel. 96/361–74–59. From Pl. del Ayuntamiento,*

Bus 19 over Puente de Aragon to Av. de Puerto. Midnight curfew, lockout 10–5. Closed Oct.–June.

FOOD Although paella is Valencia's passion, restaurants squeeze every peseta they can (about 1,000 ptas) out of visitors for a plate of the stuff. Choose from paellas *de mariscos* (seafood), *carne* (meat), and *mixta* (mixed). There are a number of cheap places to eat on Calles de Bailén and Pelayo, west of the train station. Hit up the market (open Mon.–Sat. 8–2), a five-minute walk north of Plaza del Ayuntamiento, or the hippie-trippy **J. Navarro Herbolario** (C. de Padilla 5, tel. 96/352–28–51), a health-food store with more.

Cafetería Duero. Locals swarm in for reasonably priced tapas (250 ptas–350 ptas), cheap breakfasts, and nice-size raciones and platos combinados. Combo 13 (525 ptas), made of a quarter roast chicken, fries, fried egg, and salad, could be your lucky number. *C. de Játiva 12, near train station, tel. 96/352–96–41.*

Cafetería Roma. Facing the back of a cathedral in Plaza de la Virgen, this unpretentious, quiet outdoor café does a brisk business with both tourists and locals. Raciones of calamari (500 ptas) or a ham bocadillo (350 ptas) should satisfy moderate appetites, and the truly hungry can have a pork chop, tortilla, and salad combo for 600 ptas. *Pl. de la Virgen 4, tel. 96/392–24–72. From Pl. del Ayuntamiento, walk north, take right fork (Pescadería) to Pl. de la Reina, and walk around left side of cathedral.*

La Utielana. You'll probably wait in line for a table in the small dining room, but tough it out—food here is cheap, tasty, and truly traditional. Gazpacho (200 ptas) and *fabadas asturias* (pork and bean stew with sausage; 325 ptas) makes a good combo. *Pl. Picadero Dos Aguas 3, tel. 96/352–94–14. From Pl. del Ayuntamiento, west on C. Barcas, left on C. Poeta Querol, left on tiny alley Procida. Closed Mon.–Sat. 4–9, Sun.*

WORTH SEEING Nearly all of the town's 18 museums and seven gardens are free, free, free! The **Museo de Bellas Artes** (C. San Pío V, tel. 96/360–57–93; open Tues.–Sat. 10–2 and 4–6) and the **Centro de Artesana Comunidad Valenciana** (C. Hospital 7, tel. 96/351–30–90; open Tues.–Sat. 10–2 and 5–8) constitute the bulk of free art on display. The former is a treat for Goya fans, the latter a haven for sociologists, ethnologists, or the just-plain-interested-in-folk-art crowd. A side chapel of Valencia's 14th-century **catedral** (Pl. de Zaragoza, tel. 96/391–81–27; open daily 10–1 and 4–7) contains a purple agate chalice said to be the Holy Grail. The **Museo de la Catedral** (admission 100 ptas; closed Sun.) contains two Goya paintings, various chalices, and a 1,300-kilogram gold, silver, platinum, and diamond-encrusted *custodia* used to carry the holy host through the streets during the Semana Santa parade. You can climb the 207 steps to the top of the cathedral's tower, **El Miguelete** (admission 100 ptas), a whopping 70 meters above the city. While you're up here, watch the hammer hit the 1,100-kilogram Miguel-Vicente bell on the hour. The **Museo Histórico Municipal** (Pl. del Ayuntamiento 1, tel. 96/352–54–78; open weekdays 9–2), inside the very cool, very big city hall building, and the **Museo Paleontológico Municipal** (Arzobispo Mayoral 3, tel. 96/352–54–78; closed Sun.–Mon.) fill you in on the city's recent and ancient history. Go to the **Jardín Zoológico** (C. Beato Gaspar Bono, 1 block east of Puente Glorias Valencianas, tel. 96/391–16–57; admission 50 ptas, students free) to see a hell of a lot of trees, bushes, ferns, cacti, and feral cats. The most bizarre sight in town is the **Parque Gulliver** (in Túria riverbed park at Puente Angel Custodio, tel. 96/393–39–91; open Tues.–Sun. 10–7), with a huge, climbable sculpture of the legendary guy that makes Kareem Abdul-Jabbar look Lilliputian.

AFTER DARK On weekends, **Plaza Fray Luis Colomer,** in the university district just north of Avenida de Vicente and east of Avenida de Aragon, fills with bar-hopping students. **Bar Penalty** (C. Artes Gráficas at Av. Suecia, no phone) has cheap drinks as well as late-night snacks. Both gay and straight people hang out at the many bars around **Plaza Calderers,** roughly north of the Mercat at the north end of C. Bolgería. Cool vibes and cheap beers are on tap at the **Café Infanta** (Calderers 4, no phone). Funky people hang out at **Cola-Caos** (C. Alta 6, no phone), and good late-night snacks are available from the **Bocatería Pepito** (C. Alta 3, no phone) across the street.

NEAR VALENCIA

Along the 250 km of coastline along the Costa Blanca, south from Valencia to Cartagena, you can discover some of the cleanest, most unspoiled beaches on the east coast. Towns like **Elche,** famous for its ancient palm trees, and **Benidorm,** the British vacation spot of choice after Málaga or Marbella, are not indicative of the serene beauty found in smaller villages. The HI hostel **Mar I Vent** (C. Doctor Fleming, tel. 96/289–34–25 or 96/289–37–48), in the village of Piles, 10 km from Gandía, is actually right on the beach—you open the door, and there's the sand.

GANDIA The sleepy village of Gandía is so small and insular that backpackers draw puzzled stares from locals. Tourism, bolstered by a 1992 European Community commission award to the town for having the most pristine continental beach, is something of a recent phenomenon. Luckily, tourists have yet to ruin the place; the sand is so white that the beach almost looks like a snow-covered hillside. The town, where the **train station** (tel. 96/287–18–06) is, and the beach are separated by a 3-km stretch of farmland, traversed by a single bus that departs from the front of the **tourist office** (C. Marqués de Campo, tel. 96/287–77–88). Trains from Valencia (1 hr, 370 ptas, 425 ptas weekends) arrive every half hour. **Pitiusos** (tel. 96/284–45–00) has summer-only ferry service to San Antonio, Ibiza (8 hrs) and Formentera (11 hrs via Ibiza) for 5,220 ptas.

➢ **WHERE TO SLEEP** • The town has lots of cheap places to stay: **Requena** (Tirso de Molino 30, tel. 96/286–58–63) and **La Inmaculada** (Duque Carlos de Boria, tel. 96/287–31–04) offer mushy beds in double rooms for 2,200 ptas. **L'Alquería** (Carretera Gandía–Playa de Gandía, km 2, tel. 96/284–04–70; 420 ptas per person, 460 ptas per tent), along the main road to the beach, is one of three campgrounds near the waterfront.

Barcelona
Catalan poet Joan Maragall dubbed Barcelona *la gran encisera* (the great enchantress), and most visitors to this gorgeous city fall quickly under its intoxicating spell. No matter who you are—history hound, hedonistic partyer, architecture buff, beach bum, or disco queen, you'll find what you seek in this city that's still glowing from the 1992 Olympic spotlight. From the cool, dark dampness of its Barri Gòtic (Gothic Quarter) and the breezy splendor of the broad, geometric avenues of the Eixample (Enlargement) to Las Ramblas, Barcelona's famous, flower-lined pedestrian street, Barcelona has become everyone's favorite city.

Well, almost everyone's favorite city. The Madrileños have long competed with the residents of Barcelona for economic, cultural, and political supremacy. By the Middle Ages, Barcelona had been built up from wealth generated by brisk trade with the rest of the world. However, the conquest of the New World and Madrid's new wealth from plundering it, as well as the switch of focus from the Mediterranean to the Atlantic, resulted in Barcelona's eventual loss of economic primacy.

During the 19th century the industrial revolution found a home in Barcelona, and the city developed into the industrial capital of Spain, which was still overwhelmingly agrarian. The industrial revolution set the stage for the beginning of a golden period in Barcelona's (and Catalunya's) history known as the Renaixenca (Renaissance). As artists and architects began to redesign the burgeoning city, the growing spirit of Catalisme, Catalan nationalism, was expressed in the artistic style known as *modernisme,* emphasizing traditional Catalan building techniques such as stained glass, tilework, and iron grills. To this day, the city has remained on the cutting edge of design, and architecture students from around the world still come here to study (and play) in this unique, open-air classroom.

BASICS

VISITOR INFORMATION Barcelona has several tourist offices to serve the masses. If you arrive by train, go to the oficina de turisme (open daily 8–8) at Estació Sants or the office (open daily 8–2 and 4–10) at Estació França. The **main oficina de turisme** (Gran Via de les Corts Catalanes 658, tel. 93/301–74–43; open weekdays 9–7, Sat. 9–2) has loads of info. From June 15 to September 15, city-sponsored tourist guides (decked out in red and white uniforms) hang out in key locales like Las Ramblas and the Barri Gòtic. For information about cultural events in Barcelona, go to **Palau de la Virreina** (Las Ramblas 99, at Carrer del Carme).

AMERICAN EXPRESS *Passeig de Gràcia 101, at Carrer Rosselló, tel. 93/217–00–70. Metro: Diagonal. Open weekdays 9:30–6, Sat. 10–noon.*

BUCKET SHOP The best spot for cheap bus, train, and plane tickets is the **Oficina de Turisme Juvenil.** They dole out advice on cheap travel and sell tickets, ISIC cards, and hostel cards. They also have a ride-sharing bulletin board. Try to come as early as possible to avoid the lines. In the evening, they only give out info, not tickets. *Carrer Gravina 1, tel. 93/302–06–82. Metro: Universitat. Take Carrer Pelai off Pl. Universitat. Open June–July, weekdays 9–2 and 4–8, shorter hrs off-season.*

CHANGING MONEY Several casas de cambio are on Las Ramblas; they don't charge commission, but their rates are worse than banks. The only advantage is they stay open late—until 11 PM or midnight. **Exact Change** (La Rambla 85 and 130, tel. 93/302–23–51) seems to have the best rates by a small margin.

EMBASSIES **Australia.** *Gran Via Carles III 98, tel. 93/330–94–96. Open weekdays 10–noon.*

Canada. *Via Augusta 125, tel. 93/209–06–34. Open weekdays 9–1.*

Great Britain. *Av. Diagonal 477, tel. 93/419–90–44. Open weekdays 9:30–1:30 and 4–5.*

Ireland. *Gran Via Carles III 94, tel. 93/491–50–21. Open weekdays 10–1.*

United States. *Passeig Reina Elisenda 32, tel. 93/280–22–27. Open weekdays 9–12:30 and 3–5.*

EMERGENCIES The police station on Las Ramblas (La Rambla 43, across from Pl. Reial; open in summer 24 hours, off-season 7 AM–midnight) has visitors' assistance and counseling services available in English. In spring and summer the special tourist police number is 93/01–90–60. The central police office is at Via Laietana 43. In an emergency, call 092 (Municipal Police) or 091 (National Police).

PHONES AND MAIL The main telephone office, **Telefónica** (Carrer Fontanella 4, open Mon.–Sat. 8–1 and 5–9), is right off Plaça de Catalunya. You'll also find a telephone office (open daily 7:45 AM–10:45 PM) at Estació Sants.

The main post office, **Correos,** has telegram services and holds mail; write the addressee's name (preferably in capital letters), Lista de Correos, 08002 Barcelona Central. They also sell stamps. *Pl. d'Antoni López s/n, tel. 93/318–38–31. Metro: Jaume I or Barceloneta. Open weekdays 8 AM–9 PM, Sat. 9–2.*

COMING AND GOING

Barcelona is a major transportation hub, and you can hop a plane, bus, or train to virtually anywhere your heart desires. For advice on the best and cheapest ways to travel go to the **Centre d'Informació i Assessorament per a Joves** (Carrer Ferràn 32, at Carrer d'Avinyó, tel. 93/402–78–03; open weekdays 10–2 and 4–8); you can browse through their vast collection of maps, travel guides, and brochures, or talk to their peppy staff. Another key stop is the **Oficina de Turisme Juvenil** (*see* Bucket Shop, *above*). Also talk to **Nouvelles Frontières** (Carrer Balmese 8, tel. 93/318–68–98) about cheap ways out of Barcelona.

Berlin

Vallespir

Josep Tarradellas

Paris

Corcega

C. Rosselló

Provença

Estació
Sants

Av. Roma

Mallorca

Creu Coberta

Tarragona

Valencia

Arago

Consell de Cent

Llansá

Enlença

Rocafort

Calabria

Viladomat

Comte Borrell

Comte d'Urgell

Villarroel

Casanova

Muntaner

Aribau

Enric Granados

Balmes

Av. Diagona

Diputacio

Plaça
d'Espanya

Plaça
Universitat

Gran Vía de les Corts Catalanes

Rc

Av. Reina M. Cristina

Sepulveda

Rda. Sant Antoni

C. Pelai

Tallers

Mistral

Floridablanca

Av. Paral·lel

Tamarit

Joaquim Costa

Manso

Rda. de Sant Pau

C. del Carme

Av. de l'Estadi

Hospital

⑪

⑫

Carreres

C. de la Unió

Sant Pau

⑱

⑲

②

Av. Miramar

②

Nou de la Rambla

㉕

㉒

③

Drassanes

Escu

Estació
Funicular

④

Passeig de Montjuïc

Parc
de
Montjuïc

⑤

Montjuïc
Funicular

Jardins
de
Miramar

Transbordador

Plaça
Portal
de la Pau

ℹ

Pc

㉝

Moll c
(M

Aeri

Moll de
Sant Bertrán

Estació
Marítima

(cable c

Moll de la Costa

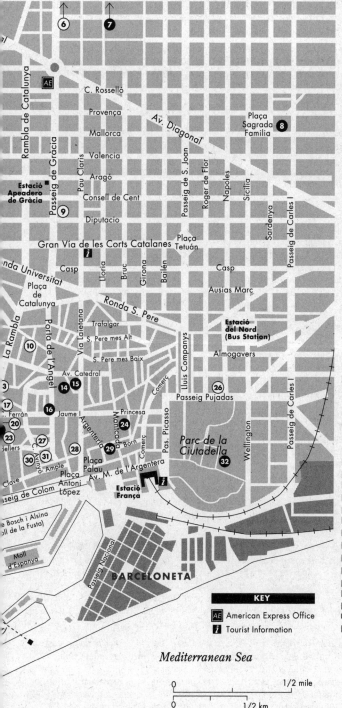

Barcelona

Sights ●

Castell de
Montjuic, **5**

Catedral, **14**

Estadi Olímpic
de Montjuic, **3**

Fundacio
Joan Miró, **2**

Gran Teatre
del Liceu, **18**

Monument a
Colom, **33**

Museu d'Art
Modern, **32**

Museu Frederic
Marès, **15**

Museu Picasso, **24**

Palau Güell, **25**

Parc d'Attraccions
de Monjuic, **4**

Parc Güell, **7**

Plaç de
Sant Jaume, **16**

Plaça Reial, **21**

Santa María
del Mar, **29**

Temple Expiatori de
la Sagrada
Familia, **8**

Tibidabo, **1**

Lodging ○

Albergue Verge de
Montserrat (HI), **6**

Hostal Campi, **10**

Hostal de Joves
(HI), **26**

Hostal New York, **31**

Hostal Oliva, **9**

Hostal Paris, **13**

Hostal-Residencia
Europa, **17**

Hotel Roma, **23**

Kabul Youth
Hostel, **22**

Pensión Alamar, **27**

Pensión Avinyo, **30**

Pensión Colón 3, **20**

Pensión Flores, **11**

Pensión
Macarena, **19**

Pensión Nueva
Orleans, **28**

Pensión Venecia, **12**

KEY

AE American Express Office

i Tourist Information

Mediterranean Sea

0 — 1/2 mile

0 — 1/2 km

BY TRAIN Barcelona has two train stations, Estació Sants, northwest of the city center, and Estació França, near the port and Barri Gòtic. Most arriving trains stop at both. For train information, call 93/490–02–02.

Estació Sants is the larger of the two stations and serves most national and international destinations. Trains rumble daily to Madrid (9–10 hrs, 4,500 ptas–7,000 ptas), Tarragona (1½ hrs, 500 ptas), and Valencia (7 hrs, 2,600 ptas). The ticket office is open 6 AM–11 PM. There's not much going on near the station, so hop on the Metro inside the station pronto. Take Line 3 (direction Montbau) to get to Las Ramblas (Metro: Liceu or Drassanes). For late-night arrivals, night buses N2, N12, and N14 will whisk you and your pack to Plaça de Catalunya.

Estació França (open 6 AM–11 PM) has trains to Paris (14½ hrs, 10,000 ptas), Geneva, Milan, and Zurich. Tickets are sold 6:30 AM–10 PM. França is only 10 minutes away from the budget accommodations in the Barri Gòtic. Walk southwest (toward the Columbus monument) along Avenida Marquès de l'Argentera and turn right onto Via Laietana, or further down on Las Ramblas. The Metro stop Barceloneta is just behind the station toward the port.

BY BUS The bus system is complicated; head to the nearest tourist office, find out which of the many bus companies serves your destination, and then go to a travel agency or the bus company itself to purchase tickets. **Cetransa** (tel. 93/412–00–00; open weekdays 7:30 AM–10 PM) can give you extensive information on all bus routes, prices, and hours. Most buses arrive and depart from the central bus station, **Estació del Nord** (Av. Vilanova; Metro: Arc de Triomf). The station's info booth is open daily 8 AM–10 PM. Companies operating out of this station are: **Enatcar** (tel. 93/245–25–28) for Madrid (2,660 ptas) or Valencia (2,650 ptas); **Bacoma** (tel. 93/231–38–01) for Granada and Sevilla; **Irbarsa** (tel. 93/265–60–61) for San Sebastián and Pamplona; and **Sarfa** (tel. 93/265–78–45 or 93/265–77–95) for towns along the Costa Brava such as Cadaqués (1,625 ptas), and L'Escala (1,450 ptas). Two major companies that don't leave from Estació del Nord are **Auto Transport Julià-Via** (Plaça Universitat 12, tel. 93/317–64–54) and **Carrer Viriato** (tel. 93/490–40–00), located just to the left as you exit Estació Sants. Both these companies have international buses to Paris (9,300 ptas) and London (13,450 ptas); they give a 10% discount to students and those under 26. **Alsina Graells** (Ronda Universitat 4, tel. 93/302–65–45) has buses for Lleida, La Seu d'Urgell, and Andorra. **Iberbus-Linebus** (Av. del Paral-lel 116, tel. 93/242–33–00) is another line specializing in European destinations outside Spain, with discounts for those under 26, and students under 29.

BY PLANE Barcelona's airport is 12 km south of the city in the suburb of El Prat de Llobregat. Trains (240 ptas) head to **Estació Sants** every 30 minutes 6 AM–10:45 PM, and from there you can take the Metro. After 11 PM, a bus heads to Plaça de Catalunya for 400 ptas; it runs until 3:15 AM, but only once an hour, so you may want to splurge on a taxi into town (about 2,000 ptas–2,500 ptas). For airport information, call 93/478–5000. You can get a round-trip flight to Paris for as little as 30,000 ptas and to London for 27,000 ptas with **Iberia Airlines** (Passeig de Gràcia 30, tel. 93/401–33–00) if you're willing to book at the last minute. Always ask about youth discounts.

BY FERRY Ferries for the Balearic Islands arrive and depart from **Estació Marítima** (tel. 93/412–2524) at the port south of Las Ramblas (Metro: Drassanes). **Trasmediterránea** (tel. 93/317–7211) has the monopoly on the ferries. Their boats leave daily for Palma, Ibiza, and Menorca in the summer, usually around 10 or 11 PM—5,700 ptas will get you a chair for the eight- to nine-hour trip. Beds are about 2,000 ptas more. In summer book ahead. Go to **Oficina de Turisme Juvenil** (*see* Bucket Shop, *above*) for a discount ticket (10% off) if you're under 26.

HITCHING If you want to thumb it to France, the Costa Brava, or other northern destinations, take the Metro to the Fabra i Puig stop. This puts you on Avinguda Meridiana, which leads to the A-7 freeway. To head east toward Madrid take Bus 7 from Plaça de Catalunya to its terminus at Avinguda Diagonal, which leads to the A-2 freeway. **Barnastop** (Carrer San Ramon 29, off Nou Carrer de la Rambla, tel. 93/443–06–32; open summer, weekdays 11–2 and 5–7, Sat. 11–2, no evening hrs in winter) is a helpful ride-sharing office.

GETTING AROUND

Many of Barcelona's attractions and hotels are within easy walking distance of the street **La Rambla** (more commonly known as **Las Ramblas**), but the city also has an excellent public transportation system. If the Metro didn't close at 11 PM on weekdays, just when people are revving up for the night, you couldn't ask for anything more efficient. Luckily, after the Metro closes, many buses fill the gap. Taxis are plentiful and relatively cheap. Call 93/412–00–00 for general info about public transport.

BY METRO Five Metro lines cover most of the city frequently—you'll never have to wait more than five minutes for a train. Tickets cost 115 ptas. If you're going to be here for even a few days, the multiride T-2 (Tarjeta Multiviatge) card is the way to go—it's good for 10 rides on the bus, Metro, or local train (Ferrocarriles de la Generalitat) and costs 590 ptas. If you need to cover a *lot* of ground in a day, you can get a ticket for one day of unlimited public transport for 400 ptas. The Metro runs weekdays 5 AM–11 PM; weekends and holidays it stops at 1 AM.

BY BUS The bus will take you wherever the Metro won't, and night buses run from 10:30 PM to 4:30 AM, long after the Metro shuts down. Night buses are blue (day buses are red), and usually start or end up in Plaça de Catalunya. The fare is 115 ptas, or you can use your T-2 card (*see above*). Get a free brochure with route information at the tourist office.

BY TAXI Yellow and black taxis can be hailed from most key spots in the city for about 250 ptas for the first five minutes and 100 ptas for each additional kilometer. Watch out when taking a taxi from Estació Sants late at night—they charge extra. If you think you're getting ripped off, ask for a *recibo* (receipt). Call 93/357–77–55, 93/358–11–11, or 93/300–38–11 for a taxi.

WHERE TO SLEEP

The great thing about cheap sleeps in Barcelona is that they're mostly concentrated around Las Ramblas and the Barri Gòtic—places packed with sights. The only problem is that the Barri Xinès, *the* hangout area for prostitutes, heroin addicts, and other lost souls, is right next to these central areas. If you're anxious about this sort of thing, look for lodging by heading away from the port, toward the Eixample and the newer parts of the city. If you've arrived late at Estació França and don't feel like walking, try **Hostal Residencia La Hipica** (Carrer Gen. Castanyos 2, bet. Pl. Palau and França station, tel. 93/315–13–92), where basic doubles fetch 2,990 ptas.

➤ **UNDER 2,500 PTAS • Hostal New-York.** Don't come for the dark, gloomy, *Addams Family* feeling, but for rock-bottom prices and friendly owners. Doubles 2,000 ptas, 2,450 ptas w/bath. *Carrer Gignàs 6, near post office, tel. 93/315–03–04. Metro: Jaume I.*

Pensión Avinyo. Not well marked, but a very welcoming spot in Barri Gòtic. Owner is rightfully proud of recent renovations. Doubles 2,000 ptas, 2,500 ptas w/bath. *Carrer Avinyó 42, just west of Carrer dels Escudellers, tel. 93/318–79–45.*

➤ **UNDER 3,500 PTAS • Hostal Campi.** Very secure (you buzz for entry both at the front door and your room floor), and a primo locale right near Plaça de Catalunya. Roomy doubles and triples, though slightly cramped singles. Doubles 3,300 ptas, 4,500 ptas w/bath. *Carrer Canuda 4, tel. 93/301–35–45. Metro: Plaça de Catalunya.*

Hostal Paris. Overlooking Las Ramblas at Plaça de la Boqueria. Large place with clean, spacious rooms with new tiles. Check out groovy TV room with bad oil paintings of Catalunya. Doubles 3,200 ptas, 4,200 ptas w/bath. *Carrer Casanyes 4, on Pl. de la Boqueria, tel. 93/301–37–85.*

Hostal-Residencia Europa. Quiet, small rooms near Las Ramblas. Friendly management. Hot water in showers, but low, low pressure. Doubles 3,000 ptas, 3,500 ptas w/bath. *Carrer Boqueria 18, tel. 93/318–76–20. Metro: Liceu.*

Pensión Alamar. Staying here with owner Maxi Hernandez is like visiting your Spanish uncle. Access to a kitchen and washing machine. It's a bitty place, so call ahead in high season. Doubles 3,000 ptas. *Carrer Comtessa de Sobradiel 1, tel. 93/302–50–12. Take Metro to Liceu or Drassanes and take Carrer Escudellers off Las Ramblas to Carrer Avinyó; Carrer Comtessa de Sobradiel is at their intersection.*

Pensión Flores. Great location right on Las Ramblas. Embarrassing inconvenience of shower being right next to front desk. Clean, well-kept rooms. Doubles 3,000 ptas, 4,500 ptas w/bath. *La Rambla 79, tel. 93/317–16–34. Metro: Liceu.*

Pensión Macarena. Handy location just off Las Ramblas, with beautiful, plant-filled patio where you can hang laundry. Basic, clean rooms. Doubles 2,600 ptas, 3,200 ptas w/bath. *Carrer de la Unió 9, tel. 93/412–56–95. Metro: Liceu. ½ block from Las Ramblas.*

Pensión Nueva Orleans. Right behind post office off Carrer Ample; good for access to Estació França. Flowery bedspreads, new bathrooms, very clean rooms, most with TVs. Call ahead if possible. Doubles 3,000 ptas, 4,500 ptas w/bath. *Carrer Ancha 53, tel. 93/315–34–07. Take Metro to Barceloneta or Estació França and take Carrer de la Fusteria away from port to Carrer Ample. MC, V.*

Pensión Venecia. Off Las Ramblas near Liceu Metro. Fluorescent lighting and smallish rooms compensated for by sparkling new bathrooms, nice owners, and quiet nights. Doubles 2,600 ptas, 3,500 ptas w/bath. *Carrer Junta de Comerç 13, tel. 93/302–61–34. Take Metro to Liceu and take Carrer de Hospital to Carrer Junta de Comerç.*

➤ **UNDER 5,000 PTAS** • **Hostal Oliva.** A most respectable uptown address on Passeig de Gràcia near Plaça de Catalunya with gorgeous courtyard and an old wooden elevator. Reservations taken with one night's deposit. Doubles 4,770 ptas, 5,800 ptas w/bath. *Passeig de Gràcia 32, tel. 93/488–01–62 or 93/488–17–89. Metro: Plaça de Catalunya.*

➤ **UNDER 6,000 PTAS** • **Hotel Roma.** Popular, if not particularly atmospheric, hotel right on Plaça Reial. Come here for central locale, quiet rooms (request one off the plaça), and new bathrooms. All rooms with telephone and bath. Doubles 5,500 ptas. *Pl. Reial 11, tel. 93/302–03–66 or 93/302–04–16. AE, MC, V.*

HOSTELS **Albergue Verge de Montserrat (HI).** Beautiful, Moorish-style building makes up for slightly inconvenient location out near Parc Güell. HI cards can be purchased here. Dorm beds and breakfast 1,000 ptas (1,500 ptas for those 26 and over). Reservations for groups only, so come between 8 AM and 9 AM to get a spot. Curfew at midnight, but doors open again at 1 AM and 2 AM sharp. *Carrer Mare de Déu del Coll 41–51, tel. 93/210–51–51. Take Metro to Vallcarca, then take Av. República Argentina over bridge to the right to Carrer Mare de Déu del Coll (a 15-min walk). Lockout 9:30 AM–1:30 PM, laundry, luggage storage, sheets 350 ptas. Closed Christmas.*

Hostal de Joves (HI). Across the street from Parc de la Ciutadella and convenient to Estació França. Dorm bed including breakfast and hot shower 975 ptas. Gets very busy in summer, so come before 10 AM and be persistent. They don't insist on an HI card. *Passeig de Pujades 29, tel. 93/300–31–04. Take Metro to Arc de Triomf, then take Carrer Nàpols to Passeig de Pujades. Midnight curfew, lockout 10 AM–3 PM, kitchen facilities, sheets 225 ptas.*

Kabul Youth Hostel. Privately owned hostel on Plaça Reial. Their ads boast "great party atmosphere." Don't come looking for peace and quiet, but it's friendly, casual, and a great place to schmooze. No curfew, lockout, or meals. Dorm bed 800 ptas. *Pl. Reial 17, tel. 93/318–51–90. Metro: Drassanes or Liceu. Laundry 500 ptas, luggage storage 75 ptas, sheets 150 ptas, pool tables, TV.*

Pensión Colón 3. On noisy Plaça Reial. No curfew or lockout. Dorm beds 900 ptas. Private rooms (singles 2,000 ptas, doubles with shower 3,600 ptas) also available. Reservations for private rooms only. *Carrer Colón 3, tel. 93/318–06–31. Metro: Drassanes or Liceu. Laundry, sheets 200 ptas.*

CAMPGROUNDS To reach the campgrounds south of the city take Bus 93 (runs 8 AM–9 PM) from Plaça Universitat; most sites are either on the main highway, Autovia Castelldefels, or just off it. The closest site to Barcelona, **Cala Gogó** (Carretera de la Platja s/n, El Prat de Llobregat, tel. 93/379–46–00), 10 km to the south, is very near the airport and noisy as hell. For general camping info, call **Asociación de Campings de Barcelona** (Gran Via de les Corts Catalanes 603, 3rd floor, tel. 93/415–59–55), or go to the tourist office for a list of campgrounds.

La Ballena Alegre. One of the biggest in the area, with space for 1,850 happy campers. It's 12.5 km south of the city. Clean, family-vacation type place. Like most campgrounds near Barcelona, it squats between the ocean and the freeway. Tent site for two people 2,000 ptas. *Autovia Castelldefels, Viladecans, tel. 93/658–05–04. Bus 93 from Pl. Universitat. Wheelchair access. Closed Oct.–mid-May.*

FOOD

Dining in Barcelona is done in characteristic Catalan style, late into the night and with exuberance. Although prices are, in general, a little higher than in other parts of Spain, it's not difficult to eat cheaply and well. The largest concentration of budget bars and restaurants is around Las Ramblas, the Barri Gòtic, and the currently hip neighborhood of Gràcia. You can also cut costs by going to one of the excellent open markets. The best is **Mercat Sant Josep,** a.k.a. **La Boqueria** (Metro: Liceu; open Mon.–Sat. 8–8), housed in a grand modernista structure. The meat section is truly a sight—bloody slabs of meat, eyeballs, and innards are enthusiastically displayed. Vegetarians should look to the self-service restaurant **Self Naturista** (Carrer de Santa Anna 13, tel. 93/318–23–88; closed Sun.). For a quick bite, there's an excellent falafel/*shawarma* (gyro) stand in Plaça Reial.

➤ **UNDER 800 PTAS • Blues Bar.** A bar with pictures of rock icons and American-style kitsch on walls. Bocadillos named after musicians like Bob Dylan and Lou Rawls. Also, try salads and *torrades* (grilled, open-face sandwiches), each for about 475 ptas–650 ptas. *Carrer Comerç 23, no tel. Metro: Jaume I. Closed weekdays 4–7 and dinner weekends.*

La Cova Fumada. Small and popular hole-in-the-wall in Barceloneta. There's no sign: Look for big wooden doors on south side of square. Grilled artichokes 150 ptas, fabulous calamari with garlic 280 ptas. Cheap beer. *Carrer Baluarte 56, no phone. Metro: Barceloneta. Closed Sun.*

Restaurant Borràs. Beautifully tiled, this busy lunch spot near Parc Ciutadella is popularly known as "Económico." Excellent 775 ptas menú del día, including beef stew, grilled chicken, and soups and salads. If you fancy liver, order the *hígado de ternera* (beef liver) prepared with garlic. *Pl. de Sant Agustí Vell 13, tel. 93/319–64–94. Head north off Carrer Princesa to Carrer Tantarantana to Pl. de Sant Agustí Vell. Lunch only; closed weekends.*

Velodromo. Open since 1909, this vast, high-ceilinged joint is the perfect place to stop for beer and tapas while out exploring the Eixample. Grilled octopus, artichokes, sardines, tortilla, and other tapas 150 ptas–350 ptas. *Carrer Muntaner 213, tel. 93/230–60–22. Metro: Diagonal. Closed Sun.*

El Xampanyet. Popular, bustling tapas bar just down the street from Picasso Museum. Famous for seafood tapas and *cava*, the local champagne (100 ptas a glass). *Carrer de Montcada 22, tel. 93/319–70–03. Metro: Jaume I. Closed Sun. night and Mon.*

➤ **UNDER 1,000 PTAS • Gran Bodega.** In the Eixample not far from Passeig de Gràcia, this atmospheric bar is famous for its tapas. Pics of the original owner with celebrities line the walls—find the one where he and Muhammad Ali are pretending to box. Lunch menú is 800 ptas. *Carrer Valencia 193, tel. 93/258–10–53. Metro: Passeig de Gràcia.*

La Llesca. Just north of Plaça del Sol in Gràcia. Friendly, with checkered-tile floor and collection of old radios in back room. Specializing in grilled meats, including *butifarra* (thick, Catalan sausage; 550 ptas) and *conejo* (rabbit; 880 ptas). *Carrer Terol 6, no phone. Metro: Joanic. Closed 4:30–8:30.*

Els Quatre Gats. Just off Avinguda Portal de l'Angel. Started in 1897 by Pere Romeu as a place for modernista artists to hang out and display their works. Picasso had his first exhibition here in 1901. A la carte items and the menú del día are pricey, but you can chow on tapas and beer for under 1,000 ptas. *Carrer Montsió 3, tel. 93/302–41–40. Metro: Catalunya. Closed Sun. lunch.*

➤ **UNDER 2,000 PTAS** • **Flash Flash.** Near Avinguda Diagonal just east of the Eixample; large menu specializing in that Spanish staple, tortilla (500 ptas–1000 ptas), a thick omelet usually filled with potatoes or spinach. The decor must be seen to be believed—sort of Andy Warhol meets Cher in a room from Kubrick's *Clockwork Orange. Carrer de la Granada de Penedes 25, tel. 93/237–09–90. Metro: Diagonal. Closed 5–8.*

La Fonda. This restaurant near Plaça Reial cannot be recommended highly enough. This chic, airy place seems out of place on the often congested Carrer dels Escudellers; it's less expensive than it looks, with very reasonable prices for generous portions of fantastic Catalan and Spanish specialties (400 ptas–950 ptas). If you splurge just once, this should be it. No reservations; come before 9 PM or stand in line. *Carrer dels Escudellers 10, tel. 93/318–87–29. Metro: Drassanes. Closed 3–8:30, and Mon.*

CAFES With its long, tree-lined Ramblas, countless plaças, and fundamentally social nature, Barcelona revels in café culture. One of the best cafés is the immensely popular **Café de l'Opera** (La Rambla 74, across from Gran Teatre del Liceu), a classy place to gulp your morning coffee (125 ptas), or a late night beer. **Café Valenciana** (Aribau 1) is another turn-of-the century spot, this one overlooking Plaça Universitat and specializing in wonderfully refreshing *horchatas* (a sweet, milky-colored drink made from nuts) and *granizados* (a Slurpee-like drink, usually flavored with lemon; 280 ptas). Out in Gràcia, try **Café del Sol** (Pl. del Sol 29), the most happening of several cafés and bars that line the plaça.

WORTH SEEING

With the exception of its two mountainous parks, **Montjuïc,** in the southwest corner, and **Tibidabo,** towering over the western border of the city, Barcelona is a flat, sprawling area. Most of the major sights are centrally located in the **Ciutat Vella** (Old Town), or on and around Las Ramblas. Take advantage of Barcelona's impressive transportation system to check out some of the more far-flung sights, such as Parc Güell and the Sagrada Familia (*see below*).

LAS RAMBLAS Everybody's favorite street, Las Ramblas is the hammering heartbeat of Barcelona. Technically, it's not one street but a series of five connected streets leading up from the port to the Plaça de Catalunya. Waiters from the cafés whisk glasses efficiently off the outside tables, while flamenco dancers, mimes, bird and flower vendors, folk singers, families, tourists, pickpockets, and cops all do their thing up and down its long, shady expanse. There are some sights to keep an eye out for while strolling along. Barcelona's opera house, the **Gran Teatre del Liceu** (La Rambla 61, tel. 93/318–79–80), with extravagant Baroque detail on every surface, is a gorgeous building housing the largest auditorium in Europe. Guided tours run weekdays at 11:30 AM and 12:15 PM for 200 ptas, 100 ptas students. Another building worth a peek is **Palau Güell** (Carrer Nou de la Ramba 3, tel. 93/317–39–74, just off Las Ramblas; open Mon.–Sat. 10–1 and 5–6), originally a private residence built around 1888 for the Güell family by Barcelona's favorite son, Antoni Gaudí. Now it's a museum, so waltz in for a look at the luxurious interior with high vaulted ceilings. Close by is the graceful **Plaça Reial,** designed according to Napoleonic city plans, with several entrances facing side streets and Las Ramblas. Despite the seedy characters hanging around, the palm trees, central fountain, and balconies overlooking the square make it quite lovely. Lively clubs and bars (*see* After Dark, *below*) line the plaça, and on Sunday and holidays there's a flea market with old coins, postcards, and books. Off Las Ramblas is

Barcelona's central food market, **La Boqueria** (*see* Food, *above*), a sensory overload of edibles. Look for the tile design by Joan Miró at Plaça Boqueria, near the market.

BARCELONETA AND THE HARBOR Las Ramblas peters out at the port at the **Monument a Colom,** with Columbus pointing ambitiously (greedily?) out to water. Stroll down the new, post-Olympic waterfront boardwalk, **Moll de la Fusta,** to get to the former fishing village of **Barceloneta.** While most of the port has been renovated with newly planted trees, immaculate stretches of lawn, and a lot of cement thrown in for good measure, Barceloneta itself still has a small neighborhood feel once you're off Passeig Nacional, the main drag. On the side streets, you'll stumble into some great little seafood restaurants. Barcelona's crowded beaches are just behind this strip of land; they're not the best you'll see in Spain, to be sure, but are welcome enough on a hot day. There are a couple of scenic ways to view the harbor. The **Teleférico** (cable car), open daily noon–8:15, heads from near the Columbus statue to the docks (850 ptas), or all the way up to Montjuïc (975 ptas). For far less dramatic (but cheaper) views, you can take sightseeing boats with **Las Golondrinas al Rompeolas** (330 ptas; daily 11–8) from near the Columbus statue.

PARC DE LA CIUTADELLA This large city park near Estació França has lots of trees (all labeled by variety) and lots of grass—perfect for sprawling and vegging out. The Catalunya Parliament meets here in a building that also houses the **Museu d'Art Modern** (tel. 93/319–57–28; admission 500 ptas; open Mon. 3–7:30, Tues.–Sat. 9–7:30, Sun. 10–3), with a great collection of works from the modernisme period. If you're into Gaudí, this is where you can get a look at what other Catalan artists (Fortuny, Casas, and Rusinyol) were doing at the same time. At the other end of the park is a monumental fountain designed by a young Gaudí as one of his first projects in Barcelona; note the extravagant detail that would become a hallmark of his work.

PARC DE MONTJUIC Montjuïc is another one of Barcelona's oasis-like parks that manages to thrive amid the tangled buzz of the city. This one allows you to escape the city by literally rising above it. Its prime location overlooking the city made it a favorite spot for the military. The fortress-like **Castell de Montjuïc** is where Franco's troops executed the president of the Catalan Generalitat. It now houses the **Museu Militar** (tel. 93/329–86–13; open Tues.–Sat. 10–2 and 4–8, Sun. 10–8), with an extensive collection of weapons, uniforms, and medals. The **Parc d'Attraccions de Montjuïc** is an amusement park with your basic harem-scarem rides—but did you really come all the way to Spain to ride a roller coaster? Montjuïc was also an important Olympic Games address, and you'll find the renovated **Estadi Olímpic de Montjuïc** (open weekends 10 AM–6 AM) and the impressively modern **Palau Sant Jordi,** both just off Avinguda de l'Estadi, a major road cutting through Montjuïc. To get to Montjuïc, take Metro Line 1 to Plaça d'Espanya from Plaça de Catalunya, then walk up the hill toward the **Palau Nacional** (National Palace). You can also hop on Bus 61 from Plaça d'Espanya or take the funiculars from near the Metro Paral-lel or near the port.

➢ **FUNDACIO JOAN MIRO** • This beautifully designed building in the Parc de Montjuïc with a light and airy feel and views of Barcelona houses the most important works of Joan Miró, an internationally known Catalan artist; Miró donated many of his works to this museum. You can trace the development of his distinctive art, heavy with abstract symbols and bright colors. *Pl. Neptú, on Av. Miramar, tel. 93/329–19–08. Admission: 500 ptas, 250 ptas students. Wheelchair access. Open Tues.–Sat. 11–7, Thurs. until 9:30, Sun. 10:30–2:30.*

TIBIDABO There is no better way to appreciate Barcelona's massive, sprawling splendor than by heading west to the mountain of Tibidabo, Barcelona's highest point. Views are fantastic, particularly when Barcelona's nasty smog has blown somewhere else for the day. You'll also find an odd pairing of a church and amusement park (admission 950 ptas; open Wed.–Fri. 11–7, weekends and holidays noon–10 PM). The basilica has some interesting frescoes depicting nautical scenes. To get up here, take Ferrocarriles Catalanes to Avenida Tibidabo; then take Bus "Tramvia Blau" at JFK Plaça, which brings you to the funicular (200 ptas–250 ptas one way) to make the final ascent.

BARRI GOTIC Most of Barcelona's oldest and most-visited sights are all packed into the Barri Gòtic's (Gothic Quarter's) tiny, winding streets, where the day's laundry hangs down over everything like banners. When Barcelona was a walled city, this densely populated area was built up story by story because people had no room to go but up. The Barri Gòtic revolves around the **Catedral** (*see below*), and **Plaça de Sant Jaume,** home to the impressive **Ajuntament** (Town Hall), and bordered by Las Ramblas and Via Laietana. Crossing Via Laietana, you enter the area known as **La Ribera,** with a similar look and feel to the Barri Gòtic except with a lot more air and light. Here you'll find Museu Picasso and the church of **Santa María del Mar** (open daily 10–12:30 and 5–8), an excellent example of Catalonian-Gothic architecture with beautiful stained glass.

➤ **CATEDRAL** • Construction of this impressive Gothic structure began in 1298, but the main facade wasn't completed until 1890. The gloomy interior is brightened by candles blazing away in the 20-odd chapels—one chapel contains a replica of the famous Black Virgin icon found in Montserrat (*see Near Barcelona, below*). Enter the **museum** (admission 40 ptas; open daily 11–1) from the lovely, tropical cloister with palm trees, gardenias, fountains, and geese. *Pl. de la Seu. Open daily 8–1:30 and 4–7:30.*

➤ **MUSEU FREDERIC MARES** • Downstairs, you'll browse through an extensive collection of sculptures of Christ, particularly of the Crucifixion. Look for the unusual 14th-century carving of Christ and Joseph of Arimathea, where Joe appears to be, um, giving Jesus a hand. It's a wonderful collection, but a bit heavy. The delightful upstairs section provides some much-needed comic relief, with the eccentric personal collection of local sculptor Frederic Marès. This guy was a collector extraordinaire, hoarding everything from turn-of-the-century keys, watches, photographs, cigarette cases, pipes, cards, stamps, shells, and more. *Near the cathedral, off Carrer dels Comptes, tel. 93/310–58–00. Admission: 300 ptas, 150 ptas students under 25. Open Tues.–Sat. 10–5, Sun. 10–2.*

Modernisme and Antoni Gaudí

Thanks to the home-grown genius of architect and visionary Antoni Gaudí, wandering around Barcelona can be a surreal experience—his wavy, elaborate, fantastical buildings pop up all over the place. In the late 19th and early 20th centuries, during the Catalan Renaissance, Gaudí helped popularize the style of "modernisme" in art and architecture. Gaudí, who was killed when hit by a streetcar in 1926, continues to be the city's favorite son, but other brash Catalan architects and designers of the period include Domènech i Muntaner and Puig i Cadafalch.

The parts of town hoarding the majority of the modernista works are the Eixample and Gràcia. An obligatory stop on the Gaudí route is the Casa Milà, a.k.a. La Pedrera (Passeig de Gràcia 92, tel. 93/488–35–92; tours Tues.–Sat. at 10, 11, noon, and 1), an entire apartment block built in 1905–1910 as Gaudí's last project of civil architecture. The building's nickname means "rock pile," owing to its organic, chipped-rock exterior; the interior is just as wild, with every normally mundane detail of a building—railings, chimneys, columns, doors—a mix of the functional and the surreal. One of Gaudí's first works hides in the neighborhood of Gràcia. Casa Vicens (Carrer de les Carolines 22, Metro: Fontana) is a beautiful brick-and-tile Mudéjar-style building. Many other modernista works are scattered about town. Pick up the free, highly informative guide, "Discovering Modernist Art in Catalonia," from the tourist office.

➤ **MUSEU PICASSO** • The museum's two medieval palaces contain one of the world's best collections of Picasso's work. Barcelona is a fitting host—Picasso spent many of his formative years here, including his Blue Period from 1901 to 1904. The collection is particularly strong on his earlier work, including some incredibly sharp portraits of his father that Picasso painted when he was a mere lad of 14. *Carrer de Montcada 15, off Carrer de la Princesa, tel. 93/319–63–10. Admission: 500 ptas, students free. Open Tues.–Sat. 10–8, Sun. 10–3.*

TEMPLE EXPIATORI DE LA SAGRADA FAMILIA You'll visit countless cathedrals while in Spain, but you'll never see anything like this. This fantastical, Dr. Seuss-ish building was Gaudí's all-consuming project until he died—he left it unfinished, and cranes still hover around various parts of the cathedral. The design involves complex symbolism, with 18 towers (of which only four, representing the Apostles, the Evangelists, the Virgin, and Christ, are completed). You can take an elevator up for 100 ptas, but climb the stairs to get a view of the unfinished inside. A small museum chronicles the work on the building. *Pl. Sagrada Familia s/n, tel. 93/255–0247. Metro: Sagrada Familia. Admission: 500 ptas. Open daily 8 AM–9 PM.*

PARC GUELL Commissioned by Eusebi Güell in 1900 as a kind of garden-city intended for single-family residences, Parc Güell ended up instead as a whimsical city park with fine views and a curvy wonder of a park bench adorned with colorful ceramic tiles. A modernista-style house (once Gaudí's residence) is now a museum, **Casa Museu Gaudí** (tel. 93/214–64–46; admission 150 ptas; open Apr.–Oct., daily 9–2 and 4–8, shorter hrs off-season), with furniture built with the same imaginative flair as the building. *Carrer d'Olot. Bus 24 from Passeig de Gràcia. Open May–Aug., daily 10–9; shorter hrs off-season.*

CHEAP THRILLS

The tradition of campy drag performance positively flourishes in Barcelona, with a very Pedro Almodóvar/John Waters flair. The best place to see a free, fun-for-the-whole-family drag show is at **Marsella** (Carrer Sant Pau 65, no phone; Metro: Liceu), Thursday and Sunday nights at 12:30 AM. Unfortunately, they don't do shows in July and August—"It's too hot," they say. The audience is packed with mostly young, middle-class people slumming it in the Barri Xinès to enjoy the silly fun of it. Just a few blocks away toward the port is the **El Cangrejo** (Carrer Montserrat 9, tel. 93/301–85–75; closed Mon.), which serves up its own tacky, flashy drag show for free on Thursday and Saturday nights.

FESTIVALS Barcelona is a city that lives for fun and socializing; tons of festivals—both secular and religious—fill the streets. Big ones to look out for are **Sant Jordi's Day** on April 23, celebrating Catalunya's patron saint with everyone exchanging books and roses; and **Sant Joan's Day** (June 23), with firecrackers, bonfires, and partying all night. In August, the neighborhood of Gràcia is the site of the biggest celebration of the **Assumption of Mary,** with dancing, fireworks, and street decorations. In September, the **Festa de la Mercè** (Our Lady of Mercy) goes down with music, fireworks, and parades of papier-mâché giants. Finally, there is the state-sponsored **Grec Summer Festival,** a series of cultural events from June through September ranging from rock concerts to opera and theater productions. Get program info at Palau de la Virreina (*see* Visitor Information, *above*).

AFTER DARK

Take advantage of the midday siesta; you're going to need some extra sleep to do as the natives do—start late, and stay out until dawn. Locals head out for a drink or two around 11:30 PM or midnight, and eventually scoot on over to a club or disco. The only real difference between a bar and a disco is that the former stays open until 2 or so, while the latter stays open until 5 AM or later. Some discos and music clubs charge a cover, though whether it's enforced depends entirely on the whims of the doorman.

Generally speaking, you'll find the swanky designer spots out near Avinguda Diagonal in the Eixample, in Gràcia, and along Carrer de Marià Cubí, just off Via Augusta. The funky, shabby places are in and around the Barri Xinès. The *Guia del Ocio*, sold at many newsstands for 60 ptas, has listings of music, cinema, and theater.

BARS **Casa Quimet.** Known more popularly as the "Guitar Bar," this famous old bar in Gràcia has guitars galore hanging from the ceiling, which you are free to play; sessions develop. Beer 300 ptas. *Carrer Rambla del Prat 9, off Carrer Gran de Gràcia, tel. 93/227–87–81. Metro: Fontana.*

El Gato Rojo. Good rocking music, dart boards, and great Guinness on draught (350 ptas) in this small place run by an English woman. International crowd of young hipsters. *Carrer Vigatans 13, tel. 93/319–71–69. Just off Carrer Argenteria. Metro: Jaume I. Closed Mon.*

London Bar. Opened in 1910, this famous bar was once the hangout (so to speak) of circus performers, which explains the trapeze over the bar. Stage in back for jazz performances and drag shows. *Carrer Nou de la Rambla 34, tel. 93/318–52–61. Metro: Drassanes. Closed Mon., Tues.*

Mirablau. On the way up to or down from Tibidabo, stop here where you can sit and drink with nothing between you and the steep hill below. Amazing view and cheaper drinks than you would expect (beer 225 ptas, wine 200 ptas). *Final Av. Tibidabo, tel. 93/418–58–79. Take Tramvia Blau from Pl. JFK to the end at the base of the funicular to Tibidabo.*

LIVE MUSIC AND CLUBS Most of these places don't get going until at least midnight.

La Boîte. Great live jazz and blues in this low-ceilinged, mirrored club in the Eixample. On weekends after 2 AM, a DJ plays funk and everyone shakes their butts until 6 AM. Cover including drink is usually 1,000 ptas–1,500 ptas. *Av. Diagonal 477, tel. 93/419–59–50. Metro: Diagonal.*

Gay Nightlife: How to Score

Barcelona has a thriving gay scene—here are some of the best places, and the hour(s) in which to make your appearance. First, start at the barnlike Punto BCN (Carrer Muntaner 63–65), where everyone starts out their night with a couple of drinks. From midnight to 1:30 AM, it's the place to be. Next, head around the corner to Este Bar (Carrer Consejo de Ciento 257), where all the prettiest men in Barcelona are to be found. Small and well-lit, this bar is where you can check everyone out and make that crucial eye contact. Stay here until 2:30 AM, or until you're tired of flirting. Now, slide just down the road to Satanassa (Carrer Aribau 27; closed Sun.) to join in some sweaty dancing on the crowded floor. For the grand finale, head to Marten's Disco (Passeig de Gràcia 130), the biggest gay disco in town. If you're ready for more when is closes at 5 AM, go to Distrito-Distinto (Av. Meridiana 140), a mixed disco that's a tad off the beaten track, but open until 9 AM.

Unfortunately, lesbians don't have as many options because the scene is smaller and more underground. However, Daniel's (Carrer de Santa Peronella 7, bet. Carrer de Marià Cubí and Carrer de la Forja) is a very cool, low-key women's club with free snacks and a small but groovin' dance floor. Ring the buzzer for entry.

Karma. If you just want to dance your ass off and aren't concerned with atmosphere or attitudes, come to this thumping, loud disco on Plaça Reial; 1,000 ptas cover is usually not collected. *Pl. Reial 10, tel. 93/302–56–80. Closed Mon.*

Pipe Club. You don't have to smoke a pipe to get in—just ring the buzzer for entry. Dim lighting, comfy chairs; 500 ptas cover for live blues, jazz, and Irish music. *Pl. Reial 3, next to Cervecería Glaciar, tel. 93/302–47–32. Closed Wed.*

Near Barcelona

MONTSERRAT

Barcelona may be the undisputed cultural and political capital of Catalunya, but the spiritual home of the region is definitely the monastery of Montserrat, perched high atop bizarre rock formations. Poet Joan Maragall wrote that "Montserrat is the Catalan miracle," and the mountain truly seems miraculous—until you read the brochures with dry, scientific explanations about limestone and ocean drainage some 10 million years ago. The monastery dates back to the early 11th century, and has long been intimately associated with Catalan identity and the preservation of the Catalan language. During Franco's reign, when Catalan was officially banned, the monastery was one of the few places allowed to perform mass in the language. As well as being one of the most breathtaking symbols a region could ask for, Montserrat is famous beyond Catalunya on account of the Black Virgin icon housed in the **basilica** (open daily 8–8). The Black Virgin sits high atop a silver throne, encased in a protective Plexiglass shield. (Thoughtfully, one hand has been left exposed for the pilgrims to kiss.) Try to time your visit to the basilica so that you can hear the heavenly **Montserrat Boys' Choir** sing the *Salve Regina* (daily at 1 PM) in truly angelic voices.

Pilgrimages aside, hiking around the mountain can be a religious experience in itself, offering awe-inspiring views of the plains below and the weird rocks above. You can walk to the highest point, Sant Jeroni, or take the **funicular** (700 ptas round-trip, 620 ptas students; open daily 10–7) up to Sant Joan, near the summit. The **tourist booth** (Pl. de la Creu, tel. 93/835–02–51 ext. 586; open daily 10–6) is right across from the funicular.

While Montserrat makes a fine day trip, it's damn inspiring to wake up perched on this awesome mountain. You can stay in the dorm rooms adjoining the monastery at **Cel-les de Montserrat** (Monestir de Montserrat, tel. 93/835–02–51 ext. 630) for as little as 1,200 ptas per person.

COMING AND GOING **Ferrocarriles Catalanes trains** (EurailPasses aren't accepted) leave from Barcelona's Plaça d'Espanya. They connect at the Montserrat rail station with the Montserrat Aeri (cable car) for a hair-raising ride up to the monastery (total travel time 1½ hrs, 1,050 ptas round-trip). If dangling over the mountain makes you nervous, **Julia Tours buses** (Ronda Universitat 5, tel. 93/316–64–54) leave from Barcelona's Estació Sants.

SITGES

In Sitges, a small beach resort 36 km south of Barcelona, you can enjoy both quiet days vegging out on beautiful beaches and frenetic nightlife in countless bars and discos. There are a series of fine beaches all along the main Passeig Marítim; if you want a tad more seclusion, walk up behind the church and city hall to the smaller **Platja de Sant Sebastià**. Walk 2 km south to **Platjas del Muerto** for sunbathing in the buff.

Carrer Primer de Maig, dubbed "The Street of Sin," is stuffed with bars; all night the tanned masses spill out into the street while music thumps in the background. Also try along both Carrer San Francisco and Carrer San Buenaventura for gay, mixed, and straight bars and clubs. **Carnival** in Sitges is one of the wildest anywhere. It's like a mini-Rio de Janeiro, with nonstop partying, parades, and lots of men in high-style drag.

Trains from Barcelona (30 min, 240 ptas) arrive at the **station** (Pl. E. Maristany, tel. 93/894–98–89), a 10-minute walk from the center of town and the beach. The **oficina de turisme** (Oasis complex, tel. 93/894–1230; open July–Sept. 15, daily 9–9, shorter hrs off-season) is down the hill and to your right as you exit the station.

WHERE TO SLEEP AND EAT Cheap lodging can be problematic in July and August. Hunt around the streets in the center of town; from the oficina de turisme, head down Passeig de Vilafranca. **Hostal Casabella** (Av. Artur Carbonell 12, tel. 93/894–27–53; doubles 3,450 ptas) has rooms reminiscent of summer camp: spartan, yet homey. The rooms at **Hostal Internacional** (Carrer San Francisco 52, tel. 93/894–40–52) are the cheapest around at 3,250 ptas for a double in high season, and 1,600 ptas in the off-season. For eats, the cozy **Bar Baron** (Carrer Sant Gaudenci 17) is a good, central spot for a cheap bocadillo (230 ptas–250 ptas) and tapas.

Around Catalunya

Don't limit your stay in Catalunya to Barcelona; this autonomous region has other charms that deserve exploration. The beaches along the Mediterranean coast have long been a popular destination; the Greeks were here a good 2,000 years ago, leaving behind fascinating ruins at **Empúries.** Where the Greeks went the Romans followed, and now cities like **Tarragona** offer impressive evidence of their civilization. Part of the spectacular Pyrenees mountain range is also in Catalunya, though visiting means conquering some transportation challenges. For information on the Catalan Pyrenees, *see* Northern Spain, The Pyrenees, *below.*

Costa Brava

This rugged stretch of coastline between the French border and Barcelona is Catalunya's most obvious—and subsequently overvisited—attraction. The hotel-building spree of the 1960s may have marred the beauty of some of the more developed resorts, but a number of small fishing villages have hung onto their traditional appearance.

PORT BOU

A tiny fishing village before the international rail barreled through in 1878, Port Bou, edging right up to the French border, still retains a bit of that old-fashioned flavor. Here you can enjoy characteristic Costa Brava scenery—small cove beaches with jutting cliffs surrounding them—without having to share the views with too many tourists.

The **train station** looms above the town; head down any street and you'll hit downtown. Hourly trains go to Barcelona (2½ hrs, 1,100 ptas). For RENFE info, call 972/39–00–99. From the train station, Carrer del Mercado will take you directly to Passeig de la Sardana, the beach boardwalk.

WHERE TO SLEEP AND EAT Happily, lodging in Port Bou is less expensive than in some of the more showy beach resorts. **Hostal Juventus** (Av. Barcelona 3, tel. 972/39–02–41), just half a block off Passeig de la Sardana, is an excellent value, with big, bright, airy doubles for 2,600 ptas. If they're full, ask about rooms in the pizza place next door. **Hostal Comercio** (Rambla Catalunya 16, tel. 972/39–00–01) is not quite as nice, but it's cheaper (doubles 2,000 ptas) and sits on the peaceful tree-lined street near the **oficina de turisme** (Passeig de la Sardana, off the boardwalk, tel. 972/39–02–84).

On the boardwalk, you'll find a bunch of cafés and restaurants with surprisingly cheap menús del día (about 900 ptas). Hordes of waiters hover about and serve good food at **Restaurant España** (Passeig de la Sardana 4, tel. 972/39–00–08). For cheaper eats, head up Carrer Miguel Cabre off Passeig de la Sardana for some quiet, local tapas bars.

FIGUERES

The spirit of Figueres's favorite son, Salvador Dalí, permeates life in this pleasant, relatively untouristed town. Dalí was born here in 1904, and in 1974 he opened the **Teatre-Museu Dalí** (Pl. Gala-Salvador Dalí 5, tel. 972/51–19–76; admission 600 ptas, 400 ptas students; closed Mon. in winter) on the spot where he held his first public exhibition in 1918. One of the most popular museums in all of Spain, it's a fantastical building full of the whimsical and macabre. If you leave the Dalí museum wondering what inspired his mad vision, go to the **Museu del Joguets** (Rambla 10, tel. 972/50–45–85; admission 300 ptas; closed Feb. and Tues. in winter) for an answer. This museum contains an eccentric collection of antique toys, games, and dolls from Catalunya and elsewhere in Spain; the mask of a laughing head with a snail crawling up its nose is not too far a jump from Dalí's car with snail-covered passengers. Also worth a visit is the **Castle Sant Ferran,** where Dalí did his time in the military. You can't actually go inside, but the views from atop the hill are wonderful.

BASICS The **American Express** office is at Viatges Figueres (Carrer Peralada 28, tel. 972/50–91–00; open Mon.–Sat. 9–1 and 4–8). The well-stocked **oficina de turisme** (Pl. del Sol, tel. 972/50–31–55; open weekdays 8:30–8, Sat. 9–1:30 and 3:30–8) is just past the Rambla up Carrer Lasuca.

COMING AND GOING Both the bus and train stations are a 15-minute walk from the town center. From the stations, go straight up Carrer Sant Llàtzer to Carrer Nou and turn right towards the Rambla and the museum. The **train station** (tel. 972/50–46–61) has trains to Barcelona (2 hrs, 870 ptas), Port Bou (30 min, 200 ptas), and Girona (1 hr, 250 ptas). The **bus station** (tel. 972/30–06–23), just west of the train station, has buses to Cadaqués (1½ hrs, 350 ptas) and other Costa Brava destinations. Buy tickets at the station's **SARFA** window; they offer a 10% discount for folks under 25 years. Student discount train tickets and RENFE tickets are also available in town at **Viajes del Sol** (Carrer Lasauca 20, tel. 972/50–86–00).

WHERE TO SLEEP AND EAT The streets around the Dalí museum yield the most lodging and dining possibilities. There are two cheapish places right off Carrer del Castell: **Pensión Mallol** (Carrer Pep Ventura 9, tel. 972/50–22–83), with large, nicely tiled doubles for 2,800 ptas; and, next door, **Pensión Victoria** (Carrer Pep Ventura 5, tel. 972/51–05–10), with spartan but clean doubles for 2,550 ptas. If they're full, ask about rooms at the bar next door. For a splurge, try **Hotel Los Angeles** (Carrer Barceloneta 10, tel. 972/51–06–61; doubles 3,800 ptas, 4,800 ptas in Aug.), with big bathrooms, comfy beds, and Dalí prints in the hallway. The centrally located **HI hostel** (Carrer Anicet Pagés 2, tel. 972/50–12–13; beds 1,000 ptas, 1,500 ptas 26 and over; closed Oct.–mid Nov. and Christmas) is just a block away from the oficina de turisme. You'll find clusters of cheap restaurants along Carrer de la Jonquera behind the museum. **Crostó** (Carrer de la Jonquera 3) is one of the best, with yummy vegetarian paella served in a dining room adorned with the *pan de tres crostons* (bread with three crusts) that also decorates the Dalí museum's exterior; Dalí was apparently obsessed with bread, and it's a common symbol in his works.

CADAQUES

Come play expatriate artist in this picturesque town of whitewashed houses and cobblestone streets. Cadaqués is the place to hang out and savor both natural beauty and an artsy, bohemian atmosphere that is the legacy of the likes of Dalí, Picasso (who lived here while developing his Cubist style), and García Lorca. The beach itself is small and pebbly, but

At night, go to L'Hostal, a bar on Passeig Marítim, and try to imagine the scene on the night sometime in the '70s when Dalí brought Mick Jagger in for a drink.

there are excellent hikes around the coast and the surrounding hills. Dalí groupies should make a pilgrimage to his house, soon to be converted into a museum, about 1 km away in Port Lligat. Definitely worth a visit is the **Museu Perrot Moore** (Carrer Vigilant, tel. 972/25–80–76; admission 400 ptas, 250 ptas students; open daily 10:30–1:30 and 4–8, Sun. 10:30–1:30), boasting the earliest painting by Dalí, done when he was eight years old, as well as 42 studies and sketches for Picasso's famous *Guernica* painting. The **oficina de turisme** (Carrer Cotxe 2, tel. 972/25–83–15; open Mon.–Sat. 10–1 and 4–7) is just off Plaça de Federico Rahola. There's no train service to Cadaqués, but **SARFA** bus company (tel. 972/25–87–13) has buses to Figueres (1½ hrs, 350 ptas). Buses arrive and depart on Carrer Sant Vicens, a five-minute walk from the town center.

WHERE TO SLEEP AND EAT Your only problem here is finding a cheap room in high season. Call ahead in July and August. Try the big **Hostal Marina** (Carrer Riera 3, tel. 972/25–81–99) just off the main square with doubles for 3,500 ptas. **Pensión Ranxo** (Carrer Riera, next to supermarket, tel. 972/25–80–05) has pleasant, spacious doubles with bathrooms and breakfast for 4,500 ptas. A cheaper option is the small, family-run **Fonda Encarna** (Carrer Tórtola 5, tel. 972/25–80–19), with doubles for 3,000 ptas. Carrer Miquel Roset, which runs parallel to Passeig Marítim, is restaurant row with a number of cheap and moderate places. Also try **Restaurant Vehi** (Carrer de l'Esglesia 6, tel. 972/25–84–70), where the owner will remind you of your favorite aunt and stuff you with excellent seafood (menús 900 ptas–1,200 ptas).

Tarragona

South of Barcelona and the popular Costa Brava resorts, often-overlooked Tarragona is a former Roman stronghold that preserves impressive Roman ruins, a lovely beach, and a massive, magnificent cathedral. Well-preserved Roman sites are clustered in the upper part of town, bordered by remains of Roman walls on three sides, while the newer section of town and the beach and port spread out below.

To get into the Roman thing, check out the well-preserved **Amfiteatre** (Parc del Miracle; admission 400 ptas, students free; closed Mon., also Sun. in winter). It dates from the 1st century AD and has fine views overlooking **Platja Miracle,** Tarragona's main beach. **Museu Arquelógic** (Pl. del Rei, tel. 977/23–62–06; admission 100 ptas; closed Mon.) has an excellent collection of mosaics from the 1st through 3rd centuries AD. The **Museu d'Art Modern** (Carrer Santa Anna 8, tel. 977/23–50–32; admission 100 ptas; open Tues.–Sat. 10–8, Sun. 11–2) is a light, airy building with classically styled sculptures by Catalan artist Julio Antonio, as well as a large, multicolored tapestry by Joan Miró, a gift to the Tarragona Red Cross after his daughter was in a car accident here. The **Catedral** (Pl. de la Seu, tel. 977/23–86–85; admission 300 ptas; closed Sun. in winter) is a magnificent hulking monster made from a mix of architectural styles. Inside, the chapels are elaborately decorated and tapestries hang in the naves. Be sure to look up and check out the big, bad organ, one of the largest in Catalunya.

VISITOR INFORMATION Oficina de Turisme de la Generalitat (Carrer Fortuny 4, just off Rambla Nova, tel. 977/23–34–15; open Tues.–Sun. 9–2 and 4–7) has lots of info, as do the two other offices at Rambla Nova 46 (tel. 977/23-21–43) and Carrer Major 39 (tel. 977/29–62–24).

COMING AND GOING Frequent trains arrive from Barcelona (1½ hrs, 465 ptas) and Valencia (3 hrs, 1,490 ptas). The **train station** (Passeig d'Espanya, tel. 977/24–02–02) is a 10-minute walk east and slightly south of Rambla Nova. There's a bus stop to your left as you exit the station. If you arrive by bus you're near the hostel but a longer walk from the old town and other lodgings. Take Bus 9 from outside the station to Rambla Vella and you'll be in the heart of town. The **bus station** (Pl. Imperial Tárraco, tel. 977/22–91–26) has daily buses to Barcelona (800 ptas) and Valencia (1,970 ptas).

Most sights are clustered in and around the old part of the city, but the "Circular A" and the "Circular B" buses circle around the city, stopping at the train and bus stations, the port area of El Serrallo, and Rambla Nova. To get to the beach, either walk a short distance down Via Augusta from Rambla Nova, or take Bus 9. Most lines run until about 10:30 PM, and the cost is 75 ptas per ride.

WHERE TO SLEEP Budget accommodations are concentrated in front of the train station and in the old part of town around Plaza de la Font. A five-minute walk from the train station down Carrer Barcelona is **Hostal Residencia Abella** (Carrer Apodaca 26, tel. 977/23–42–24;

doubles 2,700 ptas). It's not in the most picturesque part of town, but the owners are friendly. The rooms at **Pensión Marsal** (Pl. de la Font 26, tel. 977/22–40–69) are small but cheap
(doubles 3,000 ptas) and have ceiling fans; some rooms overlook a pretty plaça. The well-
maintained **Sant Jordi hostel** (Av. President L. Companys at Carrer Marquès de Guad-el-Jelu,
tel. 977/24–01–95) has dorm beds for 1,000 ptas, 1,500 ptas for those over 25. Walk up
Avinguda President L. Companys from Plaça Imperial Tarraco. You can **camp** north of the

Andorra

*Andorra, a tiny semiautonomous principality, is squeezed into the scenic mountains
between the borders of Spain and France. Andorra's claim to fame is that it imposes
no taxes on luxury items such as booze, cigarettes, perfume, and electronic gear
(imagine one huge duty-free airport shop and you'll get the picture). The result is that
on the main shopping strips of the capital, Andorra la Vella, you'll witness unbridled
capitalism and a total sacrifice of aesthetics for the convenience of the consumer.
The assault of shops would not be so offensive if it were not taking place in such a
gorgeous location: The mountains tower on either side of you, and there is a rushing
river curving through the center of town. Luckily, the older part of town has been
spared much of the madness, and a walk through this quarter gives you an idea of
what, until recently, was a charming little town.*

*Andorra la Vella is the best spot to base yourself for checking out the rest of Andorra.
Most cheap accommodations are centered along the main streets of Avinguda Meritxell and its continuation, Avinguda Princep Benlloch. Just off Plaça Guillemó, where
the bus from La Seu d'Urgell drops you off, is Residència Benazet (Carrer la Llacuna
19, tel. 8/20698), with bright rooms, lacy curtains, and firm beds at 1,300 ptas per
person. The charming hostess gives a 10% discount to students. You can find heaps
of cheap eats around the shopping district. The Viena Restaurant (Carrer la Vall 32,
tel. 8/29233; closed Nov.) serves yummy escalivada (marinated eggplant and peppers) for 450 ptas.*

*A mere 20-minute jaunt from the capital by local bus takes you to the smaller, less-
developed towns of Ordino, Canillo, and El Serrat, where you can hike around the
Pyrenees. The mountain range is filled with truly gorgeous scenery, verdant green
hills, snow-capped mountains, rivers, and hordes of wild flowers, including the daf-
fodil, which is the symbol of the country—not the Camel cigarette logo, as you might
otherwise assume based on its prevalence on billboards and buildings. You can get
hiking maps and information about places to stay from the tourist office in Andorra la
Vella (Av. Meritxell at Carrer Bisbe Princep Iglesias, tel. 8/27117). The American
Express office (Carrer Roc dels Escolls 12) is right off Avinguda Princep Benlloch.*

*You can get to Andorra by direct bus (4 hrs, 2,105 ptas) from Barcelona with the Alsi-
na Graells bus company (Ronda Universitat 4, tel. 93/302–65–45), or by bus from
other cities in Catalunya.*

city along the beach. **Tarraco** (C-340, tel. 977/23–99–89; 450 ptas per person and 450 ptas per tent; closed Oct.–Mar.), 2 km north, is the closest; take Bus 3A.

FOOD There aren't many inexpensive restaurants in Tarragona, but a few cheap comedors dot the streets leading away from the train station. The port neighborhood of **El Serallo** has a bunch of restaurants with the fresh catch of the day at moderate prices. Try **El Varado** (Carrer Santa Andreu and Trafalgar) for delicious *pulpito en salsa* (octopus; 675 ptas). Closer to the center of town, try **Restaurant Delicias** (Carrer August 8, tel. 977/23–21–04; closed Sun. night) for a 1,100-ptas menú with the regional dish *pescado Romesco* (fish prepared with tomatoes, hazelnuts, almonds, onions, and garlic). Plaça de la Font, just above Rambla Vella, yields cheaper options. **Can Peret** (Pl. de la Font) is a café that serves cheap, scrumptious croissants and empanadas. Before leaving Tarragona, you *must* try the incredible churros at the stand near the main tourist office. Get a big, hot bag (150 ptas) and you'll be addicted. For some night fun, get a drink at **El Cau** (Carrer del Trinquet Vell, just off Pl. de la Font), a Roman-era underground cave turned into a bar with aquariums and good-looking patrons.

Balearic Islands

For most Europeans, the Balearic Islands repre-sent the height of hedonistic vacationing. Los Baleares are an autonomous Spanish province, and each of the four main islands—Ibiza, Formentera, Mallorca, and Menorca—has been gradually replacing Castilian Spanish with the Catalan language that dominated before Franco banned its use. **Ibiza** is the wildest resort island in the Balearics, if not the world. Cross-dressers, hippies, the ultra cool, the utterly normal, and everyone else meet on the streets of Ibiza's main town every night. Off Ibiza's southern tip, **Formentera** is the smallest of them all and has absolutely spectacular beaches and nature trails. **Mallorca,** the biggest, most-visited, and best-known island, is the home of the capital of the archipelago, Palma. **Menorca,** the most easterly of the group, is pretty mediocre for nightlife, but has a cool countryside and some out-of-the-way beaches.

Your biggest challenge as a traveler to the Balearic Islands will be the battle to find a place to stay. Rooms are sometimes booked weeks in advance, and even if they're available, you'll have to pay inflated prices. The rugged traveler will rent a moped and crash on a deserted beach. Camping in unofficial campsites is forbidden, but in practice, few people ever get moved along from obscure beaches. The next-greatest cost will be transportation between islands and to the mainland. The small number of companies conspire to keep prices high, but some flights on Aviaco—Iberia's sister line—from Palma to Ibiza or Palma to Mahón are as much as 900 ptas cheaper than ferry tickets, and flights take only 25 minutes.

Ibiza

Visitors come to Ibiza (known to locals as Eivissa) to do just one thing: whatever the hell they want. This island rivals all other Mediterranean resorts in the quality and variety of nightlife. On Ibiza you'll find dancing and partying as well as hiking and biking trails. And, in case you're overwhelmed by Ibiza, nearby Formentera (*see below*) offers a convenient escape.

The town of **Ibiza** is a lively spot, filled with bars, restaurants, and fashion boutiques. Built into a mountain, it maintains some 16th-century walls and a small old quarter, but for the most part is a modern, characterless tourist mecca. You have to take a bus to get to the nearest beach, **Playa d'En Bossa.** Further away, the beach at **Santa Eulàlia** (northeast of Ibiza) is lined with hotels but is not nearly as frenetic or developed as the resort of **Sant Antoni de Portmany,** on the west coast. **Portinatx,** along the island's north coast, is a series of small coves with sandy beaches, of which the first and last, Cala Xarraca and Caló d'Es Porcs, are the best. If you tire of the crowds at any of these places, you can take a boat that circles the island and hop off at any beach along the way—some are only accessible by water. Boats leave from the ferry port in Ibiza, and most companies charge around 1,000 ptas.

BASICS Ibiza Town greets visitors with an **tourist office** (Passeig de Vara de Rey 13, tel. 971/30–19–00) and an **American Express office** (C. Vicente Cuervo 9, tel. 971/31–11–11).

COMING AND GOING **Transmediterránea** (Av. Bartolomé Vicente Ramón, tel. 971/31–41–73) ferries serve Barcelona (3–6/week, 8 hrs, 5,700 ptas), Valencia (5/week, 8 hrs, 5,700 ptas), and Palma (2–3/week, 5 hrs, 4,200 ptas). **Flebasa** (Puerto Maritimo, tel. 971/31–20–71) has between three and six daily trips to Formentera (30 mins, 1,600 ptas) and two weekly ferries to Alicante (8 hrs, 5,860 ptas). **Maforsa** (tel. 971/32–23–10) and **Transmapi** (tel. 971/31–44–86) also go to Formentera several times daily (1 hr, 1,070 ptas). The two major carriers at Ibiza's **airport** (tel. 971/30–03–00) are **Iberia/Aviaco** (tel. 971/30–03–00) and **Lufthansa/Condor** (tel. 971/30–33–90). An hourly bus connects the airport to Ibiza Town (15 min, 250 ptas).

Buses leave from the station on Avinguda Isadora Macabich. **H.F. Vilas** (tel. 971/31–21–17) runs to local beaches. **Autobuses San Antonio** (tel. 971/31–20–75) runs a night "Disco Bus" service to San Antonio and Playa d'En Bossa hourly from midnight to 5 AM. A Bonobus pass (600 ptas) gives you access to all buses all night long. **Ribas** (C. Vicente Cuervo 3, tel. 971/30–18–11) has a wide selection of scooters for under 3,000 ptas per day.

WHERE TO SLEEP AND EAT If you're coming here in the summer, try to get here before the end of July or at least come midweek, when there are fewer people arriving. There are a number of casas de huéspedes in the streets just parallel to Passeig de Vata de Rey, identifiable by the standard blue sign with the CH on it. At **Avenida** (Av. Bartolomé Vicente Ramón 26, tel. 971/30–33–14) you get a clean room with mediocre beds for 2,000 ptas a double. The same goes for the **Sol Paris** (C. Vicente Cuervo 8, tel. 971/31–12–22). The snazzier, newer **Hostal Residencia Sol y Brisa** (Av. Bartolomé Vicente Ramón, 15, tel. 971/31–08–08; doubles 2,800 ptas) has better beds and lots of backpackers.

There is no shortage of fast-food places in the old town, south of the marina. For a real meal, go to **Casa Gallega Machiño** (Av. Isidoro Macabich 24, tel. 971/31–64–74), where you can sit down to a whopper of a calzone with ham (550 ptas) or just grab a whole roast chicken to go (750 ptas). For a more esoteric experience, head over to **Es Pas Café** (C. Xeringa 7, tel. 971/31–18–57) and sample one of their fresh-squeezed juices (300 ptas) or have a light cheese and tomato bocadillo (250 ptas).

AFTER DARK Tease your hair, squeeze into that slinky skirt (girls *and* guys), and prepare to hit the streets. Ibiza exists for nightlife. The first thing everybody does here is go to the bars. From 10 to midnight, the old town/marina area becomes jam packed with people hanging out at tables and checking one another out. Most bars see a very mixed crowd. **Liberty Bar** (Pl. Gradigo 12, no phone), a British-owned hole-in-the-wall near the lighthouse at the eastern end of the marina waterfront, plays a good selection of modern rock. At no earlier than 2 AM, people head out to the discos. They charge roughly 4,000 ptas for admission, but if you pick up discount coupons in bars you can save a few pesetas. The big five discos are: **Pachà** (Paseo Maritimo, Ibiza), **Amnesia** (Carretera San Antonio), **Kiss** (Carretera San Antonio), **Space** (Carretera San Jose), and **Ku** (Playa d'En Bossa). All of these are on the Disco Bus line except Pachà, which is a 20-minute walk north of the Estación Maritimo. All these discos are replete with fly girls and guys, bizarre murals, and great sound and lights.

NEAR IBIZA

FORMENTERA Just 30 km south of Ibiza is the tiny, unassuming island of Formentera, home to only about 500 permanent residents. Less than 20 km from east to west coast, Formentera is better suited to day trips than spending the night. Every beach on the island features cobalt-blue water that is as clear as glass, perfect for snorkeling. The main port is **La Savina**, at the northern end of the island. Ferries from Ibiza come every hour (1 hr, 1,070 ptas), and hydrofoils every two hours (30 min, 1,600 ptas). Buy your ticket on the boat; there's no need to reserve in advance. The **oficina de turismo** (Edificio Junta Puertos, tel. 971/32–20–57) is at the port.

The best way to get around the island is by bicycle, but if you're not up for the hills, you'll want to rent a moped. Several companies in front of the port, including **Isla Blanca** (tel. 971/32–25–58) and **Moto Rent Mirada** (tel. 971/32–83–29) rent bikes (500 ptas–1,000 ptas) and mopeds (1,700 ptas–2,000 ptas). **Autocares Paya** (tel. 971/32–25–14) runs the island's single, infrequent bus line around the island.

Mallorca

By far the largest of the four islands, Mallorca makes an ideal intermediary stop on a tour of the Balearic Islands. Of all Balearic towns, the capital city of **Palma** comes the closest to approximating a real city. It's a big transport hub with a modern section and a large old town. The old town is dominated by a huge, dark Gothic cathedral which clashes nicely with the white, stucco walls of surrounding homes. A trip from Palma to **Cala d'Or,** a port town on the southeastern coast, is nearly 65 km—about as far as you can go from Palma and not end up in the drink. In the summer, the island is overrun by Germans, who rent homes in villages west and north of Palma; Brits, who descend on the coastal town of Peguera, 23 km west of Palma; and the French, who flood Alcúdia and swarm the nearby HI hostel (*see* Where to Sleep, *below*). So just where on this curiously horse-head-shaped island can a traveler go that is untrammeled by hundreds of others? In summertime, nowhere. But that doesn't mean you can't have a good time. Take a ferry to an otherwise inaccessible beach, or take a hike in the mountains on the peninsula northeast of Alcúdia. And besides, those foreign tourists are good about picking up hitchhikers, so you can't complain too much.

BASICS There are two principal **tourist offices** in Palma: one is in the Plaça Espanya (tel. 971/71–15–27), and the other is at Carrer Sant Domingo 11 (tel. 971/72–40–92). There's an **American Express office** (Passeig d'es Born, tel. 971/72–67–43) in Viajes Iberia.

COMING AND GOING Most people come here by air, since plane tickets are sometimes competitive with ferry ticket prices. Iberia/Aviaco (tel. 971/26–42–12 or 971/21–01–40) has several flights daily between Palma's **airport** (tel. 971/26–46–24) and Barcelona, Madrid, Valencia, Alicante, Ibiza, and Mahón. Bus 17 (30 min, 300 ptas) runs between Palma's airport and the bus station. **Transmediterránea** (tel. 971/40–50–14) runs ferries to Mallorca from Barcelona (7–10/week, 6,000 ptas, 9 hrs), Valencia (6/week, 5,700 ptas, 8 hrs), and Ibiza (2/week, 6 hrs, 5,700 ptas).

The cheapest way to get around is by bus. **Transports a Palma** (tel. 971/71–13–93) runs local buses from Plaça Espanya. Ask the tourist office for info on bus service around the island. Slow trains depart from Plaça Espanya, carting tourists to **Inca** and **Sóller.** Both towns are quite touristy, but Sóller is also cute and historical. If you can afford it, rent a car. **Hasso** (Camí Ca'n Pastilla 100, tel. 971/26–02–19 or 971/49–12–76) is cheap enough to warrant a bus ride to the town of Ca'n Pastilla, about 15 minutes east of Palma (Bus 100). Prices start at 3,300 ptas per day, but they charge less if you rent for more than three days or pay by cash at the time of rental. Reserve your car a week in advance for the best deal.

WHERE TO SLEEP The few cheap hostales in Palma are just west of Plaça Reina, in the narrow lanes of the old part of town. The cheapest beds period are at the **Hostal Goya** (C. Estanc 7, tel. 971/72–69–86), which features clean showers and an amiable staff for only 1,800 ptas per double. Only slightly more are the rooms at **Hostal Pons** (C. Ví 8, tel. 971/72–26–58), where for 2,400 ptas you can interact with bizarre but friendly Spanish Fawlty Towers–esque staff and sleep in huge, antique beds. The British proprietress at the **Hostal Ritzi** (C. Apuntadores 6, tel. 971/71–46–10) charges 2,700 ptas for big doubles. She'll also fix a full English breakfast for 375 ptas. There are two **HI hostels** on the island, but neither is in Palma. The nearer is at the beach of **Sometimes** (Costa Brava 13, tel. 971/26–08–92), about 20 minutes by bus from Palma. The farther, about 8 km west of the town of Alcúdia (Carretera a Cabo Pinar, km 4, tel. 971/54–53–95; beds 1,000 ptas), on the opposite side of the island, has an amazing view of Playa La Victoria. Unfortunately, there's no public transportation to the hostel. Head toward the hills, then follow signs to Ermita de la Victoria/Camí de la Victoria. Book about a week in advance to assure yourself a spot.

FOOD Finding food to your liking should be no problem—just remember that all restaurants close at midnight. West of Plaça Reina, Calle Apuntadores and Calle Vallseca are rife with restaurants of all shapes and sizes. For a slice of the good life without slicing into your budget, head to **Giovanini Pizzería** (C. Apuntadores 4, tel. 971/72–85–89), an Italian-food mecca where you can eat a Texas-size calzone, filled with tomato, ham, cheese and mushrooms, or spinach tortellini in a heavy cream sauce for only 700 ptas. For traditional Spanish café fare in a tiny bar reminiscent of a vintage Denny's diner, stop into **Bar Tomás** (Baron de Pinopar 2, tel. 971/71–26–18), at the north end of Passeig de la Rambla. A tortilla or tuna bocadillo costs 225 ptas, and a whopping plate of fresh calamari is 520 ptas.

AFTER DARK In Palma, near the marina, there are hip bars and clubs along **Passeig de Sagrera**, between Plaça Llotja and Plaça Reina. The coolest bar is **Abaco** (Sant Joan 1, no phone), a stately home that has been transformed into an experience in design, with marble columns, high ceilings, a cobblestone floor, and huge candelabras. Dress in your nicest clothes and be prepared to nurse that 700-ptas soda pop for a while.

Menorca

Menorca somehow got a reputation for being an isolated paradise, leading every middle-class British family with a few extra pounds to rush here to fill the gap—after all, those sun-deprived Brits have to get their vitamin D somewhere. By August, the locals in **Mahón** (the east-coast capital town also known as **Maó**) and **Ciutadella** (the west coast's largest town) tend to be pretty fed up with English-speaking guests. If you know any Spanish at all, use it. As on all the islands, the best beaches are as far from the towns as possible. If you have a scooter, hit up the beaches west of **Fornells,** on the north coast, or east of **Cala Morell,** in the northwest.

VISITOR INFORMATION Mahón's **oficina de turismo** (tel. 971/36–37–90) is at Plaça Explanada 40, and **American Express** (tel. 971/36–28–45) is at Carrer Nou 35.

COMING AND GOING **Trasmediterránea** (tel. 971/36–29–50) ferries go from Mahón to Valencia (15 hrs) via Palma (8 hrs), charging 5,700 ptas for either stop. **Flebasa** (tel. 971/48–00–12) connects Ciutadella to the port of Alcúdia, in the northeast of Mallorca (5 hrs, 2,950 ptas). In general, **buses** stick to the main road connecting Mahón and Ciutadella (45 min, 400 ptas), and you'll need your own wheels to seek out more remote areas, like the north coast beaches. The cheapest scooter rentals (about 2,500 ptas per day) are at **Valls** (Pl. Real, tel. 971/36–25–13); call two days before you arrive for the best selection.

WHERE TO SLEEP Finding a place to stay in Mahón can be a challenge, especially if you arrive without a reservation. The cheapest place in town is the **Casa de Huéspedes Company** (C. Rosari 27, tel. 971/36–22–67), with standard rooms for about 2,500 ptas. The next place to check is the very nice **Hostal Residencia Orsi** (C. Infanta 19, tel. 971/36–47–51) for 3,700 ptas doubles; book a week in advance. Alternatively there is one official campsite, **La Atalana** (Carretera Ferreries–Santa Galdana, km 4, tel. 971/37–42–32), about 22 km from Mahón. A night's stay will set you back 700 ptas. To get here, catch the bus to Cala de Santa Galdana and ask the driver to stop at *la parada más cerca de La Atalana* (the closest stop to La Atalana).

Northern Spain

The northern regions of the Iberian Peninsula— the principality of Asturias, the small province of Cantabria, the collection of Basque provinces (called Euskadi in the Basque language), and Navarra and Aragón, with their gorgeous Pyrenean mountain scenery—don't fit the stereotypical conception of Spain as a hot, dry expanse of plains. In fact, most of this part of the country is lush and verdant from the frequent rains, and it is anything but flat: The countryside is dominated by rolling green hills, climaxing in the stunning Pyrenees bordering France, and the Picos de Europa in Asturias and Cantabria.

The Pyrenees

The Pyrenees mountains, stretching 450 km from the Basque province of Guipúzcoa on the Atlantic all the way across to Catalunya on the Mediterranean, form an imposing, natural barrier between Spain and France. The Pyrenees have contributed, along with other geographical, political, and cultural factors, to the Iberian Peninsula's historic tendency toward isolation. Today, however, they don't serve as a barrier to isolate Spain so much as they tempt foreigners to visit for some of the best hiking, skiing, and river-rafting in Europe. Fine old monasteries, Romanesque buildings, and small, friendly towns are almost as much of a draw as the natural setting.

Editorial Alpina puts out the best maps for hiking in the Pyrenees. You can find these maps in most bookstores in mountain towns, or sometimes in tourist offices.

The Pyrenees are basically divided into three regions: the Navarrese, Aragonese, and Catalan. Of these, the Aragonese are the most rugged, have the highest peaks, and are the most visited. The most out-of-the-way but rewarding section of the Catalan Pyrenees is the Vall d'Aran in the far northwest corner.

CATALAN PYRENEES

Besides its enviable Mediterranean coast and hip capital, Catalunya has some of most breathtaking mountains in Spain. The only problem you may have is getting to, from, and around them. Sometimes buses are few and far between and schedules are erratic; consider renting a car. In winter, the Catalan Pyrennes are a skier's paradise, with 19 resorts in operation. In summer, hikers and river-rafting enthusiasts head for the tremendous peaks and valleys. For hiking, get the indespensible maps (around 500 ptas) put out by Editorial Alpina.

The final two rail connections to the Catalan Pyrenees are Puigcerdà, served from Barcelona and France, and La Pobla de Segur, accessible from Lleida. After that, it's the bus and your thumb. Luckily, rides are frequently offered by drivers who realize that the bus service sucks. Bus "hubs" of a sort include La Seu d'Urgell and El Pont de Suert (*see below*).

PUIGCERDA The only reason to be in this town—where entertainment means watching old guys play chess in the main plaza—is to make bus and train connections for the mountains. It's the first Spanish stop on the Toulouse–Barcelona line, and it's the farthest the rail penetrates into the mountains from Barcelona. The town is up on a plateau; the **train station** (tel. 972/88–01–65), unfortunately, is not. With a big backpack, it's a grim walk up the stairs that lead to town and the **tourist office** (C. Querol at Pl. Ajuntament, tel. 972/88–06–50; open Tues.–Sat. 10–1 and 4–7, Sun. 10–2). If you're stuck here, try **Pensió Cardanya** (C. Ramon Cosp 7, tel. 972/88–00–10; 1,900 ptas per person). Five daily trains come from Barcelona (820 ptas). **Buses** leave from an unmarked bus stop on Paça de Barcelona for La Pobla de Segur (1,900 ptas) and Lleida.

LA POBLA DE SEGUR This is another blink-and-miss-it kind of town. It sits at the confluence of the La Noguera Pallaresa and Flamiell rivers, once navigated on log rafts. A wild festival rocks the town in the first week of July in honor of the rafters; the drink of choice is a local herbal liquor called Ratafia dels Raiers—strong stuff. The people are friendly, and asking for directions can lead to the kind of spontaneous tour that only happens in towns where tourists are still the exception, rather than the rule. While you're wandering around town, be sure to walk past the **Town Hall,** an unlikely modernisme building with beautiful tile work.

The **oficina de turisme** (Av. Verdaguer 35, tel. 973/68–02–57) has plenty of rafting and hiking information. If you need to stay the night it doesn't get cheaper than **Casa El Mano** (C. Llorens 1 Torres 17, tel. 973/78–08–41; 1,000 ptas per person), though the showers are not always a hot-water experience. **Camping Collegats** (tel. 973/68–07–14) is a campground 3 km from town on the road to Gerri de la Sal.

➤ **COMING AND GOING** • La Pobla de Segur is the last stop on the train from Lleida; make connections here for the bus to the Vall d'Aran, El Pont de Suert, and other pretty towns along the river such as **Sort** and **Llavorsi** (both renowned white-water rafting spots in spring). In June–October, two buses head daily to Viella (1,005 ptas) in the Vall d'Aran; the one at 9:30 AM goes through the tunnel; the other at 11:40 AM heads north via Sort and Llavorsi. Buses also head to El Pont de Suert and Barcelona. The **bus station** (Av. Verdaguer 1, tel. 973/68–03–36) is near the center of town; the **train station** (Av. Estació, tel. 973/68–04–80) is a 10-minute walk from town.

EL PONT DE SUERT At El Pont de Suert, you're finally getting close to the good nature stuff. This pleasant town sits on the River Ribagorcia in a green valley. If you walk behind the surprisingly modern church where the bus lets you off, you'll find a crumbling medieval quarter—still inhabited—with cool, winding streets. The **tourist office** (tel. 973/69–00–05; open July–Sept., daily 10–2 and 4–6) is in the square behind the church. Family-run **Pensió Isard** (C. de Sant Aventi 29, tel. 973/69–01–39) has 2,000 ptas doubles; they serve hearty, inexpensive food in the dining room, and mounted deer heads watch you eat.

➤ **COMING AND GOING** • Buses leave El Pont de Suert for Viella (1,470 ptas) in the Vall d'Aran at 11 AM and 7:10 PM, and for Lleida and Barcelona at 6:15 AM and 2:30 PM. El Pont de Suert is also close to the **Vall de Boí** (there's a bus at 11 AM or it's an easy hitch), a secluded valley boasting both important Romanesque churches. From the town of Boí, it's a 7-km walk to the western entrance to the magnificent Aigüestortes Park.

VALL D'ARAN The big payoff for all this changing buses business is the gorgeous, isolated valley of Vall d'Aran, at the western corner of Catalunya. The River Garonne rushes though the postcard-perfect scenery of deep greens, wild flowers, and snowcapped mountains. The valley is formed by a break in the Pyrenees mountains, which have cut it off from its French and Catalan neighbors for much of its history. Indeed, until 1948 when a tunnel was hacked 6 km through the mountains in the direction of Lleida, the Vall d'Aran was snowbound and cut off from the rest of Catlunya during winter. The valley even has its own language, Aranés, an odd mix of Gascon, Catalan, and Basque that belongs to the Langue d'Oc family.

Viella is the largest town in the Vall d'Aran. The older area of town is made up of traditional Alpine-style stone buildings on the banks of river, and there's one main street, Avenida Castiero (it becomes Avenida Pas d'Arró, which cuts through the center). Just off this road, try the wonderful cabinlike rooms with lace curtains and beautiful woodwork at **Pension Puig** (C. Reiau 6, tel. 973/64–00–31; 1,000 ptas per person). The rooms at **Habitacions de Miguel** (Avinguda Castiero 1, tel. 973/64–00–63; doubles 3,000 ptas) aren't quite as cozy, but they're big and have new furniture. **Camping Artigane** (tel. 973/64–01–89; around 400 ptas per person; closed Oct. 18–Mar. 21) is 2½ km from town on the road to France. The **HI hostel** (Carretera de Viella, tel. 973/64–52–71; beds 900 ptas) is in nearby Salardú. The bus from Pobla de Segur via Sort passes by Salardú; ask the driver to drop you off at hostel.

➤ **COMING AND GOING** • One bus in winter (9 AM) and two in summer (9 AM and 5 PM) leave from Lleida for the 3½-hour journey to Viella, passing through the town of El Pont de Suert about midway. In summer, two daily buses leave La Pobla de Segur (9:30 AM and 11:40 AM) and Barcelona (6:30 AM and 2:30 PM) to travel up here. Three buses daily (5:30 AM, 11 AM, and 1:45 PM) leave Viella for Barcelona and Lleida.

PARQUE NACIONAL DE ORDESA

Even if you don't have much time to spend in the Pyrenees, you really should give it the old college try and get up to this indescribably beautiful park. The park encompasses some of the most dramatic and varied scenery around, from alpine meadows, forests, waterfalls, and rivers to sheer cliffs and treeless peaks covered in snow year-round. This variety of terrain makes the park popular with both serious hikers and families with small children and picnic supplies. The park is sometimes crowded, but even in summer it's still possible to find your own trail and play Grizzly Adams.

You can hike into the park from Torla (*see below*) on a trail that starts just to the left of the Hostal Bella Vista. Follow it left along the river for an easy, beautiful, two-hour hike. The trail eventually deposits you at a parking lot and a cheapish restaurant (tel. 974/48–60–82). The **park information center** (tel. 974/48–62–12; open July–Oct. 8:30–8:30), where you can get free maps of the park's hiking trails, is five minutes farther up the main road. One steep trail leads up to the **Refugío Góriz** (tel. 974/48–63–7; beds 800 ptas including breakfast), the only place to sleep in the park. You can, however, **camp** at elevations above 2,100 meters, and around the grounds of the Refugío if it's full. If you're whipped by the day's hiking, you'll be glad to know it's an easy hitch back into Torla on the one main road that cuts through the park.

TORLA The bus from Sabiñánigo (*see below*) lets you off in this tiny, pretty town, the closest (8 km) you can get to the park by public transport, and the best place to use as your base for the park. The cheapest beds are at **Refugío L'Atalaya** (C. Francia, tel. 974/48–60–22; beds 900 ptas; closed Nov.–Easter), with rustic dorms offered by the French owners who cook up the most delicious food in town at the attached restaurant (1,100-ptas menú). Just past here up the hill to the left you'll find **Fonda Ballarín** (C. Capuvita 11, tel. 974/48–61–55; doubles 2,330, 2,540 ptas in summer), with cozy, clean rooms. You can camp at either **Camping Río Ara** (tel. 974/48–62–48; 350 ptas per person and 350 ptas per tent; closed Nov.–Mar.), just off the same foot path you take to the park, or **Camping Ordesa** (tel. 974/48–61–46; 425 ptas per person and 425 ptas per tent; closed Dec.–Easter), about 1 km past Torla on the main road. One daily bus leaves Sabiñánigo for Torla at 11 AM, continuing on to Ainsa.

SABINANIGO This is only a transportation junction, nothing more. Try not to get stuck here; if you do, the cheapest beds are at **Fonda Laguarta** (C. Serrablo 21, tel. 974/48–00–04; doubles 2,800 ptas), with an attached restaurant serving 1,000-ptas menús. Three daily trains (20 min, 70 ptas) or buses (15 min, 140 ptas) head to Jaca. One small mail bus leaves daily at 11 PM for the one-hour trip to Torla.

JACA

This town in the Aragonese Pyrenees was one of the first stops religious pilgrims made on their long hike through Spain to Santiago de Compostela. Today, modern-day hikers come to Jaca looking for another sort of spiritual experience in the beautiful surrounding mountains. Jaca itself is not so quiet, with hopping bars and cafés. Perhaps it's all the testosterone in the air— Jaca is where many young Spanish army recruits are stationed to train in the mountainous terrain.

Jaca makes a good base for exploring the Aragonese section of the Pyrenees, including the awe-inspiring Parque Nacional de Ordesa. There are a couple of things worth seeing in Jaca itself, reflecting its history as a pilgrim's stop and as a military base. The **cathedral** isn't particularly stunning, but it's historically and architecturally important as one of the first Romanesque churches (around 1060) built in Spain; it influenced designs further along on the pilgrim route. The **Museo Diocesan** (tel. 974/36–18–41; admission 200 ptas; closed Sun. and Mon.) inside the cathedral houses well-preserved Romanesque frescoes from the surrounding area. **La Ciudadela** (admission 150 ptas; daily tours at 11 and 5) is a testament to Jaca's past military importance as one of the first defenses of the Spanish frontier. Dating from 1590, the fort has five bastions that are still intact.

VISITOR INFORMATION The **oficina de turismo,** tucked into a row of shops just below the Paseo Generalismo Franco, is the place to stock up on good skiing, hiking, and Parque Nacional de Ordesa info. *Av. Regimiento Galicia 2, tel. 974/36–10–81. Open July–Aug., weekdays 9–2 and 4:30–8, Sat. 10–2 and 5–8, Sun. 10–2; shorter hrs off-season.*

COMING AND GOING The **bus station** (Av. Jacetania, tel. 974/22–70–11) has buses to Sabiñánigo (15 min, 140 ptas), Huesca (1¼ hrs, 600 ptas), and Pamplona (2 hrs, 650 ptas) via Puente La Reina. The **RENFE station** (end of Av. de Juan XXIII, tel. 974/36–13–22), northeast of town, has trains to Sabiñánigo (20 min, 70 ptas), which continue on to Huesca (2 hrs, 600 ptas), and trains to Madrid (6½ hrs, 3,700 ptas). You can catch a bus to the train station every half-hour before a train departure in front of the **Ayuntamiento** (City Hall) on Calle Mayor.

Jaca is a good place to rent a car for mountain exploration. **Jacacar** (Av. Jacetania 60, tel. 974/36–07–81) offers the best deal at 3,500 ptas per day, 25 ptas per mile, with no age restrictions.

WHERE TO SLEEP AND EAT You should have no problem finding decent, cheap lodging; look along Calle Mayor and around the cathedral. The cheapest rooms in town are at **Hostal Paris** (Pl. San Pedro 5, tel. 974/36–10–20; 2,750 ptas per person; closed Sept.), near the cathedral. For a little more comfort and your very own bathroom, head to the end of Calle Mayor to **Casa Paco** (C. la Salud at Av. Jacentia, tel. 974/36–16–18), where the restaurant is pricey, but the rooms aren't—you pay 3,200 ptas for smallish doubles with checkered bed-spreads. The HI hostel, **Albergue Juvenil de Vacaciones** (Av. Perimetral 6, tel. 974/36–05–36; closed Oct.–Nov.) is a little too cute, with flowers, red shutters on white cottages, and lots of children running around in the summer; no HI card is necessary. Beds cost 1,000 ptas, 1,200 ptas for those 26 and over, and 1,250 ptas for those without a card. Take a bus from the train station to the *pista de hielo* (ice skating rink), and the hostel is just to the right. The closest campsite is **Camping Victoria** (tel. 974/36-03–23; 400 ptas per person), 1½ km from the town center.

Thank all the young military dudes stationed here for the town's lively bars and restaurants. You'll find most of the eating and drinking action near Calle Mayor. **El Viejo Rancho** (C. Belli-do II, tel. 974/36–10–32) has a large selection of raciones in the 400 ptas–600 ptas range; try the spinach or Roquefort pie. One of the best deals in town is at the homey **Meson La Fragua** (C. Gil Berges tel. 974/36–06–18; closed Wed.), where you can chow on grilled meats of all sorts; a plato combinado will set you back 450 ptas–750 ptas. Buy your own food at the funky, cheap **Autoservicio Descuento** (Av. Jacetania 34), right by the bus station.

Pamplona

Pamplona (Iruña in the Basque language), a quiet city in the Basque region of northern Navarre, positively explodes every year from July 6 to 14 for the world famous (and infamous) festival of **Los San Fermínes.** During San Fermínes all mundane matters are abandoned in favor of nonstop partying in the streets, while the star event takes place every morning at eight sharp when huge, angry bulls are let loose into the street behind an adrenaline-and-alcohol-infused crowd of runners. While this reckless tradition was seemingly dreamed up one night after one too many, it's actually a festival honoring Pamplona's patron saint San Fermín, who died a martyr after being dragged through the streets by bulls.

Even if you don't participate in any of the bull-oriented activities, the seven-day, city-wide party involving parades of gigantic papier-mâché figures, dancing, bands, fireworks, and more is reason enough to come. The rest of the year, Pamplona displays its usual dignity, with several important churches, **San Saturino** and **San Nicolás,** both dating from the 13th century, and the **cathedral** with a beautiful Gothic cloister. The city park **Parque de La Taconera** has deer, rabbits, chickens, turkeys, and peacocks all living together in harmony in the surrounding moat.

BASICS The small **oficina de turismo** near the Plaza de Toros can be an invaluable source of info. During the festival, little old ladies hang around outside offering to let you stay in a room in their homes for extortionate prices (about 5,000 ptas). *C. Duque de Ahumada 3, tel. 948/22–07–41. Open June–Sept., daily 10–7; shorter hrs off-season.*

➤ **BUCKET SHOP • TIVE** has a friendly staff to hook you up with the cheapest deals to get out of town. *C. Paulino Caballero 4, 5th floor, bet. C. Arrieta and C. Roncesvalles, tel. 948/21–24–04. Open weekdays 9–1:30.*

➢ **PHONES AND MAIL** • **Telefónica** (C. Cortes de Navarre, tel. 948/22–86–02; open Mon.–Sat. 9–2 and 4–9, later hrs during San Fermínes) is across the street from the bullring. The main **post office** (Paseo de Sarasate 9, tel. 948/22–12–63) sells stamps weekdays 8–9 and Saturdays 9–2. Pick up Lista de Correos around the corner at Calle Estella 10.

COMING AND GOING Pamplona is better (and more cheaply) connected to the rest of the world by bus than by train. The **bus station** (Av. Conde Oliveto 8, tel. 948/22–38–54) is centrally located near the Parque de la Ciudadela, about a 10-minute walk from the Plaza del Castillo. Many companies are in operation here, including **Conda** (tel. 948/22–10–26), with buses to Madrid (5 hrs, 2,800 ptas); **Ibarsa** (tel. 948/22–09–97), with buses to Barcelona (5½ hrs, 1,860 ptas); and **Roncalesa** (tel. 948/22–20–79), with buses to San Sebastián (2½ hrs, 660 ptas).

Avoid the hassle of going all the way to the train station for train reservations by heading instead to the **RENFE office** (C. Estrella, tel. 948/13–02–02), around the corner from Paseo Sarasate. The **train station** (Av. San Jorge s/n tel. 948/13–02–02) is outside the city center to the northwest, with connections to Barcelona (7–8 hrs, 3,200 ptas–3,900 ptas), Madrid (5 hrs, 2,500 ptas), San Sebastián (2–3 hrs, 1,100 ptas), and Zaragoza (2 hrs, 1,600 ptas).

GETTING AROUND The old section of Pamplona centers around the Plaza del Castillo, with the two large city parks, Parque de la Taconera and Parque de la Ciudadela, bordering the city center to the west. From the train station, take Bus 9 to Paseo Sarasate, near budget

Run for Your Life

To see the encierro (running of the bulls), get a spot behind the fences set up at the beginning of the course near the Plaza Santo Domingo, or near the end of it just before the bull ring. You can see the end of the run into the ring (through the narrow entrance known as the "tunnel of death") by getting one of the free spots reserved on the lower level (arrive by 6 AM for these), or by paying 1,500 ptas or more for a seat higher up. The advantage of being inside the ring itself is that you can check out the action at greater length, as the actual running through the streets from start to finish lasts only about three minutes, and it all flashes by in a flurry of scared runners and thundering bulls.

Make sure you watch a run and know the course before you decide to tempt fate and try it yourself. It's always dangerous, but it's much less dangerous when the bulls stay together and run as a pack; when they get separated, they get confused, panic, and start goring the crowd. Another factor to keep in mind is when to run; don't, whatever you do, attempt to run with the huge weekend crowds when all the extra bodies create an extra hazard. On one weekend in 1993 a bottlenecked wall of terrified flesh formed; no one was able to move and the bulls plowed through and over the crowd. Once you're running, there are many possible escape points along the way. Women are traditionally barred from running, but there are always some who do it every year anyway; just keep a low profile and avoid contact with officials at the beginning of the course. You can see the same bulls that ran in the morning at the bullfights that take place every night at 6:30. The cheapest seats begin at about 1,400 ptas. Buy them at the ticket windows at the bullring after the previous night's fight is over.

lodging and the city center. Buses (75 ptas) normally run until 11 PM, but service is extended until 5:30 AM during San Fermínes.

WHERE TO SLEEP During the week of San Fermínes Pamplona's rooms are booked up a year in advance. You might get lucky and find a bed in a *casa particular* (private home) by looking in the local paper, *Diario de Navarra,* but they're not cheap; expect to pay 3,000 ptas–6,000 ptas. To get to the closest official campsite, **Ezcaba** (tel. 948/33–03–15; 400 ptas per person and per tent; closed Oct.–May), 7 km north of town, take the Bus "La Montañesa" from Calle Arrieta near the Plaza de Toros. Alternatively, you can do what everybody else does and use the parks and streets of Pamplona as your campground. Avoid the area behind the city walls to the northeast of the old town, and check your pack and valuables for 200 ptas at the special 24-hour luggage storage office set up at the bus station during the festival.

The rest of the year, look for cheap pensions and hostales on Calle San Nicolás and Calle San Gregorio, or Calle Estafeta and the streets near the cathedral. The nice lady who runs **Angeles Arrondo Lizarraga Pensión** (C. Estafeta 23, tel. 948/22–18–16; 1,000 ptas per person, 4,000 ptas during San Fermínes) prides herself on the shrine to San Fermín in the living room and on her balconies overlooking the bull route below. Brave your way past the dark entrance of **Pensión Santa Cecilia** (C. Navarrería 17, tel. 948/22–22–30; doubles 3,000 ptas) because the gigantic rooms inside are much nicer. A little more upscale are the rooms with hardwood floors at **Pensión Monton** (C. Mayor 46, tel. 948/22–24–26; doubles 4,000 ptas, 6,000 ptas during San Fermínes).

FOOD Besides the usual bocadillos, there's a frustrating lack of cheap eating in Pamplona. If you feel like sitting down to eat, try Calle Jarauta and its continuation, Calle San Lorenzo, for cheap and moderate possibilities; **Bar Gallego** (C. Jarauta 57), a basic comedor popular with locals, has a menú for 900 ptas. San Nicolás has many lively bars, some with tapas. Near here, just off Plaza San Nicolás, **Casa Paco** (C. Lindachiquia 20, tel. 948/22–51–05) is busy at lunch, serving salads and entrées for 500 ptas–800 ptas, and a very tasty 1,200-ptas menú. The **market** is just behind the Plaza de los Burgos.

San Sebastián

Simply put, San Sebastián (Donostia in the Basque language), capital of the Basque province of Guipúzcoa, is a gorgeous town. Unlike other beach resorts, the city hasn't wrecked its beaches or sense of aesthetics to cater to tourists. Part of the city's self-assured beauty comes from the fact that it has been the privileged frolicking ground of the rich and famous for over a hundred years. You can practically smell the money when you get off the train—beautiful fountains, gardens, trees, and parks are everywhere. Not surprisingly, San Sebastián is not cheap. You'll find yourself dropping painful sums of money on lodging in July and August. A night or two shouldn't clean you out entirely, though, since you can find cheap eats in the literally hundreds of tapas bars.

BASICS The **main tourist office** (C. Reina Regente, tel. 943/48–11–66) is on the river near the older part of town. From the RENFE station, cross Puente María Cristina, turn right, and walk along the water; it's on the left just before Puente Zurriola. A second tourist office operates out of a booth on the bay at Paseo de Mollard. The **TIVE office** (C. Tomás Gros 3, tel. 943/27–69–34; open weekdays 9–2), selling student and hostel cards and cheap bus tickets, is on the east side of the river, near Plaza de Euskadi off Calle Miracruz. The **post office** (C. Urdaneta, tel. 943/46–49–14; postal code 20080) is just behind the cathedral. The **Telefónica** (C. San Marcial 29; open Mon.–Sat. 9:30 AM–11 PM) is a few blocks away toward Avenida de la Libertad.

COMING AND GOING San Sebastián is a major point of entry from the rest of Europe, particularly France. It hosts an **airport** (tel. 943/64–22–40), two train stations, and numerous private bus companies.

➤ **BY TRAIN** • The main RENFE station, **Estación del Norte** (Av. Francia, tel. 943/28–35–99), is on the east side of the river at Puente Maria Cristina, and serves international and domestic destinations. Trains head to Madrid (7½ hrs, 3,600 ptas–6,200 ptas); Barcelona (9 hrs, 3,500 ptas–4,700 ptas) via Pamplona (2 hrs, 800 ptas); Burgos (3–4 hrs, 1500 ptas); and Paris (11 hrs, 7500 ptas). For trains to the surrounding region and Bilbao (2–3 hrs, 575 ptas), go to the **Estación de Amara** (Pl. Easo 9, tel. 943/45–01–31), also known as ET. These trains aren't part of RENFE service, so InterRail and EurailPasses aren't valid.

➤ **BY BUS** • The **Estación de Autobuses** is a 10–15 minute walk south of the city center at Plaza de Pio; Avenida Sancho el Sabio leads north from the station straight into town. The various bus companies sell tickets along Avenida Sancho el Sabio. **Continental Auto** (Sancho

"Euskadi ta Askatasuna"
(Basques and Freedom)

Isolated in the mountainous areas of southern France and northern Spain, the residents of the Pais Basco (Basque Country) are perhaps the last remnants of Europe's original indigenous population, predating the vast waves of migration from the East over 3,000 years ago. Their complex language, called Euskera or Euskara, is not related to any other known language, as far as linguists can tell. While philologists puzzle over their language, biologists focus on the fact that even their blood type marks them as genetically different from other Europeans—they have a higher proportion of blood types B and Rh+.

The Basques have always fiercely resisted foreign domination or influence. They were the last people in this area of Europe to be converted to Christianity, and even when they were incorporated into the Spanish state in the 16th century, they maintained an enviable level of autonomy. Basque nationalism resurged in the early 20th century, but was then interrupted in a big way during the Spanish Civil War, with the coastal Basque provinces of Guipúzcoa and Biscay defending the Republic, while Alava and Navarra sided with Franco. The brutal punishment that Biscay and Guipúzcoa received both during and after the war set the stage for the organized resistance to Franco's regime in the early '60s by ETA (which stands for "Euskadi ta Askatasuna" (Basques and Freedom). Over the last 30 years ETA has organized terrorist activities, from the assassination of Franco's chosen successor, Admiral Carrero Blanco, to the brutal 1987 bombing of a supermarket in Barcelona in which 21 people were killed. It's this kind of attack, coupled with the fact that the death of Franco in 1975 ushered in an era of increased autonomy for the Basques, that has greatly eroded the support ETA used to enjoy. Finally, a heavy postindustrial recession in the region also contributes to the wish of the majority of Basques for a negotiated resolution as soon as possible, as fear of terrorism has kept investment out the region. The arrest in February 1993 of many key ETA members had many speculating that the demise of the organization was inevitable. However, when two car bombs rocked rush-hour Madrid in June 1993, killing one and injuring many others, it was clear that it would take a lot more to make ETA to disappear.

el Sabio 31, tel. 943/46–90–74) buses rumble to Madrid (7–8 hrs, 3,235 ptas), Vitoria (2–3 hrs, 800 ptas), and Burgos (4 hrs, 1,600 ptas). **Pesa** (Sancho el Sabio 33, tel. 943/46–39–74) buses head to Bilbao (925 ptas) and Biarritz (620 ptas).

GETTING AROUND The town wraps itself around a pretty bay called La Concha (meaning "the shell"), and the Urumea River snakes through the city to the east of the bay. Most of the sights are concentrated on the west side of the river. The old quarter squeezed into the strip of land between the bay and the river near Monte Urgull is where you'll probably do your eating, drinking, and sleeping.

San Sebastián is quite easily managed on foot. Lots of city buses zip around town, though, with service until 10 or 11 at night; a ticket is 75 ptas. For city bus info call 943/28–71–00.

WHERE TO SLEEP Fierce competition for rooms in July and August means that even dumps can charge ridiculously high prices. Most of the cheaper places cluster around the cathedral and in the small, busy streets in the old town. **Pensión Kaia** (C. Puerto 12, tel. 943/43–13–42), near Iglesia Santa Maria, has doubles with shining bathrooms down the hall for 4,200 ptas in summer and 2,500 ptas in winter. Another possibility is the spotless rooms at **Pensión Urkia** (C. Urbieta 12, near cathedral, tel. 943/42–44–36; doubles 3,000 ptas, 4,500 ptas July–Aug.). The owner of **Pensión San Jerónimo** (C. San Jerónimo 25, tel. 943/28–64–34) is a real Basque character; his rooms (4,000 ptas) are decorated with funky posters. To get to the great **HI hostel** (El Paseo de Igueldo 25, tel. 943/31–02–68; beds 1,300 ptas, 1,500 ptas July–Aug.), take Bus 24 (direction Antiguo) from the RENFE station, or Bus 16 (direction Igueldo) from Alameda del Boulevard to Playa de Ondarreta. Walk about 10 minutes up Avenida de Satrustegui to Paseo de Igueldo and turn left. **Camping De Igüeldo** (Igüeldo Village, tel. 943/21–45–02; 2700 ptas per site for 4 people) is near Monte Igüeldo about 4 km from the town center. Take Bus 16 (direction Igüeldo) from Alameda del Boulevard.

FOOD Tapas have been raised to the level of high art here, and nearly every bar you stumble upon will have its bite-size offerings temptingly laid out; each tapa costs about 150 ptas–250 ptas. Try **Bar Aralar** (C. Puerto 10, tel. 943/42–63–78), a noisy, popular bar/restaurant offering *pimientos rellenos* (red peppers stuffed with cod) for 250 ptas, and many other delicious *pinchos* (the regional name for tapas). At least once you should try the Basque specialty *chipirones en su tinta* (squid in their ink). **Casa Vergara** (C. Mayor 21, tel. 943/42–79–10; closed Thurs. except in July and Aug.) has them for 900 ptas.

WORTH SEEING The **old quarter**'s lively, dingy streets bordered by Alameda del Boulevard to the south, Monte Urgull to the north, and the bay and ocean to the west and east, contrast markedly with the wide, regal boulevards in the rest of town. Bars pack the streets, encouraging noisy crowds and lots of drinking, eating, and general partying. Besides bar-hopping around here, you should also pop into the over-done Baroque church of **Santa María** (cnr. of C. Mayor and C. Treinta y Uno de Agosto). Sugary cherubs mark the outside, but the interior is more subdued. Also check out the beautiful Gothic church of **San Vicente** a couple blocks east of Santa María.

An easy climb up the hill **Monte Urgull** behind the old town will get you to an enormous statue of Jesus Christ and commanding views of both the bay and sea. This vantage point has made Monte Urgull strategically important, and you'll find old cannons and the remains of a castle fortress up here. At the foot of the hill the **San Telmo Museum** (Pl. Zuloaga 1, tel. 943/42–49–70; admission 350 ptas, 200 ptas students; open Mon. 3:30–7, Tues.–Sat. 9:30–1:30 and 3:30–7, Sun. 10:30–2) houses an interesting collection of artwork in a 16th-century monastery. The view from **Monte Igüeldo** is even better than the view from Monte Urgull, but the climb is more of an effort. The road starts just to the left of the tennis courts at the bottom of the mountain near the beach. If you're feeling lazy, there's a **funicular** that will carry you to the top.

Oviedo

Oviedo is the political and administrative capital of the Principality of Asturias, the only Spanish kingdom not conquered by the Moors, thanks in part to the handy, imposing natural barrier of the Picos de Europa (Europe's Peaks). It was here that the Reconquista of Spain began, and remnants of its important past are still felt. Today, however, Oviedo's importance is derived (more mundanely) from being an industrial center, albeit with unusually happy, helpful inhabitants. Oviedo has a dignified, noble feel to its *casco antiguo* (old quarter), with pleasantly lived-in, grand-looking, ochre buildings smudged by factory smoke.

Oviedo also has the distinction of having its very own architectural style: Asturian Pre-Romanesque. As Europe began to grope its way out of the Middle Ages, one of the brightest lights shining in Europe was the building going on in Asturias in the 9th century. Buildings were totally innovative in design, mixing elements of Visigothic, Muslim, and Romanesque architecture, even though the Romanesque style wouldn't hit it big for two centuries. Two churches within walking distance of the city are perfect examples of this style. **Santa María del Naranco** (tel. 98/529–67–55; admission 200 ptas, free Mon.) was originally built as a royal residence for King Ramiro I, but was eventually used as a church instead. It sits atop a hill 3 km northwest of the city, offering beautiful views from its high, arched windows bordered by a ropelike design called *sogueado*. A five-minute walk farther up the road brings you to **San Miguel de Lillo** (free entry with ticket from Santa María), a quiet 9th-century masterpiece in a similar style. The church's sense of proportion is graceful and unusual; the height is three times the width of the nave. It's decorated with beautiful, delicate latticework on the windows, as well as with unusual carvings of circus performers on the door jamb at the entrance. To get to the churches, you can either take Bus 6 from Calle General Yagüe (near the park), or walk up Calle Nicolás Soria (under the bridge between the two train stations), take a left on Calle L. Abruñedo, and then a right on Avenida de los Monumentos—a pleasant 45-minute walk. Back in town, visit the Gothic **cathedral** (tel. 98/522–1033; open daily 9–1 and 3:30–6), with its **Cámara Santa** (Holy Chamber; admission 250 ptas; closed Sun.) built by Alfonso II to house holy relics when this was the only spot safe from the ever-pesky Moors.

BASICS The **tourist office** (Pl. de Alfonso II 6, tel. 98/521–3385; open weekdays 9:30–1:30 and 4:30–6:30, Sat. 9–2), on the plaza right in the front of the cathedral, hands out pathetic maps of the city. The **American Express office** (C. Uria 6, Oviedo, 33003, tel. 98/522–52–17) is open weekdays 9:30–1 and 4:30–7, Saturday 9:30–1.

COMING AND GOING The cathedral and surrounding old quarter are to the east of the strollable, fountained city park, **Campo de San Francisco.** The RENFE and FEVE train stations and the bus station are all within spitting distance of each other about a five to 10-minute walk northwest of the park. The **bus station** (Pl. Primo de Rivera, tel. 98/528–12–00) has connections to León (2 hrs, 900 ptas), Madrid (6 hrs 3,300 ptas–5,485 ptas), and Santiago (5 hrs, 3,500 ptas). Buses run by **Economicos Easa** (tel. 98/529–00–39) will take you to Picos de Europa jumping-off points such as Covadonga and Arenas de Cabrales. The

It's No Use Crying over Spilled Cider

Asturian bartenders are excellent marksmen, pouring cider from a bottle high above their heads into a glass held as far below their waists as possible—the real hotshots don't even look. Not surprisingly, cider often misses the glass or just splashes out. No matter—the whole purpose of this ritual is to oxygenate the cider and give it a good head, anyway. When you order cider, you'll get three separate shots (about 200 ptas each). You're supposed to polish off each shot in one swig, but don't drink the last few drops—dump them on the ground if you want to look like a pro. Finally, never pour the cider yourself; it's the waiter's or bartender's job.

RENFE station (Av. de Santander, tel. 98/525–02–02) has trains to León (800 ptas), Madrid (3,300 ptas), Burgos (2,600 ptas), and Barcelona (6,400 ptas). Right next door, the **FEVE station** (Av. de Santander, tel. 98/528–40–96) sends trains to Santander (1,420 ptas), where you can connect to head farther east to Bilbao or San Sebastián.

WHERE TO SLEEP AND EAT Lodging is cheap and plentiful; most of the budget digs are conveniently near the train stations, around Calle Uría, or around the nearby commercial district by Calle Pelayo. Just off Calle Uría, you'll find **Pensión Oriente** (C. Melquiades Alvarez 24, tel. 98/521–22–82; doubles 2,500 ptas), with unadorned but clean rooms (some with balconies) all under the attentive care of the nice couple who run it. Throw down a little more cash for the pleasant rooms with rugs, fluffy beds, and sparkling bathrooms at **Fonda Riesgo** (C. Nueve de Mayo 26, tel. 98/521–8945; doubles 3,000 ptas, 3,400 ptas July–Aug). West of the center of town you can stay at the hostel, **HI Residencia Juvenil R.M. Pidal** (C. Julián Clavería 14, tel. 98/523–20–54; 650 ptas, 850 ptas 26 and over). Take Bus 2 from Plaza Primo de Rivera or from the corner of Avenida Santander and Calle Nicolás Soria.

Definitely try out Oviedo's *sidrerías* (cider saloons), a wonderful Asturian variation on a cervecería; you may actually be too busy watching the cider-pouring ritual (*see box, above*) to eat the cheap raciones, bocadillos, or menús that most of them offer. To try the Asturian specialty, *fabadas asturias,* a hearty stew made of beans, ham, and sausage, head for **Bar Gonzalez** (C. San Bernabé 3, near C. Covadonga, tel. 98/522–00–80; closed Sun.), a small place where they serve huge, steaming bowls (enough for two) of this filling fare for 850 ptas. The **market** (C. Fierro) is just off Plaza Mayor near the City Hall.

Galicia

Brushing aside the raindrops as you hike through a forest, savoring ribeira wine and fresh octopus, or lying on a beautiful beach where you hear only Spanish or Gallego voices, you may begin to understand why Gallegos, the Galician natives, take so much pride in their land, history, and culture. The sea exerts a powerful influence in Galicia, an area bordered by the Atlantic Ocean and the Rías Altas and Bajas, a series of tidal estuaries along the Galician coast. It was from here that many Spanish colonists left for the New World, and fishing still dominates the economy; here you'll find some of the best seafood in Europe. Beaches such as

Gallegos Are Galled by Castilian

The Gallegos' unique language has been both a source and a symbol of the region's tense relationship with the rest of Spain. Eighty-five percent of the population speaks Gallego, described by the father of Galician nationalism, Alfonso Castelao, as "the son of Latin, brother of Castilian, father of Portuguese." After having been suppressed for decades by the most famous Gallego of this century, Francisco Franco, the language has recently reemerged on street signs and newspapers, in university lectures, and on one TV station. Though the resurgence of Gallego gratified most people's ethnic sympathies in the '80s, its success brought new problems to the fore. Years ago, you were considered really cool if you defaced Castilian signs, scrawling in the appropriate Gallego counterpart to any message. These days, Gallego signs are targeted by hardcore Galician nationalists who consider modern Gallego a Castilian-infested perversion of the real thing. A significant minority here wants not only a return to an antiquated form of Gallego, but also full political independence from Spain. Such radicals stand out in what is otherwise one of the most politically conservative regions in Spain.

Bayona, El Grove, Noya, and **Miño** are still unspoiled by international tourism, though the Spanish have long been coming here to sun, swim, and even surf.

Santiago de Compostela

The name Compostela means camp of the stars; the region was so named because it was here that a great light appeared, leading the hermit Pelayo to the tomb of St. James (Santiago). As if this weren't miracle enough, Santiago then rose from the dead and disguised himself as a knight on a white horse, leading the Catholics to victory over the Moors. These legends inspired the growth of a cult around the apostle, making Compostela the goal of once-in-a-lifetime pilgrimages.

Santiago today is an alluring combination of the sacred and the profane. Though its origins and its essence are profoundly religious, here one encounters such things as a *tetilla*—a block of cheese molded to the shape of a woman's breast—shamelessly displayed in countless restaurant and shop windows. This combination seems manifest in the pilgrimage itself: While it's a serious religious undertaking, when pilgrims and locals alike revel in a giant, unrestrained party every year on St. James' Day (July 25).

VISITOR INFORMATION The main **oficina de turismo** (Rúa del Villar 43, tel. 981/58–40–81) is down the street from the cathedral.

COMING AND GOING The **train station** (tel. 981/59–60–50) sits at the south end of Santiago, a 15-minute walk up Calle del Hórreo to Plaza de Galicia and the ciudad vieja. Trains travel to La Coruña (1 hr, 570 ptas), Vigo (2 hrs, 630 ptas), Madrid (9 hrs, 4,800 ptas), and Pamplona (10 hrs, 5,800 ptas). The **bus station** (tel. 981/58–77–00) is in the San Caetano district, a half-hour hike east of the town's center; take Bus 10 to Plaza de Galicia. Some destinations include Madrid (9 hrs, 4,900 ptas) and La Coruña (50 min, 675 ptas).

GETTING AROUND Wedged between the ciudad vieja to the north, the more generic ciudad nueva to the south, and the pretty Alameda park to the west, **Plaza de Galicia** is a good point of reference. The old city is dominated by the cathedral and several large plazas. The most important streets in the old city are those leading up to the cathedral from the south, like Rúa del Villar, the oldest street in Santiago, and the Rúa do Franco (named for the tax that pilgrims entering Santiago once had to pay, *not* the dictator).

WHERE TO SLEEP AND EAT Even on St. James' Day, when Santiago packs in the greatest number of pilgrims, it is still fairly easy to find a room here. Rúas da Raiña, do Franco, and del Villar have plenty of hostales and hospedajes, many of them atop street-level bars and restaurants. **Hospedaje Ramos** (Rúa da Raiña 18, tel. 981/58–18–59; doubles 2,200 ptas) is in the center of old city action, so you can hear all the street music and big concerts from your bed. **Hostal-Restaurante El Rápido** (Rúa do Franco 22, tel. 981/58–49–83) has large doubles, all with bath, for 3,000 ptas–3,500 ptas. **Hostal Real** (C. Calderena 49, tel. 981/56–52–39; doubles 3,500 ptas) has bright, pretty rooms and homey corridors. From Plaza de Galicia, head up Huérfanas, which becomes Calderena.

Still-moving *mariscos* (shellfish), erotically shaped cheese, and sweets of all sorts beckon the hungry from windows all over the city. The streets south of the cathedral contain the most bars and restaurants. **Café-Bar Platerias** (Rúa da Raiña 1), like most bars in Galicia, serves fresh *mejillones* (clams) in oil and vinegar; a plate of them, plus bread and a glass of wine, costs only 225 ptas. Some wonderful local tapas bars lie to the east and northeast of the cathedral. **A Gamela** (Rúa de Olivera 5; closed Mon.), in a tiny alley between the Santa Maria do Camiño church and the clothes shop, specializes in *setas* (mushrooms). Once the hangout of Galician poets, **Café Derby** (Huérfanas 29, tel. 981/58–65–71) remains a nice place to go for coffee and pastries. And don't miss Santiago's **mercado** (Plazuela de San Fiz, near Travesia de Universidad), an unusual market set up in a centuries-old stone complex where you can watch the merchants fondling their tetillas.

WORTH SEEING At night, when the Baroque facade is lit up and music pours in from all over the old city, the **catedral** seems to be itself a miracle. It's not hard to believe that it was at this spot in 813 that a hermit saw a great light, which led him and Bishop Teodoro to the tomb of the apostle St. James buried beneath the undergrowth. Pilgrims have been trekking here since the 10th century, coming to embrace the statue of the apostle in the chancel, and to kneel before his mortal remains in the crypt. The **Pórtico de la Gloria,** the work of Maestro Mateo in the 12th century, glorifies Christ with the joyful representation of his resurrection in the central arch. Commenced in the Middle Ages, the **Botafumeiro** ceremony is breathtaking (and more than a little scary). At the end of the daily midday pilgrim's mass (around 12:45), huge urns of flaming, smoking incense fly wildly through the cathedral. The dignity of the cathedral can't prevent everyone from applauding afterward. The **Museo de la Catedral** (admission 150 ptas; open daily 10–1:30 and 4–7:30) holds tapestries based on works of Goya and Rubens. *Pl. del Obradoiro. Open daily 7 AM–9 PM.*

A work in the Museo de la Catedral entitled Castigo de los Lugurios (Punishment of the Luxurious), depicts the fate of the profane in a world governed by divine justice; she gets her breasts ripped off by a snake— and you can guess what they do to him.

The **Bazo de Xelmirez,** a magnificent work of 12th- to 15th-century civic architecture, was built to be the Palace of Xelmirez, the first archbishop of Compostela. Because it was built onto the cathedral in the 12th century, you can see parts of the cathedral's original Romanesque shell from its entrance. In the main hall, the Sala de Fiestas, the sculptures actually seem to be moving, playing music and indulging in Galican food and wine. *Pl. Obradoiro. Admission: 150 ptas. Open daily 10–1:30 and 4–7:30.*

A bunch of talented young Tunas (roving groups of male student musicians) once lived in the **Casa da Troia.** A. Pérez Lugín made it the subject of his 1915 novel *Casa da Troia,* a Galician classic. The still-relevant Tuna symbols and the photographs gathered in this museum, not to mention the proud, rowdy boys at the door, hint that nothing, really, has changed. *C. de la Troia 5. Admission: 200 ptas, 150 ptas students. Open Tues.–Sat. 11–2 and 4–8, Sun. 11–2.*

AFTER DARK Santiago's many students ensure a dynamic nightlife. Competitive drinkers join in "Paris to Dakar," starting out at **Paris** (at the beginning of Rúa do Franco, on the edge of the old city), drinking a copa at every bar (there are about 30) on the way to **Cafetería Dakar** (Rúa do Franco 13, tel. 981/58–19–66). For those who prefer to stay in one place, have a couple of shots of *tumba,* a special Galician concoction, at the bar by the same name on Rúa del Villar. Within the ciudad vieja, bars and pubs are concentrated around Vía Sacra and the streets shooting off from the Praza de Cervantes.

NEAR SANTIAGO DE COMPOSTELA

Its cosmopolitan luxury and Castilian bent make La Coruña atypical of Galicia, but its history (the Spanish Armada sailed from here), popular surfing beaches, and distinctive glass-facade buildings make the City of Crystal deserving of its status as one of Galacia's four regional capitals. Famed for the revelries surrounding the annual mid-August festival in which everyone parties on flower-laden boats, **Betanzos** warrants a visit at any time. It was from here that the brothers García left for South America to make their fortune. Wanting to spread their newfound capitalist ideology, they came back and sponsored the building of a **pasatiempo,** a kind of early-20th-century amusement park intended for the entertainment and edification of the townspeople. Its surreal ruins are on the edge of town, though you might have to climb a wall to see the assortment of Art Nouveau fountains and fake caves that hold fake dinosaurs.

VIGO Sitting on the harbor formed by the Ría de Vigo (Vigo Estuary), this graceful city is worth visiting for two reasons. First, its port, a landing spot for sailors from all over the world and marketplace for many fishermen, teems with salty delights. West of the tourist office, in **Mercado de la Piedra,** which extends from the Praza de Piedra to the narrow alleys of Rúa de Teófilo Llorente, merchants hawk their wares, while women prepare plates of fresh octopus. The second reason to come here is that lodging is cheap and available, making it a good base for excursions to the many beaches and towns nearby. Some of the bright rooms at **Hostal Mendez** (Rúa Real 4, tel. 986/43–60–07; doubles 2,500 ptas) overlook the water. From Porta do Sol, cut through Praça da Constitución to Rúa Triunfo, and go left on Rúa de Palma, which turns into Rúa Real. Otherwise, look on **Rúa Carral,** where you'll find a number of hostales.

Vigo's **tourist office** (Praza do Rei, tel. 986/81–01–44) is just outside the port. The **train station** (tel. 986/43–11–14 or 986/43–68–83) is southeast of the port. To get to Porta do Sol, the center of town, walk 20 minutes up Principe Urzáiz or hop on any bus—all of them stop there. The **Estación de Autobuses** (tel. 986/37–34–11), at the south end of town, services most of the little towns nearby, plus Santiago, Bilbao, Barcelona, and Madrid. From the station, take Bus 7, 12, or 21 to get to Porta do Sol.

SWEDEN

By Marisa Gierlich

Sweden's history goes back to pre-Viking days, and before the United States was even a glimmer in Uncle Sam's eye, Sweden had risen and fallen as the greatest power in northern Europe. Vikings sailed from Svea (the early name for Sweden) and along the way collected booty that has made for some incredible archaeological finds. Once a land of plundering Vikings and bellicose monarchs, Sweden has been experimenting with peace for the past few centuries. With a spirit of cooperation inbred in the population, collective thinking has crept into every aspect of society, from parliamentary debates to the use of hiking trails.

In southern Sweden, culture gets the big emphasis, while in the north, nature reigns supreme. Throughout the country, though, the two are invariably integrated. From the parks and waters of Stockholm to the dense forests of the north, the natural world is respected, well tended, and actively appreciated. The great outdoors is not just a weekend warriors' playground, but an integral part of Swedish heritage. Stockholm's professionals who scale ice peaks on the weekend feel as strongly for the "energy of the mountains" as do the Sami reindeer herders who have lived with Mother Nature since time immemorial. For all this tree-hugging, though, the Swedes are a pretty cultured bunch. Carl von Linné (Linnaeus), Alfred Nobel, and Anders Zorn hardly grew up with daisies in their hair, and the large University of Uppsala was founded before Christopher Columbus even hit the first grade.

Uncertainty, however, is looming on Sweden's horizon. In 1991 the Social Democratic party, in power since 1932, was ousted by the rightist Conservative Majority. Since then, the economy has been on a constant slide and the unemployment rate, at 4%, is the highest in many years. But the economic and political woes that may provoke heated discussions and restless nights are definitely not apparent in the Swedish lifestyle. The standard of living is high, the crime rate is low, and it's not unusual to see university students enjoying a restaurant that may seem exorbitantly priced to non-Scandinavians. Luckily for the traveler, though, everything in Sweden is seeming a little less extravagant these days as the kronor continues to fall, putting Sweden's incredible natural beauty and rich cultural heritage well within reach.

KEY

⊢—⊦ Rail Lines

*Norwegian
Sea*

Abisko

Kiruna

Gällivare

Luleälven

Jokkmokk

Arjeplog

Töre

Tornea

Tärnaby

Kalix

Sorsele

Arvidsjaur

E79

Luleå

Storuman

95

Piteå

Lycksele

Skellefteå

342

Åsele

Umeälven

90

92

Strömsund

Umeå

Åre

Östersund

Tännäs

E75

NORWAY

Ljungan

Sundsvall

84

*Gulf
of
Bothnia*

Idre

Hudiksvall

70

Bollnäs

Sälen

Söderhamn

Mora

62

Falun

Gävle

Klarälven

Leksand

80

Borlänge

Avesta

FINLAND

Fagersta

E4

Uppsala

Karlstad

Västerås

Mälaren

Stockholm

Gulf of Finland

E18

Mellerud

Örebro

Strömstad

Vänern

*Gotska
Sandön*

Uddevalla

Trollhättan

Vättern

Norrköping

ESTONIA

Göteborg

Linköping

*Baltic
Sea*

Borås

Jönköping

40

Visby

*Gulf of
Riga*

Falkenberg

Nässjö

E66

Gotland

Värnamo

E6

Oskarshamn

Halmstad

Växjö

Öland

23

LATVIA

Helsingborg

Kalmar

Malmö

Karlskrona

DENMARK

Lund

Kristianstad

Trelleborg

Ystad

LITHUANIA

400

N

0 ——— 50 miles

0 ——— 75 km

Basics

MONEY $1 = 7 kronor and 10 kronor = $1.42. The krona is divided into 100 öre. Banks in major cities are open weekdays 9:30–5; in small towns they often close at 3 PM. Most banks charge 3% per exchange or 50kr, whichever is greater. Post offices offer the best exchange rates and lowest fees; they're generally open weekdays 9–6, Saturday 10–1. The most convenient place to exchange money is usually at a **Forex** office, most open daily until 9 PM; their rates are better than the banks', and they'll exchange kronor back into dollars at no charge if you have your receipt.

➤ **HOW MUCH IT WILL COST** • Sweden is by no means as cheap as Spain or Portugal, but it is the cheapest of the Scandinavian countries. Hostels cost around 90kr a night, hotels start at 450kr for a double, and you can get a decent meal for about 70kr. Service is included in restaurant bills, but taxi drivers expect some sort of a tip, especially if you have luggage. Staying in hostels you can probably get by on $35–$40 a day.

COMING AND GOING If you don't have a rail pass, you might want to consider flying to Sweden; flights from most European cities cost no more than train and ferry tickets to the country. EurailPass holders get a discount on most ferry lines.

➤ **BY BUS AND TRAIN** • **Eurolines** (tel. 020/98–73–77 in Stockholm) is the major international bus company, with service to France, Germany, the Netherlands, and England. Trains from major European cities head to Stockholm via Hamburg and Copenhagen (the trains actually get right on the ferries). Some train routes, especially from Finland and Norway, are supplemented by buses; in this case, rail passes are honored by the bus line.

➤ **BY FERRY** • The key piece of info for ferry folks is the *Färjenyckel*, a brochure available at tourist offices and travel agents with the carriers, times, and prices for all routes to and from Sweden; the routes are endless. The major carriers are **Silja Line** (tel. 08/22–21–40), **Stena Line** (tel. 031/75–00–00), **Scandinavian Seaways** (tel. 08/679–8880), and **Viking Line** (tel. 08/743–6400).

➤ **BY PLANE** • Traveling by plane may be a better deal than you think. **SAS airlines** (tel. 020/910–150 in Stockholm) offers regular service to Stockholm and Göteborg from most European cities for $300 round-trip. Planes that fly to Copenhagen often have connecting buses to Malmö, Göteborg, and Stockholm for a small supplement (about 85kr).

GETTING AROUND Nearly all **trains** in Sweden are state-run SJ (Statensjärnväg) trains. Pendeltåg trains are smaller ones that make short trips to a city's surrounding areas. Eurail and InterRail are valid on all train lines. For Scandinavian travel only, the Nordturist card (1,480kr) offers unlimited travel for 21 consecutive days. The Scanrail pass, available only outside Scandinavia, is good for four days of travel completed within 15 days ($199 first class, $149 second class), for nine days within 21 days ($339 first class, $254 second class), or for one month of unlimited travel ($499 first class, $374 second class). With a Reslust card (150kr), available from any train station, you get a 50% discount on all fares in Sweden for a year.

Buses are sometimes cheaper than the trains and are equally comfortable. Discounts and specials vary according to season and day of the week; the cheapest fares are on weekdays September–May. Swebus and Svenska Buss are the major carriers in the south; Linjebuss is big in the north. Tourist offices can hook you up with the local offices and help you plan itineraries. Bus stations are usually situated conveniently next to or within train stations.

WHERE TO SLEEP **Hostels** and **campgrounds** are by far the cheapest places to stay in Sweden. **Hotels** are pricey, even on weekends when discount rates are in effect, and are rarely much nicer than hostels. Luckily, Sweden's hostels are better than almost any others in Europe. They are run by Svenska Turistföreningen (STF), part of Hostelling International, so HI membership cards are valid. Prices listed in this chapter, usually about 90kr, are for HI members. Nonmembers will pay more, often about 125kr. Most hostels have fully equipped kitchens, laundry facilities, TV rooms, and luggage storage. Doubles are usually available if you call far enough in advance. Reservations are standard protocol, so it's good to call ahead.

Campers will be happy to know that *allemansratt* (every man's right) is the law in Sweden, so you can pitch a tent for one night anywhere in the open, as long as you are 100 meters from the nearest dwelling. Campgrounds are usually well located, clean, and full of conveniences, but also full of family vacationers with cars, caravans, and barbecues.

Hosteling in Sweden is not just for the young. Don't be surprised if you find yourself brushing your teeth with a six-year-old (and strawberry-flavored toothpaste) on one side and a 60-year-old (and dentures) on the other.

FOOD Sweden follows the rest of Europe in eating the main meal in the middle of the day. The *dagens rätt* (daily special) is usually served in restaurants between 11 AM and 2 PM and consists of a main dish, salad, bread, and coffee for around 70kr. Most places offer several choices: *biff* (beef), *fläsk* (pork), *vegetarianisk* (vegetarian dish), and some sort of pasta. Fish and potatoes are the true Swedish staples. *Lax* (salmon) can be had for less than $10 at most restaurants and *sill* (herring) is always cheap. The legendary Swedish smorgasbords are few and far between (not to mention unaffordable), but pizzerias are cheap and plentiful. *Smorgås* (open-faced sandwiches), topped with *räkor* (shrimp), *skinka* (ham), or *tonfisk* (tuna) can be found at any café for about 20kr. The Swedes love their coffee dark, strong, and plentiful. *Patår* (refills) are usually included in the average 10kr price tag. **ICA** and **Konsum** supermarkets will come to the rescue of frugal, hungry travelers, but they generally close at 6 PM weekdays, on Saturday afternoons, and all day Sunday.

BUSINESS HOURS Swedish businesses are usually open weekdays 9–5. In the summer, tourist offices often stay open until 8 PM, restaurants until 1 AM; museums have varying extended hours. Banks are open 9–4:30, and post offices are almost always open weekdays 9–6, Saturday 10–1.

FESTIVALS AND HOLIDAYS Midsummer's Eve is *the* festival in Sweden, far surpassing Christmas and New Year's. It's celebrated on a weekend around the summer solstice in late June. Many stores close early on Friday, and virtually everything is shut on Saturday and Sunday, while the Swedes recover from a nationwide hangover. Dalarna is the most popular region in which to celebrate.

VISITOR INFORMATION Swedish tourist offices, called *turistbyrån* or *turist information* and marked with green signs with a big white I, are usually near the train station and always have an English-speaking staff. Most stock information about the entire country, sell tickets to local events, and arrange guided tours.

De Handikappades Riksidrottsförbund (Stora Nygatan 4, Box 2053, 10312 Stockholm) has books and brochures in English for travelers with disabilities.

PHONES Country Code: 46. You can make an international call from any pay phone in Sweden via an international operator. For **AT&T**, dial 020/79–56–11; for **MCI**, 020/79–59–22. To dial direct, dial 009 and then the country code and number. Pay phones use either coins (50 öre, 1kr, or 5kr pieces) or phone cards (45kr for 50 units or 80kr for 100 units). Each unit is equivalent to 1kr in the phone. Calls within a city cost 2kr, and long-distance calls take an additional krona every 50 seconds. The nationwide **Telebutiks** have phone booths where you can make a call before paying the cashier; prices are the same as at pay phones. For directory information within Sweden, dial 07975 (the operators speak English). For info for anywhere else in Europe, dial 0019.

MAIL Letters to the United States cost 6kr and take about a week. For the rest of Europe, letters cost 5kr and take four working days. You can buy stamps everywhere postcards are sold, at all Pressbyrån stands, and, of course, at the post office. To send poste restante mail to any sizable city, address it to: name of city, poste restante, Central Post Office, postal code, Sweden. In small towns, it's best to have mail sent to the tourist office or youth hostel.

EMERGENCIES Call 90000 for all sorts of emergencies. *Nattapoteks* (night pharmacies) are few and far between, so for late-night emergencies go to the local *vardcentral* (medical center) or *sjukhuset* (hospital).

LANGUAGE As well as Swedish, a Germanic language, Finnish and Lappish are spoken in parts of northern Sweden. Virtually everyone speaks at least a little English, or is happy to find someone who does. German is spoken almost as commonly as English.

Stockholm

The water surrounding the 11 islands that make up greater Stockholm is as vital to the city as its magnificent buildings and historical parks and gardens. The wealthy Birger Jarl knew what he was doing when he founded Stockholm as a trading port in 1252; its location on Sweden's southeast coast means access to the Baltic and protection by the vast *skärgården* (archipelago) made up of 24,000 islands. Today the archipelago is used more for pleasure than protection by Stockholm's one million or so city dwellers. The islands are easily reached by boat from near the city center and are chock-full of beaches, hiking paths, hostels, and camping spots that you can find out about from Stockholm's main tourist office.

Almost everyone in Stockholm speaks English, sometimes so perfectly that you feel you're the one with the accent.

Even travelers who don't actually take to the islands feel the effect of Stockholm's waterways while exploring the city. The sterile, modern city center is easily escaped by bridge: to Gamla Stan (the Old Town), wooded Djurgården, and Södermalm, with its casual cafés and galleries. All of this gives Stockholm much more character than your average modern metropolis.

BASICS

VISITOR INFORMATION The **Sverigehuset** (Sweden House) distributes information, sells tickets to events, and books trips to other Swedish destinations. There's also an in-house Forex exchange desk. *Kungsträdgården, across from NK shopping center, tel. 08/789–2490. Open weekdays 9–7, weekends 9–5.*

The **Hotell Centralen**, on the bottom level of the train station, doles out information and books hostel and hotel rooms for 12kr per person and 30kr per room respectively. They book rooms for free if you call instead of stop by. *Tel. 08/24–08–80. Open June–Aug., daily 8 AM–9 PM; Sept.–May, daily 8–7.*

Stockholm This Week (it actually covers a whole month), available at tourist offices and most hotels, has a good map and info on museums and sights.

AMERICAN EXPRESS *Birger Jarlsgatan 1, tel. 08/679–7880, 24-hr hotline 020/79–51–55. Mailing address: Box 1761, 11187 Stockholm. Open weekdays 9–6, weekends 10–1.*

CHANGING MONEY The **post offices** have the best rates. **Forex** has offices in the train station, airport, Silja ferry terminal, and Sverigehuset (*see* Visitor Information, *above*).

EMBASSIES **Australia.** *12 Sergels Torg, tel. 08/613–2900. Open weekdays 8:30–12:30 and 1:30–4:30.*

Canada. *4 Tegel Backen, tel. 08/23–79–20. Open weekdays 9–5.*

United Kingdom. *6 Skarpögatan, tel. 08/667–0140. Open weekdays 9–5.*

United States. *101 Strandvägen, tel. 08/783–5300. Open weekdays 9–6.*

EMERGENCIES For the police, an ambulance, or the fire department, dial 90000. The hospital **City Akuten** (tel. 08/11–71–02 or 08/644–9200 after 5 PM) always has doctors on duty. **C.W. Scheele** (64 Klarabergsgatan, tel. 08/24–82–80) is a 24-hour pharmacy.

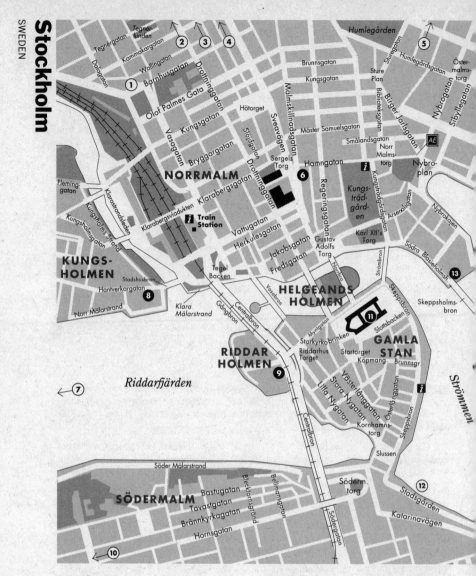

Sights ●

Kulturhuset, **6**
Kungliga Slottet, **11**
Millesgarden, **17**
Moderna Museet, **16**
National Museum, **13**

Nordiska Museet, **19**
Riddarholms-kyrkan, **9**
Skansen, **20**
Stadhuset, **8**
Vasamuseet, **18**

Lodging ○

af Chapman and Skeppsholmen's Vandrarhem (HI), **14**
Brygghuset, **3**
Café Bed and Breakfast, **4**
Columbus Hotell, **15**

Gustaf af Klimt, **12**
Hotell Danielson, **1**
Hotell Gustav Vasa, **2**
Hotell Östermalm, **5**
Långholmen (HI), **7**
Zinkens (HI), **10**

ÖSTERMALM

Kommendörsgatan

Karlaplan

N. DJURGÅRDEN

Karlavägen

Banérgatan

Narvavägen

Linnégatan

Linnégatan

Oxenstiernsgatan

Gardesgatan

Skarpögatan

Linnégatan

Storgatan

Styrmangatan

Grevgatan

Skeppargatan

Artillerigatan

Riddargatan

Strandvägen

Strandvägen

Djurgårdsbron

Djurgårdsbrunnsviken

Rosendalsvägen

Sirishovsvägen

DJURGÅRDEN

SKEPPSHOLMEN

Svensksundsvägen

Alkärret

Djurgårdsvägen

Falkens G.

Allmänna Gränd

Djurgårds Slätten

Sollidsbacken

Singelbacken

KASTELL-
HOLMEN

Saltsjön

BECKHOLMEN

N

KEY

AE American Express
Office

i Tourist Information

├─┤ Rail Lines

0   500 yards

0   500 meters

PHONES AND MAIL The main **Telebutik** (open daily 8 AM–9 PM) is on the bottom floor of the train station. The main **post office** is an enormous brick building at the corner of Vasagatan and Mäster Samuelsgatan, across from the train station. The mailing address for poste restante is GPO, S-10110 Stockholm, Sweden.

COMING AND GOING

BY TRAIN Trains head from Stockholm's **Central Station** (tel. 08/762–2000) to Paris (15 hrs, 1,839kr), Copenhagen (5 hrs, 437kr), Amsterdam (11 hrs, 1,379kr), and Frankfurt (15 hrs, 1,453kr). Underneath the train station is a T-bahn station (see Getting Around, below) and several grocery stores open until the wee hours.

BY BUS The **City Terminalen** (main bus station) is in the World Trade Center across from the train station. **Swebus** (tel. 020/640–640) and **Svenska Buss** (tel. 020/676–767) handle bus trips within Sweden, and **Eurolines** (tel. 020/987–377) is the international carrier. Buses are generally cheaper than trains and only slightly slower. Prices for one-way trips are 1,370kr to Paris, 800kr to Amsterdam, and 420kr to Copenhagen.

BY FERRY Five ferry companies float in and out of Stockholm's waterways; each has its own terminal. **Viking Line** (tel. 08/743–6400), the biggest company, has daily boats to Åbo, Finland (99kr–200kr) and to Riga, Latvia (200kr–500kr). Boats leave from the Viking Line terminal on Södermalm (take the T-bahn to Slussen and then a free Viking Line bus). **Baltic Express Line** (tel. 020/290–029) has biweekly service to St. Petersburg, Russia (26 hrs, 200kr), and leaves from Frihamn (take the T-bahn to Ropsten and then a free shuttle). **Birka Cruises** (tel. 08/714–5520) has six boats weekly to Mariehamn, Finland (9 hrs, 129kr), and leaves from Hjorthagen (take the T-bahn to Ropsten and then take Bus 63). **Estline AB** (tel. 08/667–0001) has boats to Tallinn, Estonia (16 hrs, 385kr), and leaves from Frihamn. **Silja Line** (tel. 08/22–21–40) goes daily to Åbo, Finland (12 hrs, 115kr), and to Helsinki, Finland (24 hrs, 300kr), and leaves from Hjorthagen (take the T-bahn to Ropsten and take a free Silja bus). Eurail holders often travel free on Silja Line, and get generous discounts with other ferry companies.

BY PLANE **Arlanda International Airport** is 40 minutes from Stockholm via Flygbuss airport buses (50kr one-way). The buses leave every 10 minutes from City Terminalen. Most flights within Sweden and to Copenhagen, Oslo, and Helsinki are run by **SAS** (tel. 020/910–150) and **Finnair** (tel. 08/679–9330).

GETTING AROUND

The entire city spreads over 11 islands, but only seven of them are part of the city center. **Norrmalm** is the biggest island, with the train station on its eastern edge. The western part of the island, called **Östermalm**, has plentiful shops and apartments. Next in size is **Södermalm** to the south, where you'll find cheap hotels and restaurants and good nightlife. Between Östermalm and Södermalm, from west to east, are **Riddarholmen,** punctuated by the lacey spire of Riddarholm church; **Gamla Stan,** home to the old royal palace; **Skeppsholmen,** marked by the masts of the 17th-century ship af Chapman; and **Djurgården,** the woodsy old hunting grounds. **Kungsholmen,** west of the train station, is marked by the massive brick tower of the Stadhuset on the southeastern tip.

The T-bahn (subway) and buses can tote you around town in no time at all. Local trains run from the city outskirts to neighboring towns; local train routes are marked on the T-bahn map. The T-bahn, local trains, and buses all use coupons that cost 6.50kr and are valid for one hour. For some trips, two or three coupons may be required. You can buy a book of 20 coupons for 85kr at tourist offices and T-bahn stations. A 60kr **tourist card** is valid for 24 hours and is good on all forms of local transportation. The 115kr card is good for 72 hours and gets you into Skansen (see Worth Seeing, below) for free. The **Stockholm Card** (150kr) gives you unlimited rides on public transportation and free admission to about 50 museums for 24 hours. All cards are available at tourist offices, many hotels, and at the Hotell Centralen office (see Visitor

Information, *above*) at the train station. For general public-transportation info, call 08/600–1000.

BY T-BAHN The T-bahn system is not that convenient (trains run only every 15 minutes, and stations are few and far between), but the system is handy at times. Tickets cost 13kr (two 6.50kr coupons) for travel within Zones 1 and 2 and an additional 6.50kr for Zone 3. Tickets are available in each station. All four T-bahn lines run through T-Centralen at the Central Station (*see* Coming and Going By Train, *above*). You can get a map of the system at most T-bahn stations.

BY BUS Red buses cruise the city from 5 AM to 11 PM, stopping at nearly every corner every five minutes. Tickets, available from the driver, are good for one hour and are valid on the T-bahn. Buses 48, 55, and 59 go to Södermalm via Gamla Stan, Bus 65 goes to Skeppsholmen, and Bus 47 goes to Djurgården. The main bus hubs are at Sergels Torg in front of the train station and at Slussen on Södermalm.

BY BOAT **Stockholm Sightseeing** (tel. 08/24–04–70) has various tours (1–3 hrs, 70kr–200kr) of Stockholm. The one- and two-hour tours are free with the Stockholm Card (*see above*). **Strömma Kanalbolaget** and **Waxholmsbolaget** (tel. 08/789–2415) both have boats that travel around the archipelago, leaving from Stromgatan and from in front of the Stadhuset. **Djurgården** shuttles cruise between Djurgården and several other points in the city from 6 AM until midnight. They cost 10kr a shot if you get on at the main port on Stromgatan, but are free if you just hop on at any other point. Boat info is available at the tourist offices or in front of the ticket booths on Stromgatan.

WHERE TO SLEEP

Stockholm has a slew of hotels and hostels in all price ranges. Even people who prefer hotels should consider staying in a hostel—they're clean, well located, and usually have doubles if you call far enough in advance. Hotel prices drop by about 100kr on weekends and in summer, but the hotels still aren't cushy enough to justify the high price tags. **Hotell Centralen** (*see* Visitor Information, *above*) books rooms and gives out a useful hotel guide. If you don't stick close to the city center, your bus and T-bahn fares will add up.

➢ **UNDER 400KR • Hotell Danielson.** Mike is the friendly owner of this hotel on the second floor of an old apartment building near small theaters and plenty of pizzerias. Easy walk to the city center and train station. Doubles 390kr, including breakfast. *31 Wallingatan, tel. 08/11–10–76. From train station, walk north on Vasagatan 6 blocks past City Conference Center and turn left.*

Hotell Gustav Vasa. An eclectic set-up with '70s decor and marginally clean rooms. Close to antiques shops, affordable restaurants, and a major T-bahn station. Doubles 375kr, 450kr with bath. *61 Västmannagatan, tel. 08/34–38–01 or 08/34–13–20. From Odenplan T-bahn stop, go west on Karlbergsvägen and take a left; it's behind the church.*

Hotell Östermalm. Within walking distance of city center and near a T-bahn stop. Nice building feels luxurious without being too pricey. Doubles 390kr, 460kr with bath. *57 Karlvägen, tel. 08/61–04–71. From Karlaplan T-bahn stop, take Bus 41 or 54 or walk west.*

➢ **UNDER 500KR • Columbus Hotell.** Nicely renovated hotel/hostel (it used to be a prison) in Södermalm near cheap food, good nightlife, and a major T-bahn stop. Hotel rooms aren't any nicer than hostel rooms, but they do include breakfast. Doubles 490kr in hotel, 250kr in hostel; dorm beds 110kr. *11 Tjärhovsgatan, tel. 08/644–1717. From Medborgarplatsen T-bahn stop, go east on Tjärhovsgatan.*

Gustaf af Klimt. An old boat turned into a comfy hotel and youth hostel. Rooms small but clean. On Södermalm, just across the bridge from Gamla Stan. Doubles 480kr, dorm beds 120kr. *153 Stadsgårdskajen, tel. 08/640–4077. From Slussen T-bahn stop, cross Stadsgårdsleden to the blue-and-white boat.*

HOSTELS **Af Chapman** and **Skeppsholmen's Vandrarhem (HI).** These two jointly run hostels almost always have beds. The af Chapman is an 18th-century sailing rig that's now a cozy hostel. Bathrooms are big and lack privacy. Beds 90kr. Skeppsholmen is an old military building. Dorm beds 60kr, doubles 90kr per person. The most popular hostels in Stockholm, great for meeting other travelers. Rooms locked and reception closed daily noon–3. *Skepp-sholmen, tel. 08/679–5015 or 08/679–5017. From train station Bus 65 to Skeppsholmen. 2 AM curfew.*

Brygghuset. Not-so-friendly hostel in the university area off Odenplan. Near transportation, cafés, and nightlife. Dorm beds 110kr, doubles 150kr per person. *12N Norrtullsgatan, tel. 08/31–24–24. Take T-bahn to Odenplan. 2 AM curfew, no lockout, sheets 30kr, reception open daily 7–noon and 3–11.*

Café Bed and Breakfast. Dorms on the bottom floor of a woman's house. The bathrooms beautifully done in wood. A stone's throw from the Hard Rock Cafe in the university area. Beds 110kr. Negotiable curfew around 2 AM. *21 Rehnsgatan, tel. 08/15–28–38. Just off Sveavågen, catercorner to Rådmansgatan T-bahn.*

Långholmen (HI). On a green island just across from western end of Södermalm. Not really within walking distance of the heart of the city, but near transportation. A prison for 250 years, this place is now an upscale hostel. Beds, most in doubles, 90kr. *Kronohäktet, tel. 08/668–0510. From Hornstull T-bahn stop, go left on Högalidssgatan and turn right across the Långholmsbron bridge. Laundry, kitchen facilities, reception open 24 hrs.*

Zinkens (HI). Woodsy spot on Södermalm a fair distance from the city center, but an easy walk to nightlife. Family-oriented, with kitchen facilities and a TV room. Beds 90kr. *20 Zinkens Väg, tel. 08/668–5786. From Zinkensdamm T-bahn stop, walk south on Ringvägen and make a right.*

CAMPGROUND **Bredäng Camping.** Ten km south of Stockholm, squished between Lake Mälaren and high-rise apartments. Near hiking and beaches, and five minutes from a T-bahn station and supermarket. 65kr for tent sites, 125kr for caravans. *Stora Sälskapets Väg, tel. 08/97–70–71. From Bredäng T-bahn stop, go left under tunnel and head straight. Laundry, kitchen facilities, café/store.*

FOOD

Stockholm's size and international flair make for a veritable smorgasbord of dining choices. Generally, hot meals can be found for less than 70kr, especially at lunchtime, when a daily special goes for around 50kr at most cafés. If a kebab or hot sausage on a bun is enough to make you happy, you'll be eating well at every corner *gatukökk* (snack kitchen) for around 20kr. Most cheap eats are found outside the city center; to the south, Södermalm has plenty of neighborhood cafés and pizzerias with artsy patrons. North, along Drottninggatan and Odenplan, you'll find lots of ethnic restaurants and a slew of Asian markets.

➤ **UNDER 60KR • Da Costa.** Right across from train station. Pseudo-Italian restaurant that serves up daily specials of pizza, pasta, salad, bread, and coffee for lunch (48kr) and dinner (58kr). If you're craving the exotic, try the pizza tropicana with banana and curry. *8 Vasagatan, tel. 08/10–10–29.*

Herman's. Great vegetarian food in upbeat local place in Gamla Stan. Daily specials at lunch (48kr) and dinner (58kr) come with salad and homemade bread. Spicy Yogi tea 12kr. *11 Stora Nygatan, tel. 08/411–9500. Closed lunch weekends.*

Silverhästen. Late-night post-party hangout near Sergels Torg. Looks like a typical counter-service café, but serves up heaping hot dishes of lasagna (47kr), salmon (56kr), and roast beef (56kr), all with salad and unlimited bread. *21 Mäster Samuelsgatan.*

Zinkens Krog. In the western part of Södermalm, near the Zinkensdamm T-bahn station. Neighborhood bar with great outdoor tables dishes out hearty daily lunches (steak, fish, salads), including salad, bread, and coffee and biscuits for dessert, for 47kr. Dinners around 70kr. *14 Ringvägen, tel. 08/668–2856.*

➤ **UNDER 150KR • Hot Wok Cafe.** Psychedelic graffiti art and '70s funk music give this place a great vibe, and a family of Malaysian cooks gives it the most authentic stir-fry this side of Kuala Lumpur. A bit pricey, but absolutely worth it for spicy Satayanic chicken (120kr) or the veggie deluxe Greenwich Spaceage (98kr). *78 Hantverkargatan, tel. 08/654–4202. From Fridhemsplan T-bahn, walk west.*

Zum Franziskaner. Great place for a splurge. Founded in 1421, it's the oldest restaurant in Stockholm. French bistro food in upscale beer-hall environment. Sits waterside in Gamla Stan. *44 Skeppsbron, tel. 08/11–83–30.*

CAFES **Cafe Art.** Vaulted, candlelit café in a brick cave in Gamla Stan. Wall next to the pastry counter is part of the 12th-century fortifications that surrounded the city. Coffee is expensive (19kr, with free refills), but the apple cake with vanilla sauce (26kr) is awesome. *60 Västerlånggatan. From Gamla Stan T-bahn, walk north.*

Stortorgets Kaffestuga. Kerstin and Linus Edberg run this cozy café where locals stop on their way to church for hot porridge, boiled eggs, and café au lait; 38kr for a full breakfast. *22 Stortorget, tel. 08/20–59–81. In Gamla Stan, across from Storkyrkan. Open daily 7–3.*

WORTH SEEING

Stockholm can seem overwhelming at first, with so much water, so many spires, and so many gorgeous buildings. As well as the blockbuster sights, Stockholm has a number of small museums showcasing everything from 18th-century musical instruments in the **Musikmuseet** (2 Sibyllegatan; open Tues.–Sun. 11–4) to mailboxes of the world in the **Post Museum** (6 Lilla Nygatan; open. Tues.–Sun. 11–4). The thorough *Stockholm's Museums,* available from the tourist office, will help you choose. If you plan on hitting a ton of museums and sights, it's a good idea to buy a 150kr **Stockholm Card** (*see* Getting Around, *above*). If you're on the last leg of a European tour and the idea of going to another museum makes you want to retch, never fear. A large part of Stockholm's appeal lies in its physical beauty. The harbor at **Nybroplan** hosts a constant flow of nautical activity, and **Djurgården,** once the royal hunting grounds, has a slew of explorable fields and trails. The island's paths, flanked by trees, ambassadors' mansions, and great views of the Feather Islands (the first islands of Stockholm's archipelago), make for some of the most beautiful strolling in Europe. Take Bus 47 from Sergels Torg to Walkdernarsudde or Bus 69 from the Central Station to Blockshusudden (the very tip of Djurgården).

MUSEUMS If you're tired of just visiting museums and want in on the art action yourself, visit the **Kulturhuset** (Sergels Torg 3, tel. 08/700–0100; open Tues.–Sun.). As well as viewing contemporary Swedish art, you can get creative and paint and make collages at their art table.

➤ **MODERNA MUSEET •** Stockholm's museum of modern art is a great mix of "traditional" modern art (Picasso, Miró, Kandinsky) and cutting-edge, weird-o-rama stuff. Several rooms are dedicated to photography and avant-garde Swedish works. *Skeppsholmen, tel. 08/666–4250. From train station Bus 65. Admission: 20kr, free Thurs. Open Tues.–Thurs. 11–8, Fri.–Sun. 11–5.*

➤ **NATIONAL MUSEUM •** The marble building is a masterpiece and makes a wonderful home to Swedish artwork from the 17th century to the present. No big-name artists here— just a tremendous collection of works by Swedes like Zorn, Larsson, and Eriksson. *Södra Blasieholmshamen, just before the bridge to Skeppsholmen, tel. 08/666–4250. Admission: 40kr, 20kr students. Open Tues. 11–9, Wed.–Sun. 11–5.*

➤ **NORDISKA MUSEET** • This magnificent, palatial museum celebrates the history of Sweden, with displays so saturated with props, films, and visual aids that you almost forget it's all in Swedish. The top floor has life-size models of typical Swedish houses of the 18th century. *Djurgårdsvägen, tel. 08/666–4600. Bus 47 from Norrmalmstorg. Admission: 50kr, 30kr students. Open Tues., Wed., and Fri. noon–5, Thurs. noon–8, weekends 10–5.*

➤ **VASAMUSEET** • After sinking on her maiden voyage in 1628, the flagship *Vasa* sat on the bottom of Stockholm's harbor for 333 years until she was lifted in one piece to be towed to port on her own keel. The restored ship and the accompanying displays on its sinking and retrieval made this Sweden's "Museum of the Year" in 1991. *Galärvarvet, Djurgården, tel. 08/666–4800. Bus 47 from Norrmalmstorg or take Djurgården ferry. Admission: 40kr, 25kr students. Open June–Aug., daily 9:30–7; Sept.–May, daily 10–5.*

PARKS AND GARDENS

➤ **MILLESGARDEN** • Fifteen km north of Stockholm, the enchanting house and garden of Swedish sculptor Carl Milles are filled with his own whimsical works and his private collection of classical Greek and Italian pieces from which he drew inspiration. *2 Carl Milles Väg, tel. 08/731–5060. From Ropsten T-bahn stop, take any bus to the first stop across the bridge and follow the signs. Admission: 30kr, 25kr students. Open May–Sept., daily 10–5; Oct.–Apr., daily 11–4.*

➤ **SKANSEN** • The world's first and biggest open-air museum, Skansen is a must-see for visitors who aren't going any farther than Stockholm. Skansen is a huge expanse of land scattered with historic homes, farms, shops, and churches (from 50 to 600 years old) that have been brought here from all over Sweden. With reindeer, a Sami camp, and a workman's village (you can see glassblowers, potters, and bakers in action and buy their wares), this is like doing Sweden in a day. *Djurgården, tel. 08/442–8000. Bus 44 or 47 from city center. Admission: 35kr. Open May–Aug., daily 9 AM–10 PM; Sept.–Apr., daily 9–5.*

PALACES AND CHURCHES

➤ **DROTTNINGHOLM PALACE** • On the island of Lovön in Lake Mälaren, Drottningholm has been the permanent residence of the royal family since 1981, when the king and queen decided that their tykes should grow up in the countryside. The part of the palace open to the public was decorated largely in the 17th century by King Gustav III and Louissa Ulrika. In the southeast corner of the estate, across from the enormous Baroque garden, is a Chinese pavilion with a colorful display of theater sets; the eccentric Gustav III liked to perform here when he wasn't busy being king of the country. The boat ride (50 min, 30kr) to the palace is possibly the most enjoyable part of the adventure. Boats leave every hour from in front of the Stadhuset. *Tel. 08/759–0310. Admisson: 30kr, 10kr students. Open June–Aug., daily 11–4:30; Sept.–May, daily 1–3:30.*

➤ **KUNGLIGA SLOTTET** • This big, boxy royal palace built in 1760 is today used mostly for formal royal affairs and by scores of tourists; the royal family has been living in Drottningholm since 1981. The palace is divided into three separate sections, each with its own claim to fame. The **Royal Apartments** (admission 30kr, 15kr students) give you a peek at the kingly and queenly living arrangements; the **Armémuseum** (admission 40kr, 30kr students) has a good collection of armor, weapons, and stagecoaches; and the **Skattkammaren** (Royal Treasury; admission 25kr, 15kr students) has a dazzling display of crowns, orbs, and scepters. *Slottsbacken, tel. 08/789–8500. Take T-bahn to Gamla Stan. Open May–Sept., daily 10–4; Oct.–Apr., daily 11–3.*

➤ **RIDDARHOLMSKYRKAN** • The lacy spire of Riddarholm is probably Stockholm's most distinctive roof topper, and below is undoubtedly Stockholm's most distinctive church. Finished in the 14th century, Riddarholm's original floor was made of cobblestones, but today consists of the graves of more than 200 Swedish kings and nobility. If you hear the church bells ringing, you know it's serious—they only sound when a duke or king has gone to his throne in the sky. *Riddarholmen, tel. 08/789–8500. Take T-bahn to Gamla Stan. Admission: 10kr. Open June–Aug., Mon.–Sat. 10–3, Sun. noon–3; shorter hrs off-season.*

➢ **STADHUSET** • Stockholm's brick city hall, capped with the three-crown symbol of Sweden, is one of Sweden's most important buildings for several reasons. Completed in 1923, it was designed by Ragnar Ostberg, one of the founders of the Swedish national romantic movement. With a dark, brick, onion-shaped look, the building is a powerful example of the style. It's also the headquarters of Stockholm's city council, and the place where some of the world's geniuses congregate every December 10 for the Nobel Prize award dinner. The Stadhuset's history is related during the required, amusing guided tour. *1 Hantverkargatan, tel. 08/785–9074. Across Stadhusbron bridge from train station. Admission: 20kr. Daily tours at 10, noon, and 2.*

AFTER DARK

Stockholm has a rousing party scene. Kungsträdgården has a host of techno-funk clubs, Södermalm is a great place to find 20kr beers before the prices go up at 9 PM, and the university area around Odenplan and Sveavägen is dotted with cheap student bars. Jazz and blues are big; look for posters or check out the *Nöjesguide,* a free monthly paper that lists the happenings in theater, music, and film; it's in Swedish, but decipherable.

Glenn Miller Cafe. Old musical instruments and signed pictures of jazz greats cover the walls, and if you score the table in the corner by their record player, you get to play DJ for the night. Beer 37kr, wine 35kr. *21 Brunnsgatan, tel. 08/10–03–22. 1 block north of Kungsgatan.*

King's Cross. Lacks charm, but full of students who like to hear live bands and suck down the cheapest beers in town; 17kr for a pint until 9 PM, 28kr after. *40 Malmskillnadsgatan, no tel. At Mäster Samuelsgatan, just east of Sergels Torg.*

Pelikan. High, painted ceilings, tiled floor, and carved wood furniture reminiscent of Europe in the '20s. Borderline bohemian crowd. Piano is there for the playing. Beer 25kr until 8 PM, 35kr after. *40 Blekingegatan, tel. 08/743–0695. From Medborgarplatsen T-bahn, walk south on Götgatan and turn left.*

CHEAP THRILLS

For a peaceful adventure out of the city, take the T-bahn to the Skogskyrkogården cemetery, where chapels by Gunnar Asplund compliment the landscape of Sweden's most beautiful final resting place. The **Moderna Museet** (*see* Worth Seeing, *above*) has summer concerts in their gardens. Grab a six-pack, crash on the grass, and enjoy the tunes outside.

FESTIVALS The **Stockholm Water Festival** is *the* big deal in Stockholm. People from all over Europe come for the concerts, races, light shows, and general partying that takes place during the festival, held in early August. The first week in July is Skeppsholmen's **Jazz and Blues Festival,** where big names play on outdoor stages; the cost is about 150kr a night. Book lodging in advance during both festivals.

Near Stockholm

UPPSALA

Uppsala is a serene combination of old and new. History seeps through the walls of the 600-year-old university and the cafés where Carl von Linné (a.k.a. Linnaeus, inventor of the genus-species classification system) and Olof Rudbeck (inventor of the anatomical theater) used to get their caffeine fixes before making earth-shaking discoveries. From the Domkyrkan, Scandinavia's largest church, to Ofvandahl's Cafe, which supplied bread to kings and queens in the 18th century, everything in Uppsala seems to exude historical vibes. This isn't to say that Uppsala feels old; 25,000 students attend classes taught in these centuries-old buildings. Even the Viking burial mounds in Gamla Uppsala (Old Uppsala) don't look so ancient, with half-naked picnickers on their slopes and joggers and bikers cruising around their base. Hard-core sightseers can make Uppsala a day trip from Stockholm (it's only an hour by train), but it really deserves an overnight stay.

BASICS The **tourist office branch** in the castle (open mid-Apr.–June and Aug., Mon.–Sat. 11–3, Sun. 11–4; July, daily 11–5) has smaller crowds than the **main office** (8 Fyris Torg, tel. 018/27–48–00; open mid-Aug.–mid-June, weekdays 10–6, Sat. 10–2, mid-June–mid-Aug., closed Sat.), which is just south of the cathedral. The **main post office** (tel. 018/17–96–30), across from the train station on the second floor of the Svava mall, changes money for a 35kr fee.

COMING AND GOING The **train station** is on the east side of town, a block from the shopping district. All trains south from Uppsala head through Stockholm (1 hr, 50kr), and all trains north go through Gävle (1 hr, 104kr). The **bus station** (tel. 018/14–14–14) is next to the train station, but buses are necessary only for going to the Arlanda airport (35 min, 70kr).

GETTING AROUND In about 10 minutes, you can stroll from the modern shopping district to the hilltop castle in the older part of town via one of the old bridges across the tree-lined Fyris canal. **Bredgrändgatan** runs southwest from the train station, across the canal and into the old part of town. Most tourist sights are clustered near the cathedral.

All city buses leave from Dragarbrunnsgatan, one block southwest of the train station. You can also catch a bus on any of Uppsala's major thoroughfares. Tickets, available from the driver, cost 12kr and are valid for one hour.

WHERE TO SLEEP In summer, there are a number of hostels and campgrounds, but some hotels close for either the whole summer or on summer weekends. The hotels that are open, however, have super cheap rates. Places outside town tend to be nicer than the ones in the center and are often cheaper, but the 15kr fare for buses into the suburbs and limited weekend service make them a bum deal. **Hotell Årstagård** (14 Jordgubbsgatan, tel. 018/25–35–00; doubles 550kr, 470kr weekends and summer) is a charming yellow house with a rose garden in the suburb of Årsta, 10 minutes from town by bus. Take Bus 19 (52 on weekends) to the end of line and walk three blocks northwest. Near the train station, **Samariterhemmet** (tel. 018/10–34–00) is part of a hospital, but doesn't have any sterile hospital vibes. The new section (4 Kungsängstorg) has spic-and-span doubles with bath for 650kr, 520kr weekends and summer. Doubles in the old section (16 Hamnesplanaden) cost 650kr, 450kr weekends and summer, and have a bit more character but no private baths. From the train station, walk left on Kungsgatan and take a right after the hospital.

KFMU (YMCA) Interpoint Tunet Youth Hostel (2 Torbjörns Torg, off Svartbäcksgatan, tel. 018/15–63–04; closed Sept.–June), 1½ km north of town, has plenty of cheap beds in big dorm rooms, but only two showers. Beds are 70kr plus 25kr for KFMU membership (good for a year). From the train station, take Bus 10 or 25 (50 on weekends). **HI Sunnersta Herrgård** (24 Sunnerstavägen, tel. 018/32–42–20; closed Sept.–Apr.), in a beautiful green suburb 8 km south of town, has two- and four-person bungalows with bathrooms for 83kr and an all-you-can-eat breakfast for 25kr. From the train station, take Bus 14 (20 or 50 on weekends). **Fyrishov Camping** (Fyrisfjädern, tel. 018/23–23–33), just 1 km north of town, has tent sites for 70kr, cabins with kitchens for 325kr. Take Bus 26 or 36, Bus 56 on weekends.

FOOD It's pretty easy to get decent food without spending a lot of cash. Pizzerias here are among the cheapest in Sweden; try along Sysslomansgatan. In the summer, pubs and bars often have menus that include the daily special and a beer for around 55kr. Student bars, or nations (see After Dark, below), are also good for filling plates of grub, but don't expect more than glorified cafeteria food. A favorite student pastime is to grab a sandwich or kebab at **Saluhallen** (St. Eriks Torg, across from cathedral) and then sit outside in the adjacent **Akanten Cafe** and have a 32kr beer. A century-old student dining hall, **Barowiak** (3 Nedre Slottsgatan, north of the castle, tel. 018/12–40–30) is now one of the hottest night spots in town. For less than 70kr you get gourmet food served on the patio or in the 19th-century house. The daily special, served until 10 PM, is 55kr.

WORTH SEEING Although much is made of the **Gustavianum** (behind the cathedral, tel. 018/18–20–84; open daily 11–3), one of only three anatomical theaters in the world, the place is less than thrilling. Med students might be interested, though, in seeing the theater built in 1663 to accommodate 200 people during a human dissection. The large number of seats was important since corpses were so hard to come by—only criminals executed in Uppsala could be used. More interesting is the **Universitet** (University Building; behind the cathedral, tel. 018/18–25–00; admission 10kr), constructed in 1887 to commemorate the university's 400th anniversary. The beautifully decorated rooms are used today for faculty meetings, student assemblies, and to display the university art collection, the second largest in Sweden.

➤ **CAROLINA REDIVIVA** • Finished in 1841, this is the oldest university library in Sweden. You can't get to any of the four million books unless you're a university student, but the display hall has manuscripts by the scientific likes of Darwin, Carl von Linné, and Curie; texts dating back to the 9th century; and the much-glorified Silver Bible, written in AD 895 on silver and gold leaf. *At the south end of Drottninggatan, next to the castle, tel. 018/18–39–00. Admission: 5kr weekend afternoons, otherwise free. Open weekdays 9–7, Sat. 9–6, Sun. 1:30–3.*

➤ **DOMKYRKAN** • It's cathedrals like this—ornately decorated with incredibly lofty arches—that give chiropractors a booming business. Consecrated in 1435, after 175 years of construction, it is Sweden's oldest coronation church. The interior, however, is bright and shiny, following a thorough cleaning with white bread supplied by Ofvandahl's Cafe in 1976. Apparently, something in the bread removes the dirt but leaves the old paint unharmed. Among the dead here are Gustav Vasa, Johan III, Carl von Linné, and St. Erik. *Open Sept.–May, daily 8–6; June–Aug., daily 8–8.*

➤ **GAMLA UPPSALA** • Four km north of Uppsala lie these massive Viking burial grounds. In 1874, excavators confirmed that these three mounds were the final resting place for the crematorium urns of three kings who ruled over Svea (ancient Sweden) around AD 500. The 12th-century church next to the mounds was probably built on the former site of a pagan temple. *From train station, take Bus 14, 24, or 20, or Bus 54 on weekends. Admission free.*

➤ **LINNETRADGARDEN** • The botanical gardens originally planted by Olof Rudbeck in 1650 are today arranged according to the plan of its more famous caretaker, Carl von Linné, inventor of the genus-species classification system. Linné used the 1,300 species of plants here, along with his collection of bottled snakes, fish, and birds, to give lectures when he taught botany at the university in 1745. The gardens are free, but if you want to see the zoological collection and Linné's home and working environment, you'll have to shell out 10kr. *27 Svartbäcksgatan, tel. 018/13–65–40. Gardens open daily 9–9; museum open daily noon–4.*

AFTER DARK Even in the summer, when most university towns are dead, Uppsala has a raging nightlife. Student bars called nations (each one represents a different "nation" or region of Sweden) take over libraries and school buildings to serve cheap beer and food and host occasional live music. To enjoy the fun you have to buy a student guest card (30kr) from the student union (Ovre Slottsgatan 7, tel. 018/10–59–54) on Thursdays. You can also try flashing your own student ID with a smile and you might get in. You can get a list of all the nations when you buy the guest card; some of the more popular ones are **V-Dala,** on Sysslomansgatan, and **Smålandsnation,** behind the university off St. Olofsgatan.

Southern Sweden

makes it the least Swedish part of the country. Sweden's typical red-and-white houses don't start until Dalarna, and you'll rarely see any trace of Sami culture south of Arvidsjaur. This doesn't mean you should skip the region, though; the countryside is still picturesque, and the people still go out of their way to make travelers feel welcome. **Helsingborg** is the only exception to this rule; industry and heavy ferry traffic make this an international eyesore.

Göteborg

Göteborg, just a short ferry hop from Denmark, wouldn't attract many travelers if it weren't so convenient to the Continent. There's not a lot to do here, but the energy on the streets exuded by a young population and many Euro tourists makes up for the city's lack of traditional tourist sights. On summer nights, the main boulevard, Kungsportsavenyn, teems with people strolling to the sounds of funky street bands playing in the sidewalk cafés. Probably the biggest draw for travelers, though, is Göteborg's relatively low prices—especially for liquor.

From the 10th century, when the Vikings sailed from Göteborg's shores, to the 17th century, when the Swedes decided to annex the city to avoid paying Danish tolls on cargo traveling the Göta canal, life in Göteborg has revolved around the sea. Today, Göteborg is Scandinavia's largest port and home to Stena Line, the world's largest ferry company. On top of that, Göteborg is also home to Nordstan, Europe's largest indoor shopping mall; Liesberg, Scandinavia's biggest amusement park; and Scandinavium, which, until recently, was Europe's biggest indoor arena.

BASICS The main **tourist office** (Kungsportsplatsen 2, tel. 031/10–07–40; open July–Aug., daily 9–8, shorter hrs off-season) books private rooms. You can change money at the **American Express office** (35 Ostra Hamngatan, tel. 031/13–07–12; open weekdays 10–1:30 and 2:30–6) or, for slightly better rates, at the **main post office** (6 Drottningtorget, next to the train station, tel. 031/15–09–30). The post office also books hotel and hostel rooms, sells InterRail passes, and has a *Resebyrå* (reservation bureau) for boat, bus, and plane reservations.

Bag the touristy ferry excursions and join the Göteborg locals in a day trip to the archipelago west of the city. Take Tram 4 to its final stop at Saltholmen, show the ferry captain your tram ticket, and sail for free to the different islands.

COMING AND GOING You can get anywhere from Göteborg's central **train station,** including Oslo (4½ hrs, 350kr), Helsinki (3 hrs, 250kr), Stockholm (4 hrs, 425kr), and Berlin (16 hrs, 500kr). Swebus and Sun Eurolines **bus companies** share an office in the train station.

The Resebrå in the main post office (*see above*) has mounds of info on all the ferry lines. Most prices double on weekends. **Stena Line** (tel. 031/775–3030 or 031/775–0000) services Frederikshavn (60kr) and Kiel (380kr–440kr). Ferries leave from Packhuskajen, at the harbor; take Tram 3 or 4 to Masthuggstorget. **Scandinavian Seaways** (tel. 031/80–55–10) has ferries to Harwich (895kr), Newcastle (895kr), and Amsterdam (445kr), all leaving from the northern side of the Göta Canal. A complimentary shuttle leaves from in front of the train station 1½ hours before each ship's departure.

GETTING AROUND Almost everything is within walking distance or an easy tram ride away. Göteborg has three main centers of activity: Nordstan shopping center, Kungsportsplatsen (where the tourist office is), and Götaplatsen (the cultural hub where the big museum and theaters are). The streets (particularly Kungsgatan) that run perpendicular to Ostra Hamngatan/Kungsportsavenyn make up the city's main shopping and strolling area.

Efficient **trams** run Sunday–Thursday 5 AM–12:55 AM, Friday and Saturday until 2:15 AM. Tickets cost 14kr from the driver. A good map of the seven main tram routes is in the tourist office brochure. **Buses** (12kr) are not as useful as trams because they often head directly out of the

city. The main bus info center is on Drottningstorget, near the train station. If you're planning to do the tourist thing full force, it's worthwhile to get the **Göteborg card** (24 hrs, 120kr; 48 hrs, 200kr; 72 hrs, 250kr), which gets you free use of trams of buses and entrance to museums. You can buy the card from the tourist office, Pressbyrån kiosks, and hotels.

WHERE TO SLEEP There are several good, cheap sleeps scattered around town, and the hostels and pensions lurking on the edges of the city are all easily reached by tram or bus. In the heart of Göteborg, **Aveny Turist Hotel** (2 Sodra Vägen, tel. 031/20–52–86) is a real find, with crystal chandeliers, Oriental rugs, and fresh flowers. Call ahead to stay in their 375kr doubles or their four- and five-person rooms that cost 125kr per person. Take Tram 4 or 5 to Berzeliigatan. Old but well kept and in an ideal location just off Kungsportsavenyn, **City Hotel** (6 Lorensbergsgatan, tel. 031/18–00–25) has doubles for 375kr, breakfast included. Take Tram 1, 4, 5, or 6 to Valand and walk a block west on Vasagatan.

Kärralund Vandrarhem (Olbersgatan, tel. 031/25–27–61; dorm beds 90kr, doubles 250kr, campsites 75kr) is like a woodsy summer camp, with a campground, hostel, main reception lodge, general store, and lots of rowdy teenagers. Take Tram 5 to Welandergatan and walk up the small hill past the Dat Max market. The **M/S** *Seaside* (8 Packhuskajen, next to Maritime Center, tel. 031/10–10–35; dorm beds 100kr, singles 250kr), an old boat-cum-youth hostel, is moored right in the middle of Göteborg's harbor. The three-bed cabins are small but comfy. Take Tram 5 to Lilla Bommen, walk to the harbor, and go right.

FOOD If Göteborg's many restaurants were as cheap as they are plentiful, we'd all be happy and stuffed. As it stands, though, the most affordable way to eat in Göteborg is in the cafés, most of them around Nordstan and on Kungsgatan. A favorite Göteborg lunch is a cheese sandwich on homemade bread washed down by a café au lait at **Mauritz Kaffe** (2 Fredsgatan, no tel.), in the maze of shops between Kungsportsplatsen and Nordstan. **Cafe Norrland** (20 Västra Hamngatan, no tel.) is a beat-generation café with live jazz Thursday nights and occasional poetry readings. Fresh soups are 34kr, salads 42kr. **Solrosen** (cnr. of Kaponjärgatan and Haga Östergatan in Hagaram) serves up some of the best vegetarian food in Sweden in a very mellow atmosphere. The daily special is 45kr, and everything comes with a trip to the monster salad bar.

WORTH SEEING Much of Göteborg's heritage revolves around the sea, and a stroll down by the **harbor** can turn into an all-day excursion. Göteborg's main art museum, the **Konstmuseet** (Götaplatsen, tel. 031/61–29–80; admission 25kr; open May–Aug., daily 10–5, shorter hrs off-season) has an impressive collection of works by Sweden's most famous painters and sculptors, as well as a few pieces by Picasso, Degas, Rubens, and Rembrandt. Take Tram 4 or 5 to Berzeliigatan. The **Röhss Museum** (37–39 Vasagatan, tel. 031/18–46–92; admission 25kr; open weekdays 11–4, weekends 10–5) is the only museum in Sweden to specialize in arts and crafts and industrial design. The permanent exhibit of furniture, glass works, and art from the Renaissance to the present includes a great collection of Bauhaus stuff. **Liseberg** (admission 35kr; open summer,

At Goteborg's Liseberg amusement park you'll see plenty of the over-40 set getting in touch with their inner child at the game booths and at the Polka Pavilion.

daily 11–11; winter, daily 11–6), Sweden's biggest amusement park, is packed with roller coasters, spinning rides, and carnival games. You can buy an unlimited use ticket for 125kr, or shell out 3kr–9kr each time you want to play or ride. Take Tram 5 to Liseberg.

In **Haga,** Göteborg's oldest suburb, the 19th-century wood-upon-concrete houses (built to bypass a restrictive fire law) now hold cafés, antiques shops, and secondhand stores. To get here, take Tram 1, 3, or 4 to Jarntörget and walk south from the canal. Across Linnegatan from Haga is an unnamed neighborhood where students and antiques hounds congregate among alternative music stores, ethnic cafés, and antiques shops. Stop in at **Viktoriahuset** (13–21 Linnegatan), an old brick schoolhouse that is now home to Göteborg's solidarity-movement offices as well as a café and a foreign-film theater.

AFTER DARK Göteborg's nightlife, especially on Kungsportsavenyn, is great. **Magasinet** (14 Magasinsgatan) is a local favorite. Bands play nightly, and there's no cover on weeknights. Hang out with friendly students at **Chez Ami** (cnr. of Västra Hamngatan and Park Gatan).

Malmö

Look up as you ride or sail into Malmö and you'll see an unusual skyline—the bulky steel of massive cranes at the loading docks, the modern glass structure of Malmö's navigation center, and enough domes and spires to make you think that every other building in the city must be a church. As Sweden's third-largest city, Malmö borders on the metropolitan, complete with fast-food chains, shopping malls, and people asking for spare change.

Scandinavia's gateway to the Continent, Malmö is an easy day trip from Copenhagen, just a hop, skip, and a ferry ride away. And as capital of the province of Skåne, Malmö boasts a comprehensive **history museum** that tells the tale of southern Sweden. This museum, along with the city's art collection, a natural-history museum, an aquarium, and a tropicarium (housing lemurs, lorises, and bush babies), is in **Malmöhus Slott** (Malmöhusvägen, tel. 040/34–10–00; open Tues.–Sat. noon–4, Sun. noon–4:30), a moated castle built in the 16th century. An outstanding collection of contemporary artwork is displayed at the **Rooseum Center for Contemporary Art** (Gasverksgatan 22, tel. 040/12–17–16; open Tues.–Sun. 11–5). To get an eyeful of Swedish architecture, check out the powerful **St. Petri Kyrka**, a Gothic church behind Stortorget, and **Radhuset,** the city hall on the northeast corner of Stortorget.

BASICS The **tourist office** (Skeppsbron 2, tel. 040/30–01–50; open weekdays 9–5, Sat. 9–1) is across from the train station. The handiest place to change money is at the **Flygbåtarna ferry terminal** (next to the train station; open Mon.–Sat. 7:30–7, Sun. 9:30–5), because of its good rates and long hours. The main **post office** (Skeppsbron 1, tel. 040/14–90–00; open weekdays 8–6, Sat. 9:30–1) has an exchange counter and a hotel reservation center (40kr fee).

COMING AND GOING Malmö is a mere 25 km across the Öresund from Copenhagen. The **Flygbåtarna hydrofoil** (tel. 040/10–39–30) will whisk you across in 45 minutes for 93kr. The **Pilen Line** ferries are just as fast, but cost only 39kr (49kr weekends). The **"Shopping" Line** (tel. 040/11–00–99) ferry takes 1½ hours but costs only 25kr. All three lines depart from the ferry terminal north of the train station on Skeppsbron.

Malmö has daily trains to Göteborg (4 hrs, 340kr) and Stockholm (6½ hrs, 520kr). The purple regional trains run from an adjoining station and make trips to Lund (15 min, 25kr) and Helsingborg (40 min, 60kr).

GETTING AROUND Malmö is easily manageable on foot or by bus. Heading south from the train station, you'll cross the canal via the **Mälar bridge** to **Stortorget,** the city's main hub. From the southwest corner of the main square branches **Lilla Torget,** which is lined with 16th-century half-timbered houses. **Sodergatan,** leading away from the southeast corner, is the main pedestrian street.

City buses leave from the south side of the train station and cost 12kr. Bus 21 goes to Gustav Aldophs Torget and Trianglen. Bus 20C runs to Malmöhus Slott, west of the train station via busy Norra Vallgatan. For a view of the city by boat, try the canal boat tour (45 min, 50kr) that leaves every hour, across from the south side of the train station.

WHERE TO SLEEP AND EAT The **HI Youth Hostel Södergarten** (tel. 040/82–22–00; beds 90kr) is as industrial and impersonal as the part of town it's in. Since it costs 12kr a pop for the bus ride out here, it's cheaper to stay at the hostel in Lund (*see below*) if you have a rail pass. To get to the Malmö hostel, take Bus 21A to the Vandrarhemmet stop and follow Eriksfältsgatan around the right until it dead-ends. An alternative is the shaggy but conveniently located **Pallas Hotell** (88 Norra Vallgatan, 3 blocks west of station, tel. 040/11–50–77), where the rooms without bath are 345kr for a single and 445kr for a double.

Eating in Malmö is boring but cheap. At lunchtime, you can easily grab a quick fix at one of the many kiosks on Södergatan or Sodra Forstadsgatan. For a tad more atmosphere, try **Saluhallen** (open weekdays 10–6, Sat. 10–2), an indoor market with a host of groceries and prepared food, at the northwest corner of Lilla Torget. Near the train station, the **Olympus Pub and Restaurant** (89 Norra Vallgatan) serves Greek dishes, pasta, and pizza for less than 60kr.

Lund

Sweet little Lund is a fun stop for a night or two. It's filled with a slew of historical buildings and museums to keep you busy during the day, and a hopping university nightlife to amuse you at night. Its proximity to Copenhagen makes it a perfect spot to visit if you want to get a glimpse of Sweden but are short on time and cash.

The **Domkykran** (Kyrkogatan; open weekdays 8–6, Sat. 9:30–5, Sun. 9:30–6) still acts as a center of social and religious activity in Lund. Consecrated in 1145, the cathedral is declared (by the town of Lund, funnily enough) to be "the finest Romanesque building in Scandinavia." It's a personal judgment call, of course, but it's still undisputedly worth visiting at noon or 3 PM (1 PM on Sundays) to watch the 14th-century astronomical clock do its swinging version of "In dulci jubilo." The **Student Union Archives Museum** (Sandgatan 2, in the basement of the Student Union, tel. 046/13–79–92; open Tues.–Thurs. 4–6) has a colorful collection of photos, drawings, and insignia tracing the history of the university from its founding in 1666 to the present. To traipse through Lund's history, stop by **Kulturen** (Tegnérsplatsen, behind the cathedral, tel. 046/15–04–08; admission 30kr, 20kr students; open daily 11–5). The vast collection of military uniforms, weapons, textiles, folk costumes, and a huge courtyard of replicated Swedish houses will wow you. The **Skissernas Museum** (Museum of Sketches; Finngatan 2, north of the cathedral, tel. 046/10–72–83; open Tues.–Sat. noon–2, Sun. 1–5) is a lofty warehouse gallery with working sketches and models of pieces by Marc Chagall, Pablo Picasso, and Diego Rivera, among others. It's absolutely worth the 10kr admission.

BASICS The **tourist office** (Kyrkogatan 11, tel. 046/35–50–40; open May–Aug., weekdays 10–5, weekends 10–2, shorter hrs off-season) doles out lots of helpful info. The deluxe **post office** (Knut den Storegata 2, across from the train station; open weekdays 9–6, Sat. 10–1) changes money for the best rates in town.

COMING AND GOING Local trains run to Copenhagen (2 hrs, 70kr), Helsingborg (1½ hrs, 50kr), and Malmö (20 min, 25kr). For longer trips, pick up the national SJ trains in Malmö. Life in Lund centers around three main areas: the University and Domkyrkan, Stortorget, and Mårtenstorget, which all form an easily walkable triangle.

WHERE TO SLEEP AND EAT It's almost worth coming to Lund just to stay in **STF Vandrarhem Tåget** (Vävareg 22, tel. 046/14–28–20; beds 90kr), an old wooden train that has been converted into a youth hostel. The extra-close quarters are made up for with spectacularly clean bathrooms, a fully equipped kitchen, and a TV room. To get here, take a right out of the tunnel as you get off the train and follow the sign.

Food prices are moderate, especially around the university and Stortorget. A favorite student hangout is the Student Union building, where **Cafe Tua** (open daily 9–2) and **Chrougen** (open daily 11:30–2 and 6–midnight) serve up hearty lunches and a do-it-yourself buffet for less than 40kr. Tua is the place for café goers, while Chrougen is more pub-like, with live entertainment most weekends.

Gotland

In the Baltic Sea, five hours from the Swedish mainland, lies the island of Gotland, a big-time Swedish summer haven. Roughly 100 km long, Gotland boasts archaeological finds, limestone rock formations, reconstructed Viking settlements, and kilometer upon kilometer of rocky cliffs and sandy beaches. Linking the whole shebang together is an amazing system of bicycle trails, hostels, and campgrounds. Highlights for those who want to do some exploring include the

12th-century monastery of **Roma,** in the middle of the island; **Torsburgen,** the largest fortification in Scandinavia, on the east side of the island; and the limestone cliffs and rock formations of **Stora Karlsö,** a little island off the southwest coast of Gotland, with a killer, though isolated, **hostel** (tel. 0498/24–05–00). In the summer prices are painful, but if you camp or stay in hostels and stick to the remote eastern and northern parts of the island, a trip to Gotland is well worth the 85kr (115kr on weekends) for the ferry ride.

VISBY

The main town on the island of Gotland, Visby is about as storybook perfect as any place. A 13th-century city wall encloses a collection of cobblestone streets that wind crookedly under vaulted passageways, through ancient church ruins, and past small cottages and half-timbered houses whose gardens burst with color in the springtime. The city squats on a steep hill, so the ocean view, over a jumble of tiled roofs and cathedral spires, is sensational. Half a day can easily be spent walking the perimeter of the wall and checking out the history of different gates, towers, and outcroppings, all explained on placards at various points along the wall. The history of Visby and of Gotland is presented in the **Gotlands Fornsal** (14 Strandgatan, across from the tourist office, tel. 0498/24–70–10; admission 35kr; open daily 11–6). Definitely check out the **Silversmederna** (Silversmith Shop, 28 Strandgatan; open weekdays noon–6, Sat. 11–1), where artists create silver and gold jewelry in a merchant's house built in 1250. The **Domkyrkan St. Maria,** where you can hear organ recitals on Saturdays at noon, is the only one of Visby's 17 medieval churches that isn't in ruins. If you're feeling claustrophobic, bust out of the city wall and head north for a walk along the water or a swim in the Baltic.

BASICS Visby's main tourist office, **Turistbyrån Burmeisterska Huset** (9 Strandgatan, tel. 0498/21–09–82; open weekdays 8–6, weekends 10–8), is in a 16th-century, half-timbered building. Down the street at the **Turistbyrån** (4 Hamngatan, tel. 0498/21–09–82; open daily 10–6) you can book private rooms and make ferry and bus reservations for 35kr. The best exchange rates are at the **post offices** (2 Norra Hansegatan, outside the Oster port; and inside the ICA market at 6 Söderväg).

COMING ANG GOING **Gotlandslinjen** (tel. 0498/29–30–00) has a monopoly on the ferry business. Boats from Nynäshamn (south of Stockholm) run nightly at 11:30 PM (135kr, 85kr students). From June 6 to August 15, an additional boat (175kr, 115kr students) heads out at 12:40 PM Friday–Monday.

Once you arrive, get your hot little hands on the bus schedule, available at the tourist office, for info on how to get around the island. Buses leave from **Visby Busstation,** just outside the city wall of Söderport, and cost 20kr–80kr.

GETTING AROUND There's no rhyme or reason to Visby's streets, and even the detailed map that the tourist office doles out doesn't do much good. Buses meet the ferry for the short ride up to the bus station for those who want to head straight out of town or to the hostel. Otherwise, head north from the ferry terminal and make a right on Hamngatan to get to the tourist office.

WHERE TO SLEEP AND EAT Accommodations in the center of town are expensive, but the only buses to lodgings on the outskirts cost 20kr a shot and run only until 6 PM. The best bet is the **STF Vandrarhem** (tel. 0498/26–32–58; dorm beds 60kr, doubles 260kr; closed Aug. 16–June 9). To get here from the bus station, walk east up Artillerigatan, past the cemetery and the soccer field, and it's on your right. **Norderstrands camping** (tel. 0498/24–87–87), 1 km north of town on the water, has tent spots for 40kr and four-bed cabins for 240kr. Prices go up to 70kr and 360kr from June 12 to August 15.

Visby doesn't have much to offer in the way of affordable food. Most of the budget pizza joints and falafel stands are down by the harbor and along Adelsgatan just inside Söderport. For a change of pace, sup on coffee and pastries (22kr) at **St. Hans Konditori** (St. Hansplan), whose garden consists of the enormous stone ruins of the St. Hans, St. Per, and St. Carin churches. Well worth the extra kronor is the homemade pasta at **Kors and Tvärs** (51 St.

Hansgatan, tel. 0498/28–28–28; open Tues.–Sun. 11:30–2 and 6–midnight), where *pasta pesto toscana* (pasta with pesto and bacon) is 80kr.

Central and Northern Sweden

You can get a taste of Sweden's culture and history behind glass or at the Skansen open-air museum in Stockholm, but not until you've seen the villages of Dalarna or the vast mountain ranges and Sami villages of Lapland can you really know what Sweden is all about.

It's hard not to sound like a cheesy tourist brochure when discussing this part of the country. The rolling green hills dotted with farms and maypoles, and the pristine lakes and mountains of Norrland (nothern Sweden) are a nature lover's wet dream. The Sami people of Lapland now use motorcycles and snowmobiles to herd their reindeer, but their culture is still very much alive. The climate up here is extreme: Long, dark winters with temperatures below –40°F are followed by beautiful green summers with enough mosquitos to drive you crazy with itching.

Trains service central Sweden efficiently, but if you want to get up to most towns north of Östersund without going all the way up to Kiruna, you have to take the Inlandsbanan train route (*see below*), which can be expensive (Eurailers and InterRailers get a 50% discount) and slow. But to see Sweden's roots, it's well worth the extra time and money and a couple (okay, hundreds) of skeeter bites.

Dalarna

Curving around the shores of Lake Siljan in central Sweden, the cluster of villages that form the province of Dalarna are as typically Swedish as you'll find. The area's handicrafts and natural landscape attract big crowds of outdoor enthusiasts and older tourists looking for quaint villages and idyllic picnic spots. To disillusioned 20th-century travelers, the folk costumes and artisan workshops may seem like a tourist show, but, in fact, Dalarna is about as close as you can get to the real Sweden without knowing any Svensons or Petersons personally. If you skip tacky tourist shops and go wandering in the hills, you'll see that birch bark and sod are still used in making roofs, and every red-and-white-painted village has a maypole in its church yard.

Fäbodars (traditional farms) dating from the 16th century and *gammelgards* (open-air museums) are the main attractions of the region, offering ample opportunity to buy handcrafted artwork and see artisans in action making pottery, yarn, woodwork, and traditional food. In the

The Fairytale Origin of the Vasaloppet

Once upon a time, in 1521, the daring young Gustav Vasa arrived in Mora to tell the locals of the gruesome slaughter of Swedish noblemen in Stockholm that had been ordered by the Danish King Christian. "Yeah, right," said the Mora skeptics, who convinced the town that Vasa was full of crap. So, Vasa set out on skis to Norway, where he planned to live out the rest of his days in exile, free from the hand of Danish rule. Pretty soon, news came to Mora confirming Vasa's story. They hurriedly sent two strapping young skiers to catch up with Vasa at Sälen. The three men returned to Mora, recruited an army, and marched south to drive the Danes out of Sweden. Gustav Vasa lived happily ever after as king and founder of modern Sweden, and today the Vasaloppet cross-country ski race traces the path that Vasa took. The End.

summer, you'll find loads of hiking paths (free) and water sports (not even close to free) on and around Lake Siljan. After the snow falls, hikers put on cross-country skis, and picnics are replaced by hearty meals at cozy fireside inns.

Dalarna's major towns are accessible by train from Uppsala (3 hrs, 150kr), and several trains a day (about 20 min, 28kr) connect the smaller towns. Dalatrafix buses cost the same as the train but run more frequently between towns. Campgrounds are plentiful, and *rum* (room) signs mean a cheap bed and a hearty breakfast in someone's house.

MORA The northernmost town of importance on Lake Siljan, Mora lives for two men: Gustav Vasa and Anders Zorn. The Vasaloppet (*see box* The Fairytale Origin of the Vasaloppet, *above*), now the world's largest cross-country ski race, was begun in 1922 and inspired by the action of Swedish hero Gustav Vasa. Beginning in Sälen, toward the Norwegian border, the "way of the suffering thousands" ends 90 km later in Mora amid cheers, tears, and much partying. Awards, memorabilia, and a great video celebrating the race can be seen at the **Vasaloppsmålet** (Vasagatan; open daily 10–5). Except for the week of the race (usually in early March), Gustav Vasa takes a back seat to the impressionist painter Anders Zorn, Mora's most acclaimed citizen. His house, called **Zorngården** (Vasagatan; admission 20kr; open Mon.–Sat. 10–5, Sun. 11-5; tour in English at 3 PM), has been preserved as it was when he lived here with his wife until his death in 1920. Next door is the **Zornmuseet** (tel. 0250/16560; open Mon.–Sat. 9–5, Sun. 11–5), with many of his oils and watercolors. A tourist office representative meets trains in the summer, and the **main tourist office** (Ångbåtskajen, tel. 0250/26550; open weekdays 9–5, Sat. 9–1; in summer, daily until 8 PM) is on the lake about 800 meters from the station.

➢ **WHERE TO SLEEP AND EAT** • There is no hostel in Mora, but the **Hotell Kung Gösta Annex** (1 Kristinebegsgatan, across from train station, tel. 0250/15070) has doubles for 320kr and dorm beds for 95kr. **Mora Camping** (tel. 0250/26595) is across from Zorn's house and has tent spots for 60kr and cabins for 250kr–350kr. There is a **Konsum** market on Kyrkogatan, and **Ströms** (cnr. of Moragatan and Köpmangatan; open daily 9–9) is a good spot for sandwiches (22kr).

LEKSAND Leksand is one of the most picturesque of Lake Siljan's major towns, and its gammelgard, **Hembygdsgärdar**, is one of the most authentic. In summer (when it's open daily 11–5), you can see locals baking bread and weaving birch baskets. The **Kulturhuset** (Cultural Center; 29 Norrsgatan; open weekdays 9–7, weekends 9–5) has a good display of local art and doesn't charge admission. During the summer, a number of activites take place in the large, grassy areas that cling to a cliff above the confluence of the Osterdaläven River and Lake Siljan's southern waters. Leksand's **tourist office** (cnr. of Norsgatan and Kyrkallén, tel. 0247/80300; open summer, Mon.–Sat. 9–9, Sun. noon–9; shorter hrs off-season) sells tickets to all events and festivals.

➢ **WHERE TO SLEEP AND EAT** • The awesome **HI Vandrarhem** (Parkgården, tel. 0247/10186) is 3 km south of the town center on a restored farm. Cabins go for 84kr, and the kitchen and common room are straight out of *Heidi*. To get here, go south through town, over the bridge, and left on Insjövagen. For a hearty lunch, try the pasta (45kr) at **Goldis** (cnr. of Faluvagen and Leksandsvägen, tel. 0247/10502), the locals' favorite pizzeria, bar, and disco.

The Inlandsbanan

The Inlandsbanan (Inland train) runs from Mora up to Gällivare, right through the middle of Sweden. The railway reopened in 1993 after being defunct for some years and is now more a form of entertainment than a mode of transportation. Guides relate anecdotes and tidbits of natural history, and should the train pass by a reindeer too quickly, don't worry—they'll back up so you can take a photo. Hell-bent travelers who cringe at the high prices and slow pace should stick to the normal SJ trains that run parallel along Sweden's east coast and intercept the Inlandsbanan at Gällivare.

The small towns along the route pretty much revolve around Inlandsbanan tourism; it's easy to make an overnight stop in any one of them—accommodations are near the train station, and tourist office representatives meet each train. If you just want to get into the woods, you can hop off the train anywhere north of Sorsele and be near mountains and lakes. Purists will want to head east of the train route to one of the towns near the Kungsleden, a 500-km hiking trail that ends at Abisko, at the northern tip of the country. The Inlandsbanan–Kungsleden combo is a popular one, so there are good bus connections from Sorsele, Jokkmokk, and Gällivare.

The official starting point of the Inlandsbanan is Mora, but to save a few kronor, take the normal SJ train to Östersund and start from there. The two legs of the Inlandsbanan route are the **Vildmarkstäget** (Wildlife Express), which runs from Östersund to Arvidsjaur, and the **Räls-bussen**, which goes the rest of the way up to Gällivare. Inlandsbanan ticket prices change throughout the year: From June 5 to June 24, the Östersund–Arvidsjaur route costs 150kr and Arvidsjaur–Gällivare costs 75kr; the prices go up 25kr on June 25 and another 25kr on July 3 and then drop 25kr on July 19. Eurailers and InterRailers get a 50% discount, and tickets, available on board, are good for a month.

OSTERSUND Östersund's bustling, shop-lined streets snuggle up to the northeast side of Storsund (Big Lake), and its small harbor and lakeside park make for beautiful 11 PM sunset strolling. The open-air museum of **Jamtli** (Museiplan; admission 50kr; open June–Aug., daily 11–5) has farms and cabins from the 18th and 19th centuries where people go about their daily chores as if the 20th-century were still a futuristic farce. The SS *Thomée*, Sweden's oldest steamboat still in regular service, leaves from the harbor at the west end of Biblioteks-gatan for one- to five-hour cruises (40kr–75kr). A thousand feet across the water, the mountainous island of Fröson, where Viking gods held court 1,000 years ago, is now home to loads of skiing and hiking trails, the **sommarhagen** (summer home) of composer Wilhelm Peterson-Berger (admission 15kr; open daily 11–3, in July until 6 PM), and the 12th-century wooden Frösö Church. Take Bus 3 or 4 to get to the island. For more info, talk to the **tourist office** (44 Rädhusgatan, tel. 063/14–40–01; open June–Aug., Mon.–Sat. 9–9, Sun. 10–7, shorter hrs off-season).

➤ **COMING AND GOING** • There are two train stops in Östersund: The first is 1 km south of the town center and the second is two blocks west of the town center via Samuel Permans Gata. Get off at the first only if you're headed for the HI hostel. Buses leave from Gustav III's Torg on Radhusgatan and cost 10kr a shot, 28kr after 11 PM.

➤ **WHERE TO SLEEP AND EAT** • All the cheap options are here: hostels, camping, pensions, and small hotels. The tourist office books rooms for a 40kr fee, but you're better off using the thorough list of places on the tourist map and calling yourself. The centrally located **HI Vandrarhem** (12 Tingsgatan, east of Järnvagen train station, tel. 063/10–23–43; beds 90kr) is open only June–August. At lunchtime, check out Storgatan and Prästgatan for sit-down eateries with a 45kr daily special. If you're wondering why the streets are empty after 7 PM, it's because everybody is at **Café Brunkullan** (5 Postgränd, tel. 063/10–14–54) having beers (36kr) and dinner (cheese enchiladas 72kr, curry shrimp pasta 80kr).

ARVIDSJAUR The main reason to stop in Arvidsjaur is to go white-water rafting. The two-hour, 210kr trip (including bus transportation to the river, equipment, and, of course, coffee) on the Piteälaven River leaves four times a day from the train station and the tourist office. It's not exactly a raging white-water adventure, but the scenery is spectacular. If you can get a reservation, stay at **Lappugglans Turistviste** (9 Vastra Skolgatan, tel. 0960/12413), where you sleep in old Sami cabins for 90kr a night and sit around the open fire in the front yard. The small wooden **tourist hut** at the train station is good for getting a map and finding a place to stay, but for regional info and rafting reservations, go to the **main tourist office** (4 Garvaregatan, north of train station via Stationsgatan, tel. 0960/17500; open daily 10–6).

JOKKMOKK If you only make one stop on the Inlandsbanan, Jokkmokk is a good one. On the Arctic Circle, Jokkmokk is the gateway to Lapland. A longtime winter meeting place for Sami reindeer herders, the town was officially founded in 1602 as part of a trading chain meant to expand population and, more importantly, taxation northward. Jokkmokk's Winter-market, held the first Thursday, Friday, and Saturday in February, has been held every year since 1605. The **Gamla Apotek** (Old Apothecary Building; 15 Västra Torggatan, tel. 0971/17276; open daily 10–7) has an elegant display of local artists' wares. The town's biggest attraction is the new **Ajtte Swedish Mountain and Saami Museum** (3 Kyrkogatan, east of the tourist office, tel. 0971/12057; admission 20kr; open weekdays 9–6, weekends 11–6). Along with hands-on displays, there is a beautiful film studio showing a 1940s documentary on the Sami lifestyle. A tourist office representative meets the train, and the **main tourist office** (4 Stortorget, 2 blocks south of train station, tel. 0971/12140; open daily 9–7) has good topographic maps.

➣ **WHERE TO SLEEP AND EAT** • As you head south on Stationsgatan from the station, the first two houses on your right have cozy double rooms for 85kr per person. The **HI Vandrarhem** (east on Storgatan, tel. 0971/11977; beds 85kr) has a well-equipped kitchen. **Jokkmokks Turistcenter** (tel. 0971/12370), 3 km east of town, has doubles for 225kr and cabins with bathrooms for 525kr. Campers can pitch a tent for 60kr. Even the town pizzeria, **Restaurang Milano** (Berggatan, tel. 0971/10085), can run well over 70kr for dinner, so your best bets are the **ICA** and **Konsum** supermarkets, both on Storgatan.

GALLIVARE Gällivare, the northernmost stop on the Inlandsbanan line, is kind of a letdown. Still, it makes a good base for exploring the surrounding mines. For a gander at the town, head to Gällivare's open-air museum. To get to the museum, follow the signs marked KULTURSTIGAN (culture path) for a 2-km tour around town. The path starts at the school building that houses the **tourist office** (16 Storgatan, tel. 0970/16660; open May–Aug., daily 9–8; Sept.–Apr., weekdays 9–4:30), winds back toward the train station, crosses the railway station bridge, and heads along the water past an 18th-century church. The path finally reaches the **Hembygdsomiade** (open daily 11–6) with a Sami camp, bakery cottage, and Sweden's northernmost windmill. For a great view of the midnight sun, hike up the ski trails (in summer, of course) to the top of Dundret Mountain, 3 km south of the city past the hostel. The beautiful 19th-century wooden **train station** (tel. 0970/11000) is on the southwest edge of town.

The mines surrounding Gällivare are worth a look but pricey since they're only viewable by guided tour. **Aitik,** Europe's largest copper mine, is 13 km northeast of Gällivare. An environmentalist's nightmare, the mine consists of a canyon 4 km by 8 km by 500 meters. It's worth the 135kr for the three-hour guided bus tour (daily at 1:30 from the tourist office) that takes you down into the pit. The tour also includes a stop at Malmberget, a mining town founded in 1888. Catch the bus at Gällivare's tourist office.

➣ **WHERE TO SLEEP AND EAT** • The *Guld Guiden,* handed out by the tourist office, has a list of private homes with rooms that run about 100kr per person. The **HI Vandrarhem** (tel. 0970/14380; reception open 8–10 and 5–10:30), 500 meters southwest of the train station, has beds for 84kr in spacious cabins, each with its own bathroom and kitchen. The **Hembygdskaféet** (tel. 0970/15509; open weekdays 9–7, weekends 9–5), in the tourist office building, has sandwiches (20kr) and baked goodies (15kr).

SWITZERLAND

24

By Katherine Stechschulte

It's a wonder that Switzerland's trademark orderliness and efficiency could devel-op amid its chaos of languages, religions, and impassable mountain ridges. On this canvas of fresh alpine meadows, sparkling blue lakes, and dizzying peaks, a wide assortment of Euro-peans have left their marks. Four languages—German, French, Italian, and Romansch—rub shoulders here today, despite the fact that the country's population is only 6 million.

A decentralized political system doesn't make it any easier for residents to develop a national identity. The federal government takes care of international affairs, but local administrations handle schools, road construction, taxation, and town planning. Sovereign power seems, at least, to rest very much with the people, who vote on everything from what color official trash cans should be to whether Switzerland should join the Euro-pean Union. (They decided against membership by a slim margin, most no votes coming from German-speaking resi-dents who feared joining would destroy their unique grass-roots democracy and weaken the economy.)

Against all odds, the political and ethnic hodgepodge has resulted in one of the highest standards of living in Europe, a national income divided evenly among citizens, and—perhaps most surprisingly—a long-standing policy of neutrality during the wars that have rocked the European continent. Of course, Switzerland doesn't have *all* the bases covered. As Orson

Although they haven't engaged in war for the past 300 years, the Swiss remain prepared, with extensive underground airports and shelters that store enough food to feed the entire country for six months.

Welles said in *The Third Man,* "Hundreds of years of peace, and what did it produce? The cuck-oo clock." It's true that the country lacks an exciting cultural heritage, but it has produced a couple famous artists, including Paul Klee and Alberto Giacometti, and its neutrality during World War II attracted many talented refugees, among them James Joyce, Hermann Hesse, Thomas Mann, and Max Beckmann. That said, you won't get a heavy dose of culture on your visit to Switzerland. You will find loads of bucolic charm, mountain scenery that astounds, and peaceful lakeside cities that could lull you into staying for months if this weren't one of the most expensive countries in Europe.

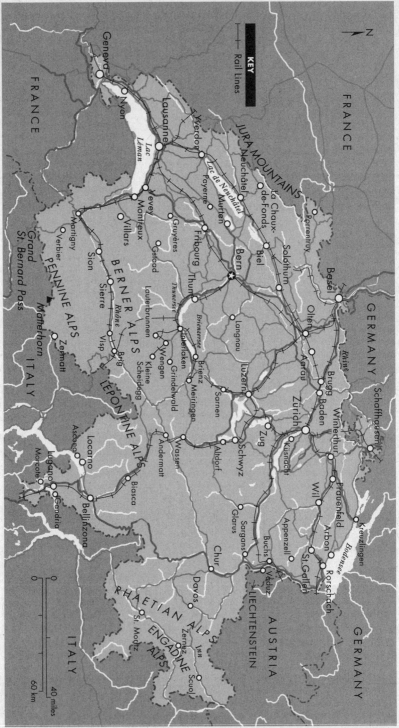

N

KEY
Rail Lines

FRANCE

FRANCE

GERMANY

GERMANY

AUSTRIA

ITALY

ITALY

LIECHTENSTEIN

JURA MOUNTAINS

PENNINE ALPS

BERNER ALPS

LEPONTINE ALPS

RHAETIAN ALPS

ENGADINE ALPS

Geneva
Nyon
Lausanne
Yverdon
Neuchâtel
Lac de Neuchâtel
La Chaux-de-Fonds
Porrentruy
Basel
Lac Léman
Vevey
Montreux
Villars
Gruyères
Payerne
Lac de Murten
Fribourg
Biel
Solothurn
Bern
Olten
Brugg
Baden
Schaffhausen
Rhine
Winterthur
Martigny
Verbier
Gstaad
Thun
Thunersee
Brienzersee
Langnau
Aarau
Zürich
Zug
Frauenfeld
Kreuzlingen
Bodensee
Sion
Sierre
Lauterbrunnen
Kleine Scheidegg
Wengen
Grindelwald
Interlaken
Brienz
Meiringen
Luzern
Küsnacht
Wil
Arbon
Rorschach
St. Gallen
Grand St. Bernard Pass
Matterhorn
Zermatt
Visp
Brig
Andermatt
Wassen
Sarnen
Altdorf
Schwyz
Glarus
Appenzell
Rhône
Ascona
Locarno
Biasca
Sargans
Buchs
Vaduz
Morcote
Lugano
Bellinzona
Gandria
Chur
Davos
St. Moritz
Zernez
Scuol
Inn

0
20
40
60 km
0
20
40 miles

Basics

MONEY $1 = 1.24 Swiss francs and 1 Swiss franc = 80¢. The Swiss franc (SFr) contains 100 centimes. You can exchange money at banks, usually open weekdays 8–noon and 2–6:30 and sometimes open Saturday mornings. Bureaux de change at train stations (look for GELDWECHSEL signs) offer rates comparable to the banks' and have longer hours. ATM machines are becoming more common, but most accept only European cards.

➤ **HOW MUCH IT WILL COST** • Switzerland is one of the costliest countries in Europe. Food is especially pricey: Lunch at an inexpensive sit-down restaurant runs about $10, and even the food at snack stands often costs $7. Trains are expensive, so get a Eurail-Pass or a Swiss pass if you plan to stay long. If you sleep in hostels (SFr14–SFr21) and eat at inexpensive cafés, you can probably get by on $50 a day.

GETTING AROUND Train stations rent **bikes** for about SFr16 per day, SFr64 per week, and you can pick up from one station and return to another. Reserve the bike at 6 PM the day before you want it. **Hitchhiking** on major highways is illegal, so you should try to catch a ride by standing at the on-ramp. **Mitzfahrcentrale** (tel. 01/261–68–93 in Zürich) is an organization that pairs drivers with riders; you'll pay about SFr35 to the agency and a small per-km fee to the driver.

➤ **BY TRAIN** • The rail system is quintessentially Swiss: clean, orderly, and always on time. *Schnellzuge* (express trains) race between major cities, while *regionalzuge* (local trains) chug slowly from town to town. An official timetable (called "Kursbuch" or "Horaire") covering all the rail and bus lines costs about SFr14 at train stations. White booklets listing schedules and prices between major cities are free. EurailPasses are good on most trips, but not on mountain railways.

The **Swiss Pass** (SFr410), available inside or outside Switzerland, is good for one month of travel on most trains, buses, and ferries, but it only gets you a 25%–50% discount on certain mountain railways and cable cars. Unless you move quite fast, it may not be worth the price. The **Half-Fare Travel Card** (SFr90), available at Swiss train stations, gives you a 50% discount on trains, buses, and steamers and a free round-trip to the airport. With this card you can buy the Swiss Pass for only SFr300. Regional passes, most valid for five days of travel and a further 10 days of half-price travel, are useful if you're exploring one part of the country in depth. Swiss Pass and Half-Fare Travel Card holders get a 20% discount on these passes.

➤ **BY BUS** • Yellow **PTT postal buses** link cities with off-the-beaten-track villages and are as prompt as trains. Swiss passes are good on many buses, but EurailPasses aren't. Get free timetables at post offices.

WHERE TO SLEEP Try to stay in Switzerland's clean, orderly **Jugendherbergen** (hostels) whenever possible. HI members pay around SFr14; nonmembers get tagged with an extra SFr7 charge. Mandatory sleep sheets rent for around SFr2. Book in advance between June and September if possible (for a small fee, your hostel can book you a room at the next hostel you plan to visit). **Camping** opportunities abound in the spectacular Swiss outdoors. Many campgrounds close between October and April; the higher the altitude, the shorter the open season. Prices average SFr3–SFr6 per person and SFr4–SFr9 per tent.

For names of good budget **hotels,** ask a tourist office for the *E&G Hotel Guide,* which specializes in cheap but atmospheric inns outside major cities. In rural areas, **privatzimmer** (rooms in private homes) are plentiful and can be booked through local tourist offices. For a real local experience, try staying on a farm with a Swiss family. Contact **Schweizerischer Bauernverband** (CH-5200 Brugg, tel. 056/42–32–77), which keeps a list of host families.

FOOD Bountiful supermarket/restaurants like **Migros** and **Co-op** provide the cheapest, healthiest meals. Otherwise you'll have to stick to produce markets and street stands, unless you want to leak Swiss francs at a phenomenal rate. Your main fallbacks will be burgers and pizza slices, as well as *Wurst* (sausage) in German-speaking areas. Restaurants are quite expensive, though you can make a filling lunch of fondue for a relatively affordable SFr12–SFr18. German specialties include *geschnetzeltes* (veal in cream and white-wine sauce) and *rösti* (fried potatoes, usually topped with cheese or baked ham). French Switzerland boasts famous cheese fondues, and the Ticino region rarely strays from standard Italian cuisine.

PHONES AND MAIL **Country code: 41.** Local calls cost 40 centimes. Phones take 10- and 20-centime and SFr1 and SFr5 coins. Many phones also take PTT phone cards (SFr10–SFr20), available at post offices and train stations. Make international calls from phone booths or from the post office, where cash and credit cards are accepted. Dial 111 for directory assistance, 191 or 114 for an English-speaking operator, 155–00–11 for AT&T USA Direct, and 155–02–22 for an MCI operator. Calling the United States costs about SFr2 per minute.

You can have mail sent poste restante (or *postlagernde*) to any post office in Switzerland. In French Switzerland, address it: Name, Poste Restante, 1 (city name) Hauptpost, Switzerland. Everywhere else, write: Name, Postlagernde Briefe, 1 (city name) Hauptpost, Switzerland. Post offices are generally open weekdays 7:30–noon and 2–6, Saturday 7:30–noon.

EMERGENCIES Dial 117 for the **police,** 144 for an **ambulance.**

LANGUAGE AND CULTURE Two-thirds of the population speak some German dialect, though Swiss German is like nothing you ever learned in school. In the west, locals speak French, and in the south, a small part of Switzerland's population speaks Italian. A mere 1% of residents use Romansch, a linguistic relic preserved in the eastern Alps; Italian and German should also work here if you haven't brushed up lately on obscure European languages.

German Switzerland

In most respects, the Swiss resemble their efficient German neighbors to the north more than the French or Italians to the south. The country's notorious coziness is everywhere tempered by strict control and state-of-the-art technology—you'll see liquor measured with scientific precision into 2-centiliter glasses, and high-tech stereo speakers cleverly concealed behind oversize cowbells. Switzerland's fastidious side is especially apparent in the German-speaking regions. Bern, for example, preserves its medieval arcades and towers to an to an errie perfection, while fast-paced Zürich has drawn on a strict Protestant work ethic to become one of the world's best-organized financial centers. Even quirky Basel moves 27,500 French and German commuters into Switzerland every day with clockwork efficiency.

Zürich

Switzerland's largest city, which straddles the banks of the Limmat River on the northern shore of Zürichsee (Lake Zürich), is a major center of international finance that provides almost one-fifth of Switzerland's income. But considering its worldwide reputation as an economic giant, Zürich seems surprisingly small and intimate. Wealthy, cosmopolitan galleries and tearooms are interspersed with friendly coffee houses and bars, where locals have hung out for years watching the tourists come and go. And if you look hard enough, you may find a wild streak in this city of conservative bankers. Lively political banter has resounded in some bars since the days when Lenin lived here.

Portrait of the Artist as a Dead Man: James Joyce, who once lived at Universitätstraße 38, is immortalized in stone in Flutern Cemetery.

BASICS At the train station **tourist office** (Bahnhofpl. 15, tel. 01/211–40–00; open Nov.–Feb., weekdays 8–8, weekends 9–6, Mar.–Oct., weekdays 8 AM–10 PM, weekends 8 AM–8:30 PM), you can pick up *Züri Tip,* a free newspaper listing concerts, bars, restaurants, cinemas, and exhibits. The **American Express** office (Bahnhofstr. 20, tel. 01/211–83–70) is open weekdays 8:30–5:30, Saturday 9–noon. The **post office** (Kasernenstr. 95–99, tel.

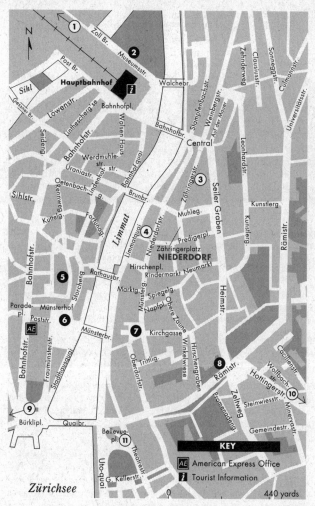

Sights ●
Fraumünster, **6**
Großmünster, **7**
Kunsthaus, **8**
Peterskirche, **5**
Schweizerisches
Landesmuseum, **2**

Lodging ○
Fällanden, **12**
Foyer Hottinger, **10**
Heilsarmée, **1**
Hotel Splendid, **4**
Martahaus, **3**
Vorderer
Sternen, **11**
Zürich-Wollishofen
(HI), **9**

KEY

AE American Express Office

ℹ Tourist Information

0 ━━━━━━ 440 yards

Zürichsee

01/245–41–11; open weekdays 7:30–6:30, Sat. 7:30–11 AM) holds poste-restante mail; address it to Sihlpost, Kasernenstr. Postlagernde Briefe, CH-8021 Zürich. If you're in need of a **consulate,** the U.S. office (Zollikerstr. 141, tel. 01/422–25–66) is open weekdays 9–11:30 and 1:30–4, and the U.K. office (Dufourstr. 56, tel. 01/261–15–20) is open weekdays 9–noon and 2–4.

COMING AND GOING Trains arrive at the **Hauptbahnhof** (tel. 01/211–50–10) in the city center. Zürich has express connections to Basel, Geneva, Bern, and Lugano at least once an hour from 6 AM to midnight. **Kloten** (tel. 01/812–12–12) is Switzerland's most important airport. A train terminal beneath the airport has direct service into the Hauptbahnhof (10 min, SFr4.50).

GETTING AROUND To orient yourself, remember that the two towers of the Großmünster are on the east side of the Limmat River, while the copper spire of the Fraumünster is on the west side. These structures mark the center of the Altstadt (Old City), which stretches to the

Hauptbahnhof in the north, Zürichsee in the south, Bahnhofstraße to the west, and Zähringerplatz and Rämistraße to the east. You can hoof it to most destinations in this part of town, but Zürich's **trams** and **buses** are hardly ever crowded, and they're a breeze to use. Single rides start at SFr2 and a day pass costs SFr6. Get a system map from the tourist office, but watch out for lines that change routes at night. All lines stop at midnight. If you prefer **biking,** it's easy to ride around here; rent a bike from the station for SFr19 a day, SFr76 a week.

WHERE TO SLEEP Prices in the center of town are no worse than those out in the boonies; doubles generally run SFr80–SFr110. Only men can stay at the ultracheap **Heilsarmée** (Dienstr. 76, tel. 01/242–48–11; dorm beds SFr15, singles SFr20, doubles SFr36). Get a private room here; you never know who'll crash next to you in this neighborhood. To reach the Heilsarmée from Paradeplatz near the AmEx office, take Tram 8 to Helvetiaplatz and walk east on Langstraße to Dienstraße. Women, married couples, and families can stay at the cozy **Foyer Hottinger** (Hottingerstr. 31, 2 blocks from Kunsthaus, tel. 01/261–93–15; dorm beds SFr20, singles SFr50, doubles SFr80). From the Hauptbahnhof, take Tram 3 to Hottingerplatz.

The tidy rooms at **Vorderer Sternen** (tel. 01/251–49–49) are a great value on the well-located Bellevueplatz. Singles go for SFr60, doubles for SFr80, and triples for SFr105; the hotel accepts credit cards. To get here, take Tram 4 or 11 from Hauptbahnhof to Bellevueplatz. **Martahaus** (Zähringerstr. 36, tel. 01/251–45–50), right in the Altstadt, has a cool breakfast room and dorm beds for only SFr30. Singles are SFr60, doubles SFr90, and triples SFr105. You may think the **Hotel Splendid** (Rosengasse 5, tel. 01/252–58–50) is misnamed when you see the run-down common areas, but the rooms (all with sinks) are okay. Singles run SFr55, doubles SFr90, and triples SFr120. There's an American bar on the ground floor.

➢ **HOSTELS • Fällanden.** The cheapest bed around (SFr10), and on the edge of the lake to boot. Quiet and peaceful location a half-hour from town. *Maurstr. 33, tel. 01/825–31–44. From Hauptbahnhof, Tram 7 to Stettbach, then transfer to Bus 743 to Jugendherberge.*

Zürich-Wollishofen (HI). Central location makes this the most popular hostel in town. Filling breakfast included, hearty dinners SFr10. Don't get too comfy: They may throw you out at a moment's notice to make room for large groups. Beds SFr22, SFr30 nonmembers. *Mutschellenstr. 114, tel. 01/482–35–44. From Hauptbahnhof, Tram 7 to Morgenthal, follow signs 10 min.*

FOOD Eating out in Zürich will eat a hole through your wallet; meals in restaurants start at SFr10 and go way up. Your best bet is to pack a lunch from **Metzgerei Traiteur Deli** (Hirschenpl.) or the **Co-op Supermarket** (across from Hauptbahnhof) and settle down to a picnic. **Rene's Hard Rock Café** (Hirschenpl.) will let you bring food to their outdoor tables as long as you wash it down with one of their beers. Some spots in the Niederdorf neighborhood sell pizzas for around SFr10, and in cafés you can get a small *shinken und käse* (ham and cheese) sandwich for about SFr9 or a bowl of soup with bread for SFr5. The **Berner Bakery** across from Hottingerplatz (east of Rämistr. on Hottingerstr.) has pizza slices, quiche, and sandwiches for around SFr4 each. Get cafeteria food and a taste of Swiss student life at **Mensa der Universität Zürich** (Rämistr. 71). Students hang out all day at the café next door.

Blockhaus Spezialitäten Restaurant. Friendly owner serves delicious Italian meals (SFr13–SFr20) in the Altstadt. Cozy, calm atmosphere draws locals. *Schifflände 4, near cnr. Limmatquai and Rämistr., tel. 01/252–14–53.*

Gran Café. Loud café with tables lining the sidewalk. Hot sandwiches with salad only SFr10. *Limmatquai 66, tel. 01/252–31–19.*

Rheinfelder Bier Halle. Locals and an occasional tourist pile up on rickety benches for hearty meals (about SFr13) in a lively setting. *Niederdorfstr. 76.*

WORTH SEEING A walk through Zürich should provide your full daily dose of churches and museums. For a taste of the former, head to **Peterskirche,** on a tranquil medieval square west of the river. It's most famous for its 16th-century clock, the largest in Europe—the minute hand alone is 12 feet long. Directly to the south, you'll see the elegant copper spire of the **Fraumünster,** built in the 13th century. The impressive stained-glass windows in this church's choir were added much later by Marc Chagall. Competing for attention across the Münsterbrücke, the **Großmünster** features modern stained-glass windows by Giacometti. The interior, like the Protestant reformers' beliefs, is somewhat austere. The Großmünster is dedicated to Zürich's patron saints (Felix, Regula, and Exuperantius), who, after drinking molten lead and being beheaded, still found the energy to carry their heads uphill and bury themselves to the right of the church.

A feast for the eyes but an insult to the wallet is **Bahnhofstraße,** the fanciest shopping street in the country. This strip is loaded with jewelry, watches, and boutiques. If all the upscale merchandise makes you tired, head to the south end of the Altstadt for a rest at the **Uto-quai,** a leafy lunchtime gathering place with views of the lake.

➤ **KUNSTHAUS** • This eclectic museum has it all: works by famous Swiss artists like Ferdinand Hodler; big, bright spaces filled with Constructivist art; a serene upper room displaying Giacometti's works; and some Matisse and Rodin sculptures thrown in for good measure. Also check out one of the largest Edvard Munch collections outside Norway and many works by Marc Chagall. *Heimpl. 1, tel. 01/251–67–55. Admission: SFr12, SFr6 students. Open Tues.–Thurs. 10–9, Fri.–Sun. 10–5; shorter hrs off-season.*

➤ **SCHWEIZERISCHES LANDESMUSEUM** • In an eccentric 19th-century building behind the train station, the Swiss National Museum holds the country's most important national treasures. The collection starts with Stone Age relics and doesn't quit until it reaches modern times—along the way, you'll see costumes, furniture, early Swiss watches, and thousands of toy soldiers reenacting battle scenes. *Museumsstr. 2, tel. 01/221–10–10. Admission free. Open Tues.–Fri. and Sun. 10–noon and 2–5, Sat. 10–noon and 2–4.*

AFTER DARK Niederdorfstraße is filled with bars, cafés, and dance clubs, and the adjacent Hirschenplatz hosts periodic live performances of every sort. An eclectic crowd hangs out at **Café Zähringer** (Spitalgasse, off Niederdorfstr.), and **Bar Füsser** next door has a gay clientele. **Casa Bar** (Münstergasse 30, up hill from Hirschenpl.), Zürich's oldest and best jazz club, plays great tunes, but beer is a high SFr9. Walk toward Bellevueplatz to reach the gorgeous, Art-Nouveau **Bar Odeon** (Limmatquai 2), filled with Zürich's stylish high rollers. Lenin frequented this place while sitting out World War I. After-hours crowds congregate at **The Spaghetti Factory** (Theatrestr. 10, at Bellevuepl.) and munch on pasta until 2 AM.

Basel

At first glance, Basel doesn't seem to offer much; the complacent town lacks Zürich's glitter and Geneva's Latin grace. But once you enter the Altstadt, Basel comes alive with street musicians, markets, and visitors. Although the town lies at the convergence of France, Germany, and Switzerland, its personality is firmly its own: Basel prides itself on being different from "Züri," mocks the French during Carnival, and revels in its reputation as a center for art. From Jean Tinguely's great mechanical sculpture at the train station to the huge Hammering Man at Aeschenplatz to the modern pieces hidden in parks or tacked onto freeways, Basel's mania for the arts is obvious. The university where Friedrich Nietzsche once taught feeds this interest, and an outlandish variety of museums saves everyone from too-serious cultural contemplations.

So rare are discounts in Switzerland that residents have a hard time figuring out how to give them. Here's the bizarre deal some of Basel's hotels have come up with: In July and August, if you're under 26, a room costs your age times the number of stars the hotel has.

BASICS The small information office in the Hauptbahnhof (tel. 061/271–36–84) books rooms, but the **main tourist office** (Schifflände 5, tel. 061/261–50–50; open weekdays 8:30–6, Sat. 8:30–1) is better located on the Rhine near Mittlere Brücke. From the Hauptbahnhof, take Tram 1 or 8 to Schifflände. The **American Express** office (Aeschengraben 10, tel. 061/272–66–90) is open weekdays 8:15–6, Saturday 9–noon.

COMING AND GOING Basel has a French, a German, and a Swiss train station. Be sure to get off at the Swiss station, **Schweizerische Bundesbahnen (SBB)** (tel. 061/272–67–67); many weary travelers have walked a long hour from the German side of town. Basel's extensive pedestrian zone covers nearly the entire Altstadt. **Klein-Basel** (Small Basel), east of the Rhine in German territory, is an industrial center; the more affluent **Gross-Basel** (Greater Basel) on the western side contains the Altstadt. To reach outlying areas, take the **tram.** Tickets cost SFr1.20–SFr4, and a day pass is SFr6.60.

WHERE TO SLEEP Basel's hotels are clean and full of character, but they don't come cheap. Singles usually run SFr50–SFr60, doubles SFr100–SFr130. The best choice in town is the no-frills **Stadthof Hotel** (Gerbergasse 84, tel. 061/261–87–11; doubles SFr100–SFr130), centrally located in Barfüsserplatz above a popular restaurant. The homey, spotless **Hotel Rochat** (Petersgraben 23, tel. 061/261–81–40), next to the university, is terrific, especially if you can snag a SFr150 triple. Singles start at SFr65, doubles at SFr110. The restaurant downstairs has good meals for SFr10–SFr18. Take Tram 3 to Lyss and walk downhill to reach the hotel.

The almost-cozy **HI Jugendherberge** (St. Alban–Kirchrain 10, tel. 061/272–05–72; beds SFr20), a short walk from the town center, has a garden where you can eat breakfast. From the train station, take Tram 2 to Kunstmuseum, then walk down St. Alban–Vorstadt and turn left on Mühlenberg Castellio, following the signs. About 6 km outside the city, **Camp Klaldhort Basel** (Heideweg 16, tel. 061/711–64–29; open Mar.–Oct.), has a grocery store, warm showers, and a swimming pool. Sites are SFr5 per person, SFr6 per tent. From Aeschenplatz, take Tram 11 to Landhof.

FOOD Most students find refuge from Basel's expensive restaurants at the self-service joints in **Migros Market** (Clarapl.). Pick up pizza slices (SFr3.50) and great pastries at **Ziegler Bakery** (Freiestr. 8), or grab sliced ham and mortadella at the meat market across the street. On Marktplatz, a big daily market sells fruit, bread, cheese sandwiches, and even egg rolls. If you come here, stop in at Basel's oldest tearoom (open since 1870), the **Schiesser Café.** You can buy beautiful chocolates on the bottom floor and have coffee and a sumptuous pastry with a polite local crowd upstairs.

Restaurant Fischerstübe (Rheingasse 45; closed Sun.), a block from the river in Klein-Basel, serves typical Swiss meals and fresh fish for SFr9–SFr13. At night it becomes a beer hall. **Restaurant St. Alban Stübli** (St. Alban–Vorstadt 74), a great family-run place near the hostel, offers healthy portions of rösti for SFr8 and ham and eggs for SFr9. At the bustling **Restaurant Kunsthalle Basel** (Theatrepl.), meals (SFr12–SFr30) include a range of brochettes, and you eat under low trees in a courtyard full of classical sculpture.

The mechanical fountain on Theatreplatz, with imaginative metal creatures spouting water, is the work of Basel's favorite local artist, Jean Tinguely, the creator of the huge mechanical piece that greeted you at the Hauptbahnhof.

WORTH SEEING The Altstadt's three main plazas—Münsterplatz, Marktplatz, and Barfüsserplatz—claim the best sights and the most action. The colorful **Marktplatz,** in the middle of the pedestrian zone, is dominated by the bright-red, fancifully overdone **Rathaus** (Town Hall). The front of the building is covered with colorful frescoes; the interior coutyard features more frescoes and a gilded statue of Basel's founder, Munatius Plancus. Several blocks south of Marktplatz, people and trams jam the small **Barfüsserplatz** ("Barefoot Plaza"), home to businesses and restaurants. Bordering the square to the west, the **Historisches Museum** (tel. 061/271–05–05; open Wed.–Mon. 10–5) is filled with relics from medieval Basel and mementos of Erasmus, who died here in 1536.

A never-ending list of museums can satisfy anyone's art appetite. The **Kunsthalle** (Steinenberg 7, near Theatrepl., tel. 061/272–48–33; admission SFr9, SFr6 students; open Tues. and Thurs.–Sun. 10–5, Wed. 10–9) displays experimental work by contemporary artists. Behind the hostel, the **Museum für Gegenwarts Kunst** (St. Alban–Rheinweg 60, tel. 061/272–81–83; admission SFr8, SFr5 students; open Tues.–Sun. 11–5) showcases art from the past few decades in a modern glass structure overlooking the Rhine.

➤ **MUNSTER** • Basel's main attraction towers over the Rhine on Münsterplatz. The relief-covered facade of this red sandstone cathedral dates back to the 12th century, and the carved portal is worth a visit by itself. Inside you'll find some pretty impressive dead folk, including Erasmus and the Habsburg queen Anna. You can view the square and a good chunk of Basel from the Gothic towers for SFr2.

➤ **KUNSTMUSEUM** • In the courtyard outside this museum, you see Rodin's *Burghers of Calais* and sculptures by Hans Arp and Alexander Calder—only a preview of the incredible art inside. The first floor contains works by local artists Konrad Witz and Nilaus Manuel Deutsch. Also look for modern art by the likes of Degas, Van Gogh, Gauguin, Renoir, and Rodin, and a room full of Cézanne sketches. The second floor is rich in Giacomettis, Klees, Mondrians, Chagalls, and Kandinskys, and two rooms are devoted to Braque, Picasso, and Leger. *St. Alban-Graben 16, tel. 061/271–08–28. Admission: SFr6, SFr4 students, Sun. free. Open Tues.–Sun. 10–5.*

AFTER DARK Nightlife centers around Barfüsserplatz, where the **Rio Bar** is an established local hangout. On warm nights, crowds gather on the stairs of Theatreplatz, and the busy outdoor **Kunsthalle Restaurant** (Theatrepl.) bubbles over with Basel's literati. **Atlantis** (behind Theatrepl.) is popular with students, but it costs SFr8 to enter and drinks aren't cheap. **Arche** (across from Kunsthalle) serves cheap beer to bankers, bikers, and other locals.

Luzern

The mountains surrounding Luzern (Lucerne in French) are spooky and beautiful when the fog rolls in—the views are dramatic even for Switzerland. But once you've had your fill of scenery (which could take quite some time), you may as well clear out of this dull town, a sea of video cameras and pushy sightseers. Head instead into the mountains, or onto Luzern's beautiful lake for one of Switzerland's best boat rides. Among the few features worth seeing in town are the murals scrawled across the facades of many buildings. You can learn their stories by madly sifting through brochures or by taking a guided tour (SFr12) from the **tourist office** (Frankenstr. 1, next to station, tel. 041/51–71–71). **American Express** (Schweizerhotquai 4, tel. 041/50–11–77) is open weekdays 8–noon and 2–6, Saturday 8–noon.

COMING AND GOING Express trains run to Luzern from Zürich (50 min) and Geneva (3½–4 hrs, change at Bern). For rail information, call the **Hauptbahnhof** (tel. 041/21–31–11), on the lake just south of the Reuss River. Everything in Luzern is completely accessible on foot. Most sights are north of the river and south of Museggmauer, the old fortified walls. To get to the hostel and a few faraway sights, take the **bus;** tickets (SFr1–SFr1.50) are available at automated machines at each stop.

WHERE TO SLEEP If you've got a sleeping bag, the best deal in town is a SFr10 dorm bed or a SFr5 site (plus SFr2 per tent) at the lakeside **campground** (Lidostr., tel. 041/31–21–46). From the Hauptbahnhof, take Bus 2 to Verkehrshaus or walk a half-hour along the lake. Otherwise, stay at the impersonal **HI Jugendherberge am Rotsee** (Sedelstr. 12, tel. 041/36–88–00; beds SFr21, SFr28 nonmembers) unless you want to fork out SFr30 for a pension or SFr50 for a hotel. To reach the hostel from the Hauptbahnhof, take Bus 18 to Gopplismoos and follow the signs, or, after 7:30 PM, take Bus 1 to Scholossberg, walk up Freidentalstraße, and follow the signs. Dorm beds at the **Tourist Hotel** (St. Karliquai 12, tel. 041/51–24–74) go for SFr43 with breakfast and shower, 10% less with an ISIC card. Doubles are SFr55. The hotel is on the northern riverbank, about 15 minutes' walk west of the Hauptbahnhof.

FOOD Don't even peer into those restaurant windows. Hit supermarkets like **Migros** (Hertensteinstr. 40) or eat at the hostel. The **Bell Market,** just outside the train station to the left, has premade salads, meats, and pizza slices for SFr4. At the buffet-style **Schiffländi** (exit station, go through gate, and turn right), you can enjoy the view while munching on chicken legs with fries (SFr8). A short walk from town, vegetarian **Karibia** (Obergrundstr. 3, at Pilatusstr., tel. 041/23–61–10) has appetizers starting at SFr9 and a veggie burger for SFr11. **Mr. Pickwick's** (Rathausquai 6, tel. 041/51–59–27) serves snacks and is the most popular nightspot in an otherwise quiet town.

WORTH SEEING Begin a quick walk around town at Kornmarkt, site of the old grain market and the **bakers' guild,** a white building with a mural of a baker's family tree. The nearby **Picasso Sammlung** (Furrengasse 21, tel. 041/51–17–73; admission SFr5, SFr3 students; open Apr.–Oct., daily 10–6, shorter hrs off-season), housed

At the Picasso museum, you'll see tons of photos of the modern master doing just about everything but clipping his toenails.

in the 17th-century Am Rhyn Haus, has a collection of Picasso's paintings and drawings. A bit farther east, Kapellplatz contains Luzern's oldest church, **St. Peterkirche.** From here, you can cross the wooden **Kapellbrücke,** built in 1333. The paintings by Heinrich Wagmann along the bridge were meant to educate illiterate townspeople about Swiss history. The south side of the bridge ends at the **Jesuit-enkirche,** built by the Jesuits with a light, cheery interior to lure wayward Catholics to mass. In Weinmarkt, a former execution site just west of Korn-markt, the **Hôtel des Balances** displays paintings of patrician families on its exterior. The colorful Hirschenplatz, immediately northeast, contains the **Hotel Alder,** where Goethe stayed when he came to town.

The **Hofkirche** (Schwanenpl., north of Nationalquai), dedicated to the town's patron saint, Leger, houses a famous 4,950-pipe organ. It's a well-known city symbol, as is the **Löwen-denkmal** (Lion of Lucerne), a massive lion sculpted into the side of a mountain. The work is dedicated to the Swiss soldiers who died defending Louis XIV and Marie Antoinette in Paris. Just above the lion, the **Gletschergarten** (Denlemalstr. 4, tel. 041/51–43–40; admission SFr6, SFr4.50 students; open May–mid-Oct., Tues.–Sun. 8–6, shorter hrs off-season) is a group of 30-foot potholes dramatically etched by the glacier that formed the Reuss River.

The **Verkehrshaus** (Lidostr. 5, tel. 041/31–44–44; admission SFr12; open Mar.–Oct., daily 9–6, shorter hrs off-season) is a knockout survey of every type of transportation imaginable, from stagecoaches to spaceships. The **Richard Wagner Museum** (Wagnerweg 27, tel. 041/44–23–70; admission SFr5; open Apr.–Oct., Tues.–Sun. 10–noon and 2–5, shorter hrs off-season) displays letters, pictures, Wagner's piano, and some original music in the house where he lived and composed from 1866 to 1872. Get here on Bus 6 or 8.

OUTDOOR ACTIVITIES Boating on the lake is one of Luzern's best activities, and boat trips are free with a EurailPass. They last anywhere from one to four hours; some go to lakeside resorts, some into the Alpine ranges. Boat trips start at around SFr20 for those without a EurailPass. **Mt. Pilatus,** supposedly haunted by the spirit of Pontius Pilate, offers outstanding views, and you can reach the peak on the world's steepest cog rail (a special train for mountains). Take the ferry to Alpachstad and transfer to the train. You can descend by cable car and take Tram 1 back to town, or brave the 4½-hour walk from Pilatus to the town of Kriens. If you don't walk, the entire round-trip from Luzern costs SFr50 with a EurailPass, SFr66.20 without.

Some find the view from **Mt. Rigi** as beautiful as the view from Pilatus. Mark Twain trekked up here, but slept through the sunrise when he reached the top. You can make the trip more easily: From Luzern, take a boat to Vitzhau and transfer to the cog rail. The whole trip costs SFr41.20 with Eurail, SFr68.60 without. For info on transportation and weather conditions for mountain excursions, call 041/51–71–71. Some popular peaks, including Pilatus, have restaurants, but pack a lunch to be on the safe side.

Interlaken

The first thing to do when you get to Interlaken is leave—get out into the mountains or blow some money on the multitude of activities offered in the area, including paragliding, mountain biking, rock climbing, river rafting, and bungee jumping. There's not much to the town itself except some bustling nightspots, but its location at the foot of the mighty Jungfrau (*see* Near Interlaken, *below*) makes it an excellent entryway to some of the country's most beautiful landscape. The **tourist office** (Höheweg 37, tel. 036/22–21–21) at the bottom of Hotel Metropole can give you the scoop on planning trips.

COMING AND GOING Two train stations serve Interlaken: **Westbahnhof** and **Ostbahnhof**, at opposite ends of the major street, Höheweg. Trains run hourly from Geneva (2¾ hrs) and once an hour from Bern, sometimes with a change at Spiez. From Zürich, a scenic trip over the Golden Pass through Luzern takes about two hours. Cheap hotels and nightlife center around the Westbahnhof; you'll probably use the Ostbahnhof only to catch trains into the mountains or to board the bus to the hostel.

WHERE TO SLEEP The easiest way to find lodging is to look on the board at either station that lists rooms and prices; the phone by the board links you directly to the hotels for free. The **Happy Inn Lodge** (Rosengasse 17, off Centralpl., tel. 036/22–32–25) offers straightforward dorm beds (SFr20) and doubles (SFr70). **Hotel Aarburg** (Unterseen, tel. 036/22–26–15; doubles SFr80–SFr110), a sweet chalet on the river next to the Altstadt, adjoins a restaurant that serves big traditional meals for SFr12.

Popular with Americans is the raucous **Balmer's Herberge** (Hauptstr. 23, tel. 036/22–19–61; dorm beds SFr16, doubles SFr52, triples SFr63). If the beds are full, they'll put you on a spare mattress or in the tent outside. Take Bus 5 from the Westbahnhof or Bus 1 from the Ostbahnhof, or pick up the hostel's bright yellow brochure at the tourist office and follow the map. The **Alp Lodge** (Marktgasse 59, tel. 036/22–47–48; dorm beds SFr19–SFr21, doubles SFr50) has more spacious dorm rooms than Balmer's. Most have views of the river and mountains, and all come with a choice of breakfast or a beer at the Riverside Bar next door. From the Westbahnhof, turn left and follow the tracks to Marktgasse. From the Ostbahnhof, follow Höheweg to the PTT in the center of town and take a right on Marktgasse. For a more tranquil experience, try

Trekking from Interlaken

Strike out in just about any direction from Interlaken and you're guaranteed some awesome sights. The trip outlined here offers dramatic views of the Alps, good hiking, and a visit to the incredible Trümmelbach Falls. From Interlaken's Ostbahnhof, take the train to Lauterbrunnen (SFr15 round-trip). You can check out waterfalls, snowy mountains, and the rock walls of the Lauterbrunnen Valley as the train snakes its way through the trees. From Lauterbrunnen, a funicular (SFr8) heads up to Mürren, where you'll see the dramatic Eiger, Mönch, and Jungfrau peaks rising nearly 13,000 feet above sea level. From Mürren, walk about 45 minutes to Gimmelwald for more superb views of the rocky monsters. You can stay overnight here in the Mountain Hostel (tel. 036/55–17–04; beds SFr7), but bring food to cook, since dinner's not offered. From Gimmelwald, take the gondola (SFr6.20) and then walk 20 minutes to the tremendous Trümmelbach Falls (admission SFr8; open daily 9–5), which cut a stormy path through the rocks. Take the postal bus or walk 3 km from Trümmelbach back to the Lauterbrunnen train station.

HI Jugendherberge Böningen (Aareweg 21, tel. 036/22–43–53; beds SFr18) on the Brienzersee. Go left out of the Ostbahnhof, and turn right along the Aare for a 20-minute walk.

FOOD Go to **Migros,** to the right of the Westbahnhof, to grab a picnic for your excursions. **Tea Room Spatz** (Spielmatte 49, tel. 036/22–97–22) has affordable meals on a terrace overlooking the Aare River. **Mercato Restaurant** (tel. 036/22–27–81), a popular pizza and spaghetti joint, is open until midnight. From Centralplatz, go to Postplatz and walk up Postgasse. Nightlife centers around the **Riverside Bar,** with live music on Marktgasse near the river, and **Buddy's** (Höheweg 37), a crowded pub that serves cheap beers.

NEAR INTERLAKEN

Eurailers and Swiss Pass holders can cruise for free along Thunersee and Brienzersee, the lakes immediately west and east of Interlaken, respectively. **Thunersee** is the more popular of the two excursions. Besides great views, you'll get a look at the **castles** at Thun and Spiez, and you can stop at Beatushöhlen, where a 20-minute walk from the landing leads to the eerie stalagmites and stalactites of the **St. Beatus caves** (admission SFr8, SFr7.50 students; open Apr.–Oct., daily 9:30–5). On the **Brienzersee,** stop at the tranquil town of **Brienz** (worth a stay if you want to relax by the lake); the beautiful **Geissbach Falls,** with plenty of hiking; and the **Freilichtmuseum Ballenberg** (admission SFr12; open Apr.–Oct., daily 10–5), accessible by bus from Brienz. This open-air museum features an impressive collection of traditional Swiss buildings.

JUNGFRAUJOCH You can't see the whole continent from the Jungfraujoch, Europe's highest accessible peak, but it sure seems like you can. The train from Interlaken's Ostbahnhof passes through Grindelwald or Lauterbrunnen before arriving at Kleine Scheidegg, just below the mountain. Here you transfer to the famous Jungfraubahn, which winds its way slowly uphill through a rock tunnel, stopping twice for views from lookout windows. At the top, the lack of oxygen and the otherworldly landscape will make you feel like you're on the moon. For the real adventurer, there's a hut where you can spend the night when the weather's right; ask at regional tourist offices for more info. Unfortunately, prices for the entire trip are as high as the peak itself: SFr150, SFr97 if you catch the 6:34 AM train from Interlaken, the 7:05 AM train from Lauterbrunnen, or the 7:18 AM train from Grindelwald. If you plan to spend some time in the region, look into a regional rail pass for SFr155. Dial 036/22–52–52 for climatic conditions—bad weather will ruin the trip. And always bring a jacket; even on warm days, there can be snow at the top.

Wherever you walk, you can't escape the treacherous north face of the Eiger, which some call the most difficult mountain in the world to scale. World-class climbers drool at its base, preparing to accept the challenge.

GRINDELWALD The tiny town of Grindelwald is framed by the sculpted edges of the Eiger peak. From here, you can hike past lakes and waterfalls, or through icy glaciers and precipitous gorges, all for the price of a good pair of walking shoes and some sore muscles. The town consists of a single street of touristed shops and a smattering of wood-timbered houses and finely trimmed farms. Hostels offer great views—you might have a hard time getting your butt off the back porch, which usually faces the mountains. Still, you should motivate yourself to take a gondola ride; you'll see overwhelming mountain vistas set to a symphony of cowbells. Without a bit of physical effort, visitors can reach the most remote points, thanks to Swiss engineers and their cog-wheel trains, gondolas, and buses. The **tourist office** (Hauptstr., near Hauptbahnhof in Sportzentrum, tel. 036/53–12–13; open weekdays 8–noon and 2–6, also Sat. 8–noon and 2–5 July–Sept.) is your source for hiking and gondola info. Get a map from here before you attempt any hikes.

One popular hike leads from the **First** ski area down into town. The Firstbahn (about a 10-minute walk up the main road from the Grindelwald station) will take you up for SFr25. From First you can hike straight down to Grindelwald or take a detour to the vantage point at **Faulhorn.** A three-hour hike from First leads to the village of Grosse-Scheidegg. If you want to avoid paying for a gondola ride, hike from the Grindelwald station to Grosse-Scheidegg (3 hrs), or take a bus (40 min, SFr14) to the town and walk back. A hike also goes from Grindelwald to the **Obergletscher** (1 hr), a fast-moving glacier with access to the famous **Blue Ice Grotto.** If you still feel energetic once you get here, walk up a steep incline to the base of **Mt. Schreckhorn** (1½ hrs from Obergletscher); from there, about two hours of scenic strolling will take you back to Grindelwald. Balmer's Herberge (*see* Where to Sleep, in Interlaken, *above*) arranges trips in this region at decent prices.

For a dramatic close-up view of the mountains, take a gondola ride (SFr25 one-way) from Grund (15-min walk from the Grindelwald station) to Männlichen. From here, it's an hour's walk to **Kleine Scheidegg,** where you'll come face to face with the Eiger, Mönch, and Jungfrau peaks. A string of bratwurst stands and some cheap Chinese food places are here. From Kleine Scheidegg, you can catch the Jungfraubahn up to Jungfraujoch (*see* Near Interlaken, *above*).

➤ **WHERE TO SLEEP AND EAT** • Grindelwald's hostels are great, so don't even bother with expensive hotels. **HI Jugendherberge die Weid** (Terrassenweg, tel. 036/53–10–09; beds SFr15) is an inviting wooden house with a deck that looks straight into the mountains and a comfy common room. From the Hauptbahnhof, walk straight, then take the first alley on the right and follow the signs; it's a steep 20-minute climb. To hold a spot, write your name on the list and come back between 5 and 6 PM or 7:30 and 8:30 PM. The crowd is slightly older, the hikers a little more serious at **Naturfreundhaus** (tel. 036/53–13–33; beds SFr20, SFr22 nonmembers, doubles SFr58), just up Terrassenweg from the hostel. You'll find clean, wood-paneled dorm rooms, friendly sitting rooms, and a small garden out back where smokers and beer drinkers (beer SFr3) congregate after dinner and take in the views. Ask your hostel proprietor for a free **Visitors Card,** good for discounts on gondolas and many activities.

Pick up supplies at **Co-op,** three minutes from the Hauptbahnhof. Across the street, the **Sportzentrum** (tel. 036/53–33–66) has a rustic dining room and okay food; with dinners from about SFr15, it's one of the cheapest places in town. The **Espresso Bar** in the Hotel Spinne (tel. 036/52–23–41) and the **Gepsi-Bar** (tel. 036/53–21–31) across the street are two night-time hot spots.

Bern

Sophisticated Zürichers say Bern (Berne in French) is too much like its mascot, the slow, clumsy bear. Bern is the federal capital, but it's a modest place: The local cuisine features fatback and sauerkraut, the annual fair celebrates the humble onion, and the president of the Swiss Confederation takes the tram to work. The slow-paced, well-preserved town has an almost medieval character. Bern's cobblestone streets are the domain of old men playing chess and vendors hawking fruit under the spires of 13th-century towers; only when you check out the interesting museums and the university do you remember that this has been the seat of the modern Swiss government since 1848. But the city's down-to-earth approach works—you can't help but be intrigued by a place where residents farm small gardens in the town center while well-behaved heroin addicts do their thing on the terrace of the parliament building.

BASICS The train station **tourist office** (tel. 031/22–76–76) is open weekdays 8 AM–8:30 PM and Sunday 9–8:30 from May to October, weekdays 8–6:30 and Sunday 10–5 from November to April. **American Express** (Bubenbergpl. 11, tel. 031/22–94–01) is open weekdays 8:30–6, Saturday 9–noon. The **Schanzenpost** (Schanzenstr. 4, behind station, tel. 031/65–61–11) holds poste-restante mail; send it to Name, Schanzenpost 13000, Bern 1.

GETTING AROUND Bern is easy to navigate. From the station the main shopping street, **Spitalgasse,** leads straight through **Bärenplatz;** this square and the adjacent **Bundesplatz** mark the center of town. Most sights are on or near Spitalgasse (or one of its aliases). **Trams** and **buses** (tel. 031/22–14–44) are handy for getting outside the Altstadt. Before boarding, buy a SFr4 ticket, good for 24 hours, at the machines near each stop. Single-ride tickets cost SFr1–SFr2.

Bern

SWITZERLAND

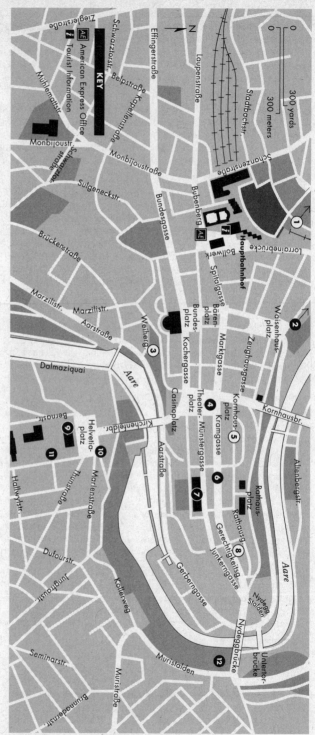

Sights ●

Bärengraben, **12**
Bernisches
Historisches
Museum, **9**
Einnstein-Haus, **6**
Kunsthalle, **10**
Kunstmuseum, **2**
Münster, **7**
PTT Museum, **11**
Zeitglockenturm, **4**

Lodging ○

Hospiz zur
Heimat, **8**
Hotel Goldener
Schlüssel, **5**
Jugendherberge, **3**
Marthahaus, **1**

KEY

AE American Express Office

i Tourist Information

WHERE TO SLEEP As usual in Switzerland, hotel rates are awful. Stick with the run-of-the-mill **Jugendherberge** near the river (Weihergasse 4, tel. 031/22–63–16; beds SFr14–SFr21), or the clean, well-run **Heilsarmée** (Muristr. 6, tel. 031/43–46–96; beds SFr11), Switzerland's version of the Salvation Army, accessible on Bus 12 to Liebegg. **Camping Kappelenbrücke** (Wohlenstr. 62C, Hinterkappelen, tel. 031/36–10–07 or 031/36–15–01) is a new campground on the shores of Wohlensee. From the station, take the yellow postal bus marked WOHLEN/AARBERG to Eymatt.

Hospiz zur Heimat (Gerechtigkeitsgasse 50, tel. 031/22–04–36) has simple, tidy rooms right in the Altstadt. Singles run SFr60, doubles SFr88, and triples SFr117, including breakfast. The **Hotel Goldener Schüssel** (Rathausgasse 72, tel. 031/22–02–16) has big rooms and a great location. Singles are SFr60, doubles SFr96. Both hotels accept credit cards. A bit out of the town center, **Marthahaus** (Wyttenbachstr. 22A, tel. 031/42–41–35) has clean rooms and a nice reception area. Singles are SFr55, doubles SFr85, and triples SFr120. From the station, take Bus 20 toward Haltestelle and exit at Gewerbeschule.

FOOD A **Migros** market is near the station, a **Co-op** is on Spitalgasse near Bärenplatz, and **Vatter,** a health-food store, is across from the Co-op. **Bell Market** (Spitalgasse 34) has such goodies as tofu salad, corn salad, and chicken legs. Locals flock to **Restaurant Manora,** across from the train station (look for the green alligator), for pastries, cheap coffee (SFr1.90), pasta (SFr9.50), and an extensive salad bar (SFr8.50). **Restaurant Marzilibrücke** (Gasstr., at Brückenstr.), around the corner from the hostel, is popular with Bern's hip crowd. Great waiters serve relatively cheap meals (chicken legs SFr7.50, veggie dishes SFr12.50) on an outdoor terrace Tuesday–Sunday. **Kornhaus Keller** (Kornhauspl. 18, tel. 031/22–11–33), in a huge, barrel-vaulted hall, is a throwback to earlier centuries. Have a meal for SFr15–SFr35 if you can afford it, or just grab a drink in the well-known wine gallery. You can catch live folk music every night here.

WORTH SEEING Bern's oldest and most famous landmark, the 13th-century **Zeitglockenturm** (Clock Tower), puts on a little show four minutes before every hour. Originally at the western gate of the city, it now marks the western boundary of **Zähringerstadt,** the oldest part of town, which was built by the German duke of Zähringer. Tours (SFr5) daily at 4:30 show you what makes the clock tick. Legend has it that Duke Zähringer named Bern after the first animal he killed in a hunt—by now you've seen enough bear memorabilia to know what that animal was. Five live bears hang out at the **Bärengraben** (Bear Pits), clowning around pitifully for snacks.

The Gothic **Münster** (Münsterpl.), built between 1421 and 1893, was conceived as a Catholic church but became Protestant during its construction. The main portal vividly illustrates what awaits the damned in hell and the elect in heaven (notice which side has the majority of the women). The central window over the choir, known as the Passion Window, is done in warm blues and reds. A climb up the tower leaves you SFr2 poorer, but you get a great view.

More than 40 oil paintings and 2,000 drawings at the **Kunstmuseum** (Hodlerstr. 8–12, tel. 031/22–09–44) allow you to trace Paul Klee's development from draftsman to abstract artist. You'll also find works by 14th-century Italian painters, impressionists, and surrealists. The **Einstein-Haus** (Kramgasse 49, tel. 031/21–00–91; admission SFr2; open Tues.–Fri., 10–5, Sat. 10–4), where Einstein discovered his theory of relativity in 1905, has some interesting exhibits, including the scientist's report card and an advertisement in which he looks for work.

A whole slew of museums lines Helvetiaplatz. The **Kunsthalle** (Helvetiapl. 1, tel. 031/43–00–31; admission SFr4, SFr2 students; open Tues. 10–9, Wed.–Sun. 10–5) gives emerging artists a chance to show their stuff. The **Bernisches Historisches Museum** (Helvetiapl. 5, tel. 031/43–18–11; admission SFr3, SFr1.50 students; open Tues.–Sun. 10–5), housed in a 16th-century castle, displays booty from Swiss victories over Burgundy. The **PTT Museum** (Helvetiastr. 16, tel. 031/62–77–77) has one of the largest and most valuable stamp collections in the world.

CHEAP THRILLS On a clear day, treat yourself to a great SFr3 cup of coffee at the **Belle-vue Hotel** (Kochergasse 3, at Theaterpl., tel. 031/22–45–81), and sit with the diplomats gazing at the Alps on a beautiful terrace overlooking the Aare River. Don't linger too long, though: At night the price of coffee goes way up. Ask at the tourist office about **concerts** at Theaterplatz. The music is classical, the hall's Baroque, and the dress is fancy—but it's free! Also free is a jump into the Aare River at the **River Bath Marzili** swimming pools (open week-days 8:30–8, weekends 8:30–7) on Aarstraße, one block from Brüjckenstraße.

AFTER DARK Nightlife centers around **Bärenplatz**, where locals gather for beer (SFr3–SFr4) at outdoor cafés. **Bar Big Ben** (Zeughausgasse 12, tel. 031/22–24–28), around the corner from Bärenplatz, is packed with English speakers from various parts of the world. Next door, **Restaurant BZ** (Zeughausgasse 14) has indoor and outdoor seating for students and a young working crowd. The cheapest beers are at **Restaurant Marzili** (Weihergasse), across from the funicular and down the block from the hostel. A big beer goes for SFr3, and you can get it to go. At the end of Gerechtigkeitsgasse, the inconspicuous **Club Ursus** (Junkerngasse 1, tel. 031/22–74–06) hosts a gay crowd; you could walk by a couple of times before finding it. Women are admitted only if accompanied by a man.

Liechtenstein

A dot on the map between Austria and Switzerland, Liechtenstein is one of the small-est independent sovereign states. A prince, a princess, and a measly 28,500 citizens share about 60 square miles of castles and alpine villages in this prosperous country, which is closely tied to Switzerland. In 1959, Switzerland became Liechtenstein's diplomatic representative abroad, and the tiny country shares Switzerland's high stan-dard of living. A whopping 25% of Liechtenstein's income comes from its famous postage stamps.

There's not much to Vaduz, the main town, except a one-lane street packed with tourist shops and a castle that's inaccessible to visitors. Pictures of the prince and his wife plaster the shop windows and postcard stands. The royal residence, high over the city, contains a valuable art collection, including some of Rubens's most famous works. Plebeians can see some of the loot at the Staatliche Kunstsammlung (Städtle 37, near tourist office; admission SFr3, SFr2 students; open daily 10-noon and 1:30–5). On the other side of the tourist office, the free Briefmarkenmuseum (Stamp Museum) has rotating exhibits of some of the country's most famous stamps.

Liechtenstein has no trains; to get here, catch a bus from the train stations in Switzer-land's Sargans or Buchs. If you've just come to collect another passport stamp, the tourist office (Städtle 37, tel. 075/2–14–43) will give you one for SFr1, but if you're looking to stay overnight, the bucolic HI Jugendherberge (tel. 075/2–50–22; beds SFr16.30) in Schaan is an ace attraction of the region.

Chur

At the head of the Rhine Valley, Chur mixes Latin and German influences. The capital of Graubünden, the canton that includes the Engadine Valley and parts of the Rhine and Inn rivers, dates from about 3000 BC, making it the oldest town in Switzerland. More important, it's a transit point for destinations higher in the mountains, and also for Germany and Austria. Many of the most scenic **railway** lines start here, including the Rhätische Bahn to St. Moritz. For a good walking tour, pick up a map at the **tourist office** (Grabenstr. 5, tel. 081/22–18–18; open weekdays 8–noon and 1:30–6, Sat. 9–noon); to get here from the station, walk down Bahnhofstraße and turn left on Grabenstraße. The **Kunstmuseum** (Postpl.) contains works by local favorites, including Giovanni Segantini, known for his scenes of Engadine life. Also look for Giacometti, E. L. Kirchner, Die Brücke (leader of the German Expressionists) and H. R. Giger, the eccentric creator of the monsters from the movie *Alien*.

WHERE TO SLEEP AND EAT The diligent woman who runs the **HI Jugendherberge** (Berggasse 28, tel. 081/22–65–63; beds SFr16) almost makes up for the lack of modern facilities. From the station, walk down Bahnhofstraße, turn left on Grabenstraße, and follow signs (a 15-minute walk), or take Bus 7 or 8 to Berggasse and walk uphill. The run-down **Hotel City** (Martinspl. 4, tel. 081/22–54–44; doubles SFr80) has views of the elegant Kirche St. Martin (St. Martin's Church). Also in the old town, **Hotel Franziskaner** (Unteregasse 29, tel. 081/22–12–61; doubles SFr90) has a little more local flavor than Hotel City.

The **Co-op** supermarket and restaurant is at Quaderstraße and Bahnhofstraße. For more relaxed dining in quiet surroundings, go to **Leh Restaurant and Bar** (Arcas 3, 1 block from Kirche St. Martin, tel. 081/22–03–10) and sit outside in the quiet plaza. Pizzas start at SFr10, and cheesy lasagna is SFr14. For nighttime entertainment, the outdoor bars and cafés around Kornplatz are a sure bet. You can also enter into the imagination of Chur native H. R. Giger (*see above*) at the bizarre **Giger Bar** (Comercialstr. 23, tel. 081/23–75–06), a half-hour walk or a SFr10 taxi ride from town.

St. Moritz

The healing, iron-rich waters of St. Moritz (San Murezzan in Romansch) put it on the map some 3,000 years ago, but now the town is best known as one of the world's most chic ski resorts. The train ride from Chur in summer may be the most interesting part of your visit here: Along the way, you pass lush green valleys, golden fields with round haystacks, and ravines spanned by arched bridges. After such a ride, the town itself, a schizophrenic mix of traditional Engadine buildings, stone churches, and boxy modern atrocities, may be a disappointment. It does harbor a few cultural attractions, though, including the **Engadine Museum** (Via dal Bagn, tel. 082/3–43–33; admission SFr5), packed with traditional furniture in elegant rooms. For more info on the town and the region, head to the tourist office, **Kur-And Verkehrsverein** (Via Maistra 12, tel. 082/3–31–47; open weekdays 9–noon and 2–6, Sat. 9–noon).

The skiing aristocrats clear out of St. Moritz in summer, leaving the town feeling empty; you might want to follow their lead and take off for some hiking in the Engadine and Bregaglia valleys. Ride the gondola to **Piz Corvatsch** (SFr19 one-way, SFr27 round-trip), where the seemingly infinite white peaks make you feel you've hit the top of the world, or take the funicular (SFr20, SFr30 round-trip) from the tourist office to glorious **Piz Nair** and walk back down (3 hrs). Get off the funicular at Corviglia, the second stop (SFr13, SFr20 round-trip), to shorten the hike to two hours. For a more strenuous hike (6 hrs, 19 km one-way) past lakes and mountains, take **Via Engadina** to the town of Maloya. Or rent bikes (SFr14) from the shop around the corner from the train station and ride along the lake to **Sils,** the town where Nietzsche spent his summers from 1881 to 1888. Residents have turned his house into a small museum with eclectic mementos.

GETTING AROUND St. Moritz is divided into two parts: ritzy St. Moritz-Dorf and modern, ugly St. Moritz-Bad. Blue-and-white local buses connect the two parts of town, and yellow regional buses stop at the train station. You can stay in **Pontresina,** 20 minutes northeast by bus, or **Maloya,** 30 minutes southwest by bus, if St. Moritz is full.

WHERE TO SLEEP AND EAT The **HI Jugendherberge** (Via Surpont 60, tel. 082/3–39–69; dorm beds SFr30.50, SFr37.50 nonmembers, doubles SFr80; closed Nov.–mid-Dec. and May–mid-June) is on the other side of the lake from the train station. The high price fortunately includes breakfasts and good dinners. To get here, take the yellow postal bus toward Sils, Corvatsch, or Maloya, exit at Hotel Sonne, and follow signs to the left. Next to the hostel, **Sporthotel Stille** (tel. 082/3–69–48) offers utilitarian doubles with showers for SFr80. Down the block (turn right at the bus stop), **Hotel Sonne** (tel. 082/3–35–27) has nicer doubles without showers for SFr90–SFr110. Pontresina, 20 minutes away by bus, has a low-key **HI Jugendherberge** (tel. 082/6–72–23) next to the train station that charges the same as St. Moritz's hostel. For relatively uncrowded camping, go to **Camping Plauns** (tel. 082/6–62–85), a 15-minute walk along a well-marked path from the train station in Pontresina.

Food is expensive in this upscale resort, so get used to packing picnic lunches. One of the cheaper restaurants in town, **Au Reduit** (Piazza Mauritius, tel. 082/3–66–57) in St. Moritz-Dorf, has an upstairs terrace with a view of the mountains. Pizzas start at SFr12, and a big *aelpler-rösti* (potato with ham, eggs, and cheese) can feed two not-terribly-hungry people for SFr18.

French Switzerland

The French Swiss differ noticeably from their German-speaking compatriots—in dress, sense of humor, and the unexpected flashes of joie de vivre that liven up their calm and orderly towns. French Switzerland centers around grand, romantic Lac Léman (Lake Geneva). Stravinsky wrote *The Rite of Spring* in Montreux, on the east side of the lake, now the site of one of the world's hottest jazz festivals. To the west, Geneva, headquarters of the International Red Cross, has long been a sedate city of humanity and enlightenment, but even she lets down her discreet chignon once a year (December 11) to celebrate the Escalade, a 17th-century battle.

Geneva

A harbor filled with slender sailboat masts, backed by the white mists of the Jet d'Eau fountain, is the first image that strikes most visitors upon arrival in Geneva (Genève in French). You'll find plenty of sights to match it, from the opulent mansions and flowery promenades that wrap around Lac Léman to the copper spire of the cathedral at the apex of the old town. Placid Geneva may say "Switzerland" on the outside, but the town is French at the core—it wasn't until 1815, after the collapse of the Napoleonic empire, that Geneva joined the Swiss Confederation. As the second seat of the United Nations (after New York City), it has remained cosmopolitan. Jean-Jacques Rousseau and Voltaire are two of many famous residents who've left their marks on the city, but Calvin's influence is perhaps most solidly entrenched. The Protestant reformer preached here against theater, dancing, and wine consumed for pleasure. His puritanical presence remains: If you're looking for wild nightlife, catch the next train to Paris.

BASICS Pick up the useful guides *What's on in Geneva* and *This Week in Geneva,* with listings of clubs, restaurants, and events, at the train station **tourist office** (tel. 022/738–52–00; open mid-June–Aug., daily 8–8, Sept.–mid-June, Mon.–Sat. 9–6). The **Centre d'Accueil et de Renseignements (CAR)** has an information bus outside the station on rue du Mont-Blanc that helps budget travelers daily 8 AM–11 PM from June 15 to September 15. Have your mail sent to **American Express** (7 rue du Mont-Blanc, Box 859, Geneva 1, CH-1208, tel. 022/731–76–00); they'll hold it for two months. Otherwise, the **main post office** is a block from the station on rue du Mont-Blanc, in the Hôtel des Postes.

COMING AND GOING Most trains arrive at the **Gare de Cornavin,** on the northern edge of town; a few, mostly from the French Alps, arrive at the **Gare Genève Eaux-Vives** on the city's eastern edge. The **Compagnie Générale de Navigation (CGN)** (tel. 022/722–39–16) runs boat trips to and from Geneva that are free with a EurailPass. Boats depart from the quai du Mont-Blanc for Lausanne (3½ hrs, SFr38) and Montreux (5 hrs, SFr46).

GETTING AROUND The Rhône River divides Geneva into two parts: the **Rive Gauche** (Left Bank) and the **Rive Droite** (Right Bank). The Rive Gauche, to the south, comprises the **vieille ville** (old town), the Jardin Anglais, and the university. The Rive Droite includes the St-Gervais district, the quai du Mont-Blanc, and the important parks. Pont du Mont-Blanc, the main bridge, connects the two areas. From the bridge, you can see the copper steeple of Cathédrale St-Pierre in the old town.

➤ **BY BUS AND TRAM** • You won't need Geneva's extensive public transportation system to see most sights. If you want to take buses or trams, look for the vending machines at each station, which spit out different types of tickets depending on the length of the ride. All-day tickets, available from agents listed on the signs at the stops, cost SFr6 for one day, SFr11 for two, and SFr14 for three. Tickets must be validated at automatic machines.

WHERE TO SLEEP Geneva has decent hotel rooms at reasonable prices—for Switzerland, at least. Student-housing options are plentiful and cheap, though not always very comfortable. The **Accueil de Nuit–Salvation Army** (4 chemin Galiffe, tel. 022/344–91–21) offers the cheapest beds in town (SFr10, breakfast and shower included), but expect small two-cot rooms in a barracks-like building. If the places below are full, **Hôtel des Tourelles** (2 blvd. James-Fazy, tel. 022/732–44–23) offers quiet, sunny rooms with brightly colored bedspreads for SFr60 per single, SFr84 per double, and SFr100 per triple. Most rooms have hardwood floors and a view of the lake, and the hotel takes credit cards.

Hôtel de la Cloche. Easy to find, 10 minutes from the station off quai du Mont-Blanc. Some rooms are big with hardwood floors, others small with carpet, but most have balconies and big windows. Singles SFr40, doubles SFr65, triples SFr85, quads SFr110, showers SFr2, breakfast SFr5. *6 rue de la Cloche, tel. 022/732–94–81.*

Hôtel du Beau-Site. Fairly central, in an old building with spacious rooms, big windows, and eclectic furnishings. Bright breakfast room and friendly owner. Singles from SFr45, doubles SFr70 (SFr80 w/shower), triples SFr90, quads SFr100. Students get SFr5–SFr15 off rooms without sinks. *3 pl. du Cirque, tel. 022/328–10–08. From station, Bus 1 to Cirque stop. AE, MC, V.*

Pension St-Victor. The best bet in Geneva. Big, sunny rooms overlook quiet streets. Mme. Claire Pittet has created a warm atmosphere in a quiet residential neighborhood two minutes from the vieille ville. Singles SFr45, doubles SFr70–SFr75. *1 rue Lefort, tel. 022/346–17–18. From station, Bus 8 or 3 to Museum stop, then walk down blvd. des Tranchées, turn right on rue Charles-Galland and left on rue Lefort.*

➤ **HOSTELS** • **Auberge de Jeunesse (HI).** Big, clean, modern, and well-equipped. Great doubles with shower and balcony for SFr66. Dorm beds SFr18, SFr25 nonmembers. *28 rue Rothschild, tel. 022/732–62–60. From station, walk 10 min on rue de Lausanne, turn right on rue Rothschild. Midnight curfew, lockout 10–4, reception open 6:30–10 AM and 5–11 PM, laundry, kitchen.*

Hôme St-Pierre. In the center of the old town, facing the cathedral. A great place to stay but only accepts women. Rooms are a little cramped, but there's a communal room, a rooftop sitting area with a view of the lake, and cooking and laundry facilities. Dorm beds SFr16, singles SFr29, the rare double SFr44, breakfast SFr7.50, sheets SFr2. *4 cour St-Pierre, tel. 022/310–37–07.*

➤ **STUDENT HOUSING** • **Cité Universitaire.** Cheap, but far from town. Decent dorm rooms (12 beds per room) for SFr14 in a high-rise building. Doubles SFr48–SFr54. In winter, only groups allowed. *46 av. Miremon, tel. 022/346–23–55. From pl. de Cantons near station take Bus 3, direction rte. de Champel, to the last stop. 11:30 curfew, lockout*

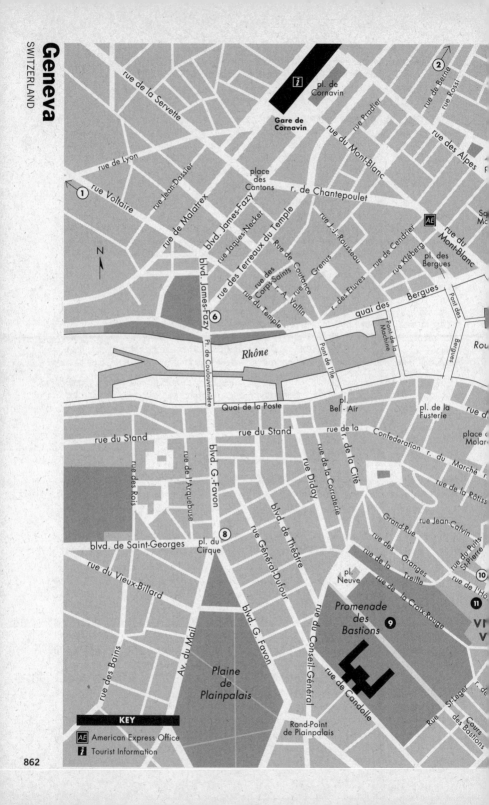

rue de la Servette

rue de Lyon

rue Voltaire

① rue Jean-Dassier

rue de Malatrex

blvd. James-Fazy

Pl. de Coulouvrenière

② rue de Berne

rue Rossi

rue Pradier

rue du Mont-Blanc

rue des Alpes

pl. de Cornavin

Gare de Cornavin

i

place des Cantons

r. de Chantepoulet

blvd. James-Fazy

rue Jaques-Necker

rue des Terreaux du Temple

Rue de Coutance

rue des Corps-Saints

r.-A.-Vallin

rue du Temple

Grenus

rue J.-J.-Rousseau

r. des Étuves

rue de Cendrier

rue Kléberg

AE

rue du Mont-Blanc

pl. des Bergues

Bergues

quai des

Pont des Bergues

Pont de la Machine

⑥

Rou

Rhône

Pont de l'Ile

Quai de la Poste

pl. Bel - Air

pl. de la Fusterie

rue d'

rue du Stand

rue du Stand

rue de la

r. de la Cité

Confederation

r. du Marché

place de Molar

r.

rue de la Rôtiss

rue des Rois

rue de l'Arquebuse

blvd. G.-Favon

rue de la Corraterie

rue Diday

rue de la

rue Jean-Calvin

rue du Puits-St-Pierre

⑩

blvd. de Saint-Georges

pl. du Cirque

⑧

rue Général-Dufour

blvd. de Théâtre

Grand-Rue

rue des Granges

rue de la Treille

rue de l'Hô

⑪

rue du Vieux-Billard

pl. Neuve

rue de la Croix-Rouge

Promenade des Bastions

V

V

⑨

rue des Bains

Av. du Mail

blvd. G. Favon

rue du Conseil-Général

rue de Candolle

Plaine de Plainpalais

Rue St-Léger

r. de

Cours des Bastions

Rond-Point de Plainpalais

KEY

AE American Express Office

i Tourist Information

N

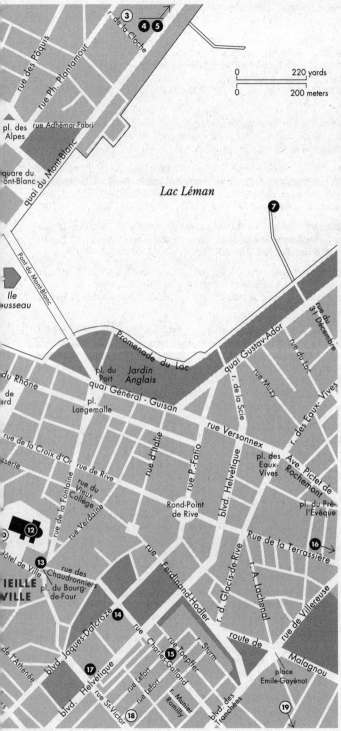

Sights ●

Cathédrale
St-Pierre, **12**

Jet d'Eau, **7**

Hôtel de Ville, **11**

Musée d'Art et
d'Histoire, **14**

Musée de
l'Horlogerie, **16**

Musée des
Instruments Anciens
de Musique, **15**

Musée du Petit
Palais, **17**

Musée International
de la Croix-Rouge et
du Croissant-
Rouge, **5**

Palais de
Justice, **13**

Palais des
Nations, **4**

Promenade des
Bastions/Monument
de la Réformation, **9**

Lodging ○

Accueil de Nuit-
Salvation Army, **1**

Auberge de
Jeunesse (HI), **2**

Cité
Universitaire, **19**

Hôme St-Pierre, **10**

Hôtel de la
Cloche, **3**

Hôtel des
Tourelles, **6**

Hôtel du
Beau-Site, **8**

Pension
St-Victor, **18**

8:30–6, reception open weekdays 8–noon and 2–10, Sat. 8–noon and 6–10, Sun. 9–11 and 6–10.

FOOD Cosmopolitan Geneva offers a refreshing variety of cuisines: If you crave Indian, Korean, or Thai food, you're in the right place, provided you're padded with cash. Those who just want a good deal can choose from 17 different **Migros** self-service restaurants. Pick up a restaurant guide (free at the tourist office or CAR) for all the locations. Right outside the train station, **L'Age d'Or** (11 rue Cornavin, tel. 022/731–30–93) offers a small pizza, salad, and a drink for SFr9.50.

Les Armures. Geneva's oldest café has outdoor seating in a picturesque alley around the corner from the cathedral. Great fondue is SFr19; cheapest pizza in the vieille ville starts at SFr11. *1 rue du Puits-St-Pierre, tel. 022/28–34–42.*

Nouvelle Post. An attractive interior, with high ceilings and a bar in the corner, makes you feel like you're sitting in a French postcard. Friendly waiters, piano music after 9 PM. Dinners such as steak tartare with melon start at SFr14. *7 rue du Vieux-Collège, tel. 022/311–56–31. From Jardin Anglais, walk south on Longemalle.*

Pizzeria da Paolo Restaurant. The town's hot spot, packed with people and fast-moving, fast-talking Italian waiters. Vaulted stone interior and outdoor terrace. Pizzas start at SFr14. *3 rue du Lac, 1 block from Jet d'Eau, tel. 022/736–30–49.*

Le Rive-Gauche. Bubbly French lady serves filling dinners in a friendly restaurant with pink tablecloths. *Plats-du-soir* (evening specials) go for SFr14. Five-minute walk from Jet d'Eau or vieille ville, near place des Eaux-Vives. *9 rue des Eaux-Vives, tel. 022/736–64–52. Closed Sat. until 6 PM and Sun.*

WORTH SEEING You could easily spend an afternoon watching the boats sail across Lac Léman. Check out quai du Mont-Blanc, on the lake's north bank, where hotels, shops, and cafés vie for space with impressive mansions. Across Pont du Mont-Blanc in the **Jardin Anglais,** the **Horloge Fleurie** (Flower Clock), on a neatly sculpted bed of flowers, keeps accurate time in good Swiss fashion. Next to the Jardin Anglais, along quai Gustave Ador, the impressive **Jet d'Eau** shoots 500 liters of water per second 140 meters into the air. The fountain has become Geneva's premier landmark, and you can see its misty sprays shooting up above rooftops all around the city. On a hot day, walk underneath the fountain and let the spray revive you.

The spunky old lady who runs the Musée d'Instruments Anciens de Musique (23 rue Lefort, tel. 022/746–95–65; admission SFr2; open Tues. afternoon, Thurs., and Fri. evening) makes sure you touch the musical instruments inside, and if you have any talent, you'd better be ready to play.

Also worth exploring is the **vieille ville,** with its cobblestone hills and narrow streets. The busiest area here is place du Bourg-de-Four, first a Roman forum and later a medieval town square. Outdoor cafés, a fountain covered with flowers, historic buildings, and art galleries make it a popular hangout for tourists and dapper Genevoises. The **Palais de Justice** was built on the south side of the square in 1707. A short walk up rue de l'Hôtel de Ville will bring you, appropriately enough, to the **Hôtel de Ville** (Town Hall), the site of the first convention of the Red Cross in 1864. Across from here, the **Arsenal** shows off cannons and colorful murals. If you can't get enough of Switzerland's most famous product, head east to the free **Musée de l'Horlogerie** (15 rte. de Malagnou, tel. 022/736–74–12; open Wed.–Mon. 10–5), where sand timers, sundials, and loads of watches from the 17th and 18th centuries are on display.

➤ **CATHEDRALE ST-PIERRE** • This cathedral, constructed mostly in the 12th and 13th centuries, radiates plain Swiss strength and common sense. But like the Genevoises themselves, it displays a little unexpected zest, especially in the colorful Gothic chapel on the south side, built in the 15th century, and in the neoclassical facade, added in the 18th century. Underneath the church is an impressive archaeological site, the **Site Archéologique de St-Pierre** (admission SFr5), complete with a baptistry, a crypt, 4th-century mosaics, and sculptures covering over 2,000 years of history. *Cour St-Pierre, tel. 022/29–75–98. Admission to tower: SFr2. Cathedral open June–Sept., daily 9–7; Mar.–May and Oct., daily 9–noon and 2–6; Nov.–Feb., daily 9–noon and 2–5.*

➤ **PROMENADE DES BASTIONS** • Below the walls of the vieille ville stands the impressive, unadorned **Monument de la Réformation.** Forbidding sculptures of four local Protestant reformers (Calvin, Farel, Bèze, and Knox) and other reliefs flank this 100-yard wall. The surrounding park, Promenade des Bastions, contains the university. It's a great daytime hangout, complete with students, Frisbee players, and sidewalk chess games.

➤ **MUSEE D'ART ET D'HISTOIRE** • In a posh residential neighborhood next to the vieille ville, this museum displays an impressive collection of archaeological finds from Egypt, Greece, and Rome on the ground floor. The best works in the painting collection are landscapes by Swiss artist Ferdinand Hodler that capture strong light on the mountains. The museum also has a good collection of period furniture and weapons. *2 rue Charles-Galland, tel. 022/29–00–11. Take Bus 3 from station. Admission free. Open Tues.–Sun. 10–5.*

In a pleasant 19th-century town house behind the museum, the small **Musée du Petit Palais** (2 terasse St-Victor, tel. 022/46–14–33; admission SFr10, SFr5 students) displays impressionist and surrealist works, among others, with a few pieces by Renoir, Picasso, Cézanne, Utrillo, and Chagall.

➤ **PALAIS DES NATIONS** • The imposing United Nations building, beautiful in its stark features, sits in a garden filled with gifts from different countries (the United States donated a bronze sphere in honor of President Wilson, Russia an obelisk commemorating space travel). The interior is worth a visit for its works by international artists and for the famous assembly rooms seen on TV, but you have to go through an exhausting tour to see it all. *14 av. de la Paix, tel. 022/734–60–11. Take Bus 8 from station. Admission: SFr8, SFr6 students. Tours daily 9–noon and 2–5:15. Closed mid-Dec.–Jan 1.*

Across from the Palais des Nations lies the small but impressive **Musée International de la Croix-Rouge et du Croissant-Rouge,** where exhibits, films, and slides chronicle the founding and heroic activities of the Red Cross. Jean Henry Dunant, a local businessman, began the organization after witnessing the inhumane treatment of prisoners and wounded in the 1859 Battle of Solferino. *17 av. de la Paix, tel. 022/734–52–48. Admission: SFr10, SFr5 students.*

CHEAP THRILLS Gardens galore make Geneva a great place for picnicking, strolling, and admiring finely pruned flower beds. **Parc Mon Repos, Parc Perle du Lac,** and **Parc Villa Barton** are three connecting parks that form an extensive green area north of the train station, at the end of quai Wilson. Wander here and around the botanical gardens next door to see a multitude of plants, a rock garden, a deer pen, and an aviary. **Parc de la Grange,** on the opposite bank, has a rose garden that's especially colorful in June. In early August, look for the **Fêtes de Genève,** which brings fireworks, live music, and flower parades to the city.

AFTER DARK Nighttime entertainment centers around the place du Bourg-de-Four and surrounding alleys. **Cafe la Clémence** takes up a large chunk of the plaza, and a good-looking international crowd lounges here day and night. **Post Café** (7 rue de Berne, tel. 022/732–96–63), off rue du Mont Blanc near the train station, draws a lively English-speaking crowd into its two small rooms. You can get hamburgers for SFr10, and during happy hour (5 PM–10 PM) half-liters of beer are SFr3.50. **Au Chat Noir** (13 rue Vautier, tel. 022/43–49–98) offers jazz every night in rooms decked out with murals. Employees from the United Nations show up at **Mr. Pickwicks** (80 rue de Lausanne, north of station, tel. 022/731–67–97), an English-style pub. Lesbians should contact **Centres Femmes** (tel. 022/789–26–00) and gay men **Dialogi** (tel. 022/340–00–00) for listings of gay clubs.

NEAR GENEVA

You can take boat rides from Geneva to nearby towns, including beautiful **Yvoire,** loaded with restaurants, flowers, and tourists. EurailPasses are valid on all cruises run by **CGN** (*see* Coming and Going, *above*). **Swiss Boat** also gives tours of villas near Geneva. Two-hour trips (SFr18) depart at 10:15 and 3; one-hour tours (SFr12) leave at 3:15 and 5:15. EurailPasses are not valid.

Mt. Saleve, 6 km south of Geneva in France, makes a great half-day excursion. From this 4,000-foot ridge, you can see Geneva on one side and the fabulous French Alps and Mt. Blanc on the other. Take time to wander under the sails of sky-high parasailers, or hang out with some contented cows. From Geneva, take Bus 8 to Veyrier, where you'll go through passport control, and then take the cable car (SFr15 round-trip) up to the peak.

Lausanne

Heavyweight writers like Voltaire, Rousseau, Byron, and Victor Hugo have waxed passionate about Lausanne's beauty—Hugo described the graceful tiered city as "a staircase where my thoughts climbed step by step and broadened at each new height." But Lausanne has a certain sterile feel: It's less cosmopolitan than Geneva to the west, and less charming than Montreux to the east. Flower beds, fountains, and shady promenades abound, but the atmospheric alleys and narrow streets that once filled the town were mostly demolished after World War II for the sake of progress and hygiene; they remain only in the painstakingly restored vieille ville, around the cathedral. The **tourist offices** in the train station (tel. 021/23–87–94) and near the water in Ouchy (2 av. de Rhodanie, tel. 021/617–14–27) can help you get your bearings.

COMING AND GOING Lausanne lies on a major **train** route between Bern (1 hr) and Geneva (30 min), with express trains running from Basel and Zürich. High-speed TGV trains connect the town with Paris (3 hrs 40 min). **CGN boats** (tel. 021/617–06–66) leave from place du Port, behind the Château d'Ouchy, for Montreux (1½ hrs, SFr15 one-way), Vevey (1 hr, SFr11 one-way), and Geneva (3 hrs, SFr27 one-way). All trips are free with a EurailPass.

Lausanne is divided into the **haute ville** (upper town), where the vieille ville is, and the **basse ville** (lower town), which contains Ouchy, the lakeside resort area. The vieille ville and Ouchy are easily seen on foot, but you'll need the bus or Metro to traverse the steep streets from one to the other. Buy **bus** tickets at automatic dispensers before boarding. Fares, based on zones and starting at SFr1, are posted at stops. Get 24-hour tickets (SFr6) at major stops. The **Metro** swooshes from place St-François, just below the heart of the vieille ville, through the train station and down to place de la Navigation at the Ouchy port.

WHERE TO SLEEP Many places that cater to local students rent out extra rooms to travelers. The clean **Pension Bienvenue** (2 rue du Simplon, behind station, tel. 021/26–29–86; singles SFr29, doubles SFr44) rents to women only. The elderly proprietress at **Hôtel le Chalet** (49 av. d'Ouchy, tel. 021/26–52–06; doubles SFr80) keeps a beautiful garden and rents out big, sunny rooms in a 19th-century house. Breakfast overlooking the garden is SFr10. For a funkier experience, try **Villa Cherokee** (4 chemin des Charmilles, tel. 021/37–57–50; doubles SFr50–SFr60), where the hostess greets you with an armload of bracelets and an earful of stories. Take Bus 2 to Presbytere and turn left on chemin des Charmilles.

The **HI Auberge de Jeunesse** (1 chemin de Muguet, tel. 021/26–57–82; beds SFr18, SFr25 nonmembers) isn't the most exciting Swiss hostel, but at least it's close to the water and the meals are pretty good. From the station, cross the street and catch Bus 1 (direction Matadière); get off at La Batelière and follow the signs to the hostel. **Jeunotel** (36 chemin du Bois-de-Vaux, tel. 021/626–02–22; dorm beds SFr20, doubles SFr50–SFr60), a big new complex with spotless rooms around a courtyard, is a great alternative to the hostel. Take Bus 2 to Bois-de-Vaux, then backtrack and turn right toward the water on chemin du Bois-de-Vaux.

FOOD In the center of the vieille ville, **L'Etrier Pizzeria** (2 rue de la Madeleine, off pl. de la Palud, tel. 021/23–41–56) serves hearty pizza (SFr10 and up) on a busy terrace or in a cozy wooden dining room. **Le Barbare** (27 Escalier du Marché, tel. 021/312–21–32), under the cathedral next to a covered stairway, also serves pizza (SFr10 and up), and its terrace is quieter. You can eat fondue with locals at **Pinte Besson** (4 rue d'Ale, tel. 021/312–72–27; closed Sun.). **Manora Restaurant** (17 pl. St-François) is less atmospheric but a better value, with a great self-service salad bar and cheap steaks and pastas. In Ouchy, you're stuck with expensive waterfront restaurants or cheap fast food. Your best bet is the **Ouchy White Horse Pub** (66 av. d'Ouchy, tel. 021/26–75–75), with good food, moderate prices, and a local crowd.

WORTH SEEING The cobblestone streets above the train station lead through the vieille ville, a haven for wandering pedestrians, shoppers, and café seekers. Place de la Palud, a center of activity, contains the **Fontaine de la Justice** (1726). Also check out the facade on the building next to this fountain; animated clock figures do their thing on the hour between 9 AM and 7 PM. In summer, the arcades of the 17th-century **Hôtel de Ville,** on the southern end of the plaza, are filled with vendors selling crafts.

On Place de la Riponne, just north of Place de la Palud, the early 20th-century **Palais de Rumine** once housed the university and now contains a host of free museums. The **Musée Cantonal des Beaux-Arts** (tel. 021/312–83–32) has paintings by 19th-century Swiss artists, as well as works by Matisse, Degas, Bonnard, and Utrillo. In summer, most of the permanent exhibition is taken down to make way for temporary exhibits.

➢ **CATHEDRALE DE NOTRE-DAME** • The doors of Switzerland's most famous Gothic cathedral are ornamented with fanciful reliefs; and a stunning 13th-century rose window, *Imago Mundi,* depicts the elements, seasons, and signs of the zodiac. It's worth a climb up the 232 steps (admission SFr2) for a view of the town, Lac Léman, and the Alps. Next door, the **Ancien-Evêché** (4 pl. de la Cathédrale, tel. 021/44–72–85), the former bishop's palace, now houses the **Musée Historique de Lausanne,** with exhibits on the history of the city. *Pl. de la Cathédrale, tel. 021/44–72–85. Open Apr.–Sept., weekdays 7–7, Sat. 8–7, Sun. 2–7; Oct.–Mar., weekdays 7–5:30, Sat. 8–5:30, Sun. 2–5:30.*

➢ **MUSEE DE L'ART BRUT** • This fascinating collection of "outsider art" gathered by the famous painter and sculptor Jean Dubuffet is kept in the former stables of the 18th-century Beaulieu Château. The collection consists of imaginative and individualistic works from people on the fringes of society—schizophrenics, the criminally insane, and reclusive eccentrics. *11 av. des Bergières, northwest of vieille ville, tel. 021/37–54–35. Admission: SFr5, SFr3 students. Open Tues.–Fri. 10–noon and 2–6, weekends 2–6.*

➢ **OUCHY** • At this lakeside resort area you can rent boats, stroll along the river on quai d'Ouchy and quai de Belgique, or walk west to the **Bellerive Beach and Pool** (23 av. de la Rhodaine, tel. 021/617–81–31; admission SFr4). The International Olympic Committee has been based in Lausanne since 1915, and the modern **Musée Olympique** (1 quai d'Ouchy; open May–Sept., Tues.–Sat. 10–7, Oct.–Apr., Tues.–Sat. 10–6) shows the history of the Olympics from antiquity to the present. Videos of famous Olympic moments will bring tears to your eyes—but so will the SFr12 admission. You can see clips of any recorded event from the Olympics.

CHEAP THRILLS Start your day off right with the locals and plenty of tourists at the **wine fair** in nearby Vevey, open every Saturday until about noon. Buy a small wine glass for SFr4.50, or a large glass for SFr6; refills are free all morning. Boats from quai d'Ouchy take about 1 hour, trains about 25 minutes.

Montreux

Spilling down steep hillsides into a sunny bay, Montreux has maintained its Edwardian dignity in the face of considerable development. It's been a resort for wealthy tourists since its casino opened in 1883, but today Montreux's big draw is the **Jazz Festival** (tel. 021/963–82–82), for which the entire town heats up during early July. Tickets run a high SFr50–SFr150 and sell out quickly, but if you're lucky you may snag standing-room tickets (SFr65) at the concert venues the day of the performance. If you miss out, take a trip instead to the vineyards that surround the town; ask at the **tourist office** (pl. du Débarcadère, on lakefront near boat landing, tel. 021/963–12–12; open weekdays 8–noon and 2–6, Sat. 8–noon) for more info.

Montreux's must-see sight is the **Château de Chillon,** an awe-inspiring 13th-century castle on the shore of Lac Léman less than 3 km from the city (take Bus 1). Check out the festival hall, with a roof in the form of an inverted ship's hull, and the elaborate bedrooms, some of which were used as torture chambers in the 17th century. The underground vaults were once the prison that held François de Bonivard, who was chained to a pillar for four years after he tried to introduce the Reformation in Geneva. *Tel. 021/963–39–12. Admission: SFr5, SFr4 students. Open July–Aug., daily 9–6:15; shorter hrs off-season.*

WHERE TO SLEEP AND EAT   The hostel is a bit out of the way, but most hotels are central. **Hotel Elite** (25 av. du Casino, tel. 021/963–67–33), near the action in the center of town, has comfortable doubles for SFr80–SFr90. From the station, walk down avenue des Alpes and turn left at place de la Paix onto avenue du Casino. **Hostellerie du Lac** (12 rue du Quai, tel. 021/963–32–71; doubles SFr85 and up) has a great location right on the lake. The **Auberge de Jeunesse Haut Lac** (8 passage de l'Auberge, tel. 021/63–49–34; beds SFr16), 30 minutes' walk along the lake from town, accepts only HI members. Take Bus 1 toward Villeneuve, exit at Territet-Gare, and follow the signs downhill. Montreux's restaurants are superexpensive; instead, use the **Co-op** (80 Grand Rue) or the **Migros** (av. du Casino).

NEAR MONTREUX

If even Montreux seems like too much of a modern metropolis, take the train to nearby **Aigle.** From here, another train (SFr8) makes the steep climb to the hilltop village of **Leysin,** and you can walk back toward Aigle to the right of the tracks (2–3 hrs), passing meandering cows, woods, and vineyards. Amid the vines, the **Château d'Aigle** (tel. 025/26–21–30; admission SFr6, SFr3 students; closed Mon. Sept.–July) houses a wine-making museum, with labels, goblets, info on the wine-making process, and impressive wooden contraptions used for pressing grapes. Wine tasting (SFr12.50 per person) can be arranged for groups upon request.

Italian Switzerland

Newcomers to Europe, a little weak on their geography, might hear the names Lugano, Locarno, and Ascona and assume they're in Italy. The photos in the tourist brochures for this region certainly wouldn't set them straight: Nearly every publicity shot shows palm trees, red roofs, and loggias. But behind the wavering date palms are the telltale signs: the surgical neatness, the fresh paint, the geometric gardens, the timely trains. There's no mistake about it—it's a little bit of Italy, but the region is Swiss at heart.

Lugano

Bella Italia! Well . . . almost. Wedged between the gently rounded peaks of Mt. Bré and Mt. San Salvatore, the Italian Swiss city of Lugano offers hot weather, densely wooded slopes to explore, and sparkling water that begs you to take a boat ride to a neighboring village. The **main tourist office** (Riva Albertoli 5, tel. 091/21–46–64) can help you plan your visit; take almost any bus to Piazza della Riforma in the town center, walk to the water, and turn left. A booth at the train station also gives hotel information and directions.

The **Cattedrale di San Lorenzo** (Via Cattedrale), with its copper dome, greets you as you exit the train station. Its main attractions are three decorated Renaissance portals, an elegant facade and Baroque interior, and a 16th-century tabernacle designed by the Rodari brothers of Maroggia. The terrace has a good view of the lake and Lugano. **Chiesa di Santa Maria degli**

Angeli (Piazza Luini, at Via Nassa) is a simple, elegant church with two beautiful frescoes painted by Bernardino Luini: The 1529 *Crucifixion* and the *Virgin and Child with St. John* have been compared with the work of Leonardo da Vinci. **Museo Cantonale d'Arte** (Via Canova 10, tel. 091/22–93–56; admission SFr5, SFr3 students; open Tues. 2–5, Wed.–Sun. 10–5) has works by Klee, Renoir, and the early 20th-century Russian painter Alexei von Jawlensky. Once you've done your cultural duty for the day, plop down in the shade in **Parco Civico** on Lake Lugano. A little beach is right next to the park.

COMING AND GOING Trains connect from Zürich (3 hrs) and Milan, Italy (1½ hrs); if you're coming from Geneva, catch the Milan Express and change at Domodossola and Bellinzona. From the **train station** (tel. 091/22–65–02), a funicular runs to Piazza Cioccaro, north of **Piazza della Riforma**, the main square. The central quay, departure point for many boat trips, is just south of Piazza della Riforma. **Buses** are useful for getting to accommodations, many of which are just outside town. Prices are posted at stops; SFr4 day passes will save you money if you're going to get on the bus more than twice.

WHERE TO SLEEP As usual, the cheapest bed is at the hostel, **Albergo per la Gioventú** (Via Cantonale, tel. 091/56–27–28). The big grounds here feature tropical plants and a swimming pool. What the hostel lacks in Swiss fastidiousness, it makes up threefold in charm; the only bummer is the ridiculous 10 PM curfew. Dorm beds go for SFr14.50 (SFr20 nonmembers), singles for SFr30, and doubles for SFr40. Sheets are SFr2. From the station, cross the street, take Bus 5 toward Vezia, get off at the Crocifisso stop, and follow signs up Via Cantonale (the street right before the stop). The hostel is closed mid-October–mid-March.

Ostella Montarino (Via Montarino 1, tel. 091/56–72–72; closed Dec.–Feb.), behind the train station, offers dorms for SFr20, singles for SFr50, and doubles for SFr75. It's not nearly as nice as the hostel, though, and you'll know when every train is coming and going. **Pensione La Santa** (Via Merlina 2, tel. 091/51–61–45), a bit farther out, has doubles for SFr60. A bunch of locals play chess and drink wine on the outside terrace. Take Bus 10 to La Santa from the train station. Women can get a bed at **Casa delle Giovane** (Corso Ilvezia 34, tel. 091/22–95–53) for SFr20. **Hotel Ceneri** (Via Nassa 44, tel. 091/23–33–40), in a great location at the center of town, has pleasant SFr80 doubles overlooking a cobblestone street.

FOOD The best deals cluster around Piazza Cioccaro. **Restaurant INOVA** (Piazza Dante 2, tel. 091/21–38–88; open 7 AM–10 PM), in the Innovations department store, cooks huge plates of pasta (SFr8) right before your eyes, and there's a great salad bar (SFr4 small, SFr9.50 large). Another location, with windows overlooking the lake, is on Via Canove near Piazza della Riforma (look for the INNO LAGO sign). The colorful corner of Via Pessina and Piazza Cioccaro has a meat store, a bakery, and a fruit and vegetable market. Pick up some wurst or delicious tortes and pack a picnic. Piazza della Riforma has lots of cafés, but at most of them you'll only be able to afford the beer—pizzas run about SFr15. **Bar la Piazza** (Piazza della Riforma, tel. 091/23–31–34), a local hangout, is the exception, serving pizza for only SFr9.

NEAR LUGANO

VILLA FAVORITA This lakeside villa (admission SFr12, SFr8 students; closed Oct.–Apr.), surrounded by beautiful gardens, houses the **Thyssen-Bornemisza art collection,** the private holding of a family of wealthy German steel industrialists. Unfortunately, they've recently carted the most famous works—including some by Raphael, Titian, and Rembrandt—to Madrid's Villahermosa Palace. The museum still displays a good collection of 19th- and 20th-century paintings by cubists, German expressionists, Russian Constructivists, Dadaists, and surrealists. To get here, take a boat (SFr8 round-trip) from Lugano's central quay by Piazza Manzioni, or take Bus 2.

GANDRIA Restaurants hover over the water, small cobblestone streets climb the hill, and lush vegetation is everywhere—ample reward for your efforts to get to Gandria. It's so attractive that many popular postcards of Lugano really picture this village. You can pay SFr13 for a round-trip boat from Lugano's central quay, or buy a one-way ticket (SFr9) and then pay

SFr4 for a boat to Castagnola, where a walk through gardens leads to Villa Favorita (*see above*); from here, it's SFr2 for a ticket back to Lugano. You can also walk to Castagnola along the lake in less than an hour—follow signs from Gandria.

MORCOTE An excellent bike ride (1 hr) takes you from Lugano through small lakeside towns to the beautiful old fishing village of Morcote. When you arrive, you can climb the hill to the **Church of Madonna del Sasso** for a cool rest amid 16th-century frescoes and calming organ music. Walk through the cemetery next door—you'll be amazed by the pains they took to bury local bigwigs. The **Parco Scherrer** (tel. 091/69–21–25; admission SFr4; open Mar. 15–Oct. 31, daily 9–5) contains colorful gardens and paths lined with sculpture. Eat next door at **Ristorante del Grotto**, housed in an old stone bulding, or try one of the restaurants on the water (you can always find pasta for SFr14). If you're wiling to shell out SFr100 for a double, you can stay overnight in an Italian-style country home, **Hotel Rivabella** (tel. 091/69–13–14). Boat fare from Lugano to Morcote is SFr20 round-trip, SFr12 one-way. You can also combine a visit to Morcote with a trip to the top of **Mt. San Salvatore**—it just takes a little foot power. Take the funicular to the top of San Salvatore (SFr10 one-way), check out a great view of the lakes and the Alps, and then walk $2^1/_2$ hours down the mountain to Morcote (the path is marked next to the self-service restaurant).

LOCARNO Cooled by breezes from Lago Maggiore (Lake Maggiore), Locarno strikes a balance between resorty Ascona to the west and citified Lugano to the south. The town became famous in 1925, when the Disarmament Conference took place here following World War I. Since then, Locarno has attracted German retirees, who hang out in cafés downing afternoon coffee and a torte. Unfortunately, Locarno's waterfront is not as appealing as Ascona's, and swimming spots in the lake are hard to find. Still, the town hosts plenty of musical events during summer, and a **film festival** lights up Piazza Grande in the first two weeks of August. For more info, go to the **tourist office** (Largo Zorzi 1, off Piazza Grande, tel. 093/31–03–33; open Apr.–Oct., weekdays 8–7, weekends 9–noon and 1–5, Nov.–Mar., weekdays 8–noon and 2–6). If you're staying overnight, try to get a dorm room (SFr20–SFr28) at **Pensione Città Vecchia** (Via Torretta 13, tel. 093/31–45–54), north of Piazza Grande.

Ascona

Small Ascona is a resort town through and through, good for a day trip but not worth a long visit. Ice-cream stands, outdoor cafés, and pedestrians line the busy lakefront. Colorful houses and cobblestone streets attract small crowds of wanderers—boyfriend in one hand, gelato in the other. Join them in shuffling along the lake; stop by Piazza San Pietro, where musicians take advantage of good acoustics; or visit the Renaissance courtyard of the **Collegio Pontificio Papio**. The church of **Santa Maria della Misericordia** next door has some worthwhile frescoes. Unfortunately, swimmers take a back seat to boats here, and those who can't resist the waters have to head to the south side of the lake. The **Ente Turistico di Ascona e Losone** (Piazza San Pietro, near San Pietro tower, tel. 093/ 35–00–90) dispenses visitor information Monday–Saturday 8–7. No trains run between Ascona and Locarno, but a **PTT bus** (20 min, SFr2) does. You can also catch a boat (SFr4.60) at the Locarno ferry terminal every hour until 6:30 PM. Piazza Motta is Ascona's most bustling area. Via Borgo connects this stretch of waterfront with Via Papio, where bus passengers disembark. The public beach is at the south end of the lakefront.

WHERE TO SLEEP AND EAT **Garni Silvia** (Via Circonvallazione 7, tel. 093/35–13–14; doubles SFr80–SFr90) is pretty much the Motel 6 of Ascona, but the rooms are at least big and clean, and they're the cheapest in town. Most of the plain rooms at **Hotel La Perla** (Via Collina, tel. 093/35–35–77; doubles SFr95–SFr110) come with balconies and TVs. If you want to live large, go to **Villa Verantum** (Via Locarno, tel. 093/35–35–77; doubles SFr140), a welcoming old villa with a pleasant garden. You can eat in an outdoor courtyard to the sound of jazz music at **Al Torchio** (Contrada Maggiore 1, tel. 093/35–71–26), where spaghetti is a good bargain at SFr10 but a full meal could cost you SFr30. The most happening waterfront restaurant is **Osteria Nostrana** (Via Albarelle, tel. 093/35–51–58), where pasta is SFr10–SFr14 and main courses start at SFr15.

TURKEY

25

By David Poole and Oliver Schwaner-Albright

If you're planning on popping into western Turkey, forget about fezzes, sultans, harems, and camels. Turkey looks more like Western Europe than you might think, despite its dramatically different architecture—buildings with bold, Byzantine colors and swirling patterns. The young people, in particular, look to the West, listening to pop music played on classical Turkish instruments and watching Turkish game shows and MTV. The lifestyle of Turkish parents and grandparents is different from that of their children, especially young women, many of whom have traded in their traditional dresses and *türbans* (black veils) for jeans and T-shirts.

Despite the modernization, though, Turkey remains an Islamic nation, and you'll notice the influence of religion wherever you go, especially in the east. The effect of Islam goes far beyond the call to prayer that rings through the streets five times daily. Although religion is less a force here than it is in the Middle East, many parents still arrange marriages for their children and enforce strict rules of behavior.

Turkey first grew powerful under the Hittite Empire, which rivaled Egypt in importance during the Bronze Age; but most of what you see today are remains of the Greek, Roman, Seljuk, and Ottoman empires. The great archaeological sites, mainly Roman, are among the most spectacular of the classical world. Despite a history that dates back 10,000 years, though, Turkey has experienced some of its most sweeping changes very recently. In 1922, Kemal Atatürk and his army fought the greedy victors of World War I to win the country's independence, and an almost complete overhaul of Turkish language and culture followed. Atatürk became president and westernized the country in an effort to encourage trade with Europe. He is revered as a national hero, and you'll see photos and statues of him all over. Today Turkey's first woman president, Tanşu Ciller, is faced with an 80% inflation rate and terrorism in the east from separatist Kurdish factions, but the country's tourist industry is booming, as vacationers increasingly choose the Turkish Aegean over Greece.

Basics

MONEY $1 = 19,000 Turkish liras and 1,000 Turkish liras = 5¢. The Turkish lira is constantly being devalued, so don't hold on to too much currency. Exchange money every week or so. We've quoted prices in U.S. dollars. Banks, generally open weekdays 9–noon and 1:30–5, are everywhere, and you'll usually find at least one teller who speaks English. All banks change cash and traveler's checks, although commissions vary. In most cities, PTTs

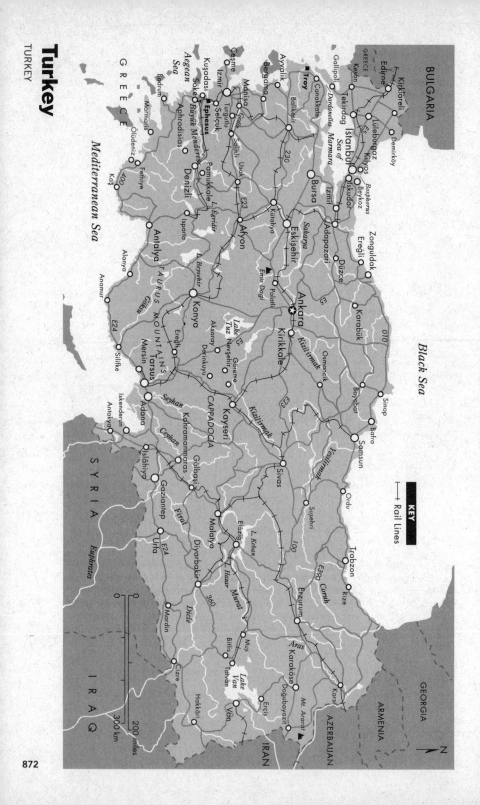

Turkey

TURKEY

(*see* Phones and Mail, *below*) also offer competitive rates. Outside bank hours, nearly any hotel owner or merchant will change cash for a commission, at rates similar to the banks'.

Most banks give cash advances on Visa and MasterCard, and many ATMs accept credit cards. The best place to go for Visa cash advances is Türkiye Iş Bank, which doesn't charge for the service. Otherwise, a 2%–5% fee, plus $3 for the telephone call for verification, is usual.

➤ **HOW MUCH IT WILL COST** • Turkey is the cheapest Mediterranean country; you can easily get by on $20 a day or less. Budget hotels are $4–$10 per person ($8 and up in Istanbul), and meals at most restaurants cost about $3. You can travel long distances for very little: A 100-km journey on a bus is usually no more than $1. Museums and archaeological sites charge $2–$4, but students often get a 50% discount. Nightspots don't charge a cover, and beer costs 50¢– $2.

VISA AND ENTRY REQUIREMENTS U.S. and Canadian citizens don't need visas for stays of less than three months. Visas are routinely issued to citizens of the U.K. and Australia on entry to the country.

COMING AND GOING If you've looked at a map recently, you'll realize how far Turkey is from most European destinations. Flying into Istanbul will save you a long overland journey. Call **Turkish Airlines (THY)** (tel. 124/82631) for fares. The trip from Paris is about $200, from London $270, although students can get up to a 50% discount.

You can travel as far as Istanbul with a EurailPass, and the InterRail pass is good throughout Turkey. The Athens–Istanbul **train** ride, though, is a hellish 24 hours. The trip from Sofia, Bulgaria (12 hrs) is a little better. **Buses** are faster than trains but aren't much fun. Alexandroúpoli in Greece and Sofia in Bulgaria are popular points for picking up the bus. If you're coming from Greece, try taking the **ferry** and island-hopping your way to Turkey if you have time. Frequent ferries sail from Lésvos to Ayvalık, from Híos to Çeşme, from Sámos to Kuşadası, from Kós to Bodrum, and from Ródos to Marmaris. The ferries cost about $20–$25 each, but tack on another $8–$10 for port tax.

GETTING AROUND In general, you're best off taking buses, many of which put Greyhound to shame with their efficient, frequent, and cheap service. Although trains are slightly cheaper, they're often painfully slow.

➤ **BY TRAIN** • Eurail will get you only as far as Istanbul, but InterRail is valid throughout the country. The Turkish rail system connects all major cities; take advantage of the express service between Istanbul and Ankara (7 hrs, $10).

➤ **BY BUS** • Buses come so frequently that you don't need reservations. Walk into the *otogar* (bus station), pick your destination, and hawkers will usually put you on a bus within the hour. You can also stop any bus on the road and pay the rate from the last stop—a good option for stranded hitchhikers. Buses are clean, and although most don't have toilets, you can make a dash at almost any stop (ask the driver how long he's pausing). Prices don't vary much between companies. You'll pay about $1 for a 100-km trip. If you ask for the student rate and complain a lot, you may get a discount of about 15%.

➤ **BY DOLMUŞ** • For shorter journeys between or within towns, wave down a *dolmuş* (shared taxi, often a Ford Transit or Mercedes van) on any main road; you needn't go to the station. Most journeys cost no more than 30¢. Destinations are displayed in the front window, and you pay on board the van.

➤ **HITCHING** • *Otostop* (hitching) is relatively easy, although it can be exhausting in the intense summer heat. Truckers in particular will usually stop. The thumb signal is considered rude, so just put a hand out when cars pass. Women are likely to get hassled and probably shouldn't hitch alone. Men will get rides much more quickly by hitching with a woman.

WHERE TO SLEEP Budget hotel rooms generally cost $4–$10 per person (higher in Istanbul) without a private shower. Hotels in the east are a few dollars less. *Pansiyons* (pensions) usually have cooking and washing facilities, but otherwise aren't substantially different from *otelis* (hotels). You can sleep on a mattress on a roof terrace for $2, although on a breezeless night you may not be able to see the stars for all the mosquitoes. Campsites also cost about $2, but the Turkish sun will bake you and wake you at 8 AM, so look for shade. Few people camp rough, although you're unlikely to be disturbed while doing it. Beaches are an option, but tides, thieves, and beach flies make them a hassle.

FOOD The language barrier shouldn't be a problem in restaurants; just look at the trays of food and point at what you want. You can even go into the kitchen for a closer look. Restaurants generally charge $1 for cold starters in olive oil and $2 for warm entrées; at hyped-up resorts and in Istanbul you'll pay more. *Kebaps* (roasted lamb), served with either *pide* (pita bread) or salad, is a budget standard. Turkish pizza, often topped with cheese and tomato, will bail out vegetarians, as will cold starters like *dolmas* (vegetables, including eggplant, bell pepper, and tomato, stuffed with rice or bulgur and spices). *Pastanesis* (bakery-cafés) serve trays of baklava, cakes, chocolate mousse, and *lokum* (Turkish delight). Coffee is expensive ($1), and usually you can find only instant coffee or strong *kahve* (Arabic coffee). Teahouses are the refuge of old men who smoke pipes, play backgammon or dominoes, and sip strong black tea called *çay*, or *çi*, of which Turkey has hundreds of varieties, served in little glasses on steel saucers with a small spoon and two lumps of sugar. A cup is 10¢.

Take advantage of pansiyon cooking facilities by buying groceries. Fresh produce costs little, and the peaches, apricots, cherries, bananas, eggplants, onions, and garlic are excellent. A loaf of Turkish white bread is bland but cheap (30¢); it's served free with every meal. Whole-wheat options are scarce. Efes Pilsen, a light lager, is the most widely available beer. The national cocktail is *raki*, an aniseed liqueur that turns milky white when diluted with water.

BUSINESS HOURS Normal business hours are Monday–Saturday 9–7, but shops sometimes stay open until midnight if business is good. Some pious merchants close on Friday evening. Most restaurants are open daily from early morning to midnight, and clubs and bars in resorts keep going until 4 AM. Museums are usually open daily 9–5, although they sometimes close for lunch and on Monday.

VISITOR INFORMATION All but the tiniest towns have a tourist office (sometimes called Turizm Danişma Bürosu), with free brochures in French, German, and English and local and regional maps. Offices are generally open weekdays 8:30–5:30, sometimes with an hour-long lunch break at about 12:30.

PHONES AND MAIL Country code: 90. Go to the PTT, the combination postal and phone office, for long-distance calls or to get 100-unit phone cards ($5) with which you can make national and international calls at yellow phones scattered around most towns. Otherwise, you'll have to use one of three tokens (available at PTTs and some stores) at inferior coin phones. Collect calls are cut off every few minutes, and you'll pay about $20 for three minutes to the United States—double the direct-dial rate. For the local operator, dial 011. For international calls, hit 9 and wait for the tone, then dial 9, the country code, and the number; you'll usually get an immediate, clear connection. For the AT&T operator, dial 9, wait for a dial tone, then dial 9800–122–77. For calls within Turkey, dial 9 before the city code and phone number. All city codes are in the process of being changed. We've tried to give the most up-to-date information, but don't be surprised if some codes are different when you arrive.

Mailboxes are found outside PTTs, and you can buy stamps inside. The central branch in each city has poste restante (10¢ per item). Address letters Poste Restante, PTT, and the name of the city. You can mail postcards for 25¢ to Europe, and for 35¢ to the United States. Letters cost another 5¢.

CRIME AND PUNISHMENT You may see police hanging out together and drinking raki, but don't be fooled by their laid-back attitude. You'll get a minimum of six months for drug possession, and if you're caught smuggling drugs out of the country, you can make that 1½ years. In case of arrest, notify your consulate before all else—the staff can provide you with a list of lawyers and assist in having money wired to you.

EMERGENCIES **Police** (tel. 055 or 666–666), **fire** (tel. 000), **ambulance** (tel. 077). Istanbul's emergency numbers are different (*see below*). For the **Istanbul Tourist Police**, call 1/527-45-03.

STAYING HEALTHY Travelers to Turkey rarely report major health problems, but cautious doctors recommend that your diphtheria-tetanus, typhoid, gamma-globulin, and polio vaccinations be up-to-date before you go. Antimalaria pills are recommended for those heading to eastern Turkey. Tap water is generally safe, although it may not taste too good in big cities. If you'll only be in Turkey for a few days, you might want to drink bottled water. The food is almost always safe; Turkish kitchens are very clean and open for your inspection. The biggest health risks are overexposure to the summer sun, and the occasional scorpion or adder in undeveloped areas.

Condoms, available at any eczane (pharmacy), are only 30¢ each, but there's a reason they're so cheap—they're small, thin, and often unlubricated. Shop around if you don't want to end up with mediocre South Korean imports, or, better yet, pack some from home.

LANGUAGE English is widely spoken in the more touristed areas, but knowing a little German or French helps. Try to learn at least a few Turkish words, like *merhaba* (hi), *teşekkür ederim* (thank you), *lütfen* (please), *hayır* (no), *evet* (yes), *sören yok* (no problem), and *tamam* (OK), as well as numbers to help you haggle.

CULTURE Though many Turks consider themselves "secular" and "European," Turkey is 99% Muslim and very different from the rest of Europe. Visitors to mosques should cover their arms and legs and try to avoid prayer times. Women should dress modestly at all times to avoid unwanted attention, although shorts and bikinis are the norm in highly touristed resort towns. Only a few men will persist in harassing a woman accompanied by a man. Gays are not likely to be hassled, although the average Turk's attitude was summed up as follows by one university student: "Gays are human like us and have thoughts, too." Give them another 100 years.

Istanbul

Istanbul is in the midst of remaking itself, a process that has continued on and off for the past 1,600 years, throughout the city's history as Roman Constantinople, Byzantium, and Ottoman and Turkish Istanbul. Today the city is asserting its influence in the eastern Mediterranean and around the Black Sea, as evidenced by an onslaught of opportunity-seeking immigrants from Eastern Europe and mystically inclined tourists from the West. The current attempt to pull Istanbul into the financial ranks of the Western European capitals involves tearing up streets and bringing the bridges up to at least 19th-century standards. Despite these heady stabs at making Istanbul a city of the future, the town is incorrigibly old-fashioned. Some avenues carry massive amounts of whirring traffic, but back streets are filled with artisans, vendors, children playing, and old men discussing the past over glasses of *çi* (tea). Domes and minarets fight hotels and telecommunications towers for skyline space.

The recent changes have left the city somewhere between charmingly fragmented and frustratingly unworkable. Muezzins, the Muslim criers who once called the faithful to prayer, have been replaced by recordings and public-address systems; pilgrims pile out of air-conditioned buses to camp by the walls of Topkapı Palace, and you can stand between the glorious Blue Mosque and the wondrous Hagia Sophia as you withdraw lunch money from the Yapı Kredi 24 ATM. Contradiction has always been one of Istanbul's defining characteristics, and locals take these latest developments in stride. So don't be disappointed if you find yourself sipping an espresso at a pseudo-French café off İstiklâl Caddesi rather than a drink poured from an ornate pot strapped to a man's back in the Sultanahmet. They're equally authentic Istanbul experiences.

HALICIOĞLU

Çakırbeyler Sok.

Kumbarahane Cad.

Bypass

İstanbul

Ayvansaray Cad.

AYVANSARAY

Demirhisar Cad.

BALAT

Müselpaşa Cad.

FENER

Draman Cad.

EDİRNEKAPI

Fevzipaşa Cad.

Akşemsettin Cad.

Akdeniz Cad.

Haliçılar Cad.

Vatan Cad.

TO TOPKAPI TERMINUS

Millet Cad.

Cerrahpaşa Cad.

AKSARAY

Namık Kemal Cad.

HASKÖY

Haşköy Cad.

Okmeydanı Cad.

Kasımpaşa

KULAKSIZ MEZARLIĞI

Kulaksız Cad.

Tay Sokağı

Hacıhüsrev Cad.

İpliçi Sok.

YEN

Yenişehir Cad.

Tarlabaşı

İstiklal C.

BEYC

Haşköy Yolu Melez Sok.

KASIMPAŞA

Bahriye Cad.

TEPEBAŞI

Asmalı Mescit Sok.

Refik Saydam Cad.

Postacılar S.

Yeniçarşı C.

İstiklal Cad.

Haliç (Golden Horn)

Evliyaçelebi Cad.

Yolcuzade Cad.

THY

Kemeraltı Cad.

Necatibey Cad.

Kemankeş

Tersane Cad.

Voyvoda Cad.

Atatürk Bridge

GALATA Cad.

Tünel Subway Line

Postacılar S.

Fe Do

Yavuz Selim Cad.

Tabak Yunus

Haliç Caddesi

Abdülezel paşa Cad.

Karadeniz Cad.

Cibali Cad.

Salihpaşa Cad.

UNKAPANI

Galata Bridge

Eminönü Ferry Docks

Macarkardeşler Cad.

İftaiye Cad.

Atatürk Bulvarı

Hatbar Cad.

Şehzadebaşı Cad.

KÜÇÜKPAZAR

Ragıp Günüşpala Cad.

Yeni Postahane Cad.

Kalpakçılar Cad.

Katipvefa Cad.

LÂLELİ

BEYAZIT

Ordu Cad.

Besim Ömer paşa Cad.

Fuatpaşa Cad.

Uzunçarşı Cad.

Mustafa Kemal Cad.

Tiyatro Cad.

Gediкpaşa Cad.

Türkeli Cad.

Kadırgalimanı Cad.

KUMKAPI

Yeniçeriler Cad.

ALEMDAR

Divanyolu Cad.

Üçler Sok.

Mehmet

Kennedy Cad.

SULTANAHMET

Kennedy Cad.

Sea of

Kennedy Cad.

EMİNÖNÜ

Sirkeci Station

SİRKECİ

CAĞALOĞLU

Ankara Cad.

Yerebatan

③

⑤

⑦

⑥

⑧

⑨

⑩

⑬

⑭

⑮

④

Ahırkapı

Kabasakal

Alemdar

Kurtuluş C.

YEN

①

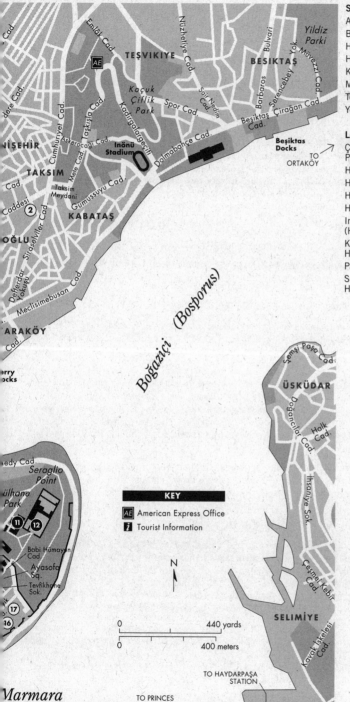

Sights
Arkeoloji Müzesi, **11**
Blue Mosque, **13**
Hagia Sophia, **10**
Hippodrome, **6**
Kapali Çarşi, **4**
Misir Çarşisi, **3**
Topkapi Sarayi, **12**
Yerebatan Sarayi, **8**

Lodging
Çelik Guest House
Pension, **14**
Hotel Ayasofya, **5**
Hotel Nomade, **7**
Hotel Pelikan, **1**
Hotel Şark, **2**
Interyouth Hostel
(HI), **9**
Konyali Youth
Hostel, **17**
Pansiyon Ilknur, **16**
Sultan Tourist
Hostel II, **15**

TEŞVIKIYE

BEŞIKTAŞ

Yildiz
Parki

Nüzhetiye Cad.

Bulvari

Yok. Müvezzi Cad.

Enlât Cad.

Koçuk
Çiflik
Park

Şair Nedim
Cad.

Barbaros

Serencebey

Çirağan Cad.

Beşiktaş
Cad.

Spor Cad.

Kadırgalargeçit

Dolmabahçe Cad.

Beşiktaş
Docks

TO
ORTAKÖY

İnönü
Stadium

dere Cad.

Cumhuriyet Cad.

Askerocağı Cad.

Taşkışla Cad.

Mete Cad.

NİŞEHİR

TAKSIM

Taksim
Meydani

Gümüşsuyu Cad.

Caddesi

②

Siraselviler Cad.

KABATAŞ

OĞLU

Defterdar
Yokuşu

Meclisimebusan Cad.

ARAKÖY

Cad.

erry
ocks

Boğaziçi (Bosporus)

Şemşi Paşa Cad.

ÜSKÜDAR

Doğancilar Cad.

Halk
Cad.

İhsaniye Sok.

edy Cad.

Seraglio
Point

ülhane
Park

⑪ ⑫

Babi Hümayan
Cad.

Ayasofa
Sq.

Tevfikhane
Sok.

⑰

⑯

KEY

AE American Express Office

🛈 Tourist Information

N

Çeşmel Kebir
Cad.

SELIMIYE

Kavak İskelesi
Cad.

0   440 yards

0   400 meters

Marmara

TO PRINCES
ISLANDS

TO HAYDARPAŞA
STATION

BASICS

VISITOR INFORMATION The tourist agents in the Sultanahmet district (Sultanahmet Meydanı 3, at north tip of Hippodrome, tel. 1/518–18–02; open Mon.–Sat. 9–5) are much friendlier than those at the airport information kiosk. There are other offices at the Karaköy ferry docks and near the junction of Istiklâl Caddesi and Yeniçarşı Caddesi in the Beyoğlu district.

AMERICAN EXPRESS **Türk Ekspres** holds mail and can help you with American Express traveler's checks and credit cards. *Lobby of Istanbul Hilton Hotel, 80200 Harbiye-Istanbul, tel. 1/241–02–48 or 1/241–02–49. Bus 74 from Eminönü to Hilton. Open weekdays 9–5.*

CHANGING MONEY Recently, a boom of exchange agencies has effectively replaced the black market. Agencies usually offer better rates than banks, but they charge a commission on traveler's checks, while most banks don't. Yapı Kredi 24 and AkMatik ATMs litter the city, giving you access to your Visa, Cirrus, or Plus account. **Ak Bank** has a currency-exchange machine open 24 hours at the Istiklâl Caddesi branch. From Taksim Meydanı, walk south one block on Istiklâl Caddesi.

CONSULATES **Australia.** *Tepecik Yolu Uzeri 58, Etiler, tel. 1/257–70–50.*

Canada. *Büyükdere Cad. 107, Gayrettepe, tel. 1/272–51–74.*

United Kingdom. *Meşrutiyet Cad. 34, Beyoğlu, tel. 1/244–75–40.*

United States. *Meşrutiyet Cad. 104–108, Tepebaşı, tel. 1/251–36–02.*

EMERGENCIES **Ambulance** (tel. 112), **fire** (tel. 110), **police** (tel. 155).

Tourist Police. These well-armed, English-speaking police can help out 24 hours a day with minor tourist catastrophes like theft and harassment. Their most convenient representative is the guy with the machine gun on the corner of Divanyolu Caddesi and Yerebatan Caddesi (also called Hilâliahmer Caddesi), near Hagia Sophia. *Tel. 1/527–45–03.*

PHONES AND MAIL You can dial direct anywhere in the world from a yellow PTT pay phone. Some phones accept cards, some accept tokens; buy either from the ubiquitous PTT stations (most open daily 9–5), from an orange street kiosk, or—for a nominally higher fee— from a newsstand or hawker. The cards run out quickly when you call abroad. For credit-card calls, dial your long-distance company's access code (*see* Basics, *above*) on a token-operated phone.

The stamp-vending machine near the Yapı Kredi 24 ATM in front of Hagia Sophia is especially handy when the schedule of current postal rates is tacked up. The main post office offers poste-restante service: Address letters to Büyük PTT, Yeni Postahane Caddesi, Sirkeci.

COMING AND GOING

BY TRAIN Istanbul has two train stations. **Sirkeci** (tel. 1/527–00–51), on the Golden Horn, serves Europe and is an appropriately exotic terminus for the *Orient Express.* You can reach the station by bus, by Tramvay, or on a ferry bound for the Eminönü district. A train runs daily at 11:30 PM to Athens (23 hrs, $45). **Haydarpaşa** (tel. 1/348–80–20), across the Bosporus, serves the east with two trains daily to Ankara (7½ hrs, $8.50). The quickest way to Haydarpaşa is via ferry from the Karaköy docks, northeast of the Galata Bridge.

BY BUS Comfortable, well-equipped Turkish buses are a much better bet than trains. The **Topkapı Terminus** (not to be confused with Topkapı Palace) handles all bus traffic; it's west of the city center. There are daily departures for Athens (20 hrs, $48), and several buses run daily to Edirne (4 hrs, $9). Students get a 15% discount on most tickets. Buy your ticket at the terminal or at a travel agency in town; tickets are pretty much the same price no matter where you get them.

BY PLANE The depressing **Atatürk International Airport** (Yeşilköy, tel. 1/574–83–00) has domestic and international flights through two terminals. To get into Istanbul, board the hourly bus ($2) operated by Turkish Airlines, and get off at Aksaray. From there you can take the Tramvay (20¢) to the Sultanahmet.

GETTING AROUND

Istanbul is constantly on the move, but don't expect to reach your destination quickly—the city simply goes nowhere at a breakneck pace. The public transportation system is massively disjointed, with trolleys, buses, and trains working near but not exactly in sync with each other. Walking can be just as frustrating: Sidewalks narrow to 2 feet on busy throughways, and taxis refuse to slow down or swerve to avoid foot traffic.

The worst thing you can do in Istanbul is stop moving. Standing still amid the city's perpetual motion could result in pandemonium.

The **Boğaziçi** (Bosporus) strait divides European Istanbul, where all the sights are, from Asian Istanbul. The **Haliç** (Golden Horn) waterway creates a peninsula where sightseers spend most of their time. If you stay in the **Sultanahmet,** the region nearest the tip of the peninsula, well-known sights are within easy walking distance. **Taxis** become useful at night, when most public transport stops running. Hail one as you would a cab at home, and be sure the driver turns on the meter. The **Tünel** is a subway with two stops; the one known simply as "Tünel" is at the base of Istiklâl Caddesi, and the other is at the Karaköy docks. It's good for a quick zip up the hill in this part of town; purchase tokens (40¢) at either end.

BY BUS Buses are the best way to get across the Haliç from the Sultanahmet. They operate out of various stations, including Eminönü and Taksim, scattered throughout the city and recognizable by the mass of people looking expectantly up the road. Buy tickets from the white kiosks at stations (40¢) or from a street vendor (50¢), and establish the destination and route of a bus with the list of neighborhood names to the right of the bus door.

BY DOLMUS Dolmuş, shared taxis traveling specified routes, are a common and convenient form of transport throughout most of Istanbul—*if* you have a map or know the routes by heart. Otherwise, you'll have to ask a lot of questions, since routes are marked only at the first and last stops. Catch dolmuş at stops or hail them like taxis. They're especially useful at night for moving between clubs.

BY FERRY Istanbul's ferry system moves tens of thousands of people between Europe and Asia every day. Destinations are spelled out at the dock terminals. Most ferries depart from Eminönü, shipping out about every five minutes. It costs 50¢ for a token to get through the turnstile. There are also ferry docks at Karaköy, across the Galata bridge from Eminönü.

BY TRAMVAY The Eminönü–Topkapı Tramvay is smooth and quick and covers a wide range of districts. The antique cars of the Taksim–Tünel line are less efficient, but they're good for a joy ride along Istiklâl Caddesi. In major stations you can purchase tickets (20¢) at kiosks; at small stations you have to pay a street vendor 10¢ more.

WHERE TO SLEEP

The lodging situation in Istanbul has changed in the past few years. The **Lâleli** and **Aksaray** districts, once perfect for budget travelers, are still cheap and central, but now you'll meet mostly prostitutes and families looking for deals on knockoff Lacoste T-shirts. The districts of **Taksim** and especially **Sultanahmet** are a better bet. Most hotels throw in breakfast with the room price. During summer (or winter for the hardy), many budget hotels offer rooftop accommodations—involving anything from a cement slab to chairs and cushions—for about $4.

SULTANAHMET The sunny Sultanahmet district offers an ever-growing number of modest hotels within a short distance of the best historical sights. Particularly central is the tidy **Hotel Ayasofya** (Yerebatan Cad. 33, near Hagia Sophia, tel. 1/522–71–26; doubles $15–$20).

➤ **UNDER $15 • Pansiyon Ilknur.** Manager's charm more than compensates for her lack of English skills. Stunning view of the sea from rear balcony. Two four-bed rooms $10, top-floor dorm beds $2.50. *Terbıyık Sok. 22, across from Konyalı Youth Hostel (see below), tel. 1/517–68–34.*

➤ **UNDER $25 • Celik Guest House Pension.** New and central, next to carpet bazaar in little row of stores and cafés. Standard furnishings, helpful front desk. Singles $10, doubles $20. *Mimar Mehmetağa Cad. 22, tel. 1/518–96–75. From Sultanahmet plaza in front of Blue Mosque, southeast on Mimar Mehmetağa Cad.*

➤ **UNDER $35 • Hotel Nomade.** Tastefully decorated with carpets from the shop downstairs. Stunning view of Blue Mosque and Hagia Sophia from rooftop terrace. Enthusiastic staff. Singles from $20, doubles from $30. *Ticarethane Sok. 7–9, tel. 1/511–12–96. From Sultanahmet Tramvay station, 1 block east on Divanyolu Cad., left on Ticarethane Sok.; red building on west side of street. AE, MC.*

TAKSIM On the other side of the Haliç, the Taksim district offers a vibrant nightlife and café scene, but the hotels here tend to be cramped, dirty, noisy, and overpriced.

➤ **UNDER $15 • Hotel Pelikan.** Large, older hotel in the heart of the Istiklâl Caddesi area. Street-side rooms are sunny in the afternoon. All rooms with private shower. Doubles $12. *Asmalı Mescit Sok. 44, tel. 1/251–89–34. From Taksim Meydanı, south on Istiklâl Cad., right on Asmalı Mescit Sok.*

Hotel Sark. Bare-bones accommodations if you need a cheap bed in the area. Not a hangout for prostitutes, but it can be loud at night nonetheless. Close to popular nighttime cafés. Doubles $6. *K. Parmakkapı Sok. 40, tel. 1/243–48–67. From Taksim Meydanı, south on Istiklâl Cad. 2 blocks, left on K. Parmakkapı Sok.*

HOSTELS **Interyouth Hostel (HI).** Well-run, safe, and clean. Incredible location near Hagia Sophia. Popular after-hours café downstairs features an occasional belly dancer. Reservations by fax only. Beds $6.50. *Caferiye Sok. 6, tel. 1/513–61–50 or 1/513–61–51, fax 1/512–76–28. Laundry, luggage storage.*

Konyalı Youth Hostel. Front rooms are noisy by day, back rooms by night. Cat-loving owners share kitchen and washing machine with well-mannered guests. Simple, clean rooms; backyard terrace serves 80¢ beer. Singles $4, doubles $9, dorm beds $2.50–$3. *Terbıyık Sok. 15, tel. 1/518–94–68. From Hagia Sophia, southwest on Babi Hümayun Cad., left on Tevfikhane Sok., left on Kutlugun Sok., right on Adliye Sok. to dead end, right on Terbıyık Sok.*

Sultan Tourist Hostel II. Popular hangout for backpackers of all breeds, especially Kiwis and Australians. Share your wisdom on graffiti-covered wall in backyard beer garden. Reserve ahead during high season. Doubles $10, singles $8, dorm beds $4. *Terbıyık Sok. 3, near Konyalı Youth Hostel (see above), tel. 1/516–92–60.*

CAMPGROUNDS **Ataköy Tatil Köyü.** Full facilities in slightly wooded location some distance from center. Staff speaks little English, but they try their best. Sites $3. *Ataköy, tel. 1/572–35–42 or 1/572–35–43. Bus 82 from Eminönü to Ataköy.*

FOOD

For such a cosmopolitan place, Istanbul's food scene is strikingly unimaginative. The day's major meal is a dinner of soup, salad, and vegetables. Lunch means a sandwich, and breakfast is virtually nonexistent.

SULTANAHMET In general, you should avoid the Sultanahmet's hastily prepared, over-priced food. A few places can bail you out if you're staying in the area, however.

➤ **UNDER $5** • **Doy-Doy.** Some of the cheapest, freshest Turkish food around—a favorite with budget travelers. Kebaps $1.70, drinks 60¢; you can stuff yourself for less than $3.50. *Sifa Hamamı Sok. 13, tel. 1/517–15–88. From south end of Hippodrome, south on Nakil-bent Sok., east on Sifa Hamamı Sok.*

Meshur Halk Köftecisi. Food and ambience at this local joint defy its touristy location. Floor covered with sand, walls with letters from famous Turks. Great *köfte* (spicy meatballs; $1.50) and zingy salads (80¢). *Divanyolu Cad. 12, 2 blocks east of Sultanahmet Tramvay station.*

➤ **UNDER $10** • **Kathisma.** A nice treat in the midst of the Sultanahmet hotels. Owner seems to have gotten hooked on high-concept design during his training in Vienna, so you get to eat among exposed brick and brushed aluminum. Salads $2, kebaps $4.50. *Yeni Akbıyık Cad. 26, 1 block from Sultan Tourist Hostel II, tel. 1/518–97–10.*

Yerebatan/Ciçekler. Standard Turkish fare served with astounding grace. German-trained owner bursts with pride over his full bar. Try cold starters ($1) with hot, crisp bread baked on the premises. *Yerebatan Cad. 15, 1 block north of intersection of Yerebatan Cad. and Divanyolu Cad, tel. 1/527–44–98.*

You'll be offered shot-size glasses of çi, a potent tea, at every juncture, whether someone's trying to get you to buy a kilim (carpet) or celebrating your excellent Australian accent. Locals bolt it all day long, and recent horror stories about drugged tea shouldn't entirely dissuade you from having a glass, although you should use common sense about the situation.

TAKSIM/BEYOGLU The popular, pleasant sidewalk restaurants along **Nevizade Sokak,** near Istiklâl Caddesi and the Ciçek Pasaji (Flower Market), serve meals for about $5. On **Sahne Sokak** west of Istiklâl Caddesi you'll find a bunch of good restaurants, including **Mercan Cafe Birahane** (Sahne Sok. 13 and 18, tel. 1/245–55–74), where you can feast on fried mussels and beer for $2.50.

➤ **UNDER $5** • **Bereket Döner & Köfte Salonu.** Fairly orthodox Muslims serve up damned fine food. Well-known to locals, but the obscure location keeps it off the tourist track. Good selection of vegetables ($1.50) and rice dishes. *Fuat Uzkinay Sok. 17/A, 1 block east of Istiklâl Cad.*

➤ **UNDER $10** • **Cati.** Traditional Turkish food prepared better than usual, seven stories above the city. Filled with plants and boisterous conversation; popular with Istanbul's literati. Meals $8. *Orhan A. Apaydın Sok. 20, tel. 1/251–00–00. 1 block northwest of Istiklâl Cad.; enter lobby on north side of street, take elevator to 7th floor.*

Papirus. A truly great restaurant that pays homage to Istanbul's cosmopolitan history. Playbills from around the world cover the walls. Beautifully prepared food includes $7 steaks that are worth every lira. Special requests often honored. Call for reservations. *Ayhan Isik Sok., Erman-han 5, tel. 1/251–14–28. From Istiklâl Cad., east on Ayhan Isik Sok.*

WORTH SEEING

ARKEOLOJI MUZESI One of the oldest ancient-art collections open to the public outside Western Europe and the United States, the Archaeological Museum houses a stunning collection of Mediterranean and Near Eastern art. Under Ottoman intellectual Osman Hamdi Bey's direction, the museum unearthed what many believe is the tomb of Alexander the Great, at an unmarked site in Egypt. Along with the tomb, the museum's collection includes a lion from the mausoleum at Halicarnassus, pottery from ancient Troy, and an exceptional gathering of athletes, nymphs, poets, and soldiers made immortal in marble. In 1993 the museum received the prestigious Council of Europe award for its displays, although it appears the prize was given as much for what the museum will become as for what it is today—like much of Istanbul, the building is undergoing renovation. *Topkapı Palace, tel. 1/520–77–40. Admission: $2.50, $1.25 students. Open Wed.–Mon. 8:30–5.*

BLUE MOSQUE In the middle of the Sultanahmet sits the Blue Mosque, or Sultan Ahmet Camii, a stone mountain of domes, half-domes, and minarets rising out of the trees opposite Hagia Sophia. The structure was built in the early 17th century under the patronage of Ottoman ruler Sultan Ahmet, who wanted to prove that Islam could produce a building as beautiful and impressive as Christendom's Hagia Sophia. Architect Mehmet Aga designed a structure that not only fits in well with its regal neighbors, but exhibits a harmonious relationship between exterior and interior.

The mosque gained its name from the thousands of blue tiles covering the inside, which create a dazzling symphony of Arabic script and patterns. The interior of the mosque is most graceful at night, when electric chandeliers cast brilliant lights and severe shadows throughout the building. The exterior hosts an almost nightly light show with accompanying dialogue in Turkish, English, French, and German. If you're wearing shorts or a short-sleeved shirt, you'll have to don a muslin cloth at the door, where you must also leave your shoes—it's polite to give the shoe holder a nominal tip. Don't sit with your feet pointing toward Mecca (the altar). *Sultanahmet. Admission free. Open daily from first to last prayer, except during prayer and ceremonies.*

HAGIA SOPHIA One of the most magnificent buildings ever constructed, Hagia Sophia (also known as Aya Sofya) has been both the central church of Christendom and the major inspiration for the mosques of Islam. Built in 532 under the patronage of Emperor Justinian, the church was designed by the mathematician Anthemius and the scientist Isidorus, who used their scientific skills to create a dome 108 feet in diameter, a size that remained unsurpassed until the construction of Michelangelo's dome at St. Peter's in Rome 1,000 years later. The seemingly impossible stability of Hagia Sophia awed the faithful; the unfaithful had their day when the dome partially collapsed in 558. The next dome was higher than the first, but stress caused by lateral pressure forced repairs in 989 and again in 1346. After that, the dome held up pretty well until recently, when it again underwent renovation.

Once the Turks conquered Constantinople in 1453, the church was converted into a mosque. In the mid-15th century, its mosaics were plastered over in accordance with the Islamic belief that the physical world shouldn't be represented in religious art. The bodies and legs of angels on the pendentives were turned into a mess of wings; the effect is psychedelic. Atatürk ended the religious career of the building in 1936, uncovering some of the original mosaics and

The Blue Mosque According to Freud?

A current topic of academic discussion is the combination of phallic and mammary forms in traditional Islamic architecture. Put simply, mosques look like a series of breasts and penises stacked next to each other. The Blue Mosque is a fine subject for this sexually charged interpretation—six minarets stand in rigid contradiction to the dome's curvaceous mass. Much could be said about Islam's ability to bring strong male and female forms into structural and visual harmony, and about the mosque's shape as a symbol for the highest ideals of Muslim society. Whether you agree with this revisionist version of the building's significance, or whether you think architects used domes because they were impressive and minarets because they were practical places from which to call people to prayer, the potential symbolism does make titillating conversation with a stranger.

establishing it in its present role as a sight only. *Sultanahmet, tel. 1/522–17–50. Admission: $4, $2 students. Open Tues.–Sun. 9:30–4:30.*

ORTAKOY Far removed from the city center and the white kneecaps of tourists is the tiny waterfront district of Ortaköy. In the shadow of the Boğaziçi Bridge, Ortaköy is a 10-block area whose cobblestone streets have recently been taken over by cafés, baked-potato stands, and poetic graffiti composed in endearingly dysfunctional English. Mellow during the day, the district fills up at night with Istanbul's young bohemian crowd, thirsting for an alternative time. Sundays the streets are overrun with an arts-and-crafts bazaar, drawing shoppers from all over the city. *On the river, south of Boğaziçi Bridge. Bus 22, 22A, or 22C from Eminönü; Bus 23B from Taksim.*

TOPKAPI SARAYI Overlooking the Sea of Marmara, Topkapı Palace is an eclectic, sumptuous collection of landscaped courtyards and elegant buildings. Construction began in the mid-15th century, and the palace was enlarged according to the tastes of Ottoman sultans and their mothers for 400 years, until Sultan Abdül Mecit abandoned it for more Western-looking digs in an attempt to get accepted by European royalty as one of the gang. Topkapı Palace today contains a series of museum galleries that unfold over four courtyards and the *Harem* (Forbidden). The Harem, a sort of gilded cage composed of hundreds of salons, baths, and bedrooms, held the sultan and his mother—the second most powerful person in the empire—as well as his wives, brothers (kept in virtual isolation lest they aspire to the throne prematurely), children, concubines, and female slaves. Although only a fraction of the Harem is open to the public (by guided tour only; admission $1), you'll see enough inlaid furniture and silk-lined domes to get a taste of its royal flavor.

The four courtyards of the palace are flanked by former kitchens and janissary quarters, now watch museums and manuscript galleries. The treasury in the third courtyard holds such booty as an 86-karat diamond (mounted on a motorized velvet cushion to better catch the light), an over-full bucket of emeralds, clippings from the beard of the prophet Mohammed, and the occipital bone of St. John the Baptist. If you're not up for a museum visit, the arcades, marble terraces, and incredible views of the palace grounds make for a pleasant afternoon on their own. *Sultanahmet, tel. 1/512–04–80. Behind Hagia Sophia, to the southeast. Admission: $5, $2.50 students. Open Wed.–Mon. 8:30–5.*

YEREBATAN SARAYI Rumbling trams and carpet salesmen shouting in the streets contrast with the almost churchlike peacefulness of this expansive underground sanctuary. The Yerebatan Sarayı is a subterranean water reservoir built by Emperor Justinian in the 6th century to keep a steady water supply for imperial Constantinople. The cistern was used until the mid-1980s, when it was drained and opened to the public. Water continues to drip from the vaulted brick ceiling, cooling the columned space and adding a soothing accompaniment to the piped-in arias. *Yerebatan Cad., north of intersection with Divanyolu Cad., across from Tourist Police. Admission: $5. Open daily 9–5.*

CHEAP THRILLS

The annual **Istanbul Festival** runs from mid-June through July, hosting the likes of Sting, Joan Baez, and John Scofield in an ever-growing collection of outdoor and indoor concert halls. Buy tickets ($1–$30) at the Atatürk Cultural Center (Mete Cad., at Taksim Meydanı, tel. 1/251–56–00).

A Turkish bath is the most glorious torture you can inflict upon yourself. The ritual of being scalded, beaten, and cooled down causes physical (and sometimes spiritual) rebirth. The Sultanahmet harbors several notorious baths, but you'll get a better deal at **Tarihi Galatasaray Hamamı** (24 Turnacıbaşı Sok., 1 block east of Istiklâl Cad., tel. 1/144–14–12 for men, 1/149–43–42 for women), where the works cost about $10.

Brooding old men contemplate a broken fountain while sucking on ancient hookahs and sipping çi (30¢) at **Erenler Nargile Salonu** (36 Yeniçeriler Cad., Beyazıt, tel. 1/528–37–85), one of Istanbul's last traditional tea gardens, in the overgrown courtyard of an old mosque.

The most beautiful, cost-efficient way to see Istanbul is from the deck of a city-transit ferry (*see* Getting Around, *above*). Although rush-hour crowds and smoke can be less than romantic, a sunset view of the city's minarets and parks is worth the minor discomfort. You can take any ferry; the Eminönü–Kadiköy line is leisurely and usually less crowded than others.

SHOPPING

Most travelers to Istanbul do their shopping, for better or worse, in the **Kapalı Carşı** (Grand Bazaar) in Beyazıt, open Monday–Saturday 8:30–6:30. The bazaar dates from the 1450s; these days it's a hangout for tourists, who are smug about having negotiated $1 off the price of a cardboard fez. The bazaar is better for sightseeing than shopping; if you want to actually buy something, try the smaller, quieter **Mısır Carşısı** (Spice, or Egyptian, Bazaar), in Eminönü south of Yeni Mosque. Open Monday–Saturday 8–7, it offers excellent deals on nuts, dried fruits, spices, and the occasional cardboard fez.

AFTER DARK

BARS Istanbul's youth have the makings of good rockers—they have the right hair, jeans, and attitude and a working knowledge of the Doors and the Velvet Underground. Proto-bohemians hang at **Café Guitar** (Ayhan Isik Sok., 1 block east of Istiklâl Cad.), drinking Efes Pilsen ($1) and playing darts until the live music kicks in, all the while maintaining their disdainful cool. Off the northern end of Istiklâl Caddesi, along **Aptullah Sokak,** a number of mellow café-bars offer backgammon, beer, and conversation as alternatives to the Taksim discos.

Istanbul's clubs fall in and out of fashion as rapidly as Italy changes its government. What's here today will be here tomorrow, but all the hip people will be somewhere else.

With live music, a dance floor, and a full bar (beer $2–$3), the **Sis Bar** (Yapur Iskelesi Sok. 4, Ortaköy, in southwest corner of pedestrian district) attracts many of Ortaköy's Beautiful People. Closer to the Sultanahmet, the rooftop bar of the **Orient Youth Hostel** (Akbıyık Cad. 13, in middle of hotel district) does an admirable job of keeping the music loud in an otherwise quiet neighborhood. In addition to countless Dutch and Kiwis buzzed off large 75¢ beers, the bar is known for the occasional belly dancer. If you're too lazy to move, almost every hotel offers at least a chair and a refrigerator stocked with beer.

MUSIC AND CLUBS A good resource for clubs is *The Guide,* a bimonthly English-language magazine available at newsstands for $3. The famed **Andromeda** (call 1/246–01–68 for current location), an almost grotesque mix of lasers, lights, and faux-marble columns, is touted as Europe's largest disco. Like most Istanbul clubs, Andromeda spends winter in Taksim and summer in larger outdoor quarters on the Boğaziçi—at all times of the year, taxi drivers know where to find it.

Northwestern Turkey

The northwestern corner of Turkey, bordering Bulgaria to the north and Greece to the west, isn't the most popular region for today's travelers, nor was it for history's conquerors. Although every general within marching distance hoped to get hold of Istanbul, most passed through the inhospitable northwest, which sizzles in summer and turns bleak in winter. Still, with the Black Sea to the north and the Saros Gulf and Sea of Marmara to the south, the region can hardly avoid having some beautiful, pebbly coastline. And if you're tired of hanging out with rowdy Americans in nearby Greece, you'll be able to escape them here. Your traveling companions will most likely be Eastern European day-trippers, especially in Edirne, home of the largest mosque outside Mecca and world capital of the sport of grease wrestling.

Edirne

Edirne makes a great stopover on a journey from Greece or Bulgaria to Istanbul. Here you'll find the second-largest mosque in the world, in the center of a market town that caters to Bulgarians and Romanians on shopping expeditions for Western clothes and electronics. The market Semiz Ali Paşa Çarşısı has burned down, but remaining markets include **Arasta,** in front of Selimiye Camii, and **Bedesten,** in front of Eski Camii. Don't get too excited by the spectacular market buildings; the merchandise inside is pretty tacky. Locals dress in jeans and T-shirts, and only a few women wear the türban.

Weekending soldiers wander through Edirne's markets, choosing among postcards of naked women with nipples censored by black stars.

Edirne's major mosque, **Selimiye Camii,** designed by Mimar Sinan in 1569, has minarets 235 feet high and a dome that surpasses that of Istanbul's Hagia Sophia in diameter. The interior was repainted in bright, contemporary colors in 1989, and the tiles and stonework are spotless. Edirne has a few other mosques worth exploring. The dramatic calligraphy on the walls of **Eski Camii** is still visible, although the mosque is undergoing restoration. **Muradiye Camii,** north of the town center on a hill, has impressive Iznik tiles but is open only sporadically.

Behind Selimiye Camii, the **Archaeological and Ethnographical Museum** and the **Turkish Islamic Art Museum** (both open Tues.–Sun. 9–5) store calligraphy, Greek artifacts, and photos on the history of *yaǧli güreş* (grease wrestling). During the yearly **Kırkpınar Festival** at the end of June or beginning of July, people pour into town to dance and listen to Gypsy music for four days and watch yaǧli güreş for three.

BASICS At the **tourist information office** (Talatpaşa Cad. 17, near Hürriyet Meydanı, tel. 181/51518), you can get a map of Edirne and assistance with hotels. At the **PTT** (Saraçlar Cad. 17), you can exchange money without commission and use phone and mail services 24 hours a day.

COMING AND GOING Buses are the most efficient way to get to and from Istanbul, 230 km east (4 hrs, $6). They leave from the otogar, 2 km southeast of Edirne. Buses to the Bulgarian border, 18 km away, leave from behind Eski Camii. If you plan to cross the border, you'll have to first stop by the **Bulgarian Consulate** (Talatpaşa Asfaltı, tel. 181/51069) for a visa. The Greek border crossing, 6 km south of Edirne, is open 8 AM–1 PM only. Buses leave from behind Eski Camii and stop at **Karaağac.** From there it's a 3-km walk or $3 taxi ride to the border. Trains depart from a station 1 km from the otogar, and take seven hours to reach Istanbul.

The main street, **Talatpaşa Caddesi,** runs from the **Tunca River** east through town, intersecting with **Saraçlar Caddesi,** the biggest north–south street. There's a fountain and café in the central square, **Hürriyet Meydanı,** near the intersection of the two streets.

WHERE TO SLEEP AND EAT **Konak Hotel** (Maarif Cad. 6, tel. 181/51348; doubles $7), off Talatpaşa Caddesi near the tourist office, is the best budget choice, with a rose garden, a fountain, and grand marble steps. **Saray Otel** (Eski Istanbul Cad. 28, tel. 181/21457; doubles $8), southeast off Saraçlar Caddesi, is lit by neon and decorated in apple green. **Rüstempaşa Hotel Kervansaray** (immediately south of Eski Camii, tel. 181/12195; doubles $25), in a building designed by Sinan 400 years ago with beautiful arches and a shady garden, houses a loud, seedy disco. The campground **Fifi Mocamp** (tel. 181/11554), 9 km along the E5 toward Istanbul, charges $4 per person.

You'll find great desserts and Turkish delight at the pastanesis along Saraçlar Caddesi, and markets all over town sell picnic fixings. *Ciǧer* (deep-fried liver), a ubiquitous local specialty, is available at most restaurants. **Restaurant Uçler** (behind PTT, tel. 181/52776) has good veggie options, including *imam bayıldı* (literally, "the Imam fainted"), eggplant stuffed with tomato and onion and spiced with jalapeño and paprika. A full meal is $2. **Park Restaurant** (Maarif Cad., tel. 181/55657) serves cheap kebaps and *ezo gelin* (rice and vegetable soup).

Bursa

Below the northern slopes of the Ulüdağ peak lies the elongated city of Bursa. The town grew when Romans flocked to nearby Cekirge and the baths of Ulüdağ northwest of the city, which are still popular with Arabs today. In 1326 Bursa became the first Ottoman capital, and remained so until Edirne assumed the role in 1402. The first six Ottoman sultans are buried here. Ottoman architectural styles were developed in Bursa, too, laying the foundation for more elaborate works found in Edirne and Istanbul. The minarets of more than 100 mosques make an impressive skyline, although today Bursa's urban sprawl mars its beauty.

The magnificent **Yeşil Camii** (Green Mosque), east of the Heykel area, is an example of the first purely Turkish architecture. The unfinished mosque (admission free) is covered with blue and green Iznik tiles. Next door, **Yeşil Türbe,** the Green Tomb (admission free; open daily 8:30–noon and 1–5:30), contains the enormous green-tiled sarcophagus of Mehmet I, who ordered work on the mosque to begin in 1421. The 14th-century **Bedesten** (Covered Bazaar) was carefully restored after a massive earthquake flattened it in 1855. Here you can find *ipek* (silk cloth), and camel-skin puppets used as props in a comic theatrical form called *Karagöz,* named after a legendary clown from the 14th century. In Cekirge, **Eski Kaplucaları,** the restored ancient marble baths next to Kervansaray Temal Hotel, are a decadent place to spend the afternoon soaking ($5) or getting a scrub and massage ($20).

BASICS You'll find **tourist information** booths at the otogar and west of Heykel on Atatürk Caddesi (tel. 24/112–959). Both booths are helpful, but neither has a good city map. The **PTT** (200 meters west of Heykel) is the destination of poste-restante letters.

COMING AND GOING The **otogar** is 2 km north of Heykel; a dolmuş to the center of town costs 30¢. Hourly buses go to Istanbul (4 hrs, $6), Ankara (7 hrs, $9), and Izmir (6 hrs, $8). Express **ferries** from Istanbul (3 hrs, $4) arrive five times each weekday. Bursa's dock is at Yalova, a $1, 20-minute dolmuş ride from the city.

GETTING AROUND The main road runs 4 km from the northwest to the southeast and changes names five times, eventually turning into Atatürk Caddesi at the city center. **Heykel,** the area at the center of town near the intersection of Atatürk Caddesi and Inönü Caddesi, is where you'll find the Atatürk statue. The city climbs the Ulüdağ slopes to the south. Walking is the best way to get almost everywhere except the thermal baths in **Cekirge,** a dolmuş ride from Heykel. To picnic or camp on Ulüdağ, take a funicular dolmuş from Heykel and then a cable car (1 hr, $5 round-trip) up to **Sarialan,** a crowded and littered park. You'll find pretty lakes nearby and mediocre skiing December through March ($20 per day for equipment and passes).

WHERE TO SLEEP Avoid the cheap hotels near the otogar and head instead for places just south of Heykel or farther out in Cekirge. Near Atatürk Caddesi is the recently renovated **Hotel Bilgiç** (Ressam Sefik, Bursalı Cad. 30, tel. 24/20–31–90), where you'll pay $11 per person with bath. **Hotel Camlıbel** (Inebey Cad. 71, southwest of PTT, tel. 24/11–25–65), with doubles for $12, is quieter. Next door, look for the friendly **Hotel Cağlayan** (Inebey Cad. 73, tel. 24/21–14–58), where doubles go for $12. In Cekirge, the well-kept **Konak Palas Oteli** (Birinci Murat Camii Arkası 11, tel. 24/36–51–13) has doubles for $12 and thermal baths. **Huzur Oteli** (tel. 24/36–80–21) next door, with doubles for $11, is similar to Konak Palas Oteli, but the rooms have no sinks.

FOOD Famous for its *Iskender kebaps* (mutton kebabs), Bursa is a great town for carnivores. *Inegöl köfresi,* a rich meat patty, is another specialty, as are candied chestnuts, often used in pastries. **Kebapci Iskenderoğlu** (Atatürk Cad. 60), open for lunch only, sells Iskender kebaps for $2. Posh **Ciçek Izgara** (Belediye Cad. 5) has good service, but meals are pricey at $4.

Canakkale

As you approach the naval town of Canakkale, on the Dardanelles straits, by ferry, you see little more than a 2-km sweep of blocky high-rises. Between the buildings, though, you'll discover the narrow streets of a busy old town and to the south, **Cimenlik,** whose name means "fortress hidden by grass." Here a castle houses the naval museum, **Askeri Ve Deniz Müzesi** (tel. 196/71707), and the grounds contain a large collection of artillery guns from the Gallipoli campaign. The mine-laying ship *Nusrat* adjoins the castle museum. The site is open every day but Monday and Friday 9–noon and 1:30–5; buy tickets ($1) at the naval museum.

The small **Archaeological Museum** (Atatürk Cad., tel. 196/73252; open Tues.–Sun.), 2 km from the town center toward Troy, has great jewelry and gold laurel wreaths. To get there, look for a dolmuş marked SEHIRICI in the town center by the cannon monument. After you've done your museum duty for the day, join the locals in walking the waterfront promenade, eat a strawberry ice cream from one of the pastanesis, or watch a soccer match just north of the central **PTT.** You can change money at the PTT, which is near the ferry docks, and get a town map from the **tourist information kiosk** (Iskele Meydanı 67, tel. 196/71187).

COMING AND GOING Dolmuş from Bursa (6 hrs, $6), Istanbul (5 hrs, $8), and other towns arrive at the otogar on Atatürk Caddesi, about a 15-minute walk from the ferry docks. Hourly ferries from Eceabat (50¢) arrive at the docks near the middle of town.

To visit **Kilitbahir,** the fortress opposite Cimenlik, take a motorboat (10 min, 30¢) from the ferry dock. The two fortresses, which flank one of the narrowest points in the Dardanelles, were built by Fatih Sultan Mehmet in 1451 to control the passage of ships into Istanbul (the name *Kilitbahir* means "padlock on the sea").

WHERE TO SLEEP AND EAT Around April 25 (Anzac Day) and during mid-August, when the Troy Festival is held, rooms are hard to find. At other times you can bargain and get a bed for $4. The budget hotels are clustered south of the clock tower near the ferry dock. **Hotel Kervansaray** (Fetvahane Sok. 13, no phone; $4 per person), with high ceilings and a long garden, was a Turkish pasha's mansion 200 years ago. Nearby, the efficiently run **Otel Efes** (Aralık Sok. 5, tel. 196/73256; doubles $8) has less character but is quieter. The more expensive hotels are north of the dock along the esplanade. The best value is the **Berlin Otel** (Kayserili Ahmet Paşa Cad. 18, tel. 196/11986; doubles $12), where rooms come with large, clean bathrooms and terraces. From May to September, **Pansiyon Seru Palas** (Cimenlik Sok. 11, tel. 196/26500; doubles $4) has four rooms opposite the castle. Many campsites lie off the beach along the road to Troy.

Restaurants along the waterfront charge about $5 for a full meal. Try **Entellektüel** (Rihtim Boyu 17, tel. 196/78474) or **Sehir** (Yalı Cad. 24, tel. 196/71070) for good seafood. **Aussie and Kiwi Restaurant** (Yalı Cad. 32, tel. 196/21722) is owned by Kemâl, a hospitable Turk who speaks good English and serves up excellent mackerel and fried eggplant.

NEAR CANAKKALE

TROY If you come to Troy (Truva in Turkish) expecting to see the great city from Homer's *Iliad,* you're bound to be disappointed by this small set of ruins. All that remains is the wall's foundation and a small theater. In front of the archaeological site, a wooden Trojan horse appeases package tourists and gives the kids something to play on while the adults look at the rubble. A short video in German or English covers the site's excavation, from the destructive treasure hunt of Heinrich Schliemann in 1871 to reverential dusting with toothbrushes by university students. As much damage as Schliemann did, his excavation was important. Previously, Troy was the only site in Homer's poems that archaeologists had been unable to locate, and the town was thought to exist in legend only. Eleven plaques, one at each building, give the complicated history of the nine levels of settlement, built on top of one another from 3000 BC to AD 300. It's worth checking out the various city plans in the video room before walking around, to get a sense of how the nine developments were laid out. *Tel. 196/31061. Admission: $2. Open daily 8–5.*

➤ **COMING AND GOING** • Dolmuş (80¢) travel the 20 km to Troy from the cannon monument in the center of Canakkale, although you'll probably have to change cars along the way. Lots of truckers take the route and pass the Troy exit, so hitching is easy. **Troy Anzac Tours** (near Çanakkale's clock tower, tel. 196/15847) offers three-hour guided tours of Troy, but don't bother; plenty of information is available at the site.

GALLIPOLI Aussies and Kiwis make a patriotic pilgrimage to this peninsula (called Gelibolu in Turkish), touring the battlefields and graveyards of the Allies' catastrophic World War I campaign to gain control of the Dardanelles and destroy Istanbul. Between them, the attacking Allies and defending Turks suffered a half-million casualties during the nine-month campaign (1915–1916). At the outset of the Allied attack, General George Hamilton placed a marker at **Brighton Beach,** an ideal landing point with flat country beyond. During the night, Turks moved the marker to **Anzac Cove,** a shallow beach with steep cliffs behind which Turks waited with German machine guns. Allied forces followed Hamilton's beacon and landed during the night in full view of the Turks. More than 1,500 Allied soldiers were slaughtered on the first day. Lieutenant Colonel Mustafa Kemal (better known as Atatürk), who later became Turkey's president, led the Turkish force.

Look out at the Aegean and the Dardanelles from Colonel Atatürk's small bunker, 760 feet above the Allied landing point in Gallipoli, and you'll understand why the attack was virtual suicide. The morbid, depressing battleground should make a pacifist of any visitor.

Near **Lone Pine Cemetery,** you can walk along trenches that were once 10 feet deep but are now covered with young pine trees. The Australians dug tunnels beneath the Turkish trenches and blew them up from below. The tunnel entrances are still visible near **Johnston Jolly's Cemetery.** (The Aussie Captain Johnston got his nickname because he used to jolly the Turkish troops by throwing over supplies of chocolate to them. The Turks threw back greatly needed supplies of water to thirsty Australians.) Gallipoli's **Kabatepe Museum** (Millipark, Müdürkigu, tel. 196/41297; admission $1) displays uniforms, ammunition, medals, coins, and soldiers' letters. A tray of cartridges wrapped around each other, with holes where bullets passed right through, is testament to the intensity of the barrage of deadly metal.

Aside from testifying to the idiocy of war, the area has hot, pebbly beaches and great views of the islands of Greek **Samantreka** and Turkish **Gökçeada.** The canopy of pine trees on the peninsula provides shade, and the *papatya,* an aromatic yellow flower, offers sweet scents.

➤ **COMING AND GOING** • Ferries (50¢) travel from Canakkale to Eceabat. If you have some time, you can take a bus from Eceabat to the southern end of the peninsula and walk the 7 km around the sites. Anil gives informative guided tours of the area to groups of four for $6 per person. To arrange a tour, ask Kemâl at the Aussie and Kiwi Restaurant (*see* Canakkale, *above*); he'll tell Anil to meet you at the ferry in Eceabat in his green taxi. **Troy Anzac Tours** has the monopoly on official tours, charging $15 per person for minibus expeditions with one guide for as many as 50 people.

Aegean Coast

Travelers come here in droves to enjoy the sun and swim in the clear blue Aegean, but many are shocked to find out how overdeveloped and sleazy the resorts are, especially south of Izmir, the region's main hub. Despite the ugly hotels and tacky restaurants, the south offers beaches within a short distance of the Greek islands of Sámos, Pátmos, and Ródos, as well as some of the country's most famous archaeological sites, including Ephesus and Aphrodisias. The northern Aegean, where the beaches are rocky and chillier than in the south, is less developed. After high season (July–Aug.), many towns here actually become pleasant, as the package tourists flee and the residents return to a life of fishing and agriculture.

Ayvalık

Entering the town of Ayvalık, on the northern Aegean coast, you see a typically busy resort with expensive waterfront restaurants and shops. Head up the hill, though, and you'll find yourself in a maze of cobbled lanes and alleys leading to olive groves and pine trees, on a hill with a view of the Greek island of Lésvos. The best views are from **Seytan Sofrası** (Satan's Table), a lookout point high on the rocks south of the town center (take a dolmuş there for 25¢). **Alibey Adası** (Cunda Island), home to a small fishing community of Greek descent, is a 25¢ ride north across a causeway. A 4,000-year-old hot spring lies in a pine forest in the **Kosak Mountains,** 20 km from town and accessible by taxi. **Sarımsaklı** (Garlic Beach), 6 km south of town, is jam-packed with glitzy resort hotels and Jet Ski rentals. It's a 25¢ dolmuş ride away; pack a lunch and don't plan on spending the night unless you want to pay a fortune.

BASICS The **PTT** (Inönü Cad., near yacht harbor, tel. 663/21003) offers currency exchange and postal and phone services. The town's most convenient **tourist information office** (Yat Limanı Karşısı, tel. 663/22122) is at the Cunda ferry dock. Banks crowd the central square near the Atatürk statue.

COMING AND GOING Buses arrive at the otogar, 1 km north of town, from Canakkale and Izmir. Ferries to Lésvos are expensive ($30 one-way, $35 round-trip). **Jale Turizm Acentesi** (Gümrük Cad. 41/A, tel. 663/22740) runs boats on Monday, Wednesday, and Friday, and **Yeni Istanbul Tur** (Talatpaşa Cad. 67/A, tel. 663/26008) has service on Tuesday, Thursday, and Saturday. Ferries run May 15 through September and leave Ayvalık at 9 AM, returning from Mitilíni, Lésvos's port town, at 5 PM. Port tax is about $17.

WHERE TO SLEEP AND EAT Prices nearly double from July 1 to September 10, but bargains are available at other times of year. The cheapest choice is **Hotel Sehir** (Merkez, tel. 663/21569; $4 per person). The mattresses are rickety, the mosquitoes legion, and the hot water nonexistent, but the hotel is centrally located behind the expensive waterfront restaurants. **Hotel Canlı Balık** (Gümrük Cad. 20, tel. 663/22292; $5 per person) has clean rooms with sturdy beds, but the few rooms with windows have views of a brick wall. **Ayvada Pansiyon** (Atatürk Cad., Yat Limanı Karşısı 63, tel. 663/22929; $7.50 per person) has immense, pristine rooms with high ceilings and views across the bay, and a downstairs bar with a Club Med feel. For a more homey stay, book one of six stylish rooms at **Villa Lila** (Edremit Cad. 48, tel. 663/27291; $10 per person), where Monika offers tours of the area.

Right on the waterfront, **15 Brothers Restaurant** (Inönü Cad., tel. 663/26015) serves good soups and kebaps to a local crowd. A stall in the fish market offers fried-fish sandwiches for $2. On Alibey Adası, **Poseidon Restaurant** (Selamet Cad. 2/2, tel. 663/71227) charges about $10 a meal, but the excellent seafood is worth it.

Bergama

On a hill inland from the Aegean coast, the ancient city of Pergamon was a base for Lysimachus, a general under Alexander the Great, in the 4th century BC. At the time, the town was a trade center and home to many artists, but it fell into ruin after a Goth invasion in AD 262 and wasn't rediscovered until 1873, when German engineer Karl Humann took its well-preserved Altar of Zeus back to Berlin. These days, in addition to extensive remains, you'll find some attractive neighborhoods in Bergama, especially if you look past the prominent modern buildings that clutter the town. Houses on hillsides to the west and north are painted in pastel shades and Greek-style white and blue, and weathered, round cobblestone streets curve upward to meet walls on either side.

BASICS Stop by the **tourist information office** (Izmir Cad. 54, tel. 541/21862) for a simple map and other info. The **PTT** (Izmir Cad.) offers currency exchange and postal and phone services until midnight.

GETTING AROUND Buses arrive at the otogar, near the Asclepion, from Izmir and Ayvalık. The main road, Izmir Caddesi, winds from the Acropolis in the north to the Asclepion in the south. Taxi drivers extort $12 to drive you to the ruins, so it's worth taking the time to walk to the sights yourself. For the Asclepion, walk along the twisting narrow streets behind the police station and up a steep incline—this route is more scenic than the road behind the tourist information office. To get to the Acropolis, you'll have to climb a winding 2-km road north of town. Take a detour along the old, grassy road that zigzags up the southeast face of the hill; you'll see peripheral ruins and local wildlife—tortoises, snakes, butterflies, and dragonflies.

At the bar behind and to the right of the police station (look for the Tuborg Gold sign), you can see Turk-pop on TV and watch the men's club knock back liters of raki. The bartender has elevated beer-pouring to an art, removing the froth with a spatula and filling glasses to the brim with Turkey's best beer, Tuborg Gold.

WHERE TO SLEEP AND EAT Although there are plenty of budget hotels near the otogar, the pensions in the more secluded old town at the foot of the Acropolis are far preferable. The best option is **Nike Pension** (Talatpaşa Mah., Tabak Köprü Cıkmazı 2, tel. 541/23901; $6 per person), with a gold-painted staircase leading up to neat rooms. Their garden, near the foot of the hill, boasts 74 types of flowers. Slightly nearer town is **Pension Athena** (Barbaros Mah., Imam Cıkmazı 5, tel. 541/33420; $6–$8 per person), in a restored Ottoman house. **Pergamon Pension** (Bankalar Cad. 3, tel. 541/32395; $4 per person) has no hot water, but it's conveniently located and comfortable. Expect to be awakened by a loud 5 AM call to prayer, and be sure to check out by 11 or you'll pay for an extra night.

Expensive restaurants along the main road are used to dealing with (and conning) tourists; check your bill carefully. The best is **Meydan Restaurant** (Istiklâl Meydanı 4, tel. 541/31797), where you can get stuffed bell peppers, rice, eggplant salad, and beer for $3. To beat the heat, sit under the fans at **Café Manolya** (Izmir Cad., near the PTT, tel. 541/34488) and have a baklava topped with vanilla ice cream ($1).

WORTH SEEING The **Arkeoloji Müzesi** (Archaeological Museum) on Izmir Caddesi (admission $1) has a variety of jewelry, swords, pistols, old costumes, and ornate rifles. The statue collection consists of good local finds, including a bust of Zeus, muscular centurions, and noseless deities. A Roman sarcophagus at the entrance, barely 1½ meters long, is a reminder of how short people used to be. The dramatic **Kızıl Avlu** (Red Basilica), built as a pagan temple and later dedicated to St. John, is famous for being called the throne of the devil in the Book of Revelation. One section is now a small mosque with a pink interior. You'll find the basilica where the river crosses Izmir Caddesi; admission is $1.

The ancient health spa **Asclepion** (admission $2; open daily 8:30–5:30) attracted moneyed Greeks in search of a hedonistic holiday. Much of the medical treatment at the Asclepion consisted of dream analysis, but patients would also be told to run barefoot, eat particular foods, take mud baths, or soak in mineral waters to cure their ills. These days you enter the site from the **Sacred Way,** a sunken street overgrown with grass. Nearby, the **Temple of Telesphorus** is linked by an underground corridor to the **Sacred Spring.** What were once mud baths are now algae-covered pits, home to camouflaged tortoises. Above the ancient theater, a shaded walkway offers a view of the site and surrounding hills. Unfortunately, the site is close to military buildings, and the original theater is being converted into a modern concert arena. You'll have to ignore the tour groups coming through, too.

On the hill north of town, the Selinus River passes beneath the **Acropolis** (admission $2), hangout of the ancient kings of Pergamon. Most of the **Altar of Zeus,** the site's main attraction, was carted to Germany during the 19th century, but the chalky white pillars remain, overlooking a **theater** dug into the hill. The **library** once housed 200,000 books, until Mark Antony gave most of them to Cleopatra.

Izmir

Izmir, Turkey's third-largest city, is a modern urban mass with most of the evils of big Western cities. Sterile buildings dominate the business district, and blocks of concrete apartments spread out in a depressing urban sprawl. If you look closely, though, you'll find twisting alleyways and older houses hugging Mt. Pagos, where each turn reveals scenes of kids constructing kites out of newspaper and parents mellowing out with water pipes on terraces, as the inevitable call to prayer echoes around the city.

Izmir, formerly known as Smyrna, is thought to have been home to the epic poet Homer in about 850 BC. Alexander the Great also left a permanent mark on the city. He dreamed that he should build a fortress here, and with the support of the oracle of Apollo at Claros he constructed **Kadifekale** (the Velvet Fortress) on the flat top of Mt. Pagos on the southern edge of the city. Only the western and southern walls remain, but the fortress's view of the Aegean and the islands of Híos and Lésvos is spectacular.

As foreign merchants and foreign ideas began to flow through Izmir during the 1500s, the port became known as the City of the Infidel. Izmir is still a center for merchants, and its **bazaar** is renowned. Once you enter the maze of stores selling clothes, shoes, and kitchenware, it's easy to lose your sense of direction. Anafartalar Caddesi, with the important stores and banks, is the area's main street, curving along the southern edge to **Konak,** the central square. Just southeast of Konak are the **Arkeoloji Müzesi** (Archaeological Museum), with a colossal statue of the emperor Domitian, and the **Etnoğrafya Müzesi** (Ethnographic Museum), with quirky displays on folk arts and daily life. Admission to each is $1.

Directly east of Konak, the large, open **agora** (admission $1; open daily 9–5) was built by order of Alexander the Great, destroyed by an earthquake in AD 178, and rebuilt by Marcus Aurelius. The market, once a many-storied complex of arches and columns, is now largely buried by scorched earth and yellowed grass. To the east lie sections of columns, statuary, and gravestones.

BASICS Of the four **tourist information offices,** the one on Gaziosmanpaşa Bulvarı (tel. 51/84–21–47) is most central. The nearby 24-hour **PTT** (Cumhuriyet Meydanı) is the quietest in town, but there are branches in each district.

COMING AND GOING **Basmane train station,** just south of the Kültürparkı, has daily service to Ankara (16 hrs, $5, $20 with sleeping car) and Istanbul (9 hrs, $8). Dolmuş run from the train station to the **otogar,** 2½ km northeast of the city center, for 30¢. Taxi fare is $2. Buses to Ankara (9 hrs, $8) are faster and cleaner than the train. Buses also travel to Istanbul (9 hrs, $8) and Selçuk (90 min, $1). Several companies provide frequent service; just show up at the otogar when you want to travel.

GETTING AROUND The most interesting area is roughly a square, with the train station in the northeast corner, the fortress of Kadifekale in the southeast, museums in the southwest, and the bazaar in the northwest. The agora is in the center. Local buses leave from Konak, near the museums; buy 35¢ tickets at the white kiosks before you board.

WHERE TO SLEEP AND EAT Just west of Basmane station, hundreds of similar hotels charge $2–$6 per person. For your own shower (a rare extra) you'll pay $2 more, but many rooms have sinks. The closer to the minaret you are, the louder your 5 AM wake-up call will be. **Otel Saray** (Anafartalar Cad. 635, tel. 51/83–69–46; $5 per person) has clean, quiet rooms that open onto an atrium. The helpful manager speaks good English. **Otel Konak** (945 Sok. 15, tel. 51/82–06–94; $4 per person), south of Fevzipaşa Bulvarı near the train station, has tall windows and new wallpaper. It's one of the better choices on this street, which is packed with hotels. You might actually meet a few Turks at the nearby **Güzel Konya Oteli** (1296 Sok. 37, tel. 51/83–69–39; $2 per person), oddly decorated with stained glass, pink window frames, and red Christmas lights over the door.

The cheapest eats are near the budget hotels. **Zeybek Mongal Restaurant** (1368 Sok. 61/A, tel. 51/83–52–31), off Fevzipaşa Bulvarı, has good kebaps. Crowded **Sandal Restaurant** (Iknici Kordon 22–24, no phone) has good seafood and is open late. A smart pine veneer and shiny brass decor draw a wealthy crowd to the pastanesi **Bolulu Hasan Usta** (853 Sok. 13, tel. 51/25–13–80) for *aşure* (sweet-pea pudding topped with walnuts, apricots, and raisins).

NEAR IZMIR

ÇEŞME Finnish and English bus-tour types stroll along the seafront of Çeşme, preparing to fork over some liras at overpriced restaurants and Euro-style boutiques. The town has a pretty promenade and clear blue water—that is, until the tide brings restaurant refuse (soggy rolls and napkins) into the harbor. Çeşme's **castle** (admission $1; open 8:30–11:45 and 1–5:15), used by Sultan Beyazit II to defend the city against the Crusaders, and the meager **Museum of Ottoman Arms** inside aren't enough to make the town an attractive destination. If you're not using Çeşme as a transit point for Híos, leave it to package tourists and Izmir weekenders; better beaches and fishing villages can be found elsewhere along the coast.

The best budget-lodging deal is **Tani Pansiyon** (Carşi Sok. 15, behind Kervansaray, tel. 549/26238; $5 per person). The town's open-air restaurants cater to tourists and charge $5 and up for meals, but joints along the main drags sell pizza for $1.50. Buses run to Çeşme from Izmir about every 20 minutes (2 hrs, $1.80). Talk to the **Ertürk travel agency** (near tourist office, tel. 549/26768) about ferries to Híos ($25, $30 round-trip), which leave at 10 AM every day but Monday from mid-July to August. The **tourist office** (on seafront southwest of castle, tel, 549/26653; open daily 8–8) has thick bilingual brochures.

Selçuk

Many people come to Selçuk planning to stay one night and visit Ephesus, then end up staying for weeks. Although you'll find the usual tourist schlock in the modern part of town, Selçuk also has a few great ancient sites, an intriguing Ephesus-related museum, and the rarely visited remains of the **Temple of Artemis,** one of the Seven Wonders of the Ancient World. Great beaches are a short hitch or dolmuş ride away.

Penis pendants hung on wires get giggles from Japanese tourists at the **Ephesus Museum** (Agora Carşisi, no phone; admission $2.50; open daily 8:30–6:30). The Priapus statue is a disappointing few inches high, but two interesting statues of Artemis are decorated with eggs (or breasts, or testicles, depending on your interpretation). Orgies were once held in the name of Priapus and Artemis, god and goddess of fertility, at the Temple of Artemis. Only a single column remains, behind the Ephesus Museum on the road to Ephesus. **St. John's Basilica** (St. Jean Sok.; admission $1.50; open daily 8–5), where St. John is thought to be buried, is also well worth a peek. The barrel-vaulted roof collapsed long ago, but a few walls have been heaved back into place, so you can get a general idea of what the place looked like originally. The mosque **Isa Bey Camii** (St. Jean Sok.; open daily 9–5), next to the basilica, is built of a hodgepodge of stones: marble blocks with Latin inscriptions, chunks of the altar from the Temple of Artemis, and black granite columns from Ephesus. The **tourist information office** (Atatürk Mah., Agora Carşisi 35, tel. 5451/1328) doles out maps and Ephesus brochures.

COMING AND GOING The **E24 highway** divides the small market town. To the west is the old town, with most of the sights and the best pensions. On the east side are the otogar, train station, and market. From the **otogar,** you can pick up buses to Kuşadası (20 min, 80¢) and Izmir (about 2 hrs, $3).

WHERE TO SLEEP AND EAT Hotels in the old town charge $4–$5 per person and are quieter than those on the east side of town. Stay in **Homeros Pension** (Asmalı Sok. 17, tel. 5451/3995; $5 per person), which is kept clean by hard-working Ayşa. The carpeted, covered rooftop has nice views and is a great place to relax and enjoy the breeze when it's hot outside. Cheaper **Abasix Pension** (Turgut Reis Sok. 13, tel. 5451/1367; $2.50 per person) has basic rooms and a small garden.

The standard kebaps in pita are sold for $1 all around town. If you call **Pamukkale Pide** (next to market, tel. 5451/3662), they'll deliver a pizza ($1) to you in 15 minutes. Live large and order meat toppings for 20¢ extra (feta cheese, parsley, and lemon are free).

NEAR SELCUK

EPHESUS This ancient city, built on a bay where the Küçük Mederes River met the sea, is the most visited place in Turkey after Istanbul, but it's been a hot spot since long before the first tour buses rolled into town. The Ionians settled in Ephesus (Efes in Turkish) during the 11th century BC. Like most Ionian cities in Asia Minor, Ephesus later became a Roman city and eventually a Christian one. It remained an important commercial center even after the river silted up, cutting off direct access to the sea. St. John, St. Paul, and the Virgin Mary all set up camp here and left behind churches and tombs that attest to their presence.

Unfortunately, many of the buildings have been restored with cheap concrete, and the crowds can be unbearable. But Ephesus is massive—2 km across—and depending upon how much of its 3,000-year history you want to absorb, the city could hold you for a few hours or for weeks. If you really want to understand it all, it's worth shelling out some money for a special guidebook about the site. Ephesus is open daily 8–5:30; admission is $4.50, but people have been known to sneak in for free when large tour groups congregate around the gate. Try to arrive early in the day or as the sun sets, when you have the city to yourself and the stone turns pink. The place is hot and packed during the day.

The broad **colonnade** leads to the 25,000-seat **stadium,** now used as an open-air concert arena for stars like Sting. Walking south on the paved road, you'll approach one of the largest buildings, the **Harbour Baths.** South is the **Library of Celsus,** with a reconstructed sculpted facade. Twelve thousand scrolls were kept dry in galleries between its walls, now alleys for bats. The **Marble Road** leads uphill from the library. Thousands of years ago, people emptied their water stores onto the road every evening to wash the day's refuse away. A heavy rain today causes the same effect, with soda cans rather than broken amphorae as the jetsam.

➤ **COMING AND GOING** • Ephesus is an easy 15-minute walk from Selçuk. Most dolmuş from Kuşadası or Selçuk (80¢) stop 1 km from the site. From here, follow the paved road. You can slip through a gap in the fence at the sign for the **Grotto of the Seven Sleepers,** a necropolis where seven murdered boys were supposedly resurrected after 200 years. A rough, thistle-covered path above and behind the stadium starts here, leading through the baths and city walls.

KUSADASI Once a quiet port and a base for seeing Ephesus, Kuşadası is now perhaps the most repugnant, overtouristed town in Turkey. The town's only sights are a Genoese **castle,** along a causeway south of the harbor, and the requisite **Kervansaray,** a caravansary restored as a hotel. If you're amused by seedy, Europop meat markets, you might get some enjoyment out of **Pub Lane** (near the Kervansaray), which is lined with discos open until 4 AM. Beer is $1, sex about $50 an hour. Otherwise, avoid Kuşadası altogether and make Selçuk your base for visiting Ephesus.

The **tourist information office** (Iskele Meydanı, by docks, tel. 636/11103) has a great map of town. The **otogar** is 1 km inland. Selçuk (20 min, 80¢) is 10 km north. If you're headed for Sámos, catch a boat at 8:30 AM or 5 PM for $35. If you get stuck here overnight, stay at **Hülya Pension** (Ileri Sok. 39, 10 min uphill from tourist office, tel. 636/42075), at the highest point in the old town. Beds are $4 per person, $2 if you sleep on the roof.

PAMUKKALE You may have already seen the white cliffs of Dover, or the chalky formations off the coast of Normandy, but the landlocked cliffs at Pamukkale (Cotton Castle) are unique. What looks like a landslide from far away and like ski slopes close up is solidified calcite, blooming from natural terraces that rise 330 feet above the plain. The cliffs were formed when a calcium-rich spring flowed downhill and evaporated. You can still sit under a small waterfall that runs over the cliffs, or wade knee-deep through milky pools, but the area's beauty has been marred by development, and the cliffs are eroding under tourist feet.

The **museum** (tel. 6218/2034; admission $1; open Tues.–Sun.) at the top of the cliffs houses a meager collection of finds from **Hierapolis** (admission $3 but rarely collected), the site just behind the museum. Hierapolis was a Roman spa where the rich bathed in mineral waters, thought to cure various ailments. Visitors still arrive from all over, but the waters, instead of flowing freely over the cliff, are now channeled into swimming pools at the overpriced cliff-top resort hotels. At the **Pamukkale Motel** (Orenyeri, in front of Hierapolis, tel. 6218/2024), nonguests can swim for $3 per hour in uncomfortably hot mineral water in a huge pool full of columns and smooching couples. If you want to smooch in private, come at about 8 PM, one hour before the pool closes. Don't open your eyes in the water—they'll itch.

➢ **BASICS** • The well-marked **tourist information office** (tel. 6218/2077; open daily 8–noon and 1:30–5:30) gives out a useless map and brochure depicting romantic sunsets on the cliffs and showing you what the place must have looked like before it became so touristy. Change money at **Halkbank** (at start of road leading up cliff, tel. 6218/2124), which is within sight of the tourist office.

➢ **COMING AND GOING** • Buses arrive at Denizli, about 12 km from Pamukkale. From there, it's an 80¢ dolmuş ride to Pamukkale Köyü (the village at the bottom of the cliffs) or the cliff-top resorts.

➢ **WHERE TO SLEEP AND EAT** • All of the affordable accommodations, most charging $4–$5, are in the village at the bottom of the cliffs. **Coban Pension** (at base of cliffs to west, tel. 6218/1045; $4 per person) is the best budget choice, with clean, quiet rooms and a platform that looks up at the cliffs. Camping here is $3. This place is less pretentious than central, overtouristed pensions like **Motel Mustafa** (main junction, tel. 6218/2240), where the jaded owner offers good rooms overlooking a courtyard for $5 per person. If you must stay on the cliff, try **Bel-Tes** (next to museum, tel. 6218/2019), where you can pitch a tent for $4 per person or get an A-frame bungalow for $12.50 per single, $15 per double. The place is noisy and the bathrooms grungy, but the bar has superb views. **Harem Restaurant** (center of town, tel. 6218/2252) offers good kebaps and beef chili.

APHRODISIAS Aphrodisias makes an excellent day trip from Pamukkale. The city walls encircle several ancient buildings that have remained relatively untouched. Grass grows between the seats of the 30,000-seat oval **stadium** that hugs the northern wall. The whole remote, untouristed place is a nice break from the manicured ruins of more popular sites.

Aphrodisias's **museum** (admission $2; open daily 8–5:30) houses a mediocre collection of statuary; your time is better spent walking around the site. Most remains are in the center of the walled city. A wire fence restricts access to the **Temple of Aphrodite,** where Romans held orgies in the name of the goddess of fertility until the prudish Byzantines converted the temple into a church. Only a few columns remain of the **Tetrapylon,** the huge gate east of the temple. Next to the **Bishop's Palace** is the cozy **Odeon,** a theater with nine rows of seats. In the largest building, the **Baths of Hadrian** adjoin the **Double Agora.** The black-and-white floor tiles are still intact. The **theater** is backed by five chambers with legal inscriptions. Admission to the site is $2.50; it's open daily 8–5:30.

➢ **COMING AND GOING** • Buses (90 min, $7) depart from Pamukkale at 9:30 AM and drop you near Aphrodisias's museum. They leave Aphrodisias at 1:30 PM and stop 1 km away at the mediocre restaurant-hotel **Chez Mestan** (tel. 6379/8046; meals $2.50, rooms $6) for an hour before continuing. You can walk to Chez Mestan and pick up the bus at 2:30 if you want another hour at the site.

Bodrum

Like Kuşadası, Bodrum is a Club Med–style venue for debauchery on the Mediterranean, filled with discos and resort schlock. Spend two hours in the castle and its museum, 10 minutes at the mausoleum, and you'll be done. Bodrum (the name means "dungeon"), known as Halicarnassus in antiquity, is most famous for its **castle.** An excellent **Underwater Archaeology Museum** inside displays treasures discovered on ships wrecked off the Aegean coast. The museum also has an extensive display of amphorae that includes examples of the foods people stored in these clay vessels and explains how the goods were then stacked in ships. A wine room offers a glass of red for $1. *Tel. 614/61095. Admission: $2. Castle open daily 10–7; shorter hours off-season.*

On the other side of the harbor lies the **mausoleum** (admission $2; open daily 8–5), one of the Seven Wonders of the Ancient World. The tomb of Mausolus, built by his wife (who was also his sister), was once a massive structure with 36 Ionic columns, but the pile of rubble that remains is hardly worth the $2 admission. A **gallery** beside the mausoleum has some replica carvings. The **theater,** marked ANTIK TEATRO, is north of the town's main road, Kibris Sehitler. It's now used by local soccer players and by cows, who graze around the seats.

If you want to attract attention from the locals, pay $5 for a cheesy five-minute camel ride along the water. The incongruous animals are hard to miss; just watch out for camel spit.

BASICS Visit the **tourist information office** (next to castle on waterfront, tel. 614/61031; open daily 8–7:30) for a map of the town and a list of hotels. The 24-hour **PTT** (tel. 614/61560) is on Cevat Sakir Caddesi.

GETTING AROUND Dolmuş leave from the **otogar** on Cevat Sakir Caddesi, the main drag, and pick up passengers along the road to Bodrum's peninsula resorts. Bodrum has good connections to Selçuk and Marmaris.

WHERE TO SLEEP AND EAT Pensions lie inland, west of the PTT, but there are no single rooms; solo travelers have to sleep on the roof or shell out $10–$15 for a double. Two good places behind the waterfront to the west are generally full: **Menekşe Pansiyon** (Neyzen Tevfik Cad. 34, tel. 614/ 63416; doubles $12) and **Yenilme Pansiyon** (next door, tel. 614/61520; doubles $12). For better values, stay in one of the villages on the peninsula (*see below*), where camping and pensions are easy to find but nightlife is nonexistent.

Local produce is pricey, restaurants even worse: Pizza and kebaps run about $4. The kebap house across from the otogar is an exception, with excellent pizza or *pide kebap* (grilled meat in pita) for $1.80. Also try **Salonu** (behind PTT) for cheap Turkish pizza. **Han Cafe** (off Cevat Sakir Cad., tel. 614/62802) makes good apricot ice cream ($1).

NEAR BODRUM

The beaches in Bodrum are pretty grim, so head farther out on the peninsula if you want a clean patch of sand. Only 3 km from Bodrum, **Gümbet** has a decent beach, but you can hardly see it for all the bodies. **Turgutreis,** toward the western tip of the peninsula, has grainy beaches, light surf, and the most evolved hotel scene this side of Bodrum. Try the central, reasonably priced **Kadir Pansiyon** (Domaian Cad. 141/B, tel. 614/22485; doubles $15). The north coast is generally more secluded, but **Yalıkavak** has its share of crowds.

Marmaris

Once a small fishing village, Marmaris is now home to 10,000 people. As the city has grown, so has the tourist trade, and now the marina teems with yachters, package tourists, and rich Turks. Overpriced restaurants, bars, and banks crowd the waterfront. At least Marmaris makes a good transit point for the Greek island of Ródos, and it's useful as a base for exploring nearby beaches and forested hills. **Kumlubük, Turunç,** and **Phosphorus Cove** offer some of the best beaches a short dolmuş or boat ride away. Day trips for fishing and swimming can be arranged with the guys at the waterfront. They usually leave midmorning and charge $6 for the day with lunch. If you take a dolmuş past İçmeler into the steep hills that surround the immense resort development, you can hike or mountain bike in the shade of pine trees.

BASICS Visit the **tourist information office** (tel. 612/11035) by the ferry dock for a brochure on the region and information on chartering yachts. The owner of Interyouth Hostel is more helpful, though, for budget-travel info. The **PTT** (Fevzipaşa Sok., 1 block east of Atatürk statue) is open 24 hours.

GETTING AROUND The town is divided by a major street, Ulusal Egemenlik Caddesi, which begins at the Atatürk statue at the harbor and runs north. West of Ulusal Egemenlik Caddesi, between the water and the covered bazaar, lies a barren **otopark**, a rubbly parking lot full of minibuses. Beyond are some 20 pensions scattered among modern buildings, waterfront stalls, and a market. The **otogar** is a 10-minute walk northeast of the otopark, but most buses pick up passengers at central offices near the Atatürk statue. Everything in town is within walking distance. If you want to go to the beach, catch a dolmuş from the otopark, since the beaches near town are dirty.

WHERE TO SLEEP Pensions charge generally $8–$15 for a double, and many places offer rooftop beds for $3 per person. One of the best places to stay is the modern **HI Interyouth Hostel** (Kemeraltı Mah., Iyiliktaş Mevkii, behind waterfront at Garanti Bank, tel. 612/23687). Doubles are $6 per person, dorm beds $5, and roof spots $3. West of the otopark, **Omür Pansiyon** (K. Altı Mah. 25, tel. 612/25376; doubles $8) is one of the cheapest places. Two of the few hotels that offer singles are **Günel Aile Pansiyonu** (Hacımustafa Sok. 105, tel. 612/14676; $5 per person) and, in the bazaar, **Kordon Pension** (Kemeraltı Mah. 24, tel. 612/24762; $6 per person).

FOOD Stay away from the waterfront, where people hassle you to come into their restaurants. **Yiğit Restaurant** and **Oz 49,** both near the hostel, have meals for $3; try the latter's *izkender* (lamb kebab). **Greenhouse** (Tepe Mah., Mustafa Sok. 39 [a.k.a. Bar La.], tel. 612/25071; open until 4 AM) serves giant tuna sandwiches ($2) and is *the* nightspot, with a mix of music and people. **Uğur Pasta Firini** (Carşisi Meydanı Sok. 29, no tel.) offers vegetarian pide with sweet bread and a *börek* (flaky cheese pastry) baked by a gnomelike fellow.

Mediterranean Coast

Stretching 1,025 km from the resort town of Marmaris in the west to the Syrian border in the east, the Mediterranean coastline has some of Turkey's best beaches, most of them (if you believe what you read) enjoyed by Cleopatra and Mark Antony while they carried on their torrid love affair. You won't find as many slick, sleazy resorts here as on the Aegean, and tourism has not yet developed to the point where every restaurant serves fish and chips. Still, this is by no means virgin territory, especially in the west. Fethiye and Kaş are developed vacation towns, used by British and German travelers as bases from which to explore the beaches. **Alanya,** with its magnificent fortress, is also overdeveloped, but it marks the beginning of less touristed eastern Turkey, which is mainly used as an overland route to Syria or as a terminus for ferry departures to Cyprus (pick up a boat in Mersin or Tarsus).

Fethiye

Fethiye is at its best at night, when the residents come out to promenade along the harbor or sip tea in their gardens. In the daytime, it's a little too obvious that most of the city's original buildings were replaced after a devastating 1957 earthquake. The town almost completely encircles Fethiye Bay, and the streets of the old town wind up the hill west of the touristy shopping area. East of the PTT is a new **Fethiye Museum** (open daily 9–5), with a trilingual inscription (in Lycian, Persian, and Greek) on a block of stone dating from the 4th century BC and a beautifully carved church door. The **tomb of Amyntas,** a 4th-century bigwig, is the most impressive of a cluster of rock tombs carved into the cliff that looms above town.

Fethiye is most heavily developed on the southeast side of Fethiye Bay. Here the main road, Atatürk Caddesi, runs along the waterfront and east to the **otogar** 1 km outside town. On Atatürk Caddesi you'll find the 24-hour **PTT** (tel. 615/41498). At the boat landing, the **tourist information office** (Iskele Meydanı 1, tel. 615/41527; open daily 8–noon and 1–6) distributes an excellent map and a comprehensive hotel list. Dolmuş stop all along the main roads and at the water. Many head to Olüdeniz (15 min, 80¢), a resort 12 km southeast of Fethiye.

WHERE TO SLEEP AND EAT **Derelioğlu Pansiyon** (Fevzi Cakmak Cad., tel. 615/45983; doubles $14) is the best of five adjacent pensions on a busy road. **Ateş Pansiyon** (Karagözler Cad., behind Prenses Oteli, tel. 615/16291; doubles $8) is quiet and cheap, and **Yeşilçam Pansiyon** (Yat Limanı Karşısı 91, tel. 615/21126; doubles $12) has terraces on all four levels and the best bay view. With rooms backing onto a quiet alley, **Oztürk Pansiyon** (Çarşı Cad., Depboy Sok. 16, tel. 615/41418) has rare single rooms for $5. **Ulgen Pension** (Cumhuriyet Mah., Paspatır Mekvii Merdiven 3, tel. 615/13491) has lots of options, with $8 doubles, $4 singles, and $3 rooftop spots.

The cheapest restaurants are on the busy main road. On the waterfront, popular **Pizza 74** (Atatürk Cad. 4, tel. 615/41869) has a variety of appetizers for $1.50 each and goulash for $3. For a French-food blowout, try the **Castle** (Karagözler Yokuşu 49, above boat landing, tel. 615/20985), run by a French chef who whips up an extensive menu for $15.

NEAR FETHIYE

OLUDENIZ Come to this resort town, on a beautiful lagoon, for nightlife and pebbly beaches. You'll find a rope swing that dangles from an overhanging tree, and rock cliffs from which the adventurous dive 23 feet into the water. Day cruises ($10) take you to a variety of coves and beaches. On the downside, swarms of mosquitoes thrive in the lagoon's still water, and swarms of hotel keepers and restaurant owners charge jacked-up prices.

On the dolmuş ride from Fethiye you'll pass a small tourist village with pensions and restaurants, and Olüdeniz itself offers more restaurants and bars along the water. **Shiny's Place** (no phone) has camping and tree-house mattresses for $2. **Harry's Bar and Disco** (tel. 615/66097) sells chicken-and-garlic pide for $2 and tuna and prawns for $4. **Safran Restaurant** (side street past Harry's, tel. 615/66315) has many veggie options. Lasagna is $4.

Kaş

Kaş, once a fishing village of 4,000, now relies on tourism for its living. During the summer season, families leave town to tend apple orchards and pastures in the cooler highlands, turning their houses into pensions run by young daughters and grandmothers. One of the smallest resorts in the area, Kaş offers restaurants, nightlife, history, and stunning ocean views without overwhelming travelers in the way Marmaris and Bodrum do. East of the main square with the Atatürk statue are old streets lined with shops and cafés with carved woodwork terraces. One street, which slopes up from the tourist office, leads to a **sarcophagus** decorated with four regal lion heads. On the opposite side of town, about 1 km west of the main square, lies a restored 28-row **theater,** the last significant remnant of the ancient town of Antiphellos.

BASICS The **tourist office** (Cumhuriyet Meydanı 6, tel. 322/61238) is conveniently situated on the main square. The **PTT** (Cukurbağli Cad., tel. 322/61430; open daily 8:30–5:30) is a few blocks north.

COMING AND GOING The **otogar** is a five-minute walk from the center of town; follow Cukurbağli Caddesi, the pedestrian shopping street, downhill to the main square. From there it's only a few blocks to the harbor. Frequent dolmuş arrive from Antalya. The route to Fethiye (2½ hrs, $4) is winding but scenic.

WHERE TO SLEEP AND EAT Kaş is packed with pensions renting doubles for $8–$10. Many are clustered around the otogar, but some of the nicer places are in older buildings east of the main square. **Otel Andifli** (Hastane Cad., tel. 322/61042; doubles $10) has a stellar sea view. **Aphrodite Pansiyon** (Yaka Mah., near otogar, tel. 322/61216; doubles $10) has modern rooms, all with balconies. The most central choice is **Huzur Pansiyon** (Cukurbaǧli Cad., tel. 322/61160; doubles $10), between the otogar and main square. Just beyond the Antiphellos theater, **Kaş Camping** ($2 per person, $10 double in a bungalow) offers a rock platform to sunbathe on and clear water for swimming. The on-site **Rock Bar** has great views of Kaş's lights at night.

Try **Cinar Restaurant** (Sube Sok., up from main square on left, tel. 322/61735) for garlicky eggplant yogurt and a beer ($2). An American who has lived in Kaş for years recommends two restaurants on the main square: **Eriş** because it's cheap, and **Derıya** because the food is especially fresh. Another good bet is **Ferah** (near main square), where enough stir-fry for two costs $3. **Red Point Bar** (open until 3 AM), in the center of town near the Atatürk statue, is a pickup joint popular with young Turks.

Antalya

The outskirts of Antalya, a big city of 250,000, are absolute hell. Dirty beaches line the coast for miles, and grim apartments house a recent influx of the working-class people and retirees. But attractive **Kaleiçi,** the historic harbor area, still preserves narrow streets with restored Ottoman timber houses and lots of pensions, restaurants, and shops. Everything worth seeing is in this historic area, except for the **Antalya Müzesi** (admission $2.50; open Tues.–Sun. 9–6), accessible by a westbound dolmuş from the city center. The museum has an overwhelming quantity of statuary and attention-grabbing, human-size amphorae. Most fun are the laudatory dedications on the statue pedestals in the garden, where Roman gods, Muslim gravestones, Ottoman cannons, and a modern version of a Roman theater mix in a collage of historical periods. Back toward the main square is the **Yivli Minare** (Fluted Minaret), a 13th-century tiled tower commissioned by Seljuk sultan Alaeddin Keykubat. At the eastern entry to Kaleiçi, **Hadrian's Gate** was constructed in honor of the Roman emperor in AD 130. The **Kesik Minare** (Broken Minaret) is a central Kaleiçi landmark plopped on top of 5th-century church ruins. At the south edge of Kaleiçi, **Hıdırlık Kulesi** (Hıdırlık Tower) overlooks the bay, next to a grassy promenade perfect for sunset strolls.

Soothe your homesickness with Hollywood escapism at Cine Oscar (just north of Kesik Minare), where the latest films are played with Turkish subtitles for $3 ($1.50 students). Films usually start at 7 PM and 9 PM.

BASICS The main **tourist information office** (Cumhuriyet Cad., tel. 31/21–17–47) is west of the central square, which contains the Atatürk statue. More conveniently located is **Kaleiçi Tourist Information** (Selçuk Mah., Mermerli Sok., tel. 31/27–05–41). A 24-hour **PTT** is near Kalekapısı Square.

COMING AND GOING The otogar (Kazım Ozalp Cad.) is 1 km north of the main square. Frequent dolmuş leave for Fethiye (8 hrs, $6), Konya (7 hrs, $6), and other major destinations.

WHERE TO SLEEP The Kaleiçi district is packed with pensions in old, renovated houses with views. Most charge $8–$15 for a double. **Pansion the Garden** (Hesapçı Sok. 44, near Kesik Minare, tel. 31/21–08–16; doubles $10), run by an old sergeant, has a large walled garden of fruit trees inhabited by a few pet sheep. **Ertan Pansiyon** (Uzunçarşi Sok. 9, tel. 31/41–55–35; doubles $10) is above town. **Kleopatra Pansiyon** (Kaledibi Sok. 6, tel. 31/42–21–11; doubles $10) has a large roof terrace.

FOOD East of Kaleiçi is **Eski Sebzeciler İçi Sokak,** a covered pedestrian street lined with hard-sell restaurants, most offering *tandir kebap* (fatty, roasted mutton served with a huge piece of pita bread) for about $4. The street to the west has better options without the aggressive sales pitch. At **Hisar** (Cumhuriyet Meydanı, tel. 31/21–52–81) you pay $10 for an above-average meal and great atmosphere. The restaurant is built into the retaining walls of an old fortress, and the terrace has a view of the harbor. For reasonable prices, quick service, and a comfortable sunset view, try **Villa Park Restaurant** (in front of Hıdırlık Kulesi, tel.

31/48–03–09). At pastanesis, look for crystallized fruit, including orange, lemon, watermelon, fig, and tasty eggplant.

Alanya

East of Antalya on a rocky peninsula, Alanya is another overpriced resort, but the ruins of a magnificent castle above the city almost redeem it. Nearly 8 km of wall and 150 buttresses surround a covered bazaar and the **İç Kale**, or Inner Fortress (admission $2; open daily 9–5:30), which contains the remains of a Byzantine church. Buses leave the **tourist office** (Carşi Mah, Kalearkası Cad., tel. 323/11240; open daily 9–5:30) every hour for the castle; make the steep one-hour walk past old houses if you have time, though. Behind Damlataş Restaurant where the road heads up to the castle, you'll see the entrance to the **Damlataş Magarasi**, or Cave of Dripping Stones (admission $1; open 10 AM–sunset), the muggy home of a poor collection of stalactites and stalagmites. It may be worth the $10 to take a boat tour of other caves—haggle at the dock near **Kızıl Kule** (Red Tower).

Buses from Antalya (2 hrs, $3) arrive at the otogar 3 km west of town. From here, a bus (30¢) totes you into town every 10 minutes. For lodging, **Akdeniz** (one block west of museum, tel, 323/32811; doubles $8) is central and has a restaurant downstairs. The quiet **Gürkan Pansiyon** (Damlastaş Cad., Taşçıali Sok. 9, tel. 323/32798; doubles $10) is in an ugly modern building, but it has nice enough rooms. **Rain Man Restaurant** (Damlataş Cad. 109/A, tel. 323/35164) serves pancakes with your choice of filling for $3, and **The Brothers Restaurant** (on seafront near tourist office) has grilled meats for $5.

Central Turkey

A triangle 200 km on each side, with Konya in the south, Cappadocia to the east, and Turkey's dull capital, Ankara, in the north, forms the central Anatolian plateau. Ankara has one of the best museums in Turkey but little else of interest. You can usually avoid it if you're traveling by bus, although it's a transport hub for trains. Konya is worth a stop only to break up the journey between the Mediterranean and Göreme's fairy castles. Cappadocia, however, is great. Sixty million years ago, two volcanoes spewed ash over a large area that since has been eroded into weird, often phallic shapes by wind and rain. You need at least three days to walk around the unique valleys, explore the abandoned underground cities, and look into churches and homes carved into rocklike sculptures.

Ankara

Turkey's capital city, Ankara, is a modern, polluted, noisy nightmare. Apart from the museum, there's little reason to visit, although you might get stuck here for the night waiting for a connection to someplace more interesting. The historic Ulus district, north of the train tracks, is the most colorful part of the humdrum city. At the top of a hill, the crumbling, 1,100-year-old **Hisar** (Citadel) dominates Ulus. Within the walls you'll find a rambling, old-fashioned Turkish town with cobblestone streets and bits of broken columns and slabs taken from Roman ruins. In an old covered market south of the Hisar, the **Ankara Anadolu Medeniyetleri Müzesi**, or Museum of Anatolian Civilizations (Kadife Sok., tel. 312/324–31–60; admission $4; open Tues.–Sun. 8:30–5:30) has the best collection of Hittite artifacts in Turkey, including coins and sculpture. **Anıt Kabir**, Atatürk's mausoleum, is a massive, colonnaded building containing a 40-ton sarcophagus. Enter respectfully: The shrine houses the remains of Turkey's national hero. There's also a museum with a collection of Atatürk memorabilia. The mausoleum, open Tuesday–Sunday 9–5, is in a park 3 km southwest of Ulus; take Bus 63.

BASICS For the essential city map, try the **tourist information offices** at the otogar, the airport, and Ulus (Istanbul Cad. 4, tel. 312/311–22–47; open weekdays 8:30–7:30, weekends 9–5:30). The **American Express** office (Cinnah Cad. 9, opposite Kavaklidere PTT, tel. 312/467–73–34) holds travelers' mail but won't cash checks. Each district has its own PTT office, but **Ulus PTT** (Atatürk Bulvarı, south of Atatürk statue; open 24 hrs) is the main one.

It charges 10¢ for each poste-restante item held. The information desk is run by a helpful English-speaking woman.

COMING AND GOING At the western corner of Gençlik Park, 1 km southwest of the hotels in Ulus, the **central station** (Hipodrum Cad., tel. 312/311–05–20) has trains to Istanbul (8 hrs, $10) and Izmir (15 hrs, $30). From the station, walk east through the park and cross Atatürk Bulvarı to reach the hotel district. Buses to Ankara are more frequent than trains. The **otogar** is 1 km west of the hotels in Ulus, a 25¢ dolmuş ride. Buses go just about everywhere from here, including Istanbul (8 hrs, $7), Antalya (10 hrs, $10), and Nevşehir (4 hrs, $6). Check the kiosk windows to find out when the next departure is—the hawkers will try to put you on their bus regardless of whether another leaves earlier. The otogar is massive and ugly like the city. If possible, leave your bags in a bus firm's office, take a taxi to and from the museum ($2 each way), and catch another bus out of town.

➤ **BY PLANE** • **Esenboğa Airport** is 33 km north of town. Havaş buses ($2) leave the **Turkish Airlines** office (Talat Paşa Bulvarı, opposite train station, tel. 312/321–40–00) 1½ hours before flight departures. Most domestic flights cost only $40 with a student ID card; hourly planes go to Istanbul.

GETTING AROUND Atatürk Bulvarı divides Ankara into east and west. Buses (25¢) cruise the street. Most sights are in the **Ulus** district, in the northern part of town. Walking is hot, dirty work, but nothing is far from Atatürk Bulvarı, so shuttle up and down the street and then walk east or west (rarely more than 1 km to any sight). You can pay aboard some buses, but try to buy tickets from kiosks before you board. To travel from the north side of town to the south by taxi costs $3—worth it in midday heat or if you're far from the buses that run down Atatürk Bulvarı.

WHERE TO SLEEP Hotels, mostly east of Ulus and as far south as the opera house, are expensive—$6–$9 per person at best. Many places lock the showers and charge you $2 when you have the urge to take one. Forget about laundry and cooking facilities, and look for rooms high above the smog, noise, and sweat—worth the climb upstairs. The five-floor **Otel Sönmez Pamukkale** (Işkılar Cad. 9, tel. 312/310–74–16; $4 per person) is conveniently located between the PTT and the castle. The northern rooms have city views, but a chimney from a kebap kitchen leaks smoke through the open windows. Noisy, central **Hisar Oteli** (Hisarpark Cad. 6, tel. 312/311–98–89; $7 per person) is about 600 feet east of the Atatürk statue. The rooms have sinks, but the locked showers encourage you to use the adjacent Hisar Hamam ($3). **Otel Pınar** (Hisarpark Cad. 14, tel. 312/311–89–51; $8 per person), next to Hisar Oteli, is tidier and a step farther from the junction's traffic noise. **Sembol Otel** (Sümer Sok. 28, tel. 312/231–82–22; singles $20, doubles $30), south of the train tracks in the café-laden Kızılay district, is expensive, but it gets you out of crowded Ulus.

FOOD Greasy kebap joints abound, and travelers homesick for a burger can get one for $2 at Wimpy's, McDonald's, or one of the other fast-food restaurants that greet you at every corner. Since most hotels lack cooking facilities, vegetarians have nowhere to make their own meals and only fruit, raw vegetables, and yogurt to fall back on. The "If it's crowded, it's good (or at least cheap)" rule works in Ankara. Ulus has the cheapest eats (meals about $6); things get ritzier the farther south you go. **Madencioğlu Pasta ve Piknik** (Anafartalar Cad. 25/B, near Hisar Oteli, tel. 312/312–39–54) makes great *peynir börek* (cheese pastry) and is packed in the morning. **Sinema Bar** (Olgunlar Sok. 18, near Metropol Cinema, tel. 312/425–47–31) stays open until 2 AM in a city where everything else shuts down at midnight. The music videos are drowned out by live hard-rock guitar.

CHEAP THRILLS Kill time browsing in Kızılay's bookstores and music shops or hanging out in the cafés, where you might meet some university students mimicking European student fashions. The air-conditioned boutiques in the southern neighborhood of Kavaklidere are a good escape from the heat. Three cinemas in Kızılay and two in Kavaklidere are great for a siesta. American films in English, with Turkish subtitles, show for about $1.50. Halfway through the film, the lights go on, a Coke sign flashes on the screen, and the whole audience goes out for a soda.

Cappadocia

Cappadocia is like another planet with its bizarre rock formations, made of volcanic dust compacted by wind and rain. Since the time of the Hittites, people have carved houses into the soft, crumbly stone. Cappadocia stretches 150 km from **Ihlara Gorge** in the west to the 5,000-room underground city of Derinkuyu and ancient **Kayseri** in the east. **Nevşehir** is the dreary transport hub, and nearby Zelve has a large monastery. **Avanos** is the pottery center, making use of red clay taken from Kızılırmak River, the longest in Turkey, which runs across the northern part of Cappadocia.

GOREME A rural village where locals and tourists alike sleep in rock houses, Göreme, 9 km east of Nevşehir, is the best place to stay. From here you can walk south into **Pigeon Valley** (where pigeon droppings are used as fertilizer) or 6 km north to Zelve (*see below*), a canyon filled with chimneys and churches. For **tourist information,** see the travel agents near the otogar. The **PTT** is on the north side of town toward Avanos.

The overrated **Açik Hava Müzesi** (Open-Air Museum), 1 km east of town, has more than 30 rock churches with defaced 1,000-year-old Byzantine frescoes. It's open daily 8:30–5:30, and admission is $4.50. The museum is on every package-tour itinerary, but all over Cappadocia there are hundreds of similar spots for which you don't have to pay. One is the 10th-century **Tokalı Kilisi** (Church of the Buckle), about 50 yards from the museum, which contains scenes from the life of St. Basil.

The valleys are full of apricot trees, vines, and unused rock houses that you can camp in for free. Noisy cows and donkeys remind you that you're in a farming community.

➤ **GETTING AROUND** • The small otogar at the center of town has frequent direct service to most places in Turkey (Ankara 4 hrs, Konya 3 hrs). Most dolmuş pass through Nevşehir, and you might have to change there. The best way to travel in this area, though, is to walk through the valleys to Cavuşin and Zelve (*see below*), following the trails between vineyards and orchards.

➤ **WHERE TO SLEEP AND EAT** • Göreme has lots of great pensions, many built into the hillside. All cost $4 per person. **Keleş Cave Pension** (east above village, tel. 4857/2152) has four floors of cool rooms with beds and windows carved from rock. Like all rock rooms, they're cold, damp, and have little natural light, but you shouldn't miss the experience. At **Special Motel** (southwest of center, tel. 4857/2347), the easygoing staff will lend you blankets for camping trips into the valley. Ask the owner, Ali Baba, to do some magic tricks for you. There are three campgrounds on the way to the Açik Hava Müzesi, all charging $2 per tent, but camping on the top story of a rock warren is a cooler experience. Just head out to any of the rock formations that encircle the town and look for a place to crash.

Prices at **Ataman** (in Pigeon Valley, tel. 4857/1310) are on the high end for a restaurant (meals are about $10), but the place is built into the rock face, and tourist guide Abbas and his wife Sermin serve good traditional Turkish fare. For music, fresh trout, and excellent dolmas, try **Hacinin Yen Restaurant** (tel. 4857/1392), slightly out of town. Head down the road to Nevşehir about 300 yards and look left.

CAVUSIN This little village, 3 km from Göreme in the direction of Zelve, has only one sight—the **Cavuşin Kilese,** a church guarded by frescoes of the angels Michael and Gabriel. Still, it's a peaceful place to stay and a good base from which to explore the region on foot. **In Pansion** (tel. 4861/7070; doubles $8) has free hiking maps of the area.

ZELVE The **monastery complex** (admission $2.50; open daily 8:30–6) at Zelve is composed of cave churches built over a thousand years ago and a more recent mosque. Here, Muslims and Christians used to live in a horseshoe-shape valley surrounded by sheer cliffs. It's a nice three-hour walk from Göreme, but getting down to the monastery requires lots of controlled slipping down gravel-strewn hills. The museum is a warren of unlit rooms (bring a flashlight if you can) and precarious tunnels. Scaling the stone walls, which are chiseled with dusty handholds, is a real adrenaline rush.

DERINKUYU From Nevşehir you can catch a dolmuş 29 km south to the 3,000-year-old underground city of **Derinkuyu** (admission $2.50; open daily 8–7), one of Cappadocia's blockbuster sights. The 5,000 rooms are spread over 16,000 square feet and sink to 180 feet deep. The eight excavated levels contain a crucifix-shape church, a wine press, and dining areas. Take a flashlight to explore the tiny side tunnels and 52 ventilation shafts that allow air down and smoke up.

Konya

Although Konya is a major religious center with 11 mosques and two museums, it attracts surprisingly few tourists. Those who do come here make a beeline for the **Mevlâna Müzesi** (Mevlâna Meydanı; admission $2), a museum that occupies the monastery of the Whirling Dervishes. The group's original leader, Celaleddin Rumi (1207–73), known as Mevlâna, wrote the 25,000-verse poem *Mesnevi* and initiated a ritual dance symbolizing union with God. The dervishes spin in white robes and conical red hats that represent their tombstones. They dance for Allah but encourage people of all faiths to join them. Both robe and hat are draped over symbolic tombs in the museum, which also contain 1,100-year-old Korans, 990-bead rosaries, books with floral lacquer covers, and stone receptacles for Holy April Rain. In front of the museum, **Selimye Camii** (Selim Mosque) has a carpet that mirrors the pattern of its dome. **Koyunoğlu Müzesi** (about 800 yds east of Mevlâna Müzesi; admission $1) has a mediocre collection of coins, carpets, fossils, and stuffed birds. The mosque in the **Sahib Ata** complex at the southern edge of town has a wood ceiling and minaret. Opposite is the small **Arkeoloji Müzesi** (Archaeological Museum), with a 3rd-century-BC sarcophagus depicting the 12 labors of Hercules. Admission is $1.

BASICS You'll find the **PTT** (tel. 33/54–16–10) near the central square, Hükümet Alani. The **tourist information office** (Mevlâna Cad. 21, tel. 33/11–10–74; open daily 8:30–5) can arrange for you to meet families and students or, on weekends, to attend circumcision or marriage ceremonies.

GETTING AROUND Most attractions are between **Alaeddin Tepesi,** a raised circular park to the west, and **Mevlâna Caddesi** to the east. The **otogar** is 1 km north of town on Ankara Caddesi. Dolmuş shuttle people from the otogar to **Hükümet Alani** in the center of town. The town has a good tram system, but dolmuş (25¢) or your own two feet are better, since nothing is ever more than 2 km away.

WHERE TO SLEEP AND EAT Budget hotels are behind the PTT and to the east. Clean, central **Hotel Ulusan** (Kurşuncular Sok. 2, behind PTT, tel. 33/11–50–04) is the best choice. **Otel Mavi Köşk** (Bostançelebi Sok. 13, tel. 33/50–19–04) has a good view of the mosque, and **Otel Mevlâna** (Cengaver Sok. 1, tel. 33/51–24–44) is on a quiet side street.

Most restaurants in Konya close early, often at 9 or 10. The popular **Sifa Restaurant** (Mevlâna Cad. 29/B, tel. 33/52–05–19) serves pizza for $1.30. **Damla Restaurant** (Alladin Cad., tel. 33/51–37–05) has great appetizers and a range of Turkish dishes. **Sahin Bar** (Hükümet Alani 6, tel. 33/51–33–50), one of the few nightspots in town, sells beer for $2. Expect red neon and uppity service.

Architectural Primer

Temple of Venus and Rome in Rome

There's no getting around the fact that Europe is a cultural blitzkrieg of items covered in Art History 101. And the only way to ease the pain—excluding a bottle of cheap wine—is to understand the styles and ideas that congest Europe's streets, museums, and cathedrals. This primer is just to get you started.

ROMAN ARCHITECTURE

Even if you never set foot in Rome you're likely to see a little Roman architecture in your ramblings across Europe. From about the 2nd century BC to the 6th century AD, the Romans were busy rampaging through western Europe and northern Africa, establishing colonial settlements all along the way. The Romans needed an efficient method of communicating with and defending their far-flung colonies. Rome's fleets were mighty, but traveling by sea was not sufficient to maintain control over an empire that spanned from England and Germany to Libya and Egypt. So the Romans developed a complex system of **roads.** While it's an exaggeration to say that all roads led to Rome, it's true that the Roman network spanned most of the empire. The Via Appia, which ran from Rome south to Campania, was the road most admired, made of smooth blocks cushioned by crushed gravel. Government officials—particularly the *cursus publicus,* the ancient version of a UPS driver—traveled by horse and could cover up to 120 miles a day. The less fortunate had to plod along by horse-drawn wagon or on foot. According to the poet Horace, even the strongest walkers could cover no more than 20 miles before collapsing at a roadside inn.

> *To Romans, beauty was a product of utility and order, not necessarily of decoration. Roman architects considered a structure beautiful only if it presented an elegant solution to a practical problem.*

Another of the Romans' engineering feats was the **aqueduct,** which was used to transport water from distant sources to large towns. The earliest aqueducts were underground tunnels dug by slaves. Water didn't flow through these aqueducts at enough of an angle, though; they could carry water only short distances and were unable to supply large cities such as Rome, which had an estimated population of 1.2 million in 45 BC. These problems were solved by above-ground aqueducts: The water flowed down a gentle gradient through a channel that was carved along the tops of interconnected arches. An aqueduct had to have a gentle slope—no matter what the terrain—so Roman engineers often constructed multitiered aqueducts to span valleys and steep slopes. According to Frontinius, an ancient engineer, Rome in the 1st century AD was

Trajan's column in Rome

supplied with more than 250 million gallons of water every day. Happily, you don't have to visit Rome to see an aqueduct; some of the most impressive examples are in Nîmes (France) and Segovia (Spain).

The Roman **baths** were as important as the forum to a city's social life. According to a 3rd-century AD survey, Rome had an estimated 800 public bathhouses. Admission was cheap, and men and women bathed in the nude at different times to ensure at least some decorum. Construction of the baths, however, presented a few technical problems. Owing to the heat and humidity of the *caldaria* (steam rooms) and the *laconica* (sweating rooms) architects had to use concrete instead of wood (which tends to rot when exposed to moisture). Roman advances in the use of concrete—laboriously made of pulverized earth mixed with limestone—set the foundation, so to speak, for architectural innovations throughout Europe.

Another of the Romans' important architectural developments was the **round arch,** which allowed engineers to build bigger and more varied buildings than the Greeks, who generally stuck to cylindrical columns and rectangular floor plans. Round arches were especially handy when building elliptically shaped **amphitheaters,** which were used as arenas for spectacles like gladiator combat and the slaughter of Christians (c.f., *Spartacus,* starring the inimitable Kirk Douglas). Occasionally, amphitheaters were flooded for "sea combat," with dozens of ships and hundreds of sailors battling for supremacy in crocodile-infested waters. Amphitheaters were on the architectural cutting edge in their day, with rows of round arches on the exterior and tiers of seats—which often accommodated as many as 50,000 spectators—inside. Although they were more about function than form, some amphitheaters—like those in Rome and in Orange, France—have decorative Greek Ionic, Doric, and Corinthian columns.

The **triumphal arch** and **column** are other uniquely Roman monuments usually mastermined by some megalomaniacal conqueror who wanted to ensure that his accomplishments were properly commemorated. Trajan's Column in Rome is a fine example. Triumphal arches and columns were decorated with all sorts of bas-relief sculpture; horse-drawn chariots were among the most popular motifs.

BYZANTINE ARCHITECTURE

Constantine I moved the capital of the Roman Empire to Byzantium in AD 330, ultimately inciting an east–west split between Rome and what would later be called both Constantinople and—since 1930—Istanbul, in modern Turkey. Comprising the Balkan Peninsula, Greece and its islands, and most of Asia Minor, Constantine's Byzantine Empire was a unique blend of Hellenic and Roman culture transfigured through the lens of Christianity (Constantine legalized Christianity with the AD 313 Edict of Milan). The Byzantine influence, however, was not limited to the east: Venice, Ravenna, Sicily, and western Russia all displayed heavy touches of the Byzantine aesthetic, particularly after the fall of the western Roman Empire in AD 476.

Byzantine architecture is heavily indebted to the designs and technical achievements of Rome, which explains why Christian churches in Turkey are built on a north–south axis with a central nave and transept. The primary example of this is Hagia Sophia, in Istanbul, built by Justinian between AD 532 and AD 537. Unlike some of its western counterparts, Hagia Sophia has a central dome flanked by smaller domes and half-domes, each decorated with colorful tile mosaics—an art form at which Byzantine artists excelled. Nine times out of 10, the most central dome of a Byzantine church has a vast mosaic of the Pantocrator, a stylized image of Christ, surrounded by lesser religious and political figures.

Another Byzantine development was the eight-sided church; the textbook example is Ravenna's 6th-century San Vitale, which features a central Pantocrator figure as well as scads of colorful mosaics bereft of any human likeness. Other examples of Byzantine design are Basilica San Marco, in Venice, which preserves dozens of intricate Byzantine mosaics, and Charlemagne's chapel in Aachen, Germany.

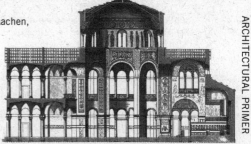

ROMANESQUE ARCHITECTURE

Working primarily in the 11th and 12th centuries, Romanesque architects employed many of the Roman forms—particularly round arches and the basilica layout, hence the clever name Roman-esque—in revolutionary ways.

Church of San Vitale in Ravenna

Almost without exception, a church or cathedral was the largest and most important building in any community in the Middle Ages; it symbolized solidity and permanence, as well as the promise of a glorious afterlife, to people, who spent most of their days trudging knee-deep in manure and mud. During times of upheaval—which the Middle Ages had aplenty—the massive, blocky Romanesque churches were transformed into well-defended refuges. As a result, your first impression of a Romanesque cathedral is likely to be that of a heavy, solid, somber place—one that's firmly rooted to the ground. Prime examples of Romanesque architecture include Vezelay in France, Aix-la-Chapelle in the German town of Aachen, Durham Cathedral in England, and the fortresslike duomo in the Italian town of Lucca.

Many Romanesque churches have a **basilica floor plan;** that is, they're shaped like Roman basilicas, with the addition of a perpendicular **transept.** This layout is known as "cruciform" because of its likeness to a cross, and there's hardly a medieval church in Europe that doesn't embody such a plan. A major aspect of cruciform churches is the central **nave,** the vast open space where worshippers stand during services. The **aisles** on either side allow people to move throughout the church without disrupting services. The **altar**—at the intersection of the nave and the transept—stands over the **crypt,** in which the sacred bones of some saint are often buried. (Some churches display the preserved bones, fingers, and shriveled hearts of saints, not to mention pieces of The One True Cross and maybe even a thorn from Christ's crown.)

The entrance to a Romanesque church is usually at the west end and is often flanked by two towers. Sometimes a number of smaller recessed **apses,** each with its own altar dedicated to a saint, protrude from the east end of the church, which gets the lion's share of morning sunlight—the prime reason for colorful stained-glass panels above many altars.

Cathedral and Tower of Pisa in Piazza dei Miracoli

Perhaps the most characteristic features of Romanesque architecture are barrel vaults and groin vaults, both of which were adopted from the Romans (who adopted them from the Etruscans). A vault is essentially a curved ceiling built of brick or stone that's shaped to form a tight, compact arch over a rectangular space. Earlier Romanesque churches, in particular, used the simple **barrel vault**—which is named for its straightforward half-barrel shape—to create a heightened sense of space (though, by today's standards, barrel vaults look austere and blocky). A later Romanesque feature is the **groin vault,** a complicated way of describing the intersection of two barrel vaults at right angles. Both types of vaults exert an enormous amount of pressure outward and downward; to avoid collapse they had to be hedged in with heavy stone walls. As a result, architects could incorporate only a few small windows into their designs, lest the walls crumble under the intense pressure.

Other than thick walls and round arches, Romanesque churches had few common characteristics, largely because of regional differences in taste. Many Romanesque interiors are austere, but that's because Romanesque architects were typically commissioned by church leaders who felt that decoration was frivolous and blasphemous. Other interiors, however, are richly decorated, according to the principle that art should be employed simultaneously for the glory of God and for the edification of the church's largely illiterate masses. Whether it's the painted monasteries of Romania or the brilliant Byzantine frescoes of Siena and Ravenna, medieval art was nothing if not didactic: Scenes of gargoyles tormenting lost souls, of hellish monsters devouring the wicked, and of the blessed gathered by Christ's side (next stop, paradise) abound.

GOTHIC ARCHITECTURE

When Abbot Suger, an adviser to Louis VI, decided in AD 1140 to build a cathedral in St-Denis, near Paris, he set out to create a towering structure full of heavenly light—an unfettered monument that would reach to the heavens and encourage worshippers to do likewise. During the 12th century, however, building a church with voluminous interior spaces and wide decorative windows wasn't a simple thing. Massive stone walls were required to support the traditional barrel vaults used in Romanesque churches. At St-Denis, however, you'll find a catalogue of Gothic innovations: **pointed arches, rib vaults,** and **flying buttresses.** (The pointed arch and rib vault were generally known to Romanesque architects but were employed to a much greater degree and in more daring ways starting in the 12th century.)

Gothic architecture got its name from Renaissance snobs who thought Gothic cathedrals looked awkward and unstable; the name itself comes from the barbarian Goths, who sacked Rome in the 5th century AD.

Rib vaults are essentially groin vaults with X-shaped arches exposed on the underside—an innovation that, via the crisscrossing ribs, distributed the weight of the roof outward instead of downward. This freed up space between the ribs for all sorts of decorative designs. More important, the outward thrust produced by groin vaulting could be counterbalanced by a complex system of buttresses and flying buttresses—essentially, external stone supports that absorbed the thrust of the nave wall. Buttresses allowed architects to reduce the thickness of walls and to place windows of different shapes and sizes into walls that were no longer solely responsible for the stability of the overall structure. The upshot is that Gothic cathedrals are uniformly bright and voluminous, with arching ceilings and tall towers that command attention for miles. Even the interior vaulting directs the eye upward instead of around and down, an effect that exemplifies the ideal of Gothic architecture.

Gothic Spire

Textbook examples of Gothic design include Rheims, Rouen, Chartres, and Amiens cathedrals, in France; Lincoln and Salisbury cathedrals in England; the Cologne cathedral in Germany; and the Toledo cathedral in Spain.

RENAISSANCE ARCHITECTURE

The Renaissance, or "rebirth," was not based on a newfound set of aesthetics or artistic skills, but rather on a re-evaluation of classical ideals. Renaissance architects studied the works of ancient Rome and attempted to recapture the solid, earthly, and symmetrical tendencies that had been abandoned in the Gothic extravagances of the

Middle Ages. Artists studied the proportions of ancient temples, anatomists carved open and catalogued the human body, and engineers and scientists set out to discover and manipulate the complex laws of nature. Art and architecture were no longer myopic fields, but rather poignant aspects of interrelated disciplines—among them poetry, philosophy, anatomy, engineering, and astronomy—that promised a new understanding of the universe.

During the 15th century, Florence was the cradle of Renaissance architecture. After spending several years studying in Rome, **Filippo Brunelleschi** (1377–1446) returned to his native Florence in 1420 and began work on the dome for the city's massive Gothic cathedral. Brunelleschi's octagonal dome wowed the Florentines (who were skeptical that such a thing could be built) and paved the way for a revolution in architectural design. Though it made use of vaulting techniques developed by Gothic architects, Brunelleschi's dome was of a scale and technical design previously unseen, and after its completion it became the standard for countless Renaissance architects. Brunelleschi's other major works include the churches of San Lorenzo and Santo Spirito, in Florence.

Leone Battista Alberti (1404–1472) was the Renaissance's other architectural luminary. Author of the first architectural treatise since Roman times, the *De re Aedificatoria* (1452), Alberti argued that architecture should imitate nature and incorporate the ideals of symmetry and order. He felt that buildings, much like music, should conform to certain harmonic proportions and embody specific ratios.

Outside of Florence, Renaissance ideals were slowly but surely embraced in Urbino, Mantua, Milan, and Naples, Italy, and to a lesser extent in France, Spain, and England.

Duomo di Santa Maria del Fiore in Florence

Speaking in Tongues

Here's a handy list of architectural terms to consider before passing through the next church portal (front door):

- **Chancel:** The space around the altar that is off-limits to everyone but the clergy. It's usually at the east end of the church and is often blocked off by a rail.
- **Choir:** The section of the church set off to seat the choir. It's either in the chancel or in a loft in another part of the church.
- **Clerestory:** The upper part of the church walls, typically lined with windows (often of the stained-glass variety) to bathe the nave with light.
- **Narthex:** A hall or small room leading from the main entrance to the nave.

- **Nave:** The main section of the church that stretches from the chancel to the narthex.
- **Transept:** The part of the church that extends outward at a right angle from the main body, creating a cruciform (i.e., cross-shaped) plan. Both ends of the transept are usually punctuated with stained glass, as at Chartres in France and at Salisbury in England.
- **Tympanum:** A recessed triangular or semicircular space above the portal, often decorated with sculpture.

Throughout Europe, however, many Renaissance churches abandoned the Romanesque cruciform floor plan in favor of the **Greek cross plan.** The essential characteristics of the Greek cross were the polygonal central chamber (as opposed to a rectangular nave) abutted by four arms of equal length, a nod to the Renaissance obsession with symmetry. The finest examples of this style are **Donato Bramante's** (1444–1514) Tempietto in Rome and his original design for St. Peter's in Vatican City.

Renaissance ideals also influenced secular architecture, especially French châteaux, such as those in the Loire Valley. These buildings are characterized by ruthless symmetry and the use of repetitive geometrical forms. Pointed arches were replaced with traditional Roman round arches, and vaulting was replaced with coffered ceilings, decorated with square or octagonal recessed panels. Fontainebleau and Chambord are perhaps the most pure examples of French Renaissance architecture, with Pierre Lescot's Louvre (AD 1547) coming a close third.

BAROQUE ARCHITECTURE

During the High Renaissance, in the late 16th century, architectural tastes reverted to a heavy decorative style. Although the symmetry and solidity remained, architects began dressing up their staid Renaissance buildings with all sorts of ornaments, curlicues, and lavish paintings. Interiors were well-lighted—either by candles or the sun—so that worshippers could ponder the wealth of expensive marble and gold leaf used to cover every nook and cranny. The architect became a conductor of emotional intensity and used swirling lines and light to give the buildings' interiors a sense of movement intended to engulf the viewer.

Church of San Carlo alle Quattro Fontane in Rome

Church of St. Ignatius in Rome

While order is the foremost feature in Renaissance buildings, willful confusion is the primary characteristic of Baroque architecture. The reason for this shift, at least in parts of Europe, may be traced to changing religious ideals. Theologians began to argue that trying to come closer to God through the exercise of the intellect was futile, and that faith was a far superior attribute. Chaotic church architecture was supposed to encourage worshippers to abandon their reason in favor of raw emotional response.

This effect was achieved through complex, massive floor plans, through unfamiliar undulating facades adorned with puffs of sculpted plaster and marble, and through the novel use of vivid, contrasting colors. The big names to remember in this context are **Francesco Borromini** (1599–1677), who designed the church of San Carlo alle Quattro Fontane in Rome; **Gianlorenzo Bernini** (1598–1681), the Naples-born architect who dominated Italy's Baroque scene; and **Johann Balthasar Neumann** (1687–1753), who designed late Baroque churches in Würzburg and Rothenburg-ob-der-Tauber in Germany.

Index

THE BERKELEY GUIDES
1995 "Big Bucks and a Backpack" Contest

Four lucky winners will receive $2,000* cash and a Jansport® World Tour backpack to use on the trek of a lifetime!

HOW TO ENTER:

Complete the official entry form on the opposite page, or print your name, complete address, and telephone number on a 3" x 5" piece of paper and mail it, to be received by 1/15/96, to: "Big Bucks and a Backpack" Contest, PMI Station, P.O. Box 3562, Southbury, CT 06488-3562, USA. Entrants from the United Kingdom and the Republic of Ireland may mail their entries to: Berkeley Guides Backpack Contest, Random House Group, P.O. Box 1375, London SW1V 2SL, England.

You may enter as many times as you wish, but mail each entry separately.

* One Grand Prize — £1,000 and a Jansport® World Tour backpack — will also be awarded to entrants from the United Kingdom and the Republic of Ireland.

Prizes: On or about 2/1/96, Promotions Mechanics, Inc., an independent judging organization, will conduct a random drawing from among all eligible entries received, to award the following prizes:

(4) Grand Prizes—$2,000 cash and a Jansport® World Tour backpack, approximate retail value $2,180, will be awarded to entrants from the United States and Canada (except Quebec).

(1) One Grand Prize — £1,000 and a Jansport® World Tour backpack, approximate retail value £1,090, will be awarded to entrants from the United Kingdom and the Republic of Ireland.

Winners will be notified by mail. Due to Canadian contest laws, Canadian residents, in order to win, must first correctly answer a mathematical skill testing question administered by mail. Odds of winning will be determined from the number of entries received. Prize winners may request a statement showing how the odds of winning were determined and how winners were selected.

To receive a copy of these complete official rules, send a self-addressed, stamped envelope to be received by 12/15/95 to: "Big Bucks and a Backpack" Rules, PMI Station, P.O. Box 3569, Southbury, CT 06488-3569, USA.

Eligibility: No purchase necessary to enter or claim prize. Open to legal residents of the United States, Canada (except Quebec), the United Kingdom, and the Republic of Ireland who are 18 years of age or older. Employees of The Random House, Inc. Group, its subsidiaries, agencies, affiliates, participating retailers, and distributors and members of their families living in the same household are not eligible to enter. Void where prohibited.

General: Taxes on prizes are the sole responsibility of winners. By participating, entrants agree to these rules and to the decisions of judges, which shall be final in all respects. Winners must complete an Affidavit of Eligibility and Liability/Publicity Release, which must be returned within 15 days or prize may be forfeited. Each winner agrees to the use of his/her name and/or photograph for advertising and publicity purposes without additional compensation (except where prohibited by law). Sponsor is not responsible for late, lost, stolen, or misdirected mail. No prize transfer or substitution except by sponsor due to unavailability. All entries become the property of the sponsor. One prize per household.

Winners List: For a list of winners, send a self-addressed, stamped envelope to be received by 1/15/96 to: "Big Bucks and a Backpack" Winners, PMI Station, P.O. Box 750, Southbury, CT 06488-0750 ,USA.

Random House, Inc., 201 East 50th Street, New York, NY 10022

Complete this form and mail to:

"Big Bucks and a Backpack" Contest, PMI Station, P.O. Box 3562, Southbury, CT 06488-3562.

Entrants from the United Kingdom and the Republic of Ireland, mail to: Berkeley Guides Backpack Contest, Random House Group, P.O. Box 1375, London SW1V 2SL, England.

Mail coupon to be received by 1/5/96.

NAME

ADDRESS

COUNTRY   **TELEPHONE**

WHERE I BOUGHT THIS BOOK

A T-SHIRT FOR YOUR THOUGHTS . . .

After your trip, drop us a line and let us know how things went. People whose comments help us most improve future editions will receive our eternal thanks as well as a Berkeley Guides T-shirt. Just print your name and address clearly and send the completed survey to: The Berkeley Guides, 515 Eshleman Hall, U.C. Berkeley, Berkeley, CA 94720.

Your Name _____

Address _____

_____ Zip _____

Where did you buy this book? City _____ State _____

How long before your trip did you buy this book? _____

Which Berkeley Guide(s) did you buy? _____

Which other guides, if any, did you purchase for this trip? _____

Which other guides, if any, have you used before? (Please circle)
Fodor's   Let's Go   Real Guide   Frommer's   Birnbaum   Lonely Planet
Other _____

Why did you choose Berkeley? (Please circle as many as apply)
Budget information   More maps   Emphasis on outdoors/off-the-beaten-track
Design   Attitude   Other _____
_____

If you're employed: Occupation _____

If you're a student: Name of school _____ City & state _____

Age _____ Male _____ Female _____

How many weeks was your trip? (Please circle) 1 2 3 4 5 6 7 8 More than 8 weeks

After you arrived on your trip, how did you get around? (Please circle one or more)
Rental car   Personal car   Plane   Bus   Train   Hiking   Biking   Hitching
Other _____

When did you travel? _____

Where did you travel? _____
_____

The features/sections I used most were (please circle as many as apply):
Basics   Where to Sleep   Food   Coming and Going   Worth Seeing   Other

The information was (circle one):
Usually accurate   Sometimes accurate   Seldom accurate

I would _____ would not _____ buy another Berkeley Guide.

These books are brand new, and we'd really appreciate some feedback on how to improve them. Please also tell us about your latest find, a new scam, a budget deal, whatever—we want to hear about it.

For your comments:

_____

_____

Notes

Notes

Notes

One destination fits all.

Switzerland is Downtown Europe.
From here, on a clear day, you can see people squeeze grapes in France or schmooz
with girls in Italy; see them curtsie in
Austria, or cut Wurst in Germany.

Balair/CTA, Switzerland's second most
famous airline takes you to Zurich. With
friendly service and a brand new fleet of jets.

And to make it even more attractive, we
offer Relax Class. Our version of business
class, with prices actually lower than many
airlines' coach fares.

For details call us at: 1-800-322-5247

balair cta
The leisure line of Swissair.